THE AMERICAN NEGRO
HIS HISTORY AND LITERATURE

THE
ATLANTA UNIVERSITY PUBLICATIONS

Nos. 1, 2, 4, 8, 9, 11, 13, 14, 15, 16, 17, 18

ARNO PRESS and THE NEW YORK TIMES

NEW YORK 1968

General Editor
WILLIAM LOREN KATZ

27051

LIST OF PUBLICATIONS
IN THIS VOLUME

PRESIDENT HORACE BUMSTEAD OF ATLANTA UNIVERSITY and George Bradford, a trustee, influenced by a series of Tuskegee conferences (which had begun in 1891) on rural Negro problems, started a program of annual conferences at Atlanta University on urban Negro problems in 1896. In 1897 Dr. W. E. Du Bois was called to Atlanta to direct this series of conferences as well as supervise the university's sociology program.

American social science was in its infancy at this time and was enamored with theory, with laws of limited validity, and with inaccurate speculation. Du Bois, an empiricist, had just completed work on *The Philadelphia Negro: A Social Study* (1899), the first scientific sociological study in the United States (at the University of Pennsylvania). He had studied economics, history and sociology under Adolf Wagner, Heinrich von Treitschke and Gustav Schmoller at the University of Berlin and was familiar with the scientific methods of social research. His inductive method was to study all the facts and by measurement, comparison and research to work up valid conclusions. He came to Atlanta thinking not merely of conferences but of carrying out an ambitious and comprehensive plan for studying aspect after aspect of the group life of Negroes for a decade; then repeating the whole series every decade with improved methods and objectives for a hundred years. As the main address at the November 1897 meeting of the American Academy of Political and Social

Science in Philadelphia, Du Bois read a brilliant paper entitled "The Study of the Negro Problem," which was published in *The Annals* of the Academy for January 1898.

The proceedings of the first two Atlanta University conferences, held in 1896 and 1897 (*Mortality Among Negroes in Cities* and *Social and Physical Condition of Negroes in Cities*) had been published before Du Bois became the director of the conferences. He immediately tightened up the series and set up a long-range, more intensive research program, and made the studies as thorough as his limited resources permitted. The *Atlanta University Publications*, consisting of 18 monographs published between 1896 and 1914, were the first attempts to study scientifically the problems of the American Negro anywhere in the world: the first studies to make factual, empirical evidence the center of sociological work on the Negro. Du Bois was the first sociologist of the South (probably of the nation) and his studies gained international attention. But underlying his scholarly efforts was his primary aim and objective: to reform and uplift the Negro people; he hoped for social reform through social science. Virtually all of the monographs (with five bibliographies) were the first real studies of their subjects. They did not touch on politics, sexual race relations or Negro civil rights, since these subjects were considered too controversial. But biographers of Dr. Du Bois concede that the studies were impressive and laid to rest many of the myths about U. S. Negroes and about Africa.

The first publication, *Mortality Among Negroes in Cities*, deals with the causes of a very high adult and infant Negro mortality rate as compared to whites. The second study, *Social and Physical Condition of Negroes in Cities*, continues the discussion of the public and personal health of Negroes and their social environment; of the care of children, of the prevention of illnesses, the care of teeth and general personal hygiene.

The third study, *Some Efforts of American Negroes for*

Their Own Social Betterment (1898), with which Dr. Du Bois began his editorship of the series, has been left out of this volume since virtually all of the material in it can be found in the fourth study, *The Negro in Business* (1899). *The Negro in Business* contains much useful data on the various types of Negro business enterprise, as well as material on the many problems of Negro business. It also calls for the establishment of a national "Negro Businessmen's League," which Booker T. Washington formed the next year.

The fifth study, *The College-Bred Negro* (1900), the sixth, *The Negro Common School* (1901), and the seventh, *The Negro Artisan* (1902), have been omitted since their material has been included in the fifteenth, sixteenth and seventeenth studies, respectively.

The eighth study is *The Negro Church* (1903). Several histories of Negro denominations had been published, but this was the first overall study of the Negro church and religion. Starting with early African religious beliefs, the monograph covers Negro religion under slavery, the attitudes of white religious sects to bondage, early Negro churches and preachers, and the Negro church in 1890. There are brief accounts describing Negro churches in various localities, the status of the various Negro church denominations, the training of Negro ministers and the moral status of Negroes. This book-length study and C. G. Woodson's *The History of the Negro Church* (1921) were the only scholarly studies of the Negro church until the later monographs of Benjamin E. Mays, E. Franklin Frazier and others.

The ninth study is *Some Notes on Negro Crime Particularly in Georgia* (1904). Although the understanding of Negro crime was not as clear in 1904 as it is today and much blame for crime was placed on the Negroes themselves, this study points up poverty and all of its ramifications as a major cause of Negro crime. Other causes detailed are the convict-lease system for southern prison labor, a double standard of justice in the courts (one for Negroes, another for whites), prej-

udiced judges, discriminatory laws, the denial of rights to
Negroes either by law or custom, the defenselessness of Negro
women through law or custom against the aggressions of white
men, and the enforced caste system which humiliated Negroes
and crushed their self-respect.

The tenth study, *A Select Bibliography of the Negro American* (1905), is 71 pages long and very good for its time. This
was the third edition of the bibliography (the other two
smaller editions were published in 1901 and 1903), but since
it is very dated and has quite limited usefulness today, it has
been omitted. Also omitted is the brief, five-page special report, *Some Notes on the Negroes in New York City*, published in January 1903.

The eleventh study, *The Health and Physique of the Negro
American* (1906), is an excellent monograph with chapters
on the races of men, the Negro race, the Negro brain, the
Negro American as a racial type, physical measurements, psychological considerations of the Negro problem, the Negro's
population increase, illness, mortality rate, insurance, hospitals, medical schools, physicians, dentists and pharmacists.
Dr. W. Montague Cobb of the Howard University School of
Medicine called this study the "first significant scientific approach to the health problems and biological study of the
Negro. . . . But," said Cobb, "neither the Negro medical
profession nor the Negro educational world was ready for it.
Its potential usefulness was not realized by Negroes. Whites
were hostile to such a study" which embraced the anthropology, psychology and physical health of the Negro. "This
study, Du Bois's single excursion into the health field, was,"
said Cobb, "an extraordinary forward pass heaved the length
of the field, but there were no receivers."

The twelfth study, *Economic Co-Operation Among Negro
Americans* (1907), has been omitted, as its subject matter is
included in the fourteenth.

The thirteenth study, *The Negro American Family* (1908),
is a continuation of the second study, dealing with social con-

ditions with the family group as focal point. Negro marriage, the home, and family economics are studied from their origins in Africa through slavery to freedom in the early 1900's. This study was an early and worthy forerunner of E. Franklin Frazier's *The Negro Family in the United States* (1939), although it naturally lacked Frazier's approach to the family as a natural human association and as a social institution subjected to the severest stresses and strains of social change.

The fourteenth study, *Efforts for Social Betterment Among Negro Americans* (1910), presents important facts on Negro real estate and personal property, churches, schools, philanthropy, charity, clubs of various sorts, hospitals, orphanages and homes for the elderly and for women, YMCA's and YWCA's, libraries, newspapers, settlement houses, day nurseries and kindergartens. These uplift activities were and are very important, and have long been ignored by many whites who still do not know about this phase of Negro life and activity.

Monographs fifteen through eighteen were co-edited by Du Bois and Associate Professor A. G. Dill of Atlanta University. When Du Bois began *The Crisis* magazine of the NAACP in 1910, Dill became the business manager. (Later the two formed a publishing company and brought out *The Brownies' Book* for Negro children in 1920 and 1921.) The fifteenth study, *The College-Bred Negro American* (1910), takes up the problems of the Negro colleges, their curricula and students, as well as the problems of Negro students in white colleges and universities. It discusses what happens to Negro college alumni in terms of occupations, property ownership, and avocations and the education of their children. This Negro college survey and the Phelps-Stokes Foundation-United States Bureau of Education's big, two-volume survey, *Negro Education* (1916), laid the groundwork for the Negro colleges of today.

The sixteenth study, *The Common School and the Negro American* (1911), after brief sections on the history of Negro public schools, Negro illiteracy, enrollment and general educational conditions, goes into a state-by-state description of Negro elementary education in the southern states and the District of Columbia. The study shows that the southern Negro child received a vastly inferior education. There is material on high schools and the significant relationship of Negro disfranchisement to Negro public education. The study also disproves the common belief that whites paid for Negro education by showing that sizable monies accrued from Negro taxes plus federal funds and public lands sales.

The seventeenth study, *The Negro American Artisan* (1912), is a sound, thorough research monograph. It begins with the African artisan, takes up the southern Negro slave artisan on the plantations and in the towns, and includes a state-by-state rundown for the whole country of the occupations of Negroes after Emancipation. It also covers organized labor's treatment of the Negro and the training of Negro artisans and their economic future. It was an important, book-length, ground-breaking study.

The eighteenth and last study in this series, *Morals and Manners Among Negro Americans* (1914), is a review and continuation of sections in *The Negro Church* (the eighth study) on the moral and religious status of Negroes ten years later. This monograph covers good manners, sound morals, cleanliness, personal honesty, home life, the rearing of children, amusements for young people, care of old people, the church and present conditions, compared with the past, with comment on the state of each one in virtually all of the states where Negroes lived. It concludes that much of the real work of social uplift and moral awakening was carried on by Negro women amid insult and race discrimination, and says that the hope of the future in moral uplift rests in a thorough education for Negro children, respect and protection for Negro women, widened industrial opportunity for Negro men and systematic efforts to lesson race prejudice.

The *Atlanta University Studies* were indeed a pioneering,

ground-breaking series and, although they never received wide circulation among Negroes or whites, they were reviewed in important magazines and metropolitan newspapers. Economic historian Frank W. Taussig said that no better work was being done anywhere in the country. (More prejudiced reviewers of these studies who could not accept their conclusions had to belittle them in one way or another. They insisted that Negroes were emotional, not scientific.) Of course, these studies could not improve the conditions of Negroes; much more drastic action was necessary, as Dr. Du Bois soon discovered. The Negroes' political and social conditions actually worsened during this period. But these studies did help Negro morale and group pride by showing Negro achievements and advances and by giving valid sociological explanations and reasons for the Negroes' low status in American society.

Ernest Kaiser
SCHOMBURG COLLECTION
NEW YORK PUBLIC LIBRARY

ATLANTA UNIVERSITY PUBLICATIONS,

No. 1.

MORTALITY AMONG NEGROES IN CITIES.

PROCEEDINGS OF THE CONFERENCE FOR INVESTIGATION OF CITY PROBLEMS,

HELD AT

ATLANTA UNIVERSITY, MAY 26–27, 1896.

ATLANTA, GA.

ATLANTA UNIVERSITY PRESS.

1896.

CONTENTS.

PROCEEDINGS OF THE CONFERENCE.

INTRODUCTION.

Atlanta University always has drawn its students extensively from the cities and large towns, and a great proportion of its graduates are now holding positions at these centers of influence. From these workers information has come to the faculty and trustees of the University from time to time that has led them to believe that there exists a great need for a systematic and thorough investigation of the conditions of living among the Negro population of cities. So, at the annual meeting of the trustees, July 1, 1895, President Bumstead brought the subject before the Board, and it was decided to inaugurate such an investigation, and provision was made for holding the first of a series of conferences at the University. The plan at that time was to hold this conference in November, 1895, during the Atlanta Exposition. But upon further consideration, it was deemed wise to change the time to the Commencement in May, 1896.

It was not expected that much in the line of scientific reports based upon accurate data could be presented at this first conference, but it was believed that much information could be gathered from the ordinary experiences and observations of graduates and others, and that the subject could be considered in such a manner as to arouse interest and enthusiasm, and so pave the way for collecting and digesting extensive and accurate data. Such, it is believed, has been the result of the conference held.

Fortunately for the cause, there was elected as a trustee of the University, in 1895, Mr. George G. Bradford of Boston, a graduate of Harvard University, who for several years has been making the study of the Negro the occupation of his leisure time. He entered heartily into this plan of investigation, and has taken the lead in it by preparing blanks, opening up correspondence, and in other ways. In his efforts he has had the assistance of Mr. Edward Cummings, Professor of Sociology in Harvard University. It was thought best to begin with the topic of mortality among the Negro population in cities, and so most of the papers and discussions at the conference were upon that subject.

The conference was organized Tuesday evening, May 26, by the election of President Horace Bumstead as chairman, and George A. Towns ('94) and James W. Johnson ('94) as recording secretaries. The addresses, papers and resolutions in this pamphlet furnish a sufficiently detailed account of the proceedings at the two sessions of the conference. Provision for work during the coming year was made by the election of Mr. Geo. G. Bradford of Boston, as corresponding secretary, and an executive committee, consisting of Professor Thomas N. Chase of Atlanta, Butler R. Wilson, Esq. of Boston, Rev. Joseph E. Smith ('76) of Chattanooga, and S. P. Lloyd, M. D. ('89) of Savannah.

REMARKS OF PRESIDENT BUMSTEAD.

This conference has its origin in several striking facts. One of these is the large proportion of the Negro population of the land now found to be living in cities, viz: one-sixth, or a million and a quarter out of the whole number of seven and a half millions. Whatever we may think of the wisdom or unwisdom of this drift to the cities, the fact presents a condition that must be met and provided for. For we must remember that the condition and circumstances of Negroes living in cities differ widely from those of the plantation Negroes. They are thrown much more closely together in large masses on narrower areas of land and in more contracted tenements. Negro slums are already beginning to be found. The employments of city Negroes are different from those of the rural brethren, agriculture being replaced by the trades, or the various forms of personal service, and to some extent by mercantile and professional pursuits. Their social life is also different.

Very little attention, too, has yet been given to the specific problems arising out of the changed conditions under which this large proportion of Negro population is now sharing the city life of their white brethren. The Negro has been thought of chiefly as a tiller of the soil, as in fact he is; and much has been done, and very properly, for the improvement of his plantation life. But the problems connected with his life in the cities and larger towns need even more careful study and thorough treatment.

In view of these considerations, it is important to note another fact, and that is that nearly all the graduates of Atlanta University are living and working in the cities and larger towns of the South. This fact is very suggestive, for the problems of Negro city life must be settled largely by Negroes themselves, and the body of our alumni are in some respects specially fitted for this task. Not only are they familiar with the conditions of life in cities, but they have acquired, in their training in this Institution, some degree of accurate observation and careful reflection, some acquaintance with high standards of living, some familiarity with measures of reform and of social and economic improvement that are indispensable for dealing with such matters. Herein is the great opportunity of Atlanta University and of this conference of its alumni for the investigation of city problems which we inaugurate this evening.

Let us not forget that the general subject of this and succeeding conferences—the study of Negro city life—and the particular subject of this year—the mortality of Negroes in cities—constitute a human problem far more than a Negro problem. We shall use the words "Negro" and "colored," not to emphasize distinctions of race, but as terms of convenience. We are simply to study human life under certain conditions—conditions which, if repeated with any other race, would have practically the same result. Patient, painstaking and persistent work in gathering reliable statistics and other data will be necessary for our success. It is no gala day enterprise that we have begun. Courage and honesty in the search for real facts are called for, and we must be ready to face and deal with even the disagreeable facts and those which upset our previous theories, which our investigations may compel us to recognize as facts.

And let me remind you, as I close this brief introduction to the work of our conference, that the richest rewards await the result of our undertaking if we are successful. Dr. Parkhurst has said that it is in the great cities that the life of the nation beats and throbs itself out. What the cities are, that in large degree will the country that surrounds them be. The connection between the two is intimate. So the improvement of Negro life in cities will make itself felt in the improvement of Negro plantation life. And the improvement of Negro life anywhere will be a blessing to the life of the nation as a whole, regardless of race or color.

OCCASION AND PURPOSE OF THE CONFERENCE, AND AN OUTLINE OF THE PLAN OF WORK.

BY MR. GEORGE G. BRADFORD OF BOSTON.

The rapid growth of our great cities, within recent years, is one of the phases of modern life which brings with it problems whose solution calls for the best efforts of the leading men in the city communities, whether white or black. Special courses for the study of these problems have been established in the Northern colleges, and it is felt that the time has come when Atlanta University must take up the study of those problems of city life which its graduates are called upon to meet and solve. It is none too soon to begin this work, for each year a larger proportion of the colored race are concentrating in the cities.

In 1860, only 4.2 per cent of the colored population of the United States were living in the cities. By 1880, the number had increased to 8.4 per cent of the whole colored population, while by 1890, it had increased to 12 per cent. This process of concentration in the cities has been relatively much more rapid among the colored people than among the whites, the figures for whites during the same period being 10.9 per cent in 1860, and 15.7 per cent in 1890, or an increase of 4.8 per cent, as against 7.8 per cent for colored. How rapid this increase in the city population really is, may be illustrated by the growth of the colored population in the city of Atlanta, where the increase has been at a rate three times as great as for the country at large. For decade 1870–1880, the increase was 64 per cent; for 1880–1890, 72 per cent; while the average increase of colored population for the whole country during the same period was only 20 per cent in each decade.

In taking up the study of city problems, we feel that we cannot do better than begin by an inquiry into the physical and moral condition of the people. It is a line of inquiry which has not been previously pursued on any systematic or

extensive scale. Up to the present time, students and investigators of the problems confronting the colored race have
confined themselves principally to the study of problems of
country life or directed their attention towards economic or
educational questions. Of the physical condition of the Negro
under the trying conditions of city life, we have little accurate
information. Many of the Southern cities have not had, until
within a few years, any city boards of health, and, as a result,
there has not been hitherto sufficient official data from which
any broad generalizations could be drawn, and such data as
have been obtainable have not yet been brought together into
available form. We have, however, some few data that are
sufficient to prove the necessity of the inquiry upon which we
have begun.

From the United States census for 1890, we have the mortality for the white and colored population of five of our largest
cities—Washington, Baltimore, New Orleans, Louisville and
St. Louis—as given in a paper published by the trustees of
the Slater Fund:

	┌─RATES PER 1,000.─┐	
	WHITE.	COLORED.
Washington	19	36
Baltimore	22	36
New Orleans	22	37
Louisville	18	32
St. Louis	17	35

The excess of colored over white is 100, 63.6, 68, 77 and
106 per cent.

By special report from Washington, these figures would appear to be for that city 19 whites, 34.7 colored; excess of colored over white, 83 per cent. The death-rate among the
whites in these five cities ranged from 17 to 22 per thousand,
and among the colored from 32 to 37 per thousand, or from
63 per cent to 106 per cent greater among the colored than
among the whites. In the city of St. Louis, the death-rate
among the colored was more than twice that among the whites.

The significance of this excessive mortality can be appreciated only when we come to study the causes of destitution in
out great cities. There are some very valuable figures on thi

point in a comprehensive treatise by Amos G. Warner, Ph.D., entitled "American Charities." (See table annexed.) In his analysis of causes of destitution among the colored people of Baltimore, we find 38 per cent of all cases of destitution are due to sickness. We have no official figures on this point for Washington or any other Southern city. But a similar report for New York shows 37 per cent from sickness, and for Boston 45.6 per cent. These are among cases of destitution of which there is official record. The result might be different, could we obtain the facts for all cases. Among the whites, also, sickness is one of the chief causes of destitution, but the percentage is much smaller, averaging about 20 per cent, while the average among the colored people is 39 per cent, or nearly twice as great. We see, therefore, that one of the first things we must do in improving the condition of the masses of the poorer colored people crowded together in the great cities is to try to lighten the heavy burden of sickness now weighing them down. This will involve an inquiry not only into physical or economic conditions, but into moral conditions as well. We feel, therefore, that in beginning our study of city problems by an inquiry into the causes of the excessive mortality among the colored people, we are striking right at the root of many of the evils that we have been trying to reach.

Important as is the industrial education of a state, it is evident that no rapid economic advance can be made by a race physically or morally weak. It is evident that both physical and moral as well as the economic conditions should be carefully studied, and we shall see later that they should be studied together, as each one acts upon the other. The task, then, which we have undertaken is the inquiry into the exact conditions, physical, moral and economic, affecting life in city communities. Later, when we have gathered sufficient information, we may be able to point out how those conditions may be improved. But at present our chief aim must be to make a thorough and searching investigation.

The method which has been adopted for making this investigation is as follows: In order to gather the necessary data, uniform sets of blanks have been prepared and put in the hands of graduates of this University, and of educated colored men and women located in different cities. These sets consist of three different blanks, known as blanks Nos. 1, 2 and 3. Blank Nos. 1 and 2 are to serve the purpose of a permanent record by which to measure the progress of each city community from year to year. As in many cities the official records from which the data for these blanks must be gathered, have been in time past very incomplete, we shall be unable to review the past progress of those cities as we should like to, but these records are being made more complete each year, so that in the future we shall be able to measure progress made with some degree of accuracy. Blank No. 3, called the Family Budget blank, provides for a more intimate inquiry into the conditions of life existing in a particular community, and is intended to bring out the causes of results shown in blanks Nos. 1 and 2. The points of inquiry covered by this blank, No. 3 are :

First—General conditions of the home life, the size of the homes, their sanitary conditions, and the amount of sickness in the family.

Second—Economic conditions, occupations of family, the amount of income, etc.

Third—The expenditure of family for food, rent, intoxicants, etc., showing habits of life in the community.

The results of an investigation carried on along the above lines will be brought out in later papers.

In regard to the conferences: It is proposed each year to take up the discussion of certain phases of city life most deserving attention. Just what will be the subjects for these discussions will be determined by the results of investigations already begun, and announcements will be made later. The general plan of conference will be not unlike that of the National Conference of Charities and Corrections, and some of the subjects taken up will be similar to those discussed there, such as home life, child saving, district nursing, scientific study of social problems, municipal and county charities; or economic questions, such as diversity of employment, co-operation, loan associations, savings institutions, mutual insurance, etc. It will probably be found advisable to have at the conference next year section meetings where special topics can be discussed more freely and fully than in the general conference. This is, in general, an outline of the plan upon which the investigation and the conference will be conducted. As the work develops, and we gain more experience, the plan will be modified to meet the needs of the time.

The work of investigation will no doubt prove difficult, and will require not only patient and accurate work, but the willing co-operation of a large number of individuals. But we believe that there is no body of men and women so well able to do this important work for their communities as the graduates of Atlanta University and similar institutions. They are scattered through all the principal cities of Georgia and the neighboring States; they are all in positions where they have special facilities for the gathering of valuable data, and their zeal and industry will more than compensate for any lack of scientific statistical training. No one of these graduates can prosecute this work alone. His investigation would necessarily be too limited to produce any accurate results. It is only by comparing and compiling data from many different sources that accuracy can be insured. Co-operation, therefore, is essential. Though the results accomplished by each individual may seem to him incomplete and insignificant, the combined results of all will prove of the utmost value.

A word of caution : Some of the information brought out by this investigation may prove very unpleasant for us to contemplate. It may seem as if much of our work for the last twenty-five years had been of no avail. We may be tempted to shut our eyes to the real facts, or to doubt their existence. But if we are to make any progress, we must have the courage to look unpleasant facts in the face. We are not attempting to prove or disprove any theory, but we are trying to get at the most unfavorable conditions affecting our communities, in order that we may improve those conditions. Accuracy is the first essential in an investigation as important as that upon which we have begun. It is well for us all to keep this in mind, that we may not be tempted by our previous theories or predilections to suppress or distort the information we are called upon to furnish. We need have no fear of the results. The past we cannot mend. It is the future we must look out for, and we need all the knowledge and informatiou we can gather for the solution of the difficult problems before us.

[Table Annexed. See page 9.]

TABLE NO. IX, ON "CAUSES OF DESTITUTION," FROM

"AMERICAN CHARITIES."

BY AMOS G. WARNER, PH. D.

COLORED.

Causes.	New York		Boston.		Baltimore.		New Haven.	
	NO.	PER CT.	NO.	PER CT.	NO.	PER CT.	NO.	PER CT.
Matters of Employment	19	35.18	24	17.39	96	29.62	9	30 00
Sickness	20	37 03	63	45.65	126	38.88	7	23.33
Drink	4	7.40	11	71.97	16	4.93	3	10.00
Shiftlessness and Inefficiency	3	5.55	6	4.34	21	6.48	1	3.33
All Causes	54	2.02	138	6.65	324	15.86	30	6.72

REPORTS FROM THE CITY OF WASHINGTON.

BY MR. GEORGE G. BRADFORD.

The following is a summary of reports received from the City of Washington. We are indebted to Mr. L. M. Hershaw of the class of '86, for a very complete report for blanks Nos. 1 and 2, and to the courtesy of Dr. W. Bruce Evans of Howard University, who at very short notice made up for us a small group of family budgets. The results of the investigations made by these two gentlemen, in their own city, may prove helpful to workers in other cities, and may also serve to show how far the blanks serve the purpose for which they were intended. Blanks Nos. 1 and 2 were to serve as an index to mark the progress of the community. Let us see, therefore, what Mr. Hershaw's reports, in these two blanks, show as to the progress which has been made in Washington during the last ten or fifteen years:

Taking first the death-rate, we see by blank No. 1 that the average death-rate among the colored people for the two five-year periods, 1878–1882 and 1888–1892, were respectively 37.12 per thousand and 32.8 per thousand, showing a smaller death-rate for the second period.

	WHITE.	COLORED.
Average 1878–1882.........	18.61	37.12
Average 1888–1892.........	19.19	32.08

Turning to blank No. 2, where we have the death-rate for the years 1880, 1890 and 1895, as well as the causes of death, we find the same result, namely a constantly decreasing death-rate:

	WHITE.	COLORED.
1880....................	17.6	35.5
1890....................	12.3	34.7
1895....................	15.8	28.1

The excess of colored over white is 103, 83 and 78 per cent.

Comparing the number of deaths for the series of years in each of the four groups into which the blank is divided, we

see a steady decrease in each group without exception, and
that in most instances it is a decrease both actually as to number of deaths, and relatively as compared with whites.

BLANK II.   CAUSES OF DEATH.   RATE PER THOUSAND.

	CROUP I,				GROUP II.	
	White.	Colored.	Excess of Colored.	White.	Colored.	Excess of Colored.
1880......39.5	101.6	157 per ct.	1890......21.6	65.7	204 per ct.
1890......33.4	86.3	158 per ct.	1895......16.8	56.3	250 per ct.
1895......28.9	63.4	119 per ct.			

	CROUP III.				GROUP IV.	
	White.	Colored.	Excess of Colored.	White.	Colored.	Excess of Colored.
1890......17.04	33.6		1880.....117.88		
1895......13.35	18.2	37 per ct.	1890.....117.00	161.5	
			1895.....100.06	143.6	43 per ct.

The conclusion we should come to is that there has been a
general and continued improvement in the condition among
the colored people in Washington during the last fifteen years.
The only exception to this shown by the blanks is found in
blank No. 1, under heading "Illegitimate colored births."
Comparing the averages for the two five-year periods given in
1878-1882 and 1888–1892, we find the number of illegitimate
births per thousand inhabitants to be 5.1 and 5.9, and the per
centage of total births to be 18.3 and 25, showing a slight increase for the second period in the actual number of such
births per thousand inhabitants, and quite a considerable increase in the proportion of such births to the total number of
births (colored), the figures being 18.3 per cent for the first
period, and 25 per cent for the second period.

So much, then, for the two blanks as a record of the progress of the community. Let us see how far they give us any
indication of the character of the population or of the causes
of some of the results to be noticed.

One very striking fact is to be noted in blank No. 1, bringing out in a most graphic way the peculiar and abnormal character of the population of Washington, both white and colored.
In comparing the death-rate and birth-rate, we find the death-
rate actually larger than the birth-rate; that is, more persons
die in Washington every year than are born there, and yet the

population is steadily increasing. This paradoxical state of things is due to the fact that Washington is our national capital and its population largely transient.

	1880.		1890.	
	WHITE.	COLORED.	WHITE.	COLORED.
Average death-rate	18.61	37.12	19.19	32.08
Average birth-rate	17.16	24.47	14.89	25.02
Excess in death-rate	1.45	9.65	4.30	7.06

But it is to be noticed that so far as these figures indicate, the colored population is becoming more permanent, while the white population is becoming more transient.

It would be interesting if that conclusion could be verified in any way.

For causes of the high mortality still prevailing among the colored people, we turn first to blank No. 2. Although considerable progress has been made in the last fifteen years, the death-rate among the colored people in 1895 was still 78 per cent greater than among the whites. Analyzing the causes of death, we see that the greatest excess is found in Group II, which includes the three causes of infant mortality. In 1895, the number of deaths from these three causes was 250 per cent greater among colored than among whites, and we find that there has been an increase in that respect since 1890, when the excess was only 204 per cent. We also find that the proportion of the whole number of deaths due to these three causes was greater in 1895 than in 1890, the figures being respectively 20 and 18.9 per cent.

We are able to show still more conclusively to what an extent the excessive death rate among the colored people is due to the great infant mortality, for we have for the five years 1888–1892 a report of the number of deaths under five years of age:

	1888–1892.		
	WHITE.	COLORED,	EXCESS COLORED.
Deaths under 5	5.7	15.0	163.0 per cent.
Deaths over 5	13.4	17.8	32.8 per cent.
Total deaths	19.1	32.8	

This shows that the rate of deaths of children under five years of age was 15 per thousand of population among colored, as against 5.7 among the whites, or nearly three times as many for the colored. This difference we may partly attribute to the more permanent character of the Negro population in Washington, and to the fact that there is consequently a larger proportion of children among them than among the whites, but there are other causes, some of which have to do with the social conditions prevailing in that community indicated by the exception to the general progress noted in an early part of this paper, viz: increase in illegitimate births.

Following the investigation made by Mr. Hershaw, through official records, we have that made by Dr. W. Bruce Evans, by the family budget method. This latter method is intended to give us an intimate knowledge of the conditions of life among the individual members of the community. Groups of families are selected representing a single neighborhood, trade or class in the community, and accurate information is obtained in regard to the families in each of these groups. By combining, comparing and classifying the information obtained from several groups, we are enabled to come to very accurate conclusions as to the most favorable as well as to the most unfavorable conditions affecting life in that community, and are thus able to determine on the most feasible measures of reform.

Dr. Evans has furnished us the information in regard to one group of twenty-one families, and although it is impossible for us to make from this one group any generalization in regard to the colored population of the City of Washington, a community of 86,000 persons, the information is very interesting as representing the generally well-to-do character of the twenty-one families represented.

The neighborhood in which they live is reported as being fair or good, and this is confirmed by the following figures deduced from the report, thus:

Thirteen of the twenty-one families own their own houses. The houses for the most part are supplied with modern conveniences, nineteen having city water, nine sewer connection, etc. The average number of rooms occupied by a family is between five and six, the smallest number being four, while over half have from six to eight.

The average number of persons occupying the same sleeping room is two, although in four instances there are four to a room, and in one instance, five.

There are only four cases of sickness reported, while twelve families report no sickness at all.

Only ten families report as to income, but the average for the ten is high, being $664 a year, and in seven families out of the ten the husband entirely supports the family by his sole labor. It is interesting to note the occupations of these seven men. The largest income is earned by a carpenter, who reports his earnings as $780 ; next comes a barber, earning $720 a year ; a teacher, earning $650; a janitor, $560 ; a laborer, $480 ; a steward, $390 ; and laborer, $250.

This matter of the occupations of city residents is one deserving a special line of inquiry, and it is hoped that some one will undertake to make a report on this subject at the next conference. The data obtained, by a continuation of the family budget investigation, will be found very useful for such a report.

The largest income of one family is that of a family of nine, the father and mother both dead, and the eldest brother and two sisters supporting the family. The brother is an expressman, earning $500 a year ; the two sisters are teachers, earning $450 each, making a total of $1,400 a year. This family owns its own house, having eight rooms, with city water, sewer connections and other conveniences. Five of the families report savings averaging $123.52 per family.

In concluding this report for the City of Washington, I wish to express regret that the very limited time within which the investigation had to be made should have prevented its being carried through on a more extensive scale, and I wish also to acknowledge once more the valuable assistance rendered by Mr. Hershaw and Dr. Evans.

REPORT FROM ATLANTA.

An attempt was made to fill out blank No. 2 from the records in Atlanta, but the data obtainable were not sufficiently
full or accurate for an extended report.

The following are the returns for the year 1890, figured on
the basis of the census population for that year. For purposes of comparison, the census figures for population are the
only reliable ones to use :

⁀1890.⁀

	WHITE.	COLORED.
Population	37,416	28,117
GROUP I.—Consumption and pneumonia, total	126.0	225.0
Rate per 10,000	33.7	80.0
Excess for colored		137.0 per cent.
GROUP II.—Cholera infantum, convulsions and still-born, total	123.0	230.0
Rate per 10,000	32.8	81.8
Excess for colored		149.0 per cent.
GROUP III.—Contagious diseases, total	90.0	78.0
Rate per 10,000	24.0	27.7
Excess for colored		15.0 per cent.
GROUP IV.—Other causes, total	369.0	374.0
Rate per 10,000	98.0	133.0
Excess for colored		35.0
Grand total	708.0	907.0
Rate per 10,000	489.0	322.0
Excess for colored		70.0 per cent.

In looking for causes for excessive death-rate among colored
people, we see at a glance by this table that the cause is not to
be found under heading of Group III, "Contagious diseases,"
as the excess there is only 15 per cent, as against 70 per cent
excess for total death-rate. We see that it cannot be found
under heading of Group IV, "Other causes," as excess there
is only 35 per cent. It must be found, therefore, among the

five diseases included under Groups I and II. Looking there we find that 50 per cent of all deaths are due to those five diseases. From consumption and pneumonia there were 225 deaths, or 24.8 per cent of the whole number. From the three children's diseases there were 230 deaths, or 25.4 per cent of the whole number, making for the two groups 50.2 per cent of the whole.

We also see that the excess under Gronp I was 137 per cent, and under Group II it was 149 per cent. These figures are sufficiently startling, but they are still more so when compared with the figures for 1880. The death-rate for consumption and pneumonia that year among the colored people was 60 in 10,000, being 19 per cent. of the whole number of deaths, and 91 per cent in excess of rate among whites. Comparing these figures with those for 1890, we see that the latter year shows a greater actual and relative death-rate from those diseases. The conclusion to be drawn from this comparison would be that consumption and pneumonia were on the increase among the colored people for the decade 1880–1890. The causes for that increase are to be sought by such investigations as that planned in blank No. 3, the "Family Budget," which are being made, and will furnish data for the next annual conference.

NEGLIGENCE A CAUSE OF MORTALITY.

BY H. R. BUTLER, M. D., ATLANTA.

For many years great questions have arisen concerning the colored people in this country, many of which, regardless of strong and powerful arguments to the contrary, have been beneficial to them.

It was once argued by some that the Negro had no soul, but after many hotly contested theological and anatomical discussions, it was finally agreed that since he resembled man so closely, he must therefore have something like a soul. Hence from that day, so far as man's admissions are concerned, we have had something like souls.

It was also declared that the Heavenly Father had made him to be forever a slave. But when England emancipated her slaves, and Toussaint L'Ouverture, by his own mighty arm, whipped the French and liberated his own people, and when the sainted and immortal Abraham Lincoln, by the stroke of his pen, gave freedom to the four millions of slaves then in this country, that proposition fell.

It was then announced that the Negroes were dying out and that soon the race would be gone. But only one generation has passed, and from four millions they number to-day nearly eight millions. It is therefore evident to us all that this proposition, too, has collapsed.

Now comes the charge that, while we are not dying out, we are dying faster than the white race. This proposition is true, and will stand until the conditions and causes which produce death more readily among us than among the whites are removed. I refer to those causes and conditions that have been so ably discussed here during this conference, such as poverty, ignorance, intemperance, etc., and among these negligence holds a prominent place.

We have already learned by this investigation what diseases cause more deaths among our people than among the whites.

We have found these to be pneumonia, convulsions, cholera infantum, and consumption. It has also been discovered that there are more still-born among our people than among the whites. But there are causes for these things—yes, more causes than the time alloted will allow me to discuss.

As convulsions and cholera infantum are largely caused by ignorance and poverty, and since these two diseases were discussed at some length under those causes, I will pass over them, pausing only long enough to say that it is true that hunger and the want of proper food, as well as the ignorance of how to prepare it, when to eat it and how to eat it, often cause convulsions, cholera infantum and other diseases of the alimentary canal.

As to still-births: Why should we be surprised at the great number of still-births among our women, since they do most of the work that is liable to produce this state of things? They do the cooking, the sweeping, the lifting of heavy pots; they carry the coal, the wood, the water; they carry heavy burdens on their heads; they do heavy washing, make beds, turn heavy mattresses, and climb the stairs several times during the day, while their more favored white sister is seated in her big arm-chair, and not allowed to move, even if she wanted to. In these things, my friends, you have the causes of the excess in this trouble.

The average colored laborer is exceedingly neglectful. He will drive or walk all day in the rain or snow, come home and go to bed with his wet clothes on, with the belief firmly fixed in his mind that unless he lets these clothes dry on him he will contract a cold, and no argument we might use will convince him otherwise. Again, since the colored people here compose the majority of the laboring classes, it stands to reason that they are more exposed than the whites, and are therefore more susceptible to those diseases that may be caused by exposure. The colored man sweeps the streets and fills his lungs with the dust and dried bacteria expectorated on the streets a few hours since from the lungs of some consumptive; he drives the garbage carts, he digs the sewers, drives hacks and drays, and in fact does most of the work involving exposure which naturally makes him more liable to contract such diseases as pleurisy, bronchitis, pneumonia and consumption.

It has been said by some that the Negro did not die with consumption until he became free, and that this new life brought also a new cause of death to him.

But this statement in itself is sufficient proof to me that in those dark days of slavery the colored people as a race, received little or no attention. Any case which calomel, bluemass or castor oil could not reach, was left to take its own course, with few exceptions. The main cause of their sickness was often neglected, and when death came it was simply a Negro gone—that was all. No record was left to show what the cause of death was, and there the matter was dropped. I believe, reasoning from what I see to-day relative to the causes that produce consumption, that there were more graves filled with the victims of that disease thirty years before the war closed than there have been for a similar period of time since. The only difference* is that now the deaths and their cause are recorded, and we know; then they were not recorded and we did not know.

Again, experience has taught me that most of the deaths due to consumption among our people were the result of consumption contracted, and not to congenital consumption, as our enemies invariably put it down.

The city has neglected and is still neglecting the colored people, and especially that class of them which is dependent upon its charity in times of sickness. It has millions to build prisons with, but not a dollar with which to build charitable institutions. It allows money grabbers to build small huts and crowd into them five times the number of people that should be allowed ; it has no law by which the owners of this property can be made to keep it clean. The houses are never painted, the wells are filled with the filth of the neighborhood and the fences are never white-washed, and the city is powerless to interfere. Family after family move into these places, and often only one or two are left to tell the story. My friends, it is one thing to stand here in this clean, well-lighted hall and read papers on this subject, but it is altogether different to go down into those dark, poor and humble homes and see death going through destroying the old and the young because of the negligence on the part of those in authority.

Some of the white physicians neglect the colored people. I wish it to be understood, however, that I mean some, not all, for there are some honorable exceptions to the statement just made. I say they neglect our people, and we cannot blame them. Doctors can no more afford to work for nothing than a teacher or any other person who is working for an honest living. Hence he refuses to go to these people ; first, because they are not able to pay, and secondly, because the city has appointed physicians whose duty it is to attend the poor in their various wards. These physicians are paid from $600 to $800 a year to do that work, and then they neglect it, especially such cases as diphtheria.

While this city has furnished physicians, it has furnished no medicine. It has no free dispensaries, as it should, nor does it pay the physician money enough to furnish medicines applicable in every case, and at the same time care for himself and family. Hence, when he is called to see a patient, it matters not what the disease may be, it is either compound cathartic pills, calomel, Epsom salts, blue-mass or castor oil. Any case these remedies don't reach is left to get well if it can or die if it must. I ask, then, in all candor : Is it any wonder that we die so fast when we get such good attention, doctors, such excellent nursing, such fresh medicines applicable in every case of our diseases?

Here in this city of push, pluck and Christian progress, there is not a decent hospital where colored people can be cared for. At the Grady Hospital, which takes about $20,000 of the city's money annually to run it, is a small wooden annex down by the kitchen, in which may be crowded fifty or sixty beds, and that is all the hospital advantages 40,000 colored citizens have. But, on the other hand, our white friends, with a population of about 70,000, have all the wards and private rooms in the entire brick building at this hospital, together with a very fine hospital here, known as St. Joseph's Infirmary. Hence, my friends, you can see that one of our greatest needs is a first-class up-to-date hospital, where the colored people can not only get proper treatment, but can also have all necessary operations performed. However, this excessive death-rate among us may be best for us. God moves in mysterious ways. He purged us in the burning fires of slavery for more than two hundred and fifty years, preparing us for the great responsibilities of freedom, and now who knows but what He is cleansing us with His fan of death, ridding us of the worthless elements of the race, and thus fitting us for that higher brighter and nobler citizenship which is yet to come? All we can do is to work, watch, pray and wait.

Again, the educated and the more highly favored of our people often neglect their own race. They neglect the poor, they will not support race enterprises, they fail to support their own business and professional men, and yet they want to pose as big men and leaders of their people. But, as I see it, that is not carrying out the idea of a truly educated person. Education does not mean that we must stop work, but it rather means that we must go to work with greater energy to help elevate our people along all lines, and thereby make them better citizens and better Christians. Neither does to graduate and get a diploma mean to separate us from our people, but it rather means to bind us closer to our race, our country and our God. It matters not whether we be preachers, teachers, lawyers, doctors, or whether we are engaged in business, we should remember that God has made us the pillar of cloud by day and the pillar of fire by night to lead our people, which we cannot do unless we keep near to them. I speak of these things because they have much to do with the health of the people. If we patronize race enterprises, if we patronize our preachers, teachers, lawyers, dentists and business men, it will increase our wealth, with which we can help the poor of our race; it will open other avenues of labor for our people, we will be able to build health resorts and hospitals for them, and do many other things beneficial to their health that we are not able to do now because we fail to support each other.

Taking all things into consideration, I don't think the death-rate of the colored race is so far in excess of the whites. Is it any wonder that we die faster than our white brother when he gets the first and best attention, while we are neglected on all sides? They have the best wards and treatment at the hospital, while we must take it second-hand or not at all; they have all the homes for the poor and the friendless, we have none; they have a home for fallen women, we have none; they have the public libraries where they can get and read books on hygiene and other subjects pertaining to health, we have no such privileges; they have the gymnasiums where they can go and develop themselves physically, we have not; they have all the parks where they and their children can go in the hot summer days and breathe the pure, cool air, but for fear we might catch a breath of that air and live, they put up large signs, which read thus: "For white people only"; they live in the best homes, while we live in humble ones; they live in the cleanest and healthiest parts of the city, while we live in the sickliest and filthiest parts of the city; the streets on which they live are cleaned once and twice a day, the streets on which we live are not cleaned once a month, and *some* not at all; besides, they have plenty of money with which they can get any physician they wish, any medicine they need, and travel for their health when necessary; all of these blessings we are deprived of. Now, my friends, in the face of all these disadvantages do you not think we are doing well to stay here as long as we do?

In conclusion, I would say that even to remove all the causes of death due to negligence will take ages. We may remove ignorance, we may remove intemperance, we may remove poverty and negligence, but in order to decrease this mortality among our people we must have our own physicians and a plenty of them, we must have parks and public baths, we must have free dispensaries, and we must have good hospitals, and until these things are accomplished very little headway will be made in reducing this excessive death-rate. It is the duty of every Christian citizen to see that these things are done.

INTEMPERANCE AS A CAUSE OF MORTALITY.

BY MRS. GEORGIA SWIFT KING ('74).

Alcohol sustains a double relation to disease and death, that of direct or immediate cause and that of indirect or remote cause, and the peculiar nature of this relation confines the writer on this subject to facts rather than to figures. To ascertain the truth concerning the relation of intemperance to mortality, it is necessary not only to enumerate the deaths due to acute alcoholism, such as delirium tremens and the various sudden congestions and paralyses consequent upon the taking of excessive quantities of strong drink, together with the great majority of homicides, suicides and accidental deaths, which may be traced directly to the use of alcoholics; but it is necessary also to inquire into the real causes of the deaths ascribed to the ordinary acute and chronic diseases, the contagious and infectious diseases, indeed, the whole category of classified diseases. There is a condition known as fatty degeneration, which the medical scientist recognizes not only as a distinct and formidable disease of itself, but because it renders the tissues unable to resist the ravages of other diseases, and because of its general distribution throughout the body, it is known to furnish for all diseases a most fruitful soil. Says Dr. Monroe of England, in his lecture on "The Physiological Action of Alcohol": "Alcoholic narcolization appears to produce this peculiar condition more than any other agent with which the medical scientist is acquainted," and quotes from Dr. Lees as saying "that alcohol should produce in the drinker fatty degeneration of the blood follows as a matter of course, since we have an agent that retains waste matter by lowering the nutritive and excretory functions, and a direct poisoner of the vesicals of the vital stream." Dr. Monroe continues: "This devitalization of the nutritive fluid is probably the first step to the devitalization of the tissue which it feeds," and credits Dr.

Chambers with the assertion: "Three-quarters of the chronic diseases which the medical man has to treat are occasioned by this disease." Fatty degeneration is evidently coextensive with the drink habit, whether excessive or moderate, appearing to follow as surely the glass of beer at dinner as the glass of strong drink three times a day. To this disease is due a very great majority of the sudden deaths of persons apparently in perfect health.

With reference to death from contagious and infectious diseases, it is the unanimous testimony of the leading authorities that during the scourges of cholera, yellow fever and smallpox, it is the drinker who falls victim, the moderate drinker being no exception to the rule, while the total abstainer is less liable to contract the disease, and if affected, is far more likely to survive. The fact holds good in such diseases as scarlet and typhoid fevers, when there is no known antidote to the specific poison, and the quality of the tissues is relied upon to resist or survive the disease.

Alcohol, as a remote cause of death, is none the less effective in cases in which the victim is not himself addicted to the use of strong drink, but inherits from drinking parents a weak constitution, which renders him an easy prey, an inviting field for disease. To inherited weakness is due a large per cent of the alarming rate of infant mortality resulting from cholera infantum, measles, scarlet fever, diphtheria, etc. Says our own Dr. Orme: "If it were possible to separate deaths due to alcohol, from the classified diseases to which they are ascribed, the facts would be astounding." Dr. Kellogg, at the head of the Battle Creek Sanitarium, the largest in the world, agrees with other great authorities that the brain, liver and kidneys are the organs having greatest affinity for alcohol, and that it is the disease of these organs and of the heart, of which alcohol is the most common cause; while in pneumonia, the ordinary febrile diseases, such as bilious and malarial fevers, as well as the infectious and contagious diseases, such as cholera, smallpox, yellow, scarlet and typhoid fevers, etc., the question often is, whether alcohol is the real cause, the occasion, or simply a great factor. Alcohol is mentioned among the causes of rheu-

matism and gout. It is one of the chief causes of insanity and
idiocy. Alcohol and its twin evil, tobacco, are very generally
responsible for paralysis and other diseases of the nervous
system. If we accept the unanimous testimony of the leading
medical scientists of the world, we can but conclude that intemperance is one of the chiefest, if not the chiefest, among
causes of mortality. The great Gladstone declares that intemperance has more victims than the three great scourges—
war, famine and pestilence—combined.

That intemperance is one of the principal factors in the terrible death-rate among the Negro population in the cities,
there can be no question. It is in the cities that intemperance
prevails. I believe that no one at all informed would hesitate
to assert that ninety-nine per cent of the city population are
addicted to some extent to the use of strong drink. No one
will deny that the Negro is no exception to this rule. It is
well known that that class of the Negro population which furnishes the excessive death-rate is that class most addicted to
the use of whiskey and beer in their vilest forms. It is this
ignorant, drunken class of Negroes which furnish ninety per
cent of the criminals which crowd our jails and penitentiaries,
and who, poorly clad and fed, exposed to great extremes of
heat and cold, working rain or shine at most laborious tasks,
while serving terms in the chain-gangs, contract diseases and
die by hundreds annually. Those who live to be released
flock to the cities to finish their remaining weeks or months,
and add their quota to the death-rate. If this were the end
alone of men and women, old and hardened criminals, it
would not be so serious, but this is the end of hundreds of
boys and girls arrested for misdemeanors.

How long shall our poor and untaught children, tempted
on every corner by the cigarette seller, the beer shop and the
brothel, be arrested and placed in the chain-gangs with hardened criminals, to be steeped in iniquity and schooled in
crime, and hastened to death of body and soul? What can
we do to lessen this enormous death-rate? I answer, remove
the causes, chief among which is intemperance. And among
the causes which lead to intemperance is the use of tobacco,

and innutritious and poorly cooked food. A volume might be written on the responsibility of the teacher, the preacher and the physician with relation to this subject. It is a fact that the conscientious up-to-date physician seldom or never prescribes alcoholics. The preacher or teacher who suffers himself or those whom he serves to be uninformed on this vital question is recreant to his highest trust. Let Georgia lessen the death-rate among the Negro population by establishing at once a reformatory for juvenile offenders.

I beg your aid in the attempt to secure the pledge of the representatives of the approaching legislature to enact a law providing a State reformatory.

POVERTY AS A CAUSE OF MORTALITY.

BY MRS. ROSA MOREHEAD BASS ('80).

Slavery left the colored man the rich inheritance of a log cabin and patch of turnip greens. This log cabin is a piece of architecture that will soon be entirely relegated to the barbarous past. Peace be to its ashes! It has disappeared in the towns and cities, and is found only in the poverty-stricken rural districts. Cannot you recall the picture of that poor family who worked hard all day in the field while their little ones, almost nude, played around the door until the sun dropped behind that hill studded with beautiful trees? See the mother return and prepare her evening meal; the fire is lighted, the children, hungry and crying; behold the repast—fried bacon, poorly-cooked bread, and black molasses. A pine torch illumines the room that serves as a kitchen, dining-room, bed and bath-room. After supper the little ones are off to bed without being properly bathed and dressed, and after the usual chair-nap, the father and mother retire. There they are all in a row, and only one small window and door to let in nature's life-giving air that keeps them from suffocating. The out-door work, good water and a plenty of latitude curtail the rural death-rate, but the pine torch has ruined so many eyes. Now let us pass hastily the sparkling spring of cool water, the rosy-cheeked peach and apple, the browsing cow in meadows green and fair, the brawny-armed farmer, humming his mournful song, and visit an alley in our city whose church spires point heavenward, and whose inhabitants boast of being the most cultured people of the South. I say pause a moment and look down that alley, and near that branch of stagnant water, and see that long row of tenement houses, poorly built—out of old lumber, that has never been disinfected—and not even plastered. The inmates are poorly clad, poorly fed, and, strange to say, the poorer they are, the more filthy we find them. Disease and death are rivals. Whenever an epidemic of smallpox and fever visit us, they find these unfortunates their favored victims. Their poverty maddens their brain, and they strew disease and death in their pathway.

Summer is their favorite season, and the death-rate is somewhat diminished, but when the autumn days come, "the saddest of the year," the wailing winds their open houses invade and the majestic king of winter carpets the earth, and the poor shiver from want of clothes, food and fire, and the grim monster claims them as his favorite subjects. Their poverty rendered them unable to prepare like the wise ant, and when they become ill they have neither friends nor money, and actually die from the want of attention, medical, physical and spiritual.

We find great mortality among the children of the poor. Even before they can make their wants known, the mother is compelled to leave them daily, and a surprising number are burned to death. The older children are taught to go out and pick up trash to burn, rags, bones and iron to sell, thereby inviting disease and death. It is a strange fact, yet true, that all work that is obnoxious, dangerous and laborious is given the poor Negro at pay that would kill some people even to think of having it to do for a living. These people in buying food, etc., always seek *quantity* and not *quality;* hence the butcher, fisherman, fruiterer, dairyman and merchant are careful to anticipate their wants. (The health officer is occasionally heard of when the rich are imposed upon.) The manner in which they live breeds discontent, hatred and envy, and consequently they fight, kill each other, and rob and murder the more fortunate. Their misery is one of the devil's workshops, and they are his tools.

The coffers of the landlord are being filled with the blood of his neighbor, and not until the crowded alleys are consigned to the log-cabin era will health and life take an onward march, and as the X rays of the Atlanta University are turned on, will cleanliness, thrift, industry, happiness and hygienic living add their quota to the life-rate; and last, but not least, not until the whole Christian world plays her part in the Samaritan drama, will the life-rate in Heaven be increased, and the death-rate on earth diminished!

IGNORANCE AS A CAUSE OF MORTALITY.

BY PROF. W. B. MATTHEWS ('90).

Among the many causes which produce death in our large cities, it is by no means an easy matter to distinguish between ignorance, poverty and negligence. However, it is safe to assert that no few of the deaths which occur in our large cities are the result of ignorance, either directly or indirectly.

It will be seen from the outset that city life requires a more accurate observance of the laws of health than country or village life. With this fact in mind, all cities have established their boards of health to look after and remove any and all causes which in their minds might produce sickness or death. These boards are usually composed of the best informed physicians who, from time to time, make and publish rules which are to be observed and obeyed by all the citizens. These rules the ignorant classes do not obey, not because they are willfully disobedient, but because they are ignorant. They cannot read, they have no interest in public affairs; they know but little about the causes which bring sickness and disease among them, and hence are the easy prey of epidemics and contagions.

As to the laws of hygiene, they are generally ignored because they are unknown, but this does not excuse. The laws of nature and of health are as unvarying in the case of the ignorant as in the case of the intelligent. The violation of certain rules governing the health of our bodies brings the same results to all men alike. Our aim will be to show that the ignorant violate the rules of health, and are therefore more frequently the victims of disease and death.

Many suffer on account of improper ventilation, not knowing that impure air is the parent of every lung trouble known to the human family. Pure air is one of the freest and best gifts bestowed upon man by our beneficent Father; but alas! how many thousands in our large cities die every year from failing to use this gift! Men and women, through ignorance, shut the doors and windows to their houses, thus barring out God's life-giving atmosphere, and inviting consumption and death. Pure air gives life, foul air brings death.

Thousands of men, women and children are sick and dying in the slums of our large cities from liver and kidney troubles. These troubles have come to them because the proper care has not been taken of the skin. Would it be true to say that through ignorance of the true functions of the pores in our bodies, and their relation to good health, certain classes of people fail to keep their bodies clean and the pores of the skin open? Whoever closes these millions of doors, the inlets of life and outlets of death, will sooner or later succumb to the pangs of disease, for by so doing they shut out life and let in death.

But what of appetite, and what people are less liable to control their appetites? Are not the most ignorant? The glutton, through ignorance of the evil result of his intemperate habit, overloads his stomach and impairs its capacity to properly discharge its functions, thereby inducing many diseases which shorten life.

With the light that we have on the evil effects of alcohol upon the system, it would scarcely be permissible to say that men who take it are ignorant of its destructive elements. Yet I venture the assertion that there are many among the ignorant classes of our large cities who are entirely unconscious of the fact that the indulgence of the appetite for strong drink shortens life and cuts off the days of their posterity.

Thus we see, looking at the matter briefly from a hygienic point of view, that the body may be kept in a healthy state by obedience to the laws of health, but when they are neglected, the inevitable result is disease and death. Can men ignorant of such laws live in accordance therewith, or avoid the consequences of their disobedience?

Turning from the persons to the locality in which they live, we may find many things which will have the same effect upon health as the failure to obey hygienic laws. It must be admitted that a filthy home, unclean bedding and wearing apparel, not changed at proper intervals, are as productive of disease and death as any other cause. As a general rule, ignorant people live together in very thickly populated communities. Such communities are usually freighted with impure air, and the germs of disease are in the very water which they drink. Not knowing how much damage filth and impure water can do to health and life, the ignorant flock to these communities, sicken and die, and never inquire into the cause. In such places, water containing foreign matter from soiled clothes, slops, etc., is thrown indiscriminately at the back door, front door or under the bed-room window, and nothing more is thought of it. People who know the results of such acts of indiscretion do not often commit them. Disobedience to the laws of hygiene brings a curse with every broken law. The body is weakened, the human system impaired, and finally death seizes its victims. No person can live in accordance with laws of which he is ignorant. Knowing that many all around us are ignorant of the proper care and use of their bodies, is it a matter at which we should wonder when we note the daily deaths that are caused from impure air, unclean bodies, unwholesome food, excessive appetites and ungoverned passions? These are the fruits of ignorance which are to be found in our large cities, and they bring death to no small number. A filthy house, an unclean yard, a soiled bed, all invite disease; they are harbingers of death. Those persons who keep such homes cannot themselves keep well; their children cannot be well born, and all who accept such surroundings do so because they are ignorant of the effect upon themselves and their posterity. To learn and obey the laws of health, to understand and observe the rules of sanitation, men must be intelligent.

GENERAL CONDITIONS OF MORTALITY.

BY MISS LUCY LANEY ('73).

"Birds of a feather flock together." In Augusta, as in most cities of America, there are parts of the city occupied exclusively by Negroes, except a few whites, usually German or Irish, keepers of small stores, who live among the Negroes for the sake of their trade. Although some do not believe it, yet it is true that there are grades of society among Negroes, as among other races, and the lines of distinction are drawn for as wise and as silly reasons as are those among the more favored people. As in other things, this grading is seen in the choosing of a locality for a home. The poorest, most untidy and the most ignorant seek each other. They always find homes in the same neighborhood, if not in adjoining houses. As each city has its Negro settlements, and as the great rank and file of the race belong to the grade or class called the poorest and most ignorant, of this kind are the largest settlements. These people have small wages, many with nothing to do a great part of the year, and the majority have no steady employment. For food, rent, fuel and clothing they are dependent upon the odd jobs that pay not more than fifty cents per day for two or three days in a week. To eke out a living on such an income requires, they know, the strictest economy, but how to economize they know not, yet thinking they know, in their way they set about it. The first step is to cut down the expense of living by taking no more house room than barely enough in which to turn around. A small family, parents and two or three children, take one room. The landlord will not agree to have this cleaned before they move in, although it has not been cleaned or repaired in a score of years, and during that time as many different families, with each a different disease, have lived in it. The tenant can't afford to have it cleaned, so he contents himself by sweeping the floor before his household goods are brought in. The truth is, he does not see the importance of having the house thoroughly cleaned before occ ipying it, and if the rent is cheap he does not parley, but p ays the installment and takes possession.

In this room, 15x15, sometimes smaller space, are placed a bedstead, a three-quarters bed, sometimes two (but in these days of cheap furniture and installment sales, a folding lounge very often takes the place of the second bedstead), one or two tables, a trunk, bureau, not less than four chairs, tubs, boards, etc. for laundrying, cooking utensils, and a lot of odds and ends. These, with the family, give breathing space scarcely sufficient for one, yet by some means it is hoped to get enough for the whole family. It is not long before hypostatic pneumonia or tuberculosis visits them, and finding the atmosphere congenial, abides with the family.

It may be that the work of the mother of the family requires that she be away from the home all day. Leaving at 6 a. m., without giving any care to the house or children, she returns at 8 or 9 o'clock at night. The children are asleep, in the street, or at some neighbor's, where they have been all day. The tired mother, after a few words, goes to bed. She awakes next day only to carry out the same program. Perhaps there are no children; then the uncleaned house is securely fastened. Perhaps once in several months, time is spared for house cleaning, or it may be put off till moving day.

A family in which the father has steady employment at fifty or seventy-five cents per day, and the mother and girls are doing the washing of one or two families, numbering six or seven persons each, bed and table linen included, for 75 cents to $1.25 per week, furnishing the soap, starch and fuel for the same, rents a house of two or three rooms. Yet the above wages will give but scanty living for parents, five or six children and grandmother. Rent, fuel, food, clothing, books for the children if they are in school, the minister's salary, and the assessment for the new church building, and during the summer an excursion—all of these must be paid for out of the wages of the family. Inferior material for clothing, if stores that deal in second-hand apparel are not patronized, most inferior food, the most dilapidated houses must be used.

Another class, there is, some of whom from choice are idle,

others, from inability to obtain work, have no visible means of support. These manage, by living in groups something after the Italian manner, to exist. Four to six occupy one room, in which there is little or no furniture. One or two meals a week, with a little food here and there, serve to sustain life and nourish disease, moral and physical. There is another class more noble than those mentioned. It is composed of persons anxious to own a home, and although they receive but scanty wages, they are not easily discouraged and go to work determined to own some land. Of course, they must buy the cheapest land and on the easiest terms—the low places surrounded by ponds outside the city limits, in the city beyond the extension of the sewers and other sanitary arrangements, places where you can see the miasma rise and touch it, as it were, with your hands. The houses put up are but apologies for houses. The people of these localities spend a good portion of the fall fighting the chills and the fever, till alas! poor, earnest, honest, simple folk, when they think their systems are enured to exposure and malaria, disease has laid fast hold upon them.

Another class, who have learned something of cleanliness and hygiene, are forced by their poverty, for the sake of cheap rents, to live in most sickly and unclean neighborhoods, with but scanty food and no money for medicines or nourishment when they are sick, which is quite often.

There is yet another class who, by their perseverance, intelligence and economy, have made for themselves better houses, comfortable homes in healthy localities; these see hearts ache with alarm at the devastation that is being made, but how to stop it is to them the unsolved problem of their race.

College settlements they cannot have, for the mighty lever of modern civilization, money, is wanting to them. The planting of factories, shops, etc., to furnish employment is for the same cause, at this time, to them an impossibility.

That the moving spirit of these meetings may be a Moses come to lead out of the wilderness is greatly to be hoped. That from these meetings may be evolved plans that will bring some relief, is the prayer and aim of all concerned.

INFANT MORTALITY.

BY FRANK S. CHURCHILL, M. D., CHICAGO.

The late Oliver Wendell Holmes said that the treatment of a patient ought to begin with the treatment of his ancestors three generations preceding, and the practicing physician is constantly and daily reminded of the truth of this observation, so often does he see the influence of heredity, and in many instances, alas! the sins of the fathers visited upon the children of the third and fourth generations.

But while it is of course impossible for us wholly to undo what has been done, wholly to eradicate from ourselves what of evil has come down to us from our ancestors, yet we can do much, by careful and temperate living, to counteract any such weaknesses, and thereby contribute, in a considerable degree, to the health and happiness of our offspring. It is the future of humanity that we must attemp to benefit, and this we can best do by regulating our own lives and those of our children, recognizing the weak points which we must combat, and cultivating to a still higher degree the traits of virtue which, fortunately, have also come down to us through the ages. And I propose to suggest briefly in this paper a few of the, to me, important points in the treatment and management of our children, careful observance of which will, I believe, tend to reduce the mortality among them, to promote in them a physical condition of good health, and thus render the task of a higher moral, mental and social life more easy of accomplishment.

In considering the subject, I shall ask your attention to a discussion of the child from the momeut of birth; for, while we might well begin with a consideration of the management of a pregnant woman, yet that is a subject too vast to be considered in a paper of this length and kind. Suffice it to say, that from the earliest moment pregnancy is suspected, a woman should place herself at once under the charge of a competent physician, placing upon him the responsibility of directing fully the period of gestation. The child, once launched into what is for most of us a life of struggle and work, is at the point where we may discuss his career. What are we to do with him? How guide him and fit him for the battle of life, that he may make the most of himself, and contribute his mite towards the improvement of the world and the evolution of the race?

The first point upon which I would insist is that his entry into the world shall be accomplished with all the care possible, exerted by a careful, conscientious and thoroughly-trained doctor. It is a most unfortunate and common practice among the poor and ignorant to employ midwives to attend their women in labor; they seem not to realize the great danger to themselves and their children, of having for attendance at such a time women wholly ignorant of human anatomy and physiology, totally untrained in habits of care and cleanliness, utterly unfit for the work they presume to do. I cannot too strongly insist upon the great danger arising from this practice of employing midwives, and would urge upon each and every one of you, whose work leads you in any way among the poor and ignorant, to warn them against this practice, and urge them to seek proper medical aid and assistance. By so doing you will do much towards decreasing the mortality among the new-born and insuring a better state of health and vigor among the mothers.

Improvement in this direction is the more easily accomplished on account of the numerous hospitals and dispensaries now found in all cities. It is safe to say that, as a general thing, the best physicians of the city will be found on the staffs of these hospitals; medical aid and advice are invariably free; with one or more of them is generally connected an obstetrical department, and by merely applying at these institutions, a woman can be attended, either at the hospital or at her home, during labor and convalescence, by a physician properly prepared, by a long course of study, to do thoroughly scientific obstetrical work.

I would then suggest to you that in all cases possible you urge these people to seek such institutions, and thus free themselves from the great dangers inevitably arising from attendance by a midwife. It seems to me a practicable way of saving life among the new-born and preserving health and strength among mothers.

The high rate of mortality among infants is a subject well worthy the consideration of all thoughtful men and women, and naturally leads one to enquire as to causes and possible remedies. Prominent among the causes of this high rate must be mentioned bad heredity and injudicious and harmful management of these little ones by their parents. As a result of these two causes, many children are ill-prepared to meet and battle with the acute diseases almost inevitably before them ; they are more apt to contract disease than a healthier child ; they are more apt to die from it, when once contracted, as their resisting power is weakened by their heredity and their management since birth.

Now what is the remedy? What can we do to counteract hereditary weakness? How manage our children so as to give them the best health and greatest resisting power possible? While the most successful solution of these problems necessitates the assistance of a trained physician, yet much aid can be furnished by the parents, and indeed without their constant and hearty co-operation, little can be done by their medical adviser. The general directions as to details must be given by the doctor ; the patient, daily, hourly, minutely execution of these details must devolve upon the parents. What, then, are the practical steps to be taken? you will ask. First, as to the question of heredity. Humanity is not perfect ; we all of us, even though we do not admit it, are conscious of certain defects in our own characters—physical, mental or moral. The tendency towards these defects we transmit to our own children, and though by care and wise management the growth of these defects may be held in check, or they may not even be apparent, or may exist only as a blemish, yet let us not blind ourselves to the fact that the *seed* is there, and that without keen watchfulness on our part it may grow and develop into the glaring defect which we seek to avoid. Tell your physician of the weakness there may be in yourself, of the hereditary taint which may exist, actively or passively, that you may have his help in the training of your child, his assistance in fighting the weak points, and developing the strong traits which fortunately also exist, hereditary and self-developed.

For example, to particularize, take the well-known disease of consumption. You yourself may be free from it, your parents or some members of your family may have been or may now be afflicted with it. Tell your doctor of this fact, show him your infant or child, that he may examine him thoroughly, that in the future, in illness or in health, he may be constantly on the lookout for signs which may escape your notice, not through carelessness on your part, but merely because it is not the business of your life to be looking for these signs. Consumption is not, of course, the only disease or defect which may exist in us; there may be a weak heart, a week stomach, weak bowels, weak kidneys, weak brain, weak nerves. By frankly facing such facts, and by care and watchfulness such as I have mentioned, we may do much either to strengthen the weak point, or often to crush out the bad seed altogether.

Nor do I hesitate to speak thus to you who must be considered the van guard of humanity, when you may think that this paper has to do with mortality among the infants of our less fortunate brethren.

There is so much in these thoughts that you and I, each and every one of us, can take home to himself and herself; we are all human, and though in the course of ages, by the process of evolution, we have arrived at the top of the animal scale, we are not yet perfect, and *must* transmit to our descendants our vices as well as our virtues. And I would suggest that you urge upon those needing your help, as I have sought to urge upon you, the importance of early and constant attention to the points mentioned above. Do not be discouraged by thinking that these poor helpless infants cannot have the medical aid and advice which I suggest. *They can.* It is in the cities that the most of this work can be done. And as I have already

said, it is in the cities that such advice and aid can be had at
the hospitals and dispensaries. So, if the necessity arise, if
their children be not thriving, urge them to seek these institutions where, I am sure, much good will be done them.

Much that has been said in the discussion of heredity of
course applies in speaking of the management and training of
infants, but a few more points seem to me to be of importance.
When shall we begin the active training of infants? To this
question I would answer most emphatically, at the moment of
birth. This, perchance, will cause you to smile. What, discipline a baby just born! How? The whole question is
summed up in a nut-shell in the three words, regularity of
habit. Come with me on my daily rounds, and see how quickly
and easily that small bundle of humanity becomes the tyrant
of the household; many of you, perchance, realize this in your
own families. It is all the more lamentable, because it can be
prevented. Fortunately, the moral and physical are so intimately blended in the young human animal that the training
of the one unconsciously involves the training of the other.
The new-born babe does nothing but eat, sleep and cry; at
least manage it that he shall eat with regularity, at stated
times, as you do yourselves, but of course oftener, and his
other occupations will regulate themselves; he will sleep
properly and regularly, and if healthy will cry but little.
Fixed, regular habits of thought and action in our own daily
lives are of an importance too well known to need more than
a passing mention. They are of equal importance in infancy
and childhood, but unfortunately this fact is rarely appreciated, and we cannot begin too early to start the young life in
habits of regularity, which once applied in the first weeks, in
the only way possible, i. e. in the matter of food and sleep,
will gradually extend themselves in other directions with the
growth and development of the child, and will do much to
strengthen and bring out a well-rounded and well-disciplined
character.

The quality and character of an infant's food has, of course,
much to do with his physical, and therefore with his nervous
condition, and though this question is one to be settled by the

doctor, yet a few words on the subject may be of interest. The natural and best food for an infant during its first year of life is, of course, its own mother's milk, if that be a good milk. If for any reason the infant cannot have such, what he shall have must be determined by a doctor. But I cannot refrain from warning all of you, and would urge you in turn to warn all others, mothers especially, against all the well-known patent baby foods. They have all been examined by educated men, and it has been found that none are good food for babies; some are too rich and make the baby sick; most are not rich enough, and so the baby's bones and flesh do not grow hard enough. No well-educated doctor will to-day advise you to use them. But he will show you how to make cows' milk just like mothers' milk, and that is the food which infants should have when they can't have mother's milk.

One more point on the food question, one which you do not need yourselves, but one as to a common practice among the ignorant, viz., tea and coffee. No infant, no child till he is eighteen years old ought to touch tea and coffee; they are bad for the stomach, bad for the nerves, and make infants and children cross and fretful. You will have opportunity to do much good by discouraging their use among the young. The same is true about beer and all forms of alcoholic drinks.

All that I have hitherto said has been in the way of suggestions to *prevent* sickness, to keep the infant strong and healthy. When an acute sickness, like scarlet fever, measles, or "summer complaint," actually comes, the infant must, of course, be carefully treated by a doctor. Much help in these cases is derived from a trained nurse, if one is to be had. As is well known, in many of our large cities there are charitable organizations, which will send to the sick poor, nurses who have by hard and long study fitted themselves to do this scientific work. In my practice in Chicago, these nurses have been of the greatest help, and many lives have been saved by their devotion and careful work. They can generally be had by going to some hospital or dispensary.

I have, ladies and gentlemen, thus very briefly attempted to suggest to you some of the actual practical steps which it is possible for you, even though not physicians, to take to reduce the mortality among and improve the physical condition of our infants and children. The work of elevating and ennobling the human race is a grand and inspiring one. Much has already been and is constantly being done among adults and youths; much, it seems to me, can be done by careful and intelligent work in infancy and early childhood. It is then that mind and body are in the most pliable and receptive condition, and that good seed, carefully sown, is most apt to bear fruit, and while I am far from deprecating the good and noble work done among adults, and would bid those engaged in it God-speed, yet I cannot help thinking that even greater good and greater strides forward will be made by the race, if we begin at the earliest possible moment to train the young human animal in the way he should go. His moral condition is greatly influenced by his nervous condition, which in turn is dependent on his general physical well-being. Hence, I have thought it important to dwell on those points which will tend to promote a condition of good health, believing that thereby the moral and social elevation of the individual and so of the race will be the more easily accomplished.

What I have said applies with equal force to the poor and ignorant of all kinds and conditions of men. I make no distinction as to race or color. But each of us is more apt to be influenced by those of his own race and kindred, and who better than yourselves, graduates of Atlanta University, are better fitted to help in the elevation of the poor and ignorant of your own race? I know of none, and would urge upon each and every one of you the duty you owe to your race and to humanity, and bid you do what you may in the common evolution and elevation of the human family. Especially to those of you who purpose taking up the "City Problem Investigation," now the subject of discussion before this conference, will there be a rare opportunity to do much for the physical improvement of the helpless infants coming in contact with your own lives.

REMARKS OF BISHOP L. H. HOLSEY.

I did not expect to say anything to-night, but came to hear what was going to be said. I am intensely a race man, and I am intensely humanitarian. I am a race man because I believe our race needs attention ; I am a humanitarian because I want to do good to all people. I am a part of the old and the new, and I know about both.

There is one idea that strikes me strongly. It is how the colored man is dying out. One of the chief causes is that he is in a state of transition. He has passed out of one state into another. He must get adapted to a climate which he is not used to. In olden times the men lived in barn houses, and they always had air. The colored man also slept out of doors, with the ground for his bed and the heavens for his cover, and hence he had fresh air. Take this colored race, keep them in close houses. They do not know anything about hygiene ; they crowd and pack things under the beds and hang things behind the doors, and if nothing disturbs them they will stay there from generation to generation. What is the remedy ? You will say that this is the remedy and that is the remedy, but there is but one great remedy—that of education. They do not need any of these fashion fandangles, These people knew nothing of the study of science, but they had religion, because they didn't have time and sense enough to have anything else.

Some one said to-night that they did not keep any record of the death of slaves. But my master kept a good record. A physician was paid annually to see to the slaves. There are a great many people now that die for want of something to eat. The doctor says he must not touch this thing and must not touch the other thing, but if he get anything to eat he will get up and work. Many of the colored people die of starvation. They say the colored people are dying with consumption. I have seen black men die of consumption, but when I traced them down, I have found that there was white blood in them. I have never known of a full-blooded Negro dying of consumption. I, however, heard of a white man who had consumption, and he had a Negro boy, and the boy died with consumption. He afterwards hired another Negro boy, and the man and this boy also died with consumption. Both boys' grandmothers had white blood in their veins.

It has been said that there is not as much intemperance in the country as there is in the city. In the city they drink every night, but in the country they drink all day Saturday and all day Sunday. They drink more in these two days than the others drink all the week. The father, mother and all the children drink. Once while I was in the country the preacher was too drunk to preach the sermon. They wanted me to read the sermon, but I said I would not. I really believe that there is as much intemperance in the country as in the city.

I want to say that my heart is in this work. I hope that you will find out remedies for these evils. We must teach our people to begin to think about these things, and to learn the laws of hygiene.

LETTER FROM PROFESSOR EDWD. CUMMINGS OF HARVARD UNIVERSITY.

Permit me to express my interest in the contributions which graduates of Atlanta University are making to the vital statistics of city life. Such inquiries are everywhere commanding the attention of sociological students, and it is a gratifying tribute to the spirit of your University that her students are so prompt in entering this field. It is in cities that the great problems of life and labor press most earnestly for solution, and anything which throws light upon the commonplace but obscure conditions of every-day life, must help us better to understand the progress which has been made and the evils which have still to be overcome. The home is the unit of our civilization; it is the nursery of social virtues, the source from which must flow those regenerating moral influences which help society at large to realize that ideal of fraternity which has always been the goal of civilization. Whatever strikes at the integrity of the home, strikes at the integrity of our civilization. Whatever ministers to the health and beauty of family life, tends to sweeten the fountains of our social life. Sound economic and sanitary conditions are the only environment in which social virtues may thrive. Industry, economy, cleanliness, plain living and high thinking are the source no less of individual happiness than of social welfare.

It is especially gratifying to observe the promptness with which the recent call for information has been met in the city of Atlanta. If the same spirit of enterprise and co-operation can be relied upon to carry on the work in other places, there is every reason to hope that these investigations may prove not only a valuable contribution to our knowledge of the progress which has been made, but an incentive and a guide to future effort. All who are interested in our common welfare will await with interest the results of these investigations by men and women who are so well acquainted with the conditions and so well equipped for the work. I shall consider it a privilege to be of assistance in any way I that can.

LETTER FROM MR. R. R. WRIGHT, PRESIDENT OF GEORGIA STATE INDUSTRIAL COLLEGE.

I am unable to express to you my regret at not being able to be present with you and those interested in the "City Problem Investigation" in your first conference at Atlanta University.   *   *   *   *   *   *
For a number of years I have thought that the greatest danger to the real progress of the colored people lies in this sociological condition in the large cities.   It is difficult, however, to get the facts.   There is very little attention given in the South to the vital statistics of Negroes.   In fact the census is neither full nor altogether reliable.   The facts, if gotten at all, must be searched out by conscientious persons specially interested in this kind of work.   Nevertheless, any one who will give the least observation to this matter will see that the cities are the hot beds of crime, misery and death among the colored people.   Here the people are huddled together, with often two or three families in one room.   Without employment for more than half the time, they are consequently insufficiently fed and poorly clothed.   When sick they are unable either to employ a physician or to buy medicine.   At least twenty-five per cent of them die without medical aid.   In the city of Savannah, during the year 1894, 251 colored persons died without medical attention.   This is $33\frac{1}{3}$ per cent of the total number of deaths among these people for that year.   About 60 per cent of this number of deaths were children under the age of ten.   Twenty-four thousand of the 52,000 population of Savannah are Negroes.   Hence it will be seen that whatever affects these people, affects at least nearly half the population of our chief seaport.   What is true of Savannah, I judge to be approximately true of all the cities of Georgia and of most of the cities of the South.

The city colored people drift into crime because they are idle and hungry far oftener than because they are purposely vicious. All cities furnish far too large a proportion ot crime, ignorance and misery of the colored people.

Any movement, therefore, that will bring to light the facts, lay bare the causes, and suggest the remedies in relation to this crime, misery and death which affects our people in the cities, will merit universal applause.

LETTER FROM GEORGE W. CABLE TO BUTLER R. WILSON, ESQ.

Your letter of May 8, which has gone long unanswered for reasons too tedious to recount to you, reminds me pleasantly of our earlier acquaintance.

The blanks and circulars of which it speaks, and which are now before me, did not reach me promptly. I think very highly of your undertaking to get accurate information of the sociological conditions of the Negro race in America. I hope you may gather a strong body of men so selected as to guarantee by their personal reputation the authenticity of whatever is put forth. It seems to me, from the highest, broadest, most patriotic and cosmopolitan point of view, to be one of the best enterprises that could be undertaken at this time.

RESOLUTIONS OF THE CONFERENCE.

Resolved, That the papers presented by the graduates of the Atlanta University and others show an alarming increase in the death-rate of the Negro population of cities and large towns, from such diseases as consumption and pneumonia, due in a great degree to ignorance, poverty, negligence and intemperance.

Resolved, That the investigations thus far made show the necessity for continuing the search for exact data on a larger scale, with a view to ascertaining more definitely the causes and seeking out and applying remedies for existing conditions.

Resolved, That the corresponding secretary and executive committee of this conference be and are hereby instructed to continue the investigations on these and other lines pertaining to the welfare of the Negro population in cities, and invite the hearty co-operation of all the graduates of the Atlanta University, and of others interested in the investigation and solution of city problems.

The following also participated in the general discussions : Butler R. Wilson, Esq. ('81) of Boston, Mass.; Mr. F. H. Henderson ('79) of Cuthbert; Rev. G. W. F. Phillips ('76) of Marshallville; Mr. George A. Towns ('94) of Atlanta; Professor Thomas N. Chase of Atlanta; and Rev. T. G. Hazel of Charleston, S. C.

ATLANTA UNIVERSITY PUBLICATIONS,
No. 2.

SOCIAL AND PHYSICAL CONDITION OF NEGROES IN CITIES.

REPORT OF AN INVESTIGATION UNDER THE
DIRECTION OF ATLANTA UNIVERSITY:

AND

PROCEEDINGS OF THE SECOND CONFERENCE FOR THE
STUDY OF PROBLEMS CONCERNING NEGRO CITY LIFE,
HELD AT
ATLANTA UNIVERSITY, MAY 25–26, 1897.

ATLANTA, GA.
ATLANTA UNIVERSITY PRESS,
1897.

CONTENTS.

INTRODUCTION.

The papers presented in this report were written exclusively by colored men and women, and are based upon statistical investigations made by them under the direction of Atlanta University.

The investigation was begun by an inquiry on the part of three graduates of Atlanta University into the causes of the excessive mortality among Negroes. A conference was held on the subject at Atlanta University in May, 1896, and the facts brought out at that conference were so significant that the investigation was continued for another year along similar lines, but on a more extensive scale, and a second conference was held in May, this year. The co-operation of graduates of other institutions was invited. The present investigation, therefore, is the result of the joint efforts of graduates of Atlanta University, Fisk, Berea, Lincoln, Spelman, Howard, Meharry and other institutions for the higher education of the Negroes.

The conclusions which these men and women have reached as a result of their investigations are, in some respects, most surprising; especially their conclusions as to the effect of environment and economic conditions upon the vital energies of the race. Their conclusions were, in substance, that the excessive mortality of their people cannot be attributed in any large degree to unfavorable conditions of environment, but must be chiefly attributed to the ignorance of the masses of the people and their disregard of the laws of health and morality. The significance of this conclusion is tersely expressed by one of the writers, who says:

"This last fact, that the excessive death-rate of the colored people does not arise from diseases due to environment, is of vast importance. If poor houses, unhealthy localities, bad sewerage, and defective plumbing were responsible for their high death-rate, there would be no hope of reducing the death-rate until either the colored people became wealthy, or philanthropic persons erected sanitary houses, or municipalities made appropriations to remove those conditions. But since the excessive death-rate is not due to these causes, there is reason for the belief that it may be reduced without regard to the present economic condition of the colored people."

The attention of the members of the conference seemed to be mainly directed to a consideration of the social questions affecting the progress of the race. The sentiment of the conference was voiced by one writer in these words:

"If we are to strike at the root of the matter, it will not be at sanitary regulation, but at social reconstruction and moral regeneration."

The solution of the problem will be found in the wise direction of the numerous charitable, religious and educational organizations of colored people already established. As a means towards that end, the University will continue the City Problem Investigation along the lines upon which it was begun, and will hold a third conference at Atlanta next May. The subject of the next conference cannot now be announced, but in accordance with the expressed wish of members of the last conference, it will be some subject dealing with the social conditions of the people.

The result of the present investigation has been, on the whole, distinctly encouraging. In the opinion of the committee having the investigation in charge, the Negro has nothing to fear from a most rigid and searching investigation into his physical and social condition, but such an investigation can be made most helpful and valuable.

RESULTS OF THE INVESTIGATION.

[Note: The three following papers on the results of the investigation were written by the three members of the conference who individually collected the most data: Mr. Butler R. Wilson, a member of the committee who gathered data relating to one hundred families that had migrated from North Carolina to Cambridge, Mass.; Prof. Eugene Harris of Fisk University, who made an extensive investigation in Nashville; and Mr. L. M. Hershaw of Washington, D. C., who had in charge the very laborious work of analyzing the reports of the boards of health for the past fifteen years.–Ed.]

GENERAL SUMMARY.

BY MR. BUTLER R. WILSON ('81), BOSTON, MASS.

In making this investigation of the habits, morals and environment of Negroes living in cities, three things have been kept constantly in view, viz.:

First– To obtain accurate information without regard to cherished theories or race pride;

Second– To make the inquiry practical and helpful, and not merely for scientific results; and,

Third– To induce the people to apply the remedies which they have in their own hands for the evils which are found to exist and which retard their progress.

The results to be gained depended entirely upon the intelligence and fitness of the investigators, who were selected with great care from the ranks of well-known colored educators, ministers, physicians, lawyers and business men, living among the people covered by the investigation. All the data were gathered by this body of trained colored leaders, and they are believed to be, perhaps, more than usually accurate because of the investigators' knowledge of the character, habits and prejudices of the people, and because of the fact that they were not hindered by the suspicions which confront the white investigator, and which seriously affect the accuracy of the answers to his questions.

The work of the investigators was entirely voluntary and was done with a willingness and industry highly gratifying.

The cities embraced in the investigation, with a single exception, are located in regions of heaviest Negro population, and are fairly representative of other cities containing large numbers of Negroes.

The data obtained were published in the May Bulletin of the U. S. Department of Labor, and cover so wide a range of useful information, that only a few things can be pointed out here.

Referring to the tables of this Bulletin, we find one noticeable fact in table 3*, namely, that the size of colored families is much smaller than is commonly supposed, the average being 4. 17 persons.

Tables 5 and 6, giving household conditions by families,—the average persons per sleeping room, and the number of rooms per family,—show that the general belief that the tenements and houses occupied by colored people are greatly over-crowded is not founded on facts. These tables do not show that any great over-crowding exists, on the whole, although for certain individual families and groups the averages are somewhat larger. It also appears that the average number of living rooms is much larger than has been thought to be the case. An average of 2. 22 persons to a sleeping room in Atlanta, 2.44 persons in Nashville, and 1. 96 persons in Cambridge, and 2. 05 persons in all the other cities covered by the investigation, is an unexpected and important showing, and reverses the idea that the number of families having but one room each for all purposes was very large and was the rule instead of the exception. Out of a total of 1,137 families investigated, only 117, or 10. 29 per cent, had but one room each for their use for all purposes.

Table 7, giving number of families and means of support, shows a large proportion of females who either support families unaided, or who contribute to the support of families.

Of the male heads only 26.7 per cent were able to support their families without assistance from other members. Of the 1,137 families 650, or 57.17 per cent, were supported wholly or in part by female heads.

In comparison with white female heads of families and those contributing to family support, there is quite a large excess on the part of colored women.

---

*Table 3 in appendix A. The appendixes contain selected tables from the May Bulletin of the Department of Labor.—Ed.

This table calls attention to the enforced absence of mothers from their homes, and the daily abandonment, by these mothers who are compelled to aid in earning the family support, of their young children to the evil associations, the temptations, and vicious liberty of the alleys, courts and slums.

To attempt to prove from the showing of this table that Negro men are unwilling to support their families, and that they are lazy and shiftless, would be unfair. Careful inquiry by a number of the investigators indicates very strongly that the comparatively small support given by these men to their families is not due to unwillingness, but to their inability to get work as readily and constantly as the women. At the South white men refuse to work at the bench, in the mill and at other employments with colored men, who, for this reason, are denied work, and therefore unable to earn means with which to support their families.

This fact was found to exist in the city of Cambridge, where a large per cent of the men in the hundred families investigated, in reply to an inquiry, said that they had been refused work because they were colored, and a number of them said that they were unable to follow their trades, but had to "job around" with unsteady employment for the same reason.

The women in these families find steady employment as domestic servants and laundresses, and at the South find but little competition from white women.

The investigation gives a great many data on this industrial side of the question, which want of space will not now allow us to consider.

Tables 8 and 9, giving the number and per cent of persons sick during the year, and the number and per cent of deaths during the past five years by causes, show that the diseases most fatal to the colored people are consumption and pneumonia. While the average length of time of sickness from it is short, malarial fever is shown to be one of the most prevalent diseases. Rheumatism is also shown to be quite prevalent. Both of these diseases, as well as typhoid fever and pneumonia, may, to a great extent, be kept in abeyance by the observance of hygienic rules and a proper care of the health.

In the 100 Cambridge families it was found that many of the men work in the water department, and after the day's work eat the evening meal without changing their damp clothing, often going to sleep in their chairs for an hour or more and then going to a lodge or "society meeting," remaining not infrequently until 11 and 12 o'clock.

These tables also show that the difference between the death-rate of the white and colored people from diarrhœa, diptheria, scarlet fever, malarial fever and typhoid fever, all diseases chiefly affected by environment, is very slight.*

Table 10, giving sickness by sanitary condition of houses, shows that while sanitary conditions have a very important bearing, they are not important enough to account for the difference of per cent in the death-rate between the white and colored people.

Great caution must be observed in making deductions from this table. While it is intended to show the bearing of sanitary conditions on the health of the community, the results obtained are not conclusive. It would be erroneous, for instance, to attribute to bad sanitary conditions the increased amount of sickness in families, and leave out of consideration such factors as irregular habits, indifference to healthy living quarters and the intimate relation between poverty and ill health.

By reference to the table it will be seen that the number of persons sick in Atlanta was 163 out of a total of 577, or 28.25 per cent, where the light and air were good ; and that out of 367 persons living where the light and air were bad, 120, or 32.70 per cent, were sick, a difference of only 15 per cent between houses with good and bad conditions as to light and air.

One hundred and twenty-eight persons living in houses with good light and air lost 5,819 days by sickness, or an average of 45.46 days each; while 102, or 26 persons less, lost, under bad conditions of light and air, only 4,361 days, or an average of 42.75 days each, a difference of 6 per cent, the average days of sickness being more in houses with good light and air than in those where the light and air were bad.

This table further shows that out of 537 persons living in Atlanta in houses with good ventilation, 153, or 28.49 per cent, were sick during the year, losing, for the 124 reporting, 5,927 days, or an average of 47.80 days each ; while out of 427 persons living in houses with

---

*The tables bearing upon diseases most prevalent will be particularly discussed in the paper following.—ED.

bad ventilation, 154, or 36 per cent, were sick during the year, 133 of whom lost 6,050 days, or an average of 45.49 days each, a difference of only 26 per cent between the per cent of persons sick where ventilation was good and where it was bad, the average number of days again being greater for those under good conditions than for those under bad.

Table XV,* giving general description of houses, shows that a large proportion of the houses occupied by the 1,137 families were wooden structures, detached and located in neighborhoods of fair character. Of the 1,031 houses but 43 had bath-rooms, and 183 had water-closets, 95 of which were in the Cambridge houses. In Atlanta and Cambridge the houses with bad outside sanitary conditions predominated. In all the other cities the houses with good outside sanitary conditions predominated, the latter being greatly in excess for the entire territory covered.

This paper may be summarized as follows:

First—All the data in the investigation have been gathered by intelligent colored men and women living in the communities covered. These investigators were not hindered by obstacles which make it difficult for a white man to get accurate information of the family life, habits and character of the colored people. These colored investigators cannot be charged with prejudice and designs against the interests of the colored people. For these reasons, their work is thought to be more than usually accurate and reliable.

Second—Over-crowding in tenements and houses occupied by colored people does not exist to any great extent, and is less than was supposed.

Third—In comparison with white women, an excess of colored women support their families entirely, or contribute to the family support, by occupations which take them much of their time from home, to the neglect of their children.

Fourth—Environment and the sanitary condition of houses are not chiefly responsible for the excessive mortality among colored people.

Fifth—Ignorance and disregard of the laws of health are responsible for a large proportion of this excessive mortality.

_____

*Not in appendix, but in May Bulletin of Department of Labor.—Ed.

SOCIAL AND PHYSICAL PROGRESS:

A COMPARATIVE ANALYSIS OF THE REPORTS OF THE BOARDS OF
HEALTH OF ATLANTA, BALTIMORE, CHARLESTON,
MEMPHIS AND RICHMOND.

BY MR. L. M. HERSHAW ('86), WASHINGTON, D. C.

The study of vital statistics is one of the most important subjects that can engage the attention. The death-rate, taken in connection with the birth-rate, determines the natural increase or decrease of population, the growth or decline of a people, and the strength of nations. Dr. William Farr, late Registrar-General of Births, Deaths and Marriages in England, states the whole matter in the following language: "There is a relation betwixt death, health, and energy of body and mind. There is a relation betwixt death, birth and marriage. There is a relation betwixt death and national primacy; numbers turn the tide in the struggle of population, and the most mortal die out. There is a relation betwixt the forms of death and moral excellence or infamy."

It has been known for a number of years to health officers and students of vital statistics that the death-rate of the colored people was larger than that of the white people; that the colored people were dying in larger numbers in proportion to the colored population than the white people were in proportion to the white population. Of late years these facts have become known to most intelligent persons, and great interest attaches to the degree of the excess of the colored death-rate, and to the causes of it.

This paper will deal with the vital statistics of the cities of Atlanta, Ga., Baltimore, Md., Charleston, S. C., Memphis, Tenn., and Richmond, Va. Each of these cities contains a large colored population, surrounded by social, economic and moral conditions such as exist in other cities where colored people are congregated in considerable numbers, if Philadelphia is excepted. The cities selected are, therefore, thoroughly representative for the purpose in hand, and the conditions found to prevail in them may be fairly presumed to prevail in the other cities having a large population of colored people.

The average annual death-rate per 1,000 of the living population in these five cities for the fifteen years from 1881 to 1895 was 20.74 for the whites and 36.13 for the colored, showing a percentage of excess for the colored of 73.8.

The average annual death-rate per 1,000 by race for each of the five cities under consideration for the past fourteen or fifteen years is as follows :

	White.	Colored.	Per cent excess of colored.
Atlanta (1882–95)	18.50	34.71	87.6
Baltimore (1880–94)	20.69	32.71	58.1
Charleston (1881–94)	23.19	44.08	90
Memphis (1882–95)	20.58	31.15	51.3
Richmond (1881–95)	20.73	38.02	83.4

An inspection of the table just given shows that the highest death-rate among the colored is in Charleston (which is also true as to the whites), and that the lowest death-rate among the colored is in Memphis, the lowest among the whites being in Atlanta. Comparing the white and colored death-rates, it is to be seen that the greatest excess of colored over white is in Charleston, where it reaches 90 per cent; the excess in Atlanta being 87.6 per cent, and that in Richmond 83.4 per cent. The least excess is found in Memphis, which is 51.3 per cent, Baltimore having 58.1 per cent. These figures seem to justify the conclusion that the worst physical conditions among the colored people are to be found in Charleston, Atlanta and Richmond, and the best in Memphis and Baltimore.

Having found the average death-rates of the two races in these five cities for the past fourteen or fifteen years, and having compared them with each other, and drawn a conclusion as to the relative physical conditions of the colored populations in the cities under consideration, it will conduce to a better understanding and a fuller knowledge of these conditions to divide the fourteen or fifteen years which this investigation covers into three periods as nearly equal as possible. By pursuing this method we shall be able, in a measure, to decide whether the physical condition of the colored is better or worse in 1894 or 1895 than in 1880 or 1881.

CITIES.	FIRST PERIOD.			SECOND PERIOD.			THIRD PERIOD.		
	White.	Col-ored.	Per cent excess of colored.	White.	Col-ored.	Per cent excess of colored.	White.	Col-ored.	Per cent excess of colored.
Atlanta......	18.22	37.96	108.4	19.25	33.41	73.5	18.03	32.76	81.6
Baltimore.....	22.60	36.15	59.9	19.46	30.52	56.8	20.01	31.47	57.2
Charleston...	25.40	44.08	73.5	22.30	46.74	109.6	21.88	41.43	89.3
Memphis......	26.08	43.01	64.9	21.49	29.35	36.5	14.17	21.11	48.9
Richmond....	22.42	40.34	79.9	21.37	38.83	81.7	18.42	34.91	89.5

The tabular statement contains, in addition to the average annual death-rate, the percentage of the excess of the colored death-rate. Lest these percentages of excess mislead somebody, it is necessary to explain that, in comparing the three periods, they merely show whether or not the colored death-rate has decreased as rapidly as the white death-rate, and not the actual increase or decrease of the colored death-rate. To illustrate: Comparing the second and third periods in Richmond, it is to be seen that the percentage of excess for the second period is 81.7 per cent, and for the third period 89.5 per cent. Without looking at the matter carefully the conclusion is likely to be drawn that the colored death-rate is greater for the third period than for the second, when, as a matter of fact, it is less, the rates being 38.83* for the second, and 34.91 for the third.

An inspection of the above table shows that there has been a constant decrease in the colored death-rate from period to period in Atlanta, Memphis and Richmond.

In Atlanta the colored death-rate for the first period is 37.96, for the second 33.41, and for the third 32.76 ; in Memphis, 43.01 for the first period, 29.35 for the second, and 21.11 for the third; and in Richmond, 40.34 for the first period, 38.83 for the second, and 34.91 for the third. While Baltimore and Charleston do not show the constant decrease from period to period noted in the other cities, they do show a lower death-rate for the third period than for the first; the death-rates

---

*Note.—The death-rate is generally expressed in terms of one thousand. The phrase "rate of 38.83" means that there were thirty-eight and eighty-three one-hundredths deaths per thousand of population. For brevity, the words "per thousand" are omitted.—Ed.

in Baltimore being 36.15 for the first period, 30.52 for the second, and 31.47 for the third; and those in Charleston, 44.08 for the first period, 46.74 for the second, and 41.43 for the third. Memphis shows the greatest improvement, the average death-rate at the end of the third period being 50.9 per cent lower than at the end of the first, and Charleston shows the least improvement, 6 per cent. In Atlanta the improvement is 13.9 per cent, in Richmond, 13.4 per cent, and in Baltimore, 12.9 per cent.

Of the five cities with which this paper deals, but two have a registration of births—Baltimore and Charleston.* Richmond had such a registration, but it was discontinued some years ago. The registrations of Baltimore and Charleston are admittedly incomplete. No view of the vital statistics of a community is complete without a knowledge of its birth-rate. The birth-rate is closely related to the death-rate. The natural increase of population depends upon the excess of the birth-rate over the death-rate. It would be highly interesting to know what the birth-rate of the colored population in the five cities under consideration is. Is it as great as the death-rate? Is it greater than the death-rate? These questions cannot be answered satisfactorily because the health reports do not supply the information. The United States Census of 1890 gives the colored birth-rate of the United States as 29.07 per thousand, but owing to the incompleteness of the records of births by the municipal and state authorities, these figures are not reliable, and are probably much too small. Four European countries have birth-rates which exceed the colored death-rate in the cities that we have under consideration. In view of the well-known fecundity of the Negro race, it is fair to infer that his birth-rate is certainly as high as that of the Italian, the German, the Austrian, or the Hungarian. If this is so, then the death-rate in these cities has not reached the point where population begins to decrease. It is well-nigh useless to pursue this branch of the subject further, because of the lack of data.

Having established the fact that the average colored death-rate for the past fourteen or fifteen years in the five cities is 73.8 per cent in excess of the white death-rate in the same cities for the same period, and having shown, by dividing these years into three equal periods and

---

* See for Baltimore table f, appendix B.—ED.

comparing the rates of previous with succeeding periods, that the colored death-rate shows an improvement over fifteen years ago, it remains to set forth the causes of this excessive mortality.

The principal causes of the excessive mortality of the colored people are the same in all the cities ; therefore, it will serve our purpose to know the average death-rate of the three cities, Charleston, Memphis and Richmond, combined, for a period of fifteen years, for certain classes of diseases, and to give in full the same facts concerning Atlanta. The table which follows shows for Charleston, Memphis and Richmond, combined, the average death-rate per 10,000, by specified causes, for a period of fifteen years, from 1881 to 1895 :

	White.	Colored.	Per cent excess of colored.
Consumption and Pneumonia	32.76*	75.48	130.4
Typhoid, Malarial and Scarlet Fevers, Diarrhea and Diphtheria	20.16	26.22	30
Cholera Infantum, Convulsions and Still-born	14.87	39.43	165.1
Scrofula and Syphilis	.81	4.72	482.7

It is to be seen from the table above that for all classes of diseases the colored death-rate exceeds the white. The greatest excess is found under scrofula and syphilis, where it is 482.7 per cent in excess of the white death-rate. The next greatest excess is due to infantile diseases,—cholera infantum, convulsions and still-born,—the excess being 165.1 per cent. The third greatest excess is due to pulmonary diseases, and is seen to be 130.4 per cent. We see also that the least disparity between the white and the colored death-rate is found under the group of diseases most affected by environment, including typhoid and malarial fevers and dipththeria, where the excess is only 30 per cent. As to syphilis and scrofula, it is to be observed that the number of deaths is small. The white death-rate during fifteen years in Charleston, Memphis and Richmond has been less than one per 10,000 of the population, while the colored was somewhat less than five. The per cent of the excess of the colored over the white is, however, startling, and furnishes much food for reflection as to the morals of the colored people.

The two principal causes of the excessive mortality of the colored people are pulmonary diseases,—consumption and pneumonia,— and

---

* These death-rates for specified causes are per *ten* thousand.—Ed.

infant mortality. The excessive prevalence of consumption and pneumonia among colored people is brought out very plainly in the foregoing table, where the excess in these cities is shown to be 130.4 per cent.

The following table containing the total average annual number of deaths, and the average annual number of deaths of children under five years of age, with distinction of race, will serve to show the extent of the infant mortality among colored people :

ATLANTA, GA.

Total average annual number of deaths.		Average annual number of deaths under 5 years of age.			
White.	Colored.	White.	Colored.	Per cent of white.	Per cent of colored.
1882–85... ....470	751... 172		.........313... ....38.7		..........41.6
1886–90............644	845.............224		.........348............34.7		............41.1
1891–95............804 ....1086...... 257			.........386....... .....31.9		............35.5

CHARLESTON, S. C.

| 1885–89.............525 ....1394.............148 | | | ....558............28.0............40.0 | | |
| 1890–94.............529.........1316.............141 | | | ....518............26.4.............39.3 | | |

MEMPHIS, TENN.

| 1886–90.............678..........742.............180 | | | ....263............26.5............35.4 | | |
| 1891–95............619........ ..741............ .145 | | | ....232............23.4...... .....31.1 | | |

There is an enormous waste of child-life among both races, not only in the cities under consideration, but in all cities. But from the data at hand the conclusion is justified that the mortality among colored children is not alarmingly in excess of the mortality among white children, unless it be for children under two years of age. The figures which we have presented on this subject show that the mortality among children of both races has decreased constantly since 1881 in Atlanta, Charleston and Memphis.

Of the diseases which are excessively prevalent among colored people, the most important, and the one which should be the occasion of the greatest alarm, is consumption. We have seen already that consumption and pneumonia are among the causes of excessive mortality of the colored people, the excess per cent of Charleston, Memphis and Richmond being 130.4.

The table following shows the rate per 10,000 of deaths from consumption in all the cities investigated :

ATLANTA, GA.

	White.	Colored.	Per ct. excess of colored.
1882–85	18.40	50.20	172.83
1886–90	18.83	45.88	143.65
1891–95	16.82	43.48	158.50

BALTIMORE, MD.

1886	25.65	58.65	128.65
1887	22.23	55.42	149.30
1891	20.00	46.32	131.60
1892	20.10	49.41	145.82

CHARLESTON, S. C.

1881–84	27.52	72.20	162.35
1885–89	20.05	68.08	239.55
1890–94	17.71	57.66	225.58

MEMPHIS, TENN.

1882–85	34.25	65.35	90.80
1886–90	24.29	50.30	107 08
1891–95	15.90	37.78	137.61

RICHMOND, VA.

1881–85	25.57	54.93	114.82
1886–90	21.27	41.63	95.72
1891–95	18.54	34.74	87.38

It is to be seen that in all of the cities the death-rate for consumption is high among the colored people, the lowest rate being 34.74 per 10,000 in Richmond, and the highest, 72.20, in Charleston. The greatest disparity between the white and the colored death-rate for this cause is also in Charleston, where the excess per cent of the colored is as high as 239.5. The important fact must not be lost sight of that the death-rate from this cause has constantly decreased in all the cities except Charleston, and in Charleston the death-rate for the period 1890–94 is lower than for the period 1881–84. There is reason, however, for great concern and anxiety as to the excessive prevalence of this disease among the colored people. Unless checked and reduced to a normal state, it may, in the course of years, be a deciding factor in the ultimate fate of the race. The prevalence of tubercular and scrofulous diseases, consumption, scrofula, syphilis and leprosy, has caused the weaker races of the earth to succcumb before the rising tide of the Christian civilization. The Carib of the West Indies, the noble red man of these shores, the natives of the Sandwich Islands, and the aborigines of Australia and New Zealand have all disappeared or been greatly reduced in numbers as the result of the ravages of these diseases. It should be an object of first importance, then, to get control of these diseases before they reach the point where control is impossible.

It will be of interest to know somewhat in detail the physical condition of the population in Atlanta for the fourteen years from 1882 to 1895, and the tables which follow set forth quite fully this fact.

DEATH-RATE PER 1,000, ATLANTA, GA.

Period.	White.	Colored.	Per ct. excess of colored.
1882–85	18.21	37.96	108.4
1886–90	19.25	33.41	73.5
1891–95	18.03	32.76	81.6

It is seen that the death-rate of the colored population, though greatly in excess of that of the white, has constantly decreased, the average death-rate per 1,000 for the first period being 37.96, for the second 33.41, and for the third 32.76. Relatively, as compared with the whites, the death rate of the colored shows much improvement. Though the percentage of excess of colored for the third period is greater than that for the second, the percentage for both of these periods shows a marked decrease from that of the first period.

The following tables show for three periods, 1882 to 1885, 1886 to 1890, and 1891 to 1895, the average annual death-rate per 10,000, Atlanta, Ga., by specified causes.

CONSUMPTION AND PNEUMONIA.

Period.	White.	Colored.	Per ct. excess of colored.
1882–85	27.43	76.89	180.3
1886–90	30.13	72.14	139.4
1891–95	28.48	75.75	165.9

CHOLERA INFANTUM AND STILL-BIRTHS.

1886–90	26.78	56.09	109.4
1891–95	24.99	53.86	115.5

TYPHOID, SCARLET AND MALARIAL FEVERS, AND DIPHTHERIA.

1882–85	11.58	19.31	66.7
1886–90	14.58	17.17	17.7
1891–95	10.72	12.48	16.4

OTHER CAUSES.

1882–85	a143.15	a283.44	a98.0
1886–90	121.05	188.67	55.8
1891–95	116.15	185.50	59.7

a Including deaths from cholera infantum and still-births.

It is observed that in all these groups of causes the colored death-rate has decreased from period to period, except for consumption and pneumonia, where the death-rate for the period 1891–95 is greater than for the period 1886–90, though slightly less than for the period 1882–85.

The statistics presented in the various tables which this paper contains, viewed candidly and dispassionately, shows results favorable to the physical improvement of the colored race. If the mortality rate had remained stationary for a period of fifteen years, it would have been a lasting evidence of the physical strength and endurance of the race. But we have shown that the rate has decreased in that period, and that, too, as is well known, in the face of hard, exacting and oppressive social and economic conditions. When all of the facts in the colored man's case are taken into consideration, the wonder is, not that the death-rate is as high as it is, but that it is not even higher. The history of weak and inferior races shows that they begin to decrease in number after one generation's contact with Anglo-Saxon civilization. The native population of the Sandwich Islands a hundred years ago was estimated to be 100,000. The latest census taken on the Islands shows the native population to be 35,000. We do not witness this decay and decrease in numbers in the colored race anywhere in the Western Hemisphere.

In studying any phase of Negro life in the United States, the fact must be kept constantly in view that the Negro has been subjected to degrading and blasting slavery for more than two centuries. While slavery did its victims a great wrong in depriving them of the fruits of their toil, it did them a greater wrong in denying them opportunities for moral and mental improvement. Those who sit in judgment upon the Negro and study his frailties and shortcomings must not forget these previous conditions.

To recapitulate, it has been shown:

First—That the colored death-rate exceeds the white, the excess averaging for five cities, during a period of fifteen years, 73.8 per cent.

Second—That the death-rate of the colored population in five cities is lower for the period 1890–95 than for the period 1881–85.

Third—That the principal causes of the excessive mortality among the colored people of five cities are pulmonary diseases and infant mortality.

Fourth—That the least disparity between the white and colored death-rates is for those diseases due to unwholesome sanitary conditions; typhoid, malarial and scarlet fevers, diphtheria and diarrhea.

This last fact, that the excessive death-rate of the colored people does not arise from diseases due to environment, is of vast importance. If poor houses, unhealty localities, bad sewerage and defective plumbing were responsible for their high death-rate, there would be no hope of reducing the death-rate until either the colored people became wealthy, or philanthropic persons erected sanitary houses, or municipalities made appropriations to remove these conditions. But since the excessive death-rate is not due to these causes, there is reason for the belief that it may be reduced without regard to the present economic conditions of the colored people.

NOTE.—For further data compiled by Mr. Hershaw, see appendix B.–Ed.

THE PHYSICAL CONDITION OF THE RACE; WHETHER DEPENDENT UPON SOCIAL CONDITIONS OR ENVIRONMENT.

BY PROF. EUGENE HARRIS, FISK UNIVERSITY, NASHVILLE, TENN.

The social conditions of the American Negro are two-fold; those which he makes for himself, and those which the white people make for him. The latter class cannot affect the physical status of the Negro except in a very indirect and unimportant way. Separate apartments in public conveniences, such as hotels, theatres, or railroad trains, social ostracism, exclusion from political preferment and the spoils of office, the suppression of his ballot, and the other discriminations which are made against the black man, have at least no immediate bearing on his health, vitality, or longevity. The Negro may eat and wear what he pleases, as much as he pleases, and as often as he pleases. The provision shops and dry goods stores do not discriminate against him in the matter of food and wearing apparel. After a hard day's work he may carouse at night just as late as he pleases. There is not a black law upon our statute books regulating his private habits, or imposing upon him unsanitary surroundings, or restricting him to deleterious occupations, or forcing him to immoderate indulgences.

It is true that in public conveniences the Negro must take separate apartments; but the air in them is just as invigorating, the water is just as healthful and pure, and the food is just as nourishing as in the apartments for the whites. Regular bathing will throw off dead matter through the skin, and control of the appetites will contribute largely to health in Negro quarters as well as anywhere else. The laws of health have no regard for artificial social barriers. They know no color line. Civilly, socially, and politically, the Negro of this country is under many cruel and unjust restrictions; but he is at perfect liberty to be abstemious or intemperate, chaste or licentious, cleanly

or filthy. In the struggle for recognition and preferment he is at a
great disadvantage ; but in the struggle for *life*, apart from those im-
pediments for which he himself is responsible, he has almost, if not
altogether, an equal chance with the whites.

It is true that if the colored people in our larger towns are bent
upon living near the center of the city, they cannot rent or buy property, except in the less desirable or abandoned parts. But it is not
necessity, it is only convenience that leads them to live over stables, in
dark, damp cellars, and on back alleys, in the midst of stench and pu-
trefaction. They can, if they would, go to the suburbs, where they
can get better accommodations for less money. I have been in families in Nashville ranging from seven to ten, living on a back alley,
with a rivulet of filth running before the door of the one room in
which they bathed and ate and slept and died. Two miles further out
all of these families might have secured for the same money shanties
of two and three rooms, with purer air and water, and had a garden
spot besides. Among the colored people, convenience to the heart of
the city often overrides considerations of health, and that the white
people offer them hot-beds of disease for homes is no excuse for their
taking them. It is better to live in the suburbs than to die in the city.
The Negro is induced, but not forced, to accept the bad accommodations of down-town life. Apart from this apparent exception in the
matter of rented houses, no race discrimination affects in the least the
Negro's physical condition ; and it is for this very reason that I am
hopeful of a change for the better in the vital statistics of our people.
If the large death-rate, the small birth-rate, the susceptibility to disease, and the low vitality of the race were due to causes outside of our
control, I could see nothing before us but the "blackness of darkness
forever." But because the colored people themselves are responsible
for this sad state of affairs, it is to be expected that time and education
will correct it.

The conclusions which I shall draw in this paper are based largely
upon my study of the problem in Nashville.

In the first place, then, the excess of colored deaths over white is due
almost entirely to constitutional diseases and infant mortality. According to health statistics, the constitutional diseases which are mainly responsible for our large death-rate are pulmonary consumption, scrofula,

and syphilis, all of which are alike in being tuberculous. A large number of the colored convicts in our state's prison at Nashville are consumptives or syphilitics. Out of 92 deaths in a certain territory in Nashville, 19 deaths, or over 20 per cent, were due to consumption. The other 73 deaths were due to 35 different causes. In the recent Atlanta investigation, according to the mortality report of Cambridge, Mass., consumption was the cause of 15 per cent of the deaths.

DEATHS FROM CONSUMPTION IN NASHVILLE FOR THE PERIOD 1893-95.

	1893	1894	1895	
White	124	91	82	A reduction of nearly 34 per cent.
Colored	177	159	218	An increase of over 23 per cent.

Alarming as are the facts set forth in the preceding table, they are not the whole truth. They would be occasion for serious concern if the races were numerically equal; but when we remember that the colored people of Nashville are only three-fifths as numerous as the whites, it is all the more startling. For the year 1895, when 82 white deaths from consumption occurred in the city of Nashville, there ought to have been only 49 colored, whereas there really were 218, or nearly four and one-half times as many as there ought to have been. It is an occasion of serious alarm when 37 per cent of the whole people are responsible for 72 per cent of the deaths from consumption.

Deaths among colored people from pulmonary diseases seem to be on the increase throughout the South. During the period 1882-85, the excess of colored deaths from consumption for the city of Memphis was 90.80 per cent. For the period 1891-95, the excess had arisen to over 137 per cent. For the period of 1886-90, the excess of colored deaths from consumption and pneumonia for the city of Atlanta was 139 per cent. For the period 1891-95, it had arisen to nearly 166 per cent.*

From these facts it would appear that pulmonary consumption is the "destroying angel" among us, and yet I am told that before the war this dread disease was virtually unknown among the slaves. Fortunately Charleston, S. C., kept even before the war the mortality statistics of the colored people, and, consequently, we are able to ascertain with some accuracy how their death-rate from consumption before

---

* See table d. appendix B.–Ed.

the war compares with their death-rate afterwards. What are the facts in the case? From 1822 to 1848, the colored death-rate from consumption was a trifle less than the white. Since 1865 it has been considerably greater, and is still increasing. According to F. L. Hoffman, the white mortality from that cause has decreased since the war 134 per hundred thousand. The colored mortality has increased over 234 per hundred thousand.*

The question arises, How do we account for this change? Is it because the Negro is inherently more susceptible to pulmonary diseases, or is it because of his changed environment,—his different social conditions? If his tendency to consumption is due to his inherent susceptibility, what was it that held it in check until after the war? It seems that this fact alone is sufficient to fix the responsibility upon the conditions which have arisen since emancipation. Mr. F. L. Hoffman claims that the Negro's lungs weigh four ounces less than a white man's, and that though his normal chest measure is greater, his lung capacity is less; and that here we have a cause for the Negro's tendency to consumption which no environment, however favorable, can affect. Even if this be a fact, it is hard to see how it began to operate as a cause of consumption only since the war.

Let us turn for the present to another cause of the excessive mortality among us; namely, the increased prevalence of scrofula and venereal diseases. For the period 1882–85, the colored death-rate in Memphis from scrofula and syphilis was 205.8 per cent in excess of that among the whites; but from 1891 down to the present time, the excess has been 298 per cent. For the period 1893–95, there were in the city of Nashville 8 white deaths from scrofula and syphilis, and 35 colored. In proportion to the population, there ought to have been only 5. Of course allowance must be made for the fact that, on account of the scandal and disgrace, white physicians are reluctant to report white deaths from these causes; whereas such motives rarely, if ever, influence them in reporting colored deaths.

According to the May Bulletin of the Department of Labor, out of 1,090 colored people canvassed this year in the city of Nashville, 18

---

* See "Race Traits and Tendencies of the American Negro," by F. L. Hoffman. —Ed.

were suffering from scrofula and syphilis.* One whose attention has not been called to the matter has no conception of the prevalence of these diseases among the Negroes of Nashville. I have looked for it in both races as I have walked the streets of my city, and to come across the loathsome disease in the colored passers-by is not an uncommon occurrence. This state of affairs can be accounted for when I tell you that there is probably no city in this country where prostitution among colored people is more rampant and brazen, and where abandoned colored women are more numerous or more public in their shameful traffic.

In the families canvassed by me this year, among 50 sufferers from rheumatism, 8 were so badly crippled as to be bed-ridden invalids. When we consider the fact that some forms of rheumatism are syphilitic in their origin, and that in these same families there were 18 suffering from scrofula and syphilis, it would appear that venereal poisoning was responsible for a considerable share of the rheumatism.

There is one obstacle to the race's reproducing itself that has some connection with venereal diseases, and hence I speak of it now. I refer to the enormous amount of still births and infant mortality, prevalent everywhere among colored people. For the period of 1893–95, the still and the premature births in the city of Nashville were 272 for the white, and 385 for the colored; or, in proportion to the population, $2\frac{1}{3}$ times as many as there ought to have been. This relative state of affairs obtains in Memphis and Atlanta, and in all the large cities of the South. From the health reports of all our large Southern cities we learn that a considerable amount of our infant mortality is due to inanition, infantile debility, and infantile marasmus. Now what is the case in regard to these diseases? The fact is that they are not diseases at all, but merely the names of symptoms due to enfeebled constitutions and congenital diseases, inherited from parents suffering from the effects of sexual immorality and debauchery. Translated into common speech, they are nothing more than infant starvation, infant weakness, and infant wasting away, the cause of which is that the infants' parents before them have not given them a fighting chance for life. According to Hoffman, over 50 per cent of the Negro chil-

---

* See table 8, appendix A.—Ed.

dren born in Richmond, Va., die before they are one year old.

The number of still and premature births among us is a matter of great alarm, not only because it seriously interferes with the numerical increase of the race, but because it involves the fecundity, the health, and even the moral character of large numbers of our women. The support of the family often falls very heavily upon our poor washer-women; and since they find it hard to get the husks to feed and the rags to clothe their already large number of little folks, living in one room like stock, rather than to add to their burden, they resort to crime. An official on the Nashville Board of Health, who is also proprietor of a drug store, tells me that he is astonished at the number of colored women who apply at his store for drugs with a criminal purpose in view.

The 16 Atlanta groups in the recent investigation showed that the female heads of families are considerably in excess of the male, and out of 324 families 31 were wholly supported by the mother, and 205 were supported by the mother altogether or in part.* In such social con-ditions as these, where the burden of bread-winning is borne largely, and often altogether, by the mother of the household, it is not surpris-ing that poor, laboring women who are ignorant of its ruinous effects upon both health and character, should resort to prenatal infanticide.

The average family for the eighteen cities covered by our recent in-vestigation numbers only 4.1, which means that in these eighteen cities the race is doing barely more than reproducing itself.† The large colored families of a few decades ago are becoming more and more scarce. I know a grandmother who was the proud mother of over a dozen children; the daughter could boast of nine; and not one of sev-eral granddaughters, though married for a number of years, is the mother of more than one child. This family is but an illustration of many others just like it. Such facts go to show that the Negro is no longer the "prolific animal" that he once was termed. The race, like the women of whom Paul once wrote to Timothy, must be "saved through child-bearing."

I take it that the excess of infant mortality from cholera infantum and convulsions means nothing more than that the Negro mothers do

---

* See table 7, appendix A.—Ed.

† See table 3, appendix A.—Ed.

not know so well how to feed and care for their offspring. They need instruction in infant dietetics and baby culture.

I have now covered the ground to which our excessive death rate is mainly due: namely, pulmonary diseases, especially consumption and pneumonia, scrofula, venereal diseases, and infant mortality. If we eliminate these diseases, our excessive death rate will be a thing of the past.

Let us now inquire, What is there in the Negro's social condition that is responsible for the prevalence of these diseases, and the consequent mortality? In the first place then, be it known by all men that we to-day in this conference assembled are not the enemies of our people because we tell them the truth. We shall know the truth, and the truth shall make us free not only from the bondage of sin, but from vicious social conditions and consequent physical death. Sanitary regulations and the social reconstruction of Israel formed a large part of Moses' religious duty, and why may it not of ours?

While I do not depreciate sanitary regulations, and a knowledge of hygienic laws, I am convinced that the *sine qua non* of a change for the better in the Negro's physical condition is a higher social morality. I do not believe that his poverty or his relation to the white people presents any real impediment to his health and physical development. Without going into the reasons for it, it is well known that the poor laboring classes often enjoy better health, are freer from disease, have larger families, and live longer lives than the rich.

I am convinced that for the causes of the black man's low vitality, his susceptibility to disease, and his enormous death-rate we must look to those social conditions which he creates for himself. What are they? I have already referred to the social causes of our excessive infant mortality, namely, the frequency with which the partial or the entire maintenance of the household devolves upon the mother; and especially the impaired chance for life which a debauched and immoral parentage bequeaths to childhood. The infants in their graves will rise up in judgment against this evil and adulterous generation and condemn it.

The constitutional diseases which are responsible for our unusual mortality are often traceable to enfeebled constitutions broken down by sexual immoralities. This is frequently the source of even pulmonary consumption, which disease is to-day the black man's scourge.

According to Hoffman, over 25 per cent of the Negro children born in Washington City are admittedly illegitimate. According to a writer quoted in "Black America," "In one county of Mississippi there were during 12 months 300 marriage licenses taken out in the county clerk's office for white people. According to the proportion of population there should have been in the same time 1,200 or more for Negroes. There were actually taken out by colored people just three." James Anthony Froude asserts that 70 per cent of the Negroes in the West Indies are born in illegitimacy. Mr. Smecton claims that " in spite of the increase of education, there has been no decrease of this social cancer." My attention has been called to a resort in Nashville within less than two blocks of the public square where a large number of abandoned women and profligate men often congregate in the underground basement, which is lighted and ventilated only through the pavement grating; and there in debauchery and carousal they make the night hideous until almost morning. What are they sowing but disease, and what can they reap but death?

It is true that much of the moral laxity which exists among us to-day arose out of slavery. It is due to a system which whipped women, which dispensed with the institution of marriage, which separated wives from their husbands and assigned them to other men, which ruthlessly destroyed female virtue, and which made helpless women the abject tools of their masters. This is the correct explanation of our social status to-day, but to explain it is not to excuse it. It is no longer our misfortune as it was before the war: it is our sin, the wages of which is our excessive number of deaths. Always and everywhere, moral leprosy means physical death. Wherever the colored people are guilty of the immoralities of which James Anthony Froude and W. L. Clowes of the London Times accuse them, if they continue in them they will be destroyed by them root and branch. Rome was destroyed because the empire had no mothers, and Babylon was blotted out because she was the "mother of harlots."

A few years ago I said in a sermon at Fisk University that wherever the Anglo-Saxon comes into contact with an inferior race, the inferior race invariably goes to the wall. I called attention to the fact that in spite of humanitarian and philanthropic efforts, the printing press, the steam engine and the electric motor in the hands of the Anglo-Saxon were exterminating the inferior races more rapidly and more surely than shot, and shell, and bayonet. I mentioned a number of races that have perished not because of destructive wars and pestilence, but because they were unable to live in the environment of a nineteenth century civilization; races whose destruction was not due to a persecution that came to them from without, but to a lack of moral stamina within; races that perished in spite of the humanitarian and philanthropic efforts that were put forth to save them.

To that utterance let me now add this thought: that where shot, and shell, and bayonet, and the printing press and the steam engine, and the electric motor have slain their thousands; licentious men, unchaste women, and impure homes have slain their tens of thousands: and I speak the words of soberness and truth when I say that if the charges of sexual immoralities brought against us are true, unless there be wrought a social revolution among us, the handwriting of our destruction even now may be seen on the wall. The history of nations teaches us that neither war, nor famine, nor pestilence exterminates them so completely and rapidly as do sexual vices.

If the cause of our excessive death-rate be, in its ultimate analysis, moral rather than sanitary, then this fact ought to appear not only in our vital, but in our criminal statistics as well. Prof. Starr, of Chicago University, claims that in the State of Pennsylvania, where there is little opportunity to assert that the courts are prejudiced against colored criminals, though the Negroes form only 2 per cent of the population, yet they furnish 16 per cent of the male prisoners, and 34 per cent of the female. The race has such great privileges in Chicago and it is dealt with so fairly and justly that the colored people themselves have denominated it the "Negroes' Heaven;" and yet, according to Prof. Starr, while the Negroes form only 1⅓ per cent of the population of Chicago, they furnish 10 per cent of the arrests. I am convinced that the immorality which accounts for these criminal conditions is also responsible for the race's physical status; and if we are to strike at the root of the matter, it will not be at sanitary regulations, but at social reconstruction and moral regeneration.

Note: We regret being unable to print the whole of Prof. Harris' valuable paper.—Ed.

PROCEEDINGS OF THE CONFERENCE.

MINUTES.

The second Atlanta University Conference on Problems of Negro City Life convened in the Ware Memorial Chapel on Tuesday, May 25, 1897, at 8 P.M.

President Horace Bumstead, of Atlanta University, opened the conference as presiding officer; after which it was voted that George A. Towns ('94) and George F. Smith ('97) be made recording secretaries.

A letter was then read from His Excellency Gov. W. Y. Atkinson of Georgia, in which he expressed regret for his inability to deliver the address of welcome. President Bumstead then delivered the opening address.

The general purpose of the meeting Tuesday night was to set forth clearly the facts as to the physical and sanitary condition of Negroes in cities, as brought out by the investigation. In accordance with this purpose three carefully prepared papers were presented: the first a "General Summary," by Butler R. Wilson, Esq., of Boston, Mass.; the second entitled "Social and Physical Progress: a Comparative Analysis of the Reports of the Boards of Health of Atlanta, Baltimore, Charleston, Memphis, and Richmond," by Mr. L. M. Hershaw of Washington, D. C.; the third entitled "The Physical Condition of the Race, whether Dependent upon Social Conditions or Environment," by Prof. Eugene Harris of Fisk University.

Bishop L. H. Holsey, D.D., who was on the program and present, did not speak because of the lateness of the hour and his physical indisposition.

Butler R. Wilson, Esq., then introduced certain resolutions, which were referred to a committee on resolutions, consisting of Butler R. Wilson, Esq., of Boston, Mass.; Prof. Eugene Harris of Nashville, Tenn.; Rev. Dr. W. G. Alexander of Atlanta; Rev. J. E. Smith of Chattanooga, Tenn.; and Miss Lucy C. Laney of Augusta.

The meeting was then adjourned.

On Wednesday afternoon at 3 o'clock there were two simultaneous meetings of the conference. That for men was held in the Prayer Meeting Room, and had as its general subject: "Consumption; its Causes, and Means to Prevent it."

The presiding officer was Prof. Wm. H. Crogman ('76), of Clark University, who made suitable introductory remarks. Papers were then read as follows: "Ventilation, Exercise and Physical Development," by H. R. Butler, M.D., of Atlanta; "Care of the Teeth in its Relation to Health," by J. R. Porter, D.D.S., of Atlanta; "Causes of Consumption, and Practical Methods of Preventing it," by A. J. Love, M.D., of Chattanooga, Tenn.; "A Social Study of 1,000 Atlanta Homes," by Prof. F. A. Updyke of the Atlanta Baptist College, read in his absence by Pres. George Sale of that institution. A paper was also read by Dr. A. M. Brown of Birmingham, Ala., in place of the one that should have been read by Dr. R. F. Boyd of Nashville, Tenn., who telegraphed regret at his inability to attend on account of sickness.

This was followed by an animated general discussion, participated in by Butler R. Wilson, Esq., Rev. J. E. Smith, Mr. L. M. Hershaw, Rev. H. H. Proctor of Atlanta, Dr. H. R. Butler, Rev. Dr. W. G. Alexander, Prof. W. B. Matthews of Atlanta, Rev. Dr. W. J. White of Augusta, Prof. Eugene Harris, Rev. William Flagg of Atlanta, and Prof. W. H. Crogman.

A committee, of which Prof. W. H. Crogman was chairman, was chosen to prepare resolutions to be offered at the evening meeting.

The meeting was then adjourned.

The meeting for women, held at the same hour, in Ware Memorial Chapel, had as its general subject: "Infant Mortality; its Causes, and Means to Check it." After a preliminary explanation by Butler R. Wilson, Esq., a suitable introductory address was delivered by Miss Lucy C. Laney, of Augusta, who presided over the meeting. Papers were then read as follows: "Friendly Visiting," by Mrs. Minnie Wright Price of South Atlanta; "Parents' Associations," by Mrs. Dinah Watts Pace of Covington; "Mothers' Meetings," by Mrs. Georgia Swift King of Atlanta; "Need of Day Nurseries," by Mrs. Selena Sloan Butler of Atlanta; "Need of Kindergartens," by Mrs. Rosa Morehead Bass of Atlanta.

The reading of these papers was followed by an animated discussion, participated in by Miss Lucy C. Laney, Mrs. Adella Hunt Logan, Mrs. Georgia Swift King, Mrs David T. Howard of Atlanta, Mrs. Thos. N. Chase of Atlanta, Mrs. Dr. Murray of Gammon Theological Seminary, and others.

A committee, of which Mrs. Dinah Watts Pace was chairman, was appointed to draft suitable resolutions for presentation at the evening meeting; after which the meeting adjourned.

The meeting Wednesday night convened in Ware Memorial Chapel at 8 o'clock and was presided over by President Bumstead. Prayer was offered by Rev. Calvin Lane of Marietta. A paper was then read by Mrs. Adella Hunt Logan of Tuskegee, Ala., on "Prenatal and Hereditary Influences." Rev. Joseph E. Smith followed with a paper on the "Care of Neglected Children." The resolutions prepared by the committee appointed at the men's section meeting were then presented by Prof. Wm. H. Crogman and adopted by the conference.*

Rev. H. H. Proctor then spoke upon the "Need of Friendly Visiting," and Miss Lucy C. Laney upon the "Care of Children and Methods of Preventing Infant Mortality." The resolutions prepared by the committee appointed at the women's section meeting were then presented by Mrs. Dinah Watts Pace, and adopted by the conference.*

At this point Rev. J. E. Smith spoke concerning the nursery movement in Chattanooga, Tenn. Prof. Wm. E. Holmes, of the Atlanta Baptist College, spoke of the work of the Sociological Club of Atlanta. Mr. L. M. Hershaw reported concerning the Graduate Club in Washington, D. C.

---

* For these resolutions see page 32.

Butler R. Wilson, Esq., then read the following letter from Mr. George G. Bradford, of Boston, to President Bumstead:

"It is with great regret that I hereby tender my resignation as corresponding secretary of the conference. I need not assure you that only urgent necessity compels me to give up a work in which I have taken so deep an interest."

The following resolution was unanimously adopted, upon the receipt of this letter:

" *Whereas*, Mr. George G. Bradford, of Boston, a trustee of the Atlanta University, has been untiring in his efforts to make permanent the movement to obtain exact information concerning the social, physical and moral condition of the colored people living in cities;

" *Resolved*: That this conference hereby tender him the thanks of the colored people for his splendid work and instruct the secretaries of the conference to send him a copy of these resolutions."

It was then voted that an executive committee of five be appointed at some future time to make plans for a subsequent investigation, to decide the subjects to be investigated, to appoint a recorder, and to name a corresponding secretary.

Butler R. Wilson, Esq., then read the resolutions presented by the committee on Tuesday night. There was considerable discussion as to the phraseology of the first resolution, participated in by Butler R. Wilson, Esq., Rev. J. E. Smith, Prof. Eugene Harris, Dr. A. J. Love, Rev. Dr. W. J. White, Mr. L. M. Hershaw, and Prof. T. N. Chase. The resolutions as a whole were unanimously adopted.*

After remarks by Mrs. Georgia Swift King concerning a partially successful attempt by the W. C. T. U. to establish a day nursery in Atlanta, and further remarks by Mrs. Dinah Watts Pace, the conference adjourned.

GEORGE A. TOWNS, } Recording
GEORGE F. SMITH, } Secretaries.

* For these resolutions see page 33.

RESOLUTIONS ADOPTED BY THE CONFERENCE.

METHODS OF PREVENTING CONSUMPTION.

REPORTED FROM THE MEN'S SECTION MEETING.

Whereas, the chief modes of infection are:

First—By inhaling dry and pulverized expectoration;

Second—By using spoons, cups, and other articles which have not been properly cleaned after using by tuberculous patients;

Third—By kissing;

Fourth—From intermarriage of tuberculous individuals.

Therefore, *Resolved*:

First—That sputum must be destroyed and must not be allowed to become dry, and that handkerchiefs used by tuberculous persons must be destroyed;

Second—That the floors and walls of rooms occupied by tuberculous persons must be thoroughly disinfected before being used by other persons;

Third—That carpets, curtains and bedding must be exposed to superheated steam under high pressure;

Fourth—That all living rooms must be thoroughly aired daily, kept thoroughly clean, and ventilated night and day.

MOTHERS' MEETINGS, DAY NURSERIES, FAMILY SUPPORT AND KINDERGARTENS.

REPORTED FROM THE WOMEN'S SECTION MEETING.

Whereas, a race cannot rise higher than its women, and the home is the great school for the molding of character, and mothers are the most important factors in these schools ;

Therefore, *Resolved*: That a new impetus be given to the establishing and holding of mothers' meetings whenever and wherever practicable, for the instruction, development and uplifting of the motherhood of our race along practical, moral and spiritual lines.

Whereas, a very large percentage of our women, being thrown upon their own resources for a livelihood for themselves and families, are compelled daily to leave, uncared for, their little ones ;

Therefore, *Resolved*: That individuals and organizations interest themselves in the immediate establishment, on a small scale at first, of day nurseries for the care and culture of these dear little ones.

Whereas, investigation shows that a very large majority of our men are supported by their wives, and since such a condition of affairs must of necessity hinder wives and mothers from performing their higher duties, such as the careful training of families along moral and spiritual lines, and since man in failing to care for his family proves himself to be unfit to be called husband or father ;

Therefore, *Resolved*: That in order to arouse and educate such men to a full appreciation of their duties men's meetings be held whenever and wherever practicable, and that our ministers of the Gospel preach special sermons along all practical lines ; that by these two agencies the men of to-day may be aroused to a keener sense of their responsibility in this matter of family support.

Whereas, the need of kindergarten work is clearly seen for the starting of the little ones into proper channels of training, and since work in this department has been of the greatest help to teachers who lead the young minds from this into higher branches, and since the child-life in the school-room should be of vital interest to parents;

Therefore, *Resolved*: That efforts be put forth for the establishment and maintenance of such departments of educational work.

GENERAL RESOLUTIONS.

Resolved, That it appears from the result of the investigation :—

First—That the excessive mortality among Negroes is not due mainly to environment ;

• Second—That the excessive mortality among Negroes is largely due either to their ignorance or to their disregard of the laws of health and morality ;

Third—That the excessive mortality and the apparent increase of immorality among the Negroes is chiefly due to neglect of home and family life, the chief cause of which is the extent to which the mothers are obliged to go out to work ;

Fourth—That the failure of the men to entirely support their families with their earnings has a most serious effect upon the social, physical and economic progress of the race ;

Fifth—That finally, it appears that the Negro must reform himself, and that he is not dependent upon charity or municipal regulations, but has the means in his own hands.

Resolved, That the following recommendations are made:—

First—That the attention of members of the conference during the coming year be concentrated on reforms in the family life of the Negro;

Second—That greater care and attention should be given to the home training of children, and also of young men and young women, and that parents' associations and mothers' meetings should be formed for that purpose;

Third—That day nurseries should be provided for the care of infants and young children in the enforced absence of the parents;

Fourth—That friendly visiting among the poor should be more general and more systematic, and that friendly visitors should hold weekly or monthly conferences under the direction of those who are making a special study of social problems.

ADDRESSES, PAPERS, AND LETTERS,

ADDRESS OF PRESIDENT BUMSTEAD.

It has been our hope, and for a time our expectation, that the address of welcome would be given to-night by His Excellency, Governor Atkinson, but circumstances have prevented his attendance, and we must content ourselves with the expression of his interest and good wishes which he has so kindly conveyed in his letter of regret.

It seems, therefore, to fall to me to speak the word of welcome, and I do it with great heartiness. I welcome you to the interesting discussions which this conference has in store for us. I congratulate you, too, on the painstaking and highly successful work which you have carried on since our meeting a year ago, and which will form the basis of discussion at the present meeting. The results of your investigations conducted last fall and winter, as embodied in the statistical tables of the May Bulletin of the Department of Labor at Washington, have impressed me deeply. I am impressed with the enormous amount of careful, patient, discriminating, and conscientious labor which those tables represent, and I am impressed anew with the significance and importance of statistical science.

What is the significance of the statistical work in which this conference is now engaged? You and I have sometimes seen a man who attracted our attention because of his striking physical health. His figure was erect and finely proportioned, his muscles well developed, his step elastic, his eye clear, his complexion of the kind that reveals healthy blood coursing through every artery and vein. This man, however, may once have been a weak and sickly student in college. How did this transformation take place? It was the work of the director of physical culture in that college. He took the student in hand, made careful measurements of the different parts of his body, tested the action of his muscles and of his lungs and heart and other vital organs, found out where the weak points in his body were, and noted accurately the degree of weakness or of insufficient development. Then he presented certain exercises for the student to practice to secure a more vigorous or a more symmetrical development, a certain diet to follow, possibly certain medicines or tonics to take. The transformation followed, and its success all depended on the accuracy with which the real condition of that young student's physical organism was ascertained by the director of physical culture.

We are dealing with a much larger and vastly more important organism than that of any individual—the great social organism of which we all form a part, an organism of wonderful complexity, with a life peculiar to itself, and just as much subject to the laws of health and disease as the body of any individual can possibly be. It is the prime object of all sociological investigation to find out the weak spots in the social organism and to seek to remedy them. This is the work in which we are engaged, in common with all other students of social science. We are not, indeed, undertaking to do the whole of it, but only a part. We have wisely chosen for the present to confine ourselves to that constituent part of the social organism which is made up of a single race or class of people, and to those nerve-centers of modern life which are found in the cities and larger towns. But it is none the less for the benefit of the larger whole that we carry on this more limited work. And for the furtherance of the great end before us all—the perfect health of the social organism, or the body politic, as it is sometimes called, I am confident that your investigations of the past winter will prove a substantial contribution.

Before we pass to the discussion of the statistics to which I have referred, it is perhaps important that I should remind you of the two things which constitute the chief value of all statistics. One is the accuracy with which they are gathered, and the other is the honesty with which they are interpreted. The gathering of statistics is not the easy task which many people suppose, or which, possibly, you supposed before you tried it. It requires intelligence, discrimination, tact, courtesy, patience and fidelity in no small degree, and your work shows the possession of these qualities to a very gratifying extent, as it seems to me. But the correct reading and interpretation of statistics is oftentimes an almost equally delicate and difficult task. The temptation is frequently strong to close our eyes to unpleasant conclusions or to attempt to explain them away. Candor and courage are needed here in the proper interpretation of our statistical work as intelligence and accuracy were needed in their collection. Let the proceedings of this conference demonstrate that we are possessed of all these qualities.

PRENATAL AND HEREDITARY INFLUENCES.

BY MRS. ADELLA HUNT LOGAN ('81), TUSKEGEE, ALA.

The boy takes his large nose from his grandmother, the small mouth from his father, and a quick temper from his mother. This is natural, for children always inherit the characteristics of their ancestors. But where does he get red hair? No one in the family has hair of that color. And how is it that the young man seems prone to the social sin? His father has always seemed upright, and his mother is regarded as a model of purity. To be sure, the grandfather sowed wild oats, and it is charged that a great–great–grandmother was born out of wedlock, but that was generations ago and this young man has never heard those family scandals of a hundred years past.

It is well, if his ears have never listened to such unhappy stories. His parents were wise in withholding them from his knowledge. Alas! while they could easily keep the family skeleton in the closet and spare their son the humiliation of such ugly tales they could not so easily purify and change the blood that coursed in their veins; hence we see the son, in spite of fine precept and example, on the downward grade in his social tendencies.

Again, they say this young man is not very strong. His mother fears he is going into consumption. The father says: "Have no fears along that line, my dear, for there is no consumption in my family nor in yours. No danger of that, although somehow our son is rather frail!"

That red hair is hard to account for, but, no doubt, this head is an exact reproduction of one in the same family generations ago. It may be so far back, indeed, that no living person remembers having heard of the peculiarity. In the same silent way influences which affect the morals and the health of the boy have been handed down.

How rarely in the every day ordering of our lives do we give any attention to that silent, but powerful, thing known as heredity! Although its power cannot be confined in time to the earthly life of man, nor in social contact to any one race, as long as we are not reminded in some very forcible or unpleasant way of its effects, we scarcely think of its operations. At any rate, the thought expended upon it rarely ripens into such action as will regulate its influence.

In respect to time the force of heredity cannot be checked by a generation. We are to-day reaping what was sown, not by our fathers alone, but by their fathers and grandfathers. " Unto the third and fourth generation of them " was the decree thundered from Mt. Sinai by the voice of Almighty God.

There can be no suspending of the influences of heredity until the human soul has had sufficient development to appreciate responsibilities ; until it wills to be shaped by this or by that influence. No, there is no choice ! Before the body is ready to begin life as a separate being, as a new personality, it is molded and cast by the combined traits of the father and the mother from whom this new creature must draw its individual existence. And the intellectual and ethical cast will follow as closely the law, " Like begets like," as will the physical. We do not expect to find the children of white parentage having black faces or kinky hair, nor the children of black ancestry having fair brows, blue eyes, and flaxen locks. It would be just as unreasonable to expect the intellectual and the ethical characteristics of children to be radically unlike those of their ancestors as it would be to expect their physical features to be radically different.

'Tis true that the progeny of some very good parents are very bad specimens of humanity, but such cases must be like our boy's red hair which fell to him despite the fact that no other such head had ever been seen in that family. In both cases the results came through blood. Both the red hair and the weak or vicious character were transmitted. Probably through a long stream of blood, but we must know that neither came as a matter of chance. The one was just as much a legacy as the other.

Placing an inheritance is often difficult for the reason that it may be the result of complex causes and combined forces.

Possibly no one in the preceding generations had red hair, but there must have been sufficient in the aggregate of that kind of pigment to produce one such head in the family. This same principle of transmission applies to the health, the brain and the morals of the descendants. The exact ailment of body or malady of mind may not be traceable to any one source, but it has been handed down.

Legacies of money seem to fall in most cases to those who are already fortunate. This may be on the theory that " To him that hath shall be given." Not so with the more enduring legacies of body and soul. Whether we will or no they come, and, like the dreaded bacteria, fix themselves in the most fertile soil. Where there is one weakness of body or mind another is the more apt to locate ; hence, instead of having a general distribution of evil, it falls much more heavily in some places than in others.

To no one source more than the conditions attendant upon pregnant women can the cause of physical or moral evil be traced. The unborn child draws its physical and in large measure its intellectual and ethical make-up from its father and its mother. Not from the mother alone, as many suppose, but from both.

Both parents contribute to the possibilities for health, good or bad, and furnish the germs for character creation and development just as certainly as they together originate the physical life.

These are solemn truths! Yet how few people understand or regard them ! The awful sacredness of procreation has never yet dawned upon any considerable proportion of mankind.

Sadly enough, the gratification of passion is too often the only thought, while the result is given little or no consideration. Too many children come into life as mere accidents. The father is irritated at the thought of an additional one to work for. He feels his present family to be quite as much as he can decently support. His moroseness is communicated to the already regretful mother, who reasons that she is not strong enough, that children worry her so she cannot do justice to those she already has, that her time and strength are too much divided, as she in many cases is also a bread-winner. Sad plight, we see, for there is reason in the objections offered. But prudential considerations come too late to be availing. Just think how the innocent offspring must reap the evil effects of these unholy feelings and expressions, and all the sympathy that you might have felt for the parents turns into disgust, and you exclaim : " In Heaven's name, call your will to the rescue and say, 'God helping me, I will not thus prejudice the cause of my own child !' "

Few women seem to appreciate the fact that the sensitive embryo receives the impressions made upon the mind of the mother. Very strange thoughtlessness, as the most ignorant believe in birthmarks and everything that affects the body. How is it that they do not realize that a mind also is being created?

All parents love their children and most love them to the very best of their understanding. Because of this love, which we believe to be the strongest known to the human breast, most parents are willing to be taught what is best for their offspring.

In making effort to give uplift to the vitality of the Negro race the best work needs to be put into the enlightenment of present and prospective parenthood. Not necessarily into general and extended learning,—that is more or less impracticable,—but the claims of prenatal and hereditary influences need to be brought to the direct and intelligent consideration of all classes.

In the women's meetings and in the men's meetings equally there should be set forth in a plain way the important teachings of science on this important subject. This instruction may be set forth in such language as the occasion demands and the instructor chooses to employ, but, above all, let it be distinctly understood that the development of germ life depends upon the original germ and equally upon the culture and treatment of that germ:—in short, teach that the prenatal development of a child depends largely upon *whatever* affects the mother. If the pregnant woman is constantly wishing that her unborn child were dead or that the man who has given her this burden,—as she has learned in her chagrin to regard the child,—were dead; who can wonder that out of such murderous thought there should come in very truth a murderer!

Should the material wants of the mother be denied her to such an extent that she feels the necessity and yields to the temptation of supplying them by theft or by prostitution who shall think it strange that her child should be a thief or prostitute? If the father is a drunkard the son is apt to be a drunkard.

Criminals are often made years and years before they are sentenced to prison. Alas! too often made criminal before they are born.

The body may come into life as sorely doomed as the mind, unable to resist the ordinary diseases incident to childlife, because of the many neglects and abuses of the bodies of parents. This is very wrong: very unfair to the child and in many ways very hard on parents.

The creation of a strong public sentiment on these subjects seems to be an imperative necessity.

THE CARE OF NEGLECTED CHILDREN.

BY REV. JOSEPH E. SMITH ('76), CHATTANOOGA, TENN.

[NOTE: For confirmation of the facts stated by Mr. Smith, see table 7 of appendix A, showing the proportion of families partially or wholly supported by women The enforced absence of the mothers from their homes will remain a vital factor in the problem for many years to come, being due to industrial conditions which will change slowly. Mr. Smith's recommendations are therefore timely.—ED.]

"Seest thou not what they do in the cities . . . and in the streets?" I desire to call attention to some of the daily scenes in our streets and the lessons which they teach. The streets of a city are the exhibition halls of its citizens. Walking through these public halls all phases and conditions of life may be seen, and the character and civilization of its people judged. Most pleasing and inspiring evidences of well ordered and happy home life appear on the one hand; while on the other hand many and sad are the evidences of no order, no home life and no happiness for a large number of people.

It is of this *imperative* need,—orderly home life and training,—as evidenced by street and prison scenes, that I shall now more particularly speak.

One of the first scenes in our streets between the hours of five and six o'clock in the morning is, large numbers of women rushing to their places of work for the day. About eight o'clock at night they return to their homes. Many of these women are mothers with from one to eight and often more children. Unwillingly these mothers leave their children all day and part of the night in the place they call home, all alone to care for themselves. If they are awake, just before the mother leaves, as is usually the case, she gives them hastily what she may happen to have for their breakfast, sometimes a piece of bread, sometimes it is a little molasses in a tin plate or old bucket top, around which the little ones all gather and each in his turn dips in his fingers and licks them off until all the molasses is gone. To this sweetness the mother adds many sweet promises of great things for them if they will be good and stay at home until mama comes back at night. Then with great anxiety and confusion she tears herself away from them and hastens to her work while they cry for her to come back, and often they are quarreling and fighting among themselves before she is out of sight. No one but a mother knows how painful it is to leave her children all alone under these unfortunate circumstances, but there is nothing else for her to do but to go, and go she does with an aching heart.

It is not long after the mother is gone before the children, being left to themselves, leave the house, go into the streets, wander about at will from place to place, get into mischief and commit sin, often taking little things from people's houses without realizing that they have done wrong. They ramble about until tired, fall down at almost any place, go to sleep, and wake up again only to continue the ramble, sometimes until late in the night.

The anxious mother comes home at night to find that her children are not there. She does not know where they are and starts out in the dark to look for them in the streets. Often she finds them in the city jail or station house, having been arrested by some officer during the day or early night for committing some little crime. Chief Hill of the police force of Chattanooga says: "They are brought in the patrol wagon to the station house by the dozen at the time. Ask them where their parents are and they will say, 'Dead, or at work, or away from home somewhere.'"

Such is a faint representation of a part of that which is going on in our streets every day, and we need only to multiply the days and we have the awful record of years. Growing up in the midst of such daily surroundings and influences is it to be wondered at that large numbers of our young people find their way to the chain-gang and work house?

There are hundreds and thousands of our children at this very hour who are roaming about at large in the streets of our cities because they have had no orderly home life or training; growing up in the streets their idea of living is such as they get from the worse side of street life, and the inevitable result must be crime, prison and the gallows. And the saddest thing about all of this is, that unless under the providence of God a preventive is found, this most appalling state of society must continue growing worse each day to the end of time.

Is it possible to so reenforce the home as to save society and the state this awful menace? I believe it is possible and practicable. The "Day Nursery" and education as reenforcements to the home furnish the preventive.

The greatest need of Negro children is the right kind of home life and training. It is a most encouraging truth that many of our people have neat, modest, virtuous homes, and their children, being reared under intelligent and safe motherly influences, are growing up virtuous and modest, trustworthy and useful. These children are not candidates for crime, disease and prison, but for a worthy and useful citizenship. While this number is small when compared to the masses, yet it is large enough to show what can be done by that all-important agency, the home. The day nursery, as a supplement to the home, is the most *urgent need* of the great masses of Negro children. Says Mrs. Dodge in the *Outlook*: "If the child is father to the man, then the influences which surround him during childhood have the greatest effect upon his after-life, and the day nursery is, therefore, the foundation upon which to build the structure of character; for, taking the child in his earliest years, often indeed in earliest infancy, nursery training is the first in the chain of educational influences which aid the state in making the useful citizen, this influence holding sway over his mind and heart on through the kindergarten period, through the public school, and over the threshold into the whirl of life's exacting activities."

If day nurseries can be established in the cities and the little ones gathered from the streets into them; soap and fresh water, comb and brush freely and effectually used; a clean little garment furnished for a clean little body, and some wholesome food for a hungry little stomach; clean thoughts put into the little mind and heart; lessons of sympathy, kindness, honesty, industry, hope and self-respect taught; —if these things can be done for all Negro children deprived of home training a long and very effectual step will be taken toward reducing crime, disease and premature death.

THE NEED OF FRIENDLY VISITATION.

BY REV. H. H. PROCTOR, ATLANTA, GA.

An undertaker who within the last ten years has buried many of the ten thousand of our people who sleep in Southview cemetery recently made a remark to me that set me to thinking. I give it to you to-night with the hope that it may have the same effect upon you. "You have no idea," he said, "how many people are dying from the lack of sympathy." This is expert testimony, and we cannot reject it.

I suspect, however, that the idea he had in mind is capable of a more precise expression. There is a wealth of sympathy in this world. It is the exceptional heart that contains no well-spring of sympathy. The difficulty is not as to the possession of sympathy; it is as to its expression. Many people are dying because no one expresses any sympathy for them. Sympathy is like the coupon on the railway ticket,—not good if detached! Prayer may be effective, though unexpressed; but not so with sympathy.

There are many ways of expressing this sympathy so as to make it effective in elevating the home life of the poor. One way is by giving good advice in an assembly like this. Another is by contributing money to be used in judicious ways. Both of these are needed, but I am thinking of another way, which, while not necessarily independent of these, is, I think, more important than either. I refer to friendly personal visitation. Advice is cheap. We may cast a coin at a beggar to quiet a disturbing conscience. But to give ourselves,—that is the gift that costs. To go into the homes of the people and, as did Philip with the eunuch, to sit with them, costs more than to make an address or contribute a quarter. And yet that is to my mind the only solution of this great sociological problem. We must come into personal touch with the masses.

To this some will put in objections. Will not these people presume upon our social reserve? Will not the upper class be dragged down by contact with the lower? These questions are not unnatural. They demand a reasonable answer. To the first objection I would say that there is not the least danger of the plainest people mistaking our kindly interest for an invitation to our private social functions. The plain people have wonderfully keen instincts. To the other I would say that it is not contact with the lower element that injures the higher; it is the kind of contact. The distinction is vital. "He is armed without who is innocent within." Virtue is its possessor's shield. The immaculate swan comes unspotted from the vilest sewer.

If you would elevate a building you would not apply pulleys at the top. You would put jackscrews under the mudsills. You cannot elevate society by lifting from the top; you must put the jackscrews under the mudsills of society. Put the unfailing dynamics of friendly visitation under the homes of the poor and the whole people will rise a living, an exalted temple before God.

CAUSES OF CONSUMPTION, AND PRACTICAL METHODS OF PREVENTING IT.

BY A. J. LOVE, M.D., CHATTANOOGA, TENN.

Mr. President: Thinking as I do that the specific treatment of tuberculosis does not come before us for consideration at this meeting, I shall not enter into a discussion of the late discoveries for the radical cure of consumption.

In presenting to you this paper on a subject about which so much has been written and concerning the solution of which so many theories have been advanced, I shall speak more from a practical than from a theoretical standpoint.

That tuberculosis is a germ disease is no longer disputed. But a practical means of destroying this bacillus is the vexatious question of to-day.

To rightly understand some of the means of checking and preventing the growth of consumption we must first know some of its predisposing as well as some of its exciting causes.

A predisposition to tuberculosis is inherited. Not that the infant is born with the germ fully developed in his system, but being born of tuberculous parents he inherits a condition favorable to the development of the disease. He is of an inferior physique, usually slender, emaciated, nervous, easily exhausted, has a low or deformed chest, his blood is poor in quality, he is susceptible to colds, and subject to bronchial catarrh and cough. The alimentary canal is one of the most vulnerable points in his anatomy. The digestion is so feeble that the mildest diet is sometimes harmful. And yet, with all this, he is bright-eyed, intelligent and hopeful

There is an intimate relation between consumption and scrofula, which is likewise a disease of degenerative tissue metamorphosis. Whether there is a direct relation between these two diseases or not, is perhaps yet to be demonstrated, but the clinical fact that tuberculous and strumous diatheses are almost always found in the same subjects cannot be denied. That the tissues of scrofulous subjects are wanting in vital power is apparent from their great tendency to suppurate. Bartholow says that the tubercle is a product of scrofula, which would indicate that the same cause which produces scrofulosis would, through the process of pathological evolution, produce tuberculosis.

Is tuberculosis possible in a subject who has not the unfortunate legacy of a tubercular diathesis? To my mind there can be no doubt that the affirmative of this is true. The child born of healthy parents, but who is reared in the slums of a densely populated city, housed in a miserable hut in the alley, forced to sleep in a crowded apartment where the atmosphere is necessarily damp and virulent, both from the effluvia rising from the decomposing excreta from the bodies of its many inmates and from the vitiated gases exhaled from their lungs, who sleeps in the garments which he wears through many weary days, who goes for months without knowing the civilizing, Christianizing and cleansing influence of the bath, whose food is improperly cooked and wanting both in quality and quantity, and concerning the hour of whose meals there is no regularity, will almost surely present early symptoms of decay.

That constitution which at the outset was physiologically perfect has gradually degenerated into one with inferior vital tendencies. The morbific influences of his surroundings have wrought upon him a molecular modification of the tissues, which undergo a low grade of inflammation and glandular suppuration. This, with its catalogue of pathological possibilities, is scrofulosis. This fruitful soil is the rendevous for bacteria of every morbid turn of mind. The cells having lost their vital resistance, the system becomes an easy prey to disease. Here the tubercle bacillus finds a suitable pabulum on which to subsist, and amid such unfavorable surroundings our subject of unfortunate circumstances will almost inevitably succumb to this disease. But even if at this period he should not himself be overtaken by tuberculosis, still this marked tendency of constitution will gradually become permanent and capable of hereditary transmission. Thus the succeeding generations of all such individuals have a natural predisposition to tuberculosis, as also to many other diseases which are superinduced by malnutrition.

Drunkenness in parents predisposes to consumption in their offspring, because of the fact that they transmit to them the toxological effects of alcoholism, producing a general deterioration of nutrition, and because of semi-starvation due to neglect on the part of these parents while under the influence of alcohol. For it is a painful fact that mothers in the lower classes, as well as fathers, are becoming more and more addicted to strong drink, and that these unfortunate children are allowed to go for many hours without nourishment.

Puberty, with its attending susceptibility to consumption, is a critical period. The system, while undergoing the important changes of maturity, is ill-prepared to defend itself against extraneous pathological factors. This period ends the career of many youth, who in their infancy were fed on artificial food instead of mother's milk. That this has a baneful influence on the constitution during a lifetime, the emaciated frames of these unfortunate subjects will attest. Those articles of diet which purport to be elegant substitutes for mothers' milk are wanting in both nutrition and digestibility. Though they have the elements necessary for development and growth the ratio of these elements is not in keeping with the natural formula of mothers' milk and a dyspeptic condition is induced which leads to marasmus, scrofulosis, tuberculosis, and death.

It is a prevalent idea that tuberculosis is transmissible by touch, and that inhalations of effluvia emanating from the skin of tuberculous subjects will reproduce the disease. This, however, is untrue.

The most frequent cause of the direct transmission of tuberculosis is the inhalation of the bacillus arising from dried and pulverized sputum. Hence the danger of living in houses recently occupied by consumptives. They frequently spit upon the walls or the floor, and the bed-clothing and wearing apparel become contaminated with sputum, which, when dry and broken into small particles, is subject to inhalation. While it is true that this virus is of a greater specific gravity than air and therefore has a tendency to fall to the floor, yet sweeping and dusting will raise it, at which time it may be inhaled and become a nucleus around which is built that insidious and yet aggressive foe.

As long as the germ is kept suspended in fluid it is less liable to cause infection, for as moisture increases its specific gravity it cannot float in the atmosphere and therefore cannot be inhaled.

In order for this bacillus to find a lodging place in the human economy, there must be a dissolution of continuity in the mucous membrane. For in a healthy condition it is not liable to infection. It is here that these bronchial catarrhs and colds cut such a distinguishing figure ; for a catarrh indicates that violence has been done to the integrity of a mucous membrane, destroying or impairing its protective power to such an extent as to admit of inoculation and infection. This is the second whirlpool for our predisposed subject, for if possibly in his childhood he has steered clear of Scylla he has now drifted into Charybdis.

It is not likely, however, that a subject with an otherwise healthy constitution, even though he has a diseased mucous membrane, will become infected under such circumstances. For the blood in such an individual is rich in the life-giving properties of the body and the cells are so vigorous as to stand as a bulwark against an invading enemy.

Tuberculosis may also be contracted through impure alimentation ; for it has been clearly demonstrated that cows are often affected with this disease and that tubercle bacilli are found in large numbers in their milk.

When there is a lesion in the alimentary tract virus may, because of this, enter the blood and induce both local and constitutional consumption. That this source of infection is true was proven a short time ago in a swine test. Of 1,026 healthy swine fed on sour whiskey and distillery slop, all were sickened and 250 died. Autopsies on 104 showed tubercle bacilli. In an adjoining pen were 600, fed on good sweet maize. None contracted tuberculosis.

Persons whose foods are subject to acetic fermentation in the alimentary canal are liable to tuberculosis through its absorption. In those habituated to strong drink the micoderma aceti, which is an acetic ferment, is frequently absorbed through the intestinal mucous membrane, which is paralyzed by the presence of alcohol, but in the absence of this stimulant this membrane is capable of protecting against such absorption.

The death-rate from consumption in the United States is appalling. But that the spread of this disease can be checked is clearly apparent.

It is the plain duty of every city to pass ordinances prohibiting its inhabitants from living in squalor and dirt; prohibiting the conversion of homes which should be clean, wholesome and pure, into pest houses and laboratories in which are incubated every conceivable form of virulent bacteria ; directing that the premises of all be kept at all times clean, that bedding and carpets be aired and exposed to the sun, that the houses be from time to time renovated, that thorough ventilation be the rule in every household.

While it is a fact that every family is not able to wear costly garments, yet every family can wear clean ones, and have clean surroundings.

Nor do I think a course of this kind impracticable or abridging personal rights; for to live in such unwholesome abodes with such unhealthy surroundings is not only damaging to those who indulge in this loathsome practice, but is forever an abiding source of infection to the community. This is a menace which no municipality can brook without becoming weakened thereby. This is the prime source of all infectious diseases, a nuisance to the public because it is in direct opposition to the pursuit of health and happiness. A government has the same right to protect its votaries from this deadly condition as it has to quarantine against smallpox. For while smallpox is rapidly contagious and spreads dread disaster in its wake, what disease is more terrible than consumption, which like the boa constrictor is stealthily winding itself around humanity and squeezing the life out of the nations?

If we would stamp out tuberculosis we must elevate the standard of living among the lower classes. We must save them from themselves. If we have not educational facilities sufficient to civilize them fast enough, we must bring them up to the requirements by legislation. In my opinion the present condition is too appalling to wait on the slow process of evolution. More vigorous measures must be taken.

We need a more rigid system of food inspection. No animal should be killed for food without first being scientifically inspected and pronounced sound. The inspection of milk for tubercle bacilli should be made a specialty. Milch cows and animals to be killed for meat should not be fed on impure foods. Stale and tainted meats of any kind should not be eaten, for although bacteria for the most part are destroyed in the process of cooking, still the decomposition of this abnormal material in the intestines may produce infection, thus lessening the vital resistance and paving the way for consumption.

VENTILATION.

BY H. R. BUTLER, A.M., M.D., ATLANTA, GA.

[NOTE: Dr. Butler's paper included also the subjects of Exercise and Physical Development. But in this case, as also in others, we have felt obliged to abbreviate.— ED.]

In the homes of the most ignorant of our people, and some of the intelligent for that matter, ventilation is an unknown quantity. The inmates are opposed to having air enter the house when all are *well*, and if any of the family are *sick* it is believed that it means death to the patient should air, and in some cases light, enter the sick chamber.

I will not enter into a description of the various methods of ventilation; we have not the time for such here. I will simply give you a few of the many cases that have come under my observation in which ventilation was much needed.

Case 1.—This first case to which I wish to call your attention was in a one-room house; room 14x14; inmates, four. It was a case of confinement. The room was as dark and the air as foul at twelve o'clock in the day as it was at twelve at night. I had to use a small tin lamp at either hour in order to see how to care for my patient.

Case 2.—It was in a small basement room where a mother and two small children lay sick, nigh unto death. The door and window had been closed for weeks. The air was foul, damp and heavy. There they were with no friends, no water, no food, and no pure air. There they lay until found by some good women who sent the mother to the poor-house, one child to the hospital where it died, and the other to the Carrie Steele Orphans' Home, where it is recovering slowly. The mother is well and has returned to the city and is at work. Both mother and child, however, show signs of tuberculosis, which are no doubt the result of inhaling the foul air of that basement room.

Case 3.—I manage to visit the public schools of the city at least once a year. I visited one of these schools this year in which everything else was taught and practiced but ventilation. The air in some of the rooms of that building was not at all conducive to good health.

Case 4.—It was a two-room house; inmates, two,—a man and his wife. The husband lay dying with consumption and would, in his delirium, spit any and every where. The wife, who was a kind and tidy woman, did all in her power, under the circumstances, to keep her little home clean. To do this she was continually sweeping, in which process she kept bacilli on the move, endangering not only her health but my health and the health of all her friends who might call.

Being a woman of some intelligence a brief explanation that she must keep the air of the room fresh and free from dust was all that was necessary to have her see the danger. I then began to care for my patient hygienically and antiseptically.

Thus I could go on and multiply case after case to show the great necessity of a better understanding among our people concerning ventilation; but it is not necessary. We all are satisfied that much improvement is needed in our homes along those lines and that is why we are here.

Preaching the laws of health and hygiene in this age has about the same effect that preaching the gospel has. They hear willingly, but heed slowly. Many hear, but only a few will believe; a few will be saved and many will be lost.

In conclusion, I would ask that this organization petition Congress to make an appropriation to help push forward this well-begun work.

With that aid we would be able to place one or two physicians in every large city, at least, whose duty it would be to push these investigations, and as they would go from home to home they could instruct the people as to ventilation and in the laws of health and hygiene. This is, indeed, necessary if we wish to have the masses instructed in those things that are indispensable in order to have strong and healthy bodies as well as strong and vigorous minds.

THE CARE OF THE TEETH IN ITS RELATION TO HEALTH.

BY J. R. PORTER ('86), D.D.S., ATLANTA, GA.

In working out our health problems we often fail to recognize certain factors which are highly important. We hardly ever figure on the effect of diseased teeth on the general health, and their permanent handicap on our energies. Many a trouble that has been assigned to some remote cause, and that has called forth learned disquisitions, should have been placed at the door of some abscessed tooth of long standing, and the diagnosis punctuated with the forceps.

Many a case of facial neuralgia is the progeny of uncared-for teeth. Many an injured eye owes all its troubles to the root of some offending tooth that reaches the floor of its orbit by using the Antrum of Hymore as a go-between ; while fever, hysteria, muscular neuralgia and apparent heart trouble, that are plainly due to these unclean members, are not infrequently met with.

There are two classes of evils that may arise as a result of diseased tooth tissue : those that come from actual contact with the poisonous matter generated in the affected member, and those that result from the constant irritation of the nerve tissues.

Each one of these may be serious in its consequences, and may force upon us evils that will run their allotted third and fourth generation, or may leave permanent marks on our physical appearance and health.

Lessons should be taught in the schools on the care of the teeth, as well as of other portions of the body. People do not neglect treating a fever, removing a splinter or caring for a sprain, and yet they pass unnoticed these long-suffering members, until one of them, after long endurance, suddenly wakes them to a sense of their duty.

There is a truth that rings through the pages of the Bible, in so many forms and varieties that it has become impressive. " Cleanliness is next to Godliness," is that truth. In it we have our first lesson in hygiene, and around it clusters all our physical and spiritual comfort.

There is nothing useless in that sacred volume, nothing written for mere ornament, nothing engrafted in the wonderful schemes of creation and redemption that has not a "because" attached to it, and that is not a link in God's economy, whether of man towards his Creator, or of man towards himself.

This beautiful truth is therefore pregnant with a deeper meaning than is at first apparent. Not only does it teach that we should keep the body pure and clean as the fit temple of the living God; but more, it teaches that if we would more nearly live the allotted span of human life, we should recognize that cleanliness is the panacea for all our ills, and that sanitation, external and internal, is our best safeguard against disease.

ADDRESS BEFORE THE WOMEN'S MEETING.

BY MISS LUCY C. LANEY ('73), AUGUSTA, GA.

Ladies : A little more than a quarter of a century ago this Ameri-- can Republic, after much painful travail, brought forth the youngest child of civilization—the Negro citizen. To-day we, the offspring of that birth, stand upon the entrance of a glorious future if we will accept and faithfully comply with the conditions upon which we may claim the boon.

To find out and to discuss some of these conditions is the object of this conference and the women's section of it. For a long time many were disposed to think that the condition of most importance was politics, and for years politicians, honest and dishonest, ignorant and wise, struggled in vain to bring about that consummation devoutly to be wished, true manhood in our race. Some vainly hoped that that mis-- erable deformity wrongly called education, viz., the conning of a few facts from text-books, was *the* condition to be complied with. Still another class said honestly and devoutly that the condition and the only condition to be met was the development of our religious nature. A fourth class united the second and third conditions, and after some-- what modifying the third, gave to the world as the watchword of Negro development " the Bible and the spelling-book." Any *one* of these made the rule of life, made the only condition to be met, has been to those who followed it an *ignis fatuus*, for it has misguided them and led them into dangerous places. Each by itself is but a part of a grand total.

No person is responsible for his ancestors ; nor should he be held responsible for their sins and short-comings, though he bear about in his body the marks and scars of those sins ; but every woman can see to it that she gives to her progeny a good mother and an honorable ancestry. I care not how humble may be the house in which two loving hearts may set up their household gods, if blessed with a manly and God-fearing husband, a womanly and God-fearing wife, intelligence and health, that place is a *home*, the nearest approach on earth to heaven. The chief joy of home is mother. You may place upon the brow of a true mother the greenest laurel or you may give into her keeping the highest civic honors, but these to her will be found wanting if weighed in a balance over against her home. To her the blessedness of motherhood is the greatest joy, a crown more costly than pearls of royalty.

Marriage, the beginning of home, is a matter of great importance and should not be carelessly entered into. It is the place to take the proverbial stitch in time. From this point a shadow may be cast which will darken the pathway of coming generations. This is not a question that can be settled on a basis of gain or convenience, but as has been said: " A tie that only love and truth should weave and nothing but death should part."

Motherhood, honored by our blessed Master, is the crown of womanhood. This gives her not only interest in the home and society, but also authority. She should be interested in the welfare of her own and her neighbors' children. To woman has been committed the responsibility of making the laws of society, making environments for children. She has the privilege and authority, God-given, to help develop into a noble man or woman the young life committed to her care. There is no nobler work entrusted to the hands of mortals.

Faithful mothers, mothers who know their duty and perform it,—such must have been the mother of the Gracchi,—such a mother we read of in holy writ: "All nations shall rise up and call her blessed."

Will not the intelligent mother gather to her heart her sons and daughters and teach them to be pure in life and chaste in conversation, and see to it that there be no double standard set up in her home, and none in her community if she be able to tear it down?

Too often that mother who is careful of her daughter's environment, the formation of her girl's character, is negligent as to her son's. He may choose his own company,—be the molder of his own character. If the daughter should drag the robes of her womanhood in the dust that mother would be covered with shame and grief,—but the son of that mother may trample down his manhood and there will scarcely be a blush ; only the old but false cry, and pernicious as it is false, " Boys must sow their wild oats."

Our boys need the careful, loving hand of mother ; perhaps not more so than the girls—but certainly not less.

Shall the boys be left to the tender training of the saloons and the fascinations of women degraded by sin? God forbid it! Women of to-day, awake to your responsibilities and privileges.

The Mothers' Congress recently held at Washington was not only a most unique gathering, but as the years roll on and men and women study more carefully that most important of all questions,—the children of the nation,—it will be found to be the working out of the noblest ideas of the noblest minds and most loving hearts of the age. That vast assemblage of men and women discussing questions most vital to the welfare of their children shows how great is the lamentation in Rama, Rachel weeping for her children, refusing to be comforted because they are not.

Shall we not catch inspiration from that Congress and in our literary societies, ladies' clubs, and even in our churches study our children by the search-light of the new psychology and with the spirit of the true and loving mother?

FRIENDLY VISITING.

BY MRS. MINNIE WRIGHT PRICE ('88), SOUTH ATLANTA, GA.

Life would not be worth living did we not have friends to rejoice with us when we are glad, and to weep with us when we mourn.

As the babe looks to his mother to laugh when something has particularly pleased him and expects that same mother to kiss away his tears when trouble has befallen him, so we, who are grown to womanhood, like to feel that we have earthly friends to sympathize with us in joy or grief. But what do we think of a near friend who never visits us?

All of us have our friends, especially while we live in the place of our birth ; for there are men and women there who knew us when we were babies, who are our friends for our mother's or father's sake, if not for our own.

There are boys and girls who grew up with us on the play-ground and in the school-room, who, in remembrance of the associations of our youth, will always be our friends. But not all spend their lives on their native heath, some are continually moving, they spend a few months here and then, when they have just begun to make friends, move on to another place. They are often strangers in a strange land and then it is that they feel the loneliness and emptiness of life without friends.

Our neighborhoods are filled with families which need the sympathy and cheer that a friendly visit from you would give, but you withhold yourself because they are a little lower in the social scale than you are, or if they are higher, you fear that they will think you are seeking their recognition. How much better off we would be if we would cease to draw these lines of caste and each of us as we climb the ladder reach down and assist a struggling sister!

What a spiritual help we would be to each other, if we would make more friendly visits ! Just a word of cheer and hope to the low-spirited, a word of sympathy to the sick, would show forth the Holy

Spirit who dwells in all Christian hearts.

Women are naturally kind and friendly. About woman has ever clustered the affection, the romance and even the comfort of human existence. Wherever women are found there is almost always cheerfulness and kindness; they are generally obliging, and even among savage tribes they are not as distant and suspicious as men. However poor their hospitality may be, they can safely be relied upon by the stranger.

Mungo Park in the midst of Africa, when robbed of his baggage and suffering from fever, was sheltered by a Negro woman, who watched and cared for him with a mother's tenderness. If cold, wet, hungry or sick, woman never stops to consider aught but the stranger's needs and will sacrifice her last stick or crumb to relieve him.

It was a poor widow who fed Elijah in the time of famine. It was the kindness of woman that led her to commiserate the sufferings of the numerous criminals, herded in the dark, unwholsome cells of the English prisons, and the work of Elizabeth Frye among the vile in Newgate will be remembered with reverence while the world lasts.

Not many of us are permitted to feed an Elijah, but how many are daily letting the opportunity slip by when we might visit some of our poor neighbors, carrying a bit of the family breakfast or dinner, and while the food satisfies their hunger, our cheering words will give them hope, courage and strength to toil on.

Very few of us are called to bring about great reforms, but each and all of us by making friendly visits among our neighbors, can teach them the lessons of purity, cleanliness, and economy in their persons and in their homes. We can also carry to them the message of Christ, while we will get in return some very valuable lesson.

In visiting those of our own station in life we gain by the exchange of ideas and our children and homes profit thereby; while friendly visits with those better situated than we will inspire us to climb higher.

We need to cultivate a habit of making friendly visits because of the help, the cheer, the inspiration we may give to others, and because of the help we may be to ourselves, for in this way we may learn to be content when comparing our lot with that of the more unfortunate;

or if discontented, it will be, not to grumble or complain of Providence, but to put forth efforts to better our condition, and also because of the help we may be to the Church and to civilization.

When we visit our neighbors, giving them spiritual cheer or physical assistance, we are teaching the lesson of Christianity by example, we are walking in the footsteps of our Master and building up His Church on earth. And as we inspire others to make home pure, comfortable and happy, we are making the men and women of the future, who will lead honest, industrious Christian lives. Thus we will rid the country of its chain gangs and prison houses, and build up a civilization such as the world has never yet seen.

MOTHERS' MEETINGS.

BY MRS. GEORGIA SWIFT KING ('74), ATLANTA, GA.

If it is true, that of the three main factors in the make-up of the individual,—the home, the school and the church,—the greatest is the home, and since it is true that the home is what the parents make it, the mother by nature having the larger share in the making, then it follows that the destiny of the Negro race is largely in the hands of its mothers.

Statistics resulting from recent investigations indicate with respect to the Negro population of the United States; first, a general decrease in the birth-rate; second, an alarmingly excessive infant death-rate; third, because of inherited tendencies and defective education,—physical, intellectual and moral,—a greatly excessive death-rate among adults; fourth, that so little does the birth-rate exceed the death-rate that the race is doing little more than reproducing itself. These indications furnish food for thought, and reason for investigation and action.

The alarming increase of infanticide (without reference to the immoral, brutal class) seems to result from the overworked, discouraged, desperate state of many *laboring* mothers, upon whom the burden of family support so largely rests.

The large death-rate of both infants and adults, I believe, may be traced to poverty and ignorance of the laws of health; an ignorance not confined to the illiterate, for how many highly intelligent people there are who have almost no knowledge of the symptoms of ordinary diseases; who do not know when to send for the doctor, nor how to care for the sick. I recall several instances during the present year where promising lives in intelligent homes have been sacrificed on the altar of ignorance and the most extravagant economy; what wonder that the illiterate and poor die in so great numbers!

Does this excessive death-rate indicate a corresponding mental and moral decay? What is the remedy for such conditions?

The blood of the fallen is required at the hands of the intelligent class. The demand is apparent for preachers who study the signs of the times and deal practically with the needs of the hour; for teachers, capable, conscientious, consecrated; for physicians, skilled, honorable, philanthropic. But these agencies alone can not meet the demands and should be supplemented by other methods.

Observation and experience lead me to conclude that a most excellent medium for effectual instruction of the masses, is "Mother's Meetings," where all questions of human interest are pertinent and may be freely discussed ; where all classes of women may become better informed ;where even the illiterate, by regular attendance, may gain much essential knowledge of such vital subjects as: The laws of sanitation ; Selection of foods ; Economic cooking ; Proper and wholesome dress ; Care of infants : Needs (physical, mental and moral) of childhood ; Care of boys and girls through the critical period between childhood and maturity ; How to fortify young men against the follies of immorality and young women against the dangers of imprudence.

The science of health and heredity and prenatal influences, and all that pertains to household morality and economy, may be handled with such simplicity in these meetings, that not only the mothers but the whole people may receive real benefit.

When difficulty is experienced in getting the mothers to these meetings I have met with some success by taking the meetings to the mothers, that is, to their immediate neighborhood.

NEED OF DAY NURSERIES.

BY MRS. SELENA SLOAN BUTLER, ATLANTA, GA.

Among the important questions of to-day is the need of day nurseries in cities and towns where children of parents who, by force of circumstances, are obliged to earn a living by working in service, may receive good and wholesome influences during that period of life when impressions are easily made and character readily molded, either for good or bad.

Many parents in cities must do work which calls them away from home, and often they toil from early dawn till a late hour to keep the wolf from the door, and, because of their small wages, their children often are forced to do work too hard for them that their meager earnings may add to the support of the still smaller children left at home during the day without the care of a poor but loving mother; left alone during that most important period of their lives when good or evil principles will, by cultivation, become the ruling passion through life; left alone to grow up amid a multitude of unfavorable surroundings. With these existing circumstances, it does not need a prophet to tell what the result will be.

It is a daily experience to find a child of tender years left to tend the baby with but a scant meal of meat and bread, while the widowed mother is out at work. At a late hour the mother returns, tired and almost exhausted; she proceeds at once to satisfy the hunger of her unfortunate children, and then, in her humble way, as best she can, with their bowed heads at her side she teaches them to lisp the " Lord's Prayer," then all are lost in sleep. The majority of the children who would be glad to find protection in a day nursery are not blessed with even this limited knowledge of a good moral training.

Such circumstances are not only unfavorable to the physical condition of the children, but detrimental to the parent, because such a state of constant activity and anxiety exhausts the vital force. Do you ask the result? Why, the mother dies at an early age, leaving little children in the hands of chance, to be brought up, quite likely, among the weeds of vice and sin, going from bad to worse, until they become a menace to society. If there had been a day nursery with good conscientious persons at its head, in which these children could have had their physical, mental and moral natures properly cared for at a small cost to the mother, they would have developed into characters with sufficient magnitude to lift humanity to a higher plane, instead of degrading it; and the mother would have no doubt lived out her three score years and ten.

If you will examine the records of the mortality of the Negroes of this city, you will find that about one-third of the deaths occurred among the children, and a closer investigation will disclose the fact that the majority of these deaths occurred in families where parents were obliged to work out and therefore could not detect disease in their little ones until too late to be relieved by medical aid.

I will relate only two of the many cases coming under my observation which make a strong appeal for the establishment of day nurseries. A widowed mother, who worked for a family in this city, had a boy about six years of age. This mother left her little boy alone, asking each morning the family in the adjoining room to have an oversight over him during the day. For several nights when the mother returned from her work between the hours of eight and nine, she found her boy with flushed cheeks, sleeping restlessly. Being tired she did not investigate the cause of this abnormal condition, but attributed it to exhaustion from play. Finally the child's condition became alarming, and one night about nine o'clock the mother took it to the office of a physician. After a careful examination, the mother was told that her child was in the third stage of typhoid fever, and recovery depended upon immediate attention and good nursing. Then the mother, with tears in her eyes, related her sad story.

The other case is that of a boy who went into a physician's office crying, and with his clothes covered with blood. What was the matter? Why, the same old story. The boy had had an artery cut with a stone that was thrown by another boy whose mother was obliged to work away from home, that she might be able to pay her house rent and feed and clothe her children: and but for the interest the physician took in the case, there might have been a dead boy, a lawsuit, and a juvenile criminal; all because of the need of day nurseries.

Another evidence of the need of day nurseries is the large number of boys, almost babies you might say, to be found not only loitering and making mischief in the alleys, but even in the chain-gangs. Many are there because in early childhood they had no one at home to hold them in check, and, yielding to the influences about them, their minds became steeped in sin and vice ; and they grew wise only in the knowledge of petty crimes.

If the absence of day nurseries affected the physical nature only it might not be so alarming, but seeing the effect daily upon the mental and moral natures, and not knowing to what extent these natures may be transmitted to coming generations, we ought to see plainly the necessity of administering the ounce of prevention by establishing day nurseries.

We need an institution where mothers who are obliged to be away from home in order that they may earn an honest living may leave their children and have the satisfaction of knowing that their little minds are lifted above the miry slough and prepared to shun the pitfalls that have been the destruction of many a young life born to be useful.

NEED OF KINDERGARTENS.

BY MRS. ROSA MOREHEAD BASS ('80), ATLANTA, GA.

[NOTE: A movement has already been started among the influential colored people of Atlanta to establish a kindergarten. The plan of the conference has been to discuss only such reforms as were immediately practical and would be dependent only on local co-operation and support.—ED.]

I could perform no pleasanter duty than to plead for kindergarten schools for the Negro children.

Some twelve years ago we had in Atlanta a model Jones kindergarten, under the care of the A. M. A., so it will not be an experiment with us. Unfortunately it had to be discontinued for want of means. It would have been self-supporting by this time, and would have accomplished untold good.

What a blessing a kindergarten would be to the tired mother who could feel that her little darling was safely housed from harm while she performs her daily duties! For the poor woman who is busy the entire week washing and ironing, it is an impossibility to care properly for her children. A kindergarten would be a rock of refuge to her; and to that mother who goes from home early in the morning and does not return till dark, for her children such a school would be a castle of escape.

I wish to give the " testimony " of three mothers, who are graduates of Atlanta University, and whose husbands are prominent in educational work. These have representative homes—homes of intelligence. Mrs. Wm. E. Holmes, whose husband is a professor in the Atlanta Baptist College, says :

" As I see it, we need kindergarten schools:

" First—Because, as a race, we are incompetent to give our children the training such schools furnish;

" Second—Because such tuition gives the teacher a foundation on which to build. We speak much concerning our progress and it must be admitted that it is great, but if we had had at the beginning of our career such preliminary education we should be considerably in advance of our present condition;

" Third—Because the impressionable years of early childhood should be turned to matters of importance and permanent value. This is a training which if neglected then can never be supplied. And if we are ever to be an *educated* race that training we must have, for education is our *greatest* need."

Mrs. Crogman, the wife of Prof. Crogman of Clark University, and the mother of eight children, says:

" In my opinion one of the greatest needs of our people is the establishment of kindergarten schools for the training of our young. In them they can be trained younger than in the primary schools ; and in them they are prepared to take hold better of the primary work."

Mrs. Edgar J. Penney, whose husband is pastor at the Tuskegee Normal and Industrial Institute, says :

" I am a kindergarten enthusiast, because I believe it is the mother's greatest help. It opens its doors at the very time when children are most restless and active, and turns that activity, which is miscalled mischief at home, into innocent and pleasant instruction, and thus the process of development of the mind and physical nature begins early. *The State is generous, I know, in educating the young, but she makes the mistake that many parents make in letting the child become bad and then trying to reform it.* The natural order ought to be for the youth to graduate from the kindergarten, then from the primary schools, and so on until the college is reached.

" What a God-send would these children-gardens be to the poor who have little or no time to give to the training of their little ones! I am praying and longing to see the day when free kindergartens will be on the corner of every alley. What a strange idea to wait until a child is six or seven to begin its education, which means books as so many think!

" There are hundreds of things and ideas that a child gets in a kindergarten which are really the beginning of its education, and yet it does not know the book language. It gets acquainted with nature. I cannot tell you how it rejoices me that this most important subject is to be discussed. I wish I could arouse every mother and teacher in this Southland to see the need of saving our children before they become steeped and dyed in vice, and then attempt to reform them."

The Catholics ask but the first seven years of a child, the formative period, asserting that ideas inculcated during that season cannot be supplanted. Let us apply the wisdom of their experience to our case. The years that need most careful instruction are those entrusted to the tender mercies of the rabble. Innocent eyes read and observe the animate illustrations of vice, innocent ears listen to the rendition of collections of depravity. With these lessons learned the school teacher has to begin to uneducate, but trace what she may upon the palimpsest the first record remains uneffaced.

The Atlanta *Journal* recently said: "This work seems to be the sweetest, the best, the most far-reaching good work that we can do for humanity. Teach a little child goodness and truth, useful facts and bright bits of knowledge, and the father and mother in the lowly homes will soon learn the same lessons from the baby lips."

With all the ardor of an anxious mother I repeat that day homes or kindergartens are a glaring need, an absolute necessity if the masses are to be raised.

Friends, I plead most earnestly for such a school at once, there are so many little children ready and eager to go to the school. Who, oh, who is ready and willing to help us to administer to their wants?

REPORTS FROM CITIES.

[NOTE: It is hoped to make the reports from cities one of the main features of the next conference. A movement has already begun in several cities to form local organizations to make investigations and work along lines suggested by the Atlanta conference. Another year one of the section meetings could be profitably devoted to reports and discussions by the delegates from such organizations. This year we print brief reports from three of these organizations located respectively in Atlanta, New Orleans and Washington.—ED.]

ATLANTA.

This report was presented to the conference by Prof. Wm. E. Holmes, of the Atlanta Baptist College.

Deeply concerned about the condition of the poor people in Atlanta, for some time Mrs. Georgia Swift King, in a quiet way, had been laboring to better it. Into homes neglected by the fortunate few she had again and again made her way to help the needy. Finding the work growing in dimensions, it occurred to her to enlist the sympathy and assistance of others.

Accordingly, early in the spring, at her suggestion a meeting was called at the residence of Rev. Dr. W. G. Alexander. A number responded, the object of the meeting was stated, discussion was engaged in and an organization was effected, of which Prof. William B. Matthews is the president.

Like similar societies, the object is to study the condition of the lowly and in all possible ways to improve it. The society intends to awaken interest in good reading, to look after female criminals, to seek to raise the standard of home life, and thus tone up the morals and decrease the mortality of the race.

Already mothers' meetings have been held, children have been looked after, and helpful suggestions have been made to the people.

NEW ORLEANS.

Reported by letter by Rev. George W. Henderson to the corresponding secretary of the conference, Mr. George G. Bradford.

I sent you newspaper clippings containing reports of our first two meetings. The third was equally successful. We were fortunate in securing the co-operation and assistance of the mayor of the city and other equally distinguished citizens of the white race.

These meetings were somewhat experimental. Their success was such as to encourage the continuance of the movement. A committee was appointed to form a permanent organization for the continued investigation and discussion of the various questions concerning our moral and material progress. The central principle of the undertaking differs somewhat from the Atlanta enterprise.

With us the fundamental thing is education. The causes and remedies of mortality are a part of this larger subject. In our city we have little doubt but that the bad sanitary condition of those sections where our people live has much to do with the high death-rate. For this the city is largely responsible. So far as the people themselves are responsible, it is due to poverty and ignorance. Hence our object is to impart knowledge and create the desire for improvement and arouse the spirit of self-help, and our method is to hold popular meetings from time to time in different parts of the city on the one hand, and also affect public sentiment on the other through the press and by committees who shall represent us before the Board of Education, the City Council and the Legislature, and ultimately we hope to extend the movement to all parts of the state.

As to the question of mortality, I hope something may be done along the lines pursued in Atlanta and other cities. My first aim has been to create an interest. I think now I see the way clear to do this particular kind of investigation, and I hope some report may be sent to your third conference next year.

WASHINGTON.

This report was presented to the conference by Mr. L. M. Hershaw.

The Graduate Club of Washington, D. C., is an organization composed of colored graduates of several Northern and Southern colleges. The object of the club is to stimulate study and research among its members. The work outlined so far lies within the province of sociology. During the year just closed the club has been studying the works of Giddings and Fairbanks on sociology. The program for next year contains studies on various phases of the Negro problem, and also several topics of a broadly sociological interest. Prof. Kelly Miller, professor of mathematics in Howard University, is president of the club, which has a membership at present of thirty-three.

EXTRACTS FROM LETTERS.

[The following are extracts from a few of the many encouraging letters received from those who sympathize deeply with the purpose of the conference.—ED.]

From His Excellency, W. Y. ATKINSON, Governor of the State of Georgia:

I have delayed replying to your kind invitation to be with you, hoping that I would be able to comply with your request, but I regret to say that I am now forced to write you that it will be impossible for me to accept.

I sincerely trust that the "Conference on City Problems" will be both profitable and enjoyable.

From MELVILLE W. FULLER, Chief Justice of the U. S. Supreme Court:

I sincerely regret that I find it impossible to attend the conference with reference to the condition of the colored population in our cities, to be held May 25th and 26th.

From FREDERICK HOWARD WINES, LL.D., Editor of the *Charities Review*:

I am very much obliged for your invitation to attend the second conference with reference to the condition of the colored population in the cities of the United States. I regret that my official duties will not permit my absence from home at the date of this meeting.

My word to the conference is simply this: that if the Negro race is ever to be elevated in the social scale, as I believe that it will be, it can only be by self-culture and self-control. Help from the outside will go but a little way. The Negro must realize his manhood and his responsibilities as a man and citizen, and meet them, if he wishes to survive in the struggle for existence. It is absolutely essential that he should receive not only a literary education, but manual training; and that he should cultivate in himself the virtues of industry, thrift, chastity, honesty and temperance. When he learns to respect himself, his women, the rights of others, and especially the rights of property; to meet the reasonable expectations of his employers, and to fulfill his contracts both in letter and in spirit, he will command the respect of the world, and his advancement will be both sure and rapid. If race prejudice on the part of the white people towards the colored is to be deplored, so also is race prejudice on the part of the colored people towards the white. The two races must live in peace and harmony, or the weaker race will inevitably go to the wall.

———

From Hon. C. A. COLLIER, Mayor of the City of Atlanta:

I shall be gone until June 1st, or about that time; consequently I shall be compelled to forego the pleasure of making the address which you desire at your conference on the 25th and 26th of May.

———

From JOHN F. CROWELL, Professor of Economics and Sociology in Smith College:

I am very deeply interested in the conference proposed to consider the condition of the colored population in our cities, at Atlanta, May 25 and 26. It is a step in the right direction—a step looking toward the selection of the socially safe and the scientifically sound means by which the colored people may avoid the dangers and yet secure the benefits of what is an essentially sympathetic civilization. Though my duties here will prevent my being present I hope that its proceedings will be given widest publicity.

I hope that those who meet to discuss these problems may, if deemed advisable, provide for permanent organization of this movement, so that from year to year the methods and results may be considered in conference. If so, please enroll my name among its members.

———

From SAMUEL M. LINDSAY, Professor of Finance and Economy, University of Pennsylvania:

I am very glad to know of your Conference on City Problems. The results of your investigation as published in the Bulletin of the Department of Labor are extremely interesting and this conference should be very helpful. I would like to be present, but my duties here at the close of the term are such that I cannot get away now.

Appendix:—A.

The data from which the following tables were compiled were gathered exclusively by representative colored men and women under the direction of Atlanta University, Atlanta, Ga. At the suggestion of Col. Carroll D. Wright, Commissioner of the U. S. Department of Labor, the data gathered were turned over to the Department of Labor for tabulation and at his request the university permitted the tables to be published in full in the May Bulletin of the Department of Labor. We reprint here summaries and extracts from these tables.

There were invited to take part in the investigation about 50 graduates of Atlanta University, 30 of Fisk University, and 15 of the colored graduates of Berea, besides the prominent colored doctors, ministers, lawyers, and teachers of the States of Georgia, South Carolina, Alabama and Tennessee, including representatives from all the more prominent institutions for the higher education of the Negro. In all, something over 300 were invited, of whom about 100 volunteered, and of the latter 50 were able to complete their part of the investigation within the time allowed them, which, unfortunately, was very short.

Great credit is due to the investigators for their work in the investigation, for through them its success has been possible. As previously stated, they are all representative colored persons. The following statement shows in detail the name of each person engaged in the work of securing the data, the number of groups investigated by each, and the total number of groups, families and individuals canvassed.

Investigators.	Group No.	Investigators.	Group No.
Athens, Ga.		*Jacksonville, Fla.*	
Dr. C. S. Haynes	15	Dr. W. C. Smalls	4
Atlanta, Ga.		Rev. W. E. Partee and L. B. Robinson.	5
Selena S. Butler	1	Prof. William F. Jackson	24
Emma L. Holmes	2	*Louisville, Ky.*	
Laura C. Davis	3	Prof. Frank L. Williams	6
Lilla E. Badger and Mary E. Brittain.	4	*Macon, Ga.*	
Mary F. Pullin	5	Dr. C. McCarthy	{ 7, 30, 31, 32
Prof. William B. Matthews	6, 7		
Dr. H. R. Butler	8	*Macon, Miss.*	
George A. Towns and Adrienne E. Herndon	9	Dr. Daniel W. Sherrod	8
Julia M. Brown	10	*Nashville, Tenn.*	
Mattie A. Ford	11	Prof. Eugene Harris	{ 1, 2, 3, 4, 5, 6, 7, 8, 9
Alice D. Carey	12		
Georgia S. King	13	Hon. J. C. Napier	10
Rev. Henry H. Proctor	14	*Orangeburg, S. C.*	
Nellie E. Crawford	15	N. J. Frederick and Chas. H. Johnson.	9
Mary E. Keller	16	Frank B. Johnson	10
Birmingham, Ala.		*Sanford, Fla.*	
Dr. A. M. Brown	1, 16	William C. McLester	11
Cambridge, Mass.		*Savannah, Ga.*	
Butler R. Wilson	1	Dr. C. McKane	12
Cartersville, Ga.		Sarah J. Butler	21
Albert B. Cooper	2	Rev. R. R. Downs	25, 26, 27
Chattanooga, Tenn.		*Tuskegee, Ala.*	
Rev. Joseph E. Smith	17	Rev. E. J. Penney	13, 28
Columbia, S. C.		*Washington, D. C.*	
Dr. C. C. Johnson	18, 19, 20	Dr. Furman J. Shadd	14
Jackson, Tenn.		Maggie R. Bowen	22
Prof. A. R. Merry	3	Dr. W. Bruce Evans	23
		C. L. Franklin	29

NUMBER OF GROUPS, FAMILIES, AND INDIVIDUALS CANVASSED.

City.	Gro'ps.	Fami-lies.	Indi-vidu'ls.	City.	Gro'ps.	Fami-lies.	Indi-vidu'ls.
Atlanta, Ga.	16	324	1,292	Orangeburg, S. C.	2	22	109
Nashville, Tenn.	10	246	1,090	Sanford, Fla.	1	24	116
Cambridge, Mass.	1	98	366	Athens, Ga.	1	16	73
Savannah, Ga.	5	96	380	Cartersville, Ga.	1	10	53
Washington, D. C.	4	66	293	Louisville, Ky.	1	15	70
Macon, Ga.	4	30	90	Macon, Miss.	1	17	64
Jacksonville, Fla.	3	77	327	Chattanooga, Tenn.	1	21	89
Columbia, S. C.	3	15	81	Jackson, Tenn.	1	22	67
Birmingham, A'a.	2	17	63				
Tuskegee, Ala.	2	21	119	Total	59	1,137	4,742

The investigation was carried to completion in 18 cities, all except one of which are located in the Southern States. The effort to secure schedules for several groups of colored people in each of the smaller cities and for a larger number of groups in cities of greater size and importance was quite successful, as the preceding statement shows. Great care was taken in the selection of groups and in securing data in Atlanta, Ga., Nashville, Tenn., and Cambridge, Mass., and it is to the tabulation for these cities that we must look for the most representative and accurate showing of the condition of the Negro so far as this investigation is concerned. The tabulation of the data for 32 groups in the other cities canvassed is presented mainly for the value it may have in corroborating the facts presented for the 16 groups in Atlanta, the 10 groups in Nashville, and the single group in Cambridge. The data for the 32 groups in other cities have doubtless been gathered with quite as much care in most cases, but the same care could not be exercised in the selection of the 32 groups to be investigated as in the cities for which a separate statement is made.

Allusion has been made to "groups" in some of the previous statements, and an explanation is probably necessary in order that the reader may have an accurate knowledge of just what is meant by the term in this connection. It was not possible to secure data from any large portion of the population or for any large section of the cities involved in the investigation, owing to the fact that in no instance was there any remuneration given to investigators for the work performed, it being purely voluntary and usually performed by persons with so many other interests that but a part of their time could be devoted to this work. For this reason it was decided to select one or more groups of from 10 to 20 houses standing together in the portions of the city which were thought to be representative of the various conditions of the Negro in that locality. Each of these collections of houses has been termed a group.

In the tabular presentations which follow, the cities embraced in the investigation have been arranged in four divisions in each summary table, and the same order is followed in the tables which give more detailed information, as follows: Sixteen groups in Atlanta, Ga.; 10 groups in Nashville, Tenn.; 1 group in Cambridge, Mass.; and 32 groups in other cities. Under each of these divisions the groups have been arranged according to their condition and the character of their surroundings, whether good, fair, or bad. In the first division, comprising the 16 groups for Atlanta, Ga., groups 1, 2, 3, 4, and 5 may be classed as good; groups 6, 7, 8, 9, 10, and 11 as fair; and groups 12, 13, 14, 15, and 16 as bad. In the second division, comprising 10 groups in Nashville, Tenn., group 1 may be classed as good; groups 2, 3, 4, 5, 6, 7, 8, and 9 as fair; and group 10 as bad. In the third division, the single group in Cambridge, Mass., may be classed as fair. In the fourth division, groups 1 to 14 are classed as good; groups 15 to 23 as fair; and groups 24 to 29 as bad; the condition of groups 30, 31, and 32 not being reported. The groups in this fourth division are located as follows: Group 1 in Birmingham, Ala.; group 2 in Cartersville, Ga.; group 3 in Jackson, Tenn.; groups 4 and 5 in Jacksonville, Fla.; group 6 in Louisville, Ky.; group 7 in Macon, Ga.; group 8 in Macon, Miss.; groups 9 and 10 in Orangeburg, S. C.; group 11 in Sanford, Fla.; group 12 in Savannah, Ga.; group 13 in Tuskegee, Ala.; group 14 in Washington, D. C.; group 15 in Athens, Ga.; group 16 in Birmingham, Ala.; group 17 in Chattanooga, Tenn.; groups 18, 19, and 20 in Columbia, S. C.; group 21 in Savannah, Ga.; groups 22 and 23 in Washington, D. C.; group 24 in Jacksonville, Fla.; groups 25, 26, and 27 in Savannah, Ga.; group 28 in Tuskegee, Ala.; group 29 in Washington, D. C.; and groups 30, 31, and 32 in Macon, Ga.

TABLE 1.—NUMBER AND PER CENT OF PERSONS OF EACH RELATIONSHIP.

Relationship to head of family.	Atlanta, Ga., 16 groups.		Nashville, Tenn., 10 groups.		Cambridge, Mass., 1 group.		Other cities, 32 groups.		All groups.	
	Number.	Per cent.	Number.	Per cent.	Number.	Per cent.	Number.	Per cent.	Number.	Per cent.
Heads of families	537	41.57	442	40.55	178	48.63	817	40.97	1,974	41.63
Children	609	47.14	486	44.59	152	41.53	920	46.14	2,167	45.70
Parents	22	1.70	30	2.75	4	1.09	44	2.21	100	2.11
Brothers and sisters	33	2.55	46	4.22	17	4.65	42	2.11	138	2.91
Grandchildren	33	2.55	25	2.29	1	.27	54	2.71	113	2.38
Nephews and nieces	13	1.01	20	1.84			37	1.85	70	1.47
Boarders	26	2.01	9	.83	1	.27	16	.80	52	1.10
Lodgers	12	.93	24	2.20	11	3.01	44	2.21	91	1.92
Other relationships	7	.54	8	.73	2	.55	20	1.00	37	.78
Total	1,292	100.00	1,090	100.00	366	100.00	1,994	100.00	4,742	100.00

TABLE 2.—NUMBER AND PER CENT OF FAMILIES OF EACH SPECIFIED SIZE.

Size of families.	Atlanta, Ga., 16 groups.		Nashville, Tenn., 10 groups.		Cambridge, Mass., 1 group.		Other cities, 32 groups.		All groups.	
	Number.	Per cent.	Number.	Per cent.	Number.	Per cent.	Number.	Per cent.	Number.	Per cent.
1 person	22	6.79	5	2.04	5	5.10	22	4.69	54	4.75
2 persons	65	20.06	44	17.89	25	25.51	84	17.91	218	19.17
3 persons	76	23.46	38	15.45	23	23.47	103	21.96	240	21.11
4 persons	48	14.82	46	18.67	18	18.37	86	18.34	198	17.41
5 persons	42	12.96	53	21.55	14	14.29	57	12.15	166	14.60
6 persons	27	8.33	21	8.54	2	2.04	36	7.68	86	7.56
7 persons	22	6.79	18	7.32	4	4.08	38	8.10	82	7.21
8 persons	9	2.78	12	4.88	5	5.10	17	3.63	43	3.78
9 persons	8	2.47	5	2.03			13	2.77	26	2.29
10 persons	5	1.54	3	1.22	2	2.04	12	2.56	22	1.94
Over 10 persons			1	.41			1	.21	2	.18
Total	324	100.00	246	100.00	98	100.00	469	100.00	1,137	100.00

TABLE 3.—AVERAGE SIZE OF FAMILY, BY CITIES.

Cities.	Total families.	Total persons.	Average size of family.
Atlanta, Ga	324	1,292	3.99
Nashville, Tenn	246	1,090	4.43
Cambridge, Mass	98	366	3.73
Other cities	469	1,994	4.25
Total	1,137	4,742	4.17

It will be seen from the above table that for all the families investigated the average number of persons per family in Atlanta, Ga., was found to be 3.99; in Nashville, Tenn., 4.43; in Cambridge, Mass., 3.73; in the other cities, 4.25; and in all the cities covered by the investigation, 4.17. Comparison with the returns of the census of 1890 in the cases of the first three cities, returns for all the others not being given, shows that for the entire population of these cities, including both white and colored, the average size of family was considerably larger, viz., for Atlanta 4.91, Nashville 4.92, and Cambridge 4.95.

TABLE 4.—NUMBER AND PER CENT OF PERSONS UNDER EACH AGE PERIOD.

Age periods.	Atlanta, Ga., 16 groups.		Nashville, Tenn., 10 groups.		Cambridge, Mass., 1 group.		Other cities, 32 groups.		All groups.	
	Num-ber.	Per cent.	Num-ber.	Per cent.	Num-ber.	Per cent.	Num-ber.	Per cent.	Num-ber.	Per cent.
Under 10 years............	290	22.44	212	19.45	90	24.59	419	21.01	1,011	21.32
10 to 19 years............	315	24.38	274	25.14	67	18.31	452	22.67	1,108	23.37
20 to 29 years............	235	18.19	190	17.43	91	24.86	404	20.26	920	19.40
30 to 39 years............	209	16.18	141	12.94	64	17.49	280	14.04	694	14.64
40 to 49 years............	112	8.67	115	10.55	32	8.74	222	11.13	481	10.14
50 to 59 years	70	5.42	91	8.35	18	4.92	119	5.97	298	6.28
60 years or over..........	56	4.33	66	6.05	3	.82	72	3.61	197	4.15
Age unknown............	5	39	1	.09	1	.27	26	1 31	33	.70
Total...........	1,292	100.00	1,090	100.00	366	100.00	1,994	100 00	4,742	100.00

TABLE 5.—AVERAGE PERSONS PER SLEEPING ROOM.

Cities.	Families having to each sleeping room an average of—						Total fami-lies.	Aver-age pers'ns to a sleep-ing-room.
	Under 1 per-son.	1 or under 2 per-sons.	2 or under 3 per-sons.	3 or under 4 per-sons.	4 or under 5 per-sons.	5 per-sons or over.		
Atlanta, Ga	6	94	119	65	26	14	324	2.22
Nashville, Tenn...	1	54	114	35	21	21	246	2.44
Cambridge, Mass. (a)	....	34	49	11	1	1	96	1.96
Other cities (a)	14	147	177	81	31	17	467	2.05
Total (b).................	21	329	459	192	79	53	1,133	2.17

a Not including 2 families not reporting sleeping-rooms.
b Not including 4 families not reporting sleeping-rooms.

TABLE 6.—ROOMS PER FAMILY.

Cities.	Families living in—											Total fami-lies.
	1 ro'm.	2 ro'ms.	3 ro'ms.	4 ro'ms.	5 ro'ms.	6 ro'ms.	7 ro'ms.	8 ro'ms.	9 ro'ms.	10 ro'ms or over.	Not re-port-ed.	
Atlanta, Ga.....	a58	a116	84	25	17	16	4	2	1	1	..	324
Nashville, Tenn.	9	55	124	34	14	5	1	2	1	1	..	246
Cambridge, M's.	5	7	28	21	18	7	6	4	..	..	2	98
Other cities.....	45	98	72	117	63	33	18	9	5	6	3	469
Total........	117	276	308	197	112	61	29	17	7	8	5	1,137

a Including one family having an additional half-room.

The following extract is from Table IV of the May Bulletin of the U. S. Department of Labor, showing method of compilation of data on household conditions of Negroes; giving the condition of each family in detail. The complete table includes 1,137 families.

EXTRACT FROM TABLE IV.—HOUSEHOLD CONDITIONS, BY FAMILIES.

ATLANTA, GA.—16 GROUPS.

GROUP 1.

[O. H. indicates that the family own the house in which they live.]

| Family No. | Persons. | | Rooms. | | Monthly rent. | Family No. | Persons. | | Rooms. | | Monthly rent. |
	Male.	Female.	Sleeping.	Other.			Male.	Female.	Sleeping.	Other.	
1........	2	2	2		$3.00	11........	4	1	3	3	$13.50
2....	3	1	1	1	3.00	12........	1	2	3	3	13.80
3........	1	1	1	1	4.00	13........	1	3	2	2	6.40
4........	1	1	1	1	4.00	14........	2	3	2	1	6.40
5........	2	3	4	2	10.00	15........	1	1	1	3	O. H.
6........	1	2	2	2	8.30	16........	3	2	3	3	O. H.
7........	1	2	2	2	O. H.	17........	2	2	2	1	10.00
8........	2	1	4	5	O. H.	18......	3	4	3	2	O. H.
9......	5	5	4	3	O H.	19........	2	5	3	3	O. H.
10.......	1	1	2	3	O. H.						

The following extract is from Table V of same report showing same data by groups. For complete tables see above-mentioned report.

EXTRACT FROM TABLE V.—HOUSEHOLD CONDITIONS, BY GROUPS.

ATLANTA, GA.—16 GROUPS.

| Group number. | Families. | Persons. | | Rooms. | | | | Families. | | | Average monthly rent per family. |
| | | Male. | Female. | Sleeping. | | Other. | | Owning house. | Paying rent. | Not reporting as to rent. | |
				Number.	Average persons to each.	Number.	Average persons to each.				
1.....	19	38	42	45	1.78	41	1.85	8	11	....	$7.49
2.....	27	52	58	49	2.24	41	2.07	16	10	1	5.10
3.....	19	31	43	30	2.47	21	2.57	4	15	....	4.60
4.....	15	25	35	23	2.61	4	3.25	....	15	....	3.27
5.....	25	37	49	46	1.87	38	1.89	10	15	....	4.50
6.....	17	36	39	35	2.14	9	3 67	....	17	....	3.29
7.....	18	36	36	40	1.80	25	2.40	11	7	...	5.04
8.....	24	35	58	41	2.27	18	3.50	....	24	....	5.83
9.....	26	50	54	59	1.76	42	2.21	9	16	a 1	5.85
10.....	21	44	44	38	2.32	10	3.20	6	15	....	4.00
11.....	21	48	51	42	2.36	23	3.65	7	14	....	3.32
12.....	24	39	50	30	2.97	3	3.00	....	24	....	2.59
13.....	20	42	41	37	2.24	10	3.30	1	19	....	4.79
14.....	16	14	35	19	2.58	2	2.00	....	16	....	2.55
15.....	16	32	35	25	2.68	13	3.62	....	16	....	3.63
16	16	25	38	22	2.86	6	3.33	1	15	....	3.70
Total.	324	584	708	581	2.22	306	2.54	73	249	b 2	$4.25

a Rent free.   b Including one family living rent free.

The following extract is from Table VI of same report showing in detail occupation and earnings by families for the 1,137 families covered by the investigation.

EXTRACT FROM TABLE VI.—OCCUPATIONS AND EARNINGS, BY FAMILIES.

ATLANTA, GA.—16 GROUPS.

GROUP 1.

Fam-ily No.	Head of family.				House wife.	At work.	At work and at school.	Earn-ings for the year.	At sch'ol.	At h'me.
	Occupation.	Weeks em-pl'yed.	Aver-age weekly earn-ings.	How sub-sisted when unem-ployed.						
							Children.			
1	Seamstress (a).......	a 16	a $4.00	Savings...	....	1	2	$258	....	....
2 ...	Bricklayer............	50	12.00	Savings...	1	....	....	....	....	2
3 ...	Employee, printing office.	26	6.00	Savings...	1	....	....	....	....	....
4 ...	Drayman............	50	5.00	Savings...	1	....	....	....	....	....
5 ...	Merchant, wood (b)..	b 24	b 7.00	....	1	c 1	....	c 40	....	2
6	Tailor (d)............	d 44	d 3.50	....	1	1	....	(e)	....	....
7 ...	Coachman............	52	5.00	....	1	....	....	....	1	....
8	Waiter...............	52	10.00	....	....	f 2	....	f 594	....	....
9	Teacher, private sch'l	52	10.00	....	1	....	1	16	6	1
10	Physician	52	25.00	....	1	....	....	....	....	....
11...	Clergyman............	52	12.50	....	1	....	....	....	3	....
12....	Dentist..............	52	20.00	....	1	....	....	....	....	c1
13 ...	Waiter..............	52	5.00	....	1	....	....	....	....	2
14 ...	Waiter...............	52	5.00	....	1	....	....	....	....	3
15....	Wheelwright	52	11.00	....	....	g 1	....	g 132	....	....
16....	Hack owner and cap-italist.	52	300.00	....	1	....	....	....	2	1
17....	Porter....	49	8.00	Savings...	1	c 1	....	c 130	1	....
18....	Bishop A. M. E. Ch..	52	41.66	....	1	1	1	261	3	....
19....	Proprietor, restau-rant (h).	h 12	h 17.00	....	1	c 1	....	c 364	2	i 2

a Also employed 36 weeks as sick nurse, no pay. e Not reported.
b Also employed 28 weeks as waiter at $10 per f Wife and child.
week.   g Wife.
c Mother.   h Also employed 40 weeks as bank porter at
d Also employed 8 weeks as hotel waiter at $10 per week.
$3.50 per week.   i Child and mother.

The following is a valuable summary as showing the industrial position of women.

TABLE 7.—NUMBER OF FAMILIES AND MEANS OF SUPPORT.

By whom supported.	Atlanta, Ga., 16 groups.	Nash-ville, Tenn., 10 groups	Cam-bridge, Mass., 1 group.	Other cities, 32 groups.	Total families.
Head, male	73	60	40	131	304
Head, male, and male children..................	10	14	4	15	43
Head, male, and female children.................	4	3	1	8	16
Head, male, and male and female children.....	7	4	..	8	19
Head, female....	31	13	4	41	89
Head, female, and male children...	11	7	3	11	32
Head, female, and female children.	10	4	1	16	31
Head, female, and male and female children....	12	5	1	5	23
Heads, male and female.....................	84	51	22	98	255
Heads, male and female, and male children.....	12	19	1	19	51
Heads, male and female, and female children....	5	7	..	19	31
Heads, male and female, and male and female children..	4	2	1	18	25
Head, male, and others	18	21	9	24	72
Head, female, and others	22	8	2	23	55
Heads, male and female, and others............	14	15	8	21	58
Others, male	1	7	1	4	13
Others, female	6	6	..	8	20
Total	324	246	98	469	1,137

6

TABLE 8.—NUMBER AND PER CENT OF PERSONS SICK DURING THE YEAR.

Name of ailment.	Atlanta. Ga., 16 groups. Number.	Per cent.	Nashville, Tenn., 10 groups. Number.	Per cent.	Cambridge, Mass., 1 group. Number.	Per cent.	Other cities, 32 groups. Number.	Per cent.	Total. Number.	Per cent.
Consumption...	2	0.45	5	1.07	......	......	7	1.08	14	0.84
Pneumonia......	20	4.53	14	2.99	4	3.74	10	1.54	48	2.88
Total...............	22	4.98	19	4.06	4	3.74	17	2.62	62	3.72
Cholera infantum........	...	......	.....	......	......	......	...	......	...	......
Convulsions...............	2	.45			1	.93	3	.46	6	.36
Total......	2	.45			1	.93	3	.46	6	.36
Typhoid fever...............	10	2.27	5	1.07	5	4.68	2	.31	22	1.32
Scarlet fever.........	2	.45	1	.21	......	......			3	.18
Malarial fever...............	50	11.31	43	9.19	1	.93	195	30.09	289	17.36
Diarrhea.			6	1.28	3	2.81	2	.31	11	.66
Diphtheria...............			5	1.07	1	.93			6	.36
Total..	62	14.03	60	12.82	10	9.35	199	30.71	331	19.88
Syphilis...............			2	.43	......	......			2	.12
Scrofula...............	3	.68	16	3.42	.....	......	2	.31	21	1.26
Total...............	3	.68	18	3.85	......	......	2	.31	23	1.38
Other ailments...............	353	79.86	371	79.27	92	85.98	427	65.90	1,243	74.66
Grand total.........	442	100.00	468	100.00	107	100.00	648	100.00	1,665	100.00

TABLE 9.—NUMBER AND PER CENT OF DEATHS DURING PAST FIVE YEARS, BY CAUSES.

Causes.	Atlanta, Ga., 16 groups. Number.	Per cent.	Nashville, Tenn., 10 groups. Number.	Per cent.	Cambridge, Mass., 1 group. Number.	Per cent.	Other cities, 32 groups. Number.	Per cent.	Total deaths. Number.	Per cent.
Consumption...............	17	9.34	32	24.06	8	15.38	35	12.77	92	14.35
Pneumonia...............	23	12.64	7	5.26	8	15.38	19	6.94	57	8.89
Total...............	40	21.98	39	29.32	16	30.76	54	19.71	149	23.24
Cholera infantum.........	7	3.84	4	3.01	1	1.92	10	3.65	22	3.43
Convulsions...............	3	1.65	2	1.50	3	5.77	9	3.28	17	2.65
Still-births...............	4	2.20	5	3.76	10	19.23	10	3.65	29	4.53
Total...............	14	7.69	11	8.27	14	26.92	29	10.58	68	10.61
Typhoid fever...............	5	2.74	3	2.26	2	3.85	4	1.46	14	2.19
Scarlet fever...............	..	......	......	......	......	......	2	.73	2	.31
Malarial fever......	3	1.65	7	5.26	..	......	15	5.47	25	3.90
Diarrhea...............	2	1.10	......	......	......	......			2	.31
Diphtheria...............	4	2.20	.....	......	......	......			4	.62
Total	14	7.69	10	7.52	2	3.85	21	7.66	47	7.33
Syphilis..	..	......	......	......	......	......	......	......		
Scrofula...............	3	1.65	2	1.51	2	3.85	1	.37	8	1.25
Total	3	1.65	2	1.51	2	3.85	1	.37	8	1.25
Other causes...............	111	60.99	71	53.38	18	34.62	169	61.68	369	57.57
Grand total...........	182	100.00	133	100.00	52	100.00	274	100.00	641	100.00

NOTE :—The following table is very instructive, but deductions from it should be made with great care. It is intended to show the effects of sanitary conditions upon the health of the community, but the results obtained are not conclusive, for the increased amount of sickness in families living under unfavorable sanitary conditions can not be attributed entirely to such conditions, as a certain proportion of it must be attributed to the more irregular habits of life of those families which are content to live under such unfavorable conditions. The same incompetency which prevents a family from making material progress and securing for itself good accommodations also prevents its resisting disease. We generally find ill health and poverty together, one the cause of the other, but quite as often both the result of a common cause, such as intemperance, immorality, ignorance, or some moral or intellectual weakness.

TABLE 10.—SICKNESS, BY SANITARY CONDITION OF HOUSES.
ATLANTA, GA.—16 GROUPS.

Sanitary condition of houses.	Number of persons.	Persons sick during year.		Days of sickness.		
		Number.	Per cent.	Persons reporting.	Total.	Average.
Light and air:						
Good	577	163	28 25	128	5,819	45.46
Fair	348	126	36.21	104	6,268	60.27
Bad..........................	367	120	32.70	102	4,361	42.75
Ventilation:						
Good	537	153	28.49	124	5,927	47.80
Fair..........................	328	102	31.10	77	4,471	58.06
Bad..........................	427	154	36.07	133	6,050	45.49
Cleanliness:						
Good	426	122	28.64	97	5,259	54.22
Fair	527	177	33.59	141	5,588	39.63
Bad	339	110	32.45	96	5,601	58.34
Outside sanitary condition:						
Good	439	122	27.79	103	4,941	47.97
Fair..........................	264	80	30.30	61	2,676	43.87
Bad	589	207	35.14	170	8,831	51.95

NASHVILLE, TENN.—10 GROUPS.

Light and air:						
Good	489	194	39.67	99	3,284	33.17
Fair..........................	404	172	42.57	114	3,734	32.75
Bad	197	76	38.58	46	1,414	30.74
Ventilation:						
Good	471	181	38.43	92	3,346	36.37
Fair..........................	290	106	36.55	61	2,103	34 48
Bad.......	329	155	47.11	106	2,983	28.14
Cleanliness:						
Good	381	144	37.80	73	2,078	28.47
Fair..........................	345	131	37.97	79	3,026	38.30
Bad	364	167	45.88	107	3,328	31.10
Outside sanitary condition:						
Good	413	158	38 26	86	2,879	33.48
Fair....	452	191	42.26	116	3,929	33.87
Bad	225	93	41.33	57	1,624	28.49

CAMBRIDGE, MASS.—1 GROUP.

Light and air:						
Good....	159	29	18.24	25	1,214	48 56
Fair..........................	173	47	27.17	39	1,623	41.62
Bad..........................	34	6	17.65	6	492	82.00
Ventilation:						
Good	133	28	21.05	26	1,073	41 27
Fair..........................	102	19	18.63	16	1,162	72.63
Bad.......	131	35	26.72	28	1,094	39.07
Cleanliness:						
Good	80	14	17.50	12	697	58 08
Fair..........................	225	57	25.33	48	2,129	44.35
Bad....	61	11	18 03	10	503	50.30
Outside sanitary condition:						
Good	116	29	25.00	27	988	36.59
Fair..........................	78	11	14.10	11	819	74.45
Bad..........................	172	42	24.42	32	1,522	47.56

[Three groups and three families are not included, as sanitary condition of houses was not reported.]

Sanitary condition of houses.	Number of persons.	Persons sick during year.		Days of sickness.		
		Number.	Per cent.	Persons reporting.	Total.	Average.
Light and air:						
Good	1,081	246	22.76	173	7.861	45.44
Fair	547	211	38.57	143	4,566	31.93
Bad	308	114	37.01	86	4,450	51.74
Ventilation:						
Good	1,087	271	24.93	194	8,849	45.61
Fair	536	180	33.58	116	3,577	30.84
Bad	313	120	38.34	92	4,451	48.38
Cleanliness:						
Good	1,127	257	22.80	171	6,458	37 77
Fair	483	192	39.75	132	5,000	37 88
Bad	326	122	37.42	99	5,419	54.74
Outside sanitary condition:						
Good	919	230	25.03	165	5,638	34.17
Fair	689	215	31.20	147	7,141	48.58
Bad	328	126	38.41	90	4,098	45.53

TABLE 11.—SANITARY CONDITION OF HOUSES.
ATLANTA, GA.—16 GROUPS.

Group number.	Number of houses having—											
	Light and air.			Ventilation.			Cleanliness.			Outside sanitary condition.		
	Good.	Fair.	Bad.	Good.	Fair.	Bad.	Good.	Fair.	Bad.	Good.	Fair.	Bad.
1	14	....	1	14	1	....	14	1	....	14	1	....
2	20	1	1	17	4	1	15	6	1	18	4	....
3	9	5	1	9	5	1	9	2	4	9	3	3
4	....	15	....	....	15	....	6	4	5	....	....	15
5	5	12	7	5	12	7	9	12	3	16	6	2
6	....	....	17	....	....	17	....	....	17	....	....	17
7	15	....	....	15	....	....	....	15	....	....	15	....
8	1	9	5	1	10	4	1	10	4	1	3	11
9	22	....	....	21	1	....	....	18	2	18	3	1
10	4	5	9	1	5	12	5	10	3	8	1	9
11	18	....	....	17	1	....	11	7	....	11	7	....
12	5	3	14	5	4	13	6	4	12	1	6	15
13	3	8	7	....	....	18	6	6	9	....	3	15
14	1	15	....	4	7	5	5	4	12	4	....	12
15	....	....	15	....	....	15	....	13	2	....	....	15
16	3	7	5	3	8	4	1	9	5	....	....	15
Total	120	80	82	112	73	97	98	105	79	96	56	130

NASHVILLE, TENN.—10 GROUPS.

	Light and air.			Ventilation.			Cleanliness.			Outside sanitary condition.		
1	14	4	5	17	3	3	8	7	8	11	9	3
2	13	5	7	12	6	7	11	7	7	10	10	5
3	13	9	3	11	12	2	11	11	3	11	13	1
4	10	11	4	11	10	4	9	7	9	10	6	9
5	14	10	1	15	8	2	12	10	3	13	10	2
6	8	11	2	9	9	3	7	8	6	9	5	7
7	18	3	3	16	....	8	16	1	7	16	8	....
8	11	11	2	11	1	12	11	2	11	12	11	1
9	9	11	5	5	8	12	5	10	10	6	14	5
10	....	18	7	....	9	16	....	11	14	....	13	12
Total	110	93	39	107	66	69	90	74	78	98	99	45

9

Group number.	Light and air.			Ventilation.			Cleanliness.			Outside sanitary condition.		
	Go'd.	Fair.	Bad.	Go'd.	Fair.	Bad	Go'd.	Fair.	Bad.	Go'd.	Fair.	Bad.
1	43	46	8	37	29	31	25	56	16	30	21	46

OTHER CITIES—32 GROUPS.

Group number.	Light and air.			Ventilation.			Cleanliness.			Outside sanitary condition.		
1	8	....	....	8	....	....	7	1	....	4	4	....
2	5	4	....	6	3	....	4	4	1	4	4	....
3	7	8	2	6	8	3	9	7	1	8	9	....
4	18	....	....	18	....	....	17	1	....	17	....	1
5	26	1	....	27	....	....	27	....	....	27	....	....
6	10	2	1	8	4	1	11	1	1	11	1	1
7	1	9	....	....	9	1	....	9	1	3	1	6
8	6	5	6	8	3	6	8	7	2	11	5	1
9	11	4	1	6	9	1	10	4	2	4	10	2
10	....	6	....	6	....	....	1	4	1	....	6	....
11	4	15	5	7	12	5	13	6	5	13	6	5
12	14	4	1	3	16	....	14	5	....	13	6	....
13	4	....	2	4	....	2	4	....	2	4	....	2
14	15	....	....	15	....	....	15	....	....	....	15	....
15	8	6	2	10	4	2	9	4	3	7	8	1
16	2	....	2	2	....	2	2	....	2	3	....	1
17	8	5	3	10	4	2	5	8	3	5	4	7
18	4	....	....	3	1	....	....	3	1	2	1	1
19	3	....	1	4	....	....	....	3	1	2	2	....
20	1	3	1	4	....	1	1	2	2	3	1	1
21	....	13	5	....	13	5	4	8	6	....	13	5
22	13	2	....	13	2	....	13	2	....	13	2	....
23	9	4	2	9	3	3	12	2	1	10	3	2
24	6	13	....	18	....	1	14	....	5	....	19	....
25	11	4	1	10	5	1	12	4	....	3	13	....
26	a 2	a 2	a 4	a 3	a 1	a 4	a 4	a 2	a 2	a 1	a 7	(a)
27	(a)	a 4	a 17	a 1	a 3	a 17	a 4	a 8	a 9	(a)	(a)	a 21
28	10	1	2	11	....	2	12	....	1	12	....	1
29	8	1	1	....	8	2	3	6	1	3	5	2
30	(b)	(b)	(b)	(b)	(b)	(b)	(b)	(b)	(b)	(b)	(b)	(b)
31	(b)	(b)	(b)	(b)	(b)	(b)	(b)	(b)	(b)	(b)	(b)	(b)
32	(b)	(b)	(b)	(b)	(b)	(b)	(b)	(b)	(b)	(b)	(b)	(b)
Total	c 214	c 116	c 59	c 220	c 108	c 61	c 235	c 101	c 53	c 183	c 145	c 61

a Not including one house, not reported.
b Not reported.
c See preceding notes.

Appendix:—B.

A compilation of data from the health reports of various cities, made by Mr. L. M. Hershaw, of Washington, D. C., an alumnus of Atlanta University, follows, and it is believed that they afford very accurate information concerning the deaths, etc., in the cities for which the necessary official reports were available.

Mr. Hershaw's work included the cities of Atlanta, Baltimore, Charleston, Memphis and Richmond. We print in full the tables for Atlanta, one table for Charleston and one for Baltimore; for lack of space we omit other tables. For explanation of these tables see paper by Mr. Hershaw, page 10.

This work is to be continued by Mr. Hershaw during the coming year.

TABLE a.—AVERAGE ANNUAL DEATH RATE PER 1,000 AND EXCESS AND PER CENT OF EXCESS OF COLORED FOR THREE PERIODS OF YEARS, BY CITIES.

City.	First period.				Second period.				Third period.			
	W'ite.	Col-ored.	Excess of colored.		W'ite.	Col-ored.	Excess of colored.		W'ite.	Col-ored.	Excess of colored.	
			No.	Per cent.			No.	Per cent.			No.	Per cent.
Atlanta......	18.22	37.96	19.74	108.41	19.25	33.41	14.16	73.51	18.03	32.76	14.73	81.65
Baltimore...	22.60	36.15	13.55	59.92	19.46	30.52	11.06	56.87	20.01	31.47	11.46	57.24
Charleston ..	25.40	44.08	18.68	73.52	22.30	46.74	24.44	109.63	21.88	41.43	19.55	89.39
Memphis....	26.08	43.01	16.93	64.95	21.49	29.35	7.86	36.59	14.17	21.11	6.94	48.95
Richmond....	22.42	40.34	17.92	79.98	21.37	38.83	17.46	81.74	18.42	34.91	16.49	89.54

TABLE b.—POPULATION, DEATHS, AND DEATH RATE PER 1,000, ATLANTA, GA.,

1882 TO 1895.

Year.	Population.		Total deaths.		Deaths per 1,000.			
	White.	Colored.	White.	Colored.	White.	Colored.	Excess of colored.	
							No.	Per cent.
1882........	23,639	18,202	392	630	16.58	34.61	18.03	108.75
1883..............	25,034	19,217	500	735	19.97	38.25	18.28	91.54
1884	26,511	20,289	497	785	18.75	38.69	19.94	106.35
1885..............	28,075	21,420	492	854	17.52	39.87	22.35	127.57
Average.....	25,815	19,782	470	751	18.22	37.96	19.74	108.41
1886..............	29,732	22,615	446	541	15.10	23.92	8.82	58.41
1887..............	31,486	23,876	680	815	21.60	34.13	12.53	58.01
1888..............	33,344	25,207	646	886	19.37	35.15	15.78	81.47
1889	35,311	26,613	653	949	18.49	35.66	17.17	92.86
1890..............	37,416	28,098	793	1,032	21.19	36.73	15.54	73.34
Average.....	33,458	25,282	644	845	19.25	33.41	14 16	73.51
1891..............	39,623	29,665	827	1,167	20.87	39.34	18.47	88.50
1892............ ...	41,961	31,319	805	1,085	19.18	34.64	15.46	80.60
1893	44,437	33,066	813	1,107	18.30	33.48	15.18	82.95
1894......	47,058	34,910	691	947	14.68	27.13	12.45	84.81
1895	49,835	36,857	884	1,126	17.74	30.55	12.81	72.21
Average.....	44,583	33,163	804	1,086	18.03	32.76	14.73	81.65

Year.	Total deaths.		Deaths per 1,000.			
	White.	Colored.	White.	Colored.	Excess of colored.	
					Number.	Per cent.
1882	163	264	6.90	14.50	7.60	110.15
1883	194	339	7.75	17.64	9.89	127.61
1884	163	319	6.15	15.72	9.57	155.61
1885	167	329	5.95	15.26	9.41	158.15
Average	172	313	6.65	15.81	9.16	137.74
1886	160	257	5.38	11.36	5.98	111.15
1887	264	332	8.38	13.91	5.53	ſ65.99
1888	206	337	6.18	13.37	7.19	116.34
1889	205	364	5.81	13.68	7.87	135.46
1890	287	451	7.67	16.05	8.38	109.26
Average	224	348	6.71	13.77	7.06	105.22
1891	264	403	6.66	13.59	6.93	104.05
1892	276	403	6.58	12.87	6.29	95.59
1893	251	421	5.65	12.73	7.08	125.31
1894	218	303	4.63	8.68	4.05	87.47
1895	276	401	5.54	10.88	5.34	96.39
Average	257	386	5.76	11.65	5.89	102.26

TABLE d.—AVERAGE ANNUAL DEATH RATE PER 10,000, ATLANTA, GA., FOR THE PERIODS 1882 TO 1885, 1886 TO 1890, 1891 TO 1895, BY CAUSES.

Causes.	1882 to 1885.				1886 to 1890.				1891 to 1895.			
	W'ite.	Col-ored.	Excess of colored.		W'te.	Col-ored.	Excess of colored.		W'te.	Col-ored.	Excess of colored.	
			Number.	Per cent.			Number.	Per cent.			Number.	Per cent.
Consumption	18.40	50.20	31.80	172.83	18.83	45.88	27.05	143.65	16.82	43.48	26.66	158.50
Pneumonia	9.03	26.69	17.66	195.57	11.30	26.26	14.96	132.39	11.66	32.27	20.61	176.76
Total	27.43	76.89	49.46	180.31	30.13	72.14	42.01	139.43	28.48	75.75	47.27	165.98
Cholera infantum	(a)	(a)	(a)	(a)	12.43	23.10	10.67	85.84	7.63	15.26	7.63	100.00
Still-births	(a)	(a)	(a)	(a)	14.35	32.99	18.64	129.90	17.36	38.60	21.24	122.35
Total	(a)	(a)	(a)	(a)	26.78	56.09	29.31	109.45	24.99	53.86	28.87	115.53
Typhoid fever	8.64	17.09	8.45	97.80	10.70	11.07	.37	3.46	7.31	9.83	2.52	34.47
Scarlet fever	.31	.15	b .16	b 106.67	1.25	.32	b .93	b290.63	1.61	.12	b 1.49	b1,241.67
Malarial fever	.97	1.92	.95	97.94	1.61	5.46	3.85	239.13	.45	2.17	1.72	382.22
Diphtheria	1.66	.15	b 1.51	b1,006.67	1.02	.32	b .70	b218.75	1.35	.36	b .99	b 275.00
Total	11.58	19.31	7.73	66.75	14.58	17.17	2.59	17.76	10.72	12.48	1.76	16.42
Other causes	c143.15	c283.44	c140.29	c 98.00	121.05	188.67	67.62	55.86	116.15	185.50	69.35	59.71
Grand total	182.16	379.64	197.48	108.41	192.54	334.07	141.53	73.51	180.34	327.59	147.25	81.65

a Included in "Other causes."

b Excess of white.

c Including deaths from cholera infantum and still-births.

TABLE e.—AVERAGE ANNUAL DEATH RATE PER 10,000, CHARLESTON, S. C., FOR THE PERIODS 1881 TO 1884, 1885 TO 1889, AND 1890 TO 1894, BY CAUSES.

Causes.	1881 to 1884.				1885 to 1889.				1890 to 1894.			
	W'ite.	Colored.	Excess of colored.		W'ite.	Colored.	Excess of colored.		W'ite.	Colored.	Excess of colored.	
			Number.	Per cent.			Number.	Per cent.			Number.	Per cent.
Consumption.	27.52	72.20	44.68	162.35	20.05	68.08	48.03	239.55	17.71	57.66	39.95	225.58
Pneumonia	8.18	19.00	10.82	132.27	8.32	18.51	10.19	122.48	6.78	17.06	10.28	151.62
Total	35.70	91.20	55.50	155.46	28.37	86.59	58.22	205.22	24.49	74.72	50.23	205.10
Cholera infantum	(a)	(a)	(a)	(a)	7.90	15.43	7.53	95.32	7.20	9.63	2.43	33.75
Convulsions...	(a)	(a)	(a)	(a)	3.48	13.01	9.53	273.85	4.30	13.60	9.30	216.28
Total	(a)	(a)	(n)	(a)	11.38	28.44	17.06	149.91	11.50	23.23	11.73	102.00
Typhoid fever	8.83	11.36	2.53	28.65	4.93	8.38	3.45	69.98	4.38	6.68	2.30	52.51
Malarial fever	6.22	6.50	.28	4.50	2.55	6.04	3.49	136.86	3.06	6.23	3.17	103.59
Diarrhea	b 4.78	b 11.72	b 6.94	b145.19	5.43	11.60	6.17	113.63	3.56	9.38	5.82	163.48
Diphtheria ..	6.96	2.59	c 4.37	c168.73	4.25	1.21	c3.04	c 251.24	.83	.25	c .58	c 232.00
Total	d 26.79	d 32.17	d 5.3s	d 20.08	17.16	27.23	10.07	58.68	11.83	22.54	10.71	90.53
Scrofula	b .30	'b 2.95	b 2.65	b883.33	.43	6.98	6.55	1,523.26	.16	2.14	1.98	237.50
Syphilis	.44	2.13	1.69	384.09	.59	6.10	5.51	933.90	.83	3.15	2.32	279.52
Total	e.74	e 5.08	e 4.34	e586.49	1.02	13.08	12.06	1182.35	.99	5.29	4.30	434.34
Other causes	f190.81	f312.36	f121.55	f 63.70	165.03	312.05	147.02	89.09	169.96	288.55	118.59	69.78
Grand total	254.04	440.81	186.77	73.52	222.96	467.39	244.43	109.63	218.77	414.33	195.56	89.39

a Included in "Other causes."
b Not including deaths in 1884.
c Excess of white.
d Not including deaths from diarrhea in 1884.
e Not including deaths from scrofula in 1884.
f Including deaths from cholera infantum and convulsions, and from diarrhœa and scrofula in 1884.

The table following shows for each of the ten years from 1884 to 1893 the total and the illegitimate births and the birth rate per 1,000 of total population of both white and colored; also the average births and birth rates per 1,000 for the two five-year periods 1884 to 1888 and 1889 to 1893:

TABLE f.—TOTAL AND ILLEGITIMATE BIRTHS AND BIRTH RATE PER 1,000 OF TOTAL

POPULATION, BALTIMORE, MD., 1884 TO 1893.

Year.	Total births.		Births per 1,000.				Illegitimate births.		Illegitimate births per 1000.			
					Excess of white.						Excess of colored.	
	W'ite.	Col-ored.	W'ite.	Col-ored.	Num-ber.	Per cent.	W'ite.	Col-ored.	W'ite.	Col-ored.	Num-ber.	Per cent.
1884	6,899	1,136	22.18	19.31	2 87	14.86	124	173	0.40	2.94	2 54	635.0
1885	6,632	1,108	20.74	18.41	2.33	12.66	112	171	.35	2.84	2.49	711.4
1886	6,481	1,213	19.72	19.70	.02	.10	103	155	.31	2 52	2 21	712 9
1887	7,765	1,262	22.98	20.04	2.94	14 67	146	224	.43	3.56	3.13	727.9
1888	7,500	1,225	21.59	19.04	2.55	13.39	134	220	.39	3.42	3.03	776.9
Average	7,055	1,189	21.45	19.31	2.14	11.09	124	189	.38	3.06	2.68	714.6
1889	8,102	1,263	22.69	19.19	3.50	18.24	156	205	.44	3.12	2.68	609.1
1890	8,226	1,172	22.41	17.47	4.94	28.28	180	229	.49	3.41	2.92	595.9
1891	8,238	1,101	21.83	16.04	5.79	36.10	224	246	.59	3.58	2.99	506.8
1892	8,087	1,347	20.84	19.18	1.66	8.65	261	359	.67	5.11	4.44	662.7
1893	7,914	1,221	19.84	17.00	2.84	16.71	224	387	.56	5.39	4.83	862.5
Average	8,113	1,221	21.48	17.76	3.72	20.93	209	285	.55	4.15	3.60	650.4

Of total births, the excess of births per 1,000 of population is seen to be in favor of the whites. For the first five-year period this excess is 2.14, the percentage of excess being 11.09; for the second five-year period the excess is 3.72, the percentage of excess being 20.93.

The illegitimate births for the colored population show a very large excess over the illegitimate births for the white. While there is an increase in the excess of colored birth rate from 2.68 in the first five-year period to 3.60 in the second, the per cent of excess shows a decrease from 714.6 in the first period to 650.4 in the second.

...The Negro in Business...

REPORT OF A SOCIAL STUDY MADE UNDER
THE DIRECTION OF ATLANTA UNIVERSITY;
TOGETHER WITH THE PROCEEDINGS OF
THE FOURTH CONFERENCE FOR
THE STUDY OF THE NEGRO PROBLEMS, HELD
AT ATLANTA UNIVERSITY, MAY 30-31, 1899.

Edited by
W. E. BURGHARDT DuBois, Ph. D.,
Corresponding Secretary of the
Conference.

ATLANTA, GEORGIA.
1899.

The work of the Atlanta Conference, like the other work of Atlanta University, depends mainly upon voluntary contributions.

CONTENTS.

INTRODUCTION.

Atlanta University is an institution for the higher education of Negro youth. It seeks, by maintaining a high standard of scholarship and deportment, to sift out and train thoroughly talented members of this race to be leaders of thought and missionaries of culture among the masses.

Furthermore, Atlanta University recogizes that it is its duty as a seat of learning to throw as much light as possible upon the intricate social problems affecting these masses, for the enlightenment of its graduates and of the general public. It has, therefore, for the last four years, sought to unite its own graduates, the graduates of similar institutions, and educated Negroes in general, throughout the South, in an effort to study carefully and thoroughly certain definite aspects of the Negro problems.

Graduates of Fisk University, Berea College, Lincoln University, Spelman Seminary, Clark University, Wilberforce University, Howard University, the Meharry Medical College, Hampton and Tuskeegee Institutes and several other institutions have kindly joined in this movement and added their efforts to those of the graduates of Atlanta, and have, in the last four years, helped to conduct four investigations: One in 1896 into the "Mortality of Negroes in Cities"; another in 1897 into the "General Social and Physical Condition" of 5,000 Negroes living in selected parts of certain southern cities; a third in 1898 on "Some Efforts of American Negroes For Their Own Social Betterment." Finally in 1899, inquiry has been made to ascertain the extent to which the Freedman and his sons are entering into business life.

The results of this last investigation are presented in this pamphlet. Next year some other phases of the economic situation of the Negro will be studied. It is hoped that these studies will have the active aid and co-operation of all those who are interested in this method of making easier the solution of the Negro problems.

Beside these regular investigations by the Atlanta Negro Conference, the University pursues its sociological work in several other directions. *First*, it offers for its students and all others interested in these lines of work the following courses of study:

1. The Theory of Economics, one term.
2. The Economic History of the American Negro, one term.
3. Statistics and Sociology, one term.
4. Present Social Condition of the Negro, one term.
5. Elementary Civics, one term.
6. Civil Government in the United States, one term.
7. Political Science, one term·

Theses and library work are required in connection with the more advanced courses.

Secondly, members of the Department of Sociology of this institution have, from time to time, published the following studies and essays on various phases of the Negro problem:

Suppression of the Slave Trade. 335 pp, Longman's, 1896.

The Philadelphia Negro, 520 pp, Ginn & Co., 1899.

The Negroes of Farmville, Va., 38 pp, Bulletin U. S. Department of Labor, Jan., 1898.

Condition of the Negro in Various Cities, 112 pp, Bulletin U. S. Department of Labor, May, 1897.

The Negro in the Black Belt, 17 pp, Bulletin U. S. Department of Labor, May, 1899.

The Study of the Negro Problems, 21 pp, Publications of the American Academy of Political and Social Science, No. 219.

Strivings of the Negro People, *Atlantic Monthly*, August, 1896.

A Negro Schoolmaster in the New South, *Atlantic Monthly*, January, 1899.

The Negro and Crime, *Independent*, May 18, 1899.

The Conservation of Races, 16 pp, Publications of the American Negro Academy, No. 2.

Thirdly, the regular University publications are as follows:

Annual Catalogue, 1870-1899.

Bulletin of Atlanta University, 4 pp, monthly; 25 cents per year.

No. 1.　Mortality of Negroes, 51 pp, 1896, (out of print).

No. 2.　Social and Physical Condition of Negroes, 86 pp, 1897; 20 cents.

No. 3.　Some Efforts of American Negroes for Social Betterment, 66 pp, 1898; 20 cents.

No. 4.　The Negro in Business, 1899; 20 cents.

List of Negro Newspapers; 2 cents.

Programme of Social Betterment; 2 cents.

Fourthly; Bureau of Information:

The Corresponding Secretary of the Atlanta Conference undertakes, upon request, to furnish correspondents with information upon any phases of the Negro problem, so far as he is able; or he points out such sources as exist from which accurate data may be obtained. No charge is made for this work except for actual expenses incurred. During the past year professors in several northern and southern institutions, students of sociology, philanthropic societies and workers, and many private persons have taken advantage of this bureau.

The following is a partial list of recipients of such information within the last two years:

Hon. Carroll D. Wright, of U. S. Bureau of Labor.

Professor Walter F. Wilcox, of U. S. Census Office.

Professor Katharine Coman, of Wellesley College.

Edward Atkinson, of Boston.

Walter R. Lambeth, Missionary Secretary, M. E. Church, South.

Miss Jane Porter Scott, of the Social Settlements Association.

Dr. David J. Fuller, of Brooklyn.

Rev. Daniel Merriman of Worcester.

Rev. Edward L. Pell, Editor *Bible Reader*, Richmond, Va.

Hon. E. D. Bassett, Haytian Légation, New York; and others.

Graduate and other students in Harvard University, Mass.

"	"	"	"	"	The Catholic University, D. C.
"	"	"	"	"	Wellesley College, Mass.
"	"	"	"	"	Wooster University, Ohio.
"	"	"	"	"	University of Texas, Texas.
Professors	and	Teachers		in	Hampton Institute, Va.
"	"	"		"	Tuskegee Institute, Alabama.
"	"	"		"	Mercer University, Georgia.
"	"	"		"	Trinity Park High School, N. C.

City Physicians in eight different cities.

The *Insurance Press* of London.

The Penn Mutual Insurance Company.

Boston Children's Aid Society.

Social Settlement, Topeka, Kansas.

Northern Inter-Collegiate Oratorical League.

The Afro-American Council.

The American Negro Academy.

The American Missionary Association.

Members of the Legislature of Georgia.

McClure's Magazine.

New York Independent, etc.

Fifthly. The Atlanta Negro Conference beside its investigations has an annual gathering of those interested in its work in May of each year when the results of the year's investigation are first reported. The attendance in these meetings is largely local, but they also bring together many persons from abroad to discuss and add to the facts collected. An attempt is here made especially to encourage all movements toward social betterment, and several enterprises of this sort have had their inception here.

Such is the work which Atlanta University is doing for the social uplifting of the American Negro, and for it we ask an endowment which will insure its permanent usefulness.

RESULTS OF THE INVESTIGATION.

BY THE EDITOR.

1. *Scope of the Inquiry.*—The general idea of the Atlanta Conference is to select among the various and intricate questions arising from the presence of the Negro in the South certain lines of investigation which will be at once simple enough to be pursued by voluntary effort, and valuable enough to add to our scientific knowledge. At the same time the different subjects studied each year have had a logical connection, and will in time form a comprehensive whole. The starting point was the large death-rate of the Negroes; this led to a study of their condition of life, and the efforts they were making to better that condition. These efforts, when studied, brought clearly to light the hard economic struggle through which the emancipated slave is to-day passing.

The general method of making these inquiries is to distribute among a number of selected persons throughout the South, carefully prepared schedules. Care is taken to make the questions few in number, simple and direct, and, so far as possible, incapable of misapprehension. The investigators to whom these blanks are sent are usually well-educated Negroes, long resident in the communities; by calling on the same persons for aid year after year, a body of experienced correspondents has been gradually formed, numbering now about fifty.

In this investigation the object was to find in each locality the number and kind of Negro business men. The following blank was sent out:

Negro Merchants in..............State of..............Reported by.....................

Name.	Street & No.	Kind of Business.	Years in Business.	Capital.
....	....	....	....	....
....	....	....	....	....
....	....	....	....	....
....	....	....	....	....
....	....	....	....	....
....	....	....	....	....
....	....	....	....	....
....	....	....	....	....
....	....	....	....	....

With this was sent an explanatory letter defining the term "business man," and urging particular care in getting at the capital invested. Thus a large number of reports were secured. Then some of the chief merchants reported were written to and more particular inquiry made into their lives and experiences. The returns represent,therefore, the reports of business men themselves, interpreted and commented upon by an intelligent investigator of some experience. They can, therefore, on the whole, be depended upon as substantially accurate. The item of "capital invested" is naturally apt to contain the largest amount of errors since it is in most cases an estimate. Yet the estimate was either made by a disinterested person on data furnished by the merchant, or given directly by the merchant. In some cases the amount may have been exaggerated from motives of pride, in others underestimated for fear of taxes or jealousy. All doubtful estimates have been omitted when discovered.

It is hardly possible to place too great stress on the deep significance of business ventures among American Negroes. Physical emancipation came in 1863, but economic emancipation is still far off. The great majority of Negroes are still serfs bound to the soil or house-servants. The nation which robbed them of the fruits of their labor for two and a half centuries, finally set them adrift penniless. It would not have been wonderful or unprecedented if the Freedman had sunk into sluggish laziness, ignorance and crime after the war. That he did not wholly, is due to his own vigor and ambition, and the crusade of education from the North. What have these efforts, seconded by the common-school and to a limited extent the college, been able to accomplish in the line of making the Freedman a factor in the economic re-birth of the South?

Of the various answers that might be made to this question, none is more interesting than that which shows the extent to which the Negro is engaging in the various branches of business. Naturally business, of all vocations, was furthest removed from slavery. Even the ante-bellum plantation owner was hardly a good business man, and his slaves were at best careless sharers in a monarchical communism and, at worst, dumb driven cattle.

For a Negro then to go into business means a great deal. It is, indeed, a step in social progress worth measuring. It means hard labor, thrift in saving, a comprehension of social movements and ability to learn a new vocation—all this taking place, not by concerted guided action, but spontaneously here and there, in hamlet and city, North and South. To measure such a movement is difficult, and yet worth the trial. We need to know accurately the different kinds of business venture that appear, the order of their appearance, their measure of success and the capital invested in them. We need to know what sort of men go into business, how long they have been engaged and how they managed to get a start. Finally, we should know where this economic advance is being most strongly felt, and what the present tendencies are.

2. *Territory Covered by the Inquiry.*—In the census of 1890, the following Negro business men are returned:[*]

---

[*] Eleventh Census. Population, Vol. II, pp 355, ff.

Hotel-keepers	420
Saloon-keepers	932
Livery-stable Keepers	390
Druggists	135
Grocers	1 829
Retail Merchants, unspecified	4 490
Publishers	20
Total	8 216

There are many obvious errors in these returns; the first three items are greatly exaggerated without doubt, containing many lodging-houses misnamed "hotels;" employees in saloons erroneously returned as "saloon-keepers;" and hostlers returned as "livery-stable keepers." The unspecified retail merchants also probably include some clerks, hucksters and restaurant-keepers. With some allowances for these errors, it is probable that there are in the United States at least 5,000 Negro business men. Of these the following study has returns from something less than one-half, living in 30 different states and territories as follows:

TABLE No. 1   NEGRO BUSINESS MEN BY STATES.

Alabama	136	Maryland	49
Arkansas	94	Mississippi	78
California	43	Missouri	49
Colorado	8	New Jersey	36
Delaware	16	New York	80
District of Columbia	50	North Carolina	98
Florida	78	Ohio	14
Georgia	324	Oklahoma	7
Indiana	4	Pennsylvania	47
Indian Territory	7	South Carolina	123
Illinois	23	Tennessee	131
Kansas	30	Texas	159
Kentucky	72	Virginia	105
Louisiana	11	Washington	10
Massachusetts	14	West Virginia	9
Total			1,906.

Condensing this table we have reported from

The north, east of the Mississippi	218
The south, east of the Mississippi	1 281
West of the Mississippi	407
Total	1 906

The value of this comparison is somewhat spoiled by the fact that the Negroes in the states of Georgia and Alabama and the middle South were more thoroughly canvassed than those in other parts of the country, since the Conference had more correspondents there. Nevertheless, it is clear that it is density of Negro population in the main that gives the Negro business-man his best chance.

There were, of course, wide gaps and large omissions in such an inquiry. Small towns in considerable numbers, and country stores, were not returned, and many minor enterprises in larger towns. Of the large cities, the most important omission was the city of New Orleans from which returns came too late for insertion. With the latter exception it would seem, after careful inquiry, that the returns represent fully 75% of the more important business enterprises among Negroes, and consequently give a fair picture of their economic advance in this line.

2. *Kinds of Business Enterprise.*—The term "business man" in this study has been interpreted to include all with stocks of goods to sell, and also all other persons who have at least $500 of capital invested; for instance, while the ordinary barber should be classed as an artisan, a man with $500 or more invested in a shop, with several hired assistants, is a capitalist rather than an artisan, and 162 such men have been classed as business men. So, too, it seemed best to include 31 blacksmiths and wheelwrights who had considerable capital invested and kept stocks of wagons or other goods on sale. In several other cases there was some difficulty in drawing a line between artisans and business men, and the decision had to be more or less arbitrary, although the investment of considerable capital directly in the business was the usual criterion.

The different kinds of business reported were as follows:

TABLE NO. 2. NEGRO BUSINESS MEN,

ACCORDING TO OCCUPATIONS.

Grocers	432	Caterers	24
General merchandise dealers	166	Plumbing, tinware, and hardware shops	17
Barbers with $500 or more invested	162	Shoe dealers and repairers	17
Publishers and job printers	89	Fish dealers	15
Undertakers	80	Furniture dealers	13
Saloon-keepers	68	Building and loan associations	13
Druggists	64	Jewelers	11
Restaurant-keepers	61	Market gardeners and planters	11
Hackmen and expressmen, owning outfits	53	Clothing-dealers	10
Builders and contractors	48	Wall-paper and paint-shops	10
Dealers in meat	47	Bakers, with shops	10
Merchant tailors	40	Dry-goods dealers	9
Dealers in fuel	27	Cotton gin proprietors	9
Dealers in real estate	36	Steam laundries	8
Wagon-makers and blacksmiths	32	Proprietors of machine shops	8
Hotels	30	Cigar manufacturers	8
Green grocers, dairymen, etc,	30	Photographers	8
Livery-stable keepers	26	Brokers and money lenders	8
Confectioners	25	Dealers in feed	7
Milliners	5	Dealers in fruit	6

TABLE NO. 2.—CONTINUED.

Banks.
Second-hand stores.
Harness-shops.
Employment agencies. } Businesses With Four Persons Engaged in each.
Florists.
Crockery-stores.
Carpet-cleaning works

Ice-cream depots.
Wire goods man'fr's. } Two Persons in Each.
Dressmaking shops.
Private cemeteries.
Bicycle-stores.
M'ch'ncs with shops

Upholstering shops.
Hair goods stores.
Lumber mills. } Three Persons In Each.
Cl'n'ng & dyeing shops.
Brick contractors.
Dealers in cotton.

Shirt factory.
Toilet supply shop
Broom manufactory
Cotton mill.
Assembly hall.
Naval stores dealer. } One Person In Each
School of music.
Fan manufactory.
Carpet manufactory
Handle factory.
Rubber goods shop.
Book-store.

Miscellaneous, undesignated,.................. ....82.

Total... ....1,906.

It must be remembered in scanning these figures, that on most lines of business here reported, only establishments of considerable size and success have been reported. There are, for instance, large numbers of ice-cream dealers, pool-rooms, cleaning and dyeing shops, employment agencies, and the like among Negroes; most of these however are small and shortlived and only a few well-established businesses in these lines have been reported. Again, under the method employed in gathering these facts, it is hardly possible that the real proportion between the different kinds of businesses is correctly pictured, and there are doubtless large omissions here and there.

Perhaps the most instructive way of studying these businesses would be in the light of their historic evolution from the past economic condition of the Negro. For example,it is easy to see how the Barber, the Caterer and the Restaurant keeper were the direct economic progeny of the House-servant, just as the Market-Gardener,the Sawmill Proprietor, and the Florist were descended from the Field-hand. We may, indeed,divide the business men in the above table as follows:

(a) HOUSE SERVANT CLASS: Barbers, Restaurant-keepers, Expressmen, Butchers, Caterers, Liverymen, Bakers, Milliners, etc.,—462.

(b) FIELD-HAND CLASS: Market-Gardeners, Green-grocers, Dairymen, Cotton-gin owners, Florists, Lumber-mill owners, etc.,—61.

(c) PLANTATION MECHANIC CLASS: Builders and Contractors, Blacksmiths, Brickmakers, Jewelers, Shoe-dealers and Repairers, Machinists, Cigar manufacturers, Tinners, Paperhangers and Painters, Harness dealers, Upholsterers, etc.,—176.

(d) THE TRADERS: Grocers, General merchants and Dealers in Fuel, Fish, Clothing, Furniture, Feed and Dry-goods, and Second Hand Dealers,—695.

(e) THE CAPITALISTS: Banks, Real Estate dealers, Money-lenders, Building and Loan Associations, etc.,—67.

(f) THE MANUFACTURERS: Makers of Shirts, Brooms, Fans, Carpets, Handles and Rubber Goods; and the Cotton Mill,—9.

(g) CO-OPERATIVE EFFORTS: Undertakers, Druggists, Publishers, Cemetaries, Printers, etc—189.

(h) EFFORTS FOR AMUSEMENT: Saloons, Pool-rooms, Photographers, Bicycle dealers, etc.,—101.

No economic development is altogether accidental—previous occupation, enforced co-operation, the natural instinct to barter, and the efforts for recreation,explain among American Negroes,as among other people,their present occupations. Let us take up the classes in order as indicated above.

34. *House Servant Class.*—It is a well-known fact that the aristocracy of the plantation slaves were the house servants—those who,for appearance, ability and intelligence, were selected from the mass of the slaves to perform household duties at their master's house. Often such servants were educated and skillful; some times they were the natural children of their masters, and at all times they were the class which, when emancipation came, made the first steps toward independent livelihood. The master's valet set up his barber-shop in town and soon had a lucrative trade; the cook became proprietor of a small eating-stand or restaurant, or, if he was exceptionally efficient and noted for certain dishes, he became a caterer. It was in this way that the famous guild of black caterers arose in Philadelphia. In similar ways, but more slowly, a little saving of capital transformed the driver into the expressman, the coachman into the livery-stable keeper, the laundress into the proprietress of a public laundry. The most successful of these ventures hitherto have been those of the barber, the restaurant-keeper, the caterer and the expressman. There were, in 1890, some 17,480 Negro barbers reported. Most of these were journeymen working for wages and the rest were largely proprietors of small shops, either entirely without assistants or with one helper on Saturday nights. Neither of these classes would come under consideration here. There are, however, a number of barbers, 162 of whom are reported here, and whose actual number may be 300 or more, who are really business men. They own large, elegant shops with costly furniture, hire from three to eight assistants and do a lucrative business. The 162 reported have nearly $200,000 capital invested as follows:

$500—1,000	60
$1,000—2,500	63
$2,500—5,000	12
$5,000—10,000	3
Others over $500	24

Of the restaurant-keepers 19 had from $1,000—2,500 invested,and 12 from $2,500 to $5,000; 14 had from $500 to $1,000. The caterers, as a class, are well-to-do men of intelligence. It is difficult to discriminate in these cases between their capital and their accumulated wealth. Their reported capital is:

$100-500 1
$500-1,000 1
$1,000-2,500 5
$2,500-5,000 5
$5,000-10,000 4
$10,000-50,000 2
Unknown 6

The expressmen and hackmen have considerable business in several southern cities. The fifty reported had capital as follows:

$ 500-1,000 8
1,000-2,500 16
2,500-5,000 20
5,000-10,000 9

This whole class represented directly after the war, and up until about ten or fifteen years ago, the most prosperous class of Negroes. The caterers, barbers and stewards were leaders in all social movements among Negroes, and held the major part of the accumulated wealth. Lately, however, the class has lost ground. The palatial hotel and large restaurant have displaced the individual caterer in business, both white and black; the cab and transfer lines are crowding the single hackmen, and in many other lines of work the influence of aggregated capital has proven disastrous to the emancipated house-servant. The barbering business has fallen into dislike among Negroes, partly because it had so long the stigma of race attached, and nearly all barbers were Negroes, and especially because the Negro barber was compelled to draw the color-line.

35. *Field Hand Class.*—The great mass of the slaves were field hands driven to the most unskilled kinds of agriculture. This, to-day, forms the great unrisen horde of freedmen who swarm in the country districts of the South, and whose social development and economic emancipation has scarcely begun. In a few cases some of them own large plantations and have money invested in cotton gins, plantation stores, market-gardening and shipping to northern markets. Possibly they might be called business men. Eleven such are so denominated in this study, and have capital invested as follows:

$ 500—1,000 1
1,000—2,500 2
2,500—5,000 2
5,000—10,000 4
50,000 and over 1
Unknown 1

Of course this does not take account of those who are simply large land owners and farmers. These eleven and scores of others like them, not reported in this query, represent a sort of border-class—the first turning of the field-hand from pure agriculture to something like merchandising. The green grocers, dairymen, and the like, have gone a step further and established market stalls or stores for the sale of the products of their farms. Thirty of these are reported, which does not include the numerous small hucksters:

$100—500 7
$500—1,000 6
$1,000—2,500 12
$2,500—5,000 3
$5,000—10,000 2

The other callings which have developed logically from this class are few in number, and of importance chiefly as indicating tendencies. The three lumber mills have an aggregate capital of $10,000, and the four florists, $6,200. Much future interest attaches to the economic development of the former field-hand and present metayer. There is, as yet, no trace of house industries or domestic manufactures of any sort, although it would seem that theoretically the economic hope of the black South lies there.

36. *Plantation Mechanic Class.*—The *elite* of the field-hands were the slave mechanics—a class which, in some respects, rivaled the house-servants in importance During slavery they were the artisans of the South, and although emancipation brought the severe competition of better trained mechanics, and complicated the situation by drawing the color-line, still Negro mechanics continue to do a large amount of work in the South. Moreover, some, by saving money, have become capitalists on a considerable scale, especially is this true of carpenters and builders. It is difficult to estimate the invested capital of a contractor as it varies so from job to job, and from season to season. Forty-one contractors are reported as follows:

$500—1,000 10
$1,000—2,500 14
$2,500—5,000 4
$5,000—10,000 8
$10,000—50,000 5

One large brickmaker has $10,000 invested. The tin-shops usually have small investments under $2,500. Three have over $5,000. The eleven jewelers are watch and clock repairers with small stocks of goods. They have sums varying from $100 to $5,000 invested. Nearly all the other vocations mentioned as belonging to this class have small capital, and are but a step removed from the journeyman mechanic. The shoe-making business some years ago had a considerable number of large enterprises making shoes to order. The ready–made machine shoe has driven all but a few of these shops out of business, leaving only the small repair shops. A few of the older shops, of which six are reported, still do a large custom business, and to these are now being added regular shoe-stores of which eleven are here reported. The great industrial schools are trying to make these enterprises, and the mechanical industries whence they sprung, their especial field of work and, eventually, their efforts will undoubtedly bear fruit. As yet there is, however, little trace of this movement.

37. *The Traders.* So far we have considered three great classes of business venture, the logical origin of which are plainly seen in the house-servant, the field-hand and the slave-mechanic. Of course this does not say that every individual green-grocer was a field-hand before the war, or every barber a house-servant. It merely serves as a rough indication of a social evolution, and is true when applied to the great mass of the Negroes.

We now come to the traders — the merchants proper. The African Negro is a born trader, and despite the communism of the slave plantation, considerable barter went on among the slaves, and between them and the whites. The Negroes, under the better class of masters, enjoyed a *peculium* earned by working over-time, and expended as they wished In some cases they owned quite a little property and were able to buy their freedom. In most cases they merely kept themselves in a little pocket money.

While then trade and property was not unknown to slaves, yet the Negro merchant is distinctly a *post-bellum* institution. The Negro grocery and general merchandise store is the direct descendant of the "store-house" on the old plantation. Here the "rations" were distributed every Saturday to the assembled slaves. After emancipation these "rations" became "supplies" advanced to the black tenant, and the "store-house" developed into a store with a variety of goods. Finally, merchants outside the plantations began to furnish supplies for the various plantations round about. In this development, the Negro who had saved a little capital was easily attracted into the grocery and general merchandise business; if he had tenants on his own farm, he set up a little store to "furnish" them. If not, he set up a little store in town and caught the transient trade of farmers and laborers. In this way the business has spread until there is scarcely a town or hamlet in the South which has not its grocer. The 598 grocers and general merchants reported here form, therefore, only a small part of the total merchants thus engaged. The 6,319 retail merchants reported by the census of 1890 perhaps approximates the truth.

Combining the grocers and general merchants we find that those reported represent a total investment of $1,828,243, in sums as follows:

Under $500	174	32%
$500—1,000	164	30%
$1,000—2,500	171	31%
$2,500—5,900	23 }	7%
$5,000 and over	15 }	

A little less than a third of these stores are small shops with a few hundred dollars worth of shelf goods bought on credit. Another third are stores worth $1,000 to $2,500 invested in a considerable variety of goods. They have Negro clerks and usually make a good appearance. Seven per cent. are large ventures. It is a question as to what, under present conditions, is to be the future of such stores. Certainly it would seem that they may form a very important field of enterprise in the future, especially when the black peasant becomes emancipated, and the present cry of "Negro money for Negro merchants" continues to grow louder.

The other merchants deal principally in wood and coal, fish, new and second-hand furniture and clothing, dry-goods, feed and fruit. Taking the dealers in these eight articles, we find they have $251,994 invested as follows:

Under $500	15
$500—1,000	17
1,000—2,505	32
$2,500—5,000	13
$5,000 and over	14
Unknown	8

It would seem probable that we might expect a considerable increase in these minor businesses among Negroes in the future. The great drawback is the little knowledge of business methods among Negroes. Their whole training, their idealistic temperament is against them. Moreover, it is difficult to overcome these defects because it is so hard to get openings for Negro youth to learn business methods. Even in the North how many firms stand ready to allow a bright black boy to come into their counting-rooms and learn the difficult technique of modern commercial life?

38. *The Capitalist.*—It is a difficult thing for those unused to the notion of property to learn to save. Moreover the national crime perpetrated in the mismanagement of the Freedman's Bank had wide-spread influence in discouraging the saving habit. As it is to-day, there is not among all these millions any far-reaching movement to encourage or facilitate saving except such local efforts as have arisen among themselves. While their extravagance and carelessness in the expenditure of their incomes is characteristic of the race, and will be for some time, yet there is some considerable saving even now, and much money is invested. Land and houses are naturally favorite investments, and there are a number of real estate agents. It is difficult to separate capital from accumulated wealth in the case of many who live on the income from rents or buy and sell real estate for a profit. Thirty-six such capitalists have been reported with about $750,000 invested. There are four banks,— in Washington, D. C., Richmond, Va. and Birmingham, Ala., and several large insurance companies which insure against sickness and death, and collect weekly premiums. There are a number of brokers and money-lenders springing up here and there, especially in cities like Washington where there is a large salaried class.

The most gratifying phenomenon is the spread of building and loan associations, of which there are thirteen reported:

Philadelphia, Penn.,	3
Washington, D. C.,	1
Hampton, Va.,	1
Ocala, Fla.,	1
Sacramento, Cal.,	1
Wilmington, N. C.	2
Augusta, Ga.,	1
Little Rock, Ark.,	1
Portsmouth, Va.,	1
Anderson, S. C.,	1

There are probably several more of these associations not reported. The crying need of the future is more agencies to encourage saving among Negroes. Penny savings banks with branches in the country districts, building and loan associations and the like would form a promising field for philanthropic effort. The Negroes, themselves, have as yet too few persons trained in handling and investing money. They would, however, co-operate with others, and such movements well-started would spread.

39. *The Manufacturer.*—If the general training of the Negro was unfavorable to general business enterprise, it was even more ill-suited to impart-

ing the technical knowledge which the manufacturer needs. It will, therefore, be many years before the Negro will enter this field. Still there are even now some interesting ventures which must be regarded as experiments. There is the Coleman Cotton Mill, spoken of in the Atlanta University Publications, No. 4. During the past year machinery has been installed, but the mill has not started yet. The foundry described among the contributed papers is small but successful, and looks as though it might survive. There are several broom factories, one of which is reported here, and a number of minor manufactures which partake something of the nature of handicrafts. As yet there is little or no trace of house industries. Here is another field for philanthropic effort. If, throughout the South, the Negro peasant proprietor could eke out the scanty earnings of the farm by home manufactures it would solve many vexed problems: it would establish the country home, elevate the Negro womanhood from the rough unsexing work of the field, lessen the temptation to migrate to cities, and decrease idleness and crime. Lack of profitable congenial occupation for the rising middle class of Negroes is the central economic problem of the South to-day, and house industries would, in a measure, solve it.

310.   *Co-operative Efforts.*—Under co-operative effort have been grouped a number of business ventures whose existence is due primarily to the peculiar environment of the Negro in this land. Segregated as a social group there are many semi-social functions in which the prevailing prejudice makes it pleasanter that he should serve himself if possible. Undertakers, for instance, must come in close and sympathetic relations with the family. This has led to Negroes taking up this branch of business, and in no line have they had greater success. Twenty-three of those reported had over $5,000 in capital invested, and there are, in fact, many more than this. Probably $500,000 is invested by Negroes in this business. Then, too, the demand for pomp and display at funerals has compelled these undertakers to equip their establishments unusually well. In Philadelphia, Baltimore, Atlanta and other cities there are Negro undertaking establishments equal in most of their appointments to the best white establishments. The advent of the Negro physician and undertaker naturally called for the drug-store. Sixty-four drug-stores are reported, forty-seven of which have over $1,000 invested. They are especially popular in the South for the social feature of the soda fountain and for their business partnership with sick-benefit societies. They are usually neat and well conducted, and are a favorite venture for young Negro physicians. There are many private cemeteries owned by companies and societies, only two of which are reported here. They arose from the color line in burial and the poor condition of the public burial grounds for colored people. Finally, a demand for news and books among themselves has led to the establishment of many hundred newspapers, of which over a hundred still survive, and to three or four publishing houses. The more successful publishing houses are connected with the large Negro church organizations, as the African Methodist at Philadelphia and Nashville, the Methodist Zion at Charlotte, N. C., and the Baptist at Nashville. These publish denominational literature, papers and books. They own four buildings in all, and the largest has a plant valued at $45,000. There are some other small publishing establishments of no great importance.

The newspapers are dealt with in another place.*

These enterprises are peculiar instances of the "advantage of the disadvantage"—of the way in which a hostile environment has forced the Negro to do for himself. On the whole he has begun to supply well some of the needs thus created.

311. *Efforts for Amusement.*—Efforts to supply the large social demand for recreation and amusement are a large part of the co-operative efforts noted above. The Negro church has, until recently, been the chief purveyor of amusement to the mass of Negroes, and even now it supplies by far the larger part of social intercourse and entertainment for the masses. At the same time, there is a large unsatisfied demand for recreation natural to a light-hearted people who work hard. The saloon and the poolroom supply a part of this demand, and of the 68 saloons reported, 54 have over $1,000 invested. The abuse of alcoholic liquors is not one of the especial offenses of the Negro, and yet he spends considerable in this way, especially during the Christmas holidays. The saloon among these people, even more than among the Irish and other city groups, is a distinct social centre. In the country towns of the black belt, the field-hands gather there to gossip, loaf and joke. In the cities a crowd of jolly fellows can be met there and in the adjacent pool-rooms. Consequently, the business has attracted Negroes with capital in spite of the fact that the Negro church distinctly frowns on the the vocation, which means some social ostracism for the liquor dealer. Next to saloons in importance come the traveling Negro vaudeville shows. None of these are reported here, for having no permanent headquarters they were difficult to reach; but there are known to be some three or four successful companies of this sort traveling about the country. Most of them are compelled to have white managers in order to get entree into the theatres, but they are largely under Negro control, and represent a considerable investment of Negro capital. Other caterers to amusements are the bicycle dealers, photographers and the like.

There is a large field for development here, and for considerable education and social uplifting. Few people, for instance, have stronger dramatic instincts than Negroes, and yet the theatre is almost unknown among them. Much could be done to elevate and enlighten the masses by a judicious catering to their unsatisfied demand for amusement. Here is a chance for philanthropy and five per cent for black and white capitalists.

312. *Capital Invested in Business.*—As has been said before, there is probably a considerable amount of error in these returns. Every effort has been made, however, to reduce mistakes to a minimum, to eliminate exaggerations and misstatements, and to present as nearly as possible an approximately true statement of the capital invested. The table is as follows:

* See page 72.

TABLE NO. 3.   KINDS OF BUSINESS ACCORDING TO CAPITAL INVESTED.

KINDS OF BUSINESS.	Under $100	$100 to $500	$500 to 1000	$1,000 to 2,500	$2,500 to 5,000	$5,000 to 10,000	$10,000 to 50,000	$50,000 and Over.	Capital Unknown	Actual Total.
General M'd'se.	....	29	39	57	18	4	2		17	$1,423,075
Real Estate.........			4	6	8	10	3	5	.....	742,700
Groceries...............	8	137	125	114	5	5	4		34	405,038
Liquor Saloons.....		6	6	25	15	13	....	1	2	291,300
Banking and Insurance...				1	2	4	....	3	1	270,900
Undertakers...		.9	4	21	11	19	4	....	12	229,450
Publishers and Printers......	1	18	17	25	15	4	4		5	226,975
Market Gardeners, Planters, etc.			1	2	2	4	....	1	1	205,700
Barbers..............			60	63	12	3	....	....	24	197,325
Building and Loan Ass'ns........				....	2	....	6	1	4	165,000
Builders and Contractors........			10	14	4	8	5	....	7	140,200
Hall, for renting, etc., ...							... .	1	.....	120,000
Drugs and Medicines		5	9	35	9	2	1		3	119,150
Hotels.......		5	1	13	7	2	2	....	6	92,200
Fuel-dealers........	1	4	8	10	5	3	2		4	81,500
Caterers...............		1	1	5	5	4	2	....	6	79,395
Expressmen and Hackmen.....		8	16	20	9	....	....	....	.....	78,875

TABLE No. 3.—CONTINUED.

KINDS OF BUSINESS.	Under $100	$100 to $500	$500 to 1000	$1,000 to 2,500	$2,500 to 5,000	$5,000 to 10,000	$10,000 to 50,000	$50,000 and Over.	Capital Unknown	Actual Total.
Fish-dealers	1	2	4	4	1		2		1	$ 67,744
Livery-stables		3	2	14	2	3	1		1	62,860
Miscellaneous		8	18	25	2				3	59,355
Restaurants		4	14	19	12	5			7	51,925
Plumbing and Tin-shops and Hardware stores		3	4	5	1	1	2		1	45,250
Green Grocers, Dairymen, etc.,		7	6	12	3	2				43,475
Tailor-shops		12	10	9	3	1			5	37,125
Furniture, New and 2nd Hand		2	1	6	2	1	1			32,800
Wagon-makers, Blacksmiths and Wheelwrights		8	11	9	3	1				31,700
Meat-shops	3	13	9	13	2				7	31,055
Dry-goods			1	4	1	3				28,200
Brokers and Money-lenders		1		2	1	1	1		1	27,500
Cotton Factory							1			25,000
Shoe-dealers	1	1	4	9	1	1				23,210
Cotton Gin Proprietors				2	4	1			2	21,000
Confectioners	1	9	6	4	1	1			3	19,175
Jewelers		2	3	2	1		1		2	18,850

THE NEGRO IN BUSINESS.

TABLE No. 3.—CONCLUDED.

KINDS OF BUSINESS.	Under $100	$100 to $500	$500 to 1000	$1,000 to 2,500	$2,500 to 5,000	$5,000 to 10,000	$10,000 to 50,000	$50,000 and Over.	Capital Unknown	Actual Total.
New and 2nd Hand Clothing...	....	1	2	3	2	1	....	....	1	$ 17,050
Bakers	....	3	3	3	1	....	....	....	.....	13,250
Steam Laundries...	....	1	2	1	3	....	....	.. ..	1	15,300
Feed-stores..........	....	1	1	2	1	1	....	....	1	12,700
Fruit-stores	.. ..	2	.....	3	1	....	....	....	1	12,000
Machine-shops	....	......	4	3	1	....	....	....	.....	11,000
Paper-hanger and Paint-shops	....	1	3	2	....	1	....	....	3	10,750
Brick Contractors	....	.....	....	....	....	....	1	....	2	10,000
Second-hand Stores.................	....	......	.....	1	1	1	....	....	.....	10,000
Lumber Mills	....	......	.....	1	1	1	....	....	.....	10,000
Stationers and Newsdealers	....	1	4	2	1	....	....	....	1	8,950
Photographers	....	2	1	3	1	....	... .	....	1	7,600
Cigar Man'fc'rs...	....	2	......	5	....	....	....	....	1	7,450
Wire-goods Manufactory	....	.....	......	1	....	1	....	....	.....	7,000
Carpet Man'fct'ry	....	.....	.....	....	....	1	....	....	.....	7,000
Florists	....	......	1	2	1	....	....	....	.....	6,200
Hair-goods..........	....	1	......	3	....	....	....	....	1	5,350
Handle Factory...	....	.....	.....	....	....	1	....	....	.....	5,000

Summarized, this table shows the following investments:

Under $100 16
$100—500.. 312
$500—1,000 415
$1,000—2,500 586
$2,500—5,000 183
$5,000—10,000 115
$10,000—50,000 45
$50,000 and over 12

 Total actual amount invested .... $5,691,137.
Capital unknown.. 170
  Estimated capital of the unknown cases * ....$93,500.
  Possible capital ** of 3,094 unreported businesses......$3,000,000.
  Estimated total capital invested by the American
  Negro in business...$8,784,637.

Compared with the immense sums of money invested in American business, this showing seems meagre enough; but when one considers the poverty and training of the Freedmen, the saving and investment of six or eight millions in enterprises managed by themselves is a most creditable accomplishment. The great bulk of these investments, 79%, is in sums less than $2,500, showing the popular character of the business movement: only twelve establishments reach the sum of $50,000 or more.

A list of some of the larger investments is as follows:

$10,000—2 real estate dealers, Houston, Texas,
  1 real estate dealer, New York city,
  1 builder and contractor, Brooklyn, N. Y.,
  1 builder and contractor, Carlisle, Penn.,
  1 builder and contractor, Raleigh, N. C.,
  1 builder and contractor, St. Louis, Mo.,
  1 publishing house, Nashville, Tenn.,
  1 publishing house, Jackson, Tenn.,
  1 undertaker, Washington, D. C.,
  1 merchant and planter, Dougherty county, Ga.,
  1 banker and merchant, Kinston, N. C.
$12,000—1 building and loan association, Brooklyn, N. Y.
$15,000—1 proprietor of transfer wagons, Nashville, Tenn.
$20,000—1 brick contractor and druggist, Durham, N. C.,
  1 club house, New York city,
$25,000—1 real estate agent, New York city,
  1 hardware and crockery store, Mobile, Ala.,
  1 undertaker, Chicago, Ill.,
  1 hotel, Chicago, Ill.,
  1 fish dealer and capitalist, Concord, N. C.,
  1 caterer, Chicago, Ill.,
  1 banking association, Jacksonville, Fla.
$30,000—1 planter and contractor, Dougherty county, Ga.,
  1 merchant and planter, Dougherty county, Ga.,

---

* This estimate is based on a consideration of the several cases, and is not far from the truth.

** This estimate approaches guess work, but it can hardly be an overstatement if the census of of 1890 is to be depended upon.

   1 publishing house, Nashville, Tenn.,

   1 bank, Richmond, Va.

$50,000—1 real estate dealer, Houston, Tex.,

   1 bank, Birmingham, Ala.,

   1 building and loan association, Washington, D. C.

$60,000—1 relief society, New York city.

$100,000-1 dealer in real estate, Cleveland, O.,

   1 bank, Richmond, Va.

$120,000-1 public hall association, New York city.

$150,000-2 real estate agents, New York city,

   1 savings bank, Washington, D. C.

One Negro church in New York city is reported as having an endowment of over $200,000. This has not been added in the totals given, however, as it seemed more of a philanthropic than business enterprise. However, it rents out considerable property to tenants.

There is considerable Negro capital invested in enterprises conducted by whites. Of the wealthy Negroes in one northern city only a fifth invested their capital in purely Negro enterprises. So, too, in the South, Negro business ventures have not yet begun to attract the bulk of Negro savings.

314. *Tendencies of Business Ventures.*—The next question of interest is how long the different enterprises reported have been in existence, and what the average age of each sort of business venture is. Full reports as to the length of time in business were not obtained, but this was reported in the majority of cases. The table is as follows:

TABLE NO. 4. KINDS OF BUSINESS ACCORDINC TO THE NUMBER OF YEARS ENGAGED.

KINDS OF BUSINESS.	UNDER 1 YR.	1–3 YR'S	3–5 YR'S	5–10 YR'S	10-20 YR'S	20-30 YR'S	30 and OVER	Actual Av'rge
General Merchandise.....	5	26	21	44	34	9	....	9
Real Estate	1	1	1	7	14	3	1	14
Groceries........................	26	80	67	110	78	20	2	12
Liquor Saloons...............	5	20	9	6	15	8	....	7
Banking and Insurance..	....	....	....	6	....	....	....	7
Undertakers	2	11	8	11	15	8	1	10
Publishers and Printers	....	7	6	16	10	3	....	8
Market Gardeners, etc.,	....	....	....	2	7	1	....	15
Barbers	....	7	8	27	53	46	13	16
Building & Loan Ass'ns	....	....	....	3	2	....	....	10
Builders and Contractors	....	1	13	6	20	8	5	17
Drugs and Medicines......	....	12	14	14	5	2	4	8
Hotels.............................	....	5	3	6	7	2	....	8
Fuel-dealers	1	2	4	10	8	8	....	10
Caterers	....	....	1	3	5	4	3	19

Table No. 4.—Continued.

KINDS OF BUSINESS.	UNDER 1 YR.	1–3 Y'RS	3–5 YR'S	5–10 YR'S	10–20 YR'S	20–30 YR'S	30 and OVER	Actual Av'rge
Expressmen and Hackmen	....	4	6	15	15	7	1	3
Fish-dealers	....	4	1	2	3	3	....	9
Livery-stables	....	....	6	6	6	3	....	9
Restaurants	2	8	7	19	8	2	1	7
Plumbing and Tin-shops and Hardware-stores	....	1	2	5	3	1	2	12
Green-grocers and Dairymen	....	....	5	8	14	5	2	13
Tailor-shops	1	8	3	10	5	5	1	8
Furniture, new and second-hand	....	2	1	6	2	....	....	8
Meat-shops	....	7	....	11	3	4	4	12
Dry-goods	....	2	1	3	2	....	....	7
Brokers, etc.,	....	1	....	2	1	....	....	8
Shoe-dealers	1	4	....	1	....	2	1	4
Cotton Gin Proprietors	1	1	1	4	1	....	....	6
Confectioners	1	6	7	7	1	1	....	5
Jewelers	....	3	....	1	5	....	1	11
Clothiers	....	....	1	1	4	....	....	10
Bakers	....	2	2	1	1	4	....	14

TABLE No. 4.—CONCLUDED.

KINDS OF BUSINESS.	UNDER 1 YR.	1–3 YR'S	3–5 YR'S	5–10 YR'S	10-20 YR'S	20-30 YR'S	30 and OVER	Actual Av'r'ge
Stationers and News-dealers	....	1	....	2	1	1	....	9
Photographers	....	....	....	3	2	....	....	9
Cigar Manufacturers	1	....	....	....	2	....	....	8
All other manufactures	1	....	....	....	....	1	3	....
Florists	....	....	....	....	1	2	1	17
Dealers in Hair-goods	....	1	....	1	1	1	1	12
All other businesses	....	11	16	28	29	11	5	....

Of all the businesses reported:

32% had been established under 1 year,
16% "   "   "   " 1-3 years,
14.7% "   "   "   " 3-5 years,
24.9% "   "   "   " 5-10 years,
25.9% "   "   "   " 10-20 years,
11.8% "   "   "   " 20-30 years,
3.5% "   "   "   " 30 years or more,

Or, in other words:

One-fifth of them were established since 1895
One-third   "   "   "   " 1893,
Three-fifths   "   "   "   " 1888,
Four-fifths   "   "   "   " 1878.

Those enterprises that show the longest average number of years of establishment are:

> Barbers,
> Caterers,
> Builders and Contractors, } Over 15 years established.
> Market Gardeners,
> Florists,

All these are the kinds of business towards which the Freedmen most naturally turned. Next come:

> Real Estate Dealers,
> Grocers,
> Undertakers,
> Building and Loan Associations,
> Fuel Dealers,
> Expressmen,
> Hardware,   } Over 10 and less than 15 years established.
> Green-grocers,
> Butchers,
> Clothiers,
> Bakers,
> Jewelers,
> Dealers in Hair-goods,

These represent most of the successful business which are the enterprises of the Freedmen's sons in the majority of cases rather than of the ex-slaves themselves. Those businesses towards which capital has but recently turned are, among others:

General Merchandise Stores,
Liquor-Saloons,
Banks and Insurance Societies,
Publishing Houses and Newspapers,
Drug-stores,
Hotels,
Dry-goods Stores,
Shoe-stores,
Confectionery-stores,
Photographic Galleries, etc.

Businesses like the Grocery business, conducting Restaurants, Fish-dealing, Tailoring, Second-hand Stores, and the like, have a large number of both old and new ventures. On the whole, then, it may be said that the tendency is to venture more and more boldly into the purely commer-cial lines where capital and experience are the determining factors, and where a severe test of the Negro's ability to enter modern competitive business life will be made.

The great obstacle to be encountered here is the fact that while the Ne-gro is learning the A B C of business as it is now conducted, the charac-ter of commercial life is slowly but significantly changing. The large in-dustry, the department store and the trust are making it daily more difficult for the small capitalist with slender resources and limited knowl-edge to live. This will have an unfortunate effect on the Negro, for not only will he, with his white brother, lose ground in much of the retail business, but he, unlike the other, will not be so readily admitted to posi-tion of direction and co-operation in the large business. A Negro can to-day run a small corner grocery with considerable success. To-morrow however, he cannot be head of the grocery department of the depart-ment store which forces him out of business.

15. *Characteristics of Localities.*—A closer study of the geographical dis-tribution of Negro business is instructive.

Cities having twenty or more Negro merchants are as follows:

Birmingham, Ala., 32.

Grocers	8
Barbers	6
Banks and Brokers	5
Druggists	4
Tailors	4
Miscellaneous	5

Mobile, Ala., 25.

Grocers	2
Fuel-dealers	2
Barbers	2
Saloon	1
Hardware-store	1
General Merchandise	1
Cohfectionery	1
Fish and Oysters	1
Undertakers	2
Publisher	1
Hotels	2
Shoe-store	1
Drug-store	1
Miscellaneous	7

Montgomery, Ala., 20.

Grocers	6
Undertakers	2
Drug-stores	2
Butcher	1

Dry-goods	1
Builder and Contractor	1
Miscellaneous	7

Little Rock, Ark., 42.

Grocers	14
Tailors	3
Confectioners	3
Publishers	3
Hotels	2
Jewelers	2
Druggists	2
Fuel-dealers	2
Undertakers	2
General Merchandise	2
Wholesale Grocer	1
Shirt Manufacturer	1
Miscellaneous	5

Washington, D. C., 49.

Grocers	9
Druggists	4
Restaurants	2
Undertakers	3
Caterers	2
Newspapers	2
Job Printers	2
Saloons	2
Coal-dealers	2

Green Grocers............ 2
Hardware............... 1
Fish-dealer 1
Photographer.......... 1
Hotels 2
General Merchandise.................... 1
Undertaker 1
Book-store 1
Grain and Feed............. 1
Miscellaneous 7

Atlanta, Ga., 50.

Grocers 19
Meat-markets............................... ·6
General Merchandise.......... 5
Fuel-dealers................. 5
Undertakers................. ....·........ 2
Real Estate 2
Tailor 1
Drug-store 1
Publisher 1
Wagon Builder 1
Miscellaneous............................... 7

Savannah, Ga., 30.

Grocers 7
Saloons............... 5
Meat Markets......................... 7
Plumber 1
General Merchandise...................... 1
Printer................... 1
Cotton Merchants............ 2
Miscellaneous................................ 6

Macon, Ga., 27.

Grocers 7
Broom Manufacturers 2
General Merchandise...................... 3
Contractors and Builders..... 2
Real Estate........ 1
Tailor 1
Coal-dealer 1
Druggist.................... 1
Saloon... 1
Barbers 4
Miscellaneous.................................. 7

Louisville, Ky., 35.

Grocers 5
Expressmen 4
Saloons.. 3
Feed-stores 3

Publishers 2
Restaurants 2
Real Estate........................ 2
Undertakers 2
Drug-stores 2
Milliner 1
Furniture.............................. 1
Fish-dealer...................................... 1
Photographer 1
Miscellaneous................................. 6

Baltimore, Md., 31.

Undertakers 5
Caterers.. 5
Furniture 3
Butchers 2
Printers 2
Green Groceries............................... 2
Coal and Wood 2
Pork Butcher 1
Tailor 1
China Store......................... 1
Ice Cream Manufactory 1
Stationery.. 1
Cigar Manufacturer................... . 1
Grocer... 1
Miscellaneous....................,.............. 3

Vicksburg, Miss., 21.

Saloons.. 2
Jeweler 2
Clothiers and Tailors.................. 2
Drug-stores 2
Newspapers 2
Dry-goods 2
Undertaker 1
Confectioners 2
Upholsterer 1
Butcher 1
Fish and Oysters............................. 1
Miscellaneous.................................. 3

St. Louis, Mo., 12.

Grocers... 3
Express 2
Coal-dealers 2
Stock-dealer 1
Painter and Paper-hanger......... 1
Paving Business............... 1
Wall Paper.......................... 1
Tailor 1

Contractor and Builder................. 1
Undertaker 1
Publisher 1
Miscellaneous................................... 5
New York City, N. Y., 63.
Caterers.. 6
Express 5
Intelligence Offices 4
Real Estate...................................... 4
Undertakers 4
Newsdealers 3
Printers... 2
Hotels 2
Restaurants...................................... 2
Machinists.. 2
Coal-dealer 1
Saloons 2
Grocer 1
Tailors... 2
Fuel-dealer 1
Publisher 1
Manufacturer of Wire Goods 1
Bicycle Manufacturer..................... 1
Druggist 1
Miscellaneous..............................18
Wilmington, N. C., 20.
Grocers 5
Undertakers 4
Druggists 2
Merchant Tailors............................. 2
General Merchandise 1
Broker 1
Contractor and Miscellaneous........ 5
Philadelphia, Penn., 45.
Caterers... 5
Undertakers 4
Grocers 4
Building and Loan Associations..... 3
Saloons 3
Bicycle Shops.................................. 2
Real Estate 2
Crockery-stores............................... 2
Publishers 2
Printers 2
Cigars and Tobacco......................... 2
Upholsterers 2
Expressman 1
Steam Carpet Cleaning................... 1
Restaurants...................................... 2

Rubber Goods Dealer..................... 1
China-store 1
Market.. 1
Dairy 1
Fancy Goods.................................... 1
Florist 1
Miscellaneous................................. 2
Charleston, S. C., 58.
Undertakers 7
Barbers 6
Green Grocers 6
Tailors 5
Grocers.. 4
Contractors 4
Fruit and Vegetables....................... 3
Printers... 3
Livery Stables................................. 3
Shoe-store 2
Wheelwrights 2
Photographer 1
Fan-maker.. 1
Drug-store 1
Steam Dye Works 1
Miscellaneous................................. 9
Nashville, Tenn., 45.
Contractors...................................... 9
Grocers 6
Undertakers 2
Saloons 2
Drug-stores 2
Second-hand Stores......................... 2
Livery-stables 2
Publishers 2
Tailors 2
Coal and Ice,.................................... 1
Produce Merchant 1
Furniture 1
Transfer Wagons.............................. 1
Restaurant and Grocer.................... 1
Grocer and Saloon........................... 1
Second-hand Furniture.................... 1
Miscellaneous.................................. 9
San. Antonio, Tex., 24.
Saloons 8
Expressmen...................................... 3
Real Estate...................................... 1
Newspaper....................................... 1
Tailor 1
Contractor 1

Green Grocer..................................... 1   Miscellaneous.................................. 9
Miscellaneous.................................. 8   *Richmond, Va.,* 28.
Houston, Tex , 37.   Insurance Societies........................ 5
Grocers...10   Grocers.. 4
Real Estate...................................... 6   Undertakers 4
Contractors 4   Fish-dealers 4
Saloons.. 3   Banks 2
Dairy 1   Druggist 1
Coal and Wood-dealers................... 2   Newspaper 1
Pawn Broker................................... 1   Dry-goods....................................... 1
Caterer.. 1   Miscellaneous................................ 6

Some of these plans deserve to be studied in detail. Washington, D. C.
is the capital of Negro population of America, even more than of the
whites, and here in most directions one can see the Negro's best development. At the same time, sharp competition and lack of capital have
made development in business enterprise here slow. The following statistics, compiled by the members of the Colored Normal School, are typical;

NEGRO MERCHANTS IN WASHINGTON, D. C.

KINDS OF BUSINESS.	YEARS IN BUSINESS.	CAPITAL INVESTED.
Ice Cream Manufacturer and Restaurant.	5 years.	$ 700
Undertaker,	15 "	10,000
Groceries and Provisions,	10 "	15,000
Jeweler and Watchmaker,	9 "	800
Newspaper Publisher,	18 "	700
Job Printer,	6 "	500
Undertaker,		
Druggist,	8 "	1,000
Druggist,	5 "	1,500
Restaurant,	8 "	500
Grain and Feed,	25 "	2,000
Pork Business,	7 "	3,000
Vegetable Business,	25 "	5,000
Grocer,	4 "	1,000
Green-grocer,	4 "	700
Fish-dealer,		15,000
Grocery,	12 "	5,000
Tinner and Hardware work,	3 "	5,000
Coal,	15 "	8,000
Caterer and Confectioner,	22 "	5,000
Grocery,	13 "	300
Grocery,	5 "	500
Wood, Coal and Fertlizers,	12 "	10,000
Undertaker,	20 "	10,000
Undertaker,	6 "	5,000
Restaurant,	1 "	3,000
Sign Writer,	15 "	5,000
Barber,	15 "	500

KINDS OF BUSINESS.	YEARS IN BUSINESS.	CAPITAL INVESTED.
Barber,	15 "	500
Grocery,	6 "	800
Grocery,	7 "	500
Confectioners, Caterers, Bakers, &c.,	11 "	3,000
Old Books, Documents, Magazines, &c.,	7 "	1,000
Photographer and Artist,	12 "	1,200
Bakery,	6 "	800
Saloon and Restaurant,	½ "	5,000
Saloon and Restaurant,	4 "	5,000
Newspaper,	6 "	3.500
Saloon, Cafe and Hotel,	½ "	6,000
Hotel,	2 "	1,000
Book and Job Printer,	13 "	1,200
Druggist,	5 "	1,500
Dying and Cleaning,	30 "	700

The eleven year old confectionery store is a large and complete establishment. The book store makes a specialty of rare editions and bindings. One newspaper has 15 persons on its pay roll, and the largest hotel has 18 well furnished bed-rooms, dining and reception rooms and steam heat.

With this, one may compare the situation in the far southwest:

NEGRO MERCHANTS OF HOUSTON, TEXAS.

KINDS OF BUSINESS.	YEARS IN BUSINESS.	CAPITAL INVESTED.
Grocery,	4 "	$ 1,500
Grocery,	3 "	1,000
Grocery.	5 "	2,000
Grocery,		1,000
Real Estate Dealer	15 "	10,000
Real Estate Dealer,	18 "	50,000
Contractor,	12 "	10,000
Contractor,	12 "	8,000
Barber,	20 "	1,000
Barber,	18 "	1,200
Barber,	16 "	1,000
Saloon,	14 "	4,000
Hair Dressing,	20 "	1,000
Real Estate Broker,	3 "	6,000
Real Estate Broker,	20 "	40,000
Real Estate Broker,	30 "	75,000
Grocer,	5 "	350
Grocer,	15 "	1,200
Contractor, Builder,	6 "	7,000
Grocer,	3 "	200
Contractor, Builder,	30 "	5,000
Grocer,	10 "	3,000
Grocer and Real Estate Broker,	10 "	15.000

Grocer,	4 "	500
Grocer,	3 "	500
Barber,	10 "	2,000
Barber,	15 "	3,000
Real Estate Broker.	10 "	14,000
Dairyman,	14 "	2.000
Real Estate	6 "	7.000
Real Estate	8 "	4.000
Tailor	6 "	5,000
Huckster	12 "	2,000
Barber	9 "	2,500
Contractor and Real Estate	15 "	12,000
Wood-dealer	10 "	900
Saloon Business	3 "	6,000
Caterer,	15 "	1,000
Blacksmith and Wheelwright,	12 "	1,800
Pawn Broker,	8 "	3,500
Saloon,	17 "	5,000

A few of the larger enterprises in the capital of Virginia are:

NEGRO MERCHANTS OF RICHMOND, VA.

Insurance and Banking	$ 75,000
Insurance and Banking	135,000
Fish-dealer	3,000
Fish-dealer	2,000
Dry-goods Store	2,000
Insurance Society	1,000
Undertaker	2,000
Undertaker	10,000
Undertaker	8,000
Photographer	1,500

From the middle west we have the following report:

NEGRO MERCHANTS OF KANSAS CITY, KAN.

KINDS OF BUSINESS.	YEARS IN BUSINESS.	CAPITAL INVESTED.
Coal, Wood, Flour, Feed, etc.,	9 "	$ 500
Drug Store,	3 "	1,500
Grocery,	2 "	300
Builders and Owners of a Hall,	9 "	2,500
Bridge Contractor,	10 "	1,000
Grocery,	2 "	
Newspaper	10 "	500
New and Second-hand Furniture and Stoves,	3 "	1,200
Dry-goods and Groceries,	10 "	1,500
Meat Market,	2 "	250
Confectioner,	1 "	100
Dairyman,	3 "	1,000
Confectioner,	9 "	500
Restaurant and Hotel,	3 "	1,000

Restaurant and Hotel,   1 "   1,000
Barber,   8 "   500
Jeweler,   10 "   2,000

The coal and wood dealers do a business of $2,000 a month, and the drug-store, of $500 a month. The hall rents for $50 a month; the paper is a daily.

A small Georgia town has this report:

NEGRO MERCHANTS OF GRIFFIN, GA.

KINDS OF BUSINESS.	YEARS IN BUSINESS.	CAPITAL INVESTED.
Grocer,	12 "	$ 500
Barber,	18 "	600
Liveryman,	20 "	7,000
Drayman,	16 "	800
Grocer and Baker,	10 "	600
Grocers and Undertakers,	2 "	400

The grocer does a "paying business;" the barber has $2,700 of assessed property; the liveryman, $18,000, and the dairyman $6,000. The last business is co-operative, and is managed by a society. It has been very successful so far.

From a border state comes this report for one of the smaller cities:

NEGRO MERCHANTS OF LEXINGTON, KY.

KINDS OF BUSINESS.	YEARS IN BUSINESS.	CAPITAL INVESTED.
Drug Store,	5 "	$ 2,000
Barber,	20 "	1,000
Tinner,	16 "	2.000
Brick Contractor,	20 "	10,000
New and Second-hand Furniture.	16 "	1,500
Stock Company,	27 "	5,000
Undertakers, Livery Stable,	6 "	5,000
Undertakers,	2 "	1,500
Barber,	25 "	700
Dressmakers and Milliners,	2 "	500
Barbers,	18 "	500

The drug-store is well run, and keeps the proprietor and one clerk busy. The contractor employs thirty or forty men, and is now working on the new county court house which is to cost $20,000. The agricultural society holds annual fairs, which are largely attended. One of the undertakers is very successful, and does a large business. The report concludes: "We have also many more barbers, restaurant-keepers, grocers, etc., of minor importance."

The following report has especial interest, as the town is composed entirely of Negroes, and is governed by them from the mayor down:

NEGRO MERCHANTS OF MOUND BAYOU, MISS.

KINDS OF BUSINESS.	YEARS IN BUSINESS.	CAPITAL INVESTED.	ASSESSED REAL ESTATE
General Merchandise,	10	$ 5,000	$ 3,000
Merchandise aed Ginning,	8	1,000	2,000
General Merchandise,	2	300	500
General Merchandise,	8	150	800
General Merchandise,	3	750	.....
Merchandise and Blacksmith,	7	150	800
Merchandise and Saw Mill,	10	1,000	10,000

The new territory of Oklahoma has a few business men:

NEGRO MERCHANTS OF GUTHRIE, OKLAHOMA TERRITORY.

KINDS OF BUSINESS.	YEARS IN BUSINESS.	CAPITAL INVESTED.
Grocery,	8 years.	$ 3,000
Grocery,	7 "	1,000
Grocery,	3 "	800
Grocery,	5 "	700
Newspaper,	6 "	500
Newspaper,	8 "	800
Barber,	4 "	500

Here is a report from an old Virginia town:

NEGRO MERCHANTS OF PETERSBURG, VA.

KINDS OF BUSINESS.	YEARS IN BUSINESS.	CAPITAL INVESTED.
Grocery,	34 years.	$ 300
Boots, Shoes and Books,	6 mos.	1,250
Grocery,	12 years.	500
Grocery,	13 "	500
Grocery.	28 "	50
Grocery,	7 "	200
Druggist,	12 "	500
Confectioneries,	10 "	200
Grocery,	8 "	150
Grocery.	20 "	250
Butcher,	10 "	1,000
Butchers,	10 "	750
Grocery,	10 mos.	100
Grocery,	6 years.	75
Grocery,	15 "	150
Grocery,	4 "	200
Grocery,	1 mo.	50
Grocery,	30 years.	100

"No account has been made here of hucksters, fish-dealers and other small tradesmen."

When the shameful riot occurred in North Carolina last year, it was given as an excuse that the Negroes there had made little or no progress since the war.

The following report contradicts this statement:

NEGRO MERCHANTS OF WILMINGTON, N. C.

KINDS OF BUSINESS.	YEARS IN BUSINESS.	CAPITAL INVESTED.
Grocer,	15 years.	$ 2,000
Grocer,	— "	1,800
Grocer,	— "	800
Grocer,	— "	2,000
Grocer,	— "	1,200
Druggist,	— "	1,500
Druggist,	15 "	1,000
Contractor and Paint-dealer,	— "	2,500
Undertaker,	— "	2,800
Undertaker,	— "	2,000
Undertaker,	— "	1,500
Broker,	— "	3,000
Merchant Tailor,	— "	1,200
Merchant Tailor,	— "	1,500
Grocer,	— "	1,600
Grocer,	3 "	2,000
Building and Loan Association,	8 "	20,000
Building and Loan Association,	7 "	11,000
Wood Yard,	— "	2,000
Wood Yard,	— "	2,500

Beside this we must not forget that these Negroes hold $500,000 in real and personal property, own fifteen churches, five of which are worth $90,000; own two public halls worth $20,000, and have four physicians and four lawyers.

An Alabama city, which has a large number of merchants send a partial list as follows:

NEGRO MERCHANTS OF MOBILE, ALA.

KINDS OF BUSINESS.	YEARS IN BUSINESS.	CAPITAL INVESTED.
Hardware, Crockery, Glassware, etc.,	32 years.	$ 25,000
Funeral Director and Livery Stable Keeper,	5 "	3,000
Grocer,	30 "	2,500
Wholesale and Retail Candy Manufacturer,	9 "	2,200
Grocer,	20 "	1,500
Undertaker.	5 "	5,000
Printing Establishment,	5 "	1,000
Coal and Wood,	4 "	1,600
Wood and Coal,	6 "	2,000
Restaurant,	18 "	2,500
Restaurant,	6 "	1,200
Barber,	22 "	2,000

No other city has so many Negro business men as the metropolis of the state of South Carolina. A partial list of the more successful follows:

NEGRO MERCHANTS OF CHARLESTON, S. C.

KINDS OF BUSINESS.	YEARS IN BUSINESS.	CAPITAL INVESTED.
Steam Dye Works,	7 years.	$ 1,500
Undertakers,	21 "	5,000
Undertakers,	16 "	2,000
Undertakers,	3 "	300
Undertakers,	3 "	700
Undertakers,	1 "	400
Undertakers,	6 mos.	500
Groceries and Provisions,	2 years.	800
Groceries and Provisions,	— "	400
Groceries and Provisions,	1 "	1,000
Groceries and Provisions,	— "	600
Groceries and Provisions,	5 "	700
Fish, Oysters and Game,	30 "	30,000
Livery Stables,	— "	20,000
Livery Stables,	— "	5,000
Livery Stables,	— "	2,000
Wagon Maker and Wheelwright,	15 "	5,000
Wagon Maker and Wheelwright,	2 "	500
Printing Office,	8 "	———
Printing Office,	8 "	———
Job Office,	— "	———
Drug-store,	5 "	3,000
Shoe-store,	1 "	1,000
Fan Maker,	30 "	———
Tailor-shop,	20 "	500
Upholsterer,	— "	———
Barber,	12 "	600
Barber,	5 "	600
Contractors,	— "	———
Stair Builder,	30 "	———
Contractor,	— "	———
Contractor,	25 "	———
Green Grocer,	10 "	2,500
Photographer,	12 "	———
Green Grocers,	30 "	2,000
Green Grocers,	25 "	3,000
Green Grocers,	25 "	1,500
Stone Cutter,	15 "	1,000
Contractor,	— "	———
Tailor,	6 "	300
Truck Farm,	30 "	100,000
Tailor-shop,	25 "	400
Barber,	25 "	700
Green Grocer,	4 "	500
Tailor,	— "	———
Green Grocer,	— "	500

Fruit and Vegetables,	11 years.	2,000
Fruit and Vegetables,	10 "	2,000
Fruit and Vegetables,	—	500
Shoes,	1 "	500
Undertaker,	—	300
Tinner,	—	———
Paint Store,	10 "	1,000
Barber,	—	1,000
Barber,	—	500
Barber,	—	700
Tailor-shop.	8 "	500

For a small place, this Georgia town has a good representation of business men:

NEGRO MERCHANTS OF AMERICUS, GA.

KINDS OF BUSINESS.	YEARS IN BUSINESS.	CAPITAL. INVESTED.
Grocery and Farming,	14 years.	$ 1,500
Grocery and Restaurant,	10 "	1,200
Grocery,	9 "	1,500
Druggist,	5 "	1,000
Grocery,	2 "	225
Grocery,	6 "	300
Furniture,	7 "	3,000
Grocery,	4 "	300
Grocery,	10 "	270
Grocery,	8 "	300
Grocery,	8 "	375
Grocery,	5 "	300
Grocery,	12 "	1,000
Restaurant and Barber-shop,	9 "	500
Market,	7 "	1,000
Wood Yard,	22 "	1,000
Grocery,	9 "	500
Cigars and Tobacco,	4 "	500

"It is not the custom among retail grocery merchants to carry large stocks on account of the convenience to wholesale dealers. So the amount given here conveys but little idea of the volume of business done."

At the capital of Alabama are a number of merchants with large investments:

NEGRO MERCHANTS OF MONTGOMERY, ALA.

KINDS OF BUSINESS.	YEARS IN BUSINESS.	CAPITAL INVESTED.
Hacks and Undertakers, Coal & Wood, etc.	— years.	$ ———
Dry Goods,	9 "	8,000
Groceries,	12 "	4,000
Groceries,	11 "	———
Groceries,	5 "	3,000

Drug Store,	10 "	5,000
Drug Store,	4 "	3,000
Undertaker,	—	2,000
Undertakers,	—	———
Manufacturers of Boots and Shoes,	18 "	500
Harness Maker,	15 "	700

The dry goods store did a business of $35,000 last year—"a fine store."

Florida has some thriving little enterprises. :

NEGRO MERCHANTS OF JACKSONVILLE, FLA.

KINDS OF BUSINESS.	YEARS IN BUSINESS.	CAPITAL INVESTED
Dry Goods and Millinery,	7 years.	$ 5,000
Groceries,	2 "	1,000
Millinery,	3 "	700
Tinware,	6 "	1,000
Cement-Work,	5 "	———
Curios, Jewelery Store, etc.,	2 "	3,000
Commission Merchants,	9 "	3,000
Shoe Store,	5 "	7,000
Lumber Mill,	5 "	———
Newspaper and Jobbing,	3 "	5,000
Drug Store,	4 "	1,000
Contractor and Builder,	15 "	6,000

The dry goods store did a business of $15,000 last yeor.   It employs five women clerks.   The commission merchants do $25,000 worth of business annually, and employ fifteen clerks.   The capacity of the lumber mill is 20,000 feet a day ; it sells to northern and southern markets.

NEGRO MERCHANTS OF TALLAHASSEE, FLA.

KINDS OF BUSINESS.	YEARS IN BUSINESS.	CAPITAL INVESTED.	SALES PER YEAR.
Groceries and Dry Goods,	— years.	$ 1,500	$ 6,000
Meat Market,	—	1,000	4,680
Meat Market,	—	250	832
Groceries,	—	400	1,500
General Merchandise,	—	150	
General Merchandise,	—	150	

The few Negroes who live in the far West make an unusually good showing:

NEGRO MERCHANTS OF SAN FRANCISCO, CAL.

KINDS OF BUSINESS.	YEARS IN BUSINESS.	CAPITAL INVESTED.
Hairdressing, Toilet Articles, etc.,	22 years.	$ 8,000
Expressing,	3 "	2,000
Electrician,	3 "	500

Weekly Newspaper,	5 years.	3,000
Barber,	2 "	500
Expressman,	15 "	2,000
Expressmen,	15 "	3,000
"Nabob" Restaurant,	5 "	5,000
Stove Store,	30 "	2,000
Barber Shop,	17 "	3,000
Barber Shop,	4 "	2,500
Restaurant,	4 "	4,000
Groceries and Fruit,	2 "	1,500
Cleaning Suits,	3 "	500
Newspaper and Printing,	5 "	1,000
Newspaper and Printing,	13 "	800
Fancy Goods, Embroidery,	1 "	500
Real Estate,	25 "	100,000

The hair-dressing store is one of the leading businesses — "fine store, good location." The electrician does "all kinds of electric light wiring" and electrical contracting. He is an "expert workman." The first restaurant runs day and night, and takes in about $25 a day. The first store has a "good trade." The second restaurant has the eating privileges at a race track, and employs fifteen persons. The real estate owner lives in the east, and rents large properties in the city.

"There are a great many Negroes in janitor, house-cleaning and white-washing work; also a number of Negro clubs and saloons which are of no great benefit to the community, as the same amount of capital invested in some other line would be more beneficial."

NEGRO BUSINESS MEN OF SEATTLE, WASH.

KINDS OF BUSINESS.	YEARS IN BUSINESS.	CAPITAL INVESTED.
Real Estate,	5 "	$ 10,000
Stock Broker,	3 "	2,500
Hotel,	2 "	1,500
Club House,	2 "	700
Barber,	6 "	3,000
Saloon,	2 "	1,000
Barber,	3 "	500
Restaurant,	4 "	900
Restaurant,	9 "	1,000
Newspaper,	6 "	2,000

Ohio has some enterprising business men:

NEGRO MERCHANTS OF CLEVELAND, OHIO.

KINDS OF BUSINESS.	YEARS IN BUSINESS.	CAPITAL INVESTED.	MEN EMPLOYED.
Barber Shop,	11 years.	$ 10,000	18 men.
Barber Shop,	20 "	5,000	20 "

Barber Shop,	10 years.	$ 6,000	12 men.
Hair Workers, Wigs, etc.,	10 "	2,000	5 "
Grocers,	1 "	600	5 "
Baker and Grocer,	30 "	1,500	3 "
Druggist,	2 "	300	2 "
Groceries,	2 "	800	4 "
Builder and Contractor,	12 "	3,000	15 "
Plasterer,	7 "	500	4 "
Merchant Tailor,	45 "	3,000	5 "
Blacksmith and Wagon Builder,	10 "	1,500	5 "

Two Virginia coast towns make an interesting showing:

NEGRO MERCHANTS OF NORFOLK, VA.

KINDS OF BUSINESS.	YEARS IN BUSINESS.	CAPITAL IVNESTED.
Undertaker,	18 years.	$ 5,000
Undertaker,	9 "	2,500
Coal and Wood,	5 "	3,000
Grocer,	15 "	2,500
Groceries,	1 "	1,000
Florist,	6 "	1,500
Groceries,	6 mos.	1,000
Publishers,	6 years.	2,000
Restaurant,	28 "	3,000
Bakery,	10 "	2,000
Undertaker,	4 "	1,500
Undertaker,	25 "	1,500

"These are doing an excellent business. There are many more smaller ones. The people are waking up and are trying to support their business enterprises. They still lack leadership, however, and are not urged sufficiently to support the efforts of the race."

NEGRO MERCHANTS OF PORTSMOUTH, VA.

KINDS OF BUSINESS.	YEARS IN BUSINESS.	CAPITAL INVESTED.
Huckster,	42 years.	$ 400
Barber,	35 "	1,500
Grocer,	20 "	2,300
Wood-dealers & Contractors for Sand & Shells,	16 "	1,500
Loaning Money on Real Estate, etc.,	16 "	11,000
Huckster,	15 "	300
Undertaker and Embalmer,	12 "	6,500
Grocer,	8 "	1,000
Liquors and Tobacco,	7 "	3,600
Grocer,	5 "	2,400
Druggist,	3 "	2,000
Oyster Planter,	40 "	1,500

The first two mentioned own considerable real estate. Four others own the buildings where their business is conducted. The building association is chartered, and owns $6,000 in improved real estate, and has $5,000 in loans outstanding. The undertaker owns a cemetery.

A small Georgia town furnishes the following figures:

NEGRO MERCHANTS OF ATHENS, GA.

BUSINESS.	YEARS IN BUSINESS.	CAPITAL.	LARGEST DAILY INCOME.	AVERAGE DAILY AM'NT.
Grocery..............	2	$300	$ 70 50	$25
Grocery..............	4	650	350 00	35
Grocery..............	8	150	12 00	6
Barber............ ..	25	500	85 00	7
Livery-stable ...	3	360	15 00	6
Barber..............	4	350	63 35	10

The extreme northeast has its quota of business enterprises. New Bedford was a centre for fugitive slaves and refugees:

NEGRO MERCHANTS OF NEW BEDFORD, MASS.

KINDS OF BUSINESS.	YEARS IN BUSINESS.	CAPITAL INVESTED.
Merchant Tailor,	14 years.	$ 1,000
Drug store,	17 "	4,000
Portrait Photographer,	10 "	3,000
Expressman,	—	——
Expressman,	—	——
Baker, bread, pies, cake. &c.,	4 "	1,000
Shoe dealer,	2 "	1,500
Druggists,	3 "	3,000
Hair store,	35 "	——
Hair store,	20 "	——

The tailor employs eleven men and women. He "does the largest business in the city, in refitting men's and women's garments, and makes ladies' tailoring a specialty. The majority of lady patrons are of the best class of people. About half of the employees are white". The largest Drug store is "one of the best appointed in the city," and is patronized largely by the wealthy. It is prominently located. The photographer commenced as errand boy, and eventually bought out the leading photographer in southeastern Massachusetts. The shoe dealer sells shoes and does a large repair business. The Hair store is the largest in the city. The proprietor of the second Drug store is also a large real estate holder. Beside these merchants there are "several conducting business on a small scale; grocers, news-dealers, restaurant keepers, clothes cleaners, tailors, expressmen, ice cream dealers, etc."

This section can best close with one of the curious coincidences which the rise of the Negro often involves; not far from Jamestown where in

1619 the first slaves were landed, is Williamsburg, the quaint old capital of Virginia, one of the most picturesque of the older American towns. In this place the largest and in every way the chief general store is a Negro's, situated on the main broad thoroughfare—the Duke of Gloucester street—and it commands the patronage of white and black for miles around:

NEGRO MERCHANTS OF WILLIAMSBURG, VA.

KINDS OF BUSINESS.	YEARS IN BUSINESS.	CAPITAL INVESTED.
General Merchant,	26 years.	40,000
General Merchant,	2 "	3,000
General Merchant,	6 "	2,000
General Merchant,	5 "	1,500
Restaurant,	12 "	1,200
Barber,	12 "	300

16. *Some Typical Business Men.*—Some 200 business men sent in detailed accounts of their lives and experiences. A few typical cases will illustrate the success and difficulties of this class of merchants. Says one:

"I was born a slave at Petersburg, Va., in the year 1845. My early surroundings were the same that nearly all the race at the South in those days had to face. We were considered chattels and as such had no right to life, liberty and the pursuit of happiness. Unrequited service was my lot. After the outbreak of the civil war the old home lost its attraction for me. During part of '64 and '65 I was employed along with the 13th O. Cavalry. In '68 I came to Baltimore. For about 18 years I was engaged in the furniture moving business in which I had some success. My next venture was to open an upholstering establishment in the fall of '84. Desiring a permanent location I purchased property at ——st. which, with the improvements since added is now worth five thousand dollars. Besides my shop, I operate a storage ware house in the rear on my premises. I was married in '74. Have one son who is working at the trade with me. I have been a member of Sharo St. M. E. Church for about 26 years. I regret to say that I am not an educated man. All the time spent at school would not exceed a week. The small learning obtained was picked up here and there at odd times and ways. I learned my trade by first watching mechanics hired to work for me. I have made it a rule to profit by observation.

I had but little capital to begin with. I thought it expedient to proceed cautiously. I had some appreciation of the importance of building up a reputation which requires time as well as work. I made it my aim not simply to get a customer, but to hold him as long as possible. I employed competent workmen and gave strict attention to all the details. I planned to deal on a cash basis. Work was paid for promptly and bills were not allowed to go beyond the time. I have adhered to this course ever since. I determined not only to use my best judgement but also to seek guidance from the Lord. He has aided me.

Considering everything I think I have had fair success. I have been able to save some money and besides, I can boast of having obtained creditable footing among men of business. My shop is never idle. I do not regard quick and large profits as always indicative of success in business. The gain that has not integrity and merit to justify it, may be looked upon with suspicion. I have received considerate treatment at the hands of the white people. The larger part of my patronage comes from that source. They confide in my skill and honesty. They visit my store and I am frequently called to their houses. The contact is friendly, both parties understanding that it is of a business rather than a social character.

Negro business men are situated pretty much as are business men of the other race. What helps or hinders in the one case has like effect in the other case. We must study the laws of business. We must demonstrate that we can be trusted for integrity of conduct and efficiency of service. Absolute trustworthiness will go farther than color. Instead of making our shops and stores a rendezvous for loafers, it must be understood that business only is in order during business hours. We must not make the mistake of trying to give attention to business one half the day and spending the remainder in looking after political matters. Negro business men must have one aim."

A colored jeweler writes as follows:

"I was born on the island of Barbadoes, British W. I., in the town of Bridgetown. My life has been rather uneventful. My father was a man in fair circumstances and was enabled to give his children some education and provide well for them. Most West Indian parents have their boys to learn some trade after leaving school, even though in some cases they take a profession afterwards, the object being to provide them with a means of earning a living with their hands if they fail to succeed otherwise. So to follow the bent of my mind—mechanics, I was put apprentice to a watchmaker, where I spent five years at the bench, until I had a fair knowledge of the trade. I then came to this country in the spring of '85 where I have remained since.

The popular system of education in the West Indies in my time was private tuition especially for primary instruction. And so I went to several pay schools, and last to a public school, receiving what would be called here a good grammar course. Some reading in later life has been of much benefit to me.

My first venture was in Kansas City. About four months after my arrival in this country, I applied for work at some of the leading jewelry stores of the above city and found out for the first time that the roads to success in this country for the black man were not so free and open as those of his brother in white. So I worked as porter for two years, and then encouraged by the success of pleasing my friends with private work done for them during my leisure hours at my room, I bought a small frame building, opened a watch repairing shop and became Kansas City's first Negro jeweler.

With close attention to business, by observing frugality, and by manifesting a disposition to please my patrons with courteous treatment and efficient work I have succeeded so my critics say "well." I had the misfortune to lose $500 in a bank failure and the good fortune to have saved enough to be notated in four figures. As regards the second question, it is rather difficult to tell how a white man really regards a Negro, especially when there is something to be gained to the former from the latter. A white man has a remarkable power of self concealment. Those whom I deal with treat me well. Those whom I do not deal with do not molest me. I don't know how they regard me.

Negro business men are helped by competing with inferior white businesses and by the prejudice which some white businesses have to Negro patronage. The average Negro business man is hindered by his neglect to keep his business in such a manner as to invite the patronage of the better class of white and black patrons, and the inability to find efficient and trustworthy partners in a good business. In fine the envy, distrust and lack of patronage of his own race greatly hinders the progress and success of the Negro business man.''

One member of a firm of merchant tailors writes:

"I was born in Huntsville, Ala., in 1876. My parents were in comfortable circumstances, and I led a typical village boy's life. My father was a brick contractor. In 1894 I left Huntsville, Ala., and came to this city and was employsd by Mr. Rotholz (white), of the People's Tailoring Co., and remained in his employ until I went in business for myself. My partner was born in Huntsville, Ala., in 1877. His father was a mattress maker and being quite successful, was then, and now is in comfortable circumstances. He came to Birmingham one year later than I did, and was employed by the same firm, but resigned to go into business with me.

I was educated at the city school and the A. and M. college, from which I graduated, at Normal, Ala. My partner also attended the same school.

Having received excellent training from my employer, I determined to go in business for myself, and after a consultation with my partner we started our business, September 1st, 1897, under the firm name of The Artistic Tailoring Co. We estimate our business to be worth $3,500.

Our success is shown by the steady increase of our business. Our motto, Never to promise that which we cannot fulfill, has made itself felt, and by sticking to it we have won hundreds of customers. While we have competition in the form of two more colored and fourteen white establishments I think we have no cause to complain. Each season calls for an increase in our force, and many times we are compelled to send away for workmen. We keep one cutter and six tailors at regular work, while my partner, our salesman, and myself are almost continually on the road. Competition notwithstanding, we have a fair share of the white patronage. We are regarded by the whites as respectful law abiding citizens, and first class tailors, having been called into court as expert witnesses on cloth.

The helps and hindrances of Negro business men are two extremes; while we have little or no help we have hindrances ten-fold. The business tact and integrity of a Negro in business is doubted to such an extent, that from his creditors he gets little or no consideration on his bills, while the white competitors have their own time. I find there is *no* outside help for the Negro in business; it is only by his untiring energy and push, together with the class of work which he turns out that speaks for him."

A florist writes:

"I was born in Anne Arundel County, Maryland, ten miles from Annapolis. I was raised on a farm, my grandfather and mother served as father and mother. When I was 21 years old, I came to Annapolis and was employed by a doctor to drive for him and to serve as waiter-boy. I married when I became 22 years old. I left the doctor when I was about 24 years old and went to work on the rail road. I soon stopped working there and went to work at gardening. Soon after I went to work at flowering.

I went a little while to night school, but on account of not being able to hear well and speak plainly, I stopped without securing an education.

I was working for a white woman pruning trees and looking after the garden. One day I picked up a bouquet of flowers that had been thrown out on an ash-pile. I untied the seemingly dead flowers and found a rosegeranium which seemed to have a little life in it by its smell and I carried it home and planted it. It lived and I have been growing flowers ever since. I have had good success notwithstanding I have had many drawbacks. I am living off my flowers. The whites visit my place, buy flowers from me and speak kindly of me. The leading florist here is white and has said "I studied three years and paid a good sum of money for my education but Queen's knowledge of flowers has been given him by his Maker." He comes around some times and I give him a few points.

My business is a little hampered by my difficulty to hear and speak plainly and lack of means. But I will never give it up until God calls me so to do. I could use a good boy now, teach him the business and help him to make an honest living for himself, but cannot find one who is ready and willing to accept the offer I make."

A cooperative grocery store gives the following account:

"Four men were the prime movers in the organization of the Excelsior Mercantile & Investment Company that is now operating a successful business in the city of Anniston, Ala. It was organized September 6th, 1898.

Only two of these men could be called educated. One was educated at Selma University, the other in a northern college. They were helped some by their parents, but depended mostly on themselves for their education.

We started with about one hundred dollars in a grocery business. We were moved to organize the company, which is chartered, by talking over the duty of the fathers to open business for their children as well as it is to educate them; this talk was done in a little meeting of the male members of Galilee Baptist church to listen to a lecture by the minister.

We have good success. The whites regard us as a worthy business organization. The wholesale men honor our orders right along.

The idea is now becoming general that the Negro must unite and rise, or remain down. This is a great help to Negro business. The crop lien system is a great hindrance to Negro business. Exclusion from the commercial clubs is another; imperfection in the knowledge of keeping a first class set of books is also a great hindrance. The lack of confidence in each other is the greatest hindrance."

A dry goods merchant writes:

"I was born in Lowndes County, Alabama, June 15th, 1867. I left there in 1880 and have been a citizen of Montgomery ever since. I have worked on a farm, in a saw-mill, and on a rail-road previous to engaging in my present business.

I was educated in the common schools of Lowndes and at a private night school since settling in Montgomery.

After working for several years in the dry goods business with a Mr. J. J. Levy, I felt that there was a good opening for colored men along that line; so I left him and rented a small store on one of the principal streets. After paying the first mont's rent in advance, and giving notes for the balance I found that I had spent one-third of my capital. The balance went for goods.

My success has been all that could be expected. The whites regard me just as they do any other business mon, as far as I am able to judge.

The Negro business man having once gained the confidence of the people will obtain patronage in direct proportion to his business ability."

A successful lumber merchant writes:

"I was born in Monmouth Co., N. J., in 1862, of parents in extremely humble circumstances. I attended public school about twelve months of my life. I could read and write when I left school in 1874. I had to work for a livelihood and not attend school. My father was a white man and died in the civil war a few months before I was born. I was reared on a farm. I came to Florida thirteen years ago. I did not have $3 in cash when I arrived here. I did not have a friend or acquaintance in this state. I hewed cross ties for ten cents apiece. I have laid up no money. I have spent all I have made in my business. I own a saw mill and planing mill, grist mill and novelty works, cost about $6000, (I have added $1000 this year). I own over 1000 acres of land, some improved. I own eight mules and three horses. The gross earnings of my business are about $25,000 per year. I had $125 in cash and had no experience when I began.

I do not consider myself educated, only practically; I am my own shipping clerk, chief engineer, blacksmith, bookkeeper, solicitor of work and collector. I do all the best sort of work. I learned all this in Florida.

I had $125 in cash and mortgaged my home for $850 which I paid before it was due. I worked for another company as foreman in the woods and hired my work done; at night I repaired anything that was broken during the day.

I have more friends among the whites than the colored. I sell most of my products to whites. They treat me well in business. I attend strictly to my business and do not visit or go to social gatherings. In the mill or work shop I am happy, while in large gatherings I am miserable. I am plain and straightforward in my manners and treat all alike both white and colored. In my mill both white and colored are employed.

The lack of capital has been my greatest trouble. There is no discrimination in my business. I aim to equal and excel in quality of work and material; I furnish good material, well manufactured. I have a spendid trade—at present I am building two miles of iron track."

An undertaker writes:

"I was born in the city of Galveston, Texas, in 1862. I followed various occupations. I came to New York at the age of 20 years and married when I was 22 years old. I now have a large family. I worked in Club-houses for many years in New York.

I had only a common school education. I would advise every young man to seek for knowledge as I find that very essential in any or every vocation of life.

I accumulated a little money with the intention of being my own master. I was somewhat puzzled as to what business I should select but finally made up my mind to become an undertaker. I went to an embalming school and learned the art of embalming. I am now a licensed undertaker of New York city, N. Y.

I have been pretty successful. I do very little white work. I depend entirely on the Negro support. I am the official undertaker for seven societies. I have been in business one year and seven months.

I have gained the confidence and respect of the majority of the Negroes in New York city. Therefore they and self-respect are the most helpful to me as a business man. The hindrances are lack of capital and education."

A publisher writes that he was born in Maybinton, S. C. in 1859, and was a slave. At a very early age he worked his mother's farm, and being the oldest boy he was obliged to help support her. In 1870 his family moved to Columbia, S. C., where he entered the public school. He occupied his time when not in school by doing jobs of work; his uncle being a member of the S.C.Legislature, in 1871-2, succeeded in getting him the position of page in the Legislature. Afterward he worked for a while in a dry goods store as porter and in the Columbia Central National Bank as messenger.

His opportunities for education were few and meagre, he did not enter school until he was eleven years old. Through many difficulties he pursued with zeal the school training which he received. He had a great desire to obtain a thorough education but was not able.

His intense convictions lead him to support all movements designed to elevate or ameliorate the conditions of his people; so he decided in 1894 to go to work with pen and tongue and arouse the people to action. With a partner therefore he started the paper known as "The People's Recorder." He is also proprietor of a large grocery store known as "Our Store," which filled a long felt want in the the city of Columbia. This store was open for three years when it was moved to Orangeburg, S. C.

The firm is doing a great work in the paper business. The paper is strictly a race paper. It is sent in the homes of the people as a welcome visitor, and there are many white families who are subscribers. He was not very successful in the store business in Columbia, so moved to Orangeburg where it is doing a goo work, it is regarded as the leading Negro store there.

The Negro in business has many disadvantages to contend against, especially from the intelligent class of people who regard themselves as the "best class" of Negroes. Experience teaches that the poorer class, or what is commonly called the "common people" are more inclined to support race enterprises, and our professional men than the first class named. The Negro business man scarcely receives any help outside of his race.

17. *Education and Source of Capital.*—The education of 185 Negro business men was obtained as follows:

From Institutions of Higher training.............................. 41
From Public Schools in Towns or Cities..... 35
From Public Schools in the Country.. 32
From Grammar Schools...... 15
From Normal Schools 14
From Night Schools... 13
From Private Instruction....... 9
From Instruction at Home............... 3
With little or no education....... 23

Total....... 185

This would seem to be a fair sample of the training these merchants received.

It is of interest to know at what sort of work these merchants were engaged when they saved enough to enter business, or how else their capital was obtained. To questions on these points men answered as follows: Borrowed their capital, 30.

Saved money from work as follows:

Keeping boarders, 4	Drayman, 2	Barber, 2	Steward, 3
Railroad hand, 1	Messenger, 1	Miner, 1	Teacher, 5
Lunch counter, 2	Blacksmith, 1	Bartender, 1	Farmer, 5
Working at a trade, 11	Seamstress, 1	Laborer, 6	Clerk, 4
Government service, 2	Fruit stand, 1	Porter, 5	Pedlers &c., 6

From such sources capital was obtained so as to start business as follows:

$ 1 50—1	$ 1 60—1	$ 2 20—1	$ 5 00—3	$ 6 00—1	$ 10 00—4
10 45—1	15 00—1	20 00—1	25 00—6	25 45—1	27 00—1
28 00—1	30 00—1	35 00—1	40 00—2	45 00—1	50 00—2
57 00—1	60 00—1	65 00—1	75 00—3	90 00—2	100 00—3
105 00—1	120 00—1	150 00—2	200 00—3	235 65—1	250 00—1
300 00—4	460 00—1	500 00—3	700 00—2	900 00—1	1000 00—1
1500 00—1	2350 00—1	5000 00—1			

PART II.

PROCEEDINGS OF THE FOURTH ATLANTA CONFERENCE.

The Fourth Annual Atlanta Conference to study the Negro problems, was called to order at 8 o'clock, P. M. of May 30, 1899, in the Ware Memorial Chapel, with President Horace Bumstead, D. D., of Atlanta University in the chair, and Mr. J. A. Henry of Chattanooga as secretary. An earnest prayer for divine guidance was offered by Rev. F. H. Means of Connecticut.

An address of welcome was then made by the President who clearly set forth the necessity for, and the great good accomplished by, these conferences at Atlanta.

Following the address of President Bumstead, His Excellency, Gov. Candler of Georgia made an address. (See p. 52)   Prof. John Hope of the Atlanta Baptist College was then introduced and read a scholarly paper on "The Meaning of Business." (See p. 56)

The next paper on the program was to have been one from Dr. R. F. Boyd of Nashville, Tenn., on "The Negro and Real Estate." President Bumstead read a letter of regret from Dr. Boyd, stating that illness prevented his attendance. Mr. W. O. Murphy of Atlanta was then introduced and presented an interesting paper on the "Negro Grocer." (See p. 64)

A committee on resolutions was appointed as follows:

Mr. M. V. Lynck, Jackson, Tenn., Publisher.

Rev. J. E. Smith, Chattanooga, Tenn., Pastor.

Mr. C. H. Fearn, Chattanooga, Tenn., Manager of Iron Foundry.

Mr. W. E. B. DuBois, Atlanta, Ga., Teacher.

Mr. W. O. Murphy, Atlanta, Ga., Grocer.

There were two special sessions Wednesday afternoon, the first a symposium upon practical business questions, and the second a General Mothers' Meeting. The programmes were as follows:

At 3 P. M.

SYMPOSIUM.

1. How can we induce young men to go into business?
2. What hindrances have Negroes in business?
3. What helps have Negroes in business?
4. What is the outlook?

Five Minute Speeches.

4:30 P. M.

GENERAL MOTHERS' MEETING.

SUBJECT: "What shall our children do for a living?"

Mrs. I. M. Henry, Presiding.

"The necessity of work," Miss Lucy H. Upton, Dean of Spellman Seminary.
"How the Public School may train business men,"   [nary.

Mrs. Alice D. Carey, Principal Mitchell Street School.
"The need of Negro Merchants," Miss H. Escridge. (See p. 61).
"The habit of saving," Mrs. M. A. Ford.

The third session of the Atlanta Conference was called to order by President Bumstead at 8 o'clock P. M., May 31st. The first paper of the evening was one by Dr. M. V. Lynk of Jackson, Tenn., on "The Negro Publisher."

Mr. C. H. Fearn of Chattanooga, Tenn., then read a paper on the "Southern Stove and Hollow-ware Company," near Chattanooga. (See p. 66). President Bumstead called attention to the interesting lessons to be drawn from the papers read. They evidenced the fact that the race was branching out into new industries. The unavoidable absence of Mr. J. C. Dancey of Wilmington, N. C. was announced by the president who stated that his paper on "The Negro in the West Indies," would be read by H. M. Lee of the University. The interesting paper was enjoyed by the conference.

Mr. P. H. Williams read a number of biographies sent in by correspondents, designed to show how they had been led to engage in business and the success attained. The biographies were full of encouragement and profitable lessons. President Bumstead then announced the question open for general discussion.

Dr. Butler, President of the Sociological Club of Atlanta, was called upon and responded in a brief but forcible address. Mr. R. J. Henry, an insurance agent in the city, was also introduced and spoke upon the general subject, The Negro in Business. Mr. Hugh Young an elderly business man of New York city and a trustee of Atlanta University, was called upon and spoke in favor of the principle of doing for yourselves. Capital, said he must be accumulated by saving. "It is obtained either by earning more than you spend or in spending less than you earn. The white people complain that as you advance you become saucy. You must remember that 'The meek shall inherit the earth.' "

Mr. Bedford of the board of trustees of The Tuskegee Normal and Industrial Institute was introduced and spoke words of encouragement.

Mrs. Rosa Bass of Atlanta was invited to address the conference. She spoke of the wisdom of colored grocers and hucksters putting forth an effort to make their goods presentable and so more saleable.

Some interesting statistics as compiled and exhibited upon the walls of the room in which the conference was held were then explained by the corresponding secretary. The committee on resolutions then reported through Prof. DuBois. On motion the resolutions were adopted.

After a brief closing address by President Bumstead the conference was declared adjourned.

J. A. HENRY, SECRETARY.

RESOLUTIONS ADOPTED BY THE CONFERENCE

The resolutions passed at the last session of the conference were as follows:

1. Negroes ought to enter into business life in increasing numbers. The present disproportion in the distribution of Negroes in the various occupations is unfortunate. It gives the race a one-sided development, unnecessarily increases competition in certain lines of industry, and puts the mass of the Negro people out of sympathy and touch with the industrial and mercantile spirit of the age. Moreover the growth of a class of merchants among us would be a far-sighted measure of self-defense, and would make for wealth and mutual cooperation.

2. We need as merchants the best trained young men we can find. A college training ought to be one of the best preparations for a broad business life; and thorough English and high school training is indispensable.

3. Negroes going into business should remember that their customers demand courtesy, honesty, and careful methods, and they should not expect patronage when their manner of conducting business does not justify it.

4. The mass of the Negroes must learn to patronize business enterprises conducted by their own race, even at some slight disadvantage. We *must* cooperate or we are lost. Ten million people who join in intelligent self-help can never be long ignored or mistreated.

5. The 1,900 business men reported to the conference are to be congratulated. They are pioneers in a great movement, and some of them have made a creditable record. We earnestly ask Negroes—and especially the better class of thinking Negroes—to patronize these establishments and encourage them in every way.

6. The most advisable work for the immediate future would seem to be:
(a) Continued agitation in churches, schools, and newspapers, and by all other avenues, of the necessity of business careers for young people.
(b) Increased effort to encourage saving and habits of thrift among the young that we may have more capital at our disposal.
(c) The organization in every town and hamlet where colored people dwell, of Negro Business Men's Leagues, and the gradual federation from these of state and national organizations.

M. V. LYNK.
J. E. SMITH.
C. H. FEARN.
W. E. BURGHARDT DuBois.
W. O. MURPHY.

PART III.

PAPERS SUBMITTED TO THE CONFERENCE.

The following eight papers were among those submitted to the Conference. All of them, except the first, were written by Negroes who have special knowledge of their subjects. Professor John Hope is a teacher in one of the Atlanta institutions, and a graduate of Brown University. Miss Hattie G. Escridge is a graduate of Atlanta University and is book-keeper in her father's grocery-store. Mr. H. E. Lindsay is a very successful Negro merchant and Mr. W. O. Murphy, also a graduate of Atlanta University, is junior partner in one of the oldest Negro firms of this city. Mr. C. H. Fearn is the manager of a very interesting co-operative venture among Negro mechanics of Chattanooga, Tenn. Messrs. Porter and Seabrooke were seniors in Atlanta University last year. The latter has, since graduation, gone into the shoe business in Charleston, S. C

OPENING ADDRESS OF THE HON. ALLAN D. CANDLER,
GOVERNOR OF GEORGIA.

MR. PRESIDENT, LADIES AND GENTLEMEN OF THE CONFERENCE:— I have come before you tonight with no prepared oration or speech. My duties are so exacting, that I have no time really to prepare such an address as this occasion merits. I have come because I am a friend to this old institution, and because I want you to know that the State of Georgia through its chief executive, recognizes the usefulness of this institution to the State. (Applause) And first, I want to endorse as my sentiments, and the sentiments of all good men in this commonwealth, the remarks which have been made by your distinguished President. All good men, fair men, philanthropic men in this State endorse every one of those remarks. "The Negro In Business". It is a theme worthy of the attention of every patriot in this and every other State in the greatest Republic of all the ages.

Unfortunately in our portion of the great Republic, there have been too few avenues to successful effort open even to the white race, and much fewer avenues to successful effort open to the colored race. A generation ago we emerged from one of the most cruel, and I would be pardoned to say, that in my judgment, one of the most unnecessary wars that ever devastated the face of the earth. The result of this war was the freeing of the colored race, and like the young child which has not long had an opportunity to be taught, a new world was opened to this race. The position that they occupied prior to that time was entirely changed. They became in the eyes of the law the equals of the other races that inhabit this Republic. They were clothed not only with all the privileges, but all the responsibilities of citizenship. The scenes that surrounded them were new scenes; they had never been accustomed to them. They were like a child that is transported in a day from the scenes of his birth to other scenes, entirely different, if you please, on another continent. Necessarily, those things which attracted their attention at that time being novel, not only attracted, but riveted their attention. Yet the things which they saw, the conditions that existed were abnormal conditions. The people of the entire South were in a state of turmoil, in an abnormal state. In other words, everybody talked about the war, and about the results of the war, and especially did everybody talk about politics.

The young men of my own race at that time saw things that I had never seen; saw things that the men who had controlled the destinies of this State prior to that time, had never seen. They saw a riot at the polls they saw methods employed by political parties, and I exempt none—all were guilty—they saw methods employed by political parties, in party elections, which were perfectly abhorrent to the men who had controlled the destinies of this State prior to that time; and these young men of my race, and the colored men, seeing these things, concluded that that was politics, legitimate politics, and hearing nobody talk about anything but politics, they concluded that politics was the chief end of life; but in this conference to-day, in the discussion of the problems, we are realizing the fact that there are other things besides politics. Those men as a rule, no matter in what class or race they belong, who regard politics as the chief end of life, are always unsatisfactory citizens of the country, no matter to what race they belong.

. . . .

But it is not astonishing that the young men of thirty years ago,—the young men of both races, who had aspirations, who desired to make for themselves a name in the world,—concluded and looked upon politics as the only avenue to distinction, because that is all they discussed. Nobody talked anything else. Up on the farms you would hear the old colored men and the white men talk about their cotton crops; you would hear that, but there was no distinction in that. Those that desired to make for themselves a name, saw no avenue except through politics. Now other avenues are open, and in the future still other avenues will be opened. It is more honorable to be a successful merchant, or to be a useful, intelligent mechanic, than it is to be a third rate member of the American Congress. A man serves his God better, because Congressmen, when I was in Congress didn't serve God much; they served the other fellow. He can serve his fellow citizens better, and he will serve his God better than any man who stands in the arena of partisan politics.

Now it has been demonstrated in this old institution. Thirty years ago I was a teacher. I took an interest in educational matters. I came here when they were founding the Atlanta University for the training of the youth of the Negro race for usefulness and good citizenship, because I had an interest in it. From that time to this, I have not been on this ground. During that thirty years I know that this institution has done more, (and I do not desire to disparage other institutions; I do not intend to disparage them) so far as my information has gone, to elevate the colored race than any other institution in the bounds of this State.(Applause) You have done a good work; you have been a conservative people; and there is a great work ahead of you yet,— a great work especially for all the teachers of this country, of both races.

I do believe that education properly so called, training in arts and science and literature, and morality, and especially in morality, is the most potent, indeed the only education that can make us citizens worthy of the great Republic in which we live, and thus believing, I came here tonight to lend whatever encouragement I can to this institution which, I repeat, is doing more, in my judgment, and has done more for the elevation of the race for which it is intended than any other institution in Georgia.

I want you to know that I am in full sympathy with you. I want you to know that I represent 90 per cent of the people of my race in this State. I want you to know that while there are men in Georgia who do not feel as I do about this matter—who do not feel that institutions like this, intended for the colored race, should receive the encouragement of every white man in Georgia—the per-centage of those is very small.

I want to say to-night in all sincerity, that the only consoling feature and reflection in connection with some of the horrid scenes that have been enacted in this State in the past,— the only consoling reflection is, that those men who have engaged in these things constitute a very small percentage of both races. The man who would denounce the entire colored race for the act of one member of that race, or a few members of that race, is unjust. The man who would denounce the entire white race of this State because of the lawless acts of a few, is unjust. The people of Georgia are made of the same flesh and bones as their brethren in New England. Georgia was one of the old Thirteen. Massachusetts was one, and so was Connecticut, and so was New York. We were one people, with one common cause, and established the greatest Republic that has ever existed in the annals of the world; and we are now one people, and if crimes are committed here in Georgia now by my race, don't blame me. Don't blame the teachers, and the law-abiding people of this State; they are not responsible for them. If crimes are committed by the colored race, don't blame the entire colored race for it, for I tell you before God to-night that I believe that 90 per cent of the colored race of Georgia desire to be law-abiding citizens. They are as patriotic as I am, and there is a very small proportion of the races that are responsible for these troubles. I was reared among the colored race. I have lived with them all my life, and I know that there are good white people and I know that there are good colored people, and I know that there are bad white people, and I know that there are bad colored people. I would advise all of my fellow citizens of both races to draw a line, separating the virtuous and intelligent on the one side, from the vicious and ignorant on the other, and when we have drawn that line, and arrayed ourselves on both sides of it, let those who love order, and who love justice, and who love equity, fair play, let's be careful that those who are allied on one side, on the side of ignorance and vice, let's be careful that they do not pull us over on their side. We will reach our hands to them, good white men and colored men,—we will stretch out our hands to those fellows on the other side, and pull them over to us if we can, but let's not allow them to pull us over on their side.

I know that the colored man is as loyal to his friends as I am. I know that he loves law and order. I know this, that it has taken my race six hundred years to get up to the point where we are. I know it is unreasonable to suppose that a race emerging from a state of servitude should accomplish in one generation what it has taken our race six hundred years to accomplish. But at the same time, I know that these same colored men and women in Georgia are just as loyal to their convictions, and to their duties, and as God-serving and as God-loving as my race are, and we want to teach one thing, not the law of hate, but the law of love. Hate never benefitted anybody; love benefits everybody. Because, I repeat, I believe the only real happiness ever enjoyed in this world is in an effort to make other people happy.

But I have spoken to you longer than I intended. I would not have gone anywhere else to-night but to the Atlanta University. I have some visitors at my house that I have not seen for forty years, and I excused myself, telling them that I felt it my duty to come over to Atlanta University and lend my assistance in the effort to elevate and benefit the race among whom I have been born and reared, and for whom I have nothing but the kindest feeling and regard, and for whose elevation I have the most earnest desire; and besides, one of my guests told me to come, and I have come. I have delivered my little message. I have spoken sincerely, and I wish you God speed in this work, and I believe that useful as the Atlanta University has been in the past, that on the line of this discussion, that the colored race will be crowned with abundant success. God grant that it may be. (Applause).

THE MEANING OF BUSINESS.

Paper Submitted by Professor John Hope, of the Atlanta Baptist College.

The Negro status has changed considerably since the Civil war, but he is to-day to a great extent what he has always been in this country—the laborer, the day hand, the man who works for wages. The great hiring class is the white people. The Negro develops the resources, the white man pays him for his services. To be sure some few Negroes have accumulated a little capital. But the rule has been as I have stated: the white man has converted and reconverted the Negro's labor and the Negro's money into capital until we find an immense section of developed country owned by whites and worked by colored.

However, the Negroes multiply and the succeeding generations, though wiser, show no alarming signs of physical weakness. Therefore, if we still have a demand for our services as laborer, the wolf can be kept from the door. We can still eat, drink and be merry with no thought of to-morrow's death. But in that contingency we perceive a portent. To say, "if we still have a demand for our services" implies a doubt. Already the Negro has no monopoly of the labor market. The white man is his competitor in many fields; and in some of the humbler walks, here in the South where honest toil has been held in reproach, white men are crowding Negroes out of places which in my childhood belonged to the Negro by right of his birth. For in the matter of inheriting work the Negro has been a prince. But we are already opening our eyes to the fact that we are not employed South because we are loved, but because we are a necessity, and that as soon as white capital can secure competent white labor for the same money with which it secures Negro labor, white capital is seized with a violent attack of race sympathy, and refuses to hire Negroes where white men are obtainable. To say nothing of high grade artisans like brick-masons and carpenters who are crowding Negroes, you now see white porters, ditchers, news-boys, elevator-boys and the like getting positions once the exclusive property of our people.

Let me say here, that while ignorance and incompetency may in some sense explain the mysterious departure of the Negro white-washer, carpenter, news-boy and washer-woman in many quarters, I have seen too many competent Negroes superceded by whites,—at times incompetent whites,—to lay so much stress on ignorance and incompetency as a total explanation. This change of affairs in the labor market south, is due to competition between the races in new fields. The labor prince finds himself losing some of his old estate. Industrial Education and labor unions for Negroes will not change this condition. They may modify it, but the condition will not be very materially changed. The white man will meet the Negro on the same ground and work for the same wages. That much we may as well take for granted, calculate the consequences of it, and strive by every means to overcome this falling off in our old-time advantages.

We must take in some, if not all, of the wages, turn it into capital, hold it, increase it. This must be done as a means of employment for the thousands who cannot get work from old sources. Employment must be had, and this employment will have to come to Negroes from Negro sources. This phase of the Negro's condition is so easily seen that it needs no further consideration. *Negro* capital will have to give an opportunity to Negro workmen who will be crowded out by white competition; and when I say Negro workmen I would include both sexes. Twenty-five years from today it will be a less marvelous phenomenon for colored girls and women to see white girls and women pushing baby carriages and carrying clothes-baskets than it is today for white women to see colored women performing on the piano. Employment for colored men and women, colored boys and girls must be supplied by colored people.

But supposing there should remain our oldtime monopoly of labor; suppose we should do all the tearing down and building up and draw our wages, man by man and there should be no press for bread, no fear of the winter's blast from the winter's poverty; could we as a race afford to remain the great labor class, subject to the great capitalist class? The wage-earner, the man on a salary, may, by rigid self-denial, secure for himself a home, he may besides husband his earnings so carefully as to have a small income, but the wage-earner and man of salary seldom save a competence. It is exceedingly rare that they can retire from labor and spend an old age of leisure with dignity. It is usually the case that their last and feeblest days mark their most desperate struggle for sustenance. At that time of life when men ought to be most able to provide for themselves and others, these men are least able. There is little or no independence in the wage-earner, because there is no practical security. Bread is a great arbiter in this world. Say what you will of liberty and religion, back of the shrillest, most heart-rending cries this hard old world has ever heard has been the need of bread. The name of the cry may have been liberty, it may have been taxation without representation, it may have been vested rights, but much of the truth is that men have wanted the bread conditions to be easier. Millions of empty stomachs made the French Revolution possible. There is not much race independence for the race that cannot speak its mind through men whose capital can help or harm those who would bring oppression. We need capital to dictate terms. This notion is old enough but bears repetition.

However, suppose the wolf is kept from the door, and suppose the Negro has such independence as the law now grants white men. Suppose he can go and come as other men do; suppose he is molested in no political or civil rights, and suppose he gets a fair trial under the most unfavorable circumstances, is all this the *summum bonum*, is this the end of life—that it brings man to the point where he has his bread and his rights? It seems to me that the highest privilege, the greatest blessing, and the highest point of development which any man could seek is that of being an interested and controlling member in the foremost matters of his own country and through this interest and control becoming a partner in the world's activity. We are taught in Holy Writ that we cannot live by bread alone and that life is more than raiment. Nor has man gained all that appeals

to him as worth possession when he has his rights.   Rights, every man
ought to have equal with every other man.   But we are infinitely better
off when we not only have the rights but comprehend their significance,
the cause and the use of them.   To attain to this position of dignity and
manhood, we must get into the world current.   We cannot stem it by
standing on the shore, nor can we ever know its power until we have
leaped into the rushing stream.

   This partnership in the world's business, to be sure, is fostered by the
guarantee of fair enforcement of equal laws.   But the desire for partnership, and the ability to be partner, must be in the man himself.   The law
and public sentiment may protect a business man, but they cannot make
him.   The making is largely with the man himself.   Now the age in
which we are living is an economic one ; manufacturing and merchandising claim the world's attention.   No doubt this remark in a modified form
has been made time and time again, ever since Jacob of old carried on his
little business transactions.   But as we scan history, it does appear that,
through combinations and inventions, we are now under the immediate
sway of business, more than humanity has ever been before.   Life and
progress are most perceptible to-day in business activities.   To be sure
there are religious, moral and educational movements, glorious, noble and
far-reaching.   But the greatest, at least in its immediate consequences on
the world, is the business movement, and nobody can tell to what extent even the moral, religious and educational efforts are influenced by
business motives.   Education and philanthrophy often find their explanation in terms of business.   Whenever an enterprise is proposed, the
question arises, not is it right, is it best, but does it pay, how much will it
bring?   Empires have their reason for being, not through abstract form-
ulae of political principles, not through religious creeds, but through their
value to the world's business.   It is not thirst for Christianity that is
joining Russia with the Chinese Sea, and the historic shores of northern
Africa, with the diamond fields of the south.   And much suspicion
attaches to the sympathy of the United States for "bleeding Cuba" as we
behold our army bleeding the poor Philipinos.   The struggle for business,
buying and selling and owning are actually to-day the most daring and
gigantic undertakings that have marred and made this world.   I am not
here to defend these motives, but to point out this existence, and to say,
that our temporal, I say nothing of spiritual, salvation depends on our
aptitude for conceiving the significance of present day movements and
becoming a conscious, positive, aggressive party to them.

   This idea of business is a *large* one I admit.   And many a man accumulates thousands of dollars without realizing his relations to the rest of
the world, his dependance on the world and his independence of it as a
result of his accumulations.   But it is this idea that ought to be promoted
among us in order that men of education and power may know that outside of the learned professions there is a vast field for personal honor, and
emolument, and for doing a great public good.   In fact we can have very
few really learned professional men, until we do have some capital, for a
professional man must have time and facilities for increasing his knowledge.   These cannot be obtained without money.   This money must come

from Negroes. Wage-earners alone cannot supply enough money. I therefore regard it as a menace to the the progress and utility of professional men that business enterprise among us increases so slowly. We have not enough of teachers, preachers and physicians. In fact there is still room, even under present conditions, for a few more lawyers. But none of these make sufficient money to supply them advantages necessary to their highest development and usefulness. More money diffused among the masses through Negro capital will alter this unfavorable state of things. No field calls for trained minds and creative genius to a greater extent than does business To calculate prices months hence, to see what will be the result with such and such a factor removed or introduced, call for men of large parts and superior knowledge, no matter where gained. I know of no men who as a class go so far for the good of others as do Negro men for the good of the race. There is a big lump of public spirit among us. All we need is to be shown how to use this public spirit. From now on, for many years it must be employed in business channels, if it would do most and immediate service.

I do not believe that the ultimate contribution of the Negro to the world will be his development of natural forces. It is to be more than that. There in him emotional, spiritual elements that presage gifts from the Negro more ennobling and enduring than factories and rail-roads and banks. But without these factories, railroads and banks, he cannot accomplish his highest aim. We are living among the so-called Anglo-Saxons and dealing with them. They are a conquering people who turn their conquests into their pockets. The vanquished may not always recognize this as true, but the fact remains. Now our end as a race most likely will not be of the same nature as that of the Anglo-Saxon. In the long run each will play a very different part; but, for the present, for the sake of self-preservation and for the sake of grasping the meaning of the civilization in which we live, we must to a large extent adopt the life and use the methods of this people with whom we are associated. Business seems to be not simply the raw material of Anglo-Saxon civilization—and by business I mean those efforts directly or indirectly concerned with a purposive tendency to material development and progress, with the point in view of the effort bringing material profit or advantage to the one making the effort; and I would include all such efforts whether made in peace or war. I was saying, business seems to be not simply the raw material of the Anglo-Saxon civilization, but almost the civilization itself. It is at least its mainspring to action. Living among such a people is it not obvious that we cannot escape its most powerful motive and survive? To the finite vision, to say the least, the policy of avoiding entrance in the world's *business* would be suicide to the Negro. Yet as a matter of great account, we ought to note that as good a showing as we have made, that showing is but as pebbles on the shore of business enterprise.

Ladies and gentlemen, I have talked on for some minutes without giving you the name of the talk. I once heard a scholarly Massachusetts congressman lecture, and he said the subject of his lecture was "Whence and Whither," but that the subject had nothing to do with the lecture. In refusing to christen my remarks I may escape the charge of irrelevence.

Yet, if you force me to a confession, I dare say I had in mind "The business man's contribution to the development of our race."

All of us know that material wealth is not the test of highest development and manhood. Yet, in as much as this highest development is dependent on the material foundation, the man who lays that foundation is as great a benefactor to the race as that man or generation that will in the end present that final gift, which shall yield the rich, ripe fruit of the emotions and the soul—the consummation of those aspirations that look beyond material things to the things that are abiding and eternal. In some such noble form as this the vocation of the business man presents itself to me; and were I a vender of peanuts or an owner of a mill, I should feel that I, along with preachers and teachers and the rest of the saints, was doing God's service in the cause of elevation of my people.

THE NEED OF NEGRO MERCHANTS.

Abstract of Paper Submitted by Miss Hattie G. Escridge, N. '98.

One way, I think, toward the solution of the much-talked-of Negro Problem is for us to enter into business. Let us keep our money among ourselves. Let us spend our money with each other. Let us protect each other, as the other races do.

Every Negro who successfully carries on a business of his own, helps the race as well as himself, for no Negro can rise without reflecting honor upon other Negroes. By Negroes sticking together and spending whatever they have to spend with their own race, soon they would be able to unite and open large, up-to-date, dry-goods, millinery, hardware and all other establishments as run by their white brothers, thereby giving employment to hundreds who otherwise have nothing to do. *All the young people who are graduating from our schools to-day, cannot be school teachers and preachers.* Of course education is used in all avocations of life, but it looks like a loss of time to spend a number of years in school, to do just what any common laborer has to do. The Negro has helped to make rich every race on earth but his own. They will walk three blocks or more to trade with a white man, when there is a Negro store next to their door. They say the Negro does not have as good material as the white man. In all cases that is not true, for they have both bought from the same wholesale grocer and have the same material. If there is any difference give the advantage to the Negro, for he is doing no more than the white merchant has done before. If there are weak points in the race, we should help to make them strong. It will be only by our coming together that we shall ever succeed. The different commodities that are brought into market by the Negro could be disposed of with the Negro merchants and by bartering as they do with the white merchants, benefit themselves, and aid the Negro merchant, and thereby the farmer and the grocer would be building each other up, and giving strength financially to both.

We have aided the Jew from the time he came into our neighborhood with his store on his back, consisting of tin-ware, laces, table cloths, cotton handkerchiefs, cheap window curtains and the like, until now he has a large brick building, a number of clerks, and he and family ride in a fine carriage drawn by expensive horses, and they driven by a Negro. Why can we not help our brother who is struggling with all the odds against him, and has been since the day of his birth? I am sure what we might buy from the Negro could be no more inferior than some of the things we have bought from the Jew, and I suspect his recommendation of the article would be as truthful as that of the Jew.

NEGRO BUSINESS MEN OF COLUMBIA, S. C.

Paper Submitted by Mr. H. E. Lindsay.

Columbia has a population of over twenty thousand people, half of these being colored. The Negroes here, as in most Southern cities and towns, are well represented in the various mechanical trades. As to what they are doing in business can best be understood from the following:

We have about twenty-five grocery, dry goods and clothing stores in the city, varying in size from the little surburban shop, with its assortment of wood and shelf goods, to the well stocked and neatly kept store, whose only difference from other stores is the color of its clerks.

Possibly the business that represents the largest outlay of capital, is conducted by Mr. I. J. Miller the clothier. His store is located in the heart of the business center of the city. Besides giving his business his strict personal attention he is aided by three clerks.

During last fall his estimated stock was $10,000 at one time. Mr. Miller about fifteen years ago, commenced this enterprise with scarcely a shelf of goods: through toil and perseverance he has succeeded in establishing a business, that not only reflects credit upon himself and the race, but stands comparison with the most favored enterprise of its kind in the city.

The next I shall mention is the well-known Merchant Tailor, Mr. R. J. Palmer. Mr. Palmer on account of his thorough knowledge of his business, has for many years been the recognized leader in his line. He occupies his own building, valued at eight thousand dollars; it is located in one of the best business blocks in the city.

He carries in connection with his tailoring business, a complete line of clothing and gent's furnishings,—his stock representing some thousands of dollars. He visits the northern markets as often as twice a year to select his stock.

The enterprise of which I have the honor to be head, is younger than the two mentioned above, and much the junior of many other enterprises of the race here, and we feel indeed gratified at occupying even third place.

Our enterprise is a grocery and provision store, with one branch business at its old stand, near the western suburbs. I was placed in charge of the business before reaching my maturity, and since completing a normal course at Allen University in '92, I devoted my entire attention to its management.

Our beginning was certainly humble. We opened up with a few dozen canned goods, wood, etc; our stock valued at about forty dollars. In five year's time we made three additions to our building, and out of a little shop had grown a general merchandise store, where we sold from a paper of pins to a suit of clothes, from a pound of bacon to a barrel of flour.

We conduct our business with five clerks and a delivery with each store. Some of the other enterprises worthy of mention are Mr. J. P. Evans, grocer, Mrs. Caroline Alston, dry goods, Mr. Richard Bell, grocer.

Mr. Evans has been conducting his business at the same old stand for over twenty years,—his patrons are about equally divided between the two races. Mrs. Caroline Alston, a lady who conducts a dry goods store, has met with much success in her more than twenty years experience in business, and enjoys the esteem and confidence of the white race as well as her own.

Mr. Richard Bell, a comparatively young man, has succeeeed well in his business, and in point of neatness and cleanliness, his store is a model after which anyone might pattern.

We have one drug store, Dr. James J. Leggett, a graduate of Howard University, in charge; two harness and saddlery shops; five confectioners; no saloons; seventeen boot and shoe repair shops, six blacksmith and wheelright shops, two butchers, three newspapers with two job printing offices.

The "People's Recorder," a paper published and edited by Holmes and Nix, has a creditable circulation throughout the state, and is the most influential paper of the three. They have a creditable job department in which are employed several printers.

The next is the "South Carolina Standard;" J. R. Wilson is one of its editors. The Standard is a neatly printed paper; their job department is second to none in the city, as their work will testify. The "Christian Soldier" is a bright little paper edited by Rev. Richard Carrol, founder of the new orphan home.

We have twenty barber shops, the leading shops are all colored; we have three lawyers, and three physicians: Dr. C. C. Johnson, Dr. C. L. Walton and Dr. Matilda Evans.

Dr. Evans is an example to all women of our race, who are standing aside and allowing the men to monopolize all the professions. She has won many friends since her coming to our city, less than two years ago, and has met with constant success.

We have two undertaking establishments, two mattress manufacturies, three tailoring establishments Among the carpenters and brickmasons we have fully a dozen contractors, many of which are worthy of mention, being honest and reliable and have accumulated wealth. Ninety per cent of the carpenters and brickmasons are colored.

Rev. M. G. Johnson represents a building association that does a majority of the business among colored people. The above is but a partial list of the many enterprises among the Negoes of Columbia.

THE NEGRO GROCER.

Paper Submitted by W. O. Murphy, '91.

Were the question asked,   What is at this moment the strongest power in operation for controlling, regulating, and inciting the actions of men? What has most at its disposal the conditions and destinies of the world? we must answer at once BUSINESS, in its various ranks and departments, of which commerce, foreign and domestic, is the most appropriate representation.   In all prosperous and advancing communities—advancing in arts, knowledge, literature, and social refinement—BUSINESS IS KING.

Other influences in society may be equally indispensable, and some may think far more dignified, but nevertheless, BUSINESS IS KING.

The statesman and the scholar, the nobleman and the prince, equally with the manufacturer, the mechanic, and the laborer pursue their several objects only by leave granted, and means furnished by this potentate.

These facts were true a hundred years ago and they are true to-day and we as propressive, up-to-date citizens must push our way in and share the fruits of commercial effort.

Well has it been said that "Man is the only animal that buys and sells or exchanges commodities with his fellows. Other animals make an attempt at least, to do every other thing that men can do except trade ; and among them are types of every profession except the merchant. The beaver, the bee, and the bird, can build as well as some of our mechanics ; the fox surpasses some lawyers in cunning ; musicians are content to be called nightingales of song ; the tiger is an uneducated warrior ; lions are the lords of the forest ; but the merchant who buys from one people to sell to another has no representative in the animal creation."

Civilization depends upon the activity of the merchant who by his zeal and acumen not only supplies the wants of the trade but seeks out new products of other climes and furnishes a new market for commodities more or less unmarketable in regions where they are indigenous.

So we see that a business man is at once a leader, a servant, and a benefactor to the community, if he is a thorough business man.

This brings me to my subject "The Negro Grocer." I do not know that I can be considered as authority on this subject as I am only 28 years old, yet 27 of these years have I spent in this business ; so when I look backward in the dim past it seems, sometimes, that I now know less about "The Negro Grocer," in particular, and business in general, than when I was born a Negro in business.

There are in the city of Atlanta about 600 licensed grocers, of whom 49 are Negroes. It has been estimated that the grocery trade of Atlanta amounts to approximately $1,000,000 per month, or $250,000 per week.

The population of Atlanta is placed at 100,000 of whom 40,000 are Negroes, allowing 5 persons to each family, gives us 8,000 Negro families.

If each family expends $3.00 per week for groceries, and I think such is a fair estimate, we have $24,000 spent each week, by Negroes, for Negro consumption.

If the 49 Negro grocers of Atlanta furnished the 4000 Negroes this $24,000 worth of groceries each week, every one of these faithful 49 would have the pleasure of receiving over his counters nearly $500 each week.

You need not ask me Are they doing it?

In addition to the $24000 spent each week by Negroes for Negro consumption, a large sum is spent daily by servants who in a great measure are able to carry this trade whither they will. You need not inquire, Do they take it to the Negro Grocer?

So much for the reality. We all know that the Negro eats, and eats, not always sumptously, but certainly, at times, to his utmost capacity.

We know that these goods are paid for; i. e. most of them; We also know that these 49 Negro grocers do not sell one-half of the goods purchased and consumed by Negroes in Atlanta.

Now for "the why."

That is the problem that confronts the Negro Grocer of Atlanta, some of whom, years ago, embarked in business, with no capital, save a few dollars, his honest heart and his necessity; no established credit; ignorant of most of the ordinary rules of business, many of them, at the start would not have known an invoice from a bill of lading; with nothing to guide him but his native shrewdness and nothing to save him from disaster, save what he might accumulate by the strictest economy.

Yet in spite of all these drawbacks some of the of the 49 have managed to establish a fair credit and accumulate a few dollars and a little property.

The need is not so much for more Grocers, but for younger and more intelligent ones and we are looking to our schools for suitable material, so as to at least capture the $24000 spent weekly by Negroes, for groceries, in Atlanta.

It was this idea that induced me to accept the invitation to speak to you on this occasion, I thought I might drop a word which would be the means of inducing some young man to make an earnest attempt to engage in some kind of business in Atlanta, and help these poor, struggling, hopeful 49 Negro grocers capture that $24,000 spent here each week by Negroes.

With the same ambition that sustained you in scholastic efforts; with the same energy and push that prompted you in your athletic contests; with the same pride that makes you prize your degree; with the same love that makes you boast of your Alma Mater; with the same economy and fidelity that actuated your forefathers and with the same persistence that controls the 49 now struggling in the grocery business in Atlanta, we can capture our share not only of the $24,000 spent by Negroes, but we can have a fighting chance for the $250,000 spent by Atlanta Citizens regardless of their race.

A NEGRO COOPERATIVE FOUNDRY.

Paper Submitted by Mr. C. H. Fearn, Manager.

The Southern Stove Hollow-ware and Foundry Company was temporarily organized on the 15th day of February, 1897, and was permanently organized and incorporated at Chattanooga, under the laws of the State of Tennessee, on August 15, 1897. Our charter provides for a capital stock of $5,000 to be divided into shares of $25 each, which are sold only to colored people, either for cash or upon monthly payments, but in no case is a certificate of stock issued until fully paid for.

The Foundry was built and began operations on a small scale on or about October 27th, 1897, and has now increased and been perfected until we manufacture stoves, hollow-ware of all kinds, fire grates complete, boiler grate bars, refrigerator cups, shoe lasts and stands and other kinds of castings generally made in foundries. We also do a repair business which has now grown until it has become a business that pays well and is one of our chief sources of revenue.

The land, buildings, machinery and all patterns are fully paid for except part of the stove patterns and these we are paying for in products of our foundry; and we can say that we are virtually free from debt. Of the capital stock authorized we have sold $1466 worth, and this has all been used strictly in equipping the plant; but this sum does not represent now the worth of our plant, as all our profits have been allowed to accumulate and have been used in the business.

By a unanimous vote at the various meetings of the directors of the Company, it has been decided to draw no dividends until we shall have a fully perfected plant and one upon a paying basis.

Our stockholders, or the majority of them, are active members of the Company and are men who are masters of different trades which are needed to successfully operate a foundry. We have men who have in the past been the mainstays of other foundries—men who for years have followed the business of pattern makers, moulders, cupola tenders, engineers, repair workers, stove mounters and blacksmiths. And we boast that to-day we are fully able to do work that any other men can do.

The objects in forming and operating the Southern Stove Hollow-ware and Foundry Company are many. First, we believe if we can now invest our capital, together with our labor, that we will build up a business that will in years to come furnish us our means of support; a business that we can increase and build up until we shall look on it with pride and have the satisfaction to know that we are the owners and masters of the same.

We believe that to solve the great problems that confront us, there is no better way for our race to attain the position they deserve than to become masters of the art of manufacturing. If we as colored men, are able to run and operate the foundries that are built with the white man's capital, why can't we do the same with ours? When other races see that we are able to become the masters of the different trades and to employ our own capital, direct and control our own industries, then the time will come that we will cease to be the serfs, but we will be the brother laborers in the great struggle of life.

We believe that by establishing foundries and work-shops by the older men of our race, and the successful operation of the same, that it will be to the betterment of the young men of our race. They will follow our example and, being able to have a place to learn the higher trades and to invest the savings of their labor, it will stop the roving disposition of our race and make them better citizens. It is our duty to watch, protect and guide our young men. It is our duty to establish places where they can learn to be masters of all trades.

We believe it is our duty to our race to produce as well as to buy. No race or people can be prosperous who always buy and never produce. We must make if we expect to own and what we make must be for ourselves instead of for others.

There is no doubt but what the South will be the work-shop of the world; and as the South is the home of the colored man, why can't he own and control the shops? Gentlemen, I tell you the Southern Stove Hollow-ware and Foundry Company is a young plant but I say it is a success. It to-day stands out to the world as an evidence that the colored man can manufacture. To-day we are offered orders that will take us months to complete. We need more capital; we need more men and we can say to you that if we had the necessary capital to operate our plant as it should be, that we can do the rest; and we would show to the world that the Southern Stove Hollow-ware and Foundry Company was an industry that is not only a pride to our race, but an honor to the people of the country in which we operate.

We would be pleased to have any one come and inspect our plant. It is a worthy enterprise and deserves support. We believe the time is not far distant when the name of the Southern Stove Hollow-ware and Foundry Company will adorn the lists of the best and most prosperous manufacturing plants of the United States of America and then, and not until then, will the object of this institution be attained.

NEGRO BUSINESS VENTURES IN ATLANTA, GA.

Compiled by the Editor from the Senior theses of
G. F. Porter, '99, and J. P. Seabrooke, '99.

According to the United States Census of 1890 there were in Atlanta, Ga., 28,117 Negroes. At present there are probably from thirty-five to forty thousand. Among this population the class in Sociology of Atlanta University counted 61 business enterprises of sufficient size to be noticed. These were as follows:

Grocery-stores	22
General Merchandise stores	5
Wood-yards	6
Barber-shops, with hired employees and over $300 invested	6
Meat-Markets	7
Restaurants	2
Undertakers	2
Blacksmiths and Wheelwrights, with stock	2
Saloons	2
Tailor, with stock	1
Drug-store	1
Creamery	1
Pool and Billiard Parlor	1
Loan and Investment Company	1
Carriage and Wagon Builder	1
Real Estate Dealer	1
Total	61

There are some of the above that combine several businesses; e. g., one of the grocery-stores has a meat-market, in connection; two others have wood-yards; one a coal and wood-yard; and one combines a grocery, restaurant, wood and coal-yard and a meat-market. In one of the above mentioned wood-yards, coal is also sold; in another there is a restaurant.

The capital invested in these businesses is as follows:

GROCERY STORES.

CAPITAL.	NUMBER OF STORES.	CAPITAL.	NUMBER OF STORES.
$100	1	$ 600	1
150	1	800	4
200	2	1 000	2
250	2	1 275	1
300	1		
400	1	Total	61
500	6	Total capital invested $11,925	

OTHER ENTERPRISES.

BUSINESS.	AMOUNTS INVESTED.							TOTAL.
General Md'se.	$3 800	$2 000	$1 000	$ 500	$ 500	$......	$......	$ 7 800
Wood-yard,	500	500	400	200	150	50	......	1 800
Barber-shop,	3 000	2 500	2 000	1 800	400	300	......	10 000
Meat-market,	500	200	150	80	75	75	30	1 110
Restaurant,	500	125						625
Undertaker,	7 000	6 000						13 000
Blacksmith,	800	600						1 400
Saloon,	1 500	1 200						2 700
Tailor,	200							200
Drug-store,	1 900							1 900
Creamery,	300							300
Pool-room,	1 600							1 600
Investment Co.,	4 000							4 000
Carriage-builder,	900							900
Real Estate.	5 000							5 000

Total..$52 335

This makes a total investment of $64,260 in all businesses.

Nearly all these investments have grown from very small beginnings, as, for instance:

CAPITAL AT START.		CAPITAL AT PRESENT.
Drug-store,	$ 900	$1 900
Restaurant,	50	500
Grocer,	150	600
Tailor,	75	200
Undertaker.	0	6 000

At present three firms have an investment of $5,000 and over; four be- tween $2.500 and $5,000; eleven from $1,000 to $2,500; twenty from $500 to $1,000 and twenty-three under $500.

The number of years in business is as follows:

YEARS IN BUSINESS.

BUSINESS.	UNDER 1 YR.	1-3 YRS	3-5 YRS	5-7 YRS	7-10 YRS	10-12 YRS	12-15 YRS	15-18 YRS	20-25 YRS	25-30 YRS
Grocery,	1	1	2	3	2	5	3	....	2	1
Gen'l Md'se,	....	2	....	....	....	....	1	1	....	1
Wood-yard,	....	2	....	1	1	....	....	....	1	....
Barber-shop,	....	....	1	....	1	2	....	1	1	....
Meat-market,	....	1	1	1	2	....	2	....	....	....
Restaurant,	....	1	1	....	....	....	....	....	....	....
Undertaker,	....	....	....	....	....	1	1	....	....	....
Blacksmith,	....	....	1	....	1	....	....	....	....	....
Saloon,	1	....	....	....	....	1	....	....	....	....
Tailor,	....	....	....	....	....	....	1	....	....	....
Drug-store,	....	....	1	....	....	....	....	....	....	....
Creamery	....	....	....	1	....	....	....	....	....	....
Pool-room,	....	1	....	....	....	....	....	....	....	....
Inves'nt Co.,	....	....	....	1	....	....	....	....	....	....
Car'ge Bldr.,	....	....	1	....	....	....	....	....	....	....
Real Estate	....	....	....	....	....	1	....	....	....	....
Total,	2	8	8	7	7	10	8	2	4	2

The oldest business is a general merchandise establishment, 29 years old; next comes a grocery, 25 years old, and two groceries and a barber-shop, each 20 years old.

A comparison of the years in business and the invested capital is of interest:

	UNDER $500.	$500-1,000.	$1,000-2,500.	$2,500-5,000.	$5,000-OVER.
UNDER 3 Yr's	6	2	2	......	......
3-5	3	4	2	......	......
5-10	5	8	......	1	......
10-15	3	5	5	......	3
15-20	1	......	......	2	......
20-30	2	1	2	1	......

The general merchandise store, which is 29 years old, has $1,000 invested; the grocery-store, which is 25 years old, has the same amount invested; contrasting with these is a grocery with the same investment, three years old. The two 20 year-old groceries have respectively, $400 and $500 invested; the general merchandise store, which has the largest investment, $3,800, is fifteen years old. The undertaking firm, with $7,000 invested, has been in operation 14 years; while the $6,000 firm has been running 10 years. Thus we can see that in the main there has been a growth in capital, due to the saving of profits; at the same time, there are a number of old shops which show no growth, but continue to live, and there is also evidence of ability to begin new businesses with some considerable capital.

The next question is as to the manner in which these establishments are conducted and their special advantages and disadvantages. Most of them must, of course, depend primarily on Negro patronage. Of 25 firms especially studied in 1898, none depended wholly on white trade; 9 had considerable white patronage, and two some white trade; the rest depended wholly on Negro trade. Much depends naturally on the character of the business; a drug-store would get white trade only by chance or in an emergency; a grocery-store might get a little transient white now and then; wood-yard might get trade of both races; restaurants and barber-shops must draw the color-line without exception and either serve all whites or all Negroes; undertakers can serve Negroes only. All these considerations make, of course, a vast difference between white and Negro business men. A Negro undertaker in Atlanta is in a city of 35,000 people, chiefly of the laboring class: a white undertaker has a constituency of, perhaps, 80,000, largely well-to-do merchants and artisans. The white grocer has not only the advantage of training and capital, but also of a constituency three times as large, and ten times as rich as his Negro competitor. Moreover, 75% of the Negro firms are compelled by custom to do business largely on a credit basis, and, too, have fewer means of compelling payment. Finally, the Negro merchants, as a class, are poorly trained for the work. The 25 studied in 1898 were educated as follows;

College Training.. 1
Common School 9
Read and Write only 12
No Education.. 3

THE NEGRO NEWSPAPER.

By the Editor.

There are in the United States to-day the following periodicals published by Negroes in the interest of the colored people:

MAGAZINES.

A. M. E. Church Review, quarterly, Philadelphia, Penn.

A. M. E. Zion Church Review, quarterly, Charlotte, N. C.

Howard's American Magazine, monthly, Harrisburg, Pa.

DAILY PAPERS.

The Daily Recorder, Norfolk, Va.
American Citizen, Kansas City, Kan.

The Daily Record, Washington, D. C.

WEEKLY PAPERS.

Alabama.

Baptist Leader, Montgomery,
Mobile Weekly Press, Mobile,
Christian Hope, Mobile,

National Ass'n Notes, Tuskegee,
Southern Watchman, Mobile,
Christian Age, Mobile,

Educator, Huntsville.

California.

Western Outlook, San Francisco.

Colorado.

Statesman, Denver,

Sun, Colorado Springs,

Western Enterprise, Colorado Springs.

District of Columbia.

Bee, Washington,

Colored American, Washington.

Florida.

Sentinel, Pensacola,
Evangelist, Jacksonville,
East Coast Banner, Interlacken,

Forum, Ocala,
Recorder, Orlando,
Samaritan Ledger, Sanford,

Herald, Live Oak.

Georgia.

Appeal, Atlanta,
Baptist Truth, Savannah,
Tribune, Savannah,
Georgia Baptist, Augusta,
Progress, Athens,
Dispatch, Albany,
So. Christian Recorder, Atlanta,
So. Georgia Baptist, Waycross,
Aurora, Atlanta,

Age, Atlanta,
Weekly News, Savannah,
Union, Augusta,
Clipper, Athens,
Herald, Brunswick,
Enterprise, LaGrange,
Guide, LaGrange,
Voice of Missions, Atlanta,
Iconoclast, Albany,

Spectator, Darien,
Monitor, Columbus,

Sentinel, Macon,
Investigator, Americus.

Index, Carpentersville.

Illinois.

Conservator, Chicago.

Indiana.

World, Indianapolis,

Freeman, Indianapolis,

Recorder, Indianapolis.

Kansas.

Plaindealer, Topeka.

Kentucky.

Lexington Standard, Lexington,
Bluegrass Bugle, Frankfort,

American Baptist, Louisville,
Major, Hopkinsville.

Louisiana.

S. W. Christian Advocate, New
Orleans,

Republican Courier, New Orleans.

Massachusetts.

Courant, Boston.

Maryland.

Weekly Guide, Baltimore.,
Baptist Voice, Baltimore,
Republican Guide, Baltimore,
Afro-American, Baltimore,

Messenger, Baltimore
Crusader, Baltimore,
Ledger, Baltimore,
Signal, Cumberland.

Michigan.

Informer, Detroit.

Mississippi.

New Light, Columbus

Missouri.

American Citizen, St. Louis.

Minnesota.

Appeal, St. Paul.

Nebraska.

Enterprise, Omaha,

Afro-American Sentinel, Omaha,

Progress, Omaha.

New Jersey.

Public Record, Newark,
W. T. Patterson's Weekly, Asbury
Park.

Union, Orange,
Public Record, Atlantic City.

New York.

Spectator, Albany,
Presbyterian Herald, N. Y.

Age, New York,
Methodist Herald, N. Y.

North Carolina.

Defender, Raleigh,
Gazette, Raleigh,
Star of Zion, Charlotte,
Eastern Herald, Edenton,
Neuse River Herald, Waldron,

Blade, Raleigh,
Baptist Sentinel, Raleigh,
Afro-American Presbyterian, Charlotte,
True Reformer, Littleton,

Cotton Boll, Concord.

Ohio.

Gazette, Cleveland,

Observer, Xenia,

Rostrum, Cincinnati.

Oklahoma Territory.

Constitution, Oklahoma,

Guide, Oklahoma

Pennsylvania.

Christian Recorder, Philadelphia,
Christian Banner, Philadelphia,

Tribune, Philadelphia,
Odd Fellows Journal, Philadelphia.

Symposium, Philadelphia.

South Carolina.

Peedee Educator, Bennettsville,
People's Record, Columbia,
Christian Soldier, Columbia,

Piedmont Indicator, Spartanburg,
Standard, Columbia,
Observer, Charleston.

Texas.

Weekly Express, Dallas,
City Times, Galveston,
Elevator, Wharton,
Helping Hand, Oakland,
Advance, San Antonio,
Herald, Austin,
Reporter, Marshall,
New Idea, Galveston,
Spectator, Yoakum,
Paul Quinn Weekly, Waco,
Bugle, Navasota,

Rising Sun, Rockdale,
Star, Fort Worth,
Guide, Victoria,
Gazette, Galveston,
Item, Dallas,
Searchlight, Austin,
Teacher, Caldwell,
X Ray, San Antonio,
Southern Herald, Waco
Sequin, Navasota,
Enterprise, Bellville

Monitor, Marshall.

Tennessee.

Ship, Bristol,

Christian Index, Jackson.

Virginia.

Richmond Planet, Richmond,
Reformer, Richmond,
Leader, Alexandria,

Virginia Baptist, Richmond,
National Pilot, Petersburg,
Colored Churchmam, Bedford City.

West Virginia.

Pioneer Press, Martinsburg.

SCHOOL AND COLLEGE PAPERS.

Lane College Reporter, Jackson, Tenn.   College Arms, Tallahassee, Fla·
Argus, Biddle Univ., Charlotte, N. C.   College Record, Talledega, Ala·
Aurora, Morris Brown College, Atlanta.   Courier, Clark Univ., Atlanta.
Scroll, Atlanta Univ., Atlanta, Ga.   News, Brick Ins., Enfield, N. C.
Tuskegee Student, Tuskegee, Ala.   Fisk Herald, Nashville, Tenn.
University Herald, Howard Univ., Washington, D. C.

SUMMARY.

Magazines	3
Daily papers	3
School papers	11
Weekly papers	136
Total	**153**

The sixty-six leading newspapers were established as follows:

1839	Christian Recorder	Philadelphia, Pa.
1865	Southwestern Christian Advocate	New Orleans, La.
1870	Christian Index	Jackson, Tenn.
1876	Star of Zion	Charlotte, N. C.
1877	Conservator	Chicago, Ill.
1880	Georgia Baptist	Augusta, Ga.
	Leader	Alexandria, Va.
	American Baptist	Louisville, Ky.
1881	New York Age	New York, N. Y.
1882	Washington Bee	Washington, D. C.
	Pioneer Press	Martinsburg, W. Va.
	Indianopolis World	Indianapolis, Ind.
1883	Gazette	Cleveland, O.
	Richmond Planet	Richmond, Va.
1884	Philadelphia Tribune	Philadelphia, Pa.
	A. M. E. Church Review	Philadelphia, Pa.
1885	Tribune	Savannah, Ga.
	Elevator	San Francisco, Cal.
1886	The Brotherhood	Natchez, Miss.
1887	Florida Sentinel	Pensacola, Fla.
	National Pilot	Petersburg, Va.
1888	Southern Christian Recorder	Atlanta, Ga.
1889	Augusta Union	Augusta, Ga,
	American Citizen	Kansas City, Kan.
	Statesman	Denver, Col.
1890	Christian Banner	Philadelphia, Pa.
1891	Southern Watchman	Mobile, Ala.
	Raleigh Blade	Raleigh, N. C.
	Constitution	Guthrie, Oklahoma.
1892	Afro-American Sentinel	Omaha, Neb.
	Afro-American	Baltimore, Md.
	Lexington Standard	Lexington, Ky.
1893	Colored American	Washington, D. C.
	People's Recorder	Columbia, S. C.

	Defender	Raleigh, N. C
	Guide	Guthrie, Oklahoma.
1894	Weekly Express	Dallas, Texas.
	Western Outlook	San Francisco, Cal.
	Weekly Press	Mobile, Ala.
1895	The Ship	Bristol, Tenn.
	Enterprise	La Grange, Ga.
	Baptist Sentinel	Raleigh, N. C.
	Spectator	Albany, N. Y.
	Kentucky Standard	Louisville, Ky.
1896	Forum	Ocala, Fla.
	South Georgia Baptist	Waycross, Ga.
	Association Notes	Tuskegee, Ala.
	Public Record	Atlantic City, N. J.
	Guide	Baltimore, Md.
	Monitor	Jacksonville, Fla.
1897	Evangelist.	Jacksonville, Fla.
	Informer	Detroit, Mich.
	Herald	Brunswick, Ga.
	Elevator	Wharton. Tex.
	Advance	San Antonio, Tex.
	Helping Hand	Oakland, Tex,
	American Eagle	St Louis, Mo.
1898	Atlanta Age	Atlanta, Ga.
	Enterprise	Omaha, Neb.
	Appeal	Atlanta, Ga,
	Union	Orange, N. J.
	Symposium	Germantown, Penn.
	Observer	Macon, Miss.
	Republican Guide	Baltimore, Md.
	Baptist Voice	"
	Gazette	Galveston, Tex.

The following papers, among others, own their own buildings:

Star of Zion, Charlotte, N. C.

Pioneer Press, Martinsburg, W. Va.

Planet, Richmond, Va.

Christian Recorder & A. M. E. Church Review, Philadelphia, Penn.

Florida Sentinel, Pensacola, Fla.

Forum, Ocala, Fla.

The Ship, Bristol, Tenn.

Public Record, Atlantic City, N. J.

Symposium, Germantown, Penn.

Bee, Washington D. C.

Christian Index, Jackson, Tenn.

The buildings are valued as follows:

$ 700
900
1,500
1,700
3,500
5,500
8,000
10,000
12,000
17,500

Total valuation $ 61,300

Forty-four papers own printing plants:

VALUE.	NUMBER.
Under $ 500	6
$ 500—1,000	14
1,000—2,500	12
2,500—5,000	9
$5,000 and over	3

Total actual valuation $89,450.

These papers are published by the following agencies:

Single Individuals	39
Firms	18
Religous societies	10
Secret or other Societies	3

The Negro newspaper has not yet gained an assured footing, but it is rapidly becoming a social force. Nearly all Negro families read them and while the papers are not yet strong enough to mould opinion, they are beginning to play a peculiar part in reflecting it.

There exists today no better means of forming, directing and crystalizing Negro public opinion than by means of the press. A strong, fearless, national newspaper or magazine which the Negroes could feel was their own, with sane views as to work, wealth and culture, could become, in years, a vast power among Negroes. Here is a chance for a peculiar sort of philanthropic work, and one hitherto little tried—the endowed periodical. Fifty thousand dollars might, with care and foresight, launch a social force in the American world which would be of vast weight in guiding us toward the proper settlement of many vexed Negro problems.

THE NEGRO CHURCH

Report of a Social Study made under the direction of Atlanta
University; together with the Proceedings of the Eighth
Conference for the Study of the Negro Problems,
held at Atlanta University, May 26th, 1903

EDITED BY

W. E. BURGHARDT DU BOIS

CORRESPONDING SECRETARY OF THE CONFERENCE

The Atlanta University Press
Atlanta, Ga.
1903

THE Negro Church is the only social institution of the Negroes which started in the African forest and survived slavery; under the leadership of priest or medicine man, afterward of the Christian pastor, the Church preserved in itself the remnants of African tribal life and became after emancipation the center of Negro social life. So that today the Negro population of the United States is virtually divided into church congregations which are the real units of race life.

Report of the Third Atlanta Conference, 1898.

CONTENTS

PREFACE

A study of human life to-day involves a consideration of conditions of physical life, a study of various social organizations, beginning with the home, and investigations into occupations, education, religion and morality, crime and political activity. The Atlanta Cycle of studies into the Negro problem aims at exhaustive and periodic studies of all these subjects so far as they relate to the American Negro. Thus far, in the first eight years of the ten-year cycle, we have studied physical conditions of life (Reports No. 1 and No. 2), social organization (Reports No. 2 and No. 3), economic activity (Reports No. 4 and No. 7), and Education (Reports No. 5 and No. 6). This year we take up the important subject of the NEGRO CHURCH, studying the religion of Negroes and its influence on their moral habits.

Such a study could not be made exhaustive for lack of funds and organization. On the other hand, the United States government and the churches themselves have published a great deal of material and it is possible from this and limited investigations in various typical localities to make a study of some value.

This investigation bases its results on the following data:

> United States Census of 1890.
> Minutes of Conferences.
> Reports of Conventions, Societies, etc.
> Catalogues of Theological Schools.
> Two hundred and fifty special reports from pastors and officials.
> One hundred and seventy-five special reports from colored laymen.
> One hundred and seventeen special reports from heads of schools
>   and prominent men, white and colored.
> Fifty-four special reports from Southern white persons.
> Thirteen special reports from Colored Theological Schools.
> One hundred and nine special reports from Northern Theological
>   Schools.
> Answers from 1,300 school children.
> Local studies in—

Richmond, Virginia.	Atlanta, Georgia.
Chicago, Illinois.	Greene County, Ohio.
Thomas County, Georgia.	Deland, Florida.

> General and periodical literature.

In the preparation of this report the editor begs to acknowledge his indebtedness to the several hundred persons who have so kindly answered his inquiries; to students in Atlanta University and Virginia Union University, who have made special investigations; and particularly to Professor B. F. Williams, Mr. M. N. Work, Mr. R. R. Wright, Jr., and Mr. W. H. Holloway, all of whom have given valuable time and services to this work. The Rev. F. J. Grimke has kindly allowed the use of his unpublished report, made to the Hampton Conference in 1901; Mr. J. W. Cromwell has loaned us the results of his historical researches, and Dr. A. M. MacLean has given us the results of a valuable local study. The proof-reading was largely done by Mr. A. G. Dill.

Atlanta University has been conducting studies similar to this for the past seven years. The results, distributed at a nominal sum, have been widely used.

Notwithstanding this success the further prosecution of these important studies is greatly hampered by the lack of funds. With meagre appropriations for expenses, lack of clerical help and necessary apparatus, the Conference cannot cope properly with the vast field of work before it.

We appeal therefore to those who think it worth while to study this, the greatest group of social problems that has ever faced the Nation, for substantial aid and encouragement in the further prosecution of the work of the Atlanta Conference.

<hr />

SELECT BIBLIOGRAPHY OF NEGRO CHURCHES

A brief statement of the rise and progress of the testimony of the religious society of Friends against slavery and the slave-trade. Philadelphia: Joseph and William Kite. 1843.

Ernest H. Abbott. Religious life in America. A record of personal observation. New York: The Outlook, 1902. XII, 730 pp. 8o.

Nehemiah Adams. A South side view of slavery. 8o. Boston, 1854.

Richard Allen, first bishop of the A. M. E. Church. The life, experience and gospel labors of the Rt. Rev. Richard Allen. Written by himself. Philadelphia, 1833.

Richard Allen and Jacob Tapisco. The doctrine and discipline of the A. M. E. Church. Philadelphia, 1819.

Matthew Anderson. Presbyterianism and its relation to the Negro. Philadelphia, 1897.

A statistical inquiry into the condition of the people of color of the city and districts of Philadelphia. Philadelphia, 1849, 1856 and 1859.

Samuel J. Baird. A collection of the acts, deliverances and testimonies of the Supreme Judiciary of the Presbyterian Church, from its origin in America to the present time, with notes and documents explanatory and historical, constituting a complete illustration of her polity, faith and history. Philadelphia: Presbyterian Board of Publications.

J. C. Ballagh. A history of slavery in Virginia. Johns Hopkins University Studies. Extra vol., No. 24. Baltimore, 1902.

Albert Barnes. Inquiry into the scriptural views of slavery. Philadelphia, 1857.

John S. Bassett. History of slavery in North Carolina. Johns Hopkins University studies. Baltimore, 1899.

   Slavery and servitude in the colony of North Carolina. Baltimore: The Johns Hopkins Press, April and May, 1896.

David Benedict. A general history of the Baptist denomination in America and other parts of the world. Boston, 1813.

Edward W. Blyden. Christianity, Islam and the Negro race. With an introduction by the Hon. Samuel Lewis. 2d edition. London: W. B. Whittingham & Co. 432 pp. 8o.

George Bourne. Man-stealing and Slavery denounced by the Presbyterian and Methodist Churches. Boston: Garrison and Knapp.

Jeffrey R. Brackett. Notes on the progress of the colored people of Maryland since the war. A supplement to the Negro in Maryland, a study of the institution of slavery. Baltimore: J. Hopkins Univ., 1890. 96 pp. 8o.

   The Negro in Maryland. A study of the institution of slavery. Baltimore: N. Murray. (6) 268 pp. 8o. (Johns Hopkins University studies in historical and political science.) Extra vol. 6.

William Burling. An address to the elders of the church upon the occasion of some Friends compelling certain persons and their posterity to serve them continually and arbitrarily, without regard to equity or right, not heeding whether they give them anything near so much as their labor deserveth. 1718. In Lay, All Slave Keepers Apostates. pp. 6–10.

Rev. Dr. R. F. Campbell. The race problem in the South. Pamphlet, 1899.

W. E. Burghardt DuBois. 1900. The religion of the American Negro. New World, vol. 9 (Dec. 1900) 614–625.

   The Philadelphia Negro. A Social Study. Philadelphia, 1899: Ginn & Co.

   The Negroes of Farmville, Va. 38 pp. Bulletin U. S. Department of Labor, Jan. 1898.

   Some efforts of American Negroes for their own social betterment. Report of an investigation under the direction of Atlanta University, together with the proceedings of the third Conference for the study of the Negro problems, held at Atlanta University, May 25–26, 1898. Atlanta, Ga. (Atlanta University, 1898. 66 pp.)

   The Souls of Black Folk. Chicago, 1903.

William Douglass. Sermons preached in the African Protestant Episcopal Church of St. Thomas. Philadelphia, 1854.

   Annals of St. Thomas's Church. Philadelphia, 1862.

Bryan Edwards. History, civil and commercial, of the British Colonies in the West Indies. London, 1807.

Friends. A brief testimony of the progress of the Friends against slavery and the slave-trade. 1671–1787. Philadelphia, 1843.

William Goodell. The American slave code in theory and practice. Judiciary decisions and illustrative facts. New York, 1452.

H. Gregoire. Enquiry concerning the intellectual and moral faculties, etc., of Negroes. Brooklyn, 1810.

L. M. Hagood. The Colored Man in the Methodist Episcopal Church. Cincinnati.

Bishop J. W. Hood. One Hundred Years of the A. M. E. Zion Church.

Edward Ingle. The Negro in the District of Columbia. Johns Hopkins University studies. Vol. XI. Baltimore, 1893.

Samuel M. Janney. History of the religious society of Friends. Philadelphia, 1859–1867.

Chas. C. Jones. The religious instruction of the Negroes in the United States. Savannah, 1842.

Absalom Jones. A Thanksgiving sermon on account of the abolition of the African slave-trade. Philadelphia, 1808.

Robert Jones. Fifty years in the Lombard Street Central Presbyterian Church. Philadelphia, 1894. 170 pp.

Fanny Kemble. A journal of a residence on a Georgia plantation. New York, 1863.

Walter Laidlow, editor. The Federation of Churches and Christian Workers in New York City. New York, 1896–1897.

Lucius C. Matlack. The history of American slavery and Methodism from 1789–1849. New York, 1849.

Holland McTyeire. A history of Methodism, comprising a view of the rise of this revival of spiritual religion in the first half of the eighteenth century. Nashville, Tenn.: Southern Methodist Publishing House, 1887.

Minutes, Annual Conferences, A. M. E. Church.

Minutes, Annual Conferences, C. M. E. Church.

Minutes, Annual Conferences, M. E. Church.

Minutes, Annual Conferences, A. M. E. Z. Church.

Minutes, General Conferences, A. M. E. Church.

Minutes, General Conferences, C. M. E. Church.

Minutes, General Conferences, M. E. Church.

Minutes, General Conferences, A. M. E. Z. Church.

Minutes, National Baptist Convention.

Edward Needles. Ten years' progress or a comparison of the state and condition of the colored people in the city and county of Philadelphia from 1837–1847. Philadelphia, 1849.

Daniel A. Payne. History of the A. M. E. Church. Nashville, 1891.

I. Garland Penn and J. W. E. Bowen. The United Negro: his problems and his progress. Containing the addresses and proceedings of the Negro Young People's Christian and Educational Congress, held August 6–11, 1902. Atlanta, Ga.: D. E. Luther Publishing Co., 1902, XXX, 600 pp. Plates, portraits. 12o.

Reports, Freedmen's Aid Society, Presbyterian Church.

Robert R. Semple. History of the rise and progress of Baptists in Virginia. Richmond, 1810.

William J. Simmons. Men of Mark, Eminent, Progressive and Rising. Cleveland. Ohio.

Slavery as it is; the testimony of a thousand witnesses. Publication of Anti-Slavery Society. New York, 1839.

George Smith. History of Wesleyan Methodism. London, 1862.

David Spencer. Early Baptists of Philadelphia. Philadelphia, 1877.

William B. Sprague. Annals of the American Pulpit. New York, 1858.

Benjamin T. Tanner. An outline of history and government for A. M. E. Churchman. Philadelphia, 1884.

An apology for African Methodism. Baltimore, 1867.

H. M. Turner. Methodist Polity. Philadelphia.

United States Census, 1890. Churches.

A. W. Wayman. My Recollections of A. M. E. Ministers. Philadelphia, 1883.

S. D. Weld. American Slavery as it is: testimony of thousands of witnesses. New York, 1839.

Stephen B. Weeks. Anti-slavery sentiment in the South. Washington, D. C., 1898. Southern Quakers and Slavery. Baltimore, 1896.

George W. Williams. History of the Negro race in America. New York, 1883.

White The African Preacher.

THE NEGRO CHURCH

1. Primitive Negro Religion. The prominent characteristic of primitive Negro religion is Nature worship with the accompanying strong belief in sorcery. There is a theistic tendency: "Almost all tribes believe in some supreme god without always worshiping him, generally a heaven and rain god; sometimes, as among the Cameroons and in Dahomey, a sun-god. But the most widely-spread worship among Negroes and Negroids, from west to northeast and south to Loango, is that of the moon, combined with a great veneration of the cow."* The slave trade so mingled and demoralized the west coast of Africa for four hundred years that it is difficult to-day to find there definite remains of any great religious system. Ellis tells us of the spirit belief of the Ewne people; they believe that men and all Nature have the indwelling "Kra," which is immortal. That the man himself after death may exist as a ghost, which is often conceived of as departed from the "Kra," a shadowy continuing of the man. So Bryce, speaking of the Kaffirs of South Africa, a branch of the great Bantu tribe, says:

"To the Kaffirs, as to the most savage races, the world was full of spirits—spirits of the rivers, the mountains, and the woods. Most important were the ghosts of the dead, who had power to injure or help the living, and who were, therefore, propitiated by offerings at stated periods, as well as on occasions when their aid was especially desired. This kind of worship, the worship once most generally diffused throughout the world, and which held its ground among the Greeks and Italians in the most flourishing period of ancient civilization, as it does in China and Japan to-day, was, and is, virtually the religion of the Kaffirs."

The supreme being of the Bantus is the dimly conceived Molimo, the Unseen, who typifies vaguely the unknown powers of nature or of the sky. Among some tribes the worship of such higher spirits has banished fetichism and belief in witchcraft, but among most of the African tribes the sudden and violent changes in government and social organization have tended to overthrow the larger religious conceptions and leave fetichism and witchcraft supreme. This is particularly true on the west coast among the spawn of the slave traders.

There can be no reasonable doubt, however, but that the scattered remains of religious systems in Africa to-day among the Negro tribes

---

* Professor C. P. Thiele, in Encyclopedia Britannica, 9th ed., XX, p. 362.

are survivals of the religious ideas upon which the Egyptian religion was based, and that the basis of the religion of Egypt was "of a purely Negritian character." *

The early Christian church had an Exarchate of fifty-two dioceses in Northern Africa, but it probably seldom came in contact with purely Negro tribes on account of the Sahara. The hundred dioceses of the patriarchate of Alexandria, on the other hand, embraced Libya, Penta-polis, Egypt, and Abyssinia, and had a large number of Negroid mem-bers. In Western Africa, after the voyage of Da Gama, there were several kingdoms of Negroes nominally Catholic, and the church claimed several hundred thousand communicants. These were on the slave coast and on the eastern coast.

Mohammedanism entered Africa in the seventh and eighth centuries and has since that time conquered nearly all Northern Africa, the Soudan, and made inroads into the populations of the west coast. "The introduction of Islam into Central and West Africa has been the most important if not the sole preservation against the desolations of the slave-trade,"† and especially is it preserving the natives against the desolations of Christian rum.

2. Effect of Transplanting. It ought not to be forgotten that each Negro slave brought to America during the four centuries of the Afri-can slave trade was taken from definite and long-formed habits of social, political, and religious life. These ideas were not the highest, measured by modern standards, but they were far from the lowest, measured by the standards of primitive man. The unit of African tribal organization was the clan or family of families ruled by the pat-riarch or his strongest successor; these clans were united into tribes ruled by hereditary or elected chiefs, and some tribes were more or less loosely federated into kingdoms. The families were polygamous, com-munistic groups, with one father and as many mothers as his wealth and station permitted; the family lived together in a cluster of homes, or sometimes a whole clan or village in a long, low apartment house. In such clans the idea of private property was but imperfectly devel-oped, and never included land. The main mass of visible wealth be-longed to the family and clan rather than to the individual; only in the matter of weapons and ornaments was exclusive private ownership generally recognized.

The government, vested in fathers and chiefs, varied in different tribes from absolute despotisms to limited monarchies, almost republi-can. Viewing the Basuto National Assembly in South Africa, Mr. Bryce recently wrote:

---

* Encyclopedia Britannica, 9th ed., XX, p. 362.

† Blyden, *Meth. Quar. Review*, Jan. 1871. See also his Christianity, Islam and the Negro Race.

"The resemblance to the primary assemblies of the early peoples of Europe is close enough to add another to the arguments which discredit the theory that there is any such thing as an 'Aryan Type' of institutions." *

In administering justice and protecting women these governments were as effective as most primitive organizations.

The power of religion was represented by the priest or medicine man. Aided by an unfaltering faith, natural sharpness and some rude knowledge of medicine, and supported by the vague sanctions of a half-seen world peopled by spirits, good and evil, the African priest wielded a power second only to that of the chief, and often superior to it. In some tribes the African priesthood was organized and something like systematic religious institutions emerged. But the central fact of African life, political, social and religious, is its failure to integrate—to unite and systematize itself in some conquering whole which should dominate the wayward parts. This is the central problem of civilization, and while there have arisen from time to time in Africa conquering kingdoms, and some consolidation of power in religion, it has been continually overthrown before it was strong enough to maintain itself independently. What have been the causes of this? They have been threefold: the physical peculiarities of Africa, the character of external conquest, and the slave-trade—the "heart disease of Africa." The physical peculiarities of the land shut out largely the influence of foreign civilization and religion and made human organization a difficult fight for survival against heat and disease; foreign conquest took the form of sudden incursions, causing vast migrations and uprooting of institutions and beliefs, or of colonizations of strong, hostile and alien races, and finally for four centuries the slave-trade fed on Africa, and peaceful evolution in political organization or religious belief was impossible.

Especially did the slave-trade ruin religious evolution on the west coast; the ancient kingdoms were overthrown and changed, tribes and nations mixed and demoralized, and a perfect chaos of ideas left. Here it was that animal worship, fetichism and belief in sorcery and witchcraft strengthened their sway and gained wider currency than ever.

The first social innovation that followed the transplanting of the Negro was the substitution of the West Indian plantation for the tribal and clan life of Africa. The real significance of this change will not appear at first glance. The despotic political power of the chief was now vested in the white master; the clan had lost its ties of blood relationship and became simply the aggregation of individuals on a plot of ground, with common rules and customs, common dwellings, and a certain communism in property. The two greatest changes, however, were, first, the enforcement of severe and unremitted toil, and, second,

---

* Impressions of S. Africa, 3rd ed., p. 352.

the establishment of a new polygamy—a new family life. These social innovations were introduced with much difficulty and met determined resistance on the part of the slaves, especially when there was community of blood and language. Gradually, however, superior force and organized methods prevailed, and the plantation became the unit of a new development. The enforcement of continual toil was not the most revolutionary change which the plantation introduced. Where this enforced labor did not descend to barbarism and slow murder, it was not bad discipline; the African had the natural indolence of a tropical nature which had never felt the necessity of work; his first great awakening came with hard labor, and a pity it was, not that he worked, but that voluntary labor on his part was not from the first encouraged and rewarded. The vast and overshadowing change that the plantation system introduced was the change in the status of women—the new polygamy. This new polygamy had all the evils and not one of the safeguards of the African prototype. The African system was a complete protection for girls, and a strong protection for wives against everything but the tyranny of the husband; the plantation polygamy left the chastity of Negro women absolutely unprotected in law, and practically little guarded in custom. The number of wives of a native African was limited and limited very effectually by the number of cattle he could command or his prowess in war. The number of wives of a West India slave was limited chiefly by his lust and cunning. The black females, were they wives or growing girls, were the legitimate prey of the men, and on this system there was one, and only one, safeguard, the character of the master of the plantation. Where the master was himself lewd and avaricious the degradation of the women was complete. Where, on the other hand, the plantation system reached its best development, as in Virginia, there was a fair approximation of a monogamic marriage system among the slaves; and yet even here, on the best conducted plantations, the protection of Negro women was but imperfect; the seduction of girls was frequent, and seldom did an illegitimate child bring shame, or an adulterous wife punishment to the Negro quarters.

And this was inevitable, because on the plantation the private home, as a self-protective, independent unit, did not exist. That powerful institution, the polygamous African home, was almost completely destroyed and in its place in America arose sexual promiscuity, a weak community life, with common dwelling, meals and child-nurseries. The internal slave trade tended to further weaken natural ties. A small number of favored house servants and artisans were raised above this—had their private homes, came in contact with the culture of the master class, and assimilated much of American civilization. Nevertheless, broadly speaking, the greatest social effect of American slavery was to substitute for the polygamous Negro home a new polygamy less guarded, less effective, and less civilized.

At first sight it would seem that slavery completely destroyed every vestige of spontaneous social movement among the Negroes; the home had deteriorated; political authority and economic initiative was in the hands of the masters, property, as a social institution, did not exist on the plantation, and, indeed, it is usually assumed by historians and sociologists that every vestige of internal development disappeared, leaving the slaves no means of expression for their common life, thought, and striving. This is not strictly true; the vast power of the priest in the African state has already been noted; his realm alone— the province of religion and medicine—remained largely unaffected by the plantation system in many important particulars. The Negro priest, therefore, early became an important figure on the plantation and found his function as the interpreter of the supernatural, the comforter of the sorrowing, and as the one who expressed, rudely, but picturesquely, the longing and disappointment and resentment of a stolen people. From such beginnings arose and spread with marvellous rapidity the Negro Church, the first distinctively Negro American social institution. It was not at first by any means a Christian Church, but a mere adaptation of those heathen rites which we roughly designate by the term Obe Worship, or "Voodoism." Association and missionary effort soon gave these rites a veneer of Christianity, and gradually, after two centuries, the Church became Christian, with a simple Calvinistic creed, but with many of the old customs still clinging to the services. It is this historic fact that the Negro Church of to-day bases itself upon the sole surviving social institution of the African fatherland, that accounts for its extraordinary growth and vitality. We easily forget that in the United States to-day there is a Church organization for every sixty Negro families. This institution, therefore, naturally assumed many functions which the other harshly suppressed social organs had to surrender; the Church became the center of amusements, of what little spontaneous economic activity remained, of education, and of all social intercourse.

3. The Obeah Sorcery. Let us now trace this development historically. The slaves arrived with a strong tendency to Nature worship and a belief in witchcraft common to all. Beside this some had more or less vague ideas of a supreme being and higher religious ideas, while a few were Mohammedans, and fewer Christians. Some actual priests were transported and others assumed the functions of priests, and soon a degraded form of African religion and witchcraft appeared in the West Indies, which was known as Obi,* or sorcery. The French Creoles

---

* Obi (Obeah, Obiah or Obia), is the adjective : Obe or Obi, the noun. It is of African origin, probably connected with Egyptian Ob, Aub, or Obron, meaning serpent. Moses forbids Israelites ever to consult the demon Ob, i. e., "Charmer, Wizard." The Witch of Endor is called Oub or Ob. Oubaous is the name of the Baselisk or Royal Serpent, emblem of the Sun, and, according to Horus Appollo, "ancient oracular Deity of Africa."—Edwards, West Indies, II, pp. 106–119.

called it "Waldensian" (Vaudois), because of the witchcraft charged against the wretched followers of Peter Waldo, whence comes the dialect name of Voodoo or Hoodoo, used in the United States. Edwards gives as sensible an account of this often exaggerated form of witchcraft and medicine as one can get:

"As far as we are able to decide from our own experience and information when we lived in the island, and from the current testimony of all the Negroes we have ever conversed with on the subject, the professors of Obi are, and always were, natives of Africa, and none other; and they have brought the science with them from thence to Jamaica, where it is so universally practiced, that we believe there are few of the large estates possessing native Africans, which have not one or more of them. The oldest and most crafty are those who usually attract the greatest devotion and confidence; those whose hoary heads, and a somewhat peculiarly harsh and forbidding aspect, together with some skill in plants of the medical and poisonous species, have qualified them for successful imposition upon the weak and credulous. The Negroes in general, whether Africans or Creoles, revere, consult, and fear them. To these oracles they resort, and with the most implicit faith, upon all occasions, whether for the cure of disorders, the obtaining revenge for injuries or insults, the conciliating of favor, the discovery and punishment of the thief or adulterer, and the prediction of future events. The trade which these imposters carry on is extremely lucrative; they manufacture and sell their Obeis adapted to the different cases and at different prices. A veil of mystery is studiously thrown over their incantations, to which the midnight hours are allotted, and every precaution is taken to conceal them from the knowledge and discovery of the White people."*

At first the system was undoubtedly African and part of some more or less general religious system. It finally degenerated into mere imposture. There would seem to have been some traces of blood sacrifice and worship of the Moon, but unfortunately those who have written on the subject have not been serious students of a curious human phenomenon, but rather persons apparently unable to understand why a transplanted slave should cling to heathen rites.

4. Slavery and Christianity. The most obvious reason for the spread of witchcraft and persistence of heathen rites among Negro slaves was the fact that at first no effort was made by masters to offer them anything better. The reason for this was the widespread idea that it was contrary to law to hold Christians as slaves. One can realize the weight of this if we remember that the Diet of Worms and Sir John Hawkins' voyages were but a generation apart. From the time of the Crusades to the Lutheran revolt the feeling of Christian brotherhood had been growing, and it was pretty well established by the end of the sixteenth century that it was illegal and irreligious for Christians to hold each other as slaves for life. This did not mean any widespread abhorrence of forced labor from serfs or apprentices and it was par-

---

*Edwards: West Indies, II, 108-109.

ticularly linked with the idea that the enslavement of the heathen was meritorious, since it punished their blasphemy on the one hand and gave them a chance for conversion on the other.

When, therefore, the slave-trade from Africa began it met only feeble opposition here and there. That opposition was in nearly all cases stilled when it was continually stated that the slave-trade was simply a method of converting the heathen to Christianity. The corrollary that the conscience of Europe immediately drew was that after conversion the Negro slave was to become in all essential respects like other servants and laborers, that is bound to toil, perhaps, under general regulations, but personally free with recognized rights and duties.

Most colonists believed that this was not only actually right, but according to English law. And while they early began to combat the idea they continually doubted the legality of their action in English courts. In 1635 we find the authorities of Providence islands condemning Mr. Reshworth's behavior concerning the Negroes who ran away, as indiscreet, "arising, as it seems, from a groundless opinion that Christians may not lawfully keep such persons in a state of servitude during their strangeness from Christianity," and injurious to themselves. *

The colonies early began cautiously to declare that certain distinctions lay between "Christian" inhabitants and slaves, whether they were Christians or not. Maryland, for instance, proposed a law, in 1638, which failed of passage. It was:

"For the liberties of the people" and declared "all Christian inhabitants (slaves only excepted) to have and enjoy all such rights, liberties, immunities, privileges and free customs, within this province, as any natural born subject of England hath or ought to have or enjoy in the realm of England, saving in such cases as the same are or may be altered or changed by the laws and ordinances of this province."†

The question arose in different form in Massachusetts when it was enacted that only church members could vote. If Negroes joined the church, would they become free voters of the commonwealth? It seemed hardly possible.‡ Nevertheless, up to 1660 or thereabouts it seemed accepted in most colonies and in the English West Indies that baptism into a Christian church would free a Negro slave. Massachusetts first apparently attacked this idea by enacting in 1641 that slavery should be confined to captives in just wars "and such strangers as willingly sell themselves or are sold to us," meaning by "strangers" apparently heathen, but saying nothing as to the effect of conversion. Connecticut adopted similar legislation in 1650 and Virginia declared

---

* Sainsbury : Calendar of State Papers, 1574–1660, ¶ 262.

† Williams' History of the Negro Race, I, 239.

‡ *Ibid* I, 190.

in 1661 that Negroes "are incapable of making satisfaction" for time
lost in running away by lengthening their time of service, thus imply-
ing that they were slaves for life, and Maryland declared flatly in 1663
that Negro slaves should serve "*durante rita.*" In Barbadoes the Council presented, in 1663, an act to the Assembly recommending the
christening of Negro children and the instruction of all adult Negroes
to the several ministers of the place.

At the same time in the ready-made Duke of York's laws sent over
to the new colony of New York in 1664 the old idea seems to prevail:

" No Christian shall be kept in bondslavery, villenage, or captivity, except such
who shall be judged thereunto by authority, or such as willingly have sold or
shall sell themselves, in which case a record of such servitude shall be entered in
the Court of Sessions held for that jurisdiction where such masters shall inhabit,
provided that nothing in the law contained shall be to the prejudice of master or
dame who have or shall by any indenture or covenant take apprentices for term of
years, or other servants for term of years or life." *

It was not until 1667 that Virginia finally plucked up courage to
attack the issue squarely and declared by law:

" Baptisme doth not alter the condition of the person as to his bondage or freedom, in order that diverse masters freed from this doubt may more carefully
endeavor the propagation of Christianity." *

Following this Virginia took three further decisive steps in 1670, 1682,
and 1705. First she declared that only slaves imported from Christian
lands should be free. Next she excepted Negroes and mulattoes from
even this restriction unless they were born of Christians and were
Christians when taken in slavery. Finally only personal Christianity
in Africa or actual freedom in a Christian country excepted a Virginia
Negro slave from life-long slavery.†

This changing attitude of Christians toward Negroes was reflected in
Locke's Fundamental Constitutions for Carolina in 1670, one article of
which said:

"Since charity obliges us to wish well to the souls of all men, and religion ought
to alter nothing in any man's civil estate or right, it shall be lawful for slaves as
well as others to enter themselves and to be of what church or profession any of
them shall think best, and thereof be as fully members as any freeman. But yet
no slave shall hereby be exempted from that civil dominion his master hath over
him, but be in all things in the same state and condition he was in before." ‡

So much did this please the Carolinians that it was one of the few
articles re-enacted in the Constitution of 1698. In 1671 Maryland was
moved to pass "An Act for the Encouraging of the Importation of
Negroes and Slaves." This law declared that conversion or the holy

---

* Williams I, 139.

† Ballagh, pp. 47–52.

‡ Bassett: Slavery in Colony of N. C., p. 41.

sacrament of baptism should not be taken to give manumission in any way to slaves or their issue who had become Christians or had been or should be baptized either before or after their importation to Maryland, "any opinion to the contrary notwithstanding."

It was explained that this law was passed because "several of the good people of this province have been discouraged from importing or purchasing therein any Negroes or other slaves; and such as have imported or purchased any there have neglected—to the great displeasure of Almighty God and the prejudice of the souls of those poor people— to instruct them in the Christian faith, and to permit them to receive the holy sacrament of baptism for the remission of their sin, under the mistaken and ungrounded apprehension that their slaves by becoming Christians would thereby be freed." * This law was re-enacted in 1692 and 1715.

It is clear from these citations that in the seventeenth century not only was there little missionary effort to convert Negro slaves, but that there was on the contrary positive refusal to let slaves be converted, and that this refusal was one incentive to explicit statements of the doctrine of perpetual slavery for Negroes. The French Code Noir of 1685 made baptism and religious instruction of Negroes obligatory. We find no such legislation in English colonies. On the contrary, the principal Secretary of State is informed in 1670 that in Jamaica the number of tippling houses has greatly increased, and many planters are ruined by drink. "So interests decrease, Negroes and slaves increase. There is much cruelty, oppression, rape, whoredoms, and adulteries."†

In Massachusetts John Eliot and Cotton Mather both are much concerned that "so little care was taken of their (the Negroes') precious and immortal souls," which were left to "a destroying ignorance merely for fear of thereby losing the benefit of their vassalage."

So throughout the colonies it is reported in 1678 that masters, "out of covetousness," are refusing to allow their slaves to be baptized; and in 1700 there is an earnest plea in Massachusetts for religious instruction of Negroes since it is "notorious" that masters discourage the "poor creatures" from baptism. In 1709 a Carolina clergyman writes to the secretary of the Society for the Propagation of the Gospel in England that only a few of 200 or more Negroes in his community were taught Christianity, but were not allowed to be baptized. Another minister writes, a little later, that he prevailed upon a master after much importuning to allow three Negroes to be baptized. In North Carolina in 1709 a clergyman of the Established Church complains that masters will not allow their slaves to be baptized for fear that a Christian slave is by law free. A few were instructed in religion, but not baptized. The Society for the Propagation of the Gospel combated

---

* Brackett, p. 29.

† Sainsbury's Calendars, 1669–74, ¶ 138.

this notion vigorously. Later, in 1732, Bishop Berkeley reports that few Negroes have been received into the church.* This state of affairs led to further laws, and the instructions to some of the royal Governors contain a clause ordering them to "find out the best means to facilitate and encourage the conversion of Negroes and Indians to the Christian religion."† New York hastened to join the States which sought to reassure masters, declaring in 1706:

"Whereas, Divers of her Majesty's good subjects, inhabitants of this colony, now are, and have been willing that such Negroes, Indian and Mulatto slaves, who belong to them, and desire the same, should be baptized, but are deterred and hindered therefrom by reason of a groundless opinion that hath spread itself in this colony, that by the baptizing of such Negro, Indian or Mulatto slaves, they would become free, and ought to be set at liberty. In order, therefore, to put an end to all such doubts and scruples as have, or hereafter any time may arise about the same:

"Be it enacted, etc., That the baptizing of a Negro, Indian, or Mullatto slave shall not be any cause or reason for the setting them, or any of them, at liberty.

"And be it, etc., That all and every Negro, Indian, Mullatto and Mestee bastard child and children, who is, are, and shall be born of any Negro, Indian, or Mestee, shall follow the state and condition of the mother and be esteemed, reputed, taken and adjudged a slave and slaves to all intents and purposes whatsoever."‡

In 1729 an appeal from several colonies was made to England on the subject in order to increase the conversion of blacks. The Crown Attorney and Solicitor General replied that baptism in no way changed the slave's status.§

5. Early Restrictions. "In the year 1624, a few years after the arrival of the first slave ship at Jamestown, Va., a Negro child was baptized and called William, and from that time on in almost all, if not all, the oldest churches in the South, the names of Negroes baptized into the church of God can be found upon the registers." ‖

It was easy to make such cases an argument for more slaves. James Habersham, the Georgia companion of the Methodist Whitefield, said about 1730:

"I once thought it was unlawful to keep Negro slaves, but I am now induced to think God may have a higher end in permitting them to be brought to this Christian country, than merely to support their masters. Many of the poor slaves in America have already been made freemen of the heavenly Jerusalem and possibly a time may come when many thousands may embrace the gospel, and thereby be brought into the glorious liberty of the children of God. These, and other considerations, appear to plead strongly for a limited use of Negroes; for, while we can buy provisions in Carolina cheaper than we can here, no one will be induced to plant much."

---

* Brackett, p. 31. Bassett: Slavery in Colony of N. C.; p. 46.

† Instructions of Lord Cornbury of Va., 702. Williams I, 140.

‡ Williams I, p. 141.

§ Brackett, p. 30.   ‖ Archdeacon J. H. M. Pollard.

In other cases there were curious attempts to blend religion and expediency, as for instance, in 1710, when a Massachusetts clergyman evolved a marriage ceremony for Negroes in which the bride solemnly promised to cleave to her husband "so long as God in his Providence" and the slave-trade let them live together!

The gradual increase of these Negro Christians, however, brought peculiar problems. Clergymen, despite the law, were reproached for taking Negroes into the church and still allowing them to be held as slaves. On the other hand it was not easy to know how to deal with the black church member after he was admitted. He must either be made a subordinate member of a white church or a member of a Negro church under the general supervision of whites. As the efforts of missionaries, like Dr. Bray, slowly increased the number of converts, both these systems were adopted. But the black congregations here and there soon aroused the suspicion and fear of the masters, and as early as 1715 North Carolina passed an act which declared:

"That if any master or owner of Negroes or slaves, or any other person or persons whatsoever in the government, shall permit or suffer any Negro or Negroes to build on their, or either of their, lands, or any part thereof, any house under pretense of a meeting-house upon account of worship, or upon any pretense whatsoever, and shall not suppress and hinder them, he, she, or they so offending, shall, for every default, forfeit and pay fifty pounds, one-half toward defraying the contingent charges of the government, the other to him or them that shall sue for the same."*

This made Negro members of white churches a necessity in this colony, and there was the same tendency in other colonies. "Maryland passed a law in 1723 to suppress tumultuous meetings of slaves on Sabbath and other holy days," a measure primarily for good order, but also tending to curb independent religious meetings among Negroes. In 1800 complaints of Negro meetings were heard. Georgia in 1770 forbade slaves "to assemble on pretense of feasting," etc., and "any constable," on direction of a justice, is commanded to disperse any assembly or meeting of slaves "which may disturb the peace or endanger the safety of his Majesty's subjects; and every slave which may be found at such meeting, as aforesaid, shall and may, by order of such justice, immediately be corrected, without trial, by receiving on the bare back twenty-five stripes, with a whip, switch, or cowskin," etc.† In 1792 in a Georgia act "to protect religious societies in the exercise of their religious duties," punishment was provided for persons disturbing white congregations, but "no congregation or company of Negroes shall upon pretense of divine worship assemble themselves" contrary to the act of 1770. Whether or not such acts tended to curb the really religious meetings of the slaves or not it is not easy to know. Probably they did, although at the same time there was probably much disorder and

---

* Lapsed in 1741. See Laws of 1715, Ch. 46, Sec. 18; Bassett: Colony, p. 50.
† Prince's Digest, 447.

turmoil among slaves, which sought to cloak itself under the name of the church. This was natural, for such assemblies were the only surviving African organizations, and they epitomized all there was in slave life outside of forced toil.

It gradually became true, as Brackett says, that "any privileges of church-going which slaves might enjoy depended much, as with children, on the disposition of the masters." * In some colonies, like North Carolina, masters continued indifferent throughout the larger part of the eighteenth century. In New Hanover county of that state out of a thousand whites and two thousand slaves, 307 masters were baptized in 1742, but only nine slaves. The English are told of continued indifference in Massachusetts, the Connecticut General Assembly is asked in 1738 if masters ought not to promise to train slaves as Christians, and instructions are repeatedly given to Governors on the matter, with but small results.†

6. The Society for the Propagation of the Gospel.‡ "The Society for the Propagation of the Gospel in Foreign Parts" was incorporated under William III, on the 16th day of June, 1701, and the first meeting of the society under its charter was the 27th of June of the same year. Thomas Laud, Bishop of Canterbury, Primate and Metropolitan of all England, was appointed by his majesty the first president.

This society was formed with the view, primarily, of supplying the destitution of religious institutions and privileges among the inhabitants of the North American colonies, members of the established church of England; and, secondarily, of extending the gospel to the Indians and Negroes. The society entered upon its duties with zeal, being patronized by the king and all the dignitaries of the Church of England.

They instituted inquiries into the religious condition of all the colonies, responded to "by the governors and persons of the best note," (with special reference to Episcopacy), and they perceived that their work "consisted of three great branches: the care and instruction of our people settled in the colonies; the conversion of the Indian savages, and the conversion of the Negroes." Before appointing missionaries they sent out a traveling preacher, the Rev. George Keith (an itinerant missionary), who associated with himself the Rev. John Talbot. Mr. Keith preached between North Carolina and Piscataqua river in New England, a tract above eight hundred miles in length, and completed his mission in two years, and returned and reported his labors to the society.

The annual meetings of this society were regularly held from 1702 to 1819 and 118 sermons preached before it by bishops of the Church of

---

* Brackett, pp. 108-110.　　　† Bassett: Colony, p. 49; Williams I, p. 188.

‡ This section is taken largely from Charles Colcock Jones' "The Religious Instruction of the Negroes," Savannah, 1842.

England, a large number of them distinguished for piety, learning, and zeal.

In June, 1702, the Rev. Samuel Thomas, the first missionary, was sent to the colony of South Carolina. The society designed he should attempt the conversion of the Yammosee Indians; but the governor, Sir Nathaniel Johnson, appointed him to the care of the people settled on the three branches of Cooper river, making Goose creek his residence. He reported his labors to the society and said "that he had taken much pains also in instructing the Negroes, and learned twenty of them to read." He died in October, 1706. He was succeeded by a number of missionaries.

"In 1709 Mr. Huddlestone was appointed school-master in New York city. He taught forty poor children out of the society funds, and publicly catechised in the steeple of Trinity Church every Sunday in the afternoon, 'not only his own scholars, but also the children, servants and slaves of the inhabitants, and above one hundred usually attended him.'

"The society established also a catechising school in New York city in 1704, in which there were computed to be about 1,500 Negro and Indian slaves. The society hoped their example would be generally followed in the colonies. Mr. Elias Neau, a French Protestant, was appointed catechist, who was very zealous in his duty, and many Negroes were instructed and baptized.

"In 1712 the Negroes in New York conspired to destroy all the English, which greatly discouraged the work of their instruction. The conspiracy was defeated, and many Negroes taken and executed. Mr. Neau's school was blamed as the main occasion of the barbarous plot; two of Mr. Neau's students were charged with the plot; one was cleared and the other was proved to have been in the conspiracy, but guiltless of his master's murder. 'Upon full trial the guilty Negroes were found to be such as never came to Mr. Neau's school; and, what is very observable, the persons whose Negroes were found most guilty were such as were the declared opposers of making them Christians.' In a short time the cry against the instruction of the Negroes subsided: the governor visited and recommended the school. Mr. Neau died in 1722, much regretted by all who knew his labors." He was succeeded by Rev. Mr. Wetmore, who afterwards was appointed missionary to Rye in New York. After his removal "the rector, church wardens, and vestry of Trinity Church in New York city" requested another catechist, "there being about 1,400 Negro and Indian slaves, a considerable number of whom had been instructed in the principles of Christianity by the late Mr. Neau, and had received baptism and were communicants in their church. The society complied with this request and sent over Rev. Mr. Colgan in 1726, who conducted the school with success."*

* Cf. Atlanta University Publications, No. 6.

The society looked upon the instruction and conversion of the Negroes as a principal branch of its care, esteeming it a great reproach to the Christian name that so many thousands of persons should continue in the same state of pagan darkness under a Christian government and living in Christian families as they lay under formerly in their own heathen countries. The society immediately from its first institution strove to promote their conversion, and inasmuch as its income would not enable it to send numbers of catechists sufficient to instruct the Negroes, yet it resolved to do its utmost, and at least to give this work the mark of its highest approbation. Its officers wrote, therefore, to all their missionaries that they should use their best endeavors at proper times to instruct the Negroes, and should especially take occasion to recommend zealously to the masters to order their slaves, at convenient times, to come to them that they might be instructed.

The history of the society goes on to say: "It is a matter of commendation to the clergy that they have done thus much in so great and difficult a work. But, alas! what is the instruction of a few hundreds in several years with respect to the many thousands uninstructed, unconverted, living, dying, utter pagans. It must be confessed what hath been done is as nothing with regard to what a true Christian would hope to see effected." After stating several difficulties in respect to the religious instruction of the Negroes, it is said: "But the greatest obstruction is the masters themselves do not consider enough the obligation which lies upon them to have their slaves instructed." And in another place, "the society have always been sensible the most effectual way to convert the Negroes was by engaging their masters to countenance and promote their conversion." The bishop of St. Asaph, Dr. Fleetwood, preached a sermon before the society in the year 1711, setting forth the duty of instructing the Negroes in the Christian religion. The society thought this so useful a discourse that they printed and dispersed abroad in the plantations great numbers of that sermon in the same year; and in the year 1725 reprinted the same and dispersed again great numbers. The bishop of London, Dr. Gibson, (to whom the care of plantations abroad, as to religious affairs, was committed,) became a second advocate for the conversion of Negroes, and wrote two letters on the subject. The first in 1727, "addressed to masters and mistresses of families in the English plantations abroad, exhorting them to encourage and promote the instruction of their Negroes in the Christian faith. The second in the same year, addressed to the missionaries there, directing them to distribute the said letter, and exhorting them to give their assistance towards the instruction of the Negroes within their several parishes."

The society were persuaded this was the true method to remove the great obstruction to their conversion, and hoping so particular an application to the masters and mistresses from the See of London would have the strongest influence, they printed ten thousand copies of the letter to the masters and mistresses, which were sent to all the colonies on the continent and to all the British islands in the West Indies, to be distributed among the masters of families, and all other inhabitants. The society received accounts that these letters influenced many masters of families to have their servants instructed. The bishop of London soon after wrote "an address to serious Christians among ourselves, to assist the Society for Propagating the Gospel in carrying on this work."

In the year 1783, and the following, soon after the separation of our colonies from the mother country, the society's operations ceased, leaving in all the colonies forty-three missionaries, two of whom were in the Southern States—one in North and one in South Carolina. The affectionate valediction of the society to them was issued in 1785. "Thus terminated the connection of this noble society with our country, which, from the foregoing notices of its efforts, must have accomplished a great deal for the religious instruction of the Negro population."

7. The Moravians, Methodists, Baptists, and Presbyterians.* The Moravians or United Brethren were the first who formally attempted the establishment of missions exclusively to the Negroes.

A succinct account of their several efforts, down to the year 1790, is given in the report of the Society for the Propagation of the Gospel among the Heathen, at Salem, N. C., October 5th, 1837, by Rev. J. Renatus Schmidt, and is as follows:

"A hundred years have now elapsed since the Renewed Church of the Brethren first attempted to communicate the gospel to the many thousand Negroes of our land. In 1737 Count Zinzendorf paid a visit to London and formed an acquaintance with General Oglethorpe and the trustees of Georgia, with whom he conferred on the subject of the mission to the Indians, which the brethren had already established in that colony (in 1735). Some of these gentlemen were associates under the will of Dr. Bray, who had left funds to be devoted to the conversion of the Negro slaves in South Carolina; and they solicited the Count to procure them some missionaries for this purpose. On his objecting that the Church of England might hesitate to recognize the ordination of the Brethren's missionaries, they referred the question to the Archbishop of Canterbury, Dr. Potter, who gave it as his opinion 'that the Brethren being members of an Episcopal Church, whose doctrines contained nothing repugnant to the Thirty-nine Articles, ought not to be denied free access to the heathen.' This declaration not only removed all hesitation from the minds of the trustees as to the present application, but opened the way for the labors of the Brethren amongst the slave population of the West Indies, a great and blessed work, which has, by the gracious help of God, gone on increasing even to the present day.

"Various proprietors, however, avowing their determination not to suffer strangers to instruct their Negroes, as they had their own ministers, whom they paid

---

* This section is largely based on Jones. See ¶6.

for that purpose, our brethren ceased from their efforts. It appears from the letters of Brother Spangenburg, who spent the greater part of the year 1749 at Philadelphia and preached the gospel to the Negroes in that city, that the labors of the Brethren amongst them were not entirely fruitless. Thus he writes in 1751: 'On my arrival in Philadelphia, I saw numbers of Negroes still buried in all their native ignorance and darkness, and my soul was grieved for them. Soon after some of them came to me, requesting instruction, at the same time acknowledging their ignorance in the most affecting manner. They begged that a weekly sermon might be delivered expressly for their benefit. I complied with their request and confined myself to the most essential truths of scripture. Upwards of seventy Negroes attended on these occasions, several of whom were powerfully awakened, applied for further instruction, and expressed a desire to be united to Christ and his church by the sacrament of baptism, which was accordingly administered to them.'"

At the request of Mr. Knox, the English Secretary of State, an attempt was made to evangelize the Negroes of Georgia. "In 1774 the Brethren, Lewis Muller, of the Academy at Niesky, and George Wagner, were called to North America and in the year following, having been joined by Brother Andrew Broesing, of North Carolina, they took up their abode at Knoxborough, a plantation so called from its proprietor, the gentleman above mentioned. They were, however, almost constant sufferers from the fevers which prevailed in those parts, and Muller finished his course in October of the same year. He had preached the gospel with acceptance to both whites and blacks, yet without any abiding results. The two remaining Brethren being called upon to bear arms on the breaking out of the war of independence, Broesing repaired to Wachovia, in North Carolina, and Wagner set out in 1779 for England."

In the great Northampton revival, under the preaching of Dr. Edwards in 1735-6, when for the space of five or six weeks together the conversions averaged at least "four a day," Dr. Edwards remarks: "There are several Negroes who, from what was seen in them then and what is discernible in them since, appear to have been truly born again in the late remarkable season."

Direct efforts for the religious instruction of Negroes, continued through a series of years, were made by Presbyterians in Virginia. They commenced with the Rev. Samuel Davies, afterwards president of Nassau Hall, and the Rev. John Todd, of Hanover Presbytery.

In a letter addressed to a friend and member of the "Society in London for promoting Christian knowledge among the poor" in the year 1755, he thus expresses himself: "The poor neglected Negroes, who are so far from having money to purchase books, that they themselves are the property of others, who were originally African savages, and never heard of the name of Jesus or his gospel until they arrived at the land of their slavery in America, whom their masters generally neglect, and whose souls none care for, as though immortality were not a privilege common to them, as with their masters;

these poor, unhappy Africans are objects of my compassion, and I
think the most proper objects of the society's charity. The inhabitants of Virginia are computed to be about 300,000 men, the one-half
of which number are supposed to be Negroes. The number of those
who attend my ministry at particular times is uncertain, but generally about 300, who give a stated attendance; and never have I been
so struck with the appearance of an assembly as when I have glanced
my eye to that part of the meeting-house where they usually sit,
adorned (for so it has appeared to me) with so many black countenances,
eagerly attentive to every word they hear and frequently bathed in
tears. A considerable number of them (about a hundred) have been
baptized, after a proper time for instruction, having given credible
evidence, not only of their acquaintance with the important doctrines
of the Christian religion, but also a deep sense of them in their
minds, attested by a life of strict piety and holiness. As they are
not sufficiently polished to dissemble with a good grace, they express
the sentiments of their souls so much in the language of simple nature and with such genuine indications of sincerity, that it is impossible to suspect their professions, especially when attended with a
truly Christian life and exemplary conduct. There are multitudes of
them in different places, who are willingly and eagerly desirous to be
instructed and embrace every opportunity of acquainting themselves
with the doctrines of the gospel; and though they have generally very
little help to learn to read, yet to my agreeable surprise, many of
them by dint of application in their leisure hours, have made such
progress that they can intelligibly read a plain author, and especially
their Bibles; and pity it is that any of them should be without them.

"The Negroes, above all the human species that I ever knew, have
an ear for music and a kind of ecstatic delight in psalmody, and there
are no books they learn so soon or take so much pleasure in as those
used in that heavenly part of divine worship."

The year 1747 was marked, in the colony of Georgia, by the authorized introduction of slaves. Twenty-three representatives from
the different districts met in Savannah, and after appointing Major
Horton president, they entered into sundry resolutions, the substance
of which was "that the owners of slaves should educate the young
and use every possible means of making religious impressions upon
the minds of the aged, and that all acts of inhumanity should be
punished by the civil authority."

Methodism was introduced in New York in 1766, and the first missionaries were sent out by Mr. Wesley from New York in 1769. One
of these says: "The number of blacks that attend the preaching
affects me much." The first regular conference was held in Philadelphia, 1773. From this year to 1776 there was a great revival of religion in Virginia under the preaching of the Methodists in connection
with Rev. Mr. Jarratt of the Episcopal Church, which spread through

fourteen counties in Virginia and two in North Carolina. One letter states "the chapel was full of white and black;" another, "hundreds of Negroes were among them, with tears streaming down their faces." At Roanoke another remarks: "In general the white people were within the chapel and the black people without."

At the eighth conference in Baltimore in 1780 the following question appeared in the minutes: "Question 25. Ought not the assistant to meet the colored people himself and appoint helpers in his absence, proper white persons, and not suffer them to stay late and meet by themselves? Answer. Yes." Under the preaching of Mr. Garretson in Maryland "hundreds, both white and black, expressed their love for Jesus."

The first return of colored members distinct from white occurs in the minutes of 1786: White 18,791, colored 1,890. "It will be perceived from the above," says Dr. Bangs in his history of the Methodist Episcopal Church, "that a considerable number of colored persons had been received into the church, and were so returned in the minutes of the conference. Hence it appears that at an early period of the Methodist ministry in this country it had turned its attention to this part of the population."

In 1790 it was again asked: "What can be done to instruct poor children, white and black, to read? Answer. Let us labor as the heart and soul of one man to establish Sunday-schools in or near the place of public worship. Let persons be appointed by the bishops, elders, deacons, or preachers, to teach gratis all that will attend and have a capacity to learn, from 6 o'clock in the morning till 10 and from 2 p. m. till 6, where it does not interfere with public worship. The council shall compile a proper school-book to teach them learning and piety." The experiment was made, but it proved unsuccessful and was discontinued. The number of colored members this year was 11,682.

The first Baptist church in this country was founded in Providence, R. I., by Roger Williams in 1639. Nearly one hundred years after the settlement of America "only seventeen Baptist churches had arisen in it." The Baptist church in Charleston, S. C., was founded in 1690. The denomination advanced slowly through the middle and Southern States, and in 1790 it had churches in them all. Revivals of religion were enjoyed, particularly one in Virginia, which commenced in 1785 and continued until 1791 or 1792. "Thousands were converted and baptized, besides many who joined the Methodists and Presbyterians. A large number of Negroes were admitted to the Baptist Churches during the seasons of revival, as well as on ordinary occasions. They were, however, not gathered into churches distinct from the whites south of Pennsylvania except in Georgia."

"In general the Negroes were followers of the Baptists in Virginia, and after a while, as they permitted many colored men to preach, the great majority of them went to hear preachers of their own color, which was attended with many evils."

"Towards the close of 1792 the first colored Baptist Church in the city of Savannah began to build a place of worship. The corporation of the city gave them a lot for the purpose. The origin of this church —the parent of several others—is briefly as follows:

George Leile or Lisle, sometimes called George Sharp, was born in Virginia about 1750. His master sometime before the American war removed and settled in Burke county, Georgia. Mr. Sharp was a Baptist and a deacon in a Baptist church, of which Rev. Matthew Moore was pastor. George was converted and baptized under Mr. Moore's ministry. The church gave him liberty to preach."*

About nine months after George Leile left Georgia, Andrew, surnamed Bryan, a man of good sense, great zeal, and some natural elocution, began to exhort his black brethren and friends. He and his followers were reprimanded and forbidden to engage further in religious exercises. He would, however, pray, sing, and encourage his fellow-worshippers to seek the Lord. Their persecution was carried to an inhuman extent. Their evening assemblies were broken up and those found present were punished with stripes! Andrew Bryan and Sampson, his brother, converted about a year after him, were twice imprisoned, and they with about fifty others were whipped. When publicly whipped, and bleeding under his wounds, Andrew declared that he rejoiced not only to be whipped, but would freely suffer death for the cause of Jesus Christ, and that while he had life and opportunity he would continue to preach Christ. He was faithful to his vow and, by patient continuance in well-doing, he put to silence and shamed his adversaries, and influential advocates and patrons were raised up for him. Liberty was given Andrew by the civil authority to continue his religious meetings under certain regulations. His master gave him the use of his barn at Brampton, three miles from Savannah, where he preached for two years with little interruption.

The African church in Augusta, Ga., was gathered by the labors of Jesse Peter, and was constituted in 1793 by Rev. Abraham Marshall and David Tinsley. Jesse Peter was also called Jesse Golfin on account of his master's name—living twelve miles below Augusta.

The number of Baptists in the United States this year was 73,471, allowing one-fourth to be Negroes the denomination would embrace between 18,000 and 19,000.

The returns of colored members in the Methodist denomination from 1791 to 1795, inclusive, were 12,884, 13,871, 16,227, 13,814, 12,179.

The Methodists reported in 1796, 11,280 colored members. The recapitulation of the numbers for 1797 is given by states:

---

*See infra.

Massachusetts	8	Maryland	5,106
Rhode Island	2	Virginia	2,490
Connecticut	15	North Carolina	2,071
New York	238	South Carolina	890
New Jersey	127	Georgia	148
Pennsylvania	198	Tennessee	42
Delaware	823	Kentucky	57

Making a total of 12,215 Negroes; nearly one-fourth of the whole number of members were colored. There were three only in Canada.

The year 1799 is memorable for the commencement of that extraordinary awakening which, taking its rise in Kentucky and spreading in various directions and with different degrees of intensity, was denominated "the great Kentucky revival." It continued for about four years, and its influence was felt over a large portion of the Southern States. Presbyterians, Methodists, and Baptists participated in this work. In this revival originated camp-meetings, which gave a new impulse to Methodism. From the best estimates the number of Negroes received into the different communions during this season must have been between four and five thousand.

In 1800 there were in connection with the Methodists 13,452 Negroes. The bishops of the Methodist Episcopal Church were authorized to ordain African preachers in places where there were houses of worship for their use, who might be chosen by a majority of the male members of the society to which they belonged and could procure a recommendation from the preacher in charge and his colleagues on the circuit to the office of local deacons. Richard Allen, of Philadelphia, was the first colored man who received orders under this rule.

"The fact, however, is worthy of remembrance that, while the Indians—some of whom received us as guests and sold us their land at almost no compensation at all, and others were driven back to make us room, and with whom we had frequent and bloody wars, and we became, from time to time, mutual scourges—received some eminent missionaries from the colonists, and had no inconsiderable interest awakened for their conversion; the Africans who were brought over and bought by us for servants, and who wore out their lives as such, enriching thousands from Massachusetts to Georgia, and were members of our households, never received from the colonists themselves a solitary missionary exclusively devoted to their good, nor was there ever a single society established within the colonies, that we know of, with the express design of promoting their religious instruction!"

8. **The Sects and Slavery.** The approach of the Revolution brought heart-searching on many subjects, and not the least on slavery. The agitation was noticeable in the legislation of the time, putting an end to slavery in the North and to the slave-trade in all states. Religious

bodies particularly were moved. In 1657 George Fox, founder of the
Quakers, had impressed upon his followers in America the duty of
converting the slaves, and he himself preached to them in the West
Indies. The Mennonite Quakers protested against slavery in 1688, and
from that time until the Revolution the body slowly but steadily
advanced, step by step, to higher ground until they refused all fellowship to slaveholders. Radical Quakers, like Hepburn and Lay, attacked
religious sects and Lay called preachers "a sort of devils that preach
more to hell than they do to heaven, and so they will do forever as
long as they are suffered to reign in the worst and mother of all sins,
slave-keeping."

In Virginia and North Carolina this caused much difficulty owing to
laws against manumission early in the nineteenth century, and the
result was wholesale migration of the Quakers.*

Judge Sewall, among the Massachusetts Congregationalists, had
declared, in 1700, that slavery and the slave-trade were wrong, but his
protest was unheeded. Later, in 1770 and after, strong Congregational
clergymen, like Samuel Hopkins and Ezra Stiles, attacked slavery,
but so democratic a church could take no united action. Although
Whitefield came to defend the institution, John Wesley, founder of
the Methodists, called the slave-trade the "sum of all villanies," and
the General Conference in America, 1780, declared slavery "contrary
to the laws of God, man, and nature and hurtful to society." From
this high stand, however, the church quickly and rather ignominiously
retreated. By 1780 it only sought the destruction of slavery "by all
wise and prudent means," while preachers were allowed to hold their
slaves in slave states. In 1787 the General Conference urged preachers
to labor among slaves and receive worthy ones into full membership
and "to exercise the whole Methodist discipline among them."
Work was begun early among the slaves and they had so many members that their churches in the south were often called Negro churches.
The church yielded further ground to the pro-slavery sentiment in
1816, but in 1844 the censure of a bishop who married a slaveholder
rent the church in twain on the question.

The Baptists had Negro preachers for Negro members as early as
1773. They were under the supervision of whites and had no voice in
general church affairs. The early Baptists held few slaves, and they
were regarded as hostile to slavery in Georgia. The Philadelphia Association approved of abolition as early as 1789, and a Virginia Association urged emancipation in the legislature about the same time. In
Kentucky and Ohio the Baptist Associations split on the question.
The Baptists early interested themselves in the matter of slave marriages and family worship, and especially took spiritual care of the
slaves of their own members. They took a stand against the slave-

---

* Cf. Week's Southern Quakers and Slavery ; Thomas : Attitude, etc.

trade in 1818 and 1835. After the division on the subject of missions the Missionary Baptists began active proselyting among the slaves.

The Presbyterian Synod of 1787 recommended efforts looking toward gradual emancipation, and in 1795 the question of excluding slave-holders was discussed, but it ended in an injunction of "brotherly love" for them. In 1815, 1818, and 1835 the question was dismissed and postponed, and finally in 1845 the question was dropped on the ground that Christ and the Apostles did not condemn slavery. At the time of the war the church finally divided.

9. Toussaint L'Ouverture and Nat Turner.

"The role which the great Negro Toussaint, called L'Ouverture, played in the history of the United States has seldom been fully appreciated. Representing the age of revolution in America, he rose to leadership through a bloody terror, which contrived a Negro "problem" for the Western hemisphere, intensified and defined the anti-slavery movement, became one of the causes, and probably the prime one, which led Napoleon to sell Louisiana for a song; and, finally, through the interworking of all these effects, rendered more certain the final prohibition of the slave-trade by the United States in 1807." *

The effect of the revolution on the religious life of the Negro was quickly felt. In 1800, South Carolina declared:

"It shall not be lawful for any number of slaves, free Negroes. mulattoes, or mestizoes, even in company with white persons, to meet together and assemble for the purpose of mental instruction or religious worship, either before the rising of the sun or after the going down of the same. And all magistrates, sheriffs, militia officers, etc., etc., are hereby vested with power, etc., for dispersing such assemblies." †

On petition of the white churches the rigor of this law was slightly abated in 1803 by a modification which forbade any person, before 9 o'clock in the evening, "to break into a place of meeting wherein shall be assembled the members of any religious society in this State, provided a majority of them shall be white persons, or otherwise to disturb their devotions unless such persons, etc., so entering said place [of worship] shall first have obtained from some magistrate, etc., a warrant, etc., in case a magistrate shall be then actually within a distance of three miles from such place of meeting; otherwise the provisions, etc., [of the Act of 1800] to remain in full force."‡

So, too, in Virginia the Haytian revolt and the attempted insurrection under Gabriel in 1800 led to the Act of 1804, which forbade all evening meetings of slaves. This was modified in 1805 so as to allow a slave, in company with a white person, to listen to a white minister in the evening. A master was "allowed" to employ a religious teacher for his slaves.§ Mississippi passed similar restrictions.

---

* DuBois' Suppression of the Slave-Trade, p. 70.   ‡ Stroud, 93-4 ; Goodell, 329.

† Goodell, 329.   § Stroud, 94 ; Ballagh, 95.

By 1822 the rigor of the South Carolina laws in regard to Negro meetings had abated, especially in a city like Charleston, and one of the results was the Vesey plot.

"The sundry religious classes or congregations, with Negro leaders or local preachers, into which were formed the Negro members of the various churches of Charleston, furnished Vesey with the first rudiments of an organization, and at the same time with a singularly safe medium for conducting his underground agitation. It was customary, at that time, for these Negro congregations to meet for purposes of worship entirely free from the presence of whites. Such meetings were afterwards forbidden to be held except in the presence of at least one representative of the dominant race. But during the three or four years prior to the year 1822 they certainly offered Denmark Vesey regular, easy and safe opportunities for preaching his gospel of liberty and hate. And we are left in no doubt whatever in regard to the uses to which he put those gatherings of blacks.

"Like many of his race, he possessed the gift of gab, as the silver in the tongue and the gold in the full or thick-lipped mouth are oftentimes contemptuously characterized. And, like many of his race, he was a devoted student of the Bible, to whose interpretation he brought, like many other Bible students not confined to the Negro race, a good deal of imagination and not a little of superstition, which, with some natures, is perhaps but another name for the desires of the heart. Thus equipped, it is no wonder that Vesey, as he poured over the Old Testament scriptures, found many points of similitude in the history of the Jews and that of the slaves in the United States. They were both peculiar peoples. They were both Jehovah's peculiar peoples, one in the past, the other in the present. And it seemed to him that as Jehovah bent his ear, and bared his arm once in behalf of the one, so would he do the same for the other. It was all vividly real to his thought, I believe, for to his mind thus had said the Lord.

"He ransacked the Bible for apposite and terrible texts whose commands in the olden times, to the olden people, were no less imperative upon the new times and the new people. This new people was also commanded to arise and destroy their enemies and the city in which they dwelt, ' both man and woman, young and old, with the edge of the sword.' Believing superstitiously as he did in the stern and Nemesis-like God of the Old Testament he looked confidently for a day of vengeance and retribution for the blacks. He felt, I doubt not, something peculiarly applicable to his enterprise and intensely personal to himself in the stern and exultant prophecy of Zachariah, fierce and sanguinary words, which were constantly in his mouth: 'Then shall the Lord go forth and fight against those nations as when he fought in the day of battle.' According to Vesey's lurid exegesis 'those nations' in the text meant beyond peradventure the cruel masters and Jehovah was to go forth to fight against them for the poor slaves and on whichever side fought that day the Almighty God on that side would assuredly rest victory and deliverance.

"It will not be denied that Vesey's plan contemplated the total annihilation of the white population of Charleston. Nursing for many dark years the bitter wrongs of himself and race had filled him without doubt with a mad spirit of revenge and had given to him a decided predilection for shedding the blood of his oppressors. But if he intended to kill them to satisfy a desire for vengeance he intended to do so also on broader ground. The conspirators, he argued, had no choice in the matter, but were compelled to adopt a policy of extermination by the necessity of their position. The liberty of the blacks was in the balance of fate against the lives of the whites. He could strike that balance in favor of the blacks only by the total destruction of the whites. Therefore the whites, men, women, and children, were doomed to death."*

The plot was well-laid, but the conspirators were betrayed. Less than ten years after this plot was discovered and Vesey and his associates hanged, there broke out the Nat Turner insurrection in Virginia. Turner was himself a preacher.

" He was a Christian and a man. He was conscious that he was a Man and not a 'thing;' therefore, driven by religious fanaticism, he undertook a difficult and bloody task. Nathaniel Turner was born in Southampton county, Virginia, October 2, 1800. His master was one Benjamin Turner, a very wealthy and aristocratic man. He owned many slaves, and was a cruel and exacting master. Young 'Nat' was born of slave parents, and carried to his grave many of the superstitions and traits of his father and mother. The former was a preacher, the latter a 'mother in Israel.' Both were unlettered but, nevertheless, very pious people. The mother began when Nat was quite young to teach him that he was born, like Moses, to be the deliverer of his race. She would sing to him snatches of wild, rapturous songs and repeat portions of prophecy she had learned from the preachers of those times. Nat listened with reverence and awe, and believed everything his mother said. He imbibed the deep religious character of his parents, and soon manifested a desire to preach. He was solemnly set apart to 'the gospel ministry' by his father, the church, and visiting preachers. He was quite low in stature, dark, and had the genuine African features. His eyes were small, but sharp, and gleamed like fire when he was talking about his 'mission' or preaching from some prophetic passage of scripture. It is said that he never laughed. He was a dreamy sort of a man, and avoided the crowd. Like Moses he lived in the solitudes of the mountains and brooded over the condition of his people. There was something grand to him in the rugged scenery that nature had surrounded him with. He believed that he was a prophet, a leader raised up by God to burst the bolts of the prison-house and set the oppressed free. The thunder, the hail, the storm-cloud, the air, the earth, the stars, at which he would sit and gaze half the night all spake the language of the God of the oppressed. He was seldom seen in a large company, and never drank a drop of ardent spirits. Like John the Baptist, when he had delivered his message, he would retire to the fastness of the mountain or seek the desert, where he could meditate upon his great work." †

In the impression of the Richmond *Enquirer* of the 30th of August, 1831, the first editorial or leader is under the caption of "The Banditte." The editor says:

"They remind one of a parcel of blood-thirsty wolves rushing down from the Alps; or, rather like a former incursion of the Indians upon the white settlements. Nothing is spared; neither age nor sex respected—the helplessness of women and children pleads in vain for mercy. . . . The case of Nat Turner warns us. No black man ought to be permitted to turn preacher through the country. The law must be enforced—or the tragedy of Southampton appeals to us in vain." ‡

Mr. Gray, the man to whom Turner made his confession before dying, said :

---

*Grimke : Right on the Scaffold (Pub. American Negro Academy), pp. 11-12.

† Williams II, pp. 85-86.   ‡ Quoted in *Ibid*, p. 90.

"It has been said that he was ignorant and cowardly and that his object was to murder and rob for the purpose of obtaining money to make his escape. It is notorious that he was never known to have had a dollar in his life, to swear an oath or drink a drop of spirits. As to his ignorance, he certainly never had the advantages of education, but he can read and write, and for natural intelligence and quickness of apprehension is surpassed by few men I have ever seen. As to his being a coward, his reason as given for not resisting Mr. Phipps, shows the decision of his character. When he saw Mr. Phipps present his gun, he said he knew it was impossible for him to escape as the woods were full of men. He, therefore, thought it was better for him to surrender and trust to fortune for his escape.

"He is a complete fanatic or plays his part most admirably. On other subjects he possesses an uncommon share of intelligence, with a mind capable of attaining anything, but warped and perverted by the influence of early impressions. He is below the ordinary stature, though strong and active, having the true Negro face, every feature of which is strongly marked. I shall not attempt to describe the effect of his narrative, as told and commented on by himself, in the condemned hole of the prison; the calm, deliberate composure with which he spoke of his late deeds and intentions; the expression of his fiend-like face when excited by enthusiasm, still bearing the stains of the blood of the helpless innocence about him, clothed with rags and covered with chains, yet daring to raise his manacled hand to heaven, with a spirit soaring above the attributes of man. I looked on him and the blood curdled in my veins." *

The Turner insurrection is so connected with the economic revolution which enthroned cotton that it marks an epoch in the history of the slave. A wave of legislation passed over the South prohibiting the slaves from learning to read and write, forbidding Negroes to preach, and interfering with Negro religious meetings. Virginia declared, in 1831, that neither slaves or free Negroes might preach, nor could they attend religious service at night without permission. In North Carolina slaves and free Negroes were forbidden to preach, exhort or teach "in any prayer-meeting or other association for worship where slaves of different families are collected together" on penalty of not more than thirty-nine lashes. Maryland and Georgia had similar laws. The Mississippi law of 1831 said: It is "unlawful for any slave, free Negro, or mulatto to preach the gospel" upon pain of receiving thirty-nine lashes upon the naked back of the presumptuous preacher. If a Negro received written permission from his master he might preach to the Negroes in his immediate neighborhood, providing six respectable white men, owners of slaves, were present.† In Alabama the law of 1832 prohibited the assembling of more than five male slaves at any place off the plantation to which they belonged, but nothing in the act was to be considered as forbidding attendance at places of public worship held by white persons. No slave or free person of color was permitted to "preach, exhort, or harrangue any slave or slaves, or free persons of color, except in the presence of five respectable slaveholders or unless the person

---

* Williams II, pp. 91-92.

† Williams II, 163.

preaching was licensed by some regular body of professing Christians in the neighborhood, to whose society or church the Negroes addressed properly belonged."

In the District of Columbia the free Negroes began to leave white churches in 1831 and to assemble in their own.

10. Third Period of Missionary Enterprise. The efforts to convert Negroes in America fall in three main periods. The first period was early in the eighteenth century after it was decided that baptism did not free slaves. Results at this time were meagre, and the effort spasmodic. A second period came about the time of the Revolution, and had larger results. C. C. Jones says of the conditions, 1790–1820, that:

"It is not too much to say that the religious and physical condition of the Negroes were both improved during this period. Their increase was natural and regular, ranging every ten years, between 34 and 36 per cent. As the old stock from Africa died out of the country the grosser customs, ignorance and paganism of Africa, died with them. Their descendants, the country-born, were better looking, more intelligent, more civilized, more susceptible of religious impressions.

"On the whole, however, but a minority of the Negroes, and that a small one, attended regularly the house of God. and taking them as a class, their religious instruction was extensively and most seriously neglected."

The third period followed after the depression of the thirties. This depression was severe, and lasted nearly twenty years.

The Presbyterian Synod of South Carolina and Georgia, in 1833, published a statement in which they said of the slaves:

"There are over two millions of human beings in the condition of heathen and some of them in a worse condition. They may justly be considered the heathen of this country, and will bear a comparison with heathen in any country in the world. The Negroes are destitute of the gospel, and ever will be under the present state of things. In the vast field extending from an entire state beyond the Potomac, [i. e., Maryland], to the Sabine river [at the time our southwestern boundary] and from the Atlantic to the Ohio, there are, to the best of our knowledge, not twelve men exclusively devoted to the religious instruction of the Negroes. In the present state of feeling in the South, a ministry of their own color could neither be obtained nor tolerated. But do not the Negroes have access to the gospel through the stated ministry of the whites? We answer, no. The Negroes have no regular and efficient ministry : as a matter of course, no churches; neither is there sufficient room in the white churches for their accommodation. We know of but five churches in the slaveholding states, built expressly for their use. These are all in the state of Georgia. We may now inquire whether they enjoy the privileges of the gospel in their own houses, and on our plantations? Again we return a negative answer. They have no Bibles to read by their own firesides. They have no family altars; and when in affliction, sickness or death, they have no minister to address to them the consolations of the gospel, nor to bury them with appropriate services." *

The Presbyterian Synod of Kentucky, in 1834, said :

---

* Goodell, pp. 333-5.

"Slavery deprives its subjects, in a great measure, of the privileges of the gospel. The law, as it is here, does not prevent free access to the scriptures; but ignorance, the natural result of their condition, does. The Bible is before them. But it is to them a sealed book. Very few of them enjoy the advantages of a regular gospel ministry."*

The Synod of South Carolina and Georgia returned to the subject, in 1834, and declared:

"The gospel, as things now are, can never be preached to the two classes (whites and blacks) successfully in conjunction. The galleries or back seats on the lower floor of white churches are generally appropriated to the Negroes, when it can be done without inconvenience to the whites. When it cannot be done conveniently, the Negroes must catch the gospel as it escapes through the doors and windows. If the master is pious, the house servants alone attend family worship, and frequently few or none of them, while the field hands have no attention at all. So as far as masters are engaged in the work [of religious instruction of slaves], an almost unbroken silence reigns on this vast field."*

To this the Rev. C. C. Jones, of Georgia, adds:

"We cannot cry out against the Papists for withholding the scriptures from the common people, and the keeping them in ignorance of the way of life, for we withhold the Bible from our servants, and keep them in ignorance of it, while we will not use the means to have it read and explained to them."*

In 1838 the Methodist Conference of South Carolina appointed a missionary to labor among the colored people, but the enterprise was soon suppressed by the principal citizens. The Greenville (S. C.) *Mountaineer* of November 2, 1838, contained the particulars: A committee was appointed, who addressed a note to the missionary, requesting him to desist. This was backed up by James S. Pope and 352 others. The document argues at length the incompatibility of slavery with the "mental improvement and religious instruction" of slaves. "Verbal instruction," say they, "will increase the desire of the black population to learn. We know of upwards of a dozen Negroes in the neighborhood of Cambridge who can now read, some of whom are members of your societies at Mount Lebanon and New Salem. Of course, when they see themselves encouraged, they will supply themselves with Bibles, hymn books, and catechisms! Open the missionary sluice, and the current will swell in its gradual onward advance. We thus expect that a progressive system of improvement will be introduced, or will follow, from the nature and force of circumstances, and, if not checked (though they may be shrouded in sophistry and disguise), will ultimately revolutionize our civil institutions. We consider the common adage that 'knowledge is power,' and as the colored man is enlightened, his condition will be rendered more unhappy and intolerable. Intelligence and slavery have no affinity with each other." The document refers to the laws of the state, and hopes that "South Carolina is yet true to her vital interests," etc., etc.†

---

* Jones, 167-8; Goodell, p. 335-6.   † Goodell, p. 336-7.

Bishop Capers testifies about this time that there was the most urgent need for preaching among Negroes. Of the Negroes around Wilmington, N. C., he says: "A numerous population of this class in that town and vicinity were as destitute of any public instruction (or, probably, instruction of any kind as to spiritual things) as if they had not been believed to be men at all, and their morals were as depraved as, with such a destitution of the gospel among them, might have been expected." To this state of things the masters were indifferent; for, adds the bishop, "it seems not to have been considered that such a state of things might furnish motives sufficient to induce pure-minded men to engage, at great inconvenience or even personal hazard, in the work of improving them." Such work, on the other hand, seems to have been regarded as unnecessary, if not unreasonable. Conscience was not believed to be concerned.

As the result of such appeals a reaction set in about 1835, and the Methodists and Baptists especially were active among the slaves. A minister in Mississippi testified that he had charge of the Negroes of five plantations and three hundred slaves; another in Georgia visited eighteen plantations every two weeks. "The owners have built three good churches at their own expense, all framed; 290 members have been added, and about 400 children are instructed." Another traveling minister declared, in 1841, that in many places, like Baltimore, Alexandria, and Charleston, the Negroes had large, spacious churches, and he thinks there were 500,000 Negro church members at the time, which is probably an exaggeration.

Charles C. Jones writes, in 1842, that:

"The Negro race has existed in our country for two hundred and twenty-two years, in which time the gospel has been brought within the reach of, and been communicated to, multitudes.

"While there have been but few societies, and they limited in extent and influence, formed for the special object of promoting the moral and religious instruction of the Negroes, and while there have been comparatively but few missionaries exclusively devoted to them, yet they have not been altogether overlooked by their owners, nor neglected by the regular ministers of the various leading denominations of Christians, as the facts adduced in this sketch testify.

"Yet it is a remarkable fact in the history of the Negroes in our country that their regular, systematic religious instruction has never received in the churches at any time that general attention and effort which it demanded, and the people have consequently been left, both in the free and in the slave states, in great numbers, in moral darkness, and destitution of the means of grace."

"In 1848 an enterprise was begun for the more thorough-going evangelization of the colored people in Charleston, S. C., under the auspices of the Rev. Dr. J. B. Adger and the session of the Second Presbyterian church. In 1859 a church building costing $25,000, contributed by the citizens of Charleston, was dedicated. From the first the great building was filled, the blacks occupying the main floor, and the whites the galleries, which seated two hundred and fifty persons. The Rev. Dr. J. L. Girardeau, one of the greatest preachers in the South, was for years the pastor of this church. The close of the war found it with exactly five hundred colored members, and nearly one hundred white."*

There were thirteen colored churches in Baltimore in 1847, supported largely, but not altogether, by free Negroes. In 1854 one-fourth of the slaves of South Carolina were said to be Methodists; one-third of the Presbyterians of that state were black, and one-half of the Baptists of Virginia. In 1859 there were 468,000 Negro church members reported in the South, of whom 215,000 were Methodists and 175,000 Baptists.†

Even at this time many restrictions on Negro religion remained. In Maryland camp-meetings were forbidden, and all meetings save at regular churches and with the consent of white preachers. There were also many local laws restricting worship. In other states the laws of the thirties remained in force or were strengthened. Moreover, even the church organizations working among Negroes were careful in their methods. The North Carolina Baptist Convention adopted a report concerning the religious instruction of the colored people, with a series of resolutions, concluding as follows:

"*Resolved,* That by religious instructions be understood verbal communications on religious subjects?"‡

Moreover, the masters clung to the idea that the chief use of religion among slaves was to make them "obey their masters." When it was charged that slaves were not allowed to read the Bible, one naive answer was that it was read to them, especially "those very passages which inculcate the relative duties of masters and servants."

An intelligent Negro, Lundsford Lane, thus describes the religious instruction of slaves:

" I was permitted to attend church, and this I esteem a great blessing. It was there I received much instruction, which I trust was a great benefit to me. I trusted, too, that I had experienced the renewing influences of divine grace. I looked upon myself as a great sinner before God, and upon the doctrine of the great atonement, through the suffering and death of the Savior, as a source of continual joy to my heart. After obtaining from my mistress a written permit, a thing always required in such cases, I had been baptized and received into fellowship with the Baptist denomination. Thus in religious matters I had been indulged in the exercise of my own conscience; this was a favor not always granted to slaves. There was one hard doctrine to which we as slaves were compelled to listen, which I found difficult to receive. We were often told by the ministers how much we owed to God for bringing us over from the benighted shores of Africa and permitting us to listen to the sound of the gospel. In ignorance of any special revelation that God had made to master, or to his ancestors, that my ancestors should be stolen and enslaved on the soil of America to accomplish their salvation, I was slow to believe all my teachers enjoined on this subject. How surprising, then, this high moral end being accomplished, that no proclamation of emancipation had before this been made! Many of us were as highly civilized as

---

* Campbell : Some Aspects, etc.; and Jones.

† Cf. Ingle Side Lights, pp. 273-74.

‡ Goodell, p. 336.

some of our masters, and as to piety in many instances their superiors. I was rather disposed to believe that God had originally granted me temporal freedom, which wicked men had taken from me—which now I had been compelled to purchase at great cost. There was one kind-hearted clergyman whom I used often to hear; he was very popular among the colored people. But after he had preached a sermon to us in which he urged from the Bible that it was the will of heaven from all eternity that we should be slaves, and our masters be our owners, many of us left him, considering, like the doubting disciple of old, 'This is a hard saying; who can hear it?'"*

So, too, Dr. Caruthers says although many of the slaves were pious they owed for this "no thanks to slavery or the slave laws." Even after the war the reconstruction legislation of states like Mississippi sought especially to restrain Negro preachers and imposed, in 1865, upon Negroes exercising the functions of a minister without a license from a regularly organized church a fine of $10–$100, and liability to imprisonment not more than thirty days.†

11.　The Earlier Churches and Preachers, (by Mr. John W. Cromwell).

The original colored churches in different sections of the country came about in one of the following ways:

1. They were in some cases the result of special missionary effort on the part of the whites.

2. They were brought about by direct discrimination against the blacks made by the whites during divine worship.

3. They were the natural sequence, when, on account of increase in members, it became necessary for congregations to divide, whereupon the blacks were evolved as distinct churches, but still under the oversight, if not the exclusive control, of the whites.

4. They were, in not a few cases, the preference of colored communicants themselves, in order to get as much as possible the equal privileges and advantages of government denied them under the existing system.

The establishment of these churches took place about the same time in sections more distant from each other then than now, for it was before the time of the railroad, the use of the steamboat or the telegraph; so that their coming into existence at the same time must be attributed to a correspondence of general causes.

The first regular church organization of which I know was a Baptist Church at Williamsburg, Va., in the year 1776. Following it were three Baptist Churches in the year 1778, one in Augusta and two in Savannah, Ga.; the Episcopal Church, St. Thomas, in Philadelphia, in 1791; Bethel Church, Philadelphia, in 1794; Zion Methodist Church, New York city, in 1796; Joy Street Baptist Church, Boston, in 1807; Abyssinian Baptist Church, New York, in 1808; First Baptist, St. Louis, 1830.

---

* Bassett: State, pp. 51-52.

† Garner: Reconstruction, p. 115.

So far as the establishment is concerned of those colored Methodist Churches which evolved the A. M. E. and the A. M. E. Zion denominations, persecution by the whites was the moving cause. They were compelled to protect themselves against the yoke sought to be imposed on them, by worshipping among themselves. The one movement in Philadelphia, the other in New York, moved in parallel, often in rival lines. New York and Philadelphia were soon in free states and their methods were those of free men, in name at least, while the establishment of colored Methodist Churches in the South, as in Maryland, under the direction of the whites, illustrated one of the instances of special missionary effort.

The colored Baptist Church in the South came mostly into existence mainly through the third inciting cause mentioned.

The Presbyterian Church, as found among the colored people, came about through the operation of two causes: the desire of the colored people to be by themselves and that of the whites to strengthen their denomination among this class.

The first colored Episcopal Churches, both in New York and Philadelphia, resulted directly from causes similar to those which gave rise to the Methodist Churches in the same localities.

Of the men mainly instrumental by reason of their position as pioneers in organizing these first churches in the different colored denominations a word is needed.

First in order came Richard Allen. He was one of the leaders in the free African Society. From the members of this body came the leaders, almost the organization itself, both of the Bethel Methodist and the St. Thomas Episcopal Churches in the city of Philadelphia.

Richard Allen was born February 12, 1760, old style, a slave in Philadelphia. At an early age he gave evidence of a high order of talent for leadership. He was converted while quite a lad and licensed to preach in 1782. In 1797 he was ordained a deacon by Bishop Francis Asbury, who had been entrusted by John Wesley with the superintendence of the work in America. April 11, 1816, at the general conference of the African Methodist Churches, held in the city of Philadelphia, he was elected their first bishop. Under his administration the work was vigorously prosecuted in all directions. He died in 1831, universally lamented.

He possessed talents as an organizer of the highest order. He was a born leader and an almost infallible judge of human nature. He was actively identified with every forward movement among the colored people, irrespective of denomination, and died, leaving a greater influence upon the colored people of the North than any other man of his times. He was one of the promoters, as well as one of the chief actors, in the first national convention of colored men in the United States ever held, which was in Philadelphia in the year 1830.

Absalom Jones, who certainly comes next in point of time, was born a slave in Sussex, Del., November 6, 1746. At the age of sixteen he was taken to Philadelphia. He was married in 1770, purchased his wife, and afterward succeeded in obtaining his own liberty. Like his co-laborer, Richard Allen, with whom he was associated in the African Society, he was quite thrifty and became the owner of several pieces of real estate. His education was quite limited, so much so that a dispensation was necessary to admit of his ordination, to which a condition was annexed that this church (St. Thomas) should not have the power of sharing in the government of the Episcopal Church in the diocese of Pennsylvania. Rev. Wm. Douglass, subsequently a rector of this church, in his "Annals of St. Thomas Episcopal Church," says of Absalom Jones, that he was impressive in his style of preaching, though his forte was not in the pulpit. It was his mild and easy manners, his habits as a pastor, his public spirit, that strengthened him in public estimation. He says that "he was of medium height, dark complexion, with stout frame, bland and open countenance, yet indicative of firmness. Whenever he appeared in public he donned the costume of the profession, black dress coat, breeches and vest of the same color, with top-boots or shoes with buckles and black stockings." After a ministry of twenty-two years, he died February 13, 1818, aged 71 years.

Rev. John Gloucester, the first colored minister to act as pastor of the first colored Presbyterian Church, was a man thoroughly consecrated to his cause. He possessed a fair English education, which he received from private sources. He was a pioneer of Presbyterian ministers; four of his own sons, Jeremiah, John, Stephen, and James, became Presbyterian ministers, and from the Sunday-school of his church three other well known ministers went forth—Rev. Amos to Africa, Rev. H. M. Wilson to New York, and Rev. Jonathan C. Gibbs, who died in Florida after having been Secretary of State and State Superintendent of Schools.

Mr. Gloucester, like Allen and Jones, was born a slave, in Kentucky, about the year 1776. Such was his intelligence that he was purchased by Rev. Gideon Blackburn, one of the leaders of the Presbyterian denomination in Kentucky. The records show that when Rev. Gloucester was ordained, Dr. Blackburn was the moderator of the presbytery. On the appointment of Rev. Gloucester to the first African Presbyterian church his master liberated him. One of the attractions of Rev. Gloucester was his rich musical voice that was pronounced as something phenomenal. In prayer his power was manifest.

His character was so simple and Christian that he won many friends of both races. He was not only preacher, but pastor and adviser of his people in their temporal matters. He traveled extensively North and South and in nearly every city, raising the money with which he liberated his wife and children.   He even crossed the ocean, where he met with great success.

After fifteen years of service in the church, during which time it rapidly increased in members, from 22 to 300, he died May 2, 1822, a victim of consumption, in the forty-sixth year of his age.

Now it is not to be inferred that these were the only men deserving of special notice as pioneers.   By no means.   We allude to them because of their relation to the historical churches.   There were Harry Hosier, who travelled with Bishop Asbury, and who often filled appointments for him; Rev. Daniel Coker of Baltimore, and Rev. Peter Spencer of Delaware, who organized the Protestant branch of colored Methodism.

Circumstances were somewhat similar in other parts of the country. With the increase of the colored population and its distribution to other centers, other religious societies sprang up, so that wherever you find any number of these people in the earlier decades of the republic you find a church, often churches, out of all proportion to the population.

In the West, it may be stated, that colored churches were not the result of secessions or irregular wholesale withdrawals from the white churches as in the East.   They sprang up directly in the path of the westward migration of colored people from the South and the East.

In the South the whites were in complete and absolute control, in church as in state.   Colored people attended and held membership in the same church as the whites, though they did not possess the same rights or privileges.   They either had special services at stated times or they sat in the galleries.   There may have been deep protests against such un-Christian treatment, but we may rest assured that these were by no means loud, however deep.   It was when this membership increased to very large numbers that separate churches for colored people, rather than of the colored people, were established.   In the South, as in the North, this membership was principally in the Baptist and Methodist churches, and to these denominations did these separate colored churches belong, with exceptions so rare that they may be named as to cities or districts where it was otherwise.

Outside of the few ministers of the A. M. E. and the A. M. E. Zion churches in the border states, it is doubtful if there were a score of colored pastors in full control of colored churches in the South before the war.   Nevertheless, there were a few colored ministers so very conspicuous by their work as pioneers as to deserve special notice here.   It is possible to refer briefly only to a few.

Taking them in the order of time there was the Rev. George Lisle, a native of Virginia, the slave or body servant of a British officer. Throughout that struggle he preached in different parts of the country. As one of the results of his labors we find one of the very first colored churches of any denomination in the country organized, especially that in 1788 at Savannah, Ga., by Rev. Andrew Bryan, whom Lisle had baptized. Compelled to leave the United States at the close of the war, Lisle went to Jamaica, where he organized a church with four members in 1783. By 1790 he had baptized more than 400 persons on that island. In 1793 he built there the very first non-Episcopal religious chapel, to which there were belonging, in 1841, 3,700 members. That white Baptist missionaries subsequently went to the West Indies is to be attributed to Rev. Lisle's work, for they were brought there as a direct result of his correspondence with ecclesiastical authorities in Great Britain.

Next we have Lott Carey, also a native of Virginia, born a slave in Charles City county, about 1780. His father was a Baptist. In 1804 Lott removed to Richmond, where he worked in a tobacco factory and from all accounts was very profligate and wicked. In 1807, being converted, he joined the First Baptist Church, learned to read, made rapid advancement as a scholar, and was shortly afterwards licensed to preach.

After purchasing his family, in 1813, he organized, in 1815, the African Missionary Society, the first missionary society in the country, and within five years raised $700 for African missions.

That Lott Carey was evidently a man of superior intellect and force of character is to be evidenced from the fact that his reading took a wide range—from political economy, in Adam Smith's Wealth of Nations, to the voyage of Captain Cook. That he was a worker as well as a preacher is true, for when he decided to go to Africa his employers offered to raise his salary from $800 to $1,000 a year. Remember, that this was over eighty years ago. Carey was not seduced by such a flattering offer, for he was determined. His last sermon in the old First Church in Richmond must have been exceedingly powerful, for it was compared by an eye-witness, a resident of another state, to the burning, eloquent appeals of George Whitefield. Fancy him as he stands there in that historic building ringing the changes on the word "freely," depicting the willingness with which he was ready to give up his life for service in Africa.

He, as you may already know, was the leader of the pioneer colony to Liberia, where he arrived even before the agent of the Colonization Society. In his new home his abilities were recognized, for he was made vice governor and became governor, in fact, while Governor Ashmun was absent from the colony in this country. Carey did not allow his position to betray the cause of his people, for he did not hesitate to expose the duplicity of the Colonization Society and even to defy their authority, it would seem, in the interests of the people.

While casting cartridges to defend the colonists against the natives in 1828, the accidental upsetting of a candle caused an explosion that resulted in his death.

Carey is described as a typical Negro, six feet in height, of massive
and erect frame, with the sinews of a Titan. He had a square face,
keen eyes, and a grave countenance. His movements were measured;
in short, he had all the bearings and dignity of a prince of the blood.

12. Some Other Ante=Bellum Preachers. Six noted Negro preachers
have been mentioned: Nat Turner, the revolutionist; Richard Allen, the
founder of the African Methodists; Absalom Jones, the first Negro
Episcopal rector; Harry Hosier, the companion of Bishop Asbury;
George Lisle, the West Indian missionary, and Lott Carey, the African
missionary. To these may be added the names of Lemuel Haynes,
John Chavis, Henry Evans, James Varick, Jack of Virginia, Ralph
Freeman, and Lunsford Lane, forming thirteen remarkable characters.
"Lemuel Haynes was born in Hartford, Conn., July 18, 1753. His
father was an African, his mother a white woman. He received the
honorary degree of A. M. from Middlebury College in 1804. After
completing a theological course he preached in various places and
settled in West Rutland, Vt., in 1788, where he remained for thirty
years, and became one of the most popular preachers in the state. He
was characterized by subtle intellect, keen wit, and eager thirst for
knowledge. His noted sermon from Genesis 3:4 was published and
passed through nine or ten editions. His controversy with Hosea
Ballou became of world-wide interest. The life of Lemuel Haynes
was written by James E. Cooley, New York, 1848."* John Chavis was
a full-blooded Negro, born in Granville county, N. C., near Oxford, in
1763. He was born free and was sent to Princeton, and studied privately under Dr. Witherspoon, where he did well. He went to Virginia to preach to Negroes. In 1802, in the county court, his freedom
and character were certified to and it was declared that he had passed
"through a regular course of academic studies" at what is now Washington and Lee University. In 1805 he returned to North Carolina,
where he in 1809 was made a licentate in the Presbyterian Church and
preached. His English was remarkably pure, his manner impressive,
his explanations clear and concise. For a long time he taught school
and had the best whites as pupils—a United States senator, the sons
of a chief justice of North Carolina, a governor of the state and many
others. Some of his pupils boarded in his family, and his school
was regarded as the best in the State. "All accounts agree that
John Chavis was a gentleman," and he was received socially among
the best whites and asked to table. In 1830 he was stopped from
preaching by the law. Afterward he taught a school for free Negroes
in Raleigh.†

---

* Report U. S. Bureau of Edacation, 1900–1, p. 857.

† Bassett, State, North Carolina, pp. 73-6.   Cf. also Ballagh : Slavery in Virginia.

Henry Evans was a full-blooded Virginia free Negro and was the pioneer of Methodism in Fayetteville, N. C. He found the Negroes there, about 1800, without religious instruction. He began preaching and the town council ordered him away; he continued and whites came to hear him. Finally the white auditors outnumbered the black, and sheds were erected for Negroes at the side of the church. The gathering became a regular Methodist Church, with a white and Negro membership, but Evans continued to preach. He exhibited "rare self-control before the most wretched of castes! Henry Evans did much good, but he would have done more good had his spirit been untrammelled by this sense of inferiority." *

His dying words uttered us he stood, aged and bent beside his pulpit, are of singular pathos:

"I have come to say my last word to you. It is this: None but Christ. Three times I have had my life in jeopardy for preaching the gospel to you. Three time I have broken ice on the edge of the water and swam across the Cape Fear to preach the gospel to you; and, if in my last hour I could trust to that, or anything but Christ crucified, for my salvation, all should be lost and my soul perish forever." †

Early in the nineteenth century Ralph Freeman was a slave in Anson county, N. C. He was a full-blooded Negro, and was ordained and became an able Baptist preacher. He baptized and administered communion, and was greatly respected. When the Baptists split on the question of missions he sided with the anti-mission side. Finally the law forbade him to preach.‡

Lunsford Lane was a Negro who bought his freedom in Raleigh, N. C., by the manufacture of smoking tobacco. He later became a minister and was intelligent, and had the confidence of many of the best people.§

James Varick was a free Negro of New York, and is memorable as the first bishop of the Zion Methodists.

The story of Jack of Virginia is best told in the words of a Southern writer:

"Probably the most interesting case in the whole South is that of an African preacher of Nottoway county, popularly known as 'Uncle Jack,' whose services to white and black were so valuable that a distinguished minister of the Southern Presbyterian Church felt called upon to memorialize his work in a biography.

"Kidnapped from his idolatrous parents in Africa, he was brought over in one of the last cargoes of slaves admitted to Virginia and sold to a remote and obscure planter in Nottoway county, a region at that time in the backwoods and destitute particularly as to religious life and instruction. He was converted under the occasional preaching of Rev. Dr. John Blair Smith, president of Hampden-Sidney College, and of Dr. Wm. Hill and Dr. Archibald Alexander of Princeton, then young theologues, and by hearing the scriptures read. Taught by his mas-

---

* Bassett, State, North Carolina, pp. 58-9.   † Ibid., loc. cit.

‡ Ibid., p. 64.   § Ibid., p. 50. Cf. p. 29.

ter's children to read, he became so full of the spirit and knowledge of the Bible that he was recognized among the whites as a powerful expounder of Christian doctrine, was licensed to preach by the Baptist Church, and preached from plantation to plantation within a radius of thirty miles, as he was invited by overseers or masters. His freedom was purchased by a subscription of whites, and he was given a home and a tract of land for his support. He organized a large and orderly Negro church, and exercised such a wonderful controlling influence over the private morals of his flock that masters, instead of punishing their slaves, often referred them to the discipline of their pastor, which they dreaded far more.

"He stopped a heresy among the Negro Christians of Southern Virginia, defeating in open argument a famous fanatical Negro preacher named Campbell, who advocated noise and "the spirit" against the Bible, winning over Campbell's adherents in a body. For over forty years, and until he was nearly a hundred years of age, he labored successfully in public and private among black and whites, voluntarily giving up his preaching in obedience to the law of 1832, the result of 'Old Nat's war.' . . . .

"The most refined and aristocratic people paid tribute to him, and he was instrumental in the conversion of many whites. Says his biographer, Rev. Dr. Wm. S. White: 'He was invited into their houses, sat with their families, took part in their social worship, sometimes leading the prayer at the family altar. Many of the most intelligent people attended upon his ministry and listened to his sermons with great delight. Indeed, previous to the year 1825, he was considered by the best judges to be the best preacher in that county. His opinions were respected, his advice followed, and yet he never betrayed the least symptoms of arrogance or self-conceit. His dwelling was a rude log cabin, his apparel of the plainest and coarsest materials.' This was because he wished to be fully identified with his class. He refused gifts of better clothing, saying, 'These clothes are a great deal better than are generally worn by people of my color, and besides if I wear them I find I shall be obliged to think about them even at meeting.' " *

13. The Negro Church in 1890. (From the Eleventh United States Census). There were in the United States in 1890, 23,462 Negro churches. Outside of these there were numbers of Negroes who are members of white churches, but they are not distinguished from others:

---

* Ballagh, pp. 110-112. Cf. White: The African Preacher.

SUMMARY OF COLORED ORGANIZATIONS

DENOMINATIONS.	Organizations.	Church Edifices.	Approximate Seating Capacity.	Halls, etc.	Seating Capacity.	Value of Church Property.	Communicants or Members.
Total	23,462	23,770	6,800,035	1,358	114,644	$26,626,448	2,673,977
Denominations	18,835	19,631	5,791,384	940	78,719	20,389,714	2,303,151
Organizations in other denominations	4,627	4,139	1,008,651	418	35,925	6,236,734	370,826

DENOMINATIONS.	Organizations.	Church Edifices.	Approximate Seating Capacity.	Halls, etc.	Seating Capacity.	Value of Church Property.	Communicants or Members.
Regular Baptists	12,533	11,987	3,440,970	663	45,570	$ 9,038,549	1,348,989
Union American Methodist Episcopal	42	35	11,500	7	250	187,600	2,279
African Methodist Episcopal	2,481	4,124	1,160,888	31	2,200	6,468,280	452,725
African Union Methodist Protestant	40	27	7,161	13	1,883	54,440	3,415
African Methodist Episcopal Zion	1,704	1,587	565,577	114	15,520	2,714,128	349,788
Congregational Methodist	9	5	585	4	450	525	319
Colored Methodist Episcopal	1,759	1,653	541,464	64	6,526	1,713,366	129,383
Zion Union Apostolic	32	27	10,100	1	100	15,000	2,346
Evangelist Missionary	11	3	1,050	9	2,650	2,000	951
Cumberland Presbyterian	224	183	52,139	34	3,570	195,826	12,956
Regular Baptists (North)	406	324	92,660	72	7,245	1,087,518	35,221
Regular Baptists (South)	7	5	1,900	2	80	3,875	651
Freewill Baptists	5	3	800	2	200	13,300	271
Primitive Baptists	323	291	96,699	33	1,700	135,427	18,162
Old Two-Seed in the Spirit Predestinarian Baptists	15	4	1,025	11	825	930	265
Roman Catholic	31	27	8,370	3	60	237,400	14,517
Christians (Christian Connection)	63	54	16,495	7	800	23,500	4,989
Congregationalists	85	69	19,360	11	1,925	246,125	6,908
Disciples of Christ	277	183	41,590	75	5,850	176,795	18,578
Lutheran Synodical Conference	5	5	1,050			13,400	211
Lutheran United Synod in the South	5	3	550	2	250	1,750	94
Methodist Episcopal	2,984	2,800	635,252	165	12,925	3,630,093	246,249
Methodist Protestant	54	50	11,545	4	200	35,445	3,183
Independent Methodists	2	2	725			4,675	222
Presbyterian (Northern)	233	200	56,280	21	3,100	391,650	14,961
Presbyterian (Southern)	45	29	6,190	7	565	22,200	1,568
Reformed Presbyterian (Synod)	1	1	300			1,500	76
Protestant Episcopal	49	53	11,885	2	100	192,750	2,977
Reformed Episcopal	37	36	5,975	1	100	18,401	1,723

Organizations by States

STATES.	Organizations.	Church Edifices.	Approximate Seating Capacity.	Halls, etc.	Seating Capacity.	Value of Church Property.	Communicants or Members.
The United States.....	23,462	23,770	6,800,085	1,358	114,644	$ 26,626,448	2,673,977
Alabama..................	2,395	3,425	717,989	113	8,925	1,880,656	297,161
Arizona...................	2	2	450			8,000	155
Arkansas.................	1,375	1,432	378,056	94	6,885	962,149	106,445
California................	29	23	5,879	8	2,000	65,300	3,720
Colorado.................	10	8	2,900			73,800	1,171
Connecticut.............	23	20	6,000	3	350	116,950	1,624
Delaware................	82	91	21,310	7	570	187,825	6,595
District of Columbia.......	77	65	38,325	14	1,400	1,182,650	22,965
Florida..................	657	729	172,412	47	3,806	506,970	64,337
Georgia.................	2,878	3,134	953,873	102	7,085	2,171,267	341,433
Illinois.................	192	207	53,744	14	2,075	566,885	15,635
Indiana.................	121	126	39,725	11	825	347,950	13,404
Indian Territory.........	27	31	4,580			5,598	780
Iowa....................	45	43	10,795	2	250	121,990	2,643
Kansas.................	149	136	32,699	21	1,675	270,145	9,750
Kentucky...............	816	734	212,795	84	6,880	1,143,380	92,768
Louisiana...............	1,340	1,343	323,311	27	2,525	1,228,617	108,872
Maine..................	1			1	150		45
Maryland...............	463	473	122,379	22	1,840	1,118,040	58,566
Massachusetts..........	34	30	12,050	5	950	285,700	3,638
Michigan...............	49	47	12,520	7	1,750	107,085	3,957
Minnesota..............	10	9	3,700			62,500	958
Mississippi.............	2,309	2,354	614,681	91	7,120	1,434,102	224,404
Missouri................	549	515	133,809	72	4,700	919,427	42,452
Montana................	3	2	350	1	100	14,000	32
Nebraska...............	4	4	1,350			62,000	399
New Jersey............	136	140	40,076	10	1,448	405,490	12,720
New Mexico...........	3	3	550			3,300	62
New York..............	110	94	39,340	17	2,113	1,023,750	17,216
North Carolina	2,191	2,205	668,588	64	4,845	1,592,596	290,755
Ohio....................	250	214	66,515	31	1,750	576,425	19,827
Oklahoma..............	4			3	270		100
Oregon.................	3	2	900			20,000	291
Pennsylvania...........	228	234	77,865	25	3,025	1,156,408	26,753
Rhode Island...........	16	11	4,800	5	1,218	148,100	1,999
South Carolina..........	1,731	1,959	599,544	55	5,660	1,770,504	317,020
Tennessee..............	1,328	1,350	399,568	71	4,740	1,690,946	131,015
Texas..................	2,323	2,126	551,965	244	19,810	1,455,507	186,038
Utah...................	1			1	50		7
Virginia................	1,360	1,346	449,972	52	4,139	1,735,873	238,617
Washington.............	2	1	400			4,000	66
West Virginia	27	96	24,045	31	3,415	154,768	7,160
Wisconsin..............	5	4	550	1	200	40,400	268
Wyoming	4	2	325	2	200	5,500	154

We may now consider these organizations by denominations:

Regular Baptists (Colored)

The colored Baptists of the South constitute the most numerous body of Regular Baptists. Not all colored Baptists are embraced in this division; only those who have separate churches, associations, and state conventions. There are many colored Baptists in Northern States, who are mostly counted as members of churches, belonging to white associations. None of them are included in the following tables.

The first state convention of colored Baptists was organized in North Carolina in 1866, the second in Alabama, and the third in Virginia in 1867, the fourth in Arkansas in 1868, and the fifth in Kentucky in 1869. There are colored conventions in fifteen states and the District of Columbia.

In addition to these organizations the colored Baptists of the United States have others more general in character: The American National Convention, the purpose of which is "to consider the moral, intellectual, and religious growth of the denomination," to deliberate upon questions of general concern, and to devise methods to bring the churches and members of the race closer together; the Consolidated American Missionary Convention, the General Association of the Western States and Territories, the Foreign Mission Convention of the United States, and the New England Missionary Convention. All except one are missionary in their purpose.

The Regular Baptists (colored) are represented in fifteen states, all in the South, or on the border, and the District of Columbia. In Virginia and Georgia they are very numerous, having in the latter 200,516, and in the former 199,871 communicants. In Alabama they have 142,437, in North Carolina 134,445, in Mississippi 136,647, in South Carolina 125,572, and in Texas 111,138 members. The aggregate is 1,348,989 members, who are embraced in 12,533 organizations, with 11,987 church edifices, and church property valued at $9,038,549. There are 414 associations, of which 66 are in Alabama, 63 in Georgia, 49 in Mississippi, and 39 in North Carolina.

Regular Baptists (Colored)

SUMMARY BY STATES AND TERRITORIES

STATES AND TERRITORIES	Organizations.	Church Edifices.	Approximate Seating Capacity.	Halls, etc.	Seating Capacity.	Value of Church Property.	Communicants or Members.
The United States	12,533	11,987	3,440,970	663	45,570	$ 9,038,549	1,348,989
Alabama	1,374	1,341	376,839	50	3,365	795,384	142,437
Arkansas	923	870	243,395	51	3,310	585,947	63,786
District of Columbia	43	33	18,600	10	1,150	383,150	12,717
Florida	329	295	61,588	37	2,270	137,578	20,828
Georgia	1,818	1,800	544,540	58	3,460	1,045,310	200,516
Kentucky	378	359	109,030	26	2,025	406,949	50,245
Louisiana	865	861	191,041	13	1,480	609,800	68,008
Maryland	38	34	12,389			150,475	7,750
Mississippi	1,385	1,333	371,115	59	3,695	682,541	136,647
Missouri	234	212	60,015	26	1,225	400,518	18,613
North Carolina	1,173	1,164	362,946	14	750	705,512	134,445
South Carolina	860	836	275,529	37	3,685	699,961	125,572
Tennessee	569	534	159,140	41	1,860	519,923	52,183
Texas	1,464	1,288	282,590	180	12,000	664,286	111,138
Virginia	1,001	977	358,032	32	1,955	1,192,035	199,871
West Virginia	79	50	14,175	29	3,340	50,090	4,233

African Methodist Episcopal

This branch of American Methodism was organized in Baltimore in 1816 by a number of colored members of the Methodist Episcopal Church. They withdrew from the parent body in order that they might have larger privileges and more freedom of action among themselves than they believed they could secure in continued association with their white brethren. The Rev. Richard Allen was elected the first bishop of the new church by the same convention that organized it. In the year 1787 Mr. Allen had been made the leader of a class of forty persons of his own color. A few years later he purchased a lot at the corner of Sixth and Lombard streets, Philadelphia, where the first church erected in this country for colored Methodists was occupied in 1794. This site is now covered by an edifice, dedicated in 1890, valued at $50,000.

In doctrine, government, and usage, the church does not essentially differ from the body from which it sprang. It has an itinerant and a local or non-itinerant ministry, and its territory is divided into annual conferences. It has a general conference, meeting once every four years; bishops or itinerant general superintendents, elected for life, who visit the annual conferences in the episcopal districts to which they are assigned, and presiding elders, who exercise sub-episcopal oversight in the districts into which the annual conferences are divided; and it has the probationary system for new members, with exhorters, class leaders, stewards, stewardesses, etc.

The church in its first half century grew slowly, chiefly in the Northern States, until the close of the war. At the end of the first decade of its existence it had two conferences and about 8,000 members. In 1856 it had seven conferences and about 20,000 members; in 1866, ten conferences and 75,000 members. Bishop B. W. Arnett, the ardent and industrious statistician of the church, in noting a decrease of 343 members in the decade ending in 1836, in the Baltimore conference, explains that it was due to the numerous sales of members as slaves. According to elaborate figures furnished by him the increase in the value of church property owned by the denomination was not less than $400,-000 in the decade closing in 1866, or nearly fifty per cent. In the succeeding ten years the increase was from $825,000 to $3,064,000, not including parsonages, which seem to have been embraced in the total for 1866. According to the returns for 1890, given herewith, the valuation is $6,468,280, indicating an increase of $3,404,280 in the last fourteen years, or 111.11 per cent.

The church is widely distributed, having congregations in forty-one states and territories. The states in which it is not represented are the two Dakotas, Idaho, Maine, Nevada, New Hampshire, and Vermont, the territories being Alaska, Oklahoma, and Arizona. Its members are most numerous in South Carolina, where there are 88,172. Georgia comes second, with 73,248; Alabama third, with 30,781; Arkansas fourth, with 27,956; Mississippi fifth, with 25,439. Tennessee has 23,718, Texas 23,392, and Florida 22,463. In no other state does the number reach 17,000. The eight Southern States above given report 315,169 members, or considerably more than two-thirds of the entire membership of the church. It will be observed that of the 2,481 organizations only thirty-one worship in halls, school-houses, etc. All the rest, 2,450, own the edifices in which their meetings are held.

African Methodist Episcopal

SUMMARY BY STATES AND TERRITORIES

STATES AND TERRITORIES.	Organizations.	Church Edifices.	Approximate Seating Capacity.	Halls, etc.	Seating Capacity	Value of Church Property.	Communicants or Members.
The United States	2,481	4,124	1,160,838	31	2,200	$ 6,468,280	452,725
Alabama..................	145	274	77,600	4	200	$ 242,765	30,781
Arkansas................	173	333	77,585	.....	....	233,425	27,956
California................	13	15	2,929	.....	....	24,300	772
Colorado.................	8	6	2,300	.....	....	63,500	788
Connecticut	4	4	1,275	.....	....	16,000	158
Delaware.................	16	33	7,025	.....	....	39,500	2,603
District of Columbia.....	6	7	5,500	.....	....	117,500	1,479
Florida..................	152	269	63,445	.....	....	168,173	22,463
Georgia.................	334	654	184,592	7	250	601,287	73,248
Illinois	74	105	23,799	.....	....	310,985	6,383
Indiana	36	51	16,450	.....	....	138,280	4,435
Indian Territory..........	14	22	1,680	.....	....	2,618	489
Iowa....................	29	29	7,115	.....	....	87,365	1,820
Kansas..................	48	58	14,309	.....	....	153,530	4,678
Kentucky................	90	106	39,100	.....	....	181,201	13,972
Louisiana................	81	115	36,150	.....	....	193,115	13,631
Maryland................	58	93	29,881	.....	....	266,370	12,359
Massachusetts	12	11	5,950	1	75	119,200	1,342
Michigan	21	26	7,155	.....	....	72,185	1,836
Minnesota	6	6	2,350	.....	....	30,000	489
Mississippi...............	122	255	59,833	1	50	226,242	25,439
Missouri	87	126	27,870	.....	....	281,289	9,589
Montana.................	3	2	350	1	100	14,000	32
Nebraska................	4	4	1,350	.....	....	62 000	399
New Jersey...............	54	68	19,510	1	300	159,850	5,851
New Mexico..............	3	3	550	.....	....	3,300	62
New York................	34	29	12,900	6	325	231,500	3,124
North Carolina...........	61	147	42,350	.....	....	112,998	16,156
Ohio	111	113	40,965	1	50	318,250	10,025
Oregon..................	1	......	....	.....	....	....	16
Pennsylvania	87	112	39,900	5	600	605,000	11,613
Rhode Island.............	4	3	2,050	1	....	95,000	595
South Carolina...........	229	491	125,945	.....	....	356,362	88,172
Tennessee................	144	236	61,800	.....	....	461,305	23,718
Texas...................	138	208	82,850	.....	....	233,340	23,392
Utah....................	1	......	....	1	50	....	7
Virginia.................	67	102	34,375	.....	....	187,245	12,314
Washington	2	1	400	.....	....	4,000	66
West Virginia.............	3	3	1,050	.....	....	11,000	216
Wisconsin................	3	3	400	.....	....	40,000	118
Wyoming................	3	1	200	2	200	4,000	139

African Union Methodist Protestant

This body, which has a few congregations divided among eight states, came into existence at about the same time the African Methodist Episcopal Church was organized (1816), differing from the latter chiefly in objection to the itinerancy, to a paid ministry, and to the episcopacy.

SUMMARY BY STATES

STATES.	Organizations.	Church Edifices.	Approximate Seating Capacity.	Halls, etc.	Seating Capacity.	Value of Church Property.	Communicants or Members.
The United States.............	40	27	7,161	13	1,883	$ 54,440	3,415
Delaware...........................	6	4	1,250	2	270	$ 9,600	368
Maine.............................	1			1	150	....	45
Maryland.........................	8	7	2,255	1	240	5,600	1,546
New Jersey.......................	8	6	836	2	108	5,940	281
New York.........................	3			3	568	....	60
Pennsylvania.....................	8	8	2,140			32,100	852
Rhode Island.....................	1			1	148	....	49
Virginia..........................	5	2	680	3	399	1,200	214

Congregational Methodist (Colored)

Dissatisfaction with certain features of the system of polity led a number of ministers and members of the Methodist Episcopal Church, South, to withdraw and organize a body in which laymen should have an equal voice in church government, and local preachers should become pastors.

This body consists of congregations of colored members organized into conferences by presidents of the Congregational Methodist Church, to which it corresponds in all particulars of doctrine, polity, usage. The only difference between the churches of the two bodies is, that they are composed of white and colored persons, respectively.

SUMMARY BY STATES

STATES.	Organizations.	Church Edifices.	Approximate Seating Capacity.	Halls, etc.	Seating Capacity.	Value of Church Property.	Communicants or Members.
The United States..............	9	5	585	4	450	$ 525	319
Alabama...........................	7	5	585	2	250	525	215
Texas.............................	2			2	200	....	104

African Methodist Episcopal Zion

A congregation of colored people, organized in New York city, in 1796, was the nucleus of the African Methodist Episcopal Zion Church. This congregation originated in a desire of colored members of the Methodist Episcopal Church to hold separate meetings in which they "might have an opportunity to exercise their spiritual gifts among themselves, and thereby be more useful to one another." They built a church, which was dedicated in 1800, the full name of the denomination subsequently organized being given to it.

The church entered into an agreement in 1801 by which it was to receive certain pastoral supervision from the Methodist Episcopal Church. It had preachers of its own, who supplied its pulpit in part. In 1820 this arrangement terminated, and in the same year a union of colored churches in New York, New Haven, Long Island, and Philadelphia was formed, and rules of government adopted. Thus was the African Methodist Episcopal Zion Church formally organized.

The first annual conference was held in 1821. It was attended by nineteen preachers, representing six churches and 1,426 members. Next year James Varick was chosen superintendent of the denomination, which was extended over the states of the North chiefly, until the close of the civil war, when it entered the South to organize many churches.

In its polity lay representation has long been a prominent feature. Laymen are in its annual conferences as well as in its general conference, and there is no bar to the ordination of women. Until 1880 its superintendents or bishops were elected for a term of four years. In that year the term of the office was made for life or during good behavior. Its system is almost identical with that of the Methodist Episcopal Church, except the presence of laymen in the annual conference, the election of presiding elders on the nomination of the presiding bishop, instead of their appointment by the bishop alone, and other small divergences. Its general conference meets quadrennially. Its territory is divided into seven episcopal districts, to each of which a bishop is assigned by the general conference.

The church is represented in twenty-eight states and the District of Columbia. It is strongest in North Carolina, where it has 111,949 communicants. Alabama comes next, with 79.231 communicants; South Carolina third, with 45,880, and Florida fourth, with 14,791. There are in all 1,704 organizations, 1,587 church edifices, church property valued at $2,714,128, and 349,788 communicants.

EIGHTH ATLANTA CONFERENCE

African Methodist Episcopal Zion

SUMMARY BY STATES AND TERRITORIES

STATES AND TERRITORIES.	Organizations.	Church Edifices.	Approximate Seating Capacity.	Halls, etc.	Seating Capacity.	Value of Church Property.	Communicants or Members.
The United States	1,704	1,587	565,577	114	15,520	$ 2,714,128	349,788
Alabama	336	315	118,800	17	2,500	$ 305,350	79,231
Arkansas	29	23	8,800	6	750	17,250	3,601
California	13	6	2,600	7	1,950	37,200	2,627
Connecticut	12	10	2,900	2	150	79,350	1,012
Delaware	2	1	115	1	200	500	158
District of Columbia	6	6	3,400			298,800	2,495
Florida	61	61	23,589			90,745	14,791
Georgia	70	62	19,775	9	200	52,380	12,705
Illinois	5	5	2,000			13,400	434
Indiana	5	5	2,400			54,700	1,339
Kentucky	55	52	13,075	3	250	86,830	7,217
Louisiana	21	19	5,200	2	350	12,920	2,747
Maryland	13	10	2,375	3	400	17,350	1,211
Massachusetts	7	6	2,050	1	75	58,800	724
Michigan	6	4	650	2	500	3,200	702
Mississippi	64	50	22,350	14	2,375	22,975	8,519
Missouri	6	6	3,900			6,000	2,037
New Jersey	25	24	7,400	1	150	107,700	2,954
New York	47	47	17,000			371,400	6,668
North Carolina	541	527	171,430	14	1,300	485,711	111,949
Ohio	8	5	1,160	3		13,000	194
Oregon	2	2	300			20,000	275
Pennsylvania	62	55	17,625	7	275	256,150	8,689
Rhode Island	3	1	400	2	870	2,000	401
South Carolina	130	128	66,770	2	250	126,395	45,880
Tennessee	55	52	21,093	3	250	78,813	12,434
Texas	47	38	11,500	9	1,775	26,450	6,927
Virginia	72	66	16,770	6	950	68,449	11,765
Wisconsin	1	1	150			400	102

Colored Methodist Episcopal

The Colored Methodist Episcopal Church was organized in 1870 of colored members and ministers of the Methodist Episcopal Church, South.

Before the late civil war the Methodist Episcopal Church, South, did a large evangelistic work among the Negroes. Bishop McTyeire, of that body, in his "History of Methodism," says:

"As a general rule Negro slaves received the gospel by Methodism from the same preachers and in the same churches with their masters, the galleries or a portion of the body of the house being assigned to them. If a separate building was provided, the Negro congregation was an appendage to the white, the pastor usually preaching once on Sunday for them, holding separate official meetings with their leaders, exhorters, and preachers, and administering discipline, and making return of members for the annual minutes." For the Negroes on plantations, who were not privileged to attend organized churches, special missions were begun as early as 1829. In 1845, the year which marks the beginning of the separate existence of the Methodist Episcopal Church, South, there were in the Southern conferences of Methodism, according to Bishop McTyeire, 124,000 members of the slave population, and in 1860 about 207,000.

In 1866, after the opening of the South to Northern churches had given the Negro members opportunity to join the African Methodist Episcopal, the African Methodist Episcopal Zion, and other Methodist bodies, it was found that of the 207,742 colored members which the church, South, had in 1860 only 78,742 remained. The general conference of 1866 authorized these colored members, with their preachers, to be organized into separate congregations and annual conferences, and the general conference of 1870 appointed two bishops to organize the colored conferences into a separate and independent church. This was done in December, 1870, the new body taking the name "Colored Methodist Episcopal Church." Its rules limited the privilege of membership to Negroes. The Colored Methodist Episcopal Church has the same articles of religion, the same form of government, and the same discipline as its parent body. Its bishops are elected for life. One of them, Bishop L. H. Holsey, says that for some years the body encountered strong opposition from colored people because of its relation to the Methodist Episcopal Church, South, but that this prejudice has now almost entirely disappeared.

Colored Methodist Episcopal

SUMMARY BY STATES AND TERRITORIES

STATES AND TERRITORIES.	Organizations.	Church Edifices.	Approximate Seating Capacity.	Halls, etc.	Seating Capacity.	Value of Church Property.	Communicants or Members.
The United States...	1,759	1,653	541,464	64	6,526	$1,713,366	129,383
Alabama	222	220	69,200	....	.....	$ 264,625	18,940
Arkansas	116	104	31,059	13	1,200	60,277	5,888
Delaware	6	3	430	3	100	1,125	187
District of Columbia	5	4	3,500	1	100	123,800	939
Florida	36	26	7,000	5	1,236	14,709	1,461
Georgia	266	256	100,495	7	1,075	167,145	22,840
Illinois	2	2	800	....	.....	1,250	56
Indian Territory	13	9	2,850	....	.....	2,975	291
Kansas	17	15	3,625	....	.....	14,400	713
Kentucky	91	63	16,000	12	1,225	140,330	6,908
Louisiana	138	131	43,220	2	100	134,135	8,075
Maryland	2	2	205	....	.....	475	44
Mississippi	293	292	72,150	....	.....	230,490	20,107
Missouri	35	31	5,554	3	100	22,140	953
New Jersey	5	3	625	2	140	7,500	266
North Carolina	26	20	7,725	6	.....	23,120	2,786
Pennsylvania	6	2	310	4	1,050	1,400	247
South Carolina	34	33	15,045	1	100	65,325	3,468
Tennessee	206	205	67,900	....	.....	258,120	18,968
Texas	222	216	88,330	3	.....	147,075	14,895
Virginia	18	16	4,850	2	100	33,150	1,351

Cumberland Presbyterian (Colored)

This body was organized in May, 1869, at Murfreesboro, Tenn., under the direction of the General Assembly of the Cumberland Presbyterian Church. It was constituted of colored ministers and members who had been connected with that church. Its first synod, the Tennessee, was organized in 1871, and its general assembly in 1874. It has the same doctrinal symbol as the parent body and the same system of government and discipline, differing only in race. It has twenty-three presbyteries, and is represented in nine states and one territory. It has 224 organizations, 183 church edifices, 12,956 communicants, and church property valued at $195,826.

Cumberland Presbyterian (Colored)

SUMMARY BY STATES AND TERRITORIES

STATES AND TERRITORIES.	Organizations.	Church Edifices.	Approximate Seating Capacity.	Halls, etc.	Seating Capacity.	Value of Church Property.	Communicants or Members.
The United States	224	183	52,139	34	3,570	$ 195,826	12,956
Alabama	44	38	9,574	7	475	$ 26,200	3,104
Arkansas	2			2	300		255
Illinois	7	4	1,300	2	75	5,375	195
Kansas	6	3	650	3	150	15,000	190
Kentucky	36	31	7,730	2		31,645	1,421
Mississippi	4	4	950			1,825	278
Missouri	10	9	1,650	1	50	17,900	471
Oklahoma	4			3	270		100
Tennessee	81	72	24,125	7	825	88,660	5,202
Texas	30	22	6,160	7	1,425	9,221	1,740

14. Local Studies, 1902-3. To realize the present condition of churches and the changes in the last thirteen years, the Conference of 1903 arranged for a number of local studies of churches: one in a black belt county of Georgia, another in a county of southern Ohio, a third in the city of Chicago and the state of Illinois, a fourth in Virginia, and a fifth in Atlanta, Ga. To these studies were added the results of previous investigations in DeLand, Fla., Farmville, Va., and Philadelphia, Pa. The study in Thomas county, Ga., was made by a colored Congregational minister, the Rev. W. H. Holloway, a graduate of Talladega College. The study in Greene county, Ohio, was made by the Rev. R. R. Wright, Jr., who later made a more comprehensive study for the United States Bureau of Labor. Mr. Monroe N. Work, of the University of Chicago, studied Illinois, and the investigations in Atlanta were made by senior students in Atlanta University. Dr. Annie M. MacLean kindly furnished the study of Deland, Fla. The students of Virginia Union University, under the direction of Professor B. F. Williams, made the investigations in Virginia.

To realize just the change in moral conditions it is instructive to preface these studies with several verbatim paragraphs taken from the work of an apologist for slavery, but one who strove manfully for the uplift of the slaves.* The period referred to is generally the decade, 1830–1840:

---

* C. C. Jones: Religious Instruction of Negroes, pp. 89-176, *passim.*

"Persons live and die in the midst of Negroes and know comparatively little of their real character. They have not the immediate management of them. They have to do with them in the ordinary discharge of their duty as servants, further than this they institute no inquiries; they give themselves no trouble. The Negroes are a distinct class in the community, and keep themselves very much to themselves. They are one thing before the whites and another before their own color. Deception before the former is characteristic of them, whether bond or free, throughout the whole United States. It is habit, a long established custom, which descends from generation to generation. There is an upper and an under current. Some are contented with the appearance on the surface; others dive beneath. Hence the diversity of impressions and representations of the moral and religious condition of the Negroes. Hence the disposition of some to deny the darker pictures of their more searching and knowing friends. . . . . .

"Their general mode of living is coarse and vulgar. Many Negro houses are small, low to the ground, blackened with smoke, often with dirt floors, and the furniture of the plainest kind. On some estates the houses are framed, weatherboarded, neatly whitewashed, and made sufficiently large and comfortable in every respect. . . . . .

"It is a matter of thankfulness that the owners are few in number, indeed, who forbid religious meetings on their plantations, held either by their servants themselves, or by competent and approved white instructors or ministers. 'All men have not faith.' I have never known servants forbidden to attend the worship of God on the Sabbath day, except as a restraint temporarily laid, for some flagrant misconduct. . . . . .

"Nor can the adult Negro acquaint himself with duty and the way of salvation through the reading of the scriptures any more than the child. Of those that do read, but few read well enough for the edification of the hearers. Not all the colored preachers read. . . . . .

"Such, then, are the circumstances of the slave population, which have an unfavorable influence upon their moral and religious condition. Those circumstances only have been referred to which prominently assist us in our inquiry. In conclusion, it may be added that servants have neither intellectual nor moral intercourse with their masters generally, sufficient to redeem them from the adverse influence of the circumstances alluded to; for the two classes are distinct in their association, and it cannot well be otherwise. Nor have servants any redeeming intercourse with any other persons. On the contrary, in certain situations there is intercourse had with them, and many temptations laid before them against which they have little or no defense, and the effect is deplorable."

"To know the extent of their ignorance, even where they have been accustomed to the sound of the gospel in white churches, a man should make investigation for himself. The result will frequently surprise and fill him with grief. They scarcely feel shame for their ignorance on the subject of religion, although they may have had abundant opportunity of becoming wiser. Ignorance, they seem to feel, is their lot; and that feeling is intimately associated with another every way congenial to the natural man, namely, a feeling of irresponsibility—ignorance is a cloak and excuse for crime. Some white ministers and teachers, in their simplicity, beholding their attention to the preaching of the gospel, adapted to their comprehension, and hearing the expressions of their thankfulness for the pains taken for their instruction, come to the conclusion that they are an unsophisticated race; that they form one of the easiest and pleasantest fields of labor in the world; and that they are a people 'made ready, prepared for the Lord,' nothing more being necessary than to carry them the gospel and converts will be multiplied as drops of morning dew; yea, a nation will be born in a day. Experiment shortly dissipates these visions, and well is it if the sober reality does not frighten the laborer away in disgust and disappointment. . . . . .

"But a brief view of the prevailing vices of the Negroes will best reveal their moral and religious condition.

"*Violations of the Marriage Contract.* The divine institution of marriage depends for its perpetuity, sacredness, and value, largely upon the protection given it by the law of the land. Negro marriages are neither recognized nor protected by law. The Negroes receive no instruction on the nature, sacredness, and perpetuity of the institution; at any rate they are far from being duly impressed with these things. They are not required to be married in any particular form, nor by any particular persons. Their ceremonies are performed by their own watchmen or teachers, by some white minister, or as it frequently happens, not at all; the consent of owners and of the parties immediately interested, and a public acknowledgement of each other, being deemed sufficient.

"There is no special disgrace nor punishment visited upon those who criminally violate their marriage vows, except where they may be inflicted by owners, or if the parties be members, by the church in the way of suspension and excommunication.

"Families are, and may be, divided for improper conduct on the part of either husband or wife, or by necessity, as in cases of the death of owners, division of estates, debt, sale, or removals, for they are subject to all the changes and vicissitudes of property. Such divisions are, however, carefully guarded against and prevented, as far as possible, by owners, on the score of interest, as well as of religion and humanity. Hence, as may well be imagined, the marriage relation loses much of the sacredness and perpetuity of its character. It is a contract of convenience, profit, or pleasure, that may be entered into and dissolved at the will of the parties, and that without heinous sin, or the injury of the property or interests of any one. That which they possess in common is speedily divided, and the support of the wife and children falls not upon the husband, but upon the master. Protracted sickness, want of industrial habits, of congeniality of disposition, or disparity of age, are sufficient grounds for a separation. While there are creditable instances of conjugal fidelity for a long series of years and until death, yet infidelity in the marriage relation and dissolution of marriage ties are not uncommon.

"On account of the changes, interruptions and interferences in families, there are quarrelings and fightings, and a considerable item in the management of plantations is the settlement of family troubles. Some owners become disgusted and worried out, and finally leave their people to do their own way; while others cease from the strife ere it be meddled with, and give it as an opinion that the less the interference on the part of the master the better. A few conscientious masters persevere in attempts at reformation, and with some good degree of success.

Polygamy is practiced, both secretly and openly. In some sections, where the people have been well instructed, it is scarcely known; in others, the crime has diminished and is diminishing; it is to be hoped universally so. It is a crime which, among all people and under all circumstances, carries, in its perpetration, vast inconveniences and endless divisions and troubles, and they are felt by the Negroes as well as by others, and operate as a great preventive. Polygamy is also discountenanced and checked by the majority of owners, and by the churches of all denominations.

"*Uncleanness.* This sin may be considered universal. The declaration will be sufficient for those who have any acquaintance with this people in the slave-holding states or in the free states; indeed, with the ignorant laboring classes of people wherever they may be found. It is not my object to institute comparisons. If it were, I could point to many tongues and people, in civilized governments, upon the same level of depravity with the Negroes. The sin is not viewed by them as by those of higher intelligence and virtue, so that they do not consider character as lost by it, nor personal degradation as necessarily connected with it. A view which, however it may spring from vitiated principle, preserves the guilty from entire prostration."

"Intimately connected with this view is the crime of

"*Infanticide.* A crime restrained in good measure by the provision made for the support of the child on the part of the owner, by the punishment in case of detection, and by the moral degradation of the people that takes away the disgrace of bastardy.

"*Theft.* They are proverbially thieves. They bear this character in Africa; they have borne it in all countries whither they have been carried; it has been the character of slaves in all ages, whatever their nation or color. They steal from each other, from their masters, from anybody. Cows, sheep, hogs, poultry, clothing; yea, nothing goes amiss to which they take a fancy; while corn, rice, cotton, or the staple productions, whatever they may be, are standing temptations, provided a market be at hand, and they can sell or barter them with impunity. Locks, bolts, and bars secure articles desirable to them, from the dwelling of the master to that of the servant, and the keys must always be carried.

"*Falsehood.* Their veracity is nominal. Duplicity is one of the most prominent traits of their character, practiced between themselves, but more especially towards their masters and managers. Their frequent cases of feigned sickness are vexatious. When criminal acts are under investigation, the sober, strenuous falsehood, sometimes the direct and awful appeal to God, of the transgressor, averts the suspicion, and by his own tact and collusion with others, perhaps fixes the guilt upon some innocent person. The number, the variety, and ingenuity of falsehoods that can be told by them in a few brief moments is astonishing. Where opportunity is given they will practice imposition. Servants, however, who will neither steal nor lie, may be found, and in no inconsiderable numbers.

"*Quarreling and Fighting.* The Negroes are settled in some quarter of the plantation, in houses near each other, built in rows, forming a street. The custom is to give each family a house of its own. The houses sometimes have a partition in the middle and accommodate a family in each end. These are called double houses. Living so near each other, and every day working together, causes of differences must necessarily arise. Families grow jealous and envious of their neighbors; some essay to be leading families; they overhear conversations and domestic disagreements; become privy to improper conduct; they depredate upon each other; a fruitful source of tumult is the pilfering and quarreling of children, which involve their parents. The women quarrel more than the men, and fight oftener. Where no decisive measures are taken to suppress these practices, plantations sometimes become intolerable, might is right; the strong oppress the weak. Every master or manager has the evil under his own control.

"They come to open breaches, too, with their neighbors on adjoining plantations, or lots, if they live in towns. The Sabbath is considered a very suitable day for the settlement of their difficulties. However, with truth it may be said, there are fewer personal injuries, and manslaughters, and murders, among the

Negroes in the South, than among the same amount of population in any part of the United States; or perhaps, in the world.

"*Insensibility of Heart.* An ignorant and degraded people are not wont to exhibit much of the milk of human kindness.

"Unless the Negroes are carefully watched and made accountable for power lodged in their hands, it will be abused. Parents will beat their children, husbands their wives, master mechanics their apprentices, and drivers the people. In sickness, parents will neglect their children, children their parents; and so with the other social relations. They cannot be trusted as nurses. Hence they must be made to attend upon the sick, and then watched lest they neglect them; which ultimately brings the whole care of the sick upon the master or manager. It is a saying of their own, 'that white people care more for them than their own color,' and again, 'that black people have not the same feeling for each other that white people have.' It is an indisputable fact that when Negroes become owners of slaves they are generally cruel masters. They will overload, work down, bruise and beat, and starve all working animals committed to their care, with careless indifference. . . . . .

"The moral and religious condition of town and city Negroes, may be disposed of in a few lines.

"They admit of division into four classes: family servants, or those who belong to the families which they serve; hired servants, or those who are hired out by their owners to wait in families, or to any other service; servants who hire their own time, and work at various employments and pay their owners so much per day or month; and watermen, embracing fishermen, sailors and boatmen.

"Town and city Negroes are more intelligent and sprightly than country Negroes, owing to a difference in circumstances, employments, and opportunities of improvement. Their physical condition is somewhat improved; and they enjoy greater access to religious privileges.

"On the other hand, they are exposed to greater temptations and vices; their opportunities of attending upon places of pleasure and dissipation are increased; they have stronger temptations to theft, and idleness, and drunkenness, and lewdness; and the tendency to Sabbath breaking is equally great. Their moral and religious condition is precisely that of plantation Negroes, modified in some respects by peculiarities of circumstances. They are more intelligent, but less subordinate; better provided for in certain particulars, but not more healthy; enjoy greater advantages for religious improvement, but are thrown more directly in the way of temptation; and, on the whole, in point of moral character, if there be any pre-eminence it is in favor of the country Negroes; but it is a difficult point to decide. . . . . .

"The Honorable Charles Cotesworth Pinckney, in an 'Address before the Agricultural Society of South Carolina,' (Charleston, 1829, second edition, pp. 10-12), said:

"'There needs no stronger illustration of the doctrine of human depravity than the state of morals on plantations in general. Besides the mischievous tendency of bad example in parents and elders, the little Negro is often taught by these natural instructors, that he may commit any vice that he can conceal from his superiors, and thus falsehood and deception are among the earliest lessons they imbibe. Their advance in years is but a progression to the higher grades of iniquity. The violation of the seventh commandment is viewed in a more venial light than in fashionable European circles. Their depredations of rice have been estimated to amount to twenty-five per cent. on the gross average of crops, and this calculation was made after fifty years experience, by one whose liberal provision for their wants left no excuse for their ingratitude.' . . . . .

"The Honorable Whitemarsh B. Seabrook, in an 'Essay on the Management of Slaves,' Charleston, (1836, pp. 7, 8, 12, etc.), says: 'As human beings, however slaves are liable to all the infirmities of our nature. Ignorant and fanatical, none are more easily excited. Incendiaries might readily embitter their enjoyments and render them a curse to themselves and the community. The prominent offences of the slave are to be traced in most instances to the use of intoxicating liquors. This is one of the main sources of every insurrectionary movement which has occurred in the United States, and we are, therefore, bound by interest, as well as the common feeling of humanity, to arrest the contagious disease of our colored population. What have become of the millions of freemen who once inhabited our widely-spread country? Ask the untiring votaries of Bacchus. Can there be a doubt, but that the authority of the master alone prevents his slaves from experiencing the fate of the aborigines of America? At one time polygamy was a common crime; it is now of rare occurrence. Between slaves on the same plantation there is a deep sympathy of feeling which binds them so closely together that a crime committed by one of their number is seldom discovered through their instrumentality. This is an obstacle to the establishment of an efficient police, which the domestic legislator can with difficulty surmount.'

"The executive committee of the Kentucky Union for the moral and religious improvement of the colored race, in their 'Circular to the ministers of Kentucky,' 1834, say: 'We desire not to represent their condition worse than it is. Doubtless the light that shines around them, more or less illuminates their minds and moralizes their characters. We hope and believe that some of them, though poor in this world's goods, will be found rich in spiritual possessions in the day when the King of Zion shall make up his jewels. We know that many of them are included in the visible church, and frequently exhibit great zeal; but it is to be feared that it is often 'a zeal without knowledge,' and of the majority it must be confessed that 'the light shineth in darkness and the darkness comprehendeth it not.' After making all reasonable allowances, our colored population can be considered, at the most, but semi-heathen.' . . . . .

"C. W. Gooch, Esq., Henrico county, Virginia, in a Prize Essay on Agriculture in Virginia, said:

"'The slave feels no inducement to execute his work with effect. He has a particular art of slighting it and seeming to be busy, when in fact he is doing little or nothing. Nor can he be made to take proper care of stock, tools, or anything else. He will rarely take care of his clothes or his own health, much less of his companion's when sick and requiring his aid and kindness. There is perhaps not in nature a more heedless, thoughtless human being than a Virginia field Negro. With no care upon his mind, with warm clothing and plenty of food under a good master, is far the happier man of the two. His maxim is 'come day, go day, God send Sunday!' His abhorrence of the poor white man is very great. He may sometimes feel a reflected respect for him, in consequence of the confidence and esteem of his master and others. But this trait is remarkable in the white, as in the black man. All despise poverty and seem to worship wealth. To the losses which arise from the dispositions of our slaves, must be added those which are occasioned by their habits. There seems to be an almost entire absence of moral principle among the mass of our colored population. But details upon this subject would be here misplaced. To steal and not to be detected is a merit among them, as it was with certain people in ancient times, and is at this day, with some unenlightened portions of mankind. And the vice which they hold in the greatest abhorrence is that of telling upon one another. There are many exceptions it is true, but this description embraces more than the majority. The numerous free Negroes and worthless, dissipated whites, who have no visible means of support, and who are rarely seen at work, derive their chief subsistence from the slaves. These thefts amount to a good deal in the course of the year, and operate like leeches on the fair income of agriculture. They vary, however, in every county and neighborhood in exact proportion as the market for the plunder varies. In the vicinities of towns and villages they are most serious. Besides the actual loss of property occasioned by them, they involve the riding of their horses at night, the corruption of the habits and the injury of the health of the slaves; for whiskey is the price generally received for them.'

"These extracts, selected at random, are sufficient. A multiplication of them would be but a tiresome repetition. After all, the best testimony, is the observation and experience of all persons who are intimately acquainted with them. That the Negroes are in a degraded state is a fact, so far as my knowlege extends, universally conceded. It makes no difference if it be shown, as it might be, that they are less degraded than other portions of the human family, the fact remains true in respect to them, they are degraded, and it is with this fact which we have to do. . . . . .

"All approaches to them [the slaves] from abroad are rigidly guarded against, and no ministers are allowed to break to them the bread of life, except such as have commended themselves to the affection and confidence of owners. I do not condemn this course of self-preservation on the part of our citizens. I mention it only to show more fully the point in hand: the entire dependence of the Negroes upon ourselves for the gospel.

"While this step is taken another has already been taken, and that of a long time; namely, Negro preachers are discouraged, if not suppressed, on the ground of incompetency and liability to abuse their office and influence to the injury of the morals of the people and the infringement of the laws and peace of the country. I would not go all the lengths of many on this point, for from my own observation, Negro preachers may be employed and confided in, and so regulated as to do their own color great good, and community no harm; nor do I see, if we take the word of God for our guide, how we can consistently exclude an entire people from access to the gospel ministry, as it may please Almighty God from time to time, as he unquestionably does, to call some of them to it 'as Aaron was.' The discouragement of this class of preachers, throws the body of the people still more in their dependence upon ourselves, who indeed cannot secure ministers in sufficient numbers to supply our own wants.

"Nor have the Negroes any church organizations different from or independent of our own. Such independent organizations are, indeed, not on the whole advisable. But the fact binds them to us with still stronger dependence. And, to add more, we may, according to the power lodged in our hands, forbid religious meetings, and religious instruction on our plantations; we may forbid our servants going to church at all, or only to such churches as we may select for them; we may literally shut up the kingdom of heaven against men, and suffer not them that are entering to go in?' . . . . .

"The celebrated John Randolph, on a visit to a female friend, found her surrounded with her seamstresses, making up a quantity of clothing. 'What work have you in hand?' 'O, sir, I am preparing this clothing to send to the poor Greeks.' On taking leave at the steps of the mansion, he saw some of her servants in need of the very clothing which their tender-hearted mistress was sending abroad. He exclaimed: 'Madam, madam, the Greeks are at your door !' . . . . .

"We have colored ministers and exhorters, but their numbers are wholly inadequate to the supply of the Negroes; and while their ministrations are infrequent and conducted in great weakness, there are some of them whose moral character is justly suspected and who may be considered blind leaders of the blind."

Finally, a word must be added on the church and slave marriages in ante-bellum days. The sale of a slave away from his home and family "was a virtual decree of divorce and so recognized, not only by usage, but by the deliberate decree of the churches."

"The time will come when this statement will seem almost incredible. The usage, considered as a barbarism for which no religious defence would be possible, is bad enough. But to give it the sanction of religion, the religion of Jesus Christ, and to invoke the divine blessing upon a marriage which was no marriage at all, but simply a concubinage which the master's word might at any moment invalidate, seems at first beyond all manner of excuse. Yet it was done, and that not only by individual ministers of Christ, but by authority of ecclesiastical conventions. The resolutions to that effect went upon record in Methodist, Baptist, Presbyterian churches, declaring that the separation of husband and wife under slavery, by the removal of either party, was to be regarded as 'civil death,' sundering the bonds, and leaving both parties free to make another marriage contract. Slavery, by necessity of the case, abolished all family ties, of husband and wife, of parents and children, of brothers and sisters, except so far as the convenience of the master might be suited by their recognition. Legal sanction there was none. But the sham service which the law scorned to recognize was rendered by the ministers of the gospel of Christ. I have witnessed it, but could never bring myself to take part in such pretence.

"And yet I feel compelled by truth to say that, among all the alleviations of slavery, there was none greater than this. While the nominal relation continued at all, it mas made sacred to the slave husband and wife, and the affectionate African nature was comforted and sustained by it. It was a strong motive to good behavior, it promoted decency in social intercourse, it tended towards keeping the slave-family together, and was some restraint upon masters—a great restraint upon the better class of them—against arbitrary separation by sale; in short, it was one of the fearful anomalies of a brutal and barbarous social system existing among a civilized, Christian people.

"The question was fully discussed by the Savannah River Baptist Association of Ministers in 1835; aud the decision was, 'that such separation, among persons situated as slaves are, is civilly a separation by death, and that in the sight of God it would be so viewed. To forbid second marriages in such case would be to expose the parties to church censure for disobedience to their masters, and to the spirit of that command which regulates marriage among Christians. The slaves are not free agents, and a dissolution by death is not more entirely without their consent and beyond their control than by such separation.'

"Truly the logic of slavery was the destruction of humanity."*

---

* Eliot: Story of Archer Alexander.

15. A Black Belt County, Georgia, (by the Rev. W. H. Holloway).

Thomas county is situated in extreme southwest Georgia, within twenty miles of the northern boundary line of Florida. According to the census of 1900, the Negro population was 17,450. Among this population there are ninety-eight churches. These churches represent all denominations, Baptist predominating, there being only two Congregational and one Episcopal church. This number gives the actual churches which we have been able to learn of. It will be a safe estimate to affirm that about twenty per cent. of this number may be added, of which we failed to learn.

This will give a church for every 150 persons, and here it might be said that, unlike much of our American population, the Negro is well-churched. It is his only institution and forms the center of his public life. He turns to it not only for his spiritual wants, but looks toward it as the center of his civilization. Here he learns the price of cotton or the date of the next circus; here is given the latest fashion plates or the announcement for candidates for justice of the peace. In fact, the white office seeker has long since learned that his campaign among the Negroes must be begun in the Negro church, and by a Negro preacher.

These ninety-eight institutions in Thomas county, like those of many other counties, have interesting histories. About half this number represent the churches whose beginning has been normal, the natural outgrowth of expansion. The other half's history is checkered. Their rise can almost invariably be traced to one or two methods. First, there is the proverbial "split." A careful study of the roll of membership in many of the churches will reveal the second method. Some brother is called to preach. This call is so thunderous, and the confidence that he can "make a better preach" than the present pastor so obtrusive, till he soon finds that there is little welcome in the sacred rostrum of the old church. He therefore takes his family and his nearest relatives and moves away. Study the rolls, therefore, of many of the churches and you will find that they are largely family churches, and that the first preacher was some venerable patriarch. I think one will be perfectly safe in concluding that two-thirds of the growth in churches of the various denominations has been made in this way; and that little has been accomplished by the church executives as the result of direct effort at church extension.

It will be readily seen that churches having their origin in this way merely duplicate the old institution; often it is not a creditable duplicate. I know of no rural church in Thomas county whose inception had the careful nursing of an educated, cultured leader. Others have labored and we have entered into their labors. The largest churches and the biggest preachers in Thomas county do little home missionary work and organize no new churches.

The result, therefore, must necessarily be a constant propagation of the old regime. Standards of slavery time and directly after still prevail. It is impossible that it should be otherwise. Like begets like.

The supreme element in the old system was emotionalism, and, while we hate to confess it, truth demands that we affirm it as the predominating element to-day. The church which does not have its shouting, the church which does not measure the abilities of a preacher by the "rousement" of his sermons, and indeed which does not tacitly demand of its minister the shout-producing discourse, is an exception to the rule. This is true of the towns as well as the country. Of course we all understand that it has always occupied first place in the worship of the Negro church; it is a heritage of the past. In the absence of clearly defined doctrines, the great shout, accompanied with weird cries and shrieks and contortions and followed by a multi-varied "experience" which takes the candidate through the most heart-rending scenes—this to-day in Thomas county is accepted by the majority of the churches as unmistakable evidence of regeneration.

Now, the preachers who have had some advantages of study, who have come into contact with the learning of the schools, and have in their intelligence gotten above the ignorant preacher of the country, know that the old order of things is wrong. Talk with them and they all confess it. Confront them with the truth that it prevails in their own churches, and their reply puts the question upon the basis of supply and demand. They say: "My people have been used to it, my predecessor was thought to be the embodiment of perfection, and this was his standard; therefore, if I would succeed, if I would hold my people, I must supply this demand; and if I would make the record of my success more enduring than my predecessor I must supply this demand in greater quantities and more acceptable quality than he."

The spirit of rivalry also has much to do with the continuance of this emotional feature. Two churches in the same community—one presided over by an educated minister, with lofty ideals and correct standards, and to whose better nature the old order is repulsive, and the other presided over by a typical representative of the old school : the educated minister will often preach unseen and waste his eloquence on the desert air. He soon finds that not only is his church losing its pristine prominence, not only is his own reputation as a representative clergyman waning, but that there is soon a very perceptible diminution in the loaves and fishes. It is a problem and it is forcing young preachers who would otherwise do good work in the ministry into the old ruts which, while their better natures condemn it, they have not the power to resist. Any system which robs the man of his individuality and makes him less than a man, finds itself early bereft of its power for the highest service. Another effect is, that it is driving out of the work the young men of ability whom the work most needs. I know one promising young man in my county who is driven to desperation and vows, for none other cause than this of which we have been speaking, that he will leave the work at the next annual conference. And, too, the young men in our schools turn their faces toward other vocations.

Under this old system, which prevails in Thomas county, the question arises, is the moral condition of the people being raised?

Of the blanks which we had returned, while some said openly "No," the majority left the question in doubt.

We would conclude, however, that the moral standard of the Negroes in Thomas county is being bettered; but I seriously raise the question whether the church is the great factor in this improvement. Speaking especially now of the towns, whose condition has been studied more carefully and at first hand, the conclusion is almost inevitable that there are other factors equally potent, doubtless more so, than the church.

This question of better morals must affect not so much the older generation, who still occupy a large place in the church, as it does the newer and younger people.

If this is true, then we find certain conditions in many of the churches which give credence to the foregoing assertion.

I beg you to note that I am giving what is true of the majority of the churches of Thomas county as insinuated in the answers to the questions sent out, supplemented by my own knowledge upon the subject.

The first condition I would speak of is the relation of the church to the popular amusements. The supreme end of the church is spiritual: the bringing of the individual up to the higher ideals as exemplified in the life and teachings of Christ. When, therefore, the institution subordinates, even for a moment, this supreme end to a lower one, there can but be a perceptible lessening of the moral force of the institution. Now this is just what the church is doing. They vie with each other so strongly, the rivalry in new inventions and performances is so intense, till it has lead them into the realm of the questionable.

To a great extent the church has so entered into this business that the young people look to it more as a bureau whose object is to provide amusement than they do toward it as a holy institution whose high privilege it is to deal with eternal realities and interpret the weightier matters of the law.

Inordinate rivalries among the denominations is another condition. Rivalry is no mean motive and to its stimulating influence is traceable much of the world's progress; but when the church, in its ambition to excel, stoops to petty meannesses, then she need not complain if her moral dynamic becomes a doubtful quantity. We shall not mention examples here, for this is a condition which prevails in other churches than the Negro's.

The prominent place in church circles taken by characters whose lives in the community are a constant contradiction to the creed prescribed to when they entered the church, is another condition which lessens the moral force of the church.

True, as a race, we have had neither time nor training to establish that caste which marks the higher development in the moral code, and whose logical sequence is closer moral discrimination and segregation; yet the church, whose very motto is separation from the world, should have itself on record as being the most discriminating in this respect.

The fact is, however, that some of the churches are too lax in this matter. It is true in Thomas county that some of the secret societies, especially among women, are more vigilant as to their constituencies than the church. I am personally acquainted with people who occupy first place in all the affairs in the church whose applications to the societies have been repeatedly turned down.

The fact that their monied connections and their popularity are sufficient guarantees for the success of any church enterprise, seem to make their fitness for church membership unquestioned. Their lives may be black but no notice is paid to it.

Now what is the effect of all this? Nothing other than that the young people, and the older people who do their own thinking, lose regard for the moral standards of the church. The preacher may discourse frequently on purity of life, but if he shuts his eyes to the impurity of some of his own members, and seems to insist that they be placed at the forefront of the church's activities, then his precepts become sounding brass and tinkling cymbals; and his example, weightier by far than his precepts, becomes a barrier to the highest usefulness of his institution as a moulder of the community's morality.

Another condition which gives rise to our assertion that the church is not exercising its highest moral influence, is seen in its lax business methods. Let us give one example, which we dare assert is true of nine-tenths of the churches in Thomas county and in the South: A contract is made with every incoming minister. They promise him a stipulated sum for his year's service and when the year ends, he goes to conference with only about two-thirds of the pledge fulfilled. If he is sent back to the same field, the second year finds the church still deeper on the debit side of the ledger. If he is sent to another field the debt is considered settled, a new contract is made with the new preacher, and the same form is gone through.

As far as I have been able to learn fully 75 per cent. of the churches in the county are in debt to their former preachers, and what is worse, there seems never to arise a question as to the honesty of the religious body.

Now, this may seem a too minute selection of ecclesiastical faults, but when it is remembered that the simple virtues of honesty, truthfulness, and business promptness are the qualities most needed by the race, then that institution which represents the embodiment of all that is perfect in its precepts loses its moral force by the laxity of its example, and this laxity which is characteristic of the body must find counterpart in the individuals who compose the body.

We ventured the assertion that the church in this county is not too potent a factor in the moral betterment of the race; and we went further and raised the question as to whether there were not other factors equally potent, perhaps more so than the church.

You will notice that I have not said that the church is doing nothing toward this betterment. Some of them are, and some of the denominations more than others; but what we are talking about is the weight of the combined influence of all the churches; and we still claim that its power is small, smaller to be sure than it should be, when it has such exalted example of all that is good to draw from in the enforcement of its teachings.

We have been able to learn of about 120 preachers in the county. Of this number fully seventy-five are either ordained or licensed. The most of their names appear in the minutes of the various denominations. Now this number may be almost doubled if we search for all those who call themselves preachers and fill the function of interpreters of the word of God. This number moulds as great a sentiment for or against the church as those who hold license.

You will get some idea of the vast host who belong to this class when I tell you that the records of the last conference of the Southwest Georgia District of the African Methodist Episcopal Church show that there were forty-three applicants for admission to the conference. Note that this is only one of the four or five conferences of this church in the state. Be it said to the lasting credit of the conference that it in unmistakable terms put the stamp of condemnation upon the presumption of about thirty-five of them and sent them back to their homes disappointed men. And yet, while it sent them back home unadmitted, it did not make them less determined to preach, for in their several communities you will find them still exercising themselves in the holy calling.

Now of this vast number, so far as I have been able to learn, only four of them hold diplomas from any institution giving record of previous fitness. Only about one per cent. of them can point to any considerable time spent in school.

The course of study prescribed in the African Methodist Episcopal Church has helped some, but after all this, it can be truthfully said that for real fitness, fitness in the truest sense of the word, there is little to be found among the ministers of the county.

Putting this another way is to say, that the majority of the ministers are unlearned or ignorant men, ignorant in the sense of fitness for leadership; for, learned or unlearned, the Negro preacher is to-day the leader of the race. If they are ignorant, then this ignorance manifests itself in any number of ways:

1st. His home life as a general rule is on no higher level than that of his neighbor. In most cases he married before he began to preach and his wife is ignorant. Here, then, is no toning example for the community which he serves. I beg you to note that the pulpit is not the only place where the minister is to do powerful and eloquent preaching.

2d. In morality he has much to learn. Morality as it affects: (1) Temperance; (2) debt paying and business honesty; (3) sexual morality.

I have presented a gloomy picture. I have one consolation, however, that it is true, if it is black.

Your criticism will be that I have not brightened the picture a particle. But your conclusion will be erroneous if you decide that there is no brightness in it.

First. The greatest hope lies in the young people who go out to these darkened places and sacrifice themselves for the betterment of the people. Thomas county is dotted with these young people from the schools.

Second. Young men are seeing the need and are responding to it by entering the ministry.

Third. In every community there is a body of older men, men indeed of the old school; but during the years their ideas of the function of the church, the qualifications and requirements of the minister have all undergone a very radical change. They are thoroughly disgusted with the old order of things and besides withdrawing their own support they give their children no encouragement to support it.

Fourth. There is also a strong tendency in my county toward the newer denominations. This tendency will have two results: These newer denominations will continue to draw the young people and will continue to push the crusade for religious education. Second, this growth and popularity of the newer denominations will stimulate the older ones to greater efforts and to more intelligent worship.

In these and other ways the race is gradually coming out of the darkness into the light, and the next generation will see all of the denominations of the South exerting a stronger religious and moral influence upon the Negro than they are to-day doing.

Statistics of Three Churches, Thomas County

	C. M. E.	A. M. E.	Episcopal
Membership	120	72	149
Active membership	110	28	22
Value of church	$800.00	$700.00	$2,500.00
Expenses—			
Salaries	240.00	259.10	
On debt	.00	.00	
Running expenses	12.00	23.80	
Charity, etc	2.00	4.90	
Missions	2.50	6.00	
Support of connection	50.00	31.00	
Other expenses	10.00	3.20	
Total	$316.50	$328.00	

Negro Baptist Churches, Thomas County, Ga.

NAME.	Membership.		Value of Church Property.	
	1901.	1902.	1901.	1902.
Spring Hill	95	95	$ 750	$ 500
St. Mary	17	25	250	125
Evergreen	28	28	100	200
Ocklochnee	125	80	100	150
St. Paul	161	157	1,000	150
N. O. Grove	240	250	1,000	1,500
Centennial	35	30	322	275
Bethel	329	325	500	350
Paradise	51	54	100	100
Walnut Hill	109	112		
New Hope		38		75
Aucilla	202	169	1,000	500
Centenary	150	159		100
A. B. C., Thomasville	500	500	10,000	12,000
Richland	38	37	150	200
Mt. Pilgrim	43	48		200
Friendship	150	140		200
Antioch	83	75	85	100
St. Luke	10	15	100	100
Beulah Road	13	14	100	100
Piney Grove	65	70	500	250
Silver Hill	87	88	250	250
Mt. Olive	80	80	350	380
Mt. Calvary	113	68	600	600
Magnolia	16	19	30	600
Shady Grove	77	65	700	250
Mt. Moriah	50	44	1,500	300
Midway	50	48	250	300
Rebecca		38		150
County Line	30	30	200	200
Oaky Grove	19	22	50	50
Turner Grove		12		75
Jerusalem	120		150	
Total	3,086	3,035	$17,465	$20,320

Opinions of Intelligent Colored Laymen on Thomas County Churches

1. **Condition of the churches.**

"Well attended." "More centers for amusement than for worship." "Little spiritual life." "Half are in debt." "Not what they should be." "Lack competent leaders."

2. **Influence of Churches.**

"Influence good." "Influence bad." "Good, on the whole." "Ten per cent. of the membership is honest, pure, and upright." "Influence is bad, but there are some earnest folks."

3. **Are the ministers good?**

"No." "Out of ten, three are sexually immoral, one drinks, three are careless in money matters." "Weak in morals." "One is sexually impure and frequents disreputable places." "Lack intellect." "They fairly represent those whom they lead." "Some of them are good men."

4. **Charity work.**

"Nine-tenths believe there is but one object of charity—the minister; give all you've got to the minister and if any one is sick or in prison, give him one-half of what is left."

5. **The young people.**

"The church amuses the young people, and they pay for the amusement." "Young people join slowly." "Church support comes largely from non-members."

6. **Are moral standards being raised?**

"Cannot say; much laxity." "Standard never lower." "Raised by presence of a score or more of graduates of city schools." "Being raised." "In six years I note a change for the better." "Reaching high moral standards." "In some cases standards are being raised, in others, not." "There are fewer separations of man and wife, and fewer illegitimate children."

14. A Town in Florida. (By Annie Marion MacLean, A. M., Ph. D.)

The Negro is always an interesting subject for study in a Southern town, and one feels amply repaid for any effort made to understand his life. The town of Deland appealed to me as being an excellent place to make a study of the Negro population, both on account of its character and size. The town is largely Northern in population and sentiment, and it is small so that city problems do not need to be considered.

There are three regularly organized Negro churches in Deland. In and around these the religious life of the colored inhabitants centers, and we may study these in order of importance.

1. Missionary Baptist Church

This church, the largest and most flourishing in the community, is located on the outskirts of the town, in the best Negro district. Its founding dates back to 1883, when one of the prominent white citizens gave a lot of land and erected a small house of worship. The membership has constantly increased since that time, and in 1895 a new site was purchased and the present structure put up at a cost of about $1,000. A parsonage was bought immediately adjoining the church at a cost of $300, the necessary money for these improvements being raised by the members themselves. The church building is kept in good repair and is provided with a small organ, good, comfortable pews, and has carpeted aisles and plain stained glass windows. The seating capacity is 250, the membership 109—forty-six male and sixty-three female. The average attendance is about one-quarter of the total membership, and contrary to the usual state of affairs in white churches, men are always in the majority at the meetings. The minister's explanation of this is that the women work very hard during the week, and when Sunday comes they are too tired to leave their homes. He says that it is much easier for the women to get steady employment than for the men. No children are received into membership under the age of twelve years. The Sunday-school is well attended, and there are two fully organized missionary societies—one to aid home and the other to aid foreign missions. The other societies are a Young People's Society of Christian Endeavor and a Baptist Young People's Union, both of which meet in the church weekly, with fair attendance. The minister is a man of average intelligence, his early education having been obtained in the public schools. He is elected by the congregation, and preaches three Sundays in the month at morning and evening service. The fourth Sunday he preaches in a small country church. His regular salary is $300 a year, and from his country charge he receives $125. In addition to this he has the use of the parsonage and its furnishings. When he was called, two years ago, the church was $250 in debt. It now owes but $50.

2. Bethel Church (African Methodist Episcopal)

This is the second largest church in the community, and is located on the opposite side of the town from the one just described. It was organized in 1882, and has now its second building. The church and the parsonage immediately adjoining are valued at $800 and $400, respectively. The church has not always been self-supporting, having from time to time received aid from the Extension Board of the denomination. The building is kept in very good repair, and a large belfry has been added during the past year. Inside is a very good small organ, good, plain pews, and other necessary furniture. The seating capacity is 235, the membership ninety-three, one-quarter of which is men; and the average attendance is one-third the total membership. Children are baptized and received at any age, and later, upon confession of faith, are confirmed.

Among flourishing church organizations may be mentioned the Young People's Society of Christian Endeavor, a Christian Willing Working Club, which corresponds to a missionary society, and a Stewardesses' Board, composed of the most intelligent women in the church. This last named society has charge of all charities, church furnishings, and the like. The two former meet once a week, and are well attended. There is a well organized Sunday-school. A prayer service is held on Thursday of each week.

The pastor is a remarkable Negro in many respects. He is a little past middle age; never attended school, and yet is by all odds the most intelligent of his race in the community. He was born of slave parents, and early in life was seized with a desire to learn. As a boy he had no advantages. He educated himself, "after whistle time," to use his own words. This is his first year in his present pastorate. He was for eight consecutive years presiding elder of this, the eleventh, district, which includes the entire state of Florida. He is a good conversationalist, being well posted on the topics of the day. He spends his whole time in the work of this one church and in looking after his business interests. He pays taxes on $16,000 worth of property, and has an income of $102 per month on rentals. The church pays him about $300 per year salary, and gives him the use of the parsonage. He gave his son a college education, and sent him through a medical course of four years. The son is now a physician of large practice in St. Augustine. Under the African Methodist Episcopal form of church government the ministers are appointed to their charges at the annual conference.

There are two regular Sunday services—one in the morning and one in the evening. The debt at present amounts to about $228, which the pastor expects to pay in the near future at a "rally."

The church has a mission about two miles distant, at a Negro settlement called Yamassee. This mission has but eight members and holds services once a month, at which time communion is given. The preacher comes from a town about thirty miles distant, and is said to be a man of but average ability. There are no activities within the church, except the monthly services. The building is extremely rough and is valued at $400.

3. St. Annis' Primitive Baptist (Primitive Orthodox Zion Baptist Church)

This church is the most interesting of the three, from the standpoint of the student of sociology. It is the principal church of Yamassee, the only other being the mission just mentioned. Yamassee is the largest of the Negro settlements and lies about a mile and a half from the center of the town, but within the town limits.

Facts concerning the origin and history of the church are hard to obtain. Indeed neither the minister nor any of the members seem to know just when or how it had its beginning. The building is valued at $1,800 and it has never been painted, and is not kept in good repair. The floors are uncarpeted, the interior is finished in wood, the windows plain, and there is no musical instrument. The seating capacity is 300, the membership fifty-six, twenty of whom are male. The average attendance is two-thirds of the membership, and the men and women are about evenly divided. No children under twelve years are admitted to membership. There is an organized Sunday-school, which is fairly attended, and also a weekly prayer meeting. This is led by some member of the church. There is a society called "The Young People's Band," which corresponds to the "Young People's Society of Christian Endeavor." It meets in the church once a week, but is poorly attended and not strongly organized.

This church asserts, with much vigor, that it is the original Baptist Church; that the so-called "Missionary Baptist" (of the type described above) is a false body, which withdrew from the mother church in 1832. It points with pride to the list of the great men who were "Primitive Baptists." Its members believe in the scriptures of the Old and New Testaments, in predestination, in the fall of man, in the covenant of redemption, in justification, regeneration, in the resurrection and general judgment, baptism, the Lord's supper, and foot-washing. This last (foot-washing) is, of course, the main distinguishing characteristic. The regular communion service is held on the second Sunday of each month and after the sermon the members turn their benches so as to form two large squares on each side of the pulpit, the men on one side and the women on the other. They then wash each other's feet in turn, the preacher taking the lead. This, they say, is merely carrying out the example of Christ. The service generally ends with a kind of a dance, which they call "Rocking Daniel." No information could be gained as to the origin of this most peculiar custom. A leader stands in the center of a circle, which the members form in front of the pulpit. They begin with singing the lines:

"Rock Daniel, rock Daniel,
Rock Daniel till I die."

Gradually they move round in the circle, single file, then begin to clap hands and fall into a regular step or motion, which is hard to describe. Finally, when they have become worked up to a high state of excitement, and almost exhausted, the leader gives a signal, and they disperse. This ceremony reminds one quite strongly of an Indian war dance, except that it is on a somewhat tamer plan.

The songs sung by the church are extremely interesting, as they embody so many strange and original sentiments. These people seem to believe thoroughly in a noisy religion. They frequently interrupt the speaker with shouts of approval or disapproval and songs. The prayers are long and earnest in the extreme. The churches spoken of above are much more conventional in their services.

The minister preaches one Sunday in a month at a country church; the remainder of the time he spends with his own congregation. He was educated in the public schools of Jacksonville, Fla., and in Cookman College, and is a graduate of the Correspondence Bible College, and of the Christian University, Canton, Mo., having taken the degree

of M. A. L. (Master of Ancient Literature) at the last named institution. Bethaney College of North Carolina conferred upon him the
honorary degree of D. D. In 1895 he delivered the annual address to
the literary societies of the Southern University of New Orleans, La.
He is the author of several pamphlets, and was the general secretary
of the Eleventh Annual Sunday-school and Ministers' Convention of
the Eastern and Southern District of his church in 1901. He is considered to be a man of unusual ability and attainments by the residents
of his community.

Generally speaking, the ministers are men of good character and of
fair education. They are highly respected by their congregations and
others. They all agree that the Negro was given citizenship long
before he was ready for it; that his only salvation lies in education.
They try to impress upon their people the real extent and meaning of
the ignorance which is so prevalent among them, and also the fact that
they must look to the white inhabitants for encouragement and help.

There is very little sectarian animosity between the different denominations; union meetings and efforts are common, and much good often
results from them. The church members play almost no part in the
politics of the community, although most of them are property holders.

There is comparatively little moral or religious training in the homes
or in the schools. Family worship is not observed. The churches are
the center of social life and activity, but one finds the meetings of the
morning poorly attended, while those of the evening are full, and are
generally very lengthy.

Just how deep the every-day lives of the members are affected by
their religion it is difficult to say, but the pastors agree that it has a
decided tendency to keep them " in the straight path."

To sum up, the following brief table may be presented as an indication of the present condition of the Negro churches in the town under
consideration:

CHURCH.	Founded.	Value of Prop- erty.	Seating Capacity.	Members.
Missionary Baptist	1883	$1,900	250	106
Bethel Church (African M. E.)	1882	1,200	255	93
Primitive Baptist	?	1,800	300	56

17.   A Southern City.* There are in the city of Atlanta, Ga., the following Negro churches:

DENOMINATION.	No. Churches.	Membership Claimed.	Active Membership.	Value of Property.	Income, 1902.
Baptist	29	10,363	5,274	$ 61,273	$ 23,259.30
Methodist	21	5,015	2,571	149,235	23,101.75
Other denominations	4	883	578	42,000	5,451.79
Total	54	16,261	8,423	$ 252,508	$ 51,812.84

The Negro population of Atlanta (1900) was 35,727. This means one church to every 662 men, women, and children, or one to every 130 families. Half the total population is enrolled in the church, and probably nearly two-thirds of the adult population. The active paying membership is much smaller.

There are 29 Baptist churches, with an active membership of over 5,000, and $60,000 worth of real estate. The $23,000 raised by them annually is expended as follows:

For salaries	$ 10,811.00	........46.4%
Running expenses, etc	4,629.70	........19.9
Debt and interest	4,493.40	........19.3
Charities and missions	2,751.60	........11.9
Support of Connectional Boards	573.60	.... 2.5
Total	$ 23,259.30	100.0%

The Baptist churches may be tabulated as follows:

---

* The data in this section were gathered by students in the 3   ⁘ junior college classes in Atlanta University in 1902–3.

Baptist Churches

Serial No.	Membership Claimed.	Active Members.	Value of Buildings.	Income.
1	79	12	$ 125	$ 178.20
2	874	350	2,500	750.00
3	85	50	....	162.00
4	400	150	1,500	310.00
5	20	14	....	87.00
6	150	60	1,000	263.00
7	30	20	800	112.00
8	37	20	700	791.00
9	600	300	7,000	1,148.50
10	387	200	4,000	2,405.00
11	34	32	200	120.00
12	125	75	1,000	582.00
13	120	80	500	300.00
14	12	7	85	57.00
15	22	18	200	101.00
16	500	200	4,000	2,408.00
17	750	150	6,000	1,960.00
18	800	200	2,500	2,400.00
19	200	125	2,000	392.25
20	62	40	800	....
21	50	20	800	106.00
22	500	250	4,500	1,200.00
23	15	6	13	25.50
24	60	30	1,000	....
25	13	10	900	55.00
26	265	165	1,200	514.60
27	2,598	1,560	2,700	4,040.00
28	1,500	1,100	15,00	2,774.00
29	75	30	250	17.25
All.	10,363	5,274	$ 61,273	$ 23,259.30

The twenty-one Methodist churches are divided as follows:

Methodist Churches

DENOMINATIONS.	No.	Membership Claimed.	Active Members.	Real Estate.	Income.
African Methodist Episcopal.......	14	3,242	1,461	$ 90,200	$ 13,831.10
Methodist Episcopal................	4	1,333	910	48,500	6,927.00
Colored Methodist Episcopal.......	3	440	200	10,535	2,343.65
Total	21	5,015	2,571	$ 149,235	$ 23,101.75

Annual expenditures of these churches are approximately as follows:

Salaries......................................	$ 9,174.53	........39.7%
Debt and interest........................	7,510.02	........32.5
Charities, etc.............................	1,137.50	.... 4.9
Support of connection	1,694.00	.... 7.4
Other expenses...........................	3,585.75	........15.5
Total	$ 23,101.80	100.0%

The churches in detail are :

African Methodist Episcopal Churches

Serial No.	Membership Claimed.	Active Members.	Real Estate.	Income.
37	340	110	$ 9,200	$ 1,420.00
38	30	20	200	125.00
39	40	32	150	120.00
40	20	6	1,200	233.00
41	35	20	600	307.00
42	400	600	50,000	4,864.86
43	100	70	2,000	585.00
44	506	200	20,000	5,274.00
45	370	135	3,500	3,058.67
46	16	8	500	. . . .
47	90	50	250	740.02
48	110	100	300	587.55
49	135	85	2,000	135.00
50	50	25	300	140.00
All.	3,242	1,461	$ 90,200	$17,590.10

Methodist Episcopal Churches

Serial No.	Membership Claimed.	Active Members.	Real Estate.	Income.
33	740	500	$ 40,000	$ 3,235.00
34	227	115	1,000	542.00
35	166	100	2,500	1,425.00
36	200	195	5,000	1,725.00
All.	1,333	910	$ 48,500	$ 6,927.00

Colored Methodist Episcopal

Serial No.	Membership Claimed.	Active Members.	Real Estate.	Income.
30	100	50	$ 4,000	$ 1,543.05
31	75	25	35	20.65
32	265	125	6,500	780.00
All.	440	200	$ 10,535	$ 2,343.65

The remaining churches are four in number, one each of the Congregational, Episcopal, Christian, and Presbyterian denominations. Figures for them are :

Serial No.	Membership Claimed.	Active Members.	Real Estate.	Income.
51	485	• 400	$ 25,000	$ 2,225.00
52	180	80	10,000	1,494.00
53	68	. . . .	4,000	1,296.79
54	150	30	3,000	436.00
All.	4,125	1,971	$ 42,000	$ 5,451.79

The expenditures of three of these deserve to be given in detail :

	51	52	53
Salaries	$ 1,200	$ 244	$ 950.00
Debt and interest	0	495	44.08
Charities	300	75	5.80
Connection	25		
Other expenses	700	180	296.91
Total	$ 2,225	*$ 994	**$1,296.79

Three extracts, from the reports of first-hand young investigators, throw some general light on the general character of these churches:

From an old colored citizen of Atlanta, I learned of the marked advancement he has witnessed in the erection of church edifices and in the character of worship. Just after the war, when the colored people were in their bitter struggle for the necessities of life, he says the race worshipped in box cars frequently, for they could not always obtain houses. As conditions changed the churches were moved to better quarters. The people generally supported the church very well until finally the Negro began to pattern his churches after the white churches, building structures which were far too costly for the Negro's financial status at the time. It seemed very sad to this old man that the "worship of the good, old time" was not what it used to be.

The character of the pastors of the seven Methodist churches in my district seems, in every case, to be good. Such phrases as "you could not find any one to say anything against his character," express the sentiments of the members of these churches. The education of the pastors is fair, although there are exceptions. Among the schools represented by the different pastors, are : Bennet College, Clark University, Turner Theological Seminary (Morris Brown Theological Department), and Gammon Theological Seminary.

The education of the members seems to vary from fair to very poor. In the case of my largest church (membership 740) a large number of the members were graduates of Clark University, and nearly all have a fair education. However, in the smaller churches, having from 16 to 277 members, the education of the congregations was very meagre.

A great majority of the members of the smaller churches are common laborers and are quite poor. The members of the larger churches are in moderate circumstances, and although most of them are laborers, there is a fair per cent. of artisans and business men among them.

The total expenses for the respective churches for last year varied from $6 to $5,274. The salaries paid by churches varied from $500 to $1,240, not considering a case where there was no fixed salary and one where the church had no preacher last year, the pulpit being supplied by "local" preachers.

Four of the seven churches are in debt. The debts ranged from $35 to $600, the latter of which was incurred by the building of a new church.

---

* To this the general church adds $500 for salaries.

** Only partially raised by members themselves.

Most of the churches have relief societies to look after the charity and relief work. Some churches did no special relief work. One church, however, has a deaconess, who devotes her time to such work. The money expended in such work varied from nothing to $100 in the different churches. That spent for missions varied from nothing to $200.

The government of all Baptist churches is extremely democratic. Each member has the power of taking part in any of the general meetings and of voting. The financial and business matters of the church are attended to by the deacons' board. The power of the pastor varies somewhat according to the different congregations, and the difference of esteem in which the pastor is held sometimes governs his influence and sway over them.

All Baptists agree that each church is complete in itself and has the power, therefore, to choose its own ministers and to make such rules as it deems to be most in accordance with the advancement of its best interest and the purpose of its existence. The time that a pastor is to serve is not fixed but varies according to the wishes of the people. If the people like the pastor, he is kept as long as he desires to remain, but if they do not, he is put out immediately.

The general condition of the ten Baptist churches in this part of the city shows that on a whole their work is not progressing very fast. Over half of them are very small, with very small memberships, and very ignorant and illiterate pastors. And certainly where there are ignorant leaders of ignorant people not very much progress or good influence can be expected to follow. The places of meeting are not comfortable, being poorly lighted and unclean most of the time, and in some cases the church was situated in an unhealthy place. These, however, represent the worst half; and on the other hand, the larger churches are progressing very fast and their influence is gradually but surely spreading far and wide, and includes all grades of society. Many of the most influential and wealthy Negro churches of the city are Baptist.

The pastors of the Congregational, Episcopal, and Presbyterian churches have excellent characters, and are doing much towards lifting the moral standard and religious life of the people. Not only are they earnest workers, but they are also well equipped for their work. They are well educated, one being a graduate of Fisk and Yale Universities, another is a graduate of St. Augustine College, Raleigh, N. C., and took a post graduate course at Howard University, Washington, D. C., and one is a graduate of Lincoln University, who completed both the college and theological courses. They have excellent reputations, and are held in high esteem by their Alma Maters. The Yale graduate is well known North and South. The character of the members of these churches is good. They are quiet and intelligent, and there is no emotionalism in the churches. Most of the members of these churches are at least high school graduates, and a large per cent. is composed of business and professional men and women.

The best picture of Atlanta churches can be obtained by studying certain typical congregations now existing in the city. The primitive Negro congregation as it emerged from slavery was of two types: the large group, led by a masterful personality; the small democratic group, led by one of their own number. This latter group is of interest as approximating conditions in the early Christian church. In the case of the Negro, however, the communicants were ignorant people, with largely perverted, half-mystical ideals, and liable to become the victims of mountebanks and rascals. A few such groups still survive, although they are dying out rapidly. Here is an example:

No. 24.   Primitive Baptist—Active members thirty.

The pastor can read and write, but is not well educated. His character is good, but he will not do laborious work, which the members think he ought to do outside his church work. Most of the members were slaves, and the church is about twenty-eight years old. It has no influence except among its members and it began where it now stands, and was organized by most of the present members. No collection is taken except on communion day. The building is an old wooden one of rough lumber, raised about five feet from the ground. I looked through one of the cracks to get a view of the interior. Its seating capacity is about seventy-five. The benches are of rough lumber. The lamps (four oil lamps) are hanging from the shabby ceiling. I saw a large Bible upon an altar of dressed lumber. One of the oldest members told me that he gave all the coal and oil used this year. He said that the church had a meeting once a month, and every three months communion and washing of feet. They believed in having no music, save singing. They believed in the pastor's working for his living just as the members did, and because the present pastor would not do this they were going to let him go. I could not find the pastor nor could they tell me where he or any of the other members lived.

This is an example of church communion among lowly ignorant and old people—a survival from the past. Such groups tend to change—to absorption into some larger group or to degenerate through bad leaders and bad members. Two other specimens of this type follow:

No. 5.   Baptist—Fourteen active members.

The old store, which is used for church purposes, is a very shabby building. A few chairs, two lamps, and a small table and a Bible make up the furniture. All of the members are old and ignorant. There is no Sunday-school connected with the church. The church government is a pure democracy, the pastor and the active members governing the church. The members are ignorant and of questionable character. The pastor is an old and ignorant man, but is fairly good. He went away two years ago and left his flock because they did not give him the proper support. The church did not split but degenerated. Very little charitable work is done. When one of the members is sick he is given aid if he asks to be aided. There are several ignorant Negroes living in the vicinity of the church.

No. 25.   Baptist—Six active members.

The pastor has a fairly good education, but there seem to be some serious doubts as to his character. In the church there seem to be three classes of members: some with good character, some with questionable character, and some about whose character there is no question. There is no charitable and rescue work done. The building is simply a small room house which is not used regularly for worship, but is used sometimes when the people in the neighborhood desire to meet there and can get the pastor to attend. They hold no regular meetings.

The other type of church, with a strong leader and a number of followers, is a more effective organization, but its character depends largely on its pastor. Here is one:

No. 26.   Baptist (Missionary)—165 active members.

The education of the pastor is fair, but his character is not good. He has the reputation of being very immoral. He is, however, a good speaker. There are a few intelligent members, but the larger portion of the members are very illiterate.

There is connected with the church an organized body of women (Woman's Mission) which looks after the poor, the old, and the sick. The church was organized in 1878, in the old barracks of this city. It has had eight pastors since its organization, and it is very influential over a large number of people in the vicinity. The church building is large and was once a beautiful wooden structure, but at present it is very much in need of repairs. It is furnished fairly well on the inside, and is situated in one of the black belts of Atlanta. There is an official board appointed by or elected by the church. This official board attends to the affairs of the church. The pastor presides over the meetings. The pastor now in charge was once forced to give up his charge and leave the city, so the general report goes, because of his immorality. There were seven preachers called during his absence and two church splits, brought about through the pastors who were leading. Then the first pastor was recalled. While many of the members and the pastor bear the reputation of being immoral, they are also said to be very good to the poor. The entire collection of every fifth Sunday goes to the poor. There is a fairly good Sunday-school connected with the church, and this Sunday-school has recently purchased an organ for the church. The church debt is $400.

To reform a perverted group like this is extremely difficult, and yet the work is slowly going on. If the reform is attempted through a change in the type of pastor the result at first is likely to be the substitution of a less forceful personality and the consequent loss of enthusiasm and interest among the mass of members.

No. 8. Baptist—Twenty-five active members.

The pastor, from the report of the clerk and two or three other members, is an upright man. He attended the Atlanta Baptist College, but did not graduate. He is a tailor, with a place of business on Edgewood Avenue, near Ivy Street. He does not depend on the church to support him, but is supported entirely by his business. The majority of the members are hard-working people. The men are employed as day laborers and the women do house-work. There is a lack of interest among the members. The Sunday-school is held at 3 o'clock each Sunday afternoon, and is composed of about ten or twelve children. The pastor is planning an organization, a B. Y. P. U., to meet each Sunday afternoon after Sunday-school. There is now being carried on a revival at the church. This church building is one story, and has about twenty-five or thirty benches in it. There are four windows on each side and a seating capacity for about 150 or 175. It has a small organ, and is lighted by one large kerosene lamp with a few lamps on the walls. It is situated in an unhealthy spot, but the pastor is contemplating changing the locality. As soon as the debt is paid he says that he and the deacons intend to sell and move to a more desirable locality, where they can do more effective work.

No. 49. African Methodist Episcopal—Eighty-five active members

The church was built about fourteen years ago. It was organized in a small house, where the meetings were held for about three years. The present building was then erected and a pastor called, but the church was so poor that after a few years there was no pastor sent. In January of this year the present minister was sent, but he is pastor of two other small churches. The influence of the church depends largely on the activity of the minister, yet its location would restrict its influence in any case. It is bounded on one side by Oakland cemetery and all others by a small settlement of Negro hovels, while back of these for a long way extend only white residences. The building is a wooden structure, with basement, fairly large. It is kept fairly clean on the inside, and was recently whitewashed. Outside the woodwork is unpainted.

When, however, inspiration comes from without through the larger churches or the church connection these small groups often show renewed activity and grow into influential churches.

No. 30. Colored Methodist Episcopal—Fifty active members.

The church was first begun with one family, at the old barracks, in a one-room cabin. From there it was moved to Peters street, to Shell hall, where it was joined by a second family. Then it was moved to Markham street, where it was joined by others; then to Hunter street, in a white church, where it was burned. It was then re-established at Taylor street, in a store house, from whence it was moved to its present site. It now has a fair brick building, which cost about $3,000, and is fairly well furnished inside. The present building and parsonage were built largely by the co-operative labor of its own members. The pastors are noisy, but of pretty good education.

No. 34.- Methodist Episcopal—115 active members.

The pastor has attended Clark University, and is a graduate of Gammon. He is well liked by his parishioners. The church recruits its members from the railroad hands and their families, who are for the greater part uneducated. Some charitable work is done by different societies in the church. Such, for instance, as aiding paupers. The church is nineteen years old. It is not in debt, and has a large membership. Its influence is wide-spread, being one of the largest churches in this particular section. The church has connected with it a Woman's Home Missionary Society and an Epworth League. Through the missionary society, and through the help department of the league, much charitable work is being done in the community. I am told that during this year a poor woman was taken and given a decent burial, whereas otherwise the county would have had it to do. There is also a parsonage adjoining the church, which, together with the church, is estimated to be worth $1,500.

The services in churches of this type are calculated to draw the crowd, and are loud and emotional. A student thus describes a sermon in a large Baptist church of 500 active members on the occasion of the annual sermon before the Knights of Pythias. "He began by telling the history of the Knights of Pythias. This was interesting and I could understand him; but when he shut the Bible and began to preach I could not understand him at first. As soon as I could distinguish between the words and the peculiar sound made by the intaking of his breath, I found myself listening to what the people called 'a good sermont.' During his talk he spit behind the altar many times, and often raised his voice to a veritable yell. I could not keep any record of his exact words. After the sermon there were speeches by several laymen and then the deacons, gathering around the table in front of the pulpit, began to call for the collection. The choir then sang, but the calls of the deacons so interrupted that I could not hear the singing well. Twenty-three dollars were finally collected, each bringing forward his collection and placing it on the table."

Such churches grow into large and influential organizations, losing many of their unconventional features and becoming very much like churches in any part of the land.

No. 42. African Methodist Episcopal—600 active members.

The pastor is of good character and education, a graduate of Howard University Theological School. The members vary from the old, poor, and respectable, to the young and well educated. In 1866 this church was organized by Rev. J. J. Wood; the membership increased steadily until 1868. The church moved into a new building. This old structure itself is yet sufficiently well preserved to show what a nice building it was. In 1891 the present structure was begun. In a short while the building went up, but owing to poor workmanship it was condemned. For this reason one wall had to be torn away at a loss of about $5,000. This meant a great blow to the congregation for the edifice was constructed at a great cost and as a result of much sacrifice on the part of many people. This left the people under the burden of a heavy debt, and the ministers who have succeeded have worked hard to pay it. The present structure is a handsome one, with a beautiful interior. The building is granite and is finished inside in yellow pine. Beautiful glass windows adorn the church and there are electric light fixtures and theatre chairs in the auditorium, while a $2,500 pipe organ also adds to the beauty. The church is very large, having a seating capacity of 3,000. The total membership is about 1,400, and is composed of some of the most influential and cultured colored people of the city, a considerable number being school teachers and property owners and respected people. The church is valued at $50,000 and a statement of the money paid out during the previous year shows a total of $4,964.86, which includes $984.86 for salary to the pastor and $3,020 for the church debt. This church does a great deal of relief work among the indigent members. Last year the amount expended was $200 for such work and $360 for missions; $500 was given to the general connections.

The growth of such great Negro institutions involves much effort and genius for organization. The greatest danger is that of the "split;" that is, the withdrawal of a dissatisfied minority and the formation of a new church. The government of the Methodist churches hinders this, but the Baptist churches are peculiarly liable to it. A case in the Methodist church follows:

No. 37. African Methodist Episcopal—110 active members.

The pastor is educated and respected and the grade of membership is fairly high. The church property, building and parsonage, is worth about $9,200. On this there is a debt of $2,800, but as this was loaned by one of the church members, no interest is charged on it. The church is a nice brick structure, with stained glass windows, galleries, choir, and organ. In the basement is a Sunday-school room. The church was founded in 1870 by members of No. 44, who had moved too far from their own church to attend services. As the church grew a cleft appeared between the richer and poorer members and the result was that some thirty or more members of the poor class withdrew and formed:

No. 54. Christian—Thirty active members.

The leader and pastor is a man of questionable character. The members are mainly the middle working classes of average intelligence. Very little charitable and relief work is done because the church has a hard time to keep on its feet. The church drew out of No. 37 in 1897 and established this church, and since that time the young church has been struggling for existence. The church building is a large barn-like structure, roughly finished on the outside and rather crudely furnished on the inside. It will accommodate about 400 people.

Such splits in the Negro church have been numerous in the past, but as the churches grow stronger this method of protest is less effective. Of the present fifty-four churches, eleven represent withdrawals from older churches. In some cases this represents only natural growth; in others the establishment of more convenient local churches; in others quarrels and differences. Since splits are so easy in the democratic Baptist churches a large church of this denomination is evidence of great cohesion and skilled leadership:

No. 57.   Baptist—1,560 active members.

The character of the pastor is good and he is educated. The membership includes some of the best people of the city, less than 100 are illiterate; there are many business men, property owners and steady laborers and servants. The church supports two missions, and has a committee for charitable work and general relief. The organization dates back to 1870, when a few members of No. 28 formed a small church. To-day the church is out of debt and has a bank account; has the largest Sunday-school in the state and one of the largest congregations in the city. It occupies a large plain building, furnished comfortably but not elaborately. It has two organs and a piano. It has had but three pastors, the second retiring on account of age, with a pension paid by the church.

Another type of church is the Negro church which is an organization in one of the great white denominations. The Episcopal Church, for instance, has had Negro communicants from early times, but while it helps them there is the feeling that the church wants them to keep in their "place," and their churches are not growing.

No. 53.   Protestant Episcopal—Sixty-eight communicants.

The character of the rector is excellent. He was educated at St. Augustine College, Raleigh, N. C., and at Howard University, Washington, D. C. The membership is small, quiet, and intelligent. Charity and relief work is done by distributing clothing to the needy; periodicals are also distributed and visits made to the sick. The present structure was erected in 1893. It is a frame building, painted, of moderate size, and neatly but plainly furnished on the interior. There is under the auspices of the church and in an adjoining building a primary school with an enrollment of 120 students and three teachers.

The Methodist Church has treated its Negro members with much consideration and sympathy and has in consequence many large and influential churches. One of the best of these in Atlanta is:

No. 33.   Methodist Episcopal—500 active members.

The pastor is a "gentleman and honest man." The membership is composed of the best class of working people with a large number of educated people and graduates of the schools. The church supports a salaried deaconess to take charge of its charitable work and spends nearly $300 a year on this work outside of salaries. The church was organized in 1870 with thirty members. The present building was owned by white Methodists, but they gave it up after the war and it was turned over to the Negroes, and has become the leading church of this denomination in the South. The church is especially noted for its harmonious work and lack of "splits." It does much for its young people, having a large Sunday-school besides classes in cooking and sewing and a week-day class in religious training.

The Congregational Church is virtually independent and its growth and influence is due almost entirely to Negroes.

No. 51. Congregational—400 active members.

The membership presents the highest average of intelligence of any colored church in the city. The charitable work is regularly and efficiently organized and a mission is maintained in the slums. The church was founded thirty-eight years ago by two white missionaries. The church became self-supporting under its present pastor and exerts a wide-spread influence in the city. The building is plain but substantial and well located. The church raises $2,225 a year and has no debt. Three hundred dollars is given in charity annually.

A word may be added here as to the character of pastors and the finances of churches. In several of the smaller churches the pastors are ignorant and immoral men, who are doing great harm. In the larger churches there is not in the city a man of notoriously immoral life. Against a few ministers there are rumors of lapses here and there, but it is difficult to say how far such gossip is trustworthy and how far it is the careless talk of a people so long used to a low standard among ministers that they hardly realize that there has been any change. That there has been a change, however, is certain. The older type of minister who built up the great churches of twenty years ago had a magnetic personality, great eloquence, and a power of handling men. In private life he varied in all degrees from an austere recluse to a drunkard and moral leper. This type of man has passed away and his place has been gradually taken by a quiet, methodical man, who can organize men and raise money. Such men are usually of good average character and are executive officers of organizations strong enough to hold together with or without a pastor. They, however, fall behind the present demand in two particulars: they are not usually highly educated men, although they are by no means illiterate, and their goodness is the average goodness of every day men and not the ideal goodness of a priest, who is to revivify and reinspire the religious feelings of a rapidly developing group.

While the salaries paid ministers are still small, there has been a great improvement in recent years. The ministers of the fifty-four Atlanta churches are paid as follows per annum :

$1,000 and over	7
750–1,000	3
500–750	10
300–500	7
100–300	8
50–100	6
Under $50	5
No fixed salary	8
Total	54

The greatest change in the last decade has come in the forming of the church groups. Ability to organize and systematize, arrange a regular income and spend it effectively is demanded more and more of ministers and church officials. There is still much looseness and waste in money matters and some dishonesty in the smaller churches. Over $12,500 was paid out in interest and principal of debts last year. This probably represents a total indebtedness of $50,000 to $75,000 on a quarter of a million dollars worth of property.

18. **Virginia.***   There are twenty-four Negro churches in Richmond,† nineteen of which are Baptist. The active membership of these churches is nearly the same as that of the fifty-four churches in Atlanta. As the Negro population of the two cities is nearly the same, this shows a striking concentration in church fellowship and is probably the result of longer growth in the older city, eliminating the smaller churches. The statistics of membership and expenses are:

DENOMINATION.	No. of Churches.	Membership Claimed.	Active Members.	Value of Church Property.	Expenses of Last Year.
African Methodist Episcopal	1	236	78	$ 25,000	$ 3,810.00
Methodist Episcopal	1	97	50	3,500	1,490.00
Baptist	19	14,802	6,949	291,400	40,653.29
Presbyterian	1	83	60	11,000	732.00
Episcopal	2	143	138	10,800	1,210.70
Totals	24	15,361	7,275	$ 341,700	$ 47,895.99

The expenditures of these churches are distributed as follows:

DENOMINATION.	ITEMIZED EXPENSES.						
	For Salaries.	For Interest and Principal Debt.	For Running Expenses.	For Charity and Relief Work.	For Missions.	For Support of the Connection.	For other Expenses.
African Methodist Episcopal	$ 600.00	$ 4,100.00	$ 1,500.00	$ 90.00	$ 20.00	$	$ 500.00
Methodist Episcopal	500.00	750.00	100.00	20.00	20.00	30.00	70.00
Baptist	15,278.22	14,843.79	5,859.94	1,667.02	1,042.46	446.81	4,616.08
Presbyterian	570.00	....	150.60	....	12.00	....	....
Episcopal	600.00	360.00	190.00	54.20	.50	....	6.00
Total	$ 17,548.22	$ 14,053.79	$ 7,699.91	$ 1,831.22	$ 1,094.96	$ 476.81	$ 5,191.08

Richmond is noted for its large Baptist churches. If we divide the twenty-four churches according to active membership, we have:

---

* The data on which this paragraph is based were collected by students of Virginia Union University.   † Including Manchester.

Over 1,000 active members	2
750–1,000 active members	1
500–750 active members	3
250–500 active members	2
100–250 active members	8
Under 100 active members	8

The three largest churches claim a total membership of 6,169 persons, and an active membership of 3,134. They are all Baptist churches with interesting histories. Over one the noted John J. Jasper was stationed for years. The largest church has a total membership of 2,553, of which one-half are active. This church raises $5,229 a year and spends nearly $700 in charity and mission work. It has no debt. Ninety-four persons joined the church last year, of whom sixty-two were under twenty years of age. The pastor is a college graduate. Another church has 1,058 active members. It raises $5,000 a year and spends $270 in charities. It paid nearly $3,000 on its debt last year. A third church, with 800 active members, raises $3,250 a year. They paid off the last indebtedness on a $3,000 church last year. The Protestant Episcopal Church has 133 communicants and raises $1,200 a year. It spends $243 a year in charity.

The present condition of Richmond churches seems, on the whole, to be good. While the standard of the ministry is not yet satisfactory, the proportion of upright and moral men is increasing. There is considerable work among the sick and the poor, and this kind of work is increasing.

For a picture of the condition of churches in Farmville, Va., in 1898, we may quote the following : *

"The church is much more than a religious organization: it is the chief organ of social and intellectual intercourse. As such it naturally finds the free democratic organizations of the Baptists and Methodists better suited to its purpose than the strict bonds of the Presbyterians or the more aristocratic and ceremonious Episcopalians. Of the 262 families of Farmville, only one is Episcopalian and three are Presbyterian; of the rest, twenty-six are Methodist and 218 Baptist. In the town of Farmville there are three colored church edifices, and in the surrounding country there are three or four others.

"The chief and overshadowing organization is the First Baptist Church of Farmville. It owns a large brick edifice on Main street. The auditorium, which seats about 500 people, is tastefully finished in light wood, with carpet, small organ, and stained glass windows. Beneath this is a large assembly room with benches. This building is really the central club-house of the community, and in greater degree than is true of the country church in New England or the West. Various organizations meet here, entertainments and lectures take place here, the church collects and distributes considerable sums of money, and the whole social life of the town centers here. The unifying and directing force is, however, religious exercises of some sort. The result of this is not so much that recreation and social life have become stiff and austere, but rather that religious exercises have

* Bulletin of the United States Department of Labor, No. 14, pp. 34–35.

acquired a free and easy expression and in some respects serve as amusement-giving agencies. For instance, the camp-meeting is simply a picnic, with incidental sermon and singing; the rally of the country churches, called the 'big meeting,' is the occasion of the pleasantest social intercourse, with a free barbecue; the Sunday-school convention and the various preachers' conventions are occasions of reunions and festivities. Even the weekly Sunday service serves as a pleasant meeting and greeting place for working people, who find little time for visiting during the week.

"From such facts, however, one must not hastily form the conclusion that the religion of such churches is hollow or their spiritual influence bad. While under present circumstances the Negro church can not be simply a spiritual agency, but must also be a social, intellectual, and economic center, it nevertheless is a spiritual center of wide influence; and in Farmville its influence carries nothing immoral or baneful. The sermons are apt to be fervent repetitions of an orthodox Calvanism, in which, however, hell has lost something of its terrors through endless repetition; and joined to this is advice against the grosser excesses of drunkenness, gambling, and other forms disguised under the general term 'pleasure' and against the anti-social peccadillos of gossip, 'meanness,' and undue pride of position. Very often a distinctly selfish tone inculcating something very like sordid greed and covetousness is, perhaps, unconsciously used; on the other hand, kindliness, charity, and sacrifice are often taught. In the midst of all, the most determined, energetic, and searching means are taken to keep up and increase the membership of the church, and 'revivals,' long continued and loud, although looked upon by most of the community as necessary evils, are annually instituted in the August vacation time. Revivals in Farmville have few of the wild scenes of excitement which used to be the rule; some excitement and screaming, however, are encouraged, and as a result nearly all the youth are 'converted' before they are of age. Certainly such crude conversions and the joining of the church are far better than no efforts to curb and guide the young.

"The Methodist Church, with a small membership, is the second social center of Farmville, and there is also a second Baptist Church, of a little lower grade, with some habitual noise and shouting."

Outside the city of Richmond, we have returns from thirty-five churches. Thirty-two of these are Baptist, one is Christian, and two Presbyterian :

Total churches	35
Total membership	18,727
Total actual membership	10,842
Total value property	$114,810.00
Total expenses	21,155.54

Total expenses		$ 21,155.54
Salaries	$ 9,738.28	
Debt and interest	862.00	
Running expenses	3,821.68	
Charity, etc.	1,247.66	
Missions	1,475.09	
Support and connection	437.68	
Other expenses	4,335.15	

The condition of the Methodist churches can be judged by the reports of the African Methodist Episcopal Churches in the Norfolk, Portsmouth, Richmond, and Roanoke districts—108 churches in all :

Ministers	77
Members	9,126
Churches	108
Parsonages	38
Value churches and parsonages	$ 168,114.09
Present indebtedness	64,739.61
Money raised for—	
Pastors' support	18,578.62
Missionary money	1,177.46
Charitable purposes	1,162.53
Educational purposes	512.40
Building and repairs	8,489.40
Current expenses	38,284.22
For all purposes	70,584.67

19. The Middle West, Illinois. (By Monroe N. Work, A. M., and the Editor).

There are approximately about 250 Negro churches in the state with a total membership of 15,177. The Negro population of the state was 85,078 for 1900. This gives about 22½ per cent. of Negro population of the state as members of the church. There is a large number of persons who have moved into the state that in their native homes were members of churches. These would raise the actual number of church communicants considerably, for they commune, etc., and to all intents and purposes are members of the churches where they happen to reside. These would in a census be returned as members and counted in the state where residing.

By denominations the membership is as follows:

African Methodist Episcopal	8,375	Episcopal	380
Baptist	8,812	Presbyterian	210
African Methodist Episcopal		Cumberland Presbyterian	65
Zion	100	Christian	50
Methodist Episcopal	360	Catholics (not ascertained)	...
Old Time Methodist Episcopal	100	Adventists (estimated)	25

The total amount of church property owned in the state was about .$445,000
The total expenses for 1902 were about 133,000

Of the above amount about $70,000 was for pastors' salaries and about $20,000 on church debt.

The following conclusions are based on my own observations and the replies to questions sent out:

The Negro church, as a result of slavery, emphasized the emotional side of mentality and the future life. Freedom, with its changed environments and opportunities, has modified these two aspects. It is found in the study of churches of this state, that there is a decided tendency away from the emotional and the emphasizing of the future life. This is especially noticeable in both Baptist and Methodist churches, which contain the bulk of the Negro communicants. In the churches of these denominations in the city of Chicago there are only a few where the emphasis is on the emotional and the future life. There are some churches where the emphasis is placed sometimes on the emotional, the future life, and sometimes on the intellectual and this present life. There is a large number of churches in which the emphasis is almost entirely on the intellectual and the things of this life. It may be said, therefore, that in general the farther the people have moved from slavery conditions the less emotional and unpractical they are religiously; the more effort there is to make religion a rule of conduct for every day life.

Historically the Negro ministry has had three distinct stages of development and appears to be passing into a fourth stage. The minister of slavery days and early freedom, for the most part ignorant, was the leader of the people along all lines—religiously, intellectually, politically, etc. The emancipated Negro had few or no church buildings. This, with the additional fact of a large emigration to the cities, caused a demand for ministers who could build large church buildings and control large congregations. The church-building, congregation-managing minister was the result. It was not necessary that he should be intellectual or morally upright if he could meet with the demands, hence the development of this type of ministry. The need of church buildings was largely met, but almost every church had a debt upon it. There arose a demand for ministers who could raise money to pay these debts and keep the church doors from being closed. This, the third type, has more business ability than his predecessors. He is stronger intellectually and better morally. There is arising a demand for still another type of ministry, viz.: the man strong intellectually and sound morally. This demand is, as yet, not very strong, mainly because there are not many churches out of debt, and the energies of the people are largely expended in raising money to pay on church debts. It is more than probable that as the people progress in intelligence and the churches are freed from debt, thus permitting them to pay more attention to internal aspects of religion, the intellectual and moral man will become more and more the leader in the churches.

The above is not intended as a full or adequate explanation of the churches in Illinois, especially in Chicago, but rather as one of the main causes in producing the present conditions of the churches in this state.

The present conditions of the churches seems to be about as follows: they are for the most part deeply in debt. Hence the energies of the people are expended in raising money to pay interest, etc., of debt, thereby causing the emphasis to be laid on the incidentals instead of upon the essentials of the religious life. The people live for the church instead of the church existing for the people. There is not as much attention given to teaching the essentials of religion as should be, but the tendency seems to be more toward this phase as the churches are freed from debt. This is best illustrated by the institution of pastors having for their purpose the ministering to the social needs of the people. The Institutional Church, established in Chicago by the African Methodist Episcopal denomination, is the most advanced step in the direction of making the church exist for the people rather than the people for the church. Because of the financial needs and other things this church has been compelled to modify its efforts to minister to the people and lay emphasis on the incidental features.

The church appears to be occupying a somewhat less prominent place in the social life of the people than it once did, although it is yet probably the most influential factor, or one of the most influential, in their social life.

The ministry has probably improved, both intellectually and morally. It is, however, not meeting the needs of the people in the best possible manner, because there are few ministers with college and theological training, and the debt-ridden conditions of the churches call for men with ability to raise money rather than for men intellectually and morally strong.

The morals of the people are probably being raised. This is best evidenced by the wide-spread dissatisfaction that is found to exist among church members and the criticism of present conditions which they make; also the increasing demand for a better ministry. This criticism is:

(1) One of the ministry.
   a. It lacks edification.
   b. It lacks morality.
   c. It lacks business ability.

(2) Of the members.
   a. Of the officers of the church who are often dishonest and lacking in business ability.
   b. The members lack moral sense and appreciation, i. e., the ethical standards are bad.

The church is probably losing its influence on the young people because of the scarcity of ministers able to meet the intellectual needs of the times and the emphasis which the church is compelled to place on eternal things. The conditions of the churches in this state, while far from being good, are probably being improved.

1. A better type of ministry is appearing (very few).
2. The business affairs of the church are being better managed. This is notably true in Chicago.
3. The people are demanding better ministers and higher morals (demand very weak and uncertain as yet).
4. Tendency appears to be toward more honest and upright living among the members.

The opinions of seventy-five intelligent colored laymen throughout the state are as follows:

The majority think that the present condition of the churches is bad. The churches' influence is, on the whole, toward better and more upright life, but there is great room for improvement. The ministers are said not usually to be the right sort of men, their faults being ignorance and immorality, and in some cases, drunkenness. Opinions are divided as to the efficiency of Sunday-schools. Not much charitable work is done and the church is not attracting young people.

The great needs of the church in Illinois are better ministers, better business management, a high standard of living among members, a larger income, and more practical work.

The standards of morality among Negroes are being slowly raised.

Detailed returns as to churches have been received directly from sixty-one Negro churches having an enrolled membership of 10,144 and an active membership of 6,172. Of this active membership, 4,969 is in the thirty-two churches in the city of Chicago. The twenty-nine churches outside of Chicago report the following statistics:

Twenty-nine Churches in Illinois

Total membership	2,143
Active membership	1,093
Cost of churches	$72,660.00
Salaries	$ 8,200.91
Debt and interest	3,206.49
Running expense	2,388.23
Charity	481.66
Missions	310.03
Support of connection	698.26
Other expenses	3,176.10
Total	$ 18,461.68

For southern Illinois we have reports of seventy-four African Methodist Episcopal Churches as follows:

Ministers	52
Members	4,085
Churches	74
Parsonages	35
Value churches and parsonages	$ 83,190.00
Present indebtedness	23,304.44
School houses	3
Money raised for—	
Pastors' support	$ 17,964.11
Missionary money	481.35
Charitable purposes	650.08
Educational purposes	243.75
Building and repairs	8,215.74
Current expenses	4,161.98
For all expenses	33,207.58

There are in Chicago thirty-two colored churches and missions. Sixteen of these own the places where they worship. There are no returns from four of them. The figures are:

The Negro Churches in Chicago

DENOMINATION.	No. Reporting.	Membership.	Active Membership.	Valuation of Church Property.	Expenses Last Year.
African Methodist Episcopal.......	9	3,549	2,080	$ * 125,800	$ 39,372.95
Baptist..............................	11	3,097	2,140	16,500	12,674.74
African Methodist Episcopal Zion .	1	500	300	20,000	....
Presbyterian........................	2	215	134	8,000	2,640.60
Christian............................	1	50	40	....	....
Episcopal...........................	1	280	125	5,000	1,811.25
Methodist Episcopal	2	310	150	3,500	1,909.00
Adventist............................	1	....	....	....	....
Total	28	8,001	4,969	$ 178,800	$ 58,408.50

[N. B.] These totals are smaller than they really should be owing to the fact that some churches were only partially reported, while the "Adventist Church" has *no* report of statistics.

*One of the African Methodist Episcopal Churches does not own property, but uses a rented building.

Four of the Baptist Churches do not own property, but use rented buildings.

One of the Presbyterian Churches owns no property.

The Christian Church uses a rented building.

One of the Methodist Episcopal Churches uses a rented building.

The active membership of these churches varies as follows:

750–1,000..	2
500–750..	2
300–500..	1
100–300..	7
Under 100........	14
Unknown....................................	6
Total.....................................	32

The pastors of these churches may be classified as follows: Of the five larger churches (300–1,000 members) the pastors are reported:

No. 1. "Reputation fair."

No. 2. "Charged with drunkenness and immorality; but charges not confirmed."

No. 3. "Charged with misuse of church funds."

No. 4. "No especial charges."

No. 5. "Character not good—immoral."

Of the pastors of churches with 100–300 members:

Nos. 6, 7, 8, 9, 10 and 12. "Character good."

No. 11. "Character not good—given to drink."

Of the pastors of the smaller churches nine are of good character. The others are :

No. 14. "Reputation not good."
No. 26. "Charged with misuse of funds."
Nos. 15 and 17. ?
No. 20. Has no pastor at present.

In the larger churches four are composed largely of ignorant or lower middle class people. One has a pretty intelligent class of people. Of the seven medium churches three have intelligent congregations of the upper class and four congregations of fair intelligence. The smaller churches consist of three rather intelligent congregations, seven of fair or medium intelligence, and five ignorant bodies.

Only one of the large churches does much charitable work. It spent last year nearly $400. One other church claims to spend considerable, but does not do very effective work. Two of the medium sized churches do charitable work of some importance. One of these was originally organized as a social settlement, but for lack of proper guidance has had but partial success. Nevertheless, it is a significant movement and indicates a drift in the right direction. It has done some good work, among other things co-operating with Atlanta University in this study. One of the smaller churches has a day nursery and kindergarten, and two others do some institutional work among the young people. The oldest of the Negro churches was established in 1850. It was for some time a station on the underground railroad. It is to-day a center of social and religious life and also of the political life of the Negroes. President McKinley spoke in the church on his last public visit to Chicago. The second oldest church was established in 1853.

The actual services in these churches can best be judged by recording the results of a series of visits. In four of the large churches we have the following results:

African Methodist Episcopal Church—700 active members.

11 a. m. Sunday service. There was a long ritualistic introduction. The singing was good and effort was put forth to make strangers feel at home. The sermon was preached especially to converts and there was much emotion prevalent. The emphasis was laid on the after life. The house was well filled and the ventilation bad.

African Methodist Episcopal Zion Church—300 active members.

Morning service. The attendance was poor and much emotion was displayed. The sermon was on "God's love." There was much insistence on money. The ventilation was bad.

African Methodist Episcopal Church—800 active members.

Special afternoon service. Discussion of the decrease of consumption by colored physicians of the city. Talks on care of the body.

Baptist Church—1,000 active members.

Evening service. The house was crowded and the sermon emotional. The service was long, running forty-five minutes over time. Sermon had some practical bearings at the close. Ventilation was good.

Ten other church services in the medium and smaller churches are reported. In nine of these there was no evidence of emotion—in some cases for lack of interest, in other cases from custom. In one case the church had white and colored members and a colored pastor. They showed much emotion at the service, but were very sincere and earnest people. The sermons varied: one was on the "Future life;" another took the theme "Get ready to leave this world," but ended with practical advice on home-owning. Another spoke of the "Blessed life," putting emphasis on both this and the future life. Another sermon was on "Self-control."

The expenditures of Chicago churches were as follows:

Thirty-two Churches in Chicago

Total membership	6,811
Active membership	4,329
Valuation of churches	$ 199,300.00
Salaries	17,895.13
Debt and interest,	17,617.39
Running expenses	12,869.32
Charity	2,760.98
Missions	609.10
Support of connection	1,550.95
Other expenses	4,267.10
Total	$ 57,569.97

The comments of intelligent Negroes and some of the pastors on the condition of the churches are worth listening to. As to the condition of the churches there is much complaint of the debts due largely to the erection of imposing edifices:

"As a rule, they are marked with inefficiency and a lack of proper regard for the moral development of the people. The emphasis placed on the financial condition is so great that the church is lacking in that which works for the moral development of the people in honesty, in sexual purity, etc."

"I have been informed that all but two of the churches in this city carry large debts. These debts range from $5,000 to $27,000. In appearance and appointments the church structures compare favorably with the edifices of the white population. One was built and completed at a cost of nearly $50,000. The Institutional Church was bought from the First Presbyterian Church for $33,000, of which sum $9,000 has been paid. The Bethel African Methodist Episcopal Church and the Olivet Baptist Church cost in the neighborhood of $30,000 each. They each owe about $15,000."

"The majority are in debt. The larger churches are largely attended by fashionably dressed people. The smaller ones have a hard struggle to exist. There is a constant demand for money at every service in all of them."

The influence of these churches is criticized :

"The thought of right doing and right living seems to be secondary. The primary idea seems to be to get the most good-paying members."

"We have many loyal and faithful members in our churches, and, I may add, altogether too many bad ones."

The ministers are especially taken to task :

"As a rule, I think the ministers are good men. There are dangerous exceptions, however."

"I know some good, pure, and upright men in the ministry, but I know some who are not good, pure, and upright. In my observations, I have noticed drunkenness, poor paymasters, lack of interest in their families, and very much tainted with sexual impurity."

"The ministers of . . . . churches are excellent Christian gentlemen, educated, and doing all in their power to raise the standard of Christian citizenship."

"So far as my personal knowledge goes, the ministers are good men. I can not deny that I have heard some ugly and persistent rumors concerning the life and character of several of the local staff of preachers. Sexual immorality and drunkenness are the offenses charged. I do not know of this from personal knowledge, however. In making this statement I am not attempting to evade whatever responsibility may rest with me in this matter. I simply do not know of my own knowledge of the correctness of these charges."

"I do not know of any specific cases of immorality such as you make mention of here. I can only judge by what I hear and that not too harshly. If I should judge strictly according to what I hear, I should not believe that there were any Christians among our ministers. This I am unwilling to accede."

"I regret to say some of those in our larger churches have not conducted themselves as Christian ministers should, numerous scandals having arisen about them. Whether false or true, it has a tendency to destroy their influence for good."

"Common rumor charges the ministers of our largest churches in this community with gross immorality—sexual impropriety and drunkenness. The ministers of the three largest Methodist churches are charged with drunkenness, and the one at another church with gross sexual immorality. According to persistent rumor, one church was robbed by a former pastor who still has a charge here."

"Several ministers whom I know have had the above charges laid at their door. I cannot say whether they are guilty or not. I know, however, that a great deal of money passes through their hands and still the churches groan under the heavy weight of debt. Some I know are positively immoral."

Several pastors write of their especial difficulties, enumerating them as follows:

"How to secure sufficient means to prosecute the work in my district, which is the 'Slum District,' and how to treat and deal with the influx now migrating here from the South."

"One is poverty. Another is to have my message received for its own sake. A third is the utter lack of moral stamina in the community, extending to everything."

"The pastor's greatest difficulty is to meet his financial obligations because of his meagre salary."

"The one great difficulty of the Negro pastor is to overcome the persistent, well nigh peremptory demand for something which appeals to the animal rather than to the human—that rouses the excitable rather than convicts the judgment.."
"Lack of competent officials in a business way."

The greatest needs of the churches, according to the pastors, are:

"More intelligence and more piety, as well as an infinitely greater degree of purified refinement."

"(1) New methods of giving, i. e., from principle; (2) harmony between inner and external life; (3) promptness in attendance; (4) true conception of the meaning of worship; (5) to keep the church out of politics."

"The greatest need is money."

The laymen think the needs are:

"I think the greatest need of our churches is good business management of funds, honest, intelligent and industrious business men on our trustee and deacon boards."

"More earnestness, higher moral tone, particularly in pulpit. To reform methods of raising money so as to preserve the quiet calm that should prevent devotional meetings from degenerating into a bargain counter session. The building of large and imposing edifices without previous monetary arrangements or its spiritual value being thought of, makes morals and religion serve as bell-ringer merely to call the congregation in order to cajole, importune or brow-beat interest money and pastor's salary."

And above all, *"Better ministers."*

Yet, that there is some good work done in matters of charity and reform by the churches, all admit.

"Yes, we have Sunday Clubs, as for instance, the Ladies' Aid of Berean Church, which did noble work during the severe cold weather just passed. They meet from house to house and sew for the poor."

"The Institutional Church and Social Settlement does the most of this kind of work. The other churches confine their charitable and reformatory work to their membership. I think this is accounted for in the small and moderate means of the membership."

"No specialized charity, but particularly generous and open-hearted in request cases"

"The Institutional, Quinn Chapel, Bethel, and others in Chicago. Special collections are lifted to bury some poor unfortunate or to relieve the wants of the destitute."

The churches are not attracting young people as they should.

"Owing to present conditions, as I see them, the young people of the intellectual class are not attracted to the church. They give very little for the support of the church."

"Not in large numbers. A few are scattered throughout all of the churches, but the vast majority seems to have no inclination toward the church."

"Taking Chicago as a whole. No! In the community of which I write, Yes! One of the largest Negro churches in the city until recently actually set a premium on ignorance, and drove the younger element from the church."

"I am sorry to have to answer No. Our young people are being educated away from the church. A very small percentage of our professional men and women are regular in their church attendance."

In spite of all drawbacks the weight of opinion is that moral stand-ards in Chicago are being slowly raised despite the influx of the new colored immigrants:

"It is my firm belief that the standards are being raised in these particulars. The accumulations in property holdings and homes, the increase in bank accounts, the visible improvement in the matter of good taste in dress, are signs which, in my opinion, confirm the belief that the standards included in this question are being raised."

"I do not think the standards are being raised by any means."

"Through the efforts of the church, Women's Clubs, and Sunday Clubs, there seems to be an improvement in morals."

"Lowered, as viewed from large numbers of marriages, which are not held in such sacredness as such tie demands and in careless rearing of children."

"I think the standard of morality is being raised. Marriages are common, every-day occurrences, and illicit and illegal cohabitation is no longer common but is very rare. The chief agencies in this work are church and school."

20. The Middle West, Ohio. (By R. R. Wright, Jr.*)

Greene County is situated in the southwestern portion of the state of Ohio, about midway between Cincinnati and Columbus. Its area is 453 square miles and its population is 31,613, of whom 4,055 are Negroes. Greene County is a typical county for the study of the Negro problem, as it refers to the Northern Negro of the country and small town, for it not only has a very varied population of Negroes, but also the largest proportion of Negroes to whites in the state; and among these Negroes are some of the oldest inhabitants of the state as well as some of the most recent immigrants from the South.

Negro Church in Ohio

Ohio has a population of 4,157,545 persons, of whom 96,901 are Negroes. Of these about 28,000, or twenty-nine per cent., are reported as church members.

Early in the last century the Negro church had its rise in this state. In 1815, when there were but few Negroes here, the first Negro church was established at Cincinnati. This was under the Methodist Episco-pal church. Rev. B. W. Arnett, now bishop of the African Methodist Episcopal Church, gives the following account in his "Proceedings of the Semi-Centenary Celebration of the African Methodist Episcopal Church of Cincinnati, 1874:" "The first religious society organized in Cincinnati by colored people was the Deer Creek Church, organized in 1815, under the auspices of the Methodist Episcopal Church. This was one year before the organization of the African Methodist Episcopal denomination in Philadelphia by Richard Allen and others. What Negroes there were in Cincinnati had been attending Old Stone Church,

---

*Cf. Mr. Wright's longer study, Bulletin United States Bureau of Labor, No. 48.

or 'Wesley Chapel' Methodist Episcopal Church; but on account of
the shouting habit they were not very much desired at this white
church. They were all crowded into one section of the church, where
with much effort they tried not to disturb their white brethren by
their frequent outbursts of praise to God. The whites tolerated them
as long as they were successful in suppressing this inclination to shout.
The crisis came, however, in 1815, when a brother, striving to suppress
his shout by muffling his mouth with a handkerchief, burst one of his
blood vessels in the attempt. After this the whites themselves took
serious steps to have a separate church for Negroes. The result was
the Deer Creek Church, whose pastor for a long while was a slave who
came over from Kentucky from time to time. This new church was
under the Methodist Episcopal connection until 1823, when, on account
of alleged discrimination and unbrotherly action on the part of the
white brethren toward the colored, many of the latter withdrew and
went over to the African Methodist Episcopal Church. Those who
remained continued in the Methodist Episcopal Church, known later
as Union Chapel. Thus began the Negro church in Ohio. Its mother
was the Methodist Episcopal Church. The first African Methodist
Episcopal Church was at Steubenville. In 1823, according to Bishop
D. A. Payne's History of the African Methodist Episcopal Church,
there were churches of this denomination at Cincinnati, Steubenville,
and Chillicothe. When the Chillicothe and Steubenville churches
were founded is not exactly known. In 1824 the report for the African
Methodist Episcopal churches was as follows: Jefferson County Circuit (composed of Steubenville, with forty-five members, Cape Belmont,
six members, Mount Pleasant, twelve members)—total sixty-three
members; Chillicothe Circuit (composed of Chillicothe, Zanesville,
Lancaster, and Cincinnati), only thirty-three members were reported
on these charges. In 1833 there were churches at twenty different
points with a membership of 690. In 1836 the membership of the
African Methodist Episcopal Church was 1,131, and in 1838 it was 1,817.
It has steadily increased until to-day it is more than 6,000.''

When the separate Negro church was established, in 1815, nearly
all the Negroes of the town joined or attended it regardless of what
denomination they had before belonged to. It was not until 1835 that
the first Baptist organization was begun—"Union Baptist Church" of
Cincinnati.

There are now in the state seven denominations maintaining separate
churches for Negroes, with a membership as follows :

Baptists....................................	16,213
Western Association......................	6,885
Eastern Association......................	3,704
Zion Association..........................	*3,500
Providence Association	2,124
African Methodist Episcopal Church......	6,308
Ohio Conference	3,179
North Ohio Conference....................	3,129
Methodist Episcopal Church, North.......'	1,645
Wesleyan Methodists......................	557
Christian (Disciples)......................	*1,000
Episcopal and Presbyterian................	2,000
Total	27,723

These with the number of Negroes who are members of white congregations among Presbyterians, Catholics, Congregationalists, Zionists (Dowieites), would make the total about 28,000, or about twenty-nine per cent. of the total Negro population of the state. Of the population over fifteen years of age—70,032—forty per cent. are church members. In 1890 there were 250 organizations in the state among Negroes, having 19,827 communicants. This was 22.8 per cent. of the total population of 87,113 Negroes, much less than in 1902. The number of church members in the country at large in 1890 was 2,673,977 or 35.7 per cent. of the total Negro population. By this we see that Ohio is now still somewhat behind what the country at large was in 1890. The following table is taken from the United States census of 1890:

STATE.	Organizations.	Edifices.	Seating Capacity.	Halls.	Seating Capacity.	Value.	Communicants.	Population.
Total for United States.	23,462	23,770	6,800,035	1,358	114,644	$26,626,488	2,673,977	7,488,788
Ohio	250	214	66,516	34	1,750	576,425	19,827	87,113

There are now over 300 organizations distributed among over 200 cities and towns in the state.

Greene County

Greene County has a population of 31,613, of whom 4,055 are Negroes. The county is favorably situated for farming, and outside of Xenia many Negroes engage in this occupation, chiefly as "hands" at odd labor, however, as the census of 1900 gave only ninety farmers among the colored population of the county. The county is one of the oldest in the State, constituted in 1802, and named for General Nathaniel

---

* Estimated by Secretary.

Greene. From its earliest days it has had Negroes among its population, as the following table will show:

POPULATION OF GREENE COUNTY BY UNITED STATES CENSUS, 1810–1900

Year.	White.	Colored.	Total.
1810.	5,834	36	5,870
1820.	10,468	61	10,521
1830.	14,639	162	14,801
1840.	17,184	344	17,528
1850.	21,292	654	21,946
1860.	24,722	1,475	26,197
1870.	24,199	3,839 a	28,038
1880.	26,774	4,575 b	31,349
1890.	25,950	4,060 c	29,820
1900.	27,554	4,055 d	31,613

a Includes 24 Indians.
b Includes 6 Chinese and 19 Indians.
c Does not include 3 Chinese and 7 Indians.
d Negroes only. Does not include 4 Chinese and Japanese.

The following table gives a partial exhibit of the general financial condition of the churches of the State:

CHURCHES.	Value of Property.	Indebtedness.	Salary of Pastor.	Paid on Debt.	Total Raised.
M. E. Church.	a$79,050.09	$10,439.00	$ 8,430.00	b$9,074.00	....
A. M. E.—					
N. O. Conference.	242,375.00	17,055.25	14,692.01	14,898.29	$37,878.57
Ohio Conference.	108,570.00	10,364.53	13,116.28	10,806.64	28,522.43
Baptist { Eastern Association.	....	....	....	....	....
Western Association.	....	....	13,380.00	d13,510.00	....
Zion Association.	....	....	....	....	....
Providence Association.	31,350.00	....	c1,414.40	....	....
Wesleyan.	9,400.00	....	1,954.99	....	3,296.52

a $12,200 for parsonages.
b $5,628 for improvements, $3,466 on debt.
c For six pastors only.
d The total valuation of church property of the Baptists is estimated at $259,200.

Greene County is noted for its many small towns, among a score of which the most prominent are Xenia, with a population of 8,696; Jamestown, 1,205; Yellow Springs, 1,371; Cedarville, 1,189; Osborn, 948; Bowersville, 370; Springvalley, 522; and Bellbrook, 352. In five of these, viz: Xenia, Jamestown, Yellow Springs, Cedarville, and Wilberforce, we find the Negro church. To describe one of these is to describe all save Xenia and Wilberforce, the latter a college community, where Wilberforce University is located.

One rides into one of the other of these little towns and here he finds two more or less neat little church buildings, with seating capacity, on an average, of about 150 or 200 persons; sometimes of brick, sometimes frame. At Yellow Springs, the seat of Antioch College, where once the great Horace Mann presided, both churches are of brick and neat. One of these churches is an African Methodist Episcopal, and the other a Baptist Church. Almost invariably you will find that the younger and more intelligent class of Negroes is at the Methodist Church, while the older contingent generally constitute the membership of the Baptist Church. At the Baptist Church one will find more fervency of speech and a more sanctimonious look on the part of both pastor and people, more of heaven and the future is talked of; at the Methodist churches there is all of this, but less in proportion. The sermons one very probably will hear at the Baptist Church will abound in much good thought, ending generally in the same way, with something foreign more or less to the text. While the Methodist pastor may not be free from digressions, yet he is in every case the more logical speaker, and now and then gives his people something out of the "same old way."\ This is natural, when we know that the pastor of the Baptist Church is generally a middle-aged man * of but meagre English and no theological training, while the pulpit of the Methodist Church is occupied by a student in the Theological Seminary at Wilberforce, who is also generally the equivalent of a high school graduate. These circumstances account for the above-named facts that the more intelligent class attends the Methodist Church. This comparison is somewhat abnormal when the whole state is considered, because the Methodist pastors are students who, were they engaged solely in preaching, would have much better churches, and leave these smaller churches to more poorly equipped men, as is the case with the Baptists now. The Baptist churches are, however, generally larger than the Methodist chiefly because they receive more time from their pastors. This was the case up to two years ago. Still there is no friction, but the most cordial feeling between both pastors and both flocks. Indeed many of the members of the Methodist Church take active parts in affairs of the Baptist Church, and *vice versa.* The pastors even change their pulpits, which once was not common. During the winter of 1902, when the revival fever had taken vigorous hold of Greene County, in order that there be no disadvantage in fighting Satan occasioned by a division of the hosts of the Lord, an agreement was made in Cedarville to the effect that one of the denominations would hold its revival and that all the members of the other church would give aid. After this first revival, then all, regardless of denomination, should combine their forces at the other church. This worked well for both. On the day

---

* The pulpit of Cedarville Baptist Church has been recently given to a young man—student at Wilberforce.

that the Methodist Church was visited by the writer, he found the pastor of the Baptist Church present to preach.

In all of these churches the chief stress is put upon "saving souls;" that is, in persuading people to forsake sin and accept the Christian religion as the guiding force of their lives. And the method is quite rational. Usually in the middle of the winter, i. e., the first thing in the new year, the churches begin their revivals. This first work of the year lasts from two to eight weeks and many come to be saved, and are converted. Some of these see visions or dream dreams, some spend weeks in mourning, and still others are converted in a few minutes. In the revivals the sermons are chiefly on hell and its terrors, the love of Christ and God as shown in the suffering and death of Christ, Christ seeking sinners, the awful doom of those rejecting Him, etc. They abound in pathetic stories, which are related with great feeling, and which seldom fail in the desired result. This result is a large number of conversions and accessions to the churches. These are in due time baptized and admitted to full membership. Then the revival has closed, not only having been of great benefit to those converted, but also a positive moral help to the community at large. The remaining nine or ten months of the year are used for strengthening and teaching the members in the Christian religion and in the doctrines of the church. The Baptists take in their members directly. The Methodists require six months of probation, during which the candidate is supposed to receive instruction in his duty as a Christian and church member by the pastor, beside the regular instruction given from the pulpit. In none of the Methodist churches of Greene County is this carried out fully, but in those where it is attempted with anything like success, the results show well in the character of the members.

If there is any criticism as to method in arousing and directing the religious consciousness it should be more severe as regards post-revival methods than revival methods. Experienced revivalists, and some men of much intelligence living in the county, state that for the average Negro congregation their method, though accompanied by much of the spectacular, is best suited for those to whom they appeal, but that after the "revival" is over the proper oversight is seldom given the young Christian and, as is quite natural, the life is far from the ideal.

WILBERFORCE.—The value of the Wilberforce church consists in the fact that many students are interested in Christian work, and are trained for larger service after leaving school. The pastor of the church is the instructor in science and a very devout man. Under his preaching from forty to eighty students are converted every year. Of these some take an active interest in the local Christian work, and of these latter some enter the ministry. In many states of the Union there are men and women earnestly engaged in church, Sunday-school, Young Men's Christian Association work, now leaders and pastors, who were converted in the Wilberforce revival and got their first interest and training here. For the training of the newly converted there is a class led by one of the instructors. Beside this the Bible classes of the ·Y. M. C. A. and Y. W. C. A., taught by professors in the University, have in the past year been successful in imparting systematic knowledge of the Scriptures more than at any previous time.

Payne Theological Seminary is at Wilberforce, and its students and teachers are local preachers in the church. Its dean is superintendent of the Sunday-school. In the Seminary are forty-five students, representing South America, South Africa, West Africa, and various states in the Union. The class of 1903 numbers eleven members.

XENIA.—Xenia is the county seat of Greene County and one of the oldest towns in the state. Its population by the census of 1900 was 8,696, of whom 1,988, or 21.7 per cent., were Negroes. These Negroes are made up of about half natives of the state of Ohio and about half immigrants from Kentucky, Virginia, North Carolina, Tennessee and other Southern states. In general the immigrants make up the lower class, being the poorer and more illiterate. The illiteracy of Xenia Negroes is 13.42 per cent. for all above ten years, and 1.57 per cent. for those between ten years and forty years. About 63 per cent. of Xenia Negroes own their homes and they pay taxes on $116,828 worth of property. The school advantages, through high school, are far above ordinary. Yet Xenia is a town of but little thrift compared with the advantages offered. The chief businesses are barbers, small groceries and an undertaking establishment. While the Negroes are not extraordinarily thrifty, they are not, on the other hand, very vicious. Composing 21.7 per cent. of the population, they furnish 29.9 per cent. of the arrests. The number for 1901-2 was ninety-eight. Among these cases were: Drunk, ten; loitering, three; disorderly, twenty; drunk and disorderly, seven; assault and battery, seven; suspicion, five; safe keeping, eleven; stealing ride, seven; petit larceny, one; lunacy, two; burglary, fugitive from justice, murder in another state, larceny, threatening, execution, one each; gambling, seven; horse stealing, two.

Xenia, then, is a slow, not good, not bad, conservative, somewhat conceited sort of a town, whose people live, in the main, comfortably, i. e., according to the general standard for Negroes.

Negroes have lived in the county ever since it has been established. The first count made in the county, in 1803, took a record only of white males over twenty-one years of age, but the United States census gives the colored population of Xenia only since 1830, as follows:

Year.	White.	Colored.	Total.
1830	902	17	919
1850	2,694	330	3,024
1860	3,856	802	4,658
1870	4,687	1,690	6,377
1880	5,077	1,949 a	7,026
1890	5,424	1,877 b	7,301
1900	6,705	1,991 c	8,696

a Includes 3 Chinese and Japanese and 3 Indians.
b Includes 3 Chinese and 6 civilized Indians.
c Includes 3 Chinese.

There are seven churches in Xenia, viz: Three Baptist, one African Methodist Episcopal, one Methodist Episcopal, one Wesleyan Methodist, and one Christian Church.

The first church in Xenia was established by the African Methodist Episcopal connection in 1833. Nothing is known of it save that it was on the Hillsboro Circuit, and Rev. Thomas Lawrence was its pastor. In 1836 Rev. William Paul Quinn, afterwards bishop of the African Methodist Episcopal Church, was pastor. In 1842 the church was called the "Greene County Mission," had twenty-five members and paid its pastor the neat sum of $7.91. The first Baptist Church was established in 1848. Henry Howe's first "History of Ohio," published in 1852, says that then Xenia contained one German Church, one Lutheran Church, one Methodist Episcopal Church, one Seceders' Church, one Associate Reformed Church, one Baptist Church, and two churches for colored people.

Membership.—The seven churches of Xenia report a total membership of 1,068, or 53.4 per cent. of the entire Negro population. The membership is as follows:

Church.	Membership.
Baptist	640
Zion	370
Middle Run	140
Third	130
African Methodist Episcopal	240
Methodist Episcopal	54
Wesleyan	9
Christian	125
Total	1,068

By a personal count of 1,832 persons made by the writer during May-June, 1902, 976, or 53.6 per cent., reported themselves as church members. These members were all persons over ten years of age. The number of persons counted who were over ten years of age was 1,505. Hence 64.8 per cent. of these were church members. The following table will show the membership as reported by the persons themselves:

AGE PERIOD.	Church Members.			Total Population.			Percent of Members.
	Males.	Females.	Total.	Males.	Females.	Total.	
10 to 19 years.............	46	102	148	142	189	331	44.7
20 to 29 years.............	52	124	176	149	168	317	55.5
30 to 39 years.............	44	106	150	104	133	237	63.3
40 to 49 years	73	119	192	112	125	237	81.0
50 to 59 years.............	64	93	157	82	103	185	84.8
60 to 69 years.............	53	47	100	73	51	124	80.7
70 to 79 years	17	15	32	25	18	43	74.4
80 years and over........	4	12	16	5	12	17	94.1
Unknown age..........	4	1	5	9	5	14	35.7
Total.................	357	619	976	701	804	1,505	64.8

This table shows very strikingly that the young people are not forsaking the church to such an extent as to discard membership. More than half for every age period above twenty years are members, and in the first period more than half from fifteen to nineteen years of age are church members. The excess is of women over men. These persons are distributed throughout all occupations, but almost invariably those in the most lucrative positions or employments are church members. As to culture, as indicated by scholastic training, it appears from a personal count by the writer that out of ninety-five high school graduates 80 or 84.2 per cent. are church members—fifty-nine out of sixty-seven women, and twenty-one out of twenty-eight men. In the African Methodist Church the principal of the high school is superintendent of the Sunday-school, and the principal of the elementary school, although a woman, is a class leader. The only college graduate in the city is also an ordained minister connected with the local African Methodist Episcopal Church. As to material standing of the church members it is noted that of the 318 families who own their homes 288, or 90.6 per cent., were connected with the church by some member of the family, and 237 of them were connected by the head of the family.

The chief means of increasing the membership is through the revival, which is substantially the same as conducted in other parts of the county. Last year there were 175 conversions, of whom sixty-nine were under twenty years of age, and eleven were over forty years, according to the report of the pastors. (See table, page 00).

Activities.—These churches make some attempt to satisfy all the legitimate social desires of their members. There are sick benefit societies, educational societies, Home and Foreign Missionary Societies, Christian Endeavor Societies, Baptist Young People's Unions, sewing circles, besides various temporary organizations for raising money and other purposes. These are in addition to the organizations fundamental to the church government, such as in the Methodist Church, the various conferences, boards of trustees, stewards, spiritual officers, Sunday-school, etc.

As before stated, the chief activity is to preach and teach Christian doctrine and morality. The method for this is preaching in all the churches two or three times on Sunday, once or twice during the week, prayer-meeting on Wednesday night, class-meeting once a week in the Methodist Church and pastoral visiting, beside monthly love feasts or covenant meetings. As a means to this end is the material side of the church life to be looked after, and this is chiefly in regard to raising funds for the pastor's salary, current expenses, the debt, improvements, general purposes, etc. This is done by way of the Sunday and weekly collections and by organizing the members into clubs to solicit subscriptions or to raise funds by concerts and other entertainments. In this way the African Methodist Episcopal Church paid its debt of some $400 last year.

The next function of the church is the purely social. This is carried forward in other organizations and as a part of the more religious and financial activity. At church service old friends are met and new ones often made, but as no part of the special program. To raise money socials are given, etc., so that as secondary through all the activity there is the purely social. Along literary and musical lines, in spite of the fact that Negroes have free access to the theatre, the University Extension Courses, and the Y. M. C. A. lecture courses, the church is still the most powerful factor in Xenia life. Here the local talent finds the best opportunity for expression and development, and here the best available talent is brought from afar. In the Baptist Church last year there were ten lectures and two high class concerts. Among the lecturers was Rev. M. C. B. Mason, one of the most distinguished Negro orators. The Methodist (African) Church had during this year Miss Flora Batson, the noted singer, and a few weeks later the Canadian Jubilee Singers to entertain the people. In this way the church fulfills a social need which neither the extension courses or the theatre would fulfill—that of bringing the Negroes into touch with some of the best of their own race.

The table below will show that there is not much charity work done in Xenia by the churches, chiefly because there is not much need for such. Last year the churches gave as follows :

Zion Baptist	$ 25.00
Middle Run Baptist	7.00
St. John African Methodist Episcopal	50.00
Total	$ 82.00

Eighty-two dollars are reported, but the amount of charity work is more. By this it is seen that Middle Run Baptist Church reports $7, but Middle Run takes care of an old woman of eighty years, granting her free rent of a small house owned by the church and furnishing her, from time to time, with other necessities. In times of sickness, in many ways the church influences charity, though it does not get credit for it. On the first Sunday of each month most of the churches take an offering called the "Poor Saints' Collection." Beside this there are connected with several of the churches sick benefit societies. For instance, connected with Zion Baptist there are two: The Ladies' Home Aid and the Ladies' Auxiliary, both of which are especially designed to help the sick. There is practically no prison work undertaken by the churches of Xenia, except an occasional visit to the workhouse or jail by one of the pastors.

Pastors.—The pastors of Xenia are all men of high moral character, as is the universal testimony of those who have given opinions. They are all men of zeal for their work, intelligent, though none are college graduates. (See table, page 105.) It seems that Xenia has always had as ministers men of good reputations and high character. A historian* of Greene County, writing in 1881, speaking of the different Negro ministers of the city, said of one: "He has always been an upright Christian man;" of another: "By his gentlemanly deportment and Christian walk, he has gained many warm friends;" of another : "A congenial, attractive man, he shows from his fruits that he practices what he preaches;" of another: "The people of this county will find it a hard matter to fill his place should he be called to some other locality."

Value of Church Properties, Indebtedness, Pastor's Salary and Total Amount Raised by Churches of Greene County

CHURCH.	Value of Property.	Indebtedness.	Pastor's Salary.	Total Raised.
Baptist—				
Zion	$ 12,000	$3,400.00	$ 500.00	$1,025.00
Middle Run	1,000	00	170.00	
Third	8,000		500.09	
Yellow Springs	3,000		210.00	
Cedarville	1,000		170.00	223.25
Jamestown	2,000		350.00	505.00
Massies' Creek	700			
Methodist Episcopal	1,500	266.00	640.00	
Wesleyan Methodist	500		25.59	42.49
Christian	3,000		300.00	600.00
A. M. E.—				
Jamestown	2,000	00	300.00	956.71
Cedarville	1,200	00	167.50	316.80
Yellow Springs	3,000	00	250.00	495.85
St. John, Xenia	6,000	00	768.00	1,178.00
Wilberforce	Use Chapel of Wilberforce University	0	250.00	624.75

Incomplete.

* Dill's History of Greene County.

General Financial Statistics

CHURCH.	Current Expenses.	For Connection.	Interest on Debt and Principal.	Charity.	Missions.	Education and Other Purposes.	Salary.	Total.
Baptist—								
Zion	$ 100.00	......	$400.00	$25.00	......	......	$500.00	$1,025.00
Middle Run	100.00	$32.60	475.00	7.00	$14.00	......	170.00	......
Third	......	......	......	......	......	......	500.09	......
Yellow Springs	......	3.83	210.00	......	22.00	$ 54.17	......	280.00
Cedarville	2.60	......	40.00	1.50	6.75	2.40	170.00	......
Jamestown	75.00	10.00	0	30.00	25.00	15.00	350.00	505.00
Massies' Creek	......							
Methodist Episcopal	72.00	......	10.00	......	2.00	......	640.00	......
Wesleyan	7.40	7.00	......	......	......	9.50	25.59	42.49
Christian	92.00	......	208.00	......	......	......	300.00	600.00
A. M. E.—								
Jamestown	89.00	37.50	448.71	12.50	9.00	60.00	300.00	956.71
Cedarville	37.20	11.50	.00	19.60	27.58	53.42	167.50	316.80
Yellow Springs	18.78	33.30	125.00	......	8.77	......	2.50	495.85
Xenia	200.00	120.00	400.00	50.00	40.00	......	768.00	1,178.00
Wilberforce	113.72	65.75	......	49.68	60.00	127.00	250.00	665.65

Incomplete.

The questions on the schedules for "Data from Negro Churches" were answered as follows by the pastors of Greene County :

I.

What do the churches need most ?

Preachers that study the Bible and teach it in its purity............ 1
Educated ministers on fire with glory of God and uplift of the people. 1
Leaders, pure, courageous, with executive ability..................... 1
Educated, experienced, courageous, and honest men as preachers... 1
Religion and good sense........................ 1
Religion and faithful ministers, and refinement..................... 1
Revival of religion and money....................................... 1
More of the spirit of Christ 1
Better attendance and support from members....................... 1
Union.. 1

II.

What is the pastor's greatest difficulty ?

Lack of conscientious Bible study on his part....................... 1
Minister too abusive and people too sensitive....................... 1
Lack of courage and ability on part of minister..................... 1
Unconverted membership.. 1
Irregular and desultory attendance of members..................... 2
Lack of co-operation on part of members........................... 1
Difficulty of getting people to live Christian lives after joining the
    church.. 1
Immorality and ignorance of the people............................ 1

III.

Are the morals of the people being raised or lowered in respect to sexual morals, honesty, home life, truth-telling, etc ?

Raised.. 5
Raised by fifty per cent... 1
Doubtful.. 1
Very little as to sexual morals, home life and truth-telling; some as
to honesty.. 1

IV.

Is the Sunday-school effective ?

Yes... 8

How can it be improved ?

By co-operation of parents... 4
Systematic visiting through the week............................... 1
Gathering the little children.. 1

V.

How many persons joined the church last year?
How many of these were under 20 years of age?
How many were over 40 years of age?

CHURCH.	Accessions.		Total.	Total Members.	Total Active Members.
	Under 20 Years.	Over 40 Years.			
Baptist—					
Zion..............................	19	....	38	370	250
Middle Run......................	30	4	81	140	45
Third.............................	0	0	2	130	27
Yellow Springs...................	....	....	....	161	....
Cedarville........................	0	3	10	40	30
Jamestown........................	8	0	9	108	75
Massies' Creek...................	0	0	0	25	14
Methodist Episcopal...............	0	0	0	58	
Wesleyan Methodist..............	....	....	....	9	9
Christian.........................	0	1	4	125	50
A. M. E.—					
Jamestown........................	18	1	20	124	85
Cedarville........................	24	0	24	47	35
Yellow Springs...................	9	0	9	75	40
St. John, Xenia...................	20	6	50	240	160
Wilberforce*......................	60†	2	80	108	55
Total..........................	188	17	327	1,760	875

* 1901. Report for 1902 not available.   † Estimated.

VI.

Is there much shouting or emotion ?

Not very much.. 8
Considerable emotion, occasional shouting........................... 1
Yes... 1
Too much for the good done.. 1

VII.

Are the younger set of educated people joining the church and helping in its work ?

Yes.. 8
To some extent... 1
Slowly; they do a little... 1

VIII.

Sketches of Pastors of Greene County

(This includes also the A. M. E. and M. E. Presiding Elders.)

Church of Which Pastor.	Age.	Birthplace.	Years of Experience.	Education.
Baptist—				
Zion.....................	45	Ohio.	14	Normal.
Middle Run............	25	Ohio.	7	High School.
Third...................	48	South Carolina.	18	Common Schools of South Carolina.
Cedarville.............	29	Ohio	1	Common School.
Jamestown	48	....	17	Common School.
Yellow Springs........	50	....	....	Common School.
Massies' Creek.........	..	No pastor.	....	
Methodist Episcopal ...	..	....	....	
Wesleyan Methodist...	..	No pastor.	....	
Christian................	54	Kentucky.......	18	"Very limited."
A. M. E.—				
Xenia..................	34	Illinois	11	High School Graduate.
Cedarville.............	36	Florida..........	3	{Common School and Member of Class '03, Theological Seminary.
Jamestown............	31	Ohio	8	{Theological and High School Graduate.
Yellow Springs........	30	Louisiana	5	{Grammar School and Graduate Theological, '03.
Wilberforce	41	Ohio	7	College Graduate.
Presiding Elder A. M. E.	47	Ohio	25	Theological.
Presiding Elder M. E...	50	Indiana.........	20	College.

Opinions of Negro Church

These opinions are from people of long residence and good standing in Greene County. They are as to occupations as follows:

Pastors...................................... 6
Presiding Elders......................... 2
Physicians................................. 2
College Professors........................ 3
Dean Theological Seminary.............. 1
Principal High School.................... 1
Principal Elementary School............. 1
Barbers.................................... 2
Grocer..................................... 1
Student.................................... 1
____
Total...................................... 20

I.

So far as you have observed, what is the present condition of the churches in .your community ?

```
Very gratifying.....................................................  1
Improving ........................................................  2
Embarrassed financially...........................................  2
Fair..............................................................  3
Good .............................................................  5
```

Some answered this question as follows:

```
Financially, poor.....  ...........................................  2
Financially, fair.................................................  1
Financially, good ................................................  1
Intellectually, fair..............................................  1
Intellectually, good.............................................  1
Spiritually, dull.................................................  1
Spiritually, fair.................................................  2
```

II.

Is their influence, on the whole, toward pure, honest living ?

```
Yes..............................................................12
Not as much as should be.........................................  3
In part, but not all.............................................  2
Largely so.......................................................  2
Generally so.....................................................  1
```

III.

(a) Are the ministers usually good men ?

```
Yes .............................................................16
Usually, not universally.........................................  2
```

(b) Their chief faults ?

```
Whiskey and women................................................  2
```

    (This does not apply to those in Greene County.)

```
Illiteracy and want of deep convictions ..........................  1
```

    (This also does not apply to those in Greene County.)

```
Desire to be popular .............................................  1
Failure to study.................................................  1
```

IV.

Of the ministers whom you know, how many are notoriously immoral? What direction does their immorality take ? Cite instances.

This question, like the third, was generally answered for the *general* condition and not as applying to Greene County in particular, as directed. One man of wide experience says he knows twenty-four notoriously immoral preachers, but there are only twenty-five in the county, including those who are idle and who preach outside of the county.

```
None..............................................................11
A few.............................................................  1
Two ..............................................................  2
Twenty-four.......................................................  1
```

"Eighty-five per cent. are good men, five per cent. dishonest in money matters, ten per cent. tinctured with sexual impurity."—A Presiding Elder.

"I know a dozen who are immoral, basing my reply upon facts given by others." —A principal of city schools.

As to kinds of immorality, see above, and also—

Sexual impurity and drunkenness...................................... 1
Sexual impurity, dishonesty in money matters, and drunkenness.... 3
Dishonesty in money matters... 1

V.

Is the Sunday-school effective in teaching children good manners and sound morals?

Yes 10
In a large degree.. 1
Generally.. 3
To some degree... 5
Not as much as might be.. 1

VI.

Do the churches with which you are acquainted do much charitable work?

Yes.. 3
Some... 6
Not much... 7
Considerable among the poor.. 1
Yes, in large cities 1

VII.

Do the young people join the church and support it?

Some do.. 4
Only a few... 2
Yes, but about one-fourth support it................................. 2
Yes.. 5
Yes, but do not support well... 3
Not all, but a fair proportion....................................... 3
Young women do, but not many young men............................... 1

VIII.

What is the greatest need of our churches?

Pure gospel and money.. 1
More enforcement of spiritual duty of the church..................... 2
Ministers of broader culture and deeper piety........................ 3
Systematic business methods, trained men in pulpits, doctrinal preaching, and an earnest desire to persuade men to serve God from choice... 1
Religious enthusiasm, sound financial basis, respect for pastor...... 1
Higher ideals and deeper Christianity................................ 1
Educated and called ministry... 1
Pure religion, money, and education.................................. 1
Fewer churches, better preachers, better religion.................... 1
More love for church and each other on part of members............... 2
Money, and instruction in race pride, and business................... 1
Good morals, home training, and piety................................ 1

IX.

Are the standards of morality in your community being raised or lowered in respect to sexual morals, home life, honesty, etc? Give instances.

Raised 14
Inclined to think raised 1
Raised very little.. 1
Raised to some extent.. 1

"Twelve or thirteen years ago the patrol was constantly called to a class of resorts which have been wiped out."

"Xenia, Jamestown, Cedarville, Yellow Springs, are 'dry.' "

"Greater condemnation of men who deceive women."

21. An Eastern City.* Philadelphia, Pa., gives an opportunity to study the growth of the Negro church for over a century. In 1800 there were in that county † 7,000 Negroes and three Negro churches, founded as follows :

1792—St. Thomas......................Episcopal.
1794—Bethel......African Methodist Episcopal.
1794—Zoar.................Methodist Episcopal.

In 1813, when there were about 11,000 Negroes in the city, there were the following churches and members :

St. Thomas, Protestant Episcopal............ 560
Bethel, African Methodist Episcopal 1,272
Zoar, Methodist Episcopal.................... 80
Union, African Methodist Episcopal........ 74
Baptist, Race and Vine Streets.............. 80
Presbyterian 300
                                          ――――
Total.......................................2,366

There were about 17,500 Negroes in 1838 :

DENOMINATIONS.	No. Churches.	Members.	Annual Expenses.	Value of Property.	Incumbrance.
Episcopalian...........................	1	100	$1,000	$ 36,000	....
Lutheran	1	10	120	3,000	$ 1,000
Methodist..............................	8	2,860	2,100	50,800	5,100
Presbyterian	2	325	1,500	20,000	1,000
Baptist................................	4	700	1,300	4,200	....
Total.............................	16	3,995	$6,020	$ 114,000	$ 7,100

In 1847 the population had grown to 20,000. There were nineteen churches; twelve of these reported 3,974 members; the property of eleven cost $67,000. After the war the population had increased to 22,000. There were the following churches in 1867 :

---

* From the more elaborate study on the Philadelphia Negro (Ginn).

† City and County are to-day co-terminous.

NAME.	Founded.	No. of Members.	Value of Property.	Pastor's Salary.
Protestant Episcopal—				
St. Thomas	1792			
Methodist—				
Bethel	1794	1,100	$ 50,000	$ 600
Union	1827	467	40,000	850
Wesley	1817	461	21,000	700
Zoar	1794	400	12,000	
John Wesley	1844	42	3,000	No regular salary.
Little Wesley	1821	310	11,.00	500
Pisgah	1831	116	4,600	430
Zion City Mission	1858	90	4,500	
Little Union	1837	200		
Baptist —				
First Baptist	1809	360	5,000	
Union Baptist		400	7,000	600
Shiloh	1842	405	16,000	600
Oak Street	1827	137		
Presbyterian—				
First Presbyterian	1807	200	8,000	
Second Presbyterian	1824			
Central Presbyterian	1844	210	16,000	

By 1880 (population 30,000) there were twenty-five churches and missions. In 1897 there were about 60,000 Negroes in the city, and the following churches:

DENOMINATION.	Churches.	Members Claimed.	Value of Property.	Expenses.
African Methodist Episcopal	14	3,210	$ 202,229	$ 27,074
African Methodist Episcopal Zion	3		25,000	5,000
Union African Methodist Episcopal	1			
Methodist Protestant	1			
Methodist Episcopal	6	1,202	49,700	16,394
Baptist	17	5,583	296,800	30,000
Presbyterian	3	633	150,000	4,473
Protestant Episcopal	6	791	130,000	6,613
Roman Catholic	1	200?		

There are three other small churches, making fifty-five churches in all, with 13,000 members, $910,000 worth of property, and an annual income of $95,000. In 1900 Philadelphia had 62,613 Negroes.

The general character of church life is thus set forth :

"Perhaps the pleasantest and most interesting social intercourse takes place on Sunday; the weary week's work is done, the people have slept late and have had a good breakfast, and sally forth to church well dressed and complacent. The usual hour of the morning service is eleven, but people stream in until after twelve. The sermon is usually short and stirring, but in the larger churches elicits little response other than an 'Amen' or two. After the sermon the social features begin; notices on the various meetings of the week are read, people talk with each other in subdued tones, take their contributions to the altar, and linger in the aisles and corridors after dismission to laugh and chat until one or two o'clock. Then they go home to good dinners. Sometimes there is some special three o'clock service, but usually nothing, save Sunday-school, until night. Then comes the chief meeting of the day; probably 10,000 Negroes gather every Sunday night in their churches. There is much music, much preaching, some short addresses; many strangers are there to be looked at; many beaus bring out their belles, and those who do not, gather in crowds at the church door and escort the young women home. The crowds are usually well-behaved and respectable, though rather more jolly than comports with a Puritan idea of church services.

"In this way the social life of the Negro centers in his church—baptism, wedding and burial, gossip and courtship, friendship and intrigue—all lie in these walls. What wonder that this central club-house tends to become more and more luxuriously furnished, costly in appointment and easy of access!

"It must not be inferred from all this that the Negro is hypocritical or irreligious. His church is, to be sure, a social institution first, and religious afterwards, but nevertheless, its religious activity is wide and sincere. In direct moral teaching and setting moral standards for the people, however, the church is timid, and naturally so, for its constitution is democracy tempered by custom. Negro preachers are condemned for poor leadership and empty sermons, and it is said that men with so much power and influence could make striking moral reforms. This is but partially true. The congregation does not follow the moral precepts of the preacher, but rather the preacher follows the standard of his flock, and only exceptional men dare seek to change this. And here it must be remembered that the Negro preacher is primarily an executive officer rather than a spiritual guide. If one goes into any great Negro church and hears the sermon and views the audience, one would say, either the sermon is far below the calibre of the audience, or the people are less sensible than they look. The former explanation is usually true. The preacher is sure to be a man of executive ability, a leader of men, a shrewd and affable president of a large and intricate corporation. In addition to this, he may be, and usually is, a striking elocutionist. He may also be a man of integrity, learning, and deep spiritual earnestness; but these last three are sometimes all lacking, and the last two in many cases. Some signs of advance are here manifest: no minister of notoriously immoral life, or even of bad reputation, could hold a large church in Philadelphia without eventual revolt. Most of the present pastors are decent, respectable men. There are perhaps one or two exceptions to this, but the exceptions are doubtful rather than notorious. On the whole, then, the average Negro preacher in this city is a shrewd manager, a respectable man, a good talker, a pleasant companion, but neither learned nor spiritual, nor a reformer.

"The moral standards are, therefore, set by the congregations, and vary, from church to church, in some degree. There has been a slow working toward a literal obeying of the Puritan and ascetic standard of morals which Methodism imposed on the freedmen, but condition and temperament have modified these. The grosser forms of immorality, together with theatre-going and dancing, are specifically denounced; nevertheless, the precepts against specific amusements are often violated by church members. The cleft between denominations is still wide, especially between Methodists and Baptists. The sermons are usually kept within the safe ground of a mild Calvinism, with much insistence on salvation, grace, fallen humanity, and the like." *

---

* Philadelphia Negro, p. 204, ff.

22. Present Condition of Churches—The Baptists.

"In the minutes of the old Savannah Association for 1812, is the following note: 'The Association is sensibly affected by the death of Rev. Andrew Bryan, a man of color and pastor of the first colored church in Savannah. This son of Africa, after suffering inexpressible persecutions in the cause of his Divine Master, was permitted to discharge the duties of his ministry among his colored friends in peace and quiet, hundreds of whom through his instrumentality were brought to a knowledge of the truth as it is in Jesus. He closes his useful and amazingly luminous course in the lively exercise of faith and in the joyful hope of a happy immortality.'

"The most of the colored Baptists were at this period identified with white churches, and in churches of mixed membership the whites were often in the minority. In the mixed churches of this period, the colored members had no voice in affairs, unless in the reception and discipline of members of their own race. After the emancipation of slaves, the Negro Baptists of the Southern states very generally separated from the white churches, and organized churches and Associations of their own. Other colored Baptist churches of that section, that were organized at an earlier period, besides the one at Savannah, above mentioned, are the Springfield Baptist Church, Augusta, Ga., 1790, and the one at Portsmouth, Va., 1841; the Nineteenth Street Baptist Church of Washington, D. C., 1832; one in Louisville, Ky., 1842; one in Baltimore, Md., 1836. In the Northern and Western states, the earliest organized colored Baptist churches are the Abyssinian of New York City, 1803; the Independent of Boston, 1805; the First of Philadelphia, 1809; Ebenezer of New York City, 1825; the Union of Cincinnati, 1827; the Union of Philadelphia, 1832; the Union of Alton, Ill., 1838.

"The Western states organized the first colored Baptist Association. The Providence Baptist Association of Ohio was organized in 1836, and the Wood River Baptist Association of Illinois in 1838. The number of colored Baptists in the United States in 1850 is reported but in part. In fifteen Southern states and four Northern states, 100 out of 336 Associations report 89,695 colored members. There is no report from 146 Southern Associations, but high authority puts the whole number of colored Baptists in this country in 1850 at 150,000. Then we have a numerical growth of Negro Baptists in America from 150,000 in 1850 to 1,604,310 in 1894; an increase of 1,454,310 in forty-four years, which is an increase of over 33,000 net each year. From one ordained preacher in 1777 to 10,119 in 1894; from one church in 1788 to 13,138 churches in 1894, or an average increase of 124 churches each year; increase in valuation of church property from nothing in 1788 to $11,271,651." *

The Baptist churches unite in Associations and State Conventions for missionary and educational work. For a long time, however, it seemed impossible to unite any large number of them in a National Convention, but this has at last been done.

The National Baptist Convention was organized at Atlanta, Ga., September 28, 1895. Its objects are missionary and educational work, and the publication of religious literature. The membership consists of representatives of churches, Sunday-schools, Associations, and State Conventions of Baptists, and of such individual Baptists as wish to join. The Convention meets annually, and has a president, vice-presidents from each state, a statistical secretary, and other officers. This Con-

---

* Growth of the Negro Baptists, by R. De Baptiste, 1896.

vention elects annually a Foreign Mission Board, a Home Mission Board, an Educational Board, and a Baptist Young People's Union Board. These boards all consist of one member from each state represented, and elect their own officers and executive committee so located as to be able to meet monthly. The Convention also collects statistics concerning the Negro Baptists throughout ·the United States. The Conventions of 1901 and 1902 follow.

These figures are not altogether accurate, but 'are probably understatements rather than exaggerations.*

The most remarkable result of the united efforts of the Negro Baptists is the Home Mission department, including the publishing house :

"It has been the policy of our Board from its incipiency to do whatever missionary work that is done in any state in co-operation with the regular state authorities or state organizations in their organized capacity.

"We believe also that when this policy of our Board is better understood, the churches, Associations and Conventions will contribute more liberally to the advancement of the work of our Board. While we have not been able to do as much in this co-operative mission work as we had hoped, yet we have done what we could. We have gone as far as our limited means would allow. The following is a summary of the missionary work done by our Board and by its co-operative policy in the United States :

COMBINED REPORTS

Sermons preached	1,550	Homes visited	1,661
Sunday schools addressed	905	Homes found without Bibles	84
Prayer–meetings attended	829	Churches visited	1,323
B. Y. P. U. meetings attended	478	Sunday-schools organized	7
Women's meetings addressed	261	Missionary societies organized	44
Other addresses made	1,495	Baptisms	70
Total number addresses made	2,376	Miles traveled by railroad	99,612
Conventions, Associations and women's meetings visited since last report	253	Cost of travel	$1,493.64
		Miles traveled otherwise	5,491
		Cost of same	$ 188.30
Number of letters and cards written	12,056	Total traveling expense	$1,681.94
Number of circulars and tracts distributed	40,703	Total amount of money sent to National Baptist Publishing Board	$1,281.36
Number of books and tracts donated	1,019	Amount of the money collected applied to salaries	$ 281.35
Books sold	$1,774.83	Total amount of money collected and left with churches	79.80
Money collected	$3,538.37		
Total amount of money received from all sources	$5,114.02	Number of Missionary Conferences held	31
Subscriptions to the Union	256	Paid on salaries	$3,839.38
Money collected for same	$ 57.20	Total paid on salaries	$4,174.73
Days of service rendered	2,223		

* A prominent church official writes:

"The statistics are not correct. For instance, you will notice New Jersey. At the time of getting the statistics from there we had only thirty-six churches. I have just returned from there, and know that they have sixty-seven. What is true of that state is true of many others.

"We have a very poor way of getting accurate statistics. We have had to depend upon the various minutes of the state meetings and, as you know, our people attend these meetings if they wish and let it alone if they please. There is no reason nor power to compel them to give statistics. A great number of our churches do not attend the Associations and a great number of our Associations do not attend the State Conventions and a number of the State Conventions are not represented in our National Convention. Therefore, you see that we only have to get such statistics as are in co-operation with us."

"It has been our custom, from year to year, to call the attention of our Convention to the work of correspondence of our Board. This is done with a view of giving the members somewhat of an idea of the magnitude of this portion of our work. For the benefit of those who may be interested, we quote the following number of first-class letters received and disposed of by answers by the Corresponding Secretary and his assistants during the fiscal year:

September, 1901................................ 4,303
October, 1901................................. 6,255
November, 1901................................ 2,243
December, 1901................................ 3,355
January, 1902................................. 5,968
February, 1902................................ 2,709
March, 1902 6,432
April, 1902.................................. 9,607
May, 1902.................................... 4,866
June, 1902................................... 8,576
July, 1902................................... 7,922
August, 1902................................. 2,720
                                            ———
Grand total for the year 64,956

General Summary of Baptists in the United States

	1901.	1902.
State Conventions...........................	....	43
Associations................................	515	517
Churches....................................	15,654	16,440
Ordained ministers..........................	14,861	16,080
Present membership in the United States.......	1,975,538	2,038,427
Meeting houses..............................	7,576	11,069
Valuation...................................	$ 11,605,891	$ 12,196,130
Sunday-schools..............................	7,466	13,707
Teachers and officers.......................	36,736	41,537
Pupils in Sunday-schools....................	473,271	544,505
Total in Sunday-schools.....................	510,007	586,042

MONEY RAISED

Church expenses.............................	....	$ 3,090,190.71
Sunday-school expenses......................	....	107,054.00
State Missions..............................	....	9,954.00
Foreign Missions	....	8,725.00
Home Mission and Publication................	....	81,658.40
Education	$ 115,809.55	127,941.00
Total raised during the year	$ 1,816,442.72	$ 3,425,523.11

"The Publishing Board of the National Baptist Convention is acting as trustees of the Convention in holding and managing the publishing concern. It is composed of a committee of nine, and the vacancies are filled by three each year. These form the charter or corporate members and are incorporated under the laws of Tennessee, and hold and operate the property in trust for the National Baptist Association, and are amenable to our Home Board. They, under the authority of our Home Board, have their regular organization of chairman, secretary and treasurer. The secretary and treasurer is one and the same person, who is required to execute and file in the courts of Davidson County a suitable and sufficient, well secured bond. This has been the requirement since this board was inaugurated in 1898.

"In order to curtail the expenses and economize in our work, the Home Missionary Board has operated its missionary and Bible work under the management of the Publishing Board, together with its publication work. The experiment has proved a profitable one, and we find that the business has been operated with less than one-half the expense of other denominations doing similar work. In fact, the Corresponding Secretary of the Home Mission Board, upon a meagre salary, has operated the missionary work, and has acted as secretary, treasurer and general manager of the National Baptist Publishing Board. By blending the four offices into one we have been able to save the salary of three other secretaries. This is one of the great causes or economical provisions that have enabled your board to give a dividend to missions each year.

"The publishing plant and offices are located at the corner of Market and Locust streets, one-half block from the Louisville and Nashville passenger depot. Market street is one of the greatest business thoroughfares in the city of Nashville. This plant occupies four brick buildings, one one-story, two two-story, and one three-story building. The scattered condition of the plant makes it very inconvenient to operate the machinery in carrying on the great volume of manufacturing that is necessary to supply the increasing demands of this institution.

"This plant consists of a large first-class steam boiler, two engines, a complete electric plant, a complete system of telephones, with a well-regulated set of the most improved power printing presses, a well-regulated bindery, with all the machinery and equipment that is commonly attached to the most modern printing and publishing plant, together with a complete composing room, with all of the modern paraphernalia, including linotype machines. This plant, with its stock, is fully worth to the denomination $100,000 and if it were in a stock company its stock, if placed at $100,000, would sell in the market at par, and its income would pay a creditable dividend.

"The board has been compelled to purchase and exchange a considerable amount of its machinery. The authorities or managers were unable to foresee the large increase of work that would be necessary to supply the necessities. They, therefore, supplied themselves with machinery and material in proportion to then present needs of the institution, but so marvelous has been the increase that the machinery and quarters were found inadequate to meet the demands. They have, therefore, been compelled to exchange old machinery and buy new at a considerable loss in the dealings. They have been compelled to lease or rent other buildings. These increased demands have also created a demand for more and better skilled laborers, and they have, therefore, been compelled to increase the wages in each department in order to secure the help needed.

"The Book Department of our work is divided into three departments. First, books bought of other publishers and dealers and sold with or without profit to supply the needs of our patrons. Secondly, books manufactured by ourselves for the exclusive use of the denomination. Third, books manufactured for the author as job work, and, at the same time, bought and retailed by our board. These three features of the book work constitute the major portion of our actual work.

"The periodical and Sunday-school departments deal almost exclusively with the rising element of our denomination. In other words, in this department we are preparing the future church. In this periodical department we are sending fresh publications to the homes of our churches each quarter, month and week. We are thereby moulding the doctrines and opinions and shaping the destiny of the future church and race. The expression that we now put forth may be criticised by some, but we give it as our opinion that it is impossible for any race of people to keep their identity, sway their influence, keep pace with other races, hold the influence over their offspring, unless they provide themselves with literature and keep before their rising generation the great men that are passing from the stage of action. Artists and poets have done more to make the Caucasian great than has the writer of prose. The Negro Baptists of this country, therefore, will be compelled to cease talking or discussing cheap literature for their children, but they must discuss, produce or provide literature capable of keeping the identity and increasing race pride of the rising generation or they must be entirely overshadowed by the dominant race of this country, and each child born of Negro parents must be brought to feel that his God has made him inferior by nature to other races with whom he comes in contact. We, therefore, feel the value of the literature produced by the National Baptist Publishing Board cannot be measured by dollars and cents.

"The following is a list and number of periodicals published and circulated by our Board during the years 1900, 1901 and 1902:

PERIODICALS.	1900.	1901.	1902.
Teachers	84,800	136,000	139,000
Advanced Quarterlies	416,000	244,000	543,000
Intermediate Quarterlies	175,000	244,000	250,000
Primary Quarterlies	275,000	380,000	332,000
Leaflets and Gems	557,000	528,000	585,000
Picture Lesson Cards	1,560,000	2,340,000	2,500,000
Bible Lesson Pictures	33,800	41,600	50,000
National Baptist Concert Quarterly	259,000	800,000	850,000
Child's Gem	6,000		
Davidson's Questions			85,000
Boyd's Questions			85,000
National Baptist Easy Lessons			90,000
Total	3,366,600	4,713,600	5,509,000

"These periodicals have been published and mailed to our Sunday-schools at such prices as in reality do not pay for the expense of producing them. In fact, our thirty-two paged magazines are retailed to our Sunday-schools, with the postage paid, cheaper than blank paper could be received through the mail. We call the attention of the Convention to this fact in order that they may see and know under what difficulties we are laboring.

"We are glad to call the attention again this year to the department of our work of issuing circulars and tracts. We still hold to the opinion that more people are influenced by tracts than by any other publications, and, as we have had occasion to say in the preface of the introductory of one of our little booklets, that the colored people, more than any other in this country, need the use of short and concise tracts; that is, they need Bible doctrine, true gospel teaching, put in plain, simple, concise form, and furnished to them in such a way that they can read it. A glance at the census of 1900 will show that the illiteracy in the South reaches over 50 per cent., but as this may be overdrawn, it is perfectly safe to say that 40 per cent. of the colored people are illiterate, and 20 per cent. of those who can read and write are not fluent readers. Sixty per cent. of those who can read are youths—children. Therefore, it is very essential that reading matter for these people must not be in large and soggy books, but must be in small books, booklets, tracts and pamphlets. Our board has endeavored to turn some attention to raising a tract fund, but has done very little as yet.

"We are in need of both money and writers to produce these tracts. Addresses, papers and sermons read or delivered before the different annual gatherings, if they were put in print and circulated among the people, would do much toward elevating them. We have been able this year to publish a few tracts for free distribution. We have been able to print and distribute through our free distribution system something over 40,000 tracts. These the writers have contributed free of charge.

RECEIPTS

BUSINESS DEPARTMENT

Balance on hand	$ 1,054.09	
Fourth quarter, 1901	12,119.01	
First quarter, 1902	10,825.69	
Second quarter, 1902	15,884.82	
Third quarter, 1902	18,782.77	
Total receipts from Business Department		$ 58,666.38

RECEIPTS FROM MISSIONARY DEPARTMENT

From Woman's Auxiliary Convention	$ 75.00	
From Home Mission Board of Southern Baptist Convention	1,800.00	
From Woman's Auxiliary of Southern Baptist Convention	50.00	
By missionary collections ....(a)	3,538.37	
By special missionary collections.............(b)	281.35	
By designated collections....................(c)	79.80	$ 5,824.52

SPECIAL DONATIONS FOR BIBLES AND COLPORTAGE WORK

From Sunday-school Board of Southern Baptist Convention	$ 121.25	
By other donations	119.00	
For colportage and book work	2,100.94	
From special periodical donations	230.90	
From special tract donations	109.36	
For special Bible work in Africa	35.71	
From general missionary and Bible donation	432.48	$ 3,149.64

SPECIAL SUBSCRIPTION, ADVERTISING, NEGOTIABLE NOTES AND OUTSTANDING ACCOUNTS

From subscriptions to *Union*	$ 499.91	
From advertisements	510.00	
From negotiable notes	738.26	
From periodicals uncollected	1,129.57	
From printing uncollected accounts	2,205.58	
Remaining in hands of colporters and missionaries unreported	1,683.78	$ 6,767.10
Grand total		$ 74,407.64

DISBURSEMENTS

BUSINESS DEPARTMENT

Wages, printing material and Editorial Department	$30,326.54
Merchandise, notes, machinery and other miscellaneous	17,073.84
Coal, ice, freight, drayage, boarding horses, etc..	2,842.54
Rents, water tax, gas, commission, insurance, traveling and special missions	2,127.92
Stamps, postage, telephone, telegrams, electricity, etc	5,360.54
To balance in hand	934.94

Total disbursements of Business Department. $ 58,666.38

MISSIONARY DEPARTMENT

In salaries of district secretaries, state and local missionaries, male and female	$ 5,824.52	
In expenses, books, Bibles, tracts and periodicals donated by them	3,149.64	
Salary of secretary, advertising, special traveling expenses, uncollected accounts, negotiable notes, manuscripts, etc	6,767.10	$ 15,741.26

Grand total....................................... $ 74,407.64

"Notwithstanding the failure of crops of 1901, by glancing over the report of the work done for the year it will be seen that this institution is not only self-supporting, but besides defraying its own expenses, has been able to spend on missionaries and their traveling expenses $11,683.19, and on machinery, notes, etc., which stand as a sinking fund, $5,352.48, making a dividend to the denomination of $17,035.67; and, if we add in the $1,601.09 deficit for running the denominational paper, and the $3,335.15 outstanding accounts for work and periodicals during the year, and $1,683.78 in the hands of agents, missionaries and colporters unreported, it will be seen that the denomination has a clear dividend arising from the work of these boards of $23,655.69."

The Negro Baptists support eighty schools, as follows :

List of Institutions by States

STATES.	INSTITUTION.	LOCATION.
Alabama	Baptist University	Selma.
"	Normal College	Anniston.
"	Eufaula Academy	Eufaula.
"	Marion Academy	Marion.
"	Opelika High School	Opelika.
"	Thomsonville Academy	Thomsonville.
Arkansas	Aouchita Academy	Camden.
"	Baptist College	Little Rock.
"	Arkadelphia Academy	Arkadelphia.
"	Brinkley Academy	Brinkley.
"	Magnolia Academy	Magnolia.
Florida	Florida Baptist College	Jacksonville.
"	Florida Institute	Live Oak.
"	West Florida Baptist Academy . . .	Pensacola.
Georgia	Americus Institute	Americus.
"	Walker Academy.	Augusta.
"	Jeruel Academy	Athens.
"	Central City College	Macon.
Illinois	Southern Illinois Polytechnic Institute .	Cairo.
Indiana	Indiana Colored Baptist University . . .	Indianapolis.

List of Institutions by States—Continued

STATES.	INSTITUTION.	LOCATION.
Indian Territory . .	Dawes Academy	
"	Sango Baptist College	Muskogee.
Kentucky	State University	Louisville.
"	Cadez Theological Institute	Cadez.
"	Female High School	Frankfort.
"	Glasgow Normal Institute	Glasgow.
"	Western College	Weakly.
"	Danville Institute	Danville.
"	Hopkinsville College	Hopkinsville.
"	Eckstein Norton University	Cane Springs.
Louisiana	Leland Academy	Donaldsonville.
"	Baton Rouge Academy	Baton Rouge.
"	Houma Academy	Houma.
"	Morgan City Academy	Morgan City.
"	Howe Institute	New Iberia.
"	Opelousas Academy	Opelousas.
"	Central Louisiana Academy	Alexandria.
"	Cherryville Academy	Cherryville.
"	Baptist Academy	Lake Providence
"	Monroe High School	Monroe.
"	Ruston Academy	Ruston.
"	Shreveport Academy	Alexandria.
"	Mansfield Academy	Mansfield.
"	North Louisiana Industrial High School	Monroe.
Maryland	Clayton Williams Institute	Baltimore.
Mississippi	Natchez College	Natchez.
"	Gloster High School	Gloster.
"	Central College	Kosciusko.
"	Greneda High School	Winona.
"	Meridian High School	Meridian.
"	Ministerial Institute	West Point.
"	Nettleton High School	Nettleton.
"	Greenville High School	Greenville.
"	New Albany High School	New Albany.
Missouri	Western College	Macon.
North Carolina . . .	Wharton Industrial School	Charlotte.
"	Latta University	Raleigh.
"	High School	Wakefield.
"	Shiloh Industrial Institute	Warrenton.
"	Thomson's Institute	Lumberton.
"	Addie Norris' Institute	Winston.
"	Training School	Franklinton.
"	Roanoke Institute	Elizabeth.
"	Albemarle Training School	Edenton.
"	Bertie Academy	Windsor.
Ohio	Curry School	Urbana.
South Carolina . . .	Mather School	Beaufort.
"	Peace Haven Institute	Broad River.
Tennessee	Howe Institute	Memphis.
"	Nelson Merry College	Jefferson City.
"	Lexington Normal School	Lexington.
Texas	Guadalupe College	Seguin.
"	Central Texas Academy	Waco.
"	Houston Academy	Houston.
"	Hearne Academy	Hearne.
Virginia	Virginia Seminary and College	Lynchburg.
"	Union Industrial Academy	Port Conway.

Total number of schools . . . 80   Valuation of property . . $564,000

Twenty of the above schools reported last year as follows:

Teachers, males	75
Teachers, females	73
Total	148
Students, males	1,833
Students, females	1,531
Total students	3,364
Total in Home Missionary Society Schools	6,198
Total in schools heard from	9,562

The value of property owned by these schools is as follows:

Alabama	$ 39,500
Louisiana	45,000
Missouri	15,000
Georgia	10,000
Mississippi	77,000
Ohio	5,000
Arkansas	70,000
Maryland	6,000
Kentucky	65,000
Florida	20,000
Tennessee	33,000
Texas	80,000
North Carolina	16,000
South Carolina	19,000
Virginia	60,000
Indian Territory	3,700
Total	$ 564,200

The total income of the schools for 1902 was:

Arkansas	$ 35,000.00
Alabama	10,500.00
North Carolina	2,700.00
Louisiana	15,000.00
Mississippi	9,100.00
Tennessee	4,300.00
Florida	16,000.00
Georgia	12,000.00
Maryland	585.00
Virginia	25,000.00
Texas	23,000.00
Ohio	3,500.00
Kentucky	20,000.00
Missouri	8,041.02
District of Columbia	400.00
Pennsylvania	857.75
Miscellaneous sources	238.00
Total	$ 186,221.97

The total number of pupils in all these schools is not given. Twenty of them report 148 teachers and 3,364 pupils. Probably there are at least 6,000 or 7,000 pupils in all the schools. The institutions are for the most part primary and secondary schools, despite their pretentious names, and supplement the public schools.

Beside, these Negro Baptists have contributed largely to the Baptist schools of higher denomination, supported by the Northern white Baptists, for Negro students. The chief schools of this class are:

Baptist Schools (Report of the United States Commissioner of Education, 1900-1)

PLACE.	SCHOOL.	Teachers.	Students.	Value of Lands, Buildings, etc.
Richmond, Va	Hartshorn Memorial College	11	120	$ 50,000
Richmond, Va	Virginia Union University	13	157	300,000
Raleigh, N. C.	Shaw University	27	511	90,000
Winton, N. C.	Water's Normal Institute	5	272	12,000
Columbia, S. C.	Benedict College	16	488	76,000
Athens, Ga	Jeruel Academy	5	221	2,500
Atlanta, Ga	Atlanta Baptist College	13	165	75,000
Augusta, Ga	Walker Baptist Institute	6	121	4,500
Jackson, Miss	Jackson College	10	102	35,000
Marshall, Tex	Bishop College	16	337	100,000
Nashville, Tenn	Roger Williams University	13	268	200,000
Little Rock, Ark	Arkansas Baptist College	9	213	25,000
Atlanta, Ga	Spelman Seminary			
Harper's Ferry, W. Va	Storer College	7	142	50,000
Hampton, Va	Spiller Academy	6	103	10,000
Windsor, N. C	Bertie Academy	2	96	1,000
LaGrange, Ga	LaGrange Baptist Academy	4	182	1,000
New Orleans, La	Leland University	11	115	150,000

In the words of the late General Morgan, secretary of the American Baptist Home Missionary Society, this society "has already spent more than $3,000,000 in their (i. e., the Negroes') behalf; the value of school property used for their benefit is not less than $1,000,000; its expenditure in their interest at present exceeds $100,000 a year. It has aided in the erection of a good number of meeting-houses."

The other departments of the church are of less relative importance. The Baptist Young People's Union Board spent $7,000 for its work; the National Board spent $8,302.29 for missions, with the following results :

SIERRA LEONE, WEST COAST AFRICA—Churches, 2; pastors and workers, 3; members, 40.

LIBERIA, WEST COAST AFRICA—Churches, 52; pastors and workers, 86; members, 3,000.

LAGOS, SOUTHWEST COAST AFRICA—Churches, 21; pastors and workers, 56; members, 2,000.

CAPE COLONY, SOUTH AFRICA—Churches, 23; pastors and workers, 80; members, 1,750.

CHIRADZULU BLANTYRE, EAST COAST AFRICA—Churches, 3; pastors and workers, 5; members, 35.

GEORGETOWN DEMERARA, BRITISH GUIANA, SOUTH AMERICA—Churches, 3; pastors and workers, 11; members, 310.

LAGWAN, EAST COAST, BRITISH GUIANA, SOUTH AMERICA—Churches, 1; pastors and workers, 2; members, 10.

SURINAM, DUTCH GUIANA, SOUTH AMERICA—Churches, 1; pastors and workers, 3; members, 30.

BARBADOES, BRITISH WEST INDIES, BRIDGETOWN—Churches, 1; pastors and workers. 5; members, 62.

There are churches at St. George, St. John, Christ Church and St. Thomas, on the island, with pastors and workers, 7, and members, 42.

There is a Convention organized separately from the regular organization. It had in 1902:

State Conventions	22
Mission Societies	4,033
Children's Bands	1,380
Sewing Circles	420
Circles of King's Daughters	120
Money raised during 1902	$ 3,800

There are the following newspapers published by Negro Baptists in the interest of that denomination:

NAME.	Where Published.
American Baptist	Louisville, Ky.
Baptist Leader	Selma, Ala.
Baptist Magazine	Washington, D. C.
The Pilot	Winston, N. C.
The Sentinel	Raleigh, N. C.
Christian Banner	Philadelphia, Pa.
Baptist Herald	Live Oak, Fla.
Florida Evangelist	Jacksonville, Fla.
Georgia Baptist	Augusta, Ga.
Western Messenger	Macon, Mo.
National Baptist Union	Nashville, Tenn.
Virginia Baptist	Richmond, Va.
Baptist Vanguard	Little Rock, Ark.
The Western Star	Houston, Tex.
The Baptist Truth	Savannah, Ga.
The Baptist Truth	Cairo, Ill.
The Christian Organizer	Lynchburg, Va.
The South Carolina Standard	Columbia, S. C.
Southern Watchman	Mobile, Ala.
The Herald	Austin, Tex.
People's Recorder	Columbia, S. C.
The Informer	Urbana, O.
The Messenger	New Orleans, La.
The American Tribune	New Orleans, La.
Negro World	Cary, Miss.
Guadaloupe College Recorder	Seguin, Tex.
Advanced Quarterly (National Baptist Convention)	Nashville, Tenn.
Intermediate Quarterly (National Baptist Convention)	"
Primary Quarterly (National Baptist Convention)	"
The Teacher	"
Child's Gems	"
Easy Lesson Primer	"
Preacher's Safeguard	
Zion Church Bulletin	Denver, Col.
The Journal	
The Clarion	Nashville, Tenn.
The Blue Grass Bugle	Frankfort, Ky.
The Moderator	Louisville, Ky.
The Mission Herald	Louisville, Ky.
The Trumpet	Washington, D. C.
The Watchman	Columbia, S. C.
The Pennsylvania Baptist	Pittsburg, Pa.
The Florida Baptist	Fernandina, Fla.

As to the general character of the churches and preachers the following statement, made by the Home Missionary Society about five years ago, seems a fair presentation :

In the few large cities and towns of the South a minister usually serves one church ; in the rural districts and small villages, where three-fourths of the Negro population are found, he has from two to four churches, and preaching "once't a month" is customary. Of the 12,000 churches in 1895, probably not 1,000 have preaching every Sunday. Except in the larger and more progressive churches ministers do very little pastoral work.

About fifteen ministers receive $1.500 or more ; one per cent. about $1,000 each ; fifteen per cent. from $500 to $700. The great majority get only $200 to $400 ; while many never see $100 in money yearly. These eke out their scanty salaries by manual labor. The people, generally, are very poor.

Many are noble, high-minded, upright, God-fearing, unselfish, sincere, self-sacrificing, who honor their high calling. Of a great number, however, it must be said in sorrow, that their moral standards are not at all in accord with those of the New Testament for the ministry. They have grown up in an environment unfavorable to the production of a high type of character. The development of a Christian conscience is a fundamental need. In some states and localities it is more difficult than formerly for unworthy men to be ordained.

Forty years ago, the minister who could read was the exception ; now, the exception is one who cannot. Many, however, were too old to learn easily and made egregious blunders and understood what they read most imperfectly. Little could they learn in the very inferior country schools, maintained for only three or four months each year. Their knowledge was "picked up." There are sixty per cent. of the ministers whose libraries do not average a dozen volumes. Many, however, take a cheap religious paper. Yet among these are preachers of much native ability.

About 25 per cent. have had approximately a fair common school education. Some spent a year or more at an academy or other higher school, where they also had a little instruction in the Bible and in preaching. A few got a start that led to intellectual and spiritual growth and power.

Possibly 20 per cent. have had something like an ordinary academic course. Full college graduates are rare ; not 100 Negro Baptist ministers have had a full collegiate and theological course.

There are able preachers, whose sermons compare favorably with the average sermons of white preachers, in substance, diction and delivery. Most of these are the products of our Home Mission schools. They are an uplifting influence to their churches, and to their less favored brethren in the ministry.

But it may be safely said that two-thirds of the preaching is of the crudest character, emotional, hortatory, imaginative, visionary, abounding in misconceptions of scripture, the close of the sermon being delivered with powerful intonations and gesticulations to arouse the audience to a high pitch of excitement, which both preacher and people regard as indispensable to a "good meeting." Two members of a ministers' class recently made these statements to their colored instructor : one had preached that Joshua never had father or mother, because he was "the son of Nun," (none) ; the other wrought up his congregation mightily by repeatedly shouting : "Mesopotamia." Such instances can be multiplied indefinitely.

The religious phenomenon of this land, if not of this age, is in the fact that while our Negro population increased slightly more than twofold in forty years, the Baptist increase among them was over fourfold. Negro preachers are remarkable evangelists in their way. Converts with weird and rapturous experiences are quickly baptized. With the survival of old-time notions concerning conversion, probably two-thirds of the churches are made up largely of "wood, hay and stubble." Nevertheless, in these are sincere, devout souls, in whom the Spirit of God seems to have wrought a genuine work and to whom he has given singularly clear views of truth. The process of emancipation from the old order of things is going on, largely under the leadership of men from our schools. Numerous churches maintain most orderly services, have good Sunday-schools, and young people's societies, and are interested in missions. Thousands of church edifices, some well equipped and very costly, bear witness to the zeal and devotion of the people, and to the persuasive power of their religious leaders.

23. The African Methodists. The greatest voluntary organization of Negroes in the world is probably the African Methodist Church. Its beginning had a tinge of romance, and this is the story :*

Between 1790 and 1800 the Negro population of Philadelphia County increased from 2,489 to 6,880, or 176 per cent., against an increase of 43 per cent. among the whites. The first result of this contact with city life was to stimulate the talented and aspiring freedmen; and this was the easier because the freedman had in Philadelphia at that time a secure economic foothold; he performed all kinds of domestic service, all common labor and much of the skilled labor. The group being thus secure in its daily bread needed only leadership to make some advance in general culture and social effectiveness. Some sporadic cases of talent occur, as Derham, the Negro physician, whom Dr. Benjamin Rush, in 1788, found "very learned." Especially, however, to be noted are Richard Allen, a former slave of the Chew family, and Absalom Jones, a Delaware Negro. These two were real leaders and actually succeeded to a remarkable degree in organizing the freedmen for group action. Both had bought their own freedom and that of their families by hiring their time—Allen being a blacksmith by trade, and Jones also having a trade. When, in 1792, the terrible epidemic drove Philadelphians away so quickly that many did not remain to bury the dead, Jones and Allen quietly took the work in hand, spending some of their own funds, and doing so well that they were publicly commended by Mayor Clarkson in 1794.

The great work of these men, however, lay among their own race and arose from religious difficulties. As in other colonies, the process by which the Negro slaves learned the English tongue and were converted to Christianity is not clear. The subject of the moral instruction of the slaves had early troubled Penn, and he urged Friends to provide meetings for them. The newly organized Methodists soon attracted a number of the more intelligent, though the masses seem at the end of the last century not to have been church-goers or Christians to any considerable extent. The smaller number that went to church were wont to worship at St. George's, Fourth and Vine. For years both free Negroes and slaves worshipped here, and were made welcome. Soon, however, the church began to be alarmed at

---

* Taken in part from " The Philadelphia Negro."

the increase in its black communicants which the immigration from the country was bringing, and attempted to force them into the gallery. The crisis came one Sunday morning during prayer, when Jones and Allen, with a crowd of followers, refused to worship except in their accustomed places, and finally left the church in a body.

Allen himself tells of the incident as follows:

"A number of us usually sat on seats placed around the wall, and on Sabbath morning we went to church and the sexton stood at the door and told us to go to the gallery. He told us to go and we would see where to sit. We expected to take the seats over the ones we formerly occupied below not knowing any better. We took these seats; meeting had begun and they were nearly done singing, and just as we got to the seats, the elder said: 'Let us pray.' We had not been long upon our knees before I heard considerable scuffling and loud talking. I raised my head and saw one of the trustees—H. M.—having hold of Absalom Jones, pulling him up off his knees and saying, 'You must get up, you must not kneel here.' Mr. Jones replied, 'Wait until prayer is over and I will get up and trouble you no more.' With that he beckoned to one of the other trustees—Mr. L. S.—to come to his assistance. He came and went to William White to pull him up. By this time the prayer was over and we all went out of the church in a body, and they were no more plagued by us in the church. This raised a great excitement and inquiry among the citizens, insomuch that I believe they were ashamed of their conduct. But my dear Lord was with us, and we were filled with fresh vigor to get a house erected to worship God in."

This band immediately met together and on April 12, 1787, formed a curious sort of ethical and beneficial brotherhood called the Free African Society. How great a step this was, we of to-day scarcely realize. We must remind ourselves that it was the first wavering step of a people toward organized social life. This society was more than a mere club: Jones and Allen were its leaders and recognized chief officers; a certain parental discipline was exercised over its members and mutual financial aid given. The preamble of the articles of association says:

"Whereas, Absalom Jones and Richard Allen, two men of the African race, who for their religious life and conversation, have obtained a good report among men, these persons, from a love to the people of their own complexion whom they beheld with sorrow, because of their irreligious and uncivilized state, often communed together upon this painful and important subject in order to form some kind of religious body; but there being too few to be found under the like concern, and those who were, differed in their religious sentiments; with these circumstances they labored for some time, till it was proposed after a serious communication of sentiments that a society should be formed without regard to religious tenets, provided the persons lived an orderly and sober life, in order to support one another in sickness, and for the benefit of their widows and fatherless children."

The society met first at private houses, then at the Friends' Negro school-house. For a time they leaned toward Quakerism; each month three monitors were appointed to have oversight over the members; loose marriage customs were attacked by condemning cohabitation, expelling offenders, and providing a simple Quaker-like marriage ceremony. A fifteen-minute pause for silent prayer opened the meetings. As the representative body of the free Negroes of the city, this society opened communication with free Negroes in Boston, Newport, and other places.

The Negro Union of Newport, R. I., proposed, in 1788, a general exodus to Africa, but the Free African Society soberly replied: "With regard to the emigration to Africa you mention, we have at present but little to communicate on that head, apprehending every pious man a good citizen of the whole world." The society co-operated with the Abolition Society in studying the condition of the free blacks in 1790. At all times they seem to have taken good care of their sick and dead, and helped the widows and orphans to some extent. Their methods of relief were simple: they agreed "for the benefit of each other to advance one shilling in silver, Pennsylvania currency, a month; and after one year's subscription, from the dole thereof then to hand forth to the needy of the society, if any should require, the sum of three shillings and nine pence per week of the said money; provided the necessity is not brought on by their own imprudence." In 1790 the society had £42 9s. 1d. on deposit in the bank of North America, and had applied for a grant of the potter's field, to be set aside as a burial ground for them, in a petition signed by Dr. Rush, Tench Coxe, and others.

It was, however, becoming clearer to the leaders that only a strong religious bond could keep this untrained group together. They would probably have become a sort of institutional church at first if the question of religious denomination had been settled among them; but it had not been, and for about six years the question was still pending. The tentative experiment in Quakerism had failed, being ill-suited to the low condition of the rank and file of the society. Both Jones and Allen believed that Methodism was best suited to the needs of the Negro, but the majority of the society, still nursing the memory of St. George's, inclined toward the Episcopal church. Here came the parting of the ways: Jones was a slow introspective man, with a thirst for knowledge, with high aspirations for his people; Allen was a shrewd, quick, popular leader, positive and dogged, and yet far-seeing in his knowledge of Negro character. Jones, therefore, acquiesced in the judgment of the majority, served and led them conscientiously and worthily, and eventually became the first Negro rector in the Episcopal church in America. About 1790 Allen and a few followers withdrew from the Free African Society, formed an independent Methodist Church, which first worshipped in his blacksmith's shop on Sixth street, near Lombard. Eventually this leader became the founder and first bishop of the African Methodist Episcopal Church of America.

Full figures as to the growth of this institution are not available, but there are enough to show its striking advance in a century from a dozen or more to three-quarters of a million members:

Growth of the African Methodist Episcopal Church

	1816.	1826.	1836.	1846.	1866.	1876.	1880.	1900.	1901.
Bishops	1	2	3	4	4	6	9	13	13
General officers						3	4		12
Presiding Elders						25	40		264
Annual Conferences									
Itinerant preachers	2	2	4	6	10	1,418	1,857		6,079
Local preachers	14	17	27	40	185	3,108	9,760		9,749
Members						172,806	391,044	561,550	688,354
Total members	3,000	7,927	7,270		285	213,469	402,638	663,746	762,580
Churches			86	198		1,833	2,051	5,630	5,715
Value of property			$43,000 00	$90,000 00	$883,000	$3,064,911		$8,718,456	$10,390,131
Parsonages						218	402	1,380	2,075
Value of total property						$3,203,711	$2,448,671	$9,300,973	$11,044,663
Schools				3			88		41
Raised for support of schools									125,650
Total money raised	$1,151 75	$1,385 88	$7,231 03	$90,000 00	$91,593(?)	$447,624			

Detailed figures showing the operations of seven fairly typical Annual Conferences follows:

Annual Conference Reports

	Virginia.	Illinois.	Indiana.	Iowa.	Ontario.	Michigan.	So. Carolina.
Ministers	102	51	74	68	7	22	100
Members	9,116	4,085	4,196	4,287	377	1,345	18,787
Churches	38	74	60	52	9	24	196
Parsonages	35	35	36	26	4	17	52
Value churches and parsonages	$161,215 00	$83,190 00	$159,658 50	$246,265 00	$15,300 00	$280,032 89	$14,147 00
Indebtedness	64,739 61	23,301 44	15,493 77	61,006 42	5,737 90	8,467 29	10,212 14
Pastors' support	18,378 62	17,961 16	17,704 32	22,252 89	1,922 67	11,251 19	31,883 16
Total raised	70,514 67	31,707 00	39,608 95	76,426 85	4,217 52	17,688 40	47,883 38

In 1818 a publishing department was added to the work of the church, but its efficiency was impaired on account of the great mass of its members being in slave states or the District of Columbia, where the laws prohibited them from attending school, and deprived them of reading books or papers. In 1817 Rev. Richard Allen published a book of discipline; and shortly after this a church hymn-book was published also. Beyond this there was little done in this department until 1841, when the New York Conference passed a resolution providing for the publication of a monthly magazine. But the lack of funds compelled the projectors to issue it as a quarterly. For nearly eight years this magazine exerted an excellent influence upon the ministers with a strong interest. It contained the news in each of the conferences; its editorials breathed a spirit of love and fellowship; and thus the members were brought to a knowledge of the work being accomplished. At length the prosperity of the magazine seemed to justify the publication of a weekly paper. Accordingly a weekly journal, named the "Christian Herald," made its appearance and ran its course for the space of four years. In 1852, by order of the General Conference, the paper was enlarged and issued as the "Christian Recorder", which has continued to be published up to the present time.

The department now publishes the *Recorder*, the *African Methodist Episcopal Review*, and various books.

The financing of so large an organization is a matter of great interest. In the quadrennium, 1896-1900, there was raised for the purposes of the general church organization on the average:

Each year	$ 236,194.79
Each month	19,682.89
Each day	656.09
Each minute	.45

The bishops receive $2,000 a year; the general officers, $1,200. In 1826 the pastors averaged $50 and $60 a year in salary, and often had other work for a livelihood. In 1900 the average salary of presiding elders was $663.72; of preachers $204.18. There is a system of pensions for the widowed and superannuated partially in force. The funds of the church are of two sorts: local monies, raised for the local churches, and "Dollar" money (i. e., one dollar per member), for the general church. The dollar money, which amounts to over $100,000 a year, is divided as follows :

Forty-six per cent. to general financial department.
Thirty-six per cent. to the annual conferences.
Ten per cent. to church extension.
Eight per cent. to education.

The total amount raised by the church in the four years, 1896–1900, was:

Dollar money	$ 403,401.62
Church extension	64,474.00
Publishing Department	71,313.83
Education	270,988.54
Sunday-school Union	77,159.46
Preacher's aid	2,605.25
Missions	64,836.39
Total	$ 954,779.09

Salaries of presiding elders	$ 139,735.37
Salaries of ministers	735,796.21
Traveling expenses	29,594.00
Salaries of bishops	18,000.00
Salaries of general officers	12,300.00
Total *	$ 935,425.58

Total raised in quadrennium, 1896–1900	$ 1,777,948.20
Total raised in quadrennium, 1892–1896	1,533,414.01
Total raised in quadrennium, 1888–1892	1,064,569.50

Turning to the various departments, we have first the Publishing Department. The *Review* is an octavo publication of about 100 pages, and is now in its twentieth year. It has a circulation of perhaps 1,000 copies. The contents of the New Year's number, 1903, were:

The Mission of the African Methodist Episcopal Church to the Darker Races of the World—By C. J. Powell.

Publications and Literature of the African Methodist Episcopal Church.—John E. Hagins.

The Flight of Hagar.—J. A. Adams.

The South Mountain Reservation.—Ralph Elwood Brock.

The Leadership of the Church and the Opportunity of the Ministry.—George W. Henderson.

The Opportunity of the Colored Young Men's Christian Association in the Work of Education.—F. D. Wheelock.

The Preacher at Hill Station.—Katherine D. Tillman.

St. Cecilia.

A New Year—Looking Before and After.—H. T. Kealing.

Joseph Parker's Prophecy.

Women—Life's Mirror; Character in Eyes; Foes to Embonpoint; Tennyson's Egotism.

Sociological.—Loves the Game; Alone in Paris; Indian Territory.

Religious.—Some Questions and Answers.

Miscellaneous.—Christmas; Christmas in the Orient; Who is Santa Claus? Keep Old Santa Claus; Winter; Music and Old Age; T. Thomas Fortune; The Strength of New England; Things to take to Church.

Editorial.—The Review for 1903; President Roosevelt; Thomas B. Reed; Dr. Joseph Parker; You Count for One; The Stars for Us; The Good Old Times Worse than Our Times.

---

* Some of the items in this table are paid wholly or in part from the dollar money above.

The *Recorder* is a weekly, eight-page paper, and is the oldest Negro periodical in the United States. It is taken up largely with church announcements and reports.

The Philadelphia house received $65,687.98 in the four years, 1896–1900. It is not self-supporting at present, although it has been at various periods in the past. The outfit, including building and land, is valued at $45,500, on which there is a debt of $15,000. The branch establishment in Atlanta publishes the *Southern Christian Recorder*, a small weekly, at an annual cost of about $1,400.

In Nashville there is located the Sunday-school Union, a publishing house for Sunday-school literature. It has valuable real estate and had an income of $77,159.46 during the quadrennium, or a little less than $20,000 a year.

The mission work at home and abroad has been vigorously pushed in recent years, and in the thirty-six years from 1864 to 1900 this church has spent $2,102,150.75 in mission work. It has to-day in Africa 180 missions and over 12,000 members, beside missions in Canada and the West Indies. Over $60,000 was raised for missions in the last four years.

There is some indebtedness on the general church property. The total value of churches and parsonages was $9,309,937 in 1900, on which there was a debt of $1,068,995.

The African Methodist Episcopal Church began in 1844 to start schools for Negroes. A committee was appointed and founded Union Seminary. Later this institution was united with Wilberforce University, which was bought by the church from the white Methodist Church. Thus Wilberforce, dating from 1856, is the oldest Negro institution in the land. The church has now about twenty-five schools in all. They are supported from three sources: 1. Tuition, etc., paid by students; 2. Donations and bequests; 3. Appropriations from the general fund of the church. From these sources about $275,000 was raised in the four years, 1896–1900; and since 1884, when the general educational department was organized, there has been raised $1,250,000 for education. The figures are :

Schools	25
Teachers	140
Average attendance, four years . .	3,693
Acres of land	1,482
Buildings	51
Value of property . . . . $	535,000.00
Raised and appropriated 1896–1900 .	270,988.54
Raised and appropriated 1884–1900 .	1,140,013.31

The schools are:

African Methodist Episcopal Schools

SCHOOLS.	Established.	Scholars.	Teachers.	Property.	Receipts, four years.
Payne Theological Seminary, Wilberforce, O...	1891	37	3	$ 13,000	$ 15,360.48
Wilberforce University, Wilberforce, Ohio.....	1856	311	20	158,000	85,923.23
Morris Brown College, Atlanta, Ga............	1880	350	17	75,000	35,248.69
Kittrel College, Kittrel, N. C.....................	1886	136	8	30,000	31,372.46
Paul Quinn College, Waco, Tex..................	1881	203	8	80,000	28,510.56
Allen University, Columbia, S. C................	1880	285	8	35,000	19,365.05
Western University, Quindan, Kan...............	......	90	10	75,000	15,637.53
Edward Waters College, Jacksonville, Fla......	1883	172	8	25,000	12,873.85
Shorter University, North Little Rock, Ark....	1887	110	4	10,250	11,929.44
Payne University, Selma, Ala....	......	233	9	3,000	5,981.00
Campbell-Stringer College, Jackson, Mo........	......	100	2	10,300	4,272.85
Wayman Institute, Harrodsburg, Ky............	1891	50	1	2,760	2,618.08
Turner Normal Institute, Shelbyville, Tenn....	1887	79	3	3,500	2,030.36
Flagler High School, Marion, S. C..............	......	161	3	1,500	700.00
Delhi Institute, Delhi, La............	......	57	3	3,000	....
Sission's High School, South McAlister, I. T....	......	35	2	....	332.78
Blue Creek and Muscogee High School, I. T.....	......	......	......	......	....
Morsell Institute, Hayti.................	......	......	......	......	....
Bermuda Institute, Bermuda..............	......	......	......	......	....
Zion Institute, Sierra Leone, Africa........	......	......	......	......	....
Eliza Turner School, Monrovia, Africa....:...	......	......	......	......	....
Cape Town Institute, Cape Town, Africa.......	......	......	......	......	....

In 1901 there were 175 teachers, 6,725 students and 6,696 graduates from forty-one schools, valued at $865,574.

The church extension work received $64,474 during the quadrennium, and there was $1,742.25 paid to preachers' widows. The total ministerial insurance in force amounted to $80,000.

The African Methodist Episcopal Church, however, is chiefly noteworthy on account of its Board of Bishops. A board of thirteen men more or less wield the power directly over 750,000 American Negroes, and indirectly over two or more millions, administer $10,000,000 worth of property and an annual budget of $500,000. These bishops are elected for life by a General Conference meeting every four years. The membership of the General Conference consists of ministerial and lay delegates: the clerical delegates are elected from the Annual Conferences, one for every thirty ministers. Two lay delegates for each Annual Conference are selected by the representatives of the official church boards in the Conference. Thus we have a peculiar case of Negro government, with elaborate machinery and the experience of a hundred years. How has it succeeded? Its financial and numerical success has been remarkable as has been shown. Moreover, the bishops elected form a remarkable series of personalities. Together the assembled bishops are perhaps the most striking body of Negroes in the world in personal appearance: men of massive physique, clear cut faces and undoubted intelligence. Altogether the church has elected about thirty bishops.

These men fall into about five classes. First, there were those who represented the old type of Negro preacher—men of little learning, honest and of fair character, capable of following other leaders. Perhaps five or six of the African Methodist Episcopal bishops have been of this type, but they have nearly all passed away. From them developed, on the one hand, four men of aggressive, almost riotous energy, who by their personality thrust the church forward. While such men did much for the physical growth of the church they were often men of questionable character, and in one or two instances ought never to have been raised to the bishopric. On the other hand, in the case of four other bishops, the goodness of the older class developed toward intense, almost ascetic piety, represented pre-eminently in the late Daniel Payne, a man of almost fanatic enthusiasm, of simple and pure life and unstained reputation, and of great intellectual ability. The African Methodist Episcopal Church owes more to him than to any single man, and the class of bishops he represents is the salt of the organization. Such a business plant naturally has called to the front many men of business ability, and perhaps five bishops may be classed as financiers and overseers. The rest of the men who have sat on the bench rose for various reasons as popular leaders—by powerful preaching, by pleasing manners, by impressive personal appearance. They have usually been men of ordinary attainment, with characters neither better nor worse than the middle classes of their race. Once in office they have usually grown in efficiency and character. On the whole, then, this experiment in Negro government has been distinctly encouraging. It has brought forward men varying in character, some good and some bad, but on the whole decency and ability have been decidedly in the ascendency, and the church has prospered.

25. The Zion Methodists. The history of the African Methodist Episcopal Zion Church has already been given.* From the 1,500 members of 1821 it has grown until it claimed, in 1904, 551,591 adherents. Some facts about the church, as given at the twenty-first quadrennial session, are :

"In May, 1896, the ordained ministry of the church numbered 2,473; this has increased in four years to 2,902, an addition of 429. The number of church edifices, which were 3,612, has increased to 4,841, an addition of 229. The membership of 409,441 has swollen to 528,461, an increase of 119,020. These, with an approximate transient membership of 12,000, and denominational adherents of 125,000, will give the church a following of nearly 668,000. The increase has been well proportioned in each department of the church. The average increase per year for the ministry is 107; of increase in church buildings, 57, and members, 29,755.

"The valuation of church property, including real estate of every description, church, parsonages, schools, general departments, and other buildings, is estimated at $4,865,372, on which rests a total indebtedness of only $758,400. The rate of

---

* P. 45.

reduction of property indebtedness slightly exceeds its increase, the financial wave of 1899 contributing largely to this pleasing result. The African Methodist Episcopal Zion is the least debt-encumbered of any of the large Negro denominations. The growth in material interests has been rapid, while the denominational indebtedness has fallen thirty per cent. A number of magnificent churches have been erected, completed, or extensively rebuilt or remodeled.

"The African Methodist Episcopal Zion Church ranks fourth in the family of Methodism; second in Negro Methodism, and thirteenth in denominational standing in the United States. Beginning in 1896 without a single denominational Christian Endeavor Society, we have to-day more than 600, with a membership of about 30,000. We are happy to say our number of societies and members is constantly increasing.

"Current expenses were per annum, $153,700; for the quadrennium, $614,800; on church debt and building new churches, per annum, $940,999; for the quadrennium, $3,763,996. This, with the general fund, missionary and other revenue to the church, will aggregate for the four years $11,449,800."

The amounts of money for general purposes raised by this connection during four years is as follows, made up of the following items:

Bishops	$ 64,378.78
Livingstone College	11,421.53
General Secretary	1,516.09
General Steward	1,162.11
Star of Zion	2,462.65
Book Concern	1,770.62
Quarterly Review	881.10
Sunday-school Department	1,077.91
Expenses General Secretary	1,230.55
Expenses General Steward	1,148.34
Mrs. J. C. Price	1,669.16
Bishop Jones' estate	417.19
Bishop Moore's estate	1,175.02
Bishop Thompson's estate	1,159.03
Funeral expenses	75.00
Superannuated ministers	1,746.99
Total	$ 93,292.07

The following sums were raised for education:

School and College Statistics

(Several of the schools had not reported when this report was read.)

NAME OF SCHOOL.	No. of Teachers.	No. of Students.	Amount Collected per Quadrennium.	Value of Plant.
Livingstone College	14	267	$ 57,193.05	$ 117,950
Clinton Institute	5	202	3,450.00	5,000
Lancaster Institute	6	277	5,038.00	4,500
Greenville College	3	125	2,705.66	3,000
Hannon and Lomax	2	80	300.00	1,500
Walters Institute	2	72	300.00	1,000
Mobile Institute			1,500.00	2,000
Jones University			530.00	
Money raised by Secretary			568.50	
Totals	32	1,023	$ 71,585.21	$ 134,950

There were the following additional schools:

Atkinson College, Madisonville, Ky.
Palmetto Institute, Union, S. C.
Edenton Industrial High School, Edenton, N. C.
Lloyd Academy, Elizabethtown, N. C.
Hemphill High School, Crockett, Ga.
Pettey Academy, Newburn, N. C.
Lomax and Rutler Academy, Tampa, Fla.
Carr Academy, North Carolina.
Lee Institute, Amite City, La.
Pettey Institute, Calvert, Tex.
African Methodist Episcopal Zion High School, Norfolk, Va.

The publishing house had an income of $30,949 in the last four years, and publishes the *Star of Zion*, a weekly paper, the *African Methodist Episcopal Zion Review*, a quarterly, and other literature. The church extension department raised but $1,400, and $2,103 was spent for missions.

26. The Colored Methodists. The Colored Methodist Episcopal Church* started with 80,000 members and two bishops in 1866, and has grown as follows:

	1872.	1896.	1900.
Bishops	3	5	6
Itinerant preachers	635	1,400	....
Local preachers	583	2,500	....
Members	67,889	200,000	....

The church collected $145,707 during the four years, 1898–1902. The bishops receive $2,000 a year, and the church supports the following educational institutions:

Name.	Expenditures, Four Years.
Lane College	$ 11,718
Payne Institute †	7,466
Haygood Seminary	1,794
Homer Seminary	1,927
Texas College	3,157

The Publishing Department expended $12,960 in the quadrennium, and has a plant worth $20,000. This church is often put on the defensive by reason of its origin, but it accepts the challenge boldly:

"The Colored Methodist Episcopal Church, organized in 1870, is, as you well know, the daughter of the Methodist Episcopal Church, South. We are not ashamed of our origin; nor do we regret the relation which we sustain to that church. We are not forgetful of the fact that the Christianity and Methodism which our fathers enjoyed were largely due to the zeal and labors of Southern Methodist pioneers. The first labors of Bishop John Early were among the slaves of Thomas Jefferson, in Bedford County, Va. Bishop Capers deserves to be called the 'Founder of Missions to the Slaves'; James O. Andrew, ninth bishop of the Methodist Episcopal Church, whose history is pretty well known to these two

---

* Cf. page 47.   † The Methodist Church, South, helps support this school.

great bodies of Methodism, frequently rose to superhuman heights of eloquence when pleading for the religious training of the enslaved Negro. Since emancipation no Southerner has done more to ameliorate the condition of the freedman than the author of 'Our Brother in Black.' Bishop Haygood, by his unselfish labors, reflected himself upon the current of the ages as the mountain mirrors itself in the gentle stream which flows at its base. These men, and many others whom I could mention, will ever live upon the tablets of our memory." *

27. The Methodists. All of the above represent branches of Methodism and agree in doctrine and discipline save in a few minor points. There was in earlier times talk of some of them rejoining the parent body; later there have been negotiations looking to the union of the African Methodists and Zionists, and negotiations are pending for a union of the Colored Methodists and Zionists. The chances are that some union will eventually take place, but how soon it is difficult to say. Meantime large numbers of Negroes have remained in the Methodist Episcopal Church, and this colored membership increases. In 1902 we have the following figures :

Methodist Episcopal Church—Negro Membership

CONFERENCES.	Full Membership.	Valuation.	Monies Raised.
Central Missouri	6,909	$ 200,606	$ 34,994
Delaware	19,288	552,251	104,055
Florida	4,490	79,943	14,674
Liberia	2,832	75,520	3,346
Little Rock	5,018	85,148	15,543
Louisiana	14,178	314,820	65,356
Lexington	9,558	301,775	49,341
Mississippi	18,042	181,070	35,907
Upper Mississippi	19,721	161,149	38,927
Washington	26,980	988,193	98,065
Atlanta	13,028	181,138	28,017
Central Alabama	5,149	65,700	11,470
East Tennessee	4,700	111,380	16,298
Mobile	5,546	71,235	11,829
North Carolina	9,912	116,170	23,481
Savannah	7,648	77,442	15,297
South Carolina	39,490	408,834	60,548
Tennessee	8,598	97,622	22,377
Texas	13,045	273,700	35,940
West Texas	11,792	193,255	31,935
Total	245,954	$4,566,951	$ 717,400

It is of interest to know how much this element contributes to the church. (1) From 1900 to 1903, inclusive, the society appropriated to colored schools $449,119. (2) The colored membership of the church gave of this amount $227,321.53, and beside this they gave as a special contribution towards buildings and debts $55,601.69. Add to this amount their other contribution for Student Help for the same period of

* Bishop Phillips, in Fraternal Address to the African Methodist Episcopal Church.

$12,599.40 and you have a grand total of $292,522.62 contributed by the colored people in this church towards their education for four years. It must be remembered, however, that the Student Help money passes through the Board of Education. (3) We raised for missions during the same period $83,131.23. The Church Extension Board spent $591,132 in aiding colored churches, 1864–1901, and has collected $81,514 from these churches. The Freedman's Aid Society has spent over $7,000,000 in Negro education. It maintains the following schools:

INSTITUTIONS.	Teachers Past Year.	Students Past Year.	Estimated Value of Property
THEOLOGICAL.			
Gammon Theological Seminary, Atlanta, Ga	4	48	$ 100,000
COLLEGIATE.			
Bennett College, Greensboro, N. C	16	205	60,000
Claflin University, Orangeburg, S. C	58	609	110,000
Clark University, Atlanta, Ga	35	603	350,000
George R. Smith College, Sedalia, Mo	15	144	50,000
Morgan College, Baltimore, Md	24	286	35,000
New Orleans University, New Orleans, La	25	503	125,000
Philander Smith College, Little Rock, Ark	17	521	30,000
Rust University, Holly Springs, Miss	40	334	125,000
Walden University, Nashville, Tenn	56	1,104	125,000
Wiley University, Marshall, Tex	30	501	64,000
Total	320	4,858	$1,174,000
ACADEMIC.			
Alexandria Academy, Alexandria, La	2	122	18,000
Central Alabama Academy, Huntsville, Ala	5	148	8,000
Cookman Academy, Jacksonville, Fla	6	194	21,000
Delaware Academy, Princess Anne, Md			
Gilbert Academy, Baldwin, La	11	219	60,000
Haven Academy, Waynesboro, Ga	3	241	5,000
La Grange Academy, La Grange, Ga	3	154	8,000
Meridian Academy, Meridian, Miss	8	404	8,000
Morristown Academy, Morristown, Tenn	27	371	75,000
Sam Houston College, Austin, Tex	16	252	48,000
Virginia Collegiate and Industrial Inst., Lynchburg, Va.			35,000
Total	81	2,105	$ 286,000
MEDICAL.			
Meharry Medical School, Walden University *		339	
Flint Medical College, New Orleans, La			$ 20,000
Sarah Goodridge Nurse-training School and Hospital, New Orleans, La	13	72	18,000
Total	13	411	$ 38,000
Total	414	7,374	1,498,000

* Faculty included in Walden University.

The history of the Negro in the Methodist Episcopal Church is, however, of far-reaching interest in any study of the relation of the races. This is the one church with a centralized episcopal government which has a large Negro membership, and the efforts to adjust the races in

this organization throw light on the problem in the whole country.
This history may be graphically illustrated as follows:

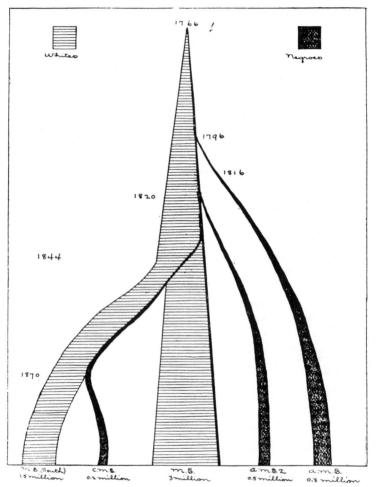

We have clearly discussed the secession of the African Methodist
Episcopal, African Methodist Episcopal Zion Church and the setting off
of the Colored Methodist Episcopal. These churches, by their individual development, have settled the question of the ability of the
Negro in self-organization and self-direction of his religious life. But
it was left to the Methodist Church to struggle with the more baffling
problem of the relation of the races in one organization. Something

has already been said of the Methodists and slavery and the split of 1844.*   Even before that serious questions of color had arisen outside the slavery problem. The General Conference of 1800 settled the first of these questions by enacting that bishops could "*ordain deacons of our African brethren* in places where they have built a house or houses for the worship of God," the only limitation being the possibility of finding suitable men. The next question arose after the secession of 1844 had left many Negro congregations in the border states without their usual white pastors; they petitioned the General Conference of 1848 for colored ministers and colored Annual Conferences; the Conference declared "that the organization of such (separate) Conferences" was "at present inexpedient," but it authorized the employment of *itinerant colored ministers* at the discretion of the bishops. No regular appointment was usually made to these congregations, but they were left "to be supplied" by the colored itinerants. In 1852, however, the General Conference directed "that the colored local preachers now employed within the bounds of the Philadelphia and New Jersey Annual Conferences be assembled together once each year by the bishop or bishops for the purpose of conferring with the said colored local preachers with respect to the best means of promoting their work and also for the purpose of assigning their work respectively."   This was virtually *a Colored Annual Conference* in all but name, and meant the dividing of identical territory with separate Conferences along the color line.

Four years later the color question rose in a different guise. The church had been working in Africa, especially Liberia, and now the members there asked for a *missionary bishop*. The General Conference assented and ordained Francis Burns, a Negro, to the bishopric of Liberia, October 14, 1856; in 1866 the Rev. John W. Roberts, another Negro, was ordained to this same bishopric. These were the first and, so far, the only Negro bishops in the Methodist Episcopal Church. The same Conference of 1856 recognized further the principle of *colored Annual Conferences* all over the land whenever "the holding of said Conference or Conferences shall be recommended by an Annual Conference, and the bishops upon due inquiry, shall deem it practicable and expedient."   At the same time it was declared that, "Our colored preachers and official members shall have all the privileges which are usual to others in Quarterly Conferences, where the usages of the comity do not forbid it," otherwise separate Quarterly Conferences could be held. The General Conference also secured Wilberforce University as a seat of Negro education, but afterward sold it to the African Methodist Episcopal Church in 1863 for a nominal sum.

In 1860 the General Conference raised the colored Annual Conferences to full powers and that of 1864 urged the extension of the system to the South, and began to organize the great work of aiding the freedmen.

---

* P. 21, ff.

Negroes first sat as *delegates in a General Conference* in 1868 in Chicago. The church spread among the Negroes of the South, many preachers were ordained, and when the General Conference of 1872 met they were faced by a *demand for a Negro bishop.* The question was shelved by declaring the eligibility of Negroes to the office but the absence of any obvious candidate. In 1876 the demand came again, but the General Conference escaped the dilemma by deciding to elect no new bishops. The committee on episcopacy at the Conference of 1880 after considerable deliberation recommended "that this General Conference elect one bishop of African descent," but the Conference postponed the matter by a vote of 228 to 137. Since this time Negroes have been elected to seven general offices, * involving the superintendence of matters concerning the Negroes, and while a Negro candidate for bishop has received a large vote, no Negro has been elected. In all probability the matter will eventually be settled by electing one or more Negroes as suffragan bishops, with special charge of Negro Conferences and churches.

This evolution has been of great interest and will be in the future as showing a peculiar process of adjustment between two groups of people in spite of strong centrifugal forces. May it not in a way prefigure the national struggle?

28. The Episcopalians. We now come to the churches where the Negro forms but a small percentage of the membership. Archdeacon Pollard gives the following facts concerning Negro Episcopalians in 1903:

The field of the work among the colored people covers twenty-one Dioceses and three Missionary Districts—all in the Southern States—and ministering specifically to 20,000 persons, of whom 8,000 are communicants, worshipping in 200 churches and chapels, and in charge of more than 100 clergymen. The workers actually number 108 clergymen, 65 laymen and 145 women, or 318 persons in all.

In the entire country to-day there are eighty-five colored clergymen engaged in the work of the church, about 15,000 communicants, and upwards of $50,000 placed annually as an offering upon the altar. As far as I have been able to trace with certainty, 146 colored men have been admitted to Holy Orders in this church, and two consecrated bishops. The Rt. Rev. James Theodore Holly, D. D., the first bishop of Haiti, was born in Washington, D. C., and consecrated bishop in the year 1874. The Rt. Rev. Samuel David Ferguson, D. D., D. C. L., the fourth missionary bishop of Cape Palmas and parts adjacent, West Africa, was born near Charleston, S. C., and consecrated in the year 1885. Forty-two (42) colored clergymen ordained in this church served their day and generation faithfully and then passed into the paradise of God. Seven (7) felt called to other lands and are now out of the coun-

---

* These officers are: Rev. M. C. B. Mason, D. D., Corresponding Secretary Freedman's Aid Society; Rev. I. B. Scott, D. D., Editor *Southwestern Christian Advocate;* Professor I. Garland Penn, Assistant General Secretary Epworth League; Rev. G. G. Logan, D. D., Field Secretary Missionary Society; Rev. Robert E. Jones, D. D., and Rev. C. C. Jacobs, D. D., Field Secretaries Sunday-school Union; Mr. W. F. Waters, Assistant Business Manager *Southwestern Christian Advocate.* The last five of these men were elected by the General Boards, the other two by the General Conference: all are official.

try, but still engaged in ministerial work, while twelve (12), for various causes, were deposed. Some of these last are to-day among the most active, learned and honorable men in the denominations around us.

Although the Episcopal Church was the first American church to receive Negro members, the growth of that membership has been small. This was the one great church that did not split on the slavery question, and the result is that its Negro membership before and since the war has been a delicate subject, and the church has probably done less for black people than any other aggregation of Christians.

What colored churchmen think of their treatment is best shown in this extract from the *Church Advocate*, one of their organs :

The Church Commission for Work among the Colored People at a late meeting decided to request the various rectors of parishes throughout the South to institute Sunday-schools and special services for the colored population "such as were frequently found in the South before the war." The Commission hope for "real advance" among the colored people in so doing. We do not agree with the Commission with respect to either the wisdom or the efficiency of the plan suggested. In the first place, this "before the war" plan was a complete failure so far as church extension was concerned, in the past when white churchmen had complete bodily control of their slaves. We are going to quote from the Journals of Conventions of the Diocese of Virginia, since Virginia is a fair type of Southern States.

The Journals of Virginia will verify the contention, that during the "before the war" period, while the bishops and a large number of the clergy were always interested in the religious training of the slaves, yet as matter of fact there was general apathy and indifference upon the part of the laity with respect to this matter.

At various intervals resolutions were presented in the Annual Conventions with the avowed purpose of stimulating an interest in the religious welfare of the slaves. But despite all these efforts the Journals fail to record any great achievements along that line.

In the Convention of 1840, a preamble recited the great and urgent need for such work, and after appealing to the final reckoning as an occasion of condemnation to the master class who have neglected the members of this "degraded race," certain resolutions were presented and adopted : a committee of seven was appointed to consider and report upon the matter. This committee consisted of the two bishops, two clergymen and three laymen. Among other things they were to report to the Convention "the most efficient system of oral religious instruction, both public and private," and further, they were to give such information as would determine the "proper subjects of baptism, both infant and adult."

In the Convention of 1841 the committee was continued.

In the Convention of 1856 the committee reported as follows:

"We commend the establishment of Sunday-schools in our bounds, by the masters and mistresses in our church for colored children, where the instruction would be exclusively oral and governed by the standards of our church:

"In connection with these, and as perhaps more important and auxiliary, the catechetical instruction of young servants by their masters and mistresses of our church, in their families, is strongly recommended. And we further distinctly approve of the plan of making such domestic arrangements as will allow and encourage servants to attend upon the public services of the sanctuary, as well as at family prayers."

Two years later, in 1858, the following action was taken:

"Resolved, That a special committee be appointed to ascertain from the parishes, and to report to the next Convention whether any, and if any, what provision is made for the instruction of the colored population of their limits."

In the Convention of 1859 resolutions were adopted looking to the maintenance of "missionary services with the slaves," and for building houses of worship for them.

In the Convention of 1860, which met at Charlottesville, a somewhat more elaborate plan of operation was presented and adopted, which in brief may be described as follows: 1. Separate and distinct congregations. 2. Provision of suitable place of worship; trustees chosen by contributors and appointed by the court. 3. A certain number to be taken from the communicants, to assist the minister in the affairs of the congregation, with special reference to the admission, supervision and discipline of church members. In the first place these were to be appointed by the minister. Vacancies to be filled by the communicants, subject to the approval of the minister. 4. The minister always to be a clergyman of the Diocese, either a rector within the bounds, or a missionary appointed by the executive committee of the Diocesan Missionary Society, with the approval of the bishop.

At this same Convention in 1860 a committee was appointed to consider the importance of more generally procuring baptism for children of slaves of members of the church.

So much for ante-bellum relations. So faithful had been the work under such conditions that as late as 1879 there were less than 200 colored communicants reported in the whole state of Virginia. The next ten years in Virginia, 1879–1889, constituted the most glorious period, so far as church extension is concerned, among colored people in the entire history of the Diocese. God richly blessed the efforts put forth so that the list of communicants was increased to nearly 1,000, a native Negro ministry of some ten clergymen raised up. With this auspicious blessing of the Almighty, on the part of some of the white brethren came the "color" question, and the work has never since advanced as before.

At the Convention of 1856, embracing the territory now included in the states of Virginia and West Virginia, there were reported, of colored people, forty-three adult baptisms, 244 infant baptisms, and forty-seven confirmed; the whole number of communicants in this territory being only 235. And four years later, 1860, instead of an increase there was a decided decrease, the figures being as follows: Adult baptisms, 12; infants, 166; confirmed, 22; total number of communicants, 114.

Bishop Johns, in his Convention address of 1860, in his Journal notes in connection with his attendance upon the General Convention which met in Richmond, Va., in 1859, says:

"October 3–23d—During the session of the Convention I was privileged, in common with several of the bishops and other clergy, to address the large and interesting congregations of colored people assembled in the Baptist and Methodist African Churches. We have no such congregations there or elsewhere in the Diocese, and for our delinquency in this I should find it hard to furnish a satisfactory excuse."

What a significant statement! The Episcopal Church, when its white members commanded even the bodies of their slaves, backed by all the prestige and influence of the church in Virginia, failed to any degree to get hold of the colored people.

In South Carolina the complete failure of ante-bellum instruction to result in definite church extension among the Negroes was even more disastrous.

The Journal of the Convention of South Carolina for 1856 shows 424 white baptisms against 975 colored baptisms, and 210 white persons confirmed against 414 colored persons confirmed. There were reported 2,971 white communicants, against 3,022 colored communicants.

In spite of this faithful ante-bellum instruction, when the colored people became free they left the church. They preferred, as they do now, the ministrations of their own, in leadership as well. We might ask the question how well has Archdeacon Joyner of South Carolina succeeded in bringing them back into the church in later days ? Let us answer by a few statistics. We take these statistics from official sources, directly from the Journals of the Convention of South Carolina.

In 1892 the total of colored communicants in that Diocese was 745. Ten years later, 1902, the total is 859. But of this 859, 356 belong to St. Mark's, Charleston, leaving a balance of 503 pertaining to the Archdeaconry of South Carolina. By this we fail to see any actual gain whatever. But taking the figures of 1903 we have in South Carolina 638 communicants exclusive of St. Mark's congregation. Hence, after deducting 237 communicants of St. Mark's from the total of 745 in 1892, we have as Archdeacon Joyner's portion then 508 communicants. Eleven years later this 508 has become 638.

The auditor who examined the accounts of the Archdeacon for 1892, certified of expenditures amounting to $11,330.25, and for the year 1903 the auditor certifies of expenditures in the neighborhood of $20,000. For the eleven years we have an increase of 130 communicants.

The method of special services for colored people, "colored Sunday-school," not only failed in ante-bellum days, but it has also failed in later years since the war. It is very far from us to contend that these efforts were in vain and without substantial good. Much good was the outcome of such efforts. They helped to mould and build solid characters. But they helped scarcely one iota in church extension or in making churchmen of colored people. The people got the instruction and the material help, and went off to the Baptists or Methodists.

Take an illustration of this same idea in the city of Baltimore. Twelve or fifteen years ago there were large and enthusiastic "colored" Sunday-schools in connection with the following white parishes in Baltimore: St. Peter's Church of the Ascension, St. Michael's and All Angels, and Emanuel Church. At Towson there was both a parish and Sunday-school; also a similar condition obtained at Claggett Chapel, Anne Arundel County, and at West River.

And yet to-day there is no indication whatever that such Sunday-schools were ever in existence, save here and there a communicant in the two exclusively colored congregations of churchmen in this city. So far as doing good is concerned, a great deal of good was done by these several schools, for many of their former pupils have become reliable and reputable men and women, Christian workers in Baptist and Methodist Churches. But with respect to church extension the idea has been a failure. Twenty years ago the late Rev. Dr. Dashiell, Secretary of the Virginia Council, said:

"In consideration, therefore, of the church's duty to the Negro, we are not deliberating concerning one who will be entirely quiescent. The colored people have the right to speak in the matter, and they will assert that right. . . . Again, I say, remember that they are human beings, and it is not in human nature to be content with subordination to those who do not thoroughly understand us, and, therefore, are not capable of complete sympathy with us."

What the church should do. Meeting the issue fairly, honestly and frankly, the church should recognize the fact that whatever may be in the future, at present it is hopelessly impossible to bring together, under one bishop, the white and colored people in Diocesan Conventions in the South. That being a fact, without crimination or recrimination, the church should practically say to the colored clergy and laity, "Organize your own jurisdictional Convention with a bishop of your own race at the head. The bishops and church people in the bounds of your jurisdictional territory are your friends, and they will help and assist you. It may be, in the distant future, when all of us on both sides have advanced more nearly to the true ideal, that this tentative arrangement may lapse, and all of us will be comprehended in one Diocesan system. Until then, although somewhat separated, let us love one another and work for the glory of God. We have confidence in you. We believe that you will accept this as a Providential opportunity and will demonstrate by your successful work in more largely and effectively reaching your race, the wisdom of the arrangement."

The church has lost so many opportunities that we are fearful lest she let slip the present one.

St. Thomas' Church, Philadelphia, was started just before the organic rise of African Methodism. If Bishop White, instead of making Absalom Jones a priest, had consecrated him bishop, to work among his African brethren in this country, the great African Methodist Church to-day would have been Episcopal and in full communion with the church. The church lost that opportunity. After the late Civil war, if the church had consecrated a colored priest as bishop to work among the African race in this country, following up the "ante-bellum" instruction given the slaves in church families, with the nucleus of former slave communicants, the church of to-day among the Negroes would be numerically large, vigorous and strong. The church lost that opportunity. For years some of us who have been branded as "up-starts," "heady," "not humble" and "ambitious," for the love that we have in our hearts for our dear Lord and His church, have been content to endure such things while we unfailingly and unflinchingly kept before the church the duty of the hour.

That the church is moving in the direction of this demand is shown by the fact that there are now three annual Diocesan convocations of colored clergy and laity: Southern Virginia, South Carolina and North Carolina. One has already been arranged for Arkansas, which will be effective just so soon as there are sufficient colored clergy and laity.

29. The Presbyterians.

The Presbyterian Church, North, began missionary work among the Negroes of the South fully a year before the close of the Civil war. Two committees were at work under the direction of the General Assembly (O. S.) as early as 1864—one with headquarters at Indianapolis, and the other at Philadelphia. The work of these two committees from necessity was confined by military lines, and was chiefly in connection with military and "contraband" camps and hospitals. In May, 1865, the General Assembly meeting in Pittsburg united these committees under one general committee, entitled "The General Assembly's Committee on Freedmen." It met by order of the Assembly in the lecture room of the First Church, Pittsburg, and was organized June 22d, 1865.

Before the re-union there was another work similar in character and purpose with headquarters in New York, carried on as a " Freedmen's Department," in connection with the Presbyterian Committee of Home Missions (N. S.). This "Freedmen's Department" existed only two years, making its second annual report in 1870. When the two Assemblies united in 1870, the work among the Freedmen as carried on from New York and Pittsburg was consolidated and a new committee appointed. This new committee was organized by direction of the Reunited General Assembly, June 10th, 1870, in Pittsburg, Pa.

This committee continued to work without change of plan or reorganization for twelve years; but the question of the ownership of property, necessary to the work, and the handling of bequests made it evident that it would be better to have the committee incorporated. In 1882 the Assembly at Springfield, Ill., sanctioned the change and the committee obtained a charter September 16th, 1882, and became a corporate body under the name of "The Board of Missions for Freedmen of the Presbyterian Church in the United States of America."

This board educates preachers and teachers; maintains ministers in their work and teachers in their schools; builds churches, school-houses, seminaries, academies, colleges and dormitories; prescribes courses of study; looks after the condition of buildings, and orders all repairs and extensions; elects professors and trustees; provides for boarding department all necessary utensils and furnishings; controls the various institutions of learning; receives monthly financial statements from all schools and audits all bills.

Out of confusion, ignorance and poverty there has arisen a system of educational and evangelistic work that commands the attention and demands the support of the entire church.

Schools, academies, seminaries and one large university have gathered within their walls young men and young women to the number of 11,000, who are brought under religious influence, and are being trained in the ways of the Presbyterian Church.

Congregations have been gathered and churches have been organized until now the board has under its watch and care 350 churches and missions containing 21,000 members. Church buildings have been erected and property secured for the use of churches valued at $350,000. School property owned and used by the board in its work is estimated to be worth $500,000. Funds permanently invested for the use of the work amount to $100,000, making almost $1,000,000 invested in property and permanent funds. This property, while absolutely necessary to the work of the board, entails a heavy annual expense in the way of repairs and insurance.

As the work has been a matter of growth, and its influence operative from the time it began, the power for good must not be measured alone by this year's work or last year's work, but by all the work that has been done through all these years. Probably 50,000 people have professed their faith in Christ under the preaching of our ministers. The enrollment in our Sabbath schools, adding year to year, must have reached 400,000, and the total enrollment of students in our day schools from the time we began would count up to 250,000.

The indirect influence of our work upon the communities in which our churches and schools have been established is hard to calculate, but the lives of thousands of our quiet, intelligent and order-loving citizens that are the product of our schools and churches must be included in the calculation, if we want to form an estimate of the amount of good that has been accomplished by the Presbyterian Church in its work among these people.

In Virginia there is one colored Presbytery; in North Carolina there are three; in South Carolina three; in Georgia two; in Arkansas one, and in Alabama and Mississippi one. In these eleven Presbyteries, containing 209 ministers, there are only seven white men and of these all are teachers except two. In Florida we have four colored ministers; in Tennessee fourteen; in Kentucky four; in Missouri one; in Indian Territory five ministers, two of whom are white. The larger part of our work lies in North Carolina, South Carolina and Southern Virginia.

In view of the past history of the work, and of the great good that is being accomplished, the board feels justified in saying that the Presbyterian Church has not yet given annually of its means an amount commensurate with the importance of this cause. The board has received from all sources (including legacies) for the last year about $160,000, whereas $250,000 would hardly begin to meet the reasonable demands of the work.

In 1902 the work of the Presbyterians was reported as follows:

Ministers	209	Ministers who preach only.	149
Churches and missions	353	Ministers who preach and teach	49
Added on examination	1,737	Ministers who teach only	11
Added on certificate	206	Laymen who teach	24
Whole number	21,341	Women who teach	188
Sunday-schools	350		
Sunday-school scholars	21,299		
Number of schools	88		
Number of teachers	272		
Number of pupils	10,715		421

SCHOOLS.

BOARDING SCHOOLS.

Biddle University, Charlotte, N. C.
Scotia Seminary, Concord, N. C.
Mary Allen Seminary, Crockett, Tex.
Ingleside Seminary, Burkeville, Va.
Mary Holmes Seminary, West Point, Miss.
Barber Memorial Seminary, Anniston, Ala.

CO-EDUCATIONAL.

Albion Academy, Franklinton, N. C.
Brainerd Institute, Chester, S. C.
Cotton Plant Academy, Cotton Plant, Ark.
Dayton Academy, Carthage, N. C.
Harbison College, Abbeville, S. C.
Haines Industrial School, Augusta, Ga.
Immanuel Training School, Aiken, S. C.
Mary Potter Memorial, Oxford, N. C.
Monticello Academy, Monticello, Ark.
Swift Memorial Institute, Rogersville, Tenn.
Oak Hill Industrial, Clear Creek P. O., I. T.
Richard Allen Institute, Pine Bluff. Ark.
And seventy-one academies and parochials.

To this must be added Lincoln University in Pennsylvania.

"The schools during this year have, almost without exception, done excellent work. Nearly 11,000 pupils have come under, not only Christian, but Presbyterian instruction. Over 1,800 young men and young women have been sheltered in our boarding schools, and have thus been given all the advantages of a Christian home training, as well as daily instruction in the ordinary branches of education."

There are the following Presbyterian churches in the North outside the Mission Board's work:

Fifteenth Street, Washington, D. C.
Madison Street, Baltimore, Md.
Grace, Baltimore, Md.
Knox, Baltimore, Md.
Gilbert, Wilmington, Del.
Pomfret Street, Carlisle, Pa.
Hope, Chambersburg, Pa.
Second, Oxford, Pa
Fifth, Chester, Pa.
Central, Philadelphia, Pa.
Berean, Philadelphia, Pa.
First African, Philadelphia, Pa.

Washington Street, Reading, Pa.
Grace, Pittsburg, Pa.
Fourth, York, Pa.
Siloam, Elizabeth, N. J.
Mission, Goshen, N. Y.
Mission, Washingtonville, N. Y.
St. James, New York, N. Y.
Mt. Tabor, New York, N. Y.
Liberty Street, Troy, N. Y.
St. James, Rochester, N. Y.
Ninth, Indianapolis, Ind.
Grace, Chicago, Ill.

"There are supposed to be from 10,000 to 12,000 Negro communicants who are members of white churches."

Beside the work of the Northern Presbyterians there is considerable work done by the United Presbyterians through the school at Knoxville, Tenn., and various missions, and the Southern Presbyterians do something. The General Assembly of 1899 of the church declared:

The Assembly is gratified at the evidence of a fresh interest on the part of our people in the religious instruction of the Negroes, as shown in the increased number of Sabbath schools for this race taught by the white people, and commends this work to all pastors and sessions.

In the judgment of this Assembly the time has come for a great forward movement in the work of colored evangelization, and in confirmation of this judgment it calls the attention of our people to the following considerations:

The work has perhaps a wider range than any other to which God has called us. "It includes the entering of a mission field, the erection of churches and manses, establishing and maintaining schools, the support of evangelists and pastors, the selection and training of a ministry—in short, every detail connected with the elevation of a race."

Statistics show the prevalence of immorality and crime among the Negroes. If we are not moved by considerations of pity for them and sympathy with our Lord in his love for the souls of all, we ought at least to remember that the temporal and spiritual welfare of our posterity is at stake. Are our children and children's children to inherit a land crying aloud to heaven because of violence and murder, and lynch law?

The Presbyterian Church believes that it is peculiarly fitted to give the Negro what he needs. His needs are, in our judgment, a soundly educated ministry, sober instruction, simple and quiet rather than ritualistic or emotional modes of worship, a simple and orderly system of church government and discipline, and a "home life in which the children will be carefully trained and instructed in the Word of God and in the faith of the church."

God has opened to us a wide door in Africa. The story of our mission on the Congo may be classed among the wonders of modern missionary annals. How are we to enlarge the work in Africa, so signally blessed with God's favor, except by enlarging the work for the Negroes at home? And how assuredly inconsistent to send missionaries to Africa while we neglect the Africans at our door.

The work of the Southern Presbyterian Church for the Negro has reached the gravest crisis in its history. The few, feeble, and widely-scattered Negro churches, heretofore in organic union with the white churches, have been organized, in accordance with our long-cherished plan, into an Independent African Presbyterian Church. The charge has been brought against us that we have taken this action because of race prejudice, and with the purpose to rid ourselves of the burden of colored evangelization.

Those who bring the charge ignore the fact that it was at the request of the colored ministers and elders in convention assembled that this step was taken. Our critics, too, wherever they are brought into ecclesiastical proximity to the Negroes, manifest the very race prejudice they charge against us. These facts serve as missiles to hurl at those who censure us, but they will not relieve us of the odium in the sight of God and man, if we allow the new-born African Presbyterian Church to perish for want of sympathy and support; we shall be made "a spectacle unto the world, and to angels and to men."

The Afro-American Presbyterian thus comments on the development of the church in the South :

The writer and his people were connected with the old Sion Presbyterian Church at Winnsboro, S. C. The very next Sabbath after Sherman's army had swept through that community like a besom of destruction, the pulpit was occupied by the then Rev. W. E. Boggs, now of Jacksonville, Fla., who had unexpectedly appeared on the scene from Virginia. His text was, "God hath spoken once; twice have I heard this; that power belongeth unto God."—Psalms 62:11. He sought to comfort the people by setting forth the superior power of God. From that Sabbath and for months the colored people occupied their accustomed place in the gallery of the church, the minister for the most part being a Rev. G. R. Brackett.

Then the Federal garrison came. The old Methodist Church building was taken possession of Sunday afternoon by a large number of Negroes who had been connected with it. They had been allowed this privilege formerly, some white man being present. Now the meetings became large and noisy. The whites became alarmed. A few Sabbaths later when we approached the entrance to the yard of the Sion Church we were confronted by a Federal soldier, who ordered all Negroes away. It was afterwards learned that the church had applied to the commanding officer for this guard to keep out the Negroes. We all turned away never to feel at home in the old church any more. It was under somewhat similar conditions that the Negroes went out from the white Presbyterian Churches generally. A few hung on, but most of them drifted away.

The Methodist and Baptist Churches among the colored people at the North were already old and strong organizations. The bishops and leaders pushed into the South and gathered in the people by the wholesale, and perhaps 70 per cent. of the Negroes who had been connected with the Southern Presbyterian Church went into these churches. Many of the intelligent and capable were made preachers and leaders. Exceptions may be pointed out, but the above describes the general condition.

This was the situation when the white Presbyterian missionaries came among the colored people of the Carolinas, Virginia, and Georgia, where nearly all the colored Presbyterians are now found. They came within reach of the scattered fragments which had either gone out or were freezing within Southern churches. They began in a small way by planting a few schools and organizing churches. The schools became centers of influence. Naturally the growth of the churches under the new conditions was rapid to a certain stage.

30. The Congregationalists. The work of the Congregationalists has been done through the American Missionary Association. The fifty-sixth annual report of that Association (1902) gives the following history of the work :

The American Missionary Association was formed in 1846. It is distinctly a Christian missionary society to spread the gospel of Christ wherever it has opportunity. It was organized with pronounced opposition to slavery, which then existed, and against all race and caste prejudice, which still exists. It was preceded by four recently established missionary organizations, which were subsequently merged into it. They were the Amistad Committee, the Union Missionary Society, the Committee for West India Missions among the recently emancipated slaves of Jamaica, and the Western Evangelical Missionary Society for work among the American Indians.

In the foreign field, 1854, its laborers numbered seventy-nine, located in West Africa, Jamaica, the Sandwich Islands, Siam, Egypt among the Copts, Canada among the colored refugees and in North America among the Indians.

The home department embraced two distinct fields, the West and the South. There were 112 home missionaries employed by the Association in 1860, fifteen of them being located in the slave states and in Kansas.

The missions in the slave states gave rise to some of the most stirring events in the history of the Association, which has the distinction of beginning the first decided efforts, while slavery existed, to organize churches and schools in the South on an avowedly anti-slavery basis.

The crisis so long impending came at length, and the Union armies, entering the South in 1861, opened the way for the instruction and elevation of the colored people. The Association felt itself providentially prepared to engage in this work, and the first systematic effort for their relief was made by it. Large numbers of "contrabands," or escaping fugitive slaves, were gathered at Fortress Monroe and Hampton, Va., and were homeless and destitute. The Association, on the 17th of September, 1861, established the first day school among the freedmen. That little school laid the foundation for the Hampton Institute which the Association founded later, and was the forerunner of the hundreds that have followed.

The Proclamation of Emancipation, dated January 1, 1863, insured the permanent freedom of Negroes who reached the Union lines. The American Missionary Association rapidly extended its work. At Norfolk the school of the previous year now numbered 1,200 pupils. Teachers were also sent to Newbern and Roanoke Island, N. C., to Beaufort, Hilton Head, St. Helena and Ladies' Island, S. C., and to St. Louis, Mo.; and its force was scattered over the field held by our armies in the District of Columbia, Virginia, North Carolina, South Carolina, Florida, Louisiana, Kentucky, Tennessee, Mississippi, Arkansas, Missouri, and Kansas.

The year 1865 was marked by the close of the Civil war, by the establishment, by act of Congress, of the Freedmen's Bureau, and by the holding of a National Council of Congregational Churches in Boston, which recommended to the churches to raise $250,000 for the work among the freedmen, and designated this Association as the organization providentially fitted to carry it forward. The Association accepted the responsibility, appointed district secretaries at Chicago, Cincinnati and Boston, and collecting agents in other portions of the Northern states. It also solicited funds in Great Britain, and succeeded in securing that year a little more than the $250,000 recommended by the Council. Its receipts from all sources ran up from $47,828 in 1861, to $253,045 in 1866, and $420,769 in 1870.

But in the South there came a reign of terror under the infamous Ku-Klux-Klans—the Thugs of America. The colored people were often assaulted by mobs, dragged from their homes at midnight, and shot down in the streets. But there was no want of courage on the part of our teachers to enter or remain in the field; the number of teachers, which was 320 in 1865, was enlarged to 528 in 1867, 532 in 1868, and 533 in 1870. It was during this very period that the beginnings were made for most of our permanent educational institutions. The Association must train the teachers and preachers for this people.

The Association now sustains as higher institutions Fisk University, Tennessee; Talladega College, Alabama; Tougaloo University, Mississippi; Straight University, Louisiana; Tillotson College, Texas; and J. S. Green College, Georgia, together with forty-three normal and graded schools and thirty common schools scattered over the South and among the mountains, six schools among the Indians, twenty among the Chinese on the Pacific coast, one in Alaska and two in Porto Rico.

Theological departments have also been established in Howard University, Fisk University, Talladega College and Straight University. Industrial instruction first began in Southern mission schools in Talladega, Ala., and was early introduced into many of our schools and has been constantly extended. Talladega College and Tougaloo University have large farms. In all the larger institutions and normal schools mechanical arts are taught to the boys, and household work, cooking, sewing, washing, nursing, etc., to the girls. From these schools go forth annually hundreds of well-qualified teachers and ministers.

Simultaneously with the founding of these permanent institutions the Association began the planting of churches among the freedmen. They were formed mainly in connection with the educational institutions, and were intended to be models of true church life. The work of church-planting has been pressed forward with a steady hand until the churches now number 254, located in nearly all the states of the South, among the Negroes, the mountaineers and the Indians, with most fruitful results. Sunday-schools, temperance efforts and revivals of religion have been marked features in the work. Christian Endeavor Societies were promptly organized and have been rapidly multiplied.

Conferences or Associations have been formed, and of these there are now nine, designated as the Conferences of North Carolina, Georgia, Florida, Alabama, Mississippi, Louisiana, Texas, South Carolina and Tennessee.

As to the churches, one of the corresponding secretaries writes:

"The Congregational Churches, aided by the American Missionary Association, are both few and small in comparison with the great number of Negro churches, but I am happy to say that they are experiencing rapid growth and development. Within the last ten years the number of our churches has increased over 60 per cent. Within the last few years the growth has been even more manifest. The peculiarity of this growth is the up-springing of these churches in a great many of the back country regions. Formerly our churches were almost entirely in the immediate neighborhood and under the shelter of our schools. But in different states new movements have arisen spontaneously towards free churches which shall be in fellowship with one another at the same time, while they are not under any centralized ecclesiastical control. Naturally these churches turn to the Congregational fellowship. The indications are that within the next twenty years the number of them will be very largely increased. In many cases they are the natural result of our educational forces. They are not 'Congregational' in any sectarian sense, but they are largely of the nature of 'Union' Churches, except that they do not submit themselves to any centralized church government. Thus they fall within what might be called 'The Congregational Ellipse,' with its two foci of independence on the one side and fellowship on the other."

The Rev. W. N. De Berry of St. John's Church, Springfield, Mass., made an interesting study of these churches in 1901, and has placed the results in our hands.* Reports were received by him from thirty-three representative colored Congregational churches, in seventeen states, both North and South. They were asked the following questions and made these replies:

1. About what per cent. of the membership of your church is above forty years of age?

ANSWERS:

Less than 10%	3	40%–49%	7
10%–19%	5	50%	3
20%–29%	7	60%	1
30%–39%	6	Not known	1

2. What proportion of your members came from churches of other denominations?

ANSWERS:

None	2	40%	1
Less than 10%	7	50%	1
10%–19%	6	75%	1
20%–29%	5	95%	1
30%–39%	5	Not stated	4

3. Do these persons continue to hold and assert doctrines or beliefs peculiar to the churches from which they came?

ANSWERS:

Yes	2	To some extent	4
No	20	May hold, but do not assert	6
Unanswered	1		

4. What is the state of feeling on the part of other denominations in your town toward your church?

ANSWERS:

Friendly	19	Jealous and antagonistic	4
Hostile	6	Unity of denominations, save	
Growing friendly	2	Baptists	2

5. Are the Congregationalists regarded as exclusive or "stuck up"? If so, what reasons do you assign for this?

ANSWERS:

Yes	22	No	6
To some extent	5		

Some reasons:

(a) Absence of emotionalism.
(b) 1. Lack of information on part of those who regard us as exclusive, and failure to seek that information.
    2. Ignorance, which always condemns the intelligent as "stuck up."
    3. The lack of Christian grace on our part which would lead us to treat with *special* cordiality these people that we might win them.
    4. The large proportion of educated people among us who naturally seek companionship and association among people of like education.

* For Mr. De Berry's report see the *Congregationalist*, January 11, 1902.

(c) Intelligence and mode of worship.

(d) Intelligence and education.

(e) High religious, moral, and intellectual standard required of our ministers and aimed at in our churches.

(f) Superiority in education and wealth.

(g) Because we condemn ignorance and superstition in pulpit and pew.

(h) Because we sometimes think and act as though we are better than others.

6. What per cent. of the money required for the current expenses of your church is raised in your own parish?

ANSWERS:

Less than 10%	1	70%–79%	2
10%–19%	1	80%–89%	2
20%–29%	2	90%–99%	2
30%–39%	6	100%	7
40%–49%	2	Pay all expenses, save pastor's sal-	
50%–59%	3	ary, and pay part of that	2
60%–69%	2	Unanswered	1

7. Do you regard the amount thus raised as in sufficient proportion to the financial ability of your parish?

ANSWERS:

Yes	9	Almost yes	2
No	19	Unanswered	3

8. In your opinion, has the progress of Congregationalism among the colored people any peculiar hindrances? If so, name them.

ANSWERS:

Yes	27	Yes, and no	1
No	4	Unanswered	1

Among the peculiar hindrances the following are mentioned: Lack of denominational knowledge, enthusiasm, loyalty, literature, and effort to increase the membership, the high standards, mental and otherwise, the mode of conducting service, the lack of emotionalism, the lack of denominational emphasis, the low average intelligence of Negro masses, lack of spiritual activity on the part of pastors, and newness of the work.

9. In your opinion, are the prospects for the growth of Congregationalism among the colored people encouraging? If so, upon what do you base your opinion?

ANSWERS:

Yes	30	Unanswered	1

The prospects are reported encouraging for the following reasons: The increased interest in, and desire for, education, the activity of the ministers, the discontent with the old order of things, the regard for the church and its methods.

Other answers are:

(a) Congregationalism must grow slowly. There is no reason to hope for phenomenal growth in the immediate future.

(b) It depends upon what we mean to do. If the denomination will make the preaching of the gospel and the planting of Congregational Churches on this Southern field its first and main work and put a reasonable portion of missionary money and many more men and women into church work directly, then the prospects are most encouraging and indeed all we can ask. Rapid growth is a foregone conclusion.

10. Suggestions:

The work is new, needs much attention and encouragement; the American Missionary Association schools need to care more about emphasizing the church; the pastors need concentrated organization. It will succeed or fail as interest in education goes.

The statistics of Congregationalism are as follows (1902) :

Number of churches	230	Added on profession	1,190
Ministers and missionaries	139	Benevolent contributions	$ 2,813.68
Church members	12,155	Raised for church purposes	39,397.82
Total additions	1,429	Sunday-school scholars	17,311

"Last year we enrolled a larger number of new churches than for any year since 1895. The present year has not been marked either by great advances or regressions. There has been steady progress in individual churches, especially in the increased responsibility about management of their own work. The general increase in the number of churches is manifest from the fact that ten years ago our Southern churches numbered 140; they now number 230.

"The improvement of the four-fifths of the Negro population who live in the rural regions is often exaggerated. It is still shadowed with an ignorance which has barely been touched by the light of a scanty school training for a few weeks of the year and with a church life peculiarly infiltrated with superstition. In vast plantation populations the old slave church still stands. Honesty, truth and purity are not taught, because neither old slave people nor preacher have come to realize that these virtues are essential to the religious life. The ethical power of Christianity is scarcely felt, and 'the plantation preacher is the curse of the people.' The time is ripe for a forward gospel campaign in this great, needy black South of the back country."

The figures above include a few white members.

EDUCATIONAL WORK.

SUMMARY.

Chartered institutions	6		Instructors	480
Normal and graded schools	43	TOTALS.	Pupils	14,048
Common schools	30		Boarding pupils	2,055

PUPILS CLASSIFIED.

Theological	95	
Collegiate	271	
College preparatory	365	
Normal	1,597	
Grammar	2,916	
Intermediate	3,245	
Primary	5,465	
Music	292	
Night	66	=14,312
Counted twice	264	
Total	14,048	

HIGHER INSTITUTIONS.

Attendance.

Fisk University, Nashville, Tenn	498
Talladega College, Talladega, Ala	534
Tougaloo University, Tougaloo, Miss	502
Straight University, New Orleans, La	709
Tillotson College, Austin, Tex	148
J. S. Green College, Demorest, Ga	498= 6

NORMAL AND GRADED.

Gloucester School. Cappahosic, Va	113
Gregory Institute, Wilmington, N. C	310
Washburn Seminary, Beaufort, N. C	156
Lincoln Academy, All Healing, N. C	251
Skyland Institute, Blowing Rock, N. C	83
Saluda Seminary, Saluda, N.C	123
Joseph K. Brick Agricultural, Industrial and Normal School, Enfield, N. C	211
Bethany School, McLeansville, N. C	90
Peabody Academy, Troy, N.C	135
Whittier, N. C	96
Avery Institute, Charleston, S. C	352
Brewer Normal School, Greenwood, S. C	264
Beach Institute, Savannah, Ga	285
Dorchester Academy, McIntosh, Ga	357
Storrs School, Atlanta, Ga	326
Ballard Normal Institute, Macon, Ga	519
Allen Normal and Industrial School, Thomasville, Ga	210
Knox Institute, Athens, Ga	291
Normal Institute, Albany, Ga	349
Lamson School, Marshallville, Ga	259
Cuthbert, Ga	224
Normal School, Orange Park, Fla	139
Fessenden School, Martin, Fla	250
Trinity School, Athens, Ala	210
Lincoln Normal School, Marion, Ala	304
Emerson Institute, Mobile, Ala	266
Green Academy, Nat, Ala	83
Normal and Industrial Collegiate Institute, Joppa, Ala	191
Cotton Valley, Ala	234
Kowaliga, Ala	195
Helena, Ark	165
Le Moyne Institute, Memphis, Tenn	612
Slater Training School, Knoxville, Tenn	172
Warner Institute, Jonesboro, Tenn	120
Grand View Academy, Grand View, Tenn	219
Pleasant Hill Academy, Pleasant Hill, Tenn	325
Big Creek Gap, Tenn	188
Chandler Normal School, Lexington, Ky	270
Williamsburg Academy, Williamsburg, Ky	277
Black Mountain Academy, Evarts. Ky	115
Lincoln School. Meridian, Miss	320
Girls' Industrial School, Moorhead, Miss	106
Mound Bayou, Miss	87=43

Common Schools .... =30

The American Missionary Association has stood firmly from the first for unlimited opportunity in education. It was a pioneer in industrial training and at the same time it has refused to abandon higher education.

"Too much emphasis cannot be laid on the work of our higher institutions, including the normal schools, which contain over 1,500 pupils. We believe in the higher education for those who show ability and aptitude. This is the most important part of the work of this Association. We utterly protest against the position that primary studies and industrial work are all that should be taught the Negro. This Association must not swerve from its object; better facilities and more advanced courses of study should be the aim. An examination of the courses of study in a large number of the educational institutions of the American

Missionary Association shows that many of them are abreast of our best Northern schools in modern methods."

31. Summary of Negro Churches 1900-1903. Dr. H. K. Carroll reports the following membership of Negro church bodies in the United States, not including foreign mission membership, for the year 1903:

DENOMINATIONS.	Ministers.	Churches.	Communicants.
Baptists.....................................	10,729	15,614	1,625,330
Union American Methodists............	180	205	16,500
African Methodists................	6,500	5,800	785,000
African Union Methodist Protestants..	68	68	2,930
African Zion Methodists.................	3,386	3,042	551,591
Congregational Methodists	5	5	319
Colored Methodists...	2,159	1,497	207,723
Cumberland Presbyterians	450	400	39,000
Total	23,477	26,631	3,228,393

To these may be added the following figures as already given :

DENOMINATIONS.	Ministers.	Churches.	Membership.
Methodists (Methodist Episcopal)........	....	....	245,954
Congregationalists.........................	139	230	12,155
Episcopalians..............................	85	200	15,000
Presbyterians *..............................	209	353	21,341
Catholics.................	....	....	....

* Not including twenty-four Northern colored churches.

This would make an approximate total of 3,522,843 communicants in Negro churches not including colored members of white congregations.· The study of the different sects brings out striking facts.

1. *Early tendencies toward race segregation.*

This is shown in the history of the secessions from Methodism. It had the advantage of showing the capabilities of the race, but the disadvantage of separating friends, helpers and co-religionists.

2. *Later tendencies toward race co-operation.*

This has taken several forms. Among the Baptists there has been simple co-operation among independent churches. Some friction has arisen : the white Baptist mission societies have failed to understand the Negro desire for home rule and autonomy, and the Negro recipients have not fully appreciated the help they have received from without; the Episcopalians have insisted on treating the Negroes as wards under age, while the Presbyterians have made them a department in the church.

3. *The failure of mere charity.*

Nothing is more striking or hopeful for the Negroes than the manifest fact that mere charity or patronage, however bountiful, has not satisfied them. The richest church has nearly the smallest Negro membership, not because it does not give to them, but because it does not treat them as equals. The church with the largest Negro membership is confronted by the strange fact that its black members have actually refused its alms, while the Methodist Episcopal Church has a hard time to keep its colored membership from secession despite pecuniary advantages.

4. *Negro ability to organize and control.*

Can Negroes rule? The experience of Hayti is not encouraging, but the experience of the African churches in America is pretty emphatic proof of the affirmative. What causes the difference? The African church is the oldest Negro organization, dating in part from Africa itself, and here Negroes have had the most liberty and experience. Political experience, on the other hand, they almost entirely lacked, and instead of teachers they had hindrances and detraction.

In fact, we have in the history of Negro churches one of the most important examples of the meaning and working of Social Heredity as distinguished from Physical Heredity that the modern world affords.

32. Negro Laymen and the Church. Some 200 Negro laymen of average intelligence, in all parts of the country, were asked a schedule of questions and answered as follows. The states represented are Georgia, Alabama, Florida, Louisiana, Mississippi, Texas, North Carolina, South Carolina, Virginia, Kentucky, Tennessee, Arkansas, Colorado, Illinois and Pennsylvania. The answers of a few ministers are included:

So far as you have observed what is the present condition of our churches in your community?

Very good	23
Good	49
Progressing, improving, prosperous	16
Heavy financial burdens hindering spiritual conditions	9
Fair financially; more spiritually; more intelligent	3
Not so well attended as formerly, but attendants more devoted	2
Good, bad and indifferent	6
Fair, with vast room for improvement	13
Well attended, but mostly in financial straights	12
Poor, bad; not what they should be	12
Here and there a sign of improvement	1
Too much involved with financial efforts	5
Lack of piety and true missionary spirit; need of earnest preachers.	2
At a standstill spirtually; not influential enough among the young.	2
As far as general improvement is concerned, would say, Congregationalists, the Methodists, then Baptists	1
Retrograding spiritually	4
Can't say, don't know; not answered	5

Is their influence, on the whole, toward pure, honest, upright living on the part of the members?

Yes 71
To a very large extent.... 13
To some extent 17
Room for improvement.. 5
Not so on account of preacher...................................... 1
Belief and doctrine advocated too much to have influence for good,
    upright living.. 1
Purport simply to bear good influence over the people.............. 1
Not sufficient emphasis laid on Christian living................... 2
Influence good, but members do not live as they should............ 2
Cannot say positively yes, though there are exceptions............. 3
No 17
Generally so; much advancement 6
Not answered 5

Are the ministers usually good men? If not, what are their chief faults? Cite some specific cases, with or without names:

Yes 37
Generally good men.. 10
Majority good; some exceptions. Faults: Intemperance, dishones-
    ty, careless living, selfish ambition, sexual impurity............ 31
Some good, some bad 9
Some good, majority bad... 4
Few good, majority bad.. 3
Not intelligent.... 6
Fairly good... 3
Chief faults: Selfishness and dogmatism 4
Fault of some: Immorality.. 8
Fault of some: Deceptiveness 1
Fault of some: Too great love for money......................... 3
Moral status low.. 1
Faults: Lack of earnestness, sexual impurity, intemperance, love
    of worldly things... 6
Proportion of good ones is increasing.... 2
Fault of some: Bigamy... 1
Only a few whom I have not heard rumors about.... 1
Appear good, but do not know how to influence the young.......... 1
"No better than they ought to be"................................. 2
Some good, but among others the chief faults are sexual impurity,
    improper attention to women, and selfishness.................... 4
No, not generally so.. 6
Miscellaneous... 7
Unanswered.. 5

Of the ministers whom you know, how many are notoriously immoral? What direction does their immorality take: sexual impurity, dishonesty in money matters, drunkenness, or what? Cite some particular instances, with or without names:

None immoral; all good men 28
Very few immoral.. 2
Some few are not what they should be; do not come up to the true
    standard 4

One or more are lax in financial matters........................... 8
Some few are sexually impure and dishonest in money matters; ma-
    jority good.. 12
Intemperate.. 3
Some intemperate; some cannot be trusted in money matters...... 1
Chief faults of some: Sexual impurity and intemperance........... 8
Chief fault: Sexual impurity.................................... 12
Many guilty of all... 6
Not answered.. 17

Some of the answers are :

Alabama

I can name a few who are said to be immoral, but cannot say from personal knowledge that they are notoriously immoral.—*Girard.*

I believe we have some ministers who are guilty of every fault named in question four, but I think that one of their worst habits is in their tearing down good church buildings; and in their rebuilding they don't seem to have any care for the strain they place upon their members.—*Mobile.*

I think proselyting and exaggerating minor doctrinal differences a real hindrance. Also the loose methods in vogue of conducting church finances—both in collecting and expending—a serious drawback.—*Mobile.*

Two at present in the city. I know others, but they are not preaching here now. Sexual impurity. They are the only ones in the city with the degree of D. D.—one a Methodist, the other Baptist. They both ruined the good names of two young women.—*Mobile.*

Colorado

I know some 500 ministers. Of that number probably about 100 are immoral; 10 per cent. of the 100 are sexually immoral, 20 per cent. dishonest, 70 per cent. drink.—*Colorado Springs.*

Florida

I know of no minister who is notoriously immoral. Yet occasionally there comes a little confusion in the churches here because when money is collected for one purpose, through the minister's influence it is used for another. Such actions always do cause church fusses which last for some time.—*Gainesville.*

I know of five around this city who are grossly immoral. Their immorality takes these directions: intemperance, sexual immorality, and dishonesty in money matters. Two cases of gross immorality came to light recently on two preachers. One preacher has recently been dropped for dishonesty in money matters.—*Jacksonville.*

Georgia

I cannot say how many; perhaps twenty. Women and unfair dealings in money matters. I have known comparatively few who drink, and still fewer who drink to excess.—*Atlanta.*

About one-tenth of all the ministers in that community (Perry, Ga..) are notoriously immoral, especially in the direction of sexual impurity, dishonesty and drunkenness.—*Atlanta.*

One of the most common and general faults against preachers is their failure to pay promptly financial obligations. I know a few who are said to be guilty of sexual impurity, some others who get drunk.—*Atlanta.*

I regret that I know some ministers who are immoral and they are publicly known to be immoral, but they manage to hold congregations and preach (?) to them.—*Augusta.*

The doubtful three might be classified as follows: Two for sexual impurity, one for general looseness, insincerity, questionable methods, etc.—*Augusta.*

I know ten and could name more if I would strain my memory who are notoriously immoral. Some of these are sexual impurity, dishonesty in money matters and drunkenness. I have seen this on the streets of Albany. I have not seen any preacher drunk on the streets here in Brunswick.—*Brunswick.*

By common report, yes. Sexual impurity, dishonesty in money matters lead in order given. I know ministers who drink, but they never to my knowledge become intoxicated.—*College.*

I could name as many as ten who drink whiskey and are untruthful. Many are dishonest in money matters. There is a preacher near my home who is a downright drunkard. He first led his members astray by indulging them in this evil habit, so that now it is a corrupt church.—*Jewells.*

About one-third of them are either sexually impure (these being perhaps in the majority), dishonest in money matters and [given to] drunkenness. These are distributed equally.—*Macon.*

I do not know many who are grossly immoral. I have in mind three, two of whom are sexually impure; the other a drunkard, thief, and he was also sexually impure. They say all Baptist preachers in the country drink.—*Newnan.*

Six: (1) three are dishonest in money matters, and are liars; (2) three, whose immorality seems to take almost every direction. I would add that nearly all of the ministers of my acquaintance in the rural districts are distrusted more or less from a moral standpoint.—*Powelton.*

I know several who do not even try to conceal their habits of drink and sexual impurity, as well as being dishonest in money matters.—*Savannah.*

Mississippi

About 10 per cent. are notoriously immoral; about 2 per cent. are sexually impure, 2 per cent. dishonest in money matters, and about 6 per cent. are liquor drinkers to a very great extent.—*Coffeeville.*

In a radius of five miles of us there are twelve ministers. Five are exceedingly immoral in sexual impurity and drunkenness.— *Westside.*

North Carolina

Confining my answer to this community and to the present time, I know only one man of bad report. He is charged with stealing church funds.—*Charlotte.*

Comparatively few. The Central North Carolina Conference is the largest one that I have—about 100 pastors. During the last ten years we have had an average of not more than one case a year, about equally divided between sexual impurity, drunkenness, and dishonesty in money matters.—*Fayetteville.*

South Carolina

About 10 per cent. are notoriously immoral. Immorality takes to sexual impurity, drunkenness, and dishonesty in money matters.—*Hartsville.*

Tennessee

Three or four. Their immorality takes all these directions.—*Memphis.*

They drink a great deal, but do not get drunk.—*Memphis.*

Texas

Fifteen notoriously immoral : nine sexually impure, four are drunkards, and two are dishonest in money matters.—*Dallas.*

There are but few notoriously immoral. Some are sexually impure, some dishonest in money matters, still fewer drunkards. The great deficiency in the minister's estimated salary causes failure upon their part to meet honest obligations, which places them in an awkward shape.—*Littig.*

About one-fifth. The greatest number belong to the class of sexually impure ; a few dishonest in money matters, and there are a few drunkards.—*Paris.*

Virginia

To the first, I say not one. While our ministers do not preach temperance as they should, yet I never heard of one being drunk.—*Frederick's Hall.*

Two of whom I know are immoral. One is not an active minister, but a kind of missionary secretary in North Carolina. The other one was in our community, but is now in Kentucky, in jail, I am informed.—*Lynchburg.*

I know a large number of ministers in this and other states. One out of every four I would regard as being morally bad. In the order named, I would say that sexual impurity holds the first place, drunkenness the next, and money matters third.—*Petersburg.*

None. Some are not careful in the use of other people's money. Some abhor total abstainence and even temperance, while some others are by no means trustworthy.—*Richmond.*

Four: Sexual impurity, 2; dishonesty in regard to money, 1; drunkenness, 1. One was excluded for over-exaction of money in connection with his mother-in-law.—*Rappahannock.*

Is the Sunday-school effective in teaching good manners and sound morals ?

Yes, it is effective 66
Fairly so. To some extent partially so............................ 29
Not as effective as it should be ; vast room for improvement........ 11
The teaching is tending more and more in that direction........... 9
These ends are sought for... 5
Not generally in manners, but they teach effectively sound morals.. 1
The Sunday-schools are doing a good work ; greatest hindrance
   lack of attendance... 1
To some extent ; depends greatly on the home training............ 2
Where we have teachers and preachers of this stamp they are...... 1
In part at least too many fail, but on the whole much good is done. 1
Sunday-school not so effective, but does much good............... 2
My own exceptionally good in this. Can not speak definitely of
   others. I think they are good................................. 2
Depends on teachers and officials................................. 2
These subjects generally neglected................................ 2
Cannot say definitely... 3
No ; it is not.. 17

Some answers were :

I fear that it is not. I think its ineffectiveness, however, is due to the lack of these in the home more than to the teaching. The hour, or hour and a half, out of 168 does not do effectively what the 167 or 166½ hours have failed to do, or undo what they have done.—*Houston, Tex.*

Most Sunday-schools in the West are merely playing at teaching. They lack purpose and thoroughness, interest and soundness.—*Denver, Col.*

It is not generally used for that purpose, but to instil sectarian animosity There are, however, some blessed exceptions.—*Jackson, Miss.*

With but one exception, the Sunday-schools do not take up questions of morals and manners.—*Troy, N. C.*

Real good manners, an almost obsolete term. Children are catching the spirit of the age. Some schools seem effective towards good manners and good morals.—*Atlanta, Ga.*

Do the churches you are acquainted with do much charitable and reformatory work among the poor in slums and jails or elsewhere ? Cite instances.

Yes, some are quite active	11
They aid the sick and the poor	17
To a certain extent. Fairly well	10
Not very much	29
Only one church here can claim any share in the charitable work of the community	17
They help the poor	2
They are attentive to the sick, and this is about as far as it goes	8
Not generally, but the number engaged in such work is constantly increasing	1
As much as they can according to their intelligence and ability	1
No, they do not	40
Do not know; cannot say definitely	3
Unanswered	4

Some answers follow:

Some of them do creditable work along this line. One pastor preaches in a tobacco factory every Saturday.—*Richmond, Va.*

Yes. First Congregational Church, poor-house and jail; Episcopal Church, Orphan's Home.—*Memphis, Tenn.*

Until the meeting of the "Young People's Congress" very little of such work was accomplished, but a goodly number are now actively engaged in such work.—*Memphis, Tenn.*

Yes. When we consider their small means, I think it can fairly be said that they do, in various ways, a large part of the charitable work. Aside from taking contributions, from time to time, for what is usually called missionary work, the churches, as a whole or body, are not doing much, I think, but individual members of churches are doing much individual charitable work in various ways. They feed, clothe, warm and pay house rent for the needy. Twelve persons paid a girl's expenses at Fisk University last year, or half of that expense. The Negro's charity, for the present, consists more in his doing for the needy than it does in his giving.—*Chattanooga, Tenn.*

They have no systematized methods nor regular general organizations for this kind of work. Pastors and individual churches, however, take up such work. We have a Home for Aged Women and an Orphan's Home which we support.—*Allegheny City, Pa.*

There is an Old Folk's Home supported by the Methodist Episcopal Churches, and another supported by the Baptist Churches. I know individuals who do prison work.—*New Orleans, La.*

We have a notable instance in a Baptist colored clergyman, who for twenty years has solicited and distributed some $500 or more in the interests of a Thanksgiving dinner for the white and colored poor in jails and asylums, and has funds left to repeat for both Christmas and New Year's dinners. Funds are given mostly by the whites, if not wholly—a marked instance of general confidence.— *Mobile, Ala.*

In one church a day nursery, a kindergarten, a gymnasium, a kitchen garden, and reading room for boys are carried on with more or less persistence and success. In another church there is a kindergarten.—*Chicago, Ill.*

Do the young people join the church and support it?

Yes; they do	48
The young join, but do not do much supporting; chief support from the older members	28
Usually. In the majority of cases they do	3
Some do, others do not	4
Many young people help to support. Many recently joined	2
Depends on the church and the minister. Some churches have large numbers of them	1
Many join, but few remain in the church. The support is meagre	1
About one-fourth	1
Only a few young members, but they support as best they can	1
Very few, a small proportion. Majority of them do not	2
They do not support the church	1
Not as much as they did a few years ago	1
To some degree. To a limited extent	4
The accessions from among the young people are increasing rapidly	1
The young are too much bent on pleasure	3
No; they do not	2
Unanswered	4

Some answers are:

The great masses who come into the church are young people. They make the best members, all things considered.—*Richmond, Va.*

I think the young people need to be disciplined a great deal along that line.— *Richmond, Va.*

They do to a degree commensurate with their home training.—*Lynchburg, Va.*

They are being trained toward supporting churches and schools.—*Bowling Green, Va.*

Not as I would wish, but more than is generally thought. About two-thirds of the girls and boys who come to our school are members of churches and support the church in a fairly good manner.—*Austin, Tex.*

Many of them join the churches and make big promises but, as a rule, do but little. Some will pray, but won't pay; others will pay, but won't pray; a large number won't pay nor pray, and a blessed few who both pray and pay.—*Chatta-nooga, Tenn.*

They join during revivals and leave at the close. They contribute often because they like to go up to the table. If this were stopped our churches would suffer financially.—*Darlington, S. C.*

The young people when they have attained the ages of fifteen or twenty join the church, but as to supporting the church, I think those of the less aristocratic churches do more in the line of support for the church. In the aristocratic churches the older folks support the church.—*Charleston, S. C.*

They delight in Sunday-school, Christian Endeavor, Young People's Union and church work. Are enthusiastic over it. The churches are largely made up of young people.—*Allegheny City, Pa.*

Fairly well, but they are hindered by the old members and often caused to become discouraged and indifferent by the actions of the leaders and influential members.—*High Point, N. C.*

Not generally among the men; more among the women. Church-going has degenerated into a fashion.—*Jackson, Miss.*

In those churches where the organization and training have been carefully done they do. In others I fear they do not systematically nor to the proper extent.—*Augusta, Ga.*

Not to the desired end, but there is being more and more thought and said concerning this very important duty.—*Atlanta, Ga.*

What is the greatest need of our churches ?

An earnest, consecrated, educated, wide-awake, intelligent ministry	24
An educated, well-trained Christian ministry	25
A good, pure ministry	6
True conversion, practical religion, true Christianity	4
Honest, upright leaders, both preachers and officers	9
Earnest, educated, consecrated Christian workers	5
Consecrated ministers and faithful members	5
More money and better preachers	5
The spirit of Christ and the Holy Ghost	2
Finance	3
Unity and practical Christian living	1
Do not know	1

Some answers are :

I think there is need of improvement in intellect and in a financial way.—*Vincent, Ark.*

A practical knowledge of right and wrong.—*Mobile, Ala.*

Regard for spiritual ideals.—*Mobile, Ala.*

A more perfect knowledge of the requirement of Jesus upon his followers.—*Colorado Springs, Col.*

Downright seriousness and actual missionary spirit and efforts.—*Denver, Col.*

High-toned Christian ministers in the pulpits and teachers of the same kind in Sunday-schools.—*Atlanta, Ga.*

Able and pure men as pastors and a warm oratory to reach and hold the masses.—*Atlanta, Ga.*

I should say more spiritual life. This lack is very general in our churches of to-day.—*Atlanta, Ga.*

First of all, better men in the ministry. It would follow that the members would be better.—*Augusta, Ga.*

They need so many things it is hard to say dogmatically what is the greatest need.—*Augusta, Ga.*

The greatest need is to live up to what we preach. Do away with so much emotion and do practical work. "If ye love me keep my commandments."—*Brunswick, Ga.*

1. Properly trained ministers. 2. Upright, cultured and Christian officers who possess business knowledge. 3. Bibles for congregational reading. 4. Song books for congregational singing.—*Macon, Ga.*

Decidedly, an educated ministry and a higher standard of morality.—*Rome, Ga.*

1. Pure ministry. 2. Less costly edifices. 3. More charitable work. 4. Practical sermons, i. e., how to live, etc.—*Savannah, Ga.*

Thoughtful workers.—*Thomasville, Ga.*

Moral ministers who are able to chastise immorality.—*Princeton, Ky.*

1. The Holy Spirit's power. 2. Clean, heroic, unselfish pastors who love God, righteousness and souls. 3. Deacons who fill the scripture standard. 4. Members who fear God because they are really new creatures in Christ.—*Jackson, Miss.*

The continued emphasizing of intelligent worship, spirituality instead of formality, and efforts to keep them from substituting respectability and high social forms for Christian piety.—*Allegheny City, Pa.*

Good preachers, who read, study, and can apply what they read. Thinkers who will make the churches attractive. Church boards composed of those who are not afraid to hold their preacher to a certain standard or get rid of him.—*Darlington, S. C.*

Less emphasis on financial matters and more practical preaching as to economy in living and home-getting.—*Florence, S. C.*

A broad, able and educated ministry, capable of entertaining the congregation, from the most illiterate to the most scholarly, with practical, common-sense doctrine.—*Houston, Tex.*

Punctuality, business sense, stability, devotion, ideals and tact, a faithful, a well-enlightened, and a religious pew.—*Littig, Tex.*

Men of high intellectual, moral and religious standings.—*Paris, Tex.*

A pure ministry rather than an educated one. Spirituality. The abolition of questionable methods of raising money, such as festivals, entertainments, excursions, etc.—*Paris, Tex.*

A large membership of solid, sensible, exemplary men, who will take a lively interest in the religious life of the church as well as its business matters.—*Prairie View, Tex.*

More liberal support on the part of the church members.—*Achilles, Va.*

Money to support pastors, and the Holy Spirit to enlighten the inner man.—*Bowling Green, Va.*

Better learned ministers and punctuality.—*Chula Depot, Va.*

Possibly education.—*Frederick's Hall, Va.*

I am of the opinion that the greatest need is morally and intellectually trained leaders, especially pastors; and when I say "morally and intellectually," I mean all that those terms can imply in the highest institutions of learning and under the best influence. Nothing that is really good for a white person is too good for a Negro. I am of the opinion that when this is recognized and the Negroes have leaders accordingly, we shall be a long distance on the way to the solution of the so-called "problem."—*Richmond, Va.*

Co-operation and sympathy with each other. This would make the work more effective and extend it more widely among the people.—*New Orleans, La.*

Are the standards of morality in your community being raised or lowered in respect to sexual morals, home-life, honesty, etc.?

They are being raised	81
They are being raised gradually	8
Raised to some extent, yet room for improvement	14
Lowered in respect to sexual morals; raised as to the other qualities	7
Cannot speak encouragingly on this line	8
The standards are being lowered	14
Do not believe they are	2
Cannot say	7
Unanswered	9

Some answers follow:

I think the standard is being raised, which is due mainly to increase in good schools.—*Augusta, Ga.*

There is less intemperance in the new-made homes than formerly existed in the old homes. This is largely the work of the school teacher.—*Augusta, Ga.*

To this question I must sadly admit it is not what it was twenty-five years ago.—*Brunswick, Ga.*

It is being raised. Young men and women coming from our colleges are marrying and are setting the standard in their communities for higher moral living. Their home life and honest dealing in the community are helpful, and are being diffused in all the homes to some degree.—*Brunswick, Ga.*

We have several homes that are models of purity and good morals.—*La Grange, Ga.*

There is some effort being made toward a higher standard which, if supported and encouraged, will result in much good in that direction.—*Rome, Ga.*

The church has influence on its members and they all live uprightly.—*Princeton, Ky.*

A good condition generally obtains in the churches, and where suspicion rests the parties are made to feel uncomfortable owing to the popular sentiment.—*Allegheny, Pa.*

As to the lower classes I do not know, but the educated few are being raised. Charleston is not as great an educational center as it ought to be and for this reason, I think, for the masses it is not doing as much in respect to sexual morals and home life as it might.—*Charleston, S. C.*

It is being raised. The church and the schools are the levers.—*Hartsville, S. C.*

The very best sign we have of the Negro's substantial progress is his rapidly increasing respect for the marriage vow, and the many living, beautiful, happy illustrations of his determination to keep that vow. There are hundreds and thousands of pure homes and beautiful, well-ordered families among us now, whereas, thirty-five years ago there were but few.—*Chattanooga, Tenn.*

Yes, positively. An able, eloquent minister was forced to leave one of our churches here recently because there were "rumors" and a "belief" that he was immoral.—*Austin, Tex.*

Yes, I think so—perhaps more through the influence of the schools than otherwise.—*Prairie View, Tex.*

Under conditions our people compare favorably with any other people.—*Petersburg, Va.*

33. Southern Whites and the Negro Church. The difficulty of getting valuable expressions on the Negro churches from Southern white people is that so few of them know anything about these churches. No human beings live further apart than separate social classes, especially when lines of race and color and historic antipathies intervene. Few white people visit Negro churches and those who do go usually for curiosity or "fun," and consequently seek only certain types. The endeavor was made in this case, however, to get the opinion of white people whose business relations or sympathies have brought them into actual contact with these churches. A few of the names in this list are of Northern people, but the great majority are white Southerners. The circular sent out was as follows:

Your name has been handed to us as that of a person interested in the Negroes of your community and having some knowledge of their churches. We are making a study of Negro churches and would particularly like to have your opinion on the following matters:

1. What is the present condition of the Negro churches in your community?
2. Is their influence, on the whole, toward pure, honest life?
3. Are the Negro ministers in your community good men?
4. Are the standards of Negro morality being raised?

We would esteem it a great favor if you would give us your opinion on these points.

Some of the answers follow :

J. M. Wilkinson, President Valdosta Southern Railway Company, Valdosta, Ga. :

1. In fair condition.
2. Good.
3. Most are.
4. Yes, I think so.

Alfred D. Mason, Memphis, Tenn. :

1. Good. I believe they are doing good, faithful work.
2. Yes.

3. Yes, all that I know are.
4. Yes, I am quite sure they are.

W. W. Dexter, Houston, Tex., publisher :

1. Very good.
2. Yes, among better class; but the greater influence is "fear of the law."
3. Many good ones; but as a class are of questionable repute.
4. Yes, possibly, on the whole.

W. T. Jordan, Colorado :

1. Fair. They average with the white churches.
2. Yes.
3. So far as I know.
4. Yes.

Rev. J. E. Ford, pastor of Zion Baptist Church, is president of the Denver Baptist Ministers' Conference, and is a first-class pastor, preacher and manager. Rev. Mr. Peck of the Methodist Episcopal Church is another minister of the same type. The Negro churches in the whole state are doing fully as well as the white churches, and many of them a great deal better.

Rev. J. M. Filcher, Corresponding Secretary Baptist General Association of Virginia, Petersburg, Va. :

1. Excellent.
2. Yes.
3. Yes.
4. No.

R. A. Morris, Austin, Tex. :

1. Fair.
2. In part.
3. Some are.
4. Not much.

The most of them voted the anti-(Prohibitionist?) ticket which, I think, is bad.

P. W. Meldrim, Savannah, Ga. :

I answer all of the foregoing questions in the affirmative, so far as a general answer may be given. To the first question I beg to say that it is too vague to enable me to reply.

James B. Gregg, minister First Congregational Church, Colorado Springs, Col. :

1. Very fair.
2. Yes.
3. Yes.
4. I can't say very definitely. There has been of late years an influx of Negroes into our town and there are more signs of immorality among them than when that population was small. But the ministers are decidedly above the earlier ministers of that race here and that, I should say, indicates a higher tone in the Negro churches, if not in the Negro population, as a whole.

R. B. Smith, County School Commissioner of Greene County, Woodville, Ga. :

1. Not good.
2. No.

3. No.
4. No.

I have given you my candid opinion of such churches and ministers that I know. There are some exceptions to the above. 1. There is a Presbyterian Church in Greensboro that has an intelligent pastor who is a good, true man. 2. I also think that the Methodist Church of same place is also doing pretty good work. A large portion of the ministers are ignorant and in some instances are bad men. I am truly sorry to have to write the above, but it is too true.

W. J. Groom, Princeton, Ky. :

1. Very slow, if any advancement.
2. No.
3. Very few.
4. No.

I regret to say, in my opinion, the Negro race has not advanced religiously, morally or financially. They have some few commendable ministers, but the majority are immoral and dishonest.

J. H. Icosh, Nashville, Tenn. :

1. They are making advancement, slowly but surely.
2. I think so.
3. So far as I know.
4. Yes.

It is not easy to give satisfactory answers to such questions without going into detail. I have answered, as seems to me, in accordance with the facts in the case. But information given in this way is not sufficient to furnish a basis for an intelligent view. Am glad to work in any way to help the Negro brothers.

James C. Stanley, Houston, Tex. :

1. Upward tendency for education, morality, and mutual advancement on American protective lines.
2. ———.
3. All I know, yes.
4. Considerably.

I have lived and been in newspaper business here for thirteen years. I have attached my answers to your questions above as to impressions made by experience. The memberships of churches are larger, the number of churches more; the schools are having greater attendance and teachers are of higher education and practical plane than when I first came here. There are 100 to one in business also. The careless pull all to a common level in race prejudice. I know of none seeking social equality, but many educational and legal and property rights equality.

J. H. Kilpatrick, White Plains, Ga. :

1. Lack of discipline and not harmonious.
2. I think so.
3. Some are and some are not.
4. I think not. I see no decisive evidence of it.

Geo. Wm. Walker, President Paine College, Augusta, Ga. :

1. A healthy spiritual condition.
2. Yes.

3. Yes.
4. Yes.

Prof. Burnell, Emerson Institute, Mobile, Ala.:
1. Improving, as I believe.
2. Yes.
3. The majority are; many notably so.
4. Yes.

Geo. Standing, South Atlanta, Ga.:
1. Their influence is, on the whole, good.
2. The ministers are good men.
3. The morality of the people generally is very good.

Wm. N. Sheats, State Superintendent Public Instruction, Tallahassee, Fla.:
1. Buildings fair, some good, some neglected and some poor. The proportion of really pious members is about on average of white churches.
2. Certainly, but like other churches, the black sheep are too numerous.
3. Some are, and some are the greatest drawback to real piety and the spread of the gospel.
4. Yes, I think so, but entirely too slow for their good and the good of all.

John D. Jordan, Pastor First Baptist Church, Savannah, Ga.:
1. Medium to good.
2. Yes.
3. Most of them; I really know no exceptions.
4. I think so.
I take pleasure in sending favorable answers to all your questions. I wish well for our Brother in Black.

J. Reese Blair, Troy, N. C.:
1. They are on the upgrade, but in need of better leaders.
2. Good.
3. Some not what they should be.
4. I think so.
In this county I consider the Negroes very much improved in the work of their teachers and churches.

J. W. Newman, Pastor Methodist Episcopal Church, South, Talladega, Ala.:
1. Fairly good.
2. Yes.
3. Generally.
4. Yes.

T. C. Moody, Marion, S. C.:
1. Good.
2. Yes.
3. Yes.
4. Very much.
I hope the above answers will satisfy you, as they are the true condition of the churches here. The Negro race is improving in every way.

J. W. Kein, Richmond, Va.:

1. Good and membership increasing.
2. Yes.
3. They are.
4. Yes.

W. L. Tillman, Columbus, Ga.:

1. They bring about idleness among the Negroes.
2. No.
3. Some may be.
4. No, getting worse.

In many churches are too many so-called preachers. They demoralize the Negroes and keep them from regular work by their constant preaching night and day, and require them to give up the last coin they have. Some of the preachers are very good, but a large portion of them are bad men. The Negroes morally are growing worse.

W. G. Bradshaw, High Point, N. C.:

1. Fairly good.
2. Yes.
3. Yes.
4. Doubtful.

E. H. Leidy, Memphis, Tenn.:

1. Good.
2. Yes.
3. Yes.
4. Yes.

On the whole, I think our Negroes will compare with those of any section in this country.

J. M. Collman, County School Commissioner, Putnam, Ga.:

1. There are too many—about three churches to one school. Buildings generally poor; creeds bitter against each other. Some churches established seemingly by local authority for "revenue only," the wandering priest dropping in and preaching and then a collection.
2. Not as a whole, but in part.
3. Some are, numbers are not.
4. Yes, but much too slow.

In my opinion, here, where the teachers are selected by the County Board of Education, they are doing more for the race than the preachers. They are far better educated and, as a whole, better men and women.

Sam Smitherman, Troy, N. C.:

1. They are, as a whole, bad.
2. No.
3. No.
4. No.

We have one good, honest and reliable Negro preacher in our community, and he is trying to raise the standard of living among his race. But he has an up-hill business to do so. The old Negroes, as a whole, are a long ways better than the young ones. The Negro preacher that I refer to is O. Faduma. Everyone that is acquainted with the Negro race knows that a Negro is better off without an education than he is with one, for when he has an education he begins then to want to do some mischief. He will either go to preaching or stealing or both. Of course there are some better than others.

John N. Rogers, Professor of Agriculture, Dahlonega, Ga.:

A large majority of the church buildings have been much improved in the past five or six years.

The good sufficiently dominates to warrant their encouragement. The majority are good men and exert an elevating influence on the people among whom they labor. A few are a disgrace to the church and to their race.

In answer to question No. 4, I would say that there is quite a noticeable improvement among the females, but among the males, young and old, there is quite a lack of regard for a high standard of virtue, either among themselves or for the opposite sex with whom they associate. The average colored man does not regard it as anything against him to be seen in company with the lowest woman of his acquaintance. In my seven years experience as school superintendent of the county, I had only two complaints of immorality of female teachers. I had four or five of male teachers.

The lowest state of morals is found on the large plantations where the houses throw the families in as close contact as is usually the case in cities. The greatest improvement is noted in families living on small farms (either rented or owned by them) where only one or two families live in close contact.

J. G. Collinsworth, Eatonton, Ga.:

I do not believe any race with the same environments could have made more progress since their emancipation. They deserve great credit for what they have accomplished, intellectually and educationally. They have two churches in Eatonton that are good buildings and in fair repair. These churches have marvelous influence for good. It is characteristic of the Negro to be scrupulous concerning his church vows. Their ministers, from external appearances, are capable, God-fearing, consecrated men.

J. J. Lawless, Richmond, Va.:

We have in our town two colored churches and they are fairly well supported by their members. They are gaining in numbers and getting stronger financially from year to year. They have in them some members whose lives are such as to impress outsiders with the sincerity of their Christian professions, but unfortunately they allow members to remain in their churches who ought to be turned out, and thus cause reproach to fall upon the whole body.

My opinion is that both of the Negro ministers in our town are good men.

The President of the City National Bank, Austin, Tex.:

I have deliberately delayed answering until now that I might more fully prepare myself to answer intelligently the several questions you ask me in your said favor of March 19th. What I write is principally the result of my own observation and reflection, but partly after conference with several intelligent colored and white men, in whose judgment and candor I have confidence. I will answer your questions in the order in which they are asked.

"1. What is the present condition of the Negro churches in your community?" To this I answer, in the main the church buildings of this community are in every way reputable. They are principally rock or brick buildings, of good architecture, and neatly, comfortably and tastily finished and furnished. As to the membership in the main it is clean and self-respecting. Most of the colored churches here are either out of debt or are paying their debts with reasonable promptness. Some of the colored churches are in debt and poorly administered, but as a rule the membership and physical condition and supervision of the Negro churches are good.

"2. Is their influence, on the whole, towards pure, honest life?" In answer to this question I will say that, on the whole, their influence is decidedly towards pure and honest life.

"3. Are the Negro ministers in your community good men?" To this I will say that, in the main, they are, but some of them are very sorry men. They are deadbeats, and have no regard for their word nor for their obligations, and they are low in their moral instincts and acts. They have neither regard for truth nor honesty. They are particularly unscrupulous in politics. But speaking of this community, I sincerely believe that this character of colored preachers is decreasing. They are greatly better men, and more intelligent men than they were ten or twenty years ago. Speaking of this community, again, I should say that the unworthy colored ministers are rather the exception than the rule, and I think I know what I am talking about.

"4. Are the standards of Negro morality being raised?" To this I will say that, in my opinion, they certainly are. I think there is a higher standard of morality amongst colored men as well as colored women.

A Real Estate Agent, Florence, S. C. :

The Methodist Episcopal Church, North, and the Baptist Church: these churches were well attended, and one reason was that the ministers were their political leaders. Of late years a good many men who have learned to read and write have been going about preaching, some I know of no character. The consequence has been that many new congregations have been started, and although not large, the tendency has been to do more harm than good. These Negro ministers (so-called) are too lazy to work, and make their money in an easy way, principally from the most ignorant Negro women. At present, I think the Negro ministers at the established Methodist Episcopal Church, North, the African Methodist Episcopal Church and Baptist Church are very good men; have not heard anything against their characters. But my opinion is that for real religious training of the Negro the Episcopal Church and Roman Catholic Church would be the best for the Negro, the first named from the example and training, and the latter the confession they would have to make to the priest—the latter more from fear. My opinion, again, is that the Negroes are more immoral, as they read and know what has been done and is being done by the immoral, unreligious white men of the country, and I believe that the example set by the white men of low character has been the greatest cause for the immorality of the Negro. Take for example that crime of rape. I don't know of a section where the whites are refined, nice people and treat the Negroes nicely, but let them know their places, where such an attempt has occurred. How can you expect the Negro women to be virtuous when the white men will continue to have intercourse with them? How can you blame the Negroes for committing murder when the example is set them by the white man?

We must face the truth. If any dirty work is to be done a white man hires a Negro to do it for him. If a member of a church does not wish to be seen going to buy whisky he sends a Negro. If these are facts, what an example to set to an inferior race! And they are facts and a shame on our white race. It seems to me that the Negroes are more immoral here than they used to be and the fault is due mostly to the example set them by the white men.

A. C. Kaufman, Charleston, S. C.:

1. There are a number of Negro churches in Charleston that are prospering. The great trouble, I apprehend, is in the multiplicity of churches with the colored as the whites. In my judgment, a church should not be established until there is actual need for it.

2. This is a difficult question for me to answer, but as far as I know their influence is for the betterment of the race.

3. I believe that the Negro ministers here are generally good men. I have no reason to state to the contrary.

4. The standard of Negro morality I am sure is being raised. The young men and women, under proper environments, are being raised along these lines. In the lower strata of society things may be different.

H. M. Willcox, Willcox Hardware Co., Marion, S. C.:

Your letter received. In answer to your questions will state:

1. That the Negro churches are in good condition here.

2. That the moral and religious trend is upward.

·3. That the present colored ministers are above the average in every way, both in relation to intelligence and as to morals. I have had business with them all, and the present incumbents seem to be a very reputable set of men. I will state that several who preceded them in the last ten years cast a moral blight by their lives while here upon their church community.

4. I think we have a very good class of colored people and that from a moral standpoint they are improving.

J. E. Woodcox, High Point, N. C.:

Replying to your favor of 22d, beg to say that the condition of the Negro churches in this community, in my opinion, is improving.

The influence of their churches is much better than formerly, with less sectarianism.

We have some Negro ministers in our town who are splendid, good men.

The standard of morality among the Negroes here is much better than formerly. The fact is, I have often remarked, that High Point is blessed with the best Negro population of any place I have seen in my life. Many of them own their own homes and have some credit and standing in the community.

A. E. Owen, Portsmouth, Va.:

1. The present condition of the Negro churches in this community is fairly good.

2. I do not hesitate to say that the influence of nearly all the Negro churches is toward a purer, honest life. Of course in many instances their teaching is above their practice.

3. The Negro preachers are fairly good men. Sometimes some suspicions rest upon them.

4. I am sure that the standards of morality, especially among the church members, are being raised.

The Negroes are doing well. I think if people who speak and write about Negroes would keep in mind the fact that Negroes *are* Negroes, it would keep them from being led astray. Negroes are religious, and many of them are faithful church members. Negroes should not be compared with the best conditions of the white race. But still the Negroes are improving. They are getting clearer ideas of purity and honesty, and I believe the Negro race, as Negroes, will rise to a higher plane of religion and integrity.

J. R. Peppers, Memphis, Tenn.:

1. The Negro churches in Memphis, so far as the buildings are concerned, are considerably better than five or ten years ago, which shows that more attention is being given to the houses of worship used by them, and their gifts are liberal.

2. My observation is that their influence is toward pure and honest lives and I think the pastors of the churches, as a rule, strive towards this end.

3. So far as I know the ministers in our community are good men. I know of no irregularities at present among them.

4. I think the standards of morality among the Negroes are being raised, though, of course, in no such degree as their friends would be glad to see.

W. H. Banks, Merchant, Hartsboro, Ala.:

In answer to your first question, will say that their houses of worship are not in very good condition. They are manifesting some spirit of improvement in this respect however, and have done what they could to improve their church buildings. The religious life of their churches is not of a high order. They are emotional and demonstrative and, I feel sure, are generally sincere. Many of them are really religious people, but they have standards of their own, and they are low standards. For instance, the average Negro Christian would consider it a grievous sin to play the "fiddle" or dance, but would regard it as a small offense to drink too much whiskey or to cover up a theft committed by some one of his race, or to do many other things that you would regard as grave violations of the moral law.

Question 2. I hope so. Progress in this direction is slow, and the Negro is not wholly to blame. Public sentiment among his own race and among his white neighbors, and the non-enforcement of law against inchastity, are great hindrances to his progress toward pure living. The laws against bigamy, seduction and adultery, are a dead letter so far as the Negro is concerned. The Negroes' religion does act more as a restraint upon them in their business dealings. Many of them pay their debts and meet their financial obligations well. In these respects the Negro has the support and stimulus of law and public sentiment.

Question 3. A few of them are, I think, but many of them I am afraid are not.

Question 4. In some respects I am sure that they are, and in all respects I hope there is some improvement.

Wm. Hayne Leavell, Minister, Houston, Tex.:

I am sorry to have to answer you that since coming to Texas I have not been able to know anything of the Negroes or their churches. Out here they seem to be a very different sort from those among whom I was brought up, and in whom I have always been interested. and by whom always been well received. Here they are altogether to themselves, and I do not think I know personally a solitary Negro minister. It is true I have for ten years been a man busily driven, but the one or two attempts I have made to help the Negroes have not encouraged me to try again. I know only that there are very many church organizations of the various denominations, but of their quality I know nothing.

W. J. Neel, Attorney at Law, Rome, Ga.:

I doubt if I am sufficiently informed on this subject to give you any definite or satisfactory information. It is a matter in which I am interested and I occasionally attend service at Negro churches, but I cannot say that I have information sufficient to meet your inquiry. However, I will undertake to answer the four questions submitted by you in their order.

1. As to the present condition of the Negro churches in Rome: It does not seem to me to be quite satisfactory. It has not been long since there was a serious split in the leading colored Baptist Church of Rome, resulting from differences between the pastor and a majority of his congregation; and within the recent past one of the leading colored Methodist Churches in this city was greatly disturbed on account of the conduct of its pastor, who was charged with misappropriating church funds. It resulted in an indictment and prosecution in the courts. So I cannot think the condition of the Negro churches here is what it should be.

2. To this question I would answer: Yes, but with a mental reservation as to individual instances.

3. For the most part, I believe the Negro ministers in our community are fairly good men but there are exceptions, and the exceptions are rather too numerous to be reassuring. Some of our Negro preachers, especially those of the cheaper sort, are too much inclined to drift into local politics, which seems to be always more or less corrupting and to leave a stain on their good name. A Negro-preacher-politic-hoss is not a very wholesome or helpful citizen in any community. But, happily, I believe his shadow is growing less.

4. To your fourth question, as to the standards of Negro morality, I would answer: Yes and no. In individual instances, I believe Negro men and women are rising in the moral scale and setting their faces firmly and hopefully to better things; but, if I am to be entirely candid, I will be compelled to say that the standards of morality among the Negroes in this section, and especially among the younger generation, do not seem to be rising. I regret to have to admit that the tendency appears to be in the other direction. I wish it were not so. The Negro is in the South, as I believe, to stay, and we of the South are mightily interested in his elevation and betterment as a citizen. He is here either to hinder or to help in the general progress and prosperity of our country, and his progress, up or down, necessarily affects us all.

A White Layman, Cuckoo, Va.:

In most of the churches the membership is very large, but, on a whole, I think they have very little conception of what true religion is. I think a number are trying to lead honest lives, but the majority do not know the meaning of true religion.

I think some of the ministers are by no means what preachers ought to be. I think a few are trying to do the best they can. I have attended the church nearest me occasionally and I regard the pastor as a man of ability and fine character and calculated to do much good. I wish I could say this for them all.

Answer 4. I am afraid not.

Clarence Cusley, Houston, Tex.:

1. The present condition of Negro churches in this state is altogether encouraging, though there is vast room for improvement in the character and education of many of the preachers.

2. Their influence, on the whole, is toward a better life, but the preaching is still too much emotional and too little addressed to the practical problems of living.

3. Of the Negro ministers of my acquaintance many are earnest and godly men, some are ignorant, and a few I fear are insincere.

4. The standards of Negro morality are being raised in many respects and being lowered in others. Among the more intelligent class, there is decidedly a

tendency toward purer domestic life. Many Negroes whom I know I believe to be thoroughly virtuous and honest. On the other hand, among the less intelligent class there is a very dangerous, not to say fatal, drift towards the worst forms of domestic vice.

On the whole, I believe that on this account the race is not multiplying at a normal rate.

A. J. McKelway, Editor, Charlotte, N. C.:

I am interested in the welfare of the Negro race, and know somewhat of their churches. The Presbyterian Churches in Charlotte, and Mecklenburg county, I commend most highly, not because I am a Presbyterian, but Charlotte is located in a Presbyterian section, and the old families were largely Presbyterian, and the best Negro stock is the same. Biddle University, near by, is a helpful influence, too, in training educated ministers. I can also commend the Congregational Church here, but the Methodist Episcopal and Baptist Churches are the average emotional congregations, with but little connection between morality and religion. Some ministers among them are good men, some are not. I think the standard of Negro morality is being raised; that is, the standard to which the best are trying to attain; at the same time there is a great tendency in the other direction among the worst element.

Rev. G. Lyle Smith, Paris, Tex.:

1. A considerable majority of adult Negroes are church members, a fair condition of peace prevails in the congregations, but denominational prejudices and wranglings are too frequent and violent, and a petty contentiousness is too common in individual organizations.

2. Yet, all in all, it may be said truly that their influence, on the whole, is toward a good, pure, honest Christian life.

3. Yes, with comparatively rare exceptions, the Negro preachers are good men so far as known to me. They certainly get into serious trouble far more frequently than white ministers, yet the general statement would stand that Negro preachers are good men.

4. Yes, it is manifest that the standards of morality are being steadily raised, especially if we take into view any considerable period of time. Advancement is as rapid as could reasonably be expected, all things considered.

E. C. Moncure, Judge County Court, Bowling Green, Va.

First, I have great sympathy with the Negro race and my opinion if anything, I fear, will be a little biased in their favor.

The Negro seems to be naturally a very religious person, full of emotion and human sympathy, mixed up with some superstition and suspicion.

The Negroes are devoted to their churches and will undergo many privations to contribute to church building. They have great pride in their churches, and to be turned out of church is the most humiliating condition in their minds. A Negro convicted of larceny will suffer under the burden of his humiliation from being "turned out of the church" much more than from his disgrace of criminal conviction. Of course that remark does not apply to those who are the leaders of the church. Twenty-five years ago the Negro churches were controlled by much inferior men than to-day. The Negro churches in any community of to-day are quite well organized, with well-attended Sunday-schools, and are progressing. They have an over-zeal in building church houses, and are striving to emulate the white people in having good and neat houses. Their church discipline is rather loose.

This, in a measure, comes from the great number of unconverted persons in their churches, for all Negroes must belong to the church; and a great many of their preachers are not educated and not of the highest character, so that they are not particular enough in receiving candidates into their communion. But, in my opinion, the Negroes are gradually improving along many lines. The trouble is with us white people, who, setting a judgment on their progress, expect and demand too much in a small space of time. But the influence toward pure, honest lives, upon the whole, is good; that is, the preponderating influence.

Of the colored registered vote lately voting on local option in my county, the abridged electorate, consisting principally of the educated and owners of property, nearly as a unit voted against whiskey.

Not all of the Negro ministers of my community are good men. In the main, they are, but some are ignorant and superstitious. But with all this, I am clearly of the opinion that the standards of Negro morality are being slowly and gradually raised.

To sum up, I do not think that Negro education and evangelization are failures by any means. In my acquaintance there are some noble examples of progress, faithfulness and devotion to principle.

C. C. Brown, Pastor, Sumter, S. C.:

1. One of the four Negro churches in Sumter is doing a good work. I seriously question whether the other three are accomplishing much. They suffer from poor leadership and from having too many preachers, who are always hanging around, seeking a pulpit in which they can preach.

2. I think the tendency is towards a better and more honest life. Too many supposed converts go into their churches upon the basis of emotion, and hence vital religion is to a large extent wanting.

3. Two Negro preachers here are unfit for their high place; four others are good and honest men, as far as I have had an opportunity to judge them.

4. Yes, among a certain class of Negroes. Good Negroes are getting better, and evil Negroes are getting worse. The great vice is adultery, which is winked at in many cases, and the social atmosphere can never be clarified until the harlot is no longer given a recognition by those whose lives are clean. The Negro needs lessons about home life far more than he does lessons about church life. The fact that Negroes have little or no confidence in each other lies at the bottom of many evils. This lack of confidence is general, and even the preacher has to contend against it. It weakens his power as a preacher and takes all authority away from his preaching and teaching.

But, on the whole, I am inclined to believe the Negroes are making strides towards a better condition. I am willing to be patient and live in hope. I am also willing to condone some existing evils, and to charge these things to the long years of history which lie in the past.

Edward S. Elliott, Savannah, Ga.:

1. The present condition of the Negro churches in this community is, on the whole, improving.

2. The influence, on the whole, is towards pure and honest life.

3. In my judgment, some of the Negro ministers in this community are good men and some are not.

4. The standards of Negro morality are being raised very slowly and among some.

I regret that I have not been able to give this matter a careful investigation, and the above opinion is expressed merely from casual observation.

Rev. J. T. Plunket, D. D., Augusta, Ga.:

1. I am not fully advised, but from all that I can hear or see I think, in the main, the present condition of the Negro churches here is very good.

2. I think the influence of the Negro churches is, on the whole, good and helpful toward purity and honesty of life.

3. So far as I have heard with few exceptions.

4. The moral improvement of any race must necessarily be gradual and slow. A fair judgment upon such an issue can only be made from broad and dispassionate observation rather than from a too narrow and prejudiced view. My judgment is that the racial standard of morality is being raised.

34. The Moral Status of Negroes. As to the mass of Negroes in the United States there is much confusion of evidence as to their moral condition. This is perfectly natural. Many of them are suffering from the effects of well-known tendencies to decadence of the second generation; at the same time their economic and educational advance is undoubted. What has been the resultant? Two answers are usually given to this question. One declares that the advance has been great and uniform in all moral relationships; the other answer is typified by the assertions of men like Thomas* that the Negro race is thoroughly corrupt and that "soberly speaking, Negro nature is so craven and sensuous in every fiber of its being that a Negro manhood, with decent respect for chaste womanhood, does not exist." For the purpose of getting some valuable opinions on these points and especially on Thomas's assertions, a committee of the Hampton Conference, in 1901, under the chairmanship of the Rev. Francis J. Grimke of the Fifteenth Street Presbyterian Church, Washington, D. C., made an investigation, a part of the results of which are here printed:

With a view of reaching those who were best qualified to give the desired information, the committee sent out to the American Missionary Association, the Presbyterian Board of Missions for Freedmen, the American Baptist Home Mission Society, the Home Mission Board of the National Baptist Convention, the Freedman's Aid and Southern Education Society of the Methodist Episcopal Church, and to many individuals of prominence in all the denominations, the following request:

"Will you be kind enough to send us a list of the teachers and preachers of your denomination laboring among the colored people in the South whose opinion touching their moral condition would carry most weight?"

The list of names thus secured was also supplemented by consultation with others who were in a condition to know, and also by consulting the History of the Medical Department of Howard University, recently published, which contains a list of all of its graduates.

We sent out in all nearly a thousand circulars. These were sent to teachers, preachers, lawyers, physicians and business men, both white and colored, located in Maryland, Virginia, West Virginia, North Carolina, South Carolina, Georgia, Florida, Alabama, Mississippi, Louisiana, Kentucky, Tennessee, Texas, Arkansas,

---

* W. H. Thomas: The American Negro.

Kansas, Missouri, the District of Columbia, and also in some of the Middle and Eastern states. Of the replies received only two agree wholly with Mr. Thomas.

One Southern white man writes from Atlanta:

Your circular letter received and in reply to your request as to whether, as far as my knowledge extends, the statements copied from the *American Negro* are true or not, I beg leave to say they are true.

The other is from a Northern white woman, who has lived for some time in the South, and who has been working among the colored people for a number of years, some dozen or more years in her present locality. She writes:

Your circular received as I am leaving for Denver. I have labored among the colored people for nearly twenty-two years in South Carolina and Tennessee. It is with sincere sorrow that I have to admit that those statements are true and correctly represent the present condition of the race.

Miss Sarah A. Collins, 110 East Center street, Baltimore, Md., writes:

Replying to you out of an experience of eighteen years among the humbler classes of the race I have not, by observation, found those statements true. Human weakness, under the unfavorable conditions of poverty and ignorance, has furnished examples of moral downfall, I must admit, but I have never considered them peculiarly racial nor have I noted any such downfall that has not had an offset under conditions equally unfavorable of noble, chaste womanhood.

Among the cultivated class my observation has had a more limited area, but those with whom it has been my good fortune to come in close contact have furnished some of the most beautiful examples of dignified, unspotted womanhood, whose lives might be read, page by page, without revealing one spot or blur. I have known, and do know, of homes among both the cultivated and ignorant whose sanctity is unbroken and whose atmosphere is as pure as true manhood, faithful womanhood, and innocent, happy childhood can make it.

Miss Nannie E. Grooms, 523 West Lanvale street, Baltimore, Md., writes:

My work in a large city has covered a period of nearly fourteen years. Thousands of girls have passed under my observation, many of them have already begun their careers, several are teachers in the Baltimore city school system, and are doing their part in life. The home life of all these individuals was not of the best kind, but with this much to be deplored in their condition I believe the per cent. of immorality to be low.

At this writing, my work is in a veritable slum. Degradation of every kind is rampant. In the next block above us houses of ill fame line both sides of the street. The occupants of these places are white. In a street parallel to this are houses occupied by both white and colored. Many of our children come from these places The greatest per cent. of degradation I have ever witnessed exists here. What the harvest shall be only Providence knows; but taken all in all, I believe that 8 per cent. would cover the mathematical reckoning as far as figures may be taken indicative of conditions of society.

I believe the statements made in the *American Negro* are false. William Hannibal Thomas must have spent his time entirely among the degraded, depraved and vicious.

Dr. Lucy E. Moten, Principal of the Normal School, Washington, D. C., writes:

I have had eighteen years' experience, with the closest observation, with girls of the race, average age eighteen, graduating not less than 400, and I am proud to say that not one, so far as I know, has in any wise cast a shadow upon her Alma Mater.

The Rev. Owen Waller, Washington, D. C., writes:

I was bred in England, during my most impressionable years, among the sturdy, moral, upper middle class, and now after ten years' work among the colored people, I can truly say that, class for class, circumstances compared, except for differences of complexion, one would not realize the change, certainly not in conduct and morals. One is especially impressed with the real modesty of the colored woman, and how she can be ingenuously assailed in this respect is both absolutely and relatively inexplicable.

Dr. H. B. Frissell, the Principal of the Hampton Normal and Industrial Institute, Hampton, Va., writes:

I have had an experience of twenty-one years with colored people, during which time I have been intimately acquainted with a large number of them at Hampton Institute. I have gone into their homes and have had perhaps as much opportunity as most any white man for knowing intimately their life.

I am glad to bear witness to my knowledge of the clean, pure lives of a large number whom I have known. I have often said, what I believe to be true, that it would be hard to find in any white institution in the North the freedom from low talk and impure life as is to be found at Hampton, where 1,000 young people of two races are brought together. The colored race is not degraded. Many of the young people who came to me years ago had no conception of the wrong of certain lines of conduct and who, since they have gained that knowledge, have lived up to what they know. I have seen young people coming from one-room cabins, where morality seems well nigh impossible, who sloughed that old life, and have made good use of the cleared knowledge which they have gained at Hampton.

I have often said that my own boy would be less likely to hear low talk here than in most Northern institutions for the whites. My own judgment in the matter is confirmed in the experience of others. For a number of weeks an English gentleman, who is making a most careful study of the race, has been staying at the school. He has mingled with the boys in their play, in their workshops and in their dormitories, and he confirms my impression and that of my disciplinarian, who himself is a colored man, living in close contact with the young people of the school.

I have seen in my years of work in the South a steady improvement in the whole community in which I live. The standards are being raised, and there is a marked improvement in the matter of purity of life.

The President of the State Normal School, Petersburg, Va., writes:

We have graduated 106 girls from our Seminary and following the lives of these graduates with careful and constant interest, we have known of only one who has gone astray.

Mr. W. McKirahan, Principal of Norfolk Mission College, Norfolk, Va., writes:

I have been laboring among the colored people for five years. The roll of our school carries about 900 names yearly, about 450 of these being girls. To my knowledge about five or six go astray yearly, or about one in each hundred.

Mrs. Orra Langhorne, a Southern white woman, 710 Church street, Lynchburg, Va., writes:

I was born among colored people, have always been surrounded by them and believe this man Thomas grossly exaggerates the actual conditions. It was the most sorrowful part of slavery that there could be no legal marriage for the slaves, no protection for the virtue of women. Even now there are no laws to protect the colored girl, such as have always existed for her white sisters. In discussing any question that relates to the Negroes, regard should be given to the rapid formation of classes among them. There is a respectable class, and this class is increasing, where married parents live virtuous lives, guard the sanctity of their homes, and strive to bring up their children in the path of virtue. I go among the colored people of all classes and see many signs of encouragement. We must all work and hope for the elevation of the race, and prove to the world the falsity of Thomas's cruel and odious book.

Rev. D. Webster Davis, colored, of Richmond, Va., writes:

I recall ten cases coming under my personal observation where mothers, living in vice, have put their children in boarding schools, Catholic homes, and in good families, when they could succeed in doing so, and these girls in most cases have been reared without having visited their mothers' homes since babyhood. In fact, it is the rule rather than the exception that mothers, leading lives of shame, do all in their power to prevent their children leading the same lives.

Dr. Charles F. Meserve, white, President of Shaw University, Raleigh, N. C., writes:

I believe that there are in every community large numbers of colored women that are as chaste and pure as can be found in communities made up of other races.

I believe that a large percentage of colored boys and girls over fifteen years of age, who have been properly trained, are clean and pure.

I have found, as a rule, that Negro fathers and mothers are more than anxious that their offspring should lead pure lives. Whatever truth there is in this statement can apply only to the degraded tenth.

I have spent over seven years in educational work among the colored people of the South, have seen them in school and at home, and in practically all of the Southern states. When I consider that they have come from 250 years of enforced slavery, with all the degradation and darkness that this means, the wonder to me is that there is such a large number of pure, refined, industrious, intelligent men and women as there is. There is, as every one knows, a dark picture, but it is only what is to be expected. It is a picture that is growing brighter year by year, and although there are discouragements and obstacles, from time to time, that come up, on the whole, the race is making substantial and remarkable progress, and the outlook ought to be considered by all careful observers and lovers of the human race as hopeful and encouraging.

Dr. D. J. Satterfield, white, President of Scotia Seminary, Concord, N. C., writes:

When a Southern white man told my predecessor that all Negro women were impure his reply was, "I suppose you know, I don't." I have seen Negro women who I have good reason to believe are living virtuous lives under conditions of trial such as our virtuous white women as a class know nothing about. Through my sainted wife I know of examples of colored women whose firmness in resisting temptation makes them worthy to represent any race.

Of those same women I can speak without reserve on all these points. Their modesty and genuine worth are conceded by white, as well as colored; their marital fidelity is above question. Many of them have passed through the stage of courtship and entered married life under my own personal observation, and even the most fastidious could find nothing but what was proper and pure. We have Negro women around us here who are for duty's sake remaining single, though sought by the very best of our young men.

One of the most touching things to come under my notice has been the many mothers who come to beg us to take their girls, saying, I know I am not what I ought to be, but I don't want her to be like me. We could fill Scotia over and over again every year with girls whose parents want them in a safe place, so that they may grow into good women. In these nearly fifteen years we have not had the basis of a scandal involving a member of this school inside of our grounds, and we believe that our record as a school, both for honesty and purity, will bear comparison with the female schools generally.

It would not be wise however in our zeal to refute the false assertions in Mr. Thomas's book to overlook the fact that many of them are in a measure true. We cannot do our duty to the Negro while we keep ourselves ignorant of his true condition, and no Thomas or any other man can overdraw the picture of the morals of the uncared for masses of the Negro in the South, not because they are Negroes, but because they are uncared for.

Prof. George A. Woodard, Principal of Gregory Normal Institute, Wilmington, N. C., writes:

I have been laboring among the colored race for sixteen years, and we have had three hundred colored youth in our Institution yearly. I cannot be made to think that the majority of them are devoid of morality. We would not keep a pupil in school known to be unchaste. The expulsions for this cause have not averaged one case per year.

Rev. A. B. Hunter of St. Augustine's School, Raleigh, N. C., writes:

I have no doubt that W. H. Thomas's picture is an overstatement and exaggeration of the facts, but the facts are such as to stimulate us all to secure a betterment.

Thirteen years' work here has convinced me of the truth of Prof. DuBois's statement (College-bred Negroes, page 57) that "without doubt the greatest social problem of the American Negro at present is sexual purity, and the solving of this problem lies peculiarly upon the homes established among them."

Dr. L. M. Dunton, white, President of Claflin University, Orangeburg, S. C., writes:

In reply to your circular letter permit me to say that I have read W. H. Thomas's book on "The American Negro". I have labored for nearly thirty years among the colored people of South Carolina, and I believe that Mr. Thomas is either wholly unacquainted with the Negro or else he has deliberately undertaken to get up a sensation, and possibly a market for his book, by the wholesale denunciation of the race. His statements cannot possibly be true.

Rev. A. C. Osborn, President of Benedict College, Columbia, S. C., writes:

I have been president of this college for six years, with hundreds of girls under my care, and I have not the remotest reason to believe or even to suspect that a single girl connected with this school has committed an act of immoralty or has led either before coming here or while here, or afterwards, other than a virtuous life.

Rev. Thomas H. Amos, D. D., Principal of Ferguson Academy, Abbeville, S. C., writes:

The statement with respect to Negro virtue cannot be true. We have 113 boys and girls in our boarding department. They range in age from fourteen to thirty years, and never have we known of any indecent conduct on the part of either sex toward the other. I frequently inspect the walls and fences that are marked in crayon or pencil and not more than twice have I seen in eight years any writing or drawing of an indecent nature. Our young men once thrashed a boy at their building for introducing some reference to a girl's character, and when I asked them about their conduct, said that they had only one rule in the whole building. It was that no one should speak of the school-girls slightingly, and whoever did so should be first, thrashed, second, reported to the faculty, and thirdly, expelled from the building. The facts I have in hand release 75 per cent. of Negro women from most of what Mr. Thomas says. At least 50 per cent. live above the slightest suspicion, and I think it fair to say 50 per cent. of those who are suspicioned are not guilty.

Miss Ellen Murray, of St. Helena Island, near Beaufort, S. C., one of the noblest of white Christian women from the North who have consecrated their lives to the upbuilding of this race, writes:

I have been for. nearly forty years the Principal of the Penn School, Superintendent of a Sunday-school, President of a Temperance Society, Leader of a Woman's Meeting among the Negroes of St. Helena Island, on the southern coast of South Carolina. There are 6,000 Negroes on the island, who were called the lowest of all the Negroes, and incapable of improvement.

In our school of 270 there are at least 100 young people from fifteen to twenty-two and they are living lives as pure as any white people, however high or refined. The age at which they marry has, since freedom, changed from fifteen to eighteen, on an average. After marriage, the rule is fidelity. I scarcely know a case in which the wife is unfaithful, and the more educated and intelligent the men grow, the more moral they become. I have talked with numbers of teachers from many of the colored schools of the freed people, and I do not believe that any such state of things as Thomas asserts can be found in them. It would be impossible. There are on this island 6,000 Negroes, thirty whites, one constable, one justice, and such a thing as an attack on a white woman has not been known in all these forty years. The mothers have steadily grown more and more careful of their daughters, providing for them a separate room, seeing that they are not out late in the evening; the churches are stricter on the matter; fathers are sterner with their sons. I do not claim that they are perfect. They were treated as brutes by their owners, who counted on their increase, as a Negro woman said to me bitterly, "just like we count for our chickens." Girls and women were alike forced into sin by the whip. In the two-roomed huts where three or four families crowded, there was no chance for modesty or decency. Hampered by heredity, burdened with poverty and contempt, and vexatious laws to oppose them, with many a stumble and many a fall, they are, nevertheless, pressing up, longing for learning, desirous of respectability, taking with eager gratitude all the help they can get. I wish those who talk of the Negro deteriorating could see, in contrast with the floorless huts of slavery, the homes of these people here. Five rooms, floors with rugs, papered walls, chairs, lounge, lamp, sewing machine, dresser with its china, table set with a white cloth and dishes, beds with white spreads and mosquito nets, plain indeed, cheap indeed, but comfortable and paid for.

Miss Mary L. Deas, 83 Morris street, Charleston, S. C., a teacher in the Avery Institute of that city, writes:

I think I may safely say that I am well acquainted with the school system of South Carolina. My work for the past fourteen years has been in one of the best known of the schools. I know nearly all of the educators of the colored people of the state, but I do not know one who would knowingly allow a girl sustaining immoral relations with any man to remain in the school, much less to have him pay her expenses. White men pay the tuition of many students, but these students are their children, not their mistresses, and many of these girls grow up honorable and pure women, in spite of their home surroundings. The lessons of chastity taught them in the schools bear fruit in their lives. Avery Institute, where I teach, has over 300 graduates, but not one of whom is living a dissolute life. During the past fourteen years there has been but one case of immorality known to the school authorities. The girl was expelled. All the schools of which I know anything make for purer lives.

Conditions are bad enough, but 90 per cent. is far too large an estimate for the immoral class. Fearing that my position would cause me to have too optimistic views, my associates being women pure in word and deed, I consulted two men whose business brings them in contact with all classes. They both said that even 50 per cent. was too large for the vicious of this city. The large class of people who move in good society here regard chastity in women as one of the essentials. The women who have been proven guilty of a fall from sexual virtue are dropped by their former friends. The men of this class show their respect for pure women by seeking them for wives, and by guarding their sisters whenever possible. It is true that fallen women sometimes marry, but they nearly always marry below their rank.

Miss Harriet E. Giles, white, President of Spelman Seminary, of Atlanta, Ga., writes:

I have been laboring among the colored people for more than twenty years. I am sure there is a steadily growing sentiment against immorality. I think of the girls who have been trained in Christian schools at least 95 per cent. live moral lives. By this, I mean those who have remained in the schools for several years.

Mr. Fred W. Foster, white, Principal of Dorchester Academy, McIntosh, Ga., writes:

There are thousands of Negroes who would fight to the death to preserve the purity of their own women or that of white women deserving their respect.

No doubt there are educated Negroes who "presume to be refined" who are licentious, but to say that education and refinement are no barriers against this evil, that there is no refined class of colored people who maintain their marriage vows unspotted, is too far-reaching and glaring a misstatement to go unchallenged.

I have lived and worked among the colored people twelve years, during which time I have tried to get as fair and just an idea of the average Negro character as possible, as well as to learn that which is best; and I have had opportunities of seeing and knowing somewhat of the worst side.

The Negro is the product of generations of entire freedom from restraint, to which has been added the effects of the unrestrained lust of a stronger race; but despite these things there are multitudes of the colored race in America whose lives are as pure, whose regard for the marriage vow as great, and "whose respect for chaste womanhood" as strong as of any other race in our land.

Miss Lucy C. Laney, Principal of Haines Institute, Augusta, Ga., writes:

I have been interested a number of years in noting, as I have passed through the country, to find what a large number of Negroes are true, and have been true, to their marriage vows. It is not an unusual thing to find those who have lived faithfully together for fifty, sixty and sixty-five years. Those of us who have worked for twenty years among the colored people note marked improvement.

Nothing cheers our hearts more than to see the large number of fathers who come and enter their children in school, make constant inquiry as to their progress, and who, accompanied by their wives and children, attend the public exercises of the school. This interest is real; they want to know the moral status of their children, they labor for and desire the best for their children, children of one wife. In our kindergarten of forty-five children there were only three illegitimate children.

T. DeS. Tucker, President of Florida State Normal and Industrial College, Tallahassee, Fla., writes:

I have been engaged for nearly thirty-five years, more or less, in duties which have brought me in close contact with our people in every walk of life. When the depths of depravity from which they emerged are taken into consideration the marvel of their advance in morals is simply phenomenal. Specimens of pure womanhood and exalted manhood are to be found among the race to-day in every village and hamlet in the land. While we have much to struggle for in generations to come, the assertion may be safely ventured that in the light of our past attainments in virtue, our future is safely assured.

Rev. R. C. Bedford, white, who is connected with Tuskegee Institute, writes:

I have been working for colored people now nineteen years. For eight years, 1882 to 1890, I was pastor of a colored church in Montgomery, Ala. I have traveled in every Southern state among the graduates of Tuskegee and have taken careful note of conditions everywhere I have gone, and instead of things being as represented by this book, I have found myself wondering all the time how they could be so good. Virtue, not vice, has been the characteristic most pronounced everywhere. In the eight years I was in Montgomery I made a thorough study of things in the city, and while there was much vice in certain localities, the marvel was that there were so many absolutely pure homes. During all the time I was there, we had not a single case of immorality connected with our church. I have been intimately associated with the work here for nineteen years. I know every graduate that has gone out of the school, and many of the 5,000 others who have been students here, and I have been constantly delighted with the freedom from anything like gross immorality on the part of a very large majority of these people. Things mentioned in the circular are the least of our troubles here. I have in mind one of our branch schools, located in a very dark county of Alabama, with eighteen teachers and about 400 students. I have just come from the Commencement exercises there and during the whole year, though fifteen of the teachers are unmarried, there has not been even a breath of scandal.

Miss Charlotte R. Thorn, white, Principal of the Calhoun Colored School, Calhoun, Ala., writes:

I have been for thirteen years working among, for and with, Negroes. The first four years' work and life were at Hampton, and I will say nothing much about that, for the Hampton teachers have a better and larger knowledge of students and graduates than I have. I would say, however, that it was because I saw such positive proof of high-mindedness and beauty of character among the Negroes and because we saw, year after year, the coming in of earnest, self-respecting boys and girls, that Miss Dillingham and I felt we must go out and show the way of light to some who lived in dark places and had never had a chance to know what really was the right in any part of life.

It was because we had firm belief in the Negro that we came, and each year but carries deeper conviction that we were then right. We came here (Calhoun) in 1892. During the nine years since I have been constantly filled with admiration of the people who, with but little to work for and with constant and deep temptations, are able to withstand the temptation and struggle on to get a precarious living, in the strength of high convictions and deep and ever-increasing self-respect. When we came we felt that the free living represented sin, but in a very few months we believed it represented the natural life of a group of people who had never been shown or taught life on a higher plane. After a few months of life among them they took hold of what little we could do and began to reconstruct their lives. Of course we found many whom we then believed, and still feel, were leading pure, good lives, merely from inborn instincts.

In regard to the morality of our girls at school, I do not want to omit a statement which, knowing the community, seems to be almost miraculous. In the last twelve months only two girls who have ever been in our school have been known to go wrong. One was of mixed Indian, Negro and white blood. She has been brought up in a house of vice and brutality, has heard bad language and low talk and seen low life and brutal living ever since babyhood; has been brutally beaten and knocked about, and it was small wonder that she died last week in sin of every sort. The other, a girl of sixteen, is feeble-minded, so that after trying to teach her for four years we found she knew but little more than when she started in school. These two cases had not been in school for several years, and are the only ones out of many hundreds who have attended who have gone astray.

Our boys and young men from sixteen to twenty-five years of age are upright and self-respecting in the majority of cases. Of course, in this community, one of the worst in the whole South, when we came here we found all kinds, good and bad, but there is daily evidence of desire and strivings for high standards of living, and victories over self that are marvelous.

The statement of William H. Thomas regarding the morals of the race, according to my knowledge, are false when applied to the Negro race as a whole. Of course, no one claims that the race has not its low and bad—all races have these—but the Negro's natural instincts are refined and sensitive.

Rev. H. N. Payne, D. D., white, President of Mary Holmes Seminary, West Point, Miss., writes:

For the past sixteen years I have been continuously engaged in Christian work for and among the colored people.

From that knowledge I say without hesitation that it is not true that "a Negro manhood with decent respect for chaste womanhood does not exist." It is untrue that "marriage is no barrier to illicit sexual indulgence."

That there is a great and saddening amount of immorality among the Negroes is frequently admitted, but that it is universal is unhesitatingly and absolutely denied. I glory in the purity of my own race, though there are some sad, yes, monstrous cases of moral degradation among white women. It has been my good fortune to be personally acquainted with many colored women who were morally as pure as any white women I have ever known. This I say with tender respect and reverence for some who have been very near and dear to me.

Rev. F. G. Woodworth, D. D., white, President of Tougaloo University, Tougaloo, Miss., writes:

The trend and tendency are very decidedly towards better things in the moral life, and it has been in existence long enough to have molded a very considerable portion of the Negro people to a nobler life than Thomas seems to know about. The more I study the matter the more I am convinced that with all the evils resultant from slavery and from the sudden freedom, the indictments brought against the race now have never been fully true, and it is less true now than formerly.

I have had fourteen years of experience and observation in teaching in the heart of the black belt of Mississippi.

There is an increasing number of men who have a high regard for chaste womanhood, who are earnest in the desire to protect women from impurity of every kind. They welcome and forward such agencies; for the promotion of purity is the White Cross with its pledge of reverence for women.

The number of girls who would resent solicitations to evil is not a small one and among those who have been carefully reared, who have had something of moral training, the percentage of those who go astray is a small one. The number of homes where the pure ideal of family life exists has increased constantly since I have been in the South. There are some pure homes among the poor and illiterate. Among those who are educated the dishonored homes are few.

Mrs. Sylvanie F. Williams, white, 1438 Euterpe street, New Orleans, La., writes:

I have been laboring among the colored people since 1870, and as far as my experience goes, I am prepared to say that there is a decided improvement in the moral status all along the line. I have consulted with other teachers of experience who have taught in public, private and prominent boarding schools, and none of them have ever discovered conditions such as Mr. Thomas names in his exploration of "Negro training schools of prominence. " As to illegitimate motherhood of Negro women, I will state that when I first began teaching among the freedmen, I was much surprised to find that in a family of several children each had a different name. I have watched that phase of the situation, having an annual register to make each year, and have been pleased to see how they have improved, until today I find, in my school, families of six or more children having the same father, and the celebration of crystal and even silver weddings is quite common. I speak of the lowly people who are laborers, whose children attend the public school up to the fifth grade, because they are not financially able to remain at school beyond that period. The school of which I speak numbers 900 pupils, ranging from six to eighteen years of age. I do not pretend to say that the entire roll is virtuous, although I have no reason to think otherwise, but I do say that the great majority of them are a living refutation of every assertion made by Thomas.

Rev. M. R. Gaines, white, President of Tillotson College, Austin, Tex., writes:

I have been nearly five years in my present position. We have had an average of 200 students a year. There are about fourteen of us white teachers in pretty close touch with this body of young people. Of course, they do not lay their secret thoughts open to us. I do not believe they are so honeycombed with moral depravity and sensuality as these extracts would lead us to suppose.
When I think over cases of known violation of laws of immorality and chastity, I am free to say that the record here will not suffer in comparison with what I could name of experience along similar lines elsewhere. My intimate acquaintance with young people as teacher covers several decades.

Rev. P. B. Guernsey, white, President of Roger Williams University, Nashville, Tenn., writes:

I personally know from letters received and conversations with parents of girls entrusted to this school, that the mothers of our girls are as deeply concerned for the morals and general reputation of their girls as any mothers could be. They have never failed to sanction unreservedly any restrictions and precautions felt to be desirable to protect the girls from even the appearance of evil. I am glad to say that this institution, which has for more than thirty years educated young men and young women side by side in the same classes and upon the same campus, has been, I can safely say, as free from scandal along that line as any co-educational institution that I know anywhere. I have worked in at least one co-educational institution in the North attended entirely by white students,where I saw more to criticise in the relation of the sexes than I have ever seen here. While the moral standards of many colored people are sadly defective, the surprise to me is that, considering all the circumstances and the institution of slavery, the standards should be as high as they are.

Rev. C. A. Isbell, United States Jail Physician and Surgeon, 723 South Sixth street, Paducah, Ky., writes:

I have been for the past ten or twelve years in contact with the Negro, and have had direct dealings with him. The statements made by W. H. Thomas, to my knowledge, are not true. The race is misrepresented. We have among us men and women of the highest character. We are not as a race at the top of the ladder in morals, but we are on the way to it.

Mr. W. H. Hunton, Secretary of the International Committee of Young Men's Christian Associations, Colored Men's Department, writes:

After fourteen years of constant laboring among my people throughout the South, especially among young men in the cities and students in boarding schools of all grades, I am firmly convinced that a heroic and successful fight is being waged against immoral tendencies inherited from centuries of debasing slavery. Of course there is much dross yet to be burned away before we can have only pure gold remaining.
I confess with great sorrow of heart that there are some members of my race, and possibly a large proportion, who could be put down as fitting one or more of the foul characteristics of Mr.Thomas, nor do I seek to cover this acknowledgment with the fact that in every other race on the earth, individuals can be found equally low in life and character. But there are various classes among the freedmen as among other people.

Born and reared in Canada, and having spent three years just prior to my coming South in 1888 as a civil servant at Ottawa, where I mingled freely in church and social life with some of the best of white Canadians, I find myself greatly encouraged as I compare my experience of the past fourteen years with those of my earlier life, and especially the three years referred to above. I have met in all sections of the country hundreds of colored women whose bearing has been as suggestive of good as that of the women of the fairer race in the North. I have also come into close contact with thousands of young men whom I know to be struggling against unfortunate inherited tendencies and unfavorable environment.

It is true that only a few of the Negro race have yet attained to the degree of perfection possible among men, but between those few and the submerged masses is a promising and inspiring host of men and women in various stages of moral, intellectual and industrial evolution.

35. Children and the Church. We turn now to the two questions of the training of pulpit and pew for the Negro church. Much might be said of home training, but perhaps the testimony of children themselves would be of some interest. In the colored public schools of Atlanta last May, 1,339 children were asked questions as follows and wrote out the following answers:

Are you a Christian?

AGE.	Yes.	No.
Seven years	7	10
Eight years	15	31
Nine years	27	50
Ten years	42	124
Eleven years	40	140
Twelve years	78	156
Thirteen years	87	142
Fourteen years	89	105
Fifteen years	62	57
Sixteen years	36	28
Seventeen years	10	2
Eighteen years	1	....
Total	494	845

One-third of the children were church members; of the more mature, 11–18 years of age, 60 per cent. belong to the church. Nearly all go to church, however.

Do you go to church?

AGE.	Yes.	No.	Some-times.	?
Seven years	14	2	....	1
Eight years	45	1	....	....
Nine years	78	1	1	....
Ten years	156	10	3	1
Eleven years	172	5	3	....
Twelve years	135	7	6	....
Thirteen years	224	2	3	....
Fourteen years	192	1	5	....
Fifteen years	138	2	....	....
Sixteen years	59	1	3	....
Seventeen years	12	....	....	....
Eighteen years	1	....	....	....
Not given	10	....	....	....

Do you like to go to church?

AGE.	Yes.	No.	Some-times.	?
Seven years	16	1		
Eight years	45			1
Nine years	75	1		3
Ten years	159	8		3
Eleven years	174	5		1
Twelve years	247	1		
Thirteen years	227			2
Fourteen years	197	1		
Fifteen years	137	2		1
Sixteen years	62		1	
Seventeen years	12			
Eighteen years	1			
Not given	10			

Nearly all like to go to church.
Nearly all go to Sunday-school and like it.

Their denominational affiliations were determined by all sorts of considerations:

Why do you like a certain church the best?

AGE.	On account of parents or relatives.	Because I am a member.	Because I have never attended any other.	Because they treat me nicely there.	Because I go there.	?	Because it helps me.	Because I think Christ was of that denomination.	Because I believe in that denomination.	Because it is a good, nice church, or very large.	Because they have good services.	Because it has the best method.	Because my girl goes there.	Because the people are good.	Because I was converted there.	Because I can do more good there.	Miscellaneous.
Seven years	13				2	2											
Eight years	35		1		5	2	3										
Nine years	54	1		4	6	7	7										
Ten years	91	3	3	5	15	26	10	1	10		2	1	1				
Eleven years	113	11	5	4	7	22	4	2	5	3	1		1	2		1	
Twelve years	131	13	4	3	28	26	8	2	19	6	2	2		2		1	
Thirteen years	121	17	3	1	32	17	3	8	14	8	5						
Fourteen years	99	19	2		17	19	3	8	16	5	2				3	2	6
Fifteen years	67	8	2		11	14	1	6	23	2			1	3	1		1
Sixteen years	23	6	1		5	4		3	19						1		1
Seventeen years	8	1			2												
Eighteen years	1																
Not given	4	2				2			1						1		

The chief interest, however, lies in their conception of Christianity, as there the answers showed plainly their training. The answers to the question, "What does it mean to be a Christian?", fall into five chief groups. First, then, are the answers which make Christianity simple, moral goodness, such as a child easily comprehends. Such answers were thirty-three in number:

ANSWERS.	AGE, IN YEARS.												
	7	8	9	10	11	12	13	14	15	16	17	18	?
To be good........................	4	10	9	49	32	53	37	18	14	5	....	....	1
To be kind, honest, etc.............	....	....	2	1	7	4	3	1	....	....	....	....	....
To live a better life................	....	....	....	`4	7	10	12	3	5	1	....	....	1
Total	4	10	11	54	46	67	52	22	19	6	....	....	2

Some others had the idea of goodness, but added the phrase, "and live for Jesus," although it is not clear just what this addition meant to them. The ages of these were:

Seven years.....................................	9
Eight years.......	19
Nine years......................................	10
Ten years......................................	8
Eleven years	7
Twelve years	5
Fourteen years.................................	1
Total......	59

Others considered Christianity as the obeying of the ten commandments:

Eight years.....................................	1
Nine years.............	2
Ten years	1
Eleven years...................................	1
Twelve years...................................	10
Thirteen years.................................	4
Fourteen years	7
Fifteen years...................................	3
Sixteen years..................................	3
Total...	32

The idea of love for persons as an expression of Christianity was mentioned. Several said it meant "To love everybody"; two said, "To save others."

Seven years..............................	1
Eight years	1
Nine years......................................	1
Ten years.....................................	3
Eleven years...................................	10
Twelve years...............................:	15
Thirteen years.................................	8
Fourteen years.............................	9
Fifteen years..................................	11
Sixteen years..................................	2
?.......	1
Total.................................	61

Others answered, "To serve God," but it is doubtful if they understood by this, ordinary work for anyone, although two said, "Work for God." Most of them probably meant church service:

Eight years	4
Nine years	14
Ten years	30
Eleven years	43
Twelve years	36
Thirteen years	29
Fourteen years	26
Fifteen years	20
Sixteen years	6
Seventeen years	2
Total	210

From this point the answers became more mystical aud figurative. Doubtless they had more or less meaning to the writers, but they were repetitions of common phrases and had a certain vagueness:

ANSWERS.	AGE, IN YEARS.												
	7	8	9	10	11	12	13	14	15	16	17	18	?
Child of God		1		5	4	6	10	6	2	3			
Christ-like						6	5	10	15	6	1		1
Follow Christ			4	7	7	4	11	12	10	3	1		
Soldiers of Christ				1	1	1							
Love God		6	10	9	14	26	26	18	7	4	1		11
Believe in Christ	1	1	7	9	18	32	44	43	31	18	7	1	1
Sins forgiven						5	1	3	1				
Total	1	8	21	31	44	80	97	92	66	34	10	1	13

These were followed by phrases which were without doubt theological and understood by few who used them. Some of these phrases were:

"To have true religion and honor God's word."
"To be a member in Christ."
"To be born again."
"To have the Love of God in your soul."
"To honor the Lord Jesus Christ."
"To keep the faith."
"To trust in the Lord."
"To honor God."

Those giving these answers were:

Nine years	2
Ten years	5
Eleven years	6
Twelve years	5
Thirteen years	13
Fourteen years	8
Fifteen years	5
Sixteen years	3
Total	47

A few looked for certain signs of Christianity, as baptism, joining the church, "getting religion," or "being changed:"

```
Seven years  . . . . . . . . . . . . . .  1
Ten years  . . . . . . . . . . . . . . .  5
Eleven years . . . . . . . . . . . . . .  2
Twelve years . . . . . . . . . . . . . .  9
Thirteen years . . . . . . . . . . . . .  5
Fourteen years . . . . . . . . . . . . .  5
Fifteen years . . . . . . . . . . . . . .  7
                                         ──
    Total  . . . . . . . . . . . . . . . 34
```

Few naturally spoke of the desire for happiness or reward: five mentioned heaven, and one child of eleven, with unconscious socialism, defined a Christian as "a poor man!"

```
Ten years . . . . . . . . . . . . . . .  2
Eleven years . . . . . . . . . . . . . .  2
Fourteen years  . . . . . . . . . . . .  2
                                        ──
    Total . . . . . . . . . . . . . . .  6
```

Thirty-seven children answered frankly that they did not know what Christianity was, and seventy-six left the query unanswered for lack of knowledge or time:

ANSWERS.	AGE, IN YEARS.									
	8	9	10	11	12	13	14	15	16	?
Don't know..	0	0	9	10	7	4	5	0	1	1
Unanswered.	4	4	12	9	16	7	9	7	6	0
Total.	4	4	21	19	23	11	14	7	7	1

Analyzing these answers further they reveal some interesting facts.

ANSWERS.	7-12 years.	13 years and over.
Moral and altruistic . . .	296	148
Higher will and phrases . .	387	505
Miscellaneous	21	19
Unanswered, etc.	123	97

The children of twelve and under had the clearer and simpler idea of the direct connection of goodness and Christianity. The older children tended more toward phrases which sought to express the fact that religion had reference to some higher will. Indeed this was the more popular idea, and 70 per cent. of the children spoke of Christianity as "Love for God," "Belief in Christ," or some such phrase. Clear as such phrases may be to some minds, they undoubtedly point to a lack in the moral training of Negro children. They evidently are not impressed to a sufficiently large extent with the fact that moral goodness is the first requirement of a Christian life.

A few typical answers, given *verbatim*, follow:

What does it mean to be a Christian?

Age 13.

(*a*) It means that you love God, the church, and the people, and all good things, but hate evil things.

(*b*) To be kind, honest, and trustworthy.

(*c*) To be a Christian means to live and die the same.

(*d*) It means to serve God in a true way and live above suspicion.

(*e*) To live as God would have you live.

(*f*) To give your heart to God.

(*g*) To praise the Lord.

(*h*) Holy and happy.

Age 14.

(*a*) To believe in God and not only be called a Christian, but to live the life of one.

(*b*) To tell the truth, to have a clean heart, and to keep the church laws.

(*c*) To change your mind to do right.

(*d*) To live for Christ and try to help others to come to Him.

(*e*) To live for Christ and obey the word of the Lord Jesus Christ, who died to save us.

(*f*) To have your sins pardoned by God and to be washed in the blood of the Lamb.

(*g*) When the Lord has forgiven you of your sins and you know it and you mean to follow Him the balance of your days and do all you can to make others come to Him.

(*h*) To keep in the right path.

(*i*) To obey the laws of the church.

(*j*) To hold love in your heart toward God and all mankind and work on earth for the upbuilding of God's cause.

(*k*) To believe that Jesus is the Son of God, and that all power is in His hand.

(*l*) A Christian means something more than praying.

Age 15.

(*a*) To be a holy person.

(*b*) To be truthful and never swear.

Age 16.

(*a*) To be true and honest.

(*b*) If I am not a Christian in the day of judgment my soul will be lost, because Christ has said that if a man is not born again he cannot enter the kingdom of God. Therefore, I serve and love the Lord.

36. The Training of Ministers. There are in the United States the following theological schools designed especially for Negroes :

Atlanta Baptist College, Atlanta, Ga., Baptist 1867
Union University, Richmond, Va., Baptist 1867
Biddle University, Charlotte, N. C., Presbyterian 1867
Howard, Washington, D. C., non-sectarian . . · 1870
Lincoln University, Pennsylvania, Presbyterian 1871
Talladega, Talladega, Ala., Congregational 1872
Stillman, Tuscaloosa, Ala., Presbyterian 1876
Gammon, Atlanta, Ga., Methodist Episcopal 1883
Braden, Nashville, Tenn., Methodist Episcopal 1889
King Hall, Washington, D. C., Protestant Episcopal . . . 1890
Fisk University, Nashville, Tenn., Congregational 1892
Wilberforce, Wilberforce, Ohio, African Methodist Episcopal 1891
Straight University, New Orleans, La., Congregational . . ?

The detailed figures as to these schools are as follows:

	Howard	Braden	Lincoln	Atlanta Baptist	Stillman	Talladega
Length of course	3, 4	3	3	3	4	3
Length of session	34	32	28	26	35	35
Teachers	*4	1	+3	2	2	2
Students	61	20	61	28	18	17
Students with A. B. and B. S. degrees	1	0	38	0	0	0
Total number graduates	199	....	330	48	60	55
Prospective graduates of 1903	7	10	16	.0	4	4
Value of grounds and buildings			$ 36,000	$ 75,000	$10,000	$ 4,500
Endowment fund	$45,100	....	144,000	1,000	0	13,000
Total income	4,261	....			2,500	2,815
Volumes in library	1,400	500		2,500	3,000	2,000

	King Hall	Fisk	Union University	Wilberforce	Biddle	Straight	Gammon
Length of course	3	3	3	3	3	....	3
Length of session	35	37	33	36	35		30
Teachers	2	2	5	2	12	1	5
Students	16	2	62	4	17	....	62
Students with A. B. and B. S. degrees	0	0	0		13	2	6
Total number graduates	17	9	150	40	102	9	177
Prospective graduates of 1903	1	0	5		2	2	12
Value of grounds and buildings	$30,000	$30.00	$ 300,000	$12,000.00	$ 200,000	0	$100,000
Endowment fund		4,033	70,000		85,000	0	562,096
Total income			6,000	3,731.89			20,000
Volumes in library	3,000	1,000	7,000	2,800	12,800	500	12,500

*Three others assist partially.   † Five others teach partially.   ‡ Two others assist partially.

This shows thirty-three teachers and 368 theological students. Of these students sixty are college graduates. The total number of theological graduates is 1,196, and sixty-three more graduated in 1903. The reported value of grounds and buildings was $797,500 and the endowment amounted to $944,229, of which $562,096 belonged to one institution. The income was reported only partially and amounted to $39,307.89. The libraries held 49,000 books. In many cases of omitted figures the items are not differentiated from the general figures relating to the institution, of which the theological school is a part. The reports from certain of the schools speak of their present condition and work.

ATLANTA BAPTIST COLLEGE.—The great difficulty in theological training is, that aspirants for the ministry, who have such literary training as would fit them to pursue a theological course with profit, find themselves able to meet the demands of most congregations without such training, and those who have not that literary training can take only the most elementary course in theology. The result is, speaking generally, that few of our students are able to complete a course in theology, and the average ability of the students of that department is not high. This means, of course, that the demand is for general culture and rhetorical ability in the pulpit rather than theological training. I think there is an increasing demand for more culture in the pulpit but not for specially theological training. In view of the fact that so large a number of the Negro ministry are uneducated, I am convinced of the fact that a most important class of theological training is that given in local ministers' institutions, of short duration, and dealing with exclusively Biblical topics.

FISK UNIVERSITY.—We have no regular Theological Department this year. Mr. Morrow taught some college students who took a theological elective in the fall term.

We have had no applications that we considered at all worth the considering. Insufficient preparation and other circumstances have turned down all that we have had.

GAMMON.—Some of the students who come to us from other institutions of theological training show that in some of them the instruction is of a very low grade. From other evidences, I believe, however, that, considering all the circumstances, a fair standard is maintained, but there should evidently be an effort made to secure more college-prepared students, and a more advanced course for them.

Wide observation and reports from our students from nearly every part of the nation convince me that the Negro's religious condition is steadily improving and that there is still room for large advance.

BRADEN SCHOOL OF THEOLOGY.—I have been engaged in the work of the Christian ministry for more than a quarter of a century, and will say without hesitation that I have never seen a more hopeful outlook for the moral uplift of our people than now. Better homes, higher appreciation of public instruction, the schools and colleges established and fostered by various religious denominations, with the constantly elevating standards of the Christian ministry are among the potential factors in the marvelous change in the religious sentiment of the Negro.

To meet the increasing demand of this transitional church and to direct the religious energies of this most emotional race, means an increasing output of our theological seminaries or schools which devote their time to this special work. But this preparation must be based upon the most enlarged views of the vast spiritual needs of the race. It must be broader than a mere denominational predilection. It involves a world-wide preparation for a world-wide salvation. While our theological schools are doing a magnificent work it must be admitted that the supply is not equal to the demands. The facilities for the kind of work required ought to be increased a hundredfold. Even then it would tax the energies of those directing affairs to meet the imperative demands for a thoroughly trained ministry.

VIRGINIA UNION UNIVERSITY.—A very small proportion of those who are entering the Negro ministry are receiving a broad, thorough training similar to that given in any Northern theological seminary. The weak points in this training are the same as in the training of Northern schools. I believe there is not enough attention given to relating the truth which is learned to life and the conditions with which the pastor will be surrounded. The theological student is not trained sufficiently in the problems of the community, the possibilities of increasing the welfare of the people, in practical ethics, in the practical hand to hand use of the Bible in effective public speaking. But, notwithstanding these failures, the record of our school shows, at least, that men with ordinary ability and such training as has been given have proved very useful in winning converts, in building up the character of the church and in improving the conditions of the communities. I think their record as useful ministers of the gospel would bear comparison with the record of the graduates of any Northern theological seminary.

As for the demand for this kind of education, our students, if they have ability, find no difficulty in securing wide fields of usefulness. We therefore feel that there is a large demand for men trained in this way. I do not believe that the character of the training should be changed, but I do believe that added emphasis should be placed on some things. I cannot see how a preacher can be a specialist in matters of religion without being able to get to the foundations of questions, without knowing how to use his Greek and Hebrew Bible, without knowing church history, theology and homiletics. I believe he needs these things, but with them he needs more knowledge of modern conditions and methods and the possibilities and ideals of individual and community life.

WALDEN.—This school was formerly known as Central Tennessee College. Rev. John Braden, who was for nearly a quarter of a century its president, organized, in 1889, a theological department which was continued under his supervision for nearly ten years. His death occurred in 1899, which closed the department. It is not possible to furnish you with correct data as to the school during the last three or four years of the life of the late Dr. Braden.

The change in the name of the school from Central Tennessee College to Walden University was followed by the election of Rev. Jay Benson Hamilton, D. D., as president to succeed the lamented Dr. John Braden. The theological department has been reorganized and is now known as the Braden School of Theology of Walden University, thus perpetuating the name of its founder.

STRAIGHT UNIVERSITY.—Most of our students take only a partial course, and for this reason do not appear among our graduates   The total attendance this year is eleven. Seven of these are pursuing studies in other departments.

I am without assistance at present. Our work is not well developed, but much good has been done and the future looks more hopeful.

My judgment is that hardly sufficient attention has been given to the education of our ministry. Still good foundations have been laid, and the importance of the subject is better understood. The demand is increasing. Churches which a few years ago were satisfied with uneducated men now search the country for men of high character and intelligence.

As to the success of the educated ministers that has been fully settled. The old assertion oft repeated that educated ministers could not preach successfully to churches of ignorant people has been thoroughly discredited in the city and the country. As to the education itself, the conception of religion as including all life within its scope and the duty of the minister to interest himself in sociology and the material and educational progress of the people should be insisted on.

KING HALL.—(a) The success of theological training in the past has been, considering the conditions, unparalleled. I doubt if history records another instance of a slave and subject population producing in so brief a space so many intelligent, progressive and high-minded men as are to be found in the pulpits of the Negro churches. It cannot be denied that there is still much ignorance and that a very lofty standard of morality is not always upheld, yet in view of historical and social convictions, the dominant emotions may be pride and thanksgiving for past achievement.

(b) The present condition of theological training gives ground for hope that conditions in the future will be superior to those in the past. The rule in former years has been that any man who evinced a slight degree of rhetorical or oratorical aptitude, or gave any promise of becoming useful to his denomination, was admitted to the ministry with little or no regard to his academic or theological preparation, but that method is the exception rather than the rule today. All of the religious denominations now demand some sort of intellectual preparation as a preliminary to ordination or licensure, and the rapid multiplication in these latter years of theological seminaries prophesies increase in the numbers of a well-trained ministry. Moreover, the diffusion of popular intelligence and the educational advance of the race will more and more demand an educated ministry, just as the steady quickening and strengthening of the ethical sense in the race will more and more demand moral purity and piety in those who minister at the altars.

(c) The direction it should take:

It should be dominantly and emphatically ethical and spiritual. The race must have clean, pure, high-minded men in her ministry, or it is doomed. Like priest, like people, and morality is the basis of the race's life. It must be soundly intellectual. . There should be broad culture and a thorough scholarship. The bombastic and pretentious must be barred, at any rate sternly discouraged. If the alternative is broad and thorough academic, or merely theological training, I would say, choose the former, for with that any deficiency in the latter can be easily remedied.

The tendency has been, and it is, to reverse this order. There is no training like that of the college and there is no people who stand in so much need of it as Negroes, and hence they must resist every effort to rob them of its advantages.

The training of the minister should also be practical. The race needs good, educated men, but it needs, and needs sorely, leadership in all that pertains to race development, and mere goodness and intelligence are not always guarantees of practical power. The Negro minister needs to know and do more than merely preach and pray. He must be possessed of public spirit and have the capacity to cooperate in educational and other social movements which promise present as well as prospective salvation. He must fit himself to preach and also practice the scripture that hath the promise of the life that now is as well as that which is to come.

The course of study at one school is subjoined as fairly typical of the courses offered in all the schools:

Virginia Union University

Bachelor of Divinity Course

FIRST YEAR.

First Term.	*Second Term.*
Biblical Introduction.	Biblical Introduction.
Hebrew Language.	Hebrew Language.
Greek Interpretation.	Greek Interpretation.
Sacred Rhetoric and Elocution.	Sacred Rhetoric and Elocution.
Vocal Music.	Vocal Music.

SECOND YEAR.

Church History	Church History.
Hebrew Interpretation.	Homiletics.
Greek Interpretation.	Christian Theology.
Sacred Rhetoric and Elocution.	Sacred Rhetoric and Elocution.
Vocal Music.	Vocal Music.

THIRD YEAR.

Biblical Introduction.	Pastoral Duties.
Homiletics and Church Polity.	Theology and Ethics.
Christian Theology.	Electives.
Sacred Rhetoric and Elocution.	Sacred Rhetoric and Elocution.

Candidates for the degree of Bachelor of Divinity, before entering upon the theological course, must have completed in a satisfactory manner the common school studies, namely: Reading, Spelling, Writing, Grammar, Geography, United

States History, and Arithmetic. They must also have done faithful work for, at least, one year of eight months, with five recitations a week in each of the following subjects and groups of subjects and must pass a satisfactory examination in at least eleven of these subjects before entering upon the theological course, two of which must be English Literature and Rhetoric and Composition. The subjects and groups of subjects are as follows: English Literature, Rhetoric and Composition, English History and General History, Physical Geography and Botany, Physics and Physiology, Algebra, Geometry, Civil Government and Ethics, and Industrial Training.

In addition to the required English studies, candidates for the degree of Bachelor of Divinity, before entering the classes in Hebrew and Greek, must pursue a course in Greek, which shall include Greek Grammar, Composition, and three books of the Anabasis.

Candidates for the degree of Bachelor of Theology, before entering upon the studies of the theological course, must possess the same English qualifications and pass the same tests upon English subjects as are required of candidates for the degree of Bachelor of Divinity.

Negroes have also attended theological schools in the North. It has been impossible to get a full account of these, but some figures are available :·

INSTITUTION.	NEGRO GRADUATES.
Christian Biblical Institute, Stanfordville, N. Y	Two.
Presbyterian Theological Seminary, Omaha, Neb.	Some.
Rochester Theological Seminary, Rochester, N. Y	One.
Tufts College, Divinity School, Tufts College, Mass.	One.
Episcopal Theological School, Cambridge, Mass.	Two.
Chicago Theological Seminary, Chicago, Ill.	Four.
Seabury Divinity School, Faribault. Minn.	Two.
New Church Theological School, Cambridge, Mass.	One.
Allegheny Theological Seminary, Allegheny, Pa.	Four.
Ryder Divinity School, Lombard University, Galesburg, Ill.	One.
Reade Theological Seminary, Taylor University, Upland, Ind.	Some.
Lane Theological Seminary, Cincinnati, O.	Few.
Princeton Theological Seminary, Princeton, N. J.	Some.
St. Joseph's Seminary, Baltimore, Md.	Four.
Union Biblical Seminary, Dayton, O.	Some.
General Theological Seminary of Protestant Episcopal Church, New York, N. Y.	Six.
Eureka College, Bible Department, Eureka, Ill.	One.
Union Theological Seminary, New York, N. Y.	About twelve
University of Chicago, Divinity School, Chicago, Ill.	Eight.
Meadville Theological School, Meadville, Pa.	One.
Oberlin Theological Seminary, Oberlin, O.	Twelve (?).
St. Mary's Seminary, Baltimore, Md.	Three.
Shurtleff College, Theological Department, Upper Alton, Ill.	One.
Yale Divinity School, New Haven, Conn.	Ten (?).
Hamilton Theological Seminary, Colgate University, Hamilton, N.Y.	Two.
Xenia Theological Seminary, Xenia, O.	Three.
Reformed Presbyterian Theological Seminary, Allegheny, Pa.	Two.
Moravian Theological Seminary, Bethlehem, Pa.	One.
Hillsdale College, Theological School, Hillsdale, Mich.	Five.
Evangelical Theological Seminary, Gettysburg, Pa.	One.
Concordia, College, Springfield, Ill.	Two.
McCormick Theological Seminary, Chicago, Ill.	Three.
Union Christian College, Theological Department, Merom, Ind.	Seventeen.
Hartford Theological Seminary, Hartford, Conn.	Eight or ten.
Newton Theological Institution, Newton Center, Mass.	Twenty-five.
Divinity School of the Protestant Episcopal Church, Philadelphia, Pa.	Ten or twelve.
Drew Theological Seminary, Madison, N. J.	Some.
Auburn Theological Seminary, Auburn, N. Y.	"
Drake University, Bible Department, Des Moines, Ia.	"
·Western Theological Seminary, Allegheny, Pa.	"
Pacific Theological Seminary, Oakland, Cal.	"
Nashotah House, Nashotah, Wis.	"
Andover Theological Seminary, Andover, Mass.	Three (?).
Boston University, School of Theology, Boston, Mass.	Ten.

The following schools in addition have had Negro students, but so far as known no graduates:

Theological Seminary of the Reformed Church................New Brunswick, N. J.
St. Vincent's Seminary...Beatty, Pa.
Kenyon College, Divinity School...............................Gambier, O.
Susquehanna University, Theological Department.............Selinsgrove, Pa.
Greenville College, School of Theology ....Greenville, Ill.
Augustana Theological Seminary...............................Rock Island, Ill.
German Evangelical Lutheran Seminary, Capital University..Columbus, O.
Crozier Theological Seminary ....Chester, Pa.
Theological Seminary of Reformed Church .. ..Lancaster, Pa.
Temple College of Philadelphia, Theological School......... ...Philadelphia, Pa.

The color line is, of course, evident in such institutions in spite of religion. The schools above admit Negroes. The following schools would admit them if they applied, but have never had applicants:

St. Paul Seminary...St. Paul, Minn.
St. Lawrence University.....................................Canton, N. Y.
St. Joseph's Seminary.......................................Yonkers, N. Y.
St. Charles's Seminary......................................Overbrook, Pa.
United Church Seminary......................................Minneapolis, Minn.
Augsburg Seminary..Minneapolis, Minn.
Western Theological Seminary...............................Holland, Mich.
Cobb Divinity School..Lewiston, Me.
Bangor Theological Seminary................................Bangor, Me.
Wartburg Seminary..Dubuque, Ia.
Charles City College..Charles City, Ia.
Union Biblical Institute ....Naperville, Ill.
Chicago Luthern Theological Seminary.......................Chicago, Ill.
Berkeley Divinity School....................................Middletown, Conn.
San Francisco Theological Seminary.........................San Anselmo, Cal.
Concordia Theological Seminary.............................St. Louis, Mo.
Redemptorist College of Ilchester..........................Ilchester, Mo.

In the following schools there have been no Negro applicants, and it is not certain whether Negroes would be admitted:

Church Divinity School of the Pacific.......................San Mateo, Cal.
Western Theological Seminary...............................Atchison, Kan.
Mt. St. Mary's Theological School...........................Mt. St. Mary's, Md.
St. John's University.......................................Collegeville, Minn.
Theological Seminary of the Evangelical Lutheran Church......Philadelphia, Pa.
Erskine Theological Seminary...............................Duewest, S. C.
Union Theological Seminary.................................Richmond, Va.
German Lutheran Seminary..................................St. Paul, Minn.
Heidelberg Theological Seminary............................Tiffin, O.
St. Bernard's Seminary ....Rochester, N. Y.
Louisville Presbyterian Theological Seminary................Louisville, Ky.
Red Wing Seminary...Red Wing, Minn.
Ursinus College School of Theology..........................Philadelphia, Pa.
St. Paul's College ....St. Paul, Minn.

The following schools are non-committal on the question :

Hartwick Seminary...Hartwick Seminary, N.Y.
Eugene Divinity School.....................................Eugene, Ore.
Kenrick Theological Seminary..............................St. Louis, Mo.

The following schools do not receive Negroes for obvious reasons of languages, etc. :

German Martin Luther Seminary............................Buffalo, N. Y.
Norwegian Danish Theological Seminary ....Evanston, Ind.
Jewish Theological Seminary...............................New York, N. Y.
German Theological School of Newark......................Madison, N. J.

The following schools do not admit Negroes:

Denver Theological Seminary . . . . Denver, Col.
St. Viateur's College . . . . Kankakee, Ill.
St. Meinrad's Ecclesiastical Seminary . . . . St. Meinrad, Ind.

Grand View College	Des Moines, Ia.
Presbyterian Theological Seminary	Danville, Ky.
Southern Baptist Theological Seminary	Louisville, Ky.
Westminster Theological Seminary	Westminster, Md.
Redemptorist Seminary of St. Louis Province	Kansas City, Mo.
Central Wesleyan College	Warrenton, Mo.
Seminary of the Immaculate Conception	South Orange, N. J.
St. Mary's College	Belmont, N. C.
St. Charles's Seminary	Carthagena, O.
Presbyterian Theological Seminary	Columbia, S. C.
Evangelical Lutheran Seminary	Mount Pleasant, S. C.
Grant University	Chattanooga, Tenn.
Southwestern Presbyterian University	Clarksville, Tenn.
Vanderbilt University	Nashville, Tenn.
University of the South	Sewanee, Tenn.
Episcopal Theological Seminary	Theological Seminary, Va.
Provincial Seminary of St. Francis of Sales	St. Francis, Wis.
Evangelical Lutheran Theological Seminary	Wauwatosa, Wis.
Theological Seminary of Eden College	St. Louis, Mo.
Mission House of the Reformed Church	Franklin, Wis.
Evangelical Lutheran Theological Seminary	Saginaw, Mich.
Christian University, Theological Department	Canton, Mo.
St. Stanislaus Seminary	Florisant, Mo.
St. Mary's Theological Seminary	Cleveland, O.
St. Vincent's Seminary	Philadelphia, Pa.
Rio Grande Congregational Training School	El Paso, Tex.
Kansas City University, College of Theology	Kansas City, Kan.

We have, therefore, a record of at least 185 Negro graduates of Northern theological schools. They have not gone to these schools in large enough number to allow any very valuable conclusions to be drawn, but the authorities of the schools have returned answers to several questions :

How have your colored students compared with others in ability?

They have been quite average in ability. Mr. —— was *quite* scholarly. Mr. —— did not take readily to accurate scholarship, but good in gaining general information. He used what he gained quite effectively.—Christian Biblical Institute.

The one student was of fair ability and compared with others in his class.— Presbyterian Theological Seminary.

Those we have had are so few in number that no conclusions with regard to the ability of the race can be drawn from them. If I were to judge only from those who have come to the Seminary I should be obliged to say that they were far below the average of our white students.—Rochester Theological Seminary.

We gave ——, a young Baptist minister, the B. D. since graduation. We felt that we owed something to his race.—Tufts College, Divinity School.

They have compared well. One was an excellent scholar, but no more than some whites.—Episcopal Theological School.

About up to average. One was an African chief, was a man of force; a second was weak as a scholar, but had unusual dramatic power; the third is a successful pastor. One, a B. A., we dismissed because he could not keep up with the work. Others left for similar reasons.—Chicago Theological Seminary.

Favorably.—Seabury Divinity School.

Favorably.—New Church Theological School.

Very well.—Allegheny Theological Seminary.

Mr.—— was an excellent student, both in scholarship and character. He has been for some years an influential member of the faculty of Guadalupe College, Seguin, Texas.—Ryder Divinity School, Lombard University.

Nearly equal.—Reade Theological Seminary of Taylor University.

Equal in diligence and regularity, superior with average in memory; below average in logical precision, and below average in orderly arrangement of knowledge.—Lane Theological Seminary.

Not unfavorably, although some of them have proven unable to pursue our course owing to lack of preliminary education.—Princeton Theological Seminary.

Two of our colored boys were among the best. The others were average students. Remember that the students of this house attend the lectures at St. Mary's Seminary, the National Seminary of the United States, in which are about 240 students, all whites.—St. Joseph's Seminary.

Their previous advantages were poor, and they themselves not of the best in natural adaptation.—Union Biblical Seminary.

They have been quite equal to the average white student in ability.—General Theological Seminary.

About average.—Eureka College, Bible Department.

This is a difficult question to answer and all the reply that is possible must be based on the individual opinion of the one entertaining it. There is no one person living who knows all of the colored students who have attended this Seminary. Personally I have known about six. Three of these were men of good ability, two of them above rather than below the medium line. Three others were below the average, two of them being distinctly inferior to the white low grade. But, on the other hand, it should be added that one of the six graduated with the diploma of the Seminary. He was above the ordinary average.—Union Theological Seminary.

Fairly well. Some of them have been able, some rather bright, but shallow, and two or three weak. A greater diversity than among whites.—University of Chicago, Divinity School.

Most of our colored students have been "specials," i. e., not members of our regular classes (Junior, Middle and Senior), but taking a partial course in connection with their service of the African Methodist Episcopal Church in this place. Their pastoral duties, of course, absorbed most of their time. Perhaps their average ability, as manifested to us, was hardly equal to that of our other students as scholars.—Meadville Theological School.

During the ten years of my teaching here the grade of men has been very good indeed. We get some of the best and very rarely any of the poorest. I mean that they grade with our other students, though no colored man has ever led the Seminary in scholarship. They have taken second and third grade scholarships, but not a first.—Oberlin Theological Seminary.

The three graduates have stood well up among the first third of their classes.—St. Mary's Seminary.

Most not up to average. One very much excelled in ability.—Shurtleff College.

They have varied greatly. It has seemed to depend largely upon the school at which they prepared.—Yale Divinity School.

They were not college men, as our students universally are, hence were at a disadvantage. Notwithstanding, they worked honestly and did well.—Xenia Theological Seminary.

These men were educated in the North; one, ——, was born in Allegheny, Pa.—Reformed Presbyterian Theological Seminary.

He compared well; was their equal in many respects, only somewhat less logical in thought and expression, and perhaps less logical and independent in ideas.—Moravian Theological Seminary.

Not above the average.—Hillsdale College.

Four of these compared favorably with the other students in some respects; the others were total failures.—Concordia College.

No difference appreciable.—McCormick Theological Seminary.

Somewhat below the average of white students.—Union Christian College, Theological Seminary.

They have not equalled the average of our other students, except perhaps in two cases, but they have not usually fallen far below.—Hartford Theological Seminary.

Their ability has been from fair to good. That of a few of the men may be called very good.—Newton Theological Seminary.

Only a few have compared favorably. One alone, if I am rightly informed, can be ranked among the *very* able men which this school has graduated.—Divinity School of the Protestant Episcopal Church.

They have maintained a good average.—Drew Theological Seminary.

In ability the average of the colored students has certainly not been below that of others.—Auburn Theological Seminary.

As far as I can learn they have.—Drake University, Bible Department.

Very favorably in most cases. During the past six years while I have been connected with the institution, we have had two colored students. One took a very high stand in the class and was elected president of the class. The other was so deficient in intellectual powers that he was dropped after six weeks' trial.—Western Theological Seminary.

This man, an ordained minister, with a church in San Francisco, took only special studies for one year. Of average ability with others of his class. But was irregular because of pastoral duties.—Pacific Theological Seminary.

He was above the average in scholarship, and took the degree of B. D.—Nashotah House.

How have they compared in character and morals ?

Very well. Quite on an average with the white students. They were respected by the white students without regard to their color.—Christian Biblical Institute.

We never knew any criticisms on either.—Presbyterian Theological Seminary.

We cannot complain of any positive infractions of immorality on their part. There has been weakness of purpose, over-sensitiveness to others' opinions, considerable vanity and love of display.—Rochester Theological Seminary.

Compared well in this respect.—Tufts College, Divinity School.

They have been without exception men of good morals and of manly character.—Episcopal Theological School.

Fairly well with others. Though in two or three cases of men who did not graduate there was a lack of determination and persistent effort. One had trouble in his family which led us to advise him to leave the Seminary.—Chicago Theological Seminary.

Favorably.—Seabury Divinity School.

Favorably.—New Church Theological School.

They were not inferior.—Allegheny Theological Seminary.

Very favorably.—Ryder Divinity School, Lombard University.

Not as strong in character.—Reade Theological Seminary of Taylor University.

Well.—Lane Theological Seminary.

Favorably.—Princeton Theological Seminary.

The blacks are just as good as the whites.—St. Joseph's Seminary.

Not so favorably with the white students.—Union Biblical Seminary.

They have been, so far as I know, uniformly excellent in character and morals.—General Theological Seminary of Protestant Episcopal Church.

Much above the average.—Eureka College, Bible Department.

As all of these men were candidates for the ministry it is to be supposed that a reply to this question is superfluous. I have no reason to make any unfavorable comparisons.—Union Theological Seminary.

Generally the equals of the whites. Two or three have been careless about financial honor, and one was dismissed for presenting for his own sermons taken from others.—University of Chicago, Divinity School.

They have compared favorably with our other students in morals and character. —Meadville Theological Seminary.

Our Seminary men have been of the very best—earnest Christians, sane, modest. Nothing in these respects has been left to be desired.—Oberlin Theological Seminary.

Very well.—Shurtleff College, Theological Department.

I have noticed no difference when each had the same chances.—Yale Divinity School.

Quite favorably. All three were earnest and devout.—Xenia Theological Seminary.

He was irreproachable in conduct and bore a good moral character.—Moravian Theological Seminary.

Well.—Hillsdale College, Theological School.

Those educated in our colored Lutheran mission schools in the South compared well. The rest proved to be unsatisfactory.—Concordia College.

No difference.—McCormick Theological Seminary.

Average, good.—Union Christian College, Theological Department.

Very well, as a rule.—Hartford Theological Seminary.

Favorably for the most part. I think it is a strain upon character for them to take their course here, since some of them are inclined to estimate themselves highly and to be ambitious for place.—Newton Theological Institution.

Equal to the white students. All of them better than some of the white students.—Divinity School of the Protestant Episcopal Church.

They have been men of good character so far as I know.—Drew Theological Seminary.

In character and morals they compare evenly in the case of the best men. In other cases they are not very uneven, except that an abnormally large number of colored men borrow money and fail to pay.—Auburn Theological Seminary.

They compare well.—Drake University, Theological Department.

Very favorably. I believe there has been only one case where discipline was necessary.—Western Theological Seminary.

During the vacation of his last year he was charged with immoral conduct by a young woman of his congregation. The matter came into the public press, but the charge was denied by student.—Pacific Theological Seminary.

What has been their success in after life ?

Good.—Christian Biblical Institute.

One of these left us at the end of his first year and we have never been able to learn anything from him since. A second was so feeble in scholarship that we had to dismiss him to another institution. The third succeeded in graduating, and has been doing useful service from that time until now.—Rochester Theological Seminary.

Mr. —— is now in his senior year in Medical School of Tufts College, Boston, Mass. He wants to be doubly prepared for missionary work.—Tufts College, Divinity School.

One is the successful minister of a colored church in Washington, where he has been for nine years, ever since graduation. Another had difficulty in getting a suitable place, but now is well settled. The third is just going out.—Episcopal Theological School.

The four graduates did well. One died in Africa, a second is a professor in a Southern college, the third is a pastor in Washington, D. C., the fourth is a pastor in the South.—Chicago Theological Seminary.

If anything, above the average man of their class.—Seabury Divinity School.

Good.—New Church Theological School.

Not especially noticeable, but very fair.—Allegheny Theological Seminary.

Quite useful.—Reade Theological Seminary of Taylor University.

Two are priests. A third teaches school under his father in New Orleans, La. The fourth is a school teacher in Oklahoma.—St. Joseph's Seminary.

Good, those who remained in the ministry.—Union Biblical Seminary.

As a rule, quite as good as the white fellow students.—General Theological Seminary.

So far as known, satisfactory.—Eureka College, Bible Department.

The one mentioned above as a graduate took a church in New York and made a success of it despite heavy odds. He worked so hard, however, that he undermined his health and died at an early age, respected and beloved by the members of the Presbytery with which he was connected. Most of the others I have not been able to trace. They have belonged to various denominations and I have not had the time to look them up specifically.—Union Theological Seminary.

Some have had marked success; some have done fairly well and a few have proved failures, but I judge as large a proportion have succeeded as among our white students.—University of Chicago, Divinity School.

So far as I have been able to judge from rather scanty information, they have had a fair degree of success in their work.—Meadville Theological School.

All, without exception so far as my own knowledge extends, have been exceptionally faithful and successful. But my personal knowledge does not cover all the cases.—Oberlin Theological Seminary.

They are all doing quite well.—St. Mary's Seminary.

Only two have had a marked success.—Shurtleff College.

Our regular graduates have been successful men.—Yale Divinity School.

So far as I know, it has been good. They are useful and influential men.—Xenia Theological Seminary.

He served as a missionary in Dutch Guiana, South America, disagreed with his superiors, became discontented and was dismissed from the church service because of unsuitable marriage connection, after it had been decided to give him a call in the West Indies.—Moravian Theological Seminary.

Fair.—Hillsdale College, Theological School.

Know not, except in case of Bishop D. A. Payne, whose history belongs to the public.—Evangelical Lutheran Theological Seminary.

Two are missionaries among their own people and, as the reports say, are doing well.—Concordia College.

Fair.—McCormick Theological Seminary.

Not striking. A limited number have made a splendid record—some as teachers, some as soldiers in the United States Army.—Union Christian College, Theological Department.

So far as we know their careers have varied greatly, but we judge that they have generally carried themselves at least with credit.—Hartford Theological Seminary.

Very creditable.—Divinity School of the Protestant Episcopal Church.

So far as I have known they have done well and have proved useful ministers of the people.—Drew Theological Seminary.

Tested numerically, too large a proportion of the colored men have either died young or have thus far failed of being distinctly successful. Of the fifteen two-thirds are successful, and some of the others may become so. The list is too short, however, and the instances too peculiar to make the numerical showing very decisive.—Auburn Theological Seminary.

The one whose name I give is reported as doing good work.—Drake University, Bible Department.

It compares favorably with that of our other graduates. Most of them are laboring under the Board of Freedmen in the South.—Western Theological Seminary.

Other schools say in general :

Of the colored men who have graduated from Boston University, School of Theology, J. W. E. Bowen, Prof. Wm. B. Fenderson, Prof. M. M. Ponton, are perhaps the most prominent. J. A. D. Bloise is a strong preacher (graduate Livingstone College) and A. W. Thomas who graduates to-morrow is a brilliant student.—Boston University, School of Theology.

Harvard has had three students. One excelled in philosophical studies. Two stood low. One of these was "of high character and morals", the other was probably an "impostor."—Harvard University.

In the last twelve years I can remember of about three, no one of whom graduated. They have not been well prepared for our work nor have they been of average ability.—Garrett Biblical Institute.

We are expecting great things of our one colored student who is now with us, and I should like to see our school become a larger factor in the solution of the race problem in the South.—Meadville Theological School.

We have never had a colored student graduate from the Theological Course, though we have had many take the course in part. The difficulty has always been that they come to the course unprepared and have fallen by the wayside. We had one colored student who very successfully completed our Law Course, but he was better prepared to begin the work.

It is very difficult to make the colored students realize that they must have a good foundation before beginning the study of theology. They desire to study theology before they know how to spell or before they have any knowledge of English grammar. So far as our observations have gone, we have never had any complaint to make of them morally, and they are generally very earnest.—The Temple College.

37. Some Notable Preachers. Certain early preachers among the Negroes have been noted in the eleventh and twelfth sections of this treatise. A word ought to be said as to some of their successors. Of the more notable preachers, the African Methodists have furnished Bishop Daniel Payne, a pure Christian and able executive officer, and perhaps the greatest of the bishops of that church; the Baptists have given us D. W. Anderson and Leonard A. Grimes, men of vigor and daring; the Episcopalians are proud of the clean character and learning of Alexander Crummell. Henry Highland Garnett was an eloquent Presbyterian, and the greatest of the Zion Methodists was the late J. C. Price. These men are all noteworthy as upright, able men, eloquent speakers and notable leaders and organizers.

Of living Negro preachers some are worthy of mention: there are the bishops of the three Methodist bodies, of which the foremost character is undoubtedly Bishop Benjamin F. Lee, a worthy successor of Daniel Payne, and a type of man too seldom put to the front; with him may be mentioned Bishop B. T. Tanner. Among the Baptists are two notable organizers, E. C. Morris, President of the National Baptist Convention, and R. F. Boyd, the head of the publishing house. The Presbyterians have in the Rev. Francis J. Grimke a man of power and upright character, and the Negro priest of longest service in the Episcopal Church is one of the most valuable social reformers of the day, the Rev. H. L. Phillips of Philadelphia. The Methodist Episcopal Church has Dr. J. W. E. Bowen, a man of ability and dignity, while the Congregationalists have the Rev. H. H. Proctor.

The men mentioned are not the better known to the public, but they are the ones who are doing the work and leading the best elements of the Negroes.*

38. The Eighth Atlanta Conference. The Eighth Atlanta Conference, to study the Negro Problems, met Tuesday morning, May 26, 1903, in Ware Memorial Chapel, Atlanta University. The subject for study was the NEGRO CHURCH, and the following programme was carried out:

---

* For the lives of these men, Cf. Simmon's Men of Mark.

President Horace Bumstead, presiding.
Subject: "Young People and the Church."
Address—Rev. W. H. Holloway, of Thomas County, Ga.
Address—Rev. Dr. Washington Gladden, President of the American Missionary Association.

Second Session, 3 P. M.

Mrs. Anna Wade Richardson, of the Lamson School, Marshallville, Ga., presiding.
Subject: "Women and the Church."
Music—By the pupils of the Mitchell Street School.
Address—Mrs. Mary Church Terrell, First President of the National Federation of Colored Women's Clubs.
"Children and the Church."—Report of the Secretary.

Third Session, 8 P. M.

President Horace Bumstead, presiding.
Remarks of President Bumstead.
"How the Religion of Negroes may become more Practical." Rev. C. B. Wilmer, Rector of St. Luke's Protestant Episcopal Church, Atlanta, Ga.
"Religion as a Solvent of the Race Problem." Professor Kelley Miller, of Howard University, Washington, D. C.
Symposium: "The Negro Church." Ten-minute speeches: Rev. J. W E. Bowen, Rev. G. W. Moore, and others.
Resolutions.

Mr. Holloway's address is printed in this treatise as section fifteen, and that of Dr. Gladden as section thirty-nine. Professor Miller's paper has been accepted for publication in the *North American Review*.

The Rev. C. B. Wilmer, representing the Southern white people, said in part that the country owed a debt to these Conferences and that it was a pleasure for him to take part:

"Religion is the chief means of uplifting mankind, but the Negro church is not the power for good that it ought to be. God never made a race incapable of responding to the motives of the gospel. Your past proves this of you, and to-day there is no higher hero than the Negro who lives a clean, upright life.

"Let the Negro preacher get God's truth into his mind and heart, and then let him get it into the minds and hearts of his hearers. This involves his understanding his people and understanding the truth as it is and as it ought to be applied to their needs.

"In general, the Negro possesses the primal virtue of loving what is above him. That virtue implies the capacity for all virtue. If I speak now of your weaknesses it is only that I may help you. They seem to be, mainly, emotionalism, sensuality, in the wide sense, and lack of perseverance. But, in particular, your having come out of the experience of slavery, exposes you to peculiar temptations. You have passed from childhood into youth, and are passing into manhood. The youth is apt to mistake 'sassiness' for courage, mannishness for manliness, and false pride for self-respect.

"What next, then, are some of the things your preachers should say to you and omit to say? Let the Negro preacher

"(1) Keep politics out of the pulpit.

"(2) Quit trying to reform white folks. Let the white minister raise a crusade against lynching and the Negro against crime.

"(3) Leave off talking about rights for a while and direct attention to duties.

"On the positive side let the Negro preacher

"(1) Inculcate good will toward all men, especially white folks. No cause is rendered easier of solution by hate.

"(2) Insist that only the truth can make you free. Sin is a worse taskmaster than any man could be.

"(3) Insist that nothing worth the having can be had by a jump, but must be climbed for. This is where perseverance comes in.

"(4) Above all, and finally, let the Negro preacher impress on his congregation that salvation does not mean acquittal from punishment, 'getting off,' nor is it the luxury of emotionalism. It is, negatively, deliverance from sin, and positively, the power of righteousness and service of our fellow men."

39. Remarks of Dr. Washington Gladden. You are citizens, by the definition of the constitution, and you are bound to be good citizens—intelligent citizens, law-abiding citizens, loyal citizens. From these obligations I am sure you do not wish to escape. You mean to do your part in contributing to the peace, the order, the security, the welfare of this great commonwealth in which you live.

In my counsels to the young people of Columbus, O., I went on to say that those to whom the duties as well as the rights of citizenship are entrusted ought not only to fit themselves for their discharge, but to discharge them solemnly and conscientiously, when the time comes for their performance. What shall I say to you who find yourselves obstructed in the performance of these duties ? I do not wish to make any inflammatory suggestions; I doubt whether the question of your political rights can be settled by violence. But this much I am safe in saying: people who are thoroughly fitted for good citizenship, and who show by their conduct that they have the disposition and the purpose to be good citizens, are not going to be permanently excluded, in any part of this country, from the responsibilities and duties of citizenship. That is as sure as tomorrow's sun-rising. It cannot be that in the United States of America, young men who are thoroughly intelligent, who know what citizenship means, who love their country, who are working to build up its prosperity and to secure its peace and who are ready to shed their blood in its defence, are going to be forbidden to take any part in its government.

What I have said, therefore, applies to you, I think, even more closely than to the young people of my own state. To you, in an exceptional and impressive way, this truth ought to come home. The more strenuously men oppose your participation in political affairs, the more zealous and dilligent ought you to be in qualifying yourselves to take part in them. You are not wholly shut out from such duties and whenever you have a chance to exercise them, let every man see that they are performed with exceptional intelligence and exceptional conscientiousness; that the black man holds the suffrage as a high and sacred trust; that he cannot be bribed or led astray by the arts of the demagogue; that he puts aside his own personal interests when he votes; that he will not even use the suffrage as a means of extorting benefits for his own race at the expense of the rest of the community, but will always keep in view the general welfare; that he is always and everywhere a patriot in his political action; that when he holds an office he discharges its duties more faithfully and honestly than the white man does. I have heard of some instances of this nature since I came to Atlanta—of men in public station whose white neighbors testify concerning them that their conduct is blameless and their service of the highest order. Let such instances be multiplied. Hold up the standard everywhere; rally round it all your people. Let it be your constant endeavor, your highest ambition to infuse this spirit, this purpose, into the thought and the life of all colored men. Before such a purpose as that the barriers of political exclusiveness are sure to go down.

Do not understand me as justifying or excusing those exclusions. I think they are utterly many. But I am pointing out to you the kind of weapons with which you can surely batter them down.

And now, very briefly, what can we say of the relations of the young people to the church? Here are these 1,210,481 young people under twenty-one. They are all citizens of Georgia; they all belong to the state. Do they all belong to the church? No; I fear not. They all belong to God; they are all His children; they owe Him love and reverence; if they are filial children, prodigal children, they are all God's children; they cannot, if they renounce and forswear it, rid themselves of the obligation of allegiance to Him. We may say of them, that they all belong in one sense to the kingdom of God. . . .

Here again I find myself in some doubt as to the fitness of these words to your peculiar circumstances. To those of you who live in Atlanta I can speak with confidence for I know that you can find a church here of which all that I say is true, in which you can find the kind of instruction and inspiration you need, to which you can attach yourselves with intelligent enthusiasm, with which you can join in the work of uplifting humanity. I suppose that there are churches of the same sort in many of the Southern cities in which you could be welcome. Doubtless there are a great many churches in all the Southern states which are far below this ideal, in which the religious instruction you would receive would be imperfect, in which the prevailing idea of religion would be one that no intelligent and conscientious person could accept. Many of you will find yourselves in communities in which the only churches are of this kind. I am not familiar enough with the situation in such communities to give you any very positive counsel respecting your conduct. I had hoped that I might be able to attend the whole of this conference, and that then I might be able to gain some information which would enable me to form a clearer judgment upon these questions. What I say about it now must be very provisional and tentative.

1. In the first place, it seems to me that you are bound to do all you can for the purification of the ideal of the Christian church. What the Christian church is, what it ought to stand for, you have some clear idea. You know that it stands, above all things, for pure conduct and high character; that its members ought to be men and women of blameless lives; that its ministers ought to be examples of virtue and honor and nobility. You know that conversion is no mere ebullition of religious emotion; that it is a change of mind and heart and life; a change from untruth to veracity, from impurity to chastity, from selfishness to unselfishness, from the spirit which is always asking, "How much am I going to get out of this?" to the spirit which is always saying, "Where can I give the most to those who are neediest?" You know that a Christian church ought not to be a company of men and women whose main business is having a good time—by getting happy and convincing themselves that they are sure of going to heaven—but whose main business is bringing heaven down to earth by showing men how to live such clean, beautiful, unselfish lives that the wilderness and the solitary place are glad for them, and that flowers of Paradise spring up in their path wherever they go. And I think it is your first duty to enforce this high and true ideal of what a church ought to be upon all the people with whom you come in contact. You will have to be wise about it. It will not do to be harsh and censorious in your judgments of the ideas and practices of those whom you are trying to lead into the light; you must persuade them by lifting up higher ideals before them, rather than by condemning and denouncing their ways. But I am sure that the young men and women who go out from such schools as this can do much, if they are wise and kind, to purify and elevate the ideals of the church in the communities where they live.

2. In some cases, doubtless, it will be found impracticable to improve the conditions of the existing churches, and it will, therefore, be necessary to organize new churches in which the essentials of Christianity can be maintained and exemplified. This will call for hard and self-condemning work. It will demand faith and courage and patience and gentleness; but it may be work of the highest value and productiveness, and you must be ready for it.

3. Finally, let me express my belief that no other kind of work can be more vital or more fruitful in the elevation of the Negro race than the work of the ministry when it is exercised with intelligence and fidelity and devotion to the highest standards of Christian conduct and character.

There are few positions in which a young man can do more harm than in the leadership of a church which is the exponent of nothing better than a mere emotional religionism; in which pietism is divorced from character and made the cover of all kinds of immoralities. But, on the other hand, there are few positions in which a young man can do more good than as the pastor of a church in which clean living and unselfish service are exemplified ; a church which stands for all the great verities of manhood and womanhood and lifts up a standard around which the elements that make for social and civic righteousness may gather and do heroic battle for God and home and native land. I do not believe that such churches as these are likely, in the present order of things, to be very popular all at once. It is probable that young men who undertake to organize and lead them will have to be content with the hard work and small compensation. They can find softer places and better salaries in churches where the standards are different. But no man can afford to lower his ideals for the sake of pelf or popularity. The elevation of the Negro race will wait a long time under such leadership. But men who are not looking for such berths, men to whom life means service, can find, in the Christian ministry, a great opportunity to serve their race and their country.

Such are the ideals which will, I trust, commend themselves to your choice as you go out to the work of life. For men and women with such purposes and aims the church has need and the state has need, and great rewards are waiting for them. I want you to win success, the true success—that which is won not by outstripping our neighbors but by helping them to get on their feet and keep in the way of life. That is not what the world means by success, but it is the only true success, believe me. Now is the time for you to get this truth firmly fixed in your own minds, not only as a pleasing sentiment, but as a working theory of life.

40. Resolutions. The Eighth Atlanta Conference is impressed by the great crying need of a strengthening of religious effort and moral inspiration among the masses of the Negro people.

We are passing through that critical period of religious evolution when the low moral and intellectual standard of the past and the curious custom of emotional fervor are not longer attracting the young and ought in justice to repel the intelligent and the good.

At the same time religion of mere reason and morality will not alone supply the dynamic of spiritual inspiration and sacrifice.

We need, then, first the strengthening of ideals of life and living; of reverent faith in the ultimate triumph of the good and of hope in human justice and growth.

We need this for the sake of the family, the moral standards of which need lifting and purifying. Upon the *women* of no race have the truths of the gospel taken a firmer and deeper hold than upon the colored women of the United States. For her protection and by her help a religious rebirth is needed.

We need it for the sake of our race, which, in the midst of repression and discouragement, is so easily apt to drift into crime and listlessness.

And finally, we need it for the sake of the state. Despite the present unrighteous denial of political rights to black men it is true, as Dr. Washington Gladden has said to this Conference, that—

"People who are thoroughly fitted for good citizenship and who show by their conduct that they have the disposition and the purpose to be good citizens are not going to be permanently excluded in any part of this country from the responsibilities and duties of citizenship. This is as true as tomorrow's sun-rising. It cannot be that in the United States of America young men who are thoroughly intelligent, who know what citizenship means, who love their country, who are working to build up its prosperity and to secure its peace and who are ready to shed their blood in its defense, are going to be forbidden to take any part in its government."

The great engine of moral uplift is the Christian church. The Negro church is a mighty social power to-day; but it needs cleansing, reviving and inspiring, and once purged of its dross it will become as it ought to be, and as it *is now*, to some extent, the most powerful agency in the moral development and social reform of 9,000,000 Americans of Negro blood.

The Negro of America needs an Age of Faith. All great ages are ages of faith. It is absolutely necessary for a new people to begin their career with the religious verities. Religious and moral qualities are independent of the eventualities of the race problem; no matter what destiny awaits the race, Religion is necessary either as a solvent or as a salve.

Religious precepts would rob the white man of his prejudices and cause him to recognize the Fatherhood of God and the brotherhood of man. Christianity is contrary to the spirit of caste—spiritual kinship transcends all other relations. The race problem will be solved when Christianity gains control of the innate wickedness of the human heart, and men learn to apply in dealing with their fellows the simple principles of the Golden Rule and the Sermon on the Mount.

(Signed)   MARY CHURCH TERRELL,
                            KELLY MILLER,
                            W. E. B. DU BOIS.

INDEX

SOME NOTES

ON

NEGRO CRIME

PARTICULARLY

IN GEORGIA

Report of a Social Study made under the direction
of Atlanta University; together with the Pro=
ceedings of the Ninth Conference for the
Study of the Negro Problems, held at
Atlanta University, May 24, 1904

EDITED BY

W. E. BURGHARDT DU BOIS

CORRESPONDING SECRETARY OF THE CONFERENCE

The Atlanta University Press
ATLANTA, GA.
1904

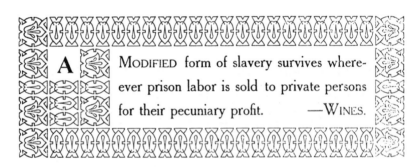

A Modified form of slavery survives wherever prison labor is sold to private persons for their pecuniary profit.   —WINES.

CONTENTS

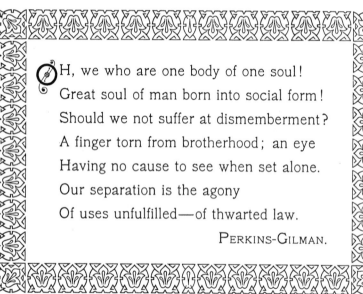

OH, we who are one body of one soul!
Great soul of man born into social form!
Should we not suffer at dismemberment?
A finger torn from brotherhood; an eye
Having no cause to see when set alone.
Our separation is the agony
Of uses unfulfilled—of thwarted law.

PERKINS-GILMAN.

PREFACE

A study of human life to-day involves a consideration of conditions of physical life, a study of various social organizations, beginning with the home, and investigations into occupations, education, religion and morality, crime and political activity. The Atlanta Cycle of studies into the Negro problem aims at exhaustive and periodic studies of all these subjects so far as they relate to the American Negro. Thus far, in nine years of the ten-year cycle, we have studied physical conditions of life (Reports No. 1 and No. 2.); social organization (Reports No. 2 and No. 3); economic activity (Reports No. 4 and No. 7.); education (Reports No. 5 and No. 6.); and religion (Report No. 8.) This year we touch upon some aspects of the important matter of Negro crime, confining our study for the most part to one state. The whole discussion of crime in the United States has usually been based on the census returns, and these are very inadequate. In this study the following sources of information were relied upon:

> Special studies of court returns and other data in Atlanta and Savannah.
> Reports from Mayors, Chiefs of Police and other officers in 37 counties of Georgia.
> Reports from colored and white citizens in 37 counties in Georgia.
> A study of arrests and commitments in 20 cities of the United States.
> Seven reports of the Georgia Prison Commission.
> Answers of 2,000 school children and students.

These data are less complete than in the case of most of our previous studies and few conclusions can be drawn until further facts and figures are available. The forthcoming government report on crime will undoubtedly be of great aid in further study.

In the preparation of this study, the editor is especially indebted to the county officials of Georgia and to a hundred or more private correspondents. He is under particular obligations to Professor M. N. Work of the Georgia State College, the Rev. Mr. H. H. Proctor of Atlanta, and Frank Sanborn, Esq., of Concord, Mass. The proof reading was largely done by Mr. A. G. Dill, who also drew the diagrams and arranged the index.

Atlanta University has been conducting studies similar to this for the past nine years. The results, distributed at a nominal sum, have been widely used. Notwithstanding this success, the further prosecution of these important studies is greatly hampered by the lack of funds. With meagre appropriations for expenses, lack of clerical help and necessary apparatus, the Conference cannot cope properly with the vast field of work before it.

Especially is it questionable at present as to how large and important a work we shall be able to prosecute during the next ten-year cycle. It may be necessary to reduce the number of conferences to one every other year. We trust this will not be necessary, and we earnestly appeal to those who think it worth while to study this, the greatest group of social problems that has ever faced the nation, for substantial aid and encouragement in the further prosecution of the work of the Atlanta Conference.

———————

A SELECT BIBLIOGRAPHY OF NEGRO CRIME

C. H. Alexander.—The Majesty of Law. University, Miss. 1900.

Benjamin C. Bacon.—Statistics of the Colored People of Philadelphia. Philadelphia, 1856.
Ibid. 2nd ed. with statistics of Crime. Philadelphia, 1859.

J. C. Ballagh.—A History of Slavery in Virginia. 160 pp. Baltimore, 1902.

J. S. Bassett.—History of Slavery in North Carolina. Johns Hopkins University Studies. Baltimore, 1899.
Slavery and Servitude in the Colony of North Carolina. Baltimore. The Johns Hopkins Press. April and May, 1896.

L. E. Bleckley.—Outrages of Negroes no Excuse for Lynching. Forum, 16:300.

J. R. Brackett.—Progress of the Colored People of Maryland. Johns Hopkins University Studies. Eighth Series.
The Negro in Maryland. 270 pp. Baltimore.
Status of the Slave, 1775-1789. Essay V. in Jameson's Essays in the Constitutional History of the United States, 1775-1789. Boston, 1889.

L. Brandt.—Negroes of St. Louis. Pub. American Statistical Society. Vol. VII., 1903.

P. A. Bruce.—Plantation Negro as Freeman. New York, 1889.

G. W. Cable.—Negro Freedman's Case in Equity. Century, 7:409.

Rev. Dr. R. F. Campbell.—The Race Problem in the South, 1899.

C. W. Chestnutt.—Thomas on the American Negro. Book Buyer, 38:350.

T. R. R. Cobb.—Inquiry into the law of Negro Slavery in the U. S. A. Vol. 1. Philadelphia and Savannah, 1858.
Law of Negro Slavery in the various States of the United States, 8vo. Philadelphia, 1858.

W. H. Collins.—The Domestic Slave Trade of the Southern States. 154 pp. New York, 1904.

Colored Statistics.—Nation, 77:400-1. Nov. 19, 1903.

Condition of the Negro in various Cities. Bulletin United States Department of Labor, No. 10.

J. Cook.—Race Riots in the South. Our Day, 5:406.

H. S. Cooley.—Slavery in New Jersey. Johns Hopkins University Studies. Baltimore, 1897.

J. E. Cutler.—Proposed Remedies for Lynching. Yale Review. August, 1904.

F. Douglas.—Treatment of Negroes: the Color-Line. North American, 13:57.
Lynching of Black People because they are Black. Our Day, 13:298.

W. S. Drewry.—The Southampton Insurrection. Washington, 1900.

W. E. B. DuBois.—Thomas on the American Negro. Dial, 30:262.
Some Notes on Negroes in New York City. Atlanta University, 1903.
The Black North.—The New York Times, 1901.
Negro and Crime. Independent, May, 1899.
Philadelphia Negro. 520 pp. Philadelphia, 1899.
Souls of Black Folk, 264 pp. Chicago, 1903.
Negroes of Farmville, Va. Bulletin United States Department of Labor, No. 14.
The Negro in Black Belt. Bulletin United States Department of Labor, No. 22.

Bryan Edwards.—History, Civil and Commercial, of the British Colonies in the West Indies. London, 1807.

R. P. Falkner.—Crime and the Census. Pub. American Academy Political and Social Sciences. No. 190.

George Fitzhugh.—Cannibals all or Slaves without Masters. Richmond, 1857.

B. O. Flower.—Burning of Negroes in the South. Arena, 7:639.

Wm. C. Fowler.—Local Law in Massachusetts and Connecticut historically considered: and the Historical Status of the Negro in Connecticut. Albany, 1872 and New Haven, 1875.

Wm. Goodell.—The American Slave Code in Theory and Practice. Judicial decisions and illustrative facts. New York, 1852.

H. W. Grady.—Reply to Mr. Cable (Negro Freedman's Case in Equity). Century, 7:909.

H. Gregoire.—Enquiry concerning the intellectual and moral faculties, etc., of Negroes. Brooklyn, 1810.

F. J. Grimke.—The Lynching of Negroes in the South. 1899.

W. Waller Hening.—Statutes at large of Virginia. Richmond, 1812.

F. L. Hoffman.—Race Traits and Tendencies of the Negro. American Economic Association. 11:1.

Hull House Maps and Papers. New York, 1895.

J. C. Hurd.—The law of freedom and bondage in the United States. Boston and New York, 1858, 1862.

Edward Ingle.—The Negro in the District of Columbia. Johns Hopkins University Studies. Vol. XI. Baltimore, 1893.
Southern Side-lights. Boston, 1896.

E. A. Johnson.—Light Ahead for the Negro. 132 pp. New York, 1904.

F. A. Kellor.—The Criminal Negro. Arena, 25:59-510; 36:20-521.
Experimental Sociology. 316 pp. New York, 1901.

Fanny Kemble.—A journal of a residence on a Georgia plantation. New York, 1863.

J. Bradford Laws.—The Negroes of Cinclare Factory and Calumet Plantation, La. Bulletin United States Department of Labor, No. 38.

George Livermore.—An historical research respecting the opinions of the founders of the Republic on Negroes as slaves, as citizens and as soldiers. Boston, 1862.

K. Miller.—Review of Hoffman's Race Traits and Tendencies of the Negro. Publications of the American Negro Academy, No. 1.

Montgomery Conference on race problems. Proceedings, 1900.

George H. Moore.—Notes on the history of slavery in Massachusetts. New York, 1866.

Edward Needles.—Ten Years' Progress, or a Comparison of the State and Condition of the Colored People in the City and County of Philadelphia from 1837–1847. Philadelphia, 1850.

Negro Problems and the Negro Crime. Harper's Weekly, 47:1050–1. June 20, 1903.

New Negro Crime. Harper's Weekly, 48:120–1. Jan. 23, 1904.

New Negro Crime considered: Southern View. Harper's Weekly, 47:1830. Nov. 14, 1903.

F. L. Olmstead.—The Cotton Kingdom. New York, 1861.
  Journey in the Back Country. London, 1861.
  A journey in the sea-board slave states. New York, 1856.
  A journey through Texas. New York, 1857.

T. N. Page.—The Negro: The Southerner's Problem. 316 pp. New York, 1904.

Present state and condition of the free people of color of the city of Philadelphia and the adjoining districts. Philadelphia, 1838.

Report of the Committee on the Comparative Health, Morality, Length of Sentence, etc., of White and Colored Convicts. Philadelphia, 1849.

Wm. Noel Sainsbury, editor. Calendar of state papers. Colonial series. America and the West Indies. 1574–1676. London, 1860–1863.

W. S. Scarborough.—Lawlessness vs. Lawlessness. Arena, 24:478.

Servitude for Debt in Georgia.—Outlook, 74:486. June 27, 1903.

Bernard S. Steiner.—Slavery and Connecticut. Johns Hopkins University Studies. Baltimore, 1893.

G. M. Stroude.—A sketch of the laws relating to slavery in the several states of the United States of America. Philadelphia, 1827.

A. Sledd.—Another View. Atlantic, 90:65–73. July, 1902.

Social and Industrial Condition of Negroes in Massachusetts. 34th Annual Report Mass. Bureau of Labor. 1904.

A Statistical Inquiry into the Condition of the People of Color of the City and Districts of Philadelphia. Philadelphia, 1849.

E. Tayleur.—Social and Moral Decadence. Outlook, 76:266–71. Jan. 30, 1904.

Walter T. Thom. The Negroes of Litwalton, Va. Bulletin United States Department of Labor, No. 37.
  The Negro of Sandy Springs, Md. Bulletin United States Department of Labor, No. 32.

Wm. H. Thomas—The American Negro. New York, 1901.

United States Census, 1870.

United States Census, 1880.

United States Census, 1890.

B. T. Washington.—Future of American Negro. Boston, 1899.

S. D. Weld.—American slavery as it is: testimony of thousands of witnesses. New York, 1839.

I. B. Wells-Barnett.—A Red Record. 1896.

W. F. Willcox.—Negro Criminality. American Journal Social Science, 37:78.

Geo. W. Williams.—History of the Negro Race in America from 1719–1880. New York, 1883.

G. B. Winton.—Negro Criminal. Harper's Weekly, 47:1414. August 29, 1903.

M. N. Work.—Crime Among Negroes in Chicago. American Journal Sociology, 6:204.

Carroll D. Wright.—Slums of Great Cities. 7th Special Report of the U. S. Department of Labor. Washington, 1894.

Richard R. Wright, Jr.—The Negroes of Xenia, Ohio. Bulletin United States Department of Labor, No. 48.

NEGRO CRIME

1. The Problem* (by FRANK B. SANBORN).

Crime is in general that portion of human depravity and passion which is regarded and punished by human laws. As distinguished from vice, it is more overt, more dreaded by the community, and held in greater abhorrence; while vice is more insidious, more general, and more ruinous to the individual, though often held in little reprehension by the community. For example, the vice of drunkenness was little censured among English-speaking persons a century ago and is still rather held in honor in some parts of the world; while the crime of parricide, though infinitely less pernicious (because it could never become common) has ever been execrated by all. But since vice is defined by conscience and opinion, and crime by law (which is the tardy result of conscience and opinion), nearly every vice comes, in some time or place, to be stigmatized as a crime, while crimes are often remanded to the catalogue of vices, and sometimes of virtues. For a two-fold reason, then, the moralist cannot regard crime precisely as it is esteemed in the popular judgment. It was once a crime where I stand to teach a slave to read, but not a crime to buy or sell that slave. We should call the first a virtue now; while the second might be held either a vice or a crime, or even a virtue, according to circumstances.

Although there are many exceptions, the mass of what we term crime is the direct or indirect result of poverty and its attendant evils. Crime from other causes, however, is also painfully common. With vice the case is different. That also is fostered by poverty and misery, but it is no less stimulated by the ease and opportunity of affluence. Between vice and crime, the distance is usually short; but pauperism is not seldom an intermediate stage. From the class of comfortable and respectable persons, men are continually lapsing, through vice, into pauperism, either in themselves or their children, and from pauperism into crime. Even when this is not its genealogy, crime may ordinarily be traced to one of the five general causes of pauperism, which in 1867 were thus assigned by me in a report to the Governor of Massachusetts, of which state I was then an official, charged with the investigation of such subjects:—

---

*Remarks to the Conference, Tuesday evening, May 24, 1904.

"The causes of pauperism are (1) Physical inferiority and degradation; (2) Moral perversity; (3) Mental incapacity; (4) Accidents and infirmities; (5) (and often the most powerful of all), Unjust and unwise laws and the customs of society. Such are the general causes,' but under the five heads come innumerable minor and proximate causes,—intemperance, profligacy, insanity, indolence, false education, ignorance, superstition, monopolies, privilege, indeed, all the enemies of human advancement. For pauperism is one of the sloughs in which the progress of mankind is arrested."

From this unhappy slough, most of the crime of the community emerges, and among the emissaries of crime are the tramps that patrol the land, especially in wealthy manufacturing communities like New England. They find in great cities the haunts of vice, and keep up a sort of circulation, like the veins and arteries of the human body, from one part of the land to another. A stationary class of vicious and criminal persons in the cities are the confederates and refuge of these wandering criminals, and vice versa,—a city criminal taking refuge in the moving army of tramps, and thus oftentimes escaping arrest.

It will readily be seen that Negro slavery, while preserving the community from an excess of technical pauperism, naturally furnished the same atmosphere of vice and crime, when the strong hand of slave law was removed by general emancipation. A similar result followed the emancipation of the serfs in the Middle Ages, and explains the outbreaks of crime and disease which marked the 14th and 15th centuries in Europe.

2. **Crime and Slavery.*** Mr. Wines, the American criminologist, has said: "A modified form of slavery survives wherever prison labor is sold to private persons for their pecuniary profit." The history of crime in the Southern states of America illustrates this. Two systems of controlling human labor which still flourish in the South are the direct children of slavery. These are the crop-lien system and the convict-lease system. The crop-lien system is an arrangement of chattel mortgages, so fixed that the housing, labor, kind of agriculture and, to some extent, the personal liberty of the free black laborer is put into the hands of the landowner and merchant. It is absentee landlordism and the "company-store" systems united. The convict-lease system is the slavery in private hands of persons convicted of crimes and misdemeanors in the courts. The object of this section is to sketch the rise and development of the convict-lease system, and the efforts to modify and abolish it.

Before the Civil War the system of punishment for criminals in the South was practically the same as in the North. Except in a few cities, however, crime was less prevalent than in the North, and the system of slavery naturally modified the situation. The slaves could become criminals in the eyes of the law only in exceptional

*First printed in slightly altered form in the *Missionary Review of the World*, Oct., 1901.

cases. The punishment and trial of nearly all ordinary misdemeanors and crimes lay in the hands of the masters. Consequently, so far as the state was concerned, there was no crime of any consequence among Negroes. The system of criminal jurisprudence had to do, therefore, with whites almost exclusively, and as is usual in a land of scattered population and aristocratic tendencies, the law was lenient in theory and lax in execution.

On the other hand, the private well-ordering and control of slaves called for careful co-operation among masters. The fear of insurrection was ever before the South, and the ominous uprisings of Cato, Gabriel, Vesey, Turner, and Toussaint made this fear an ever-present nightmare. The result was a system of rural police, mounted and on duty chiefly at night, whose work it was to stop the nocturnal wandering and meeting of slaves. It was usually an effective organization, which terrorized the slaves, and to which all white men belonged, and were liable to active detailed duty at regular intervals.

Upon this system war and emancipation struck like a thunderbolt. Law and order among the whites, already loosely enforced, became still weaker through the inevitable influence of conflict and social revolution. The freedman was especially in an anomalous situation. The power of the slave police supplemented and depended upon that of the private masters. When the masters' power was broken the patrol was easily transmuted into a lawless and illegal mob known to history as the Ku Klux Klan. Then came the first, and probably the most disastrous, of that succession of political expedients by which the South sought to deal with the consequences of emancipation. It will always be a nice question of ethics as to how far a conquered people can be expected to submit to the dictates of a victorious foe. Certainly the world must to a degree sympathize with resistance under such circumstances. The mistake of the South, however, was to adopt a kind of resistance which in the long run weakened her moral fiber, destroyed respect for law and order, and enabled gradually her worst elements to secure an unfortunate ascendency. The South believed in slave labor, and was thoroughly convinced that free Negroes would not work steadily or effectively. Elaborate and ingenious apprentice and vagrancy laws were therefore passed, designed to make the freedmen and their children work for their former masters at practically no wages. Justification for these laws was found in the inevitable tendency of many of the ex-slaves to loaf when the fear of the lash was taken away. The new laws, however, went far beyond such justification, totally ignoring that large class of freedmen eager to work and earn property of their own, stopping all competition between employers, and confiscating the labor and liberty of children. In fact, the new laws of this period recognized the Emancipation Proclamation and the Thirteenth Amendment simply as abolishing the slave-trade.

The interference of Congress in the plans for reconstruction stopped the full carrying out of these schemes, and the Freedmen's Bureau consolidated and sought to develop the various plans for employing and guiding the freedmen already adopted in different places under the protection of the Union Army. This government guardianship established a free wage system of labor by the help of the army, the striving of the best of the blacks, and the co-operation of some of the whites. In the matter of adjusting legal relationships, however, the Bureau failed. It had, to be sure, Bureau courts, with one representative of the ex-master, one of the freedmen, and one of the Bureau itself, but they never gained the confidence of the community. As the regular state courts gradually regained power, it was necessary for them to fix by their decisions the new status of the freedmen. It was perhaps as natural as it was unfortunate that amid this chaos the courts sought to do by judicial decisions what the legislatures had formerly sought to do by specific law—namely, reduce the freedmen to serfdom. As a result, the small peccadilloes of a careless, untrained class were made the excuse for severe sentences. The courts and jails became filled with the careless and ignorant, with those who sought to emphasize their new found freedom, and too often with innocent victims of oppression. The testimony of a Negro counted for little or nothing in court, while the accusation of white witnesses was usually decisive. The result of this was a sudden large increase in the apparent criminal population of the Southern states—an increase so large that there was no way for the state to house it or watch it even had the state wished to. And the state did not wish to. Throughout the South laws were immediately passed authorizing public officials to lease the labor of convicts to the highest bidder. The lessee then took charge of the convicts—worked them as he wished under the nominal control of the state. Thus a new slavery and slave-trade was established.

The abuses of this system have often been dwelt upon. It had the worst aspects of slavery without any of its redeeming features. The innocent, the guilty, and the depraved were herded together, children and adults, men and women, given into complete control of practically irresponsible men, whose sole object was to make the most money possible. The innocent were made bad, the bad worse; women were outraged and children tainted; whipping and torture were in vogue, and the death-rate from cruelty, exposure, and overwork rose to large percentages. The actual bosses over such leased prisoners were usually selected from the lowest classes of whites, and the camps were often far from settlements or public roads. The prisoners often had scarcely any clothing, they were fed on a scanty diet of corn bread and fat meat, and worked twelve or more hours a day. After work each must do his own cooking. There was insufficient shelter; in one Georgia camp, as late as 1895, sixty-one men slept in one room, seventeen by nineteen feet, and seven feet high. Sanitary conditions were wretched, there was little or no medical attendance, and almost no care of the sick. Women were mingled indiscriminately with the men, both in working and in sleeping, and dressed often in men's clothes. A young girl at camp

Hardmont, Georgia, in 1895, was repeatedly outraged by several of her guards, and finally died in childbirth while in camp.

Such facts illustrate the system at its worst—as it used to exist in nearly every Southern state, and as it still exists in parts of Georgia, Mississippi, Louisiana, and other states. It is difficult to say whether the effect of such a system is worse on the whites or on the Negroes. So far as the whites are concerned, the convict-lease system lowered the respect for courts, increased lawlessness, and put the states into the clutches of penitentiary "rings." The courts were brought into politics, judgeships became elective for shorter and shorter terms, and there grew up a public sentiment which would not consent to considering the desert of a criminal apart from his color. If the criminal were white, public opinion refused to permit him to enter the chaingang save in the most extreme cases. The result is that even to-day it is difficult to enforce the criminal laws in the South against whites. On the other hand, so customary had it become to convict any Negro upon a mere accusation, that public opinion was loathe to allow a fair trial to black suspects, and was too often tempted to take the law into its own hands. Finally the state became a dealer in crime, profited by it so as to derive a net annual income from her prisoners. The lessees of the convicts made large profits also. Under such circumstances, it was almost impossible to remove the clutches of this vicious system from the state. Even as late as 1890, the Southern states were the only section of the Union where the income from prisons and reformatories exceeded the expense.* Moreover, these figures do not include the county gangs where the lease system is to-day most prevalent and the net income largest.

INCOME AND EXPENSE OF STATE PRISONS AND REFORMATORIES, 1890.

	Earnings.	Expense.	Profit.
New England	$299,735	$1,204,029	......
Middle States	71,252	1,850,452	......
Border States	597,808	962,411	......
Southern States‡	938,106	890,132	$17,974
Central States	624,161	1,971,795	......
Western States	378,036	1,572,316	......

The effect of the convict-lease system on the Negroes was deplorable. First, it linked crime and slavery indissolubly in their minds as simply forms of the white man's oppression. Punishment, consequently, lost the most effective of its deterrent effects, and the criminal gained pity instead of disdain. The Negroes lost faith in the integrity of courts and the fairness of juries. Worse than all, the chaingangs became schools of crime which hastened the appearance of the confirmed Negro criminal upon the scene. That some crime and vagrancy should follow emancipation was inevitable. A nation cannot systematically degrade labor without in some degree debauching the laborer. But there can

---

*Bulletin No. 8, Library of State of New York. All figures in this section are from this source.

‡South Carolina, Georgia, Alabama, Mississippi, Louisiana, Texas, and Arkansas.

be no doubt but that the indiscriminate method by which Southern courts dealt with the freedmen after the war increased crime and vagabondage to an enormous extent. There are no reliable statistics to which one can safely appeal to measure exactly the growth of crime among the emancipated slaves. About seventy per cent. of all prisoners in the South are black; this, however, is in part explained by the fact that accused Negroes are still easily convicted and get long sentences, while whites still continue to escape the penalty of many crimes even among themselves. And yet, allowing for all this, there can be no reasonable doubt but that there has arisen in the South since the war a class of black criminals, loafers and ne'er-do-wells who are a menace to their fellows, both black and white.

The appearance of the real Negro criminal stirred the South deeply. The whites, despite their long use of the criminal court for putting Negroes to work, were used to little more than petty thieving and loafing on their part, and not to crimes of boldness, violence, or cunning. When, after periods of stress or financial depression, as in 1892, such crimes increased in frequency, the wrath of a people unschooled in the modern methods of dealing with crime broke all bounds and reached strange depths of barbaric vengeance and torture. Such acts, instead of drawing the best opinion of these states and of the nation toward a consideration of Negro crime and criminals, discouraged and alienated the best classes of Negroes, horrified the civilized world, and made the best white Southerners ashamed.

Nevertheless, in the midst of all this, a leaven of better things had been working, and the bad effects of the epidemic of lynching quickened it. The great difficulty to be overcome in the South was the false theory of work and of punishment of wrong-doers inherited from slavery. The inevitable result of a slave system is for a master class to consider that the slave exists for his benefit alone—that the slave has no rights which the master is bound to respect. Inevitably this idea persisted after emancipation. The black workman existed for the comfort and profit of white people, and the interests of white people were the only ones to be seriously considered. Consequently, for a lessee to work convicts for his profit was a most natural thing. Then, too, these convicts were to be punished, and the slave theory of punishment was pain and intimidation. Given these ideas, and the convict-lease system was inevitable. But other ideas were also prevalent in the South; there were in slave times plantations where the well-being of the slaves was considered, and where punishment meant the correction of the fault rather than brute discomfort. After the chaos of war and reconstruction passed, there came from the better conscience of the South a growing demand for reform in the treatment of crime. The worst horrors of the convict-lease system were attacked persistently in nearly every Southern state. Back in the eighties, George W Cable, a Southern man, published a strong attack on the system. The following decade Governor Atkinson, of Georgia, instituted a searching investigation, which startled the state by its revelation of existing conditions. Still more recently Florida, Arkansas and other states have had reports and agitation for reform. The result has been marked improvement in conditions during the last decade. This is shown in part by the statistics of 1895; in that year the prisons and reformatories of the far South cost the states $204,483 more than they earned, while before this they had nearly always yielded an income. This is still the smallest expenditure of any section, and looks strangely small beside New England's $1,190,564. At the same time, a movement in the right direction is clear. The laws are being framed more and more so as to prevent the placing of convicts altogether in private control. They are not, to be sure, always enforced, Georgia having still several hundreds of convicts so controlled. In nearly all the Gulf states the convict-lease system still has a strong hold, still debauches public sentiment and breeds criminals.

The next step after the lease system was to put the prisoners under regular state inspection, but to lease their labor to contractors, or to employ it in some remunerative labor for the state. It is this stage that the South is slowly reaching to-day, so far as the criminals are concerned who are dealt with directly by the states. Those whom the state still unfortunately leaves in the hands of county officials are usually leased to irresponsible parties. Without doubt, work, and work worth the doing—*i. e.*, profitable work—is best for the prisoners. Yet there lurks in this system a dangerous temptation. The correct theory is that the work is for the benefit of the criminal—for his correction, if possible. At the same time, his work should not be allowed to come into unfair competition with that of honest laborers, and it should never be an object of traffic for pure financial gain. Whenever the profit derived from the work becomes the object of employing prisoners, then evil must result. In the South to-day it is natural that in the slow turning from the totally indefensible private lease system, some of its wrong ideas should persist. Prominent among these persisting ideas is this: that the most successful dealing with criminals is that which costs the state least in actual outlay. This idea still dominates most of the Southern states. Georgia spent $2.38 per capita on her 2,938 prisoners in 1890, while Massachusetts spent $62.96 per capita on her 5,227 prisoners. Moreover, by selling the labor of her prisoners to the highest bidders, Georgia not only got all her money back, but made a total clear profit of $6.12 on each prisoner. Massachusetts spent about $100,000 more than was returned to her by prisoners' labor. Now it is extremely difficult, under such circumstances, to prove to a state that Georgia is making a worse business investment than Massachusetts. It will take another generation to prove to the South that an apparently profitable traffic in crime is very dangerous business for a state; that prevention of crime and the reformation of criminals is the one legitimate object of all dealing with depraved natures, and that apparent profit arising from other methods is in the end worse than dead loss. Bad public schools and profit from crime explain much of the Southern social problem.

Moreover, in the desire to make the labor of criminals pay, little heed is taken of the competition of convict and free laborers, unless the free laborers are white and have a vote. Black laborers are continually displaced in such industries as brick-making, mining, road-building, grading, quarrying, and the like, by convicts hired at $3, or thereabouts, a month.

The second mischievous idea that survives from slavery and the convict-lease system is the lack of all intelligent discrimination in dealing with prisoners. The most conspicuous and fatal example of this is the indiscriminate herding of juvenile and adult criminals. It need hardly be said that such methods manufacture criminals more quickly than all other methods can reform them. In 1890, of all the Southern states, only Texas, Tennessee, Kentucky, Maryland, and West Virginia made any state appropriations for juvenile reformatories. In 1895 Delaware was added to these, but Kentucky was missing. We have, therefore, expended for juvenile reformatories:

	1890.	1895.
New England	$632,634	$854,581
Border States	233,020	174,781
Southern States	10,198	33,910

And this in face of the fact that the South had in 1890 over four thousand prisoners under twenty years of age. In some of the Southern states—notably, Virginia—there are private associations for juvenile reform, acting in co-operation with the state. These have, in some cases, recently received state aid. In other states, like Georgia, there is permissive legislation for the establishment of local reformatories. Little has resulted as yet from this legislation, but it is promising.

This section has sought to trace roughly the attitude of the South toward crime. There is in that attitude much to condemn, but also something to praise. The tendencies are to-day certainly in the right direction, but there is a long battle to be fought with prejudice and inertia before the South will realize that a black criminal is a human being, to be punished firmly but humanely, with the sole object of making him a safe member of society, and that a white criminal at large is a menace and a danger. The greatest difficulty to-day in the way of reform is this race question. The movement for juvenile reformatories in Georgia would have succeeded some years ago, in all probability, had not the argument been used: it is chiefly for the benefit of Negroes. Until the public opinion of the ruling masses of the South can see that the prevention of crime among Negroes is just as necessary, just as profitable, for the whites themselves, as prevention among whites, all true betterment in courts and prisons will be hindered. Above all, we must remember that crime is not normal; that the appearance of crime among Southern Negroes is a symptom of wrong social conditions—of a stress of life greater than a large part of the community can bear. The Negro is not naturally criminal; he is usually patient and law-abiding. If slavery, the convict-lease system, the traffic in criminal labor, the lack of juvenile reformatories, together with the unfortunate discrimination and prejudice in other walks of life, have led to that sort of social protest and revolt which we call crime, then we must look for remedy in the sane reform of these wrong social conditions, and not in intimidation, savagery, or the legalized slavery of men.

3. Crime and the Census. Before a remedy of any kind can be applied to crime, we must know something of the extent of the evil. How far is crime prevalent among Negroes, and what sorts of crime are most common? The extreme Southern view of the situation is illustrated by the statement of Governor James K. Vardaman of Mississippi:*

1. The Negro element is the most criminal in our population.

2. The Negro is much more criminal as a free man than he was as a slave.

3. The Negro is increasing in criminality with fearful rapidity, being one third more criminal in 1890 than 1880.

4. The Negroes who can read and write are more criminal than the illiterate, which is true of no other element of our population.

5. The Negro is nearly three times as criminal in the Northeast, where he has not been a slave for a hundred years, and three and a half times as criminal in the Northwest, where he has never been a slave, as in the South, where he was a slave until 1865.

6. The Negro is three times as criminal as a native white, and once and a half as criminal as the foreign white, consisting in many cases of the scum of Europe.

7. More than seven-tenths of the Negro criminals are under thirty years of age.

The conservative Northern view may be represented by the words of Professor Walter F. Willcox in answer to the above assertions:†

"1. *The Negro element is the most criminal in our population.*" The main evidence, almost the only evidence, regarding the criminality of different classes is derived from census statistics. The most recent figures on the subject are those of 1890, an inquiry into the subject by the Census Office for the year 1904 being now in progress. The following figures show the number of prisoners in the United States in 1890 of the specified race to each 10,000 total population of that race:

Race
White.. 10
Negro.. 33
Mongolian 38
Indian 55

The preceding figures indicate that the criminality of the Negro race is much higher than that of the whites, but lower than that of the Indians and Mongolians. The Chinese and Japanese in the United States are nearly all men, from which class prisoners mainly come. For this reason such a comparison between Negroes and Mongolians is misleading, and probably more accurate comparisons would show the criminality of the Negroes to be higher than that of the Mongolians. But I see no reason for doubting the obvious inference from the figures that it is lower than that of the Indians, and therefore I do not believe the first conclusion.

"2. *The Negro is much more criminal as a free man than he was as a slave.*" Crimes committed by the Negro under the slavery system were usually punished by the master without recourse to the courts. Now there is no master, and the courts must punish the Negro criminal, if he is not in most cases to go free. Court records, if tabulated in statistical form, as they are not, would doubtless show a greater amount of recorded crime. But I do not think such statistics would prove the conclusion that he is by nature or by habit more criminal than as a slave, nor do I see how it can be established by other evidence than that derived from personal opinion. My experience does not warrant me in drawing any conclusion on this point.

"3. *The Negro is increasing in criminality with fearful rapidity, being one-third more criminal in 1890 than in 1880.*" The evidence on this point also comes from the census. In 1880 there were twenty-five Negro, Indian and Mongolian prisoners to every 10,000 persons of those races. In 1890 there were thirty-three. The Negroes are many times as numerous as the other races combined, and therefore the foregoing figures are substantially true for the Negroes alone. How far this increase is due to a change in the characteristics of the race, and how far to an increase in the number of crimes punished by the law, or to the efficacy of the judicial system in ferreting out and punishing crime, it seems impossible to say. I believe there has been an increase in Negro criminality, but that the foregoing figures do not afford an accurate measure of its amount.

"4. *The Negroes who can read and write are more criminal than the illiterate, which is true of no other element of our population.*" In 1890, among every 10,000 Negroes at least ten years of age who could read and write, there were forty-one prisoners, while among every 10,000 illiterate Negroes of the same ages there were forty-nine prisoners. The conclusion is thus shown to be incorrect. For reasons which I have not space here to state, I believe that the true difference in favor of the educated Negroes is greater than the foregoing figures indicate.

"5. *The Negro is nearly three times as criminal in the Northeast, where he has not been a slave for a hundred years, and three and a half times as criminal in the Northwest, where he has never been a slave, as in the South, where he was a slave until 1865.*" The evidence for this statement is also derived from the census. In the Southern States in 1890 there were twenty-nine Negro prisoners to every 10,000 Negroes, in the Northeast there were seventy-five, and in the far Western States ninety-five. Governor Vardaman explains this difference as a lingering effect of slavery. It certainly was not due to that. The proof is found in the fact that similar differences exist among whites. In his State of Mississippi, for example, there were fourteen Negro prisoners to 10,000 Negroes, and in my State of New York there were 100, but in Mississippi there were two white prisoners to every 10,000 whites, and in New York there were eighteen. Are we to explain the low percentage of criminals among Southern whites as also a lingering effect of Negro slavery? No; the fact is that crime and criminals are more prevalent in closely settled communities, where any sort of disorder is more likely to lead directly to the prison. Negro criminals are more numerous at the North and the West, partly because there are fewer Negro children and more adult men in those sections, but mainly because Negroes at the North live especially in the cities, while at the South they live mainly in the country.

"6. *The Negro is three times as criminal as a native white, and once and a half as criminal as the foreign white, consisting in many cases of the scum of Europe.*" Negro criminality is undoubtedly far greater than white, and I have little doubt that the foregoing statement is substantially, though not numerically, correct. Perhaps a fairer comparison than that between all Negroes and all foreign-born whites would be between the Negroes and the foreign-born living in the North. In the North Atlantic division, where recent immigrants are most numerous, the Negro prisoners relative to population are three times as numerous as foreign-born white prisoners, and in the North Central division they are more than six times as numerous.

"*7. More than seven-tenths of the Negro criminals are under thirty years of age.*" This statement is substantially correct. But it should be noticed that more than half of the white prisoners are also under thirty years of age, and that the average length of life of the Negroes is several years less than that of the whites, and therefore the proportion of them in the higher ages is small. The figures, however, do indicate a disproportionate and probably an increasing amount of juvenile crime among the Negroes.

The evidence relied upon in judging crime among Negroes is chiefly the United States Census Reports of 1870, 1880 and 1890. These reports are briefly summarized in the following pages:

White

	1870	1880	1890
Prisoners	24,845	41,861	57,310
Ratio per million	740	964	1,042

Colored (Negro, Indian, etc.)

		1870	1880	1890
Prisoners		8,056	16,748	25,019
Ratio per million		1,621	2,480	3,275
Ratio per million	Negroes			3,250
	Chinese			3,835
	Indian			5,476

How shall these figures be interpreted? First, it is certain that they cannot be given their full value because of the method of collection. The census of 1890 says:*

The increase in the number of prisoners during the last 40 years has been more apparent than real, owing to the very imperfect enumeration of the prison population prior to 1880. Whatever it has been, it is not what it might be supposed to be, if we had no other means of judging of it than by the figures contained in the census volumes.

The census method of measuring crime by counting the prison population on a certain day every ten years has been shown by Dr. Roland P. Falkner to lead to unwarranted conclusions. He says:†

If the amount of crime means the ratio between the offenses committed in a given year and the population at that time, the census volume fails to give us a correct idea of crime in the United States:

1. Because it furnishes no basis for a calculation of the increase of crime.

2. Because in depicting the geographical distribution of crime, it favors one locality at the expense of another.

3. Because it exaggerates the number of the male sex in the aggregate of crime.

4. Because it assigns to the Negroes a larger, and to the foreign-born white a smaller, share in the total of crime than belongs to each.

5. Because it distorts the picture of the relative frequency of different classes of crimes.

Mr. Falkner says further:‡

---

*11th Census, Crime, etc., Pt. I, p. 126.   †Crime and the Census, p. 66.   ‡Ibid, p. 62.

The census can here do justice to the different elements only on the supposi-
tion of a uniform distribution of sentences. If one class receive longer sentences
than another, or commit classes of crimes for which longer sentences are given,
it will appear unduly magnified in the census report. The following table
summarizes the facts of the census report, regarding sentences where a definite
term has been imposed by the courts:

Sentences of the Prison Population in 1890, by Elements of the Population

GROUPS	Average sentence, years	Prisoners with def. sentences	Sentences of under one year	Per cent of sentences under 1 year
Total	3.88	65,653	18,538	29.13
Total white	3.46	44,856	14,688	32.74
Total native white	3.67	32,076	9,141	28.50
Foreign-born white	2.97	12,434	5,425	43.63
Negroes	4.84	18,322	3,737	20.39

The variation in average sentences is quite considerable. The short term offenders really constitute the bulk of the total commitments of a year, but as we
have seen do not exercise the greatest influence upon the census totals. If the
short term sentences fall below the average, as in the case of the Negroes, that element receives undue prominence in the census. If they rise above the average,
as in the case of the foreign-born, that element has not its appropriate quota in
the census figures.

From the sentences and prisoners as reported in the census of 1890,
Mr. Falkner then proceeds to calculate the probable number of commitments and makes the following table: *

Prison Population in 1890 and Estimate of Commitments, by Elements of the Population

GROUPS	Prisoners Sentenced or Committed.			Percentages		
	1 year and over	Under 1 year	Total	1 year and over	Under 1 year	Total
SENTENCED						
Native white	22,935	9,141	32,076	50.84	49.31	50.41
Foreign-born white	7,009	5,125	12,434	15.51	29.26	19.53
Negroes	14,585	3,737	18,322	32.55	20.16	28.78
COMMITTED						
Native white	9,283	96,470	105,753	52.32	49.76	49.96
Foreign-born white	2,890	59,374	62,264	16.29	30.61	29.42
Negroes	5,445	35,036	40,481	30.69	18.06	19.12

If we compare the percentages for the prison population, we see that the long
sentences have the greatest weight in determining the average for all. In the
probable commitments the contrary is the case. Our calculations do not affect
the proportion of native white, but they reverse the positions of the Negro and
the foreign-born white.

Thus this estimate reduces the responsibility of the Negro for crime
in this land from 30% to 19%.

---

*Crime and the Census, p. 63.

4. Extent of Negro Crime. It seems fair to conclude that the Negroes of the United States, forming about one-eighth of the population, were responsible in 1890 for nearly one-fifth of the crime. Detailed figures from the censuses are as follows:

Colored* Prisoners, 1870

```
United States.........................8,056
North Atlantic States.................1,160
South        "          "         .................3,391
North Central.........................833
South        "          .....................2,640
Western...............................32
```

Colored* Prisoners, 1880

	Colored	Colored, male	Colored, female
UNITED STATES	16,748	15,500	1,248
North Atlantic Division	1,403	1,265	138
South Atlantic Division	5,579	5,057	522
North Central Division	1,708	1,580	128
South Central Division	7,394	6,938	456
Western Division	664	660	4

Offenses Charged

	Colored	Colored, male	Colored, female
ALL OFFENSES	16,562	15,381	1,181
Offenses against government	117	116	1
Offenses against society	1,072	809	263
Offenses against person	3,918	3,691	227
Offenses against property	9,510	9,027	483
Offenses on high seas	2		
Miscellaneous	315	259	56
Not stated	1,610	1,476	140

Prisoners by Sex and Geographical Divisions

1890	Males	Females	Total
UNITED STATES	22,305	1,972	24,277
North Atlantic	1,793	244	2,037
South Atlantic	8,113	750	8,863
North Central	2,528	210	2,738
South Central	9,625	756	10,381
Western	246	12	258

By Prisons

Prisons	Number	Percentages
In state prisons and penitentiaries	14,267	58.77
In county jails	5,497	22.64
In city prisons	1,068	4.30
In workhouses and houses of correction	1,327	5.46
Leased out (by counties)	1,995	8.22
In military and naval prisons	46	0.19
In hospitals and asylums for the insane	77	0.32
Total	24,277	100.00 %

* Includes Indians and Chinese.

Ratios of Prisoners to 1,000,000 of Negro Population

```
No. Atlantic Div..................... 7,547
So.     "      "   ..................... 2,716
No. Central   "       ..................... 6,351
So.      "      "   ..................... 2,984
Western        "       ..................... 9,527

United States...........................3,250
```

Out of every 10,000 Negro prisoners:

```
    5  are   under 10  years of age
1,822  "           10-19   "      "
5,078  "           20-29   "      "
1,875  "           30-39   "      "
  741  "           40-49   "      "
  327  "           50-59   "      "
  117  "           60-69   "      "
   28  "           70-79   "      "
    5  "  ,        80-89   "      "
    2  "           90-99   "      "
```

Out of every 10,000 Negroes:

```
15-19 years of age......44 are prisoners, and 11 in reformatories
20-24   "        "    .....98  "       "
25-29   "        "    .....88  "       "
30-34   "        "    .....63  "       "
35-44   "        "    .....41  "       "
45-54   "        "    .....25  "       "
55-64   "        "    .....17  "       "
65 and
over    "        "    ...... 9  "       "
```

The average age of Negro prisoners is:

```
Male .................27.73 years
Female ...............26.08   "

Total .................27.60   "
```

Negroes were incarcerated for the following offenses:

Kind of Offenses

	Both sexes	Males	Females
TOTAL	100.00 %	100.00 %	100.00 %
1. Against the government	0.70 %	0.77 %	0.08 %
2. Against society, (i. e., perjury, adultery, gambling, drunkenness, disorder, concealed weapons, vagrancy, etc.)	16.54 %	14.13 %	40.64 %
3. Against the person, (murder, rape, assaults, etc.).	25.95 %	26.72 %	18.22 %
4. Against property....................	46.65 %	48.28 %	30.33 %
5. Miscellaneous, (double crimes, infractions of municipal ordinances, witnesses, unknown)....	10.16 %	10.10 %	10.73 %

The actual number of offenses for whites and Negroes is:

OFFENSES	Whites	Negroes	Indians
ALL OFFENSES	1,000,000	1,000,000	1,000,000
1. Against the government	28,721	7,332	40,373
2. Against society	269,796	134,283	279,503
Perjury and false swearing	2,949	6,961	9,317
Incest	3,210	1,565	....
Adultery	4,886	4,407	9,317
Fornication, etc	14,849	6,591	3,105
Gambling	1,152	10,545	....
Public intoxication	99,529	16,353	52,795
Disorderly conduct	56,273	23,767	9,317
Carrying concealed weapons	2,879	14,293	....
Vagrancy	43,273	14,747	15,528
3. Against the person	179,148	277,629	388,199
Homicide	77,212	112,823	285,714
Rape	14,203	23,438	24,845
4. Against property	451,858	476,954	273,292
Burglary	120,015	114,307	40,373
Larceny	241,877	288,668	214,286
5. Miscellaneous	70,407	103,802	18,633

Average Ages of Prisoners by Groups of Crimes

	Aggregate number	Negroes
All offenses	30.65	27.60
Offenses against government	31.44	30.76
Offenses against society	33.87	27.99
Offenses against person	32.38	29.01
Offenses against property	28.35	26.60
Offenses on high seas	38.00	....
Miscellaneous	30.02	7.84

Crime and Illiteracy

NEGROES	Percentage of total population			Percentage of prison population.		
	Total	Males	Females	Total	Males	Females
Read and write	42.91	45.63	40.23	38.88	39.11	36.26
Illiterate*	57.09	54.37	59.77	61.12	60.89	63.74
Read only	6.81	6.73	6.87	6.99	6.58	11.71
Neither read nor write	50.28	47.64	52.90	54.13	54.31	52.03

From the figures of 1890 it seems fair to conclude:

1. That eight-tenths of the Negro prisoners are in the South where nine-tenths of the Negroes dwell. This is further emphasized by the fact that Negroes in the North furnish 60 to 75 prisoners for every 10,000 of population, while those in the South furnish about 30. This discrepancy is largely explained by the difference in urban and rural populations, and the migration northward.

* According to the usage of the census of 1890 the term "illiterate" includes both those who can read and not write and those who neither read nor write. Cf.

2.   While 60% of the prisoners are in State Prisons and Penitentiaries, this excess of dangerous criminals is apparent and not real and is due to the census method of computing crime.

3.   Half of the Negro prisoners are between the ages of 20 and 30 years, a fifth, 10-19 years, and another fifth, 30-40 years. This shows a lower criminal age than among whites.

4.   Nearly half of the Negro prisoners are confined for crimes against property. If commitments were tabulated, undoubtedly pilfering would be found to be pre-eminently the Negro crime. This is due to imperfect ideas of property ownership inseparable from a system of slavery.

5.   One-fourth of the Negro prisoners are confined for crimes against tl.e person. This consists of fighting and quarreling, ending at times in homicide, and also the crime of rape. Fighting is to be expected of ignorant people and people living under unsettled conditions. Of 1,392 persons confined for rape in 1890, 578 were Negroes. These figures exaggerate the apparent guilt of Negroes because the Negroes received an average sentence of 14.04 years for rape while whites received an average sentence of 12.72 years, and probably a still larger disproportion in life sentences existed. Negroes too are more easily convicted of this crime to-day, because of public opinion. Notwithstanding all these considerations there is no doubt of a large prevalence of sexual crime among Negroes. This is due to the sexual immorality of slavery, the present defenselessness of a proscribed caste, and the excesses of the undeveloped classes among Negroes.

6.   One-sixth of the criminals in jail were charged with crimes against society—gambling, drunkenness, adultery, etc.

7.   The age statistics show that among both whites and blacks the younger criminals steal; among Negroes, crimes against society and the person claim the next older set, while crimes against the government and the person come next among whites.

8.   The illiterate Negroes furnish more of the criminals than those who read and write. The difference in education between the great number who can just barely read and write and the wholly illiterate is not great, so that this does not really illustrate the full degree in which ignorance causes Negro crime. There has been so much dispute and misapprehension on this point that additional testimony is valuable. Mr. Clarence Poe says: *

But do the general, nation-wide results indicate that education is helpful? It has often been claimed that they do not. And in proof we have the oft repeated charge that the percentage of literacy among Negro criminals in 1890 was higher than that for the total Negro population—in other words, that the literate Negroes furnish a larger proportion of prisoners than the illiterate. This statement was made in an address before the National Prison Association in 1897. It was printed in one of our foremost magazines, the North American Review, in June, 1900. It was repeated by a governor of Georgia in a public message. A Mississippi

*Clarence H. Poe, a Southern white man, editor of the Raleigh *Progressive Farmer*, in the *Atlantic Monthly*, February, 1904, p. 162.

preacher has sent it broadcast over the South, and it was doubtless used in the recent campaign in that state. Scores of papers have copied it. Even now a Southern daily which I have just received has a two-column argument against Negro education, based on the alleged census figures. "To school the Negro," says the writer, "is to increase his criminality. Official statistics do not lie, and they tell us that the Negroes who can read and write are more criminal than the illiterate. In New England, where they are best educated, they are four and a half times as criminal as in the Black Belt, where they are most ignorant. The more money for Negro education, the more Negro crime. This is the unmistakable showing of the United States Census."

That such statements as these have thus far gone unchallenged should indeed excite our special wonder. It was only the desire to get the exact figures that led me to discover their falsity. The truth is, that of the Negro prisoners in 1890 only 38.88 per cent. were able to read and write, while of the total Negro population 42.90 per cent. were able to read and write. And in every division of the country save one (and that with only a handful of Negro criminals) the prisons testified that the literate Negroes were less lawless than the illiterate. To make the matter plain, the following figures have been prepared by the United States Bureau of Education. They show the number of criminals furnished by each 100,000 colored literates, and the number furnished by each 100,000 colored illiterates, according to the Census of 1890:

Criminals in each 100,000 Negroes

Section	Literates	Illiterates
North Atlantic Division	828	1174
South Atlantic Division	320	426
South Central Division	317	498
North Central Division	807	820
Western Division	542	518

When we consider that there were only 258 Negro prisoners in all the Western division (out of 24,277 in the Union), the mere accident that, of these few, seven more than the exact proportion came from the literate element loses all significance; the test is on a scale too small for general conclusions. Summing up, it appears that of our total colored population in 1890 each 100,000 illiterates furnished 489 criminals, and each 100,000 literates only 413 criminals. Even more striking testimony comes from the North Carolina State's Prison situated in the writer's own city. In the two years during which it has kept a record, the proportion of Negro criminals from the illiterate class has been 40 per cent. larger than from the class which has had school training.

Later the same writer adds to this the following data.*

From Governor Vardaman's own State of Mississippi, where, in 1890, 60.9 per cent. and in 1900 less than 50 per cent. of the colored population were illiterate, the official who sends the report writes as follows: "There are about 450 Negro convicts in the Mississippi penitentiary; about half are wholly illiterate. Of the other half less than ten per cent. have anything like a fair education." In other words, in this very state, where Negro education is pronounced a failure, the literate Negroes furnish a smaller proportion of criminals than the illiterate, and not even those literate Negro criminals are really fairly educated. Similar testimony comes from other states. In North Carolina the illiterate Negroes of the state furnished 40 per cent. more criminals, according to number, than the Negroes who could both read and write. In South Carolina, where the census of 1890 gives the Negro literates as constituting 47.2 per cent. of the entire race in the state, the

*Editorial in the Outlook, Jan. 30, 1904, pp. 246-7.

penitentiary superintendent estimates that only 25 per cent. can both read and write. In Georgia more than 60 per cent. of the Negro convicts are illiterate, while of the total Negro population only 47.6 per cent. are illiterate. In Alabama the illiterates among the Negro criminals are reported as about 70 per cent. while the illiteracy of the total colored population is only 57.4 per cent. This means that in that state the Negroes who cannot read and write furnish about 30 per cent. more criminals, in round numbers, than the Negroes who have had school advantages. It is to be remembered that the figures for illiteracy now are not quite so bad as they were ten years ago; and therefore the figures quoted do not make the facts in confutation of Governor Vardaman's theories appear as strong as they really are.

There is no doubt that the common schools for Negroes sorely need improvement; but even as they are, it is clear that these schools are factors for law, order and morality.

The following diagram illustrates the facts as to illiteracy and crime for Negroes in the United States, 1890:

POPULATION

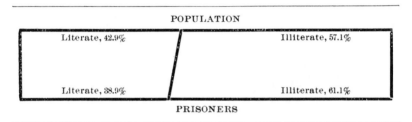

Literate, 42.9%   Illiterate, 57.1%

Literate, 38.9%   Illiterate, 61.1%

PRISONERS

So much has been said and written on the subject of lynching that it is necessary here simply to add the usually received statistics on the subject, collected by the Chicago *Tribune* [see page 19].

5. Crime in Cities (by MONROE N. WORK, A. M.). Let us now turn from the bare and partially misleading census figures to a consideration of other sources of information. The best sources available are the reports of crime in various cities together with a few states. In these places the longest periods of time for which data were available have been taken. Whenever possible, the number of prisoners received in jails, workhouses, and penitentiaries during specified periods of time have been taken. The distinction between arrests and convictions has been maintained. An analysis of crimes and offenses has also been attempted to see if particular crimes or offenses are increasing or decreasing. It is recognized that the liability to make errors has not been eliminated, but it is hoped that the method of presenting the data and of interpretation has been such as to reduce the amount of error to a minimum.

Negro crime is considered in three periods: prior to 1866-1867; from 1867 to 1880; and from 1880 to 1903. Although the data for the first two periods are somewhat meager, it enables us, however, to gain some idea of the rate of these two periods.

Lynchings by Race by Years

	1885	1886	1887	1888	1889	1890	1891	1892	1893	1894	1895	1896	1897	1898	1899	1900	1901	1902	1903	1904	Total
Negroes	78	71	80	*65	95	90	121	155	154	134	112	80	122	102	84	107	107	86	86	83	2,042
Others	103	62	43	*47	80	38	74	81	46	56	59	51	44	25	23	8	28	10	18	4	900
Totals	181	133	123	142	175	128	195	236	200	190	171	131	166	127	107	115	135	96	104	87	2,942

*Estimates. The *Tribune* was unable to furnish the figures for 1888, except the totals.

Lynchings by Crimes by Years

	1885	1886	1887	1888	1889	1890	1891	1892	1893	1894	1895	1896	1897	1898	1899	1900	1901	1902	1903	Total	%
Rape	31	30	40	*46	44	42	46	58	57	47	40	40	32	24	18	31	29	30	21	706	24.7
Murder	88	66	54	*61	64	43	79	101	79	74	68	49	69	71	56	43	42	41	55	1,206	42.2
Other crimes	62	37	29	*35	67	43	70	77	61	69	63	42	65	29	33	41	64	25	28	943	33.1
Totals	181	183	123	142	175	128	195	238	200	190	171	131	166	127	107	115	135	96	104	2,855	100.0

*Estimates.

Total Lynchings by States, 1885-1903*

State	No.	State	No.	State	No.
Mississippi	287	Oklahoma	39	Arizona	12
Texas	255	Indiana	38	Iowa	12
Louisiana	253	Kansas	34	Oregon	10
Georgia	240	California	31	Michigan	5
Alabama	221	Wyoming	31	Minnesota	4
Tennessee	184	Nebraska	30	Alaska	4
Arkansas	177	Colorado	26	Nevada	4
Kentucky	141	Montana	24	Wisconsin	3
Florida	126	Maryland	20	New York	2
S. Carolina	103	Dakota	18	Pennsylvania	2
Virginia	80	Illinois	17	Connecticut	1
Missouri	79	Idaho	16	Delaware	1
Indian Terr.	48	N. Mexico	15	N. Jersey	1
N. Carolina	48	Washington	15		
W. Virginia	43	Ohio	13		

*Figures for 1888 not included.

No special comparison of the crime rates of whites and Negroes is made. It is recognized that the crime rate of the Negroes is greater than that of the whites. In 1900 the rate of Negro arrests and commitments was from one and a half to ten times greater than that of the whites. The correct method for a comparison of crime among the whites and Negroes would be to compare the crime rate of the Negroes with the crime rate of the corresponding class or stratum of the whites. This comparison would no doubt show much less difference in the respective crime rates than is shown when the crime rate of the Negroes as a whole is compared with that of the whites as a whole. Since it is not possible to make this comparison it is probably better, as has been done in this study, to consider Negro crime in its relation to the Negro population, recognizing that the peculiar conditions of the Negro, past and present, tend to keep his crime rate high. Police arrests, jail, workhouse, and penitentiary commitments are respectively considered.

Police Arrests. Data were available for twenty representative Northern and Southern cities. Nine of these follow in detail:

Arrests per Thousand of Negro Population

CITIES	Negro population 1900	1858 A	1867 B	1872 C	1875 D	1880 E	1885 F	1890
New York	60,666	83	106					82
Philadelphia	62,613	150		94	47	69	65	80
Washington	86,702					111	161	166
Charleston	31,522					90	50	70
Savannah	28,090				79	82	65	75
Louisville	39,139						129	99
Cincinnati	14,482			163	132	106	108	225
Chicago	30,150			153	226	211	274	387
St. Louis	35,516		64	80	97	134	108	120

A—Philadelphia, 1864.
B—St. Louis, 1869.
C—Philadelphia, 1870.
D—Savannah, 1874.
E—Washington, Savannah and St. Louis, 1881; Cincinnati, 1882.
F—Louisville, 1884.

In the chart which follows a more comprehensive view of Negro arrests in the above nine cities is given. The variation in the rate of each city and the difference in the various rates of the several cities, together with what appears to be the present tendency of Negro arrests, are shown.

It appears from the following chart that, for New York and Philadelphia, the only cities for which data prior to 1866 were available, as has been shown, the rate of Negro arrests per thousand of the Negro population was about as great, or greater, prior to 1866 than in 1902. The maximum of the rate for New York, 111, was reached in 1899; the rate for Philadelphia has at no time since been as great as it was in 1864, 150. Statistics were available for Washington from 1881 to 1902. The rate of Negro arrests in 1881 was 111; in 1902, 169, and the maximum of the rate, 184, was reached in 1893. For Charleston we have data from 1880 to 1903. The rate of arrests in 1880 was 90, in 1903, 86, and

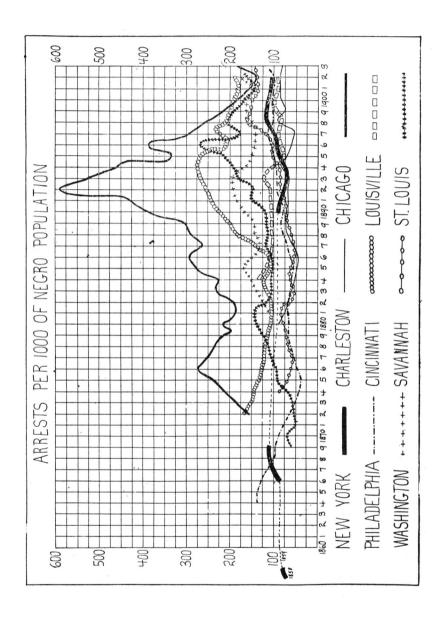

the maximum of the rate, 92. was reached in 1902. Statistics were available for Cincinnati from 1872 to 1902. The rate of Negro arrests in 1872 was 163, in 1902, 186, and the maximum of the rate, 276, was reached in 1894. For Savannah we have data from 1874 to 1903. The rate of arrests in 1874 was 79, 1903, 143. The maximum of the rate of Negro arrests for Savannah, 165, was reached in 1898. Statistics were available for Chicago from 1872 to 1903. The rate of Negro arrests in 1872 was 153, in 1903, 185. The maximum, 586, was reached in 1892.* Data were available for Louisville from 1884 to 1902. The rate of arrests in 1884 was 129, in 1902, 93. The maximum was reached in 1884. Statistics were available for St. Louis from 1869 to 1902. The rate of arrests in 1869 was 64, in 1902, 166; the maximum, 269, was reached in 1896.

The arrest rate for each particular city shows more or less variation from year to year, the greatest variation being in the case of Chicago, which also for most of the time has had the highest arrest rate. The difference in the arrest rates of the various cities has also more or less of variation. In 1879–1882, with the exception of Chicago, a minimum of difference in the arrest rates of the various cities was reached. The maximum of difference, 511, in the arrest rates was in 1892. Taking the period from 1866 to 1882 it appears that at sometime during this period the arrest rate, with the possible exception of St. Louis, for each of the cities decreased. From 1882 to 1892–1896 there was, with some exceptions, a marked increase in the arrest rates of the several cities. This was especially true of Chicago, Cincinnati, Washington, and St. Louis. From 1892–1896 to 1902–1903 there appears to have been a general tendency for the Negro arrest rates of these cities to decrease. It appears that on the whole, we are warranted in concluding that for the nine cities considered the rate of Negro arrests per thousand of the Negro population is decreasing.

Twenty cities are next considered. They are classified according to locality into Northern and Southern cities. By such a classification we have eight Northern and, including Washington, Baltimore and St. Louis, twelve Southern cities. The period of time is from 1890 to 1903. A comparison is made to see how the arrest rates of the cities of the two sections correspond in respect to variations in the individual rates of each city, the difference in the rates of the several cities of the two sections, and the tendency of the arrest rates to increase or decrease; finally the cities of which section have the highest arrest rates.

Two charts showing the comparison of police arrests in Northern and Southern cities follow [see pages 24 and 25].

An inspection of the following charts shows that variation in the individual rates of the Northern cities is greater than that of the Southern cities, with the exception of St. Louis. In 1890 the difference in the arrest rates of the Northern cities, 327, between Indianapolis and Chicago, is greater than that of the Southern cities; but in 1901 the differ-

---

*This being the year of the World's Fair, data cover the arrests of non-residents and are not therefore a measure of Chicago crime.

ence in the arrest rates of the Southern cities, 287, between Memphis and Atlanta is much greater than that of the Northern cities. In 1890 the arrest rates for four of the Northern cities were greater than those of the Southern cities, while three of the Northern cities had lower rates than any of the Southern cities except Savannah. In 1902 four 'of the Northern and seven of the Southern cities had rates above 107. This would seem to indicate that at present the rates of arrests for Southern cities is probably greater than those for the Northern cities. Observing the rates of arrests for both sections, it is seen that in the Northern section there appears to be a notable tendency for the rates to decrease. In the Southern section the tendency, while not so marked, is also apparently toward a decrease. This would be more apparent if the rates of arrests for the Southern cities were shown for a longer period of time, as was the case for Washington, Charleston, Louisville, and St. Louis.

Jail Commitments.—Data relating to jail commitments were available for three cities, Baltimore, Charleston, and St. Louis, and two states, Ohio and Michigan. Statistics for these cities and states follow:

Jail Commitments per Thousand of the Negro Population for Certain Cities and States

Year	Baltimore	Charleston*	St. Louis	Ohio	Michigan
1873				5.3	
1874					
1875					
1876				10	
1877				9	10
1878					14
1879				9	14
1880		42		9	16
1881		33	15		12
1882		32	21	9	
1883		25	14	9	
1884		24	16		
1885		22	14		13
1886		21	19	11	13
1887		20	18	11	14
1888	57	31	20		21
1889	69	30	19		29
1890	58	31	18		36
1891	57	30	24		19
1892	56	29	23		27
1893	59	21	27		28
1894	59	35	29		31
1895	56	24	28		25
1896	52	26	29	15	36
1897	60		28	12	50
1898		28		14	53
1899	55	37			33
1900	59	40			32
1901	65	38	24		23
1902		38		14	
1903		34			

* Jail commitments for Charleston include those sentenced to the chain-gang and those sentenced to pay a fine or serve a short term in jail.

By consulting the above table of statistics it is seen that in Baltimore during the year 1888 the rate of jail commitments was 57; in 1901 the rate was 65; the highest rate of commitments, 69, was in 1899. The rate of commitments for Charleston in 1880 was 42; in 1903 the rate was 34; the highest rate of jail commitments was in 1880. In St. Louis the rate

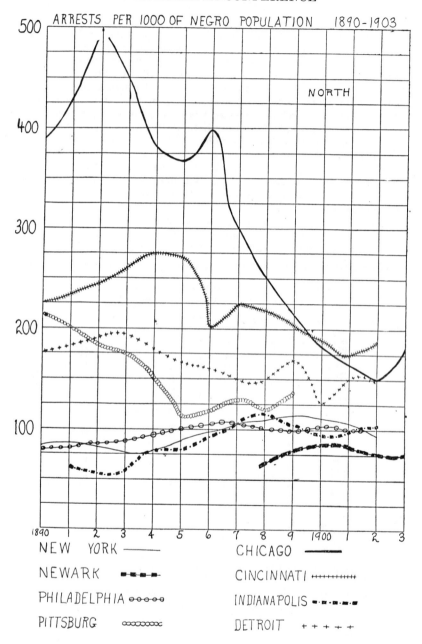

ARRESTS PER 1000 OF NEGRO POPULATION   1890-1903

NORTH

NEW YORK ———   CHICAGO ▬▬▬

NEWARK ▪▬▪▬▪▬   CINCINNATI ┼┼┼┼┼┼┼┼┼

PHILADELPHIA ◦◦◦◦◦   INDIANAPOLIS ▪▬▪▬▪▬

PITTSBURG ◌◌◌◌◌◌◌   DETROIT + + + + +

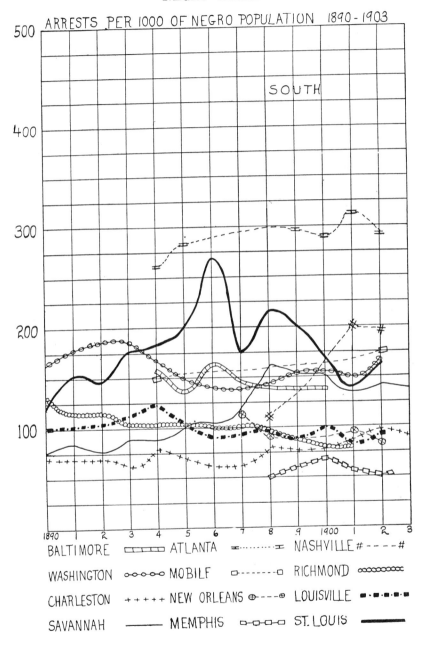

ARRESTS PER 1000 OF NEGRO POPULATION 1890-1903

SOUTH

BALTIMORE ⊏⊐⊏⊐ ATLANTA ⋆·········⋆ NASHVILLE # - - - - #

WASHINGTON ∘-∘-∘-∘ MOBILE □-------□ RICHMOND ∞∞∞∞∞∞∞

CHARLESTON + + + + + NEW ORLEANS ⊕- - -⊕ LOUISVILLE ■-■-■-■

SAVANNAH ——— MEMPHIS □-□-□-□ ST. LOUIS ▬▬▬▬

of commitments for 1881 was 15; in 1901 the rate was 24; the highest rate of commitments, 29, was in 1894 and 1896. The rate of jail commitments for the state of Ohio was 5.3 in 1873; in 1902 the rate was 14; the highest rate of jail commitments, 15, was in 1896. In the state of Michigan the rate of jail commitments for 1877 was 10; in 1901 the rate of commitments was 23; the highest rate, 53, was in 1898.

The rate of commitments for the cities of Baltimore and Charleston during the periods for which data were available do not appear to have varied very much. The rates of jail commitments for the city of St. Louis and the states of Ohio and Michigan appear to have varied considerably and are higher at the end than at the beginning of the periods considered. Their rates of commitments are not as high at the end of the periods as during some of the previous years of the periods. It appears that at present the rates of jail commitments for the cities and states considered have increased slowly since the seventies until the nineties and now apparently are beginning to decrease slightly The workhouse commitments show a similar tendency:

Negro Workhouse Commitments per Thousand of the Negro Population for Certain Cities

Year.	Philadelphia	Washington	Cincinnati	Louisville	Chicago	St. Louis
1870						16
1871						18
1872						20
1873					48	18
1874					58	29
1875			75			
1876	54				62	
1877	50				67	25
1878	45				63	
1879	37		39		36	
1880	32				33	
1881	36	21			37	21
1882	38	23			43	26
1883	34				42	24
1884	34	22	37	34	48	26
1885	40	23	33		52	28
1886	47	24	33		41	31
1887	46	19		31	42	33
1888	36	26	31	28	46	28
1889	34	32	41	28	45	36
1890	40	38	47		46	26
1891	41	41		30	38	25
1892	43	44	58	31	49	23
1893	48	44		29	54	32
1894	50	42	70	46	64	42
1895	45	35	63	42	42	38
1896			58	31	44	40
1897			68	30	31	36
1898			71		25	
1899		35	65	33	27	
1900		31	57	31	31	
1901		29	47	23	30	23
1902		30	50		24	22
1903				30		

Penitentiary commitments should be one of the best indexes of the tendencies of crime because here we have convictions for serious offenses. Some data were available for the States of Ohio, Michigan, Indiana, Illinois and Kansas, and the cities of Baltimore and Chicago. A chart showing the rates of Negroes committed annually to penitentiaries follows:

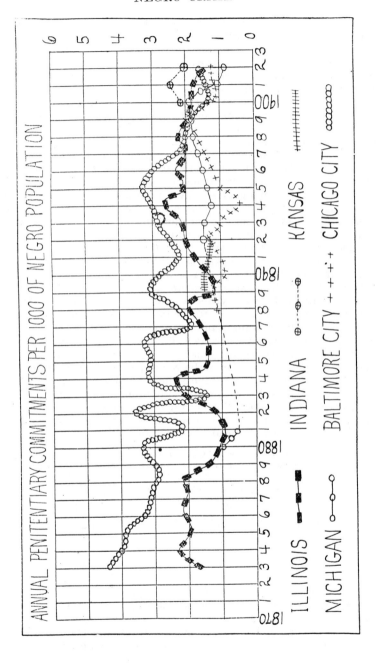

Observing the preceding chart it is seen that the period of time considered is from 1873 to 1902. The rate of annual commitments per
thousand of the Negro population for the state of Illinois in 1873 was
1.7; the rate of annual commitments for Illinois in 1902 was 1.4; the
highest rate of annual commitments for Illinois, 2.6, was in 1894. The
rate of annual commitments to the state penitentiary of Illinois from
the city of Chicago in 1873 was 4.4; in 1902 the rate was 1.6; the highest rate of annual Negro commitments to the penitentiary from Chicago was in 1873. The rate of annual Negro penitentiary commitments
for the state of Michigan in 1880 was 1.0; in 1902 the rate was 0.8;
the highest rate of annual Negro commitments to the penitentiary
from the state of Michigan, 1.9, was in 1900. The rate of annual commitments to the penitentiary from the city of Baltimore in 1888 was 1.1;
in 1902 the rate of annual penitentiary commitments from this city was
1.3; the highest rate of annual penitentiary commitments from Baltimore, 2.0, was in 1899. The rate per thousand of the Negro population
for the number of prisoners received in the Kansas penitentiary was
available for four years as follows: in 1889 and 1890 the rate of annual
Negro commitments to the Kansas penitentiary was 1.5; in 1891 and
1892 the rate was 1.3. The rate per thousand of the Negro population
for the number of prisoners received annually in the Indiana penitentiary was available for three years as follows: in 1900 the rate was 2.1;
in 1901 the rate was 2.5; and in 1902 the rate was 2.0. The rates of annual commitments for Kansas and Indiana are given merely to show
that these rates are about the same as those of the other states for the
corresponding periods of time, and show the same tendencies of rate
variation. With the exception of the Negro penitentiary commitments
from Chicago there are no great individual variations in the rates from
year to year of the Negro annual penitentiary commitments. This
will be better seen in the following table in which the difference between the lowest and the highest annual rate of penitentiary commitments is given for each of the above states and cities:

**The Difference between the Lowest and the Highest Annual Rate of Penitentiary Com-
mitments in Michigan, Indiana, Illinois, Kansas, Baltimore and Chicago**

STATES AND CITIES	Highest rate annual commitments	Lowest rate annual commitments	Greatest dif-ference in the rate of annual commitments
Michigan	1.9	0.8	1.1
Indiana	2.5	2.0	0.5
Illinois	2.6	0.9	1.7
Kansas	1.5	1.3	0.2
Baltimore ...	2.0	0.4	1.6
Chicago	4.4	1.2	3.2

As has been shown, the rate of annual Negro penitentiary commitments for no one of the states or cities was as great in 1902 as at some
previous date. Since 1894-1895 there appears to have been a continuous
decrease in the rate of annual commitments for the state of Illinois
and the city of Chicago; and since 1898-1899 there has been a decrease

in the rates of annual commitments for the states of Michigan and Illinois, and the cities of Baltimore and Chicago. This would seem to indicate that for the states and cities under consideration the rates of annual Negro commitments per thousand of the Negro population to the penitentiaries are not increasing, but on the other hand are probably decreasing.

Offenses, as is usually done, are classified as being against the person, property, society, etc. Offenses for which police arrests were made are first considered. Some data of this sort were available for the cities of Charleston and Savannah. For Charleston, offenses against the person only are given as follows:

Number of Arrests for Offenses against the Person per Thousand of the Negro Population for Charleston, S. C.

Number of Offenses per Thousand of the Negro Population by Years.

1888......... 11.0	1897..........	1899......... 8.0	1901.......... 10.7
1896......... 10.0	1898......... 9.0	1900......... 10.0	1902.......... 10.9

The above seems to indicate that in Charleston since 1888 the rate of yearly arrests per thousand of the Negro population for offenses against the person has not increased.

Classification of offenses against the person, property, and society for Negro police arrests of Savannah are next given.

Number of Police Arrests for Offenses against the Person, Property, and Society, per Thousand of the Negro Population in Savannah

Year	1874	1877	1881	1886	1895	1896	1897	1900	1901	1902	1903
Offenses against the person..	.07	3.9	6.4	5.6	10.00	13.00	11.00	16.00	10.00	9.00	7.00
Offenses against property....	10.00	7.6	7.00	5.00	24.00	19.00	22.00	25.00	23.00	23.00	21.00
Offenses against society......	68.00	45.00	67.00	48.00	79.00	66.00	84.00	110.00	103.00	111.00	115.00

From the above figures it is seen that the annual rates of arrests for offenses against the person increased from 1874 to 1900. Since 1900 there has been a decrease in the rates of arrests for offenses both against the person and property. The rate of arrests for offenses against society has increased, but not constantly, from 1874 to 1903.

It appears, from a consideration of the offenses for which arrests were made in Charleston and Savannah, that at present there does not seem to be any increase in the rate of arrests for offenses against the person. In Savannah since 1900 there has been a decrease in the rate of arrests for offenses against both the person and property. The rate of arrests for offenses against society has increased. This is due in part to more stringent legislation.

The number of commitments per thousand of the Negro population to the penitentiary from Chicago for offenses against the person and property, and for the particular offense of homicide is shown in the table which follows:

The Number of Penitentiary Commitments per Thousand of the Negro Population for Offenses against the Person, Property, and Homicide

YEAR	Total commitments	Offenses against the person	Offenses against property	Homicide	
				Manslaughter mayhem murder	Murder
1873	4.4	.44	3.9	.22	.22
1874	3.7	.00	3.7	.00	.00
1875	3.9	.19	3.7	.00	.00
1876	3.3	.00	3.3	.00	.00
1877	3.2	.35	2.8	.17	.17
1878	2.7	.17	2.5	.16	.16
1879	2.9	.16	2.7	.00	.00
1880	3.4	.30	3.0	.15	.15
1881	2.2	.41	1.8	.27	.14
1882	3.8	.37	3.4	.37	.24
1883	1.5	.22	1.3	.11	.00
1884	3.3	.41	2.8	.20	.21
1885	3.2	.09	3.2	.09	.00
1886	3.6	.26	3.4	.18	.09
1887	1.9	.33	1.5	.08	.00
1888	2.6	.63	1.9	.39	.00
1889	3.2	.66	2.6	.22	.14
1890	2.5	.63	1.8	.14	.07
1891	2.2	.31	1.9	.12	.00
1892	2.4	.51	1.8	.28	.11
1893	2.8	.73	2.0	.36	.15
1894	3.1	.53	2.5	.24	.09
1895	3.3	.50	2.8	.31	.27
1896	2.7	.50	2.2	.21	.21
1897	1.8	.31	1.5	.19	.15
1898	1.7	.44	1.2	.18	.04
1899	1.9	.21	1.6	.03	.03
1900	1.2	.23	0.9	.16	.09
1901	1.6	.44	1.2	.31	.19

Observing the rate of penitentiary commitments for the different years for offenses against the person it is seen that the rate, .44, was the same in 1901 as in 1873. The highest rate of commitments for offenses against the person, .73, was in 1894. The rate of penitentiary commitments for offenses against property in 1873 was 3.9. In 1901 the rate of penitentiary commitments for offenses against property was 1.2; the highest rate of penitentiary commitments for offenses against property was in 1873. The rate of Negro penitentiary commitments for all kinds of homicide in 1873 was .22; in 1901 the rate of commitments for homicide was .31; the highest rate of commitments for homicide, .39, was in 1888. The rate of penitentiary commitments for murder in 1873 was .22; in 1901 the rate for murder was .19; the highest rate of commitments for murder, .27, was in 1895.

It appears from a consideration of the offenses for which Negroes from Chicago were committed to the state penitentiary that: the rate of total commitments, as has already been pointed out, is decreasing; the rate of commitments for offenses against both the person and property and for homicide was less in 1901 than at times previous to this date; the rate of commitments for murder appears to show a slight decrease.

In order to secure further information respecting murder among Negroes, data from police reports of Charleston and Savannah are given.

The following figures are presented concerning arrests for murder in Charleston:

Murder in Charleston

Arrests for Murder by Years

1888	3	1898	12	1900	13
1896	4	1899	11	1901	6
		1902	12		

From the above it appears that the arrests for murder were much greater from 1898 to 1902 than they were in 1888 or in 1896. From 1898 to 1902 there does not appear to have been very much variation in the number of annual arrests for murder in Charleston. We are not warranted in concluding, however, that the crime of murder has increased among Negroes in Charleston unless it can be shown that the number of murders committed have increased annually. Police reports tell us how many persons were arrested annually for murder, but usually, as in the case of the Charleston reports, do not inform us concerning how many murders were committed annually, nor how many persons were indicted for this offense. Some of the Savannah police reports are an exception in this respect, and give information respecting the number of murders committed annually. Data relating to murder by Savannah Negroes follow:

Murder in Savannah

YEAR	Arrested for murder	Held for murder	Murders committed
1874		8	
1895		8	8
1896	18	6	6
1897	11	5	5
1900	16		
1901	17		
1902	6		
1903	9		

Observing the above figures it is seen that the arrests for murder were greater in 1896 than in any of the subsequent years for which data were available. The arrests for murder during the years 1902 and 1903 show a marked decrease under those for the previous years. The number held for murder in 1874 and in 1902 was the same and was greater than the number so held in 1896 and 1897. Since the number of murders committed by Negroes and the number of Negroes held for this offense appear to be the same for those years for which simultaneous data were available, it is probable that the number of murders committed by the Negroes of Savannah in 1874 was 8. The number of murders committed annually during those years for which data were available does not appear to vary much and what variation there is appears to be toward an absolute decrease. Since there is also somewhat of an absolute decrease in the arrests for murder, it appears that we are warranted in concluding that the crime of murder is decreasing among the Negroes of Savannah. While there appears to have been this absolute decrease in the number of murders committed annually by Negroes in Savannah during this time, i. e., from 1874 to 1903, the Negro population of the city increased 114 per cent.

Summarizing our results it is seen that police arrests, jail, workhouse and penitentiary commitments appear to have increased during the period from 1890 to 1892–1896. The highest rates of arrests and commitments were about 1893. Since 1894–1896 the tendency of both arrests and commitments to decrease has been notable. The crime rate for murder is also probably decreasing. It appears, therefore, that the conclusion that crime is probably decreasing among the Negroes of the United States is warranted. The crime rate of Negroes, North and South, appears at present to be about the same, although the rate of police arrests for some Southern cities is higher than that for the Northern cities. The claim that there is greater criminality among the Negroes of the North than those of the South is probably not true. The fallacy on which this claim was based was in comparing the criminal rate of the Negroes of the North who live almost entirely in cities with the criminal rate of the Negroes of the entire South, the great majority of whom live in rural communities.

6. Crime in Georgia. *The Prison Commission.* The second annual report of the Georgia Prison Commission says:

Previous to the year 1812, all criminals were punished by hanging, branding, public whipping, or imprisonment in the common jails. In that year the General Assembly remodeled the penal code, making most felonies punishable by confinement and hard labor, and to carry these new laws into effect appropriated money to build a penitentiary, or State prison. In 1817 this institution was completed, its location being at Milledgeville, then the capital of the State, and the new system was inaugurated and continued in effect until 1868. During this period, except the three years immediately following the Civil War, the prison population never exceeded two hundred in number, all white, the Negroes who were slaves not being amenable to the law, except for murder and other heinous offenses. These convicts were engaged in manufacturing for State account.*

A curious light is thrown on the attitude of the State toward crime when it is said, in regard to the Milledgeville State Prison, that the institution "was a financial failure. For support and maintenance $520,-000 was appropriated at different times above the income from its manufacturing enterprises, or more than $10,000 per annum net loss to the State."

After the war the number of convicts rapidly increased; the prison population has been:

---

*From 2nd annual Report of the Prison Commission of Ga., 1899, p. 3.

Prison Population, by Years

DATE	WHITE		NEGRO		Total
	Male	Female	Male	Female	
April 1, 1879	120	1	1,078	31	1,230
October 1, 1880	114	1	1,041	30	1,186
October 1, 1882	112	1	1,100	30	1,243
October 1, 1884	125	1	1,218	33	1,377
October 1, 1886	148	1	1,337	41	1,526
October 1, 1888	149	0	1,336	52	1,537
October 1, 1890	168	0	1,478	42	1,694
October 1, 1892	194	2	1,690	54	1,940
October 1, 1893	185	2	1,917	64	2,186
October 1, 1894	189	2	2,069	68	2,328
October 1, 1895	213	1	2,144	66	2,424
October 1, 1896	192	1	2,098	66	2,357
October 1, 1897	196	1	1,981	57	2,235
October 1, 1898	239	2	1,941	55	2,228
October 1, 1899	245	3	1,885	68	2,201
October 1, 1900	255	3	1,825	75	2,258
October 1, 1901	252	6	1,908	79	2,245
October 1, 1902	252	5	1,978	80	2,315
June 1, 1904	249	7	1,973	86	2,315

YEAR	Total Negro convicts	No. per 1,000 of Negro population
1879	1,109	1.54
1880	1,071	1.47
1882	1,130	1.50
1884	1,251	1.60
1886	1,378	1.71
1888	1,388	1.66
1890	1,520	1.76
1892	1,744	1.95
1893	1,981	2.17
1894	2,137	2.29
1895	2,210	2.33
1896	2,164	2.24
1897	2,038	2.07
1898	1,996	1.99
1899	1,953	1.92
1900	1,900	1.83
1901	1,987	1.88
1902	2,058	1.92
1904	2,059	1.78

It will be seen that serious crime is thus shown to have increased in Georgia up until 1895 and in the last ten years has been continually decreasing. The curve formed by these figures is characteristic of Negro crime throughout the nation, viz: an increase until about 1893–95 and a subsequent decrease.

The Prison Commission, however, taking no account of the large increase in Negro population, says :*

It was natural to expect that immediately after his emancipation, and his elevation to citizenship, with its consequent burdens for which he was wholly unfitted, that the Negro would furnish a much larger proportion of criminals than his white neighbors, who for centuries had enjoyed the blessings of freedom and education. · But it was to be expected that, after forty years of freedom and education, when his illiteracy has been reduced from 100 per cent. to 50 per cent., that his criminal record would begin to decrease. Such expectations, however, have

*7th Report.

not been realized, to the distinct disappointment of his friends, who to-day find him more criminal than when he possessed no education whatever, and who naturally wonder if his education has not been a mistake.

The premise is of course an error—Negro crime has decreased, and is decreasing. The absolute number of criminals on the other hand has increased, and as there was soon no room at Milledgeville for the large number of convicts the convict lease system was begun, convicts being leased at $10–$25 per capita from 1866–1874. In 1876 the lease was made for 20 years:

This lease was made by Governor Smith to three companies, who, under the law authorizing the lease, became corporations, known respectively as Penitentiary Companies Nos. 1, 2, and 3. No. 1 was composed of the following persons: Jos. E. Brown, Julius L. Brown, John T. and Wm. D. Grant, and Jacob W. Seaver; No. 2, B. G. Lockett, John B. Gordon, L. A. Jordan, and W. B. Lowe; and No. 3, Wm. D. Grant, John W. Murphy, W. W. Simpson, Thos. Alexander, and John W. Renfroe. The price to be paid was $25,000 per annum, irrespective of the number of convicts. There were, on April 1, 1879, when this contract went into effect, 1,230 convicts of all classes. This contract continued in force until April 1, 1896.

The act of 1897 arranged a new system. This is the same convict lease system as before, with the following changes:

1. Increasing amount paid for convict labor from $25,000 a year to $225,000, the price being settled by bidding of contractors.

2. The placing of State deputy wardens and physicians in charge of the various camps and stockades.

3. The adoption of a uniform set of rules as to diet, clothing and housing of laborers and their hours of labor.

4. The providing of a State farm for some of the women, boys and old men.

The objections to this system are manifest:

1. It still makes the income from crime rather than the reformation of the criminal of paramount importance. Special stress is laid in each report of the Prison Commission on this income; the system "is self-sustaining and nets the State large sums of money annually."* In 1899 the State received $25,000. In 1900, $61,826.32. From 1901 to 1903 the net income was about $81,000 a year. In 1904 new contracts were made:

The contracts so made will bring into the State Treasury annually, for a period of five years, beginning April 1st, 1904, the gross sum of $340,000.00 and after deducting the necessary expenses of this department estimated at $115,000.00 will leave a net amount of $225,000.00 per annum, which, under the law, will be divided among those counties not using convict labor upon their public roads, according to population, to be used for school or road purposes as may be determined by their respective grand juries. . . . .

The magnificent increase in the result of these contracts, over those of 1898, which have just expired, is not due alone to the natural increase in the value of this labor, but to several other causes, deserving mention.†

---

*5th annual Report, Prison Commission.　　†7th Report, do.

2. The effectiveness of the State control of convicts is lessened because:

There are 25 separate institutions at which convicts, not on the public roads, are confined and employed. Twenty-nine road camps, in different counties, besides 40 misdemeanor chaingangs, making a total of 94 separate institutions, containing over 4,000 convicts, which should be rigidly inspected every month.*

Besides the inspectors there are the regular deputy wardens and guards who must be furnished. The Prison Commission itself says:

The most serious objection to the present system is the division of responsibility for the care and protection of the convicts, there being at present nineteen deputy wardens in charge of as many prisons, thereby increasing the chances for acts of neglect or ill treatment, which will sometimes occur in even the best of penal systems.†

The Negro convicts were engaged in work in 1904 as follows:

```
Sawmilling...................................487 convicts
Turpentine farming .........................367    "
Brickmaking ................................307    "
Farming.....................................291    "
Mining......................................290    "
                                          ─────
                                          1,742
```

Of all the 2,315 convicts in the penitentiary in 1904:

```
594 had life sentences...........................................25.65%
234  " sentences of 20 years and over........................10.10%
164  "      "      " 15-20 years.................................7.08%
336  "      "      " 10-15 years...............................14.51%
987  "      "      " 1-9 years.................................42.63%
```

Besides the penitentiary convicts there were in Georgia in 1902:

Two thousand two hundred and twenty-one misdemeanor convicts undergoing punishment in county chaingangs, of which 103 are white males, 5 white females, 2,010 colored males and 103 colored females.

Thirty-two of these chaingangs, with an aggregate of 965 convicts, are worked for private individuals, in most cases contrary to the provisions of law. Thirty-three chaingangs, with an aggregate of 1,256 convicts, are worked on public roads or other public works.

The Commission has endeavored during the past year to give all of these gangs more frequent and rigid inspections, ... and this work has been productive of much improvement in their general condition, but many abuses continue to exist, especially in those gangs worked for private individuals, and always will exist, more or less, as long as the care and maintenance of the convicts are farmed out illegally to private individuals.‡

In 1904 there were 1,964 of these misdemeanor convicts.

Georgia has no State reformatory; two counties (those in which Atlanta and Augusta are situated) have local reformatories for white children, but none for Negroes.

7. Crime in Georgia. *Special Reports.* About 100 reports on the general criminal outlook among Negroes in Georgia were received by the conference. Reports were requested from every chief of police in the State and from various county officials, and a number responded. The following reports are from white officials and white citizens:

---

*7th annual Report, Prison Commission.   †5th Report, do.   ‡Ibid

REPORTS FROM WHITES

TOWN	COUNTY	OFFICIAL	AMOUNT	INCREASE OR DECREASE	REMARKS
Lyerly	Chattooga	Mayor	Few crimes	Decrease	Decreasing all the time
Cairo	Thomas	Citizen	Few crimes	Decrease	Apparently on decrease in this town and county
Austell	Cobb	Mayor	Few crimes	Same	Negroes, as a rule, law-abiding
Toccoa	Habersham	Mayor	....	Decrease	
Watkinsville	Oconee	Citizen	....	Decrease	Decreased 10 per cent. In last 3 years
Thomaston	Upson	Mayor	Few crimes	Decrease	Crime considerably reduced on account of prohibition
Gordon	Wilkinson	Marshal	Few crimes	Increase	
Fort Gaines	Clay	Citizen	Few crimes	Decrease	Crime for several years on the decrease on account of education
Eastman	Dodge	Sheriff	Few crimes	Decrease	Crime decreased 50 per cent. In the last 12 years; Negroes commit mostly petty crimes
White Hall	Clarke	Mayor	Little crime	Decrease	Very little crime committed
Putnam	Schley	County School Commissioner	Few crimes	Same	No perceptible increase
Hephzibah	Richmond	Justice of Peace	....	Decrease	Crimes of a serious nature are on the decrease
Yatesville	Upson	Citizen	....	Same	Cases largely of moral law among themselves
Ocilla	Irwin	Citizen	....	Decrease	Crimes less by a large per cent.
La Grange	Troup	Citizen	....	Increase	Petty crime increased
Crawford	Oglethorpe	Mayor	....	Increase	Petty crime increased some
Turin	Coweta	Postmaster	Few crimes	Same	Intemperance and immorality
La Grange	Troup	Citizen	Many crimes	Increase	Larceny is the principal crime
Sandersville / Tennile	Washington	Ordinary / Mayor	Very little	Increase	Increase since emancipation Negroes remarkably well behaved

REPORTS FROM WHITES—Continued

TOWN	COUNTY	OFFICIAL	AMOUNT	INCREASE OR DECREASE	REMARKS
Rome	Floyd			Decrease	Prohibition town
Lyons	Tattnal	Clerk			(See figures)
Macon	Bibb	Chief			(See figures)
Grantville	Coweta	Mayor			Crime among Negroes at this place is alarming; great majority of Negro population respectable and orderly.
Summerville	Chattooga	Intendant			
Brunswick	Glynn	Mayor		Same	Number of criminals same; class of crime of a minor nature
Sterling Station	Glynn	Constable		Increasing	
Dawson	Terrell	Mayor		Decreasing	
Metter	Telfair	Citizen			Crimes enormous
Greenville	Meriwether	Attorney		Increasing	Petty crimes increasing
Thomson	McDuffie	Citizen			(See figures)
Greensboro	Greene	Chief			(See figures)
Elberton	Elbert	Chief			(See figures)
	Macon	Clerk			(See figures)
Thomasville	Thomas	Mayor		Same	Normal and usual
Leary	Calhoun	Clerk			(See figures)
Jenkinsburg	Butts	Chief			(See figures)
Athens	Clarke	Chief			(See figures)

Some comments are:

BRUNSWICK—Mayor. I think the number of criminals for the present year is about the same as in former years, but the class of crime committed in our vicinity is of a minor nature. We have very few cases of a serious character during the year.

SANDERSVILLE—Ordinary. I regret to say that crime among the Negroes of the county has greatly increased since emancipation of 1865.

DAWSON—Mayor. Crime among the Negroes of my town and county is decreasing proportionally, that is while there may be as many cases or possibly more the increase in population makes the proportion less. This is due to a better understanding in our community between the races, caused by education. In our county we have many Negroes who own their farms and are out of debt, and besides have good balances to their credit in the banks. This seems to be an inspiration to the better class of Negroes to buy and save something. Whenever you hear of trouble between the races, as I see it once in a while, if you will investigate it is started by the low and uneducated Negro or white man or both.

SUMMERVILLE (Augusta)—Intendant. We have a village of only 5,000 people and comparatively few criminal cases. Most of these are for infractions of minor laws, usually disorderly conduct of some kind, although since we have declined to allow the storekeepers to sell liquor, even these offenses occur seldom. The majority of these cases, however, come from the Negro population and mostly the idle and vicious class of this race. I am glad to say, however, that the great majority of our Negro population are very respectable and orderly, and give us little if any trouble.

GRANTVILLE—Mayor. The amount of crime at this place among the Negroes is, I am sorry to say, alarming. Yet it is not of a heinous or such character that will excite the public to open indignation or unlawful violence. It is mostly of small petty crimes. I have it from reliable authority from their own statement that there have been more children born to the women out of wedlock than there have been by those who are married in this immediate section. The cause, I think, is that they employ teachers whose character is in keeping with the above statement.

THOMASVILLE—Mayor. There is about the normal and usual amount of crime committed in our town and county among the Negroes. In the last few years there has been no perceptible increase or decrease. The Negroes in the country who are engaged in farming and agricultural pursuits are generally peaceable, orderly and law abiding. Those engaged in mill work and naval stores operation are principally composed of transient labor, and their chief criminal vice seems to be gambling among themselves and skipping their employers after obtaining advances upon promises of labor. Homicides are occasionally committed by them, growing generally out of a gambling game or jealousy over and about some woman. In the towns there is a small per cent. of the Negroes who are enterprising and valuable citizens; the number is so small in proportion to the other class that they do not always in the matter of public regard receive the credit they are entitled to.

STERLING—Constable. We had two boys arrested, both colored, for brick-batting a colored woman in her house. They were sent to the chaingang for 12 months each. Two white men were sent to the chaingang for 12 months each, one for violating the game law, the other for selling whisky without a license. One colored man came here from South Carolina to hire hands; he was arrested and fined $50 and cost. He paid out. One colored man was arrested for stealing a dog; he was fined $50 and costs, and went to the chaingang for 12 months.

TENNILLE—Mayor. We have very little crime in Washington county among the Negroes, and as you know this is a large Negro county, yet they are remarkably well behaved. I have very few cases in my police court. No Negro has ever been killed in this county by a white man within my recollection. No lynchings have ever occurred here.

METTER.—In reply to your request, will say the crimes are enormous in every respect. The most crimes committed here are by our supposed-to-be-educated Negroes. In court they are treated better than they deserve.

CRAWFORD.—My observation is that the Negro is having his head educated and that his heart is sadly neglected in the home circle; the old Negro tells you plainly that his training was much better (not his education) than that of the rising generation of Negroes; he knows his place, keeps it, and is a good citizen.

EASTMAN.—In reply will say that in all the criminal courts of this county we have about fifty convictions annually, mostly minor offenses, simple larceny, etc. They all have a fair trial by white jury; in felony cases they have an impartial trial; even in cases of rape we give them a speedy justice, hanging them to the first tree if they committed the act. The Negroes of this county are peaceable and are doing well.

GREENVILLE.—It seems to me that crime among the Negroes, particularly petty crime, is on the increase among them. Many of them are tried in the courts for this class of crime, and as a rule, I think, have fair and impartial trials. It is also common for homicides to occur among them, especially on occasions when they have public gatherings. These usually result after indulgences in liquor and gambling, which the vicious element are inclined to pursue at any function, religious or social.

TURIN.—Intemperance (the love of whiskey) and immorality are the most prevalent crimes among the Negroes in this community.

PUTNAM.—There is no perceptible increase of crime among colored people in Schley county. It has been many years since a trial for murder. Crimes are generally misdemeanors, gambling, selling liquor, fights at Saturday night entertainments, an occasional case for bastardy, seduction, and for stealing little things. I am inclined to the belief that there is a tendency to a decrease of crime.

HEPHZIBAH.—I think crimes of serious nature are on the decrease, some petty crimes are brought into court in the rural districts. Those mostly occurring in this section are fighting among themselves.

YATESVILLE.—The crimes committed are almost all petty larceny. I know of no case in the county where he has not had a fair trial.

WHITEHALL.—There is very little crime committed in this portion of the county; the crimes, when any, are for simple larceny as a rule. They get fair treatment in this town and county.

THOMASTON.—As far as I can see and learn crime among the Negroes in this city is considerably reduced on account of not being able to get the use of whiskey as easily as they once did. This is a prohibition town, and therefore we are not troubled with a great deal of crime either among the whites or blacks.

AUSTELL.—The Negroes of this town are as a rule law-abiding. Their weakness is the love of liquor and some petty stealing, which is their nature.

LAGRANGE.—Fully 95 per cent. of criminals in our county are Negroes. Crime seems to be on the increase with them. Larceny is the principal crime. I think they are fairly treated in our courts.

FT. GAINES.—Crime among the Negroes of our community has been for several years on the decrease. An examination of our court records reveals this fact to the credit of the race. The violations of law are for the most part of a petty character, such as gambling, assault and battery, and carrying concealed weapons. The latter is the crying evil of the day, and the white people are equally guilty with the Negroes. The things which in my mind tend most to debauch the Negro are his propensity for strong drink, and the disposition to disregard marital vows. As a rule Negroes in our county seem to appreciate the educational advantages offered them, and in a large degree avail themselves of these opportunities. I've noticed a lack of efficiency of the teachers, and in many cases lack of character as well. This is deplorable and hurtful, and should in some way be remedied, and I suppose will in course of time.

Nearly all the white officials thought that Negroes were justly treated in the courts. This is often stated in the South, but once in a while Southern white testimony is frankly on the other side; for instance at the last meeting of the Southern Educational Convention, "two statements, perhaps, created the deepest impression. The first was made by Dr. Sherer of South Carolina, who acknowledged that the criminal courts meted out even justice in but one instance—in the case of Negro vs. Negro."

To these reports may be added the reports of Negroes. In each case these Negroes are men above the average of intelligence and reliability in their communities. They report crime as follows:

REPORTS FROM NEGROES

TOWN	COUNTY	AMOUNT	INCREASE OR DECREASE	REMARKS
Pendergrass.....	Jackson	Great deal	Increase	More than ever
Stirling	Glynn	....	Same	
Grantville	Coweta	....	Increase	
Dawson	Terrell	....	Decrease	
Lyerly............	Chattooga	....	Decrease	
Sandersville.....	Washington	Little crime	Decrease	
Leesburg........	Lee	....	Decrease	Stealing most prevalent
Greenville.......	Meriwether	....	Increase	Petty crimes increasing
Calhoun..........	Gordon	....	Decrease	Gambling and carrying weapons
Leesburg........	Lee	Little crime	Decrease	Decreased in last 10 years
Dahlonega.......	Lumpkin	Little crime	Decrease	No convictions in 2 years
Gordon	Wilkinson	Little crime	Decrease	Decreased 15 per cent.
Pearson.......,...	Coffee	....	Decrease	Three crimes in 4 years
Waynesboro.....	Burke	....	Increase	Increasing in all crimes
Elberton	Elbert	Little crime	Same	
Dalton	Whitfield	....	Decrease	Only 2 in 5 months
Adrian	Johnson	....	Same	Larceny and selling whiskey
Hoschton	Jackson	Little crime	Decrease	50 per cent less in 1 year
Statham	Jackson	....	Same	Petty crimes
Tallapoosa.......	Haralson	Little crime	Decrease	Decreased 40 per cent. in 3 years
Jefferson	Jackson	Little crime	Same	
Toccoa	Habersham	Little crime	Decrease	Crime exceedingly below other counties
Morgan	Calhoun	Very small	Decrease	Crime very small
Shady Dale......	Jasper	Great deal	Increase	Rapidly increasing
Cordele	Dooly	Very little	Decrease	Rapidly decreasing
Harmony Grove.	Jackson	....	Decrease	
Flintstone	Walker	....	Decrease	
McIntosh ...:....	Butts	....	Increase	More disorder
Turin	Coweta	....	Same	Caused by "Blind Tigers"
Newnan..........	Coweta	Very little	Decrease	Becoming less and less every year

REPORTS FROM NEGROES—Continued

TOWN	COUNTY	AMOUNT	INCREASE OR DECREASE	REMARKS
Thomaston	Upson		Same	
Jewells	Hancock			Corrupt courts
Adel	Berrien		Increasing	Forgery, larceny, etc.
Brunswick	Glynn		Increasing	Influx of Negroes from country
Columbus	Muscogee	Not extensive	Increasing	Gambling and petty larceny
Acworth	Cobb		Decreasing	Petty crimes
Newborn	Newton	Few	Decreasing	Process slow, but steady
Fort Valley	Houston		Decreasing	Petty crimes
Baxley	Appling		Decreasing	Selling whiskey and concealed weapons
Waco	Haralson	Less than average		
Crawford	Oglethorpe		Decreasing	Less than formerly
Lithia Springs	Douglas	Very little	Decreasing	Crimes very trivial
Thomasville	Thomas		Decreasing	Less crime committed
Belton	Hall	Few		
Hephzibah	Richmond		Not increasing	
Abbeville	Wilcox	Not so much	Decreasing	
Claxton	Tattnal		Decreasing	Gambling and concealed weapons
Wadley	Jefferson	Good town	Decreasing	Gambling
Marietta	Cobb		Decreasing	As many whites as blacks
Kingston	Bartow	Few	Decreasing	
Butler	Taylor	Few	Decreasing	
Brunswick	Glynn		Decreasing	Notable decrease in last 8 or 10 years
Douglasville	Douglas		Decreasing	
Baxley	Appling	25 per cent. less	Decreasing	Petty offenses
Tifton	Berrien		Decreasing	
Montezuma	Macon			Criminals: about 98 per cent. are illiterate
Pendergrass	Jackson		Decreasing	
Vienna	Dooly		Increasing	Of almost every character
Knoxville	Crawford		Same	
Rome	Floyd		Decreasing	Due to dispensary law
Oconee	Washington		Increasing	Whites and blacks both increasing in crime
Marshallville	Macon	Good, quiet	Decreasing	Good condition
Sandersville	Washington	Friendly feeling between two races	Decreasing	Criminals only 4 per cent. of voting population
Adairsville	Bartow		Decreasing	
Jasper	Pickens	Few	Decreasing	

Some comments follow:

SANDERSVILLE.—The criminality of the race in this county is the least discouraging thing, conviction being about 4 per cent. of the voting population. The majority of crimes for which they are convicted are small, a large percentage being convicted for gambling, stealing, and disorderly conduct and very frequently for dealing in blind-tiger liquor.

BRUNSWICK.—The chief causes of crime among the Negroes here are drunkenness, gambling, and sexual immorality. It is heart-breaking to see Negro women arraigned at every court for fighting about some other woman's husband; and I should not forget to mention that vagrancy among the Negro boys leads to stealing. There are now five boys in jail, all under fifteen, awaiting trial for burglary.

ADAIRSVILLE.—The general character of the Negro's crime is of a petty nature—theft, "blind tigers," fighting, saucing "Mars John," etc. He is decreasing in his amount of criminality, and whenever opportunity presents itself learns a trade or buys him a home and settles down to work out his destiny. I have noticed this in many instances. All he needs is a fair showing in life; don't despair of him.

MARSHALLVILLE.—Our best men, white and colored, think with me that we have a very quiet community. There are very few arrests. One white man said to me a few days ago: "Why, we have no need of a guard house." This is true. There has certainly not been a man in prison since Christmas. Causes: No whiskey; good schools. Of course, it is not a model community, there are evils of which we are ashamed. I think there is some gambling, but I am told by men who know that this crime is practiced by a vagrant class of men and boys who do not belong in the community. The whites tell me that these men cannot read and write and that they play cards for amusement. When they think the officers are after them they run to another settlement. This crime is most prevalent in peach season.

But the crime which is really hurting the community more than any other is sexual immorality between the races. It is of such a nature that the local courts cannot well handle it, and Negroes have not the courage to condemn it.

I am sure, however, this crime is not increasing. Within the past twenty years there have been changes for good along this line; still the subtle influence of this immorality is felt in many ways.

Causes: Poor wages and love of dress, influence of Negro preachers, lack of home training. In some portions of the county, whiskey is sold and the natural results follow—murder, stealing, drunkenness and gambling, and the county jail is, of course, well filled.

—————. I venture to give the information, but urgently insist that my name not be given publicity, because I am working in a bloody and oppressive county, and do not desire to leave by undue force because of family and business relations. Crime is rapidly increasing; blind-tigers, petty theft, concealed weapons, church disturbances. In some parts of this county absolute slavery reigns; men and women are whipped and driven cruelly from before the dawn until dark. There are men whose fines are paid and are worked at the rate of $4.50 per month. Negroes must invariably settle by books kept by men who furnish* them. Some of them with four in family make from 12 to 16 bales and fall in debt at end of year. An attempt to leave means to have corn and a clean sweep made and spurious warrants and sometimes an unmerciful beating. There are many Negroes who have lived on the same place 10 to 12 years and never been given their rent note nor a final settlement, and they are afraid to ask for either or to leave. Of those

---

*"Furnish," i. e., supply goods to them on credit.

who furnish Negroes, six out of nine confine them to bacon, meal, some flour, and strenuously object to buying sugar or too much dress. One white man in this county who had the oversight of sixty plows would go to the store, buy things for his own house and have them charged to one or the other hand's account. Social equality is forced in many places, but due to white men.

McINTOSH.—It seems to me that there is more disorder hereabouts than formerly Certainly in this immediate vicinity for the past five years there has been less safety than previously, as far as my knowledge extends. But affairs have improved somewhat of late.

NEWNAN.—Crimes of all kinds among Negroes are becoming less every year. The number of criminals in our courts this year is not half as large as that of last year. Our police court has had little to do this year, and were it not for the idlers and those inclined to gamble and run "blind tigers," it might be only a court in name. Our people are not inclined to theft as in past years. Most of the crimes are misdemeanors and arise from assaults of various kinds.

PENDERGRASS.—The amount of crime among the Negroes of my town is more than ever was known before—such as gambling and killing, and a good number of the law-breakers are bonded out of jail, and the court allows a lot of them to be paid out and they are made slaves of by the big men of our county. So far as justice being given the Negroes in court, why they never get that.

KNOXVILLE.—The criminal Negro in this county is the gang-laborer Negro, who gets employment on large plantation farms, sawmills and turpentine distilleries, where they are led and controlled by influences which are oftentimes far from being good. But Negroes may be found in most every rural district or community on their own farms, or on farms absolutely under their control, prospering. Such Negroes are as law-abiding citizens as can be found in the world.

ATHENS.—The primary cause of so much crime is drunkenness and ignorance. The state of affairs among our young men is alarming. The boys leave school between the ages of twelve and fifteen years, and they drift out into the world and learn to gamble, drink whiskey, and all other low vices. I have a boy about thirteen. At one time there were twenty boys in his class, and now there are only two. Many boys seem to be retrograding morally. They feel that it is just as high an honor to marry a deluded woman as a virtuous one. Seven marriages of that kind have occurred since Christmas in our town.

MONTEZUMA.—The clerk of the superior court informed me that 98 per cent. of the criminals were totally illiterate. It is seldom that an educated Negro gets into trouble.

These men were asked especially as to justice in the courts.

FORT VALLEY.—The persons whom I asked, seemed to think that the Negro of this county received the regulation "Georgia justice" in the courts; that is, once accused, the Negro is guilty, especially so if the controversy is with a white person, and must prove himself innocent.

AUGUSTA.—It seems to me that so many Negroes are arraigned in the courts who are innocent apparently, that it is hard too, to answer the question as to the cause of crime.

MARSHALLVILLE.—I know of no special instance where Negroes have been treated unfairly in the courts, but I think the general understanding is that the white man's word goes before everything else.

BAXLEY.—So far as a Negro is concerned, it matters not how good a law-abiding citizen he may be, or how intelligent he is, nor the amount of property he may own and pay taxes on. He has no voice in the court house except as a witness or to be tried.

NEWBORN.—Sorry to say that in our courts, a Negro's color is a brand of guilt. This refers to our county and circuit courts. Justice courts in rural districts are a mere farce. Justice to a Negro against a white man is less than a game of chance.

DAWSON.—During the August or adjourned term of the Superior Court of Terrell County 1902 one ——— was charged with vagrancy. He was a barber by trade and ran a colored barbershop. One of the police on that beat fell out with him and swore out the above warrant. The said ——— produced 85 men who swore that he shaved them from once to twice a week and cut their hair from once to twice a month, and that he sometimes did other work, such as putting down carpets, when called upon. The trial judge declared that he had never heard of Negroes shaving twice a week and did not believe any such thing: that that was as many times a week as the average white man shaved, and that the Negro's beard does not grow as fast nor come out as fast as white men's and therefore he doubted the veracity of the witnesses. The case was compromised by the said ——— paying the sum of $65.

At the November term of the Superior court held in Dawson, 1903, a boy 14 years of age was charged of helping a man or tenant steal cotton seed from his landlord. The man had pleaded guilty at the August term of the City Court and had been fined $100 or one year on the gang. The fine was paid by the landlord and the man was kept on the place. The boy refused to plead guilty and appealed his case to the Superior Court. The grand jury found a true bill and he was tried at the November term of court. At the trial the man who pleaded guilty swore that he was a cropper and worked on halves and that the boy and his father lived about three miles from him and that he learned that the boy was to be sent to town early the next morning and that he had gone to the old man who was a cripple and asked him to let the boy come by his home and carry a package to town for him and the boy's father consented as it was not much out of the way. He swore that he had the cotton seed sacked and out by the roadside when the boy came along and that he (the man) put them on the wagon and told the boy to sell them and bring him the money. He did as he was told. He also swore that the boy did not know whether he had stolen the seed or not nor where he had gotten them. The boy's parents swore to the same facts. The boy was found guilty and sentenced to twelve months in the " gang."

At the August term of the city court in Dawson, 1903, there were twenty-five young men convicted of gambling on the evidence of one who was excused because he turned state's evidence. He is known as a spotter. When he admitted his guilt the solicitor got up and recommended him to the judge as a hard working Negro, whom he knew, and who had worked for him on his place. He was excused with only a nominal fine. The other twenty-five received sentences ranging from $30 to $75 and from six to twelve months on the gang.

In the Americus city court, April term, 1904, one X——— borrowed $2 and agreed to pay $3 for the same by working it out when called upon to do so. Before Y———, from whom he borrowed the money, was ready for him or called for him, he was working out another debt which he had contracted with another party. He could not go to Y——— just at the time wanted. Y——— swore out a warrant for cheating and swindling and sent X——— up for eight months on the "gang."

SYLVANIA.—They have no voice in court. They are not treated fair in the courts at all.

THOMASTON.—The criminals do not, in my judgment, at all times have fair and impartial trials. Yet they are treated as fair as the average Negro in the South.

JEWELL.—The subject is a young man of the little town in which I teach. Christmas this young man shot a boy, for which crime he has not been punished. Of course every body in the town knows that he is a desperate character, and that he can give no cause for the crime of which he is surely guilty. And yet when tried in court he was released.

The criminal is a servant for one of the wealthiest families in the county, and of course they did their best to prevent his being brought to justice in the county court. The Negro was arrested and taken to court for trial, and as plain as the case was all the so-called best white people of the little town of Jewell met at Sparta on court day and through their influence the jurymen were bribed, and the result was that a verdict of not guilty was brought out by the jurymen, even when they knew that he was a murderer. Now, I think the court did the very worst thing that could have been done for the young man. By all means justice should have been meted out to him, not so much for his own salvation as for that of many others who will certainly be influenced by his example.

I know of three other cases where the criminals failed to receive justice in the courts, simply because they rendered good service to white people as servants.

My opinion is that the white man who makes himself a protection for the Negro's crime in one instance is simply encouraging crime in all directions.

My experience is that much of the crime among Negroes arises from the corrupt way in which the courts some times deal with criminals. Either one Negro of a certain town has been punished innocently and the others revolt, or one has not been punished for the crime he did commit, and so many others are encouraged to commit worse crimes.

ATHENS.—The races in this section work very harmoniously together, and I know of no instance where the courts have not dealt justly with the Negro. As a whole, one of the worst faults the Negro has is the concealment of crime, no matter how low the crimes are. An intelligent, law-abiding citizen in this section gets the full benefit of the law.

MONTEZUMA.—In some cases even-handed justice is meted out to both races alike. But in many cases the white man uses his power to dethrone justice.

SASSER.—As to their treatment in the courts of my county, I can without hesitation say there is some partialty shown. Do not let it be publicly known that I said we are illegally treated, that is, that we do not have a fair trial in every instance in the courts of my county. It would cause me to have enemies among the whites, and they perhaps might set snares for me.

CLAXTON.—I haven't found out definitely how they are treated in the courts. I can safely say they are tried by white juries, white lawyers and white judges, so you can judge.

WADLEY.—I don't visit the county courts, but as far as I can learn and read in the papers, Negroes don't stand any chance in them, and in our town before the mayor it is the same.

CARNESVILLE.—The Negro has very little rights here; all the white man is after is the almighty dollar. Outside of that the Negro is no more thought of.

MARIETTA.—All the officials and jurors are white, but considering the fact that our judge X—— has presided over the court for a number of years in a very impartial manner, I feel that our criminal class here is very fairly dealt with.

CALHOUN.—To my knowledge Negroes are justly treated in the courts in this county.

KINGSTON.—Now as far as courts are concerned, we do not believe that justice is altogether handed down to us. We believe that when a crime or crimes are committed that each court should do justice irrespective to creed, nationality, or color. We believe that the law should not only be enforced after election, but before as well.

WAYNESBORO.—They are treated as a rule as all Southern courts treat the Negro.

SHADY DALE.—Last year a crowd of twenty went to arrest a Negro for a debt of $22. They found six Negroes gathered there for a hunt. The man they sought got away. The six Negroes arrested were fined from $60 to $120. The white men were upheld by the law; yet they had no warrant and met no resistance.

VIENNA.—Of course, no one would expect the Negro to be dealt with justly in the courts. The judge, jury and lawyers are all whites, hence no sane man would believe that the Negro receives justice before such a prejudiced body. But so far as white men are concerned, I think the Negro is treated fairly well in the courts; that is, as well as could be expected from white men. It would not be natural for such a race as the whites, that has the superior advantage, to give the Negro justice.

ROME.—Our people as a rule get the worst of it in courts, according to my observation.

ABBEVILLE.—I do not know how the Negro stands here in the courts, but I think he has a very poor chance since the jury down here is ignorant and full of prejudice.

FOLKSTON.—We are doing very well here with the whites, only we are denied the right of jurymen on account of color.

GENEVA.—The case of a Negro always is committed, and if he hasn't got some white man on his side, he is gone to the "gang."

THOMASVILLE.—The courts, on the whole, here are inclined to give the Negro prisoners justice. In our last court 40 per cent. of the accused were acquitted. Some of the charges were very serious, but absence of sufficient evidence seemed to have been recognized by the jurors, who seemed impartial.

JASPER.—In the fall of 1903 white folks treated the colored folks very badly by white capping. They dynamited and rocked several of the Negroes' houses in this county. You know the colored people don't get justice in the courts.

MIDVILLE.—Justice is only measured out to him according to the views of that white man who is in favor of him. The Negro's word in the courts has but little weight. A Negro's word or justice to the Negro in the courts of my county depends largely upon his standing among his white friends. If a Negro has a case against a white man, it is generally held on docket until it becomes cold and thrown out. On the other hand, if a white man has a case against a Negro he is fined or imprisoned.

BLAIRSVILLE.—They are treated fairly well. They neither lynch nor take the lives of the Negro as they do further South, but we are slaves for them in a sense.

WACO.—Of course they are not treated altogether fairly in the courts, for they have no colored jurors here.

CRAWFORD.—For the most part there is a decrease in the commission of crime. We think the manner in which the law is administered has much to do with the commission of crime on the part of the Negroes. A white man here can do almost anything wrong in violation of law; if a Negro is defendant in the case justice steers clear of the Negro's side. The crime for which Negroes are most strictly held to account is that of breaking contracts. They are invariably hunted for, and when found are hand-cuffed or tied with ropes, brought back, severely whipped; now and then one is killed (self-defense or accidentally) and the murderer goes free. Negroes can run blind tigers, live in adultery and gamble on the plantation or here in the town unmolested, but he must not miss a day from work. It did actually occur in this county that a white man killed a Negro at a Negro dance without provocation. He was never bothered about it. Some time afterwards the same white man took a mule from a white farmer. He was caught, tried, and convicted of horse stealing and sentenced to the chaingang.

JEFFERSON.—There are from forty to fifty misdemeanor convictions a year in our courts. The major part of them get white men to pay their fines, for which they work double the time. These white men run kind of force labor farms. The Negroes' treatment in court is usually fair, as there is no indignant public sentiment against these petty crimes. The offender, after his arrest, is generally taken by the arresting officer to some white man, who is the Negro's choice; there a bond is made and the fellow put to work. When court convenes, the Negro and his employer appear, and after some legal formality the offender is fined. The fine is paid and the criminal goes back to work. These Negroes are nuisances to the respectable Negroes of the communities. They often give much trouble at the churches and other public gatherings, with the boast "that captain so and so will stand to me in anything." I am not a pessimist, but owing to the demand of labor in this county and the means employed by the large land owners to secure it, I truly believe misdemeanor crimes are on the increase.

PENDERGRASS.—The Negroes in general are in a bad shape here. There are about eighty criminals here out on bond, some for murder, some for selling whiskey, some for gambling, some for carrying concealed weapons, some for shooting, and most of them are guilty, too; but their captain (i. e., employer,) takes their part in court. They generally pay about $25 and work the Negro from one and a half to two years, and the Negro never knows what it cost. Some that are guilty come clear, some not guilty are found guilty just the same, for they can only swear and make a statement. The whites trade in them like slavery times or like horses. Some get their rights and some don't. There is no justice in court for the Negro, except he has money, and they will make him lose it.

STEAM MILL.—The crime of the Negro is increasing. It is two-thirds greater than ever before. The cause of this is that they are given the full extent of the law on the weakest evidence. There is such a demand down in South Georgia for turpentine hands and sawmill hands that every man who has got a sawmill or a turpentine farm in the county is bribing the courts and the lawyers to convict the Negro regardless of the evidence of the crime, because he wants to buy him for his labor, for he can shoot and force him to labor. Therefore, 98 per cent. of the convicts of the county prison are made up of the Negro race. We have got more overseers and white bosses than we had forty years ago.

WAYNESBORO.—They always get justice I believe when it is a Negro vs. a Negro, but when it is a white man vs. a Negro there seem at times to be some variations. This is putting it very mildly, too.

ADAIRSVILLE.—In reply to it, I will say that there is very little mercy shown the Negro in our circuit courts. There seems to be a premium placed on his conviction, however simple and light the charges may be. This I am at a loss to answer for, but as a general rule the pressure is upon him, and he generally gets defeated in the courts all the way from the district to circuit courts. Of course this depends on whom the Negro is in law with. If it is with another of his color, probably he may get justice; but if there is any chance for his color to figure in the matter, he is more than apt to meet squarely and promptly with sudden defeat. I have been a resident of this county since ——, and all of this time been in direct contact with the masses. We have good men on both sides—some white and some colored who strive with each other for good—and if it were not for these two classes of men this county would present a sad picture; both races would indulge more in cruel hatred for each other. I don't want to say too much right along here, but the Negro is not accorded his rights as a man, either in court, or in his domestic and commercial relations, not to say a word about his political privileges.

LAVONIA.—Of course you are acquainted with procedure of the courts with the Negroes in the South. "To be black" goes a long way in reaching a verdict and determining the fine or punishment. But it is not so bad here as in some other counties, and under these adverse circumstances the Negroes are forbearing, plodding their way onward, some with wisdom, and others with indiscretion.

OCONEE.—Crime is increasing among the whites. The whites indulge Negroes in it a great deal. A Negro kills another and he escapes punishment by getting away or some white man pays a small fine for him and he takes him and works him. The white man is already anxious for him to get into something in order that he can tie him. This is what some of them call controlling labor. There are hundreds of Negroes working on farms and public works with some white man on his bond or working out fines. A Negro seldom comes clear, no matter how weak is the evidence produced against him. It does not pay to go to court.

BRUNSWICK.—It is very difficult, if not impossible, to convict white men in the courts of crimes committed against Negroes, nor are Negroes given a fair trial when charged with offenses against the whites. Where Negroes only are involved, money or a pull will generally secure the acquittal of the Negro who has it.

ADRIEN.—Our county is very rough in many ways to work in, to the disadvantage of Negroes. We can't get a fair trial in a court of justice, and crimes can't be estimated fairly on account of injustice; especially if it is a case between the Negro and a white man, there is no hope for the Negro.

DOUGLASVILLE.—As to the treatment of the Negro in the courts, I should judge from my own observation of the proceedings of the courts for the past three years, that they are generally impartially dealt with according to the evidence. For the three years that I have been here, I don't remember any Negro complaining as to unjust treatment of his race in court. This town and county, from my observation and judgment, is an exception to most of the towns and counties that I have lived in.

BAXLEY.—Most of the crimes committed by white men are nolprossed or light fines laid when proven guilty, but there is no hope for the acquittal of a Negro; and if he is proven guilty (which is no trouble to do), he is given a long sentence or a very heavy fine. In this county we have no colored jurors, and possibly this accounts for the Negroes suffering so very much in the criminal courts.

TIFTON.—In the courts, he is usually a criminal and stands friendless before the law.

Summing up these reports we can make this rough estimate of the tendency of crime: Reports from 10 counties (11 towns) with 118,244 Negroes indicate that crime is increasing; reports from 56 counties (67 towns) with 448,117 Negroes indicate that crime is decreasing.

In 15 small towns there were, in 1903, 5,376 arrests of white and colored offenders, mostly for disorder and drunkenness. Of these, 3,113 were Negroes, 50 white, and the rest undesignated.

It seems to be fairly well proven that there is comparatively little crime in the Black Belt and in the White Belt. It is in the counties where the races meet on something like numerical equality and in economic competition that the maximum of crime is charged against Negroes.

8. **Atlanta and Savannah** (by H. H. PROCTOR and M. N. WORK).

According to the census of 1900 the total population of Atlanta was 89,872; of these 54,145 were white and 35,727 were Negroes. Approximately 60 per cent. of the population is white and 40 per cent. black. There were 14.088 arrests made in Atlanta last year; of these 5,925 were white and 8,163 black, i. e. 42 per cent. were white and 58 per cent. black. Concerning this heavy percentage of arrests three things should be said: First, that 732 of the total arrests were made on suspicion, and as all presumptions are against the Negro it may be confidently assumed that he shared largely in this class of arrests; second, that 446 of these cases were dismissed, indicating clearly that to be arrested is no sure indication of crime; and, third, that a large number of these were of that class known as "rounders," and were arrested more than once. The largest number of arrests were between the criminal period of 20 and 30. One-third of the total colored arrests consisted of women.

The principal causes of these arrests were disorderly conduct, drunkenness, idling and loitering, and suspicion. Of these arrests at least two things are noteworthy. The first is that leaving aside the blanket charge of disorderly conduct, the leading cause for arrest was drunkenness. The second is that just one man in Atlanta was arrested for rape last year and that man was white! I have been informed by the chief of police of this city that during the present year there has been but one arrest for this unspeakable crime, and that is for a white man against a colored woman.

One of the causes of Negro crime is ignorance. Thirty-five per cent. of the Negroes of Atlanta are illiterate. It should be said that this is due in part to the influx from the country districts; but the fact remains, nevertheless, that every third Negro one meets in this city is illiterate. Now, this has a close connection with crime; for ignorance and vice are twin sisters. A study of the accompanying table will show a striking thing in this connection. We have seen that the Negroes of Atlanta are about one-third ahead of the whites in crime; this table shows that they are just about one-third behind in school facilities:

Atlanta Public Schools 1902-1903

	School populat'n	Schools	Teachers	Seats	Without seats
Colored	8,118	5	49	2,445	5,673
White	14,465	20	200	10,052	4,413

But the fountain head of crime among the Negroes of Atlanta is the open saloon. There is no doubt but that the removal of strong drink from the city would decrease crime by half. In my native Southern town the abolition of the saloon has almost put the courts out of business with Negroes. In one of our Decatur street saloons 100 colored men were seen to enter within 13 minutes one rainy evening. Of the 150 colored men and boys now in the city stockade the keeper tells me that the most of them are there for drunkenness.

A strenuous effort should be made to make the home life more attractive. Too many black boys and even girls are permitted to roam the streets alone at night. A curfew law properly administered would be a splendid thing for a certain class of our young people. Another year would see fewer than 3.077 arrests between the ages of 12 and 20. We need more philanthropic agencies for the amelioration of crime among Negroes in this city. At present there are only two; they provide for less than 100 children. Day nurseries are needed for the care of the children of hard working mothers who must go out to earn the living for their children and be away from them all the day. A reformatory is needed for refractory boys, and a house of refuge for wayward girls. A fully equipped Young Men's Christian Association would be a power for good in preventing crime among young men. But the supreme need of Atlanta is a great union college social settlement established in one of the Negro centers of crime.

The figures for arrests in Atlanta since 1898 follow:

Arrests in Atlanta

	1898	1899	1900	1901	1902	1903
WHITES—						
Males	4,508	4,523	4,957	5,384	5,289	5,413
Females	418	389	474	403	449	512
Total whites	4,926	4,912	5,431	5,787	5,738	5,925
NEGROES—						
Males	6,911	7,600	7,415	8,539	7,808	7,544
Females	2,470	1,654	2,086	2,960	2,888	2,619
Total Negroes	9.381	9,254	9,501	11,499	10,696	10,163

1903

AGE	WHITES		NEGROES		Total
	Male	Female	Male	Female	
Under 12	8	0	33	1	42
Between 12 and 15	263	15	901	73	1,252
Between 15 and 20	446	89	1,321	782	2,640
Between 20 and 30	1,844	209	3,142	1,242	6,437
Between 30 and 40	1,479	130	1,362	369	3,340
Between 40 and 50	799	52	470	107	1,428
Over 50	574	17	313	45	949
Totals	5,413	512	7,544	2,619	16,088

Negro Arrests per Thousand of Negro Population

1898	274	1900	266	1902	293
1899	265	1901	322	1903	273

Savannah has 54,244 inhabitants, of whom 28,090 are Negroes (1900). The most demoralizing agencies in Savannah are some twelve or fourteen low dance houses, known as "Free and Easies," run in connection with saloons. These are a great source of crime and immorality. A large percentage of the murders and other offenses against the person are committed in them. In one month of this year two homicides occurred in them, besides numerous cutting affrays. It is probably safe to say that these low dance halls are the greatest sources of crime in the city. Another source of vice and crime is a park for Negroes on the outskirts of the city. Here a low form of vaudeville is carried on. There is a saloon inside of the park and on the outside are low drinking places and other disreputable resorts. This park, if it furnished recreation and amusements of the proper kind, could be made a great agency for good to the city's large Negro population.

Some statistics for Savannah follow:

Police Arrests in Savannah

Arrests per Thousand of Negro Population by Years.

1874... 79	1883.. 60	1887.... 65	1891... 83	1895..106	1889..153
1877... 56	1884.. 66	1888... 65	1892... 75	1896..100	1900..152
1881... 82	1885.. 65	1889... 79	1893... 85	1897..122	1901..138
1882... 68	1886.. 55	1890... 75	1894... 85	1898..1(5	1902..144
		1903.................143			

Number of Arrests for each Class of Offenses				Arrests per Thousand of the Negro Population for each Class of Offenses		
Year	Person	Property	Society	Person	Property	Society
1874	11	145	963	0.07	10.0	68.0
1877	59	114	608	3.9	7.6	45.0
1881	105	116	1,128	6.4	7.0	67.0
1886	118	112	872	5.8	5.0	43.0
1895	257	630	1,781	10.0	24.0	79.0
1896	352	512	1,732	13.0	19.0	66.0
1897	294	587	2,344	11.0	22.0	84.0
1900	462	711	3,091	16.0	25.0	110.0
1901	303	661	2,986	10.0	23.0	103.0
1902	272	687	3,243	9.0	23.0	111.0
1903	210	618	3,404	7.0	21.0	115.0

PERCENTAGE OF AGES

Ages	Males	Females	Total
0-14	27.0	25.0	26.0
15-24	21.0	27.0	24.0
25-34	23.0	21.0	22.4
35-44	16.0	13.0	14.5
45-54	7.0	6.0	6.8
55-64	2.7	3.0	2.9
65 and over	1.3	1.8	1.5
Age unknown	0.7	0.7	0.7

The sentences imposed in the city court are generally severer than those imposed in the superior court, e. g. for larceny. It is also true that the sentences imposed in the recorder's court are usually severer than those imposed in the superior court. This is a further substantiation of the fact that there is increased stringency in punishing Negroes for minor offenses. It further appears from the record of cases that the tendency is to impose severer sentence for offenses against property than for offenses against the person.

The amount of crime among the Negroes of Savannah could no doubt be reduced if all or some of the following things could be accomplished: The suppression of the Free and Easies; improved park facilities for the cólored people so that recreation and amusement which would be uplifting and helpful could be furnished; the enforcement of the law respecting minors entering saloons and other questionable places; the establishment of a juvenile court and reformatory; better house facilities; education of the mass of the Negroes respecting proper sanitary observances; an increase of the school facilities for colored children. The school census of the city for 1903 gives the number of colored children between the ages of six and eighteen as being 8,023. The total number of colored pupils enrolled during the school year of 1903 was 2,312. only 28.8 per cent. of the entire number of colored children of school age. There are four colored public school buildings in the city. They are crowded to their utmost capacity. Admission for enrollment can be obtained only by ticket. In due time some or all of the above things will be done, and then a greater lowering of the crime rate of the Negroes will take place.

Comparing Savannah and Atlanta a strange discrepancy in arrests is noticeable—143 per thousand in Savannah, and 273, nearly twice as many, in Atlanta. The cause of this is probably that the relation between whites and Negroes in Atlanta is much less pleasant than in Savannah. In Atlanta strangers have met: the mountain whites and Negroes; and the white policemen arrest Negroes on the slightest provocation, so much so that the new mayor has protested:

The idea that 17,000 cases should be tried in recorder's court in one year is appalling, Mayor Woodward said. It places Atlanta at or near the top of the list of cities of this country in criminal statistics, he says. The police department should not be run for revenue, but for justice.

He then compares Atlanta's record with that of St. Louis, Atlanta being a "sealed" city, while St. Louis is known as a wide-open town. Atlanta has a population of 100,000; St. Louis had with strangers during October and November about 700,000. Yet in Atlanta during October and November, 1904, there were 3,163 cases tried in recorder's court, while in St. Louis the number was only 5,034, the St. Louis police making only 1,871 more arrests with 600,000 more population. Atlanta, he declares, needs no such money.

Mayor Woodward said he had been informed that many policemen keep a record of the arrests which they make, the fines and sentences imposed, with the belief that the more the arrests the better their chance for promotion. He promises to make an effort to have dismissed from the force every policeman who does this.— *Atlanta Constitution, Jan. 3, 1905.*

In Savannah, on the contrary, a leaven of the old house-servant class is still living beside the sons of their former masters and the mutual understanding is far better, and perhaps runs even to laxness in cases where punishment of Negroes would be salutary.

9. Crime in Augusta (by A. G. Coombs and L. D. Davis). Augusta is a city of 39,441 inhabitants, of whom 18,487 are Negroes (1900). It has much wealth, culture and learning, and the Negroes can with just pride lay claim to some part of these. Until two or three years ago crime among the Negroes in Augusta had reached a very serious and alarming extent. The recorder's court, with its daily sessions, lasted for three or four hours disposing of drunken brawls, gambling, and similar offenses. This state of affairs, however, was due to the fact that there was no fear of the law, and not because the Negro was so bad. The punishments were slight for political reasons. The ballot of the Negro was sought for, and the city officials made themselves popular with the black population for their own political interests and welfare.

Such a condition of things demanded a reform, which was made possible by the election of a new municipality. All the courts, city, county, and superior, began to enforce the laws rigidly and punishments were meted out swift and severe, both for minor and grave offenses. The result has been quite telling, for the recorder's court seldom lasts longer than an hour, and the number of Negroes arraigned has greatly decreased. And may we hope that the decrease is due to the respect for the majesty of the law rather than for fear of punishment.

In the last half-yearly report the chief of police says that crime in the city has lessened about 30 per cent., and especially that of moral turpitude among the Negroes. And this in spite of the city's growing population.

The following table gives some statistics of criminality in Augusta for 1902 and 1903:

	1902	1903
No. of arrests	2,236	2,100
No. of reports	1,052	768
No. brought before recorder	2,506	2,366
No. fined by recorder	1,852	1,530
No. dismissed by recorder	239	227
No. turned over to city court	217	220
No. turned over to superior court	60	48
No. sent to jail without fine	16	110
No. sent to reformatory	16	25
Amount of fines imposed	$30,079	$21,093
Amount of fines collected	17,331	4,311

These figures are given for the total population of Augusta, as no separate records are kept by the officials. The Negroes, however, form three-fourths of those convicted. The average age of the Augusta criminals is about 25 years. Of the 2,868 arrested and reported for the year 1903, there were 1,490 distributed between the jail and the county farm. Those who were convicted of gambling, vagrancy, suspicious character, wife-beating, drunkenness and nuisance in general were sent to jail. Most of these were worked on the chaingang. The county farm received a less number of prisoners, these being convicted for larceny, carrying concealed weapons, assault, swindling and such grave offenses.

The jail in Augusta is a place of discipline and cleanliness. Work is required, but it is so enforced that discharged prisoners report very humane treatment. The prisoners on the county farm have more laborious work to do, and often complain of harsh and unjust treatment.

A crying need of Augusta, and one which may in a manner throw some light on the cause of Negro criminality in this city, is for increased and improved public school accommodations for the Negroes. The city has four public schools for Negroes, having twenty-seven teachers, with an enrollment of about 2,000 pupils. This leaves at least 2,000 other children unprovided for.

As to the criminals it may be said that not many girls, but a goodly number of women, are sent to jail. There are some among these who are continually brought before the recorder, and they receive their sentence with stoical indifference. Sad it is to say that among the so-classed criminals are many young boys who are not criminals in the true sense of the word. There is the offending boy caught for throwing rocks, or spinning his top, or pitching his ball in the street. While some of these young boys are pardoned, a large number are fined ; and as these fines cannot always be paid, they are therefore "sent up" and thereby classed as criminals.

According to various city officials consulted by investigators, crime among Negroes in Augusta is constantly decreasing. One official said that it was his opinion that Negroes of the ignorant type and whites of the ignorant type were those guilty of crime. Ignorant whites commit the same kind of crime that ignorant Negroes commit, and 15 per cent. of the ignorant whites were associates and co-workers in crime with the same class of Negroes.

10. What Negroes think of Crime. As a rough answer to this question, the results of written answers of Negro school children and students have been collected. A series of simple questions were first put to 1,500 Negro school children in the Atlanta public schools. The most of them were between the ages of 9 and 15 years and were city bred. Of these 583 said that laws were made " for protection ; " 315, " to keep peace " or " order ; " and 135, to " govern " or " rule " persons.

The answers classed under " For protection " include many forms of protection; e. g., protection of one's rights, of property, of person, protection of city, of state, of country. Under the hundred or more unclassified answers are many which speak of laws as a means of preventing fighting, stealing, etc.

Their ideas of courts were correct: "To determine guilt or innocence" (398) ; "to see that the laws are obeyed" (222) ; "to settle matters" (222) ; a few say for "bad people" (69). Policemen are for the purpose of "arresting people" (522), or "protecting" them (346). Policemen are usually kind to 618 of the little ones, but were considered unkind by 459 and variable by 204. Most of them say that persons are sent to the "chaingang" for breaking the law and wrong-doing, but some others say that people are sent to the chaingang because "they haven't the money to pay their fines." One boy says: "Some good people are sent to the chaingang and some bad ones. They are sent because they are convicted."

The students, 534 in number, were older (13 to 21 years of age) and come from all parts of the state. Policemen have never helped or protected most of them (408) ; and 21 declared they have been specifically wronged by policemen. Of those who have seen courts in session (134), 71 think the judge and jurors acted fairly, and 41 that they did not;

their opinions of persons sent to the "chaingang" vary: 164 think them "bad or unfortunate;" 54 think they deserve punishment "if guilty," and 46 doubt the guilt of many of them; 25 are "sorry for them," and 22 think their punishment "makes them worse," but 28 consider them "a disgrace to their race." In general, many students consider that persons who are sent to the chaingang are very unfortunate. Many say that, while they are in favor of punishment for law-breakers, they consider the "chaingang" the worst and poorest means of punishment. These also speak of and deplore the treatment of the criminals on the "gang."

Many speak of the very disastrous results upon young criminals and express the wish that reformation be provided for the youthful offenders of the law. One says along this line: "The chaingang system is discreditable. It seems to defeat the purpose of punishment. I grow indignant over the presence of young boys in the chaingang." Another says: "The intermingling of young criminals with old ones in the chaingang is one of the worst evils of the system." A third says: "I think it [the chaingang] is one of the last resorts to which the state should give itself. The treatment of the men in most cases is very severe and especially unbearable in the fierce winter months."

When asked why so many young Negroes get into the clutches of the law, 152 ascribe it to "indolence" and "laziness;" 62 say for "not attending to their own business;" 57, "disobedience;" 40, "bad company;" 39, "ignorance;" 67, "lack of home-training;" and 19, "race prejudice." Most of them have several causes why so many young colored boys get into trouble. As an example of this one student says: "Ignorance, prejudice, poverty, wrong-doing." Another says: "Idleness is almost sole cause. Race prejudice also aids, as more Negroes are handled by the courts for the same offenses than whites." A third says: "The important causes are, I think, the lack of moral training, the lack of educational privileges, and beyond all the lack of good home-training. Another cause is the difficulty Negro boys have in getting employment."

As a remedy for criminality among Negroes, 118 say "better employment;" 112, "education;" 77, "teaching them the right;" 35, "home-training;" 24, "establishing reformatories;" 22, "Christian work;" 12, "by raising their standards and ideals;" and 10, "by closing places of evil and vice." Many suggest fair trial and unprejudiced decision in courts. Many also speak of good association, while some add that "our best people should dwell on the disgrace of being confined to the chaingang."

11. Causes of Negro Crime. This study is too incomplete to lead us to many definite conclusions. Yet certain causes of crime among Negroes today seem clear. They may be briefly classified as follows:

A.—Faults of the Negroes.

1. Abuse of their new freedom and tendency toward idleness and vagrancy.
2. Loose ideas of property, petty pilfering.
3. Unreliability, lying and deception.

4. Exaggerated ideas of personal rights, irritability and suspicion.

5. Sexual looseness, weak family life and poor training of children; lack of respect for parents.

6. Lack of proper self-respect; low or extravagant ideals.

7. Poverty, low wages and lack of accumulated property.

8. Lack of thrift and prevalence of the gambling spirit.

9. Waywardness of the "second generation."

10. The use of liquor and drugs.

All these faults are real and important causes of Negro crime. They are not racial traits but due to perfectly evident historic causes: slavery could not survive as an institution and teach thrift; and its great evil in the United States was its low sexual morals; emancipation meant for the Negroes poverty and a great stress of life due to sudden change. These and other considerations explain Negro crime. They do not excuse it however and a great burden of pressing reform from within lies upon the Negro's shoulders. Especially is this true with regard to the atrocious crime of rape. This is not to be sure a crime peculiar to the Negro race. An Englishman tells us that in Jamaica justice has been dealt out impartially ; and this has not resulted in "impudence" on the part of the blacks towards the whites. Indeed, when reasonably treated they are remarkably courteous,—more so than the average Teuton. Attacks by black men on white women are absolutely unknown; a young white woman is safe anywhere, the only terror being from white sailors. There are offenses against black women and children, but not whites. He infers from this that the danger of such attacks on white women, if it exists in the United States, is not really due to race. For his own part he is sure that the evil, where it exists, is augmented by the state of frenzy with which it is met.*

But granting this and making allowance for all exaggeration in attributing this crime to Negroes, there still remain enough well authenticated cases of brutal assault on women by black men in America to make every Negro bow his head in shame. Negroes must recognize their responsibility for their own worst classes and never let resentment against slander allow them even to seem to palliate an awful deed. This crime must at all hazards stop. Lynching is awful, and injustice and caste are hard to bear; but if they are to be successfully attacked they must cease to have even this terrible justification.

B.—Faults of the whites.

1. The attempt to enforce a double standard of justice in the courts, one for Negroes and one for whites.

2. The election of judges for short terms, making them subservient to waves of public opinion in a white electorate.

3. The shirking of jury duty by the best class of whites, leaving the dealing out of justice to the most ignorant and prejudiced.

4. Laws so drawn as to entangle the ignorant, as in the case of laws for labor contracts, and to leave wide discretion as to punishment in the hands of juries and petty officials.

---

*Sidney Olivier, in the *British Friend*, Dec., 1904.

5. Peonage and debt-slavery as methods of securing cheap and steady labor.

6. The tendency to encourage ignorance and subserviency among Negroes instead of intelligence, ambition and independence.

7. The taking of all rights of political self-defense from the Negro either by direct law, or custom, or by the "white primary" system.

8. The punishment of crime as a means of public and private revenue rather than as a means of preventing the making of criminals.

9. The rendering of the chastity of Negro women difficult of defense in law or custom against the aggressions of white men.

10. Enforcing a caste system in such a way as to humiliate Negroes and kill their self-respect.

A Southern man, Professor Andrew Sledd, has perhaps best elucidated the meaning of this latter point: "If we care to investigate, evidences of our brutal estimate of the black man are not far to seek. The hardest to define is perhaps the most impressive,—the general tacit attitude and feeling of the average Southern community toward the Negro. He is either nothing more than the beast that perishes, unnoticed and uncared for so long as he goes quietly about his menial toil (as a young man recently said to the writer, 'The farmer regards his nigger in the same light as his mule,' but this puts the matter far too favorably for the Negro); or, if he happen to offend, he is punished as a beast with a curse or a kick, and with tortures that even the beast is spared; or if he is thought of at all in a general way, it is with the most absolute loathing and contempt. He is either unnoticed or despised. As for his feelings, he hasn't any. How few—alas how few—words of gentleness and courtesy ever come to the black man's ear! But harsh and imperious words, coarseness and cursing, how they come upon him, whether with excuse or in the frenzy of unjust and unreasoning passion! And his rights of person, property, and sanctity of home,— who ever heard of the 'rights' of a 'nigger'? This is the general sentiment, in the air, intangible, but strongly felt; and it is, in a large measure, this sentiment that creates and perpetuates the Negro problem.

"If the Negro could be made to feel that his fundamental rights and privileges are recognized and respected equally with those of the white man, that he is not discriminated against both publicly and privately simply and solely because of his color, that he is regarded and dealt with as a responsible, if humble, member of society, the most perplexing features of his problem would be at once simplified, and would shortly, in normal course, disappear."*

A scientific study of Southern criminal conditions says:

There is frequently collusion between lawyers and justices. A Negro asks a lawyer how much it will cost her to whip Laura Brown. The lawyer sees a justice and arranges that the fine shall be $10. She is cautioned to do no "cutting," only whipping. If her wrath is equal to $10, Laura Brown gets a whipping. The Negro is fined according to contract, but also gets classed among criminals. The justice of peace office is one which few respectable men in the South will accept. The salary is small, and the general rule is no conviction, no fee, for either jury or justice. This is a direct bribe for conviction. There is often small chance

---

*Atlantic Monthly, Vol. 90, p. 67.

for appeal, for a $100 bond is required, and few Negroes are able to secure it.
Justices and constables are often in collusion. The constable gives a Negro, called
a "striker," money to go out and play craps. He informs the constable when and
where he will gather men to play. Then the constable swoops down and arrests
them. The striker gets a dividend and the constable and justice also profit by the
transaction.*

. . . . (1) Penalties in the South are extreme and Negroes are serving life
sentences for crimes which receive penalties of from one to five years in the
North. (2) There are no agencies for preventing crime in the South. There are
no parental or vacation schools; no juvenile courts; no societies to aid discharged
convicts; no employment bureaus; no co-operative societies, and no municipal lodging houses. There are three reformatories; no manual training schools; few kindergartens; no compulsory education laws, and few Y. M. C. associations. All of these
are recognized as great forces in the prevention of crime. There are no movements
or institutions for saving the Negro women, and they largely increase the statistics
for female criminals in the United States.†

Negro women are thus peculiarly unprotected:

They constitute the domestic class, although they work in all the trades open to
them. Necessity compels them to work, and the Negro men do not discourage it.
The attitude of white women is not a protection, for many of them are indifferent
to their husbands' or brothers' relations with Negroes. This is changing as they
get farther away from the precedents of slavery. White men have little respect
for the sanctity of family life of Negroes, when they would hesitate to enter the
Anglo-Saxon's home. Negro women are expected to be immoral, and have few in-
ducements to be otherwise. Religion is more often a cause than prevention, for
the services are frequently scenes of crime. Physical senses so largely predom-
inate over the intellectual and spiritual perceptions, and but few attempts have
been made to develop the latter. The laws against immorality are laxly enforced.
Whites within their own circles would not countenance acts to which they are indifferent in Negroes. There are small opportunities for Negro women to support
themselves through occupations other than menial, which are filled with grave
temptations.‡

And again, once in jail and no attempts at reform are made throughout the Southern States:

With one exception, there are no educational influences. No trades are taught,
no schools are conducted and no reading supplied, except at mining camps in Alabama. In factories, sawmills, etc., convicts are given enough instruction to make
them productive workers, and that is equivalent to a trade. But the *idea* is not
equipment of individuals so they can support themselves when released.§

The surroundings of prisoners suggest slavery and degradation:

"About daylight convicts start off to the fields dividing into two gangs, when
they are busy. The assistant manager takes one gang, and a deputy takes charge
of the other. One gang goes to plowing and the other to hoeing. When they get
out into the field a cordon is formed by the guards, who are armed with winches-
ters. The manager stands in the midst of the gang, or rides horseback, as the
case may be, and directs the operations. He, of course, is armed with a revolver,
and carries the strap for the punishment of the refractory men. This strap is a
queer looking affair. It is a piece of leather about 6 inches wide and 2 feet long,
attached to a wooden handle. It is customary to give a refractory 'nigger' from
one to twenty-five lashes with this strap on his bare back, according to the extent

---

* Kellor: Experimental Sociology, p. 250.   †Ibid, p. 34.   ‡Ibid, p. 171.   §Ibid, p. 200.

of his offense. The occasions for punishment are comparatively rare, however. It is more often the new men who get a taste of the lash. The lash was adopted by the board some time ago, and it is regarded as the most humane yet put in use. It is impossible to cut the flesh with it, and a liberal use of it does not incapacitate a man for work. The board is also particular about too liberal use of the lash, and sergeants are compelled, among other things, to report at the end of every month the names of convicts lashed, the reason and the number of lashes."*

And finally, instead of efforts to improve workmen and to make them more efficient, one is struck by such demands as this:

Under the present status, the employing farmer has little or no redress against a breach of agreement on the part of the hands he has engaged to assist in the working and harvesting of his crop. He is at the mercy of the mercenary immigration agent or the machinations of unscrupulous planters in an adjoining county or state. . . . .

The Constitution is of the opinion, however, that outside of the aid of immigration, this bewildering problem can be largely solved in Georgia and other Southern states by the enactment of statutes making a contract between farmer and laborer even more legally binding than under existing laws. . . . .

Making a discretionary term of imprisonment the penalty for such breaches and the consistent enforcement of such a provision for two or three seasons would soon teach this floating, shiftless element to regard their obligations with greater respect and remove one of the very present menaces to the business-like management of our agricultural interests.—*Atlanta Constitution; Editorial, March 30, 1905.*

There is much difference of opinion on many of the points enumerated above, but it certainly seems clear that absolutely impartial courts; the presence of intelligent Negroes on juries when Negroes are tried; the careful defense of ignorance in law and custom; the absolute doing away with every vestige of involuntary servitude except in prisons under absolute state control, and for the reformation of the prisoner; the encouraging of intelligent, ambitious, and independent black men; the granting of the right to cast an untrammelled vote to intelligent and decent Negroes; the unwavering defense of all women who want to be decent against indecent approach, and an effort to increase rather than to kill the self respect of Negroes, it seems certain that such a policy would make quickly and decidedly for the decrease of Negro criminality in the South and in the land.

The arguments against this are often strongly urged; it is said that whites and Negroes differ so in standards of culture that courts must discriminate; that partially forced labor is necessary in the South; that intelligent Negroes become impudent fault-finders and disturb a delicate situation; that the South cannot in self-defense permit Negro suffrage; that Negro women are unchaste; and that the Negro must be "kept down" at all hazards. To all this it can only be said: These arguments have been used against every submerged class since the world began, and history has repeatedly proven them false.

---

*Quoted in Kellor: Experimental Sociology, p. 195.

12. Some Conclusions. A fragmentary study like this can, of course, come to no general conclusions. Yet confining ourselves principally to the state of Georgia and to statistics, we may distinguish certain evident forces at work: the downward tendencies are the amount of crime, the number of lynchings, and the State income from crime. The upward tendencies are the increase in population, the increase in percentage of those able to read and write, and the increase in property.

Taking these, one by one, we have:

DOWNWARD TENDENCIES

(a) *Amount of Crime.* The diagram on page 61 shows the Negro prison population of Georgia per 100,000 of total Negro population. The exact figures are given on page 33. These figures show that serious Negro crime is decreasing. Moreover, the full measure of that decrease is here but partially shown as the argument on page 11 has proven. The large proportion of life and long term sentences for Negroes makes the Negro population apparently responsible for considerably more crime than it really is. If the figures for commitments, year by year, were available the decrease in Negro crime in the last ten years would be even more striking.

(b) *Lynchings.* The absolute numbers of lynchings in Georgia, as reported by the Chicago *Tribune*, are:

Year	Lynchings	Average
1885	8	
1886	6	
1887	6	8
1889	11	
1890	18	
1891	12	
1892	16	16
1893	16	
1894	20	
1895	14	
1896	9	
1897	14	15
1898	12	
1899	28	
1900	16	
1901	14	
1902	8	12
1903	12	

Averaging these for five year periods and plotting the average number of lynchings for the half decades, we have the diagram on page 61. It is interesting to note, first, that the crest of the wave of lynching lawlessness has evidently passed, and secondly, that the crest of the wave apparently preceded the crest of the wave of crime. It would be too much perhaps to say that it caused an increase of crime, but certainly it did not lessen crime.

(c) *State Income from Crime.* From 1876–1904 the State of Georgia has received from traffic in criminals a net income over expenses of nearly nine hundred thousand dollars from the sale of criminals to private contractors. This sum has been as follows:

Net Income of State from Crime in Georgia

Year	Income per annum	Total
1876–99.............	$ 15,000.00*	$345,000.00
1900................	61,826.32	61,862.32
1901–3.............	81,000.00	243,000.00
1904................	225,000.00	225,000.00
Total	....	$874,862.32

The sinister increase of this blood money is the greatest single cause of persistent crime in Georgia, since it makes the object of the whole prison system money and not reform of criminals or prevention of crime.

Of these three backward tendencies the two first show hopeful decrease, the last dangerous increase.

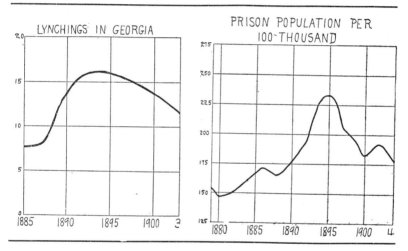

UPWARD TENDENCIES

(a) *Increase in Population.* The diagram on page 62 shows how the Negro population has grown since the war. The exact figures are:

Year	Population	Per Cent. of Increase	
		Negroes	Whites
1870................	545,142	....	....
1880................	725,133	33.0 %	27.9 %
1890................	858,815	18.4 %	19.8 %
1900................	1,034,813	20.5 %	20.7 %

This would seem to indicate a healthy, virile growth of population, equaling that of the whites with their larger prosperity and opportunity.

---

* $25,000 was received each year, but some $10,000 of this was expended for State inspection.

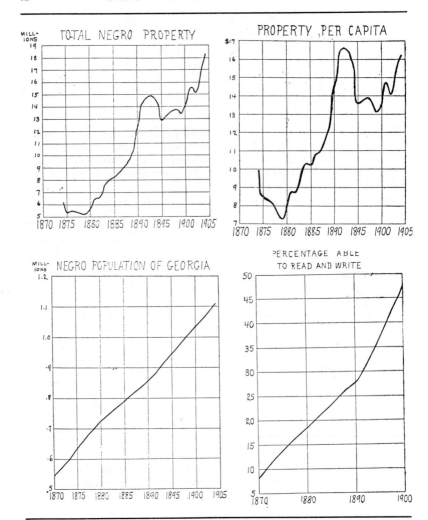

(b) *Increase in Literacy.* The diagram of those 10 years of age and over able to read and write is given above, and is based on these figures:

Year	Percentage able to read and write
1870.	7.9 %
1880.	18.4 %
1890.	32.7 %
1900.	47.6 %

This population is an ignorant population with shamefully inadequate school facilities in the country districts, and only fair facilities in the town schools. Nevertheless, the rapid growth in intelligence has been marvelous.

(c) *Property Holding.* It is continually reiterated that the Negro is lazy and shiftless. That there is a large idle class and many spendthrifts is true, but that there is a growing class of thrifty, saving Negroes is the central fact of post-bellum history, and this class cannot be ignored. The curve showing the total assessed value of Georgia property is given on page 62. The figures on which this diagram is based are:

Total Assessed Wealth of Georgia Negroes

Year	Total property	Year	Total property
1874	$ 6,157,798	1890	$12,322,003
1875	5,393,885	1891	14,196,735
1876	5,488,867	1892	14,869,575
1877	5,430,844	1893	14,960,675
1878	5,124,875	1894	14,387,730
1879	5,182,398	1895	12,941,230
1880	5,764,293	1896	13,292,816
1881	6,478,951	1897	13,619,690
1882	6,589,876	1898	13,719,200
1883	7,582,395	1899	13,447,423
1884	8,021,525	1900	14,118,720
1885	8,153,390	1901	15,629,811
1886	8,655,298	1902	15,188,069
1887	8,936,479	1903	16,714,334
1888	9,631,271	1904	18,002,500
1889	10,415,330		

To this must be added considerable property in churches and schools. Probably the market value of Negro property in Georgia to-day is close to $35,000,000. The per capita amount of property is given in the diagram on page 62. It shows a decrease from 1874 to 1879; then a rapid increase up to 1892. The financial panic and the falling price of cotton brought it down until 1899, when it began to recover, and has nearly regained its maximum. The exact figures, based on the estimated Negro population for the years between each census, are:

Property per Capita for Georgia Negroes

Year	Property per capita	Year	Property per capita
1874	$ 9.98	1890	$14.35
1875	8.49	1891	16.20
1876	8.44	1892	16.63
1877	8.09	1893	16.41
1878	7.44	1894	15.48
1879	7.33	1895	13.67
1880	7.95	1896	13.78
1881	8.77	1897	13.87
1882	8.77	1898	13.72
1883	9.91	1899	13.22
1884	10.30	1900	13.64
1885	10.21	1901	14.85
1886	10.75	1902	14.19
1887	10.92	1903	15.37
1888	11.57	1904	16.29
1889	12.32		

64 NINTH ATLANTA CONFERENCE

On the whole, then, we may say that in Georgia the tendencies are overwhelmingly in the right direction; crime is decreasing, property and education increasing. The danger lies in the environing white population with their tendency toward the unfair treatment of blacks. So far as this treatment is manifested in lynching, there is an evident decrease, but the traffic in criminal labor continues.

How far the facts true in Georgia are true for the rest of the nation, is not certain, but probably they are fairly typical.

13. The Ninth Atlanta Conference. The Ninth Atlanta Conference to study the Negro problems convened in Ware Memorial Chapel, Tuesday, May 24, 1904. President Horace Bumstead was made chairman and the Rev. Mr. H. H. Proctor was made secretary. The following program was carried out:

First Session, 10 A. M.

President Horace Bumstead, presiding.
Subject: "Causes of Crime."
Remarks—The Rev. Mr. James Bond, Nashville, Tenn.
Remarks—The Rev. Mr. A. Eustace Day, Atlanta, Ga.
"Crime in Atlanta"—The Rev. Mr. H. H. Proctor, Atlanta, Ga.
Discussion by Dr. W. F. Penn, the Rev. Mr. C. B. Wilmer, Dean L. L. Knight, and the Rev. Mr. J. E. Moorland.

Second Session, 3 P. M.

Annual Mothers' Meeting.
Mrs. Mary Tate Cater, presiding.
Subject: "Crime among Women and Children."
Music.
"Wayward Children and the School"—Miss J. F. Cutler, Atlanta, Ga.
"The School and Crime"—Miss Ruth Harris, Atlanta, Ga.
Music.
Address—Miss N. H. Burroughs, Louisville, Ky.
Music.
Reports on Social Reform:
    Juvenile Reformatory—Mrs. G. S. King.
    Women's Clubs—Miss Hattie Escridge.
Music.

(The music was furnished by children from the Leonard Street Colored Orphanage, under the direction of Miss Amy Chadwick.)

Third Session, 8 P. M.

President Horace Bumstead, presiding.
Subject: "Extent and Cure of Crime."
"Crime in Savannah as compared with Chicago, Ill."—Mr. M. N. Work, Savannah, Ga.
"Crime in Augusta"—The Rev. Mr. A. G. Coombs, Augusta, Ga.
"Co-operation among Whites and Negroes for the Cure of Crime"—The Rev. Mr. H. S. Bradley, Atlanta, Ga.
"The Problem of Crime"—Mr. Frank B. Sanborn, Concord Mass.

14. Resolutions. The following resolutions were adopted before the conference adjourned:

The Ninth Atlanta Conference, after a study of crime among Negroes in Georgia, has come to these conclusions:

AMOUNT OF CRIME

1. The amount of crime among Negroes in this state is very great. This is a dangerous and threatening phenomenon. It means that large numbers of the freedmen's sons have not yet learned to be law-abiding citizens and steady workers, and until they do so the progress of the race, of the South, and of the nation will be retarded.

CAUSES OF CRIME

2. The causes of this state of affairs seem clear:

First. The mass of the Negroes are in a transient stage between slavery and freedom. Such a period of change involves physical strain, mental bewilderment and moral weakness. Such periods of stress have among all people given rise to crime and a criminal class. *Secondly.* Race prejudice in so far as it narrows the opportunities open to Negroes and teaches them to lose self-respect and ambition by arbitrary caste proscriptions is a potent cause of carelessness, disorder and crime. *Thirdly.* Negroes have less legal protection than others against unfair aggression upon their rights, liberty and prosperity. This is particularly true of Negro women, whose honor and chastity have in this state very little protection against the force and influence of white men, particularly in the country districts and small towns. *Fourthly.* Laws as to vagrancy, disorder, contracts for work, chattel mortgages and crop-liens are so drawn as to involve in the coils of the law the ignorant, unfortunate and careless Negroes, and lead to their degradation and undue punishment, when their real need is inspiration, knowledge and opportunity. *Fifthly.* Courts usually administer two distinct sorts of justice: one for whites and one for Negroes; and this custom, together with the fact that judge and court officials are invariably white and elected to office by the influence of white votes alone, makes it very difficult for a Negro to secure justice in court when his opponent is white. *Sixthly.* The methods of punishment of Negro criminals is calculated to breed crime rather than stop it. Lynching spreads among black folk the firmly fixed idea that few accused Negroes are really guilty; the leasing of convicts, even the present system of state control, makes the state traffic in crime for the sake of revenue instead of seeking to reform criminals for the sake of moral regeneration; and finally the punishment of Negro criminals is usually unintelligent: they are punished according to the crime rather than according to their criminal record; little discrimination is made between old and young, male and female, hardened thug and careless mischief-maker; and the result is that a single sentence to the chaingang for a trivial misdemeanor usually makes the victim a confirmed criminal for life.

EXTENT AND CURE OF CRIME

3. There is no evidence to show that crime is increasing among Negroes in this state. Save in a few of the larger towns there seems to be a marked decrease since 1896.

4. The cure for Negro crime lies in moral uplift and inspiration among Negroes. The masses of the race must be made vividly to realize that no man ever has an excuse for laziness, carelessness, and wrong-doing. That these are not a cure for oppression, but rather invite and encourage further oppression. Negroes then must

be taught to stop fighting, gambling, and stealing, which seem to be the usual misdemeanors of the careless; and particularly the law-abiding must separate themselves from that dangerous criminal element among us who are responsible for murder, rape and burglary, and vigorously condemn the crime and the criminal. Four agencies among Negroes may work toward this end: the church, the school, institutions for rescue work, and the juvenile reformatory. The first step in Georgia would seem to be one toward a reformatory for Negro youth.

APPEAL TO WHITES

5. Finally, this conference appeals to the white people of Georgia for six things: Fairer criminal laws; justice in the courts; the abolition of state traffic in crime for public revenue and private gain; more intelligent methods of punishment; the refusal to allow free labor to be displaced by convict labor; and finally a wider recognition of the fact that honest, intelligent, law-abiding black men are safer neighbors than ignorant, underpaid serfs, because it is the latter class that breeds dangerous crime.

INDEX

The

Health and Physique

of the

Negro American

Report of a Social Study made under the direction of Atlanta University; together with
the Proceedings of the Eleventh Conference
for the Study of the Negro Problems, held at
Atlanta University, on May the 29th, 1906

Edited by
W. E. Burghardt Du Bois
Corresponding Secretary of the Conference

The Atlanta University Press
Atlanta, Georgia
1906

IT is the cranial and facial forms that lead us to accept the consanguinity of the African Hamites, of red-brown and black color, with the Mediterranean peoples; the same characters reveal the consanguinity of the primitive inhabitants of Europe, and of their remains in various regions and among various peoples, with the populations of the Mediterranean, and hence also with the Hamites of Africa.

Sergi.

Analytical Table of Contents

Preface

A study of human life today involves a consideration of human physique and the conditions of physical life, a study of various social organizations, beginning with the home, and investigations into occupations, education, religion and morality, crime and political activity. The Atlanta Cycle of studies into the Negro problem aims at exhaustive and periodic studies of all these subjects as far as they relate to the Negro American. Thus far we have finished the first decade with a study of mortality (1896), of homes (1897), social reform (1898), economic organization (1899 and 1902), education (1900 and 1901), religion (1903) and crime (1904), ending with a general review of methods and results and a bibliography (1905).

The present publication marks the beginning of a second cycle of study and takes up again the subject of the physical condition of Negroes, but enlarges the inquiry beyond the mere matter of mortality. This study is based on the following data:

Reports of the United States census.
Reports of the life insurance companies.
Vital records of various cities and towns.
Reports of the United States Surgeon General.
Reports from Negro hospitals and drug stores.
Reports from medical schools.
Letters from physicians.
Measurements of 1,000 Hampton students.
General literature as shown in the accompanying bibliography.

Atlanta University has been conducting studies similar to this for a decade. The results, distributed at a nominal sum, have been widely used. Notwithstanding this success, the further prosecution of these important studies is greatly hampered by the lack of funds. With meagre appropriations for expenses, lack of clerical help and necessary apparatus, the Conference cannot cope properly with the vast field of work before it.

Especially is it questionable at present as to how large and important a work we shall be able to prosecute during the next ten-year cycle. It may be necessary to reduce the number of conferences to one every other year. We trust this will not be necessary, and we earnestly appeal to those who think it worth while to study this, the greatest group of social problems that has ever faced the nation, for substantial aid and encouragement in the further prosecution of the work of the Atlanta Conference.

Bibliography of Negro Health and Physique

A large part of the matter here entered is either unscientific or superceded by later and more careful work. Even such matter, however, has an historic interest.

Bibliography of Bibliographies

Catalogue of the Library of the United States Surgeon General's Office. See *Negro*.

Bibliography

Abel, J. J., and Davis, W. S.—On the pigment of the Negro's skin and hair. J. Exper. M. New York, 1896.

Alcock, N. and others.—Negroes; why are they black? Nature, 30:501; 31:6.

Angerbliche (Die) Inferioritat der Neger-Rasse.

Atlanta University Publications.—Mortality among Negroes in Cities. Atlanta, 1896.

Social and Physical Condition of Negroes in Cities. Atlanta, 1897.

Atwater, W. O., and Woods, Chas. D. Dietary studies with reference to the food of Negroes in Alabama in 1895-1896. Washington, 1897. (U. S. Dept. Agri.)

Babcock, J. W.—The colored insane. New Haven(?) 1895.

Baldwin, Ebenezer.—Observations on the physical, intellectual, and moral qualities of our colored population. New Haven, 1834.

Ball, M. V.—The mortality of the Negro. Med. News, LXIV, 389.

Vital statistics of the Negro. Med. News, LXV, 392.

Balloch, E. A.—The relative frequency of fibroid processes in the dark skinned races. Ibid, 29-35.

Baxter, T. H.—Statistics; Medical and Anthropological, of the provost Marshall General's Bureau. Washington, 1875.

Bean, R. B.—On a racial peculiarity in the brain of the Negro. Proc. Ass. Am. Anat. Balt. 1904-5.

The Negro Brain. Century, Vol. 72, pp, 778 and 947.

Beazley, W. S.—Peculiarities of the Negro. Med. Progress, XV, 46.

Black and white ratios for eleven decades. Nation, 73:391-2.

Bodington, Alice.—The importance of race and its bearing on the "Negro question." Westminst. Rev., CXXXIV, 415-427.

Brady, C. M.—The Negro as a patient. N. Orl. M. & S. J., LVI. 431-445.

Broadnax, B. H.—New born infants of African descent. N. Y. M. Times, 1895.

Color of infant Negroes. Miss. M. Rec., VII, 174.

Broca, Dr. Paul.—The phenomena of hybridity in the genus homo. London, 1864.

Brown, F. J.—The northward movement of the colored population. A statistical study. Baltimore, 1897.

Browne, Sir T.—Of the blackness of Negroes. In his works, 2:180-197.

Bryce, Jas.—The relations of the advanced and the backward races of mankind. Oxford, 1892. 46 pp.

Bryce, T. H.—On a pair of Negro Femora. J. Anat. and Physiol., 32:76-82.

Notes on the myology of a Negro. Ibid, 31:607-618.

Buchner, M.—Psychology of Negro. Pop. Sci. Mo., 23:399.

Burmeister, H.—The black man; the comparative anatomy and physiology of the African Negro. Transl. by Julius Friedlander and Robert Tomes. New York, 1853.

Buschan, G.—Zur Pathologie der Neger. Arch. per l'antrop., XXXI, 357-375.

Byers, J. W.—Diseases of the Southern Negro. Med. and Surg. Reporter, LVIII, 734-37.

Campbell, J.—Negro-mania; being an examination of the falsely assumed equality of the various races of men. Philadelphia, 1851.

Capacity of Negroes. Spectator, 75:927.

Cartwright, S. A.—Physical characteristics of Negroes. DeBow's Review, 11:184.
Diseases of Negroes. DeBow's Review, 11:29, 331, 504.

Castellanos, J. J.—The rural and city Negro pathologically and therapeutically considered. Proc. Orleans Parish M. Soc., 1895. 111 pp., LXXX-LXXXV.

Castonnel des Fosses. La race noire dans l'avenir. Assoc. franc. pour l'avance. d. sc. 18: pt. 1, 377-380.

Causes of color of the Negro. Portfolio (Dennie's), 12:6447.

Chittenden, C. E.—Negroes in the United States. Pop. Sci. Mo., 22:841.

Clark, G. C.—The immunity of the Negro race to certain diseases and the causes thereof. Maryland M. J., XXXVIII, 222-4.

Clarke, R.—Short notes of the prevailing diseases in the colony of Sierra Leone, with a return of the sick Africans sent to hospital in eleven years, and classified medical returns for the years 1853-4; also tables showing the number of lunatics admitted to hospital in a period of thirteen years and the number treated from April, 1842, to March, 1853. J. Statist. Soc., XIV, 6081.

Coates, B. H.—The effects of secluded and gloomy imprisonment on individuals of the African variety of mankind in the production of disease. Philadelphia, 1843.

Cohn, H.—Die sehleistungen der Dahoma-Neger. Wchnschr. f. Therap. u. Hyg. d. Auges, Bresl., 1898. 2:97.

Coleman, W. L.—Some observations on consumption, diabetes, melitus and consumption in the Negro. Alkaloid Clin., III, 114-116.

The color of newly born Negro children. Lancet, 2:1419.

The colored race in life assurance. Lancet, II, 902.

Conradt, L., and Virchow, R.—Tabellarische Uebersicht der an Negern des Adeli-Landes augesfuhrten Auframen. Verhandl. d. Gesellsch. f. Anthrop., 164-186.

Corson, E. R.—The future of the colored race in the United States from an ethnic and medical standpoint; a lecture delivered before the Georgia Historical Society, June 6, 1887. XV, 193-226.
The vital equation of the colored race, and its future in the United States. Wilder quart. century book. Ithaca, 1893. 115-175.

Cowgill, W. M.—Why the Negro does not suffer from trachoma. J. Am. M. Ass., XXXIV, 399.

Crawford, J.—On the physical and mental characteristics of the Negro. Tr. Ethn. Soc. 4:212-239.

Croly, D. G., and others.—Miscegenation: theory of the blending of the races applied to the American white man and the Negro. N. Y., 1864.

Cunningham, R. McW.—The morbidity and mortality of Negro convicts. Med. News, LXIV, 113-117.
The Negro as a convict. Tr. M. Ass. Alabama, 1893. pp. 315-326.

Cureau, A.—Essai sur la phychologie des races Negres en l'Afrique tropicale. Deuxieme partie: Intellectualite. Rev. gen. d. sc. pures et appliq., 36:638-679.

Daniels, C. W.—Negro fertility and infantile mortality. British Guiana M. Ann., X, 8-17.

P. D. A propos de Negres blancs. Rev. med. de Normandie, Rouen, 1905, 441. Les Negres blancs. J. de med. de Par., 1906. XVIII, 41.

De Albertis, O.—Genesi, storia ed antropologia della razza Negra. Revista, VIII, 290-308.

Degallier, Mlle. Alice.—Notes psychologiques sur les Negres Pahouins. Arch. de psychol., IV 362-368.

8   ELEVENTH ATLANTA CONFERENCE

DeSaussure, P. G.—Is the colored race increasing or decreasing? Tr. South Carolina M. Ass., XLV, 119-121.
Obstetrical observations on the Negroes of South Carolina. Tr. Pan-Am. M. Cong., 1895, pt. 1, 917-921.
Diseases of Negroes. So. Quar. Review, 22:49.
Distinctive peculiarities and diseases of Negroes. DeBow's Review, 20:612.
Dixon, W. A.—The morbid proclivities and retrogressive tendencies in the offspring of mulattoes. Med. News, LXI, 180-182.
Dr. Cartwright on the Negro. DeBow's Review, 32:54, 238; 33:62.
DuBois, W. E. B.—The conservation of the races. American Negro Academy: Occasional Papers, No. 2.
The Philadelphia Negro. Publications of the University of Pennsylvania, Nov. 14, 1890.
Easton, Hosea.—A treatise on the intellectual character and condition of the colored people of the United States. Boston, 1837.
Edelman, L.—The Negro as a criminal and his influence on the white race. Med. News, LXXXII, 196.
Eijkman, C. The color of Negroes. Janus IV, 390.
Faison, J. A.—Tuberculosis in the colored race. Med. Rec., LV, 375.
Fehlinger.—Die Sterblichkeit der europaischen und der Neger-Rasse. Natur. Wchnschr., III, 280.
Fletcher, R. M., Jr.—Surgical peculiarities of the Negro race. Tr. M. Ass. Ala., 1898, 49-57.
Frederic.—Zur Kenntnis der Hautfarbe der Neger. Ztschr. f. Morphol. u. Anthrop., IX, 41-56.
Freiberg, A. H., and Schroeder, J. H.—A note on the foot of the American Negro. Am. F. M. Sc., CXXVI, 1033-1036.
Frissell, H. B., and Bevier, Isabel.—Dietary studies of Negroes in eastern Virginia, 1897-1898.
Gannett, H.—Are we to become Africanized? Pop. Sci. Mo., 27:145.
Giacomini, G. Annotazioni sulla anatomia del Negro; 1. memoria. Gior. d. r. Accad. di med. di Torino, XXIV, 454-470.
Annotazioni sulla anatomia del Negro; 2 memoria. Ibid., XXX, 729-803.
Annotaziona sulla anatomia del Negro; 3 memoria. Ibid., XXXII, 462-500.
Annotazioni sulla anatomia del Negro; 5 memoria. Ibid., XL, 17-64.
Notes sur l'anatomie du Negre; 4 memoire. Arch. ital. de biol., IX, 119-137.
Gilliam, E. W.—Negroes in the United States. Pop. Sci. Mo., 22:433.
Girard, H.—Notes anthropometriques sur quelquuns Soudanis occidentaux, Malinkes, Bambaras, Foulahs, Soninkes, etc. Anthropologie, XIII, 41; 167; 328.
Girtin, T. C.—Negroes, ancient and modern. DeBow's Review, 12:209.
Gould, B. A.—Investigations in the military and anthropological statistics of American soldiers. Cambridge, 1869.
Granville, R. K., and Roth, H. L.—Notes on the Jekris, Sobos and Ijos of the Warri district of the Niger Coast Protectorate. J. Anthrop Inst., 1, 104-126.
Gregoire, H.—Enquiry concerning the intellectual and moral faculties, etc., of Negroes. Brooklyn, 1810.
Guenebault, J. H., editor.—Natural history of the Negro race. From the French. Charleston, 1837.
Hamilton, J. C.—The African in Canada. Proc. Am. Ass. Adv. Sc., XXXVIII, 364-370.
Harris, S.—The future of the Negro from the standpoint of the Southern physician. Ala. M. J., XIV, 57-68. Also: Am. Med., Phila., 1901, II, 373-376.
Hecht, D. O.—Tabes in the Negro. Am. J. M. Sc., CXXVI, 705-720.
Herring, N. B.—The morphological and psychophysical intrinsicalities of the Negro race.
Herz, M. Der Bau des Negerfusses. Ztschr. f. orthop. Chir., XI, 168-174.
Higgins, R. C.—Mortality among Negroes of the South. Nation, 15:105.
Hodges, J. A.—The effect of freedom upon the physical and psychological development of the Negro. Richmond J. Pract., XIV, 161-171.

Hoffman, F. L.—Race traits and tendencies of the American Negro.
Vital statistics of the Negro. Med. News, LXV, 320-324.
Vital statistics of Negroes. Arena, 5:529.
Holcombe, W. H.—Capabilities of Negro race. Southern Literary Messenger, 33:401.
Holley, Jas. T.—Vindication of the capacity of the Negro race, etc. New Haven, 1857.
Howard, W. L.—The Negro as a distinct ethnic factor in civilization. Medicine, IX, 423-426.
Hrdlicka, Ales.—Anthropological investigations on one thousand white and colored children of both sexes, the inmates of the New York juvenile asylum, etc. N. Y., 189-(?).
Hrdlicka, Ales.— Physiological difference between white and colored children. Amer. Anthrop., 1898, II, pp. 347-50.
Hunt, Jas.—The Negro's place in nature. N. Y., 1864.
Jacques.—Contribution a l'ethnologie de l'Afrique centrale; huit cranes du Haut-Congo. Bull. Soc. d'anthrop. de Brux. XV, 188-194.
Jacques, V.—Mensurations anthropometriques de trente-neuf Negres du Congo. Ibid., 237-241.
Jarvis, Edward.—Insanity among the colored population, etc. Phila., 1844.
Johnson, J. T.—On some of the apparent peculiarities of parturition in the Negro race, with remarks on race pelvis in general. Am. J. Obst., VIII, 88-123.
Johnson, (R. H.)—The physical degeneracy of the modern Negro, with statistics from the principal cities, showing his mortality from A. D. 1700 to 1897.
Johnston, G. W.—Abnormalities and diseases of the genito-urinary system in Negro women. Maryland M. J., XX, 426-429.
Johnstone, H. B.—Notes on the customs of the tribes occupying Mombasa sub-district, British East Africa. J. Anthrop. Inst., XXXII, 263-272.
Kollock, C. W.—The eye of the Negro. Tr. Am. Ophth. Soc., VI, 257-268.
Further observations of the eye of the Negro. Tr. Pan-Am. M. Cong., Wash., 1895. Pt. 2, 1482-1484.
Kulz.—Die hygienesche Beeinflussung der schwarzen Rasse durch die weisse in Deutsch-Toga. Arch. f. Rassen-u. Gesellch. Biol., II, 673-688.
LeHardy, J. C.—Mortality among Negroes: the sanitary privileges to which they are entitled from the authorities. Sanitarian, XXXVII, 492-495.
Lehman-Nitsche, R.—Die dunklen Haut flecke der Neugeborenen bei Indianern und mulatten. Globus, LXXXVI, 297-309.
Livini, F.—Contribuzioni alla anatomia del Negro. Arch. per l'anthro., XXIX, 203-228.
Lofton, L.—The Negro as a surgical subject. N. Orl. M. & S. J., LIV, 530-533.
Macalister, A.—On the osteology of two Negroes. Proc. Roy. Irish Acad. Science, III, 347-350.
Macdonald, A.—Study of 16,473 white and 5,457 black children. Report Com. Ed., 1897-8. Chapters 21 & 25.
Colored children; a psycho-physical study. J. Am. M. Ass., XXXII, 1140-1144.
Macdonald, J. R. L.—East Central Africa customs. J. Anthrop. Inst., XXII, 99-122.
Notes on the ethnology of tribes met with during progress of the Juba expedition of 1897-9. Ibid., II, 226-250.
Mapes, C. C.—Remarks from the standpoint of sociology. Med. Age, XIV, 713-715.
Matas, R.—The surgical peculiarities of the Negro: a statistical inquiry based upon the records of the Charity Hospital of New Orleans. Tr. Am. Surg. Ass., XIV, 483; 610.
Mays, T. J.—Increase of insanity and consumption among the Negro population of the South since the war. Boston M. & S. J., CXXXV. 537-540.
McGuire, H., and Lydston, G. F.—Sexual crimes among the Southern Negroes; scientifically considered. Va. M. Month., XX, 105-125.
McIntosh, J.—The future of the Negro race. Tr. South Car. M. Ass., 1891, 183-188.
McIntosh, T. M.—Enlarged prostrate and spina bifida in the Negro. Med. Rec., LIV, 350.
McKie, T. J.—A brief history of insanity and tuberculosis in the Southern Negro. J Am. M. Ass., XXVIII, 537.

McVey, B.—Negro practice. N. Orl. M. & S. J., XX, 328-332.

Miller, J. F.—The effects of emancipation upon the mental and physical qualifications of the Negro of the South. North Car. M. J., XXXVIII, 285-294.

Miller, Kelly.—A review of Hoffman's "Race traits and tendencies." Washington, 1897.

Michel, M.—Two cervical muscle anomalies in the Negro. Med. Rec., XLI, 125.

Mitchell, Mary V.—Clinical Notes from diseases among colored children, Rep. Proc. Alumnae Ass. Woman's M. Coll., Penn., 50-58.

Morison.—Notes sur la formation du pigment chez de Negre. Cong. internat. de edrmat. et de syph. C.-r., 1889, 130-131.

Mortality among Negroes in cites. Proceedings of the conference for investigations of city problems, held at Atlanta University, May 26-27, 1896.

De Mortillet, G.—Sur les Negres de l'Algerie et de la Tunisie. Bull. Soc. d'antrop., de Par., 1890. I, 353-359.

Morton, A. S.—The color of newly born Negro children. Lancet, II, 1605.

Murrell, T. E.—Peculiarities in the structure and diseases of the ear of the Negro. Tr. IX, Internat. M. Cong., III, 817-824.

Muskat, G.—Der Plattfus des Negers. Deutsche med. Wchnschr. XXVIII, 471.

Musser, J. H.—Note on pernicious anemia and chlorosis in the Negro. Univ. M. Mag., V, 770.

Negro, equality of the races. So. Quar. Review, 21:153.

Negro Insane. Charities Review, 10:8.

Negro, The: what is his ethnological status? Cincinnati, 1872.

Olivier.—Les troupes noires de l'Afrique orientale francaise. Rev. d. troupes colon., II, 97-129.

Orr, J.—Some suggestions of interest to physicians on the scientific aspect of the race question, with particular reference to the white and Negro races. Va. M. Semi-Month., VIII, 90-95.

Oson, Jacob.—A search for truth or an inquiry into the origin of the Negro, etc. N. Y., 1817.

Paterson, J. S.—Negroes of the South: increase and movement of the colored population. Popular Science Monthly, 19:655, 781.

Patton, G. W.—An essay on the origin and relative status of the white and colored races of mankind. Towanda, Pa., 1871.

Peney, A.—Etudes sur les races du Soudan. Compt. rend. Acad. d. sc., XLVIII, 430.

Perry, M. L.—Insanity and the Negro. Current Literature, 33:467.
    Some practical problems in sociology shown by a study of the Southern Negro. Atlanta Jour. Rec. Med., IV, 459-466.

Petrie, W. M. F.—An Egyptian ebony statuette of a Negress. Man, I, 129.

Physical characteristics of the Negro. So. Quar. Review, 22:49.

Pittard, E.—De la survivance d'un type Negroide dans les populations modernes de l'Europe. Compt. rend. Acad. d. sc., CXXXVIII, 1533.

Plehn, A.—Beobachtung in Kamerun, Ueber die Anschauungen und Gehrauche einiger Negerstamme. Ztsch. rf. Ethnol., XXXVI, 713-728.
    Ueber die Pathologie Kameruns mit Rucksicht auf die unter den Kustennegern vorkommenden Krankheiten. Arch. f. Path. Anat., CXXXIX, 539-549.
    Zur vergleichenden Pathologie der schwarzen Rasse in Kamerun. Ibid., CXLVI, 486-508.
    Wundheilung bei der schwarzen Rasse. Deutsche Med. Wchnschr., XXII, 544-546.
    Die acuten Infektions Krankheiten bei den Negern der aquatorialen Kusten Westafrikas. Virchow's Arch. f. Path. Anat., CLXXIV., Suppl. Hft., 1-103.

Popovsky, J.—Les muscles de la face chez un Negre Achanti. Anthropologie, I, 413-422.

Powell, T. O.—The increase of insanity and tuberculosis in the Southern Negro since 1860, and its alliance and some of the supposed causes. J. Am. M. Aos., XXVII, 1185-89.

Pritchett, J. A.—Tuberculosis in the Negro. Ala. M. & S. Age, V, 386-421.

Ramsay, H. A.—The necrological appearance of southern typhoid fever in the Negro. Thomson, Ga., 1852.

Ratzel, F.—The History of Mankind; tr. from 2nd German edition by A. J. Butler. New York; 2 Vol., 1904.

Ray, J. M.—Observations upon eye disease and blindness in the colored race. New York M. J., LXIV, 86-88.

Regnault, F.—Pourquoi les Negres sont-ils noirs? (etude sur les causes de la coloration de la peau). Med. Mod., VI, 606.

Reinsch, P. S.—The Negro race and European civilization. Am. J. Sociol., X, 1, 145, 167.

Report of the committee on the comparative health, mortality, length of sentences, etc., of white and colored convicts. Philadelphia, 1849.

Reyburn, R.—Type of disease among the freed people (mixed Negro races) of the United States, based upon the consolidated reports of over 430,466 cases of sick and wounded free people (mixed African races) and 22,053 of white refugees under treatment from 1865 to June 30, 1873, by medical officers of the Bureau of Refugees, Freedmen and Abandoned Lands. Med. News, LXIII, 623-627.

Richardson, C. H.—Observations among the Cameroon tribes of West Central Africa. Mem. Internat. Cong. Anthrop., 199-207.

Riley, H. C.—Color of new born Negroes. Med. Brief, XXVIII, 537.

Ripley, W. Z.—The Races of Europe. New York, 1899.

Robertson, John.—On the period of puberty in the Negro. Edinburgh, 1848.

Robertson, T. L.—The color of Negro children when born. Ala. M. & S. Age, X, 413.

Rodes, C. B., Jr.—The thoracic index in the Negro. Zuschr. f. Morphol. u. Anthrop., IX, 103-117.

Rogers, J. G.—The effect of freedom upon the physical and psychological development of the Negro. Proc. Am. Méd. Psychol. Ass., XVII, 88-98.

Roscoe, J.—Notes on the manners and customs of the Baganda. J. Anthrop. Inst., XXXI, 117-130.

Further notes on the manners and customs of the Baganda. Ibid., 1902. XXXII, 25-80.

Roth, H. L.—Notes on Benin customs. Internat. Arch. f. Ethnog., XI, 235-242.

Roy, P. S.—A case of chorea in a Negro. Med. Rec., XLII, 215.

Scheppegrell, W.—The comparative pathology of the Negro in diseases of the nose, throat, and ear, from an analysis of 11,855 cases. Proc. Orleans Parish. M. Soc., III, pp. 85-88.

Schiller-Tietz.—Die Hautfarbe der neugeborenen Neger kinder. Deutsche Med. Wchnschr., XXVII, 615.

Schurtz, H.—Die geographische Verbreitung der Negertrachten. Ibid., IV, 139-53.

Schwarzbach, B. B.—The power of sight of natives of South Africa. Brit. M. J., II, 1731.

Semeleder, F.—Negroes in the Mexican Republic. Med. Rec., LVIII, 66.

Sergi, G.—The Mediterranean Race. London, 1901.

Shaler, N. S.—The transplantation of a race. Pop. Sc. Month., LVI, 513-24.

The future of the Negro in the Southern States. Ibid., LVII, 147-156.

The Neighbor: the natural history of human contrasts. (The problem of the African). Boston, 1904.

Sholl, E. H.—The Negro and his death rate. Ala. M. & S. Age, III, 337-341.

Shufeldt, R. W.—Comparative anatomical characters of the Negro. Med. Brief, XXXII, 26-28.

Simonot.—Considerations sur la coloration de la peau de Negre. Bull. Soc. d' anthrop de Par., III, 140-152.

Slavery and the diversity of the races. So. Quar. Review, 19:392.

Smith, Anna T.—A study in race psychology. Pop. Sc. Monthly, L, 354-360.

Sosinsky, T. S.—Medical aspects of Negro. Penn. Monthly, 10:529.

Steffens, C.—Die Verfeinerung des Negertypus in den Vereinigten Staaten. Globus, LXXIX, 171-74.

Stetson, G. R.—Memory tests. Psychol. Rev., 1897, IV, 285-9.

Steuber.—Ueber Krankheiten der Eingeborenen in Deutsch Ostafrika Arch. f. Schiffs-u. Tropen-Hyg., VI, 111; 1903, VII, 57.

Stevens, H. V.—Mittheilungen aus dem Frauenleben der Orang Belendas, der Orang Djakun und der Orang Laut. Bearbeitet von Max Bartels. Ztschr. f. Ethnol., XXXIII, 163-202.

Steward. T. G.—Mortality of Negro. Social Economist 9:204.

Stuhlmann, F.—Ein Wahehe-Skelet und die ethnologische Stellung der Lendu. Verhandl. d. Berl. Gesellsch. f. Anthrop., 1894, 422-424.

Stuhlmann, F., and Simon.—Anthropologische Aufnahmen aus Ost-Aurica. Ibid. 1895, 656-671.

Subgenation: An answer to miscegenation. N. Y., 1864.

Sykes, W.—Negro immunity from malaria and yellow fever. Brit. M. J., 1904, II, 1776; 1905, I, 389.

Talbot, E. S.—Negro ethnology and sociology. Illinois M. Bull., V, 124-127.

Tarbox, I. N.—The curse; or, the position in the world's history occupied by Ham. Boston, (?) 1864.

Tate, H. R.—Notes on the Kikuyu and Kamba tribes of British East Africa. J. Anthrop., Inst., XXXIV, 130-148.

Testut—Contribution a l'anatomie des races Negres; dissection de trois nouveaux Negres. Bull. Soc. d'anthrop. de Lyon, IX, 51-68.

Thomson, A.—Note on the skin and scalp of the Negro fœtus. J. Anat. and Physiol., XXV, 282-285.

Thomson, Jas., M. D.—A treatise on the diseases of Negroes . Jamaica, 1820.

Thompson, A.—Craniology (Negroid and non-Negroid skulls). Man, V, 101.

Tiedemann, F.—Das Hirn des Negers mit dem des Europaers und Ourang-Outangs verglichen. Heidelberg, 1837.

Tipton, F.—The Negro problem from a medical standpoint. New York M. J., XLIII, 549.

Trager.—Vorstellung der weissen Negerin Amanua sammt ihrer angeblichen Schwester. Verhandl. d. Berl. Gesellsch., f. Anthrop., 1902, 492.

Tria, G.—Ricerche sulla cate del Negro (contribuzione allo studio sul significato funzionale dello strato graculoso e sulla diffusione del pigmento cutaneo). Gior. internaz. d. sc. med., X, 365-369.

Turner. Sir W.—Notes on the dissection of a third Negro. J. Anat. and Physiol., XXXI, 624-626.

United States Censuses:
  Number, 1790-1900.
  Sex and age, 1820-1900.
  Defectives, 1830-1900.
  Mulattoes, 1850, 1890 (1900).
  Mortality, 1860-1900.
  Delinquents, 1880-1900.

United States Twelfth Census Bulletins.—References to the Negro-American:
  No. 1: Distribution.
  No. 4: Increase.
  No. 8: Negroes in the United States, by W. F. Wilcox and W. E. B. DuBois.
  No. 13: Ages.
  No. 14: Sexes.
  No. 15: Mortality.
  No. 22: Birth rate.

Van den Gheyn, R. P.—L'origine Asiatique de la race noire. Compt. rend. du Cong. scient. internat. d. catholiques, Sect. 8, 132-154.

Van Evrie, J. H.—Negroes an inferior race. New York, 1861.

Valenti, G.—Varieta delle ossa nasali in un Negro del Soudan. Mocitore. Zool. Ital., VIII, 191-194.

Variot, G.—Observations sur la pigmentation cicatricielle des Negres, et recherches microscopiques sur les naevi pigmentaires d'un mulatre. Bull. Soc. d'anthrop. de Par., XII, 463.

Verneau, R.—Les migrations des Ethiopiens. Anthropolozie, X, 641-662.

Virchow, R.—Kopfmaasse von 40 Wei- und 19 Kru-Negern. Verhandl. d. Berl. Gesellsch. f. Anthrop., 1889, 85-93.

Zwei junge Bursche von Kamerun und Togo. Ibid., 541-545.

Vital statistics of Negroes of the South. DeBow's Review, 21:405.

Waitz, T.—Die Negervolker und ihre Verwandten. Leipzig, 1860.

Waldeyer, W.—Ueber einige Gehirne von Ost-Afrikanern. Mitth. d. anthrop. Gesellsch. in Wien., XIV, 141-144.

Walker, F. A.—Statistics of the colored race in the United States. Pub. Am. Statist. Ass. II, 91-106.

Walton, J. T.—The comparative mortality of the white and colored races in the South. Charlotte M. J., X, 291-294.

The comparative mortality of the white and colored races in the South. Charlotte (N. C.) M. J., X, No. 3, 291-294.

Weisbach, A.—Einige Schadel aus Ostafrika. Wien, 1889.

Whitaker, D. R.—Natural history of Negro. Southern Literary Journal, 3:151; 4:87.

Why is the Negro black? Scientific American, 49:20125.

Widenmann.—Der Plattfuss des Negers. Deutsche Med. Wchnschr., XXVIII, 563.

Williams, Daniel H.—Ovarian cysts in colored women. Reprint from "Chicago Medical Record." 12 pp.

Wilser, L.—Urgeschichtliche Neger in Europa. Globus, LXXXVII, 45.

Wolbarst, A. L., Provence D. M., and March, C. J.—The color of Negro babies. Med. News, LXXIII, 844.

Wolff, B.—Deficient vulvar development in Negresses. Med. Age, XVI, 137.

Wortman, J. L.—The Negro's anthropological position. Wash., 1891.

Wyman, J.—Observations on the skeleton of a Hottentot. Boston, 1863.

Willcox, Walter F.—The probable increase of the Negro race in the United States. Quarterly Journal of Economics, August, 1905.

Addendum

Denniker, J.—The Races of Man. New York, 1904.

Negro Health and Physique

1. Races of Men

It is doubtful if many of the persons in the United States who are eagerly and often bitterly discussing race problems have followed very carefully the advances which anthropological science has made in the last decade. Certainly the new knowledge has not yet reached the common schools in the usual school histories and geographies. As Ripley says:

It may smack of heresy to assert, in face of the teaching of all our textbooks on geography and history, that there is no single European or white race of men; and yet that is the plain truth of the matter. Science has advanced since Linnæus' single type of *Homo Europæus albus* was made one of the four great races of mankind. No continental group of human beings with greater diversities or extremes of physical type exists. That fact accounts in itself for much of our advance in culture.*

In our school days most of us were brought up to regard Asia as the mother of European peoples. We were told that an ideal race of men swarmed forth from the Himalayan highlands, disseminating culture right and left as they spread through the barbarous west. The primitive language, parent to all of the varieties of speech—Romance, Teutonic, Slavic, Persian, or Hindustanee—spoken by the so-called Caucasian or white race, was called Aryan. By inference this name was shifted to the shoulders of the people themselves, who were known as the Aryan race. In the days when such symmetrical generalizations held sway there was no science of physical anthropology; prehistoric archæology was not yet. Shem, Ham, and Japhet were still the patriarchal

---

*Ripley, p. 103.

founders of the great racial varieties of the genus Homo. A new science of philology dazzled the intelligent world by its brilliant discoveries, and its words were law. Since 1860 these early inductions have completely broken down in the light of modern research; and even today greater uncertainty prevails in many phases of the question that would have been admitted possible twenty years ago.*

So, too, a leading Italian anthropologist says:

Whenever there has been any attempt to explain the origin of civilization and of the races called Aryan, whether in the Mediterranean or in Central Europe, all archæologists, linguists, and anthropologists have until recent years been dominated by the conviction that both civilization and peoples must have their unquestionable cradle in Asia.†

As illustrating the former tendency, Sergi adds:

A celebrated anthropologist, when measuring the heads of the mummies of the Pharaohs preserved in the Pyramids, wrote that the Egyptians belonged to the white race. His statement meant nothing; we could construct a syllogism showing that the Egyptians are Germans, since the latter also are fair. De Quatrefages classified the Abyssinians among the white races, but if they are black, how can they be white?‡

The new anthropology, while taking into account all the older race insignia, like color, hair, form of features, etc., has added to these exact measurements of the underlying bony skeleton and other carefully collected data. Of these new measurements the form of the head is being most emphasized today.

The form of the head is for all racial purposes best measured by what is technically known as the cephalic index. This is simply the breadth of the head above the ears expressed in percentage of its length from forehead to back. Assuming that this length is 100, the width is expressed in a fraction of it. As the head becomes proportionately broader—that is, more fully rounded, viewed from top down—this cephalic index increases. When it rises above 80, the head is called brachycephalic, when it falls below 75, term dolichocephalic is applied to it. Indexes between 75 and 80 are characterized as mesocephalic. §

Based on the new measurements and discoveries, the chief conclusions of anthropologists today as to European races are as follows:

1. The European races, as a whole, show signs of a secondary or derived origin; certain characteristics, especially the texture of the hair, lead us to class them as intermediate between the extreme primary types of the Asiatic and the Negro races respectively.

2. The earliest and lowest strata of population in Europe were extremely long-headed; probability points to the living Mediterranean race as most nearly representative of it today.

3. It is highly probable that the Teutonic race of northern Europe is merely a variety of this primitive long-headed type of the stone age; both its distinctive blondness and its remarkable stature having been acquired in the relative isolation of Scandinavia through the modifying influences of environment and of artificial selection.

4. It is certain that, after the partial occupation of western Europe by a dolichocephalic Africanoid type in the stone age, an invasion by a broad-

---

* Ripley, pp. 452-3.   † Sergi, p. 1.   ‡ Sergi, p. 35.   § Ripley, p. 37.

headed race of decidedly Asiatic affinities took place. This intrusive element is represented today by the Alpine type of Central Europe.*

What was now this Mediterranean race whence the Europeans were primarily derived? Sergi adds:

In opposition to the theory of a migration from the north of Europe to the west and then to Africa, I am, on the contrary, convinced that a migration of the African racial element took place in primitive times from the south towards the north. The types of Cro-Magnon, L'Homme-Mort, and other French and Belgian localities, bear witness to the presence of an African stock in the same region in which we find the dolmens and other megalithic monuments erroneously attributed to the Celts.†

He adds:

We have no reason to suppose that the movement of emigration in the east of Africa stopped at the Nile valley; we may suppose that it extended towards the east of Egypt, into Syria and the regions around Syria, and thence into Asia Minor. It is possible that in Syria this immigration encountered the primitive inhabitants, or a population coming from northern Arabia, and mingled with them or subjugated them.‡

Sergi's conclusions are:

1. That the primitive populations of Europe originated in Africa.
2. The basin of the Mediterranean was the chief center of the movement whence the African migration reached central and northern Europe.
3. From this great Eurafrican stock came—
    (a) The present inhabitants of northern Africa.
    (b) The Mediterranean race.
    (c) The Nordic or Teutonic race.
4. These three varieties of one stock were not "Aryan," nor of Asiatic origin.
5. The primitive civilization of Europe is Afro-Mediterranean, becoming eventually Afro-European.
6. Greek and Roman civilization were not Aryan but Mediterranean.§

This primitive race was a colored race:

If, therefore, as all consistent students of natural history hold today, the human races have evolved in the past from some common root type, this predominant dark color must be regarded as the more primitive. It is not permissible for an instant to suppose that 99 per cent of the human species has varied from a blond ancestry, while the flaxen-haired Teutonic type alone has remained true to its primitive characteristics. ‖

The types of Greek and Roman statuary:

Do not in the slightest degree recall the features of a northern race; in the delicacy of the cranial and facial forms, in smoothness of surface, in the absence of exaggerated frontal bosses and supra-orbital arches, in the harmony of the curves, in the facial oval, in the rather low foreheads, they recall the beautiful and harmonious heads of the brown Mediterranean race.¶

Of the part of this great stock which remained in North Africa, Sergi says:

The area of geographical distribution of these African populations is immense, for it reaches from the Red Sea to the Atlantic, from the equator, and

---

even beyond the equator to the Mediterranean. In this vast area we find, when we exclude racial mixtures, that the physical characters of the skeleton, as regards head and face are uniform, but that the physical characters of the skin and intermediate parts, that is to say, the development and form of the soft parts, vary. This uniformity of the cranio-facial skeletal characters, which I consider the guiding thread in anthropological research, has led me to regard as a single human stock all the varieties distributed in the area already mentioned. In the varying cutaneous coloration I see an effect of temperature, of climate, of alimentation, and of the manner of life.*

2. The Negro Race

It has usually been assumed that of all races the Negro race is, by reason of its pronounced physical characteristics, easiest to distinguish. Exacter studies and measurements prove this untrue. The human species so shade and mingle with each other that not only indeed is it impossible to draw a color line between black and other races, but in all physical characteristics the Negro race cannot be set off by itself as absolutely different. This was formerly assumed to be the case even by scientists and led to the queer *reductio ad adsurdum* that very few real pure Negroes existed even in Africa. As Ratzel points out:

The name "Negro" originally embraces one of the most unmistakable conceptions of ethnology—the African with dark skin, so-called "woolly" hair, thick lips and nose; and it is one of the prodigious, nay amazing achievements of critical erudition to have latterly confined this (and that even in Africa, the genuine old Negro country) to a small district. For if with Waitz we assume that Gallas, Nubians, Hottentots, Kaffirs, the Congo races, and the Malagasies are none of them genuine Negroes, and if with Schweinforth we further exclude Shillooks and Bongos, we find that the continent of Africa is peopled throughout almost its whole circuit by races other than the genuine Negro, while in its interior, from the southern extremity to far beyond the equator it contains only light-colored South Africans, and the Bantu or Kaffir peoples.

Nothing then remains for the Negroes in the pure sense of the word save, as Waitz says, "a tract of country extending over not more than 10 or 12 degrees of latitude, which may be traced from the mouth of the Senegal river to Timbuctoo, and thence extended to the regions about Sennaar." Even in this the race reduced to these dimensions is permeated by a number of people belonging to other stocks. According to Latham, indeed, the real Negro country extends only from the Senegal to the Niger If we ask what justifies so narrow a limitation, we find that the hideous Negro type, which the fancy of observers once saw all over Africa, but which, as Livingstone says, is really to be seen only as a sign in front of tobacco-shops, has on closer inspection evaporated from almost all parts of Africa, to settle no one knows how in just this region. If we understand that an extreme case may have been taken for the genuine and pure form, even so we do not comprehend the ground of its geographical limitation and location; for wherever dark woolly-haired men dwell, this ugly type also crops up. We are here in presence of a refinement of science which to an unprejudiced eye will hardly hold water.†

---

* Sergi, pp. 248-9.　　　　†Ratzel, II, p. 313.

Three things have been especially emphasized as characteristic of Negroes: their color, hair and features. As to color in human beings, Ripley says:

One point alone seems to have been definitely proved: however marked the contrasts in color between the several varieties of human species may be,there is no corresponding difference in anatomical structure discoverable.

Pigmentation arises from the deposition of coloring matter in a special series of cells, which lie just between the translucent outer skin or epidermis and the inner or true skin known as the cutis. It was long supposed that these pigment cells were peculiar to the dark-skinned races; but investigation has shown that the structure in all types is identical. The differences in color are due, not to presence or absence of the cells themselves, but to variations in the amount of pigment therein deposited. In this respect, therefore, the Negro differs physiologically, rather than anatomically, from the European or the Asiatic.*

The cause of this physiological difference is climate, the rays of the sun, humidity, and such natural forces:

The best working hypothesis is . . . . that this coloration is due to the combined influences of a great number of factors of environment working through physiological processes, none of which can be isolated from the others. One point is certain, whatever the cause may be—that this characteristic has been very slowly acquired, and has today become exceedingly persistent in several races. †

Sergi says of the Mediterranean race:

We may therefore conclude that as residence under the equator has produced the red-brown and black coloration of the stock, and residence in the Mediterranean the brown colour, so northern Europe has given origin to the white skin, blond hair, and blue or grey eyes. I believe we may consider this a beautiful example of the formation and variation of external characters among a section of the human race which from time immemorial has been diffused by migrations between the equator and the arctic circle, and has formed its external characters according to the variations of latitude and the concomitant external conditions.‡

As to hair, we are told that—

The two extremes of hair texture in the human species are the crisp, curly variety so familiar to us in the African Negro; and the stiff wiry straight hair of the Asiatic and the American aborigines. These traits are exceedingly persistent; they persevere oftentimes through generations of ethnic intermixture. It has been shown by Pruner Bey and others that this outward contrast in texture is due to, or at all events coincident with, real morphological differences in structure. The curly hair is almost always of a flattened, ribbon-like form in cross section, as examined miscroscopically; while, cut squarely across, the straight hair more often inclines to a fully rounded or cylindrical shape. Moreover, this peculiarity in cross section may often be detected in any crossing of these extreme types. The result of such intermixture is to impart a more or less wavy appearance to the hair, and to produce a cross section intermediate between a flattened oval and a circle. Roughly speaking, the more pronounced the flatness the greater is the tendency toward waviness or curling, and the reverse.§

---

* Ripley, p. 58.   † Ripley, p. 62.   ‡ Sergi, p. 254.   § Ripley, p. 157.

Anthropologists today are putting less stress on the development of the soft parts of the human frame—the skin, nose, cheeks and lips, but have come to regard the cranio-facial skeletal characteristics as "the guiding thread on anthropological research."* Even here the matter of absolute size and weight is of minor importance:

Equally unimportant to the anthropologist is the absolute size of the head. It is grievous to contemplate the waste of energy when, during our civil war, over one million soldiers had their heads measured in respect of this absolute size; in view of the fact that today anthropologists deny any considerable significance attaching this characteristic. Popularly, a large head with beetling eyebrows suffices to establish a man's intellectual credit; but like all other credit, it is entirely dependent upon what lies on deposit elsewhere. Neither size nor weight of the brain seems to be of importance. The long, narrow heads, as a rule, have a smaller capacity than those in which the breadth is considerable, but exceptions are so common that they disprove the rule. Among the earliest men whose remains have been found in Europe, there was no appreciable difference from the present living populations. In many cases these prehistoric men even surpassed the present population in the size of the head. The peasant and the philosopher can not be distinguished in this respect. For the same reason the striking difference between the sexes, the head of the man being considerably larger than the head of the woman, means nothing more than avoirdupois, or rather it seems merely to be correlated with the taller stature and more massive frame of the human male.†

Great stress used to be put on the facial angle, but we are told now that—

Prognathism, that is to say the degree of projection of the maxillary portion of the face, is a characteristic trait of certain skulls; however, it does not seem to play so important a part in the classification of races as anthropologists had thought twenty or thirty years ago. It presents too many individual varieties to be taken as a distinctive character of race. ‡

We have, then, in the so-called Negro races to do with a great variety of human types and mixtures of blood representing at bottom a human variation which separated from the primitive human stock some ages after the yellow race and before the Mediterranean race, and which has since intermingled with these races in all degrees of admixture so that today no absolute separating line can be drawn.

The real history of human races is unknown. A probable theory would be that the first great division of men took place at the roof of the world, the Asiatic Himalaya mountains; that here the primitive brown stock of men divided—those to southward gradually through ages becoming long-headed and tall, and those to northward broad-headed and shorter. From the southern long-headed variety developed in ages the closely allied Negro and Mediterranean races and from the Mediterranean race and the invading Asiatics came modern Europeans.

The first great step in civilization which mankind took after the Stone Age was the discovery and use of iron.

"The achievements of races are not only what they have done during

---

* Sergi, p. 249.   †Ripley, p. 43.   ‡Denniker, p. 63.

the short span of 2,000 years, when with rapidly increasing numbers the total amount of mental work accumulated at an ever increasing rate. In this the European, the Chinaman, the East Indian, have far outstripped other races. But back of this period lies the time when mankind struggled with the elements, when every small advance that seems to us now insignificant was an achievement of the highest order, as great as the discovery of steam power or of electricity, if not greater. It may well be, that these early inventions were made hardly consciously, certainly not by deliberate effort, yet every one of them represents a giant's stride forward in the development of human culture. To these early advances the Negro race has contributed its liberal share. While much of the history of early invention is shrouded in darkness, it seems likely that at a time when the European was still satisfied with rude stone tools, the African had invented or adopted the art of smelting iron.

"Consider for a moment what this invention has meant for the advance of the human race. As long as the hammer, knife, saw, drill, the spade and the hoe had to be chipped out of stone, or had to be made of shell or hard wood, effective industrial work was not impossible, but difficult. A great progress was made when copper found in large nuggets was hammered out into tools and later on shaped by melting, and when bronze was introduced; but the true advancement of industrial life did not begin until the hard iron was discovered. It seems not unlikely that the people that made the marvelous discovery of reducing iron ores by smelting were the African Negroes. Neither ancient Europe, nor ancient western Asia, nor ancient China knew the iron, and everything points to its introduction from Africa. At the time of the great African discoveries towards the end of the past century, the trade of the blacksmith was found all over Africa, from north to south and from east to west. With his simple bellows and a charcoal fire he reduced the ore that is found in many part of the continent and forged implements of great usefulness and beauty."*

Egyptian civilization was the result of Negroid Mediterranean culture, while to the south arose the ancient Negro civilization of Ethiopia, and still further south we find ruins of ancient Bantu culture.

The primitive culture of the mass of uncivilized Africans long ago reached a high grade. There was "extended early African agriculture, each village being surrounded by its garden patches and fields in which millet is grown. Domesticated animals were also kept; in the agricultural regions chickens and pigs, while in the arid parts of the country where agriculture is not possible, large herds of cattle were raised. It is also important to note that the cattle were milked, an art which in early times was confined to Africa, Europe and northern Asia, while even now it has not been acquired by the Chinese.

"The occurrence of all these arts of life points to an early and energetic development of African culture.

---

* Boas: Commencement Address at Atlanta University.

"Even if we refrain from speculating on the earliest times, conceding that it is difficult to prove the exact locality where so important an invention was made as that of smelting iron, or where the African millet was first cultivated, or where chickens and cattle were domesticated, the evidence of African ethnology is such that it should inspire you with the hope of leading your race from achievement to achievement. Shall I remind you of the power of military organization exhibited by the Zulu, whose kings and whose armies swept southeastern Africa? Shall I remind you of the local chiefs, who by dint of diplomacy, bravery and wisdom, united the scattered tribes of the wide areas into flourishing kingdoms, of the intricate form of government necessary for holding together the heterogeneous tribes?

"If you wish to understand the possibilities of the African under the stimulus of a foreign culture, you may look towards the Soudan, the region south of the Sahara. When we first learn about these countries by the reports of the great Arab traveller, Iben Batuta, who lived in the fourteenth century, we hear that the old Negro kingdoms were early conquered by the Mohammedans. Under the guidance of the Arabs, but later on by their own initiative, the Negro tribes of these countries organized kingdoms which lived for many centuries. They founded flourishing towns in which at annual fairs thousands and thousands of people assembled. Mosques and other public buildings were erected and the execution of the laws was entrusted to judges. The history of the kingdom was recorded by officers and kept in archives. So well organized were these states that about 1850, when they were for the first time visited by a white man, the remains of these archives were still found in existence, notwithstanding all the political upheavals of a millenium and notwithstanding the ravages of the slave trade.

"I might also speak to you of the great markets that are found throughout Africa, at which commodities were exchanged or sold for native money. I may perhaps remind you of the system of judicial procedure, of prosecution and defense, which had early developed in Africa, and whose formal development was a great achievement notwithstanding its gruesome application in the prosecution of witchcraft. Nothing, perhaps, is more encouraging than a glimpse of the artistic industry of native Africa. I regret that we have no place in this country where the beauty and daintiness of African work can be shown; but a walk through the African museums of Paris, London and Berlin is a revelation. I wish you could see the scepters of African kings, carved of hard wood and representing artistic forms; or the dainty basketry made by the people of the Kongo river and of the region near the great lakes of the Nile, or the grass mats with their beautiful patterns. Even more worthy of our admiration is the work of the blacksmith, who manufactures symmetrical lance heads almost a yard long, or axes inlaid with copper and decorated with filigree. Let me also mention in passing the bronze castings of Benin on the west coast of Africa, which, although perhaps due to Portuguese influences, have so far excelled in technique any European work, that they are even now almost inimitable. In short, wherever you look, you find a thrifty people, full of energy, capable of forming large states. You find men of great energy and ambition who hold sway over their fellows by the weight of their personality. That this culture has, at the same time, the instability and other signs of weakness of primitive culture, goes without saying.

"To you, however, this picture of native Africa will inspire strength, for all the alleged faults of your race that you have to conquer here are certainly not prominent there. In place of indolence you find thrift and ingenuity, and application to occupations that require not only industry, but also inventiveness and a high degree of technical skill, and the surplus energy of the people does not spend itself in emotional excesses only.

"If, therefore, it is claimed that your race is doomed to economic inferiority, you may confidently look to the home of your ancestors and say, that you have set out to recover for the colored people the strength that was their own before they set foot on the shores of this continent. You may say that you go to work with bright hopes, and that you will not be discouraged by the slowness of your progress; for you have to recover not only what has been lost in transplanting the Negro race from its native soil to this continent, but you must reach higher levels than your ancestors had ever attained.

"To those who stoutly maintain a material inferiority of the Negro race and who would dampen your ardor by their claims, you may confidently reply that the burden of proof rests with them, that the past history of your race does not sustain their statement, but rather gives you encouragement. The physical inferiority of the Negro race, if it exists at all, is insignificant, when compared to the wide range of individual variability in each race. There is no anatomical evidence available that would sustain the view that the bulk of the Negro race could not become as useful citizens as the members of any other race. That there may be slightly different hereditary traits seems plausible, but it is entirely arbitrary to assume that those of the Negro, because perhaps slightly different, must be of an inferior type."*

Other investigators emphasize these facts. Ratzel says:

In this connection the point to be most weightily emphasized is that the Negro has now passed wholly out of the stage which we are wont to denote by the "Stone Age." All their more important implements and weapons which might be of stone are now of iron.†

In alliance with stimulus from without, the interior of Africa has had a development of its own, variable no doubt, but wherever it has been undisturbed, copious. The striking point about African ethnography is that as we go towards the interior, the level of culture, so far as measured by the abundance and variety of its stock of possessions, by persistency in the conditions, by the prosperity and density of the population, is greater than in the outer districts. . . . In connection with the question of the African capacity for de-

---

* Boas, Commencement Address at Atlanta University.   † Ratzel, 2:387.

velopment, and the possible points at which higher culture may take hold, we will give a closer glance at the points where a notable superiority to the standard of inner Africa is observable. No injustice is done to the "antochthonous civilizations" of the Monbuttus, the Waganda, the Bangala, and others, if we look for their superiority primarily in the material ingredients of culture. Therein they do but maintain the inmost essence of African culture; for it is just the contrast between the high development of the material side and the backward condition of the spiritual that gives African culture as a whole its peculiar character. In that industrious pursuit of agriculture and cattle-breeding beside so limited a development of political and religious institutions there seems to be something heavy, depressing, stationary. Hence, too, the astonishing regularity of its distribution. This condition of things bears, in the first place, the mark of an inland life, but has also a deep root in the Negro disposition, of which the chief strength lies not in dash but in perseverance.*

That African culture did not go far higher than this is due to (a) climate, (b) geography, and (c) the slave-trade.

We must bear Africa in our eye if we would understand the Africans. The destinies of races are in truth dependent on the soil upon which men travel and whence they draw their food, according as it limits them or lets them spread; on the sky which determines the amount of warmth and moisture that they shall have; on the dower of plants and animals, and we may add minerals, from which they get the means of feeding, clothing and beautifying themselves, and of providing themselves with friends, helpers, and allies, but which may also raise up enemies. Africa is the most westerly portion of the mass of land which covers over a third of the Eastern Hemisphere in a vast connected system, and it extends nearly as far to the south of Australia. The southern border of the Old World encloses a great basin, whose western edge is skirted by Africa, its eastern by Australia—the Indian Ocean. In it lie the largest African and Asiatic islands, Madagascar, Borneo, Sumatra, Java, as well as the peninsulas of Somaliland, Arabia, Hither and Further India. Far beyond it, to the eastward, extend lands and islands, so far that one may well ask whether the unoccupied space between Easter Island and South America formed a permanent bar to the extension of races which had already covered a space three times as wide. When one has to speak of the ethnography of the African races one always remembers this great half-enclosed bight, which might be called the Indo-African Mediterranean. ... When we are considering the possibility of navigation between the remoter coasts of Africa and other quarters of the earth, our thoughts turn spontaneously upon its shape. We miss features favorable to navigation, gulfs and bays, peninsulas and islands. Owing to the absence from this continent of arms and inlets of the sea, the tribes of the interior have always been cut off from intercourse with Europeans; while the ruling principle of the coast tribes was to hold the position of middlemen between them and Europeans. The length of the coastline of Africa, compared with that of Europe, is little more than one-fifth. Only the northeast and the north, so far as they are bordered by the Red Sea and the Mediterranean, show a little more variety. But this is just where climatic conditions encourage the desert-formation to extend at many points as far as the coast. Madagascar, the only large island of this quarter of the earth, has led a separate life of its own.

Other forces have also had a checking effect on the development of African

---

*Ratzel, 2:254.

culture. What a great portion of the earth may lose in the way of accessibility through defective conformation in some measure be compensated for by rivers. In Africa, however, the physical geography does not allow this compensation to operate in an adequate degree; the interior, a highland region surrounded with mountains, causes the rivers to descend to the lowland, itself of no great dimensions, in cataracts. Along their more distant course in the interior, some rivers, in conjunction with the great lakes, are important aids to intercourse so far as native requirements go; but the road to the sea is cut off.*

The chief present inhabitants of Africa are classed by Denniker as follows:

Putting on one side the Madagascar islanders and the European and other colonists, the thousands of peoples and tribes of the "dark continent" may be grouped, going from north to south, into six great geographical, linguistic, and, in part, anthropological units: 1st, the Arabo-Berbers or Semito-Hamites; 2nd, the Ethiopians or Kushito-Hamites; 3rd, the Fulah-Zandeh; 4th, the Negrilloes or Pygmies; 5th, the Nigritians or Sudanese-Guinea Negroes; 6th, the Bantus; 7th, the Hottentot-Bushmen.†

It must not be thought, however, that hard and fast lines between these groups can be drawn. On the contrary, we must—

Premise the unity of by far the greatest part of the races of this quarter of the earth, and starting from this, regard the differences as varying shades. ‡

The nucleus of the populations of Africa in respect to both geographical position and of mass, is Ethiopian; dark brown skin, woolly hair, thick—or rather everted—lips, and a tendency to strong development of the facial and maxillary parts. To such races Africa, south of the Great Desert, has belonged from the earliest historical period, and the Desert itself probably once did belong. In the extreme south, in a compact group, and in small groups also in the interior, a light brown variety, of low stature. The north beyond the desert, however, is inhabited by men in general of light color, whether reddish like the Egyptians, or yellowish like the Arabs, showing curly rather than woolly hair, and a less conspicuous facial and maxillary development. The Berbers of the Atlas are even like southern Europeans. But the characteristics of the mass are not sharply opposed to the Ethiopian, deviating rather by way of mixture and attenuation.

This is more than an idle assumption as is shown by the history of the African races. From the earliest times of which we have any knowledge dark men have continually filtered through, chiefly by way of the slave-trade, to the lighter north. For this reason we may say with Fritsch that a general consideration of African ethnology shows the Soudan to have been the starting-point. It forms the middle member between dark and light Africa, apparently divided parts, out of which its mobile races have tended to make one whole. Negroes crossed the Alps with Hannibal, and fell at Worth beside MacMahon. Whatever their original nature may have been, all this population must have been alloyed with a strong Ethiopian element, as our cut of Fezzan man shows. The entire Semitic and Hamitic population of Africa has, in other words, a mulatto character which extends to the Semites outside Africa.§

---

* Ratzel, II, pp. 237-41.   † Denniker, 431.   ‡ Ratzel, 2:244.   § Ratzel, 2:245-47.

3. The Negro Brain

It is usually assumed that there are great differences between the European and African brain and that here the inevitable inferiority of the Africans shows itself. Denniker, however, says:

The weight of the encephalon varies enormously according to individuals. Topinard in a series of 519 Europeans, men of the lower and middle classes, found that variations in weight extended from 1025 grams to 1675 grams. The average weight of the brain among adult Europeans (20 to 60 years) has been fixed by Topinard, from an examination of 11,000 specimens weighed, at 1361 grams for man, 1290 grams for woman. It has been asserted that the other races have a lighter brain, but the fact has not been established by a sufficient number of examples. In reality all that can be put against the 11,000 brain-weighings mentioned above concerning the cerebral weights of non-European races, amounts to nothing, or almost nothing. The fullest series that Topinard has succeeded in making, that of Negroes, comprises only 190 brains, that of Annamese, which comes immediately after, contains only 18 brains. And what do the figures of these series teach us?

The first series dealing with Negroes, gives a mean weight not much different from that of Europeans—1316 grams for adult males of from 20 to 60 years; and the second dealing with the Annamese, a mean weight of 1341 grams, almost identical with that of Europeans. For other populations we have only the weight of isolated brains, or of series of three, four, or at most eleven specimens, absolutely insufficient for any conclusions whatever to be drawn, seeing that individual variations are as great in exotic races as among Europeans, to judge by Negroes (1013 to 1587 grams) and by Annameses (from 1145 to 1450 grams).*

On this subject Mr. Monroe N. Work, A. M., of the Savannah State College, contributes the following memorandum:

Most writers hold that the Negro brain is smaller than the Caucasian.† The first objection to this conclusion is that there has not been a sufficient number of Negro brains examined upon which to base a generalization. The total number of Negro brains which have been examined in America with reference to size is about 500. The number reported by European investigators is a little more than 200, making a total of about 700. This number is absolutely too small to base generalizations concerning the twenty or more million persons of Negro descent in the western hemisphere and the hundreds of millions in Africa, among whom are found variations as great and of the same kind as those found among white races.

But granting that the data are sufficient, another objection is that in giving the weight of Negro brains it appears that almost no account has been taken of age, stature, social class, occupation, nutrition, and cause of death; each of which separately or all together affect both the weight and structure of the brain. The following table shows brain weight in connection with age and stature.‡

---

* Denniker, p. 97.
† See Bean, "The Negro Brain," The Century Magazine, Sept. 1906.
‡ From Marshall's tables based on Boyd's records; Donaldson, the Growth of the Brain, p. 97.

AGE	MALES WEIGHT OF ENCEPHALON Stature 164 cm. and under	FEMALES WEIGHT OF ENCEPHALON Stature 152 cm. and under	AGE
20–40.........	1331 grams	1199 grams	20-40
41–70.........	1297 "	1205 "	41–70
71–90.........	1251 "	1122 "	71-90
	Stature 167–172 cm.	Stature 155–160 cm.	
20–40.........	1360 grams	1218 grams	20–40
41–70.........	1335 "	1212 ."	41–70
71–90.........	1305 "	1121 "	71–90
	Stature 175 cm. and upwards	Stature 163 cm. and upwards	
20–40.........	1409 grams	1265 grams	20–40
41–70.........	1363 "	1209 "	41–70
71–90.........	1330 "	1166 "	71–90

The third objection is that the differences in the average weight of Negro and white brains are not sufficiently great to warrant the conclusion that if an equally large number of Negro brains were taken with reference to age, stature, etc., there would be any marked differences in weight. Topinard found the average weight of 11,000 European brains to be 1361 grams for men and 1290 for women. He found the average for 190 male Negroes to be 1316 grams. Peacock found an average of 1388 grams for English from a series of 28 brains; while Boyd, from a series of 425, found an average of 1354. Hunt found an average of 1327 grams for a series of 381 United States Negro soldiers.

The following table shows what wide variations may occur among races of the same region and of fairly similar culture:

Table showing the weight of the encephalon in several transcaucasian tribes. Weight taken with pia and without drainage. (Gilchenko):*

No. of Cases	RACE	SEX	Age Years	Mean Stature	Mean weight Encephalon
10.......Ossetes............Males........21–34...........				..... Mm....	1470 grams
15.......Ingouches.........	"	........18-30...........		1704 "	1453 "
2.......Tcerkesses.........	"	....		1695 "	1532 "
3.......Daghestan.........	"	....		1650 "	1340 "
12.......Armenian.........	"	........16–60...........		1634 "	1369 "
13.......Georgian...........	"	........19–65...........		1669 "	1350 "
2.......	"	Females......25–28....		1590 "	1207 "

Broca found the mean weight of the pia to be for males 55.8 grams and for females 48.7 grams. The variation for males ranged from 38 to 130 grams.

In the most recent investigation of Negro brains, those whom the investigator classes as one-half and one-fourth white have almost as great or a greater brain weight, 1340 and 1347 grams, than those who are classed as white, 1341; and they have a greater average brain weight than the English, I and II, 1335, 1328, and the French, 1325 grams, of the European series which he presents. He found the average weight of the Negro females, 1108, to be greater than that of the white females, 1103. †

It is to be noted just here that no especial importance is to be attached to the classification by observation of Negroes as pure blacks, one-eighth, one-fourth, one-half white, etc. For popular purposes it is suffi-

* Donaldson, *loc. cit.*, p. 114.
†See Bean, Op. Cit.

cient to merely note the color of the skin, texture of the hair, etc.; but for scientific purposes it is necessary that the ancestry be investigated. The writer is acquainted with many persons who by inspection would be classed as one-fourth white, when in reality they are three-fourths and others who would be classed as three-eighths or more, when as a matter of fact they are only one-eighth white. And even if an accurate classification of American Negroes was made according to blood it would still be necessary to classify them according to age, stature, social class, etc., before any conclusion would be warranted respecting the relative brain weights of pure Negroes and those of mixed blood.

Still another objection to the conclusion that the Negro brain is smaller than the Caucasian is that the variability in the brain weight of the two races falls within almost the same limits. The following table illustrates this:

No. of Cases	RACE	SEX	Minimum wt. Encephalon	Maximum wt. Encephalon
79	Negroes (Bean)*		900 grams†	1600 grams†
381	Negro soldiers (Hunt)	Males	978 "	1729 "
190	Negroes (Topinard)	"	1013 "	1587 "
278	White (Clondenning) and others	"	964 "	1843 "
45	" Eminent men	"	1207 "	1830 "
13	" Georgian	"	1183 "	1530 "
12	" Armenian	"	1232 "	1545 "
10	" Ossetes	"	1306 "	1541 "

It is further asserted that there is much difference in the structure of white and Negro brains. The investigator mentioned above has attempted to show that the size and shape of the front end of the cerebrum is different in the two races. In proof of this, views of the frontal lobes and of the mesial surfaces of the hemispheres of a white and Negro brain and two tables of brain measurements, are presented. The weakness of this proof is that generalizations are made from too few examples; it appears to be inferred that all white brains have exactly or almost exactly the same detailed shape. The table of brain measurements, which is presented with averages, indicates that what is stated as being characteristic of Negro brains is not true of all the small number of Negro brains which he examined.‡

---

* Sex is not distinguished in connection with brain variability. See Bean, Op. Cit., p. 780. Chart of brain weight.

†"About 900" and "about 1600" grams.

‡ There are several discrepancies in this article of Dr. Bean's, e. g., he says: "The brains I have studied were accurately weighed and the weights are classified as follows," giving the number. There is a lack of agreement between the number of brains which he says he compared—103 Negro and 49 white—and the number he presents, 79 Negro and 60 white, in the table of brain weights, and 65 and 87 Negro and 45 and 51 white, in the table of brain measurements. In one table the average weight of 51 Negro male brains is given as 1292 grams. From the next table given, showing the average brain weight according to white blood, it appears that the general average of these same 51 brains is 1254 grams. The length of the section of the frontal lobe of the white brain shown is, he says, between 2 and 2.5 centimeters, for lobe of Negro brain between 1.5 and 2 centimeters. The table of brains of Negro soldiers has many errors, e. g., the table he presents is as follows:

It is also stated that the white brains have more elaborate convolutions and deeper fissuration than Negro brains. It is apparently not taken into account that fissuration and convolution depend upon several variables. As for example, a brain possessed of an extensive cortex with the elements incompletely associated can be a much folded brain, because in order to apply it to the surface of the cerebrum it must be thrown into many gyri. On the other hand, the associating fibers may be so developed as to increase the central mass, thereby giving a larger surface to which the cortex may be applied and thus tend to increase the cortical folds. These facts, with those from comparative anatomy respecting the fissuration and convolution of the brains of beasts and birds, seem to indicate that there is no certain relation between brain convolution and intelligence.

The best evidence seems to indicate that the organization and, therefore, the details of the structure of the central nervous system are continually being modified through life. That is, changes are constantly occuring. These changes, which are many and varied, are caused by age, occupation, nutrition, disease, etc. This fact of constant change makes it very doubtful whether any uniformity in the finer details of structure will be found in white brains, particularly if they are brains of different sizes from persons of different ages, statures, etc., and the cause of death not being the same. These facts, in connection with the well established fact that those characters which are said to be distinctive of particular races are found with more or less frequency in other races, seem to indicate that what has been described as being peculiar in the size, shape, and anatomy of the Negro brain is not true of all Negro brains. These same peculiarities can no doubt be found in many white brains and probably have no special connection with the mental capacity of either race.

4. The Negro=American

The transplantation of the Negro race to America was one of the most tremendous experiments in race migration the world has ever seen.

"The exact proportions of the slave-trade to America can be but approximately determined. From 1680 to 1688 the African Company sent 249 ships to Africa, shipped there 60,783 Negro slaves, and after losing

No. of brains	Grade of color	Av. brain wt
24	White	1478 grams
25........	3/4	1390 "
47........	1/2	1331 "
51	1/4	1315 "
95........	1-8	1305 "
22	1-16	1275 "
141........	Black............	1328 "

The true figures reduced from Hunt's report in Journal of Psychological Medicine and Jurisprudence, Vol. I, No. II, October, 1867, p. 182, is as follows: White, 1475; three-fourths white, 1390; one-half white, 1334; one-fourth white, 1319; one-eighth white, 1308; one-sixteenth white, 1280; black, 1331 grams.

14,387 on the middle passage, delivered 46,396 in America. The trade increased early in the eighteenth century, 104 ships clearing for Africa in 1701; it then dwindled until the signing of the Assiento, standing at 74 clearings in 1724. The final dissolution of the monopoly in 1750 led—excepting in the years 1754-57, when the closing of Spanish marts sensibly affected the trade—to an extraordinary development, 192 clearings being made in 1771. The Revolutionary war nearly stopped the traffic but by 1786 the clearances had risen again to 146.

"To these figures must be added the unregistered trade of Americans and foreigners. It is probable that about 25,000 slaves were brought to America each year between 1698 and 1707. The importation then dwindled, but rose after the Assiento to perhaps 30,000. The proportion, too, of these slaves carried to the continent now began to increase. Of about 20,000 whom the English annually imported from 1733 to 1766, South Carolina alone received some 3,000. Before the Revolution, the total exportation to America is variously estimated as between 40,000 and 100,000 each year. Bancroft places the total slave population of the continental colonies at 59,000 in 1714, 78,000 in 1727, and 293,000 in 1754. The census of 1790 showed 697,897 slaves in the United States."*

The slaves thus procured came from all parts of Africa—the Soudan, Central and South Africa. Distinct traces of Arab and even Malay blood could be seen side by side with the tall Bantu, the yellow Hottentot and the African dwarfs. The shipment of the slaves drawn from this wide area centered on the west coast of Africa along the Gulf of Guinea, and these west coast Africans were consequently most frequently represented on the slave ships.

This Negro population, which began to reach the confines of the present United States in 1619, has increased until in 1900 in the continental United States it numbered 8,833,994 souls or, today, 1906, not less than 9,500,000.

The first and usual assumption concerning this race is that it represents a pure Negro type. This is an error. Outside the question of what the pure Negro type is, the Negro-American represents a very wide and thorough blending of nearly all African people from north to south; and more than that, it is to a far larger extent than many realize, a blending of European and African blood. It is to this feature especially that this section is devoted.

In the Romanes lecture of 1902, at Oxford University, Mr. James Bryce after coming to many important conclusions concerning the darker races of men, and especially their relations to the whites, frankly acknowledges at last, that so far as intermingling of blood is concerned "one is surprised when one comes to inquire into the matter to find how little positive evidence there is bearing on it," and he further remarks that the subject "deserves to be fully investigated by men of science."

In America we have, on account of the wide-spread mixture of races

---

* DuBois: Suppression of the African Slave Trade, p. 5.

of all kinds, one of the most interesting anthropological laboratories conceivable. This is true also so far as the mingling of the two most diverse races, the black and the white, is concerned as well as·in other cases. And yet no serious attempt has ever been made to study the physical appearance and peculiarities of the transplanted Africans or their millions of descendants.

There is, of course, some reason for this, in that scientific research seldom flourishes in the midst of social struggle and heated discussion. For this reason, and from long familiarity with the strange types, we have gradually ceased to let the physical peculiarities and interesting physiognomies of these people inspire us to study them carefully. Yet this we must soon come to do. We must realize that we have brought to our very threshholds representatives of a great historic race and that, nevertheless, there is no place in the world where less systematic reliable knowledge of the Negro race exists than here. Not only is this true, but we have had going on beneath our very eyes an experiment in raceblending such as the world has nowhere seen before, and we have today living representatives of almost every possible degree of admixture of Teutonic and Negro blood.

So little attention has been paid to this blending, save in extreme controversial spirit, that we easily forget the very existence of the mixed bloods, and foreign students of our race problems appear almost totally ignorant of their existence. We ourselves do not know with accuracy even the number of mixed-bloods. The figures given by the census are as follows:

1850, mulattoes formed 11.2 pér cent of the total Negro population.
1860, mulattoes formed 13.2 per cent of the total Negro population.
1870, mulattoes formed 12 per cent of the total Negro population.
1890, mulattoes formed 15.2 per cent of the total Negro population.

Or in actual numbers:

1850, 405,751 mulattoes.
1860, 588,352 mulattoes.
1870, 585,601 mulattoes.
1890, 1,132,060 mulattoes.

These figures are, however, of doubtful validity. Those of 1850 and 1860 were probably under-statements, while those of 1890 were officially acknowledged to be so far under the truth to be of "little use" and even "misleading." Some local studies have been made, but the areas were so restricted as to form a very narrow basis of induction. I have per-

	Black	Brown	Yellow
Farmville, Va., (small town), 1897	333	219	153
Dougherty county, Ga., (country district), Black Belt, 1899	3,815	1,977	178
Albany, Ga., (village) 1899	1,319	718	238
Savannah, Ga., (city) 1900	2,658	1,521	935
Atlanta, Ga., (city) 1900	8,844	10,981	4,526
McIntosh county, Ga., (country district), Black Belt, 1900	282	208	68
Darien, Ga., (village), 1900	97	94	25
Total	17,348	15,718	6,123

sonally classified nearly 40,000 colored people. Ten thousand were in the Black Belt and in rural districts, and the rest were in cities (Atlanta and Savannah), but cities in or near the Black Belt.

Of these 17,000 were to all appearances of unmixed Negro blood; 6,000 had without doubt more white than Negro blood, while the other 16,000 were classified as "brown:" in the majority of cases they undoubtedly had some white blood—in other cases I was not sure whether their color was due to white blood or to the fact that they were descended from brown Africans.

I am inclined to think that in the light of available data and the results of fairly wide observation that at least one-third of the Negroes of the United States have recognizable traces of white blood, leaving about 6,000,000 others.* This, of course, is partial guess-work—it is quite possible that the mulattoes form an even larger percentage than this, but I should be greatly surprised to find that they formed a smaller proportion. Under such circumstances it would seem that a scientific study of types of American Negroes ought to be undertaken. This paper does not pretend to present the results of careful studies, but rather to indicate in a general way the interesting matter which is open for observation. The main types for separate study would be the full blooded Negroes and those with a quarter, half and three-quarters of white blood; in the eighths—the octoroon, the five-eighths Negro, etc. This is the regular series, but it can be and often is further complicated by the intermarriage of persons of mixed blood.

I know, for instance, a child of six with the following ancestry:

M. White—F. Negro

M. White—F. Negro   F. Mulatto—M. White

  F. Mulatto — M. White   F. Negro—M. White   M. White—F. Quadroon

   F. Quadroon—M. White   F. Mulatto—M. Negro   F. Octoroon—M. Quadroon

    M. Octoroon—F. Quadroon   M. "Colored" — F. "Colored"

     M. "Colored" — F. "Colored"   M. Mulatto—F. White

      M. "Colored" — F. Quadroon

       F. "Colored"

M. = Male.   F. = Female.

The assumption, therefore, that a mulatto has one white parent or grandparent is not always true: no full blood white may have appeared among his ancestors for four or five generations and yet he himself may be half or three-fourths white.

Amid such infinite variation in the proportion of Negro and white blood one can find a most fascinating field of inquiry. In the following pages, I have selected out of a school of about 300 young people between

* This does not mean that these 6,000,000 have no white blood—many of them have—but there are few distinct traces of it.

the ages of 12 and 20 years, 56 persons who seem to me to be fairly typical of the group of young Negroes in general. The types are only provisionally indicated here as the lines are by no means clear in my own mind. Still I think that some approximation of a workable division has been made, so far as that is possible without exact scientific measurements. Among these 56 young persons, all of whom I have known personally for periods varying from one to ten years, I have sought roughly to differentiate four sets of American Negro types:

A.—NEGRO TYPES

1. Full blooded Negroes, letters A to G, and numbers 1 to 7.
2. Brown Negroes, full-blooded or with less than one-fourth of white blood, numbers 8 to 18.

B.—MULATTO TYPES

3. Blended types, numbers 19 to 21, and letter H.
4. Negro-colored, number 25.
5. Negro-haired, numbers 23 to 26.
6. Negro-featured, number 27.

C.—QUADROON TYPES

7. The Chromatic series, numbers 28 to 32.
8. Blended types, numbers 33 to 39.

D.—WHITE TYPES WITH NEGRO BLOOD

Latin, numbers 40 and 41.
Celtic, numbers 42 and 43.
English, numbers 44 to 46.
Germanic, numbers 47 and 48.

Description of Types

For pictures see plates following p. 4

A. Dark brown in color; crisp tightly curled hair; slight in build; excellent student.

B. Very dark brown; crisp bushy hair; heavy, thick-set; quiet and serious.

C. Dark brown; curled crisp black hair; small, plump, vivacious.

D. Dark brown; crisp closely curled hair; tall and well-built; reliable.

E. Very dark brown; crisp closely curled hair; well-proportioned and well-bred; slow.

F. Very dark brown; crisp mass of hair; small and quiet.

G. Very dark brown; crisp hair; rather small; slow but earnest.

H. Light brown; black hair in small waves; medium height, slim and graceful; slow; a singer.

1. Very dark brown in color, crisp, tightly curled hair, jaw slightly-prognathous; short and stocky in build, strong; honest and reliable.

2. Very dark brown, crisp curled hair; slightly prognathous; tall and loosely jointed.

3. Brown in color, closely curled hair, tall and well built; good character.

4. Very dark brown, mass of closely curled hair, medium height and graceful.

5. Dark brown, tightly curled hair not abundant, very tall and of Amazonian build and carriage; excellent character.

6. Brown, mass of less closely curled hair, medium size; good ability.

7. Very dark brown, crisp tightly curled hair, well-formed; considerable native ability, but has had poor school advantages; sweet tempered.

8. Very dark brown, crisp tightly curled hair, medium height and slim; slow, but plodding, and perfectly reliable.

9. Brown, closely curled hair, medium height and looks frail.

10. Brown, mass of curled hair; short and plump; unusual mental ability, cheerful and good character.

11. Brown, mass of more loosely curled hair, medium size, good mental ability, mischievous.

12. Brown, tightly curled hair, slim and awkward; slow, but droll.

13. Light brown, closely-curled hair not abundant, slim; good mental ability and great application; excellent character.

14. Brown, loosely curled hair, short and well-formed; fair mental ability and a sweet singer.

15. Light brown, loosely curled hair, tall and slim; fair ability; quiet.

16. Brown, curled hair, tall and slim.

17. Brown, loosely curled hair, tall and lithe; very good mental ability; sweet tempered.

18. Brown, close curled hair, medium size; of unusual mental ability judged by any standard.

19. Light brown, curled hair, stocky build; good ability, erratic application; quick tempered. Grandson of a leading white southerner.

20. Yellow, curled and wavy hair, slight and well-formed; good mental ability; quiet.

21. Yellow, wavy hair, small and graceful; good ability.

22. Brown, straight black hair; probably has Indian blood; well built and full of fun, but with little application.

23. Light yellow, curled hair, small in size, bright mentally, and excellent in character; young.

24. Light yellow, curled hair, medium size, slim; good alto singer.

25. Light yellow, freckled, reddish curled hair, medium size; fair ability and pleasant disposition.

26. Yellow, curled and wavy hair, medium size, good form; excellent ability and application; serious.

27. Light yellow, hair glossy and curly, tall and slim; good ability and close application; quiet.

28. Smooth brown color, straight, black, slightly curly hair, long limbed and slim.

29. White face, with red freckles, giving a pinkish impression; reddish brown hair, crimped and wavy; a bashful, good girl, of fair ability.

30. A study in reds—red gold hair, crimped and fluffy, an old gold face, with reddish tinge; brilliant light brown eyes; tall, impetuous, of unusual ability.

31. Yellow in face and hair; erratic.

32. White color, dark wavy hair; sturdily built.

33. Creamy color, crimped and wavy hair, tall and graceful; well bred.

34. Yellow, with wavy long hair, short and plump; good ability and easy, good-natured character.

35. Creamy color, crimped brown hair, tall and slim; languid.

36. Light yellow, wavy hair, rather small in stature; good mind and character; quiet.

37. Light yellow, wavy hair, middle size; of unusual mental ability and excellent character; quiet.

38. Light yellow; tall, long wavy hair.

39. Light yellow, long, nearly straight hair; large and plump; slow, but willing.

40. Cream-tinted, with dark wavy hair, tall and well-formed, with very good mind and ability in several directions; musical.

41. Cream-tinted, with wavy hair, strongly built, with fair mind; rather quiet.

42. White, with freckles and long, red-gold hair; mischievous and smart.

43. White, straight brown hair, tall and thin; slow but conscientious; quiet and sensitive.

44. White, sandy hair and blue eyes, short and rather small; fair ability and good application.

45. Cream-color, dark hair, tall and slim; somewhat erratic in intellect, but conscientious; droll.

46. White, sandy hair and blue eyes, middle-size; fair ability and good character.

47. White, very light golden hair, light blue eyes, tall and stately; ordinary ability, very reliable, quiet and kind.

48. White, chestnut hair, blue eyes, plump and well-formed.

A. Negro Types

These represent, perhaps, 6,000,000 colored people of this country. The 24 pictures devoted to these are inadequate and present but a few of numerous types. A really adequate study would lead to an investigation of all the African types, most of which are represented in America, and subsequently changed by intermingling, and possibly by climate and surroundings. We can still catch glimpses of the original African—the straight-nosed, dark Nubian, as in No. 8, the tall, massive Bantu, in No. 5, the small, sturdy West Coast Negro, in No. 1, and others. All these types agree in dark color and crisp hair. The color we usually denominate black, although it is in reality a series of browns varying between black and yellow as limits. We may, for instance, arrange the first eighteen pictures by color. First come the very dark browns, 4, 7, 8, and 2, all having a certain brilliancy of coloring, although some, like 4. are dull brown. Next come the dark browns, 1, 5, and 3; then the browns, 14, 6, 9, 11, 16 and 18, in order; finally the light browns, 10, 12, 17, 15 and 13.

It would be exceedingly interesting to have a series of accurate examinations and measurements of Negro hair. If we take the first seven portraits—those which represent probably the full blooded Negro, we may distinguish several varieties which can be put in two main classes: a crisp hair in minute curls or waves with a dark grayish, black appearance, and usually scanty. This is seen in 1, 2, 5, 7 and 8; and the less closely curled and abundant hair, dead black and massive in appearance, as in 3, 4 and 6.

In general physical appearance, the first seven divide themselves into four types: the short and sturdy (1), the tall, largely built (2, 3 and 5), the medium sized, dark and more delicately featured type (8). Prognathism appears in the facial angles of 1 and 2, and slightly in 3 and 4. Numbers 3 and 6 are of good, but not striking ability, 2 and 4 are fair; the others are slow. Numbers 1, 5 and 8 are honest and reliable in character; 3 and 7 are also of good character; Nos. 4, 6 and 9 are a little more uncertain in character: only one member of the group cannot be relied upon, although he is still young and may change.

Numbers 9 to 18 have in all probability a little white blood, although this is not certain in every case. Numbers 9, 12 and 13 have the crisp hair before mentioned; 16, 17 and 18 have hair of the second variety, while 10, 11 and 14 have a still less closely curled variety, longer and more pliable. One may roughly separate three types in these persons. Numbers 9, 10, 11 and 12 are what we may call "blended" types—the variation from the stricter Negro type is not especially apparent in any one feature or characteristic, but the whole type is slightly and uniformly changed in face, hair and color, either by the even blending of white blood or by descent from tribes of Negroes different from those we have noted before. All are of medium size save No. 10, who is short and heavy. In 13 and 14 we have a different group: they show a certain delicacy of feature and melancholy cast of countenance often noticed in mixed blooded people, and associated with deep sensitiveness in both these girls. Numbers 15, 16, 17 and 18 are Bantu types—tall, long-faced and straight-nosed, with large facial angle; 16 and 17 are especially graceful in movement, while 18 is the most brilliant mentally of the whole series of 48. Numbers 10 and 17 are also of unusual ability; 11 and 19 are good, 14 and 15 fair only, and 12 and 16 poor. Numbers 10, 13, 14 and 15 are of good character; 11 and 12 are more uncertain but pretty good.

Letters A to H are pictures taken later than the others. They are well-known Negro types, although some are not usually so regarded by careless observers.

B. Mulatto Types

The ten following portraits, numbers 19 to 28, represent the mulatto types of American Negroes; they have from three-fourths to one-half Negro blood and have, in this country, to hazard a guess, about 2,500,000 representatives. I have differentiated types here chiefly in the way in which the two streams of blood have blended; the first three are blended types, where the white and Negro blood is evenly distributed in color, hair and feature, making light brown or yellow persons, with hair in small but minute curls or waves, and features rounded or half European. In the other seven persons, the Negro blood has asserted itself in some one or two characteristics and the white blood in others: in 22, for instance, the white blood (with probably some Indian) has gone into the abundant long black hair and left a dark face and full features; in Nos. 23, 24, 25 and 26, the Negro blood has asserted itself particularly in the hair, leaving the light color and European features; the hair has received a slight red tinge in 25 and the blending is more complete in 26. In 27 the Negro blood has moulded the features, leaving the light color and hair in ringlets. All this is instructive to the student of heredity as showing visibly many things which lie hidden from the eye in the blending of races of the same color and features.

In physique we have the short and sturdy (19), the short and slender

(21) and (23), the tall and slender (20, 24 and 27), and the medium sized persons, usually large boned and well built, as 22, 25 and 26. Numbers 23 and 26 are excellent in mental ability, 19, 20, 21 and 27 are good; 25 is fair, while 22 and 24 are poor. Numbers 20, 23, 26 and 27 are good and quiet in character; 25 is straightforward; 19, 21 and 24 are more uncertain, but are still young.

C. Quadroon Types

The fifteen portraits, from numbers 28 to 39, are of colored people with more than one-half and less than seven-eights of their blood white, so far as I can ascertain. They represent about 350,000 of the American Negroes, if my other estimates are correct. Here again examples of race-blending in large variety and with especial brilliancy of coloring. Sometimes the coloring is so prominent and assertive that one scarcely notices other features. Photographs, of course, fail to give any adequate idea of this group: the emphatic color may be a velvet brown in the face, as in 28, or a brownish red in the hair, as in 29, or a burst of red, red-gold and red-brown in face and hair, as in 30. Again, hair and features may both be yellow, as in 31, or all brown or dark brown and yellow, as in a number of cases, or finally the skin may be strikingly white, as in 32. These types, then, from 28 to 32, I have grouped as the Chromatic types.

Again, we may have the harmonious blending mentioned in the case of the mulattoes and illustrated in the following portraits—numbers 33 and 34, and having the most Negro blood, and number 40, having the least. The hair of the Quadroons is of almost every conceivable variety and color: it may be black and straight, as in 28, or black and waving, as in 39, or red-brown and waving, as in 30, or crimped and brownish red, as in 29, or curly and fluffy, as in 38, and so on in endless change.

In physique, 28, 30, 33, 35 and 38 are tall and slim, while 32, 34 and 37 are shorter and sturdier; 29, 31 and 40 are of slighter build and more delicate appearance. Numbers 30 and 37 have excellent minds, and 31, 34 and 36 have good ability. The group represents great varieties of character: 28 and 35 are languid in manner and work; 29 and 33 are sensitive and good; 30 is straightforward, even impetuous; 31 is uncertain, but young; 36, 37 and 39 are honest and quiet; 34 and 39 are a little erratic, but good-hearted.

D. White Types, with Negro Blood

The Octoroons and those with less than one-eighth of Negro blood pass so easily back and forth between the races that it is difficult to estimate their real numbers. In a single small city 100 colored families were estimated to have been listed as white in the census of 1890, because the Octoroon wife went to the door and the census-taker did not think or dare to ask her "color." A considerable proportion of these persons identify themselves altogether with the whites—probably several thousands in all. The census of 1890 reported 69,936 Octoroons—there may be as many as 150,000 in all. They are easily classified according to the European types they most resemble, either accidentally or because of real blood-relationship. Sergi would not need better evidence for his "Mediterranean race" theory than the distinct Latin type of the Octoroons, 40 and 41; they have, in fact, English and Negro blood. So, too, white and black blood can make as good an Egyptian type today as five thousand years ago. Numbers 42 and 43 resemble Celtic types and may have Irish blood; 44, 45 and 46 are English or Anglo-American types, and 47 and 48 are Germanic types.

Such types as these are not necessarily descended from white and colored parents, nor are they always illegitimate children as is usually assumed. In the cases of 40, 44 and 45, and probably in two other cases both parents were colored and legally married. In case of 44, 47 and 48 one parent was white. In none of these ten cases would the casual observer notice the Negro blood. An experienced person would possibly see it in 40, 41 and 45, and possibly in 42. In the others all trace is lost. In physique, 40, 41 and 48 are well-built and rather heavy; 43 and 45 are tall and slender, while 42 and 44 are slender but of medium height.

Forty is a good scholar, as are 41, 42 and 48. All are of good character, although one may succumb to unfortunate home influences.

Conclusions

It is not pretended, I repeat, that this cursory sketch can be made a basis for any very definite conclusions. Its object is rather to blaze the way and point out a few general truths. Further work must depend more largely on exact physical measurement of size, weight and head formation, as well as psycho-physical experiment. It must also be remembered that these types come from a limited class at an age before character is fully formed; this study has the advantage, however, of the author's intimate acquaintance for years with each person studied, so that the elements of character and personal peculiarities are pretty well known.

In future study the unmixed types need especial supplement. Comparisons will inevitably arise between the blacks and mixed bloods. In regard to the latter much friction and prejudice must be cleared away: today one hears, on the one hand, that mulattoes are practically all degenerates, ranking below both the parent races; and, on the other, that only the mixed blood Negroes amount to much, and this by reason of their white blood. So far as this study is concerned, neither of these theories receives any especial support. In physique, the best developed persons are 1, 2, 3, 5, 10, 16, 17, 19, 22, 32, 34, 39, 40, 41 and 48. These include all degrees of mixture and, moreover, there would seem to be in nearly all cases personal reasons for the good development outside the blood mixture; 1, for instance, is farm-bred, 2 and 5 are children of strong laboring men, 40 has been carefully reared, 41 is a baseball player, etc. Again, the members of the group who are physically weakest are of all colors—4, 12, 15 and 43. In mental ability the evidence is equally contradictory; the exceptional scholars include three nearly full-blooded Negroes, three Quadroons and one Octoroon.

Of these, a boy (number 18), with but a slight admixture of white blood, if any, is easily first.

As to moral stamina, the subjects are, of course, rather young for final judgment, and yet at the same time their tendencies are more clearly visible. Five of the 53 were born out of lawful wedlock, although in some cases the union of the parents was the permanent concubinage of slavery days, and thus not mere wantonness. Possibly one or two others are also illegitimate, but this is not certain. In the case of two girls, an octoroon and a mulatto, both now out of school, there is a rumor of sexual looseness; in the case of three (a Negro, mulatto and quadroon), there is some tendency towards habitual lying, which may not however become serious; in all the 48 there are four (a Negro boy, a mulatto girl, a quadroon boy and an octoroon girl), of whose future one may well fear. None of them are as yet hopeless.

In all these cases of physical and mental development and moral stamina, it is naturally very difficult to judge between the relative influence of heredity and environment—of the influence of Negro and mixed blood, and of the homes and schools and social atmosphere surrounding the colored people. In general, it must be remembered that most of the blacks are country-bred and descended from the depressed and ignorant field-hands, while a majority of the mulattoes were town-bred and descended from the master class and the indulged house-servants. The country schools since emancipation have been very poor, while the city schools are pretty good, and in general the difference in civilization between rural and urban districts is much more marked South than North.

For instance, if numbers 7 and 8 had had the same early training as numbers 23 and 40, they might have developed strong minds, so far as one can judge. Some of these children come from comfortable, well-to-do homes, while some were practically street waifs; some had educated—a few, college-bred—parents; others had parents who could neither read nor write, and so on. Under such circumstances, how rash it is to hazard wild statements as to the ability and desert of millions of people without waiting for exact study and careful measurements.

A word may be added as to race mixture in general and as regards white and black stocks in the future. There is, of course, in general no argument against the intermingling of the world's races. "All the great peoples of the world are the result of a mixture of races."*

Upon the whole, if we consider (1) that the most mixed and most civilized races are those which are soonest acclimatized, (2) that the tendency of races to intermingle, and of civilization to develop, goes on increasing every day in every part of the world, we may affirm without being accused of exaggeration that the cosmopolitanism of mankind, if it does not yet exist today in all races (which seems somewhat improbable), will develop as a necessary consequence of the facility of acclimatation. For it to become general is only a matter of time. †

*Bryce: Relations, etc.
†Denniker, p. 119.

At the same time there are certain bars to general amalgamation with particular races:

Nothing really arrests intermarriage except physical repulsion, and physical repulsion exists only where there is a marked difference in physical aspect, and especially in color. Roughly speaking (and subject to certain exceptions to be hereafter noted), we may say that while all the races of the same, or a similar color intermarry freely, those of one color intermarry very little with those of another.*

So far, then, as the amalgamation of the white and black races is concerned this prediction may be hazarded:

Africa will remain for many ages predominantly black.

In the West Indes the whites will be absorbed into a mulatto race.

In South America the whites will absorb the Negro. A recent writer in Brazil writes:

This racial question in Brazil has most instructive aspects. In their pride of race some visitors are disposed to despise the Brazilian people because of the manifest admixture of African blood in their make-up. This is simply because they cannot easily appreciate that taking effect before their eyes is the very process of race building that has been completed for ages past in Mediterranean lands. They do not realize that the blending of African with Aryan and Semitic elements must have been precisely the same, there and here. The swarthiness of the Italians, Spaniards, the Provencal French, etc.—these interpenetrating other European stocks—manifestly seems due to the same causes that in Brazil and other sections of Latin America and in the West Indies are producing precisely the same physical aspects . . . But though the Negro race was in itself unaffected, it has by no means been uneffective. Everywhere it has left its traces behind. All these civilizations—Egyptian, Phœnician, Grecian, Roman, Semitic, Moorish—it has in varying degrees tinged with its blood and its temperament. Its service seems always to have been that of an element in a blend.

There appears to be no saying how far this progress has gone. But there are eminent anthropologists who declare that racial characters demonstrate that the entire white race has a very high percentage of the African in its composition. The racial aspect may have a notable bearing upon the future of South America.†

In the United States the situation is far different: if slavery had prevailed the Negroes might have been gradually absorbed into the white race. Even under the present serfdom, the amalgamation is still going on. It is not then caste or race prejudice that stops it—they rather encourage it on its more dangerous side. The Southern laws against race marriage are in effect laws which make the seduction of colored girls easy and without shame or penalty. The real bar to race amalgamation at present in the United States is the spreading and strengthening determination of the rising educated classes of blacks to accept no amalgamation except through open legal marriage. This means practically no amalgamation in the near future. The available statistics of mixed marriages show in Boston, Mass., 600 such

*Bryce: Relations.
†Outlook, Vol. 84, No. 15.

marriages from 1855 to 1887; and 24 in the year 1890. The state of Massachusetts had 52 mixed marriages in 1900, 44 in 1901 and 43 in 1902. Michigan had 111 mixed marriages in 20 years (1874-93), and Rhode Island 58 in 13 years (1881-93). In the black ward of Philadelphia (the seventh) there were, in 1896, 33 mixed families.

These figures indicate comparatively few such marriages and show that the absorption of 10,000,000 Negro Americans in this way is certainly not a problem which we need face for many years.

At present those who dislike amalgamation can best prevent it by helping to raise the Negro to such a plane of intelligence and economic independence that he will never stoop to mingle his blood with those who despise him.

5. Physical Measurements

There are not many reliable physical measurements of Negroes, either in Africa or America. The following table from Denniker gives the height of the principal Africans, together with that of native Americans:

Average Height of Men

No. of Subjects	Low Statures (under 1.60 m., or 63 inches)	Height in Millimeters
38	Akkfi Negritoes of the country of the Monbuttus...............	1,378
64	Kalahari Bushmen of Angra Pequena, etc................	1,529

No.	Statures below the average (1600-1649 mm., or 63-65 inches)	H. in Mill.
50	Mzabites (Berbers of M'Zab, Algeria).........................	1,620
36	Batekes of the Congo	1,641

No.	Statures above the average (1650-1699 mm., or 65-67 inches)	H. in Mill.
32	Arabs of Algeria..	1,656
28	Mushikoegos of the Congo.........	1,658
1,103	Berbers of Tunis...	1,663
29	Abyssinians...	1,669
35	Danakils of Tajura...	1,670
52	Berbers of Biskra (Chania tribe?)...............................	1,673
244	Kabyles of Great Kabylia..	1,677
180	Berbers of Algeria...	1,680
27	Bashilanges of the Kasai...	1,680
2,020	Negroes of the United States....................................	1,681
863	Mulattoes of the United States....·..............................	1,682
28	Bechuanas	1,684
25,828	Negroes and Mulattoes of the United States (conscripts)....	1,693

No.	High Statures (1.70 m., or 67 inches and up)	H. in Mill.
315,620	Citizens of the United States (white) born in the country ...	1,719
31	Mandigans in general...	1,700
25	Bejas (called Nubians)	1,708
72	Kaffirs (Ama-Xosa and Ama-Zulu)...............................	1,715
56	Western Zandehs (Mandjas, Akungs, Awakas, etc.)	1,717
56	Somalis (Eyssa, Habis, Hwakas, etc.)...........................	1,723
30	Tonconleurs or Torodas	1,725
62	Waloss, Severs and Leybus	1,730
25	Negroes of Darfur...	1,730
35	Fulahs or Fulbes of French Sudan...............................	1,741

Measurements of cephalic index from Denniker and Ripley show these results: (Negro tribes are in italics).

Dolichocephals (73-78).

Hindus,	North Chinese,
Fulahs,	Persians,
Kaffirs,	Japanese,
Portuguese,	*Bushmen,*
English,	*Hansas,*
Danes,	South Italians,
Swedes,	Spaniards.

Mesocephals (79-81).

Chinese,
French (d. du Nord),
Central Italians.

Brachycephals (82-89).

Dalmattons,
Tartars,
Piedmontese,
Magyars.

As Ripley says, "an important point to be noted in this connection is that this shape of the head seems to bear no direct relation to intellectual power or intelligence. Posterior development of the cranium does not imply a corresponding backwardness in culture. The broad-headed races of the earth may not as a whole be quite as deficient in civilization as some of the long heads, notably the Australians and the African Negroes. On the other hand, the Chinese are conspicuously long-headed, surrounded by the barbarian brachycephalic Mongol hordes; and the Eskimos in many respects surpass the Indians in culture. Dozens of similar contrasts might be given. Europe offers the best refutation of the statement that the proportions of the head mean anything intellectually. The English, as our map of Europe will show, are distinctly long-headed."*

For Negro Americans, almost the only measurements on a considerable scale are those taken over a generation ago during the Civil war, and often since published and studied. The best available figures to-day are those from the reports of the Surgeon-General of the United States army; subjoined are tables as to the examination of recruits, their height, weight and chest measurements:

---

*Ripley, p. 40.

*Examination of recruits during the year 1901 ***

	White	Colored	Total
Total number of recruits examined	56,894	1,888	58,782
Of each 1,000 of these—			
Were accepted for service	623.93	647.78	624.70
Were rejected for under height	2.74	3.71	2.77
Were rejected for disabilities	286.66	279.13	286.42
Of each 1,000 accepted recruits the heights were as follows in inches):			
Under 61	.37		.35
61 to 62	.34		.33
62 to 63	1.69	4.09	1.77
63 to 64	15.86	17.99	15.93
64 to 65	98.54	106.30	98.80
65 to 66	124.71	148.81	125.51
66 to 67	167.16	165.17	167.10
67 to 68	166.69	178.25	167.07
68 to 69	157.14	156.17	157.10
69 to 70	123.02	96.48	122.14
70 to 71	82.31	67.05	81.81
71 to 72	35.97	37.61	36.03
72 to 73	16.76	15.54	16.72
73 to 74	6.96	5.72	6.92
74 upward	2.48	.82	2.42
Causes of rejection (exclusive of under height) expressed in ratios per 1,000 of examined recruits:			
Physical debility	2.27		2.19
Tuberculosis of lungs or other organs	2.09	3.19	2.13
Imperfect vision	41.36	24.89	40.80
Heart disease	27.54	22.25	27.37
Goiter	.28		.27
Varicose veins, varicocele, hemorrhoids	41.09	20.13	40.42
Hernia	13.02	12.18	13.00
Flat feet	2.60	5.83	2.70

Examination of recruits during the year 1902 †

	White	Colored
Total number of recruits examined	42,183	3,035
Of each 1,000 of these—		
Were accepted for service	658.80	786.16
Were rejected for under height	.95	.99
Were rejected for disabilities	255.29	171.33
Of each 1,000 accepted recruits the heights were as follows (in inches):		
Under 61	.32	.84
61 to 62	.40	.42
62 to 63	1.51	2.93
63 to 64	11.51	10.06
64 to 65	87.69	99.33
65 to 66	125.73	137.89
66 to 67	162.72	171.42
67 to 68	177.08	189.86
68 to 69	158.98	147.11
69 to 70	123.14	117.77
70 to 71	76.11	70.41
71 to 72	40.05	31.85
72 to 73	22.31	14.25
73 to 74	8.89	3.35
74 upward	3.56	2.51
Causes of rejection (exclusive of under height) expressed in ratios per 1,000 of examined recruits:		
Physical debility	1.23	.99
Tuberculosis of lungs or other organs	3.15	.66
Imperfect vision	33.31	18.12
Heart disease	21.34	11.53
Goiter	.40	.66
Varicose veins, varicocele, hemorrhoids	37.03	11.20
Hernia	11.02	8.24
Flat feet	3.80	3.63

* Report of the United States Surgeon-General, 1902.

† Ibid., 1903.

Proportion of each height per thousand of accepted colored recruits *

HEIGHT	18 yrs. and under	19 yrs.	20 yrs.	21 yrs.	22 yrs.	23 yrs.	24 yrs.	25 yrs.
5 feet 1 inch and under								
5 feet 2 inches								
5 feet 3 inches				10.4	9.9			7.5
5 feet 4 inches				72.9	108.9	61.2	64.5	37.6
5 feet 5 inches				83.3	123.8	132.6	129.0	82.7
5 feet 6 inches	1,000.0			229.2	158.4	183.7	169.4	150.4
5 feet 7 inches				218.7	198.0	122.4	145.2	233.1
5 feet 8 inches				125.0	123.8	163.3	225.8	165.4
5 feet 9 inches				114.6	113.9	153.1	161.3	135.3
5 feet 10 inches				83.3	84.2	91.8	72.6	90.2
5 feet 11 inches				31.2	49.5	51.0	16.1	45.1
6 feet				31.2	29.7	20.4	16.1	22.6
6 feet 1 inch						20.4		7.5
6 feet 2 inches and over								22.6
Total	1,000.0			1,000.0	1,000.0	1,000.0	1,000.0	1,000.0

HEIGHT	26 yrs.	27 yrs.	28 yrs.	29 yrs.	30 yrs.	31 yrs.	32 yrs.	33 yrs.
5 feet 1 inch and under								
5 feet 2 inches								
5 feet 3 inches	9.8			20.0				
5 feet 4 inches	107.8	85.7	69.4	120.0	128.2		35.7	47.6
5 feet 5 inches	186.3	114.3	83.3	160.0	51.3	241.4	178.6	
5 feet 6 inches	137.3	152.4	138.9	100.0	128.2	103.4	178.6	142.9
5 feet 7 inches	196.1	219.1	208.3	140.0	153.8	172.4	178.6	333.3
5 feet 8 inches	156.9	133.3	236.1	220.0	256.4	172.4	107.1	142.9
5 feet 9 inches	58.8	133.3	125.0	60.0	153.8	137.9	107.1	142.9
5 feet 10 inches	68.6	57.1	83.3	140.0		103.4	107.1	95.2
5 feet 11 inches	58.8	47.6	41.7		51.3		71.4	47.6
6 feet	19.6	28.6	13.9	40.0		34.5		
6 feet 1 inch		19.0			51.3		35.7	
6 feet 2 inches and over		9.5			25.6	34.5		47.6
Total	1,000.0	1,000.0	1,000.0	1,000.0	1,000.0	1,000.0	1,000.0	1,000.0

HEIGHT	34 yrs.	35 yrs.	36 yrs.	37 yrs.	38 yrs.	39 yrs.	40 yrs. and over	Total
5 feet 1 inch and under								
5 feet 2 inches								
5 feet 3 inches						83.3	24.1	7.1
5 feet 4 inches		47.6			76.9		60.2	73.0
5 feet 5 inches		142.9	272.6	200.0	153.8	250.0	144.6	123.2
5 feet 6 inches	166.7	238.1	272.6		230.8	166.7	108.4	157.8
5 feet 7 inches	250.0	238.1	363.7	100.0		83.3	216.9	192.3
5 feet 8 inches	333.3	190.5		600.0	307.7	166.7	216.9	175.8
5 feet 9 inches	125.0				230.8	166.7	84.3	117.7
5 feet 10 inches	41.7	47.6	90.9	100.0			96.4	79.2
5 feet 11 inches	83.3						24.1	38.5
6 feet		95.2				83.3	12.0	22.8
6 feet 1 inch							12.0	7.1
6 feet 2 inches and over								5.5
Total	1,000.0	1,000.0	1,000.0	1,000.0	1,000.0	1,000.0	1,000.0	1,000.0

* Ibid., 1905.

Proportion of each height per thousand of accepted white recruits

HEIGHT	18 years and under	19 yrs.	20 yrs.	21 yrs.	22 yrs.	23 yrs.	24 yrs.	25 yrs.
5 feet 1 inch and under		38.5		0.2	0.2	0.6	1.0	0.4
5 feet 2 inches		76.9		.2	.6	.3	.6	.8
5 feet 3 inches				4.2	5.9	4.2	7.9	8.5
5 feet 4 inches	50.0	230.8	66.7	69.5	73.1	68.9	70.1	69.3
5 feet 5 inches	200.0	230.8	100.0	129.1	104.5	117.9	110.3	106.7
5 feet 6 inches	200.0	76.9	200.0	162.4	160.1	138.7	146.0	144.3
5 feet 7 inches	250.0	153.8	166.7	183.8	176.4	167.3	169.9	178.4
5 feet 8 inches	100.0	38.5	266.7	168.8	166.6	182.6	169.9	164.1
5 feet 9 inches	50.0	38.5	100.0	133.1	138.2	143.6	136.5	138.9
5 feet 10 inches	50.0	38.5	66.7	82.2	94.5	90.5	92.7	101.2
5 feet 11 inches	100.0		33.3	38.0	41.7	40.8	46.5	41.1
6 feet				17.1	24.8	29.6	28.5	29.5
6 feet 1 inch				8.4	10.1	8.8	13.1	11.6
6 feet 2 inches and over		76.9		2.8	3.3	6.4	6.9	5.0
Total	1,000.0	1,000.0	1,000.0	1,000.0	1,000.0	1,000.0	1,000.0	1,000.0

HEIGHT	26 yrs.	27 yrs.	28 yrs.	29 yrs.	30 yrs.	31 yrs.	32 yrs.	33 yrs.
5 feet 1 inch and under	1.0	0.6	3.9					1.8
5 feet 2 inches	.5	1.7	2.0	0.9	1.1		4.4	1.8
5 feet 3 inches	11.4	9.4	11.1	12.6	3.3	8.8	4.4	5.3
5 feet 4 inches	78.3	74.4	72.6	64.8	70.1	75.1	91.3	63.5
5 feet 5 inches	96.4	128.3	122.2	114.3	113.5	123.7	131.1	119.9
5 feet 6 inches	154.5	149.4	141.2	140.4	153.5	166.4	137.0	158.7
5 feet 7 inches	164.3	158.8	174.5	164.7	181.3	170.8	163.5	179.9
5 feet 8 inches	170.0	169.9	147.7	159.3	153.5	173.8	166.4	179.9
5 feet 9 inches	133.8	122.8	124.2	144.9	134.6	95.7	131.1	121.7
5 feet 10 inches	96.9	101.1	104.6	94.5	85.6	94.3	82.5	74.1
5 feet 11 inches	42.5	41.1	50.3	41.4	50.1	48.6	45.7	52.9
6 feet	34.7	26.1	25.5	36.9	35.6	30.9	22.1	30.0
6 feet 1 inch	9.3	9.4	12.4	17.1	10.0	8.8	14.7	7.1
6 feet 2 inches and over	6.2	7.2	7.8	8.1	7.8	2.9	5.9	3.5
Total	1,000.0	1,000.0	1,000.0	1,000.0	1,000.0	1,000.0	1,000.0	1,000.0

HEIGHT	34 yrs.	35 yrs.	36 yrs.	37 yrs.	38 yrs.	39 yrs.	40 years and over	Total
5 feet 1 inch and under							0.9	0.6
5 feet 2 inches	1.9	2.5					2.8	.9
5 feet 3 inches	7.5	4.9	4.3	12.2	9.3	5.9	10.3	7.1
5 feet 4 inches	79.1	83.9	90.9	57.1	88.4	82.8	87.3	72.8
5 feet 5 inches	145.0	160.5	134.2	171.4	134.9	124.3	135.2	117.1
5 feet 6 inches	162.0	177.8	155.8	146.9	186.0	201.2	166.2	153.2
5 feet 7 inches	146.9	165.4	160.2	175.5	214.0	142.0	170.0	172.7
5 feet 8 inches	160.1	128.4	155.8	183.7	139.5	207.1	170.0	167.4
5 feet 9 inches	148.8	111.1	121.2	130.6	98.0	106.5	119.2	133.3
5 feet 10 inches	79.1	101.2	95.2	73.5	69.8	47.3	78.9	91.6
5 feet 11 inches	37.7	39.5	43.3	28.6	23.3	53.3	33.8	42.1
6 feet	22.6	12.3	26.0	16.3	23.3	17.8	19.7	26.1
6 feet 1 inch	5.6	9.9	8.7	4.1	9.3	11.8	2.8	10.1
6 feet 2 inches and over	3.8	2.5	4.3		9.3		2.8	5.0
Total	1,000.0	1,000.0	1,000.0	1,000.0	1,000.0	1,000.0	1,000.0	1,000.0

Proportion of each weight per thousand of accepted colored recruits.

WEIGHT	18 yrs. and under	19 yrs.	20 yrs.	21 yrs.	22 yrs.	23 yrs.	24 yrs.	25 yrs.
99 pounds and under								
100 to 109 pounds								
110 to 119 pounds					9.9	10.2	8.1	7.5
120 to 129 pounds	1,000.0			145.8	113.9	40.8	48.4	67.7
130 to 139 pounds				333.3	257.4	214.3	233.9	172.9
140 to 149 pounds				281.2	287.1	336.7	298.4	345.8
150 to 159 pounds				156.3	183.2	255.1	241.9	188.0
160 to 169 pounds				62.5	89.1	102.0	121.0	82.7
170 to 179 pounds				20.8	34.7	20.4	40.3	60.1
180 to 189 pounds					19.8	20.4	8.1	60.1
190 to 199 pounds								15.0
200 pounds and over					5.0			
Total	1,000.0			1,000.0	1,000.0	1,000.0	1,000.0	1,000.0

WEIGHT	26 yrs.	27 yrs.	28 yrs.	29 yrs.	30 yrs.	31 yrs.	32 yrs.	33 yrs.
99 pounds and under								
100 to 109 pounds								
110 to 119 pounds								
120 to 129 pounds	117.6	85.7	83.3	60.0	25.6	34.5	71.4	47.6
130 to 139 pounds	274.5	142.9	152.8	240.0	256.4	172.4	71.4	95.2
140 to 149 pounds	225.5	361.9	277.8	240.0	128.2	275.9	250.0	238.1
150 to 159 pounds	205.9	190.5	347.2	160.0	256.4	275.9	250.0	285.7
160 to 169 pounds	137.3	114.3	83.3	160.0	205.1	34.5	178.6	238.1
170 to 179 pounds	19.6	38.1	27.8	100.0	76.9	137.9	71.4	47.6
180 to 189 pounds	19.6	57.1	27.8	40.0	51.3	-69.0		47.6
190 to 199 pounds		9.5					71.4	
200 pounds and over							35.7	
Total	1,000.0	1,000.0	1,000.0	1,000.0	1,000.0	1,000.0	1,000.0	1,000.0

WEIGHT	34 yrs.	35 yrs.	36 yrs.	37 yrs.	38 yrs.	39 yrs.	40 yrs. and over	Total
99 pounds and under								
100 to 109 pounds								
110 to 119 pounds		47.6						4.7
120 to 129 pounds		47.6	90.9		153.8		60.2	79.3
130 to 139 pounds	125.0	238.1	90.9	200.0	76.9	83.3	180.7	211.9
140 to 149 pounds	250.0	142.9	454.6	100.0	230.9	416.7	228.9	283.4
150 to 159 pounds	375.0	238.1		400.0	384.6	83.3	156.6	215.1
160 to 169 pounds	83.3	47.6	181.8	100.0	153.8	83.3	132.5	109.1
170 to 179 pounds	41.7	95.2	181.8			166.7	120.5	50.2
180 to 189 pounds	41.7			100.0		83.3	36.1	29.8
190 to 199 pounds	41.7	142.9						7.1
200 pounds and over	41.7			100.0		83.3	84.3	9.4
Total	1,000.0	1,000.0	1,000.0	1,000.0	1,000.0	1,000.0	1,000.0	1,000.0

Proportion of each weight per thousand of accepted white recruits *

WEIGHT	18 yrs. and under	19 yrs.	20 yrs.	21 yrs.	22 yrs.	23 yrs.	24 yrs.	25 yrs.
99 pounds and under								
100 to 109 pounds								
110 to 119 pounds	150.0	192.3	66.7	25.1	22.1	16.5	15.7	19.0
120 to 129 pounds	300.0	230.8	166.7	177.7	153.6	111.2	129.0	109.4
130 to 139 pounds	350.0	307.6	366.7	328.4	287.7	280.6	252.8	259.9
140 to 149 pounds	150.0	153.8	200.0	256.6	282.0	279.7	274.4	273.1
150 to 159 pounds	50.0	38.5	166.7	141.8	152.8	180.7	179.8	193.2
160 to 169 pounds		38.5	33.3	50.5	72.8	93.2	95.3	91.9
170 to 179 pounds		38.5		13.8	20.4	25.9	37.7	34.9
180 to 189 pounds				4.9	6.9	9.1	10.8	11.6
190 to 199 pounds				.9	1.2	2.4	4.3	5.4
200 pounds and over				.2	.5	.6	.3	1.6
Total	1,000.0	1,000.0	1,000.0	1,000.0	1,000.0	1,000.0	1,000.0	1,000.0

WEIGHT	26 yrs.	27 yrs.	28 yrs.	29 yrs.	30 yrs.	31 yrs.	32 yrs.	33 yrs.
99 pounds and under								
100 to 109 pounds:								
110 to 119 pounds	19.2	22.2	15.0	17.1	24.5	11.8	17.7	7.1
120 to 129 pounds	117.2	116.6	118.3	103.5	103.4	107.5	98.7	97.0
130 to 139 pounds	232.8	254.9	228.1	224.1	231.4	237.1	207.7	231.0
140 to 149 pounds	280.4	255.4	260.8	262.8	244.7	256.3	268.1	262.8
150 to 159 pounds	195.4	189.9	178.4	184.5	190.2	182.5	201.8	194.0
160 to 169 pounds	93.3	98.3	128.8	119.7	120.1	100.1	109.0	100.5
170 to 179 pounds	37.8	38.3	36.6	51.3	46.7	58.9	48.6	58.2
180 to 189 pounds	17.6	14.4	22.9	21.6	30.0	26.5	28.0	26.5
190 to 199 pounds	4.1	7.2	8.5	9.9	5.6	7.4	11.8	19.4
200 pounds and over	2.1	2.8	2.6	5.4	3.3	11.8	8.8	3.5
Total	1,000.0	1,000.0	1,000.0	1,000.0	1,000.0	1,000.0	1,000.0	1,000.0

WEIGHT	34 yrs.	35 yrs.	36 yrs.	37 yrs.	38 yrs.	39 yrs.	40 yrs. and over	Total
99 pounds and under								
100 to 109 pounds								
110 to 119 pounds	16.9	14.8	8.7	24.5	32.6	17.8	27.2	20.1
120 to 129 pounds	82.9	98.8	121.2	77.6	93.0	76.9	99.5	129.1
130 to 139 pounds	252.4	207.4	190.5	253.1	176.7	218.9	166.2	263.6
140 to 149 pounds	241.1	237.0	264.0	183.7	227.9	189.4	205.6	265.6
150 to 159 pounds	184.6	175.3	181.8	216.3	176.7	159.8	149.3	172.0
160 to 169 pounds	120.5	128.4	121.2	93.9	153.5	159.8	180.5	90.6
170 to 179 pounds	45.2	74.1	56.3	69.4	65.1	76.9	93.9	34.4
180 to 189 pounds	30.1	32.1	26.0	44.9	32.6	35.6	56.3	14.9
190 to 199 pounds	11.3	14.8	17.3	24.5	27.9	41.4	36.6	6.1
200 pounds and over	15.1	17.3	13.0	12.3	14.0	23.7	34.7	3.6
Total	1,000.0	1,000.0	1,000.0	1,000.0	1,000.0	1,000.0	1,000.0	1,000.0

* Ibid.

Proportion of each measurement per thousand of accepted colored recruits *

Chest Measurement	18 yrs. and under	19 yrs.	20 yrs.	21 yrs.	22 yrs.	23 yrs.	24 yrs.	25 yrs.
30 inches and under	1,000.0			10.4	14.9	10.2	8.1	15.0
31 inches				52.1	84.2	51.0	80.6	52.6
32 inches				291.7	188.1	142.9	145.2	165.4
33 inches				354.2	356.4	377.5	266.1	308.2
34 inches				177.1	203.0	244.9	282.3	203.0
35 inches				72.9	118.8	91.8	129.0	105.3
36 inches				31.2	19.8	71.4	56.5	75.2
37 inches				10.4	14.9		24.2	45.1
38 inches						10.2	8.1	22.6
39 inches and over								7.5
Total	1,000.0			1,000.0	1,000.0	1,000.0	1,000.0	1,000.0

Chest Measurement	26 yrs.	27 yrs.	28 yrs.	29 yrs.	30 yrs.	31 yrs.	32 yrs.	33 yrs.
30 inches and under	9.8	9.5		40.0			35.7	47.6
31 inches	58.8	66.7	41.7	80.0		69.0		47.6
32 inches	264.7	123.8	152.8	60.0	102.6	172.4	107.1	95.2
33 inches	254.9	276.2	263.9	240.0	256.4	172.4	142.9	238.1
34 inches	205.9	238.1	263.9	300.0	282.1	206.9	178.6	238.1
35 inches	117.6	114.3	138.9	160.0	128.2	241.4	285.7	142.9
36 inches	39.2	85.7	83.3	80.0	153.8	137.9	71.4	142.9
37 inches	39.2	38.1	41.7		76.9		107.1	
38 inches		47.6					71.4	47.6
39 inches and over	9.8		13.9	40.0				
Total	1,000.0	1,000.0	1,000.0	1,000.0	1,000.0	1,000.0	1,000.0	1,000.0

Chest Measurement	34 yrs.	35 yrs.	36 yrs	37 yrs.	38 yrs.	39 yrs.	40 yrs. and over	Total
30 inches and under	41.7	47.6						13.3
31 inches			90.9		76.9		12.0	54.9
32 inches	41.7	142.9	181.8	200.0	153.8		120.5	163.3
33 inches	166.7	285.7	272.7		153.8	166.7	204.8	283.4
34 inches	291.7	190.5	181.8	400.0	538.5	333.3	144.6	228.4
35 inches	166.7	95.2	90.9	100.0	76.9	166.7	144.6	124.0
36 inches	83.3	95.2	181.8	200.0		250.0	192.8	75.3
37 inches	83.3	142.9					60.2	31.4
38 inches	83.3						48.2	14.9
39 inches and over	41.7			100.0		88.3	72.3	11.0
Total	1,000.0	1,000.0	1,000.0	1,000.0	1,000.0	1,000.0	1,000.0	1,000.0

* Ibid.

Proportion of each measurement per thousand of accepted white recruits—Continued

CHEST MEASUREMENT	18 yrs. and under	19 yrs.	20 yrs.	21 yrs.	22 yrs.	23 yrs.	24 yrs.	25 yrs.
30 inches and under	400.0	346.1	66.7	83.1	28.4	20.7	23.2	14.4
31 inches	100.0	115.4	166.7	98.8	88.8	68.6	57.6	56.2
32 inches	200.0	192.3	233.3	277.2	249.8	209.9	194.8	206.0
33 inches	150.0	192.3	200.0	203.3	193.3	291.3	261.3	248.6
34 inches	150.0	115.4	233.3	172.0	280.3	201.7	218.1	214.5
35 inches		38.5	66.7	80.7	100.9	127.7	140.5	143.1
36 inches			33.3	30.7	38.7	53.9	68.4	71.0
37 inches				10.6	14.5	19.2	23.9	30.6
38 inches				2.6	3.9	4.9	9.2	12.8
39 inches and over				.9	1.4	2.1	2.9	2.7
Total	1,000.0	1,000.0	1,000.0	1,000.0	1,000.0	1,000.0	1,000.0	1,000.0

CHEST MEASUREMENT	26 yrs.	27 yrs.	28 yrs.	29 yrs.	30 yrs.	31 yrs.	32 yrs.	33 yrs.
30 inches and under	14.0	15.0	15.0	9.9	17.8	13.3	8.8	12.8
31 inches	56.0	51.1	38.6	54.0	36.7	47.1	38.3	31.7
32 inches	189.2	178.2	185.0	155.7	155.7	159.0	154.6	139.8
33 inches	247.3	258.2	239.9	244.8	223.6	210.6	213.6	211.6
34 inches	215.6	211.5	218.3	209.7	200.2	201.8	194.4	201.1
35 inches	143.1	144.4	154.9	142.2	173.5	170.8	182.6	169.8
36 inches	84.5	80.0	84.3	97.2	116.8	88.4	109.0	121.7
37 inches	32.7	40.0	34.0	45.9	41.2	48.6	48.6	51.1
38 inches	11.9	15.0	21.6	30.6	28.4	32.4	30.9	44.1
39 inches and over	5.7	6.7	8.5	9.9	11.1	28.0	19.1	17.6
Total	1,000.0	1,000.0	1,000.0	1,000.0	1,000.0	1,000.0	1,000.0	1,000.0

CHEST MEASUREMENT	34 yrs.	35 yrs.	36 yrs.	37 yrs.	38 yrs.	39 yrs.	40 yrs. and over	Total
30 inches and under	16.9	19.8	8.7	12.2	27.9	29.6	5.6	21.6
31 inches	49.0	51.9	39.0	65.3	37.2	41.4	33.8	66.8
32 inches	56.5	123.5	103.9	89.8	111.6	71.0	91.1	203.6
33 inches	297.6	162.9	251.1	175.5	144.2	165.7	157.7	240.3
34 inches	192.1	237.0	255.4	187.8	209.3	147.9	170.0	218.1
35 inches	148.8	140.7	121.2	187.8	120.9	153.8	135.2	127.2
36 inches	114.9	123.5	95.2	98.0	186.1	177.5	120.2	67.5
37 inches	62.2	74.1	64.9	89.8	74.4	118.3	102.3	30.5
38 inches	32.0	29.6	39.0	53.0	37.2	35.5	74.2	14.5
39 inches and over	30.1	37.0	21.6	40.8	51.2	59.2	109.9	10.6
Total	1,000.0	1,000.0	1,000.0	1,000.0	1,000.0	1,000.0	1,000.0	1,000.0

The following figures are taken from McDonald's study of school children in the District of Columbia which included over 16,000 pupils, of whom 5,000 or more were colored. A Kansas city study is also included : *

ALL GIRLS

LIMITS OF DIFFERENT AGES				Total number of pupils	Average height	Average sitting height	Average weight	Average circumference of head
FROM—		TO—						
Yrs.	Mos.	Yrs.	Mos.		Inches	Inches	Lbs.	Inches
5	4	6	6	94	44.23	24.25	43.33	19.23
5	5	6	11	37	43.97	23.87	42.10	20.20
6	5	7	6	375	45.09	24.69	45.74	19.94
6	7	7	6	133	45.40	24.77	44.97	19.92
7	7	8	6	754	47.44	25.46	49.44	20.14
8	7	9	6	883	49.13	26.23	53.67	20.29
9	7	10	6	939	51.20	26.98	58.55	20.43
10	7	11	6	931	53.14	27.82	64.19	20.54
11	7	12	6	876	55.78	29.05	73.20	20.78
12	7	13	6	966	57.91	30.13	81.85	20.95
13	7	14	6	833	60.24	31.44	93.02	21.18
14	7	15	6	655	61.65	32.26	100.38	21.28
15	7	16	6	450	62.40	32.81	105.19	21.38
16	7	17	6	323	62.99	33.04	110.01	21.55
17	7	18	6	151	63.15	33.17	111.50	21.60
17	7	23	6	41	62.91	32.86	111.14	21.60
18	7	19	9	13	64.33	33.70	112.96	21.98
18	7	20	8	66	63.01	33 24	110.72	21.98
				8,520				

ALL COLORED GIRLS

LIMITS OF DIFFERENT AGES				Total number of pupils	Average height	Average sitting height	Average weight	Average circumference of head
FROM—		TO—						
Yrs.	Mos.	Yrs.	Mos.		Inches	Inches	Lbs.	Inches
5	10	6	6	113	43.81	23.72	42.61	19.92
6	7	7	6	248	46.61	24.70	48.63	20.50
7	7	8	6	218	47.91	25.21	53.02	20.51
8	7	9	6	209	49.02	25.74	56.89	20 72
9	7	10	6	250	50.85	26.55	62.89	20.84
10	7	11	6	266	52.94	27.35	68.89	20.87
11	7	12	6	279	54.46	27.92	77.55	20.95
12	7	13	6	270	57.42	29.09	88.40	21.14
13	7	14	6	243	59.56	30.24	98.52	21.48
14	7	15	6	167	60.06	30.74	103.10	21.51
15	7	16	6	129	61.47	31.57	106.97	21 50
16	7	17	6	83	62.25	31.91	112.96	21.74
17	7	18	6	54	62.27	32.27	115.12	21.86
18	7	19	6	20	62.73	33.21	117.75	21 78
19	7	29	11	9	60.44	31.47	109.33	22.14
				2,558				

* Report of United States Commissioner of Education, 1897-98, Vol. I, page 989, ff.

* Report of the United States Commissioner of Education, 1897-98, Vol. I, page 1085.

ALL BOYS

LIMITS OF DIFFERENT AGES				Number of pupils	Average height	Average weight	Average circumference of head
FROM—		TO—					
Yrs.	Mos.	Yrs.	Mos.		Inches	Lbs.	Inches
5	3	6	6	103	44.69	45.24	20.22
6	0	6	6	44	44.75	45.31	20.28
6	7	7	6	532	45.97	47.70	20.45
7	7	8	6	787	47.83	51.47	20.51
8	7	9	6	878	49.74	56.16	20.61
9	7	10	6	930	51.70	61.54	20.73
10	7	11	6	862	53.19	66.26	20.82
11	7	12	6	986	55.14	72.73	20.94
12	7	13	6	926	56.76	79.38	21.01
13	7	14	6	784	59.14	88.27	21.21
14	7	15	6	528	61.79	100.95	21.45
15	7	16	6	345	64.32	113.71	21.67
16	7	17	6	120	65.97	121.18	21.87
16	7	18	6	32	66.45	124.21	22.13
16	7	18	10	22	67.03	123.10	22.12
17	7	18	6	38	67.06	131.99	21.91
18	7	19	6	7	68.73	132.25	22.48
19	7	21	7	28	67.66	135.56	22.34
				7,953			

ALL COLORED BOYS

LIMITS OF DIFFERENT AGES				Total number of pupils	Average height	Average sitting height	Average weight	Average circumference of head
FROM—		TO—						
Yrs.	Mos.	Yrs.	Mos.		Inches	Inches	Lbs.	Inches
5	0	6	6	73	44.17	24.04	43.44	20.24
6	7	7	6	246	46.08	24.73	50.10	20.28
7	7	8	6	288	47.74	25.34	53.99	20.51
8	7	9	6	303	49.26	26.14	59.04	20.67
9	7	10	6	335	51.14	26.51	65.17	20.81
10	7	11	6	271	52.10	26.90	69.44	20.95
11	7	12	6	286	53.94	27.99	75.97	20.87
12	7	13	6	321	56.08	28.46	83.50	21.07
13	7	14	6	282	57.98	29.36	90.90	21.31
14	7	15	6	220	60.09	30.37	99.42	21.41
15	7	16	6	124	63.13	31.25	113.45	21.45
16	7	18	6	131	65.37	32.82	125.42	21.95
18	7	22	11	19	66.16	29.42	131.75	22.16
				2,899	....	....	....	....

RACE IN RELATION TO CEPHALIC INDEX, SENSIBILITY, ETC.*

	No. of persons	Average Age	Dolicho-cephalic	Mesocephalic	Brachy-cephalic	Least sensibility to locality		Strength of grasp		Least sensibility to heat	
						Right wrist	Left wrist	Right hand	Left hand	Right waist	Left waist
		Yr. Mo.	%	%	%	Mm.	Mm.	Kilos	Kilos	°R.	°R.
ALL BOYS:											
White............	526	12 9	11	45	44	16.4	15 5	20.9	19.6	4.17	3.89
Colored..........	33	13 3	32	53	15	14.3	13.9	19.7	18.4	2.07	1.77
ALL GIRLS:											
White............	548	13 1	12	48	40	14.9	13.9	16.8	15.8	4.43	4.06
Colored.........	58	13 1	27	52	21	15.3	14.2	17.3	16.3	2.64	2.47

Kansas City, Mo., School Children (1890)†

White Children

BOYS				GIRLS			
No.	Age	Average height	Average weight	No.	Age	Average height	Average weight
	Years	Inches	Pounds		Years	Inches	Pounds
349	10	52	67.5	400	10	51.68	65.92
395	11	53	·70.96	411	11	52.7	66.2
408	12	56	78.28	469	12	54.015	80.64
293	13	56.6	87.45	311	13	57.43	91.72
347	14	58.6	93.45	366	14	60.31	100.1
133	15	62.4	111.27	313	15	62.04	109.36
129	16	63.93	119.	186	16	65.52	111.16
77	17	64.8	126.6	87	17	62.9	117.11
24	18	66.66	136.83	52	18	63.29	118.92
				24	19	64.2	120.25

Colored Children

BOYS				GIRLS			
No.	Age	Average height	Average weight	No,	Age	Average height	Average weight
	Years	Inches	Pounds		Years	Inches	Pounds
28	10	51	72.7	30	10	49.8	74.56
36	11	53.36	78.25	52	11	52.8	79.85
44	12	53.73	83	61	12	54	82.83
51	13	56	89	62	13	56.85	97.145
29	14	58.88	93.55	44	14	58.75	103.83
33	15	61	112.3	46	15	61.54	110.13
9	16	64.44	121.1	32	16	62.8	117
5	17·	65	130	12	17	66	128

* Report of the United States Commissioner of Education, 1897-98, Vol. I, page 1010.
† Report of the United States Commissioner of Education, 1897-98, Vol. I, page 1108.

The general conclusions from these studies were:

White children have much longer bodies than colored children, and are taller, but the colored children are heavier.

The white boys are taller than the colored boys. In sitting height the difference is very striking, and it would seem to indicate that white boys have comparatively a greater length of trunk than length of legs as compared with colored boys. The colored boys are heavier from age 6 to 15. From 15 to 16 the white boys are heavier.

The colored boys are taller than the colored girls at ages 6, 9, 10, 15 and on. At other ages the girls are taller. In sitting height the boys are taller until 10 and at 12. In weight colored boys are heavier, except from 11 to 16, when the difference between boys and girls is somewhat similar to that in white children, except that this pubertal period begins about a year later and ends a year later than in white children.

The percentage of long-headedness among the colored boys is more than double that of the white boys. This is doubtless due to racial influence.

In colored children the circumference of head in the boys is superior to that of the girls at ages 6 and 11, but inferior at other ages; that is, in general the girls excel the boys in head circumference.

The white boys of American parentage have a larger head circumference than the colored boys from ages 6 to 8; again at about 12, and from 15 to 17; at other ages the colored boys excel. As the numbers compared are large this can hardly be accidental, yet we know of no reason for this alternate increase and decrease between the boys of two races, for in the case of the girls there is no such alternation.

Comparing white girls of American parentage and colored girls as to circumference of head, the colored girls show quite a marked increase from about 6 to 10 and from 14 to 15. It may be noted here that these periods of marked increase correspond to the periods of increase of colored boys over white boys; that is, from about 7 to 11 and 13 to 15. The colored girls excel the white girls in circumference of head at all ages. Comparing colored girls with all white girls, the colored girls have a larger circumference of head at all ages except at 6.

As circumference of head increases mental ability increases. (A note adds, "among those of the same race.")

Colored children are much more sensitive to heat than white children. This probably means that their power of discrimination is much better and not that they suffer more from heat.

McDonald's studies referred to above give a few psycho-physical measurements:

	BRIGHT		DULL		AVERAGE	
	Total	Per Cent	Total	Per Cent	Total	Per Cent
All boys......................	2,899	38.72	1,214	16.22	3,373	45.06
All girls......................	3,296	38.70	917	10.77	4,304	50.53
All colored boys	1,257	43.36	486	16.76	1,156	39.88
All colored girls	1,751	68.45	673	26.31	134	5.24

MENTAL DIVISIONS		All studies	Algebra	Arithmetic	Drawing	Geography	History	Language and English	Manual labor, sewing	Mathematics	Music	Penmanship	Reading	Science, botany	Spelling
		%	%	%	%	%	%	%	%	%	%	%	%	%	%
Boys of American parentage	Bright....	51	36	44	34	35	44	38	29	50	24	28	43	44	33
	Dull......	14	19	18	22	13	15	19	21	16	29	27	21	12	24
	Average..	35	45	38	44	52	41	43	50	34	47	45	36	44	43
Girls of American parentage	Bright....	45	49	37	35	36	41	46	40	34	40	40	54	45	48
	Dull......	9	11	19	17	12	15	10	9	20	10	13	11	15	14
	Average..	46	40	44	48	52	44	44	51	46	50	47	35	40	38
Colored boys	Bright....	46	61	54	47	45	51	42	....	44	36	45	49	25	41
	Dull......	23	8	20	17	13	11	17	....	31	19	17	22	43	23
	Average..	31	31	26	36	42	38	41	....	25	45	38	29	32	36
Colored girls	Bright....	69	65	60	40	62	64	63	....	....	49	54	17	31	59
	Dull......	28	19	29	25	25	22	22	....	....	14	19	21	11	23
	Average..	3	16	11	35	13	14	15	....	....	37	27	62	58	18

One manifest cause of physical differences between white and colored people in the United States is difference in physical nourishment. The studies of the United States Department of Agriculture,* although few in number, indicate the following results:

Dietaries of Negroes and Others

	Cost	Protein	Fat	Carbo-hydrates	Fuel Value
Average of 19 Negro families in Virginia......	11 cts.	109 gms	159gms	444 gms.	3.745
Average of 20 Negro families in Alabama	8 "	62 "	132 "	436 "	3.270
Average of 4 Mexican families in New Mexico	8 "	64 "	71 "	610 "	3.550
Average of 14 mechanics' families..............	19 "	103 "	150 "	402 "	3.465
Average of 10 farmers' families		97 "	130 "	467 "	3.515
Average of 14 professional men's families	28 cts.	104 "	125 "	423 "	3.325
Tentative standard for man at moderate work	....	125 "	....	....	3.500

With regard especially to the Alabama diets, which represent the diet of the Black Belt, the report says:·

Comparing these Negro dietaries with other dietary standards it will be seen that—

(1) The quantities of protein are very small; roughly speaking, the food of these Negroes furnished one-third to three-fourths as much protein as are called for in the current physiological standards and as are actually found in the dietaries of well-fed whites in the United States and well-fed people in Europe. They were indeed, no larger than have been found in the dietaries of the very poor factory operatives and laborers in Germany and the laborers and beggars in Italy.

(2) In fuel value the Negro dietaries compare quite favorably with those of well-to-do people of the laboring classes in Europe and the United States.

(3) The marked peculiarity of the Negro dietaries, namely, their lack of protein, is shown in the nutritive ratios. While the proportion of protein to fuel ingredients in the dietary standards and in the food of well-fed wage-workers ranges from 1:5 to 1:7 or 8, and is about 1:5.5 or 1:6 in the dietary

* United States Department of Agriculture, Dietary Studies, etc., in Alabama, 1897; do., in Virginia, 1899.

standards, the nutritive ratio of the Negro dietaries range from 1:7 to 1:16. Leaving out two quite exceptional cases, the lowest was 1:10 and the average 1:11.8.

6. Some Psychological Considerations on the Race Problem*

By Dr. Herbert A. Miller

Race problems are pressing hard upon most of the nations of the world. They are part of the general social question, which is growing more and more important. The first difficulty in understanding these problems is to find a clear definition of racial lines. External comparison is not enough to create a boundary between different peoples when they happen to have the same spiritual interests, i. e., the ultimate differences are psychical rather than physical. At any rate the psycho-physical comparison of races is offering facts to scientific investigation in a field as yet almost untouched. Wherever there is a heterogeneous people there is need for exact knowledge of the capacities and possibilities of its constituents.

The cause of the backwardness of the so-called lower races is variously attributed to the influence of environment of all sorts, and to natural incapacity. These points of view differ so absolutely in kind that it is necessary to make an earnest effort to analyze the relation between the two, in order that energy may not be wasted in an effort to reach common conclusions from absolutely different premises. At present both opinions are chiefly based on assumptions. Each may accord with actual conditions, but each involves a very different attitude towards the course of human development: the one assuming that, in general, equal results follow equal conditions, and that the apparent differences are due to unequal home training, economic conditions, and social ideals; the other, that, whatever the conditions, the possibilities are not the same. Between these two extremes the discussion of the Negro, and to some extent of the Indian in the United States, has been hopelessly mangled, and upon them practical educational theories have been based. Most of the sympathizers with industrial education for the Negro believe that such education is fitted to his capacity even more than to his needs.

A knowledge of the influence of environment is necessary for the understanding of a race, but it is not fundamental in drawing race lines, since environment must act upon something, and any conclusion as to its influence involves a consideration of that upon which it acts. Other facts are brought in through anthropology, in which anatomical comparisons have been supplemented with general psychological observations which have been made, unfortunately, by men of no special psychological training, and therefore have questionable value. By a purely psychological method alone can exact scientific data be obtained on what is really a psychological problem.

* Reprinted by permission from Bibliotheca Sacra, April, 1906.

Psychology has a comprehensive and a restricted field. In the former, it includes the total complex activity of mental life; in the latter, it describes only the isolated elements of the complex. The complex activity is the reaction of the psychic organism to the meaning of life. This is the popular meaning of the term "psychology." Any fact of the mind, whether intellectual, moral, or spiritual, is referred to this category. It cannot be scientific, for it does not lend itself to analysis. It is an attitude of the mind which is the result of many psychic elements working together, plus the practical theory of the universe which the individual happens to hold. This varying combination of influences which shape every attitude makes classification impossible, and to call it psychology takes one but little nearer scientific explanation. The uncertainty of complexity makes it desirable to seek relatively isolated elements. These will be component parts of the whole, but will have a meaning limited to their own functioning: e. g., the memory of legal terms to the lawyer varies with the importance of their bearing upon his cases. But memory of nonsense syllables has an interest limited solely to their interest as a memory exercise. In other words, the quality of memory may be different in different individuals, but no adequate test can be made where the interest and attention differ. Unrelated figures and letters having a minimum of interest offer an approximate condition of equality for the comparison of the memory of different individuals. The simplest element of mind that can be tested is, to be sure, more or less complex, being made up of, as yet, unanalyzable elements, but the variation of the relatively simple states is much less than that between the complex totalities. Two brothers may differ but slightly in capacity, but responsibility falling upon one will develop entirely different activity. In the simple states can be found regular and predictable variation; but in the complex, developed by the business of life, it is accidental and incalculable.

Psychophysics aims to describe these relatively simple states without relating them to their value in life. The results are meagre, but they are the only ones that can have any scientific value, because of their comparative invariability, while the larger reactions are made up of constantly changing meanings of ideals. The spirit or purpose behind the act is what determines its quality; in other words, it is the personality interpreting the value of the act to the organism as a whole. The performance of the act, on the other hand, depends on the fundamental capacity of the organ which performs it. Thus desire for study, and capacity for accomplishment, are quite different things. Again and more obviously, it is this interpretation of the value of life that makes one man moral and the other immoral, though both may have equal psychophysical capacity. To conclude, from the manifestations of immorality among the Negroes, or from their failure to recognize certain social conventions, that the Negro is incapable of morality or of adaptation to the social demand, is a conclusion based upon inadequate evidence. Morality and social adaptation are the result of the interpretation of the value of a situation, and not a necessary development of inherent capacity. Therefore, not until different races have had exactly the same history can any valid conclusion be drawn as to their relative psychophysical capacity if mere observation is used. This does not mean that there is no such a thing as race characteristics, but that there are elements in interpretation that are independent of race. This, however, is a philosophical question. My point is that there is something that cannot be put to empirical test in all practical activity.

Space fails me to give any account of the many psychological observations that have been made concerning primitive people. Suffice it to say that there have been many things said; and there are great differences of opinion,—from those who see the savage little removed from the possibilities of a brute, to those who think the difference between the highest and lowest man is very slight. It may be the uncivilized instead of the uncivilizable mind that is described. The fact that some observers find that the ideas are sensuous instead of abstract may arise out of the demands of the environment. It may not call for anything except sensuous ideas. Again, Indians and Negroes are said to lack the power of attention, and hence the door of learning is closed to them. Some travelers say that in Africa a few sentences will weary a native, and therefore conversation cannot be held with him. But attention is not merely a natural possession. In our schools the habit has to be cultivated by all sorts of subterfuges from the guardhouse to the elective system. According to the doctrine of "interest," on which the elective system is based, we find the savage giving perfect attention to his hunt. He has been under no necessity of developing the power of abstraction. Many of the arguments concerning primitive psychology arise from the logic of *post hoc, ergo propter hoc.* Africans are said to think it foolish to have manufactured articles when it would have been quite easy to get along without them, but what they *think* is no criterion of what they would think if they knew more. We can parallel that indifference in the pure Anglo-Saxons who are known as Highlanders, who find it very difficult to see the sense of the attempt to bring them back into the fold of civilization. A family in the Tennessee Mountains had but one pan, which was used for cooking, serving food, and as a family wash-basin. A new pan was presented, but was hung unused on the wall. When remonstrated with for not using it, the woman said, "Aint we uns got one pan?" The idea of progress is not inherent in any man, but is the social heritage derived from a long study of the meaning of the world.

I do not wish to be understood as claiming that race characteristics are not definite and important, but anthropologists have based their conclusion as to the difference in race levels upon the degree to which they *suppose* the race to have evolved. Their teachings have been eagerly grasped by the general public as a scientific support of their belief that the Negro is inferior to the whites.

I cannot go into the bearings of the doctrine of evolution upon the question, but, accepting the doctrine of Weissmann, would add, in the words of a writer on evolution: "Civilization and education are exter-

nal and not internal, extrinsic and not intrinsic forces. . . . Civilization has changed his surroundings, but has it changed *the man?* * This
is an important question, but progress is not evolution in the strict sense
of the word. It depends on subjective influences. As John Morley
says: "The world grows better in the moderate degree that it does
grow better because people wish that it should, and take the right
steps to make it better. Evolution is not a force but a process, not a
cause but a law. It explains the source and marks the immovable limitations of social energy. But social energy can never be superseded by
evolution or anything else." Psychology as I use it has the narrower
meaning, which makes it parallel with evolution as used by Mr. Morley.
It can aim to study the "immovable limitations," but it is utterly impossible for it to give a standard for measuring the social energy which
is the force that makes most of the visible results. We can study the
perceptions, but we can do very little with the conceptions, for they
form the unanalyzed elements.· In conception we get an ethical environment which throws light on every situation, and thus distinguishes
man from animal; we deal with every practical situation at something
more than its face value in pleasure and pain.

We find this influence as applied to the Negro summed up excellently
by one of the race speaking of his people: "They must perpetually
discuss the Negro problem, must live, move and have their being in it,
and interpret all else in its light or darkness. From the double life that
every American Negro must live as a Negro and American, as swept
on by the current of the nineteenth century while struggling in the
eddies of the fifteenth—from this must arise a powerful self-conscious-
ness and a moral hesitancy which is almost fatal to self-confidence.
Today the young Negro of the South who would succeed cannot be
frank and outspoken, but rather is daily tempted to be silent and wary,
politic and sly. His real thoughts, his real aspirations, must be guarded
in whispers; he must not criticize, he must not complain. Patience
and adroitness must in these growing black youth, replace impulse,
manliness, and courage. . . . At the same time, through books and
periodicals, discussions and lectures he is intellectually awakened. In
the conflict some sink, some rise." † This description of the conditions
of real life indicates the impossibility of drawing psychological conclusions from practical reactions. We cannot fairly compare a black and
a white artisan when the latter has pride in his work and the other an
indifference due, in part at least, to the consciousness of his social position. Still there may be differences due solely to race. I would like to
tell how I think this difference in attitude complicates any estimate of
moral and cultural possibilities, but I must hasten on to indicate briefly
my method of direct experimentation, which, though utterly incomplete, yet seems to me to be the direction in which this subject must
be pursued if we wish to get the truth unhampered by the prejudice of

---

* H. W. Conn: Method of Evolution, p. 212.
† DuBois: Souls of Black Folk.

one's geographical position. In a word I aimed to make tests of the simplest sort upon people of as nearly the same condition as possible. The subjects were pupils in schools of comparable grades, and numbered 2,488 Negroes, 520 Indians, and 1,493 whites, including 596 Highlanders in the Tennessee and Kentucky mountains. All the tests were given by myself under as nearly as possible the same conditions and without variation. I can only name the tests, and say that they were devised for the purpose of giving them to groups, and that all my subjects came in groups which would average about forty in number. A careful record of age and sex and grade was kept, and the comparison considered those facts. My word for the reliability of the work must be accepted, and I hope before very long to publish a full description of the details. The tests were: (1) quickness and accuracy of perception; (2) disconnected memory, both auditory and visual, as tested by figures and letters exposed and read; (3) logical memory, tested by reproducing a story; (4) rational instinct, as shown in the immediate detection of fallacies; (5) suggestibility, as shown by the judgment of the size of equal circles on which there were numbers of different denominations; and, finally, (6) color preference.

I can give at present only some representative averages, which are interesting, and on the whole fairly indicative of the results obtained by a more complete interpretation of the figures. With the exception of the first table, which gives the actual number, all the results are in percentages. The graphic representation of the figures shows some things that cannot appear from the mere averages. Averages for the quickness of perception:

	MALE		FEMALE	
	No.	*Av.*	*No.*	*Av.*
Whites	355	31.17	236	33.61
Indians	160	31.81	120	34.77
Negroes	377	32.35	412	34.08

The average is misleading, as the plot shows that the larger number of Indians are quicker than the larger number of either of the other races, but both aspects of the figures are consistent in showing that there is but slight difference in races in the same sex, but that there is a consistent difference in the quickness of the sexes, the females being the quicker. In disconnected memory I had five tests, and two facts are striking: the superiority of visual over auditory memory, and the consistent but slight superiority of the females, but the race differences are small. It did not seem to be unfair to combine all the persons of the same race for all the five tests in one average, and thus make it possible to multiply the number of cases by five. I do this because of the alleged superiority of the Negroes for so-called rote memory.

Male and Female		*Auditory and Visual Memory*			
No. Whites	2,960	Av. 55	Av. deviation 19		
" Indians	1,362	" 53.3	" " 17.5		
" Negroes	4,098	" 56.8	" " 19		

The conclusion seems to me to be that the differences are very slight. The variation shows that a large part of each group overlaps the others.

At the same time the similarity of the deviations shows that the averages are fairly representative.

Let me give the results of the tests for logical memory:

	No. Males	Av. %	No. Females	Av. %
Whites	343	40.27	22.)	38.9
Indians	101	37 7	88	35.17
Negroes	3.)4	40.45	427	37.49

Here the difference between the sexes is the reverse of that appearing in disconnected memory. There is almost no difference between the Whites and the Negroes; the Indians are not strictly comparable, for reasons that I cannot enter upon at this time.

Finally I would like to give you some idea of the results of the color choice test. I gave this to a larger number than any of the others. I performed these tests in two different years, and all in the same manner, except that in the second year I changed from Milton Bradley colors to Prang colors, with very interesting results. Out of the Milton Bradley colors I had 13 against 12 of the Prang. With the Milton Bradley colors 42.1 per cent of the white girls chose red and 19 per cent blue; and 42.01 per cent of the white boys preferred blue and 17.6 red. The number of persons was 380 and 112. Of the Negroes, numbering 201 girls and 267 boys, 3.6 per cent of the girls and 3.4 per cent of the boys chose red, and 57.1 per cent of the girls and 52.1 per cent of the boys chose blue. These facts are interesting, but quite different from those with the Prang colors. Putting red and red-violet together, we have the following table:

	Red and Red-Violet	Blue
W. M	11.4 %	50.4 %
W. F	27	41.4
I. M	20 6	35.5
I. F	49.4	18.5
N. M	7.3	30
N. F	17.1	41.6

Two things appear from this. That there is a racial difference in color preference, and that it makes a good deal of difference what colors are used. Preference for red does not mean for any red, and if the one presented is not quite right another color will be chosen. For the other colors than red and blue the figures are nearly parallel. It is a surprise to most people that the Negro does not take the red, but he consistently avoids it. The colors that we see in life are not so much the result of psychophysical as of social reaction. The one fact that stands out clearly in this investigation is the smallness of the differences between the Negroes and whites within the range of these experiments. In general we find the Indians somewhat lower in their averages than the other two races. I do not suggest the possible inferiority of the Indians; but there is not an iota of evidence to show that they are superior to Negroes. This is contrary to the general assumption.

We must not conclude from these tests that there are no psychophysical differences between the races; in fact, we do find some tendencies of divergence, and admit the possibility of many more. The complex of all these tendencies gives the temperamental tone, which obviously does characterize sexes and races. The differences, however, are of degree rather than of kind. It is not sufficient to make a sharp line of demarkation. In the curves which represent the figures we find that the large mass of the persons of all the races are included within the common space. So far as the original endowment of the Negro is concerned, I would conclude that there is nothing in kind to differentiate him particularly as a different psychic being from the Caucasian. I have not entered upon the prevailing difference of opinion that exists upon this point.

In estimating the psychological development of a person or race, no one should be spurned for the peculiarities that he possesses. Some racial tendencies have undoubtedly been developed by natural selection, but we are accustomed to make an assessment in contemporary psychic values, and consider primitive those that do not fit the present social order. In the process of the universe a race may have a contribution to make through its very peculiarities; and it may at least find in these peculiarities a means of working out its own salvation. Thus the vivid imagination which I found in the Negro, and the unquestioned musical genius of the Negro, are to be given a value that we cannot estimate. The transition from the morning school song of the Negroes to that of equally untrained whites is like going from a symphony to a hand-- organ. No one will question this gift of music in the Negro; and may we not expect from it, and other gifts which do not stand out so obviously, some social contribution from this and every race? We no longer hear much about the mental inferiority of women; but we are accepting the fact that the two sexes have different natural aptitudes, and are adapting the educational possibilities to meet those aptitudes. This should be the case with different races. But let us not jump to conclusions as to what these aptitudes are; for we are likely to judge from present rather than future social valuations. Perhaps from some such method as I have undertaken we can learn more of the differences between individuals.

Finally, class and race as well as sex problems arise from lack of spiritual affinity between the groups or individuals concerned. They lack "consciousness of kind." This phrase resolves itself into consciousness of the same kind of ideals or purposes. A social relation exists as soon as there are common purposes. If the ideals or purposes differ there will be antagonism. The first cause of this difference is due to some superficial accidental condition, such as the customs of the tribe or the color of the skin, which stand as symbols of the sameness of kind. That these external symbols are only accidental is proved by the ease with which they are laid aside when some deeper principle draws men together, bridging chasms that had seemed impassable. Mere propinquity will often do it. This accidental element in the race problem makes it no less real, but the purpose of science and philosophy is not to get the temporal and the accidental, but rather the universal and essential. The purpose of education and social progress is to make the accidental give way to the essential, and to let each individual stand for his true worth to society; then the problems as they now confront us will cease to exist.

7. The Increase of the Negro-American

The Negro element in the United States, classing all mulattoes as Negroes (except those who pass as white), has increased as follows:*

Negro population 1790 to 1900

CENSUS	Negro popula-tion	INCREASE OF NEGRO POPU-TION DURING—				Per cent of in-crease of the white popu-lation dur-ing—	
		Preceding 10 years		Preceding 20 years		Pre-ceding 10 yrs.	Pre-ceding 20 yrs.
		No.	*Per cent*	*No.*	*Per cent*		
Continental United States.							
1900................	8,833,994	1,345,318	18.0	2,253,201	34.2	21.2	53.9
1890 †..........................	7,488,676	....	.....	....	.....	......	......
1890 ‡..........................	7,470,040	889,247	13.5	....	....	26.7	......
1880............................	6,580,793	1,700,784	34.9	2,138,963	48.2	29.2	61.2
1870............................	4,880,009	438,179	9.9	....	....	24.8	......
1860............................	4,441,830	803,022	22.1	1,568,182	54.6	37.7	89.7
1850............................	3,638,808	765,160	26.6	....	....	37.7	......
1840............................	2,873,648	545,006	23.4	1,101,962	62.2	34.7	80.5
1830............................	2,328,642	556,986	31.4	....	....	33.9	......
1820............................	1,771,656	393,848	28.6	763,619	76.8	34.2	82.7
1810............................	1,377,808	375,771	37.5	....	....	36.1	......
1800............................	1,002,037	244,829	32.3	....	....	35.8	......
1790............................	757,208	....	.....	....	.....	......	......

Wilcox gives a simpler table derived from this, together with a correction of the erroneous censuses of 1870 and 1890, and a prophecy as to the future increase of Negroes:§

DATE	Number: Unit, 10,000	Increase in—		Per cent of increase	
		10 years	20 years	10 years	20 years
1790.......	76	....	....	....	....
1800.......	100	24	....	32.3	....
1810.......	138	38	....	37.5	....
1820.......	177	39	77	28.6	76.8
1830.......	233	56	..^........	31.4	....
1840.......	287	54	110	23.4	62.2
1850.......	364	77	....	26.6	....
1860.......	444	80	157	22.1	54.6
1870.......	541	97	....	21.7	....
1880.......	658	117	214	21.7	48 2
1890.......	770	112	....	17.0	....
1900.	883	113	225	14 7	34.2
1920.......	‖1,150	....	....	....	30.2
1940.......	1,451	....	....	....	26.2
1960.......	1,773	....	....	....	22.2
1980.......	2,096	....	....	....	18.2
2000.......	2,394	....	....	....	14.2

* Twelfth Census, Bulletin 8, p. 29.

† Includes population of Indian Territory and Indian reservations.

‡ Excludes population of Indian Territory and Indian reservations.

§ Quarterly Journal of Economics, August, 1905.

‖ These and the following figures estimated on Wilcox's percentages.

Wilcox thus thinks that there will be less than 25,000,000 Negroes in the United States at the beginning of the third millenium. Other estimates place this number as high as 60,000,000, while a conservative mean would be perhaps 35,000,000. The data upon which guesses are based are the birth and death rates. No reliable birth statistics exist. Assuming the substantial correctness of the death rate, the Twelfth Census estimates the excess of births as follows:

Increase in native population, 1890-1900, and excess of births per 1,000 of population, by classes *

	NATIVE WHITE		COLORED
	Native Parents	Foreign Parents	
UNITED STATES................	19.5	36.5	17.8
Northeastern Division	3.8	39.6	10.1
Central and Northern Divisions	20.0	36.0	10.2
Southern Division	24.1	27.4	19.1
Western Division	25.9	40.3	0.2

A more accurate method is a comparison of the number of children with the number of women of child-bearing age. For the whites these figures go back to 1830:

Number of white children under 5 years of age to 1,000 white females 15 to 49 years of age, by states and territories: 1830–1900 †

	Number of white children under 5 years of age to 1,000 white females 15-49 years of age							
	1900	1890	1880	1870	1860	1850	1840	1830
Continental United States .	465	473	537	562	627	613	744	781

For colored children the data only go back to 1850:

Number of children under 5 years of age to 1,000 females 15 to 44 years of age for the Continental United States ‡

	Total	White	§Colored	Excess of colored
1900............	474	465	543	78
1890............	485	473	574	101
1880............	559	537	706	169
1870............	572	562	641	79
1860............	634	627	675	48
1850............	626	613	694	81

* Twelfth Census, Vol. III, page 51.
† Twelfth Census, Bulletin No. 22.
‡ Ibid.
§ Negro, Indian and Mongolian.

A more detailed presentation follows:

Number and per cent of children under 10 and 5 years of age, respectively, in the Negro, Indian and Mongolian population, and decrease in per cent during the preceding 10 years, 1830-1900 *

CENSUS	Per cent of Negro, Indian and Mongolian population.		DECREASE IN PER CENT			
			Under 10 years of age during—		Under 5 years of age during—	
	Under 10 yrs. of age	*Under 5 years of age*	*Preceding 10 years*	*Preceding 20 years*	*Preceding 10 years*	*Preceding 20 years*
Continental United States.						
1900	27.1	13.6	1.1	4.8	0.2	2.9
1890	28.2	13.8	3.7	‡3.8	2.7	‡0.5
1880	31.9	16.5	‡7.5	‡1.6	‡3.2	‡0.5
1870	24.4	13.3	5.9	6.9	2.7	2.2
1860	30.3	16.0	1.0	2.9	0.5	
1850	31.3	16.5	1.9	2.9		
1840	33.2		1.0			
1830	34.2					

Number and per cent of children under 10 and 5 years of age, respectively, in the white population, and decrease in per cent during 10 years: 1800 to 1900 *

CENSUS	Per cent of white population		DECREASE IN PER CENT			
			Under 10 years of age during—		Under 5 years of age during—	
	Under 10 yrs. of age	*Under 5 yrs. of age*	*Preceding 10 years*	*Preceding 20 years*	*Preceding 10 years*	*Preceding 20 years*
Continental United States.						
1900	23.3	11.9	0.4	2.6	0.1	1.5
1890	23.7	12.0	2.2	2.7	1.4	2.1
1880	25.9	13.4	0.5	2.5	0.7	1.9
1870	26.4	14.1	2.0	2.2	1.2	0.7
1860	28.4	15.3	0.2	3.2	0.5	2.1
1850	28.6	14.8	3.0	3.9	2.6	3.2
1840	31.6	17.4	0.9	1.8	0.6	
1830	32.5	18.0	0.9	1.9		
1820	33.4		1.0	1.0		
1810	31.4					
1800	34.4					

For city and country the figures are:

---

* Twelfth Census, Bulletin No. 22.

† Increase.

Number of children under 5 years of age to 1,000 females 15 to 44 years of age in cities having at least 25,000 inhabitants and in smaller cities or country districts. by main geographic divisions, and the ratio of those numbers to the number for the whole division taken as 100: 1900 **

DIVISION OR RACE	Number of children under 5 years of age to 1,000 females 15-44 years of age: 1900			Ratio to No. in whole division taken as 100, of No.—			Difference in ratio
	Total	In cities having at least 25,000 inhabitants	In smaller cities or country districts		In cities having at least 25,000 inhabitants	In smaller cities or country districts	
Total population:							
Continental United States	518	390	572		75.3	110.4	35.1
White population:							
Continental United States	508	399	559		78.5	110.0	31.5
Negro, Indian and Mongolian populations:							
Continental United States	585	260	651		44.4	111.3	66.9

The conclusions from these figures are:

1 The Negro birth rate exceeds and has always exceeded the white birth rate.

2. The Negro birth rate decreased slightly from 1850 to 1870, then increased to 1880, and has since rapidly decreased.

It may be added that of the native stocks of America the Negro is by far the most prolific, the only exception being the Southern whites during the last decade, where increasing economic prosperity has increased marriages and children to an unusual degree, while storm and stress has harried the Negroes.

YEAR	Children under 5 and women 15-44	
	Southern whites	*Southern Negroes*
1850	695	705
1860	682	688
1870	601	661
1880	656	737
1890	580	601
1900	581	577

Turning now to the age composition of the Negro-Americans:

The simplest and probably the most significant single expression of the age constitution of the population is the median age. This is the age with reference to which the population can be divided into halves—that is, half of the population are younger and half are older than the median age. †

---

* Twelfth Census, Bulletin No. 22.

† Twelfth Census, Bulletin 13, page 21.

Median age of the population classified by sex, general nativity and race, for persons of known age in Continental United States: 1900*

CLASS OF POPULATION	Both Sexes	Males	Females
AGGREGATE	*22.85*	*23.29*	*22.43*
Native born	20.10	20.20	20.02
Foreign born	38.42	38.71	38 03
Total white	23.36	23.82	22.91
Native white	20.22	20.33	20.12
Native white—native parents	21.10	21.27	20.93
Native white—foreign parents	18.05	17.99	18.11
Foreign white	38.43	38.71	38.04
Total colored	19.70	19.97	19.46
Negro	19.45	19.45	19.44

The median age of Negroes has increased as follows:

Median age of the colored † population, classified, Continental United States: 1790 to 1900 ‡

1900...... 19.70	1870...... 18.49	1840...... 17.27
1890...... 17.83	1860...... 17.65	1830...... 16.90
1880...... 18.01	1850...... 17.33	1820...... 17.75

The general age composition is as follows by percentages: §

YEAR	NATIVE WHITES			COLORED		
	Under 15	*15–59*	*60 and over*	*Under 15*	*15–59*	*60 and over*
1880	42.6	52.9	4.9	44.2	51 2	4.6
1890	40.0	54.8	5.2	42.1	53.3	4.6
1900	39.0	55.8	5.2	39.5	55.6	4.9

A most interesting matter is a comparison of the sex distribution of whites and blacks in America:

Proportion of males and females in every 10,000 ‖

SEX

DATE	NEGROES		WHITES	
	Male	*Female*	*Male*	*Female*
1820	5,082	4,918	5,080	4,920
1830	5,074	4,926	5,077	4,923
1840	5,014	4,986	5,090	4,910
1850	4,978	5,022	5,104	4,896
1860	4,990	5,010	5,116	4,844
1870	4,905	5,095	5,056	4,944
1880	4,942	5,057	5,088	4,912
1890	4,986	5,014	5,121	4,879
1900	4,969	5,030	5,108	4,892

The influence of the slave-trade, slavery and serfdom, is here easily traced. The excess of colored women in cities is noticeable because of their greater economic opportunity there.

---

*Twelfth Census, Bulletin 13, page 21.   † Includes Indians and Mongolians.

‡ Twelfth Census, Bulletin 13, page 22.   § Ibid., p. 26.   ‖ Twelfth Census, Bulletin 14.

8. The Sick and Defective

There is much uncertainty as to the purely racial differences in human liability to disease. Ripley sums up our general knowledge today as follows: *

Three diseases are peculiar to the white race and to civilization—namely, consumption, syphilis, and alcoholism, there being marked differences in the predisposition of each of the barbarous races for them, which often vary inversely with the degree of civilization they have attained:

The European races in their liability to consumption stand midway between the Mongol and the Negro, climatic conditions being equal.

The pure Mongolian stock seems to be almost exempt from its ravages.

The Negro even in the tropics is especially subject to all affections of the lungs. The black races have in general less fully developed chests and less respiratory power than the European race.

They are consequently exceedingly sensitive to atmospheric changes, and are severely handicapped in any migration for this reason. Buchner distinguishes between "ectogenous" and "endogenous" diseases: the former due to environment, as malaria; the latter from within, as in tuberculosis. He avers that the white races more easily fall a prey to the first, the Negroes to the second. Certain facts, notably the relative immunity of the African aborigines from septicæmia, seem to give probability to this.

Almost invariably, where the European succumbs to bilious or intestinal disorders, the Negro falls a victim to diseases of the lungs even in the tropics.

The predisposition of the Negro for elephantiasis and tetanus, his sole liability to the sleeping sickness, so severe that in some localities the black is utterly useless as a soldier, his immunity from cancer and his liability to skin diseases in general, together with his immunity from yellow fever and bilious disorders, are well-recognized facts in anthropology.

[As to syphilis] probably brought by Europeans to America and to New Guinea and by them disseminated in Polynesia, this disease seems to be unknown in Central Africa to any extent. In fact, it dies out naturally in the interior of that continent even when introduced, while it kills the American aborigines at sight. The American Negroes, however, are seemingly very prone to it.

For the Negro-American the best creditable figures are those of the United States army, as follows:

Ratio per 1,000 of applicants for enlistment in the United States army rejected after physical examination

		Accepted	Rejected	Declined
1901	White	624	289	87
	Colored	648	283	69
1902	White	659	256	85
	Colored	786	172	42
1903	White	620	290	90
	Colored	636	304	60
1904	White	658	257	84
	Colored	665	275	59

The Negro candidates for admission seem to be in better physical condition than the whites.

* Ripley, p. 564.

Those rejected show the following racial differences:

Causes of rejection among candidates for United States army: ratio per 1,000 examined

1901

Number examined	White, 56,894	Colored. 1,888

CAUSES OF REJECTION	Ratio per 1,000	Ratio per 1,000
Venereal diseases	19.65	53.50
Other infectious diseases	3.50	4.77
Diseases of nutrition, general	2.27	
Diseases of the nervous system	2.88	.53
Diseases of the digestive system	20.09	15.89
Diseases of the circulatory system	39.09	28.07
Diseases of the respiratory organs	2.86	1.59
Diseases of the genito-urinary system	28.95	15.36
Diseases of the lymphatic system and ductless glands	1.27	3.71
Diseases of the muscles, bones, and joints	4.34	2.12
Diseases of the integument and subcutaneous connective tissue	5.11	5.30
Diseases of the eye	41.67	24.89
Diseases of the ear	4.15	2.65
Diseases of the nose	.90	
Hernia	13.02	12.18
Other injuries	2.50	1.06
Overheight	.02	
Underheight	2.74	3.71
Overweight and obesity	.46	
Underweight	14.40	7.42
Imperfect physique	47.84	33.37
Mental insufficiency	.47	

1902

Number examined	White, 42,188	Colored, 3,035

CAUSES OF REJECTION	Ratio per 1,000	Ratio per 1,000
Venereal diseases	21.57	34.60
Other infectious diseases	3.08	1.98
Diseases of nutrition, general	1.23	.99
Diseases of the nervous system	1.83	.99
Diseases of the digestive system	19.10	8.57
Diseases of the circulatory system	31.15	15.82
Diseases of the respiratory organs	3.15	.66
Diseases of the genito-urinary system	24.04	9.55
Diseases of the lymphatic system and ductless glands	1.49	3.29
Diseases of the muscles, bones, and joints	2.92	.99
Diseases of the integument and subcutaneous connective tissue	5.41	4.28
Diseases of the eye	33.52	18.12
Diseases of the ear	3.44	2.30
Diseases of the nose	.47	.66
Hernia	11.02	8.24
Other injuries	2.01	1.32
Overheight	.05	
Underheight	.95	.99
Overweight and obesity	.38	.66
Underweight	11.50	2.96
Imperfect physique	38.40	19.11
Mental insufficiency	.72	

1903 Number examined	White, 30,634	Colored, 1,271
CAUSES OF REJECTION	Ratio per 1,000	Ratio per 1,000
Special causes		
Physical debility	0.24	
Tuberculosis of lungs and other organs	4.67	7.08
Imperfect vision	29.83	11.80
Heart disease	30.00	14.95
Goiter	.20	
Varicose veins, varicocele, and hemorrhoids	40.96	14.16
Hernia	12.40	3.93
Flat feet	4.34	.79
General causes [Excluding those above.]		
Epidemic diseases	.03	
Venereal diseases	26.11	51.14
Other general diseases	.55	
Diseases of the nervous system	.65	
Diseases of the eye	2.42	2.36
Diseases of the ear	4.57	3.15
Diseases of the circulatory system	.76	.79
Diseases of the respiratory system	5.19	8.65
Diseases of the digestive system	16.29	8.65
Diseases of the genito-urinary system	4.77	3.93
Diseases of the skin and cellular tissue	8.00	7.87
Diseases of the organs of locomotion	12.04	8.65
Injuries (external causes)	3.46	
Overheight	.03	
Underheight	3.07	3.15
Overweight and obesity	.65	
Underweight	12.93	8.65
Imperfect physique	17.23	8.65
Mental insufficiency	1.40	3.93

1904	White	Colored
CAUSES OF REJECTION	Ratio per 1,000	Ratio per 1,000
Venereal diseases	100.46	170.78
Heart disease	94.85	68.31
Defects of vision	92.37	49.33
Varicocele	71.54	55.03
Hernia	55.92	64.51
Varicose veins	40.22	13.28
Diseases of digestive system, except hernia	38.85	7.59
Underweight	36.37	20.87
Hemorrhoids	36.13	22.77
Chest development, insufficient	29.08	37.95
Diseases of organs of locomotion, except spinal curvature	29.00	32.26
Skin diseases	27.40	20.87
Physical debility	22.67	9.49
Curvature of spine	19.31	20.87
Diseases of genito-urinary system (non-venereal)	18.59	18.98
Defects of development, except as shown in detail	17.94	15.18
Injuries	15.70	13.28
Diseases of respiratory system, except tuberculosis	15.30	22.77
Underheight	12.42	11.39
Defects of hearing	11.86	3.80
Tuberculosis	11.38	15.18
Flat feet	10.89	18.98
Diseases of the eye, except defects of vision	5.85	3.80
Diseases of the circulatory system, except as shown in detail	5.77	28.47
General diseases, except epidemic	3.28	
Diseases of the nervous system, except weakness of mind	2.88	1.90
Weakness of mind	2.16	1.90
Epidemic diseases	1.84	
Overweight and obesity	1.60	3.80
Diseases of the ear, except defects of hearing	1.52	
Overheight (cavalry and field artillery)	.16	5.69

There is among Negroes a constant excess of venereal disease among unsuccessful applicants, an excess of tuberculosis and poor chest development and a slight deficiency in stature. The whites exceed particularly in diseases of digestion, the nervous system, diseases of the genito-urinary system, deficiencies of sight, underweight, imperfect physique, heart disease, varicose veins, etc.

The general prevalence of sickness is illustrated by the following tables:

Effect of disease and injury on the army during 1901, as compared with the corresponding data for 1900 and for the decade 1890-1899

	United States Army	
	White	*Colored*
Mean strength, year 1901..............	85,357	7,134
Total admissions to sick report	152,537	13,169
Per 1,000 of mean strength	1,787.06	1,845.95
Per 1,000 for 1.00.................	2,352 60	1,841.67
Per 1,000 for decade 1890-1899	1,505.25	1,504.20
Admissions for disease	136,244	11,726
Per 1,000 of mean strength.........	1,596.18	1,643.67
Per 1,000 for previous year.........	2,157.97	1,626.57
Per 1,000 for preceding decade......	1,278.01	1,239.33
Admissions for injury....	16,293	1,443
Per 1,000 of mean strength.........	190.88	202.27
Per 1,000 for previous year.........	194.63	215.10
Per 1,000 for preceding decade......	227.24	264.87
Discharges for disability, all causes.	1,747	98
Per 1,000 of mean strength.........	20 47	13.74
Per 1,000 for previous year.........	23.09	16.87
Per 1,000 for preceding decade......	16.71	15.79
Discharges for disease	1,364	74
Per 1,000 of mean strength.........	15 98	10.37
Per 1,000 for previous year.........	18.08	13.47
Per 1,000 for preceding decade......	13.15	12.42
Discharges for injury	383	24
Per 1,000 of mean strength.........	4.49	3.36
Per 1,000 for previous year.........	5.01	3.49
Per 1,000 for preceding decade......	3.56	3.38

1901-1902

	White troops	*Colored troops*	*Filipino troops*	*U.S. Army decade 1891-1900*
Mean strength, 1902.......................	71,679	4,273	4,826	40,446
Total admissions to sick report, 1902.......	122,308	8,109	8,239	691,794
Per 1,000 of mean strength	1,706.33	1,8.7.74	1,707.21	1,710.43
Per 1,000 for 1901.......................?.....	1,787.06	1,845.95	....	....
Admissions for disease, 1902..............	107,174	7,279	7,868	602,417
Per 1,000 of mean strength	1,459.19	1,703.49	1,630.34	1,489.44
Per 1,000 for 1901......................	1,596.18	1,643.67	....	....
Admissions for injury, 1902	15,134	830	371	89.377
Per 1,000 of mean strength	211.14	194.25	76.87	220.98
Per 1,000 for 1901......................	190.88	202.27	....	....
Discharges for disability, all causes.......	1,757	114	13	7,133
Per 1,000 of mean strength..............	24.51	26.68	2.69	17.63
Per 1,000 for 1901......................	20.47	13.74	....	....
Discharges for disease.....................	1,482	107	9	5,574
Per 1,000 of mean strength	20.68	25.04	1.86'	13.78
Per 1,000 for 1901......................	15.98	10.37	....	....
Discharges for injury......................	275	7	4	1,559
Per 1,000 of mean strength	3.83	1.64	0.83	3.85
Per 1,000 for 1901......................	4.49	3.36	....	....

In the decade 1890-99 the sickness of Negro troops on account of disease was less than that of whites, since then, in 1901 and 1902, it was more and in 1903-4 markedly less, although probably foreign service may spoil the comparison:

1903-1904

Proportion per thousand of mean strength

ENLISTED MEN		Mean strength	Admitted		
			Total	Disease	Injury
White troops	⌠ 1904..	55,619	1,364.92	1,127.32	237.60
	⌡ 1903..	55,518	1,534.31	1,291.19	243.12
Colored troops	⌠ 1904	3,121	1,176.22	866.3)	309.88
	⌡ 1903..	3,183	1,025.76	770.34	255.42
Porto Rican troops	⌠ 1904..	540	1,420.37	1,253.70	166.67
	⌡ 1903.	578	1,484.43	1,275.08	209.34
Filipino troops	⌠ 1904..	4,640	1,137.09	1,023.21	113.88
	⌡ 1903..	4,789	1,372.32	1,285.03	87.2)

ENLISTED MEN		Discharged—surgeon's certificate of disability.			Constantly non-effective	Days Treated	
		Total	Disease	Injury		Each Soldier	Each case
White troops	⌠ 1904.	23.17	20.66	2.51	50.60	18.52	13.57
	⌡ 1903..	26.63	24.59	2.04	....	......	......
Colored troops	⌠ 1904.	18.07	17.45	.62	35.62	13.03	11.08
	⌡ 1903..	12.57	11.00	1.57	....	......	......
Porto Rican troops	⌠ 1904.	12.16"	7.41	5.55	61.84	22.63	15.93
	⌡ 1903..	25.15	24.22	1.73	....	......	......
Filipino troops	⌠ 1904..	5.86	5.64	.22	42.05	11.73	10.32
	⌡ 1903.	10.23	10.02	.21	....	......	......

NOTE.—Days for the year 1903 not suitably consolidated for use in this table.

For particular diseases the following tables are added, showing a smaller sick list for Negroes in nearly everything except lung troubles. Even in venereal disease the foreign service of white troops has lead to their excess—a curious commentary on imperialism:

1904

The relative prevalence of certain special diseases among white and colored troops, with the admission rates per thousand for each race, are shown in the following tables:

DISEASE	White	Colored
Typhoid fever	6.00	0.64
Measles	19.04	4.17
Malaria	51.30	21.14
Syphilis	29.60	13.78
Alcoholism	26.43	12.18
Dysentry	8.82	4.17
Gonorrhea	108.61	86.83
Insanity	1.71	1.60
Frostbite	1.30	9.61
Smallpox	.29	.64
Sunstroke	.17	.32
Pneumonia	5.12	8.65
Tuberculosis	4.41	6.41

Venereal Diseases

The following table shows the prevalence of the venereal diseases as compared with last year and the quinquennial period since the Spanish-American war:

Ratios per 1,000 of mean strength

	ADMITTED		
	White	Colored	Total
Gonorrhea:			
Year 1904.........	108.60	86.83	107.05
Year 1903.........	85.31	69.12	84.09
Years 1899-1903....			98.84
Chancroids:			
Year 1904.........	27.73	30.12	27.90
Year 1903.........	27.74	32.67	28.11
Years 1899-1903....			27.90
Syphilis:			
Year 1904.........	29.59	13.78	28.47
Year 1903.........	24.46	13.51	23.64
Years 1899-1903....			20.56
Total venereal:			
Year 1904......	165.93	130.73	163.43
Year 1903......	137.51	115.30	135.84
Years 1899-1903			147.30

Malarial Diseases

Ratios per 1,000 of mean strength

	ADMITTED		
	White	Colored	Total
Malarial intermittent fever:			
Year 1904.........	45.37	18.58	43.47
Year 1903.........	52.33	30.16	50.66
Years 1899-1903....			121.00
Malarial remittent or continued fever:			
Year 1904.........	4.07	2.24	3.94
Year 1903.........	7.96	5.97	7.81
Years 1899-1903....			16.09
Pernicious malarial fever:			
Year 1904.........	.02		.02
Year 1903.........	.08		.07
Years 1899-1903...			.18
Malarial cachexia:			
Year 1904.........	1.84	.32	1.73
Year 1903.........	2.38	1.26	2.30
Years 1899-1903....			6.63
Total malarial diseases:			
Year 1904.........	51.30	21.15	49.16
Year 1903.........	62.75	37.39	60.83
Years 1899-1903....			143.90

Statistics as to insane and defective are very imperfect and relate only to those in institutions. The census figures for 1903 are as follows:

Negro Insane in Hospitals December 31, 1903

Continental United States	9,452	North Atlantic States	1,326
Men	4,805	North Central States	1,104
Women	4,647	Western States	108
South Atlantic States	4,135		
South Central States	2,779	North	2,538
South	6,914		

By age these figures are given:

Negro Insane in Hospitals December 31, 1903

All ages	9,452	40–44	807	75–79	27
Under 15	78	45–49	637	80–84	28
15–19	662	50–54	445	85–89	7
20–24	1,477	55–59	261	90–94	4
25–29	1,377	60–64	214	95–99	0
30–34	1,195	65–69	123	100 and over	1
35–39	1,096	70–74	96	Unknown	914

To the above may be added 172 feeble minded. The census report says:

The largest representation of colored insane is found in the South Atlantic and South Central States, and in each of those states, except Delaware, West Virginia and Kentucky, the percentages which the colored constitute of the insane in hospitals are much smaller than the percentages which Negroes form of the general population. In Delaware 22.1 per cent of the insane in hospitals on December 31, 1903, were colored, yet the Negroes constituted but 16.6 per cent of the total population at the last census. In Kentucky, with 13.3 per cent Negroes in the population, 15.6 per cent of the insane in hospitals were colored. On the other hand, in Alabama and Mississippi, for instance, with respectively 45.3 and 58.7 per cent colored in their population in 1900, the percentages of colored among the insane in hospitals in 1903 were only 27.9 for Alabama and 37.4 for Mississippi. It is unthinkable that the actual ratio of insane to population among the colored of Delaware or Kentucky should so greatly exceed that of Alabama or Mississippi, or that it should be relatively much higher than in any of the other Southern states. In fact, the available statistics do not show the relative frequency with which insanity occurs among the Negroes, but merely the extent to which they are cared for in hospitals. The returns from Delaware, West Virginia, Kentucky and a number of Northern states would seem, however, to point to a ratio of insane to population among Negroes which equals if it does not surpass that among the whites.

The figures for the blind in 1900 are:

The Blind, by Degree of Blindness and Color

COLOR	Blind	Totally Blind	Partially Blind
Number:			
White	56,535	30,359	26,172
Colored	8,228	5,286	2,942
Per cent distribution by degree of blindness:			
White	100.0	53.7	46.3
Colored	100.0	64.2	35.8
Number per 100,000 population of same color:			
White	84.6	45.4	39.2
Colored	89.6	57.6	32.0

United States Census: Special Report on Insane, etc., 1904.

The Blind

	Total	Childhood (under 20)	Adult life (20 and over)	Unknown
Colored, totally blind	5,286	1,516	3,497	273
Attended school	1,034	571	436	27
Special	383	347	24	12
Other	370	154	212	4
Both	3	3		
Not specified	278	67	200	11
Did not attend school	3,780	870	2,727	183
Not stated	472	75	334	63
Colored, partially blind	2,942	913	1,861	168
Attended school	815	398	381	36
Special	157	142	12	3
Other	415	205	195	15
Both				
Not specified	243	51	174	18
Did not attend school	1,831	461	1,278	92
Not stated	296	54	202	40

There were nearly 5,000 deaf colored people reported in 1900:

Number of Deaf

	Total	White	Colored
Total	89,287	84,361	4,926
Period of life when deafness occurred:			
Childhood (under 20)	50,296	46,807	3,489
Adult life (20 and over)	35,924	34,655	1,269
Unknown	3,067	2,899	168
Degree of deafness:			
Totally deaf	37,426	34,590	2,836
Partially deaf	51,861	49,771	2,090
Ability to speak well	55,501	53,449	2,052
Imperfectly	9,417	8,902	515
Not at all	24,369	22,010	2,359
Sex:			
Male	46,915	44,223	2,692
Female	42,372	40,138	2,234

9. Mortality*

The death rate for colored† (Negroes, Indians, etc.,) and white, for the country is:

Death Rate Per Thousand Living, United States

Registration area

	1890	1900
Colored	29.9	29.6
White	19.1	17.3

Registration states

Colored	27.4	25.3
White	19.5	17.3

Cities in registration states

Colored	31.5	27.6
White	22.1	18.6

Country districts in registration states

Colored	18.1	19.0
White	15.3	15.4

* All figures in this section are from United States Census reports unless otherwise noted.

† There are no separate figures for Negroes in 1890.

While the colored death rate greatly exceeds the white, the improvement is manifest in both races. The greatest enemy of the black race is consumption. The following figures illustrate the chief diseases:

Deaths per 100,000 living Negroes	1890	1900
Consumption	546	485
Pneumonia	279	355
Nervous disorders	333	308
Malaria	72	63

The decrease for consumption is very gratifying, but the high mortality is still a menace. The increase for pneumonia is partially accounted for by the general increase in the country. *

In regard to children, these figures tell of the slaughter of the innocents:

To every 1,000 living colored children, there are each year the following number who die:

Children under 1 year of age	1890	1900
Registration states	458	344
Cities	580	367
Country	204	219

Children under 5 years of age	1890	1900
Registration states	119	112
Cities	151	132
Country	55	67

More detailed tables follow :

Color and Race in Relation to Deaths

Population, deaths and death rates, by race †

AREAS	White	Negro	Indian	Chinese	Japanese
Registration record:					
Population	27,555,800	1,180,546	14,010	48,565	8,348
Deaths	475,640	35,710	319	914	86
Death rate	17.3	30.2	22.8	18.8	10.3
Registration cities:					
Population	20,503,666	1,100,501	1,198	46,996	8,270
Deaths	367,430	34,178	60	912	86
Death rate	17.9	31.1	50.1	19.4	10.4
Registration states:					
Population	17,086,319	330,693	13,296	13,461	511
Deaths	292,618	8,650	270	129	3
Death rate	17.1	26.2	20.3	9.6	5.9
Cities in registration states:					
Population	10,034,185	250,648	484	11,892	433
Deaths	184,408	7,118	11	127	3
Death rate	18.4	28.4	22.7	10.7	6.9
Rural part of registration states:					
Population	7,052,134	80,045	12,812	1,569	78
Deaths	108,210	1,532	259	2	
Death rate	15.3	19.1	20.2	1.3	
Registration cities in other states:					
Population	10,469,481	849,853	714	35,104	7,837
Deaths	183,022	27,060	49	785	83
Death rate	17.5	31.8	68.6	22.4	10.6

The following table gives some figures for the past:

* For whites: 1890, 182.2; 1900, 184.8.
† Twelfth Census, Vol. III, page lxix.

Showing the Number of Deaths and Rate of Mortality of Whites and Blacks*

CITY	Period of Observation (SPECIFIC YEARS)	No. years	Sum of annual population — White	Colored	Total	Number of Deaths — White	Colored	Total	Living to one death — White	Colored	Total	Rate of Mortality — White	Colored	Total
Boston	1725 to 1774 and 1865 to 1861	60	2,634,585	84,678	2,719,263	71,456	5,958	77,814	36.85	14.21	34.94	2.727	7.082	2.86
New Bedford	1861, 1862 and 1863	8	66,236	4,893	71,129	1,550	179	1,729	42.73	28.78	41.35	2.343	3.652	2.43
Providence	1840 to 1863	24	940,727	35,210	975,987	20,744	1,306	22,050	45.83	26.96	45.26	2.203	3.702	2.25
New York	1821, 1824 to 1829, 1831 to 1836, 1838 to 1863	39	16,306,010	553,665	16,859,755	512,007	22,692	534,699	31.85	24.39	31.71	3.139	4.098	3.17
Buffalo	1854 to 1857 and 1859 to 1863	9	670,246	7,104	677,350	17,167	154	17,321	39.04	45.48	39.10	2.562	2.162	2.55
Philadelphia	1821 to 1863	43	12,425,719	750,308	13,185,027	283,732	27,417	311,149	43.79	27.65	42.37	2.323	3.612	2.35
Baltimore	1818,1824,1825,1827 to 1831,1833,1834,1836 to 1863	38	4,304,472	893,110	5,197,582	107,233	27,750	134,983	40.14	32.18	38.50	2.493	3.102	2.59
Washington	1849 to 1860	12	458,436	126,696	585,132	9,082	2,811	11,893	50.47	45.05	49.19	1.982	2.212	2.08
Charleston	1822 to 1860	39	533,412	624,765	1,158,177	13,950	16,860	30,810	38.15	37.05	37.61	2.612	2.692	2.66
New Orleans	1849, 1850, 8 months of 1855, 1856 and 1860	4½	538,960	119,207	658,157	32,123	6,217	38,340	16.77	19.17	17.17	5.965	5.215	5.82
Memphis	1851, 1862 and 1863	3	23,771	8,153	31,924	1,406	428	1,834	16.09	19.05	17.41	5.915	5.245	5.74
Eleven cities			38,902,644	3,216,789	42,119,433	1,070,850	111,872	1,182,622	36.33	28.75	35.61	2.753	4.472	2.87

*Eighth Census: Mortality, etc., page 280; quoted in report of Freedmen's Inquiry Commission, 1863, whence it was copied, and in Willcox: Probable increase, etc. It does not, as Willcox thinks, refer to a population of 3,000,000 Negroes and 38,000,000 whites, but to less than one-tenth of these numbers.

Causes of the Mortality Among the White and Colored Patients of the Freedmen's Bureau under Treatment from 1865 to June 30, 1872*

	WHITE		COLORED	
	Number	Rate per 1,000	Number	Rate per 1,000
Number of patients	22,053		430,466	
Deaths from all causes	785	33.3	18,027	41.9
Deaths from miasmatic diseases	288	13.1	8,364	19.4
Deaths from enthetic diseases	9	.4	160	.4
Deaths from dietic diseases	7	.8	49	.1
Deaths from constitutional diseases	65	2.9	2,371	5.5
Deaths from nervous diseases	46	2.1	765	1.8
Deaths from circulatory diseases	10	.5	357	.8
Deaths from respiratory diseases	48	2.2	1,814	4.2
Deaths from digestive diseases	59	2.7	1,302	3.0
Deaths from urinary diseases	13	.6	228	.5
Deaths from diseases of women	8	.4	184	.4
Deaths from all other causes	182	8.3	2,493	5.7

*Reyburn: Type of Disease among Freed People of United States. Wash., 1891, page 16.

The general tendency of Negro death rates is well illustrated in the case of the following cities:

Negro death rates per 1,000

YEAR	Washing-ton, D. C.	Baltimore, Md.	Boston, Mass.	New York, N. Y.	Chicago, Ill.
1875	40.74				
1876	37.39				
1877	37.63				
1878	36.98				
1879	35.71				
1880	31.27				
1881	34.54				
1882	30.69				
1883	34.61				
1884	35.99				
1885	32.80				
1886	31.25				
1887	31.59				
1888	32.97				
1889	34.20				
1890	32.68	33.57	32.04		25.79
1891	31.93	31.48		25.09	24.70
1892	32.55	29.86	32.89	24.36	28.30
1893	31.47	30.76	31.68	25.80	26.85
1894	31.47	31.60	32.34	23.90	32.75
1895	*28.18	32.06	31.14	26.61	25.30
1896	28.54	30.76	32.74	27.35	23.41
1897	28.05	28.88	28.36	27.05	20.44
1898	28.44	31.62	24.76	26.27	21.80
1899	28.98	30.60	27.66	25.13	21.25
1900	20.00	32.80	25.19	29.06	22.85
1901	29.36	32.30	26.76	29.47	21.68
1902	27.97	30.76	26.51	29.74	24.51
1903	27.17	29.45	22.97	23.42	26.56
1904	27.92	31.44	21.03		24.85
1905		31.12		28.02	23.57

Death rates of Negroes per 1,000

	1890	1900
Atlanta, Ga	33.57	31.8
Baltimore, Md	36.41	31.2
Charleston, S. C	53.94	46.7
Louisville, Ky.	31.98	28.7
Memphis, Tenn.	29.97	28.6
Mobile, Ala	43.75	30.8
Nashville, Tenn	23.92	32.8
New Orleans, La	36.61	42.4
St. Louis, Mo	34.55	32.2
San Antonio, Tex	23.24	22.4
Savannah, Ga	41.47	43.3
Richmond, Va	40.80	38.1

The following figures are for the various causes of death:

* Before 1896, by fiscal years; by calendar years, beginning with 1896.

United States: death rate per 100,000: 1900*

	White	Negro	Indian	Chinese	Japanese
Measles	13.1	15.2	61.2		
Scarlet fever	12.0	2.6	7.1		
Diphtheria and croup	45.9	32.0	7.1	6.2	
Whooping cough	12.1	28.6		6.2	
Malarial fever	6.5	63.2		2.1	12.0
Influenza	23.6	32.0	50.0		
Typhoid fever	32.4	67.5	28.6	22.7	107.8
Diarrheal diseases	129.5	214.0	171.3	43.2	47.9
Consumption	173.5	485.4	506.8	656.8	239.6
Cancer and tumor	66.7	48.0	28.6	49.4	24.0
Heart disease and dropsy	137.4	221.1	92.8	175.0	35.9
Pneumonia	184.8	355.3	228.4	282.1	59.9
Diseases of the liver	22.8	20.9	7.1	51.5	12.0
Diseases of the nervous system	213.7	308.0	135.6	57.6	47.9
Diseases of the urinary organs	99.8	157.3	78.5	142.1	35.9
Old age	53.5	66.7	50.0	16.5	

The following conclusions may be drawn:

The death rate of only one-eighth of the Negro population was recorded in 1900, and far fewer previously.

Nine-tenths of the recorded Negro death rates in 1900 refer to the city Negro population, while four-fifths of the Negroes live in the country.

Of the 7,000,000 Negroes living in the country the recorded death rates cover only districts where 80,000 live. If the death rate of these districts is true for the whole rural Negro population then the true death rate for the Negro-American is less than 22 per 1,000. In any case the death rate of 30 per 1,000 is an exaggeration and unfair for purposes of comparison with the whites.

The Negro death rate is, however, undoubtedly considerably higher than the white. It has decreased notably since ante-bellum times.

The excess is due principally to mortality from consumption, pneumonia, heart disease and dropsy, diseases of the nervous system, malaria and diarrheal diseases.

Negroes have a smaller death rate than the whites in scarlet fever, diphtheria, cancer and tumor, and diseases of the liver.

The figures for consumption follow and show a gratifying decrease, but a still large mortality:

Death Rates by Color and Nativity

CONSUMPTION	Years	Aggregate	White Total	Colored Total
Registration area	1900	187.3	173.5	490.6
	1890	245.4	230.0	546.1
Boston	1884-90		378.9	762.8
	1900			741.6
Dist. of Columbia	1890			591.8
	1900			514.0
Baltimore	1890			524.6
	1900			447.7
New York	1884-90		318.14	774.21
	1900			503.0
Philadelphia	1884-90		287.06	557.36

Figures for the other four of the chief scourges show a large increase for pneumonia with a small increase for whites, an increase for heart disease among both races and a notable decrease in diarrheal and nervous diseases:

* Twelfth Census, Vol. III, page lxx.

	Year	Aggregate	White	Colored
Pneumonia				
Registration area.............	1900	192.0	184.8	349.0
	1890	186.9	182.2	279.0
Heart Disease and Dropsy				
Registration area.............	1900	140.9	137.4	216.6
	1890	132.1	128.4	204.0
Diarrheal Diseases				
Registration area.............	1900	132.8	129.5	205 8
	1890	183.7	180.1	253.8
Diseases of the Nervous System				
Registration area.............	1900	217.2	213.7	294.6
	1890	247.4	243.0	332.9

Figures from four cities follow, in which must be noted the severe climate of Boston and the contrast in the social condition of the two races in Washington:

New York—Death rate per 100,000 : 1884-1890

	White	Colored
Diarrheal diseases.................	318.14	243.72
Consumption......	385.05	774.21
Pneumonia	287.25	324 27
Heart disease and dropsy...........	137.37	188.17
Diseases of nervous system	241.99	240.25

Boston—Death rate per 100,000: 1884-1890

	White	Colored
Diarrheal diseases................ ...	214.15	220.80
Consumption....................	378.90	762.78
Pneumonia	219.06	337.23
Heart disease and dropsy...........	148.85	224.82
Diseases of nervous system.........	243.61	248.91

Baltimore—Death rate per 100,000: 1890

	Colored
Diarrheal diseases and cholera infantum	402.70
Consumption.............................	524.55
Diseases of the nervous system...........	335.83
Heart disease and dropsy	187.23
Pneumonia............................	350.69

District of Columbia—Death rate per 100,000: 1890

		White	Negro
Diarrheal diseases and cholera infantum....................1890		....	360.65
Diseases of the nervous system.1890		....	358.01
Heart disease and dropsy.......1890		....	162.49
Pneumonia.....................1890		....	352.72
	1895	128.5	244.4
	1900	92.6	238.5
	1904	106.5	337.2
Consumption...................1890		....	591.83
	1895	197.1	468.2
	1900	183.3	492.3
	1904	164.4	492.6

Philadelphia: 1884-90		
Diarrheal diseases	155.30	175.40
Consumption	287.06	557.36
Pneumonia	158.77	293.62
Heart disease and dropsy	142.10	246.25
Diseases of the nervous system	315.86	3.30.07

The figures for suicide for the last thirty years show an increase:

1880: In every 2,000 colored deaths, one was from suicide.

1890: Death rate for suicide per 100,000 colored persons living 4.4
1900: Death rate for suicide per 100,000 colored persons living 5.8

1900: Death rate for suicide per 100,000 for years
{ 15–44 .... 8.6
{ 45–64 .... 4.1
{ 65 and over 5.9

The white rate increases in each of the above age periods from 13 to 26.1 to 30.6; the colored rate indicates the peculiar stress of the young. The rate for all accidents and injuries is:

1890: per 100,000 .... 123.3
1900: per 100,000 .... 137.4

The deaths from alcoholism are not only less than those for whites, but show a decrease for the last decade:

Total population
1890: per 100,000, colored 6.9   8.1
1900: per 100,000   " 5.0   7.2

The colored death rate is the smallest of any group except that of children of native American women:

Alcoholism

COLOR AND BIRTHPLACES OF MOTHERS	15 to 44	45 and over
White	8.2	15.6
Colored	3.7	10.4
Mothers born in United States	2.9	4.9
Ireland	18.8	27.9
Germany	6.2	12.1
England and Wales	8.4	14.6
Canada	4.4	8.0
Scandinavia	6.0	18.1

The greatest single physical fact affecting the death rate is age, as is shown by this table for the registration area:

Death rates at certain ages, per 1,000 of population

1900	Under 1	Under 5	5 to 14	15 to 24	25 to 34	35 to 44	45 to 64	65 and over
White	158.0	49.7	4.1	5.9	8.6	11.1	21.5	86.0
Males	175.9	54.2	4.2	6.2	9.0	12.0	23.5	90.4
Females	139.8	45.2	4.0	5.6	8.1	10.1	19.5	82.1
Colored	371.5	118.5	9.8	15.6	16.9	21.0	36.7	108.6
Males	403.9	127.2	9.2	17.2	18.2	21.5	38.6	119.8
Females	339.7	110.2	10.2	14.4	15.6	20.4	34.6	100.3

The death rate of Negroes is due in no small degree to the neglect and mal-nutrition of children:

Deaths under 1 year of age, per 1,000 of population

Registration Record

	Total	Cities	STATES			Cities in other states
			Total	*Cities*	*Rural*	
White........	158.0	171.1	156.0	180.4	116.0	161.4
Colored	371.5	387.0	343.8	397.2	218.9	383.8

Infant Mortality 1900

Under 1 Year of Age	Colored	Males	Females
Population..............................	21,405	10,595	10,810
Born and died in census year............	5,365	2,931	2,434
Born during census year.................	26,770	13,526	13,244
Deaths.................................	7,951	4,279	3,672
Deaths under 1 per 1,000 births..........	297.0	316.4	277.3
Death rate per 1,000 of population	371.5	403.9	339.7
Under 5 Years of Age			
Population................................	102,408	50,418	51,990
Deaths....................................	12,140	6,413	5,727
Death rate per 1,000 of population........	118.5	127 2	110.2
Deaths under 5 per 1,000 deaths at all ages	327.9	331.8	323.5

On account of the small number of children, comparison of them with Negroes is not valid, although the Negro city population also to a less degree lacks children. The following rates for cities are nevertheless instructive; they refer to 1890 and previous:

Boston (1884-90)—Death rate per 1,000, including still births

COLOR AND BIRTHPLACES OF MOTHERS	*All ages*	*Under 15 Yrs.*	*15 years and over*
White	23.71	38 71	18.68
Colored	31.92	77.67	20.95
United States (white)	21.30	37.76	14.79
England and Wales	17.75	30.36	13 62
Ireland	27.27	39.03	24.12
Hungary.................................	21.41	42.79	10.42
Bohemia.................................	22.96	45.66	9.49
Italy.....................................	20.65	44.53	8.23
Other foreign countries	10.69	33.14	8.76

Philadelphia for the 6 years ending 1884-1890—Death rates per 1,000

COLOR AND BIRTHPLACES OF PERSONS	Philadelphia		
	All ages	*Under 15 Yrs.*	*15 years and over*
White	22.69	36.68	17.27
Colored.................................	31.25	66.88	20.94
United States (white)	25.17	38.83	17.57
England and Wales	9.78	3.35	10.65
Ireland...................................	19.10	5.62	19.43

New York and Brooklyn (1884-1890)—Death rates per 1,000, including still births

COLOR AND BIRTHPLACES OF MOTHERS	New York			Brooklyn		
	All ages	Under 15 Yrs	15 years and over	All ages	Under 15 Yrs.	15 years and over
White	29 86	53.28	20.36	25.90	44.71	17.63
Colored	33.27	75.71	23.57	30.54	63.75	20.00
White mothers born in—						
United States	32.43	54.01	15.91	27.49	45.76	13.89
England'and Wales	27.67	50.53	20.78	20.51	32.42	16.95
Ireland	32.51	50.87	28.01	27.14	43.84	22.68
Scotland	26.60	43 71	21.91	19.62	29 86	16.41
France	23 28	47 01	17.86	17.22	27.81	14.43
Germany	24 27	46.97	17 04	23.18	44.31	15.46
Russia and Poland	14.85	28 67	6.21	13.93	27.03	5.85
Canada	26.57	52.06	16.71	20.04	33.44	14.33
Scandinavia	23.47	57 33	13.43	19.46	45 50	9.13
Hungary	22.43	47.21	8.45	11.27	21.16	5 20
Bohemia	43.57	82 57	29.31	52.08	90.91	31 75
Italy	35.20	76.41	12.27	24 11	53 62	7.89
Other foreign countries	21.24	40,68	13.00	27.58	56 11	18.96

There has been great improvement in Negro infant mortality during the last decade and possibly during the last two decades; the defective counting of children, however, in 1880 makes these figures for the District of Columbia and Baltimore doubtful:

Infantile Mortality

CHARACTER OF RATES	Color		Baltimore		District of Columbia	
			1890	1880	1890	1880
Number of deaths of children under 1 year of age, per 1,000 of corresponding population	White	Total	258 60	208 86	207.83	194 75
	Colored	Total	542.63	440.19	491.80	407.20
Number of deaths during the census year, per 1,000 children born within the year	White	Total	225 70	177 54	186.44	173 30
	Colored	Total	400.96	305.79	376.99	321.52
Number of deaths under 1 year of age, per 1,000 deaths at all ages	White	Total	274 36	251 44	210.58	202.68
	Colored	Total	338 75	353.85	302.80	349.67

The following comparison for registration states and their cities shows the improvement in infant mortality from 1890 to 1900:

Death rate of children under 1 year of age

COLOR		REGISTRATION RECORD					
		Total	Registration cities	Registration States			Registration cities in other states
				Total	Cities	Rural	
White	1890	249.38	278.19	241.40	297.22	137.63	260.67
	1900	158.0	171.1	156.0	180.4	116.0	161.4
Colored	1890	494.27	525.13	457.83	579.77	204.49	509.61
	1900	371.5	387.0	343.8	397.2	218.9	383.8

Death rates per 1,000 of population at certain ages, by color and sex: 1890-1900

	Registration States							Cities in Registration States						
	All ages	Under 5 years	5 to 14 years	15 to 44 years	45 to 64 years	65 years and over	Unknown	All ages	Under 5 years	5 to 14 years	15 to 44 years	45 to 64 years	65 years and over	Unknown
White:														
1890.....	19.3	63.3	5.2	9.3	21.2	76 5	35 0	21.9	78.8	6.1	10.7	26.1	88.4	21.8
1900.....	17.1	48.9	3 7	7.8	20.1	82.7	25.8	18.4	58.3	4.2	8.6	24.1	90.6	16.5
Colored:														
18:0......	27.4	118.5	10.2	14 4	28.6	84.9	16.4	31.5	151.4	12.0	16.1	33 5	98.1	6.4
1900.....	25.3	112.0	8 7	12.7	29.4	93.4	15.5	27.6	131.6	9.9	13.9	32.3	105.4	7.5

How much is the Negro death rate affected by environment? One has only to compare the wretched Negro quarters of Charleston and New Orleans, with a death rate of over 40 per 1,000, with the far better, although not ideal, conditions in Atlanta and Louisville, with a death rate of 30 per 1,000. It is further illustrated in Baltimore and Washington by these tables, giving the death rate for Negroes per 100,000 for six years (1884-90) according to the simple matter of altitude above sea level (still born excluded):

DISTRICTS	Washington		Baltimore	
	Total	Under 5 years	Total	Under 5 years
Under 25 feet above :	37.48	167.69	44.65	203.30
25-50....................	37.06	155.21	36.51	194.03
50-75....................	31.87	159 57	34.34	155.68
75-100....................	32 55	157.89	28 03	148.39
100 and over	31 23	136.11	28 21	145.53

When we remember that the highest death rate among occupations is for laborers and servants (20.2 per 1,000), we see here another contributing cause of high Negro mortality. Perhaps the army furnishes the best test of the normal Negro death rate with all disturbing factors eliminated save physical and to some extent social heredity. War and foreign service vitiate comparisons to some extent:

Effect of disease and injury on the army during 1901, as compared with the corresponding data for 1900 and for the decade 1890-1899

	United States Army	
	White	*Colored*
Mean strength, 1901........................	85,357	7,134
Per 1,000 for 1900	2,352.60	1,841.67
Per 1,000 decade 1890-1899...............	1,505.25	1,504.20
Deaths from all causes...........	1,174	115
Per 1,000 of mean strength....:.........	33.75	16.12
Per 1,000 for 1900	22.79	22.21
Per 1,000 for decade 1890-1899............	11.89	11.71
Deaths from disease......................	792	94
Per 1,000 of mean strength...............	9.28	13.18
Per 1,000 for 1900	15.86	14.97
Per 1,000 for decade 1890-1899	8.54	7.77
Deaths from injury	382	21
Per 1,000 of mean strength...............	4.48	2.94
Per 1,000 for 1900	6.93	7.24
Per 1,000 for decade 1890-1899.............	3.35	3.94

1902

	White troops	Colored troops	Filipino troops	U.S. Army decade 1891-1900
Mean strength	71,679	4,273	4,826	40,446
Deaths from all causes	1,032	103	116	5,960
Per 1,000 of mean strength	14.40	24.11	24.04	14.73
Per 1,000 for 1901	13.75	16 12		
Deaths from diseases	836	87	109	4,228
Per 1,000 of mean strength	11.68	20 36	22.59	10.45
Per 1,000 for 1901	9 28	13.18		
Deaths from injury	196	16	7	1,732
Per 1,000 of mean strength	2.74	3.75	1.45	4.28
Per 1,000 for 1901	4.48	2.94		

1903-1904

Proportion per 1,000 of mean strength

ENLISTED MEN		Mean strength	DIED		
			Total	Disease	Injury
White troops	1904	55,619	6.69	3.72	2.97
	1903	55,518	8.48	6.18	2.30
Colored troops	1904	3,121	7.79	6.54	1.25
	1903	3,183	11 31	9.42	1.89
Porto Rican troops	1904	540	3.70	3.70	
	1903	578			
Filipino troops	1904	4,610	22.34	7.59	14.75
	1903	4,789	21.51	18.17	3.34

Mr. R. R. Wright, A. M., fellow of the University of Pennsylvania, furnishes the following memorandum on the death rates of Negroes in Northern cities:

The Negro population of the North is chiefly an urban population; 70 per cent of the Negroes live in cities, and a large proportion of these in cities of 100,000 and over.

The general opinion is that the death rate of Negroes is higher in the North than in the South. This is untrue. The crude death rates of the Negroes in the Northern cities are lower than those in the Southern cities:

Crude death rates, based on census 1900

NORTHERN CITIES	Death rate per one thousand population		SOUTHERN CITIES	Death rate per one thousand population	
	Colored	Total		Colored	Total
New York	21.3	20 6	Washington, D. C	31.0	22.8
Chicago	21.6	16.2	Baltimore, Md	31.2	21.0
Philadelphia	24.3	21.2	New Orleans, La	42.4	28.9
Boston	25.5	20 1	Memphis, Tenn	28 6	25.1
Indianapolis	23.8	16 7	Louisville, Ky	28.7	20.0
Columbus, O	21.2	15.8	St. Louis, Mo	32 2	17.9
Cleveland	18.0	17.1	Atlanta, Ga	31.8	26.6
Cincinnati	29.5	18.6	Richmond, Va	38.1	29.7
Pittsburg	25.9	20.0	Nashville Tenn	32.8	25 3
Newark	29.7	19.8	Savannah, Ga	43.3	34.3
New Haven	31.8	17.2	Charleston, S. C	46.7	37.5
Buffalo	25 5	14.8	Norfolk, Va	33.8	25.2

The foregoing table shows that of the large cities, the eight highest death rates are Southern cities—Charleston, Savannah, New Orleans, Richmond, Norfolk, Va., Nashville, St. Louis and Atlanta. Thirty deaths per 1,000 seems to be the dividing line between the Northern cities and the Southern, most of the Southern cities having a rate above 30, while most of the Northern cities have a rate below 30.

Chicago, with about the same population of Negroes as Charleston and Nashville, has less than one-half as many deaths per 1,000 as the former and two-thirds as the latter. New York, with about the same population as New Orleans, has about two-thirds as many deaths per 1,000; Norfolk has twice the rate of Indianapolis.

An analysis of the Negro population in these cities, however, gives the North a decided advantage, in that the number of children is less in the North than in the South and since the first five years of life have a very high mortality, that section having a smaller proportion of children all other things being equal, ought to show the lowest general crude death rate. The United States census has a way of correcting the returns by a system of weighting which takes into consideration the varying proportions of different ages, and corrects accordingly.

Unfortunately, however, we are unable to secure extensive figures on this subject for Negro deaths but such as we have lead to confirm rather than vitiate the above conclusion that Negro death rates are higher South than North:

	Crude rate	Corrected rate
SOUTH:		
Washington, D. C....	31.0	37.2
New Orleans..........	42.4	46.6
Nashville	32.8	38.5
Charleston	46.7	54.0
NORTH:		
Boston	25.5	30.2
Cincinnati	29.5	35.0
Cleveland.............	18.0	24.7
Columbus, O..........	21.2	25.4
Indianapolis	23.8	28.3
Newark	29.7	36.2
New York............	29.3	40.0
Pittsburg	25.9	31.7

Carrying the argument further, there are two matters of evidence which can not be controverted. (1) In the diseases peculiar to manhood, the North has no advantage but a real disadvantage since a larger proportion of the Negro inhabitants in the Northern cities is between the ages of 15 and 50, than is the case in the Southern cities. (2) Tuberculosis is a disease of adult life, attacking those chiefly past 15 years of age and is most prevalent between 20 and 30.

According to a bulletin published by the Illinois state board of health (The Cause and Prevention of Consumption, 1905), 26.22 per cent of the deaths from all causes for persons between 20 and 50 in 1902-1903, were from consumption and nine-tenths of the deaths from consumption were of persons between these ages:

Death rates of Negroes in Northern and Southern cities from consumption: Census 1900

	Rate per 100,000		Rate per 100,000
NORTHERN CITIES:		SOUTHERN CITIES:	
New York	533.4	Washington	513.8
Philadelphia	458.4	Baltimore	447.7
Chicago	537.6	New Orleans	623.5
Boston	742.4	Memphis	378.5
Indianapolis	474.5	Louisville, Ky	406.2
Cleveland	393.2	St. Louis	594.1
Cincinnati	627.7	Atlanta	505.8
Pittsburg	383.8	Richmond, Va.	474.4
Newark	416.5	Nashville	638.5
New Haven	368.0	Savannah	529.6
		Norfolk	546.6

Here we see that the highest rate, to be sure, is in Boston, one of the most northernly cities, while the second, third and fourth are Southern cities. Of the 24 cities, four in the North: New York, Boston, Chicago and Cincinnati, have a rate above 1,500 per 100,000, while eight of the Southern cities, Washington, New Orleans, St. Louis, Atlanta, Nashville, Savannah, Charleston and Norfolk, Va., have a rate about this number. Only one of the Southern cities falls below the rate of 400 per 100,000, while three of the Northern cities do.

As is true of manhood it is also true of infancy, that the North has no advantage which is purely statistical, i. e. relating to age distribution. Here again the Southern cities are in excess of the Northern cities.

I have shown in the following table not the relative number of infant deaths to the total population; for that would be unfair to the South for the reason above stated—that infants form a greater percentage of the total population; but the relative number of deaths of infants under 1 year of age to the number of births in one year.

The highest mortality is represented by Savannah, Ga., with 409.3 deaths to every 1,000 births—an extreme and alarmingly high figure. The other cities come in the following order after Savannah: Charleston, Newark, N. J., Washington, D. C., Mobile, Richmond, Va., Baltimore, New York, Atlanta, Norfolk, St. Louis, Nashville, New Orleans, Memphis, Louisville, Philadelphia, Pittsburg, Indianapolis, Cincinnati, Chicago, Boston. This list is significant for being led by the South and ended by the Northern cities. Of the highest 10, 8 are Southern cities, of the highest 15, 13 are Southern:

Infantile Mortality

Death rates of colored and white under 1 year of age, per 1,000 births:
Census 1900

NORTHERN CITIES	Infantile Mortality		SOUTHERN CITIES	Infantile Mortality	
	White	Colored		White	Colored
Boston	208.3	172.4	Memphis	275.0	162.1
Chicago	211.6	133.0	Louisville	264.9	134.7
Cincinnati	246.5	151.3	New Orleans	298.6	164.4
Indianapolis	251.7	144.3	Nashville	299.1	148.6
Pittsburg	255.1	157.9	St. Louis	316.5	138.7
New York	347.6	167.0	Norfolk	316.9	167.7
Newark	374.3	158.1	Atlanta	323.9	218.3
Philadelphia	169.6		Baltimore	356.4	177.6
			Richmond	360.4	175.3
			Mobile	363.6	183.7
			District of Columbia	366.0	158.8
			Charleston	379.5	220.3
			Savannah	409.3	299.7

All of the foregoing argument shows that death rate in this country does not altogether depend upon climate; that it is a factor which can be easily overcome, and the Negroes of this generation are rapidly overcoming it. That there is something more important than climate, may be gained from the observation that almost uniformly the Northern white death rate, like the Northern Negro death rate, is lower than that of the South. Indeed the Negro Northern death rate in many places is lower than that of the whites in many Southern cities. The white death rates of Charleston and Savannah are higher than the Negro rate of Philadelphia, Indianapolis and Chicago. Charleston's white rate is higher than Boston's Negroes. The whites of New Orleans, Richmond, Charleston, Savannah, Atlanta, Mobile and Memphis are all higher than the Negroes of Chicago. And the infantile mortality among the Negroes of Pittsburg, Indianapolis, Cincinnati, Chicago and Boston, is lower than that of Savannah, Ga., among the whites; Boston's Negro mortality is lower than Atlanta's, Charleston's and Savannah's white infant mortality.

Again, we are accustomed to connect with the cold climate deaths from consumption and pneumonia and grippe (bronchitis). We need not lay much stress on consumption as that has already been discussed.

For pneumonia, Baltimore, a Southern city, leads the list, then follow New York, Pittsburg, Memphis, Richmond, Nashville, Philadelphia, New Haven, St. Louis, Savannah, New Orleans, Louisville, Cincinnati, Atlanta, Boston, Chicago, Norfolk, Newark, Washington. Indianapolis, Charleston, Mobile and Cleveland.

A Southern city leads; 3 out of the highest are Southern; 6 out of 10 9 out of 15; 11 out of 20. Boston is lower than Atlanta or Savannah or New Orleans. The coldest cities—Chicago, Boston and Cleveland—stand 15th, 16th and 22nd in the list.

For influenza, Charleston, the highest Southern city, is three times as high as the highest Northern city. The order is Charleston, Norfolk

Nashville, Richmond, Atlanta, Washington, Pittsburg, Newark, Indianapolis, New Haven, Boston. Savannah, Baltimore, Louisville, New
York. Chicago comes last, except Cleveland and Cincinnati, which do
not report any cases at all.

A study of deaths by months in Philadelphia also tends to discredit
the theory that Negroes are at a special disadvantage in the cold climate. The highest monthly average of deaths from all causes for five
years for Negroes was in April, though January for whites. The second
was May for Negroes and March for whites. The third was July for
both Negroes and whites. The lowest, September for Negroes and
October for whites, while December was next lowest for Negroes.

For the past five years—1901 to 1905, inclusive,—there were 1,589
deaths among Negroes from consumption, an average of 26.5 per month.
Strange to say the highest average for any month during these five
years was April, the next July and May, and the next October—every
one of the winter months was below the average. For the five years the
average deaths of consumption among Negroes for the month of October was less than April, December less than June, January less than
July, February slightly above August, March below September.

For pneumonia, inflammation of the lungs, we have the opposite:
For the years 1901, 1902, 1903 there were 698 deaths of 19.4 per month.
Above this average were January, February, the highest point, March,
April, November and December, while below it were the summer
months, May, June, July, August, September and October.

The point is that the season does not have any very materially different effect upon the Negroes than upon the whites, save that the total
death rate from this disease is greater among Negroes all of the year
round, but that there is not the greater difference in the winter months
which might be expected.

Let us now come to the subject of the Northern Negroes' general physical condition. For this purpose let us take a special city. That city
is Philadelphia, and for many reasons. It is the largest, the oldest and
most conservative city and is quite representative of the Negroes' progress in the North, but comparisons with other cities will be made as
are deemed necessary to the better understanding of the Philadelphia
situation.

The first thing which strikes us is the difference between the white
and Negro death rates, which are given in the following table:

Year	Total rate	Colored rate
1895	20.44	22.3
1896	20.17	20.5
1897	18.72	21.0
1898	19.18	21.4
1899	18.75	21.6
1900	19.38	26.6
1901	18.26	25.2
1902	17.67	24.3
1903	18.82	19.9
1904	16.65	19.7
1905	17.51	20.0
Total	87.15	22.02
Average	18.72	22.02 per 1,000

The average death rate for Philadelphia for ten years from 1896-1905, inclusive, was 18.72 per 1,000, while the average for colored was 22.02 per 1,000—a difference of 3.30 per thousand against the colored persons. What is shown for Philadelphia here over a course of years also holds good for every Northern city.

The colored population in 1900 comprised 4.9 per cent of the total population of Philadelphia (Negro 4.7).

In 1906, colored population was about 5.6 per cent of the entire population and composed during the entire six years 1900-1905, inclusive, an average of about 5.2 per cent. During these years there were 149,786 deaths, of which 9,514 or 6.3 per cent were of colored persons, 1.1 per cent or 165 more deaths than there normally should have been if the colored persons keep their average. What is true of Philadelphia is true of New York, Boston, Indianapolis, Chicago and all Northern cities.

Examining the table of deaths, we find out of just what diseases Negroes die to a larger extent than they comprise of the total population. This gives some idea of the diseases to which Negroes are especially susceptible:

Table showing number of Negroes dying in Philadelphia from specific causes, the percentage of such deaths to the total number of deaths from each cause, and the percentage of such deaths to the total number of Negro deaths, 1900

DISEASE	Number	Per cent of total deaths from specific causes	Per cent of total Negro deaths
Syphilis	8	20.5	.5
Marasmus	101	11.5	6.1
Whooping cough	14	11.2	.8
Consumption	287	10.7	17.2
Inanition	67	8.9	4.0
Inflammation of lungs	250	8.4	15.0
Inflammation of brain	51	8.4	3.1
Child birth	3	8.1	.2
Typhoid fever	35	7.8	2.1
Epilepsy	3	7 3	.2
Cholera infantum	52	7.1	3.1
Still born	87	7.0	5.2
Premature births	42	6.8	3.5
Inflammation of kidneys	51	6.7	3.1
Dysentry	4	6.3	0.2
Heart disease	99	5.9	6.0
Bright's disease	22	5.9	1.3
Anemia Chlorosis	3	4.8	.2
Erysipelas	4	4.8	.2
Diphtheria	36	4.0	2.2
Cancer	25	3.3	1.5
Alcoholism	3	2.9	.2
Old age	19	2.8	1.1
Diabetes	3	2.7	.2
Apoplexy	22	2.7	1.3
Sunstroke	4	2.5	.2
Fatty degeneration of heart	3	2.4	.2
Softening of brain	4	2.3	.2
Scarlet fever	2	1.2	.1
Scrofula	0	....	....
Fatty degeneration of liver	0	....	....
Other diseases	361	4.1	21.7
Total	1,665	7.2	100.00

The colored population was in 1900, 4.9 per cent of the Philadelphia population.*

The causes of death of which Negroes form more than their part are in the following order: Syphilis leads with 20.5 per cent of the total deaths;† then come marasmus, whooping cough, consumption, inanition, pneumonia, inflammation of the brain, child birth, typhoid fever, epilepsy, cholera infantum, still births, premature births, inflammation of the kidneys, dysentery, heart disease and Bright's disease.

The diseases below the line, i. e., of which the Negro population die to a less proportion than they form of the entire population are anemia, erysipelas, diphtheria, cancer, alcoholism, old age, diabetes, apoplexy, sunstroke, fatty degeneration of the heart, fatty degeneration of the liver, softening of the brain, scarlet fever, scrofula; that is, in the deaths from 17 out of about 50 diseases the Negroes form more than the percentage they form of the total population. For most of these diseases the same is general in all the Northern cities of which I have information.

But this method of comparison does not give anything as to the prevalence of diseases; therefore, we make another comparison from the point of view of prevalence, and we find that of all the deaths for the period named 17.2 per cent are of consumption, 15 per cent of pneumonia, while marasmus, heart disease, inanition, cholera infantum follow in order.

The diseases of consumption and pneumonia, infantile marasmus, cholera infantum, inanition, heart disease are the diseases which take the Negroes away. From these diseases during the years of 1900, 1901, 1902, 1903, 3,284 persons died, or 51.1 per cent of the total deaths for these four years (6,424). Each year they constituted over half of the deaths.

If deaths from these causes had been at the same rate as the whites, the Negro general death rate would have been much less than the rate for the city.

Consumption is the chief cause of excessive death rate. One out of every six Negro persons who die in Philadelphia, dies of this disease, and probably five out of every seven who die between 18 and 28 die of this disease. It attacks the young men and women just as they are entering a life of economic benefit and takes them away. This disease is probably the greatest drawback to the Negro race in this country.

In 1900 there were 1,467 babies born in Philadelphia and 25 per cent died before they were one year old. Of every five persons who die in a year two are children under five years of age. The diseases of cholera infantum, inanition and marasmus, which are simply the doctor's way of saying lack of nourishment and lack of care, cause many unnecessary deaths of children.

---

*The 1900 deaths may show a little to the disadvantage of the colored population because of the exceptionally high rate for that year.

†The comparison is not valid here as few physicians of better class patients would report syphilis as a cause of death. Hence the small white rate in part.

Not only is the death rate higher but from all available resources it seems that the sickness rate is higher. In the public hospitals of Philadelphia there are an excess of Negroes to amount to as high as 125 per cent over white. From all available sources at least 20,000 Negroes were sick in the city last year; 5.000 of these in the hospitals of the city, where the average confinement, if the records of the University of Pennsylvania and Douglass hospitals are fair samples, was about three weeks, involving an economic loss of about one-quarter of a million dollars. This sickness is heaviest among the poor and is one of the chief causes and effects of poverty.

Mr. Warner, in his American Charities, makes sickness the chief cause of poverty among colored persons in New York, Boston, New Haven and Baltimore. The percentage was twice or more as high as that of Germans, Irish and white Americans. The same is approximately true in Philadelphia.

The undeniable fact is, then, that in certain diseases the Negroes have a much higher rate than the whites, and especially in consumption, pneumonia and infantile diseases.

The question is: Is this racial? Mr. Hoffman would lead us to say yes, and to infer that it means that Negroes are inherently inferior in physique to whites.

But the difference in Philadelphia can be explained on other grounds than upon race. The high death rate of Philadelphia Negroes is yet lower than the whites of Savannah, Charleston, New Orleans and Atlanta.

If the population were divided as to social and economic condition the matter of race would be almost entirely eliminated.* Poverty's death rate in Russia shows a much greater divergence from the rate among the well-to-do than the difference between Negroes and whites of America. In England, according to Mulhall, the poor have a rate twice as high as the rich, and the well-to-do are between the two. The same is true in Sweden, Germany and other countries. In Chicago the death rate among whites of the stock yards district is higher than the Negroes of that city and further away from the death rate of the Hyde Park district of that city than the Negroes are from the whites in Philadelphia.

Even in consumption all the evidence goes to show that it is not a racial disease but a social disease. The rate in certain sections among whites in New York and Chicago is higher than the Negroes of some cities. But as yet no careful study of consumption has been made in order to see whether or not the race factor can be eliminated, and if not, what part it plays.

The high infantile mortality of Philadelphia today is not a Negro affair, but an index of a social condition. Today the white infants furnish two-thirds as many deaths as the Negroes, but as late as twenty

---

*See paper on "Housing and Sanitation:" Report Hampton Institute Conference, 1906, and So. Workman, September, 1906.

years ago the white rate was constantly higher than the Negro rate of today—and only in the past sixteen years has it been lower than the Negro death rate of today. The matter of sickness is an indication of social and economic position: Professor Du Bois, in his most valuable study of the Philadelphia Negro, gives a number of family budgets. One or the most striking things in these budgets is that the amount paid for sickness is highest among the poorer classes and lowest among the better-to-do. It seems that the sickness bill increases inversely as the wages. Benefit insurance men of Philadelphia assure me also that the time people lose at work is also approximately in inverse ratio to the wages they receive.

We might continue this argument almost indefinitely going to one conclusion, that the Negro death rate and sickness are largely matters of condition and not due to racial traits and tendencies. This condition so far as Philadelphia is concerned is caused by—

1. Lack of proper training.
2. Bad water.
3. Unskilled labor of men, which is hard and long and tends to exposure.
4. Work of women—66 per cent of Philadelphia Negro women work. This means:
5. Neglect of their children, often to care for others' children.
6. Unwholesome and improper feeding, which plays an extremely great part.
7. Ignorance.
8. Improper education. The children get a great deal of so-called mental and a little moral, and often a smattering of industrial, but the fundamentals of physical education in order to develop the bodies of the children, is criminally neglected at least among Philadelphia's poorest Negroes.

In concluding, the situation is not hopeless, but is on the contrary becoming better in nearly every city in the North. Ten years ago the death rate was twice the birth rate in New York; today they are about the same, with the death rate steadily decreasing and the birth rate increasing. Ten years ago the birth rate of Philadelphia was less than the death rate: today it is six per thousand higher. What Mr. Hoffman wrote of the Northern Negro ten years ago is not true today.

In Philadelphia the Negroes composed 4.5 per cent of the population in 1900; they now compose about 5.5 per cent. For the six years from 1900-1905, inclusive, they probably comprised an average of 5 per cent of the population. During these years there has been a total of 149,786 deaths, of which 9,514 or 6.3 per cent were Negroes. There have been 183,479 births, of which 10,266 were Negroes or 5.6 per cent, and 60,678 marriages, of which 3,708 or 6.1 per cent were Negroes. Thus it is seen that in deaths, marriages and births the Negroes have a little more than their proportion.

With the improved sanitary condition, improved education and better economic opportunities, the mortality of the race may and probably will steadily decrease until it becomes normal.

10. Insurance

We now come to the remedial measures to alleviate the burdens of sickness and death and to reduce the rate. First, there is the distribution of the economic burden by insurance. An attempt has been made to reduce this benefit by discriminting against Negro risks. In 1884 the Massachusetts legislature passed a law prohibiting discrimination by life insurance companies against Negroes. This was followed by similar laws in Connecticut (1887), Ohio (1889), NewYork (1892), Michigan (1893), New Jersey (1894) and Minnesota (1895). A few other states have laws which courts have evaded or emasculated. The argument against these laws is thus put in the leading insurance journal.* After giving some of the vital statistics for 1900, the article says:

The general conclusions deduced from these two tables would be that the most recent investigation into the subject confirms earlier investigation tending to prove conclusively that the mortality of the Negro race, especially in Northern states and cities, very largely exceeds the mortality of the white race living in the same sections of the country, and that for life insurance purposes it would be a reckless disregard of the policyholders' interest to accept the two races at the same rates of premiums or to solicit on any considerable scale this particular class of business.

It may not be out of place to conclude these brief observations on the Negro as an industrial insurance risk with two extracts from the letter of Dr. Leslie D. Ward, to the editor of *The Indicator*, published under date of September 5, 1894:

But the high mortality amongst colored persons is not the only objectionable feature to the writing of life insurance policies on their lives. We find from our office statistics, that policies on colored lives lapse in far greater ratios than policies on white persons, and that the highest percentage of lapse comes within a very few weeks of the issuance of the policy. In fact, the greater portion of the colored business issued by the Prudential is not continued on the books of the company long enough to recoup the company for the initial expenses of getting the business. In many cases those who continue their policies do not seem to value them or lay much stress upon their possession. Numerous instances are found upon our books where policies on colored people have been lapsed and revised a dozen or more times.

The argument here adduced would be stronger if similar discriminations were proposed in the case of Americans born in Germany or Ireland, or in the case of certain social classes or localities. Indeed carried to its utmost logical conclusion it would contradict the very idea of insurance, viz., the distribution of the economic burden of the unfortunate or old on the shoulders of so many of their luckier fellows that the cost will be negligible. A study of the actual experience of life insurance companies results as follows:

----

* The Spectator, September 11 and 18, 1902.

Summation—Actual and expected deaths *

Insurance Years 1-30

AGES AT ENTRY	Americans born in Germany		Americans born in Ireland		Americans born in Sweden or Norway		Negro-Americans	
	Deaths	Expected	Deaths	Expected	Deaths	Expected	Deaths	Expected
15–28..........	1,418	1,746.6	486	459.4	273	286.2	29	29.2
29–42..........	8,823	8,721.1	2,950	2,435.4	636	6.5.8	137	120.8
43–56.:........	8,776	7,557.7	3,084	2,379.4	237	228.5	70	63.9
57–70..........	1,495	1,288.7	784	580.9	28	27.9	6	9.8
15–70..........	20,512	19,314.1	7,304	5,855.1	1,174	1,238.4	242	223.7

Summation—Actual and table deaths †

Insurance Years 6-30 ⁻

AGES AT ENTRY	AMERICANS BORN IN—							
	Germany		Ireland		Sweden or Norway		Negro-Americans	
	Deaths	Table	Deaths	Table	Deaths	Table	Deaths	Table
15–28..........	783	983.8	245	256.1	103	127.0	8	12.7
29–42..........	5,857	5,716.6	1,868	1,585.8	275	322.4	53	54.6
43–56..........	6,003	5,243.4	1,933	1,571.6	120	122.9	30	31.2
57–70..........	902	790.0	412	341.5	16	15.5	4	4.7
15–70..........	13,545	12,733.8	4,458	3,755.0	514	587.8	95	103.2

The reports of the thirty-four leading companies conclude: "It has been supposed in the past that colored people have less vitality than whites, but the somewhat scanty facts here available do not prove it." In fact the Negro makes a better showing than the Irish, nearly as good as the Germans, and better than the economic class of laborers in general. To be sure these Negroes were carefully selected, but this fact only emphasizes the injustice which would have been done them had they been discriminated against merely on account of color, as the insurance companies so often do.

One result of this discrimination, particularly in industrial insurance, has been the rise of a number of Negro companies which are today doing millions of dollars worth of business among black folk.

One of these insurance societies is so important that a government report was made on it in 1902, which deserves printing in part, as the society has been called "the most remarkable Negro organization in the country." ‡

The association was organized in January, 1881, by Rev. William Washington Browne, an ex-slave of Habersham county, Ga., as a fraternal beneficiary institution, composed of male and female members with a capital of $150. On April 4, 1883, or over two years later, the circuit court of the city of Richmond, Va., granted a regular charter of incorporation as a joint stock company to Browne and his associates under the name of "The Grand Fountain of the

* Experience of thirty-four Life Companies, page 472.
† Experience of thirty-four Life Companies, page 476.
‡ United States. Bulletin of. Labor, No. 41, pp. 807-14.

United Order of True Reformers." The chief purpose of incorporation was "to provide what is to be known as an endowment or mutual benefit fund;" the capital stock was "to be not less than one hundred dollars nor more than ten thousand dollars, to be divided into shares of the value of five dollars each;" the company was to hold real estate "not to exceed in value the sum of twenty-five thousand dollars;" the principal office was "to be kept in the city of Richmond," and the officers named in the charter for the first year were Rev. William W. Browne, Richmond, Va., grand worthy master; Eliza Allen, Petersburg, Va., grand worthy mistress; R. T. Quarles, Ashland, Va., grand worthy vice-master; S. W. Sutton, Richmond, Va., grand worthy chaplain; Peter H. Woolfolk, Richmond, Va., grand worthy secretary; Robert I. Clarke, Centralia, Va., grand worthy treasurer. These, with six others, composed the board of directors for the first year. Thus the True Reformers started on their way as a full-fledged joint stock corporation whose chief aim was to provide a form of what is known as mutual beneficial insurance for its members. In 1898 the charter was amended so that a part of section 2 should read as follows; "The said corporation shall issue certificates of membership to its members and shall pay death benefits to the heirs, assigns, personal or legal representatives of the deceased members;" and section 4 as follows: "The real estate to be held shall not exceed in value the sum of five hundred thousand ($500,000) dollars."

Up to December, 1901, the last report of the organization shows that it had paid in death claims $606,000 and in sick dues $1,500,000 and that the membership was over 50,000, having increased 18,000 in the preceding year. The increase in twenty years from a membership of 100 and a capital of $150 to a membership of over 50,000 with payments to members aggregating over $2,000,000, and with real estate aggregating $223,500 in value, constitutes an excellent showing.

But it is not the growth nor even the existence of the Grand Fountain of the True Reformers as a mutual insurance association, with its small army of employees, that causes it to be considered here; it is the affiliated by-products, to use an industrial expression, that are of interest and that may prove to be of great economic value to the Negro race.

Among these are a savings bank, a real estate department, a newspaper, old folk's homes, co-operative grocery stores and a hotel.

11. Hospitals

Hospitals and careful nursing are sorely needed by Negroes. As a little North Carolina hospital reports: The hospital there has "had a wonderful effect on the death rate among our people during the last decade. The deaths used to be three to one when compared with the whites, while the colored population was only about one-half as large as the white population. But since we have had the trained nurse, there is a marked change."

In the North, Negroes are admitted to the general hospitals; in the South they have separate wards or distinct institutions; outside the public hospitals which receive colored patients there are the following private hospitals of which this Conference has knowledge:

ALABAMA.—Harris Sanitorium, Mobile; Colored Infirmary, Eufaula; Hospital, Birmingham; Hospital, Tuskegee.

ARKANSAS.—Colored Sanatorium, Little Rock.

DISTRICT OF COLUMBIA.—Freedman's Hospital, Washington.

FLORIDA.—Bruster Hospital, Faxville.

GEORGIA.—Georgia Infirmary, Savannah; Charity Hospital, Savannah; McVickar, Spelman Seminary, Atlanta; Lamar Hospital, Augusta; Burrus Sanitorium, Augusta.

INDIANA.—Colored Hospital, care of Dr. Dupee, Evansville.

ILLINOIS.—Provident Hospital, Chicago.

KANSAS.—Douglass Hospital, Kansas City; Mitchell Hospital, Leavenworth.

KENTUCKY.—Red Cross Hospital, Covington; Citizens' National Hospital, Louisville; Louisville National Medical College.

MISSOURI.—Provident Hospital, St. Louis.

MARYLAND.—Provident Hospital, Baltimore.

MISSISSIPPI.—Tougaloo University Hospital, Tougaloo.

NORTH CAROLINA.—Pinehurst Infirmary, Pinehurst; Lincoln Hospital, Durham; St. Agnes Hospital, Raleigh; State's Hospital, Winston; Good Samaritan Hospital, Charlotte; Shaw University, Raleigh.

NEW YORK.—Colored Home and Hospital, New York.

OHIO.—Colored Hospital, Cincinnati; Colley's Hospital, Cincinnati.

PENNSYLVANIA.—Douglass Hospital, Philadelphia; Mercy Hospital, Philadelphia.

SOUTH CAROLINA.—Nurse Training School, Charleston.

TENNESSEE.—Hairston Infirmary, Memphis; Mercy Hospital, Nashville; Dr. J. T. Wilson's Infirmary, Nashville; The Clinic, Memphis.

TEXAS.—Colored Hospital, Dallas.

VIRGINIA.—Richmond Hospital, Richmond; Woman's Central League Hospital, Richmond.

NAME	PLACE	Founded	Patients last year	Annual income	Graduates in nurse-training	REMARKS
Lincoln	New York, N. Y	1839	3,904	$115,115	47	Old and important charity work.
Freedman's	Washington, D. C	1862	2,918		144	A great war legacy.
Provident	Chicago, Ill	1891	*1,216	25,234	74	Endowment of $50,024.51.
St. Agnes	Raleigh, N. C	1896	137		27	Part of St. Augustine's school.
Douglass	Philadelphia, Pa.	1896	242	12,000	15	
Hospitals, etc.	Charleston, S. C	1897			18	
Burrus	Augusta, Ga	1901	232			Private.
Slater	Winston-Salem, N. C.		71			
McVickar	Atlanta, Ga.		328			Part of Spelman Sem.
Louisville	Louisville, Ky				11	Part of Nat. Med. Col.
Good Samaritan	Charlotte, N. C	1891	153	2,389		
Provident	St. Louis, Mo	1895	200	3,083	12	
Dixie	Hampton, Va	1891	249	11,151	83	Affiliated with the Hampton Inst.

Many of these hospitals have interesting histories: The Colored Hospital and Home of New York was founded by a relative of John Jay and went through the draft riots. The Freedman's Hospital grew out of the war. The Provident Hospital is one of the best organized and most efficient in the country. It has easily solved the color question, admitting both white and colored patients and employing white and colored physicians. Other institutions have been less successful. The Colored Hospital and Home of New York will not allow Negro physicians to practice in it, nor will the McVickar Hospital of Atlanta allow

* Also 4,953 patients treated in dispensary.

them to operate, although it is part of a great missionary school for Negroes.

12. Medical Schools

There are at present five medical schools for the especial training of Negro physicians. In order of size and importance these institutions are:

WALDEN UNIVERSITY.—*Meharry Medical College.* Founded 1876 at Nashville, Tenn. Endowed, and under care of the Methodist Episcopal Church.

Four buildings: The main building is constructed of brick, is 40 feet wide and 60 feet in length and four stories in height including the basement. The ground floor is used as laboratories for practical work in chemistry; the second floor for office, museum and dwelling apartments; the third floor contains a lecture room of sufficient size to accommodate 100 students, recitation room and cabinet of materia medica; the fourth story is fitted for lecture room.

The Dental and Pharmaceutical Hall, with new laboratory annex, contains a dental operatory, two dental laboratories and a reading room; three rooms for pharmaceutical work, laboratory for analytical chemistry; historical and pathological laboratory; clinical amphitheatre, with waiting rooms for patients; recitation room and museum.

The new Meharry Auditorium is located on a lot north of Meharry College and fronting on Maple street. It has an extreme width of 62 feet, with a length of 91 feet. The foundation rests on solid rock. The walls of the basement are built of stone and are 10 feet in height.

Mercy Hospital, which is located at 811 South Cherry street, is a two-story structure of 12 rooms and contains 23 beds, most of which are of the latest hospital pattern.

Courses of study:	Kinds	Months per year	Years
Medical..........	7		4
Dental	6		4
Pharmaceutical.	6		3
Nurse training..	9		2

Number of teachers, 1905-1906, 34.

Number of students,	Medical	Dental	Pharmaceutical	Nurse training
1905-1906	320	88	35	6
Number graduates..	733	74	85	15

HOWARD UNIVERSITY.—*Howard University Medical Department.* Founded 1867 at Washington, D. C. Supported by the United States government.

Buildings: The Medical College and Freedman's Hospital.

Courses of study:	Kinds	Months per year	Years
Medical..........	8		4
Dental	8		3
Pharmaceutical.	8		3
Nurse training..	9		2

Number of teachers, 44.

Number of students,	Medical	Dental	Pharmaceutical	Nurse training
1905-1906.............	147	31	26	..
Graduates, 1900	542	67	108	..

SHAW UNIVERSITY.—*Leonard Medical School.* Founded 1882 at Raleigh, N. C. Supported by the Northern Baptists.

Buildings: The Leonard Medical building is on the site donated by the North Carolina legislature. This building contains the lecture rooms, amphitheatre, laboratory, dissecting rooms, etc., and has been fitted up at some expense.

The Medical Dormitory contains rooms to accommodate 60 students.

A hospital building containing three wards affords the students clinical instruction.

A dispensary has been completed and is in operation. It has two rooms, one in which to receive students, the other in which to make necessary examinations.

Courses of study :   Kinds   Months per year   Years
Medical   7   4
Pharmaceutical.   7   3

Number of teachers, 1905-1906, 12.

Number of students,   Medical   Pharmaceutical
1905-1906   147   31
Number of graduates   236   64

NEW ORLEANS UNIVERSITY, *Flint Medical College.* Founded 1889 at New Orleans, La. Supported by Methodist Episcopal Church.

Buildings: The building has a front of 22 feet and a depth of 114 feet; it is a large three story brick structure. The lot on which the building stands, 114x 64 feet, affording room for an addition to the building. The value of the entire property is $110,000.

Courses of study :   Kinds   Months per year   Years
Medical   7   4
Pharmaceutical.   7   3
Nurse training . .   12   2

Number teachers, 11.

                        Medical   Pharmaceutical   Nurse training
Number students . . .   55   13   23
Number graduates. .   73   8   26

LOUISVILLE NATIONAL MEDICAL COLLEGE.—Founded 1887 at Louisville, Ky.

Buildings : The college building is equipped with laboratories and modern appliances.

Alumni Hall is a two story brick building in the rear of the college, which will be devoted to laboratory work in bacteriology, histology and pathology. The first floor will be devoted to chemistry and pharmacy.

The hospital is well equipped.

Courses of study :   Kinds   Months per year   Years
Medical   7   4
Pharmaceutical.   7   3
Nurse training   3

Number teachers, 1905-1906, 23.

Number of students,   Medical   Pharmaceutical   Nurse training
1905-1906   47   . .   3
Number graduates. .   83   1   11

There was a medical department at Knoxville College, Tennessee, opened in 1895, but it was soon discontinued. It had two graduates.

13. Physicians

The census reports the following Negro physicians :

1890— 909; male   794, female 115.
1900—1,734; male 1,574, female 160.
Increase per cent—90.7 per cent.

Their ages were :

	1890	1900
16-24 years	96	95
25-34 "	264	607
35-44 "	187	532
45-54 "	135	257
55-64 "	111	122
65 and over	104	105
Unknown	12	16
Total	909	1,734

From the Negro medical schools there were the following living graduates at two periods, 1895 and 1905:

Negro Physicians, 1895

	Alabama	Arkansas	Florida	Georgia	Kentucky	Louisiana	Mississippi	Missouri	North Carolina	South Carolina	Tennessee	Texas	Virginia	West Virginia	Total
Meharry Medical College	5	17	7	19	16	8	8	17	2	5	51	55			210
Howard University	3		1	9	9	2		2	2	11	1	2	12		54
Leonard Medical School	1	2	2	7					19	9			9	2	51
New Orleans University						13						6			19
Louisville National					20		1				2	1			24
Other Colleges *	4	3	1	4	8	2				1	1	1	2		27
Total	13	22	11	39	53	25	9	19	23	26	55	65	23	2	385

Negro Physicians, 1905

STATES	Howard	Meharry	Leonard	Louisville	Flint	Total
Alabama	5	37	10			52
Arizona				1		1
Arkansas	2	51	4	1	4	62
California	2	2	.1	1		6
Colorado	1	5	1	1		8
Dakota					1	1
Delaware	3					3
District of Columbia	116	4	2			122
Florida	5	33	2			40
Georgia	18	48	16		1	83
Illinois	5	18		2		25
Indian Territory	1	16	1			18
Indiana	6	3		13	1	23
Iowa	1	2				3
Kansas	5	13		1		19
Kentucky	10	52		51		113
Louisiana		16			34	50
Maine	2					2
Maryland	10		3			13
Massachusetts	3		5			8
Michigan	3	1				4
Minnesota	1	2				3
Mississippi	2	23	1		8	34
Missouri	13	35		2		50
Nebraska	1	1				2
New Jersey	9		5			14
New Mexico			1			1
New York	15	2	2			19
North Carolina	4	3	45	1		53
Ohio	17	3	1	3		24
Oklahoma	2	5		1		8
Pennsylvania	16	2	6			24
Rhode Island	3		1			4
South Carolina	12	11	17	1		41
Tennessee	1	111	1	3		116
Texas	6	71			9	86
Vermont	1					1
Virginia	17	2	48	1		68
Washington	2					2
West Virginia	13	1	8			22
South America	2					2
Central America	3					3
British West India Islands	6	2	2	1		11
South Africa		1	1			2
West Africa		2				2
Nova Scotia		1				1
Spanish Honduras					1	1
Unknown					2	
	344	579	184	83	62	1252
Known to be dead	?	72	15	?	4	

* Northern schools.

In addition to these there are, 1906, at least 213 Negro graduates of the Northern medical schools of the country.

A circular was sent to all the medical schools in the country, asking if they had Negro students or graduates and their character, etc. The Southern schools, except those for Negroes, do not receive colored students, and most of them simply stated this fact. Others replied as follows:

We have never had a Negro pupil in the Baltimore Medical College. One such pupil would, I am sure, be a great injury to our class on entering.
Baltimore, Md.   BALTIMORE MEDICAL COLLEGE.

If you are looking for "niggers" go to Boston or other "nigger" loving communities.
None, thank God!!
None, by God, sir! And what's more, there never will be any *here*.
St. Louis, Mo.   (L. C. M. McELWEE, Dean.)

The College of Physicians and Surgeons of Baltimore does not, never has, and never will admit Negroes to its lecture halls and work.
COLLEGE OF PHYSICIANS AND SURGEONS.

There are no niggers in this school and there never have been and there never will be as long as one stone of its building remains upon another.
MEDICAL DEPARTMENT UNIVERSITY OF GEORGIA.

The Hospital College of Medicine never matriculated a "coon" in all its history and never will so long as I am Dean.
HOSPITAL COLLEGE OF MEDICINE, MEDICAL DEPARTMENT OF CENTRAL UNIVERSITY.
Louisville, Ky.

The practice of some of the border states varies. The following do not receive Negroes:

University of Louisville, Louisville, Ky.
Southwestern Homeopathic Medical College, Louisville, Ky.
Baltimore University School of Medicine, Baltimore, Md.
University of Nashville, Nashville, Tenn.
Barnes Medical College, St. Louis, Mo.
Woman's Medical College, Baltimore, Md.
University Medical College, Columbia, Mo.
Hospital Medical College, Memphis, Tenn.
A. M. Medical College, St. Louis, Mo.
St. Louis University, Medical Department, St. Louis, Mo.
St. Louis College of Physicians and Surgeons, St. Louis, Mo.
University of Tennessee, Department of Medicine, Nashville, Tenn.
University of Iowa, Department of Medicine, Keokuk, Ia.

Medical College of Virginia, Richmond, Va.
Louisville Medical College, Louisville, Ky.

The following schools have never had Negro students; although some would admit them if they applied, others would not:

Johns Hopkins University, Baltimore, Md.
Medical Department, Willamette University, Ore.
The Detroit Homeopathic College, Detroit, Mich.
Saginaw Valley Medical College, Saginaw, Mich.
Medical College, Cincinnati, O.
Miami Medical College, Cincinnati, O.
The Medical Chirurgical College, Kansas City, Kans.
College of Homeopathic Medicine and Surgery, University of Minnesota, St. Paul, Minn.
Sioux City College of Medicine, Sioux City, Ia.
Wisconsin College of Physicians and Surgeons, Milwaukee, Wis.
The George Washington University, Washington, D. C.
Medical Department Washington University, St. Louis, Mo.
Medical Department of Oregon, Portland, Ore.
Georgetown University, Washington, D. C.
The American College of Medicine and Surgery, Chicago, Ill.
Hahnemann Medical College, Kansas City, Mo.
Milwaukee Medical College, Milwaukee, Wis.
Maryland Medical College, Baltimore, Md.
Army Medical School, Washington, D. C.
Eclectic Medical University, Kansas City, Mo.
Homeopathic Medical College, Baltimore, Md.

These schools have had Negro students, but no graduates:

Starling Medical College, Columbus, Ohio.
University of Kansas, Kansas City, Kans.
Medical College, Los Angeles, Cal.
Colorado School of Medicine, Boulder, Colo.

The following schools reported students and graduates as follows:

NAME OF SCHOOL	Negro Students In past	At present	Graduates	Rank of such students In Character	In Ability
Dartmouth Medical School....		1	5		Fair
Colorado School of Medicine...	5 or 6	0	0	Well	Not so well
Medical College, Los Angeles..	Several	0	0		
Cleveland Homeop. Med. Col..		1	12		Well
Medical Dep. of Univ. of Pa....		4	26 since 1882		Variable
University of Kansas............	Several	3	0	Well	Variable
Starling Med. Col., Columbus, O.	2 or 3	0	0		
Harvard Univ. Medical School		4	6		Fair
Woman's Medical Col. of Pa....		1	12	Well	Well
University of Michigan..........		4	(?)	Well	Variable
Eclectic Med. Inst., Cincinnati	20	2	8		Well
Eclectic Med. Col., N. Y. City..		0	4		
Denver Gross Medical College.		2	1		Below average
Medico - Chirurgical College, Philadelphia, Pa...............		2	5	High	Considerable
Hahneman Medical College, Philadelphia, Pa...............		2	4 or more		Well
Drake University College of Medicine, Des Moines, Ia.....			1		
Cooper Med.Col., San Francisco	1	0	1	Good	Moderate
Medical Department of Columbia University, New York....	0	1	1		Variable
College of Medicine and Surgery, University of Minnesota..	6	0	1		Variable
Hahnemann Med. Col., Chicago	2	0	0		Well
College of Physicians and Surgeons, San Francisco.........		1	0	Excellent	Average
Physio-Medical College of Indiana............................	3	0	2	Honorable	Average
Hering College, Chicago........			0	2	A good average
Cornell Univ. Med. Col., N. Y..	1	0	0		Excellent
Col. of Physicians and Surgeons of Hamlin Univ., Minneapolis	?	0	(?)		
Western Reserve University, Cleveland, O...................		0	10		Fair
Toledo Med. Col., Toledo, O....	2	0	1	Fairly	Well
College of Medicine, Syracuse University, New York.........		1	2	High	Variable
Denver Homeopathic College..		0	1		Excellent
Long Island College Hospital ..		2	12 (?)		Very well
Medical Department, University of Buffalo, New York		0	3		Average
Ohio Med. Univ., Columbus, O.		8	12		Average
Rush Medical College, University of Chicago....................		1	5		Very well
Medical Department, Western Reserve University...........		0	8 (?)		Fairly well
Kansas Medical College, Topeka		1			Well
Boston University School of Medicine.....................		4	7	Average	Fair
Ft. Wayne College of Medicine, Ft. Wayne, Ind...............		0	1		Equal footing
Detroit College of Medicine....		3	30		Fair
Homeopathic Med. Col., N. Y..		2	6		Well
Medical Department of Yale University, New Haven, Ct..		0	9		Well
Creighton Medical College, Omaha, Neb....................	Several	0	1		Below average
Northwestern University Medical School, Chicago.........		11	10	Good	Fair average
Homeopathic Department University, Michigan.............		1	1		Fair
Albany Medical College, N. Y..		0	2 or 3		
Bennett Col. of Eclectic Medicine and Surgery, Chicago....		4	?		Average
Known to be dead		66	213 ?		

A few extracts from letters received from the college officials follow:

UNIVERSITY OF PENNSYLVANIA:
The ability of these [26] graduates has been quite variable.

HARVARD:
I am unable to state how they rank in character, but in ability, I should say fair.

YALE:
One of these eight graduates I should rank as being exceptionally good, and the others as about the average of our pass men.

If the colored men had sufficient means to pay their way without being obliged to do work and drudgery for a living through college, their chances would be much better.

CORNELL:
Since the opening of the college in 1898 we have had one Negro student, who came from the West Indies. He was an excellent student but after completing three years died of tuberculosis.

LONG ISLAND COLLEGE HOSPITAL:
These students (probably a dozen) have ranked very well in character and ability; occasionally on the honor rolls.

OHIO MEDICAL UNIVERSITY:
During the past thirteen years we have graduated on an average of one or two each year. I can freely say that these young men have shown themselves to be average students in both character and ability, and we have had some exceptions in both directions.

I personally recall two men as exceptionally good students and their work in the general field since graduating has been satisfactory evidence of excellence as men and representatives of their profession.

COLLEGE OF PHYSICIANS AND SURGEONS (*Medical Department of Columbia University*):
The student who is at present in the college has a very good record, but the [one] graduate turned out very badly after leaving the college and was for a time confined in prison.

NORTHWESTERN UNIVERSITY:
The two who will graduate next June, the only colored men in the senior class, are above the average of the class: in fact, Mr. ——— ranks about fourth in the class.

THE UNIVERSITY OF MINNESOTA:
I believe there is but one colored graduate of this medical school and he was one of the best.

Perhaps, half dozen more have made the attempt and all have failed, being mediocre or worse. This is not of record, but my recollection.

WOMAN'S MEDICAL COLLEGE OF PENNSYLVANIA:
The number [12] is so small compared with the total number of alumnæ that it is not possible to make intelligent comparisons.

UNIVERSITY OF MICHIGAN (*Homeopathic Department*):
The only colored graduate in the last ten years was of the pure-looking African type; was in his classes one of the best students we have ever had. Never got a condition, always had his lessons and seemed to have ample scientific grasp.

KANSAS MEDICAL COLLEGE:

The answers to your questions regarding Negro graduates may be summed in the description of one student who is now in our graduating class. This student ranks well in his classes and in character. He has been one of our best football players, and is generally liked in school.

RUSH MEDICAL COLLEGE (*University of Chicago*):

During my connection with the college, seventeen years, the colored students that we had have ranked very well in character and ability. I am bound to say, however, that I think, as a rule, that those persons in which there is a mixture of the Caucasian blood have ranked higher than those of purely Negro descent, in that they have had better opportunities for preparation. Even in the last two or three years some of our colored students have been obliged to drop out because they felt themselves unable to keep up with the classes. This has been due, in part, to the fact that they were handicapped in being obliged to do a great deal of outside work to earn a living, and not because they were not as capable.

JEFFERSON MEDICAL COLLEGE (*Philadelphia, Pa.*):

We have five students at present of Negro descent.

The character and ability of these students has been good.

As the color is not mentioned in our alumni list, I have no means of identifying them.

WESTERN PENNSYLVANIA MEDICAL COLLEGE:

We have two students and four graduates. They have ranked very good in character and ability.

BOWDOIN COLLEGE (*Maine*):

Have only two graduates. Fairly good in ability and of good character.

In the replies from three schools the name of the school was not given:

A New York city medical school has a graduate who ranked " equal " to his fellows.

A Chicago school has eight students and six graduates. They show fair ability.

Another Chicago school has one student, and he is " first-class."

We have, therefore, by this compilation 1,252 living physicians from Negro schools and 213 from white schools, or 1,465 in all. The census figures recorded 1,734 colored physicians in 1900.

There is not space in a report like this to say much of the success of colored physicians; a few specimen cases from letters of college officials and others are added:

Dr. ———, of Newport, R. I., is the leading X-ray specialist of New England, and has been called in consultation by the best practitioners.

It may interest you to know that Dr. ———, who entered Rush as a graduate from the University of Wisconsin, and who is now practicing in Maryland, stood at the head of the list when he took the examination for licensure before the Maryland State Board of Medical Examiners. He was in competition with a number of graduates from the Johns Hopkins University Medical School.

Dr. —— received letter from examiner in surgery (State Board of Pennsylvania), complimenting him on that branch as being the best examination passed before the board in surgery and anatomy up to that time; practiced in Philadelphia for three years; then entered University of Bishop's College (McGill) Montreal, Canada; graduated spring, 1901.

Went to University of London, England, and was attached to London Hospital for two years; passed the examination of the Royal College of Surgery of London and is now a M. R. C. S. (of England) and L. R. C. P. (of London). To the best of my knowlege it's the only instance of these degrees held by a Negro in this country, and I don't suppose more than a dozen whites. Was assistant at the Royal South London Ophthalmic Hospital (London, England,) and also a registered qualified druggist (P.h. G.) in Jamaica; now practicing in Philadelphia.

Drs. —— and ——, of Barbados, are practicing there and are the leading homeopathic physicians there.

Dr. —— had a long and honorable career. He was the first to reach the prostrate form of President Garfield and alleviated his suffering when the president was shot in the depot at Washington. He is given due credit by the biographers, but not as a Negro.

The first colored graduate of the Eclectic Medical Institute (Cincinnati) was a man named Tàte. He graduated in 1880 or 1881 and went to Memphis, Tenn., where he.volunteered during the yellow fever epidemic. Made a record for himself such as to receive a medal from the city government and a handsome purse, but succumbed to the disease and died.

One of the most prominent surgeons of the West is a Chicago Negro. He was—

Born in Pennsylvania in 1858, is attending surgeon to the Cook County and Provident hospitals in Chicago, and was formerly at the head of the Freedman's Hospital in Washington. In 1893 Dr. —— operated upon a stab wound of the heart which had pierced the pericardium; the operation was successful, and the patient was known to be alive three years afterward. "Official records do not give a single title descriptive of suture of the pericardium or heart in the human subject. This being the fact, this case is the first successful or unsuccessful case of suture ever recorded." So said the *Medical Record*, of March 27, 1897. The case attracted the attention of the medical world, as have several other cases of Dr. ——. It was only last summer that the Charlotte *Medical Journal*, of North Carolina, published a violent article against Negro physicians, stating that the formation of the Negro head was such that they could never hope to gain efficiency in such a profession. About the same time the editors, Doctors Register and Montgomery, were writing the following letter to Dr. —— in blissful ignorance of his race:

"We have just read a paper of yours entitled 'A Report of Two Cases of Cesarean section under Positive Indications with Termination in Recovery' that was recently published in *Obstetrics*. You are an attractive writer. Is it possible for us to get you to do a little editorial writing for us?" *

Dr. —— was four years chief medical inspector in the Health Department of the city of Denver, and was special state inspector in contagious diseases 1899.

---

* *Booklover's Magazine,* July, 1903.

Dr. ——— is pathologist at Wesboro Insane Hospital, and one of the best men in his line of work in the state of Massachusetts.

Curiously enough the first women physicians in the South were colored. Some examples follow:

The press in general spoke highly of the brilliant state examination which ——— passed and the fact that she was the first woman to practice in Alabama: later the local press commented favorably on her ability as a physician.

I am informed by the legal authorities that I was the first and at present the only woman physician practicing in Savannah.

She graduated at the Woman's College of Philadelphia and established herself at Columbia, S. C., and was the first woman physician in the state. When she first settled in Columbia there was no hospital there. Seeing dire need of one she opened her own house as one for a time—then she rented a building where she now accommodates thirty patients (but that is crowded). This was the only emergency hospital in Columbia. The four railroads have contracts with the hospital to care for their employees when injured. She had 500 surgical operations there in two years. All of the city physicians—white—affiliate with the management and place their patients there, and hold every important consultation with her.

Some persons object to being classed as " Negroes " simply because they are of Negro descent:

——— was a colored physician, who recently died at ———. He married a white lady: two children survive. He passed as for white; went into white society, was an eminent practitioner and on visiting staff at ——— Hospital, and did not associate with colored people.

If you wish to give correct statistics on the subject you can not include the name of one who by 93 per cent belongs to another race.

The path of the Negro physician is not, however, always smooth. As a student he may be rebuffed even at the larger colleges as this letter illustrates. It was in answer to a simple inquiry as to terms of admission from a colored boy:

UNIVERSITY OF PENNSYLVANIA,
Department of Medicine.

Office of the Dean,
    Charles H. Frazier, M. D.

Philadelphia, February 10, 1906.

Mr. William J. Harvey, Jr.,
    Atlanta Baptist College.
Dear Sir:

Replying to your letter of the 5th instant, I am afraid that your being colored would handicap you very seriously in this institution, inasmuch as in all our clinical work the students are brought in close contact with the patients, and very many patients object to being examined by, or being exhibited before colored students.   Yours very truly,
                    CHARLES H. FRAZIER, Dean.

The colored physician, if successful, is in danger of the mob in certain sections, as this communication, dated December 1, 1906, shows:

We were out that evening at a tent show. The city marshal, who has known me from babyhood, appointed me deputy marshal for the night. The big show had finished when I walked up the aisle separating the two races and asked a young lady whom I accompanied there if she desired to remain to concert. She decided to remain. I turned to pass out, when a white man, who carries the reputation of being mean to Negroes, ordered me to sit down. I told him that I was not ready to be seated. He then drew back his stick and struck me. I had a stick and went for him with that. At my getting the best with stick, he drew his revolver and fired at me, the ball taking effect in the muscular part of right arm. I attacked this white man and when I jumped upon him about for other whites pounced upon me with guns, knives and clubs. Through the aid of some of the whites, I was freed from the howling mob and rushed to the jail. I received some ugly bruises about the face and head. I asked a doctor whom I knew to come up and look after me. He came and before he could dress even one wound the sheriff was notified of a raging mob of lawless white citizens. I asked the sheriff to let me out of jail that I might have an opportunity to shun the mob since I felt sure he could not protect me. He granted my request and guarded me to a dark street. I had committed no offense, neither had I violated any law. It was a matter of prejudice on the part of inefficient doctors and poor worthless whites. When I got out of the jail I decided once to go to my home and get $500.00 that I placed under my safe in my office that afternoon, but hearing the mob whoop down about there I continued out of the city. I am told that the poor scoundrels broke into my house and office and robbed them of their valuables, then went into the parlor and made up fire and completely destroyed my household affairs, office and office fixtures, including cabinet with instruments worth at least $1,000.00 and library of books worth about $1,200.00.

My house was worth about	$ 1,200.00
Household effects	1,100.00
Office library and fixtures	1,300.00
Instruments and cabinet	1,000.00
Cash and valuables destroyed	1,500.00
Total amount	$6,100.00
Amount of insurance	1,500.00
Total loss	$4,600.00

My realty and personal property I shall have to sell at a great sacrifice. What troubles me most of all is that there is no remedy for such troubles to Negroes in this section of the country. Other Negroes here are even afraid to express themselves. If they express themselves as being against such, they endanger their lives.

I must say just here, if you see any part of this letter you would like to publish, do not furnish it as coming directly from me, because it might give me more trouble.

14. Dentists and Pharmacists

The census gives the following details as to dentists:

```
1890.............................  120
1900.............................  212
Increase......................  76.5 per cent.
```

Age: Years	1890	1900
15-24........................	32	45
25-34........................	36	93
35-44........................	25	43
45-54........................	13	17
55-64........................	10	10
65 and over.................	1	4
Under.......................	3	0
	120	212

There are no separate figures as to pharmacists in 1900. In 1890 there were 139 retail "dealers in drugs and medicines" recorded. This number was probably near 300 in 1900. From the colored medical schools mentioned above dentists and pharmacists have been graduated and are located as follows:

Colored Graduates in Dentistry

NAME OF STATE	Number of Graduates		Total
	Howard	Meharry	
Alabama...	2	5	7
Arkansas..	0	2	2
District of Columbia......................	19	0	19
Florida..	0	1	1
Georgia...	2	13	15
Illinois...	1	3	4
Indian Territory..	0	1	1
Kansas..	0	1	1
Kentucky...	0	5	5
Louisiana..	0	3	3
Maryland...	1	0	1
Massachusetts...	2	0	2
Mississippi...	1	0	1
Missouri..	0	4	4
New Jersey...	4	0	4
New York...	1	1	2
North Carolina..	3	0	3
Ohio..	1	0	1
Pennsylvania...	1	0	1
Rhode Island...	1	0	1
South Carolina...	1	1	2
Tennessee..	0	20	20
Texas...	0	8	8
Virginia..	1	0	1
Wisconsin..	1	0	1
South America...	1	0	1
West Indies..	5	0	5
Total...	48	68	116

Colored Graduates in Pharmacy

NAME OF STATE	NUMBER OF GRADUATES					
	Howard	Meharry	Flint	Leonard	Louisville	Total
Alabama	1	12		3		16
Arkansas	1	3	1			5
California	2					2
Colorado	1	3				4
District of Columbia	50					50
Florida	2	7				9
Georgia	7	6		3		16
Idaho	1					1
Illinois	1	6		2		9
Indiana	1					1
Kansas		1				1
Kentucky	1	7		1	1	10
Louisiana		3	2			5
Maryland	2					2
Michigan	1					1
Mississippi	2	4	2			8
Missouri	2	3				5
New Jersey	1					1
New York	2					2
North Carolina	1			23		24
Oklahoma	1					1
Pennsylvania	3					3
Rhode Island	1					1
South Carolina	2	2		4		8
Texas	1	7	1	2		11
Tennessee	2	16		2		20
Virginia	5	2		7		14
Washington	1					1
West Virginia	3			2		5
South America	2					2
West Indies	3					3
Unknown	2					2
Total	105	82	6	49	1	243

A colored dentist has been prominent in the National Dental Association and was appointed at the head of the international dental clinics at the St. Louis fair. Southern men, however, learned that he was colored and made it so unpleasant that he resigned. The incident eventually led to the formation of a Southern Dental Association.

The pharmacists go mostly into colored drug stores, of which there are some 200. We have record of the following by states:

DRUG STORES

Alabama 10	Kansas 5	Pennsylvania 2
Arkansas 8	Kentucky 7	Rhode Island 1
Colorado 4	Louisiana 1	South Carolina 4
District of Columbia 14	Mississippi 2	Tennessee 8
Florida 16	Missouri 8	Texas 2
Georgia 21	Maryland 2	Virginia 11
Illinois 5	Massachusetts 4	—
Indiana 1	North Carolina 10	Total 160
Iowa 2	New York 5	
Indian Territory 4	Ohio 3	

Statistics of forty-three of these stores follow:

PLACE	Year established	Capital	Persons Devoting—	
			All time	Part time
Little Rock, Ark	1893	$ 3,600	3	5
Newport, Ark	1906	1,843	4	2
Portsmouth, Va	1896	5,000	3	1
Pine Bluff, Ark	1904	5,000	4	.
Helena, Ark	1904	2,500	2	5
Anniston, Ala	1892	10,000	4	2
Key West, Fla	1904	6,000	5	6
Augusta, Ga	1892	2,000	2	6
Atlanta, Ga	1904	700	3	.
Sparta, Ga	1905	2,500	2	1
Albany, Ga	1902	1,360	7	4
Columbus, Ga	1894	3,000	2	3
Washington, D. C	1903	1,300	1	1
Washington, D. C	1894	5,000	2	2
Washington, D. C	1905	3,000	2	5
Washington, D. C	1894	3,000	1	3
Washington, D. C	1905	3,000	2	3
Washington, D. C	1902	3,000	2	4
Norfolk, Va	1905	1,500	2	3
·Richmond, Va	1886	4,200	3	4
Staunton, Va	1902	8,000	3	2
Roanoke, Va	1894	3,000	3	1
Charleston, S. C	1899	2,000	2	.
Henderson, N. C	1906	1,000	3	2
Raleigh, N. C	1904	5,000	4	3
Jacksonville, Fla	1902	3,000	3	1
Pensacola, Fla	1896	800	3	2
Mobile, Ala	1902	1,650	2	.
Mobile, Ala	1905	850	1	1
Charleston, S. C	1883	2,000	2	.
Charleston, S. C	1905	5,000	1	3
Brunswick, Ga	1903	5,000	3	4
Savannah, Ga	1905	1,000	2	5
Boley, Indian Territory	1904	2,500	2	1
Muskogee, Indian Territory	1905	2,500	3	1
Topeka, Kans	1898	2,500	3	.
Chicago, Ill	1905	4,000	4	2
New Bedford, Mass	1817	3,500	2	3
Baltimore, Md	1902	1,800	3	3
Cincinnati, Ohio	1904	3,000	3	1
St. Louis, Mo	1904	3,500	2	1
Opelika, Ala	1902	4,500	2	3
Mobile, Ala	1902	6,280	3	2
Total		$139,883	115	401

The Negro drug stores of the land represent probably an investment of nearly $500,000 and employ about 800 persons.

Some comments follow:

CHARLESTON.—This community has a Negro population of about 35,000 and an adjacent Negro population coming here for medical treatment of about 100,000.

Four Negro druggists including myself.

I fill about 3,000 prescriptions a year, not including repeats. General drug business good and increasing. Bulk of my patronage from the poorer class.

MUSKOGEE, I. T.—We are doing a nice drug business, average sales about one thousand ($1,000) dollars a month.

CINCINNATI, O.—This store was opened April, 1904. The owner was forced to the wall October of the same year. A white druggist on the opposite corner bought him out. I offered him $50 more than he gave for the store. He refused. I went up town and had a Jew to buy him out for less money.

WASHINGTON, D. C.—Having started with ten dollars without fixtures, etc., since have purchased fixtures, soda fountain, etc., with stock on hand assessed at $1,300. Store now in debt $50.

WASHINGTON, D. C.—This drug store is on one of tne most popular business thoroughfares in the town, and is well patronized by the members of both races.

PORTSMOUTH, Va.—I started business with only $16 and I went in debt to get my stock. I leased the place where I did business, paying $10 per month. Now I've purchased a corner lot, paid $1,400 for same. I built on this lot a two story brick building at a cost of $2,500, all paid for.

ALBANY, GA.—Present stock paid in full $7,000. Amount of dividends paid since beginning business $3,400.

LITTLE ROCK, ARK.—First five years, discouraging, disgusting. Second five years an increase of confidence as the public saw that it was a permanent fixture and so many of our people had opened business on six months trial and quit. Last three years are record breakers.

NEWPORT, ARK.—The company is composed of twenty-six men and women. The colored people give the store hearty support, and many of the best white citizens are fast flocking in.

ANNISTON, ALA.—Wholesale and retail business.

15. The Eleventh Atlanta Conference

The Eleventh Atlanta Conference convened at Ware chapel, Atlanta University, Tuesday, May 29, 1906, and carried out the following programme:

First Session, 10 A. M.

President Horace Bumstead, presiding.

Subject: "Health of Students."

Mortality in Cities—Mr. R. R. Wright, Jr., of the University of Pennsylvania, Philadelphia.

Tuberculosis—Dr. W. F. Penn, of Atlanta.

Special Session, 11:30 A. M. (Room 15)

A Talk to Boys—Dr. W. E. B. Du Bois, of Atlanta University. (Open to Senior Preparatory boys and College men).

Second Session, 3 P. M.

Ninth Annual Mothers' Meeting.

In charge of the Gate City Free Kindergarten Association, Mrs. John Hope presiding.

Subject: "The Training of Children and Preventive Medicine."

Exhibit of Work and Exercises:

Kindergarten No. 1—Mrs. J. P. Williamson.

Kindergarten No. 2—Miss Ola Perry.

Child Training—Mrs. P. J. Bryant.

Preventive Medicine—Dr. A. G. Copeland.

President Horace Bumstead, presiding.

Remarks—President Bumstead.

Subject: "Physique, Health, etc."

Tuberculosis—Dr. S. P. Lloyd, of Savannah.

Negro Physique—Dr. Franz Boas, of Columbia University, New York.

Seeing and Hearing—Dr. C. V. Roman, of Meharry Medical College, Nashville.

The final work of the Conference was the adoption of the following resolutions. The committee consisted of R. R. Wright, Jr., fellow of the University of Pennsylvania; Franz Boas, professor of Anthropology, of Columbia University; and W. E. B. DuBois, secretary of the Conference.

RESOLUTIONS

The Eleventh Atlanta Conference has made a study of the physique, health and mortality of the Negro American, reviewing the work of the first conference held ten years ago and gathered some of the available data at hand today.

The Conference notes first an undoubted betterment in the health of Negroes: the general death rate is lower, the infant mortality has markedly decreased, and the number of deaths from consumption is lessening.

The present death rate is still, however, far too high and the Conference recommends the formation of local health leagues among colored people for the dissemination of better knowledge of sanitation and preventive medicine. The general organizations throughout the country for bettering health ought to make special effort to reach the colored people. The health of the whole country depends in no little degree upon the health of Negroes.

Especial effort is needed to stamp out consumption. The Conference calls for concerted action to this end.

The Conference does not find any adequate scientific warrant for the assumption that the Negro race is inferior to other races in physical build or vitality. The present differences in mortality seem to be sufficiently explained by conditions of life; and physical measurements prove the Negro a normal human being capable of average human accomplishments.

The Conference is glad to learn of the forty (40) Negro hospitals, the two hundred (200) drug stores, and the fifteen hundred (1500) physicians, but points out that with all this advance the race is in dire need of better hospital facilities and more medical advice and attention.

The Conference above all reiterates its well known attitude toward this and all other social problems: the way to make conditions better is to study the conditions. And we urge again the systematic study of the Negro problems and ask all aid and sympathy for the work of this Conference in such study.

COMMENTS OF THE PRESS, 1896-1906

Boston Transcript, July 8, 1896:

Atlanta University, Atlanta, Ga., has undertaken a new and most important work for the benefit of the colored people living in cities.

U. S. Bulletin of Labor, May, 1897:

Great credit is due to the investigators for their work in the investigation.

Outlook, Jan. 28, 1898:

The report of the third annual Conference is now before us and is a valuable sociological publication.

London Spectator, March 31, 1900:

The future of the Negro population of the United States is a problem charged with such serious possibilities that any light which can be shed upon it by an examination of present conditions and tendencies deserves a most cordial welcome. This work is being done with much intelligence, discrimination and assiduity at the instance and under the inspiration of the Atlanta University.

Manchester Guardian, April 26, 1901:

Careful studies of the life of Negroes in the United States.

London Speaker, June 22, 1901:

As important and interesting as the reports that have preceded it.

Biblical World, July 1, 1901:

For anyone who wishes to understand this important subject this pamphlet gives a vast amount of information gathered at first-hand.

Hartford Courant, April 5, 1901:

Based upon painstaking investigation of the facts.

Publications of the Southern History Association, Sept., 1901; July, Sept., 1902; Nov., 1904:

Most admirable investigations into this vast ethnic problem.

A most capital piece of work on that mighty race question. . . . It goes without saying that we have a most competent study based on careful historical research.

The best scientific work on the Negro question of the last two or three years.

The work done under the direction of the Atlanta Conference is entitled to the respectful and thoughtful consideration of every man interested in any aspect of the life of the American Negro.

Dial, May 16, 1902:

These studies of the Negro problem which are being made with so much intelligence by Atlanta University are of great sociological and educational value, and deserve to be widely examined.

School Review, June, 1902:

The work of this conference is constructive and merits hearty support.

New Bedford Standard, May 10, 1902:

An exceptionally valuable study of one of the most important of all the problems connected with the presence of the Negro race in America.

Outlook, July 12, 1902:

Every year since their organization in 1896 the Atlanta Conferences have published an invaluable report upon present conditions among the Negroes.

American Journal of Sociology, May, 1903:

The most exhaustive study thus far made of the economic aspects of the problem.

Boston Herald, Feb. 24, 1903:

It is not easy to estimate too highly the series of yearly reports that are coming from Atlanta University relative to the condition of the Negro population of the country. They are social studies that treat of matters about which there is to be found nowhere else so carefully gathered and trustworthy information.

Outlook, Mar. 7, 1903:

No student of the race problem, no person who would either think or speak upon it intelligently, can afford to be ignorant of the facts brought out in the Atlanta series of sociological studies of the conditions and the progress of the Negro.

Philadelphia Press, Mar. 8, 1903:

The most important study which has been made . . . in which the industrial condition of the Negro is presented with an accuracy and minuteness which has marked all the issues which have succeeded the annual conferences held in connection with the [Atlanta] university.

South Atlantic Quarterly, Oct., 1904:

They constitute, so far as the reviewer can learn, the most important body of direct evidence ever published as to moral and religious conditions of our colored people.

N. Y. Evening Post, July 3, 1905:

The only scientific studies of the Negro question being made today are those carried on by Atlanta University.

N. Y. Observer Jan. 24, 1907:

It is therefore with pleasure that we welcome a thoughtful "Social Study" of Negro crime (particularly in Georgia) prepared under the auspices of Atlanta University, which has already done such good work for society in connection with its nine "Atlanta Conferences" for the study of pressing social problems.

The
Negro American
Family

Report of a Social Study made principally by the
College Classes of 1909 and 1910 of Atlanta University, under the patronage of the Trustees of the
John F. Slater Fund; together with the Proceedings
of the 13th Annual Conference for the Study of the
Negro Problems, held at Atlanta University on Tuesday, May the 26th, 1908

Edited by

W. E. Burghardt Du Bois

Corresponding Secretary of the Conference

The Atlanta University Press
ATLANTA, GEORGIA
1908

"DIE weiblicher Tugend steht bei manchen Stämmen in viel höherer Achtung als die typischen Sittengemälde vermuthen lassen."

Schneider, on Negroes.

"THE contempt we have been taught to entertain for the blacks makes us fancy many things that are founded neither in reason nor experience."

Alexander Hamilton.

"AS fathers, husbands and brothers, you are summoned to rally around the standard of the Eagle to defend all which is dear in existence."

Andrew Jackson to the Negroes of Louisiana in 1814.

Contents

The Thirteenth Annual Conference

PROGRAMME

Subject: The Negro American Family

First Session, 10:00 a. m.

President Ware, presiding.

Subject: "The Home."

Address: Dr. G. F. Dickerman, Field Agent of the Trustees of the Slater Fund.

Address: Mr. W. T. B. Williams, Field Agent of the Trustees of the Slater Fund.

Second Session, 11:30 a. m.

Subject: "Health and the Family."

Special Talk to Men: Dr. J. W. Madison, of Atlanta.

Special Talk to Women: Miss L. S. Cathcart, of Lincoln Academy, N. C.

Third Session, 3:00 p. m.

Eleventh Annual Mothers' Meeting. (In charge of the Gate City Free Kindergarten Association), Mrs. Hattie Landrum Green, presiding.

Subject: "The Children."

1. Kindergarten songs, games and exercises by 150 children of the four free kindergartens:

> East Cain Street—Miss Ola Perry.
> Bradley Street—Mrs. J. P. Williamson.
> White's Alley—Miss Ethel Evans.
> Summerhill—Miss Hattie Sims.

2. Remarks by visitors.

3. Reports of the year's work and contributions.

Fourth Session, 8:00 p. m.

President E. T. Ware, presiding.

Subject: "The Negro American Family."

Paper: Archdeacon E. L. Henderson, of the Diocese of Georgia.

Address: Miss Jane Addams, of Hull House, Chicago.

ERRATUM

Page 122. To the table on the proportion of students paying their way, add,

$$1878\text{-}1879 \ldots\ldots\ldots 37.4\% \ldots\ldots\ldots 62.6\%$$

Preface

In 1897 the Atlanta University Negro Conference made an investigation into the "Social and Physical Condition of Negroes in Cities," which involved a study of 4742 individuals gathered in 1137 families, living in 59 different groups, in 18 different cities. These data were compiled by the United States Department of Labor and published in Bulletin number ten; and, as the editor said, "Great credit is due the investigators for their work." The object of the investigation was to study the mortality of Negroes and the social and family conditions. The study of Mortality was continued in 1906 by Atlanta University publication number eleven. The present study continues the study of social conditions from the point of view of the family group.

This study is therefore a further carrying out of the Atlanta University plan of social study of the Negro American by means of an annual series of decennially recurring subjects covering, so far as is practicable, every phase of human life. The object of these studies is primarily scientific—a careful research for truth conducted as thoroughly, broadly and honestly as the material resources and mental equipment at command will allow; but this is not our sole object : we wish not only to make the Truth clear but to present it in such shape as will encourage and help social reform. Our financial resources are unfortunately meagre: Atlanta University is primarily a school and most of its funds and energy go to teaching. It is, however, also a seat of learning and as such it has endeavored to advance knowledge, particularly in matters of racial contact and development, which seems obviously its nearest field. In this work it has received unusual encouragement from the scientific world, and the published results of these studies are used in America, Europe, Asia and Africa. Very few books on the Negro problem or any phase of it have been published in the last decade which have not acknowledged their indebtedness to our work.

On the other hand, the financial support given this work has been very small. The total cost of the 13 publications has been about $14,000, or a little over $1,000 a year. The growing demands of the work, the vast field to be covered and the delicacy and equipment needed in such work call for far greater resources. We need, for workers, laboratory and publications, a fund of $6,000 a year, if this work is going adequately to fulfill its promise. Last year a small temporary grant from the Carnegie Institution of Washington, D. C., greatly helped us, and this year our work was saved from suspension by an appropriation from the John F. Slater Fund.

In past years we have been enabled to serve the United States Bureau of Labor, the United States Census, the Board of Education of the

English Government, many scientific associations, professors in nearly all the leading universities, and many periodicals and reviews. May we not hope in the future for such increased financial resources as will enable us to study adequately this the greatest group of social problems that ever faced America ?

A Select Bibliography of the Negro American Family

Bibliography

Atlanta University Publication No. 10—Bibliography of the Negro American. 1905.
Edwards, R. H.—Studies in American Social Conditions, No. 2: The Negro Problem, 1908 (See Section 4).

Books and Pamphlets

Atlanta University Publications—Mortality among Negroes in Cities. Atlanta. 1896. 51 pp. 8vo.
Atlanta University Publications—Social and Physical Condition of Negroes in Cities. Atlanta, 1897. 72, 14 pp. 8vo.
Atwater, Wilbur Olin, and Charles Dayton Woods—Dietary studies with reference to the food of the Negroes in Alabama in 1895 and 1896. Washington, 1897. 69 pp. 8vo. (U. S. Dept. of Agri.)
Bacon, Benjamin C.—Statistics of the colored people of Philadelphia. Phila., 1856.
Bacon, Benjamin C.—Ibid. Second edition with statistics of crime. Phila., 1859. 3-24 pp. 8vo.
Baltimore Association for the moral and educational improvement of the colored people. Annual report. 2d, 3d, 1866-67. Balt., 1866. 68, v. 8vo.
Brackett, Jeffrey Richardson—Notes on the progress of the colored people of Maryland since the war. Balt., 1890. 96 pp. (Johns Hopkins University Studies. Series 8, No. 7-9.) 8vo. Supplement to the Negro in Maryland.
Buford, Mrs.—Domestic missions among the plantation Negroes. N. Y., 189—? 4 pp. 8vo.
Chestnutt, Charles W.—The house behind the cedars. Boston, 1900. 8vo.
The marrow of tradition. Boston, 1901.
The wife of his youth. Boston, 1899. 12mo.
Clowes, W. Laird—Black America. Reprint from the Times. London, 1891. xiii, 240 pp. sm. 8vo. Map.
Condition of the people of color in Ohio. With interesting anecdotes. Boston, 1839. 48 pp. 12mo
Crummell, Alexander—The black woman of the South: her neglects and her needs. Cincin., 14 pp. 8vo.
Delaware association for the moral improvement and education of the colored people. An. Reps. 1867, 1869, 1870. Wilmington, Del.
DuBois, W. E. B.—The Philadelphia Negro. Publications of the University of Pennsylvania, No. 14. Phila., 1899. 20, 520 pp. Diagrams, 3 maps.
DuBois, W. E. B.—The souls of black folk. Chicago, 1903. viii, (1), 264, (1) pp. 8vo.
Edwards, Bryan—History, civil and commercial, of the British Colonies in the West Indies. Phila., 1806. 4 vols. 8vo. Portrs. Atlas, 4to. Folded table.
Elwang, Wm. Wilson—The Negroes of Columbia, Mo. Columbia, 1904. vii, 69 pp. 8vo. Plates. Map.
Frissell, Hollis Burke, and Isabel Brevier—Dietary studies of Negroes in eastern Va. in 1897 and 1898. Wash., 1899. 45 pp. 8vo. (U. S. Dept. of Agric.)

Bibliography 7

Goodell, Will—The American slave code in theory and practice. Judicial decisions and illustrative facts. N. Y., 1853. 431 pp. 12mo.

Haygood, Atticus Green—Our brother in black, etc. N. Y., 1881. 252 pp. 12mo.

Hickok, C. T.—The Negro in Ohio. 1802-1870. Cleveland, 1896. 182 pp. 12mo.

Hrdlicke, Ales—Anthropological investigations on one thousand white and colored children of both sexes, the inmates of the New York juvenile asylum, etc. N, Y., 189—? 86 pp. 8vo.

Ingle, Edward—The Negro in the District of Columbia, Johns Hopkins University Studies. Vol. XI. Balt., 1893. 110 pp. 8vo,

Johnson, Mrs. E, A.—The Hazeley family. Philadelphia, 1894.

Jones, C. C.—The religious instruction of the Negroes in the United States. Savannah, 1842. 277 pp. 12mo.

Kemble, Fanny—A journal of a residence on a Georgian plantation. N. Y., 1863. 337 pp. 12mo

Kingsley, M. H.—Story of West Africa, 1899.
West African Studies.
Travels in West Africa.

Laidlaw, Walter, editor—The federation of Churches and Christian workers in New York City. N. Y., Sociological canvasses, 1896—. 8vo. First, 112 pp., 2d, 116 pp.

Livermore, Mrs. Elizabeth D.—Zoe; or the quadroon triumph. A tale for the times. 1st vol., 327 pp. 2d vol., 306 pp. 12mo.

Majors, M. A.—Noted Negro women. Chicago, 1893.

Miller, Kelly—Race Adjustment. 1908. 306 pp.

Minutes of the Biennial Meetings of the National Association of Colored Women. Nos. 1-6, 1897-1908.

McDonald, Arthur—Colored children. Chicago, 1899. 14 pp. 16mo.

Mossell, Mrs. N. F.—The work of Afro-American women. Phila., 1894. 178 pp. 12mo.

Needles, Edward—Ten years' progress, or a comparison of the state and condition of the colored people in the city and county of Philadelphia from 1837 to 1847. Phila., 1849.

Negro mother's appeal, The—A poem. London, 185—? 4 pp. 8vo.

Negro young people's Christian and educational congress, Atlanta, 1902. The United Negro. Atlanta, 1902. 600 pp. 8vo.

Olmstead, F. L.—A journey in the back country. N. Y., 1861. 492 pp. 12mo.

Olmstead, F. L.—A journey in the seaboard slave states. N. Y., 1856. 723 pp. 12mo.

Olmstead, F. L.—A journey through Texas. N. Y., 1857. 516 pp. 12mo.

Payne, Daniel A.—A treatise on domestic education. Cincin., 1885.

Pollard, Edward A.—Black diamonds gathered in the darkey homes of the South. N. Y., 1859. 12mo.

Richmond, Leigh—The Negro servant. Boston, 1814. 16 pp. 12mo.

Robertson, John—On the period of puberty in the Negro. Edinburgh, 1848. 8 pp. 8vo.

Schneider, W.—Die Kulturfaehigkeit des Negers. Frankfort, 1885.

Scruggs, L. A.—Women of distinction. Raleigh, 1893.

Shorter, Susan L.—Heroines of African Methodism. Xenia, O., 1891.

Smith, Mrs. Amanda—Autobiography of Amanda Smith. Chicago, 1893.

Stowe, Harriet Beecher—Uncle Tom's Cabin. 1852.

Stowe, Harriet Beecher—Dred. 577 pp.

Truth, Sojourner—Sojourner Truth's narrative. Boston, 1875.

United States Census—References to the Negro-American family:
1890: Vol. on Population, Part I: sex, conjugal condition.
1890: Vol. on Farms and Homes: ownership.
1900: Vol. II: Sex, conjugal condition, homes owned.
Vol. V, VI: Farms and Crops: ownership.
Special Reports: Statistical Atlas.
Bulletins:
No. 8: Negroes in the United States by W. F. Wilcox and W. E. B. DuBois. Wash. 1904. 333 pp.
No. 22: Birth rate.

United States Department (Bureau) of Labor Bulletins:
No. 10. Condition of the Negro in various cities.

No. 14.   The Negroes of Farmville, Va.: A social study, by W. E. B. DuBois, Ph.D.
No. 22.   The Negro in the black belt: Some social sketches, by W. E. B. DuBois, Ph.D.
No. 32.   The Negroes of Sandy Spring, Md.   A social study, by W. T. Thom, Ph.D.
No. 35.   The Negro landholder of Georgia, by W. E. B. DuBois, Ph.D.
No. 37.   The Negroes of Litwalton, Va.: A social study of the "Oyster Negro," by William Taylor Thom, Ph.D.
No. 38.   The Negroes of Cinclaire Central Factory and Calumet Plantation, La., by J. Bradford Laws.
No. 48.   The Negroes of Xenia, Ohio, by Richard R. Wright, Jr., B.D.
Webster, Noah, Jr.—Effects of slavery on morals and industry.   Hartford, 1793.

Periodical Literature

American Economic Association Publications:
    Race traits and tendencies of the Negro.   F. L. Hoffman.   11:1.
American Journal of Sociology:
    Special assimilation.   S. E. Simons.   7:539-56.
Annals of the American Academy of Political Science:
    Settlement work among colored people.   C. B. Chapin.   21:336.
Arena:
    Impossibility of racial amalgamation.   W. S. McCurley.   21:446.
Atlantic:
    Negroes: What they are doing for themselves.   S. J. Barrows.   67:805.
    Mulatto factor in the race problem.   A. H. Stone.   91:658-62.
    Intensely human.   T. W. Higginson.   93:588.
Chambers Journal:
    Family life in Negro town.   17:12.
Charities Review:
    Colored children in the District of Columbia.   H. W. Lewis.   5:94.
    The make-up of Negro city groups.   (L. Brandt.)   Charities 15:7.
    The Negro home in New York.   M. W. Ovington.   15:25.
    Fresh-air work among colored children in New York.   M. W. Ovington.   17:115.
Chautauquan:
    Negroes in Washington, D. C.   M. W. Noble.   14:183.
    Southern Negro women.   O. R. Jefferson.   18:91.
    Social life of Southern Negroes.   W. T. Hewetson.   26:295.
Educational Review:
    Social and industrial capacities of Negroes of the South.   45:383.
Lend a Hand:
    The new Negro woman.   B. T. Washington.   15:254.
Nation:
    Social problem in Baltimore.   77:497-8.
National Monthly:
    Advance of Negro women in the South.   L. S. Orrick.   21:172.
Outlook:
    Gain in the life of Negro women.   Mrs. B. T. Washington.   76:271-4.
    The Negro woman and the South.   E. H. Abbott.   77:165, 689.
    Social and moral decadence of Negro women.   E. Tayleur.   76:266.
American Statistical Association:
    The Negroes of St. Louis.   VIII.   Lillian Brandt.
Hampton Negro Conference:
    Nine reports.   1897-1905.
Slater Fund, Proceedings and Occasional Papers of:
    No. 9.   Hobson and Hopkins: Colored women of the South.

The Negro American Family

Part 1. Marriage

Section 1. The Scope of this Study. This essay is an attempt to study the family among Negro-Americans—its formation, its home, its economic organization and its daily life. Such a study is at once faced by a lamentable dearth of material. There is comparatively little exact information on many important points. Nevertheless there is perhaps enough to give a tentative outline which more exact research may later fill in. In each case an attempt has been made to connect present conditions with the African past. This is not because Negro-Americans are Africans, or can trace an unbroken social history from Africa, but because there is a distinct nexus between Africa and America which, though broken and perverted, is nevertheless not to be neglected by the careful student. It is, however, exceedingly difficult and puzzling to know just where to find the broken thread of African and American social history. Accurate scientific inquiry must trace the social history in the seventeenth and eighteenth centuries of such Negro tribes as furnished material for the American slave trade. This inquiry is unfortunately impossible. We do not know accurately which tribes are represented in America, and we have but chance pictures of Negro social conditions in those times. Assuming, however, that the condition of Negro tribes in the nineteenth century reflected much of their earlier conditions, and that central and west Africa furnished most of the slaves, some attempt has been made to picture in broad outline the social evolution of the Negro in his family relations. For past American conditions the chief printed sources of information must be sought for in the vast literature of slavery. It is difficult to get a clear picture of the family relations of slaves, between the Southern apologist and his picture of cabin life, with idyllic devotion and careless toil, and that of the abolitionist with his tale of family disruption and cruelty, adultery and illegitimate mulattoes. Between these pictures the student must steer carefully to find a reasonable statement of the average truth.

For present conditions there are, in printed sources, only the Census reports, the eight studies of the United States Bureau of Labor, the previous studies of this series, and a few other sources noted in the bibliography. To supplement this, sixteen students of the college department of Atlanta University have made a study of 32 families. These studies are based on first-hand knowledge, and are unusually accurate. They do not, however, represent properly the proportion of different types among the mass of Negroes. Most of the families studied belong to the upper half of the black population. Finally, to repeat, this study is but a sketch with no pretense toward attempting to exhaust a fruitful subject. The main cause of its limitation is lack of material.

Section 2. Africa. The data relating to African family life is fragmentary, relating to different times and places, and has all degrees of authority, from that of hurried passing travellers to that of careful students of local conditions like Ellis. In generalizing, then, one can never be very certain of his ground. Ratzel gives this general summary:

Marriage is concluded by purchase. This feature appears, to the suppression of all others, among those tribes who accumulate capital by the ownership of herds. The practice of wife-purchase is found, however, also among agriculturists, and a man's wealth is measured by the number of his wives. Polygamy is usual wherever there are means to support it. We sometimes find the young bridegroom living in his father-in-law's establishment till the birth of his first child. Only the ruling chief of the district has the right to take any man's daughter without the usual payment, just as the chief's daughter may select any man, who thereby from a peasant becomes a chief. [1] Many pretty features are met with in connection with the courtship. Among the Madis the daughter first takes the mother into her confidence, and she informs the father. He fixes the price, and the couple obey absolutely, whether "yes" or "no" be the end of the negotiations. The marriage ceremonies are almost entirely secular. Oxen are slaughtered and there is singing and dancing. Among tribes where good manners prevail, during all this time the bride never leaves the hut which her father has built for her, but sits surrounded by her new brothers and sisters-in-law, who extol the charms of married life. At the same time she may partake of the marriage-feast, but without letting herself be seen. The following picture of a ceremony in greater style is given by Cameron. First the bridegroom performed a solo-dance for half an hour; and when this was over, the bride, a girl of nine of ten years old, was placed, with all the state that could be mustered up, on the shoulders of a woman, and borne to the dancing-place, while a second woman supported her from behind. The bridegroom gave her two or three tobacco-leaves and beads, which she threw among the dancers. Then the bridegroom and bride danced together for ten minutes with very unseemly gestures, after which he snatched her up, and disappeared with her into his own hut. The dancing, yelling, and drumming went on all night.

Three pictures of betrothal and marriage may be given; the first is among the Tshi-speaking people of the west coast, after Ellis:

When a girl arrives at the age of puberty, usually in the eleventh or twelfth year, she is taken to the water-side by others of her sex, and washed. At the same time an offering, consisting of boiled ham, mashed and mixed with palm-oil, is scattered upon the banks of the stream by the members of her family, who call upon the local gods, and inform them that the child has reached a marriageable age. In Cape Coast the girl is taken to the rock of the goddess Ichar-tsirew, and there washed. After the washing, a bracelet, consisting of one white bead, one black, and one gold, threaded on white cord, is put on the girl's wrist. These three beads in conjunction are termed

---

[1] Innumerable fairy tales point to the prevalence of this rule among primitive races.

abbum, and their being taken into use is a sign to the Sassur that its protecting care is no longer required. In the interior, on such occasions, girls are streaked with white. The natives seem to judge of a girl's fitness for the married state rather by the development of the bosom, than by the fact of menstruation having commenced; for if it be not developed at the time of performing the ceremony, they wait until it becomes so before taking the next step, which is for the purpose for announcing her eligibility for marriage to the men of the community. The girl is carefully adorned with all the ornaments and finery in the possession of the family, and frequently with others borrowed for the occasion. A silk cloth, in place of the ordinary cotton one, extends from the waist to the ankle, and is carefully arranged over a neatly-made attohfo, a kind of bustle made of rolled cloth, on which infants are carried, and which is kept in position by being attached to the girdle of beads worn by all females. The silk cloth is kept in position by a silk handkerchief, which is tied over it, round the waist. The hair is covered with gold ornaments, necklets, armlets, and anklets of gold and aggry beads encircle her neck, arms, and ankles; and her bosom and the upper part of her body, which is left uncovered, is marked with white clay in very fine lines.

Of course a girl thus attired would be a daughter of a wealthy family, but even the poorest people contrive to make some show on these occasions. Thus decorated, the virgin is escorted through the streets by a number of young people of her own sex, one of whom usually carries an open umbrella over her; while the remainder sing a song in honor of her maidenhood, and inform the men that their friend is now of a marriageable age. As the natives of the Gold Coast are a far handsomer people than any other Negro race with which I am acquainted, and possess usually superb figures, and an erectness of carriage which is no doubt due to the habit of carrying articles on the head, there is frequently something very attractive about these young girls, who, in their constrained and graceful movements, seem overflowing with youth and health.

Shortly after a virgin has thus advertised herself, she is married. Perhaps she has previously been betrothed; but, if not, the public advertisement of her charms and marriageable condition seldom fails to produce suitors. If the girl's family agree to the match, the amount to be paid for her is handed over by the suitor, and he at once prepares a marriage festival. Rum, gin, and other intoxicants, together with tobacco and pipes, are sent by him to the family of the bride, for the distribution amongst their kinsmen and intimate friends, and in notification of the approaching happy event. Sometimes it is announced with greater pomp, by means of a long train of people, bearing provisions of all kinds upon their heads, who parade through the town, singing songs in honor of the occasion. These preliminaries having been completed, the bride is led to the house of the bridegroom, where a feast is prepared for the friends of both families, who keep up an orgie until long after the husband has retired to his wife. Next morning, if the husband be satisfied concerning his wife's purity, he sprinkles her over the head, shoulders, and breast with a thick powdering of dried clay; and sends her to parade the streets, accompanied by a number of young girls, who sing songs in her honor. The day following, her life as a married woman commences. Should the husband be in doubt as to the virtue of his bride, he may, under certain conditions, repudiate her. [1]

---

[1] Ellis: The Tshi-Speaking Peoples of the Gold Coast of West Africa, pp. 234-7.

The second extract is from Tylor and relates to the Zulus:

Many Zulu girls are mere flirts, but when a girl finds that her father and brothers are seeking some one to recommend to her as a husband, she suddenly disappears, having hied away to her lover's kraal. If the family approves, in a day or two a party of men appear at the home of the future bride, driving two or three cows. They all act in a friendly manner and the visitors go away leaving the cattle.

When the eventful day arrives the bride and a party of friends set out for the bridegroom's kraal, which, however, they will not enter until night, singing and dancing as they go. Early in the morning they go to the nearest stream, and about noon come up and begin a dance, the bridegroom's party looking on. When both sides have finished, a cow slaughtered by the bridegroom's party is given to the bride's party.

At night the girl wanders about the kraal, followed by the female relatives of the bridegroom. She is supposed to be trying to run away and the girls to be preventing her. The next day the bridegroom, his brothers, sisters and friends, take their seats in the cattlefold and the last part of the ceremony takes place.

The bride comes in with her party of girls, carrying in her hand a spear. One girl bears a dish of water and a calabash, and another some beads. Then, coming up singing and dancing, the bride throws the water over her husband. She also sprinkles her brothers- and sisters-in-law, striking the latter, as a symbol that from that time she assumes authority over the girls in her husband's household. After this she breaks the staff of the spear and makes a run for the gate of the kraal. If she is not stopped by a young man appointed for the purpose it is a great disgrace, and the husband has to pay a cow to get her back. The marriage rites are then finished.

The third picture is from among the Yoruba-speaking peoples of the west coast:

When a man desires to marry a girl his parents visit her parents and make proposals of marriage. If they are accepted the suiter sends a present of native cloths and kola-nuts, and after consulting a *babalawo*, a day is appointed for the wedding.

The marriage feast is held at the house of the parents of the bridegroom, and the bride is conducted there by a procession of women, who sing an epithalamium. The bride is put in bed by a female of the bridegroom's family, who remains concealed in the apartment till the bridegroom has joined the bride; after which she receives the "tokens of virginity," and coming out of the room displays them to the assembled company. She then carries them to the house of the parents of the bride, who never attend a daughter's wedding feast, and next morning they are hung on the fence for the edification of the public. In this abstention of the bride's parents from the feasting and merry-making, we perhaps find a lingering survival from marriage by capture. The producer of the "tokens" is selected from the family of the bridegroom to ensure that there is no deception, because the husband's family has no interest in falsifying the facts, while the wife's family has; but virginity in a bride is only of paramount importance when the girl has been betrothed in childhood. The marriage feast is continued on the next day.

It is not uncommon for newly wedded couples to visit some celebrated shrine and offer sacrifices together, a practice which, together with the fixing of the wedding day by a *babalawo*, shows an increasing disposition on the part of the priests to control or interfere with matters that are purely social and quite beyond the domain of religion.

Of betrothals among these people, Ellis says:

Girls of the better classes are almost always betrothed when mere children, frequently when infants, the husband *in futuro* being sometimes a grown man and sometimes a boy. Betrothal confers upon the male all the rights of marriage except consummation, which takes place shortly after the girl arrives at puberty. Since the early age of betrothal makes ante-betrothal unchastity a physical impossibility, the absence of the *primitiæ* when the marriage is consummated proves that the girl has been unchaste after betrothal, that is, after the husband *in futuro* had acquired an exclusive right to her person, and consequently he has a right to repudiate her. In such a case he may dismiss her, sending a few broken cowries to her mother, and the girl's family must return the amount paid for her, and the value of all presents made; but it is more usual to effect a compromise.

In this custom of infant child betrothal we probably find the key to that curious regard for ante-nuptial chastity found not only among the tribes of the Slave and Gold coasts, but also among many other civilized people in different parts of the world, and which certainly cannot be attributed to any feelings of delicacy, since husbands lend their wives without compunction, and often merely as a sign of friendliness. In West Africa virginity in a bride is not valued *per se*, but because it is a proof that the betrothal has not infringed the exclusive marital privileges of the husband *in futuro*; and non-virginity in a bride is only a valid ground for repudiation when the girl has been betrothed at a tender age, for unbetrothed girls can bestow favors upon whom they please. Thus no man who marries a girl without early betrothal feels aggrieved if she should prove not to be a virgin, for until she is married or betrothed she is perfectly free, and mistress of her own actions. . . .

A great deal of evidence might be adduced to show that the custom of child-betrothal leads to virginity being expected in a bride, and its absence being regarded as a just ground for repudiation.[1]

By such ceremony the African family is formed. Of the rights thus obtained Ellis says, referring to the Yorubas:

By marriage the man acquires the services of his wife in domestic affairs and an exclusive right to her embraces. That is, she may not have intercourse with other men without his knowledge and consent, but there is no objection to his waiving his right in favor of some other person, and men sometimes lend their wives to their guests or friends, though more frequently their concubines, for in a household there are both wives and concubines, the latter usually being slaves. Each wife has her own house, situated in the "compound" of the husband, and her own slaves and dependants. The wife first married is the head wife, and is charged with the preservation of order among the women. She is styled *Iyale* (Iya ile), "Mistress of the house." The junior wives are called *Iyawo* (Iya owo), "Trade-wives," or "Wives of commerce," probably because they sell in the markets.

Family relationships in Africa are usually traced through the female line, a survival of the older matriarchal family. From this there is gradual change toward the fuller patriarchal type. Ellis says of the Yorubas:

---

[1] Ellis: Yoruba-Speaking Peoples, &c., pp. 153-4, 174-188.

We find a great change from the customs of the other tribal groups of this family of nations, in the Yoruba manner of tracing descent and blood relationship; descent and consanguinity being no longer reckoned exclusively in the female line, with succession to chiefdom, office, and property from brother to brother, and then to sister's son; but in the male line as far as succession to dignities is concerned, and on both sides of the house for blood descent. The Yoruba family—using the word family as meaning a group of persons who are united by ties of blood—is thus quite a different organization to that which we found existing among the Tshi and Ewe tribes, where a family consists solely of persons who are connected by uterine ties, and in which, as two persons of the same blood may not marry, the father is never related by blood to his children, and is not considered as belonging to the family. In the Tshi and Ewe tribes the clan-name is the test of blood-relationship, and as property follows the laws of blood-descent, it ensues that property never goes out of the clan; for, with descent in the female line, a family is only a small circle of persons, all of whom bear the same clan-name, within the larger circle of the clan itself.

Among the Yoruba tribes the blood-tie between father and child has been recognized, and the result of this recognition has been the inevitable downfall of the clan-system, which is only possible so long as descent is traced solely on one side of the house, as may be readily shown. Since two persons of the same clan-name may, under the clan-system, never marry, it follows that husband and wife must be of different clans. Let us say that one is a Dog and the other a Leopard. The clan-name is extended to all who are of the same blood; therefore, directly the blood relationship between father and child comes to be acknowledged, the children of such a pair as we have supposed, instead of being, as heretofore, simply Leopards, would be Dog-Leopards, and would belong to two clans. They in turn might marry with persons similarly belonging to two clans, say Cat-Snakes, and the offsprings of these unions would belong to four clans. The clan-system thus becomes altogether unworkable, because, as the number of clans is limited and cannot be added to, if the clan name still remained the test of blood-relationship and a bar to marriage, the result in a few generations would be that no marriages would be possible. Consequently the clan-name ceases to be the test of consanguinity, kinship is traced in some other way, and the clan-system disappears; or, as appears to have been occasionally the case, descent is boldly transferred unto the male line, and marriage in the father's clan is prohibited, that of the mother being ignored. The Yorubas have adopted what appears to have been the usual course, and blood relationship is now traced both on the father's and on the mother's side, as far as it can be remembered, and marriage within the known circle of consanguinity is forbidden.

When we consider the extraordinary vitality of the system of descent through mothers possesses, so long as it is undisturbed by foreign influence, it seems probable that the acknowledgment of a father's blood-relationship to his children was brought about by the intercourse of the northern Yorubas with the Mohammedan tribes of the interior. That the Yorubas formerly had the system of female descents is known by an ancient proverb, which says, "The esuo (gazelle), claiming relationship with the ekulu (a large antelope), says his mother was the daughter of an ekulu." If the male system of descents had been in vogue when this proverb was invented, the esuo would have been made to say that his father was the son of an ekulu. Moreover, in spite of legal succession from father to son, children by different mothers, but by the same father, are by many natives still scarcely considered true blood relations.

It is no doubt in consequence of the change from kinship in the female line to kinship on both sides of the house that the family has become, to a certain extent, disintegrated. On tho Gold Coast, where the uterine family is the only one known, the family is collectively responsible for the crimes or injuries to persons or property committed by any of its members, and each member is liable for a proportion of the compensation to be paid. Similarly, each member is entitled to share the compensation received for injury to the person or property of one of the members. The head of the family can, if the necessity should arise, pawn, and in some cases sell, a junior member; while, on the other hand, the junior membeos have a right to be fed and clothed by the head of the family. Among the Yoruba tribes there is no collective responsibility in a family, except that parents are responsible for crimes committed by their children; the head of the family cannot pawn the younger members, the latter cannot claim, as a matter of right, to be supported by him.

When a man dies his sons divide all his property between them. The daughters have no inheritance in their father's house, but they divide between them the property of their mother, for here, as with the Tshi, Ya and Ewe tribes, the property of a wife is always separate and distinct from that of her husband. If a man has no sons his property falls to his brothers, or, if he has no brothers, to his sisters. From these laws of inheritance there is no departure, and a man cannot disinherit a legal heir. A man can, within certain limits, give away property during his lifetime, provided it is purely personal and not family property; but he cannot make a will, or any arrangemenr for its disposal after death. Succession to property entails the obligation of defraying the debts of the deceased.[1]

Marriages may be dissolved by divorce. Ratzel says:

Dissolution of marriage is not only rendered difficult by the business thread which runs through the band of wedlock, but apart from this, it comes into relation with legal institutions. Divorce is rare among tribes who lead a simple life undisturbed; nor is adultery so frequent among them as among those who have accumulated capital, possess numerous slaves, and have come into closer contact with Arabs or Europeans. But even among these a marriage is not dissolved without formality, as might appear on superficial observation. Among the corrupt tribes of the Gold Coast, only princesses have the privilege of separating from their husbands without coming before a tribunal. Some white clay, handed over by the husband, serves as a sign of dismissal. Common people on the other hand have to appear before the chiefs, who decide the case. If they allow the wife her divorce, her family keep the purchase money, and the chiefs present the woman with a piece of white clay, with which she marks the trees of the principal street as a sign that she is no longer a wedded wife. If the divorce is granted to the man, the wife's family have to return the sum received. An interesting example of innovation in this domain is given by Broyon in his description of Unyamwesi, where he relates how the Arabs had formerly from selfish motives introduced a law that a woman who broke anything of theirs became their slave. The Negro women had turned this to their own advantage. In order to get free from an uncongenial husband, they would break something of the chief's, and become his slaves.

Among West Coast tribes, Ellis says of the Yorubas:

---

[1] Ellis, Yoruba speaking peoples, *loc. cit.*

Adultery can only be committed with a married woman. Adultery in a wife is punishable by death or divorce, but as a rule the injured husband beats his erring wife and recovers damages (*oje*) from the adulterer. In extreme cases, where the husband is a man of rank and discovers the couple in fact, they are sometimes both put to death.

If a husband should divorce his wife for adultery, he can claim the restitution of the money he paid for her, but not if he sends her away for any other cause. When a wife is divorced or put away, no matter for what cause, the husband retains any children she may have borne him; but if a child be too young to leave the mother, it does not come to the father till ten or twelve years of age. We see here a great change from the Tshi tribes, among whom under every circumstance of divorce or separation the mother retains her children, though she is liable to her husband for a certain sum to compensate him for what he has paid for their maintenance. There children belong exclusively to the mother, but here they belong to the father, and the innovation is undoubtedly due to the alteration in the system of descents.

When a husband systematically neglects his wife and refuses to perform his marital duties, she can call upon her family to assemble and hold a palaver; when, if the husband promises to amend his ways, he is given an opportunity of retrieving his character. If after all there is no improvement, or if he refuses to treat his wife properly, she is at liberty to leave him, and sometimes, if he is of inferior rank, the indignant family tie him up and flog him.[1]

Some idea of African family government may be had from a study of the Gold Coast by a native:

The Headman, as his name implies, is the Head of a village community, a ward in a township, or of a family. His position is important, inasmuch as he has directly to deal with the composite elements of the general bulk of the people.

It is the duty of the Head of a family to bring up the members thereof in the way they should go; and by "family" you must understand the entire lineal descendants of a head *materfamilias*, if I may coin a convenient phrase. It is expected of him by the State to bring up his charge in the knowledge of matters political and traditional. It is his work to train up his wards in the ways of loyalty and obedience to the powers that be. He is held responsible for the freaks of recalcitrant members of his family, and he is looked to to keep them within bounds, and to insist upon conformity on their part with the customs, laws, and traditional observances of the community. In early times he could send off to exile by sale a troublesome relative who would not observe the laws of the community.

It is a difficult task that he is set to, but in this matter he has all-powerful helpers in the female members of the family, who will be either the aunts, or the sisters, or the cousins, or the nieces of the Headman; and as their interests are identical with his in every particular, the good women spontaneously train up their children to implicit obedience to the Headman, whose rule in the family thus becomes a simple and an easy matter. "The hand that rocks the cradle rules the world." What a power for good in the Native State System would the mothers of the Gold Coast and Ashanti become by judicious training upon native lines!

The Headman is *par excellence* the judge of his family or ward. Not only is he called upon to settle domestic squabbles, but frequently he sits as judge

---

[1] Ellis, *loc. cit.*

over more serious matters arising between one member of the ward and another; and where he is a man of ability and influence, men from other wards bring him their disputes to settle. When he so settles disputes, he is entitled to a hearing fee, which, however, is not so much as would be payable in the regular Court of the King or Chief.

The Headman is naturally an important member of his "company," and often is a captain thereof. When he combines the two offices of Headman and Captain, he renders to the community a very important service. For, in times of war, where the members of the ward would not serve cordially under a stranger, they would in all cases face any danger with their own kinsman as their leader.

The Headman is always succeeded by his uterine brother, cousin, or nephew—the line of succession, that is to say, following the Customary Law.[1]

The reasons for polygamy in Africa are social and economic:

Lichtenstein remarks of the Kaffirs that "there are fewer men than women, on account of the numbers of the former that fall in their frequent wars. Thence comes polygamy, and the women being principally employed in all menial occupation." Now, without accepting the inference that polygamy is initiated by the loss of men in war, we may recognize the fact which Lichtenstein does not name, that where the death rate of males considerably exceeds that of females, plurality of wives becomes a means of maintaining population.

Since in every society the doings of the powerful and the wealthy furnish the standards of right and wrong, so that even the very words "noble" and "servile," originally expressive of social status, have come to be expressive of good and bad in conduct, it results that plurality of wives acquires, in places where it prevails, an ethical sanction. Associated with greatness, polygamy is thought praiseworthy; and, associated with poverty, monogamy is thought mean. Hence the reprobation with which, as we have seen, the one-wife system is regarded in polygamous communities.[2]

Their ideas of right and wrong differ in no respect from our own, except in their profsssed inability to see how it can be improper for a man to have more than one wife.[3]

Parental affection is strong in Africa. Sweinfurth says:

Parental affection is developed among the Dyoor much more decidedly than among the other tribes. A bond between mother and child which lasts for life is the measure of affection shown among the Dyoor.

Parents [among the Dinkas] do not desert their children, nor are brothers faithless to brothers, but are ever prompt to render whatever aid is possible Family affection is at a high ebb among them.[4]

Ratzel says:

Agreeably to the natural relation the mother stands first among the chief influences affecting the children. From the Zulus to the Waganda we find the mother the most influential counsellor at the court of ferocious sovereigns like Chaka or Mtesa; sometimes sisters take her place. Thus even with chiefs who possess wives by hundreds the bonds of blood are the strongest. The father is less closely bound up with the family. He is indeed

---

[1] C. Hayford: Gold Coast Native Institutions, pp. 76-78.
[2] Spencer: Sociology I, pp. 671, 669.   [3] Livingstone, Zambesi, p. 309.
[4] Sweinfurth: Heart of Africa.

the head, and is recognised as such; it is said too that the Negro is in general a lover of children and therefore a good father. But even here he often rules more by force than by love. Among the institutions recalling Roman law which Hubbe-Schleiden, an expert on that subject, found among the Mpongwes, he mentions their domestic or family life: "We find among them the *patria potestas* equally comprehensive and equally strict, if not carried into such abstraction. Wives, children, servants, are all in the power of the *pater-familias* or *oga*. He alone is quite free; a degree of independence to which a woman among the Mpongwes can never attain." Yet that woman, though often heavily burdened, is in herself in no small esteem among the Negroes is clear from the numerous Negro queens, from the medicine-women, from the participation in public meetings permitted to women by many Negro peoples.

Out of some such ideas of marriage and married life the Negro was brought to America as a slave. The ideas were not those of the more highly developed modern nations. But they were definite and practicable, and evolved through long social struggle; the Africans who had invented them lived up to them and were, as Sumner shows so well, as moral as modern men; i. e., as faithful to their *Mores*.

Section 3. Slavery. The first fact which students of slavery must remember is the great disproportion among the sexes in the imported slaves. The first demand of the plantations was able-bodied male field hands. Edwards speaks

. . of the great disproportion of the sexes in the yearly importations from Africa. It has been shown from unquestionable authority, that one-third only were females. Thus, notwithstanding every allowance for the Creoles, or natives, who may reasonably be supposed to have increased according to the general laws of nature, there was in the year 1789, in Jamaica alone, an excess in its Negro population of 30,000 males.[1]

Traces of this can be found in the census reports of the United States, which unfortunately separate the sexes among Negroes only as far back as 1820. [See chart on opposite page.]

Such a social derangement through violence, war, and severe economic competition is an effective cause of wide sexual irregularity, even with a people living under their own carefully elaborated moral code; but with a transplanted and broken nation the effect was indeed disastrous. The first instinctive effort of the transplanted group was to restore the ancestral *Mores*. Edwards says:

It is a truth well known, that the practice of polygamy, which universally prevails in Africa, is also very generally adopted in the West Indies; and he who conceives that a remedy may be found for this by introducing among them the laws of marriage as established in Europe, is utterly ignorant of their manners, propensities, and superstitions. It is reckoned in Jamaica, on a moderate computation, that not less than ten thousand of such as are called Head Negroes (artificers and others) possess from two to four wives. This partial appropriation of the women creates a still greater proportion of single men, and produces all the mischiefs which are necessarily attached to the system of polygamy.[2]

---

1 Edwards: West Indies, II, pp. 175-176.   2 Edwards, *loc. cit.*

Sex of Negro Population.

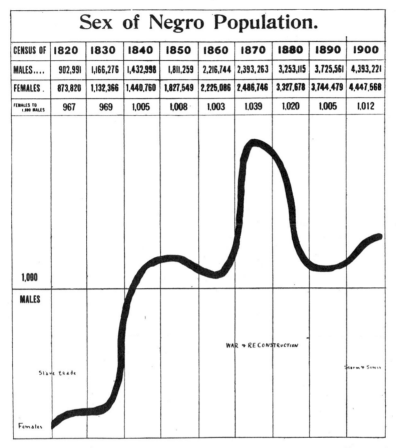

CENSUS OF	1820	1830	1840	1850	1860	1870	1880	1890	1900
MALES....	902,991	1,166,276	1,432,998	1,811,259	2,216,744	2,393,263	3,253,115	3,725,561	4,393,221
FEMALES .	873,820	1,132,366	1,440,760	1,827,549	2,225,086	2,486,746	3,327,678	3,744,479	4,447,568
FEMALES TO 1,000 MALES	967	969	1,005	1,008	1,003	1,039	1,020	1,005	1,012

1,000

MALES

WAR & RECONSTRUCTION

Slave trade

Storm & Stress

Females

Even under such conditions, however, traces of African family institutions persisted:

The men exacted a great show of respect from their families. I have often taken pleasure in watching a Negro carpenter at Guadaloupe when he ate his meals. His wife and children gathered around him, and served him with as much respect as the best drilled domestics served their masters; and if it was a fete day or Sunday, his sons-in-law and daughters did not fail to be present, and bring him some small gifts. They formed a circle about him, and conversed with him while he was eating. When he had finished, his pipe was brought to him, and then he bade them eat. They paid him their reverences and passed into another room, where they all ate together with their mother. I reproached him sometimes for his gravity, and cited him to the example of the governor, who ate every day with his wife; to which he replied that the governor was not the wiser for it; that he supposed the whites had their reasons, but they also had theirs; and if one would observe how proud and disobedient the white women were to their husbands, it would be admitted that the Negroes, who kept them always in respect and submission, are wiser and more experienced than the whites in this matter. The father says the Negroes were often very eloquent, and that they all spent much time in ridiculing the whites and their customs.[1]

When in any case these ancestral customs in family, clan, and tribal life could be preserved, revolt against slavery followed. This is the secret of the Haytian Revolution:

For many years there had been bands of runaway Negroes in the mountains under their chiefs. The earliest known of these chiefs was Polydorin, 1724; he was succeeded by Macandal, of whom the Negroes seemed to stand in superstitious dread. The great chief of these maroons at the time of the revolt was Jean Francais, and he was followed by another black called Biassou. One of their agents said to the French commissioner:

I am subject of three kings: of the King of Congo, master of all the blacks; of the King of France, who represents my father, and of the King of Spain, who represents my mother. If I passed into the service of the republic, I would perhaps be brought to make war against my brothers, the subjects of these three kings, to whom I have promised fidelity.[1]

When Christophe declared himself emperor,

Some writers have thought that this was purely an act of grandiloquence and mimicry on the part of Christophe, but it is truer to say that in it he was actuated by a clear insight into the needs and peculiarities of the people with whom he had to deal. There is nothing in the constitution which did not have its companion in Africa, where the organization of society was truly despotic, with elective-hereditary chiefs, royal families, polygamic marriages, councils, and regencies. But, undoubtedly, the form in which these things were put into writing was influenced very much by the language and systems which were known in Europe. Toussaint, Dessalines, and Christophe had ministers and others in their employ who were men educated in France.[2]

The government organized was founded on the ancient African clan:

But we have now to consider that which was the foundation of this system, which at once marks the insight of Toussaint and Christophe, and the African origin of their government. This is the system of agriculture. This system was adopted at the time of the reconciliation between the French and the blacks, under the advice of Toussaint. Some writers have called it an attempt to establish feudalism in the island, and the system does have a resemblance to it, but it also has many points of similarity with the organization of society in many African tribes. There was a division of the population into military and civil or laboring classes, the latter including both free and slave laborers. The territory was parcelled out to chiefs or lords, and the laborers were bound to the soil, which they were compelled to work under a rigorous system of inspection; for their support a part of the produce was set aside, the rest going to the chiefs, and for the support of the king or general government and the army. The army was kept under stern discipline, which made it possible to arm the free men and laborers; the women did a large part of the agricultural labor. Under Toussaint the administration of this labor system was committed to Dessalines, who carried it out with the

---

[1] Aimes; Journal of American Folk-Lore, p. 25.
[2] Aimes: Journal of American Folk-Lore, pp. 26-29.

utmost rigor, and it was afterward followed by Christophe in the same manner. The latter went so far as to import 4,000 Negroes from Africa, which he took means to bind to his person and form into a national guard, for patrolling the country. These regulations brought back for a time a large part of the prosperity which the island enjoyed.[1]

In Brazil "the Negroes brought their language and usages, which were found as original as on the coast of Africa." The patriarchal feeling remained very strong. The tribes seemed to be families, considering the prince as the father; the tie never died. "These princes are frequently seen sitting on a stone in the street, surrounded by a crowd who come to them for judgment. At the corner of the Travessa de S. Antonio, is a stone or post, for many years the throne of an African prince from Angola. . . . The natives of Congo elect a king among themselves, to whose decrees they submit in a similar manner."[2]

There is also a good account of an African funeral as practised in Jamaica. The person described above may be the Mumbo Jumbo of the Mandingoes, whose duty it was to execute public authority in the hall of the tribe upon the female offenders. The punishment was by whipping in public.[3]

In Lowndes county, Ala., in 1892, a description of a Negro country wedding tells of the chasing of the bride after the ceremony in a manner very similar to the Zulu ceremony described on a previous page. Careful research would doubtless reveal many other traces of the African family in America. They would, however, be traces only, for the effectiveness of the slave system meant the practically complete crushing out of the African clan and family life. No more complete method of reducing a barbarous people to subjection can be devised. The Indian could not be reduced to slavery because, being in his own home, he could not be permanently and effectively separated from his clan, and the clan fought for his freedom. Only in the isolated islands, then, was Indian slavery successful, and died out there for want of a slave trade. The essential features of Negro slavery in America was:

1. No legal marriage.
2. No legal family.
3. No legal control over children.

This is not inconsistent with much teaching of the morals of modern family life to slaves; the point is that the recognition of the black family from 1619 to 1863 was purely a matter of individual judgment or caprice on the part of the master. Public opinion and custom counted for much, and the law tended to recognize some *quasi* family rights—forbidding, for instance, in some cases the separation of mothers and very young infants—yet on the whole it is fair to say that while to some extent European family morals were taught the small select body of house servants and artisans, both by precept and example, the great body of field hands were raped of their own sex customs and provided with no binding new ones. Slavery gave the monogamic family ideal to slaves, but it compelled and desired only the most imperfect practice

---

[1] Aimes: Journal of American Folk-Lore, pp. 29-30.   [2] Ibid, p. 24.   [3] Ibid.

of its most ordinary morals. A few quotations will illustrate these conclusions:

A slave cannot even contract matrimony, the association which takes place among slaves and is called marriage being properly designated by the word contubernium, a relation which has no sanctity and to which no civil rights are attached.[1]

A slave has never maintained an action against the violator of his bed. A slave is not admonished for incontinence, or punished for fornication or adultery; never prosecuted for bigamy, or petty treason, for killing a husband being a slave, any more than admitted to an appeal for murder[2]

Slaves were not entitled to the conditions of matrimony, and therefore they had no relief in cases of adultery; nor were they the proper objects of cognation or affinity, but of quasi-cognation only.[3]

A necessary consequence of slavery is the absence of the marriage relation. No slave can commit bigamy, because the law knows no more of the marriage of slaves than of the marriage of brutes. A slave may, indeed, be formally married, but so far as legal rights and obligations are concerned it is an idle ceremony. . . . Of course these laws do not recognize the paternal relation as belonging to slaves. A slave has no more legal authority over his child than a cow has over her calf.[4]

In the slave-holding States, except in Louisiana, no law exists to prevent the violent separation of parents from their children, or even from each other.[5]

Slaves may be sold and transferred from one to another without any statutory restriction, as to the separation of parents and children, &c., except in the State of Louisiana.[6]

Slaves cannot marry without the consent of their masters, and then marriages do not produce any of the civil effects which result from such contract.[7]

A Brooklyn judge, in 1859, absolved a fugitive slave from bigamy,

Considering that marriage is a civil contract, which requires in the contracting parties the capacity to contract it, that slaves can not contract a regular marriage, and that the cohabitation confers no right on them or their children; (Laws of Alabama, Maryland, and North Carolina.)"[8]

Thus the right of (1) alienation, either by will or *inter vivos,* was both a cause and a consequence of the property conception. It included transfer of the whole or part of the subject's obligations, for valuable or other consideration, to other persons and places, even beyond the jurisdiction of the State.[9]

It was here that the incident of (3) separation of families, also involved in alienation, was made capable of extension until checked by law. This was finally done in 1801 by a decree of the Supreme Court of Appeals which declared that

"An equal division of slaves in number and value is not always possible and is sometimes improper when it cannot be exactly done without separating infant children from their mothers which humanity forbids and will not be

---

1 Stroud's Sketch of Slave Laws, p. 61.
2 Opinion of Daniel Dulaney, Esq., Attorney-General of Maryland. 1 Maryland Reports, pp. 561, 563.
3 Dr. Taylor's Elements of the Civil Law, p. 529.   4 Jay's Inquiry, p. 132.
5 Stroud's Sketch, p. 50.   6 Wheeler's Law of Slavery, p. 41.
7 Civil code of La., 1853.   8 Cochin: Results of Slavery, p. 392.
9 Ballagh: Slavery in Va., pp. 62-64.

countenanced in a court of equity, so that a compensation for the excess must in such cases be made and received in money." The right to separate husband and wife and larger children, however, still remained.[1]

The masters do not absolutely refuse to allow their Negroes to "marry off the place," but they discourage intercourse as much as possible between their Negroes and those of other plantations.

When a man and woman wish to live with each other they are required to ask leave of their master, and, unless there are some very obvious objections, this is always granted; a cabin is allotted to them, and presents are made of dresses and housekeeping articles. A marriage ceremony, in the same form as that used by free people, is conducted by the Negro preacher, and they are encouraged to make the occasion memorable and gratifying to all by general festivity. The master and mistress, if on the plantation, usually honor the wedding by their attendance; and, if they are favorite servants, it is held in the house and the ceremony performed by a white minister.[2]

Legal marriage is unknown among the slaves; they sometimes have a marriage form—generally, however, none at all. The pastor of the Presbyterian church in Huntsville had two families of slaves when I left there. One couple were married by a Negro preacher; the man was robbed of his wife a number of months afterwards, by her "owner." The other couple just "took up together," without any form of marriage. They are both members of churches—the man a Baptist deacon, sober and correct in his deportment. They have a large family of children—all children of concubinage—living in a minister's family.[3]

Persons who own plantations and yet live in cities, often take children from their parents as soon as they are weaned, and send them into the country; because they do not want the time of the mother taken up by attendance upon her own children, it being too valuable to the mistress. As a favor, she is, in some cases, permitted to go to see them once a year. So, on the other hand, if field slaves happen to have children of an age suitable to the convenience of the master, they are taken from their parents and brought to the city. Parents are almost never consulted as to the disposition to be made of their children; they have as little control over them as have domestic animals over the disposal of their young.[4]

One of my neighbors sold to a speculator a Negro boy about fourteen years old. It was more than his poor mother could bear. Her reason fled and she became a perfect maniac, and had to be kept in close confinement. She would occasionally get out and run off to the neighbors. On one of these occasions she came to my house. She was indeed a pitiable object. With tears rolling down her cheeks and her frame shaking with agony, she would cry out, "Don't you hear him? They are whipping him now, and he is calling for me!"[5]

Many advertisements like the following occurred:

Absconded from the subscriber, a negro man by the name of Wilson. He was born in the county of New Kent, and raised by a gentleman named Ratcliffe, and by him sold to a gentleman named Taylor, on whose farm he had a wife and several children. Mr. Taylor sold him to a Mr. Slater, who, in consequence of removing to Alabama, Wilson left; and when retaken was

---

[1] Ballagh: Slavery in Va., pp. 62-64. [2] Olmsted: Seaboard Slave States, p. 79.
[3] Quoted from Rev. W. T. Allan, of Alabama, in Slavery as it is, p. 47.
[4] Quoted from Angelina Grimke Weld, of S, C., in Slavery as it is, pp. 56-57.
[5] Quoted from Rev. F. Hawley, of Conn., in Slavery as it is, p. 97.

sold, and afterwards purchased, by his present owner, from T. McCargo and Co., of Richmond.[1]

$20 Reward for my negro man Jim.—Jim is about 50 or 55 years of age. It is probable he will aim for Savannah, as he said he had children in that vicinity.   J. G. Owens.
Barnwell District, S. C.[2]

$100 reward will be given for my two fellows, Abram and Frank. Abram has a wife at Colonel Stewart's in Liberty county, and a sister in Savannah at Capt. Grovenstine's. Frank has a wife at Mr. Le Cont's, Liberty county; a mother at Thunderbolt, and a sister in Savannah.   Wm. Robarts.
Walthourville, 5th Jan., 1839.[3]

Runaway—My negro man, Frederick, about 20 years of age. He is no doubt near the plantation of G. W. Corprew, Esq., of Noxubbee county, Mississippi, as his wife belongs to that gentleman, and he followed her from my residence. The above reward will be paid to anyone who will confine him in jail and inform me of it at Athens, Ala.   Kerkman Lewis.
Athens, Ala.[4]

$50 Reward.—Ran away from the subscriber, a negro girl named Maria. She is of a copper color, between 13 and 14 years of age—bareheaded and barefooted. She is small for her age—very sprightly and very likely. She stated she was going to see her mother at Maysville.   Sanford Thomson.[5]

Committed to jail of Madison county, a negro woman who calls her name Fanny, and says she belongs to William Miller, of Mobile. She formerly belonged to John Givins, of this county, who now owns several of her children.   David Shropshire, Jailor.[6]

$50 Reward.—Ran away from the subscriber, his negro man Pauladore, commonly called Paul. I understand Gen. R. Y. Hayne has purchased his wife and children from H. L. Pinckney, Esq., and has them now on his plantation at Goose Creek, where, no doubt, the fellow is frequently lurking.
      T. Davis.[7]

The following is a standing advertisement in the Charleston (S. C.) papers:

120 Negroes for Sale.—The subscriber has just arrived from Petersburg, Virginia, with one hundred and twenty likely young negroes of both sexes and every description, which he offers for sale on the most reasonable terms.
The lot now on hand consist of plough boys, several likely and well-qualified house servants of both sexes, several women with children, small girls suitable for nurses, and several small boys without their mothers. Planters and traders are earnestly requested to give the subscriber a call previously to making purchases elsewhere, as he is enabled and will sell as cheap, or cheaper, than can be sold by any other person in the trade.
      Benjamin Davis.[7]

One description of a separation of a family by auction will suffice:

From these scenes I turn to another, which took place in front of the noble "Exchange Buildings" in the heart of the city [Charleston, S. C.]. On the left side of the step as you leave the main hall, immediately under the windows

[1] Richmond *Whig*, July 23, 1837.   [2] Savannah *Republican*, Sept. 3, 1838.
[3] Savannah *Georgian*, Jan. 17, 1839.   [4] *Southern Argus*, Oct. 31, 1837.
[5] Lexington (Ky,) *Observer and Reporter*, Sept. 28, 1838.
[6] Jackson (Tenn.) *Telegraph*, Sept. 14, 1838.
[7] All of these advertisements are quoted in American Slavery as it is, pp. 166, 167.

of that proud building, was a stage built, on which a mother with eight children were placed, and sold at auction. I watched their emotions closely, and saw their feelings were in accordance to human nature. The sale began with the eldest child, who, being struck off to the highest bidder, was taken from the stage or platform by the purchaser, and led to his wagon and stowed away, to be carried into the country; the second and third were also sold, and so on until seven of the children were torn from their mother, while her discernment told her they were to be separated probably forever, causing in that mother the most agonizing sobs and cries, in which the children seemed to share. The scene beggars description; suffice it to say, it was sufficient to cause tears from one at least "whose skin was not colored like their own," and I was not ashamed to give vent to them.[1]

The Presbyterian Synod of Kentucky said to the churches under their care, in 1835:

Brothers and sisters, parents and children, husbands and wives, are torn asunder, and permitted to see each other no more. These acts are daily occurring in the midst of us. The shrieks and agony often witnessed on such occasions proclaim, with a trumpet tongue, the iniquity of our system. There is not a neighborhood where these heart-rending scenes are not displayed. There is not a village or road that does not behold the sad procession of manacled outcasts, whose mournful countenances tell that they are exiled by force from all that their hearts hold dear.[2]

Irregularities involved not only slaves but masters. A sister of President James Madison said:

We Southern ladies are complimented with the names of wives; but we are only the mistresses of seraglios.[3]

As it relates to amalgamation, I can say, that I have been in respectable families (so-called), where I could distinguish the family resemblance in the slaves who waited upon the table. I once hired a slave who belonged to his own uncle. It is so common for the female slaves to have white children, that little or nothing is ever said about it. Very few inquiries are made as to who his father is.[4]

Amalgamation was common. There was scarce a family of slaves that had females of mature age where there were not some mulatto children.[5]

Further proof of this is found in the statistics of mulattoes; the United States Census found 405,751 mulattoes in 1850, and 588,352 in 1860. These figures were, moreover, without reasonable doubt below the truth, as "mulatto" was probably taken to mean a person, visibly at least half white. Probably one-fifth of the slaves in 1860 had distinct traces of white blood.

---

[1] Testimony of Silas Stone, of Hudson, N.Y., 1807, in American Slavery as It is, p. 167.

[2] Address, p. 12.   [3] Goodell, Slave Code, p. 111.

[4] Testimony of Rev. Francis Hawley, of Conn., resident fourteen years in Carolina; quoted in American Slavery as it is, p. 97,

[5] Testimony of Rev. Hiram White, of N. C., *Ibid.*, p. 51.

One further quotation from a Southern student of slavery will show the best possible picture of slavery and the family:

In custom the conception of the personality of the slave tended to supplant that of property, and was recognized to·a far greater extent than accorded with the strict letter of the law. The slave was here viewed as a human being possessed of like emotions, desires and ambitions as free men and whites, many of which might be reasonably gratified without impairing any obligation of service due the master. Even practices in which damage was a possible or even certain result to the property element found a continuing sanction in custom. The common recognition of marital and family rights, for instance, was the outgrowth of a sentiment of humanity rather than of economic interest. That the ties so established were so accorded the full recognition they deserved is by no means true, but their existence, even when hampered, distinctly mitigated the conditions of slavery. So also slave-breeding, however unfortunate some of its applications may have been, had its origin in humanity. Its development prevented the introduction of the barbarous practice of the Spanish West Indies, where marriage was denied because it was cheaper to import slaves than to raise them. The abuse of breeding in the prostitution of females was not only lessened by heavy legal and social penalties, but met a natural check in the density of population, whose increase even the domestic trade, a necessity for the existence of slavery in the old States, was unable to prevent. The desire to procreate slaves when they were cheap was anything but economic in cause or effect. The damage to service in child-bearing and the cost of rearing the infant was viewed as involving a net loss, and as one of the burdens incident to a human slave system. It was upon this economic ground that conscientious anti-slavery slaveholders were wont to base their strongest arguments. Slave-breeding in the opprobrious use of the term probably had an extensive existence with a certain class, which was governed neither by economic nor moral considerations, but as this class is usually small in any civilized society and as historic evidence shows its limited extent in Virginia, the offense was kept within bounds by public sentiment and legal penalties.[1]

Section 4. Present Conjugal Condition. The United States Census has collected separate statistics of conjugal conditions among Negroes only in 1890 and 1900. The figures for whites and Negroes are:

---

[1] Ballagh: History of Slavery in Virginia, pp. 97, 98.

Negro Population at least 15 years of age and White Population at least 15 years of age, classified by Conjugal Condition, and per cent Distribution

CONJUGAL CONDITION	POPULATION AT LEAST 15 YEARS OF AGE				PER CENT DISTRIBUTION			
	Negro		White		Negro		White	
	1900	1890	1900	1890	1900	1890	1900	1890
Continental United States	5,323,591	4,295,271	44,291,080	35,489,102	100.0	100.0	100.0	100.0
Single	1,886,968	1,495,078	15,920,736	13,807,975	34.5	34.8	35.9	37.0
Married	2,806,703	2,362,947	24,775,625	19,917,695	53.9	55.0	55.9	55.4
Widowed	565,340	411,877	3,312,259	2,553,748	10.6	9.6	7.5	7.1
Divorced	38,059	15,900	164,498	104,454	0.6	0.4	0.4	0.3
Unknown	21,521	9,469	118,562	54,735	0.4	0.2	0.3	0.2

The conjugal condition by sex and age is as follows:

Per cent Distribution by Conjugal Condition, for the Negro Population by Sex and Age Periods: 1900 and 1890

PER CENT OF NEGRO MALE POPULATION

AGE PERIOD	Single and unknown		Married		Widowed and divorced	
	1900	1890	1900	1890	1900	1890
Continental United States: 15 years and over	39.8	40.0	54.0	55.5	6.2	4.5
15 to 19 years	98.2	99.1	1.7	0.9	0.1	(1)
20 to 24 years	64.9	65.8	33.8	33.4	1.3	0.8
25 to 29 years	38.4	30.3	63.3	67.3	3.3	2.4
30 to 34 years	21.4	18.7	73.7	77.7	4.9	3.6
35 to 44 years	13.5	11.5	79.1	82.9	7.4	5.6
45 to 54 years	7.4	6.5	81.4	85.1	11.2	8.4
55 to 64 years	5.5	5.2	78.6	83.2	15.9	11.6
65 years and over	5.0	5.7	69.6	74.4	25.4	19.9
Age unknown	46.7	43.8	47.4	50.8	5.9	5.4

PER CENT OF NEGRO FEMALE POPULATION

AGE PERIOD	Single and unknown		Married		Widowed and divorced	
	1900	1890	1900	1890	1900	1890
Continental United States: 15 years and over	30.1	30.2	53.7	54.6	16.2	15.2
15 to 19 years	83.3	85.0	15.7	14.4	1.0	0.6
20 to 24 years	39.9	38.3	54.6	57.3	5.5	4.4
25 to 29 years	20.8	17.7	69.4	73.1	9.8	8.6
30 to 34 years	13.1	11.8	73.1	76.4	13.8	11.8
35 to 44 years	8.2	7.5	72.3	74.7	19.5	17.8
45 to 54 years	5.3	5.0	65.3	66.3	29.4	28.7
55 to 64 years	4.4	4.7	51.6	51.6	43.7	44.0
65 years and over	4.8	4.7	28.9	29.0	66.3	66.3
Age unknown	30.1	27.7	45.6	47.7	24.3	24.6

1 Less than one-tenth of 1 per cent.

If we illustrate these percentages by a diagram we have this:

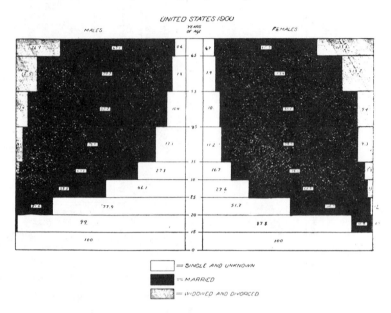

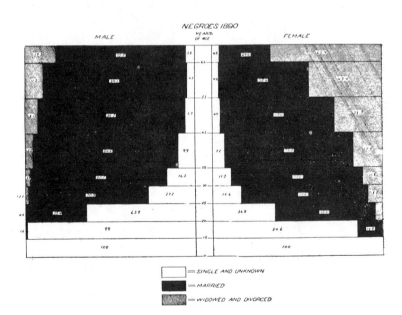

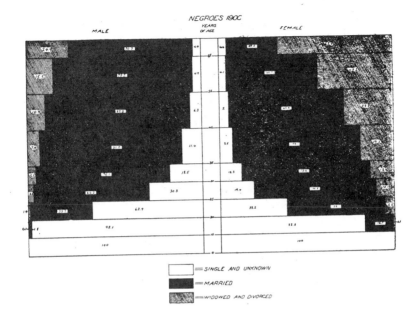

A comparison of the conjugal condition of the races in the South gives these figures:

Per cent Distribution of the Population at least 15 years of age, by Conjugal Condition, for Negro and White Races, by Sex, for the South: 1900 and 1890 [1]

CONJUGAL CONDITION	MALE				FEMALE			
	Negro		White		Negro		White	
	1900	1890	1900	1890	1900	1890	1900	1890
South Atlantic and South Central Divisions. Total	100.0	100.0	100.0	100.0	100.0	100.0	100 0	100.0
Single	38.4	39.1	39.6	40.7	29.5	29.8	30.7	31.5
Married	55.0	56.3	55.7	55 2	54.1	55 0	58.0	56.7
Widowed	5.7	4.2	4.2	3.7	15.3	14.5	10.8	11.4
Divorced	0.4	0.2	0.2	0.2	0.8	0.5	0.3	0.3
Unknown	0.5	0.2	0.3	0.2	0.3	0.2	0.2	0.1

[1] Negroes in the United States, 1904, p. 49.

A similar comparison of races in Massachusetts follows:

Conjugal Condition—Negroes of Massachusetts, 1900

MALES	Single	Married	Widowed	Divorced
Native white, native parents	52 84	41.75	4.34	0.34
Negro	57.12	38.07	3.89	0.23

FEMALES	Single	Married	Widowed	Divorced
Native white, native parents.........	.50 64	37.27	11.33	0.47
Negro	50.99	35.71	12.42	0.37

84th Report, Mass. Bureau of Statistics.

Some other comparisons follow:

Conjugal Condition of the Negroes of Xenia, of Farmville, of Sandy Spring, and of the Population of the United States, by Sex

[The per cents for Xenia, for Farmville, and for Sandy Spring are computed from schedules: those for the United States are taken from the United States census reports for 1890 and 1900.]

CIVIL DIVISION	PER CENT OF MALES 20 YEARS OF AGE OR OVER				PER CENT OF FEMALES 20 YEARS OF AGE OR OVER			
	Single	Married	Widowed	Divorced	Single	Married	Widowed	Divorced
Xenia	22.06	65.28	8.50	a4.16	15.13	57.57	21.05	a6.25
Farmville	25.00	65.44	5.15	b4.41	17.30	55.03	23.90	b3.77
Sandy Spring....	15.35	76.72	4.23	b3.70	14.36	69.31	13.86	b2.47
United States— Native whites, native parents—								
1890.............	28.54	66.08	4.74	c.64	18.75	67.88	12.79	c.58
1900	28.3	65.4	5.4	c.9	19.6	66.9	12.7	c.8
Native whites, foreign parents—								
1890..............	48.82	48.65	2.25	c.28	34.83	58.76	6.02	c.39
1900.............	43.7	52.9	2.9	c.5	31.9	60.4	7.1	c.6
Foreign whites—								
1890............	28.06	65.93	5 51	c.50	15 39	68.05	16 1	c.35
1900	25.6	67.3	6.5	c.6	14.7	68.0	16.9	c.4
Negroes—								
1890.............	25.01	69 02	5.40	c.57	15.71	65.02	18.41	c.86
1900.............	26 4	65.5	7.0	c1.1	17.4	62.5	18.8	c1.3
TotalUnitedStates								
1890............	30.95	63.83	4.65	c.57	19.92	66.35	13 19	c.54
1900............	30 1	63.6	5.4	c.9	20.5	65 5	13 2	c.8

a Including separated.   b Separated   c Including unknown.

Conjugal Condition of the Negroes of Xenia, of Farmville, of Sandy Spring, and of the Populations of Various Foreign Countries, by Sex [1]

[The per cents for Xenia, Farmville, and Sandy Spring, are computed from schedules; those for foreign are taken from Mayo-Smith's Statistics and Sociology. The figures for divorced are not shown for foreign countries.]

CIVIL DIVISION	PER CENT OF MALES 15 YEARS OF AGE OR OVER			PER CENT OF FEMALES 15 YEARS OF AGE OR OVER		
	Single	Married	Widowed	Single	Married	Widowed
Xenia	31.6	57.4	a7.4	25.1	51.0	b18.3
Farmville	41.9	50.7	c4 0	32.1	45.4	d19.4
Sandy Spring	32.5	61.2	e3.5	25 1	60.9	f 11.9
France	36.0	56.5	7.5	30.0	55.3	14.7
Germany	40.9	53.7	5.3	36.5	50.8	12.4
Great Britain	39.5	54.9	5.6	37.3	50.9	11.8
Hungary	31.5	63.7	4.7	22.0	62.8	15.0
Ireland	49.3	44.8	5.9	43.5	42 1	14.4
Italy	40.9	53.1	6.0	33.2	53.2	13.6

a Also 3.1 per cent separated and 0.5 per cent divorced.
b Also 4.6 per cent separated and 1 per cent divorced.
c Also 3.4 per cent separated.   d Also 3.1 per cent separated.
e Also 2.9 per cent separated.   f Also 2.1 per cent separated.

[1] The Negroes of Xenia, Ohio, p. 1018.

In these statistics we have striking evidence of the needs of the Negro American home. The broken families indicated by the abnormal number of widowed and separated, and the late age of marriage, show sexual irregularity and economic pressure. These things all go to prove not the disintegration of Negro family life but the distance which integration has gone and has yet to go. Fifty years ago "family" statistics of nine-tenths of the Negroes would have been impossible. Twenty-five years ago they would have been far worse than to-day, and while there is no perceptible change of moment in the statistics of 1890 and 1900, most of the tendencies are in the right direction, and a healthier home life is in prospect.

Section 5. The Size of the Family. The birth rate of the Negro American is not accurately known. It probably runs from 27 per thousand, as indicated by statistics in Massachusetts, to a birth rate of over 40 per thousand in the rural districts of the South, where the race is still massed. A table of fecundity on a sugar plantation is given as follows:

Children of each female	Females 15 to 19 years of age			Females 20 to 29 years of age			Females 30 to 39 years of age			Females 40 yrs. of age or over			Females age not reported		
	Females	Children	Children living	Females	Children	Children living	Females	Children	Children living	Females	Children	Children living	Females	Children	Children living
None.	11			7			1			1			2		
1	2	2	1	11	11	9							1	1	
2	4	8	5	6	12	9	1	2	2				2	4	2
3				4	12	6							2	6	3
4				2	8	6							2	8	5
5				1	5	2				1	5	5	3	15	6
6				1	6	6	1	6	3						
7													1	7	5
8										1	8	3	1	8	7
9							1	9	5						
10													3	30	15
11										1	11	10			
12										1	12	10	1	12	1
13													1	13	5
14															
15										1	15	6			
16										2	32	17			

Of these 80 women 58 have had children. These 58 have had 268 children, or an average of 4.62 per woman, of which 154, or 57.5 per cent are still living. In 34 cases out of the 58 the first child was still living.[1]

[1] U. S. Bulletin of the Bureau of Labor 38:103.

Comparing the number of women of child-bearing age we may get some measure of fecundity, although a distorted one on account of the large infant mortality among Negroes:

Number of children under 5 years of age to 1,000 females 15 to 44 years of age for the Continental United States:[2]

	Total	White	[3]Colored	Excess of Colored
1900	474	465	543	78
1890	485	473	574	101
1880	559	537	706	169
1870	572	562	641	79
1860	634	627	675	48
1850	626	613	694	81
1840[1]	....	744	....	....
1830[1]	....	781	....	....

[1] Women 15 to 49 years of age.
[2] Twelfth Census, Bulletin No. 22.
[3] Negro, Indian and Mongolian.

Number and per cent of children under 10 and 5 years of age, respectively, in the Negro, Indian and Mongolian population, and decrease in per cent during the preceding ten years, 1830-1900[1]

CENSUS	Per cent of Negro,Indian and Mongolian population		DECREASE IN PER CENT			
			Under 10 years of age during—		Under 5 years of age during—	
	Under 10 yrs. of age	*Under 5 years of age*	*Preceding 10 years*	*Preceding 20 years*	*Preceding 10 years*	*Preceding 20 years*
Continental United States.						
1900	27.1	13.6	1.1	4.8	0.2	2.9
1890	28.2	13.8	3.7	[2] 3.8	2.7	[2] 0.5
1880	31.9	16.5	[2] 7.5	[2] 1.6	[2] 3.2	[2] 0.5
1870	24.4	13.3	5.9	6 9	2.7	2.2
1860	30.3	16.0	1.0	2.9	0.5	
1850	31.3	16.5	1.9	2.9		
1840	33.2		1.0			
1830	34.2					

[1] Twelfth Census, Bulletin No. 22.
[2] Increase.

Number and per cent of children under 10 and 5 years of age, respectively, in the white population, and decrease in per cent during 10 years: 1800 to 1900 [1]

CENSUS	Per cent of white population		DECREASE IN PER CENT			
			Under 10 years of age during—		Under 5 years of age during—	
	Under 10 yrs. of age	*Under 5 years of age*	*Preceding 10 years*	*Preceding 20 years*	*Preceding 10 years*	*Preceding 20 years*
Continental United States.						
1900	23.3	11.9	0.4	2.6	0.1	1.5
1890	23.7	12.0	2.2	2.7	1.4	2.1
1880	25.9	13.4	0.5	2.5	0.7	1.9
1870	26.4	14.1	2.0	2.2	1.2	0.7
1860	28.4	15.3	0.2	3.2	0.5	2.1
1850	28.6	14 8	3.0	·3.9	2.6	3.2
1840	31.6	17.4	0.9	1.8	0.6	
1830	32.5	18.0	0.9	1.9		
1820	33.4		1.0	1.0		
1810	34 4					
1800	34.4					

Number of children under 5 years of age to 1,000 females 15 to 44 years of age in cities having at least 25,000 inhabitants and in smaller cities or country districts by main geographic divisions, and the ratio of those numbers to the number for the whole division taken as 100: 1900 [1]

DIVISION OR RACE	Number of children under 5 years of age to 1,000 females 15-44 years of age: 1900			Ratio to No. in whole division taken as 100			Difference in ratio
	Total	In cities having at least 25,000 inhabitants	In smaller cities or country districts	In cities having at least 25,000 inhabitants	In smaller cities or country districts		
Total population:							
Continental United States	518	390	572	75.3	110.4		35.1
White population:							
Continental United States	508	399	559	78.5	110.0		31.5
Negro, Indian and Mongolian populations:							
Continental United States	585	260	651	44.4	111.3		66.9

[1] Twelfth Census, Bulletin No. 22.

From this we may conclude:

1. The Negro birth rate exceeds and has always exceeded the white birth rate.

2. The Negro birth rate probably decreased largely until 1870; then it possibly increased somewhat and afterward rapidly decreased.

3. The Negro birth rate in the country districts is high. In the city it is low because of the immigrant character of the population.

Infant mortality among Negroes is very large but decreasing:

Death rate of children under 1 year of age

COLOR		Total	Registration cities	REGISTRATION RECORD			
				Registration States			Registration cities in other States
				Total	Cities	Rural	
White	1890..	249.38	278.19	241.40	267.22	137.63	260.67
	1900..	158.0	171.1	156.0	180.4	116.0	161.4
Colored...	1890..	494.27	525.13	457.83	579.77	204.49	509.61
	1900..	371.5	387.0	343.8	357.2	218.9	383.8

These records are but partial, and refer to city Negroes chiefly. The Atlanta University study of 1897 found 1137 city families containing 4742 individuals, composed as follows:

Heads of families	1,974	41.63%
Children	2,167	45.70%
Grandparents	100	2.11%
Uncles and aunts	138	2.91%
Grandchildren	113	2.38%
Nephews and nieces..............................	70	1.47%
Other relatives..................................	37	.78%
Boarders and lodgers.............................	143	3.02%
	4,742	100.00%

The size of the Negro family is unknown. There were, in 1900, 1,833,854 private Negro families in the United States. Such private families represent 98 per cent of the total population. Assuming that they represent 98 per cent of the Negro population—and this is pure assumption—they would contain 8,663,973 or 4.6 persons to a family, a figure probably lower than the truth. Some data bearing upon the size of the family may be found in the bulletins of the United States Bureau of Labor; by combining four tables there we have this:

Negro Families by Size in Four Towns

Members	INCLUDING ALL CHILDREN BORN		INCLUDING ALL CHILDREN LIVING		INCLUDING THE PRESENT CENSUS-FAMILY GROUP	
	No. of Families	No. of · Persons	Families	Persons	Families	Persons
1	22	22	54	54	78	78
2	108	216	209	418	191	382
3	109	327	189	567	194	582
4	109	436	152	608	154	616
5	76	380	110	550	125	625
6	59	354	90	540	91	546
7	49	343	75	525	56	392
8	58	464	70	560	45	360
9	37	333	32	288	36	324
10	45	450	24	240	19	190
11	37	407	19	209	14	154
12	24	288	10	120	2	24
13	27	351	8	104	2	26
14	26	364	2	28	2	28
15	13	195	2	30	1	15
16	7	112	....			
17	6	102	1	17		
18	3	54				
19	1	19				
20	1	20				
21	1	21				
22	1	22				
24	1	24				
25	1	25				
Total.. 821	5,329		1,047	4,858	1,010	4,342
Average	6.49			4.64		4.3

A table of Negro families by size in four small towns, a district in the black belt, and for all races in the United States, 1890 and 1900, follows in percentages:

Members in family	Georgia Country district Negroes	Ohio Town Negroes	Maryland Town Negroes	Virginia Town Negroes	United States Total families	
					1890	1900
2–6	9.09	10.18	5.45	4.96	3.63	5.00
7–10	73.95	80.84	63.64	72.90	73.33	74.70
11 and over	15.33	8.18	26.06	19.47	20.97	18.10
	1.63	.80	4.85	2.67	2.07	2.20
Total.....	100.00%	100.00%	100.00%	100.00%	100.0.%	100.00%

The sources of error in these statistics are: the broken families among Negroes, which for economic and social reasons increase the apparent families of one and two, and the absence of large hotel and institution families in the Negro group.

The economic condition of the Negro is influencing the sex morals of the race in two ways: First, present low wages and a rising economic standard is postponing marriage to an age dangerously late for a folk in the Negro's present moral development. Secondly, present economic demand draws the Negro women to the city and keeps the men in the country, causing a dangerous disproportion of the sexes, as Mr. Kelly Miller has pointed out. [1]

The enormous preponderance of colored females over males, especially in our large cities, is a persistent and aggravating factor which has almost wholly escaped the attention of our sociological philosophers. The census of 1900 gives 4,447,568 Negro females against 4,393,221 Negro males, leaving an excess of 54,347 of the gentler sex in the United States. This gives a residue of thirteen left-over women to each thousand of the male population. But this is utterly insignificant when compared with the excesses revealed by the statistics of the large cities. The predominance of the female element is perhaps the most striking phenomenon of the urban Negro population. The subjoined figures will show this excess in fifteen cities of more than 20,000 Negroes.

Excess of Colored Females, 1900

City	Females	Males	Excess of females	No. females to each 100 males
Washington	48,354	38,348	10,006	126
Baltimore	44,195	35,063	9,132	126
New Orleans	42,585	35,129	7,456	121
Philadelphia	33,673	28,940	4,733	116
New York	33,534	27,132	6,402	124
Memphis	25,359	24,551	808	103
Louisville	20,297	18,842	1,455	108
Atlanta	20,921	14,806	6,115	143
St. Louis	18,020	17,496	524	103
Richmond	17,878	14,354	3,524	123
Charleston	17,552	13,970	3,582	125
Nashville	16,775	13,269	3,506	125
Chicago	14,077	16,073	*1,996	88
Savannah	15,344	12,746	2,598	120
Norfolk	10,738	9,492	1,246	113
Total	379,312	320,221	59,091	118

* Surplus Males.

These cities, with an aggregate Negro population of 699,533, show a female excess of 59,091. Chicago is the only city where the females are not in the majority, which is doubtless due to the fact that a new city is always first settled by the men, who pave the way for a subsequent female influx. If every Negro male in these cities should be assigned a helpmeet there would still remain eighteen left-over females for every one hundred couples. In Atlanta this unfortunate residue reaches the startling proportion of 43 out of a hundred. Washington and Baltimore have respectively 10,006 and 9,132 hopeless females, for whom there are neither present nor prospective husbands. No such astounding disproportion prevails anywhere among the white race. The surplus women who give Mrs. Gilman such anxious solicitude scarcely exceed one in a hundred even in such man-forsaken cities as New York and Boston. If then the evil be a threatening one among the white race with such an insignificant surplus, what must be said of its multiplied enormity when we turn to the situation of the black race, where the excess is more than one-sixth of the male sex? Preponderance of one sex

[1] Miller: Race Adjustment, pp. 169-170.

over the other forebodes nothing but evil to society. The maladjustment of economic and social corditions upsets the scale where nature intended a balance. The argument of Mrs. Gilman is as correct as it is courageous: "Where women preponderate in large numbers," she says, "there is a proportionate increase in immorality, because women are cheap; where men preponderate in large numbers there is also immorality because women are dear."

Section 6. Sexual Morals. Without doubt the point where the Negro American is furthest behind modern civilization is in his sexual *mores* This does not mean that he is more criminal in this respect than his neighbors. Probably he is not. It does mean that he is more primitive, less civilized, in this respect than his surroundings demand, and that thus his family life is less efficient for its onerous social duties, his womanhood less protected, his children more poorly trained. All this, however, is to be expected. This is what slavery meant, and no amount of kindliness in individual owners could save the system from its deadly work of disintegrating the ancient Negro home and putting but a poor substitute in its place. The point is however, now, what has been the effect of emancipation on the *mores* of the Negro family.

The great and most patent fact has been differentiation: the emergence from the mass, of successive classes with higher and higher sexual morals. Of this, unfortunately, there is no adequate measurement. Subjoined are the figures of total and illegitimate births in Washington, D. C. :

Washington, D. C.

Year	Total Negro Births Reported	Percentage of Illegitimate Births Reported	Negro Population
1870.			43,404
1879.	1,659	18.8	
1880.	1,793	18.1	59,596
1881.	1,536	18.6	
1882	1,592	19.7	
1883.	1,397	21.1	
1884.	1,482	20.2	
1885.	1,500	22.2	
1886.	1,584	22.9	
1887.	1,761	19.5	
1888.	1,756	22.3	
1889.	1,804	26.2	
1890.	1,848	26.4	75,572
1891.	1,891	25.0	
1892.	1,910	27.1	
1893.	1,963	26.7	
1894.	2,001	25.7	
1895.	1,942	26.8	
1896.	1,842	27.0	
1897.	1,875	25.9	
1898.	2,043	25.1	
1899.	1,737	27.6	
1900.	1,867	25.5	86,702
1901.	1,735	24.3	
1902.	1,846	24.7	
1903.	1,817	22.7	
1904.	2,224	24.6	
1905.	2,275	24.7	
1906.	2,199	22.1	
1907.	2,322	21.4	

These figures are very imperfect. The total Negro births in Washington are quite unknown, being only partially reported; the illegitimate birth reports come from hospitals and city physicians, and it is impossible to say whether they are as far below the truth as the total birth reports, or not. Comparing this reported illegitimacy with other localities, we have:

Massachusetts, 1856-91	13	per 1,000
Belgium, 1900	74.5	" "
Austria, 1881-95	147.7	" "
Negroes in Washington, 1907	214	" "
Large cities of Bavaria	268	" "
Salzburg (Province, Austria)	272	" "
Kaernthen (Province, Austria)	435	" "
Jamaica, 1897	611	" "

Compared with the population the apparent illegitimate birth-rate of Washington Negroes was:

1880	5.4 per 1,000 births.
1890	6.4 " " "
1900	5.5 " " "

While these figures are a very doubtful basis of exact judgment, they point without doubt to wide-spread sexual irregularity. But this irregularity belongs to the undifferentiated mass: some of them decent people, but behind civilization by training and instinct. Above these and out of these are continually rising, however, classes who must not be confounded with them. Of the raising of the sex *mores* of the Negro by these classes the fact is clear and unequivocal: they have raised them and are raising them. There is more female purity, more male continence, and a healthier home life today than ever before among Negroes in America. The testimony supporting this is overwhelming.

A Baltimore slum-worker says:

My work in a large city has covered a period of nearly fourteen years. Thousands of girls have passed under my observation; many of them have already begun their careers, several are teachers in the Baltimore city school system, and are doing their part in life. The home life of all these individuals was not of the best kind, but with this much to be deplored in their condition I believe the per cent of immorality to be low.

At this writing, my work is in a veritable slum. Degradation of every kind is rampant. In the next block above us houses of ill fame line both sides of the street. The occupants of these places are white. In a street parallel to this are houses occupied by both white and colored. Many of our children come from these places. The greatest per cent of degradation I have ever witnessed exists here. What the harvest shall be only Providence knows; but, taken all in all, I believe that 8 per cent would cover the mathematical reckoning as far as figures may be taken indicative of conditions of society.

The principal of Hampton writes:

I have had an experience of twenty-one years with colored people, during which time I have been intimately acquainted with a large number of them at Hampton Institute. I have gone into their homes and have had perhaps as much opportunity as most any white man for knowing intimately their life.

I am glad to bear witness to my knowledge of the clean, pure lives of a large number whom I have known. I have often said, what I believe to be true, that it would be hard to find in any white institution in the North the freedom from low talk and impure life as is to be found at Hampton, where 1,000 young people of two races are brought together. The colored race is not degraded. Many of the young people who came to me years ago had no conception of the wrong of certain lines of conduct and who, since they have gained that knowledge, have lived up to what they know. I have seen young people coming from one-room cabins, where morality seems well nigh impossible, who sloughed that old life, and have made good use of the cleared knowledge which they have gained at Hampton.

I have often said that my own boy would be less likely to hear low talk here than in most Northern institutions for the whites. My own judgment in the matter is confirmed in the experience of others. For a number of weeks an English gentleman, who is making a most careful study of the race, has been staying at the school. He has mingled with the boys in their play, in their workshops and in their dormitories, and he confirms my impression and that of my disciplinarian, who himself is a colored man, living in close contact with the young people of the school.

A Southern white woman of Virginia says:

It was the most sorrowful part of slavery that there could be no legal marriage for the slaves, no protection for the virtue of women. Even now there are no laws to protect the colored girl, such as have always existed for her white sisters. In discussing any question that relates to the Negroes, regard should be given to the rapid formation of classes among them. There is a respectable class, and this class is increasing, where married parents live virtuous lives, guard the sanctity of their homes, and strive to bring up their children in the path of virtue.

The principal of a large Negro girls' school writes:

When a Southern white man told my predecessor that all Negro women were impure his reply was, "I suppose you know, I don't." I have seen Negro women who I have good reason to believe are living virtuous lives under conditions of trial such as our virtuous white women as a class know nothing about. Through my sainted wife I know of examples of colored women whose firmness in resisting temptation makes them worthy to represent any race.

Of those same women I can speak without reserve on all these points. Their modesty and genuine worth are conceded by white, as well as colored; their marital fidelity is above question. Many of them have passed through the stage of courtship and entered married life under my own personal observation, and even the most fastidious could find nothing but what was proper and pure. We have Negro women around us here who are for duty's sake remaining single, though sought by the very best of our young men.

One of the most touching things to come under my notice has been the many mothers who come to beg us to take their girls, saying, "I know I am not what I ought to be, but I don't want her to be like me." We could fill Scotia over and over again every year with girls whose parents want them in a safe place, so that they may grow into good women. In these nearly fifteen years we have not had the basis of a scandal involving a member of this school inside of our grounds, and we believe that our record as a school, both for honesty and purity, will bear comparison with the female schools generally.

It would not be wise however in our zeal to refute the false assertions in Mr. Thomas's book to overlook the fact that many of them are in a measure true. We cannot do our duty to the Negro while we keep ourselves ignorant of his true condition, and no Thomas or any other man can overdraw the picture of the morals of the uncared-for masses of the Negro in the South, not because they are Negroes, but because they are uncared for.

From the black belt of Alabama a white woman writes:

I have been for thirteen years working among, for and with, Negroes. The first four years' work and life were at Hampton, and I will say nothing much about that, for the Hampton teachers have a better and larger knowledge of students and graduates than I have. I would say, however, that it was because I saw such positive proof of high-mindedness and beauty of character among the Negroes and because we saw, year after year, the coming in of earnest, self-respecting boys and girls, that Miss Dillingham and I felt we must go out and show the way of light to some who lived in dark places and had never had a chance to know what really was the right in any part of life.

It was because we had firm belief in the Negro that we came, and each year but carries deeper conviction that we were then right. We came here (Calhoun) in 1892. During the nine years since I have been constantly filled with admiration of the people who, with but little to work for and with constant and deep temptations, are able to withstand the temptation and struggle on to get a precarious living, in the strength of high convictions and deep and ever-increasing self-respect. When we came we felt that the free living represented sin, but in a very few months we believed it represented the natural life of a group of people who had never been shown or taught life on a higher plane. After a few months of life among them they took hold of what little we could do and began to reconstruct their lives. Of course we found many whom we then believed, and still feel, were leading pure, good lives, merely from inborn instincts.

In regard to the morality of our girls at school, I do not want to omit a statement which, knowing the community, seems to be almost miraculous. In the last twelve years only two girls who have ever been in our school have been known to go wrong. One was of mixed Indian, Negro and white blood. She has been brought up in a house of vice and brutality, has heard bad language and low talk and seen low life and brutal living ever since babyhood; has been brutally beaten and knocked about, and it was small wonder that she died last week in sin of every sort. The other, a girl of sixteen, is feeble-minded, so that after trying to teach her for four years we found she knew but little more than when she started in school. These two cases had not been in school for several years, and are the only ones out of many hundreds who have attended who have gone astray.

Our boys and young men from sixteen to twenty-five years of age are upright and self-respecting in the majority of cases. Of course, in this community, one of the worst in the whole South, when we came here we found all kinds, good and bad, but there is daily evidence of desire and strivings for high standards of living, and victories over self that are marvelous.

From the black belt of Mississippi a teacher writes:

The trend and tendency are very decidedly towards better things in the moral life, and it has been in existence long enough to have molded a very considerable portion of the Negro people to a nobler life than Thomas seems to know about. The more I study the matter the more I am convinced that with all the evils resultant from slavery and from the sudden freedom, the indictments brought against the race now have never been fully true, and it is less true now than formerly.

I have had fourteen years of experience and observation in teaching in the heart of the black belt of Mississippi.

There is an increasing number of men who have a high regard for chaste womanhood, who are earnest in the desire to protect women from impurity of every kind. They welcome and forward such agencies; for the promotion of purity is the White Cross with its pledge of reverence for women.

The number of girls who would resent solicitations to evil is not a small one and among those who have been carefully reared, who have had something of moral training, the percentage of those who go astray is a small one. The number of homes where the pure ideal of family life exists has increased constantly since I have been in the South. There are some pure homes among the poor and illiterate. Among those who are educated the dishonored homes are few.

A colored Y. M. C. A. secretary of wide travel and experience says:

After fourteen years of constant laboring among my people throughout the South, especially among young men in the cities and students in the boarding schools of all grades, I am firmly convinced that a heroic and successful fight is being waged against immoral tendencies inherited from centuries of debasing slavery. Of course there is much dross yet to be burned away before we can have only pure gold remaining.

I confess with great sorrow of heart that there are some members of my race, and possibly a large proportion, who could be put down as fitting one or more of the foul characteristics of Mr. Thomas, nor do I seek to cover this acknowledgment with the fact that in every other race on the earth, individuals can be found equally low in life and character. But there are various classes among the freedmen as among other people.

Born and reared in Canada, and having spent three years just prior to my coming South in 1888 as a civil servant at Ottawa, where I mingled freely in church and social life with some of the best of white Canadians, I find myself greatly encouraged as I compare my experience of the past fourteen years with those of my earlier life, and especially the three years referred to above. I have met in all sections of the country hundreds of colored women whose bearing has been as suggestive of good as that of the women of the fairer race in the North. I have also come into close contact with thousands of young men whom I know to be struggling against unfortunate inherited tendencies and unfavorable environment.

It is true that only a few of the Negro race have yet attained to the degree of perfection possible among men, but between those few and the submerged masses is a promising and inspiring host of men and women in various stages of moral, intellectual and industrial evolution.

While, then, the tendencies are hopeful, still the truth remains: sexual immorality is probably the greatest single plague spot among Negro Americans, and its greatest cause is slavery and the present utter disregard of a black woman's virtue and self-respect, both in law court and custom in the South.

One thing further may be said, with diffidence but hearty conviction. The marriage *mores* of modern European culture nations, while in many respects superior to those of other peoples, are far from satis-

factory, as Prostitution, Divorce and Childlessness prove only too conclusively. Much has been written as to remedies and improvements,
chiefly in the line of punishing prostitution, denying divorce and
stressing child-bearing as a duty. It seems to the writer that here
the Negro race may teach the world something. Just as Olivier has
pointed out that what is termed Negro "laziness" may be a means of
making modern workingmen demand more rational rest and enjoyment rather than permitting themselves to be made machines, so too
the Negro woman, with her strong desire for motherhood, may teach
modern civilization that virginity, save as a means of healthy motherhood, is an evil and not a divine attribute. That while the sexual
appetite is the most easily abused of all human appetites and most
deadly when perverted, that nevertheless it is a legitimate, beneficent
appetite when normal, and that no civilization can long survive which
stigmatizes it as essentially nasty and only to be discussed in shame-
faced whispers. The Negro attitude in these matters is in many respects healthier and more reasonable. Their sexual passions are strong
and frank, but they are, despite example and temptation, only to a
limited degree perverted or merely commercial. The Negro mother-
love and family instinct is strong, and it regards the family as a
means, not an end, and although the end in the present Negro mind
is usually personal happiness rather than social order, yet even here
radical reformers of divorce courts have something to learn.

Part 2.   The Home [1]

Section 7.   Africa.   The general description of African homes given
in Ratzel[2] presents a good picture of the present Negro home on that
continent:

> The domiciles of the Negroes, in the widespread tendency to grouping
> round a central point, and to fencing, as well as in the prevalent light con-
> struction with grass, reeds, stalks or boughs, show a principal due to no-
> madism. Genuine nomads build temporary huts of brushwood, which they
> protect by laying mats or skins over them; a construction which extends
> from the fish-eaters of the Red Sea even to the Hottentots. The only firm
> part of these huts is some kind of stone wall carried round them to prevent
> the rain from washing away the sand, and the water from pouring into the
> house. [2]
> Among the pastoral races the individual huts are usually placed in a circle
> round an open space, into which the herds are driven and at night. Larger
> villages often contain several enclosures, hedged or palisaded, for herds and
> flocks; and the whole settlement is finally once more surrounded by a large
> hedge. This main hedge is further strengthened with a stockade, and in the
> agricultural villages a ditch is added. All the Babemba villages are thus
> fortified. But a chief point in laying out an African village is to make the
> approach difficult. This is defended, as for instance by the Fans, with poi-

---

[1] Considerable parts of sections 7-11 were first published by the editor in the *Southern Workman*, vols. 30 and 31, and are here reproduced by permission.
[2] Ratzel: History of Mankind, II; pp. 398-402.

soned splinters of reed stuck in the ground just after the Borneo fashion; or, in extreme cases, is placed in a forest stream, in the sand of which tell-tale footprints are quickly washed out.[1]

The conical style of hut-building prevails among nearly all the Negroes of Africa. The plan is circular or oval, the elevation conical or bee-hive shaped, with the entrance low; the height being that of a man, and the diameter twice as much. The bee-hive shape is the most frequent. Even the large handsome palaces of the Waganda and Wanyoro, or the regular huts of the tribes on the Upper Nile, are nothing else. Around this type are grouped the huts from the Niger to the Nile, and from Suakop to Sobat. Roomier and more comfortable huts are found especially in the Upper Nile district: as among the Bongos, whose huts run to 24 feet in height, or the Jurs; but however commodious the internal dimensions may be, the door is always low and, as a rule, there are no windows.

While the round or scattered arrangement of the village harmonises with the circular plan of this style of architecture, rectangular huts result in its being laid out in streets. A band of rectangular hut-building passes from the Manyema country through the northern Congo basin to the Cameroons. Here two rows of dwelling-huts form a street or row, closed at the two ends by council-houses, or similar "public buildings." The ingress and egress are in the longitudinal sides. The houses of one side often lie under one common roof, so as to produce two "long houses" lying opposite to each other. In this we may perhaps recognise the early state of things out of which the rectangular single premises have grown. We are still more reminded of the American or Polynesian "long houses" by the sleeping quarters for unmarried men which are found, from the Madi country westwards, through the whole region of rectangular building. In West Africa the little round huts of the restless Babongo are found intermingled with the rectangular Fan huts.

From the Fish river to Uganda and Liberia, Africa, devoid of cities, shows only slight variations in style of building and arrangement; and these are due partly to the material, partly to transmitted customs. South of the Zambesi the building is not so good because material is less abundant, and quite the best building is in the northeast; but the work is everywhere transitory, because straw, reeds, and mud are used by preference.[2]

Larger buildings, used as palaces and assembly houses, are executed in both styles. The palace huts of the Wahuma chiefs, which are over 30 feet high, and have an arched entrance 12 or more feet high; the palace-hall of the Monbuttu king, described by Schweinfurth, 50 feet high, 65 feet wide, 165 feet long, are mighty edifices for the circumstances of Central Africa. The "palaver huts" of West Africa do not fall far short of these. Cholet found the hall of a small chief in the trading village of Kosso to be 13 feet long and 65 wide. Buildings of this kind are decorated with colors, usually black, white and red, and with wood-carvings. Here, again, South Africa is behind the northern equatorial region.[3]

In East Africa we find the mud-huts, often half under ground, surrounding a large rectangular court, known as tembe, and in transition-regions like Darfour, we see stone and mud-houses mixed with the conical huts; but,wherever Moorish and Arab influences in Africa has not led to stone building, and so to the ornamental style, the village-premises in Africa are of little compactness, and correspondingly small and perishable.[4]

---

[1] Ratzel: History of Mankind, Vol. II, p. 398.
[2] Ibid, pp. 399-400.   [3] Ibid, p. 400.   [4] Ibid, p. 401.

Some villages on the west coast are described as composed of low, square, gable- roofed huts, ranging on both sides of one or more broad streets, and built always on the banks of streams—the natural highways of the land. In the rear of each house is a small kitchen garden, but the plantations, worked by the women, are a mile or so distant in the forest. [1] Further east, on the banks of the Congo, villages may be found consisting of a number of low conical grass huts, ranged round a circular common. In the center are several large shady fig trees. The doorways to the huts are very low—scarcely thirty inches in height. [2] Further down the Congo appear the long-house villages, much like similar types among the North American Indians. The long rows of houses are all connected together in blocks of from fifty to three hundred yards in length. The doorways are square apertures in the walls, two feet square and about a foot and a half above the ground. Within, the long block is divided into several apartments for the respective families forming the clan. The roof glistens with a coating of tar, and there are shelves for fuel and netting for swinging the crockery. [3] The town of Ikondu in the northern part of the Congo Free State has for homes double cages tastefully built of grass-cane, 7 feet long by 5 feet wide and 6 feet high. These cages are separate but connected by a common roof, so that the central apartments are common to both cages, and in these the families meet, perform their household duties, receive friends, and chat. "These cane cages are as cozy, comfortable and dry as ships' cabins," and are surrounded by banana trees, gardens and great tracts of waving sugar-cane. [4]

Of the homes themselves we learn that they usually consist of one and two rooms, kept in a neat and orderly manner, for the most part, and not crowded with inmates. The hut was designed primarily for sleeping and shelter in time of storm, and most of the lives of inmates were passed out of doors. A hut on the west coast is described as consisting of two rooms, one used as a kitchen and sitting-room, the other as a sleeping apartment. In the middle of the kitchen, elevated above the clay floor, was the fire-place, the smoke of which must escape by the low door. Here, from morning to night, some sort of cooking is carried on by the women—steaming cassava, boiling or roasting plantains, stewing fish or wild meat. The children have some little mess of their own to cook—an ear of maize, or some little fish. [5]

At night, when the evening meal was served, all this village seated themselves together but grouped by families, in the open air, either on low stools or on the ground, around the basin of vegetables and the little iron pot with fish and nut gravy. Plantain leaves were used as plates, and torches of the gum trees flared and lighted the night. After the meal, all drank from jugs of water, carefully cleaned mouth and teeth with their fingers, and threw away the plates on the waste heap at the end of the street. [6]

---

[1] Nassau: Mawedo, p. 31.   [2] Stanley: Through the Dark Continent, II, p. 72.
[3] Stanley: Through the Dark Continent, II, pp. 133-135.
[4] Stanley: Ibid, II, pp. 169-170.   [5] Nassau: Mawedo, p. 52.   [6] Nassau: Ibid, p. 31.

Such homes and customs vary infinitely in different parts of Africa. Among the Zulus of South Africa the huts are built in circular kraals and are made of long poles, the ends of which are fastened in the ground and the tops bent together and lashed about with a tough native vine. Thus a strong, basket-like roof is made, resting on upright posts and covered tightly with long grass. Such huts are very strong, are impervious to rain, and within, the dirt floors are often polished like a mirror.[1] At the other extreme of Africa, about the headwaters of the Nile, Schweinfurth found dwellings 30 x 20 feet, with projecting roofs, covered with grass and skins. The walls were 5 to 6 feet high, and bound together with split Spanish reed. Such huts are astonishingly strong. The doorway is large and closed by a door made of one piece. The hut is divided into two apartments. The huts of the Dinka, still further down the Nile, are conical and often 40 feet in diameter. Their foundations are of clay and chopped straw, and the supports of hard wood. Such buildings last eight or ten years.[2]

This casual glance at some of the homes of the African barbarians of today will serve to give us, perhaps, a fairly correct idea of the homes of our Negro ancestors. The slaves came from all parts of Africa, from all stages of barbaric culture, and from homes like those we have noted, as well as, probably, from others worse and better.

Section 8. Slavery. Once landed in the West Indies and "seasoned" to the new climate and surroundings, the slaves built houses not unlike those they had left at home. Nothing was provided for them save some rough building material. From this the slaves constructed their homes, driving four posts into the ground and weaving the walls of wattles so as to make a room 10 x 15 feet and 5 or 6 feet high, or possibly two rooms. There was no floor, window, or fireplace, and the roof was thatched with palms. Furniture was scanty; a rough platform raised the sleepers from the earth, and this sometimes had a mat or blanket; then there was perhaps a table, some low stools, an earthen jar for water, an iron pot for cooking and calabashes for eating. The cooking was done out of doors usually, and if the fire was made indoors there was no place for smoke to escape save through the doorway.

When slaves were few and land plentiful these rude homes were not unpleasant. They often had two rooms, could be kept clean and shady; and something like the old African life, with quasi-chief, medicineman and polygamy appeared. Such tendencies, however, quickly passed, and the cold brutality of slavery appeared, where life was nothing and sugar was all. The homes of the slaves became dirty one-room lodges where, crowded like cattle, men slept in dreamless stupor after endless hours of forced and driven toil. All pretense at marriage and the protection of black women was virtually swept away, and

---

[1] Tyler: Forty Years Among the Zulus, pp. 41-43.
[2] Schweinfurth: Heart of Africa, II, pp. 118, 119, 160.

herded and whipped like cattle, the black men existed until like beasts they fell in their tracks and died, and fresh loads of half putrid newcomers were emptied on the shores by the thrift of British noblemen and New England deacons.

When slaves were brought to the mainland of America, different building materials and colder climate substituted the square log hut for the older forms. At first the slaves were housed in rough cabins near the master, and the accommodations of the two differed chiefly in size and furniture. Thus arose the first type of slave home in America—the "Patriarchal Group." The central idea of this arrangement was distinctly mediæval and feudal, and consequently familiar to its white founders. First there was the house of the master—a large log house of two or four rooms; near it were grouped the one-room log cabins. With the light building material of the Indies it cost little more trouble to build two rooms than to build one. But with the heavy logs of Carolina pine, one room was as much as could be afforded. The room was ten to fourteen feet square, and six or more feet high; it had still the dirt floor. A cooler climate, however, made some other provisions necessary; a rough fire-place of stones was made, sometimes with a hole in the roof for the smoke and sometimes with a chimney of clay and wood. A hole in the wall, closed by a wooden shutter, served with the door for light and ventilation. The slave cabin was thus a smaller and meaner edition of the Big House; there the chimney was stone or brick, the house of logs, with board floor, and partitioned into two or four rooms and a hall. Here the group lived as master and men. At first the bond between them was almost purely legal and economic. The slaves were white and black, and the social station of the master not usually high. The condition of the bondsmen therefore depended largely on accident and whim. Here they were squalid, dirty, and driven with the lash; there a lazy, dawdling crowd, or again, simply thrifty farm-hands. Out of this chaos evolved the Virginia ideal. The white bond-servants became gradually free and migrated southward; a rigid slave-code carefully fixed the status of the black slave; he was no longer allowed to intermarry with white servants or to become a full-fledged freeman; on the other hand, excessive and wanton cruelty toward him was in some degree restrained. The slave had learned the English language and had assumed Christianity. Bonds of friendship and intimacy grew up between black and white; the physical group of Big House and cabins differentiated; some came nearer, others receded, but all formed a great feudal family of lord and retainers.

But the curse of such families, with slaves at the bottom and a privileged aristocracy at the top, ever was and ever will be, sexual debauchery. The morals of black women and white men are found to be ruined under such an arrangement, unless long-revered custom and self-respect enter to check license. But the African home with its customs had long ago been swept away, and slavery is simply a system for crushing self-respect. Nevertheless time was slowly beginning to provide remedies. White fathers could not see their black children utterly neglected, and white mothers saw the danger of surrounding their sons with vice and ignorance. Thus, gradually, the better class of slaves were brought closer into the bosom of the family as house-servants. Religion and marriage rites received more attention and the Negro monogamic family rose as a dependent off-shoot of the feudal slave regime. The first sign of this was the improvement in the Negro home; the house of the house-servants became larger, sometimes with two rooms; a more careful regard for outward decency was manifest, and the direct intercourse between the cabin and Big House brought better manners and ways of living.

One can easily imagine in this development how slavery might have worked itself out for the good of black and white. And usually those persons North and South who dwell on the advantages and training of slavery have this phase of development in mind.

The cotton-gin doomed the patriarchal slave group. Commercial slavery, which looked upon the slave primarily as an investment, meant death to the Negro home. One of the first signs of the changed condition of things was, perhaps, the "Detached Group" as I shall designate the second type of slave homes. The "Detached Group" was the group of slave cabins without a Big House—i. e., removed from the direct eye of the master, either to a far part of the same plantation or to a different plantation. The Big House has turned to brick, with imposing proportions, surrounded by trees and gardens and a certain state and elegance with which the old South was flavored. The house-servants are now either lodged in the Big House or in trim cabins near. The mass of the slaves are down at the "quarters" by themselves, under the direct eye of the overseer. This change was slight in appearance but of great importance; it widened the distance between the top and bottom of the social ladder, it placed a third party between master and slave, and it removed the worst side of the slave hierarchy far from the eyes of its better self.

From the "Detached Group" to "Absentee Landlordism" was but a step. The rich lands to the southwest, the high price of cotton, and the rapidly increasing internal slave trade, was the beginning of a system of commercial slavery in the gulf states which will ever remain a disgraceful chapter in American history. In its worst phase there was no Big House and cultivated master, only an unscrupulous, paid overseer, lawless and almost irresponsible if he only made crops large enough. The homes of the field hands were filthy hovels where they slept. There was no family life, no meals, no marriages, no decency, only an endless round of toil and a wild debauch at Christmas time. In the forests of Louisiana, the bottoms of Mississippi, and the Sea Islands of Georgia, where the Negro slave sank lowest in oppression and helplessness, the Negro home practically disappeared, and the house was simply rude, inadequate shelter.

But whither went the Big House, when so entirely separated from the slave quarters? It moved to town and with it moved the house-servants. These privileged slaves were trained and refined from contact with the masters; they were often allowed to accumulate a *peculium;* they were in some cases freed and gained considerable property, holding it in some friendly white man's name. Their home life improved, and although it was far from ideal, yet it was probably as good as that of the Northern workingman, with some manifest differences; sexual looseness was the weakest point, arising from subordination to the whites and the lessons learned therefrom by the servants themselves. They lived often in small one or two-room homes behind the masters' mansions, reached by alleys—a method which has since left the peculiar alley problem in Southern cities. Some of the slaves and the freedmen lived in a Negro quarter by themselves, although the distinctive Negro quarter of towns is largely post-bellum.

Thus we have in slavery times, among other tendencies and many exceptions, three fairly distinct types of Negro homes: the patriarchal type, found at its best in Virginia, where the housing of the slaves might be compared with that of the poorest of the Northern workingmen; the separate group and absentee type where the slaves had practically no homes and no family life; and the town group where the few house-servants were fairly well housed. In discussing slavery and incidents connected with it, these varying circumstances are continually lost sight of.

The house of the slave, which I have sought to show in its various relationships and degrees of squalor, had certain general characteristics which we must notice carefully. First, there was the lack of comfort; the Negro knew nothing of the little niceties and comforts of the civilized home—everything of beauty and taste had disappeared with the uprooting of the African home, and little had been learned to replace them. Thus, even to this day, there is a curious bareness and roughness in the country Negro home, the remains of an uncouthness which in slavery times made the home anything but a pleasant, lovable place. There were, for instance, few chairs with backs, no sheets on the beds, no books, no newspapers, no closets or out-houses, no bedrooms, no tablecloths and very few dishes, no carpets and usually no floors, no windows, no pictures, no clocks, no lights at night save that of the fire-place, little or nothing save bare rough shelter.

Secondly, and closely connected with the first, was the lack of hygienic customs: every nation has its habits and customs handed down from elders, which have enabled the race to survive. But the continuity of Negro family tradition had been broken and the traditions of the white environment never learned; then, too, the rules and exactions of the plantation favored unhealthy habits; there ensued a disgusting lack of personal cleanliness, bad habits of eating and sleeping, habits of breathing bad air, of wearing inadequate clothing—all such changes and abuses in everyday life for which the world's grandchildren must eventually pay.

Thirdly, there was in the slave home necessarily almost an entire lack of thrift, or the ordinary incentives to thrift. The food and fuel were certain, and extra faithfulness or saving could make little or no difference. On the other hand, cunning and thieving could secure many a forbidden knick-knack, far more than honest cultivation of the little garden spot which each family often had. The thriftiest slave could only look forward to slavery for himself and children.

Fourthly, there was the absence of the father—that is, the lack of authority in the slave father to govern or protect his family. His wife could be made his master's concubine, his daughter could be outraged, his son whipped, or he himself sold away without his being able to protest or lift a preventing finger. Naturally, his authority in his own house was simply such as could rest upon brute force alone, and he easily sank to a position of male guest in the house, without respect or responsibility.

Fifthly, and correlated to the last, was the absence of the mother. The slave mother could spend little or no time at home. She was either a field-hand or a house-servant, and her children had little care or attention. She was often the concubine of the master or his sons, or, if unmolested in this quarter, was married to a husband who could not protect her, and from whom she could at any time be parted by her master's command or by his death or debts. Such a family was not an organism at best; and, in its worst aspect, it was a fortuitous agglomeration of atoms.

From the following pictures of slave homes one gets varying degrees, ranging from the worst to the best:

The dwellings of the slaves were palmetto huts, built by themselves of stakes and poles, thatched with the palmetto leaf. The door, when they had any, was generally of the same materials, sometimes boards found on the beach. They had no floors, no separate apartments, except the Guinea Negroes had sometimes a small enclosure for their "god house." These huts the slaves built themselves after task and on Sundays.—Florida, 1830.

The houses for the field-slaves were about fourteen feet square, built in the coarsest manner, with one room, without any chimney or flooring, with a hole in the roof to let the smoke out.—South Carolina, 1819.

The huts of the slaves are mostly of the poorest kind. They are not as good as those temporary shanties which are thrown up beside railroads. They are erected with posts and crotches, with but little or no frame work about them. They have no stoves or chimneys; some of them have something like a fireplace at one end, and a board or two off at that side, or on the roof, to let off the smoke. Others have nothing like a fireplace in them; in these the fire is sometimes made in the middle of the hut. These buildings have but one apartment in them; the places where they pass in and out serve both for doors and windows; the sides and roof are covered with coarse, and in many instances with refused, boards.—1840.

On old plantations the Negro quarters are of frame and clapboards, seldom affording a comfortable shelter from wind or rain; their size varies from 8 by 10 to 10 by 12 feet, and six or eight feet high; sometimes there is a hole cut for a window, but I never saw a sash or glass in any. In the new country and in the woods, the quarters are generally built of logs, of similar dimensions. —1840.

Amongst all the Negro cabins which I saw in Virginia I cannot call to mind one in which there was any other floor than the earth; anything that a Northern laborer or mechanic, white or colored, would call a bed; nor a solitary partition to separate the sexes.—Virginia, 1840.

The slaves live generally in miserable huts, which are without floors and have single apartment only, where both sexes are herded promiscuously together.—Missouri, 1837.

The dwellings of the slaves are log huts, from 10 by 12 feet square; often without windows, doors, or floors, they have neither chairs, table or bedstead. —Alabama, 1837. [1]

On a very large plantation there were many exceptionally small Negro cabins, not more than twelve feet square interiorly. They stood in two rows with a wide street between them. They were built of logs with no windows —no opening at all except the doorway, with a chimney of sticks and mud; with no trees about them, no porches or shade of any kind. Except for the chimney—the purpose of which I should not readily have guessed—if I had seen one of them in New England I should have conjectured that it had been built for a powder-house, or perhaps an ice-house; never for an animal to sleep in.—South Carolina, 1859. [2]

There was a street or common two hundred feet wide, on which the cabins of the Negroes fronted. Each cabin was a frame building, the walls boarded and whitewashed on the outside, lathed and plastered within, the roof shingled; forty-two feet long, twenty-one feet wide, divided into two family tenements, each twenty-one by twenty-one; each tenement divided into three rooms—one the common household apartment, twenty-one by ten; each of the others (bedrooms), ten by ten. There was a brick fireplace in the middle of the long side of each living-room, the chimneys rising in one, in the middle of the roof. Besides these rooms, each tenement had a cock-loft, entered by steps from the household room. Each tenement is occupied, on an average, by five persons. There were in them closets, with locks and keys and a varying quantity of rude furniture. Each cabin stood two hundred feet from the next, and the street in front of them being two hundred feet wide, they were just that distance apart each way. Each cabin has a front and back door, and each room a window closed by a wooden shutter, swinging outward on hinges. Between each tenement and the next house is a small piece of ground enclosed with palings, in which are coops of fowl, with chicken hovels for nests and for sows with pig. In the rear of the yards were gardens, a half acre to each family. Internally the cabins appeared dirty and disordered, which was a pleasant indication that their home life was not much interfered with, though I found certain police regulations were enforced.—South Carolina, 1859. [3]

Section 9. The Country Home. There were reported in 1900, 1,832,818 private Negro homes in the United States Assuming that these homes are distributed approximately in the same proportion as the population, and we may conclude that 74% of these homes, or 1,350,000, are in the country districts of the South.

Here, as we would expect, the Negro home is for the most part either the actual slave home or its lineal descendant. Emancipation brought

---

[1] The above quotations are from Weld's Slavery as It Is.
[2] Olmsted: Seaboard Slave States, p. 11.   [3] Ibid, II, pp. 49-50.

at first no violent or far-reaching change in Negro country-home life. In the back districts there was no change at all. Big House and slave quarters remained and toil, though nominally on a wage basis, was really the old forced labor with a Christmas donation. Gradually, in towns and other regions, emancipation gave rise to an attempt to substitute a sort of State slavery for individual bondage. The machinery of the State judiciary, was, in many cases, after the withdrawal of the Freedmen's Bureau, used to place Negroes under the control of the State. "Vagrancy," theft, loitering, "impudence" and assault were the easily proven charges which forced large numbers of Negroes into penal servitude. The next step was to hire the labor of these persons to private contractors; thus was born the Convict Lease System. Many large planters conducted their plantations with such labor, and erected for them "barracks" and "stockades"—i. e., large enclosed quarters, guarded by high fences and crowded with inmates. These quarters were wretched, insanitary and small, and the death rate of convicts was enormous. The Convict Lease System was, however, found to be better suited to certain large operations such as brickmaking, road-building and mining, than to ordinary farming, and its use on the regular plantations was therefore limited, although not entirely discarded even to-day.

The share and rent systems of farming gradually came to replace the slave system in most cases. The best class of masters entered into contracts with their freed slaves, and the latter worked on as hired laborers. There were, however, difficulties in the carrying out of this plan. The Negroes naturally felt like seeing something of the world after freedom came. To stay on the old plantation and pursue the same dull round of toil had little attraction to a people fired with new thoughts and new ambitions. It was therefore very difficult to stop the roving instinct of the new laborers. To some extent this was accomplished by offering better wages and better houses. Frame cabins and board floors came gradually to replace the worst of the slave quarters. Still this change was but gradual and was checked by the crop-lien system or Slavery of Debt, which was soon powerful enough to keep the tenant from moving by legal process, despite his likes or dislikes. Consequently the living conditions of such freedmen were but a degree above those of former times. In the course of decades, however, a change was noticeable. The dirt-floor has practically disappeared, and fully half the log-cabins have been replaced by frame buildings, and glass windows have appeared here and there.

The great impulse toward better housing came however from the new land owners. Immediately after emancipation the Negroes began to buy land, aided somewhat by the Freedmen's Bureau, somewhat by army bounties, but mostly by the general bankruptcy. The peasant proprietors who thus arose, gradually demanded better houses. But here the anomalous situation of Southern industry showed itself: there was no ideal home-making to which the better class of freedmen could look. There were no white, green-blinded New England cottages scattered here and there, no middle class dwellings—only the Big House and the slave-pen, and nothing between. The black landholder could not think of building a mansion and he therefore built a slave cabin with some few improvements. He put a porch on the front, perhaps, cut one or two windows, and at last added a lean-to on the back for a kitchen. He beautified the yard and his wife made some tasty arrangements indoors. If he went further than this in the number of rooms or the furniture, the chances are that he got his new ideas from his friends who had moved to town.

The attraction of town life was very great to the freed slave. His few holidays and stolen pleasures in the past had centered there, and the whole aspect of concentrated life there pictured to him a long-cherished ideal of liberty. Many therefore at the first chance migrated to town, worked as mechanics or laborers and built them homes. They found in town new ideas of small comfortable dwelling places and some of them built little two, three and four-room houses such as were never seen in the country. From these patterns the country Negro learned, and two and three-room homes appeared here and there in the country. Still the reign of the one-room cabin was not seriously disputed, and an investigation in a typical black-belt county shows 40% of the families in one room, 43% in two rooms, 10% in three rooms and 7% in four or more rooms. If these figures are true for the South, 440,000 Negro rural families still live in one room.

Let us now notice more particularly what a one-room home is and means. Of course it has no peculiarly intimate connection with the Negro or the South. It is the primitive and natural method of dwelling of all men and races at some time. The cave-dwellers, the American Indians, the French peasants, the American pioneers, all lived in the one-room homes. Under certain conditions of life such homes may be fairly comfortable. Given a man and wife, the necessity of economy of heat, an active outdoor life, and a scarcity of the finer sort of building material, there can be no better home than the old roomy log hut with its great fireplace. An increase in the number of inmates, however, or a decrease in the size of the house, or a change in the manner of life, can easily transform this kind of home into a veritable pest house. This was exactly the history of the Negro's one-room cabin. Large families of children grew to maturity in it under poor moral restraint at best. There was not available building material to provide large houses, so that the original houses were built smaller and then cut in halves, with a family in either part, and then jammed closely together so as to cut off light and air. The improvements since the war have tended toward the addition of one room, more rarely two, and the changing of the building material from logs to sawn lumber. The great defects of the Negro country home, however, are still plain. They may be classed under eight chief heads:

(a) *Poor Light.* Glass windows in the country Negro homes are the exception. The light enters therefore only in pleasant weather, and then chiefly from the open door or one or two small apertures in the wall, usually of two or three square feet.

(b) *Bad Air.* A natural consequence of this is bad air and almost no ventilation. There are plenty of corners never reached by sunlight or fresh air, and as cooking, washing and sleeping go on in the same room an accumulation of stale sickly odors are manifest to every visitor. At night, when the air holes in the walls and the doors are tightly closed, from two to a dozen people sleep in a condition of air which is fatal to health. In the older log-hut the chinks in the walls admitted some fresh air. In the new board homes even this source is shut off. One of the most fruitful sources of lung disease among post-bellum Negroes is this wretched ventilation in their homes.

(c) *Lack of Sanitary Appliances.* A room so largely in use is with difficulty kept clean. The dish-water forms a pool beside the door; animals stray into the house; there are either no privies or bad ones; facilities for bathing even the face and hands are poor, and there is almost no provision for washing other parts of the body; the beds are filled with vermin. To be neat and tidy in such homes is almost impossible. Now and then one does find a tiny cabin shining and clean, but this is not the rule.

(d) *Poor Protection Against the Weather.* The average country home leaks in the roof and is poorly protected against changes in the weather. A hard storm means the shutting out of all air and light; cold weather leads to overheating, draughts, or poor ventilation; hot weather breeds diseases. The conditions are aggravated in cases where the huge old-fashioned fireplace has been replaced by a poor smoky stove.

(e) *Crowding.* So far as actual sleeping space goes, the crowding of human beings together in the Black Belt is greater than in the tenement district of large cities like New York. In one black-belt county, out of 1474 Negro families living in the country district, 761 lived in one room, 560 in two rooms, 93 in three rooms and 60 in four or more rooms. In this county there were 25 persons for every ten rooms of house accommodation, while in the worst tenement districts of New York there are not above 22.

From the single couple in one room it was an easy transition to large families with grown children occupying diminutive single-room dwellings. Sometimes married sons or daughters continue to live at home, thus introducing a second or third family. Finally the migration of young men in search of work at different seasons and in different years brings in a class of male lodgers. As a result many families entirely outgrow the physical home and use it only for sleeping and huddling in time of storm. Of real group family life there is, in such cases, little, and in this absence of group training and presence of discomfort and temptation there develop untold evils.

(f) *Poor Food.* In such homes the matter of storing and preparing food and drink is a serious problem. The well water is often tainted, or the spring so far away as to make water scarce. The cupboards for keeping food are dark, dirty and ill-ventilated. The method of preparing the meals before the fireplace or over the rickety stove is wasteful and unhygienic, filling the room with odors and making the food difficult to digest.

(g) *Lack of Privacy.* Above all, the moral and educational effect of living in one room is very bad. Of course one must not suppose that all modesty and home training disappear under such circumstances. Often there is peculiar ingenuity in guarding the children and inculcating good habits. Still, the lack of any considerable degree of privacy, the difficulty of cleanliness in a room so much used, the crowding and hurry and vulgarity of life, is bound to leave its impress on the children and to send them into the world sadly lacking in that finer sense of propriety and decency which it is the peculiar province of the home to impart.

(h) *Lack of Beauty.* Finally, it is manifest that the sense of harmony and beauty receives its first training at home. At best, the ordinary Negro country home is bare and lonely, and at worst, ugly and repelling. Out of it are bound to come minds without a sense of color contrast, appropriateness in dress, or adequate appreciation of the beautiful world in which they live. Pictures in these homes are usually confined to handbills and circus posters; the furniture is rude, tables are not set for meals, beds are not properly made. When there is an attempt at decoration it usually lacks taste and is overdone.

Such is a picture of the poorer homes of the Negro in the country districts of the South. It varies, of course, in time and place. There are sections with much more of squalor and indecency than I have pictured. There are other sections where the homes are larger and the conditions greatly improved. On the whole, however, the one and two-room cabins still prevail and the consequences are bad health, bad morals, and dissatisfaction with country life.

Section 10. The Village Home. Migration to town was one of the first results of imagination. In 1900 17.2% of the Negroes of the South lived in cities of at least 2500 inhabitants and probably one-fifth in places of at least 1000 inhabitants.

There is considerable difference in the condition of this population in the villages and in the larger cities; and as the course of urban migration is usually from the country to the village, then to the town and thence to the city, it is important that we devote some attention to the freedman's home in the villages of the South.

The village community varies in size and kind. The most primitive is a cluster of farm houses with outlying fields, something like the German *dorf.* This kind of community is not well developed in the South, the constituent homes seldom being near enough together to form farm villages like those of the old world. Nevertheless, the partial clustering of a few score of people make a community life which differs considerably from the country life proper. Two communities in DeKalb county, Georgia, will illustrate this phase of life. Doraville and a neighboring unnamed village contain in all eleven families, with an average of twelve to a family. Five of these families own their homes, while the rest rent on shares. The farms, being within twenty miles of Atlanta, are small—from one to eleven acres. Most of the houses are rudely constructed of logs or boards, with one large and one small room. There is usually no glass in the openings which serve as windows, and they are closed by wooden shutters. The large room always contains several beds, and some home-made furniture, consisting of tables, chairs and chests. A few homes have three rooms each, and one has five. Most of the homes are poverty-stricken and dirty, but a few are well-kept and neat.

Another village group is found in Israelville, Prince Edward county, Virginia. Here are 123 inhabitants, strung along in a straggling community and forming a sort of suburb to Farmville, two miles distant. Twenty-two of the 25 families own their homes, and the other three rent from colored landlords. Seven families live in one-room log cabins; nine live in two-room log cabins; i. e., in cabins with a lower room and a loft for sleeping purposes. Three families live in three-room frame houses, and six in houses of four or more rooms. The average size of the family is five, and there are, on an average, two persons to a room, or 2½ rooms to a family. These homes are distinctly of two kinds—old dirty log huts, and new neat frame houses. The Atlanta Conference of 1897 gave us a glimpse of conditions in several villages. As an example of bad conditions let us take a group of fourteen families in Tuskegee, Alabama. There were 79 persons in these families—36 males and 43 females—inhabiting 35 rooms, making an average of 2¼ persons to a room, and nearly 3 persons to each sleeping-room. Only two of these families owned their homes, the other twelve paying on an average $3.40 a month in rent. Three other groups—one in Tuskegee, one in Macon, Mississippi, and one in Sanford, Florida, present a better picture. Here 48 families of 220 persons occupy 203 rooms, 118 of which are sleeping-rooms. Thirty-five own their homes and 12 rent at an average of $3.27 a month.

Perhaps we can find in Farmville, Virginia, as good a picture as is needed of the small-town life. Farmville is near the geographic center of an old slave State and had 2471 inhabitants in 1900, of whom half or more were Negroes. Two hundred and sixty-two Negro families in 1890 occupied homes as follows:

SIZE OF FAMILY	FAMILIES OCCUPYING DWELLINGS OF				
	One room	Two rooms	Three rooms	Four rooms and over	Total
1 member	1	9	1	2	13
2-3 members	12	43	13	18	86
4-6 members	4	59	19	23	105
7-10 members	..	22	11	18	51
11 or more members	..	1	1	5	7
Total families	17	134	45	66	262
Total rooms	17	268	135	330	750

The one-room cabins are rapidly disappearing from the town. Nearly all of the 17 are old log cabins. They have one or two glass windows, a door, and a stone fireplace. They are 15 or 20 feet square. The 134 two-room homes are mostly tenements: a large, cheaply-built frame house is constructed so as to contain two, such tenements. The upper room is often used as the kitchen, and the lower as living and sleeping-room. The rooms are 15 and 18 feet square and have two windows. Three-room houses are generally owned by their occupants, and are neater than the tenements. They are usually tiny new frame structures, with two rooms, one above the other in front, and a small one-story addition at the back for a kitchen. To this a small veranda is often added. Four-room houses have either a room above the kitchen or are like the double tenements. Few of the houses have cellars and many are poorly built. The locations, however, are usually healthful and the water good. Gardens are generally attached. Six and a half per cent of the families live in one room, 51.1 per cent in two rooms, 17.2 per cent in three rooms; there are 1.6 persons to a room, and nearly three rooms to a family. Forty-three and a half per cent own their homes, mostly from two to five rooms. Of the 148 tenants, 15 rent from Negro landlords.

To the above may be added, by way of comparison, a short account of Covington, Ga., the county seat of Newton county. This is a town of 2000 inhabitants, about evenly divided between the races. In the surrounding country there are many small communities composed entirely of Negroes, which form clans of blood relatives. A few of these settlements are neat and thrifty, but most of them have a dirty, shiftless air, with one-room cabins and numbers of filthy children. Such communities furnish the emigrants for the towns. In Covington there are a few one-room cabins, but the average family occupies two or three rooms. The houses are all one-story, and a common type is that of two rooms with a hall between, and sometimes a kitchen attached to the back end of the hall. Often there is also a front porch. There are detailed statistics available for fifty of the better-class families. Forty-one of these own their homes and nine rent. The homes consist of

Two rooms, ... 9
Three rooms, ... 14
Four rooms, ... 14
Five rooms or more, ... 13

In all, 188 individuals occupy 184 rooms. There is also a lower element in the town and a great deal of idleness and loafing, arising in
part from the irregularity of work at certain seasons of the year. On
the outskirts of the town are many dives and gambling-dens where
liquor is sold. On Saturday nights there is much disorder here. The
more thrifty Negroes buy homes on installments, putting up, often, one
room at a time until they get a two or three-room home.

In Xenia, Ohio, we have these homes: [1]

Xenia, O., Families by Size of Family and Number of Rooms to a Dwelling

SIZE OF FAMILY	FAMILIES OCCUPYING DWELLINGS OF												
	One Room	Two Rooms	Three Rooms	Four Rooms	Five Rooms	Six Rooms	Seven Rooms	Eight Rooms	Nine Rooms	Ten Rooms	Eleven Rooms	Twelve Rooms	Total Families
1 member	8	12	13	12	3	3	..	..	..	..	..	..	51
2 members	1	18	34	20	15	12	10	2	..	..	..	..	112
3 members	6	11	32	31	17	12	11	2	2	1	..	..	125
4 members	..	8	16	20	11	10	2	2	1	1	1	..	72
5 members	..	3	13	17	20	4	3	1	..	1	1	1	64
6 members	1	..	10	6	9	2	1	1	2	..	..	..	32
7 members	..	1	5	2	1	2	1	2	..	..	1	..	15
8 members	..	1	2	6	2	1	1	..	..	..	..	..	13
9 members	..	3	1	2	..	..	1	..	..	..	..	..	7
10 members	..	..	3	..	1	..	..	..	..	..	1	..	6
11 members	..	..	..	1	..	..	..	..	..	..	..	..	1
12 members	..	..	1	..	..	..	..	..	..	..	..	..	1
13 members	..	..	..	..	..	1	..	..	..	..	..	..	1
14 members	..	..	..	..	..	1	..	..	..	..	..	..	1
Total Families .	16	57	130	117	79	48	30	11	5	3	4	1	501
Total Rooms	16	114	390	468	395	288	210	88	45	30	44	12	2100

In Negro village life is the growing differentiation of conditions.
Upon the country Negro just emerging from the backwoods, the village
life acts as a stimulus. Left to themselves, to chance surroundings
and chance acquaintances, and above all to chance openings for work,
the new-comers rise or fall. The successful ones give the first evidence
of awakening in improved housing—more rooms, larger windows,
neater furniture, the differentiation of sleeping-room, kitchen and
parlor, and general improvement in tidiness and taste. The worst immigrants sink into village slums, where vice by concentration and
example assumes dangerous forms. The fact is often noted that there
is more vice among village Negroes than in the country. This is true,
but needs to be supported by the additional fact that the village also
shows more civilized classes of Negroes.

[1] Bulletin of the United States Bureau of Labor, No. 48.

Between these extreme classes the mass of Negroes waver in their struggle for existence. In some towns the majority are home-owners and on the rise; in others the balance is toward the bad. If, however, the chances are against the Negro in the village, one thing is certain: he seldom returns to the farm. Quickened by the village life he passes on to the town and city to try again. Or he may have some success in the village and be fired with ambition for larger fields. Finally the taste for vice in the village slum may send criminals and degenerates to complicate the city problem, North and South. The village, then, is a clearing-house. It stimulates and differentiates; it passes no material—good, bad and indifferent—to larger centers, and unfortunately sends few back to country life to stimulate the people there. In a peculiar sense, then, the village home—the problem of housing the Negro in the smaller towns of the South—is peculiar. Good homes at this point would send out children healthy in body and soul to the city on the one hand and, with little additional effort, to the country on the other. You can with difficulty send the city boy to the country, for it is an unknown land; but the village boy knows the country partially, and properly-directed effort might be the inspiraton of neat village homes in the weird and arid waste of log cabins along the country side.

Section 11. The City Home. (a) *The Slums of Atlanta.*

Atlanta is a typical post-bellum city and had, in 1900, 37,727 Negroes. This growing city is built on the foot of the Alleghanies, a series of great round-topped mounds, which presents many difficulties in drainage and grading. The city is circular in form and over half of the Negro population is crowded into two wards, one on the east and the other on the west side of the city.

The nucleus of Negro population in Southern cities is the alley. It is seen at its worst in the slums of Charleston, Savannah, Washington, and such cities. It represents essentially a crowding—a congestion of population—an attempt to utilize for dwellings spaces inadequate and unsuited to the purpose, and forms the most crushing indictment of the modern landlord system. Attention has lately been directed to the tenement-house abominations, but little has been said of the equally pestilential and dangerous alley. The typical alley is a development of the backyard space of two usually decent houses. In the back yard spaces have been crowded little two-room dwellings, cheaply constructed, badly lighted and ventilated, and with inadequate sanitary arrangements. In Atlanta the badly drained and dark hollows of the city are threaded with these alleys, usually unpaved and muddy, and furnishing inviting nests for questionable characters. The worst type of these homes is the one-room cabin with sidings of unfinished boards running up and down; no ceiling or plastering, no windows, no paint, an open fireplace, and the whole of this cheerless box set directly on the ground, without cellar or foundation. Next to these come two-room houses, built in the same way, but with one or two windows and still without porch, blinds, or fence. Such cabins are so crowded together that they nearly touch each other, and the sun must get high before it can be seen from these alleys. Sometimes such rooms are papered inside by the inmates. They are 14 or 15 feet square and 8 or 10 feet high. The furniture is scarce—a bed or two, a few chairs, a table, a stove or fireplace, a trunk or chest. The floor is bare, and there are no pictures. Sometimes six or eight persons live in two such rooms and pay $1.50 a month or more for rent; sometimes as much as $4.00. These houses have water outside in a well or street hydrant; the out-houses are used in common by several tenants. Probably twenty per cent of the Negro homes in Atlanta fall into this class.

The surroundings of these homes are as bad as the homes. In the third ward most of the streets are in very bad condition, the longest of them having paved sidewalks only about half their length, while the shorter ones are not paved at all. The streets are of soft red clay, with-out gravel or cobble stones.

In the first ward, out of 25 typical homes,

> 4 had no water on the premises,
> 12 had wells (which are dangerous in Atlanta
>   and apt to be infected by sewage),
> 9 used hydrants in the yards or on the streets.

Only four had direct sewer connections. Conditions as to light and air vary, but in general there is less to complain of here, save that the careless construction of the houses makes the sudden changes of tem-perature in the winter peculiarly trying. This lack of protection in winter is made worse by the conditions of the foundations. Most of the houses are perched on wooden or brick pillars, allowing unchecked circulation of air beneath—a boon in summer, a danger in winter. The poor drainage of many of the hollows between the hills where these alleys lie gives rise to much stagnant water, pools and the like, and the unfinished sewer system often leaves masses of filthy sediment near these homes.

In the fifth ward, one of the poorer sections, an Atlanta University senior made the following estimates:

> 30 per cent of the families live in 1 room.
> 40 "   "   "   " 2 rooms.
> 15 "   "   "   " 3 rooms.

Of the houses,

> 60 per cent were plastered inside.
> 50 per cent were painted outside.

About half the population dwelt in districts which may be designated as "slums," although many of these were respectable people. Only 35 per cent of the homes looked clean and neat. There were five per-sons to every two rooms in the district, and three persons to every two beds. Sixty per cent of the homes had practically no yards, and 95 per cent of the homes were rented.

In the whole city of Atlanta the Negroes lived as follows in 1900:

In 1 room, ... 622 families.
In 2 rooms, ... 1654 families.
In 3 rooms, ... 1357 families.
In 4 rooms, ... 1039 families.
In 5 or more rooms, ... 1902 families.

The great majority of the one and two-room homes and some of the others are thoroughly bad as places of shelter. In other words, a third of the black population is poorly housed and, as stated before, a fifth very poorly.

The result of all this crowding is bad health, poor family life, and crime. The actual physical crowding is often great, as for example:

42 families of 6, in 1 room.
15 families of 7, in 1 room.
12 families of 8 or more, in 1 room.
21 families of 10 or more, in 2 rooms.
6 families of 12 or more, in 3 rooms.

This crowding, however, is not nearly so bad or so dangerous as the close contact of the good, bad and indifferent in the slum districts. Vice and crime spread with amazing rapidity in this way, and its spread is facilitated by the prevalent vice of Southern police systems, which make little distinction of guilt or desert among the young and old, the criminal and the careless, the confirmed rascal and the first offender, so long as they are all black. The most pitiable thing of all is the breaking up of family life, even when the mothers and fathers strive hard to protect the home. The high death-rate of the Negro is directly traceable to these slum districts. In the country the Negro death-rate is probably low. In the healthy wards of Northern cities the Negro death-rate is low; but in the alleys of Charleston, which are probably the vilest human habitations in a civilized land, the wretched inmates die in droves, while the country complacently calculates, on that abnormal basis, the probable extinction of black folk in America.

(b) *St. Louis.*[1] At present, then, almost half of the Negroes live in six wards, in which they form from 14.71 to 22.70 per cent of the population of the ward. These wards, ranked according to the proportion of Negroes, are the fourteenth, fifteenth, fifth, fourth, twenty-second, and twenty-third. Wards 4, 5, 14 and 15 form an irregular rectangle extending west from the river. Ward 4 is the mercantile section of the town and 5 contains many factories. The partial tenement-house investigation made by the Board of Health in 1897 showed that Ward 4 contained the highest number of tenement houses. Ward 14 consists of the Union Station and streets that may be considered its inevitable environment, and is no better than such sections are apt to be in an American city. Ward 15 consists partly of fine old residences that have degenerated into second and third-rate boarding houses, and partly of poor tenements and shanties that have never been anything else. . . .

In Wards 4 and 5 the dwellings are crowded in behind factories and warehouses. The white population is chiefly Italians and other south-eastern

---

[1] Brandt in Publications of the American Statistical Association, Vol. 8.

Europeans, and these districts are considered to be about the worst slums in the city. The fourteenth and fifteenth wards are not quite so bad, but the streets where the Negroes live consist of houses that are dirty and out of repair, if not actually in a tumble-down condition. Wards 22 and 23 lie west of 14 and 15, and are of a distinctly better character. They contain a better class of Negroes, the professional and successful business men. The houses in the Negro streets are comfortable and in fairly good condition, on the average, and many are owned by the occupant. This is a comparatively old section of the town, and the houses now occupied by Negroes were built by well-to-do white residents who have since moved farther west. Ward 23 includes also a poor quarter lying along the railroad tracks in low land which was once marshes. There is a considerable number of Negroes also in wards 25 and 26, which are very desirable residence sections. This number represents chiefly domestic servants, but there are also two or three settlements of well-to-do Negroes on certain streets. The 865 in Ward 18 are nearly all servants.

In general, it is true that the Negroes are almost absent from the sections of the city where there is a large foreign population, and that, with notable exceptions, they are concentrated in the worst houses of the worst sections, wherever the natural lay of the land or the unpleasant accessories of civilization, such as railroads and factories, make residence undesirable. The overcrowding of rooms is a fact for which no statistics are available, but it is none the less a fact. . . .

The hospitality of the Negroes, and their willingness to take in any friend who finds himself without a home, receives no check from the law. There are no State regulations concerning tenement houses, and the city ordinances go only so far as to class them under "nuisances" when they do not have "adequate" sewerage, drainage, ventilation, chimneys, halls, staircases, and "all reasonable precautions and provisions in every other particular, and adequate space for all occupants, so that the occupancy of said building or any apartment shall not be dangerous to life or health." Under such provisions it is not surprising that the agent of the Provident Association should find recently fourteen Negroes living in one room.

The Negroes are kept in these undesirable localities not wholly by their own faults and incompetence, but partly by the obstacles which they encounter when they try to go into a better neighborhood. No landlord wishes to have Negro tenants come into his houses, because it means a depreciation of the property sooner or later. When a Negro family moves into a street it generally happens that the white residents give place either to more Negroes or to a much inferior class of whites. To keep up the character of the street, therefore, or to reimburse himself in advance for the depreciation which he foresees, the landlord resorts to discriminating rents. A Negro going into a house previously occupied by a white family is obliged to pay from 20 per cent to 50 per cent more than his predecessor. A certain house in Ward 25, for instance, rented for $25 per month to white tenants, but a Negro was asked $40. This is true even in the poorer districts. There are some comfortless three-room flats in Ward 14 which were occupied until recently by white people paying $8.00 per month; the Negroes living there now are charged $13. Sometimes when a Negro family moves into a "white" street the residents themselves undertake to deal with the question. . . .

In the last ten years the condition of the Negroes in St. Louis has improved considerably, and general observation shows that one accompaniment of this improvement has been the acquisition of property, both for business purposes and for homes. The discriminating rents already referred to have had some influence in this discretion, for the more intelligent and more able Negroes have seen that it would be cheaper in the long run to buy their houses than to rent them.

(c) *Washington.* [1] The National Capital was evidently intended to be a city of homes. The original lots are of generous dimensions and front upon broad streets and avenues. These lots provided ample room for separate houses, with space for yards in the front and rear, and the squares were laid out in such a manner as to give access, by alleys, to the rear of each lot. This plan probably had in view the location of stables on the alleys, in the rear of each house. As the city grew the original lots were subdivided, and as land became more valuable a majority of the residences were built in blocks, with party walls, instead of being detached villas with light on all sides. Naturally, in portions of the city devoted to business, this was the usual method of building from the outset, and these dwellings and stores were, as a rule, brought to the very front of the lot, thus leaving a considerable space in the rear, as the original lots were generally from 100 to 200 feet in depth. The owners of property, as land values increased, sometimes sold off rear portions of their lots, and sometimes built small houses, facing the alleys, which they were able to let at rentals which gave them a high rate of interest on their money. These houses were often cheap frame structures, which paid for themselves within a few years. In other cases they were of brick. As a general rule, the rooms were small and the first floor was on a level with the ground, without any ventilation under it. As a result of this, the sills soon became rotten, and dampness from the ground came through the floors. As a rule, also, there was no water in the house and no sewer connections. Water was often obtained by all of the residents of an alley from a single hydrant at the corner, and box privies were in general use. Many cheap frame and brick houses were also built upon the streets and avenues of the city prior to the adoption of proper building regulations, and these exist today, in a more or less dilapidated condition, often in proximity to handsome new dwellings. Many of these old houses are on valuable ground, and they serve to pay taxes until such time as the owner can sell his ground at a figure which he considers satisfactory. . . .

The civil war brought a large influx of Negroes:

It is estimated that from 30,000 to 40,000 Negroes from neighboring States came to this city at that time. These unfortunate and ignorant people were obliged to avail themselves of any kind of shelter they could find. In many cases rough board shacks with leaky roofs were occupied for years by growing families, and rents were paid out of all proportion to the value of the property or the means of the tenant. Industrious colored men, whose labor would only command from a dollar to a dollar and a half a day, and hardworking colored women, whose lives had been spent over the washtub, have been obliged to pay, year after year, for shelter of the most indifferent kind, an amount which has yielded the landlord twenty per cent, or more, on his investment.

The following extracts from the report of the health officer will show the conditions existing ten years after the Civil War:

Leaky roofs, broken and filthy ceilings, dilapidated floors, overcrowded,

---

[1] Sternberg: Report of Committee on Building Model Homes.

below grade, having stagnant water underneath, no drainage, no pure water supply, no fire protection, having filthy yards, dilapidated, filthy privy and leaky privy box, in bad sanitary condition generally, and unfit for human habitation, described, with few exceptions, the conditions of these hovels where the poorest class of our population stay out their miserable existence, and for which they pay rents varying from $2.50 to $10.00 per month. . . .

As specific examples of overcrowding, at a later date, I quote from the report of Miss DeGraffenried, published in 1896:

One conclusion at least is evident, that rents in these alleys are dear, considering the accommodations and environment. Moreover, the moral consequences of such narrow quarters are often disastrous. Crowded sleeping rooms contribute to vice and indecency. Indeed, crowding goes on to an extent not acknowledged to the canvasser by the tenants. At night these poor roofs shelter many more people than are here reported.

I have no doubt that lodgers are harbored in these alleys whose presence, for many reasons not creditable to the occupants, is always concealed. The confessed facts are startling enough. We have here accounts of seven persons living in two rooms—the mother and her sons 21, 17 and 7 years of age, occupying one bed-chamber. Again, nine individuals live in two rooms; eleven people in four rooms. Five, almost all adults, sleep in one room—the mother 43, a son 21, and daughters 19, 17 and 14; and four persons use another room—a mother 45, an aunt 70, a son 22, and a baby 9 months old. . . .

Deanwood, East Deanwood and Burrville are scattered villages, merging into each other, and situated along the Chesapeake Beach Railway; here dwell colored people almost entirely. The villages are for the most part composed of new and respectable cottages owned by their occupants. Here and there may be seen dilapidated shacks occupied, while alongside stands a new cottage empty and for rent.

Barry Farm is situated on the outskirts of Anacostia; this is another Negro settlement, and is a curious mixture of comfortable cottages, even handsome homes, owned by well-to-do colored people, and tumbledown hovels that bring exorbitant rents.

Garfield and Good Hope are also colored communities on the order of Barry Farm; these villages are situated on the hills to the east of Anascotia. The majority of the houses here are owned by their occupants There are no public service advantages in these outlying regions, with the exception of public water supply in Ivy City; but even here the people do not have water within their houses, nearly always obtaining it from the street hydrant.

The communities just described are the only considerable aggregations of people of the laboring class to be found without the city limits. The character of old dwellings located in them is little better than we would condemn within the city. Nothing is being done to improve the quality of dwellings, and the new dwellings are of the cheapest kind. Moreover, the people who live in these suburban places are not the pick and shovel men, the cart drivers, the hod carriers, the stable men, of the city. They are for the most part more independent folk, such as messengers and skilled laborers in the departments; colored men who work from place to place as porters, waiters, or house-servants, and who keep their wives and children in these little homes. They are the kind who will not rest until they own "a little place in the country," it matters little what sort of dwelling may be upon the "place." The worst hovels are occupied by driftwood: widows who subsist by doing laundry work for the neighbors in better circumstances; old people, supported by sons and daughters in the city, and the children of the sons and daughters. . . .

The company organized under the above charter from Congress [The Washington Sanitary Housing Company] succeeded in securing stock subscriptions sufficient to justify it in commencing building operations and in October, 1904, twenty houses had been completed and were occupied by colored tenants. Seventeen of these houses were on Van Street S. W. The flats of three rooms and a bath were rented for seven dollars per month for lower and seven and one-half dollars per month for upper flats. The four-room flats were rented for eight and eight and one-half dollars per month. This is an average of $2.26 per room. It should be remembered that each of these flats has a good-sized bathroom, with a bathtub and a modern water-closet. There is a good range with water-back in the kitchen, and a small coal stove in the front room. The hot-water boiler connected with the kitchen range is placed in the bathroom and furnishes sufficient heat to make it comfortable. These flats have now been occupied by colored tenants, mostly day laborers, for nearly four years. They are in such demand that there is constantly a waiting list of applicants in case a flat becomes vacant. Many of the present tenants have occupied their flats since the houses were completed. The repairs required have not been excessive, and there has been very little loss from vacancies or failure to collect rents. . . .

In the city of Washington the death rate among the colored population, in 1875, was 42.86 per thousand. In 1906 it had fallen to 28.81 per thousand. Among the whites it was 21.04 in 1875, and in 1906 it had fallen to 15.16. To what extent this decline in death rate is due to improvement in housing conditions it is impossible to say, but no doubt there has been some improvement, and this one of the factors which accounts for one of the gradual reduction of our death rate from the disgracefully high figures of twenty-five or thirty years ago.

Section 12. City Homes of the Better Class. *Atlanta.* Scattered among other homes and gradually segregating themselves in better class districts is a growing class of Negro homes belonging to the rising groups of Negroes. These homes are often unnoticed because they are not distinguishable from corresponding white homes, and so are continually overlooked.

In an address to the Negroes of Boston, Mass., Mr. George W. Cable said: "There is a notion among Southern people, which is not confined to them, . . . but which is upon the tongues of Negro leaders—the notion that it is highly important that the Negro should be kept on the plantation. That is false. I say it because some white man ought to say it. What is civilization? The cityfying of a people or making them what a city makes them. True, the city has many temptations, and many men and women go to shipwreck there. But it only means a more energetic process of selection, and as much as some go down, others go up."

Whatever our views of the influx of Negroes into cities may be, it is clear that there alone can we find a class of Negro homes fully equal to the homes of the whites. This is significant. A determined effort has been made, especially during the reaction of later years, to judge the Negro by his worst and lowest type. Even reputed friends and leaders of the race have been zealous in laying bare the weaknesses of the race and holding its faults up to ridicule and condemnation. Some of this has been justified by a real desire to know the truth, but it has gone so far today as to obscure, almost, in the eyes of the majority of Americans, the existence of a class of intelligent American citizens of Negro blood who represent as good citizenship, as pure homes and as worthy success as any class of their fellows.

They may be found to some extent in the country. But the country was peculiarly the seat of slavery and its blight still rests so heavily on the land that the class of Negro farmers who can compare with the best white farmers of the North and West is very small. In the cities, however, the Negro has had his chance to learn. He has been quickened and taught. He has schools and contact with culture, and in those cases where he has been able to stand normal competition and abnormal prejudice he can, in a large number of cases point to homes which equal the best American homes—not, to be sure, in wealth or size, but in cleanliness, purity and beauty. This class is small and grades quickly down to homes which may be criticized; and still, as representing the best, there is good argument for calling these at least as characteristic of the race, as the alley hovels. A race has a right to be judged by its best.

To illustrate this point let us take the best Negro homes of Atlanta, Georgia. They are largely homes of the graduates of Atlanta University, and their owners are teachers, mail-carriers, merchants and professional men. These homes were thus described in the reports of the class in sociology of this institution in 1900: "They are good-sized one and two-story homes, having bathrooms and water in the house, and in many cases gas and electric-bells. There are seven or eight rooms, each with two or more windows, and both the house and furnishings are in good condition. There are from four to six occupants. The parlors and some of the other rooms have tiled hearths, and there is usually a piano or organ in the home. The walls are painted or papered, the windows have white curtains and shades. In all cases these houses are owned by the occupants." A few houses are more elaborate than this, but this is a fair description of those that are referred to in this section.

A detailed description of two or three of these homes will make the picture more vivid. Number 32 North —— Street is built on brick pillars with lattice-work between. The house is painted without and within, plastered, and the woodwork varnished. The kitchen is ceiled in yellow pine. The house is of two stories on a lot 50 by 100 feet, and has gas and water. On the first floor there is a hall 13 x 12½ x 11 feet, with two windows; a parlor 17½ x 14½, a nursery, pantry, dining-room and kitchen. The parlor has a piano, and there are open fireplaces with tiled mantles, but, as is usual in the South, no other heating apparatus. The second story is like the first, save that there is no room over the kitchen. There are four bedrooms and a bath. There are eight in this family and they own the house.

Another home, 160 ——— Street, is a frame house two stories high, with eight rooms. It is a long, narrow house, with a hall running the whole length on one side. Two rooms are papered, the rest white-finished. There is a double parlor with piano, a dining-room and kitchen on the first floor, four bedrooms and a bath on the second. The furniture is good, and all the rooms are carpeted save the kitchen. There are seven inmates, and they own the house.

The favorite type of house here for small families is one-story. The house at 260 ——— Street is one-story, weatherboarded, plastered and painted, built on a brick foundation and nicely furnished. It has five rooms: one parlor 16 x 14 with a parlor set, carpet, table, sofa, four chairs and a piano; two bedrooms with sets of furniture; a dining-room, with a nice dining-table, three chairs, a refrigerator and side-board. The kitchen has a stove, table and cupboard. There are two inmates who have owned this property for seven years. Outside is a garden, with henhouse and woodhouse.

Such homes as these are typical of the class with which we are dealing. These are, of course, exceptional, when one considers the great mass of Negroes of Atlanta; and yet, of over a thousand homes of all types studied by Atlanta University students in 1900, about forty were placed in this select class. If among the Negroes of the South two per cent of the homes of the freedmen have reached this type, it is a most extraordinary accomplishment for a single generation. In the country the percentage of comfortable homes is small, certainly not over one per cent and in many places less. In the towns and cities, on the other hand, the percentage must often rise to five per cent and sometimes more. Any more definite statements than these would be purely conjectural.

There are some criticisms that can be brought against this class of homes, although they apply equally well to the similar class of white homes in the South. First, in the economy of space there is a certain lack of coziness and convenience, which can easily be traced to climatic and social reasons. The log-cabin, so prevalent a generation since, was essentially a square box. Other rooms were made by adding, not by subdividing. So that today throughout the South the houses give one the impression of separate rooms in juxtaposition, rather than of a house subdivided according to convenience and relative use of rooms. Long draughty halls, high sombre ceilings, and stiff square walls are the usual thing. Moreover, the kitchen contains a whole social history. In New England, where the mothers and their ancestors for generations have spent most of their time working in kitchens, this important part of the house has developed into a great, clean, sunny room, with abundant ventilation and ample working and storing space. In the South, where the kitchen was the domain of an alien race and servile caste, it was actually cut off entirely from the house, and sat alone cramped and small, in the back yard. Today it has gradually fastened itself to the house again, but with an unobtrusive, apologetic air. It sticks to an out-of-the-way corner, and is usually altogether too small for its purpose. I have seen kitchens, in the homes of well-to-do people, as small as eight or ten feet square, or about the size of my grandmother's pantry. Then, again, the cupboards, closets and storing-rooms of most Southern houses are too small and are ill-arranged. Cellars, owing to the climate, are very exceptional, and good attics are seldom found. There is room for argument as to whether the one or two-story house is most convenient, but certainly for a given amount of money the two-story house furnishes considerably more room space. In a one-story house the temptation always is, among all classes of Southern people, to turn bedrooms into reception-rooms on occasions. This is always objectionable, especially where children are being trained to respect the sanctity of their private rooms. Then, too, the ventilation of the sleeping-rooms is a matter of some difficulty in a one-story house, where windows and doors near the living-rooms cannot be left open long.

The heating problem in the South is serious. Nearly all well-perfected heating systems have been developed to supply the needs of cold climates. In a large part of the South fires are only needed regularly three months or less. Consequently furnaces and base-burners are too costly. On the other hand the open grate, while delightfully cheery, is wasteful, uncomfortable and dangerous. It is responsible for a large number of fires and accidents, and above all it heats the room so unequally that it is a source of colds, rheumatism and consumption. A Southern home, even of the better class, is a dreadfully cheerless place on a cold day. Some cheap heating apparatus in connection with the open grate is really in great demand.

Outside these criticisms of the physical homes there are special moral dangers due to the environments of the best class of Negroes. The best Negro settlements are never free from the intrusion of the worst class of whites. A favorite situation for both white and colored houses of prostitution is in the Negro quarter of the town, and this often brings them near some of the best homes. I have seen a prosperous country town where a prominent white official was not tolerated in the white residence section, but allowed to build and live in a pretty home in the midst of the best Negroes. In Asheville, N. C., one of the best Negro sections is ruined by an open house of ill-fame with white inmates. Again, the Negro sections of the city are usually poorly policed (save in criminal sections), poorly paved and lighted, and, above all, the system of Southern taxation falls heavily on the middle classes: in Atlanta, books, sewing machines, furniture, bicycles, horses and wagons, and all such small luxuries are taxed.

The custom, too, of classing all Negroes together, in law and treatment, leads to carelessness in protecting the best of the Negroes from their own worst elements. A whole Negro district is put under a ban because of the lawlessness of a few, and the lack of purity in some Negro homes is sufficient excuse with many for treating the best of our women with neither courtesy nor decency.

That with such surroundings, and among the mass of poor homes there is growing up a strong beautiful family life, housed decently, and even luxuriously in some cases, is a cause of congratulation and hope.

Section 13.   A Study of Eight Homes.   The class in sociology of Atlanta University, 1908-09, made a detailed study of 32 Negro homes. Plans and descriptions of eight of these homes follow; the scale is one-fourth of that indicated:

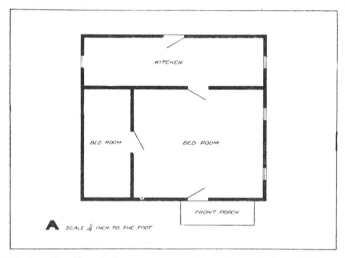

PLAN A.—Family of eleven persons (parents and nine children).

This country house is a wooden structure with the boards running up and down. The roof is shingled with large home-made shingles. None of the walls are plastered, all of the floors are bare, and the windows are without glass panes, curtains or shades. They have wooden shutters.

There are two bedrooms and a kitchen. In the large bedroom are two beds, a dresser, a sewing machine, a cupboard piled with quilts, a table with a bowl and pitcher upon it, a towel-rack and a few chairs. They have newspapers pasted upon the walls and several advertisement pictures—"Fairy Soap," "Baking Powder," "Root Beer"—tacked on. There are no books except the Bibles of the different members of the family and a few old school books. They take "McCaulay's Magazine," "The Yellow Jacket," the "Savannah Tribune," and the "North Georgian." There is a large fireplace.

The second bedroom has no windows and no fireplace. It contains three beds and nothing more. The kitchen has two windows. It contains a stove, two small tables, a cupboard and a few chairs.

The front porch is a mere platform, with no top over it. The house is kept moderately clean. There is a large front yard, bare, clean swept, which merges into woods on one side and into a large kitchen garden on the other; from the front of the yard runs a path leading to another house. The back yard is also large, bare, and clean swept. It leads into woods and cotton fields. There is no other house in sight of this one. They get their water from a spring near by.

PLAN B.—Family of twelve persons (parents and ten children).

This country house is made of pine logs 20 x 15, eight feet high; roofed with split boards. The little room on the side is made of plank 10 x 13, roofed with split boards. The floor is laid with wide plank, 1 x 10. It has one chimney, three windows 2 x 3, with board shutters, three doors 5½ x 3. The porch is just wide enough to make a passage from the

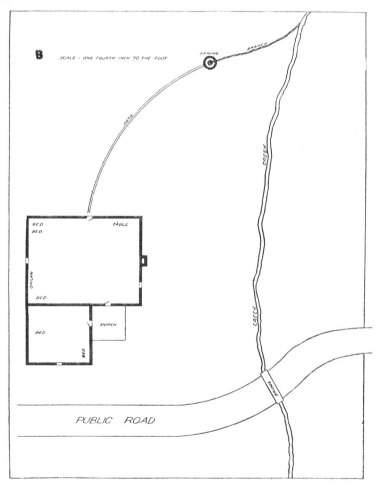

door of the main house to the room, and it is not covered. The yard is very small; cotton rows on one side run almost to the door, and in the rear are weeds and woods.

There are three beds in the main building, with the paint worn off and a large yellow organ near the rear window. There are five home-made chairs and two benches ten feet long, two small trunks, a small table for the lamp and a large one for eating purposes. The dishes are kept in a box, the surplus food is also kept in a box. The cooking utensils are kept on a shelf outside of the window. The cooking is done in this building on the fireplace. The walls are covered with newspapers, with holes showing where mice have been gnawing. The bed is bare, and the bedclothes hang from the joist. No pictures are on the walls and no carpet upon the floor. There is one glass lamp of

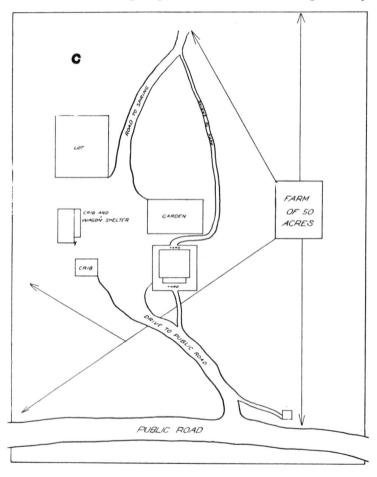

small size and a small tin lamp. A gun is hanging over the door. The water is brought from a spring about 300 yards away.

The little out-room contains two beds and a bench about ten feet long, but no pictures on the wall, no books or carpet. The beds are painted yellow, fairly new. One large box is in the corner to keep clothes packed in. This is called the guest room.

PLAN C.—Family of ten (widow and nine children).

There are four rooms in this country house. In the room that is usually used for the reception of company is a dresser, a washstand, a center-table, straight chairs, one rocker and a bed. The floor has one small rug. There is no plastering on the walls. The inside walls are just the inside of the boards that form the weatherboarding. The window has no glass, but has a lace curtain hanging over it. The other room has two beds in it, a shelf upon which quilts are kept and a big box with things packed in it. In the kitchen is a bed, with a curtain between the bed and the part where the cooking is done, a shelf where the water-bucket stands, and a cupboard where the dishes are kept. In the dining-room is a long table. Chairs are carried from the other rooms to the dining-room as they are needed. In the front room are a few pictures, and on the mantle-shelf, which is a board nailed above the fireplace, is a big clock. There is one trunk in the front room and one in the other bedroom. In the front room the furniture is comparatively new, because the family was recently burned out. Most of the water is taken from a well that is about two hundred yards from the house, and the rest is taken from a spring a little farther away.

This house is heated by fireplaces in which, principally, oak wood is used. A good part of the lighting is done by the fire in these fireplaces in winter and by kerosene lamps in summer. In the yard are flowers and one big oak tree. · The house is not painted. On the inside of the house and all around it, everything is kept extremely clean. From the appearance of the fireplace one might think that it is whitewashed three or four times each week.

The periodicals are "The Designer" and the "Delineator." The papers are "The Macon Telegraph," "The Atlanta Independent" and "The Dispatch." In the kitchen is a medium-sized stove.

PLAN D.—Family of six (parents, one child and three brothers).

This country house is a frame structure of four rooms, two on either side of a wide hall. The house is weatherboarded crosswise and painted white, with green bordering. Two windows of eight panes each admit light to each room. The front porch is comparatively wide and the back porch is very wide. The bedrooms are furnished with a wardrobe apiece, made of walnut. Each bedroom contains a bureau of walnut, and a large box upside down, covered neatly with newspaper, with a washpan, soap and towel on the top.

In the front rooms are two beds, and in the back bedroom one bed. All the beds are well kept. The front room on the right has a carpet, somewhat worn, upon the floor. Beside the fireplace is an unpainted tinder-box, containing fat lightwood, chips and wood for making fires. All the rooms have fireplaces. Though some families in that section of the country sleep upon straw-beds, this particular family has feather-beds through the house. The front room on the right has a center-table standing upon three legs with glass feet. The back rooms have lofts stored with hams and dried pumpkins. The other rooms are ceiled overhead, with plastered sides.

The walls of the front room are decked with pictures of "Noah's Ark," "Eternity," "Christ's Blessings," and to sum up the whole array of pictures, those which are not of the immediate family seem to continually impress the fact that death is near. The lights of the house are the common Miller lamps with Rochester burners. The kitchen contains a common cook-stove, a cook-table, milk cans, churn, and general milk apparatus. The bedroom on the back contains also a new food safe, made of oak with doors of flowered wirecloth. Upon the tables of the rooms may be seen copies of the "Truth," an Atlanta Negro publication; copies of cheap novels sold on trains, such as, "A Slow

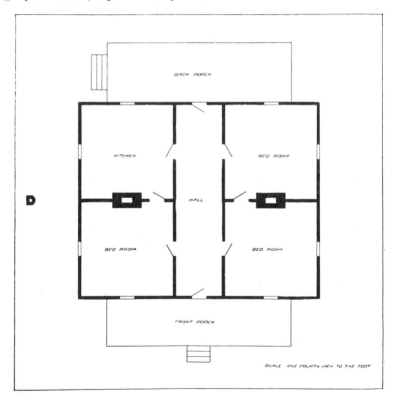

Train through Arkansas," and a book called "Stories from the Ladies' Home Journal." The Atlanta Journal is taken also. The yards are kept as free of obstruction as possible. In the front yard are a few flowers in beds, separated by cleanly-swept walks. The back yard contains a well and a side table, and perhaps half a dozen tubs made from syrup barrels. All water is carried into the house in well-polished cedar buckets.

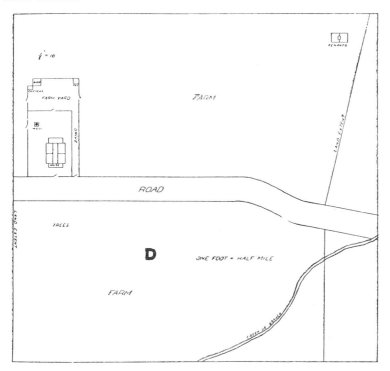

PLAN E.—Family of three (widow and two daughters).

This city house is a frame dwelling of three rooms: two bedrooms and a kitchen. One bedroom, 18 x 14½, has two windows and two doors, one leading to the next room and the other to some steps in front. The windows have no curtains nor shades. The walls are unplastered and, save for a few calendars, are bare. The floor has no covering. Within the room are a bed, a table, a bureau and a wardrobe. There is also a fireplace, with a mantel above upon which are two vases, a calendar and one or two Sunday-school cards. The other bedroom is 18 x 12. The walls are bare and the floors uncovered. There are two windows without shades and curtains. Within the room are a bed, a table and one or two chairs. There is a fireplace, with a mantel above upon which irons are kept. The kitchen, which is detached, is 12 x 7. The

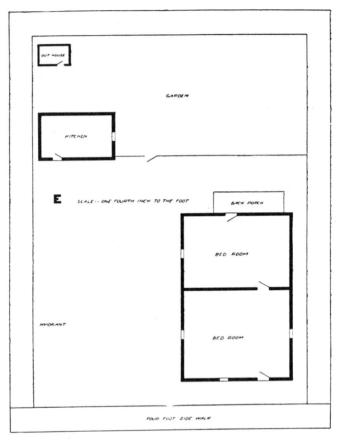

walls are bare and unplastered and the floors uncovered. In it are a
small cooking stove, a table, a food safe, a bench and four chairs.
There is one window without shade or curtain, and one door. This
family does not subscribe for any paper or magazine, and the books
consist of some school books once used by children of the family. The
yard in front is used as a place for washing, and the tubs and
clothes-lines are there. The yard in the back is used for a garden.
There are several trees and an outhouse in it. A hydrant supplies city
water.

PLAN F.—Family of four (parents and two daughters).

This city cottage is built of boards ½ x 12 in., with shingle roof and
wooden supporting pillars. The walls of the room are made out of
regular flooring lumber. The front room has paper on the walls, carpet on the floor, and curtains at the windows. On the walls are two
or three pictures of the members of the family. This room is used as

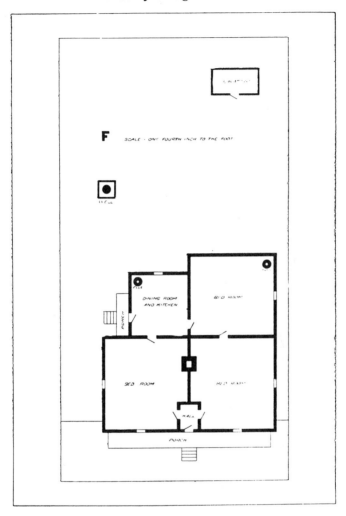

a bedroom as well as a parlor, and contains a bed, bureau, washstand, bowl and pitcher. The walls of the other two rooms and kitchen are destitute of paper, plaster and pictures, and the floors are bare. In one of these rooms is an old-fashioned bed and a bureau. In the other is an iron bed, a piano and a bureau. In the kitchen is a table, a safe and a range. There are eight chairs in the house and one rocking-chair. There are a few books in the main room, such as: the Bible, and "Life of Fred Douglas"; there is also the Atlanta "Constitution." Coal and wood is used for heating purposes. The front room has a grate and the other two have fireplaces. For light, kerosene lamps are used. The yard is inclined from the front to the back. In the back is an outhouse and a well. In the front is a rosebush and a peachtree.

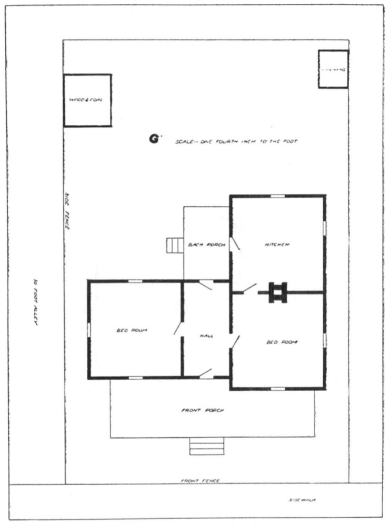

PLAN G.—Family of seven (parents, two children, grandfather, uncle and nephew).

This city house is a frame structure of three rooms, two on one side of a hall and one on the other. The house is weatherboarded crosswise and painted green. The front room on the right has two windows, the front window being a large one-pane sash, with transom. The side window has four lights in two sashes. The rest of the rooms have two and three windows each. The front porch is ten feet wide at the widest part. The back porch is five feet wide. The front room contains an oak suit of furniture, with four straight-back chairs and two rockers. There is a rug upon the oak-stained floor. The casings of the room are cherry colored. The mirrored mantel is cherry with vari-colored tile hearth, and club-house grate. The bed mattress is of cotton felt. On the under shelf of a center-table are the daily issues of the Atlanta "Georgian," an Atlanta daily, together with weekly issues of the Atlanta Independent, a Negro weekly published here. On a small bookcase are various books: novels like "Ishmael," a Webster's abridged dictionary, and the "Home Encyclopædia." The room back of this is the kitchen; it contains a common cook-stove, an iron bed used for "lounging," a cheap safe, an eating-table, a side table, a combination affair for holding flour, meal, coffee, spices, sugar, salt, etc.; the floor is kept well scoured. In the room across the hall are two beds, a washstand, a dresser, and a center-table. In this room is a small heater of ordinary style; nothing is upon the floor. Common cotton mattresses are upon the beds. The pictures are mostly of landscapes and portraits of the immediate family. In the hall is a common sideboard. The lights are Miller lamps with Rochester burners. There are three or four alarm clocks in the house. There is a stand-pipe on the back porch, furnishing water for the house. The walls are all plastered, also overhead with scratchcoat finish. The front yard has grass, but no flowers. The back yard contains a coalhouse, chicken-house, water-closet and storeroom, a washbench and three tubs.

PLAN H.—Family of eleven (parents and nine children).

A City Home:

Parlor.—The walls are kalsomined in pink and blue. There are six painted pictures on the walls, two of the mother, one of the husband and four of rural scenes. The floor is carpeted with Brussels carpet and three rugs. The furniture consists of one parlor suite, mahogany-finished and leather-bottomed, and two bookcases, one in oak and one in oil-finish, with books such as the works of George Eliot, Dickens, Shakespeare, Irving, Poe; Latin, Greek, German and French text-books, and others. The room is heated by an open grate and lighted by gas.

Reception Hall.—The walls are sand-finished, and kalsomined in blue and pink. There are six framed pictures, two of grandparents, one of sister, one of Fred Douglass, one of Booker Washington, and one rural scene. The floor is carpeted with Brussels carpet and three rugs. The furniture consists of four straw-bottomed chairs, cherry-colored, one table, and one piano ebony-finished. The books consist of collections of music. The room is heated by an open grate and lighted by gas. The woodwork of both these rooms is oil-finished.

Dining-Room.—The walls are sand-finished, and kalsomined in pink.

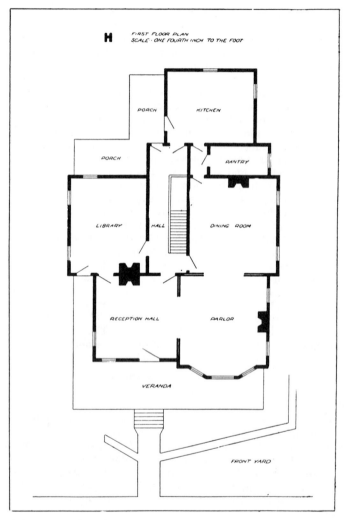

The pictures consist of four framed pictures, chiefly of fruits. The floor is painted red and has a rug. The furniture consists of twelve chairs, one table, one sideboard, oak-finished, and china closet oil-finished. The room is heated by open grate and lighted by gas.

Study.—The walls are kalsomined in blue and cream. There are four framed pictures and one framed mirror on the wall. The floor is covered with linoleum. The furniture consists of six chairs, one table, one desk and one piano. The books consist for the most part of school books—of grammar school and preparatory course—with magazines,

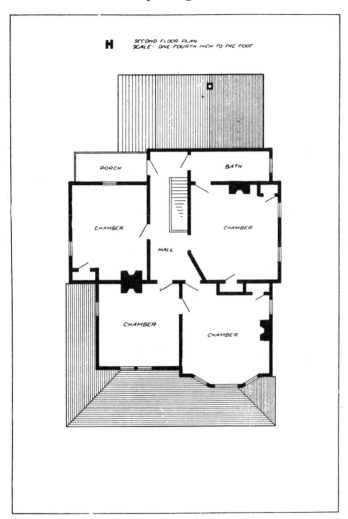

such as "The Ladies' Home Journal," "Woman's Home Companion," "Harper's," and others. The room is heated by a small heater and lighted by gas.

Kitchen.—The walls are of painted wood. The floor is bare, painted. The furniture consists of one table, range, sink, drawboard. It is lighted by gas.

Halls.—The walls are kalsomined in blue and yellow. The floors are covered with linoleum; the steps are carpeted. The halls are lighted with gas.

Bedrooms.—The bedroom over the parlor has walls kalsomined in blue and yellow. The floor is carpeted. The pictures consist of four framed pictures. The furniture consists of one bed, one washstand, table, one dresser and four chairs, oak-finished. The room is heated by an open grate and lighted by gas. The bedroom over the reception hall has similar walls, the floor is covered with matting; the pictures consist of three framed pictures, two of parents and one of country scene. The furniture consists of one iron bed, dressing-table, chiffonier and three chairs. It is heated by an open grate and lighted by gas. The bedroom over the study has similar walls, is covered with matting and has four pictures of relatives and scenes. The furniture consists of a double bed, dresser, washstand, table and three chairs. It is heated and lighted as the others. The bedroom over the dining-room has similar walls, is covered with matting, and has one framed picture of a group of boys. The furniture consists of one ordinary bed, one folding-bed and dresser. It is heated by one small fireplace and lighted by gas. Next to this bedroom is the bathroom, 5 x 10 feet.

Building Material.—The house is built of wood, with all the inside walls plastered with the exception of the kitchen. There is water through the house and in the yard. The house is lighted by gas; there is only one outhouse, the coalhouse. The house has had a recent coat of paint upon it.

Section 14. Evolution of the Negro Home. The pictures on the following pages present a series which illustrates partially the evolution of the Negro home:

No. 1—Group of African huts (loaned by the *Southern Workman*).

No. 2—Storehouse for corn—Bongo (Schweinfurth).

No. 3—Two dwelling-huts, 5-7 metres high—Bongo (Schweinfurth).

No. 4—Corn warehouses—Niam-Niam (Schweinfurth).

No. 5—Sleeping-hut for boys, kitchen-hut and dwelling-hut—Niam-Niam (Schweinfurth).

No. 6—Dwelling-hut (6 x 10 metres) and palace of the king (25 x 50 metres, 17 metres high)—Monbuttos (Schweinfurth).

Nos. 7-10—Slave-cabins, Southern United States (loaned by *Southern Workman*).

Nos. 11-13—Negro city tenements, Atlanta (photo. by A. J. Williams, '09.)

Nos. 14-19—Negro city tenements, Atlanta, poorer class (photo. by A. J. Williams, '09),

Nos. 20-27—Negro city tenements, Atlanta, better class (photo. by A. J. Williams, '09).

Nos. 28-35—Homes owned by Atlanta Negroes (photo. by A. J. Williams, '09).

No. 36—Residence of a Negro minister, Decatur (photo. by Askew).

No. 37—Residence of a Negro lawyer, Atlanta (photo. by Askew).

No. 38—Residence of a Negro tailor, Atlanta (photo. by Askew).

No. 39—Residence of a Negro working-woman, Atlanta.

No. 40—Residence of a Negro railway postal-clerk, South Atlanta.

No. 41—Residence of a Negro contractor and builder, Atlanta.

No. 42—Residence of a Negro grocer.

No. 43—Residence of a Negro business man, insurance manager and proprietor of barber shops; now building and said to be the finest Negro residence in the South. It will have electric bells and lights, fireplaces, steam-heat, roof-garden, and 15 rooms. (Photographs 39-43 by Askew).

Reproduced, by permission, from Stanley's "Through the Dark Continent."—Copyright, 1878, by Harper & Brothers.

1

Reproduced, by permission, from Stanley's "Through the Dark Continent."—Copyright, 1878, by Harper & Brothers

2

5

6

7

8

9

10

11

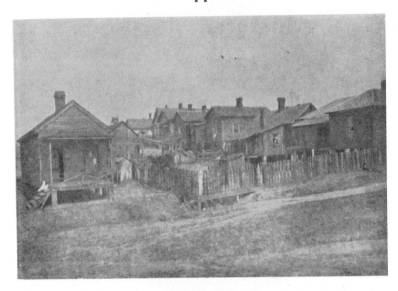

12

13

14

15

16

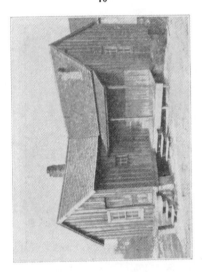

17

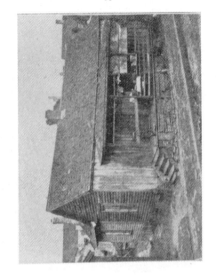

18

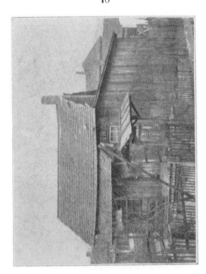

19

20

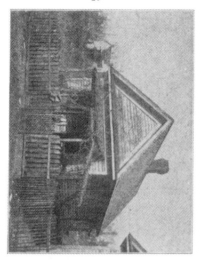

21

22

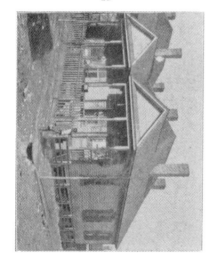

23

24   25

26   27

28   29

30   31

32

33

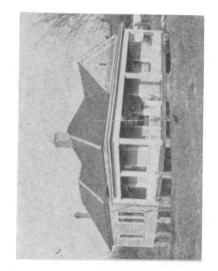

34

35

36

37

38

39

40

41

42

43

Part 3.   The Economics of the Family

Section 15.   Africa. The family economy of Africa is simple and primitive, and may be described briefly in the words of Bücher: [1]

The economy of many Negro tribes shows . . . a sharp division of the production and of many parts of the consumption according to sex; indeed even the extension of this distinction to the sphere of barter. As P. Pogge, one of our most reliable observers, says concisely of the Congo Negroes: "The woman has her own circle of duties independent of that of her husband." And in the description of the Bashilangas he observes: "No member of the family troubles himself about another at meal-times; while some eat the others come and go just as it suits them; but the women and the smaller children generally eat together." And finally he reports further regarding the Lundas: "Under ordinary conditions, when a caravan has pitched its camp in a village, the women of the place are accustomed to bring vegetables and fowl into the camp for sale, while goats, pigs and sheep are usually sold only by the men. It is similarly related by L. Wolf that in the market of Ibaushi all the agricultural products and materials, mats and pottery are sold by the women and only goats and wine by the men. Each sex is thus possessor of its special product of labor, and disposes of it independently.

The division of the labor production between the two sexes in Africa varies in detail from tribe to tribe; as a rule, however, agriculture and the preparation of all the vegetable foods are also assigned here to the woman, and hunting, cattle-raising, tanning, weaving to the man. This arrangement is often supported by superstitious usages. In Uganda the milking of the cows falls exclusively to men; a woman is never permitted to touch the udder of a cow. In the Lunda territory, again, no man is allowed to take part in the extraction of oil from the ground-nut, as his presence is thought to frustrate the success of the operation. As a rule the carriers whom Europeans engage refuse to do women's work; Livingstone even reports a case of famine among the men in a certain district because no women were there to grind the corn they had on hand. The separation of the two sexes in the preparation and consumption of food is often made still more rigid by regulations of a semi-religious character, forbidding the women the use of certain kinds of meat, which are thus reserved for men alone.

Everywhere among primitive peoples the children become independent very early in youth and desert the society of their parents. They often live then for some years in special common houses, of which there are others for married men. These common-houses for men-folk grouped according to age, and frequently also for the unmarried women grouped in the same way, are found very widely distributed in Africa and America, and especially in Oceania. They serve as common places of meeting, work, and amusement and as sleeping-places for the younger people, and are used also for lodging strangers. They naturally form a further obstacle to the development of a common household economy based upon the family, for each family is generally subdivided into different parts with separate dwellings.

It may be asserted as a general rule for primitive peoples practising polygamy that each wife has her own hut. Among the Zulus they go so far as to build a separate hut for almost every adult member of the household—one for the husband, one for his mother, one for each of his wives and other adult members of his family. These huts all stand in a semi-circle about the en-

---

[1] Carl Bücher: Industrial Evolution (translated by Wickett), chap. 1, pp. 35-38.

closed cattle-kraal in such a way that the man's dwelling is in the center. Of course it is to be remembered that a hut of this kind can be constructed in a few hours.[1]

Miss Kingsley says:[2]

The House is a collection of individuals; I should hesitate to call it a developed family. I cannot say it is a collection of human beings, because the very dogs and canoes and so on that belong to it are a part of it in the eye of the law, and capable therefore alike of embroiling it and advancing its interests. These Houses are bound together into groups by the Long ju-ju proper to the so-called secret society, common to the groups of houses. The House is presided over by what is called in white parlance, a king, and beneath him there are four classes of human beings in regular rank, that is to say influence in council: firstly, the free relations of the king, if he be a free man himself, which is frequently not the case; if he be a slave, the free people of the family he is trustee for; secondly, the free small people who have placed themselves under the protection of the House, rendering it in return for the assistance and protection it affords them service on demand; the third and fourth classes are true slave classes, the higher one in rank being that called the Winnaboes or Trade boys, the lower the pull-away boys and plantation hands. The best point in it, as a system, is that it gives to the poorest boy who paddles an oil-canoe a chance of becoming a king.

Property itself in West Africa, and as I have reason to believe from reports in other parts of tropical Africa that I am acquainted with, is firmly governed and is divisable into three kinds. Firstly, ancestral property connected with the office of headmanship, the Stool, as this office is called in the true Negro state, the Cap as it is called down in Bas Congo; secondly, family property, in which every member of the family has a certain share, and on which he, she or it has a claim; thirdly, private property, that which is acquired or made by a man or woman by their personal exertions, over and above that which is earned by them in co-operation with other members of their family which becomes a family property, and that which is gained by gifts or made in trade by the exercise of a superior trading ability.

Every one of these forms of property is equally sacred in the eye of the African law. The property of the Stool must be worked for the Stool; working it well, increasing it, adds to the importance of the Stool, and makes the king who does so popular; but he is trustee not owner of the Stool property, and his family does not come in for that property on his death, for every profit made by the working of Stool property is like this itself the property of the Stool, and during the king's life he cannot legally alienate it for his own personal advantage, but can only administer it for the benefit of the Stool.

The king's power over the property of the family and the private property of the people under this rule, consists in the right of Ban, but not arriere Ban. Family property is much the same as regards the laws concerning it as Stool property. The head of the family is trustee of it. If he is a spendthrift, or unlucky in its management, he is removed from his position. Any profit he may make with the assistance of a member of his own family becomes family property; but of course any property he may make with the assistance of his free wives or wife, a person who does not belong to his family, or with the assistance of an outsider, may become his own. Private property acquired in the ways I have mentioned is equally sacred in the eyes

---

[1] Carl Bucher: Industrial Evolution (translated by Wickett), chap. 1, p. 38.
[2] West African Studies, 2d ed., pp. 365-366.

of the law. I do not suppose you could find a single human being, slave or free, who had not some private property of his or her very own.

Section 16. Slavery. The economic revolution of slavery, so far as the family was concerned, was far-reaching. Newly imported Africans were in the West Indies often portioned off among the older slave families. These families were supposed to support themselves by food which they raised on plots of ground given them, the masters only helping out in case of drought. This, however, did not always work well, as the harder the slaves were driven the less time and inclination they had to raise food of the proper amount and kind. Gradually, therefore, on the continent, the system of "rations" came into use: every week or fortnight each slave family presented themselves at the master's storehouse and received an allowance of pork and corn-meal, and perhaps other food. Once a year, usually at Christmas-time, clothing was distributed. The following extracts will illustrate conditions:

Rev. George Whitefield, in his letter to the slaveholders of Maryland, Virginia, North Carolina, South Carolina and Georgia, published in 1739, said:

My blood has frequently run cold within me, to think how many of your slaves have not sufficient food to eat; they are scarcely permitted to pick up the crumbs that fall from their master's table.

The Maryland *Journal*, and Baltimore *Advertiser*, May 30, 1788, says:

A single peck of corn a week, or the like measure of rice, is the ordinary quantity of provision for a hard-working slave; to which a small quantity of meat is occasionally, though rarely, added.

Hon. Alexander Smyth, a slaveholder, and for ten years a Member of Congress from Virginia, in his speech on the Missouri question, said January 28, 1820:

By confining the slaves to Southern States, where crops are raised for exportation and bread and meat are purchased, you doom them to scarcity and hunger. It is proposed to hem in the blacks where they are ill-fed.

The report of the Gradual Emancipation Society, of North Carolina, 1826, speaking of the condition of slaves in the eastern part of that State, says:

The master puts the unfortunate wretches upon short allowances, scarcely sufficient for their sustenance, so that a great part of them go half-starved much of the time.

Hon. Robert Turnbull, a slaveholder of Charleston, S. C., says:

The subsistence of the slaves consists, from March until August, of corn ground into grits, or meal, made into what is called hominy, or baked into cornbread. The other six months they are fed upon the sweet potato. Meat when given is only by the way of indulgence or favor.

Others testify: [1]

The food of the slaves was generally cornbread, and sometimes meat or molasses.

[1] American Slavery as It Is, p. 28.

The slaves had no food allowed them besides corn, excepting at Christmas, when they had beef.

On my uncle's plantation the food of the slaves was cornpone and a small allowance of meat.

Angelina Grimke Weld says:[1]

Only two meals a day are allowed the house-slaves—the first at twelve o'clock. If they eat before this time, it is by stealth, and I am sure there must be a good deal of suffering among them from hunger, and particularly by children. Besides this they are often kept from their meals by way of punishment. No table is provided for them to eat from. They know nothing of the comfort and pleasure of gathering round the social board—each takes his plate or tin pan and iron spoon, and holds it in the hand or on the lap. I never saw slaves seated around a table to partake of any meal.

Mr. Eleazar Powell, Chippewa, Beaver county, Penn., who resided in Mississippi in 1836 and 1837, said:

The slaves received two meals during the day. Those who have their food cooked for them get their breakfast about eleven o'clock, and their other meal about midnight.

Philemon Bliss, Esq., a lawyer in Elyria, Ohio, and a member of the Presbyterian church, who lived in Florida in 1834 and 1835, said:

The slaves go to the field in the morning; they carry with them cornmeal wet with water, and at noon build a fire on the ground and bake it in the ashes. After the labors of the day are over, they take their second meal of ash-cake.

"The legal allowance for food in North Carolina is, in the words of the law, 'a quart of corn per day.' See Haywood's Manual, page 525. The legal allowance in Louisiana is more, a barrel [flour barrel] of corn (in the ear), or its equivalent in other grain, and a pint of salt a salt a month. In the other slave States the amount of food for the slaves is left to the option of the master." (1839.)

Thos. Clay, Esq., of Georgia, a slaveholder, in his address before the Presbytery, 1833, said:

The quantity allowed by custom is a peck of corn a week.

An observer who lived twelve years in the South says:

In lower Tennessee, Mississippi and Louisiana, the clothing of the slaves is wretchedly poor; and grows worse as you go south, in the order of the States I have named. The only material is cotton bagging, i. e., bagging in which cotton is baled, not bagging made of cotton. In Louisiana, especially in the lower country, I have frequently seen them with nothing but a tattered coat, not sufficient to hide their nakedness. In winter their clothing seldom serves the purpose of comfort, and frequently not even of decent covering. In Louisiana the planters never think of serving out shoes to slaves. In Mississippi they give one pair a year generally. I never saw or heard of an instance of masters allowing them stockings. A small poor blanket is generally the only bed clothing, and this they frequently wear in the field when they have not sufficient clothing to hide their nakedness or to keep them warm. Their manner of sleeping varies with the season. In hot weather

---

[1] American Slavery, etc., pp. 55-56.

they stretch themselves anywhere and sleep. As it becomes cool they roll themselves in their blankets, and lay scattered about the cabin. In cold weather they nestle together with their feet towards the fire, promiscuously.[1]

The masters [in Georgia] make a practice of getting two suits of clothes for each slave per year, a thick suit for winter and a thin one for summer. They provide also one pair of Northern-made sale shoes for each slave in winter.[2]

The males and females have their suits from the same cloth for their winter dresses. These winter garments appear to be made of a mixture of cotton and wool, very coarse and sleazy. The whole suit for the men consists of a pair of pantaloons and a short sailor jacket, without shirt, vest, hat, stockings, or any kind of loose garments! These, if worn steadily when at work, would not probably last more than one or two months; therefore, for the sake of saving them, many of them work, especially in the summer, with no clothing on them except a cloth tied around their waist, and almost all with nothing more on them than a pantaloons, and these frequently so torn that they do not serve the purposes of common decency. The women have for clothing a short petticoat, and a short loose gown, something like the male's sailor-jacket, without any under garment, stockings, bonnets, hoods, caps, or any kind of over-clothes. When at work in warm weather they usually strip off the loose gown, and have nothing on but a short petticoat with some kind of covering over their breasts. Many children may be seen in summer months as naked as they came into the world.[3]

The allowance of clothing on this plantation to each slave, was given out at Christmas for the year, and consisted of one pair of coarse shoes and enough coarse cloth to make a jacket and trousers. If the man has a wife she makes it up; if not, it is made up in the house. The slaves on this plantation, being near Wilmington, procured themselves extra clothing by working Sundays and moonlight nights, cutting cordwood in the swamps. which they had to back about a quarter of a mile to the river; they would then get a permit from their master and, taking the wood in their canoes, carry it to Wilmington and sell it to the vessels, or dispose of it as best they could, and with the money buy an old jacket of the sailors, some coarse cloth for a shirt, etc. They sometimes gather the moss from the trees, which they cleanse and take to market. The women receive their allowance of the same kind of cloth that the men have. This they make into a frock; if they have any under garment they must procure them for themselves. . . .

Every Saturday night the slaves receive their allowances of provisions, which must last them till the next Saturday night. "Potato time," as it is called, begins about the middle of July. The slave may measure for himself, the overseers being present, half a bushel of sweet potatoes, and heap the measure as long as they will lie on; I have, however, seen the overseer, if he thinks the Negro is getting too many, kick the measure; and if they fall off tell him he has got his measure. No salt is furnished them to eat with their potatoes. When rice or corn is given they give them a little salt; sometimes half pint of molasses is given, but not often. The quantity of rice, which is of the small broken, unsaleable kind, is one peck. When corn is given them their allowance is the same, and if they get it ground (Mr. Swan had a mill on his plantation), they must give one quart for grinding, thus reducing their weekly allowance to seven quarts. When fish (mullet) were plentiful they were allowed in addition one fish. As to meat they seldom had any. I do not

---

[1] American Slavery as it Is, p. 42.   [2] Ibid., p. 19.   [3] Ibid., p. 19.

think they had any allowance for meat oftener than once in two or three months, then the quantity was very small. When they went into the field to work they took some of the meat or rice and a pot with them; the pots were given to an old woman who placed two, poles parallel, set the pots on them and kindled a fire underneath for cooking; she took salt with her and seasoned the messes as she thought proper. When their breakfast was ready, which was generally about ten or eleven o'clock, they were called from labor, ate, and returned to work; in the afternoon dinner was prepared in the same way. They had but two meals a day while in the field; if they wanted more, they cooked for themselves after they returned to their quarters at night. At the time of killing hogs on the plantation, the pluck, entrails and blood were given to the slaves.[1]

Mr. George W. Westgate, who had been engaged in the low-country trade for twelve years, more than half of each year, principally on the Mississippi, and its tributary streams in the southwestern slave States, said:

Feeding is not sufficient—let facts speak. On the coast, i. e., Natchez and the Gulf of Mexico, the allowance was one barrel of ears of corn and a pint of salt per month. They may cook this in what manner they please, but it must be done after dark; they have no daylight to prepare it by. Some few planters, but only a few, let them prepare their corn on Saturday afternoons. Planters, overseers and Negroes have told me that in pinching times, i. e., when corn is high, they did not get near that quantity. In Mississippi I know some planters who allowed their hands three and a half pounds of meat per week when it was cheap. Many prepare their corn on the Sabbath, when they are not worked on that day, which however is frequently the case on sugar plantations. There are very many masters on "the coast" who will not suffer their slaves to come to the boats, because they steal molasses to barter for meat; indeed, they generally trade more or less with stolen property. But it is impossible to find out what and when, as their articles of barter are of such trifling importance. They would often come on board to beg a bone, and would tell how badly they were fed, that they were almost starved; many a time I have sat up all night to prevent them from stealing something to eat.[2]

Slaves belonging to merchants and others in the city often hire their own time, for which they pay various prices, per week or month, according to the capacity of the slave. The females who thus hire their time pursue various modes to procure the money; their masters making no inquiry how they get it, provided the money comes. If it is not regularly paid they are flogged. Some take in washing, some cook on board vessels, pick oakum, sell peanuts, etc., while others, younger and more comely, often resort to the vilest pursuits.[3]

This is all that good or bad masters allow their slaves round about Savannah on the plantations: One peck of gourd seed-corn is to be measured out to each slave once every week. One man with whom I labored, however, being desirous to get all the work out of his hands he could before I left (about fifty in number), bought for them every week, or twice a week, a beef's head from market. With this they made a soup in a large iron kettle, around which the hands came at meal time, and dipping out the soup would mix it with their

[1] Narrative of Mr. Caulkins on estate of John Swan, near Wilmington, N. C., 1838. American Slavery as it Is, p. 13.
[2] American Slavery as it Is, p. 30.   [3] Ibid., p. 16.

hommony, and eat it as though it were a feast. This man permitted his slaves to eat twice a day while I was doing a job for him. [1]

The custom was to blow the horn early in the morning, as a signal for the hands to rise and go to work, when commenced; they continued work until about eleven o'clock, a. m., when at the signal all hands left off and went into their huts, made their fires, made their corn-meal into hommony or cake, ate it, and went to work again at the signal of the horn, and worked until night or until their tasks were done. Some cooked their breakfast in the field while at work. Each slave must grind his own corn in a hand-mill after he has done his work at night. There is generally one hand-mill on every plantation for the use of the slaves.

Some of the planters have no corn, others often get out. The substitute for it is the equivalent of one peck of corn either in rice or sweet potatoes; neither of which is as good for the slave as corn. They complain more of being faint who feed on rice and potatoes than when fed on corn. I was with one man a few weeks who gave me his hands to do a job of work, and to save the time one cooked for all the rest. The following course was taken: Two crotched sticks were driven down at one end of the yard, and a small pole being laid on the crotches, they swung a large iron kettle on the middle of the pole; then made up a fire under the kettle and boiled the hommony; when ready the hands were called around this kettle with their wooden plates and spoons. They dipped out and ate standing around the kettle, or sitting upon the ground, as best suited their convenience. When they had potatoes they took them out with their hands, and ate them. As soon as it was thought they had had sufficient time to swallow their food they were called to their work again. This was the only meal they ate through the day. [2]

The general allowance of food was thought to be a peck and a half of meal and three pounds of bacon a week. This it was observed is as much meal as they can eat, but they would be glad to have more bacon; sometimes they receive four pounds, but it is oftener that they receive less than three. It is distributed to them on Saturday nights, or on the better-managed plantations sometimes Wednesday, to prevent their using it extravagantly, or selling it for whiskey on Sunday.

Olmsted says that the slaves take their breakfast at sunrise or a little before, then go to the field and work until noon; their dinner is brought to them, and when the work is not too pressing they have two hours to rest. Promptly at sundown they stop work and return to their cabins. Then they go to the woods, bring wood and cook their supper, which will be a bit of bacon fried often with eggs, corn-bread baked in the spider, after the bacon to absorb the fat, and perhaps some sweet potatoes roasted in the ashes. [3]

The ploughmen got their dinner at twelve o'clock: those not using horses do not usually dine till they have finished their tasks; but this, I believe, is optional with them. They commence work at sunrise and at about eight o'clock have their breakfast brought to them in the field, each hand having left a bucket with the cook for that purpose. All who are working in connection leave their work together and gather in a social company about a fire, where they spend about half an hour, at breakfast time. The provisions furnished them consist mainly of meal, rice, and vegetables, with salt and molasses, and occasionally bacon, fish and coffee. The allowance is a peck of meal or an equivalent quantity of rice per week, to each working hand old or young, besides small stores. [4]

---

1 American Slavery as it Is. p. 18. 2 Ibid., pp. 18-19.
3 Olmsted: Seaboard Slave States, I, pp. 120-122. 4 Ibid, I, p. 60

The slaves were furnished with a coat and trousers of coarse woollen, or woollen and cotton stuff for winter, and trousers of cotton osnaburg for summer. They had two pairs of shoes, or a pair of shoes and a pair of boots each year. The women have two dresses of striped cotton, three shifts, two pairs of shoes, etc.[1]

Section 17. General Economic Condition. The chief occupations of Negroes in 1890 and 1900 were as follows:

Negro Population, at least Ten Years of Age, Engaged in Specified Occupations: 1890 and 1900

OCCUPATION	1890	1900	Per cent of Increase
Continental United States:			
All occupations	3,073,164	3,992,337	29.9
Occupations giving employment to at least 10,000 Negroes in 1900	*2,917,169	3,807,008	*29.8
Agricultural laborers	1,106,728	1,344,125	21.5
Farmers, planters and overseers	590,666	757,822	28.3
Laborers (not specified)	349,002	545,935	56.4
Servants and waiters	401,215	465,734	16.1
Launderers and Laundresses	153,684	220,104	43.2
Draymen, hackmen, teamsters, etc.	43,963	67,585	53.7
Steam railroad employees	47,548	55,327	16.4
Miners and quarrymen	19,007	36,561	92.4
Saw and planing-mill employees	17,276	33,266	92.6
Porters and helpers (in stores, etc.)	11,694	28,977	147.8
Teachers, professors in colleges, etc.	15,100	21,267	40.8
Carpenters and joiners	22,581	21,113	†6.5
Turpentine farmers and laborers	‡	20,744	....
Barbers and hairdressers	17,480	19,942	14.1
Nurses and midwives	5,213	19,431	272.7
Clergymen	12,159	15,528	27.7
Tobacco and cigar factory operatives	15,004	15,349	2.3
Hostlers	10,500	14,496	38.1
Masons (brick and stone)	9,760	14,386	47.4
Dressmakers	7,586	12,569	65.7
Iron and steel workers	6,579	12,327	87.4
Seamstresses	11,846	11,537	+2.6
Janitors and sextons	5,945	11,536	94.0
Housekeepers and stewards	9,248	10,596	14.6
Fishermen and oystermen	10,071	10,427	3.5
Engineers, firemen, (not locomotive)	6,326	10,224	61.6
Blacksmiths	10,988	10,100	+8.1
Other occupations	§155,995	185,329	§32.1

* Excludes turpentine farmers and laborers.   † Decrease.
   ‡ Turpentine farmers and laborers were included in "other agricultural pursuits" in 1890.   § Includes turpentine farmers and laborers.[2]

Turning our attention specifically to the Negro farmer we may say: There was some ownership of land by Negroes before the war, but not much. During and after the war lands in Georgia and South Carolina were sold to Negroes on easy terms and Negroes bought land elsewhere. In 1875, there is reason to believe, Negroes held between two and four million acres of land; by 1880 this had increased to about six millions; to about eight millions in 1890, and to about twelve millions in 1900.

---

[1] Olmsted, I, p. 129.
[2] Bulletin No 8, p. 58.

In 1900 there were 187,799 farms in the United States owned by Negroes, comprising about 12,000,000 acres. The owned farms constitute 25.2% of all Negro farms; the private farm-owning families 25.3% of all Negro-farms families. Taking all homes, both farm homes and others, we find that 20.3% of them are owned. There were 190,111 private farm-owning Negro families in 1900, and a somewhat larger number of farm-owning families of all sorts. Since 1890 the number of Negro farmers probably increased by about 36 or 38 per cent, the number of Negro owners increased over 57 per cent, and the percentage of ownership increased by 3.5. These percentages, although based on figures which are not entirely comparable, are sufficiently exact to measure approximately the advance toward farm ownership made by the Negroes during the decade 1890 to 1900. These owners—including Indians and Mongolians, who constitute but 3% of all—have 15 million acres worth $179,796,639, and raised in 1899 products worth $57,422,983. They expended $2,624,595 for hired labor, and $1,197,180 for fertilizers. The black tenant farmer of the South is half way between slavery and free-ownership of the soil. The crop-lien system binds him in a black-belt of farming which is growing blacker. Under favorable conditions share tenants become cash renters and eventually owners, but this evolution is difficult. There are 283,614 Negro share tenant farmers in the United States and 273,560 cash tenants, and although the separate farms they cultivate are small, there is great concentration in ownership of land by the landlords. The colored tenants control 25 million acres of land and 360 million dollars of farm property; they raise 200 million dollars worth of products annually, including 3 million bales of cotton, 73 million bushels of corn, 6 million bushels of sweet potatoes, 200,000 tons of hay and forage, 1½ million bushels of wheat, 2 million bushels of oats, 31 million pounds of rice and 62½ million pounds of tobacco. The average share-tenant's farm is worth $628. It has land worth $435, $84 in buildings, $19 in tools, and $90 in live stock. It raises on an average $311 worth of products, or $7.33 worth per acre.

Considering all Negro farmers, owners and tenants, we have in the United States 746,717 farms conducted by them, with an acreage about the size of New England. Of this acreage less than a million acres are in the North and 37 millions in the South. Of these farms 716,514 were improved by buildings, and they contained 38,233,933 acres, or 59,741 square miles, an area about equal to that of the State of Georgia or that of New England; 23,362,798 acres, or 61 per cent of the total area, was improved for farming purposes. The total value of property on these farms was $499,943,734, of which $324,244,397 represented the value of land and improvements, $71,903,315 that of buildings, $18,859,757 that of implements and machinery, and $84,936,265 that of live stock. The gross value of all products on farms of Negroes in 1899 was $255,751,145. Of this sum, however, $25,843,443 represents products fed to live stock, the value of which reappears and is to that extent duplicated in the reported value of animal products, such as meat, milk, butter, eggs and poultry; subtracting this amount we have a net value of $229,907,702, or 46 per cent of the total value of farm property in farms cultivated by Negroes. This sum represents the gross farm income. The total expenditure for labor on farms of Negroes in 1899 was $8,789,792, and the expenditure for fertilizers was $5,614,844.

A third of the Negro farms yielded $100 to $250 income; another third $250 to $500 income; something over a seventh yielded over $500. The rest, 18 per cent, yielded less than $100. Estimating the net income after the rent has been subtracted, it is probable that 560,000 Negro-farm families have incomes between $150 and $170 a year, while about 200,000 families average $250 to $275 a year.

The colored farmer conducts a little less than $\frac{1}{7}$ of all the farms in the United States; controls $\frac{1}{20}$ of the total farm acreage and $\frac{1}{37}$ of all farm property in value, and raises $\frac{1}{15}$ of the products in value. In the South the Negro holds a third of the farms, a tenth of the acreage and a ninth of the property, and raises $\frac{1}{5}$ of the products. He conducts half the farms on which cotton is the chief crop, over a third of the rice farms, nearly a fifth of the tobacco farms, a seventh of the sugar farms and a tenth of the vegetable farms. Colored farmers raised, in 1899, 39.4% of the cotton on their own farms, besides what they raised as laborers on white farms; 9% of the rice, 21% of the sweet potatoes, 10% of the tobacco, and 4% of the corn. They owned 3% in value of the stock. The average Negro farm is worth 16% as much as the average white farm. The Negro is thus seen to be relatively a small economic factor according to his numbers, but nevertheless a factor that cannot be ignored and which is absolutely of great importance.

To estimate the total property held by Negroes we may quote a report of a committee of the American Economic Association based on the census of 1900:

It is the opinion of your committee that the census farm returns furnish a better basis for estimating the total accumulated wealth possessed by the Negroes in 1900 than is found in the only other source that has been used, namely, the assessors' returns for a few Southern States. The Census Bureau estimate is $200,000,000 for the value of (1) the farms, live-stock and implements on the farms owned and operated by Negroes and of (2) the live-stock on the farms rented by Negroes. This should be increased by (3) the farm property owned by Negroes and rented by them either to Negroes or to whites, and also by (4) the farm property other than live-stock owned by Negro farm tenants. It should be decreased by (1) the various unknown liabilities against this property in the hands of whites and by (2) the value of the live-stock of Negro tenants which is owned by white landlords. It is the belief of your committee that the subtractions would at least equal the additions, and that $200,000,000 may be deemed an outside estimate of the net value of the accumulated property owned by Negro farmers. Indeed it seems to us probable that this estimate would be large enough to include also the wealth owned by the 550,000 families of agricultural laborers. In other words, we believe that the total property held by these families is not greater than the legal claims held by whites against Negro farm property plus the proportion of the $50,000,000 worth of live-stock on the farms of Negro tenants which is owned by whites, of neither of which is any account taken in the Census Bureau estimate.

If this be granted, then the further assumption may be ventured that the other 500,000 Negro families in the United States are no better off on the average in the matter of accumulated wealth than are the 1¼ million families occupied in agricultural pursuits. On that assumption the total accumulated wealth of Negro families in 1900 was in the neighborhood of $275,000,000.

An inquiry into the value of the property held by Negro churches in 1890 gave as a result $26,600,000. As the Negro population of the United States increased between 1890 and 1900 by 18.0 percent and the number of Negro churches only about two-thirds as fast, the value of property held by Negro churches can hardly be supposed to have increased during the decade by more than 20 per cent. In that case the value of such property in 1900 was approximately $32,000,000. The legal claims against it owned by whites cannot be estimated. Nor does your committee see any way in which the amount of property held by Negroes other than family or church property can be approximated.

The evidence in hand leads your committee to the conclusion that the accumulated wealth of the Negro race in the United States in 1900 was approximately $300,000,000, and probably neither less than $250,000,000 nor more than $350,000,000.

Section 18. Georgia. A more detailed picture of property owned by Negroes is furnished by the reports of the Comptroller-General of Georgia:

Number of Acres and Assessed Value of Land Owned by Negroes of Georgia, 1874 to 1907

YEAR	Acres owned	Assessed value	YEAR	Acres owned	Assessed value
1874	338,769	(a)	1891	1,004,305	$3,914,143
1875	396,658	$1,263,902	1892	1,063,649	4,477,183
1876	457,635	1,234,104	1893	1,043,860	4,450,121
1877	458,999	1,262,723	1894	1,064,431	4,386,366
1878	501,890	1,294,383	1895	1,038,824	4,158,960
1879	541,199	1,348,758	1896	1,043,847	4,234,848
1880	586,664	1,522,173	1897	1,057,567	4,353,798
1881	660,358	1,754,800	1898	1,097,087	4,340,100
1882	692,335	1,877,861	1899	1,062,223	4,220,120
1883	666,583	2,065,938	1900	1,075,073	4,274,549
1884	756,703	2,262,185	1901	1,141,135	4,656,042
1885	788,376	2,362,889	1902	1,175,291	4,779,263
1886	802,939	2,508,198	1903	1,251,714	5,181,471
1887	813,725	2,508,650	1904	1,284,336	5,455,328
1888	868,501	2,822,943	1905	1,336,821	6,282,436
1889	877,112	3,047,695	1906	1,420,888	7,149,925
1890	967,234	3,425,176	1907	1,449,624	7,972,787

(a) Not reported.

An examination of the records of typical counties show that this land was distributed about as follows:

The Negro American Family

Farm Land, 1899, Approximate Distribution by Assessed Value

	Per cent of Owners	Per cent of Value
Under $100	46.9	9.4
$100 or under $300	31.1	23.3
$300 or under $500	11.3	19.2
$500 or under $1000	7.7	23.4
$1000 or under $2000	2.2	12.9
$2000 and over	.8	11.8
	100.0	100.0

Farm Land, 1906

	Per cent of Owners	Per cent of Value
Under $100	36.5	5.5
$100 or under $300	32.7	18.5
$300 or under $500	14.3	17.8
$500 or under $1000	11.2	25.1
$1000 or under $2000	4.1	17.8
$2000 and over	1.2	15.3
	100.0	100.0

Farm Land, 1899: Approximate Distribution by Acres

	Per cent of Owners	Per cent of Acreage
Under 10 acres	30.5	1.6
10 acres or under 50	32.4	12.1
50 acres or under 100	16.5	16.9
100 acres or under 300	17.4	42.2
300 acres or under 500	2.3	13.9
500 acres and over	.9	13.3
	100.0	100.0

Farm Land, 1906

	Per cent of Owners	Per cent of Acreage
Under 10 acres	30.3	1.5
10 acres or under 50	31.7	12.1
50 acres or under 100	16.4	17.1
100 acres or under 300	18.5	44.9
300 acres or under 500	2.2	12.7
500 acres and over	.9	11.7
	100.0	100.0

Georgia 109

Assessed Value of Town and City Real Estate and Per Cent of Town and City Real Estate
of Total Property Owned by Negroes of Georgia, 1875 to 1907

YEAR	Assessed value	Per cent of total property	YEAR	Assessed value	Per cent of total property
1875	$1,203,202	22.31	1892	$4,668,733	31.40
1876	1,192,609	21.73	1893	4,851,144	32.43
1877	1,154,422	21.26	1894	4,635,055	32.22
1878	1,110,147	21.66	1895	3,436,778	34.28
1879	1,094,435	21.12	1896	4,437,329	33.38
1880	1,201,992	20.85	1897	4,321,620	31.73
1881	1,323,045	20.42	1898	4,374,565	31.89
1882	1,478,623	22.44	1899	4,346,396	32.32
1883	1,657,101	21.85	1900	4,361,390	30.89
1884	1,521,801	23.96	1901	4,351,935	27.84
1885	2,098,787	25.74	1902	4,389,422	28.89
1886	2,328,962	26.91	1903	4,668,620	27.93
1887	2,499,389	27.97	1904	5,165,000	28.55
1888	2,752,024	28.57	1905	5,512,217	26.73
1889	3,103,486	29.80	1906	5,950,036	25.05
1890	3,642,586	29.56	1907	6,710,189	25.90
1891	4,131,216	29.10			

Georgia Town and City Property, 1899,
Approximate Distribution by Value

	Per cent of Owners	Per cent of Value
Under $100	26.7	4.1
$100 or under $300	38.0	19.0
$300 or under $500	16.0	17.4
$500 or under $1000	13.9	27.2
$1000 or under $2000	3.0	10.4
$2000 and over	2.4	21.9
	100.0	100.0

Town and City Property, 1906

	Per cent of Owners	Per cent of Value
Under $100	17.9	2.5
$100 or under $300	39.2	18.3
$300 or under $500	21.7	21.8
$500 or under $1000	15.4	27.2
$1000 or under $2000	4.3	15.2
$2000 and over	1.5	15.0
	100.0	100.0

Assessed Value of Horses, Mules, Cattle, and Other Stock and of Plantation and
Mechanical Tools, Owned by Negroes of Georgia, 1875 to 1907

YEAR	Assessed Value		YEAR	Assessed Value	
	Horses, mules, cattle, and other stock	Plantation and mechanical tools		Horses, mules, cattle, and other stock	Plantation and mechanical tools
1875	(a)	$20,017	1892	$3,180,322	$590,902
1876	$241,106	125,120	1893	3,130,818	547,739
1877	1,926,942	162,647	1894	2,997,587	511,316
1878	1,641,367	166,780	1895	2,288,850	402,040
1879	1,704,230	143,258	1896	2,494,390	416,091
1880	2,054,787	163,086	1897	2,676,186	491,956
1881	2,213,021	225,973	1898	2,579,770	479,520
1882	2,031,361	193,898	1899	2,213,905	433,125
1883	2,361,662	238,308	1900	2,424,674	469,637
1884	2,387,282	242,222	1901	3,078,444	645,451
1885	2,245,801	228,894	1902	2,985,831	652,583
1886	2,166,569	260,549	1903	3,531,471	810,553
1887	2,178,518	304,815	1904	3,889,441	880,599
1888	2,314,356	331,876	1905	4,633,124	1,108,534
1889	2,315,480	384,827	1906	5,880,761	1,402,083
1890	2,915,635	474,386	1907	6,080,657	1,407,865
1891	3,429,223	645,261			

(a) Not reported.

Assessed Value of Household and Kitchen Furniture Owned by Negroes of Georgia,
1875 to 1907

YEAR	Assessed value	YEAR	Assessed value	YEAR	Assessed value
1875	$21,186	1886	$858,329	1897	$1,429,247
1876	489,522	1887	901,765	1898	1,453,619
1877	535,291	1888	951,177	1899	1,434,975
1878	502,699	1889	1,017,439	1900	1,655,092
1879	448,713	1890	1,173,624	1901	1,811,113
1880	498,532	1891	1,365,468	1902	1,688,541
1881	600,892	1892	1,474,220	1903	1,822,551
1882	579,736	1893	1,486,821	1904	1,935,409
1883	676,346	1894	1,446,926	1905	2,080,444
1884	699,132	1895	1,322,694	1906	2,393,402
1885	736,170	1896	1,363,842	1907	2,581,645

Assessed Value of Total Property Owned by Negroes of Georgia, 1874 to 1907

YEAR	Assessed value	YEAR	Assessed value	YEAR	Assessed value
1874	$6,157,798	1886	$8,655,298	1898	$13,719,200
1875	5,393,885	1887	8,936,479	1899	13,447,423
1876	5,488,867	1888	9,631,271	1900	14,118,720
1877	5,430,844	1889	10,415,330	1901	15,629,811
1878	5,124,875	1890	12,322,003	1902	15,188,069
1879	5,182,398	1891	14,196,735	1903	16,714,334
1880	5,764,293	1892	14,869,575	1904	18,087,934
1881	6,478,951	1893	14,960,675	1905	20,616,468
1882	6,589,876	1894	14,387,780	1906	23,750,109
1883	7,582,395	1895	12,941,230	1907	25,904,822
1884	8,021,525	1896	13,292,816		
1885	8,153,390	1897	13,619,690		

Since 1900 Negro property in Georgia has increased 83.4%. If Negro property throughout the Nation has increased in like proportion (and this is wholly conjectural), then, to use the phraseology of the American Economic Association Committee: "The accumulated wealth of the Negro race in the United States in 1907 may be approximately $550,000,000 and possibly neither less than $550,000,000 nor more than $600,000,000."

The economic situation of Negro Americans is thus summed up:

To sum then the conclusions of this paper: half the Negro breadwinners of the nation are partially submerged by a bad economic system, an unjust admiration of the laws and enforced ignorance. Their future depends on common schools, justice, and the right to vote. A million and three-quarters of men just above these are fighting a fierce battle for admission to the industrial ranks of the nation—for the right to work. They are handicapped by their own industrial history which has made them often shiftless and untrustworthy, but they can, by means of wise economic leadership, be made a strong body of artisans and landowners. A quarter of a million men stand economically at the head of the Negroes, and by a peculiar self-protecting group economy are making themselves independent of prejudice and competition. This group economy is extending to the lower economic strata." [1]

Section 19. Income. Some ideas of the income of Negro families may be gathered from the following figures:

Number of Families by Size of Family and Annual Income. Farmville, Va., 1897

ANNUAL INCOME	FAMILIES OF									
	One Member	Two Members	Three Members	Four Members	Five Members	Six Members	Seven Members	Eight Members	Nine to Eleven Members	Total Families
$50 or less	3	..	1	..	1	..	..	..	..	5
$50 to $75	5	4	1	1	..	..	..	..	..	11
$75 to $100	1	6	..	3	..	1	..	..	..	11
$100 to $150	1	7	6	..	2	2	1	..	..	19
$150 to $200	..	8	4	5	4	3	3	2	..	29
$200 to $250	1	14	5	9	3	4	2	..	2	40
$250 to $350	..	10	7	12	5	7	6	1	5	53
$350 to $500	..	1	7	13	7	1	4	5	6	44
$500 to $750	..	2	1	3	6	7	3	8	5	35
$750 or over	..	..	..	..	1	..	..	..	5	6
Not reported	2	..	2	2	2	1	..	..	..	9
Total Families	13	52	34	48	31	26	19	16	23	262

[1] From Papers and Proceedings of the Eighteenth Annual Meeting American Economic Association, December, 1906.

The Negro American Family

Number of Families by Size of Family and Annual Income

Negroes of Xenia, Ohio, 1903

ANNUAL INCOME	One Member	Two Members	Three Members	Four Members	Five Members	Six Members	Seven Members	Eight Members	Nine Members	Ten Members or over	Total Families
Under $50	2	2	1	....	....	....	....	....	....	....	5
$50 to $75	4	3	4	....	....	....	....	....	....	....	11
$75 to $100	8	4	2	....	1	....	....	....	....	....	15
$100 to $150	7	12	8	2	2	....	....	....	....	....	31
$150 to $200	7	17	1	3	3	....	2	....	....	....	33
$200 to $250	7	8	14	12	4	1	1	3	....	....	50
$250 to $350	2	29	22	11	9	5	3	2	3	....	86
$350 to $500	3	21	35	23	18	15	3	2	2	1	123
$500 to $750	....	7	10	8	15	6	2	3	2	4	57
$750 to $1000	....	4	6	4	8	3	1	1	....	1	28
$1000 or over	....	....	3	5	3	....	2	1	....	4	18
Not reported	11	5	19	4	1	2	1	1	....	....	14
Total	51	112	125	72	64	32	15	13	7	10	501

Estimated Annual Income and Expenditure of a Family of Five

Negroes of Xenia, Ohio, 1903

INCOME		EXPENDITURE	
Items	Amt.	Items	Amt.
11 weeks @ $6.50 per week	$71 50	Rent @ $3.00 per month	$36 00
26 weeks @ 7.50 per week	195 00	Clothing (two suits)	20 00
		Underclothes	3 00
		Shoes and stockings	9 50
		Groceries and meat @ 80c. per week	93 60
		Doctor's bill and medicine	15 00
		Life Insurance for 4 @ 5c pr. wk. ea.	10 40
		Incidentals and miscellaneous	12 10
		Moving to Xenia	37 00
		Fuel and lighting	30 00
Total	$266 50	Total	$266 50

Incomes According to Size of Family in Seventh Ward. 1896. Philadelphia

Amount of Income Per Year	Size of Family											Total Number of Families
	1	2	3	4	5	6	7	8	9	10	11 to 15	
$50	7	5	1	....	....	....	1	....	....	....	....	14
100	22	18	2	2	1	....	....	....	....	....	....	45
150	31	69	19	4	6	4	....	....	....	....	....	133
200	23	105	35	12	8	4	....	....	....	....	....	187
250	32	95	46	26	7	1	5	2	....	....	....	214
300	10	108	49	33	9	3	1	....	....	....	....	213
350	9	121	46	30	11	10	2	1	....	....	....	230
400	4	95	39	34	22	9	6	....	....	....	....	209
450	1	79	40	26	14	7	3	1	1	....	....	172
500	7	115	47	37	26	17	1	3	2	....	1	256
550	....	23	12	8	4	4	1	0	3	....	....	55
600	1	17	14	8	7	3	3	....	1	....	....	54
650	1	45	26	27	11	7	4	2	1	....	1	125
700	....	10	16	12	9	5	6	3	2	....	....	63
750	3	23	19	16	13	7	9	3	1	....	....	94
800	....	7	7	7	3	2	2	1	....	1	1	31
850	....	3	2	1	3	1	4	2	2	....	....	18
900	....	5	4	8	3	3	5	9	1	1	1	40
1000 to 1200	....	1	1	1	4	....	....	....	1	3	1	12
1200 to 1500	1	3	10	3	5	7	6	2	5	3	1	46
1500 and over	2	6	10	12	6	5	10	3	2	4	5	65
Unknown	15	67	17	6	2	2	1	....	....	....	....	110
Unknown size	....	....	....	....	....	....	....	....	....	....	....	55

The income according to size of family is indicated in the next table. From this, making the family a standard of five, and making some allowance for large and small families, we can conclude that 19 per cent of the Negro families in the Seventh Ward earn five dollars and less per week on the average; 48 per cent earn between $5 and $10; 26 per cent, $10–$15, and 8 per cent over $15 per week.

Philadelphia, 1896

Average Earnings Per Week	No. of Families	Per Cent	Remarks
$5 and less	420 { 192...	8.8	Very poor.
	{ 228...	9.6	Poor.
$5 to 10	1088	47.8	Fair.
$10 to 15	581	25.5	Comfortable.
$15 to 20	91	4.0	Good circumstances.
$20 and over	96	4.2	Well-to-do.
Total	2276	100.0	

The following tables of Atlanta Negro budgets were made up in 1900:

Annual Income of 124 Representative Families of Atlanta, and Amount and Per Cent of Expenditure for Various Items

		ANNUAL INCOME		ANNUAL EXPENDITURE											
CLASSIFIED INCOME	Number of Families	Total	Average	Rent		Food		Clothing		Taxes		Other Expenses and Savings	
				Amt.	Per Cent of Total	Amt.	Per Cent of Total	Amt.	Per Cent of Total	Amt.	Per Cent of Total	Amt.	Per Cent of Total
$100 or under $200	18	$2,504	$139	$288	11.50	$928	37.06	$570	20.37	$3	0.12	$775	30.95
200 " 300	34	8,480	249	1,088	12.24	4,198	49.50	1,800	21.23	184	2.17	1,260	14.88
300 " 400	30	10,004	333	864	8.63	4,248	42.46	2,080	20.59	264	2.64	2,508	25.68
400 " 500	19	8,234	433	770	9.35	2,940	35.71	1,285	15.61	243	2.95	2,196	26.88
500 " 750	20	11,288	564	804	7.12	3,448	30.54	1,755	15.55	328	2.91	4,053	43.88
750 " 1,000	2	1,760	880			660	37.50	350	19.89	150	8.52	600	34.09
1000 or over	1	1,125	1,125			360	32.00	200	17.78	50	4.44	515	45.78

Section 20. Budgets. There follow budgets showing the expenditures of seventeen Negro families. All of these except the first three were collected in 1909 by Senior and Junior students of Atlanta University:

No. 1. Merchant's Account with a Farm Tenant. Alabama

A. B. 1898.

Dr.		Cr.	
To Balance	$59 13	By Credit	47 91
Rent	20 00	Cash	69 36
Taxes	8 71	3 bales Cotton	
Interest	17 34		
Cash	6 75		
Tools—			
3 prs. plow lines . 45			
1 plow 40	85		
Shop work...........	25		
Food—			
14¾ lbs. meat .. $13 20			
12 bu. meal.... 5 85			
4 lbs. sugar.... 28			
42 lbs. flour.... 1 40	20 73		
Carried forward ...	$138 76	Carried forward...	$117 27

A. B. 1898.

Dr.		Cr.	
Brought forward	$138 76	Brought forward.....	$117 27
Feed—Corn ... 13 85			
4 bu. Oats... 2 00	15 85		
Clothing—			
1 pr. Suspenders 10			
1 hat 75			
2 pr. pants.... 1 85			
6 pr. shoes.... 6 70			
22 yds. cloth.... 1 45	10 85		
Seeds—			
11¼ bu. cotton seed ...	1 70		
	$162 16		$117 27

No. 2. Farm-Hand,[1] Five Persons

INCOME		EXPENDITURE	
Items	Amount	Items	Amount
Man: 12 months' labor @ $12...	$144 00	Food per week @ $1.70 for 52 weeks......................	$88 40
Woman: 52 weeks' labor @ $1..	52 00	Fuel and lighting:	
Boy: 6 months' labor @ $3.....	18 00	7 cords of wood @ $3.00, $21.00; oil @ 10c. a week for 52 weeks, $5.20..........	26 20
		Clothing......................	50 00
		Miscellaneous................	10 00
		Rent..........................	18 00
		Doctor and medicine.........	10 00
		Surplus	11 40
Total......................	$214 00	Total	$214 00

No. 3. Laborer,[2] Five Persons

INCOME		EXPENDITURE	
Items	Amount	Items	Amount
Man: 39 wks. work @ $9........	$351 00	Rent 12 mos. @ $3 per mo	$ 36 00
Wife: 12 wks. cooking @ $2.50 per wk.; 18 wks. washing @ $1 per wk.......	48 00	Groceries and meat @ $4.00 per wk......................	208 00
		Dresses for wife and daughter	7 00
		2 suits for boys	4 50
		1 suit for husband............	5 50
		Shoes and stockings for all...	8 75
		Underclothes for all..........	2 00
		Doctor's bill and medicine...	21 00
		Funeral expenses.............	20 00
		Life expenses @ 25c per wk....	13 00
		Fuel..........................	33 00
		Tobacco @ 20c per wk.........	10 40
		Miscellaneous................	14 45
		On hand......................	15 40
Total......................	$399 00	Total	$399 00

No. 4. Farmer and Laborer, Four Persons

INCOME		EXPENDITURE	
Items	Amount	Items	Amount
Cotton........................	$300 00	Clothes........................	$50 00
Other work	100 00	Food	100 00
		Tax	10 00
		Amusements..........	20 00
		Other purposes.	25 00
			$205 00
		[3]Unaccounted for......	195 00
Total......................	$400 00	Total	$400 00

[1] Estimated, see U. S. Bulletin of the Bureau of Labor No. 32.
[2] Estimated, Xenia, Ohio, Bureau of the U. S. Bureau of Labor No. 48.
[3] This portion includes a part which is spent upon drink.

116   The Negro American Family

No. 5. Farmer and Teacher, Nine Persons

INCOME		EXPENDITURE		
Items	Amount	Items	Amt.	Pr. ct.
8 bales of cotton weighing 500 lbs. @ 9c......................	$360 00	Food	$230 10	41.2
2 cows @ $20....................	40 00	Fuel and light	2 50	.4
For teaching 8 months........	160 00	Clothes..................	82 00	14.6
		Sickness	25 00	} 7.1
		Other purposes............	15 00	
		Balance on hand.....	205 40	36.7
Total........................	$560 00	Total	$560 00	100%

No. 6. Laborer, Six Persons

INCOME		EXPENDITURE		
Items	Amount	Items	Amt.	Pr. ct.
Labor and income..............	$650 00	Food.......................	$250 00	38.5
		Clothes....................	100 00	15.25
		Taxes......................	13 00	2.00
		Light......................	3 00	.5
		Other things..............	284 00	43.75
Total........................	$650 00	Total	$650 00	100%

No. 7. Laborer, Five Persons

INCOME		EXPENDITURE		
Items	Amount	Items	Amt.	Pr. ct.
Labor	$625 00	Food	$250 00	40.0
		Clothes....................	125 00	16 0
		Rent and taxes............	121 00	15.75
		Fuel and light	30 00	4.8
		Family savings	27 00	4.2
		Other things..............	72 00	19.25
Total......................	$625 00	Total.....................	$625 00	100%

No. 8. Farmer, Eleven Persons

INCOME		EXPENDITURE		
Items	Amount	Items	Amt.	Pr. ct.
Cotton	$500 00	Paid out on land and stock	$200 00	} 55.6
Beans and potatoes	12 50	Balance saved up	147 50	
Chickens......................	12 50	Food	150 00	24.0
Tobacco.......................	20 00	Clothing	100 00	16.0
Peas	5 00	Church and secret orders.	25 00	4.0
Odd work on other farms.....	75 00	Taxes......................	2 50	.4
Total........................	$625 00	Total.....................	$625 00	100%

Nc. 9. Brickmason and Driver, Seven Persons

INCOME		EXPENDITURE		
Items	Amount	Items	Amt.	Pr. ct.
Average yearly returns as brickmason and driver....	$800 00	Food	$400 00	50.00
		Fuel.......................	50 00	6.25
		Clothes	75 00	9.375
		Payments on home and taxes	175 00	.875
		For amusements...........	25 00	
		Running house and payments of water bills...	25 00	
		For church purposes	6 00	} 12.50
		Sickness and tooth bill..	30 00	
		Societies	6 00	
		Books, paper, periodicals	8 00	
		Savings		21.00
Total	$800 00	Total	$800 00	100%

No. 10. Farm-hand (Georgia), 12 Persons

INCOME		EXPENDITURE		
Items	Amount	Items	Amt.	Pr. ct.
½ of 30 bales cotton $47	$705 00	Food	$329 75	40.3
5 tons cotton seeds @ 16.50......	82 50	20 bbls. flour @ $6... $120 00		
Balance due landlord	21 85	70 bu. meal @ $1.10.. 77 00		
		75 gal. molasses @ 45 33 75		
		825 lbs. meat @ 12 ... 99 00		
			$329 75	
		Clothes....	135 00	16.4
		7 suits @ 16.25.. ......$113 75		
		Sunday dresses..... 21 25		
			$135 00	
		Borrowed $25 note for	30 00	
		Mending shoes..............	5 20	
		2 boxes tobacco	6 00	
		Gun (second-hand)........	12 80	} 42.2
		Buggy (second-hand)	80 00	
		Organ	75 00	
		6 tons guano @ 22.50........	135 00	
		2 boxes shells @ 55	1 10	
		Taxes......................	9 50	1.1
Total	$819 35	Total	$819 35	100%

No. 11. Janitor, Three Persons

INCOME		EXPENDITURE		
Items	Amount	Items	Amt.	Pr. ct.
Man's salary	$520 00	Food	$369 00	41.7
Woman's sewing..........	216 00	Clothes.....................	115 00	13.0
House rent	151 00	Insurance and church	79 00	
		Amusements	3 00	} 21.2
		Medicine and toilet articles	5 00	
		Other things...............	100 00	
		Taxes......................	44 00	5.0
		Balance saved up	172 00	19.1
Total	$887 00	Total	$887 00	100%

No. 12. Brickmason, Nine Persons

INCOME		EXPENDITURE		
Items	Amount	Items	Amt.	Pr. ct.
For laying bricks..............	$907 20	Food	$278 30	29.00
For washing and ironing.....	52 00	Fuel and light.............	48 90	5.08
		Clothes.....................	85 00	8.85
		Amusements	1 20	}
		Sickness	12 00	} 7.16
		Society dues..............	55 60	}
		Taxes......................	20 25	2.10
		Savings and unaccounted	467 95	48.81
Total..........................	$959 20	Total	$959 20	100%

No. 13. Teacher, Ten Persons

INCOME		EXPENDITURE		
Items	Amount	Items	Amt.	Pr. ct.
Rent....) A	$240 00	Clothes.....................	$175 00	11.4
Nursing (	80 00	Food	432 00	27.9
Teaching) B	384 00	Taxes......................	112 00	7.2
Secretary (	60 00	Fuel	52 00	3.3
Wages) C	600 00	Repair	8 00	
Rent.. (	180 00	Insurance	54 00	}
		Amusement................	45 00	} 31.9
		Sickness	70 00	}
		Other purposes............	314 00	}
		Savings	282 00	18.3
Total	$1544 00	Total	$1544 00	100%

No. 14. Mail Carrier, Nine Persons

INCOME		EXPENDITURE		
Items	Amount	Items	Amt.	Pr. ct.
Man's salary @ $95 per month for 1 year....................	$1140 00	Food supplies @ $35 per month............./......	$420 00	26.9
Daughter's salary @ $20 per month for 1 year..........	240 00	Water and gas..	60 00	} 6.0
		Coal and fuel..............	35 00	}
Rent for 1 house @ $15 per mo..	180 00	Taxes......................	100 00	6.4
		Clothes	300 00	19.2
		Incidentals and repairs...	369 00	23.7
		Other things..............	169 00	10.9
		Savings	107 00	6.9
Total............	$1560 00	Total	$1560 00	100%

No. 15. Farmer, Eleven Persons

INCOME		EXPENDITURE	
Items	Amount	Items	Amount
Food..........................	$310 20	Food............................	$209 12
22 bu. peas @ $2.......... $44 00		15 bbls. flour $82 50	
8 gal. vinegar @ 40c..... 3 20		40 bu. corn.............. 41 62	
4 turkeys @ $1.25 .... 5 00		20 gal. syrup @ 35c.... 7 00	
400 lbs. butter @ 15c.... 60 00		330 lbs. bacon @ 11c ... 33 00	
150 gal. buttermilk @ 10c 15 00		Sugar.................... 16 00	
105 doz. eggs @ 20c 21 00		Pepper.................. 25	
225 chickens @ 20c 45 00		20 lbs. soda @ 5c........ 1 00	
Fruit 15 00		Spice.................... 20	
Watermelons.......... 17 00		2 sacks of salt @ 80c. .. 1 60	
175 gal. molasses........ 85 00		Lemon extract 30	
		2 gal. vinegar @ 40c.... 80	
Total $310 20		50 lbs. beef @ 10c...... 5 00	
Live stock	72 25	Lard.................... 6 25	
22 pigs @ $2...........,... $44 00		Ginger.................. 35	
1 cow..................... 28 25		Coffee................... 5 75	
		Grits.................... 3 75	
Total $72 25		Irish potatoes 3 73	
18 cords of wood @ $2.50. '.....	45 00		
3 tons of cotton seed @ $21....	63 00	Total $209 12	$203 90
38 bales of cotton @ $52	1976 00	Clothes........................	
		5 suits @ $15 .... $75 00	
		8 prs. shoes (Sunday)	
		@ $2.50................ 20 00	
		10 prs. shoes (everyday)	
		@ $2 .... 20 00	
		Dress goods (Sunday) 60 00	
		do (everyday) 25 50	
		Pins 15	
		Socks and stockings.. 3 25	
		Total $203 90	
		Rents and taxes..............	103 50
		Road tax $6 00	
		State tax 12 50	
		Interest 85 00	
		Total $103 50	
		Horse Food	22 70
		20 bu. oats @ 65c $13 00	
		2 bu. rye @ $1.25... ..... 2 50	
		6 sacks bran @ $1.20.... 7 20	
		Total..................$22 70	
		Medicine	66 90
		Doctor's bill (sickness) $35 75	
		Turpentine 75	
		Saltpetre 1 00	
		Alum 15	
		2 gal. whiskey @ $2.75.. 5 50	
		Patent medicine...... 5 50	
		To dentist............. 17 50	
		3 pkgs. home powder.. 75	
		Repairs	31 40
		1 watch................ $1 00	
		7 prs. shoes @ 45c 3 15	
		Shoeing horses........ 6 00	
		Mows 5 25	
		General shop work.... 10 75	
		On house dwelling 5 26	
		Total $31 40	
Total	$2466 45	Total	$637 52

No. 15 (Continued)

INCOME		EXPENDITURE	
Items	Amount	Items	Amount
Brought forward................	$2466 45	Brought forward.............	$637 52
		Personal service..............	56 60
		Field labor $50 50	
		27 hair cuts @ 20c..... 5 40	
		7 shaves @ 10c.... 70	
		Total $56 60	
		Luxuries	20 20
		60 sacks smoking to-	
		bacco.................. $3 00	
		1 doz. photos 2 25	
		½ box cigars.......... 1 00	
		Candy 1 50	
		4 doz. oranges @ 30c... 1 20	
		Jewelry 11 25	
		Total.................. $20 20	
		Farming implements..........	198 10
		Gear, harness, hoes.... $7 85	
		16 baskets @ 75c....... 12 00	
		1 disc harrow.......... 24 00	
		1 mower................ 75 00	
		1 two-horse wagon 65 00	
		2 axes @ 75c........... 1 50	
		3 buggy whips......... 1 50	
		Plows 11 25	
		Total.......... ....$198 10	
		Household purposes..........	31 50
		Furniture... .... $16 85	
		3 lamps 4 25	
		Soap.... .... 3 25	
		Matches.. 40	
		Lamp oil 6 75	
		Total.................. $31 50	
		Live animals.................	450 00
		2 mules @ $225..........$450 00	
		Seed trees.....	19 85
		20 fruit trees.......... $18 25	
		Garden seeds 45	
		Watermelon seed..... 50	
		Flower seed........... 65	
		Total.................. $19 85	
		Guano, 10 tons @ $20	200 00
		Improvements................	141 10
		Lightning rods... .....$110 00	
		28 gal. paint @ $1.10.... 30 80	
		3 qts. machine oil @ 10c 30	
		Total $141 10	
		Incidentals..................	109 55
		Church assessment... $15 00	
		School funds.......... 5 75	
		Railroad fare......... 5 55	
		Charity................ 1 50	
		Stamps and stationery 2 60	
		Books................ ... 12 75	
		Newspaper............ 6 50	
		Daughter's education. 60 00	
		Total $109 55	
		Paid on old debt..............	602 43
Total........................	$2466 45	Total	$2466 85

No. 15 (Continued)

INCOME		EXPENDITURE	
Items	Amount	Items	Amount
Brought forward...............	$2466 45	Brought forward...............	$2466 85
Balance.....................	40		
Total...........................	$2466 85		

RECAPITULATION

Items	Amt.	Pr. ct.		
Food..........................	$209 12	8.5		
Clothes.	203 90	8.2		
Rents and taxes............	103 50	4.1		
Savings (includ'g amount paid on old debt........	602 43	24.5		
Other purposes (including horse food, medicine, repairs, personal service, luxuries, farming implements, household purposes, live animals, guano, seed trees, and incidentals)	1347 90	54.7		
Total	$2466 85	100%	Total..........................	$2446 85
Income (yearly)	2466 45			
Balance.................	40			

No. 16. Farmer, Ten Persons

INCOME		EXPENDITURE		
Items	Amount	Items	Amt.	Pr. ct.
Father for one year............	$1000 00	Food @ $30 per month.....	$360 00	15.0
Two sons for one year..........	500 00	Clothes.....................	300 00	12.5
Income for rent of 600 acres @ $1.50 per acre.................	900 00	Farm labor @ $50 per mo..	600 00	
		Periodicals and papers....	5 00	
		Amusements	50 00	
		Railroad travels	100 00	45.0
		House insurance..........	75 00	
		Incidentals (house repairing, new furniture, etc.)...............	150 00	
		Money spent on wagons..	100 00	
		Taxes (State and county).	200 00	8.3
		Life insurance.............	150 00	19.2
		Family savings...........	310 00	
Total...........................	$2400 00	Total	$2400 00	100%

No. 17. Farmer, Six Persons

INCOME		EXPENDITURE		
Items	Amount	Items	Amt.	Pr. ct.
Cotton raised on farm, and fertilizer....................	$1837 50	For food	$200 00	30.37
Restaurant in town....	1825 00	Restaurant food	912 50	
		Fuel and lights	50 00	1.36
		Clothes...................	350 00	9.55
		Rent and taxes............	200 00	5.46
		Unaccounted for....▪......	1118 75	
		Amusements..............	50 00	
		Sickness.................	50 00	
		Helper in restaurant......	117 00	42.88
		For running house and keeping up rolling stock	175 00	
		Societies, church, lodges, and charity, papers, etc.	60 00	
		Savings	379 25	10.38
Total.......................	$3662 50	Total	$3662 50	100%

One indication of the strengthening of family life and sounder economic conditions is found in the proportion of students in a school like Atlanta University who are supported by their families. A search of the University records reveals the following approximate results:

ATLANTA UNIVERSITY	PROPORTION OF STUDENTS	
Date	Supported by family	Self-supported
1887–1888	42.3%	57.7%
1897–1898	51.4%	48.6%
1907–1908	68.8%	31.2%

Section 21. Rents. Two heavy items of expense for the poor are rent and food. The following tables show certain typical rents. In the country it is not possible to distinguish the rent from the wages in most cases:

Farmville, Va.

Families Owning and Renting Homes, by Number of Rooms to a Dwelling

TENURE	FAMILIES OCCUPYING DWELLINGS OF								
	One Room	Two Rooms	Three Rooms	Four Rooms	Five Rooms	Six Rooms	Seven Rooms	Eight or Nine Rooms	Total Families
Owners......................... ..	3	25	31	22	18	8	3	4	114
Renters	14	109	14	9	1	....	....	1	148
Total families...............	17	134	45	31	19	8	3	5	262

Of these 148 tenants, 15 rent from Negroes and 133 from whites. Several of the tenants own land. The rents paid by 83 typical tenants are reported in the following table, and from these the total annual rent charge of this community is estimated at about $5000.

Rents paid by Typical Families, by Number of Rooms to a Dwelling

MONTHLY RENT	FAMILIES OCCUPYING DWELLINGS OF						
	One Room	Two Rooms	Three Rooms	Four Rooms	Five or more Rooms	Total Families	Annual Rent Paid
Free	....	1	....	....	....	1	....
$1.00	2	....	....	....	....	2	$24
$1.25	1	....	....	....	....	1	15
$1.50	3	....	1	....	....	4	72
$2.00	1	9	1	....	....	11	264
$2.50	....	15	1	....	....	16	480
$2.75	....	1	....	....	....	1	33
$3.00	....	38	5	.....	....	43	1548
$3.50	....	....	1	3	....	4	168
Total	7	64	9	3	....	83	2604
Not reported	7	45	5	6	2	65	*2268

* Estimated.

Philadelphia. The inquiry of 1848 returned quite full statistics of rents paid by the Negroes. In the whole city at that date 4019 Negro families paid $199,665.46 in rent, or an average of $49.68 per family each year. Ten years earlier the average was $44.00 per family. Nothing better indicates the growth of the Negro population in numbers and power when we compare with this the figures of 1896 for one ward; in that year the Negroes of the Seventh Ward paid $25,699.50 each month in rent, or $308,034.00 a year, an average of $126.19 per annum for each family. This ward may have a somewhat higher proportion of renters than most other wards. At the lowest estimate, however, the Negroes of Philadelphia pay at least $1,250,000 in rent each year.[1]

A table of rents is as follows:[2]

Under $5 per month	490 families, or 21.9 per cent
$5 and under $10 per month	643 " or 28.7 "
$10 " $15 "	380 " or 17.0 "
$15 " $20 "	252 " or 11.3 "
$20 " $30 "	375 " or 17.0 "
$30 and over	95 " or 4.1 "

---

1 Not taking into account sub-rent repaid by sub-tenants; subtracting this and the sum would be, perhaps, $1,000,000—see infra, p. 291. That paid by single lodgers ought not, of course, to be subtracted as it has not been added in.—The Philadelphia Negro, p. 287. 2 Ibid., p. 290.

Families owning or renting their homes and living alone . ...738, or 31 per cent.
Families owning or renting their homes, who take lodgers cr sub-
renters ....937, or 38 per cent.
Families sub-renting under other families ....766, or 31 per cent.

Total individuals.......	7751	100 per cent.
Total families..	2441	
Individuals lodging with families........................... ...	1924	
Total individuals..	9675	

Families Owning and Renting Homes, by Number of Rooms to a Dwelling
Negroes of Xenia, Ohio

TENURE	FAMILIES OCCUPYING DWELLINGS OF												Total Families
	One Room	Two Rooms	Three Rooms	Four Rooms	Five Rooms	Six Rooms	Seven Rooms	Eight Rooms	Nine Rooms	Ten Rooms	Eleven Rooms	Twelve Rooms	
Owners	2	25	67	74	62	43	24	8	5	3	4	1	318
Renters	14	32	61	40	17	5	6	3	....	....	....	....	178
Not reported	....	....	2	3	....	....	....	....	....	....	....	....	5
Total.......	16	57	130	117	79	48	30	11	5	3	4	1	501

Rents Paid by Families, by Size of Dwelling
Negroes of Xenia, Ohio

MONTHLY RENT	FAMILIES OCCUPYING DWELLINGS OF								Total Families	Total Annual Rent Paid
	One Room	Two Rooms	Three Rooms	Four Rooms	Five Rooms	Six Rooms	Seven Rooms	Eight Rooms		
Free..................	2	....	1	1	1	....	....	....	5	....
$1.00	6	1	1	....	....	....	....	....	8	$96
1 50	1	1	...	....	....	....	....	....	2	36
1.75	1	....	1	....	....	....	....	....	2	42
2.00	1	10	3	....	....	....	....	....	14	336
2.25	....	1	....	....	....	....	....	....	1	27
2.50	1	10	4	1	....	....	....	....	16	480
2.75	1	1	2	....	....	....	....	....	4	132
3.00	1	4	20	10	....	....	....	....	35	1260
3.25	....	....	5	....	....	....	....	....	5	195
3.50	....	1	10	4	2	....	....	....	17	714
4.00	....	....	....	....	....	2	....	....	2	96
4.25	....	....	11	11	1	....	....	....	23	1173
4.50	....	2	1	...	....	....	....	....	3	162
5.00	....	1	1	1	....	1	2	1	7	420
5.50	....	....	1	8	4	1	....	....	14	924
6.00	....	....	....	....	....	1	....	....	1	72
6.50	....	....	....	4	6	....	1	....	11	858
7.00	....	....	....	....	2	....	2	....	4	336
7.50	...	....	....	....	....	....	1	....	1	90
8.00	....	....	....	....	..	....	....	1	1	96
8.33⅓	....	....	....	....	1	....	....	....	1	100
10.00	....	....	....	....	....	....	....	1	1	120
Total..............	14	32	61	40	17	5	6	3	178	$7765

Washington, D. C. The block of houses erected by the Washington Sanitary Improvement Company on O street, between North Capitol and First streets northwest, is rented to colored tenants. These houses contain three and four-room flats; each flat has a bathroom, with hot and cold water; a back yard with exit to an alley, and a cellar. The monthly rental (for eleven months) averages $3.18 per room. These flats have been continually occupied since their completion in 1902 by a good class of tenants, and losses as a result of vacancy or failure to pay rent have been insignificant.[1]

If we examine groups 14, 15, 16, 27, 42, 43, and 44, all occupied by colored people of the better class of laborers, except Group 43 occupied by whites, we find that there are 29 such dwellings, 13 of six rooms, 5 of five rooms, and 11 of four room. These houses are unpapered, some have no gas supply, and some have no supply of hot water; 5, Group 43, are in bad repair. The average cost of these dwellings was $1235.70 each; to which if we add 95 per cent for lot, grading, water connection, etc., we arrive at $2409.67 as the total investment. The average rental of these dwellings was $16.60; thus the gross returns on the investment may be set at 8.37 percent, practically identical with the gross returns from the better houses. It would appear, if these figures be approximately correct, that since the average rental of $16.60 for a four or five-room house, without gas, and often without hot water, furnishes only the usual return on the investment, to venture below that figure could be attempted in single brick dwellings only with the sacrifice of necessary hygienic space or sanitary equipment.[2]

Number of Dwellings	Cost per House	Sold for or Held at	Rent	Tenants
2	$2000	$3550	Owned	Colored
6	2600	....	$30.00	....
2	2000	....	$20.00 (4-room)	....
5	2000	....	$22.50 (corner)	....
....	....	....	$20.50 (inside)	....
5	2000	....	$20.50	....
19	1850	....	$25.00	....
1	1700	....	$20.00	....
2	1500	....	$20 50	....
4	1400	....	$16.50	....
7	1250	....	$16.30 (4-room)	....
2	1200	....	$14.00 (4-room)	....

Sternberg, pp. 82-83.

Other houses with Negro tenants rented as follows:

Number of Houses	Cost per House	Rooms contained	How Heated	Rent
6	$2500	4 and bath	Latrobe and range.	$20 50 / 21 00
3	2400	5 and bath	Latrobe and range.	20 50
4	2000	4 and bath	Stove and range....	15 50
7	2500	4 and bath	Latrobe and range.	15 50
8	2500	4 and bath	Latrobe and range.	15 50
5	1600	4 and bath	Latrobe and range.	15 50

Sternberg, p. 86.

Baltimore. There is no building of new dwellings for colored people in Baltimore; they occupy dwellings abandoned in the march to more fashion-

---

[1] Sternberg, p. 78.   [2] Sternberg, p. 184.

able or newer residence districts. In a section of Baltimore occupied chiefly by Negroes (Druid Hill avenue, and cross streets and alleys opening upon it) the rents were found to be comparatively high. On the larger streets, the 8, 10, or 12-room houses were occupied by very respectable and well-to-do colored people, who paid from $25.00 to $35.00 in rent. The "room to rent" sign was frequently seen, and it was thought there may be overcrowding here. In the minor streets and alleys, giving upon Druid Hill avenue, are very many houses of one type, all occupied by Negroes. These are two and three stories in height, all with basements and all two rooms deep. Occasionally such houses have running water in the kitchen, but usually there is only a hydrant in the yard. An eight-room house of this type (two rooms in the basement) rents for $15.00; a five-room house (one room in basement) rents for $12.00.

There is, also, an old type of four and five-room and cellar house to be seen in the alleys, most dark, dismal and unsanitary, which rents by the week at from $1.50 to $2.50; but even these houses seemed better structurally than the old frame houses on our main streets which bring from $12.00 to $15.00. The Baltimore house of this type is, however, so small and situated in such narrow alleys that area congestion must enter into the equation.

In general it may be said that in Baltimore, housing of the Negroes is a problem awaiting solution; the homes available for the least resourceful are unfit in many respects, and there is no building of new dwellings for colored people.[1]

Section 22. Food. Two scientific studies of Negro food have been made by the United States Department of Agriculture, from which the following examples are quoted:

Two Weeks' Food of an Alabama Field-hand Family of Four

KIND OF FOOD MATERIAL	Composition			Total Cost	Weight Used			
					Total Food Material	Nutrients		
	Protein	Fat	Carbo-hydrates			Protein	Fat	Carbo-hydrates
Animal Food	Per Cent	Per Cent	Per Cent		Grams	Grams	Grams	Grams
Bacon [1]	8.0	63.2		$3 16	17,915	1,433	11,322	....
Total animal food........				$3 16	17,915	1,433	11,322	....

Vegetable Food, Cereals, Sugar, Etc.

Corn Meal [2]	7.3	4.1	66.7	$1 26	21,005	1,533	861	14,010
Wheat Flour[2]	9.6	.8	78.3	58	19,050	1,829	152	14,916
Molasses [2]	1.3	.1	68.3	54	5,430	71	5	3,709
Total vege-table food.	....	....	....	$2 38	45,485	3,433	1,018	32,635
Total food.	....	....	....	$5 54	63,400	4,866	12,340	32,635

[1] Sternberg, p. 45.　　　[2] Average of analyses of similar Alabama foods.

Two Weeks' Food of a Negro Carpenter's Family of Six

KIND OF FOOD MATERIAL	Food Material	Nutrients			Cost
		Protein	Fats	Carbo-hydrates	
For Family, 14 days.	*Grams*	*Grams*	*Grams*	*Grams*	
Beef, veal, and mutton	2,495	392	328		$0 64
Pork, lard, etc.	5,655	269	4,433		90
Poultry	905	133	59		10
Eggs	595	79	55		10
Butter	990	12	816		44
Milk	57,140	2,000	2,400	2,971	5 04
Total animal food	67,780	2,885	8,091	2,971	$7 22
	Lbs.	*Lbs.*	*Lbs.*	*Lbs.*	
Beef, veal, and mutton	5.50	0.90	0.70		
Pork, lard, etc.	12.50	.60	9.80		
Poultry	2.00	.30	.10		
Eggs	1.30	.20	.10		
Butter	2.20		1.80		
Milk	126.00	4.40	5.30	6.50	
Total animal food	149.50	6.40	17.80	6.50	
	Grams	*Grams*	*Grams*	*Grams*	
Cereals, sugars, starches	38,050	2,838	619	29,713	$2 51
Fruits	975	12	12	235	18
Total vegetable food	39,025	2,850	631	29,948	$2 69
Total food	106,805	5,735	8,722	32,919	
	Lbs.	*Lbs.*	*Lbs.*	*Lbs.*	
Cereals, sugars, starches	83.90	6.30	1.40	65.50	
Fruits	2.20			.50	
Total vegetable food	86.10	6.30	1.40	66.00	
Total food	235.60	12.70	19.20	72.50	$9 91

Part 4. The Family Group

Section 23. Differentiation of Classes. Few modern groups show a greater internal differentiation of social conditions than the Negro American, and the failure to realize this is the cause of much confusion. In looking for differentiation from the past in Africa and slavery, few persons realize that this involves extreme differentiation in the present. The forward movement of a social group is not the compact march of an army, where the distance covered is practically the same for all, but is rather the straggling of a crowd, where some of whom hasten, some linger, some turn back; some reach far-off goals before others even start, and yet the crowd moves on. The measure of the advancement of such a throng is a question at once nice and indefinite. Measured by the rear guard there may be no perceptible advance. Measured by the advance guard the transformation may be miraculous. Yet neither of these are reasonable measurements, but rather the point which one might call the center of gravity of the mass is the true measuring point, and the determination of this point in the absence of exact measurements may be for a long time a matter of opinion rather than proof. So with the Negro American. It is easy to prove the degradation of thousands of Negroes on the back plantations of Mississippi and the alleys of Washington; it is just as easy to prove the accomplishments of the graduates of Atlanta University, or the members of St. Thomas Church, Philadelphia. The point is where, between these manifest extremes, lies today the cultural center of gravity of the race. It is begging and obscuring this question to harp on ignorance and crime among Negroes as though these were unexpected; or to laud exceptional accomplishments as though it was typical. The real crucial question is: What point has the mass of the race reached which can be justly looked upon as the average accomplishment of the group?

The exact location of this point is impossible to locate beyond doubt. Yet certain facts about it are certain: it is moving forward rapidly; this is proven by the decrease of illiteracy and the increase of property holding, both on such a scale, covering so long a period of years as to be incontrovertible evidence.

To illustrate this differentiation there follow four sections on the Negro country families, the social life of the country, the Negro Northern city home, and a study of thirteen select homes representing mostly the upper class of Negroes.

Section 24. The Negro Families of Dougherty County, Georgia.

The plantations of Dougherty in slavery days were not so imposing as those of Virginia. The Big House was smaller and one-storied, and the slave cabins set closer to it. Today the laborers' cabins are in form and disposition the same as in slavery days. They are sprinkled in little groups all over the land clustering about some dilapidated Big House where the head-tenant or agent lives. Out of fifteen hundred homes of Negroes only fifteen have five or more rooms; the mass live in one or two-room homes. The one-room cabin is painfully frequent— now standing in the shadow of the Big House, now staring at the dusty road, now rising dark and sombre amid the green of the cotton-fields. Rough-boarded, old and bare, it is neither plastered nor ceiled, and light and ventilation comes from the single door and perhaps a square hole in the wall. Within is a fireplace, black and smoky, unsteady with age; a bed or two, high, dark and fat; a table, a wooden chest and chairs or stools. On the wall is a stray showbill or a newspaper for decoration.

It is not simply in the tenement abominations of cities like New York that the world's flesh is crowded and jammed together, sometimes twenty-two persons to every ten rooms; here in Dougherty county there are often over twenty-five persons to every ten rooms of house accommodation. To be sure, the rooms are large—fifteen to twenty-five feet square. And there is the fresh air and sunshine of all outdoors to take refuge in. Still I met one family of eleven eating and sleeping in one room, and thirty families of eight or more. Why should there be such wretched tenements in the Black Belt? Timber is rotting in the forest, land is running to waste and labor is literally cheaper than dirt. Over nine-tenths of the cabins belong to the landlords yet nearly all of them let the quarters stand and rot in rude carelessness. Why? First, because long custom born in slavery days, has assigned this sort of house to Negroes. If the landlord should hire white men he would not hesitate to erect cosy three-room cottages such as cluster around the Carolina cotton-mills. Small wonder that the substitution of white for Negro labor is often profitable, since the white being better paid and better cared for often responds by doing better work. Again, the Negroes themselves, as a mass, do not demand better homes; those who do, buy land and build their own homes, roomy and neat. But the rest can scarcely demand what they have seldom thought of. As their fathers lived so they live, and the standard of the slave still lowers the standard of the quasi-freeman. In the third place, the landlords fail to see that in an increasingly large number of cases it would be a distinctly good investment to raise the standard of living among the black laborers; that a man who demands three rooms and fifty cents a day may in the end be much cheaper than a listless, discouraged toiler herding in one room at thirty cents a day. Lastly, amid such conditions of life there is little to inspire the laborer to become a better farmer. If he is ambitious, he moves to town or tries other kinds of labor; as a tenant-farmer his outlook in the majority of cases is hopeless, and following it as a makeshift or in grim necessity, he takes its returns in shelter, meat and bread, without query or protest.

That we may see more clearly the working out of these social forces, let us look within the home and scan more nearly the family that lives there. The families are large and small: you will find many families with hosts of babies, and many young couples, but few families with half-grown boys and girls. The whole tendency of the labor system is to separate the family group—the house is too small for them, the young people go to town or hire out on a neighboring farm. Thus single, lone persons are left here and there. Away down at the edge of the woods will live some grizzle-haired black man, digging wearily in the earth for his last crust; or a swarthy fat auntie, supported in comfort by an absent daughter, or an old couple living half by charity and half by odd jobs.

The boys and girls cannot afford to marry early, nor until most of the men are over twenty-five and the girls over twenty. There is little or no actual prostitution among these people and most of the families are honest, decent people, with a fairly good standard of family morals. Nevertheless the influence of the past is plain in customs of easy marriage and easy separation. In the old days Sam "took up" with Mary by leave of his master. No ceremony was necessary, and in the busy life of the great plantations of the Black Belt it was usually dispensed with. If the master needed Sam on another plantation, or was minded to sell him, Sam's married life with Mary was unceremoniously ended, and just as unceremoniously begun with Jane or Matilda elsewhere.

This widespread custom of two centuries has not disappeared in forty years. Between three and four per cent of the families are to-day separated, others have been and are remarried usually without the trouble of a divorce, while others will separate in the future. Here is the plague spot of the Negro's social relations, and when this inherited low standard of family life happens to be in the keeping of lustful whites, as it sometimes is, the result is bad indeed.

Section 25. The Social Life of the Country. A sketch of the social life of Negroes in the rural districts of the South is almost like an essay on the snakes in Ireland: it is the lack of social life that tends to depopulate the rural black belt and does draw off its best blood.

There are, however, many occasions of meeting and intercourse which may be set down thus in the order of their importance.

1. *The Saturday Visit to Town.* Practically throughout the rural South the black laborers and farmers come to town on Saturday. This is more than an occasion of marketing; it is a time of holiday, and is spent in chatting and loafing, with some liquor drinking. To thousands this forms the one glimpse of the larger world, and the merchants of many towns, indeed the towns themselves depend on the weekly pilgrimage. It reduces the working week of the rural South practically to five days save in very busy times.

2. *The Sunday Church Service.* "The Negro Church is the only social institution of the Negroes which started in the African forest and survived slavery; under the leadership of priest or medicine-man, afterward the Christian pastor, the Church preserved in itself the remnants of African tribal life and became after emancipation the center of Negro social life. So that today the Negro population of the United States is virtually divided into church congregations which are the real units of race life."[1] The typical Negro country church stands at some cross-roads and holds services once or twice a month. These meetings are great reunions and are the occasions of feasting, country gossip and preaching. The people gather from 9 a. m. to 1 p. m., and remain usually till late in the afternoon. Christenings and baptizing take place at this time.

3. *"The Christmas."* The week between Christmas and New Year's, including both days, is the great time of social rejoicing among country Negroes. Historically it was the time when the master gave his

---

[1] Atlanta University Publications, No. 3.

slaves time and license. Today it is the time when the serf receives his annual accounting with his landlord and collects his small balance due in cash. This he often spends in carousing and drinking, to pay for the hard year's work. Many honest, hard-working sober men get drunk religiously and regularly every Christmas. There are always many parties, church entertainments and excursions, together with fights and quarrels.

Later years have of course brought improvement. A resident of New Orleans writes: "Possibly there is less idleness at Christmas in Louisiana at present than formerly. My impression is that the influence of our better ministers and graduates or students from our higher institutions of learning is gradually modifying the character of the festivities and conduct of the people at the Christmas season."

4. *The "Frolic."* The occasional party given at the cabin is often called "the frolic"; it varies all the way from a pleasant little gathering with games and feasting as portrayed by Dunbar, to a scene of wild drinking and debauchery as is often the case in lumber camps.

5. *The Wedding and the Funeral.* The only distinctly family festivity is the wedding. This is celebrated with varying emphasis, being a ceremony only a generation old in the country districts. In the newer Southwest it seems to be more of a general occasion of rejoicing. A correspondent says:

The two things that interrupt our community life more than anything else in the way of home duties are the weddings and funerals, both of which seem to give the people more actual happiness and joy than anything they enter into during the whole year, but I suppose these hardly come under the head of social life. We have in our community a good many of the quiltings which appeal to the hearts of the women and during the winter is our regular form of festivities for them. This is an all-day affair with a luncheon served at midday, and sometimes we hear of as many as three or four in a single week.

6. *The Revival.* Connected with the church services comes the revival. This is a recruiting of church membership, and usually takes place in the fall after the crops are "laid by." It consists of protracted nightly meetings and brings together large numbers.

7. *School-closing.* Where the country schools are good and regular, as in Texas, there is considerable social life connected with the closing of schools; often there are examinations on this day with a free spread and an "exhibition" at night which attract large numbers.

8. *The Circus,* which visits the county-seat once or twice a year, is largely attended. So much so that such exhibitions are taxed as high as $500 for each county.

9. *Secret Societies.* In parts of Virginia and Georgia and some other States the benevolent societies, with their halls, are fast becoming the chief centers of the rural Negroes' social life. The annual installations of officers are the great social events of the year.

10. *Miscellaneous.* Besides the occasions mentioned there are summer excursions by train which take those who can get to town, the Methodist Conference and Baptist Convention which attract many to town, and a very few annual holidays like Emancipation Day, January 1st, which is often celebrated by a speech from some visiting celebrity. There are also some local celebrations, like those due to the influence of the Catholic Mardi Gras in Louisiana.

Section 26. The Negro Family in New York. (Miss Mary W. Ovington in Charities, October 7, 1905. Reprinted by permission.)

The great majority of the Negroes of New York live in poverty. Sixty-two per cent of the men, according to the last census, are in domestic and personal services, and in large stores and factories they do the work of porter or general utility man, not the better paid tasks. Only a few practice a trade. The women have not been able in any numbers to gain entrance to the factory or the shop. The result is a group of people receiving a low wage, and the character of their homes must be largely determined by their economic position.

Like all the New York poor the Negro lives in a tenement. The lower East side, famed for its overcrowding, does not know him. His quarters are West, but there he finds conditions that are often quite as bad as those among the Italians or the Jews. In the most thickly segregated Negro section, that between West Fifty-ninth and West Sixth-fourth streets and Tenth and West End avenues, the tenements are of the old double-decker and dumbbell types, with no thorough ventilation and with twenty and twenty-two families to a house. The air-shafts in these tenements are so small as to be only "culture tubes" except on the top story, where the rooms gain something of air and light. In the lower part of town, about the thirties, we still find a number of rear tenements occupied by the colored race. The sunlight enters these houses, but they are very old, impossible to keep clean, and dangerous because of their distance from the open street. Again still further south, about Cornelia street, the race lives in dilapidated former dwelling-houses. These West Side districts have little of the picturesqueness of the lower East Side, and have been more or less neglected by those interested in the moral and civil welfare of the community.

Rents are high for everyone in New York, but the Negroes pay more and get less for their money than any other tenants. Every week in the warm weather hundreds of them come from the South. They must find shelter, and the places that they may rent are few and those not tenements of the better sort. The many attractive and healthful houses that have been built since the creation of the Tenement House Department are not open to them. They are confined to certain localities, and usually to only a few houses in each block. Forced to crowd into small and uncomfortable rooms, their opportunities for making a home are much restricted.

Like the dweller on the East Side, the Negro knows enough to get out of his house and into the fresh air when he can. In the summer the streets, while not so filled with people as in the neighborhood about Rivington and Delancey streets, are well crowded. The roofs, too, offer breathing-places. Day as well as night many men and women are to be seen about, especially in the vicinity of the Sixties. The presence of men in the daytime gives an appearance of idleness among the population that is not as great as it seems, as about fifty per cent of the colored men of this city are engaged at jobs that give them leisure when other people are at their tasks.

Study closely the tenants in any of these streets and you will find every grade of social life. Their difficulty in procuring a place to live compels the colored people to dwell good and bad tögether. Ten families of pure and upright lives may be forced to rent rooms in a house where there are other ten families who are rough and noisy, often immoral. This is true of all over-crowded districts, but it is especially true in the Negro quarters; for the land-lord of a colored tenement rarely makes any attempt to discriminate among his applicants, but takes in anyone who will pay his rent. Complaints against objectionable tenants are unheeded, and the mother and father in the respect-able home have the difficult problem of rearing children in a few rooms from which there is no escape, save to the stairway and street where undesirable companions are numerous. Lines need to be drawn very sharply by such parents, and factions arise among the children that are the despair of the club worker, who gathers in her boys and girls believing that propinquity makes a harmonious group.

It is impossible to give an idea of the home of the Negro in New York without touching upon his relations with the rest of the city's population. He comes to make his home among a people who are foreign to him. He is not, to any appreciable extent, with the descendants of the men who years ago fought for his freedom; he speaks mournfully of wishing that he might take his chances with the American, but he is living among many races, the most of whom have but lately found their way to this country and are without tradition of friendliness. He has to meet the Irish, the German, the Hebrew, the Italian, the Slav. These maintain varying attitudes of animosity and friendliness. The Irish is the most boisterously aggressive, though when once the Irishman really knows the Negro he can be a very good comrade. New York seems to demand that all the laborers who come to her must endure a period of abuse and ridicule; there must be street fights and biting nick-names and the refusal to work with the detested race. All this the Negro must endure, as other races have endured before him, but his case is an exag-gerated one. There are those who wish to deny him opportunity because they believe in his inherent and eternal inferiority. This minority, for I believe it to be a minority, can prevent his obtaining a position. For where the majority of men and women will consent to have a Negro work with them, a strong caste sentiment on the part of a few will prevail against this friendly feeling which, after all, is little more than indifference.

While the Negro is an able and respected member in some of the labor unions, and while his children occasionally have playmates among the boys and girls of other races in the schools, he does not usually see the white work-ingman at his best. Too often white and colored meet only in the saloon of a low type or in the rough jostle of the street. This is a misfortune for a peo-ple who are in the process of creating a social life. To see the best among those of the same economic position as themselves would be a help and profit to them.

The contact that the colored people have with the monied people of the white race is varied. In the domestic service Negro men and women often have the opportunity to live in good and honorable homes, but it is not always so; and from people whom they are taught to regard as belonging to the upper class they learn low standards of married life. Those who are not in domestic service see from their tenement streets much that is base in the dominant race. There must be a world of irony in the heart of the seeing Negro who reads in the papers the lurid descriptions of his own crime, while he lives in the Tenderloin district and looks out upon its life. He sees the daily danger attending the attractive women of his own and other races, and he sees temptation offered where he should see high ideals. The Negro is imitative, and all this must and does have an effect upon his own home.

Yet, despite these handicaps, there is much of good and honorable living in the homes of the race. Choosing at random fifty families living in the most demoralizing neighborhood of New York, I found that seventy per cent of the mothers are known to be moral by those charitable workers who for many years had been in close touch with them. These people live a life apart from the roughness about them, but close to their church and their children. Such loose unthinking statements are made regarding the Negro and his morality that no better service could be done the race than to show us all of his homes, just as they come. For, where one would be revolting, the next would carry with it so much of worthy relationship between man and wife and parents and children that the first might be forgotten. And yet, I doubt if this would be so; for modesty like charity does not vaunt itself, and the loud colored woman who parades the streets counts for more in the minds of most of us than a dozen of the quiet women of her race who pass by without our noticing them. But for those who wish to see the whole and not merely the part that calls for censure, the majority of Negro homes, like the majority of homes of all working people, are places where good and honest men and women are striving, often against great odds, to bring up their children to lead moral and useful lives.

There is in New York, in proportion to the population, a fairly large class of professional colored men and women; and also a class of business men of some means. The homes of these do not differ essentially from the homes of all good Americans in the city. There is nothing by which to especially characterize them. Their hospitality is very pleasant and their family life is very harmonious and sweet. The young women are, perhaps, brought up in more sheltered fashion than those of the white race. Very much emphasis is laid upon education, both for the boy and for the girl. The music-loving character of the race is shown in these homes, as indeed it is in all colored households; but here we have much ability, for there are among the race in New York musicians of no mean gifts. These homes are too little known among the people of the city. Occasionally some colored high-school girl or college student will show her classmate her family circle, and thus a few in our population learn something of the wholesome life of a class of Negroes of whom one Southern woman told me that she knew less than she did of the Esquimaux. Perhaps there has never before been a race concerning which so many opinions have been written and yet of whose best life we are so ignorant. If "highest is the measure of the man," we know the highest of the New York Negro when we know the homes of the best of his race. And while from the South there comes an idle, criminal class, the industrious and intelligent come as well, and their homes are increasing and are an honor to the commonwealth.

Section 27. A Study of Thirteen Families. To illustrate this emergence of better classes, a careful description of thirteen Negro families follows. Number one represents one of the lowest type of a country family and number seven a common type of city family. The other eleven are of the higher types of Negro families. The incomes are given by the families themselves and are probably exaggerated in some cases.

No. 1. *A country family living in two rooms, with an income of $700 per year.* The whole family is very ignorant and consists of twelve members. None have had the advantage of school. A few of the younger children can write their names. No books or papers can be seen in the house.

The parents are religious fanatics; they believe in praying night and morning. The father can be heard praying on a still night for two miles. The elder boys are rough characters. They get drunk and fight, especially at church. The older girls are not wholesome characters; the two eldest have had illegitimate children, one by a white man and the other by a Negro; both children were given to relatives. The entire family is given to petty thefts, and is especially high-tempered. They do not get along with the neighbors, but tattle and tell lies and carry news to white people and Negroes.

The family consists of father, age 62 years; mother, age 61 years; six sons, ages respectively 28, 26, 22, 20, 14 and 11 years; and four daughters, ages respectively 24, 18, 16 and 8 years.

The entire family work in the field. The mother and one of the daughters leave each day in time to cook dinner. They work from sunrise or earlier until twelve, and from one until dark. The heavy farming work is done by the men and boys, the light work by the girls. The girls work from February to August and from September to December. The men and boys work the year round. When there is no work to be done on the farm, they have to report to the landlord for something to do. When it rains the bell taps and all must report at the barns to see what "Cap" wants done. For this kind of service they get no pay. The house is near the pasture and is partly surrounded with woods. The landlord's house is 300 yards away. The yard is very small, with weeds growing in the summertime into the window on the back side. The water is brought from a spring in the pasture. The house is dirty within. The bed-clothes are dingy and the doors are black with dirt. They have no bathing facilities. All bathe in a washpan, about three-quarts size, once a week. A peculiar odor is prevalent in spring and summer. They dress in gaudy colors. Their clothes are fairly good, but not well made and do not fit properly. In fact, they do not know how to wear what they have and are very hard on clothes. Only a low class of people visit them. Any decent person visiting there is branded as bad. Four of the family are members of the Baptist church. The two older daughters were members but were expelled on account of conduct. The only property is one buggy, an organ and twenty-five chickens.

Both sides are of African descent. They are very black, and it is said that their forefathers were all similarly high-tempered and immoral. Both sides of the family were in slavery, and after the war were held in peonage twenty-two years. They are much different from other colored people around in the structure of head and mouth, and in general appearance. They have three meals: breakfast before sunrise, of biscuits, pork, syrup and coffee; dinner at noon, of cornbread, syrup and pork; supper after dark, of cornbread or biscuits, and syrup. The table is too small to accommodate the entire family—seven by three feet. Some take their meals in their hands—children especially—and sit in a chair and sometimes in the door. Some of the time the food is served from the table and at other times from the cooking vessels. The dishes are common china, with some tin plates and cups. There is no tablecloth. There are two benches the length of the table on each side of the table.

No. 2. *A country family living in three rooms, with an income of $625 per year.* This family consists of eleven persons: a man and his wife and nine children; six girls and three boys. The man and his wife are both 43 years old. The oldest child is a girl of 19, the next a girl of 17, then a girl of 16, a girl of 15, a girl of 13, a boy of 11, a boy of 9, a boy of 6, and the baby, a girl of 3 years old. The people work a farm; they have never done anything else. The father is a man small in stature, about medium height, slender, with a dark brown skin, crinkly black hair and thick black mustache. He is a genial, cheerful man, always full of fun. He is very intelligent and business-like, ambitious and eager for knowledge. He is the main stay of the whole family. The mother is about medium height and corpulent. She is lighter brown than her husband, with soft and once abundant black hair. She is kind and motherly, but rather slow and sleepy; in fact, much given to deep trance-like spells of sleeping. She oversees the housework. The oldest daughter is below the medium height, with dark-brown skin and soft black hair. She is plump and vivacious, and rather restless and fidgety. She does not work much in the field, but sews and helps about the house. The next girl is about medium height, small but solid, a little lighter brown than the first, with crinkly black hair. She is strong and full of life, quick to make friends, kind-hearted, frank and winning. She does harder work in the field than any of the others. The next girl is below the medium height, about the same shade of brown, with very crinkly hair; she is somewhat inclined to be "airish" but she is lively and good-natured. She also works in the field. Next comes her inseparable companion, the girl of 15. She is of medium height and plump. She has the good looks of the family. She is the same shade of brown, with soft black hair. She has a very good opinion of herself and is somewhat high-tempered. She works in the field at the busiest season, but usually stays in the house. The girl of 13 is the scapegoat of the family. She is far below the medium height, very plump, a lighter brown than any of the others, with very crinkly black hair. She is very quiet and seldom grumbles. When she speaks she usually says something worth while. She does most of the things which the others refuse to do. She is housemaid, nurse and errand-girl. The oldest boy is about the size of the usual eleven-year-old boy. He is dark brown, with crinkly black hair; he is decidedly jolly and boyish. The next boy is his boon companion; he is nearly as large and has the same general appearance and disposition; they are often mistaken for twins. The oldest boy is his father's chief dependence in the field. He can plough as well as any man. The other one does lighter field work. The last boy is a fat child of six, dark brown, with soft black hair, and an unusually large and well-shaped head. He is very sly and quiet, but when drawn out shows great intelligence. He romps and plays all day with his baby sister. She is small, dark brown, with crinkly reddish hair. She is very droll and demure, and is well-spoiled by the whole family.

The whole family dress very simply. The girls all have calico working dresses, and the boys have calico home-made jackets and breeches. Each of the boys has a suit and cap for Sunday wear. The girls have neat, inexpensive dresses for Sunday wear. The older girls keep themselves neat and clean, but the younger members are never clean except on Sundays. The mother is not very tidy. Very few colored people live in the part of the country where these people live, and the few who live near are related to them. They often go visiting their people and receive visits from them in turn. They go to church every Sunday, unless the weather is very bad. The father, the mother and the three oldest girls belong to secret orders. There are none of the family absent except a boy who died. He came in between the boy of nine and the boy of six.

They own 165 acres of land, the house in which they live, two mules, two cows and four hogs. The family have lived in this place for sixteen years. Before that they lived about five miles away. The mother came from a family of twelve children, seven boys and five girls. All the boys are dead except one, who lives out West. Four of the girls are living, all in the same part of the country. The other is dead. The father came from a family of eight children, five boys and three girls. One of the boys is dead; all the others live in the country around. Two of the girls live near by and the other is in Milledgeville in the insane asylum. There is no school near for the children to attend.

This family has three meals every day. The food is well cooked, and they have very nice dishes but no silver. During the working season they have breakfast at 6 o'clock, dinner at 12 o'clock and supper at 6:30. During the season of rest and on Sundays they have breakfast at 7 o'clock, dinner between one and two o'clock and supper at 7:30. They raise nearly all their food. In summer they have for breakfast wheat bread and butter, milk, syrup and salt pork, varied occasionally by beef, chicken and eggs. For dinner they have vegetables, cornbread, milk, and sometimes soup and some kind of dessert. For supper they have wheat bread, butter, syrup, milk, and salt pork. In winter the breakfasts are about the same, but they have for dinner such things as peas and sweet potatoes, varied with beef and chicken. Dried fruit also plays an important part. They have tablecloths, but no napkins. They always sit at the table, and the younger ones have to wait until the older ones eat.

No. 3. *A country family living in 7 rooms with an income of $650 per year.* The family consists of six persons: the parents, two boys and two girls. The father is yellow, of moderate build—five feet four inches—weighs 156 pounds, and is 47 years of age. He has been engaged in farming since he was 19 years of age. He has a common-school education, chews tobacco but uses no intoxicants, and has good health. The mother is light brown in complexion and is rather large in build; she is 45 years of age and was born and reared in the country. She has part of a high-school education, and taught school previous to marriage. The eldest boy is 20 years old; he is five feet four inches in height, of good build, weighs 140 pounds, and has lived in the country all his life; he has a high-school education, and is still in school. The youngest boy is 19 years of age, height five feet and six inches. He is now in school and is a fairly good student; he has a high-school education. The eldest girl is 17 years of age, weighs 140 pounds; height five feet and four and a half inches, and has almost completed a high-school course. The youngest girl is 11 years old, four feet in height, and has almost completed a grammar-school course; she has some ability in instrumental music. The father supervises the farm, prepares the soil, plants the crop in the spring and during the summer superintends the working of the farm, the crop-gathering in the autumn and marketing the crop, and fertilizing the soil during winter. Also he cares for the live stock, markets $2.00 worth of wood a week, and the dairy and the poultry products ($2.00 a week). The mother does about half of the family cooking (that is, the mother and girls do the cooking by turns), sews and makes the working garments of the whole family, and all the garments of herself and girls; she cares for the poultry, cultivates the garden and supervises the garden, dairy and poultry products to be marketed; also she preserves and cans fruits. The boys prepare the fuel for family cooking and the wood for market, and assist in the farm work; also in crop-gathering during September. The girls do half of the family cooking (by turns), all of the family washing, and clean the house; and they assist some in the farm work during summer and autumn, also in gathering. The rising hour is 5:30 a. m., breakfast at 6:30. Work period from 7 to 12 o'clock; dinner at 12 m.; work hours 2 to 6 o'clock p. m., supper at 7 p. m. At 7:30 the family, except the girls who remain for dining-room duties, retire to the sitting-room for reading, study, conversation, writing, etc.; the girls join the other members of the family in the sitting-room at 8 o'clock. National holidays and family birthdays are the days of special festivity, also the first fifteen days of August, when cropmaking is over—generally called the summer lay-by. There is usually company on Sunday. The Sunday routine for the family is: Breakfast, 8:30 a. m.; bath hour, 9 to 9:30 a. m.; Sunday-school, 9:45 to 11 a. m.; church services, 11 a. m. to 1 p. m. (church three-quarters of a mile distant); dinner, 2 p. m.; company, 3 to 5 p. m.; supper, 7 p. m.; song practice, 8 p. m.; retire at 9:30. The dress of the family is as moderate as possible; the mother being a seamstress reduces the cost to a low figure. Fifty dollars ($50) is the amount which the boys find themselves together provided with in order to be clothed, and the amount for the two girls is thirty dollars (30); forty dollars clothes the parents.

The family owns $2200 worth of real estate, the estate has only been of present number of acres for six years; the original farm as owned by the father before marriage was thirty acres; six years ago at the death of the father's father he bought his father's farm of sixty acres, which adjoins his own. The land value was not as great then as now, so he profited quite a deal. At the same time, at the death of the mother's mother, her father's estate of eighty acres was sold and her realizations from the land was also used in the aforesaid transaction. The live stock value (one horse and four head of cattle) is $300; vehicles, $125; house furnishings and other incidentals, $350. So the whole value of the farm plant is approximately $3000. The estates of the grandparents were acquired by each about 1880, and was kept intact by each until their death, when they were disposed of at auction and proceeds went to their children.

At the meals the following food is used at different times: Breakfast, 6:30 a. m., bacon, ham, steak, pork, eggs, butter, hash, chicken, rabbit, liver, sausage, squirrel, etc., fish, mutton, bread-pancakes, muffins, eggbreads, rice, hominy, grits, buckwheat cakes and oatmeal. Fruits, preserves, apples, peaches, strawberries, potatoes, pears, bananas, syrup, etc. Drink: Postum and milk. Dinner, 12:00 m., Cabbage, collards, salad, peas, turnips, onions, celery, lettuce, radish, beets, soups, spinach, thyme, tomatoes, cucumbers, beans, squashes, ham, fish, beef, pork, rabbit, opossum, potatoes, chicken, partridge, duck, geese, turkey, apples, peaches, berries, lemon pies and drinks, egg custards, jams and jellies, puddings. Supper, 7:30 p. m., Postum, milk, chocolate, tea, etc. Apples, peaches, pumpkins, grapes, strawberries, blackberries, etc. Ham, eggs, chicken, rice, macaroni, cheese. Gelatine, cream, pudding, cakes, candies. Meals are cooked and served by the mother and daughters.

No. 4. *A country family occupying 9 rooms, with an income of $2500 per year.* The eleven members of this family are especially intelligent. They consist of mother and father, ages 50 and 60 years respectively, two daughters, ages 15 and 19 years, and seven boys, ages 29, 27, 25, 23, 21, 11 and 8, respectively. The deceased members of the family are two sons and two daughters; all died soon after birth. The whole family is peaceful and agreeable. The father is head, and what he says is law. The entire family is subjected to a strict discipline. The boys are allowed to visit, but they must return by sundown; if late, an excuse must be given beforehand. The girls do not leave home unless accompanied by some male member of the family. Every one on Sunday must go to Sunday-school, but there is no family prayer. No swearing is allowed. All the members of the family work on the farm excepting the mother. The boys and father do all the cutting, plowing, sometimes hoeing, repair work, and ditching, etc. The girls do the light work, such as hoeing, picking cotton, housework in general, and laundering. The mother stays at home, cooks, and looks after the children.. From July 28th to August 24th they do nothing. This is called "laying-by time." From August 24th to December 1st they gather cotton, corn, potatoes, etc. From December 1st to January 15th they do practically nothing except keep fires and hunt.

This family is situated in a peaceful community composed of white and colored people. About two hundred yards from the house on one side are woods. The house is built on a high spot with a splendid drainage. The entire yard is filled with flowers and shade trees. The barns are a convenient distance from the main building, and there is an orchard. The best people of the community visit these people, and some white people from town and the neighborhood. Everything about this house is neat and clean. Their clothes are plain and simple and well cared for. The father is a member of the Masonic order. All are members of C. M. E. Church and of all its societies. The property owned consists of 175 acres of land, 5 mules, 5 milk cows, 7 heads of cattle, 25 hogs and pigs, 3 wagons, 2 buggies, 1 syrup mill, 1 disc harrow, 1 mower and rake, and other tools; there are also 150 chickens, 8 turkeys and 12 guineas.

On the father's mother's side the descent is direct from Africa, without any mixing of blood; on the father's father's side there has been an intermingling of white blood somewhere which makes the father a shade between black and light brown, or a ginger-cake color. On the mother's side the grandfather was a white man and her father was yellow. The mother's mother had a strain of Indian blood in her, making her dark red. This makes the mother yellow. Both sides were in slavery except the mother's grandfather. Breakfast is usually about or before sunrise, with coffee, milk, butter, syrup, meat, grits or rice, chicken or beef on Sunday mornings and biscuits and eggs. Dinner comes at 12 o'clock, with boiled vegetables, cornbread, pies, syrup, milk, butter, biscuits, potatoes, etc., are served. Supper is a little after sundown, with cornbread syrup, meat, milk, butter, and cold vegetables from dinner. Of course these meals vary on different occasions, especially when company is present and on Sundays. All the members of the family assemble around one large table and the father and mother serve the food, which is put on the table before the meal. The knives, forks and spoons are made of plated silver. The dishes are china, plain, with glasses for milk and water.

No. 5. *A country family living in 8 rooms, with an income of $2000 per year.* The family which occupies this house consists of four brothers, a wife of the oldest of the brothers and his child, a boy two years of age. The oldest brother is twenty-five years of age, and tends the farm. He is a reddish-hued mulatto. The next brother; a man of twenty-three, is the life of the family. He is short and reddish, with sandy hair. The next brother, a man of twenty, is like his oldest brother. The youngest brother, of seventeen, is darker than the rest, and has straight black hair. The mother and father are both dead; they died some time ago—the mother in Augusta, the old family home, the father after they had moved to the present quarters to better family conditions. The whole family now consists of two sisters, married, living in Augusta, one brother, married, in New York city, two brothers in Atlanta, and the four brothers at home. The brother of twenty-three is the center of home life. It is he who sells the cotton, sees after all expenses, and pays the others what they have made. He does not eat at home, he runs the only down-town restaurant in the business district of a near-by town. He and his youngest brother rise about five o'clock on mornings and go to town, two miles distant, to open up and start business. There he looks after the buying of provisions, and sees that the orders are filled. The youngest brother runs errands; the other two stay at home and supervise the farm, and attend to all outdoor domestic work—sweeping, cleaning, milking, and the like. The wife cooks at home, churns, makes beds, washes, patches and scrubs. Company from town is entertained with the greatest hospitality, including buggy rides. The whole family goes to church on the second and fourth Sundays of every month. They belong to two secret orders, which meet every second and fourth Tuesday and every second and fourth Thursday nights. The farm is eighty acres in extent and is owned by the family. When dressed-up the woman wears gay-colored dresses, ordinary shoes and fancy country hats, with her hair tied with blue and yellow ribbon. All the brothers wear on Sundays red shoes, striped trousers, black coats, gay socks, and colored shirts with collars attached. The main foods are syrup, potatoes, milk and butter. As much cornbread is eaten as wheat bread, and vegetables in season. Fish comes in whenever they are caught in the nearby creek or are brought from town. Cured meat is eaten two meals a day, together with chicken and eggs. There are three meals per day: breakfast at five in the morning, dinner at twelve and supper at five. At breakfast they have corn cakes, biscuit, fried meat, coffee, and perhaps eggs. The food is served in plain semi-porcelain dishes, and sit upon the table which the family surrounds. Knives, forks and spoons are used. The dinner consists of potatoes, baked, some sort of vegetables boiled with cured meat, and cornbread served upon appropriate dishes. Supper consists of coffee, perhaps chicken or eggs, biscuit and cornbread, together with the staples, that is, syrup, butter and milk, which always have a place on the table at all meals. The table is made of white pine, and is kept well-scrubbed, for no cloth is used. The chairs are plain cane-bottom, and are also kept white with soap and water. I hardly believe that napkins are used at all meals, but they produce, when company comes, some napkins about six inches square ironed as stiff as boards.

No. 6. *A country family living in 9 rooms with an income of $1500 per year.* There are fourteen members in the family: father 58, mother 54, mother's mother 70, five sons, respectively, 35, 33, 31, 24 and 18 years of age; and six daughters, respectively, 29, 28, 26, 22, 20 and 15 years of age. Eight of the older children do not live at home. As a family they are loving and congenial. The father is a man who takes care of his family. The mother will do anything for her children. All the children do well in school and are quick to learn. The whole family dress well, and especially the girls keep up with the style. The girls have been off to school and have put aside the old-fashioned way of dressing of the community in which they live. There is not much time for dressing during the week, however, owing to household duties, but on Sunday they all appear in white dresses and straw sailor hats, or perhaps in a black skirt, a white waist and a hat trimmed in flowers. Some of the older girls have black and white silk parasols. The father wears a black suit, or sometimes a pair of striped trousers and a black coat. The mother always dresses in a plain white suit or a white waist and a black skirt. Everything is kept clean and tidy. Company call very often, sometimes to stay two or three weeks, and the guests come from neighboring cities. The family goes to church regularly. The property owned consists of 325 acres of land, very fertile, and worth fifty dollars an acre. The family has been living in the present locality for the past thirty-one years. Neither of the parents have had any education except what they have picked up themselves. All the children have been educated. Two daughters and one son are married.

Breakfast is at seven and consists of hot biscuits, cornbread, fried meat, butter and coffee. Dinner is at twelve and consists of cabbage, greens, corn (fried), pepper, fried meat, sweet potatoes, white potatoes, cornbread and squashes. For Sunday dinners there is often macaroni, cheese, chicken, and pudding in addition. Supper is at sundown, and consists of cornbread, biscuits, fried meat and syrup. Dishes and plates are all of porcelain, with steel forks and knives with wooden handles. The table is set in the week with a tablecloth of red and white flowers, on Sunday with a linen cloth. Two benches stand, one on each side of the table, and a chair is at either end.

No. 7. *A city family living in 3 rooms, with an income of $200 per year.* There are three members in this family, a mother and two daughters. The mother is fifty-one years old and wholly illiterate; she is a washerwoman and not at all neat or clean in her dress; she looks like an Indian and is very quick-tempered. The elder daughter is twenty-two years of age, very slow in thought and action. She finished the grammar schools and got as far as the second year in high school. In summer she washes and irons, in winter she cooks for a white family. Her dress is sometimes clean and neat, and sometimes just the opposite. The younger daughter is thirteen years of age and goes to grammar school. She has a very even temperament and is usually clean. They own no property except the house and lot where they live. Both daughters belong to the church, but the mother does not. They belong to no societies, and have no social life to speak of. They usually go together, except that the younger girl has some young girl friends. The father is dead. The mother's father was a white farmer and her mother a slave. The father's father and mother were slaves. He had two brothers, one of whom is dead. They know of no other relatives.

Breakfast, consisting of coffee, wheat bread, meat, bacon, sometimes beef, is eaten at half past six, and dinner, with cornbread, vegetables, now and then meats is eaten about eight at night; except on Sunday, when breakfast is eaten at nine o'clock and dinner at half past two or three o'clock. The meals are eaten from miscellaneous dishes. The table upon which the family eats has no tablecloth upon it. The food is taken from the cooking utensils and put on a plate—some of everything they have is put on a plate—and each member of the family takes her plate and sits to the table in the kitchen and eats. There are only two meals cooked. Between meals they eat what is left from the previous meal.

No. 8. *A city family living in 3 rooms, with an income of $800 per year.* This family is seven in number: husband, aged 34; wife, aged 29, their two children, both girls, ages ten and six; the husband's mother, about seventy; husband's brother, aged eighteen, and a nephew of the husband, aged fourteen. The wife before being married was orphaned and reared by her sister. She has a grammar-school education; she is red brown in color. The husband, a brown man, got a little education and then came to town in search of work. He found employment with the railroad as hostler; he was at this employment until after marriage when, under the influence of his wife, he became a brickmason. The husband's mother lived in the country until her husband died and several children, after which she moved to the city with her youngest son, a boy of eighteen, and her orphaned grandson, a boy of fourteen. The duties of the wife and the mother are to keep the home in order. The children go to school. The boy of fourteen cuts wood, brings up coal and kindling, goes to school, and spends two hours in the service of a small dairy, delivering dairy products to the neighbors, for which he receives fifty cents a week. The boy of eighteen drives a furniture wagon for a local furniture store, receiving six dollars per week for his services. The husband works at his trade, averaging about five hundred dollars a year. There have been born into this family since marriage six children, four of whom died in infancy, two of whom were twins. The dress of this family is common city dress with nothing extra. The men's suits average fifteen dollars per suit; the women's clothes, averaging five dollars per suit, being made at home. All belong to the church, although to different ones; all attend very regularly. The husband is a Mason and the wife a True Reformer. The home is now being paid for. The family is very genial in disposition, and receives some company.

The staple foods are meat, grits, rice, syrup, butter and jelly. All of this is bought from stores except the jelly, which is made in the summer. At breakfast there is rice, grits, coffee, biscuit and some sort of steak, sausage or liver, bought from the near-by market. Red damask tablecloth covers the table, with china dishes. The food is served on appropriate dishes. Common napkins are used. The whole family eat at the same time. At dinner they have baked beans, or roast, together with white potatoes, rice, and wheat bread, coffee, and some sort of cheap dessert, like pie. At supper there is something fried from the market, wheat bread, grits, cheese, coffee and tea. Breakfast is at six in the morning, dinner at twelve, and supper at six in the evening.

No. 9. *A city family living in 5 rooms, with an income of $864 per year.* The family is composed of five members: mother, father and three sons. The father, fifty-four years of age, a portly man, light yellow, with straight black hair. The mother, fifty years of age, is a heavy-built woman, with a stately and erect form, dark-brown complexion and coarse hair. The sons, of 22, 27 and 29 years, are very much alike; they have straight black hair and Indian complexion and features. The mother and father belong to the Baptist church; the sons are not church members. The mother and father are well thought of by the neighbors. The sons' habits on the whole are not of the best. The two oldest do not live at home. The mother and father wear plain clothes, the sons dress moderately and keep clean. The house is kept very clean and neat. The windows, floors and furniture are kept neat; the bedclothes are always clean and comfortable. The rooms are well-ventilated daily, and the yard is kept in good condition. The father was a country schoolteacher up to twenty-nine years ago, but from that time up to the present he has been employed as a cotton classer. The oldest son has always followed the profession of embalming; the youngest boy is a special delivery messenger at the post-office. The other boy is a common laborer. The mother and father belong to secret societies. The boys live with their parents when they are in the city. They own the house and lot they live on.

The principal foods are bread, meat, rice, grits, coffee, tea and vegetables. They cook twice a day, morning and evening, between six and seven o'clock in the morning and five and six in the evening, and serve a light cold lunch at noon. The dishes are of various sets, few in number. Common silver-plated spoons, knives and forks of different kinds are used. The mother does the cooking; at mealtime all the food is put on the table at the beginning. After the meal she clears the table and washes the dishes.

No. 10. *A city family living in 4 rooms, with an income of $560 per year.* This family is composed of nine members: father, 38 years; mother, 35 years; four girls, 16, 13, 11 and 8, respectively, and three boys, 6, 4 and 2 years, respectively. The father's father was a farmer. The man himself is a brickmason. In recent years he has been studying theology, and is now pastor of three churches. The mother's mother has been, since emancipation, a servant in the house of white families for the most part, and her daughter did the same thing until she was married. The family is thoroughly Christian, and very highly thought of in the community where it is. The dress of this family is very plain and clean. This family has no family gatherings except birthday parties. The usual company are those who belong to the same church, the same society and the school friends of the children. The older members are members of the A. M. E. Church. The four oldest children go to Sunday-school regularly, and the father is a regular church goer. The man is an Odd Fellow and a Knight of Pythias also. All the children except the youngest belong to an insurance company that collects the dues every week. This family owns three-eighths of an acre of land; one-quarter is in one place and one-eighth of an acre in another. They have a cow, a hog, chickens and ducks. The house and everything around it is kept fairly clean. The family has lived near where they now live all of their lives. When this couple was first married they rented, then they moved to a home that belonged to the mother of the man. When the family became too large to live in that three-room house, the man bought land and built the house in which the family now lives.

For breakfast the family usually has ham or bacon, grits, tea or coffee, sometimes eggs, sweet potatoes in their season, cornbread and biscuits. For dinner they usually have two kinds of vegetables—peas, collard greens, cabbage or beans—and white potatoes or rice, cornbread or biscuits; either peach, pear, apple or blackberry pie, or bread pudding for dessert; sweet potatoes for dinner in their season. For supper they have beef stew, or soup sometimes, and at other times they have ham or bacon, and rice, coffee or tea, and milk when the cow is giving milk. Syrup may be had at almost any meal, if any one desires it. This is the regular course of eating, but many times they have fish or pork for breakfast or supper. This family usually has breakfast between 5:30 and 6:30 o'clock. The man has to be at his work at seven o'clock and the children leave for school at seven-thirty o'clock. In the winter the children take their lunch to school with them, but when they get home in the afternoon they usually eat what has been left from the morning cooking, and they have supper about six o'clock when the man comes home from his work. The dishes are all very plain, but there are some silver knives, forks and spoons that are used on special occasions, or when there is special company. As a rule, everything is put on the table at one time and everybody sits down together. When the mother is at the table she usually does the serving, and when she is not there the oldest girl does it. The man serves himself, and as soon as he is through he gets up and begins reading the newspaper or a book. The table is of rectangular shape, made of pine lumber, rather small for nine people. A linen tablecloth is used all the time.

No. 11. *A city family living in 4 rooms, with an income of $1200 per year.* This is a family of three: a man 57 years old, his wife, 41, and an adopted girl 10 years old. The man is a janitor, superintending several flats. The owner furnishes him a house and all of his fuel, besides his wages in money. He was coachman for the same man before he became janitor. The woman is a fine dressmaker, and she sews and keeps house. The man is a little above medium height, slender, with dark brown skin and crinkly black hair, mixed with gray; he has a black mustache. He is jovial, usually cheerful, generous, kind-hearted, prudent and business-like. The woman is of medium height and heavy build. She might easily pass for a white woman. She has very fair skin and straight chestnut hair. She is industrious and also business like. The little girl is about the size of the average child of ten. She is a very light brown, with closely-waved reddish hair. She is the woman's niece. She goes to school, and when at home runs errands, etc. They all wear good clothes, well-made, of good material. They are very neat and clean. They are very fond of staying at home, but have friends whom they visit and who visit them. They go to church dutifully, and each one belongs to some society, insurance or secret order. There was one child, which died while an infant. Since the owner of the flats furnishes them a house, they rent out their own house, which is a wooden structure of four rooms, with a lot 25 feet by 200 feet. The woman came from a family of seven girls. The father and four of the girls are dead; the mother lives sometimes with this daughter and sometimes works out and stays where she works. Of the three other girls one—the mother of the little girl—lives in the North. She has one of her children with her, a boy, and the third child has been adopted by one of her friends. The other sister is unmarried, and teaches. The man came from a family of five children. His mother and father are dead. His three brothers live near him, and his sister lives in another city. He was reared from a small boy by the man for whom he now works and has always worked.

This family has three meals a day. The food is well-cooked and well-served. They have nice dishes, silver, and good table linen. They have breakfast at seven o'clock, dinner between two and three o'clock and a cold supper about seven-thirty o'clock. In summer they have for breakfast a cereal, fruit, flour bread, and some kind of meat (beef, fish, chicken, mutton, fresh pork). For dinner they have cornbread, vegetables, or sometimes flour bread and baked meats, rice and tomatoes, potatoes, iced tea, and some kind of dessert. For supper they have fruit, iced tea, bread and butter, and sometimes meat. In winter they have for breakfast a cereal, bread, meat, and coffee or cocoa. The dinner is about the same as that of summer, with the exception of the summer vegetables and the iced tea. They often have soup. For supper they have bread and butter, cold meats, and sometimes stewed fruit and cocoa.

No. 12. *A city family living in 9 rooms, with an income of $1300 per year.* The father's father's birthplace and age is unknown. He was a slave of some wealth when freed. He belonged to a very good taskmaster and had considerable amount of cattle and other property. Some of his money he intrusted to his master for safety, but he died without ever getting it back again. The father's mother's birthplace is unknown. She had about three-fourths Indian blood, and was married three times. She was the mother of six children: five boys and one girl. One boy died while a very small child. The mother died in 1891. The father was born December 24, 1865, and is the oldest of the six children. He has been the main breadwinner for the family since the death of his father, when he was a boy, and has had a very little chance for schooling. He had to raise the four remaining children after his mother's death. He married at twenty years of age, and has farmed fourteen years. He owns a house and a four-acre lot at ——— Texas. He moved from ——— to ——— Texas, in 1900, and was porter in a hardware store for three years, with wages at $9.00 per week. Since then he has been a porter at the depot, with wages at $35.00 per month. He has one child, a boy, age 22 years. He is now buying a quarter block at $1500. The wife was born near ———, Texas, July 13, 1867. Her father died before her birth. Her mother's birthplace was in ———, Texas, and she is still living. The mother's mother has been married twice. First husband died soon after marriage; the second husband is still living. She is the mother of two children; both are married, and both girls. The mother sells vegetables, chickens and eggs, milk and butter, to neighbors, washes and irons and sometimes cooks. She had very little chance for education, and was married at eighteen years. Neither husband nor wife possessed any property at their marriage. The boy was born at ———, Texas, and he has been in school ever since he reached school age. Only works during the summer, averaging about $5 per week. Husband belongs to Odd Fellows Lodge, and has an accident life insurance policy of $1500.

No. 13. *A city family living in 7 rooms, with an income of $1344 per year.* There are eight members in the family; father, 53 years of age; mother, 49 years of age; grandmother on the father's side, 80 years of age; eldest daughter 21, eldest son 19, younger daughter 17, youngest son 15 and the youngest girl 12. The father is a railway mail clerk and has been for years. The mother only carries on the household affairs with the aid of the three girls. The grandmother attends to the cow and sells the milk. The eldest daughter teaches in one of the public schools of the city. The oldest son works in a barber shop. The younger son attends college in the winter and works as messenger boy in one of the factories in summer. The other two girls attend school and also assist in the house work.

During vacation three meals are served: breakfast at 7:30 a. m., and dinner at 12:00 p. m. and supper at 6 p. m. But when school begins only two meals are served: breakfast, and late dinner about 4:30 p. m. They raise none of the food, everything is bought. The meals are served by the girls of the family. The dishes used on the dining-room table are china, the knives and forks silver, but those used in the kitchen are not so expensive. The table used in this kitchen is comparatively small, being only for family use. But when there is company the larger dining-room is used.

For breakfast they always have some kind of cereal, biscuits, tea and coffee; either fried steak, ham, or the like, and home-made butter. For dinner they generally have something boiled, and dessert, either pies or pudding. They always dress well and are always very neat and clean. This family was once accustomed to spending Christmas day with the grandparents—the mother's parents—but since their death they spend the holidays at home. They attend church regularly, and the mother belongs to one of the largest Methodist churches of the city. The mother and father own quite a deal of property; the mother's was left to her by her parents, the father acquired his by his own labor.

Section 20A. Expenditures of Laborers. Just before going to press the following budgets of Negro laboring people of Atlanta have been collected. Logically this section should follow Section 20 which it serves to complete, and represents more nearly the expenditures of the mass of Negroes These budgets were collected by students of Atlanta University during the current year.

No. 1. *A Wood Chopper.* Two adults. Weekly earnings: Head, $2.50; wife, 75 cents; total, $3.25. Rent, $3.00 per month, two rooms. Weekly expense: Flour, wheat, 10 lbs., 40 cents; corn and cornmeal, 2 lbs., 5 cents; potatoes (Irish, etc.), 1 quart, 5 cents; sweet potatoes, yams, etc., 1 quart, 5 cents; green vegetables, 10 cents; meat: beef (fresh), 1 lb., 10 cents; bacon, 10 cents; fish of all kinds, 10 cents; lard, 10 cents; coffee, ½ lb., 10 cents; sugar, 1 lb., 10 cents; molasses and syrup, ½ pt., 5 cents; coke, 1 bu., 10 cents; wood, 25 cents; kerosene, ½ gal. 10 cents. Total, $1.75.

No. 2. *Laborer in Paper Mill.* Seven members in family, parents and five children, two boys and three girls; ages, respectively, 19 and 15 and 18, 14 and 10 years. Weekly earnings: Head, $22.00; one boy $7.00 and one girl $1.75; total, $30.75. House owned (rent of a similar house, $10.00), four rooms. Weekly expense : Flour, wheat, 50 lbs., $1.80; corn and cornmeal, 10 lbs., 25 cents; macaroni, 2 lbs., 20 cents; rice, 3 lbs., 25 cents; Irish potatoes, 1 peck, 30 cents; sweet potatoes, yams, etc., 1 peck, 30 cents; green vegetables, 35c.; meat (fresh beef), 20 lbs., $1.75; sausage, 3 lbs., 20c.; fish of all kinds, 6 lbs., 50c.; lard, 4 lbs., 50c.; butter, 2 lbs., 40c.; cheese, 2 lbs., 40c.; milk, fresh, 8 quarts, 30c.; milk, condensed, 2 lbs., 20c.; eggs, 1 doz., 25c.; coffee, 2 lbs., 40c.; sugar, 8 lbs., 50c.; molasses and syrup, 2 pts., 20c.; coal, 480 lbs., $1.50; wood, 25c.; kerosene, 2 gal., 30c. Total, $11.20.

No. 3. *Truckman.* Parents and one child. Weekly earnings: Head $6.00, wife $3.00, total $9.00. Rent $5.00 per month, three rooms. Weekly expense: Flour, wheat 12 lbs. 50c, corn and cornmeal 10 lbs. 25c, dried peas and beans ⅓ lb. 5c, tomatoes, etc. 25c, meat, beef (fresh and corned) 2 lbs. 25c, pork (fresh and salt) 7½ lbs. 75c, bacon, ham, head cheese, etc. 6 lbs. 75c, fish of all kinds 2 lbs. 25c, lard, suet dripping 2½ lbs. 25c, cheese 1 lb. 20c, milk (fresh) 1 qt. 20c, tea 2½c, sugar 4 lbs. 25c, coal 50c, wood 50c, kerosene ⅓ gal. 10c. Total, $5.08.

No. 4. *Brickmason.* Parents and six children, four boys and two girls; ages, respectively, 19, 13, 4 and 1, 9 and 7 years. Weekly earnings: Head, $20.00. Home owned (rent of similar house $8.00), five rooms. Weekly expense: Bread, of wheat, 6 loaves, 30c.; flour: wheat 24 lbs., 90c.; rye, 5 lbs., 35c.; crackers, 2 lbs., 25c.; macaroni, 1 lb., 10c.; rice, 6 lbs., 25c.; potatoes (Irish, etc.), 3 qts., 15c.; sweet potatoes, yams, etc., 1 pk.. 30c.; dried beans, 1 qt., 15c.; tomatoes, 18 lbs., 45c.; meat: beef (fresh), 10 lbs., $1.00; ham, 2 lbs., 40c.; sausage, 1 lb., 10c.; fish of all kinds, 3 lbs., 30c.; lard, 4 lbs., 50c.; butter, 2 lbs., 40c.; cheese, 1 lb., 20c.; milk, fresh, 8 qts., 30c.; milk, condensed, 1 lb., 10c.; eggs, 1 doz., 25c.; tea, ¼ lb., 20c.; coffee, 1 lb., 20c.; sugar, 9 lbs., 50c.; syrup, 1 pt., 10c.; jams, 1 pint, 25c.; coal, 3 bu., 75c.; coke, 2 bu., 20c.; kerosene, 2 gal., 30c. Total, $7.95.

No. 5. *Railroad Employee.* Parents and one child, boy three years old. Weekly earnings: Head, $25.00. Home owned (rent of similar house, $20.00 per month), seven rooms. Weekly expense: Bread, of wheat, 8 lbs., 25c ; flour: wheat, 6 lbs., 25c.; corn and cornmeal, 6 lbs., 15c.; spaghetti, 1 lb., 10c.; rice, barley, sago, etc., 3 lbs., 25c.; oatmeal and breakfast cereals, 2 lbs., 10c.; potatoes (Irish, etc.), ½ pk., 20c.; sweet potatoes, yams, etc., ½ pk., 15c.; dried peas and beans, 1 qt., 20c.; sweet corn, 14 lbs., 35c.; green vegetables, salad, tomatoes, etc., 35c.; meat: beef (fresh), 4 lbs., 60c.; bacon, ham, head cheese, etc., 10 lbs., $1.50; fish of all kinds, 3 lbs., 45c.; lard, suet dripping, 2½ lbs., 28c.; butter, 2 lbs., 40c.; olive oil, 1 pt., 30c.; cheese, 1 1b., 20c.; milk, condensed, 2 ibs., 25c.; eggs, 6 doz., $1.20; tea, ¼ lb., 15c ; coffee, ½ lb., 15c. ; sugar, 4 lbs., 25c.; molasses and syrup, 1 pt., 10c.; Ice, 70c.; coal, 6 bu., $1.50; wood, 60c.; kerosene, 1 gal., 15c. Total, $10.88.

No. 6. *Insurance Collector.* Parents and one child, a girl, 18 years. Weekly earnings: Head $17.90, total $17.90. Home owned (rent of similar house $10.60), five rooms. Weekly expense: Bread of wheat, 10 lbs., 55c., flour: wheat, 12 lbs., 45c., corn and cornmeal 7½c., spaghetti 1 lb. 10c., rice 1½ lb. 8c., potatoes (Irish), 1 qt. 5c., sweet potatoes, yams, etc., 1 peck 20c., meat: beef (fresh), 3 lbs. 30c., pork (fresh), 2 lbs. 20c., bacon 3 lbs. 25c., lard 2½ lbs. 35c., butter 1 lb. 35c., cheese 1 lb. 20c., milk, fresh, 1 quart 5c., milk, condensed, 1 lb. 10c., eggs 1 dozen 22c., coffee ½ lb. 12½c., sugar 4¼ lbs., 25c., coal 3 bu. 75c., wood 25c, kerosene 1 gal. 15c. Total, $4.05.

No. 7. *Brickmason.* Parents and two children, ages 10 and 7 years. Weekly earnings: Head $12.00, wife $5.00; total $17.00. House owned (rent of similar house $8.00 per month), three rooms. Weekly expense: Bread of wheat, 2 lbs. 10c, flour: wheat, 12 lb. 45c, corn and cornmeal, 2 lb. 5c, crackers, 1 lb. 10c, macaroni, 1 lb. 10c, rice, 2 lb. 15c, potatoes (Irish, etc.), 1 qt. 5c, sweet potatoes, yams, etc., 2 qts. 10c, green vegetables, 10c, meat: beef (fresh), 3 lb. 25c, pork (fresh) 2 lb. 30c, ham, 1 lb. 20c., sausage, 1 lb. 10c, fish of all kinds, 3 lb. 25c, lard 2 lb. 25c, butter 1 lb. 20c, cheese, 1 lb. 20c, milk (fresh) 4 qts. 15c, milk (condensed) 1 lb. 10c, eggs, 1 doz. 25c, coffee, 1 lb. 20c, sugar, 4 lbs. 25c, molasses and syrup, 1 pt. 10c, coke 30c, wood 25c, kerosene, ½ gal. 10c. Total, $4.65.

No. 8. *City Cart-driver.* Two adults and one child, a boy one year old. Weekly earnings: Head $6.00, total $6.00. Rent $3.00 per month, two rooms. Weekly expense: Flour, wheat 24 lbs. 90c, corn and cornmeal 2 lbs. 5c, rice 1 lb. 10c, potatoes (Irish) 1 qt. 5c, sweet potatoes, yams, etc., ½ pk. 15c, dried peas 2 qts. 20c, meat: beef (fresh and corned) 6 lb. 60c, pork (fresh and salt) 1 lb. 15c, bacon 2 lbs. 25c, sausage 1 lb. 10c, lard 1 lb. 15c, butter ¼ lb. 10c, coffee ½ lb. 15c, sugar 2 lbs. 15c, molasses and syrup 1 pt. 10c, vinegar, pickles and condiments 5c, nearbeer 4 pts. 20c, coal 1 bu. 25c, wood 15c, kerosene ½ gal. 10c. Total, $3.35.

No. 9. *Drayman.* Two adults. Weekly earnings: Head $8.00, wife $1.75; total $9.75. Rent $5.00 per month, three rooms. Weekly expense: Flour, wheat 12 lbs. 45c, corn and cornmeal 4 lbs. 10c, rice 1 lb. 10c, potatoes (Irish, etc.) 2 quarts 10c, sweet potatoes, yams, etc., 3 qts. 15c, dried peas and beans 2 qts. 20c, green vegetables 30c, meat: beef (fresh and corned) 6 lbs. 60c, pork (fresh and salt) 2 lbs. 30c, ham 2 lbs. 40c, sausage 2 lbs. 20c, fish of all kinds 2 lbs. 15c, lard, suet dripping 2 lbs. 25c, butter 1 lb. 20c, eggs 1 doz. 25c, coffee 1 lb. 20c, sugar 3 lbs. 20c, vinegar, pickles and condiments 5c, spirits 2 pts. $1.60, coal 1 bu. 25c, wood 25c, kerosene ½ gal. 20c. Total, $6.40.

No. 10. *Drayman.* Two adults and two children, girls, ages 12 and 6 years. Weekly earnings: Head $6.00, wife $1.50; total $7.50. Rent $4.50 per month, two rooms. Weekly expense: Flour, wheàt, 8 lbs., 30c., cornmeal, ½ pk., 15c., dried beaⁿs, 1 qt. 10c., green vegetables—salad, tomatoes, etc., 20c., meat: beef (fresh and corned) 2 lbs. 20c., pork (salt) 4 lbs. 50c., sausage 1½ lbs. 15c., lard 15c., tea 5c., coffee 5c., molasses and syrup 2 qts. 15c., sugar 3 lbs. 15c, beer $1.00, wood 50c., kerosene ½ gal, 10c. Total, $3.85.

No. 11. *Porter in Store.* Two adults and three children, girls, ages 11, 9 and 7 years. Weekly earnings: Head $6.00, wife 75 cents, total $6.75. Rent $2.50 per month, one room. Weekly expense: Flour, wheat 24 lbs. 90c., cornmeal 1 pk. 30c., sweet potatoes 1 pk. 20c., green vegetables, salad, tomatoes, etc., 20c., pork (salt) 8½ lbs. $1.00, sausage 1 lb. 10c, fish of all kinds 4 lbs. 25c., lard 35c., butter ½ lb. 15c., coffee ½ lb. 10c., sugar 4 lb. 25c., wood 50c, kerosene 1 quart 5c. Total, $3.35.

No. 12. *Carpenter.* Three adults and one child, a girl five years old. Weekly earnings: Head $18.00, total $18.00. Rent $8.00 per month, four rooms. Weekly expense: Flour, wheat 8 lbs. 30c., cornmeal 2 qts. 10c., macaroni 1 lb. 10c., rice 1 lb. 10c., potatoes (Irish) 3 qts. 15c., sweet potatoes, yams, etc., 2 qts. 10c., dried peas and beans 1 qt. 10c., green vegetables, salad, tomatoes, etc., 40c.; meat: beef (fresh and corned) 4 lbs. 50c., pork (fresh and salt) 2 lbs. 30c., bacon 2 lbs. 25c., sausage 4 lbs. 40c., lard 3 lbs., 30c., butter 1 lb. 35c., cheese 1 lb. 20c., milk (fresh) 2 qts. 20c., milk (condensed) 1 lb. 12c., eggs 1 doz. 25c., tea ¼ lb. 15c., coffee ½ lb. 15c., sugar 5 lbs. 25c., molasses and syrup 1 pt. 5c., vinegar, pickels and condiments 1 pint 5c., fruits (fresh, dried and canned) and jams 50c., coal 250 lbs. 63c., charcoal 1 bu. 13c., kerosene 1 gal. 15c. Total, $7.68.

No. 13. *Common Laborer.* Two adults and two children, a boy and girl, ages 6 years and 9 months, respectively. Weekly earnings: Head $6.00, wife 40 cents; total $6.40. Rent $2.50 per month, one room. Weekly expense: Flour, wheat 24 lbs. 90c., cornmeal 2 qts. 10c., rice 1½ lbs. 15c., potatoes (Irish, etc.) 1 qt. 5c., sweet potatoes ½ pk. 15c., green vegetables, salad, tomatoes, etc. 25c.; pork (salt) 8 lb. $1.00, lard 3 lb. 30c. coffee ½ lb. 10c., sugar 3 lbs. 15c., coke 2 bu. 20c., wood 35c., kerosene 1 qt. 5c. Total, $3.75.

No. 14. *Stableman.* Two adults and three girls, ages 9, 4 and 2, respectively. Weekly earnings: Head $7.00, wife $2.00, total $9.00. Rent $7.60, three rooms. Weekly expense: Flour, wheat 12 lbs. 45c., rice 3 lbs. 30c., potatoes (Irish, etc.) 2 qts. 10c., dried peas and beans 2 qts. 20c., green vegetables, salad, tomatoes, etc 30c., meat: beef (fresh and corned) 6 lbs. 60c., pork 4 lbs. 50c., butter 1 lb. 25c., coffee ½ lb. 10c., sugar 3 lbs. 25c., vinegar, pickles and condiments 1 pint 5c., coal 2 bu. 50c., wood 60c., kerosene 1 gal. 15c. Total, $4.95.

No. 15. *Drayman.* Two adults and four children, two boys and two girls, ages respectively 4 and 1½, and 5 and 8 years. Weekly earnings: Head $5.00, wife $1.50; total $6.50. Rent $3.50, two rooms. Weekly expense: Flour, wheat 12 lbs. 40c., cornmeal 1 lb. 30c., rice 1 lb. 10c., dried peas and beans 20c., green vegetables, salad, tomatoes, etc., 10c., pork (fresh and salt) 9½ lbs. $1.25, fish of all kinds 3½ lbs. 25c., lard 3 lbs. 30c., tea 10c., sugar 5 lbs. 25c., fruits (fresh, dried and canned) and jams 1 lb. 10c., coke 3 bu. 30c., wood 35c., kerosene 1 qt. 5c. Total $4.05.

No. 16. *Street Sweeper.* Two adults and four children, two girls and two boys, ages respectively 14 and 3, and 17 and 10 years. Weekly earnings: Head $6.60, wife 75 cents, 1 boy $4.50; total $11.85. Rent $5.00 per month, two rooms.

Weekly expense: Flour, wheat 24 lbs. 90c, cornmeal 1 pk. 30c, rice 1 lb. 10c, sweet potatoes 1 pk. 25c, beans 2 qts. 20c, green vegetables, salad, tomatoes, etc., 25c, meat, beef (fresh) 2¼ lbs. 30c, fish of all kinds 3 lbs. 40c, lard 4 lbs. 50c, butter 1 lb. 25c, coffee ½ lb. 10c, sugar 5 lbs. 25c, syrup 3 pts. 15c, beer 60c, coal 1 bu. 25c, wood 50c, kerosene ½ gal. 10c. Total, $5.90. Meals away from home 60 cents.

No. 17. *Head Porter for Insurance Company.* Four adults and two children, one boy and a girl, ages respectively 18 and 20 years. Weekly earnings: Head $15.00, wife $4.00, total $19.00. Rent $12.60 per month, six rooms. Weekly expense: Flour, wheat 12 lbs. 55c, buckwheat and other 1 pkg. 10c, cornmeal 2 qts. 10c, macaroni 1 lb. 10c, rice 2½ lbs. 25c, oatmeal 2 pkgs. 25c, potatoes (Irish etc.) ½ bu. 60c, sweet potatoes, yams, etc. 3 qts. 15c, dried pease and beans 1 qt. 10c, green vegetables, salad, tomatoes, etc. 50c, meat, beef (corned) 2 tins 30c, pork (fresh) 6 lbs. 90c, poultry 1 chicken 65c, fish of all kinds 2 lbs. 25c, lard 3⅓ lbs. 40c, butter 1½ lbs. 45c, cheese 2 lbs. 40c, milk (fresh) 4 qts. 40c, milk (condensed) 1 lb. 12c, eggs 1 doz. 25c, tea ¼ lb. 10c, coffee 1 lb. 25c, sugar 5½ lbs. 40c, syrup 1 pt. 5c, vinegar, pickles and condiments 1 pt. 5c, fruits (fresh, dried and canned) and jams 1 lb. 10c, coal ¼ ton $1.25, coke 1 bu. 10c, wood 25c, kerosene 1 gal. 15c. Total $9.12. Meals away from home 75c; gas 25c.

No. 18. *Drayman.* Two adults. Weekly earnings: Head $5.00, wife $1.00; total $6.00. Rent $4.00 per month, two rooms. Weekly expense: Flour, wheat 5 lbs. 25c, cornmeal 4 qts. 20c, rice ⅓ lb. 5c, potatoes (Irish, etc.) ⅓ pk. 20c, green vegetables, salad, tomatoes. etc. 60c, meat, beef (fresh) 3 lbs. 30c, pork (salt) 2¼ lbs. 30c, fish of all kinds 3 lbs. 40c, lard 3 lbs. 30c, butter 1 lb. 25c, sugar 4 lbs. 20c, wood 40c, kerosene ⅓ gal. 10c. Total $3.60.

No. 19. *Common Laborer.* Two adults and three children, one boy and two girls, ages respectively 6 and 5 and 3 years. Weekly earnings: Head $7.50, total $7.50. Rent $6.00 per month, three rooms. Weekly expense: Flour, wheat 12 lbs. 40c, cornmeal 1 pk. 30c, sweet potatoes 2 qts. 10c, dried peas and beans 2 qts. 20c, green vegetables, salad, tomatoes, etc. 35c, meat, beef (fresh) 5 lbs. 60c, pork (salt) 4 lbs. 50c, fish of all kinds 2 lbs. 25c, lard 3 lbs. 30c, butter 1 lb. 25c, coffee ½ lb. 10c, cocoa 1 box 10c, sugar 3 lbs. 15c, fruits (dried) 15c, spirits ½ pt. 25c, kerosene 1 gal. 15c. Total, $4.55.

No. 20. *Stonemason.* Two adults. Weekly earnings: Head $12.00, total $12.00. Rent $6.50 per month, three rooms. Weekly expense: Flour, wheat 6 lbs. 25c, corn and cornmeal 4 lbs. 10c, sweet potatoes, yams, etc. 15 lbs. 30c, meat, beef (fresh and corned) 2 lbs. 20c, pork (fresh and salt) 1 lb. 15c, bacon, ham, head cheese, etc. 2 lb. 25c, fish of all kinds 3 lbs. 30c, lard, suet dripping 2⅓ lbs. 25c, Butter ½ lb. 15c, milk (fresh) 1 qt. 5c, milk (condensed) 1 lb. 10c, eggs 5, 10c, coffee ½ lb. 10c, sugar 1½ lbs. 10c, vinegar, pickles and condiments 1 pt. 10c, coal 100 lbs. 50c, wood 50c, kerosene ⅓ gal. 5c. Total, $3.55.

Section 28. Conclusion. Judging from family life and other conditions how far, is it fair to conclude, has the Negro American emerged into twentieth century civilization? The United States had, in 1900, 10.7% of illiteracy, 46.5% of home ownership, and perhaps 2% of illegitimate births. The Negro had, in 1900, 44.5% of illiteracy, 20.3% of home ownership and, probably though not certainly, 25% of illegitimacy.

These rough measurements would permit the following assumption: that in the Nation at large four-fifths of the citizens have at least common school training, two-thirds have reached a plane of economic independence, and nine-tenths are observing the monogamic sex *mores*. Among the Negroes probably one-third have at least common-school training, one-third have reached a plane of economic independence, and at least one-half are observing the monogamic sex *mores*.

We may conclude this study by short extracts from the remarks of two of the speakers of the Thirteenth Annual Conference.

Miss Jane Addams said, among other things:

. . . The thing I feel most strongly as the difficulty among the Italians, among the Greeks and among the Russians (for these are the ones whom I constantly see), is the contrast they find between the life they have led at home and the life they are obliged to live in Chicago. All sorts of customs fit them to walk in the old folk ways,the old ways which their ancestors have had for so many years. Now, as I take it, your difficulties are quite unlike that. The habits which you might have had from your ancestors were all broken into, they were all scattered, and especially the habits connected with family life. There are advantages and disadvantages in the lack of tradition and the lack of habits in those directions. The advantages are that you are much more ready to make your adaptation; you are much more ready to bring the results of education and the rationalistic side of life to bear directly upon the refining of the family. And the disadvantages are that you lack some of the restraints of the traditions which the people I have mentioned bring with them.

The Reverend E. L. Henderson, Episcopal Archdeacon of the diocese of Atlanta, said:

While the Negro has made a splendid beginning in the acquisition of homes, a beginning it is, and not the end. For, here and there, in country and in city, we find not only types of the ideal home but tenements and shanties which barely afford protection from wind and storm; dwellings where the laws of health are defied, where the most ordinary sanitary arrangements are unknown, and where boards of health fail to penetrate; beds innocent of clothing; human forms, even those of children, piteously clad; hunger written upon careworn faces and despair everywhere triumphant. What can be expected in such a home as this but that which often exists—an immorality as deep as its poverty; a moral atmosphere as pestilential as the physical. Again, there are homes, so-called, in which the holy ties of human affection are greatly warped, if not broken asunder, and where the old motto, "What is home without a father?" which once served as an adornment and certificate of value, is now replaced by the State's certificate of divorce. For while the Negro, being imitative, has been strengthened by the examples of the good, he has been weakened by the examples of the bad.

If the moral, economic and educational advance of the Negro race be necessary for the well-being of society; if the unit of society is not the individual, but the family; if nothing can take the place of the early influences of a true home, and the function of education be to "Prepare us for complete living," then, the Christian Church, which underlies and upholds all other institutions, and gives to each an immortal power and an eternal significance, must purify the stream at the *fountain head* by sending her ministering angels—her clergy, deaconesses, sisters, teachers, Bible women, and visitors—into the homes of the Negroes, not only to teach the importance of daily family prayer, but, in the language of one of our learned prelates, to teach, also, what is good taste in dress; the part soap and water, liberally used, plays in health and strength of mind and character; the fact that clammy bread and bad coffee are not a necessary incident of poverty; that separate and well-ventilated bedrooms, a clean tablecloth and gentle manners, belong to a polite education; that order and thrift are not a waste of time, but make time for rational enjoyment and brighten life; that nothing is lost by supplanting coarseness, vulgarity, slovenliness, with tidiness, refinement and innocent amusement; that the best elements of the highest civilization in Virginia or Connecticut are wrought in the *home*, and that the sweetness and delight of home are as possible in a plain Negro cabin as in houses of brick or marble with all modern improvements, and that the flowers and the fruits of good living are attainable wherever the disposition exists and a determined effort is made to have them.

FINALLY: If there would be a further transition from ignorance, poverty and moral darkness, to enlightenment, thrift, industry, and improvement of the individual and the Negro family, the Church and the Home must unite in a more vigorous warfare to reduce to a minimum the prevailing evil of divorce. This they must do,

(1) By teaching young women to appreciate the seriousness of marriage, its solemn import and its sacred responsibilities.

(2) By teaching young men to revere womanhood and motherhood, for the sake of their own mothers and the Mother of our Lord, so that their purity may be no mere prudential restraint, but a generous and chivalrous Christian knightliness.

(3) By teaching all that marriage and family life are not dependent upon selfish desire, or mere caprice, but are institutions ordained of God, and designed like other ordinances of God with a view to the education, the formation and discipline of character.

When the Church and the Home receive a clearer vision and use their full power; when the estate of Holy Matrimony, which has a sacramental character, be no longer entered into, as so often now, "unadvisedly or lightly," but "reverently, discreetly, advisedly, soberly, and in the fear of God," then the Church and the Home will have served their mission, and be permitted to look with satisfaction upon "Their sor- as plants grown up in their youth, and their daughters as corner-stones, polished after the similitude of a palace."

Index

The Atlanta University Publications, No. 14

Efforts for

Social Betterment

among

Negro Americans

Report of a Social Study made by Atlanta University
under the patronage of the Trustees of the John F.
Slater Fund; together with the Proceedings of the
14th Annual Conference for the Study of the Negro
Problems, held at Atlanta University on Tuesday,
May the 24th, 1909

Edited by

W. E. Burghardt Du Bois
Corresponding Secretary of the Conference

The Atlanta University Press
ATLANTA, GA.
1909

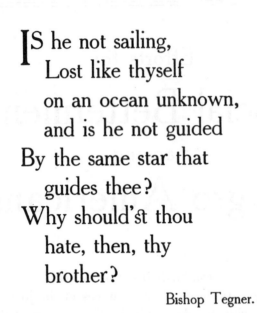

IS he not sailing,
Lost like thyself
on an ocean unknown,
and is he not guided
By the same star that
guides thee?
Why should'st thou
hate, then, thy
brother?

Bishop Tegner.

Efforts for Social Betterment among Negro Americans

Contents

The Fourteenth Annual Conference

Efforts for Social Betterment among Negro Americans

PROGRAMME

First Session, 10:00 a. m.

President E. T. Ware presiding.

Subject: "Local Charities."

Address: Mr. William A. Rogers, '99, of the State Normal School, Petersburg, Va.

Explanation of Charts: Dr. W. E. B. DuBois, Secretary of the Conference.

Second Session, 11:30 a. m.

Subject: "Health and Social Betterment."

Special Talk to Men: Dr. Stephen A. Peters, '97 (Room 16).

Special Talk to Women: Miss Anna Knight, Medical Missionary in India (Chapel).

Third Session, 3:00 p. m.

Twelfth Annual Mothers' Meeting. (In charge of the Gate City Free Kindergarten.) Mrs. David T. Howard presiding.

Subject: "The Children and Health."

1. Kindergarten songs, games and exercises by 150 children of the five free kindergartens:

    East Cain Street—Miss Ola Perry.
    Bradley Street—Miss Hattie Sims.
    Martin Street—Mrs. John Rush.
    Dover Street—Miss Leila Golden.
    Leonard Street—Miss Nannie Nichols.

2. Address: Miss Cornelia Bowen, president of the Alabama State Federation of Colored Women's Clubs.

3. Address: Mrs. J. W. E. Bowen.

4. Explanation of Kindergarten Exhibit—Miss Gertrude Ware.

5. Report of Treasurer: Mrs. Lizzie Burch.

6. Collection.

Fourth Session, 8:00 p. m.

President E. T. Ware presiding.

Subject: "Efforts for Social Betterment."

Address: "The Social Betterment of the Russian Peasant": Mr. I. M. Rubinow, Special Agent, Bureau of Labor, Washington. D. C., formerly of the Imperial Russian Civil Service.

Stereopticon Exhibit of various current methods of Social Uplift.

Errata

On page 113 insert after "Dunbar, Paul Lawrence," and before "The Sport of the Gods":

Lyrics of Lowly Life.
Lyrics of the Hearth Side.
Candle-lightin' time.
Lyrics of Love and Laughter.
Poems of Cabin and Field.

Folks from Dixie.
The Uncalled.
The Strength of Gideon.
The Love of Landry.
The Fanatics.

Preface

In 1898 the Atlanta University Negro Conference made an investigation into "Efforts of American Negroes for their own Social Betterment." As was explained in the report of that study: "To be of the highest value such an investigation should be exhaustive, covering the whole country and recording all species of effort. Funds were not available for such an inquiry. The method followed, therefore, was to choose nine Southern cities of varying size and to have selected in them such organizations of Negroes as were engaged in benevolent and reformatory work. The cities from which returns were obtained were: Washington, D. C., Petersburg, Va., Augusta, Ga., Atlanta, Ga., Mobile, Ala., Bowling Green, Ky., Clarkesville,Tenn., Fort Smith, Ark., and Galveston, Tex. Graduates of Atlanta University, Fisk University, Howard University, the Meharry Medical College, and other Negro institutions co-operated in gathering the information desired.

"No attempt was made to catalogue all charitable and reformatory efforts, but rather to illustrate the character of the work being done by typical examples. In one case, Petersburg, Va., nearly all efforts of all kinds were reported, in order to illustrate the full activity of one group. The report for one large city, Washington, was pretty full although not exhaustive. In all of the other localities only selected organizations were reported. The returns being for the most part direct and reduced to a basis of actual figures seem to be reliable."

Eleven years later the Atlanta Conference returns to the study of this subject, aided by an appropriation of $1,000 from the Trustees of the John F. Slater Fund. It is, however, again not possible to make an exhaustive study of Social Betterment among the ten million people of Negro descent in the United States. An attempt has been made, however, to secure in all parts of the country a fairly representative list of typical efforts and institutions, and the resulting picture while incomplete is nevertheless instructive.

This study is, therefore, a further carrying out of the Atlanta University plan of social study of the Negro American, by means of an annual series of decennially recurring subjects covering, so far as is practicable, every phase of human life. The object of these studies is primarily scientific—a careful research for truth, conducted as thoroughly, broadly and honestly as the material resources and mental equipment at command will allow. It must be remembered that mathematical accuracy in these studies is impossible; the sources of information are of varying degrees of accuracy and the pictures are wofully incomplete. There is necessarily much repetition in the successive studies, and some contradiction of previous reports by later ones as new material comes to hand. All we claim is that the work is as thorough as circumstances permit and that with all its obvious limitations it is well worth the doing. Our object is not simply to serve Science. We wish not only to make the Truth clear but to present it in such shape as will encourage and help social reform.

Our financial resources are unfortunately meager: Atlanta University is primarily a school and most of its funds and energy go to teaching. It is, however, also a seat of learning and as such it has endeavored to advance knowledge, particularly in matters of racial contact and development, which seem obviously its nearest field. In this work it has received unusual encouragement from the scientific world, and the published results of these studies are used in America, Europe, Asia and Africa. Very few books on the Negro problem, or any phase of it, have been published in the last decade which have not acknowledged their indebtedness to our work.

On the other hand, the financial support given this work has been very small. The total cost of the fourteen publications has been about $16,000, or a little over $1,000 a year. The growing demands of the work, the vast field to be covered and the delicacy and equipment needed in such work, call for far greater resources. We need, for workers, laboratory and publications, a fund of $6,000 a year, if this work is going adequately to fulfill its promise. Two years ago a small temporary grant from the Carnegie Institution of Washington, D. C., greatly helped us, and for two years our work has been saved from suspension by an appropriation from the John F. Slater Fund.

In past years we have been enabled to serve the United States Bureau of Labor, the United States Census, the Board of Education of the English Government, many scientific associations, professors in nearly all the leading universities, and many periodicals and reviews. May we not hope in the future for such increased financial resources as will enable us to study adequately this the greatest group of social problems that ever faced America?

A Select Bibliography of Efforts for Social Betterment among Negro Americans

Books

Annual Report of the Home Mission Board (Baptists). 14 reports.

Annual Report of the National Baptist Young People's Union Board. 10 reports.

Annual Reports of the Executive Board and Corresponding Secretary of the Woman's Convention Auxiliary to the National Baptist Convention. 9 reports. 1900(?)-1909.

Annual Reports: Published by the various institutions noted within.

Atlanta University Publications:

    No. 3. Some Efforts of Negroes for Social Betterment; 66 pp.

    No. 6. The Negro Common School; 120 pp., 1901.

    No. 8. The Negro Church; 212 pp., 1903.

    No. 11. Health and Physique of the Negro American; 112 pp.

    No. 12. Economic Co-operation among Negro Americans; 184 pp., 1907.

    No. 13. The Negro American Family; 152 pp., 1908.

Arnett, Bishop B. B. The Budget. 7 vols. 1881, 1882, 1883, 1884, 1885-6, 1887-8, 1904.

Bruce, Roscoe Conkling. Service by the educated Negro. Tuskegee, 1903; 17 pp., 12mo.

Cincinnati convention of colored freedmen of Ohio. Proceedings. January 14-19.1852. Cincinnati, 1852. 8vo.

Cleveland national emigration convention of colored people. Proceedings, August 22-24, 1854. Pittsburg, 1854. 8vo.

Cromwell, John W. The early Negro convention movement. Washington, 1904. (The American Negro Acad.) 23 pp., 8vo.

Delaware association for the moral improvement and education of the colored people. An. Reps., 1868, 1869, 1870. Wilmington, Del.

Eaton, J. Grant, Lincoln and the freemen. $2.00. 1907. Longmans.

Freedmen, Annual reports of the Presbyterian Committee of Missions for 1871-1882. (Committee incorporated under the name of Presbyterian Board of Missions for Freedmen.) An. Reps., 1883-1909. Pittsburgh. 8vo.

Freedmen's Bureau:

    Annual report of Adjutant-General's Branch of Freedmen for 1873-1877.

    Annual report of Superintendent of North Carolina for 1864, 1867; of Louisiana for 1865; of Alabama for 1867; of the District of Columbia and West Virginia for 1867.

    Report of the General Superintendent of Freedmen. Department of the States of Tennessee and Arkansas, for 1864-5.

    Report of Commissioner of Bureau of refugees, freedmen, and abandoned lands, for 1865-1871.

    Report of the Secretary of War for 1867, containing a synopsis of the report of the Commissioners of the Bureau of refugees, freedmen, and abandoned lands, for the same year.

Griggs, Sutton E. Imperium in imperio. Cincinnati, 1899; 265 pp, 8vo.

Helm, Mary. The Upward Path, the Evolution of a Race. New York, 1909. 333 pp.

Illinois State Convention of colored men. Proceedings at Galesburg, October 16, 17, 18. Chicago, 1867. 37 pp, 8vo.

Johnson, Edward A. Light ahead for the Negro. New York. 1904. 132 pp. 12mo.

Jones, C. C. The religious instruction of the Negroes in the United States. Savannah, 1842. 277 pp. 12mo.

Joyner, E. M. Missions to the colored people in the South. Hartford, 1893. 18 pp. 12mo.

Leaflets, reports, etc., Woman's Home and Foreign Missionary Society, A. M. E. Z. Church.

Mayo, Amory Dwight. The opportunity and obligation of the educated class of the colored people in the Southern States. N.p. 1899(?). 32 pp. 8vo.

Minutes of the first annual convention of the people of color. Philadelphia, 1831. Pamphlet.

Minutes of the third annual convention of the free Negroes. Phila., 1833.
Minutes of the National Association of Colored Women's Clubs. 6 reports. 1897-1909.
National convention of colored men and their friends. Troy, N. Y., 1847. 38 pp. 8vo.
National convention of colored men. Syracuse, N. Y., October 4-7, 1864. Boston, 1864.
62 pp. 8vo.
National convention of colored men of America. 1869. Proceedings. Washington,
1869. 42 pp. 8vo.
Needles, Edward. Ten years' progress, or a comparison of the state and condition
of the colored people in the city and county of Philadelphia from 1837 to 1847.
Phila., 1849.
Negroes, Charities for. Home for destitute colored children, Marylandville, Pa.
Annual reports, 1st-21st. Philadelphia, 1856-76. 2 vols. 8vo.
Negro young people's Christian and educational congress. Atlanta, 1902. The United
Negro. 600 pp. 8vo.
Penn, Irvine Garland. The Afro-American press and its editors. Springfield, 1891.
565 pp. 12mo.
Proceedings of State Federations of Colored Women's Clubs. Texas, West Virginia,
Iowa, Alabama, Colorado, Indiana, Kentucky, Maryland, Michigan, Minne-
sota, Georgia, Tennessee, Missouri, Ohio, California, Mississippi, Pennsylvania,
Illinois, Florida, Virginia.
Quadrennial conference of the Women's Parent Mite Missionary Society of the A.
M. E. Church. 4 reports.
Richings, G. F. Evidences of progress among colored people. 12th ed. $1.00. 1905.
G. F. Richings, Ashland, Ohio.
Rudd, L. E. Catholic Afro-American congresses. Cincinnati, 1893.
Smith, Mrs. Amanda. Autobiography of Amanda Smith. Chicago, 1893.

Periodicals

Appeal for hospital endowment. 68:903. Outlook.
Atlanta University conference. W. E. B. DuBois. Charities.
Conference of Negroes at Tuskegee, Ala. 1892. R. C. Bedford. 8:251. Lend a Hand.
Elevation of Tropical Races. B. Kidd. 57:545-50. Independent.
Ex-Governor Northen's work in Georgia. Independent. June 13, 1907.
Evolution of a Kentucky Negro Mission. L. J. Speed. Charities. September 21, 1907.
Fresh air work among colored children in New York. M. W. Ovington. Charities.
October 13, 1906.
Lifting of Negroes. G. Bradford. 39:462. Nation.
Negroes: What they are doing for themselves. S. J. Barrows. Atlantic. 67:805.
Negroes: how we can help them. C. A. Oliver. 42:85. Catholic World.
Negro Building and exhibit at the Jamestown Exposition. 1907. H. A. Tucker.
Charities. September 21, 1907.
Negro's up-hill climb. R. R. Moton. World's Work. April, May, August, 1907.
Progress among Negroes. E. P. Clark. 48:461. Nation.
Progress of the Negro in one county in the South. B. T. Washington. Outlook.
December 9, 1905.
Progress of the Negro. A. Walters. 53:651-2. Independent.
Race question solved in Buxton. G. L. McNutt. Independent. May 30, 1907.
Savings of black Georgia. W. E. B. DuBois. 69:128-30. Outlook.
Settlement idea in the cotton belt. P. Dillingham. 70:920-2. Outlook.
Social condition of the Negro. H. L. Phillips. 9:575. Charities.
Training of Negroes for social power. W. E. B. DuBois. 75-409-14. Outlook.
Village improvement among the Negroes. R. L. Smith. 64:733-6. Outlook.
Washington's colored population. S. C. Fernandis. Charities. September 14, 1907.
Washington's colored settlement. R. W. Buell. World To-day. August, 1906.
What the North and South have done for the Negro. 21:606. DeBow's Review.
Washington, B. T. The Free Negro. Outlook. September 18, 1909.
Washington, B. T. Law and order and the Negro. Outlook. November 6, 1909.
Work, M. W. Self-help among the Negroes. Survey. Vol. 22, No. 9.

Efforts for Social Betterment among Negro Americans

Section 1. Scope and Method of the Study. This monograph is an attempt to study efforts for social betterment among Negro Americans. By efforts for social betterment is meant mainly benevolent efforts; i. e., efforts not designed to secure direct economic return. Such activities as are usually called charitable and reformatory are the ones mainly noticed. The efforts noted are mainly those of colored people themselves directed toward their own social uplift, but some notice has also been taken of the charitable work of whites for Negroes and of the general charities of Negroes not confined to their race. The investigation was conducted as follows: In all the chief centers of Negro population the addresses of a number of persons of standing were obtained and the following letter sent them:

My dear Sir:
    I want to get a list of all charitable institutions, clubs, or organizations of any kind conducted wholly or mainly by Negroes which are doing philanthropic work among colored people. I want to omit purely business enterprises, but to include everything that can reasonably be called an effort for social betterment. Will you kindly send me such a list for ...., so far as you know, and the addresses of persons who can give me further information?
    I shall thank you very much.

To the addresses thus obtained was sent the following letter:
My dear Sir:
    I am trying to get a list of all charitable institutions, clubs, or organizations of any kind conducted wholly or mainly by Negroes, which are doing philanthropic work among colored people. The name of the .... has been handed me. I should like to know its history and all the material facts about this ...., together with a picture of the building and members, and also the figures showing the growth and present activities, and amount of property owned. I shall thank you very much.

In this way a large number of reports were obtained, and sometimes several reports of the same club or institution. For the most part, however, the only proof of the work reported was: (a) the word of a reliable resident that the institution existed and was doing some work of the kind indicated; (b) the report of the directors of the work. There is here room for some exaggeration and coloring. Some of the institutions reported may go out of existence before the report is in print and others may be started. The report is not complete or exhaustive in any sense of the word. It does, however, cover most of the larger efforts and many of the more typical ones and some of the minor ones.

Section 2. The African Background. If there is one thing in which the life of barbarians shows a decided superiority to that of civilized people it is in its solution of the problem of poverty. Under tribal communism no individual can be poorer than the tribe. This, to be sure, makes all suffer for the laziness of a few and to a degree penalizes individual thrift. It is doubtful, however, if this explains altogether the lack of accumulated wealth. At any rate it is no little thing to avoid the fearful paradox of modern life—abounding wealth and stinging poverty in the same group, with the necessity of personal charity to ward off the extremes of death and suffering. Of charity, as such, there was no need among Africans, since all shared the common fund of land and food. In the care of the old and young there was a chance for benevolence. The young were adopted by law, into the brother's family if the father died, into the care of another wife of the father if the mother died. The old did not fare so well. If the tribe was nomadic they were killed to keep them from falling into the hands of the enemy or from baser motives. Gradually the permanently settled tribes began to hold their elders in more veneration and look up to them for advice and tradition. Outside of these fundamental matters there was nothing in African life corresponding to modern benevolence.

Section 3. Slavery. No generalization is safe touching the condition of slaves in America. The plantations were self-sufficient oligarchies or monarchies, little interfered with by State or municipal law. On some of them there was severe child labor, no care in sickness, and neglect or sale of the old. On other plantations the children were well cared for, the sick nursed and the old protected. Two abstracts will illustrate these things. Frances Kemble writes:

The Infirmary is a large two-story building, terminating the broad orange-planted space between the two rows of houses which form the first settlement; it is built of whitewashed wood, and contains four large-sized rooms. But how shall I describe to you the spectacle which was presented to me on entering the first of these? But half the casements, of which there were six, were glazed and these were obscured with dirt, almost as much as the other windowless ones were darkened by the dingy shutters, which the shivering inmates had fastened to in order to protect themselves from the cold. In the enormous chimney glimmered the powerless embers of a few sticks of wood, round which, however, as many of the sick women as could approach were cowering, some on wooden settles, most of them on the ground, excluding those who were too ill to rise; and these last poor wretches lay prostrate on the floor, without bed, mattress, or pillow, buried in tattered and filthy blankets, which, huddled round them as they lay strewed about, left hardly space to move upon the floor. And here, in their hour of sickness and suffering, lay those whose health and strength are spent in unrequited labor for us—those who, perhaps even yesterday, were being urged on to their unpaid task—those whose husbands, fathers, brothers and sons were even at that hour sweating over the earth, whose produce was to buy for us all the luxuries which health can revel in, all the comforts which can alleviate sickness. I stood in the midst of them, perfectly unable to speak, the tears pouring from my eyes at this sad spectacle of their misery, myself and my emotion alike strange and incomprehensible to them. Here lay women expecting every hour the terrors and agonies of childbirth, others who had just brought their doomed offspring into the world, others who were groaning over the anguish and bitter disappointment of miscarriages—here lay some burning with fever, others chilled with cold and aching with rheumatism, upon the hard cold ground, the draughts and dampness of the atmosphere increasing their sufferings, and dirt, noise and stench, and every aggravation of which sickness is capable, combined in their condition—here they lay like brute beasts, absorbed in physical suffering; unvisited by any of those Divine influences which may ennoble the dispensations of pain and illness, forsaken, as it seemed to me, of all good; and yet, O God, Thou surely hadst not forsaken them! Now pray take notice that this is the hospital of an estate where the owners are supposed to be humane, the overseer efficient and kind, and the negroes remarkably well cared for and comfortable.

On the other hand Byron Tyson declares:

"Thus, of the three stages, youth, maturity, and old age, through which the servants pass, there is but one in which they are relied on as regular laborers. In childhood and in old age they are well taken care of, and thus the whole slave population is rendered self-supporting. So, of the 3,953,760 slaves that were in the United States in 1860, there was not one supported by a public tax. Such an instance, I presume, is unknown among an equal number of the industrial classes, anywhere in the civilized world. I will ask where else on the face of the globe could you go to find, in a population of nearly four millions, no paupers?[1]

That slaves were often neglected is shown by laws like the following law of Georgia:

"Section 1. From and after the passing of this act (December 12, 1815), it shall be the duty of the inferior courts of the several counties in this State, on receiving information, on oath, of any infirm slave or slaves being in a suffering situation, from the neglect of the owner or owners of such slave or slaves, to make particular inquiries into the situation of such slave or slaves, and render such relief as they in their discretion may think proper.

"Section 2. The said courts may, and they are hereby authorized, to sue for and recover from the owner or owners of such slave or slaves, the amount that may be appropriated for the relief of such slave or slaves, in any court having jurisdiction of the same; any law, usage or custom to the contrary notwithstanding."—Prince's Digest, 460.

Relief of suffering among slaves depended entirely on the character of the masters. That there was a great deal of relief work there can be no doubt. Indeed, the habit of direct relief to Negroes which thus grew up in slavery is now a great hindrance to organized and scientific charity in the South. Among the slaves the charitable work was chiefly in the line of adopting children and caring for the sick. The habit of adoption is still wide-spread and beneficent.

[1] Pamphlet on the Institution of Slavery, etc., by Byron Tyson, p. 8-9.

Section 4. The Present Economic Basis. How far is the Negro American to-day economically able to maintain a system of charitable relief for his own people? We can perhaps best realize these conditions by picturing a single community: Jacksonville, Florida, for instance, had 16,000 Negroes in 1900. To-day it has nine colored lawyers, eighteen colored physicians, ten colored drug stores, two sanitariums, one bank, one livery sale and feed stable, two garages, ten real estate dealers, three undertaking establishments, three denominational schools and a school for girls only, one old folks' home, one orphanage, one industrial school, one institutional church which operates a sewing class, dressmaking, bookkeeping, kindergarten, cooking, gymnasium, music—instrumental and vocal; has two paid missionaries, an assistant pastor. The church owns a full city block in the heart of the city, valued at $125,000. There are two dentists, a colored board of trade, the first and only one in the South; three cigar factories, three wholesale fish and poultry dealers; four hotels, containing twenty-five to one hundred rooms each; three weekly newspapers; one Odd Fellows Temple, valued at $100,000, and one K. of P. Temple, both paid for; several Masonic Temples of less value; one large jewelry store; one curio store; ten public school buildings; twenty-six letter carriers and postal clerks; three deputy collectors of customs; numbers of railway mail clerks; one shoe store; two industrial insurance companies that own their buildings, one valued at $35,000.

To this may be added the following general facts: a committee of the American Economic Association reported:

> The evidence in hand leads your committee to the conclusion that the accumulated wealth of the Negro race in the United States in 1900 was approximately $300,000,000, and probably neither less than $250,000,000 nor more than $350,000,000.

Since 1900 the increase of Negro property holdings has been very rapid, as the records in three States show:

North Carolina—Property listed by Negro citizens

Year	Total
1900	$ 9,478,399
1901	9,765,986
1902	11,173,227
1903	12,108,576
1904	14,339,402
1905	15,046,665
1906	17,434,844
1907	17,945,109
1908	21,253,581

Total Value of Real Estate and Personal Property Owned by Negroes in Virginia

1891

Real estate	$ 8,995,514
Personal property	3,094,451
Total	$12,089,965

1900
Real estate... ....$12,033,988
Personal property.. 3,822,582

Total..$15,856,570

1905
Real estate.. ....$16,599,152
Personal property.. 5,384,116

Total.... ....$21,983,268

1908
Real estate................................. ....$18,807,889
Personal property.. 6,920,447

Total...$25,628,336

Total Assessed Wealth of Georgia Negroes

Year	Total property	Year	Total property
1874	$ 6,157,798	1892	$14,869,575
1875	5,393,885	1893	14,960,675
1876	5,488,867	1894	14,387,730
1877	5,430,844	1895	12,941,280
1878	5,124,875	1896	13,292,816
1879	5,182,398	1897	13,619,690
1880	5,764,293	1898	13,719,200
1881	6,478,951	1899	13,447,423
1882	6,589,876	1900	14,118,720
1883	7,582,395	1901	15,629,811
1884	8,021,525	1902	15,188,069
1885	8,153,390	1903	16,714,334
1886	8,655,298	1904	18,002,500
1887	8,936,479	1905	20,616,468
1888	9,631,271	1906	23,750,109
1889	10,415,330	1907	25,904,822
1890	12,322,003	1908	27,042,672
1891	14,196,735		

Property per Capita for Georgia Negroes

Year	Property per capita	Year	Property per capita
1874	$ 9.98	1892	$16.63
1875	8.49	1893	16.41
1876	8.44	1894	15.48
1877	8.09	1895	13.67
1878	7.44	1896	13.78
1879	7.33	1897	13.87
1880	7.95	1898	13.72
1881	8.77	1899	13.22
1882	8.77	1900	13.64
1883	9.91	1901	14.85
1884	10.30	1902	14.19
1885	10.21	1903	15.37
1886	10.75	1904	16.28
1887	10.92	1905	18.37
1888	11.57	1906	20.82
1889	12.32	1907	22.37
1890	14.35	1908	23.003
1891	16 20		

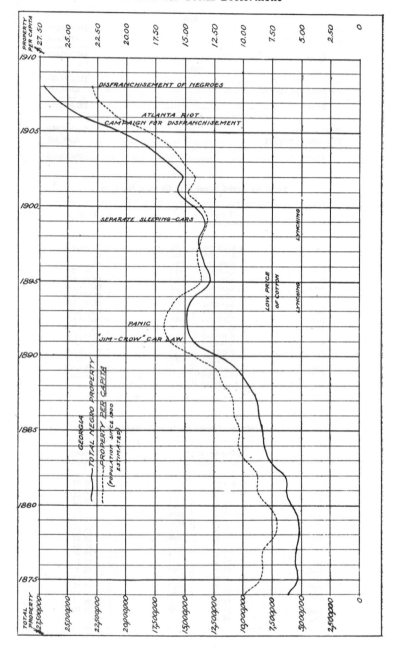

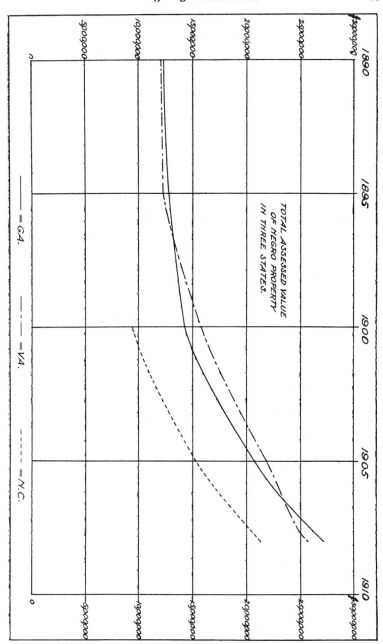

TOTAL ASSESSED VALUE
OF NEGRO PROPERTY
IN THREE STATES.

——— = GA.　——·—— = VA.　------- = N.C.

From these figures we may deduce this simpler table:

Assessed Value of Property

	1900	1908
Georgia	$14,118,720	$27,042,672
Virginia	15,856,570	25,628,336
North Carolina..	9,478,399	21,253,581
Total	$39,453,689	$73,924,589

Actual increase, $34,470,900
Increase per cent., 87⅓.

Judging from these figures and the report of the American Economic Association quoted above it would seem fair to infer that the total property of Negro Americans aggregated $560,000,000 in 1908.

Section 5. The Church. As was said in the study of 1898: It is natural that to-day the bulk of organized efforts of Negroes in any direction should center in the Church. "The Negro Church is the only social institution of the Negroes which started in the forest and survived slavery; under the leadership of the priest and medicine man, afterward of the Christian pastor, the Church preserved in itself the remnants of African tribal life and became after emancipation the center of Negro social life. So that to-day the Negro population of the United States is virtually divided into Church congregations, which are the real units of the race life. It is natural, therefore, that charitable and rescue work among Negroes should first be found in the churches and reach there its greatest development."

The statistics for Negro churches in 1906 according to the United States Census was as follows: "The total number of communicants or members, as reported by 36,563 organizations, is 3,685,097; of these, as shown by the returns for 34,648 organizations, 37.5 per cent are males and 62.5 per cent females."

According to the statistics, these organizations have 35,160 church edifices; a seating capacity for church edifices of 10,481,738, as reported by 33,091 organizations; church property valued at $56,636,159, against which there appears an indebtedness of $5,005,905; halls, etc., used for worship by 1,261 organizations; and parsonages valued at $3,727,884. The number of Sunday-shools, as reported by 33,538 organizations, is 34,681, with 210,148 officers and teachers and 1,740,099 scholars.

As compared with the report for 1890, these figures show increases of 13,308 in the number of colored organizations, 1,011,120 in the number of communicants or members, 11,390 in the number of church edifices and $30,009,711 in the value of church property.

DENOMINATION	Number of colored organizations 1906	Number of colored organizations 1890	Number of communicants or members reported 1906	Number of communicants or members reported 1890	Value of Church Property Reported 1906	Value of Church Property Reported 1890
All denominations consisting in whole or in part of colored organizations	38,770	23,462	3,685,097	2,673,977	$56,636,159	$26,626,448
Denominations consisting wholly of colored organizations	31,383	19,158	3,207,307	2,321,313	44,673,049	20,525,141
Baptist bodies:						
Baptists—National Convention	18,534	12,533	2,261,607	1,348,989	24,437,272	9,038,549
Colored Primitive Baptists in America	797	323	35,076	18,162	296,639	135,427
United American Freewill Baptists	261		14,489		79,278	
Church of God and Saints of Christ	48		1,823		6,000	
Churches of the Living God:						
Church of the Living God (Christian Workers for Friendship)	44		2,676		28,175	
Church of the Living God (Apostolic Church)	15		752		25,700	
Church of Christ in God	9		848		9,700	
Free Christian Zion Church of Christ	15		1,835		5,867	
Evangelistic associations:						
Voluntary Missionary Society of America	3		425		2,400	
Methodist bodies:						
Union American Methodist Episcopal Church	77	42	4,347	2,279	170,150	187,600
African Methodist Episcopal Church	6,647	2,481	494,777	452,725	11,303,449	6,468,280
African Union Methodist Protestant Church	69	40	5,592	3,415	183,647	54,440
African Methodist Episcopal Zion Church	2,204	1,704	184,542	349,788	4,883,207	2,714,128
Congregational Methodist				319		525
Colored Methodist Episcopal Church	2,381	1,759	172,996	129,383	3,017,849	2,713,366
Reformed Zion Union Episcopal Church	45	32	3,059	2,346	87,875	15,000
Reformed Methodist Union Episcopal Church	58	11	4,397	951	36,905	2,000
Evangelist Missionary Church						
Presbyterian bodies:						
Colored Cumberland Presbyterian Church	196	224	18,066	12,956	203,778	195,826
Denominations consisting in part of colored organizations	5,377	4,304	477,790	352,664	11,963,110	6,101,307

It was estimated in 1907 that these churches raised seven and a half million dollars a year. Most of the half million goes probably to pay high interest on a debt of five millions. The remaining seven millions goes chiefly to the support of the pastor, the maintenance of the plant and general church purposes. A large and growing share, however, goes to "mission" work. Part of this is proselyting, but the larger part of it is distinctly benevolence and work for social betterment. No complete record of this work can be obtained. Outside of these money contributions by far the larger part of the benevolent work of Negroes is the unorganized personal work of church members among the congregations. This consists of donations, visits, care of the sick, adoption of children, etc.

The missionary money raised by the churches is shown by the following figures:

A. M. E. Missionary Dept.—Total collection, April 23, 1904, to April 4, 1908, inclusive

	1905	1906	1907	1908	Total
Easter Collections:					
Received by Missionary Department, 75 per cent	$13,020.41	$18,310.00	$15,340.27	$4,922.61	
Received and disbursed by Conferences, 25 per cent	4,340.14	6,103.33	5,113.42	1,640.87	
	$17,360.55	$24,413.33	$20,453.69	$5,563.48	
Total Easter Collections, 4 years					$ 68,791.05
P. H. & F. M. Society:					
Received by Missionary Department, 40 per cent	$ 1,464.15	$ 1,762.05	$ 1,943,03	$ 2,224.15	
Received and disbursed by Conferences, 60 per cent	2,196.18	2,643.06	2,914.56	3,336.24	
	$ 3,660.33	$ 4,405.11	$ 4,857.59	$ 5,560.39	
Total P. H. & F. M. Society Collections, 4 years					$ 18,483.42
W. H. & F. M. Society:					
Received by Missionary Department, 50 per cent	$ 573.67	$ 1,101.40	$ 1,292.23	$ 1,931.35	
Received and disbursed by Conferences, 50 per cent	$ 573.67	$ 1,101.40	$ 1,292.23	$ 1,931.35	
	$ 1,147.34	$ 2,202.80	$ 2,584.46	$ 3,862.70	
Total W. H. & F. M. Society Collections, 4 years					$ 9,797.30
	1903–1904	1904–1905	1905–1906	1906–1907	
W. P. M. M. Society:					
Received by Woman's Parent Mite Missionary Society, 40 per cent	$ 2,016.91	$ 1,972.13	$ 3,202.24	$ 3,194.31	
Received and disbursed by Conferences, 60 per cent	3,025.38	2,958.18	4,803.36	4,791.43	
	$ 5,042.29	$ 4,930.31	$ 8,005.60	$ 7,985.74	
Woman's Parent Mite Missionary Society, 4 years					$ 25,963.94
Total collections for Missions, 4 years					$123,035.71

A. M. E. Church, 1864-1903

Home and Foreign Missionary Department

	Raised	Received from dollar money	Total expended
1864–1868......	$ 5,425 65	....	$ 5,425.65
1868–1872......	9,317.32	....	9,317.32
1872–1880......	12,504.22	$ 27,913.56	40,417.78
1880–1884......	34,811.83	54,510.51	89,322.34
1884–1888......	19,001.09	73,227.18	92,228.27
1888–1892......	25,675.47	187,772.45	213,447.92
1892–1896......	66,819.27	146,050.24	212,869,51
1896–1900......	58,876.36	145,226.71	204,103.07
1900–1903.......	80,815.66	136,805.15	217,620.81
Total......	$313,246.87	$771,505.80	$1,084,752.67

Seven per cent of the income of the African Methodists goes for missionary and charitable purposes. If this is true of all Negro church bodies, then their expenditure for such purposes is over half a million a year. The expenditures of the Baptists are reported as follows:

Negro Baptists, 1897-1909

Year	For Missions
1897 ....$	1,000 00
1898	2,557 41
1899	4,352 25
1900	8,920 40
1901	10,997 17
1902	15,741 26
1903	19,824 49
1904	27,520 43
1905	33,227 76
1906	49,621 90
1908	44,295 94
1909	43,396 42
Total........................	$261,565 44

The figures for Negro Baptist foreign mission work for 1907 were:

Summary by Months

September ....$	1,853 50
October	634 10
November............................	3,014 77
December...........................	553 37
January.............................	634 74
February............................	1,589 78
March	436 79
April.....	4,197 69
May.................................	1,671 73
June................................	736 26
July.................................	1,151 33
August	2,273 60
Total........................$	18,727 96

The report of activities for 1908 and 1909 follows:

Colored Baptist Missionary Work

	1908	1909
Number of missionaries, colporters, Sunday-school and Bible workers working in co-operation with our Board during the year	43	65
Days of service reported	8,678	3,812
Sermons preached	3,582	3,702
Sunday-schools addressed	1,345	1,441
Prayer-meetings attended	2,369	2,765
B. Y. P. U. Societies addressed	395	563
Missionary Societies addressed	397	481
Other addresses and public talks delivered	2,141	2,859
Total number of sermons, addresses and public talks delivered	10,229	9,046
Homes visited for Bible reading and prayer	5,853	9,410
Homes found without Bibles	507	1,788
Number of churches visited	3,221	4,755
Number of churches helped to organize	38	21
New Sunday-schools organized	42	39
Missionary societies formed or organized	58	37
Number of persons baptized by request of churches	1,260	841
Number of conventions, associations and other State and District meetings attended	1,970	1,542
Missionary and Bible conferences held	1,970	1,597
Letters and postal cards written	10,265	14,847
Number of religious tracts, pamphlets and booklets distributed	12,569	18,569
Miles traveled to perform this labor	157,363	270,639

	1908	1909
Money collected and applied to missionary work in communities where collected	$14,686 11	$16,027 24
Value of tracts, pamphlets and booklets distributed free	585 46	599 46
Money collected by missionaries and colporters and applied to their salaries	5,521 57	5,937 37
Money donated by Home Mission Board of Southern Baptist Convention on salaries of missionaries	7,262 50	9,250 00
Money collected by missionaries and applied to their traveling expenses	3,076 34	5,082 35
Salaries of female missionaries working in co-operation with our Board	980 00	950 00
Cash, commission, and books supplemented on missionaries' salaries working in co-operation with our Board	9,783 96	3,850 00
Salary, traveling, office rent, and other expenses of Field Secretary paid by Publishing Board	2,400 00	1,700 00
Total	$44,295 94	$43,396 42

"The Home Mission Board, in its general organization, is made up of fifty-three members appointed from the same number of State and Territorial conventions by your body. We have a general organization. This organization holds annually two sessions when at the sitting of the convention, for the reason that it is a financial impossibility to bring these members from the various parts of the United States and its insular possessions oftener than once a year. However, we, by the provision of the Constitution, have an Executive Board of the National Baptist Publishing Board, located at Nashville, Tenn. We co-operate with them both in the employment of a missionary or corresponding secretary, and in performing missionary work; by this method we are attempting to economize as much as possible, and use all the available means on purely missionary work. This method of operation has proven beneficial to the field and satisfactory to both boards."

One of the agencies of uplift among the Baptists is the Baptist Young People's Union. The department has in ten years accomplished the following work:

State B. Y. P. U. Conventions	38
District B. Y. P. U. Conventions	320
County B. Y. P. U. Conventions	510
City Conquest organizations	380
Local B. Y. P. U. Societies	7,600
Converts joined the churches	19,850
Number taking Bible Reader's Course	78,250
Number taking Baptist History	71,310
Number taking Baptist Doctrines	68,240

Moneys Contributed

For Christian Education	$68,200 00
" Home Missions	46,500 00
" Foreign Missions	33,460 00
" State Missions	28,210 00
" Church Repairs	69,340 00

Most of the local benevolence of Baptist churches is not reported and can be ascertained only in local associations. For instance, a West Virginia association (New River Valley) reports, July, 1908:

Fifty-eight churches gave in one year for:

State Missions	$ 31 35
Home Missions	11 87
Foreign Missions	6 45
Benevolence	1,043 80

The Baptist convention of the State of Texas reported under church support in 1903: Five schools, a chautauqua, an orphanage and an "Old Folk's" home.

The convention has raised the following sums of money:

State Mission Money

Raised by the Baptist Missionary and Educational Convention, commencing with the year 1883:

1883	$ 2,390 60
1884	116 30
1885	2,168 11
1886	3,135 82
1887	2,674 30
1888	2,588 15
1889	10,266 97
1890	13,486 71
1891	2,569 84
1891	13,085 91
1892	18,381 76
1893	6,955 63
1894	2,614 43
1895	3,721 02
1896	2,260 56
1887	1,644 79
1898	2,125 61
1899	1,059 68
1900	
1901	2,272 50
1902	1,286 17
1903	3,335 64
1904	3,782 45
1905	2,363 54
1906	3,218 52
Total	$109,554 27

Most of this money was raised among Negroes, but there were some contributions from whites. From Arkansas it is reported:

In our State (Arkansas) the Baptists support four general missionaries and a Superintendent of Missions; one college located at Little Rock, Ark., eight academies at other points in the State.

The actual amount of money raised and expended in missionary and educational work by the colored Baptists in Arkansas ranges from $45,000.00 to $50,000.00 a year—$50,000.00 for present year.

It is the women that do the larger part of the benevolent work in Negro churches.

In Mott's Sketches there is the narration of the work of a colored woman in New York city, who conceived the notion of child instruction and who carried it out under the most adverse circumstances. In the church economy of that day the child life was unconsidered, until this woman had planned and set in motion this very work. This was not long after the Revolutionary period.

In the early days of the Nineteenth Century another figure came into view—Jarena Lee. She was born in Cape May county, New Jersey, and attended school with the whites, getting the best there was to be had at that time. She was an ardent student, both of the Bible and in a general way, and possessed the gift of expression in an uncommon degree. Churches were widely scattered, and as a rule her kind, through prejudice, were without ministry or church. The need was paramount, and this woman with a will meant to fill it. She opened a Sunday-school in a private house, and the children for miles around came of a Sunday to be catechised and indoctrinated into the Bible lore. Jarena Lee had persistency, was possessed of a splendid memory and was naturally a voluble talker, and these with thorough goodness, unselfishness and large personal magnetism, made her the very one for such a crusade.

That was in South Jersey, and not only the fame but the work spread, and soon Philadelphia felt the force of her influence. Later on we find her in Pennsylvania, Delaware, Maryland, and even as far as Ohio. She first taught a secular school in Southern Jersey, but after awhile gave it up for mission effort in behalf of the church of her intelligent choice—the A. M. E. Church.

The gift of prodigious work was hers, and with the mental strength possessed by her there was a singular sweetness attached. This was attested by all the early fathers of the church, and proved how a woman could be strong in mind and action without losing the spell of her sex. The consensus of opinion from those contemporaneous with her gave her a position, for good, in the A. M. E. Church advancement, unmatched by any man of her day.

Her autobiography is a master bit of reason, and apart from its personal flavor throws much light upon the days wherein she figured, for the good of her kind, and especially for the church of her own communion.

Although the work of Mary Lewton, of Philadelphia, was more circumscribed than that of Jarena Lee, it was a valuable one. She taught the children of her neighborhood, near Fourth and Fairmount avenues, at her home, and from her endeavors the Sunday-school of Union A. M. E. Church was begotten.[1]

---

[1] Christian Recorder, 1909.

The Ninth Annual Report of the Baptist Woman's Convention shows the following cash account:

Receipts		
Balance, September 1, 1908	$	13 05
Alabama		241 18
Arkansas		167 15
California		26 25
Colorado		29 62
District of Columbia		40 95
Florida		163 41
Georgia		180 11
Indiana		143 56
Illinois		310 54
Iowa		1 45
Kansas		103 15
Kentucky		158 61
Louisiana		139 62
Maryland		39 66
Minnesota		17 45
Mississippi		347 25
Missouri		366 36
New Jersey		62 01
New York		13 70
North Carolina		26 55
Ohio		314 35
Oklahoma		234 10
National Convention—Sales		216 00
Miss C. G. Ewen		87 75
Pennsylvania		168 75
Rhode Island		1 45
South Carolina		165 15
Tennessee		227 55
Texas		893 40
Virginia		55 44
West Virginia		167 99
Borrowed Training School Fund		825 34
Treas. Finance Committee		707 10
Total, September 1, 1909		$6,756 00

Expenses		
Foreign Missions		$1,145 50
Home Missions and Education		141 55
National Bapt. Pub. Board		11 25
National Bapt. Union		8 25
Field Missionaries, salaries		839 59
Field Missionaries, traveling		624 77
Printing		458 25
Postage		276 88
Office		52 40
Supplies		749 74
Salaries		1,419 67
Traveling		131 22
Field		28 05
Stamp Day		141 18
Expense of Officers		389 45
Expressage and Drayage		49 24
Total		$6,717 70
Reported by local societies and State organizations		$6,782 09
Total received by Convention		6,756 00
Grand total receipts		$13,538 09
Total expenses National Auxiliary		$6,717 70
Total expenses local and State organizations		6,782 09
Grand total expenses		13,499 79
Balance on hand Sept. 1, 1909		$ 38 30

Besides this, $5,594.97 was raised for a girls' training school. The convention reported 326 societies and 107 children's bands. They have distributed 200,000 tracts in ten years. One tract is "The Traveler's Friend." Some of its paragraphs are:

If possible, always purchase your ticket the day before you contemplate going on a trip. If this can not be done, leave home in ample time to avoid the rush that is usual at the ticket window a few minutes before the train leaves.

If the ticket must be shown at the gate, have it in your hand, where it can be displayed when called for. Do not wait until you get up to the gate and then hunt for your ticket in your pocket-book and grip, and thus delay the other passengers.

We notice so many people paying their fares on the train. This is a very bad policy, when it is possible to secure a ticket either at the city office or at the station before train time. Then, too, the company charges more for tickets on the train. Save money by getting your ticket beforehand.

Don't stick your head out of the window at every station and hollo at somebody a block away, and don't talk so loud to your friends who may be on the platform that a person a block away may hear you. If they are not close enough for a conversation call them to you, and then talk to them, and not to everybody on the train and everybody around the waiting-room.

In States where the separate-car law is in operation we find the "crew" taking all kinds of liberties—converting the little apartment set aside for the colored passengers into a dressing-room, boot-black stand, a dump for dust-pans, pillows, lanterns, clothing to change in at the end of the journey, and indeed anything. On many of the trains baggage-men, mail-clerks, conductors, brakemen, porters—all come in to arrange their toilets in the morning; and if there is a towel provided for the colored passengers it is so thoroughly used by the "gang" that it is not fit to wipe out the basin with. Sometimes the fruit-venders, conductors and brakemen whistle and sing, and "cut shines" of all kinds in the colored-passenger cars. Always enter a respectful protest and don't forget to write the operating officials.

And now a word to those travelers who never get hungry until they see the "butcher" with his basketful of stale candies, peanuts, crackerjack, bananas, oranges, etc. There are some people who can not let the boy pass without making a purchase. These boys are generally very disrespectful to colored passengers. We have seen them uncork a bottle of smelling-salts and thrust it into the face of nearly everybody in the car. These boys have a lot of smart sayings and are a source of annoyance to respectable people. If they find that there are children on the car who will cry for fruit, or candies, they proceed to tempt them in order to force the parents to purchase something to satisfy their little ones. Those old lanterns, and pistols, full of cheap stale candy, are not worth buying, and just why so many of our people will waste their money buying circus food from these railway venders is a question.

These boys have learned that most negro passengers would rather feed their stomachs than their minds. They offer the white passengers newspapers and magazines, and offer negroes peanuts and crackerjack, candy and bananas. So many negroes eat that trash, that whenever you want to read it is necessary to make a special request of the boy to bring you a paper or a magazine. Certainly some of us have a magazine or paper at home that we could take along with us to read, and we would not have to patronize the frisky ignorant "butcher." It is certainly cheaper to purchase lunches as far from the train and railroad station as you possibly can, for the nearer you get to the station the less fruit and candy you get for your money, and these delicacies sell at a premium on a railroad train.

The writer of these pages has traveled extensively and has had many experiences with passengers, "the road gang," conductors and porters. She has suffered much because of unequal accommodation for colored passengers, and has "begged" operating officials to give Negroes who pay first-class fare first-class accommodations. Many promises have been made, but no improvement. She has also urged her own people to be careful of their deportment, look neat and clean, and thus demand what they can not hope to demand if they are boisterous and unclean.

Other activities include the donation of postage stamps, giving of Christmas boxes, the sending out of field missionaries, etc. One of the missionaries reports: Homes visited, 1,341; mothers' meetings held, 14;

churches, associations, etc.,visited, 262; money collected, not including month of August, $944.57.

The Baptist Women's Missionary Convention, which met in Harrodsburg, Ky., July 2-5, published a report of the work accomplished for the year: Pages of tracts distributed, 3,141; religious visits made, 6,597; children induced to attend Sunday-school, 1,805; sick visited, 4,052; poor and suffering aided, 1,047; garments distributed, 704; money collected, $1,931.01, of this amount $780.40 was given for local work; for State missions, $38.06; Foreign missions, $26.57.

In the A. M. E. Church the Woman's Parent Mite Missionary Society reports these sums for the four years 1903–07:

	Members	*Collected*
First District		
Philadelphia	1,400	$3,080 26
New Jersey	946	1,019 43
New York	200	936 00
New England	245	711 00
Second District		
Baltimore, Md	1,378	6,148 66
Virginia	2,896	2,764 10
Third District		
Pittsburgh	1,100	4,615 15
Ohio	600	1,672 03
North Ohio	1,300	4,712 00
Fourth District		
Indiana	727	1,509 52
Kentucky	310	524 00
Fifth District		
Kansas	210	987 83
Missouri	110	171 00
Twelfth District		
Michigan	200	480 00
Ontario	75	231 00
Total	11,697	$30,361 98

Number of Branches, 20.

The accompanying report says:

In the early days of the start of Allen's work, God directed the hearts of Bishops Campbell, Payne, Shorter, Wayman and Brown to urge the women of the A. M. E. Conference to organize. Not because there had been no effort in this direction previously, for in the early century of African Methodism women helpers were known. We find on the records Dorcas societies, women, the effect of whose unselfish labors extended broadly to alleviate the sufferings and wants of those in our immediate vicinity; also such societies as Daughters of Conference, whose interest extended over the whole of the conference and for over a quarter of a century aided the traveling ministers of the gospel. But the honored fathers, now sainted bishops, saw the necessity of not only broadening the Home work, but that the sympathies should accord with the cry of the heathen in the foreign lands and that the women of the A. M. E. Conference would push the cause to success, and that they would take great interest in the financial needs of the foreign work, and with zeal and activity at heart unite forces and willingly respond to the call which was made.

After being organized at Washington, D. C., the next meeting was called at Bethel Church, Philadelphia, Pa., at which time there was a large gathering, many of which enrolled themselves as members of the Parent Mite Missionary Society.

But it is not only in the streets of our cities of America that we see the need of this Home Missionary work, for in the streets of Cape Town, Africa, I found the need of the same practical Christian service.

From August, 1874, the organization of the Parent Society, the bishops' wives were made vice-presidents of the organization and this gave them the right, wherever they were, to organize societies and push on the work through the whole connection. I, therefore, formed in Africa four societies— the Sarah Allen, Eliza Turner, Florida Grant, and the Mary A. Campbell. With the simplest kind of constitution these societies went to work and God blessed their endeavors from the very beginning. Right in the streets of Cape Town I found my work and they found theirs. Young men that I spoke to on the streets were quite willing to go with me, and I was very glad to be able to take them to the schoolroom of the Institute, for the Temperance Society was permitted to hold its meetings there. The Colored Women's Christian Association also held its meetings there under the fostering care of the A. M. E. Church.

Therefore, we need the extended appliances of Christian Association rooms. We must take these young people while their lives are yet before them, and bring them within the protecting walls of our A. M. E. Christian Association buildings, and not wait until they have learned from bad company to become lawless and wicked, and then run after them and bring them into the church and try to wash them with floods of heavenly grace.

Years ago poor mothers who had to go out to work by the day had to leave their children at home to fall into all kinds of danger, and even wickedness; but now, thank God, by the establishment of the Day Nurseries the young are protected from these dangers, and I think the very smile of Heaven must rest upon these establishments where the innocence of the young is guarded from the snares of evil, and mothers' hearts are no longer tortured by anxiety as to what their little ones are doing while they are out striving to earn their daily bread.

Now, whether it is the Association Buildings or the Day Nurseries, God speed the day when their numbers shall increase and their wise, practical sound sense mission service shall be acknowledged by the Church of Christ the world over.

Missionary work is not alone confined to financial reports; we go a step or two farther and encourage Temperance, Mothers' Meeting, Juvenile Work, Deaconess Work, etc.

The missionary spirit, as obtained in our beloved Zion, assumed definite, tangible shape and character when, in 1824, its first missionaries laid themselves upon the altar for service in the persons of Scipio Beans and —— Robinson, and both of them came from the Baltimore Annual Conference.

These results have been obtained through the vim and earnestness put forth by those having charge of the different departments of our work, namely: the Temperance Department, the Mothers' Meeting Department, Prayer and Praise Department, seconded by our Field Organizer and Lecturer. In this connection must be mentioned the Ladies' Alliance, composed of the ministers' wives, organized for the purpose of cultivating closer social intercourse between us, amounting in reality to a Round Table Circle.

There are many factors constantly at work in drawing large numbers of non-church-going laborers and their families from Georgia, Alabama and the Carolinas, and from Middle and West Tennessee, to Chattanooga and coal mines west and east therefrom. The great attraction in Chattanooga is facility with which our people obtain positions as skilled and unskilled laborers in the large number of furnaces, foundries, pipe works, and other factories in which iron, from ore to "pig," is converted into every form in which that mineral is commercially used. In these works the wages earned by our people run from $7.50 to $21.00, and in a few instances more, per week, and are paid weekly, with a constant demand for more labor. The raw material daily worked is enormous. As a result, miners for coal, hands for the coke ovens, quarrymen for rock, miners for ore and railroad hands for freight handling, find ready employment at good wages, and in great numbers. In consequence, the rush from lands and from congested cities is very great, and brings a large number of the uncultured, low moraled aud vicious with it. These must be met and must have the Gospel preached unto them.

Not only do their brethren, through the ties of race, see this necessity and recognize its importance, but the corporations, so generally considered heartless, also recognize the necessity of the Gospel for these men and, therefore, generally at each mine and oven plant outside of the corporate limits of cities, the company has erected a church and sometimes a schoolhouse, to accommodate the preacher, but provides no funds from which to pay him for his labor. He must subsist on capricious bounty, occasional charity and meager support from Mission funds, and that, too, as a rule, which has been gathered, mite by mite and penny by penny, through the energetic solicitations of you ladies and the worthy co-laborers whom you have the honor to represent.

In the A. M. E. Zion Church is the Woman's Home and Foreign Missionary Society, which was organized in Montgomery, Ala., 1880, during the sitting of the General Conference of that year.

At first and for a long time we worked under the direction of the Mission Board of the Church. About three years ago we were set apart as one of the Church Departments. We are now putting forth every effort to get a society in every church in the congregation. We find that those women who are organized are becoming more intelligent—they have Mothers' Meeting, discuss topics on the home life, do all manner of charity work and church work. Two-thirds of the money raised by the Society is sent to the General Treasurer for Foreign work; they retain one-third for their own use and do all the local work they wish. I have no record of the local work; that is sent to the Corresponding Secretary. We are increasing every year in the two-thirds sent to me. Several years ago we only raised seven or eight hundred dollars; last year we raised over $1,200; and this year—and the year is not out until July—we have raised $1,500. We are helping two schools and five missions in Africa. One of our teachers is an African who was brought to this country and educated at Livingstone College. We have a fund in reserve to educate African girls, to return as missionaries. It is not an easy matter to get the girls, it seems, but we have almost secured one. We hope to have two come at once.

Our work is divided into districts, so that we can have meetings and help the rural districts.

In widely separated localities church work in Benevolence is mentioned, as, e. g.:

"Metropolitan Baptist Church Bureau of Information regarding respectable boarding houses, Twentieth and Tasker streets, Philadelphia."

"Church League for Work amongst Colored People, Twelfth and Walnut streets; under Episcopal Church. Organized 1897."

"All the Negro churches of any importance have their auxiliary societies, in the form of missionary societies, Epworth leagues, B. Y. P. U.'s, or C. E.'s."—Dallas, Texas.

"There are numerous efforts being made by Negroes in Virginia for their social betterment in their churches and other organizations."

"The work of our own society here is to care for the sick and needy of the town, and it also contributes toward work in foreign mission fields."—Mission Society, Henderson, N. C.

"In addition to these, there are connected with the Zion Baptist Church two boys' clubs, classified as to age; a night school with classes in gymnastics and physical culture, aside from the ordinary routine."—Phœbus, Va.

"There are also connected with nearly every church some local society which would mean at least twelve or thirteen more than the above named."—Charlotte, N. C.

"Of course I don't mention the list of organizations that are auxiliary to the churches, such as 'Willing Workers,' 'Sunshine Club,' and 'The Whatsoever Club.' Their object generally is to raise money for the churches, though they often do charitable work."—Kansas City, Mo.

We can best realize the extent of church work by considering the churches in one community—Atlanta, Georgia:

Church	Denomination	Church	Denomination
Mt. Zion	Baptist	McKinley Temple	Baptist
Prospect Baptist	"	Mt. Calvary	"
Providence	"	Mt. Moriah	"
St. Luke	"	Mt. Hermon	"
Salem	"	Frasier Street	"
Shiloh	"	Mt. Olive	"
Springfield	"	Mt. Olive	"
Tillman	"	Mt. Pisgah	"
Trinity Tabernacle	"	Mt. Gilead	"
Trinity	"	Mt. Pleasant	"
Willow Tree	"	Allen Temple	Methodist.
Tabernacle	"	Ariel Bowen Memorial	"
Zion Hill	"	Bethel	"
Wheat Street	"	Bridgeport	"
Fair Haven Tabernacle	Christian	Butler Street	"
Mission Church	"	Holsey's Temple	"
Marietta Street	Congregational	Mt. Carmel	"
First Congregational	"	Shiloh	"
St. Paul's	"	Central Avenue	"
St. Gabriel's Missions	"	Cosmopolitan	"
Butler Street Mission	Presbyterian	Pleasant Valley	"
Radcliffe Memorial	"	St. Luke's	"
Fraser Street Mission	"	St. Matthew's	"
Antioch	Baptist	St. Paul's	"
Bethlehem	"	West Mitchell	"
Beulah	"	St. Phillip's	"
Central	"	Holsey Chapel	"
Ebenezer	"	Fort Street	"
Friendship	"	St. James Mission	"
Horton Street Chapel	"	St. Mark's	"
Kelsey Tabernacle	"	Wanen's Chapel	"
Kennesaw	"	Turner's Chapel,	"
Love Street	"	Turner Monumental	"
Macedonia	"	Zion	"
Magnolia Street	"	Swedenborgian	Swedenborgian
New Hope	"		

One correspondent writes:

"I am not able to see myself (perhaps others smarter can) how we can ever hope to do much good for ourselves, in any way, so long as we foster so many different religious opinions; for doubtless you well know that nine-tenths of our differences come from our different religious opinions, which is bound to keep us divided and weak, and so long as this state of affairs continues so long will we continue to be helpless in a manner and continue to howl about the white man not giving us a chance. I believe in making our own chances, but we'll never do it until we realize the folly of trying to ape the white man in everything he does. In my mind our greatest blunder is in the fostering of the multiplicity of churches of different faiths and our fraternal organizations. We should study to have but one church, that would be adaptable to our circumstances, and but one fraternal organization likewise. Under such conditions our interests would become more mutual, and like our brother Irishman we would be united all along the line and could help ourselves."

Section 6. The School. Three questions arise in regard to Negro efforts for social betterment through schools: 1. What Negroes pay for their schools. 2. What benevolent efforts they make to improve schools. 3. What the benevolence of whites has done for Negro schools. Only the two last questions fall strictly within the scope of this report. It is, however, interesting to quote from a paper read before the twelfth annual Conference for Education in the South by a southern white man. From his tables we take the following figures:

	Virginia	N. Carolina	Georgia
Date	1907	1908	1907
Total cost of schools	$3,308,086 00	$2,958,160 00	$2,850,211 00
Cost of Negro schools	489,228 00	402,658 00	506,170 00
Per cent. of total cost going to Negro schools	14.7	13.6	17.7
Per cent. of Negroes in population	35.7	33.3	46.7
Amount of public school funds not contributed by white tax-payers; i. e., contributed by Negroes, public utility corporations, endowments, etc	$507,305 00	$429,197 00	$647,852 54

"What is true of the school funds of the three States considered above is probably true of all the others" (i. e., Southern States).[1]

The following facts are taken mainly from R. R. Wright, Jr., "Self-Help in Negro Education":

The African Methodist Episcopal Church supports twenty schools with 202 teachers and 5,700 pupils. The school property is valued at

[1] Public Taxation and Negro Schools, by Charles L. Coon, Atlanta University Publications, No. 6.

$1,132,000. The annual income of these schools is $150,000, contributed by 300,000 people. Since 1844 they have raised $3,000,000 for
education.

The A. M. E. Zion has twelve schools with 150 teachers, 3,000 students.
Value of their school property is $300,000 and they raise $100,000. In all
they have raised $1,100,000 for education.

The C. M. E. Church has six schools, and the A. M. U. Protestant
Church three.

The Baptists have 120 schools run entirely by Negroes and worth at
least $700,000. They have 613 teachers, 8,644 students. The churches
raise about $150,000 a year for their schools, and the total money raised
for these schools is $343,000 a year.

Negroes also raise $700,000 for their schools which are supported by
white Baptist churches. During the past forty years Negro Baptists
have contributed $6,000,000 to their own education. Negro members
of the M. E. Church have contributed in forty years $3,143,000 for their
own education. Negroes own 43_{10}^{9} per cent. of their schoolhouses in
155 Southern counties. Besides this, many of those owned by the county
were deeded to the county by Negroes.

In Macon county, Alabama, Negro patrons of six large schools added
207½ months to the school term and raised $6,532.44 in 1906 and 1907.

Negro students have paid in nine years $5,187,269 in cash and work to
74 Negro institutions, or 44.6 per cent of the entire running expenses.
Besides this they have raised money in other ways. For instance, the
$100,000 which built Jubilee Hall at Fisk University.

"The history of civilization does not show one other instance of a
wholly illiterate race or nation reducing its illiteracy by half in a single
generation.

"It is probably true that the Negroes pay possibly a larger percentage of the cost of their schools than any other group of poor people in
America.

"The Negroes have paid in direct property and poll taxes more than
$45,000,000 during the past forty years.

"The Negroes have contributed at least $15,000,000 to education
through their churches.

"The Negro student possibly pays a larger percentage of the running
expenses of the institutions which he attends than any other student in
the land."

A report from Virginia says:

There is in Virginia an organization known as The Co-operative Education
Commission. This is an organization for the white people. I want to briefly
mention the work of this organization because of its influence in arousing a
desire for social betterment not only among the white people but also
among the colored people. In accordance with the suggestion coming from
the commission, leagues were formed throughout the State known as School
Improvement Leagues. The first business of each member of the league was
to interest every one in the school district, both rich and poor, high and low, in
the work.

The general object of a league is to unite the friends of public schools, pupils, teachers, school officers and other citizens in an effort to secure school improvements. The specific objects include the entire circle of school interests as providing for the social, civic, and literary training of the children.

The president of this commission at that time was Dr. S. C. Mitchell, Professor of Economics and History in Richmond College. He was also Rector of the Board of Visitors of the Virginia Normal and Industrial Institute, Petersburg, Va. On one occasion when addressing the student body he mentioned the possibilities of the School Improvement League among the colored people. It was at his suggestion that there was finally organized a Negro School Improvement League. There are now local organizations in nearly every school district in the State. The money that is raised by each local organization is used as the local league may suggest. One league may raise money to lengthen the school term; another to make some improvement on their building, grounds, etc. During the school year of 1907-08 the total amount raised by the local leagues throughout the State was $7,000. During the school year of 1908-09 new leagues were organized to the number of 320. Out of this number 275 raised money for local purposes. In Farmville one school raised $180. The total amount raised by the local leagues throughout the State for 1908-09 is $15,000.

This organization is only a few years old. Its officers are in most of the large schools throughout the State. The influence of this organization is ever spreading, and plans are now on foot to make it even more influential. Nearly all the graduates of the Virginia Normal and Industrial Institute teach school, and one of the first things they are advised to do is to organize in the community where they locate a school improvement league.

To me this is the strongest organization of its kind in the State. None of the officers receive any pay, but each local league uses the money it raises for school improvement.

Mr. W. T. B. Williams, field agent of the Slater Fund, writes:

The work which these schools are doing for their communities falls generally under four or five heads: Religious work of the Y. M. C. A.; Sunday-school work and preaching in the churches; social work, such as is done by women's clubs, the visiting of homes, almshouses, jails, etc.; educational work, such as making addresses, conducting teachers' institutes, organizing school improvement leagues, holding night schools for training working girls in the line of their employment; helping farmers by means of farmers' conferences, demonstration farm work, monthly institutes, etc,; and contributing to and directing the amusements of their communities.—Southern Workman, Oct. and Nov., 1909.

The following sorts of social work are reported in different schools:

Atlanta University, Georgia.—The annual conference for the study of the Negro problems; fourteen reports published; University extension lectures; headquarters of a free kindergarten association, with five kindergartens for Negro children; fifty traveling libraries.

Hampton Institute, Virginia.—Cabin visits, jail work, poor-house work, three night schools, two settlements, song service, home garden work, annual farmers' conference, annual Negro conference, rural improvement.

Penn School, South Carolina.—Home visits, trained nurse, monthly teachers' institute, temperance work, amusements, woman's meeting, annual farmers' fair.

Clark University, Georgia.—Farmers' institutes.

Atlanta Baptist College, Georgia.—Neighborhood settlement work.

Florida Baptist Academy, Florida.—Public song service, lectures, woman's improvement association.

Americus Institute, Georgia.—Sunday-school teaching, rural visiting, teachers' institutes.

Manassas Industrial School, Virginia.—Quarterly farmers' institutes, annual teachers' institutes, summer school.

Kowaliga Institute, Alabama.—Industrial improvement, amusements.

Calhoun School, Alabama.—Mothers' meetings (semi-monthly), home visiting, dispensary, charity for the sick, amusements, lectures, annual agricultural fair, annual teachers' institute, land buying.

St. Paul Normal and Industrial School, Brunswick county, Virginia.— Farmers' conference, land buying.

St. Paul School, Lawrenceville, Va.—Increase of rural schools.

Tuskegee Institute,—Negro conference, farmers' institutes, demonstration farming, conference agent, Negro Business League, county fair, county newspaper, model village, rural school extension.

Public School, Indianapolis, Ind.—Parents' clubs, a Christmas dinner for poor pupils,Civics and Hygiene, lunches, school gardening, truant visitor, night schools and playgrounds.[1]

There are many clubs like the following:

Three Times Ten Club, Tuscaloosa, Ala.—"We meet fortnightly at the homes of club members (alphabetically), when we attend to business and a literary and musical programme is had. As our club is federated with the Alabama Federation of Colored Women's Clubs, we of course help to sustain the Colored Boys' Reformatory at Mt. Meigs; and we assist charitably those in Tuscaloosa who are deserving.

"Our main object (locally) is to establish what we sorely need and have been striving to establish—a High School. With that purpose in view we purchased a plot of land for $200, but have never been able to build. A few months ago a Tuscaloosa Educational Association, composed of citizens of the county, was formed; to which organization we have donated the plot of land, with the understanding that they are to erect a High School.

"We have about $200 in our treasury now, and as soon as a building is assured we will no doubt make a further donation, and shall continue to contribute."

Many local alumni clubs help their colleges by scholarships, funds, etc. At Fisk and Atlanta the alumni are endowing a chair by annual gifts. Other clubs like the "Eurydice Club," of Marion, Ind., the primary purpose of which is "to assist a worthy boy or girl to obtain a higher education, the secondary charity."

In some places, like Lynchburg, Va., the industrial work "in the public school is semi-philanthropic in that teachers do much extra work to make the innovations successful. Through the influence of our women this feature has been added, and the articles made go to the poor and unfortunate."

Teachers' associations are means of help. Among these are The National Association of Teachers in Colored Schools (founded 1903), R. R. Wright, president. The strongest of the State organizations are:

Kentucky State Colored Teachers' Association.

Tennessee State Colored Teachers' Association.

---

[1] cf. W. T. B. Williams in *Southern Workman,* Oct. and Nov., 1909.

Alabama State Colored Teachers' Association.
Texas State Colored Teachers' Association.
West Virginia State Colored Teachers' Association.
Nearly all of the Southern States have some such organization. The preamble of the West Virginia Association states that its object is "to elevate the character and advance the interests of the profession of teaching, and to promote the cause of popular education in the State of West Virginia."

That the Negroes are bearing an increasing part of the cost of their own children's education is shown by the following table:

Income of Atlanta University, together with the Amount Raised by Tuition; the Amount Received from the State of Georgia, and the Value of Student Labor

N. B.—The amount of tuition is included in the total amount raised; the value of student labor is not thus included.

	Total Money Raised	From Tuition	From State of Georgia	From Labor
1871	$ 83,410 75	$ 6,187 95	$ 8,000	
1871–2	28,977 85	5,697 15	8,000	
1872–3	25,627 75	6,968 95	4,000	
1873–4	24,007 96	7,600 26	8,000	
1874–5	15,162 00	7,554 75	4,000	
1875–6	21,110 30	8,483 60	12,000	
1876–7	19,268 40	6,808 75	8,000	
1877–8	17,236 25	6,663 70	8,000	
1878–9	20,166 75	7,769 45	8,000	
1879–80	30,762 65	7,619 60	8,000	
1880–81	21,584 95	10,014 30	8,000	
1881–2	27,137 35	9,982 75	8,000	
1882–3	28,950 16	11,274 85	8,000	
1883–4	28,051 17	9,365 70	8,000	
1884–5	29,326 71	9,034 96	8,000	
1885–6	28,686 88	7,965 41	8,000	
1886–7	27,210 13	8,572 60	8,000	
1887–8	27,772 11	10,318 75		
1888–9	23,199 30	8,709 37		
1889–90	46,607 06	13,685 85		
1890–91	49,325 30	16,202 26		
1891–2	58,387 91	15,650 63		
1892–3	40,495 70	13,824 99		
1893–4	35,315 95	10,279 94		$ 693 16
1894–5	32,640 79	6,569 77		497 08
1895–6	40,640 04	8,061 06		956 93
1896–7	39,228 90	8,216 55		1,245 89
1897–8	35,627 83	8,113 59		1,185 83
1898–9	45,336 43	8,140 12		1,405 25
1899–1900	44,269 38	8,212 47		1,474 45
1900–1901	40,260 24	8,835 30		1,746 17
1901–02	42,244 49	8,324 46		1,910 98
1902–03	40,822 12	8,974 04		1,930 10
1903–04	57,131 94	7,250 07		1,578 80
1904–05	55,152 97	9,119 91		1,860 70
1905–06	57,084 97	11,241 08		2,149 40
1906–07	57,478 73	12,137 80		2,305 65
1907–08	54,862 61	12,554 97		2,011 95
1908–09	48,133 33	13,567 20		1,861 48
	$1,448,696 01	$373,702 70	$132,000	$24,814 84

The total donations from colored people are unknown. The following, however, are the largest single items:

For memorial windows .... $ 260 00
For bell and clock... .... 600 00
For Alumni Fund 2,067 79

According to the Twelfth Bulletin of the Atlanta University, Negro students in nine years, or from 1898 to 1907, paid in cash to 74 Negro institutions $3,358,667, and in work $1,828,602, a total of $5,187,269; which was 44.6 per cent of the entire running expenses of these institutions. In some of them Negro students paid as much as three-fourths and in 24 of them they paid more than half of the total expense of operating the schools. In twelve institutions the average received from Negro students was more than $10,000 per year, as the following table will show:

INSTITUTION	Cash Paid by Students	Cash Value of Students' Work	Total	Average per Year
Tuskegee Institute	$217,798	$707,285	$925,083	$102,787
Hampton Institute.....	91,228	549,618	640,846	71,205
Fisk University.........	261,576	22,500	284,076	31,564
Wiley University.......	211,988	15,927	227,915	25,324
Shaw University........	168,241	5,161	173,402	19,267
Knoxville College	109,450	24,000	133,450	14,828
Clark University	116,757	7,084	123,841	13,760
Straight University....	110,702	4,916	115,618	12,846
Scotia Seminary........	64,588	48,300	112,888	12,543
Bishop College.........	81,793	12,587	94,380	10,487
Atlanta University.....	82,487	16,362	98,849	10,985

The amount given by white people for Negro education has been enormous. The Freedman's Bureau made this report for the years 1866-70:

Expenditures for Schools

YEAR	EXPENDED BY			Total
	Freedman's Bureau	Benevolent Associations	The Freedmen	
1866...............	$123,655 39	$ 82,200 00	$ 18,500 00	$ 224,359 39
1867.....	531,345 48	65,087 01	17,200 00	613,632 49
1868...............	965,806 67	700,000 00	360,000 00	2,025,896 67
1869...............	924,182 16	365,000 00	190,000 00	1,479,182 16
1870...............	976,853 29	360,000 00	200,000 00	1,536,853 29
Total			$785,700 00	$5,879,924 00

Dr. A. G. Haygood made this estimate in 1890:

Freedmen's Aid, M. E. Church............................$	2,225,000
Baptist Home Missionary................................	2,000,000
Presbyterian Home Mission.............................	1,542,746
A. M. Association, Congregational	6,000,000
The different Women's Societies........................	500,000
John F. Slater Fund.........	1,000,000
Daniel Hand Fund.......................................	1,000,000
Individual gifts...	1,000,000
Quakers and other religious bodies......................	500,000
Total gifts...$15,767,746	

The larger funds are:

1. The Peabody Fund of $2,000,000 given in 1867 and 1869. The income of this fund has gone principally to the education of the whites, but a small part has provided teachers' institutes and schools for Negroes.

2. The John F. Slater Fund of $1,000,000 given in 1882. The income of this fund has been given exclusively to Negro schools and more especially to Industrial schools.

3. The Daniel Hand Fund of $1,500,894.25 given to the American Missionary Association in 1888 for educating needy Negro students.

4. The Negro Rural School Fund, Anna T. Jeanes Foundation, is a fund of $1,000,000 given by Miss Anna T. Jeanes, of Philadelphia. The interest is to be used to help rural education among Negroes.

To this must be added the recent Stokes Fund, which is partly for Negroes.

The American Baptist Home Mission Society has spent four millions in forty years. In thirty-nine years the M. E. Church has spent $7,819,397.46, mostly from whites.

The Bureau of Education reports these receipts of Negro schools. Of the figures in the second column it is said: "Presumably the greater part of this amount should have been included under benefactions." Probably Negro schools have received over $12,000,000 from whites in the twelve years 1896 to 1908:

Negro Schools

YEAR	Benefactions	" Receipts from Other Sources "
1896	$323,718	$610,946
1897	305,050	540,097
1898	399,392	476,560
1899	433,014	625,966
1900	661,486	677,977
1901	505,244	599,602
1902	440,253	562,258
1903	446,477	814,044
1904	133,294	840,305
1905	397,289	962,127
1906	304,610	734,479
1907	470,994	1,046,872
1908	555,856	1,129,263
	$5,376,677	$9,620,496

Section 7. Miscellaneous General Efforts.—Under this head may be mentioned various national organizations:

The Niagara Movement.—Founded 1905. Organized for political rights, legal defense, publication tracts, annual chautauqua, etc.

The Negro Business League.—Founded 1900. Organized to encourage business enterprise.

National Political League.—Founded 1907. Organized for political rights.

The Committee of Twelve.—Founded in 1904. Published pamphlets and tracts.

American Negro Academy.—Founded 1897, to promote literature, science and art.

These are general organizations, the survivors of a long line of similar societies, like the Afro-American League, the Afro-American Council, and a score of general conventions and local associations. To these must be added two organizations of whites and Negroes:

The Constitution League.—Founded in ——, to agitate the enforcement of the Constitution of the United States and particularly the 13th, 14th and 15th amendments.

The National Negro Conference.—Founded in 1909; designed to unite all efforts in a general movement toward securing for the Negroes all their rights as American citizens.

Beside these there are a number of conferences:

The Atlanta Negro Conference, to study the Negro problems. Founded in 1896. Has published fourteen annual reports.

The Tuskegee Negro Conference.—Founded in 1891. Devoted to farmers and teachers.

The Hampton Negro Conference.—Founded in 1896. Devoted to general discussion and study of the Negro.

To these must be added the work of the chief Negro secret and insurance societies, like the Masons, Odd Fellows, Knights of Pythias, etc. These are more than social and business organizations. A few quotations from local reports illustrate their benevolent work:

Our city, as you may know, is small. We have about seven or eight hundred colored families, Two secret societies: Masons and K. of P., with women auxiliaries. These organizations are a wonderful help to our city. They have done and are still doing much good work, socially and financially, for the betterment of our people. We also have three women's clubs that are engaged in a good work. They have proven themselves to be philanthropic to the letter. We have no charitable institutions as yet, to boast of, but are planning for something of that nature. The Negro Masons here are preparing a building to be used by our organizations in the near future.—South Bend, Ind.

. . . We have a K. of P. Lodge. All of these organizations have done much for the social betterment of this small city.—Johnstown, Pa.

Aside from the secret organizations here in Texarkana among Negroes, all of which care for their members in sickness and death, paying sick benefits and a small death claim, there are no organizations here doing a strictly philanthropic work. These secret organizations, however, are very much in evidence and withal quite popular.—Texarkana, Tex.

The Woman's Burial Association is conducted entirely by Negroes. We have as many men in our association as women. But its name originated from a woman being the founder of it. We were organized the last Friday in August, 1902, with six societies and about 300 members. Now we number forty-one societies with 1,900 members. We pay out death-claim per member $90. We hope to pay, after our annual sitting the third week in August, $100. Our last associational year we paid out for death claims $1,876.56. This year up to the present time we have paid out $1,378, and we have four more to pay next month. It has been said by members of the other race that it is among the best steps the colored people have ever taken in this community.—Enfield, N. C.

We have any number of insurance organizations which give sick benefits, run wholly by the colored people, at least five or six operating here in the city. All of the above mentioned, in some way, do a little charity and social work for the uplift of our people.—Charlotte, N. C.

The following societies in Washington, D. C., united to celebrate the centenary of Lincoln's birth:

Crispus Attucks Relief Association.
Young Men's Protective League.
Young Men's Immediate Relief.
District Lodge No. 20, G. U. O. of O. F.
Waiters' and Ex-Waiters' Mutual Relief Association.
Bannaker Relief Association.
United Aid No. 1.
Elder Men's Relief Association.
Douglass Relief Association.

Section 8. Negro Philanthropists. Few races are more instinctively philanthropic than the Negro. It is shown in everyday life and in their group history. Some few of their larger philanthropies in America in early days have been recorded.[1]

Jasmin Thoumazeau

Was born in Africa in 1714, brought to St. Domingo and sold for a slave when he was twenty-two years of age, but afterwards, obtaining his freedom he married, and in the year 1756 established a hospital at the Cape for poor Negroes and mulattoes.

More than forty years were devoted by him and his wife to this benevolent institution, and his fortune was subservient to their wants. The only regret they felt, while their time and substance was devoted to these destitute objects, arose from a fear that after they were gone the hospital might be abandoned.

The Philadelphian Society at the Cape and the Agricultural Society at Paris decreed medals to Jasmin, who died near the close of the century.

Joseph Rachel

Joseph Rachel, a respectable Negro, resided in the island of Barbadoes. He was a trader, and dealt chiefly in the retail way. In his business he conducted himself so fairly and complaisantly that, in a town filled with little peddling shops, his doors were thronged with customers. Almost all dealt with him, and ever found him remarkably honest and obliging.

The philanthropists of England take pleasure in speaking of him: "Having become rich by commerce, he consecrated all his fortune to acts of benevolence. The unfortunate, without distinction of color, had a claim on his affections. He gave to the indigent, lent to those who could not make a return; visited prisoners, gave them good advice; and endeavored to bring back the guilty to virtue. He died at Bridgetown, on that island, in 1758, equally lamented by blacks and whites, for he was a friend to all."

John Mosely

Died—In this city, John Mosely, an aged colored man, well known from his industry, prudence, and integrity. Having no relations, he devoted his property to charitable objects. By his will he gave to the Hartford Beneficent

---

[1] From Mott's Biographical Sketches.

Society, one hundred dollars; to the American Colonization Society, two hundred dollars; to the Connecticut Bible Society, one hundred dollars; to the American Education Society, one hundred dollars; and after other legacies, the residue of his estate to the Domestic Missionary Society of Connecticut.— Hartford Courant.

Nancy Pitchford

A woman of color, died in 1824 at Hartford, Connecticut, aged 67 years. For the first forty years of her life she was a slave. She sustained an excellent character, was for many years a professor of religion, and gave satisfactory evidence of sincere and lively piety. At the time of her death she had acquired, by her industry and care, more than four hundred dollars; the whole of which, after paying the expenses of her last sickness and funeral, she left by will to charitable purposes.

The chief Negro philanthropists of our time may be noted as follows:

Primus Parsons Mason

Mr. Mason founded the Springfield (Mass.) Home for Aged Men. The first annual report says:

That the foundation for a charity like this has been laid by one man, demands that some notice of his life be placed among our records. According to the family Bible, Primus Parsons was born February 5, 1817, the youngest of seven children. His parents at that time resided in a remote part of Monson. They died when he was quite young, so that he was early thrown upon his own resources. He worked for farmers in Suffield and Monson until he had nearly attained his majority, and then came to Springfield while yet a minor. On April 21, 1837, he purchased a house on the north side of the Boston road, borrowing fifty dollars on a mortgage to the seller, Daniel Charter. Engaging in very menial occupations, he accumulated some money and started to try his fortune in California in the decade before the Civil War. This was an unprofitable venture, and he soon returned to Springfield, without money but with a decided experience in favor of consecutive enterprises, and his business life thenceforward illustrated what can be achieved by industry, prudence, foresight, and judicious investment in real estate. As a trader he was shrewd but honest, and bought where he expected a rise in values. Until the end of his life he continued to improve his estate by the construction of new houses, as his means enabled him. In these days of thrift he felt himself alone among most of his companions, and on his death-bed lamented the improvidence that, in his opinion, characterized most of his race. Not till mature life did he learn to write his name, and this was the limit of his skill in chirography; but he supplied many deficiencies of education by a well-trained memory and a keen observation. He was thrice married, and the loss of all his family, including his daughter, perhaps turned his thoughts to the charity which he has founded. Upon this he had pondered long before he embodied the plan in his will, and had advised with several practical men upon its wisdom. Throughout his life, without race prejudice of any kind, the only limitations upon the charity suggested by him to the writer are contained in the phrase that he wanted to provide "a place where old men that are worthy may feel at home." He died January 12, 1892, and is buried in Oak Grove Cemetery.

His bequest was:

Real estate valued at..$23,400 00
First mortgage, P. H. Potter... .... 8,800 00
Second mortgage, P. H. Potter 3,100 00
Cash 1,151 95
                                                                          ————
Total..$31,451 95
Deduct from this, mortgage on house, 830 State street.. 2,000 00
                                                                          ————
Net value $29,451 95

Colonel John McKee

Mr. McKee, of Philadelphia, left an estate in 1896 of upwards of one million dollars in real estate, under the following conditions:

(1) None of his real estate is to be sold, nor any of his personalty disposed of, but whole estate is to be kept intact. (2) After making provision for small annuities for children, and grand-children being children of his deceased children, all to be paid out of income, the rest of income is to accumulate until enough has been provided to (a) change certain city properties from dwellings into stores and dwellings, and otherwise to improve certain city properties; (b) to construct houses on a certain large plat of city ground and improve same. Then (3) all the net income of his estate is to accumulate until after the death of all his children and grand-children, when the residue is disposed of under the following clause and in manner following:

In order that such a number of poor colored male orphan children and poor white male orphan children born in Philadelphia County as can be trained in one institution, may receive a better education, as well as more comfortable maintenance than they usually receive from application of public funds, I order and direct that after the death of all my children and grand-children, my Trustees to devote my entire residuary estate to the erection of a college with other necessary buildings, ample and complete, to accommodate at least 200 children, to cost not over $1,000,000, on a tract of my land in Bucks County, to be called "The Colonel John McKee College," which name shall be inscribed on a large marble slab in front of the building, and in front of the building there shall be a statue of myself; all buildings and grounds to be surrounded by a stone wall. The college to supply all pupils with books and appliances. All pupils to be given a thorough naval education, similar to that given at Annapolis, my desire being that the pupils shall be equipped for service in war on sea.

In further detail, school is to have a band and the whole school turn out on the 30th of May and march to Lebanon and the Catholic Cemeteries and decorate the graves of the colored and white soldiers and sailors. All pupils to wear uniform, and the whole, in short, to be supported and carried on out of the income from his estate. Children to be between the ages of 12 and 21. The whole management is left in hands of the Archbishop of Catholic Church of Philadelphia, until after the death of children, etc. (he mentions his attorney as co-trustee), after which the school and all its affairs, being all the affairs of his estate, are to be managed by ten trustees to be appointed or elected from among the Catholic pastors in Philadelphia.

George Washington

The George Washington Educational Fund is a fund held in trust by six trustees appointed by the Circuit Court of Jersey County, Illinois, under a decree of court which established in chancery the nuncupative will of George Washington, a Negro slave who died at Otterville, a small village in Jersey county, in 1868.

This fund, after peculations of white trustees and endless litigation, now amounts to about $22,000, and under the terms of the decree above mentioned the trustees are required to use the interest arising from this fund for the purpose of educating young colored men and women of the State of Illinois. The trustees of this fund hold examinations from time to time in the city of Jerseyville. At these examinations the applicants are required to furnish satisfactory evidence to the trustees that they are residents of the State of Illinois, are of good moral character, and that they seek higher education for the purpose of fitting themselves for teachers of their race.

Another requirement is, that they shall have proceeded in their studies as far as possible in their home town.

This fund is now maintaining five students in Fisk University in Nashville, Tenn., and has educated twenty young men and women.

Thomy Lafon

The baptismal records in the archives of the Catholic Cathedral of New Orleans, at that time written in Spanish, attest that the late Mr. Thomy Lafon was born in this city on December 28th, 1810. He died at his home, corner Ursulines and Robertson streets, on December 23d, 1893, at the ripe age of eighty-three years. His body rests in the St. Louis Cemetery, on Esplanade avenue. He was a man of dignified appearance and affable manners. In early life he taught school; later he operated a small dry goods store in Orleans street, until near 1850. He was never married. Some time before the War of Secession he had started his vast fortune by loaning money at advantageous rates of interest and by the accumulating of his savings. Toward the close of his career he became attached to the lamented Archbishop Jansens, and began his philanthropies. By the terms of his will, dated April 3, 1890, he provided amply for his aged sister and some friends, and wisely distributed the bulk of his estate among charitable institutions of New Orleans. His estate was appraised at $413,000, divided in securities and realty.

In recognition of his charity the City of New Orleans named after him one of its public schools.

Before his death he had established an asylum for orphan boys called the Lafon Asylum, situated in St. Peter street, between Claiborne avenue and North Darbigny street. To this asylum he bequeathed the sum of $2,000, and the revenues, amounting to $275 per month, of a large property situated corner Royal and Iberville streets.

Other legacies were to the:

Charity Hospital of New Orleans	$10,000 00
Charity Hospital, Ambulance Department	3,000 00
Lafon's Old Folks Home	5,000 00
Little Sisters of the Poor	5,000 00
Shakespeare Alms House	3,000 00
Catholic Institution for Indigent Orphans	2,000 00

And the following properties:

1st. St. Claude street, between St. Philip and Ursulines streets, valued at	$1,500 00
2nd. Robertson street, between St. Philip and Ursulines streets, valued at	2,000 00
3rd. Burgundy street, between Hospital and Barrack, valued at	2,000 00
4th. Union street, between Royal and Dauphine streets, valued at	2,000 00
St. John Berchman Asylum for Girls under the care of the Holy Family	$2,000 00

THOMY LAFON
Negro Philanthropist of New Orleans
1810–1893

And the following property:

    1st. Burgundy street, No. 528, worth about................ $1,500 00
    2nd. Dumaine street, Nos. 2129-31, worth about.... .... 2,500 00
    3rd. Galvez street, No. 828, worth about 1,800 00
    4th. Toulouse street, Nos. 726-28, worth about............. 2,500 00
    5th. Tulane avenue, No. 1402, worth about 4,000 00
    Asylum for Old Indigents, cor. Tonti and Hospital streets 15,000 00

And the following property:

    1st. St. Andrew street, Nos. 1536-38, valued at............. $6,000 00
    2nd. Baronne street, No. 722, valued at 4,000 00
    3rd. Baronne street, Nos. 732-36, valued at 8,000 00
    4th. Canal and Villere streets, valued at...... .... 30,000 00
    And another cash gift...... .... 2,000 00
    Society of the Holy Family, Orleans street............... 10,000 00
    Straight University, of New Orleans, La...... .... 3,000 00
    Southern University, of New Orleans, La................. 3,000 00
    New Orleans University, of New Orleans, La............. 3,000 00
    Society of Jeunes Amis, of New Orleans........... .... 3,000 00
    Eye, Ear, Nose and Throat Hospital...................... 3,000 00
    Mother St. Clair of the Convent of the Good Shepherd... 20,000 00

Mr. Lafon, in his will, underestimated the value of his estate, and after an appraisement was made it was found that his estate was worth twice as much as he valued it, and consequently all his bequests were doubled by his executors. [1]

---

[1] These data were collected and furnished by Mr. J. F. Guillaume, of Straight University, New Orleans, La.

Stephen Smith

Stephen Smith (1795-1873) was a Negro lumber merchant of Philadelphia, who left nearly $100,000 to found the Home for Aged and Infirm Colored Persons.

A few other Negro donors follow: [1]

D. A. Payne to Wilberforce University	(?)$10,000 00
W. Gant to Wilberforce University	5,000 00
J. P. Campbell to Wilberforce University	1,000 00
J. A. Shorter to Wilberforce University	2,000 00
H. S. Gordon to Wilberforce University	2,100 00
F. Grey to Dooley N. & I. School	2,000 00
I. Lane to Lane College	1,000 00
G.A. and M. Walker to Straight University	1,000 00
L. Bedford to Fisk University	1,000 00
S. B. Morse to Atlanta University	5,000 00
R. F. Baptiste to Tuskegee	1,000 00
Mary Shaw to Tuskegee	38,000 00
A. Mary to Orphans' Institute, New Orleans	3,000 00
Mrs. B. Convent to Orphans' Institute, New Orleans, "bequest."	
Dr. Augustus to Oblate Sisters, Baltimore	"large bequest."
Nancy Addison to Oblate Sisters, Baltimore	$15,000 00
Louis Bode to Oblate Sisters, Baltimore	30,000 00
J. Parker to State College, Delaware	6,000 00

Section 9. Types of Benevolence.—Charity. Coming now to the more strictly benevolent work of Negroes we may distinguish the following types:

(a) General Charity.

This is the most usual form of help, and being largely unorganized is difficult to measure. It is carried on by churches, clubs and individuals.

(b) Women's Clubs.

There are thousands of these for all purposes—social and benevolent.

(c) Old Folk's Homes, and Orphanages.

These represent the first and best institutional work.

(d) Hospitals.

These are never philanthropies, and are usually supported by whites and Negroes and often receive State aid.

(e) Young Men's Christian Association.

The colored branch has been developed recently, and Negroes have been refused admission to the white branches, even in many Northern cities.

(f) Social Literary and Art Clubs.

These include philanthropy as a by-product, or encourage directly literature and art.

(g) Libraries.

Public and private Negro libraries are beginning to be started, and traveling libraries.

(h) Day Nurseries, Settlements, Kindergartens, Civic Work, etc.

---

[1] Taken in part from Wright: Self-Help in Negro Education.

These forms of specialized and scientific philanthropy are just beginning to appear among colored people.

Let us now consider a series of local reports on each of these types. First we select at random local reports on charity:

There have been other bodies organized about in the city to supply the public schools with such needs as have been omitted by the Board of Education. Very often small bodies organize temporarily to do charitable work.—Mobile, Ala.

There is a society called the Young Women's Christian Club which make it their business to look after the poor and needy in the way of clothes.—Los Angeles, Cal.

We have two charity clubs which work independently of any church. They are doing a great deal toward caring for the sick and relieving the wants of the destitute.—Dallas, Tex.

Preparing to do substantial work.—Galveston, Texas.

The Galveston Relief Association, an incorporated body, has for its object the building of a Home for Aged Colored People, at a cost of $15,000. Looking to this end the association purchased and paid for ten acres of land, and has to its credit a small bank account.

The location is on the main land thirteen miles from Galveston, hard by the little town of Lamarque, a quarter of a mile from the station of the Galveston, Houston & Henderson Railroad, and in the county of Galveston. The altitude of this plot of land is much higher than that of Galveston. This gives to it a beautiful view of several miles; the climate is genial and healthful, the soil is rich enough, by proper management, to make the Home almost self-supporting. The neighbors are generous and kind; in all, it is one of the best locations in Texas for an institution of this kind.

We believe there are three sources of moral elevation, absolutely necessary, yet to be opened to the Negro, without which we must still have the very bed of crime among us; viz.: 1. Home for the aged. 2. Industrial homes for the orphans. 3. Reform school for the incorrigible. For the aged there have been no home provisions made through private means, through denominations, or by county infirmaries, hence these people are a burden to themselves and to those who feel deeply for them.—Galveston, Tex.

One missionary or home improvement club, whose work is largely devoted to local charity.—Phœbus, Va.

One sewing-circle composed of ladies who sell their products and apply the returns to the relief of the destitute, mainly the aged.—Phœbus, Va.

Social Helpers' Club to benefit the indigent sick—Phœbus, Va.

This mission was organized by some women and men who desired to help the unfortunate. Its work is as follows:

1. Making garments for the poor and unfortunate.

2. Making garments and other articles for sale to the general public, the proceeds to go to buy articles for the support of the mission and the purchase of material.

3. Instruction is given to such children, youth and older persons as can attend and give time to study.

It is purely an effort for social betterment, and no profits accrue to individuals from any of these ventures. Many of the most prominent people in the city are members.—Lynchburg, Va.

When our members are sick we donate them fifty cents and go and tidy up their room. To-day we have in the sick treasury $25. We have in the bank $200. Since we have organized we have banked $1,579.69. We have a Christian president. She is a woman that has her race at heart, and is always ready to help those that need help. Sometimes we are called on to go to the homes of the poor and sick. We take sheets and pillow-cases and tidy up their room. Prudence Crandall Society provides poor children with shoes, that they may attend school.—Washington, D. C.

In the early part of 1900, noticing the destitute condition of some of our people and especially among the children, the question arose in my mind, what could be done to help them to better their condition? In looking through Harper's Bazaar I saw an account of the needle-work guild of America conducted by our white sisters, and being impressed with the work I opened correspondence with them. In the meantime I called some of our women together to confer with them. One day my bell rang; on answering it I found myself face to face with the president of one of the branches of the needle-work guild of America. Asking her in she inquired if this was Mrs. ———. I said it was. She said she was glad to know that I had become interested in the work, as it was "so much needed among your people," as she termed it. She said we could not have a Branch president, but might have a Section president under a white Branch. Of course you know that was not very pleasant to me. She informed me that the national president would be in Washington in a few days, and I would get all the necessary information from her. In the meantime there were about twenty-five of us meeting and planning an organization. A few weeks passed, and to my surprise who should call but the National President, a lady of refinement and culture; she expressed herself as being pleased at my efforts "to help your people," and also informed me that we could not have a Branch president of our women. After her visit we concluded to form an organization of our own.

April 20, 1900, we organized the First Branch of the National Sewing Council of the United States of America (incorporated). The first object of which is to collect new plain garments and to distribute them to men, women and children (who are needy). Men, women and children may become members by contributing two new plain garments each year or a donation of money.

We also have a Board of Directors engaged in Sabbath work, who seek and interest children in the attendance of Sabbath-schools of their denomination, in which they have been very successful. An auxiliary board was set apart April 20, 1908, to raise a fund for the establishment of a non-sectarian Old Folk's Home, which is so much needed in the District of Columbia for our people. The Council have found it very helping in distributing provisions and fuel when needed. We also organized a sewing-school for small girls.—Washington, D. C.

The Dorcas Home Missionary Society, which is connected with the Concord Baptist Church of Christ, at Brooklyn, is one of the oldest and probably the most widely known charitable organizations conducted by the women of any church among Afro-Americans in the North. During the year 1908 the society gave:

To benevolent objects.	$102 00
For the use of the Baptist Temple	50 00
For hall rent and bills	43 50
For groceries for the poor	25 00

For silverware .... $ 38 00
For printing, etc... 10 50
For delegates' fare to convention 20 00
For foreign mission work 45 00
Donated to Concord Baptist Church of Christ............. 100 00
For entertaining the National Association of Colored
    Women's Clubs.. 439 95
For miscellaneous items....................... .... 32 34
Amount in bank and on hand.............................. 498 50

Four years ago the Dorcas Society began the observance of Woman's Day on the second Sunday in March. On such occasions, by consent of the church, all the services are conducted by women. These special days have been a great blessing to the church, as well as to the women that conduct them. The collections are given to the church and have amounted to nearly $500.—Brooklyn, N. Y.

The Benevolent Society was organized in 1879. Its present aim is the care for the sick and to assist in burying its dead. Also those who may need help. Organized with ten members to aid in caring for strangers who were sick and dying. At one time there was an enrollment of one hundred and twenty-five. The present enrollment is fifty. Supported a student at Wayland Seminary. Has a bank deposit, but does not own any personal property or real estate. It is the oldest society of colored women in the State.—Detroit, Mich.

The Willing Workers Society of Detroit was organized twenty-one years ago, and is the oldest organization for charitable work among colored people in the State. The membership is limited and consists of fifty active members. The meetings are held weekly at the homes of the members, commencing on the first Thursday in October and continuing until the first Thursday in April. Although organized for work among colored people no line has been drawn, and in some instances relief has been given to worthy white people. The work of the society is carried on by various committees, who visit the sick, investigate calls for assistance, and give relief whenever possible. Food, fuel, clothing and money are distributed to persons seeking temporary relief, and regular weekly contributions are given to four persons who are worthy.

The dues consist of five cents weekly with an annual contribution of one dollar per member. Other funds are raised by making and selling quilts and other small articles which are contributed by members.

The society celebrated its twentieth anniversary last year.—Detroit, Mich.

Cornell Charity Club was organized eight years ago and had twelve members who lived in the same neighborhood, but later on this club branched out and now has sixty members living in all parts of the city. We have limited our membership to sixty. We meet every Friday and do all kinds of good work, visiting the hospitals, jails, and institutions. Also doing charity work. We assist the Home for Aged and Infirm Colored People, also Amanda Smith Home.—Chicago, Ill.

The Willing Workers Club was organized in the year 1901 for the purpose of doing philanthrophical work. The membership of the club is about twenty-five women. It has done some very good work since its organization. It has given over two thousand dollars to needy causes, including churches, out-door poor, and other purposes, until 1907, when the club decided to work up a Rescue Home for girls and a day nursery, which we hope to open in the fall.—Stamford, Conn.

We do charity work. We have sent a barrel of clothing to Sanford, N. C. One last year to New Port station. Had a rummage sale to help the Union Baptist Church of Malden, and this year we are donating fruit to the sick. Sending Easter likes to the shut-in. Our club is over ten years old, but like all clubs, they are very apt to lose interest if they do not get an active head. I have done the work for the club very faithfully, and am now acting on the sick committee. We are getting ready now to meet the necessary funds for our yearly convention which meets in Springfield.—Malden, Mass.

I suppose you understand that we are in the federation of clubs. We, of course, take care of our own sick and help bury the dead. In fact, we try to help all humanity that comes within our reach.—Boston, Mass.

The club has stood for missionary work ever since its beginning. Many families in reduced circumstances have realized the goodness of the Lucy Stone Club. One of the most important committees connected with the club is the Flower Committee. If any member hears of any of our race who is sick at one of the hospitals, or at home, they report it to the society, and then the Flower Committee goes and carries flowers or fruit to them at the hospital or home. Not only flowers and fruit, but money and provisions are often carried to the sick. At the present time the club is working hard to get enough money together to start a Home for Working Girls. It is our intention, as soon as able, to rent a house and hire a matron, and let rooms out to the young women in our city who have no home except where they work.—Worcester, Mass.

The Cambridge Charity Club is purely philanthropic and the only organization of which I know that is not in some way beneficiary.

This club originated from a Mothers' Club with a small membership. About three years ago it was reorganized and renamed, and admitted into the Federation. The work is divided between a committee of four, who look up needy cases in a quiet way, in the locality in which each lives, and report to the club. I think it unique among colored clubs, in that the work is done so unostentatiously. Names are not necessarily given in any public way to offend or humiliate, and yet many needy and worthy people are temporarily relieved. Another splendid thing they have been doing, and are still doing, is aiding a young girl to get her education at Wellesley College.

Their membership is now over a hundred. Entrance fee is fifty cents and monthly dues ten cents. It has already expended between $150 and $200 in its three years of practical helpfulness.—Cambridge, Mass.

Some general criticism is as follows:

I can say for the people out here they are trying in every possible way to help our people better their condition.—Los Angeles, Cal.

There are five Federation clubs in our city which do limited charity work; this being a small city and a thrifty people, there is little demand ordinarily of charity; however, as a secondary purpose, when needed they all work.—Marion, Ind.

Richmond, as might be naturally expected, takes the lead in the number of institutions for social betterment among the Negroes. But as was said by one of her leading citizens, "The people are not doing what they should do. I fear they are so engrossed in money-making that they have forgotten that there are some things better than money-making."—Richmond, Va.

As a rule the Negroes of this community accept charity with reluctance. A large number may be improvident, but by some means they manage to make both ends meet and only accept assistance in this connection in the last extremity.—Louisville, Ky.

In such charity Southern white people are especially willing and prominent:

There are a number of institutions of this nature in Louisville supported largely by Negroes, but not one that I know of supported entirely by them. The white people in this community are very friendly, and give very generously to charity, regardless of race or creed.—Louisville, Ky.

These organizations are doing much good, and while maintained and managed by colored people are largely and generously supported by white people. —Louisville, Ky.

Section 10. Women's Clubs. Mrs. Josephine St. Pierre Ruffin, of Boston, and Mrs. John T. Cook, of Washington, D. C., were the pioneers in the club movement among colored women, although single clubs had long existed here and there. Mrs. Josephine S. Mates, Honorary President of the National Association of Colored Women's Clubs, writes:

That organization is the first step in nation-making, and that a nation can rise in the scale no higher than its womanhood, are principles which have come to be looked upon by the sociologist and all students of the development of humanity as self-evident truth; hence it seems quite natural to speak of one in connection with the other, i. e., organization and woman.

An inquiry into existing organizations among our women reveals the fact that most of these are auxiliary societies founded and controlled by men, or by the combined efforts of men and women; also, that usually they are secret orders, or connected with various church denominations; and, furthermore, that in their respective fields much work of high order has been accomplished.

There is, however, one notable exception to the rule stated in the previous paragraph relative to organizations of women, and this is to be found in the "National Association of Colored Women," an organization founded and controlled entirely by women; and, within the scope of an article as limited as this must be, we shall confine ourselves to a synopsis of the work of this organization, composed exclusively of women, believing it to be the oldest, most completely organized, etc.; hence, affording the best test of the effectiveness of organization among our women.

The National Association of Colored Women was founded in 1896. The object, as well stated in Article II of its constitution, is, "To secure harmony of action and co-operation among all women in rising to the highest plane."

The organization has been well systematized and now contains at least fourteen well-developed departments, each under the supervision of a carefully selected superintendent. Among these departments one finds social science, domestic science, temperance, juvenile court, music, literature, Young Women's Christian Association, etc. Affiliated clubs may be found in forty or more of the States, and such clubs are rapidly increasing, as also the number of State and city federations.

The value and extent of the local work speaks for itself in the number of hospitals, homes for orphans and the aged, reformatories, kindergartens, day nurseries, and other much-needed institutions, which, through the heroic efforts of the noble and self-sacrificing women that constitute these clubs, have been established.

Illustrations of these institutions, in good working order, may be found in New Bedford, New York, Buffalo, Chicago, Detroit, Kansas City, St. Louis, Washington, Charleston, New Orleans, and probably in many other cities and towns of which we have not positive knowledge at this moment; but a glance at the work in the cities mentioned serves to demonstrate what organization in the hands of the Afro-American woman is doing, not by fine-spun theories, but by actual work; and, if matters do not miscarry, the National Association—incorporated in 1904—financially speaking, eventually will be in position to purchase land sufficient to carry out certain plans that originated with its founders and that by no means have been cast aside.

Every well-organized body has its period of growth and development, as well as of fruitage; and, with State work well under way, we may confidently look forward to the time when the National body will be "bringing in its sheaves;" meanwhile, through its State and city federations and individual clubs, it furnishes a most forcible demonstration of the value of organization among women, in the development of self-reliance, self-help and other elements so necessary to the advancement of a primitive people.

The preamble of the Association's constitution says:

We, the colored women of the United States of America, feeling the need of united and systematic effort, and hoping to furnish evidence of moral, mental and material progress made by our people, do hereby unite in a National Association.

The National Association has met as follows:

Washington, D. C., 1896—Founding.
Nashville, Tenn., 1897—First convention.
Chicago, Ill., 1899—Second convention.
Buffalo, N. Y., 1901—Third convention.
St. Louis, Mo., 1904—Fourth convention.
Detroit,, Mich., 1906—Fifth convention.
Brooklyn, N. Y., 1908—Sixth convention.

The attendance at these conventions has been as follows:

	States represented	Clubs represented	Delegates represented
St. Louis......	22	167	301
Brooklyn	28	128	176

Of the Chicago meeting the Daily News said editorially:

Of all the conventions that have met in the country this summer there is none that has taken hold of the business in hand with more good sense and judgment than the National Association of Colored Women, now assembled in this city. The subjects brought up, the manner of their treatment and the decisions reached exhibit wide and appreciative knowledge of conditions confronting the colored people.

The present departments of the Association are:

Social Science,	Rescue Work,	Literature,
Parliamentary	Music,	Young Women's Work,
Procedure,	Kindergarten,	Evangelistic Work,
Domestic Science,	Woman's Suffrage,	Juvenile Court,
Business,	Forestry,	Humane Work,
Art,	Mothers' Clubs,	Religious Work.
Church Clubs,	Suffrage.	

There is a Southern Federation and a North-East Federation and the twenty State federations:

Texas,	Kentucky,	Ohio,	Florida,
West Virginia,	Maryland,	Colorado,	Virginia,
Iowa,	Michigan,	Mississippi.	Alabama,
Minnesota,	Missouri,	California,	Georgia,
Pennsylvania,	Tennessee,	Indiana,	Illinois.

Most of the large cities like Cincinnati (twelve clubs), Kansas City, St. Louis, etc., have city federations.

A report of the clubs of Missouri is as follows:

Clubs in the Missouri Federation:

Kansas City Federation.

St. Louis Federation.

Kensington Art Club, Kansas City, Mo.—Art work and discussion, rules on parliamentary usages and household hints.

Phyllis Wheatley Club, Kansas City, Mo.

Harper's W. C. T. U. Club, St. Louis, Mo.

The Woman's Musical and Literary Club, Springfield, Mo.—Raising money for a hospital.

Josephine Silone Yates Art Club, Sedalia, Mo.—Art work, charity work and raising money for a hospital.

Woman's Club, Jefferson City, Mo.—Charity, literary and civic improvement.

Kansas City Art Club.—China painting, embroidery and charity work.

Josephine Silone Yates Club, Clayton, Mo.—Charity and missionary work.

Central Missionary Band, St. Louis, Mo.—Home, foreign and educational work.

Art Lovers' Club, St. Joseph, Mo.

Ladies' Art Club Club, Armstrong, Mo.—Art work.

Modern Prescilla, Glasgow, Mo.—Art work.

Fulton, Mo., Club.—Charity, and lifting up the fallen.

Phyllis Wheatley, Ironton, Mo.—Literary and art work

St. Paul Missionary.—Missionary work, St. Louis, Mo.

Olive Branch, Lincoln Institute, Jefferson City, Mo.—Literary work.

Young Married Women's Thimble Club, St. Louis, Mo.—Intellectual improvement and charity work.

Reading Circle, Lincoln Institute, Jefferson City, Mo.

Washington Club, Fulton, Mo.—Charity and literary work.

Colored Woman's League, Kansas City, Mo.

Booklovers' Club, Kansas City, Mo.

Home Mission Society, Sedalia, Mo.

Yates Literary and Art Club, Louisiana, Mo.

The Minnesota Clubs send this report:

The Afro-American Women's State Federation of Minnesota is composed of eighteen clubs from Duluth, Minneapolis and St. Paul, namely:

Adelphai Club, St. Paul.

Arbutus Club, Minneapolis.

Book Club, Duluth.

Dorcas Society, Bethesda Baptist Church, Minneapolis.

Florida Grant Mite Missionary Society, Minneapolis.

Inter-state Club, Duluth.

Literary and Social, St. Paul.
Monday Art, St. Paul.
M. T. C. Art, Minneapolis.
Palm Leaf, Minneapolis.
Pastor's Aid, Minneapolis.
Social Improvement, St. Paul.
Tuesday Industrial, Minneapolis.
Grant Mite Missionary Society, Minneapolis.
Sun Beam Club, Minneapolis.
Missionary Society, Minneapolis.
King's Daughters' Charity Club, St. Paul.
Zenith City Art, Duluth.

The Adelphai Club is a literary and philanthropic club. Books of poems and prose of all the leading authors are read in this club, especially those of colored authors, or anything of interest to the race is read and discussed. Quotations are given at every meeting. This club helps to care for two old ladies, giving a sum of money every month for this purpose. It has a committee to visit the city hospital every month, taking fruit and magazines for the sick. It sends one dollar a month to the Mary Miller Earl Kindergarten, at Anderson, S. C.; also sends aprons. It meets annually at Jean Brown Martin Baby Home and Attucks Home, taking clothing, etc. It gives baskets of food at Thanksgiving and Easter time. Has started a literary society, It is through this club that the room was most beautifully furnished at the Jean Brown Home by the colored citizens of St. Paul.

The Arbutus Club is a philanthropic club. Each Christmas a needy family is looked after. At different times baskets of food are given to the poor. Last summer this club took the children of the Attucks' Home to a Sunday-school picnic. All of their time and money is spent for charity.

The members of the Book Club devote some of their time to social and domestic work, although it is a literary and philanthropic club. Papers are prepared by members, and quotations are given at every meeting. The greater part of the money raised by entertainments and donations is given to St. Mark's A. M. E. Church, to aid them in erecting a new church, which will soon be finished.

The Dorcas Society is a church club. Its object is to pay the insurance money on the church property. They also assist in paying the pastor, sexton, or anything else that may come up. They aid the poor of the church, giving clothing, food and fuel. Annually they hold a sale or fair.

The Florida Grant Missionary Society works along missionary lines.

The Inter-state is a literary and philanthropic club. Papers on all the leading questions of the day are read. Quotations are given at every meeting. Some time is given to music and household economy. Each year a book of historical facts is read in the club. Most all the money they raise is given to assist in building St. Mark's Church.

The Literary and Social is a church club. Gives weekly socials, with literary and musical program, selling refreshments. They papered the basement of the church and put in new gas-lights, and have aided the church in many ways.

The Monday Art Club does all kinds of needle-work. Classes in dressmaking, china-painting and millinery were formed. Anything pertaining to home life was discussed and demonstrated, such as cooking, table-setting, etc. Have held art exhibits, entertained many noted Afro-Americans, and have given a little time to literary work.

The W. T. C. Art Club does all kinds of needle-work. Have an annual art exhibit; give many successful entertainments, give aid to the needy, and do a great deal of literary work. This club presented to the Jean Brown Martin Home a portrait of Booker T. Washington, the work of a Mr. Stepp (colored). They make annual visits to the Attucks Home and Jean Brown Home.

The Palm Leaf Club does literary and philanthropic work.

The Pastor's Aid is a church club of St. Peter's Church. They assist the officers of the church in any way they can, financially and otherwise.

The Bethesday Church contributes to Home and Foreign mission work. It has paid an apportionment to American Baptist Home Mission Society and National Training School, at Washington, and made a monthly payment toward the salary of one native African teacher. Have contributed to a fund to educate a native African doctor studying in this country. Visit the sick and help needy in their home town.

The King's Daughters' Charity Club visit the sick, help the needy, and do all the good they can to up-build God's cause.

The Zenith City Art Club does needle-work and assist in raising money to build St. Mark's Church.

The Virginia report says:

We have connected with the State Federation of Colored Women of Virginia, clubs whose members are actively engaged in home, school, church, village improvement, rescue work, and social settlement, and they are doing good work. These clubs had been organized and working long before the State Federation was organized, so that explains how we can do so much work in so short a time.

At our Second Annual Meeting, held in Richmond June 17 and 18, 1909, forty-seven clubs, representing 1,200 women, were reported.

We have succeeded in establishing a permanent organization and hope, by united and systematic effort, to give substantial evidences of the moral, mental and material progress made by our people.

The Illinois Federation has thirty-one clubs. The president's address of 1908 said:

Our clubs are indispensable factors in our elevation. As women, we must stand united for God, ourselves and our race. Some opposition has developed toward club work, someone having said that we were a set of butterflies on dress parade, but in my opinion the statement is false, for the most of our club women are the best housekeepers, the best wives and the best cooks; the most self-sacrificing women, ever on the alert to relieve suffering humanity, to the support of which they give a part of their small pittance of pin money. Our visits to the jails and juvenile courts show that many of our women are doing good work along these lines. Through organized effort, homes for working-girls, day nurseries and kindergartens are being established. Is not this progress? All this the work of our noble women. We would like here in this connection to mention: The Cairo hospital, fostered and under the supervision of the Yates Club of Cairo; the Anna Field Home for Girls, Peoria; Lincoln Old Folks and Orphans' Home, founded by Mrs. Eva Monroe and assisted by the Women's Club of Springfield; the Home for Aged and Infirm Colored People, Chicago, founded by Mrs. Gabrella Smith and others; the Amanda Smith Orphans' Home, Harvey. The last of which we mention is the Phillis Wheatley Home for Wage-Earning Girls, of Chicago.

The Colorado Federation reports:

At the last annual convention there were twenty-six clubs represented.
They are charity, art and study clubs. All help to support the colored orphanage at Pueblo. One is raising means to build a home for girls and
another to build a club house. Neither of these buildings is a certainty. The
list is as follows:

Denver:
  Life Line Club.
  Sunshine Club.
  Self-improvement and Social Club.
  Pond-Lily Art Club.
  Taka Art Club.
  Coleridge Taylor Study Club.
  Lucy Thurman W. C. T. U.
  City Federation.
  The League.

Colorado Springs:
  DuBois Reading Club.
  Twentieth Century Reading Club.
  Silver Leaf Art Club.
  Libby C. Anthony Club.
  Harper W. C. T. U.
  City Federation.
  Dahalia Art Club.
  Pond-Lily Club.
  Treble Clef Music Club.

Pueblo:
  Modeste Art Club.
  Carnation Art Club.
  Loyal Temperance Legion.
  The Mothers' Club.
  Dorcas Watson W. C. T. U.
  City Federation.

La Junta:
  N. U. G. Club.

Cheyenne, Wyo.:
  Searchlight Club.

The Women's Clubs of Arkansas report:

The first woman's club was organized February 11, 1897; first city federation June 7, 1905. The State was federated through the activities of Mrs.
B. T. Washington and Mrs. Hunton, now national organizer; two State
meetings since 1905, one in June, 1908, the other in June, 1909. In 1909 the
clubs reported twenty-five clubs with a membership of five hundred, represented by forty-four delegates at State meeting.

The city federations at Little Rock and Hot Springs are flourishing. At
Hot Springs there is an Old Ladies' Home of seven rooms costing $1,500. At
Little Rock there is an Old Ladies' Home of ten rooms costing $2,500, and
at Fort Smith one costing $1,400. There is now being planned at Little
Rock a Working Girls' Home under the auspices of the city federation. A
Reform School for Colored Youth under the auspices of the State federation has been planned, and is now being prosecuted to arouse sentiment,
influence State legislature and State officers, collect money, etc. There
are School Improvement Associations throughout the State. These assist
teachers and scholars in beautifying the grounds and school rooms, and in

systems of rewards and incentives for better school work. These clubs do philanthropic and literary work.

Some thirty clubs belong to the Ohio Federation.

Ten of them report $500 raised during the year 1908-09. They also report the following statistics:

```
Number of members.........  .....................................  165
Number married.....'..............................................  125
Number who assist in support of family......................  45
Graduates from college.............................................  7
Graduates from Normal or High School......................  39
Finished Fifth Grade .............................................  42
Can not read......................................................  0
Aggregate number of children..................................  180
Members' children graduated from college.................  8
Members' children finished Normal or High School........  31
Members' children still in school....;.........................  74
Number of children under school age.......................  .  18
Pianos ............................................................  67
Organs .................................  .........................  18
Aggregate amount of real estate .........................$282,000
Aggregate value of libraries...............  ...............  6,975
Life Insurance carried ...........................  ...........  86,049
```

One of the most successful State Federations is that of Alabama. It has forty-five clubs. Of its last session it was reported:

The State Federation of Colored Women's Clubs, which began its ninth annual session in this city last Monday, came to a close yesterday afternoon. The Federation has established and is supporting a reformatory at Mt. Meigs for Negro boys. The organization is composed of representatives from the various Negro women's clubs throughout the State, and the Negro women are very enthusiastic over the work they are doing to reform wayward Negro boys. The meeting in 1907 was held in Selma.

Since that meeting the clubs have raised and reported to the officers $2,283.72 and expended $2,236.97. At the meeting that has just closed the Federation raised cash to the amount of $1,068.92. After paying up all debts, they have now on hand $593.39.

The State Federation of Mississippi has seventeen clubs.

We have done much work toward elevating the home life among the masses by paying especial attention to plantation club work and establishing community clubs where possible.

One particular club—the Woman's Progressive Club of Alcorn College—the oldest club in the State, and the one with which I was connected for eleven years, has done much along this line, holding club meetings right in the plantation homes, showing the women of these homes how to improve themselves and their homes. We have seen many evidences of good results from this kind of work.

The Woman's Christian Union of Vicksburg and the State Federation have adopted this work as State work, and now all of the clubs are bending their energies toward its support.

The Phillis Wheatley Club of this town—a club of forty-six members—has furnished a reading-room known as the Phillis Wheatley Reading-Room.

Many clubs do literary work, studying both literature and art. At the last State Fair several pieces of work from club women took first premiums. All of our clubs do some charity work. We hold our next annual meeting at Mound Bayou—the Negro town.

Some reports from typical women's clubs throughout the country follow:

The Women's Home Progressive Club was organized October 19, 1902, with a membership of seventeen. Club work in this locality was a new feature and therefore met with considerable criticism, but, nevertheless, we went on. During the year 1903 we gave twelve dollars on a piano for the city schools besides helping a number of sick and destitute ones during the winter months. In 1905 the Club donated ten dollars to F. I. S. College. The following departments were organized: Educational, Business, Charity, and Industrial. Although our club is composed mainly of teachers or those capable of teaching, only the last three have claimed our attention so far. In our Educational Department we have only had a literary program once a month but planned to take up a regular reading course later. In the Business Department we have a saving department where each one deposits at each meeting any amount she may see fit, usually twenty-five cents. Last year our savings ran up to nearly fifty dollars.

In the Charitable Department for this year we helped to put fountains in the public schools.

Our Industrial work for this year was basketry. We made a number of beautiful baskets and hand-bags with raffia.—Paris, Tex.

E. W. Bailey, Principal of the school, in a brief talk stated that the colored women's clubs had been working for a year in order to raise $125 with which to aid the city in putting water fountains on the campus of the colored school ground. As a result of their efforts, the representatives of the federation then present had in their hands more than $100 to present to the board of education for the laudable cause. The presentation speech was made by Mrs. Hannah Simms, president of the City Federation of Colored Women. In her talk she assured the superintendent and all present that the colored women have it in their hearts to do something themselves to aid in educating the children of their race while the white people are taking such deep interest in providing the necessary facilities for their education. She further stated that the superintendent of city schools had asked for $125 and that they were ready to place with him $126. Prof. Wooten in pointed remarks accepted the contribution and he gave assurance that the amount given would be highly appreciated and that he is ever ready to help those who struggle to do something for themselves.—Paris, Tex.

There are at least ten women's clubs that are devoted to social betterment. One of these the oldest, "The Women's League" is purely charitable. They are buying a home for working girls, strangers who come to town, etc. They have paid about $700 on it so far. One club is purely literary, "The Booklover's." The others are:

> Progressive Study Club.
> Kensington Art Club.
> Phyllis Wheatley Club.
> The Hiawatha Club.
> The Crescent Club.
> The Carrie Steele Club.
> The Clionian Club.
> The Arena Club.

The last eight named do several kinds of work: some charitable, some literary, some art needlework, china painting, etc. All do some charitable work.

Nine of the ten are in an organization called the City Federation of Clubs which meets monthly, and is a sort of club clearing-house. There are over three hundred women in these clubs.—Kansas City, Mo.

Woman's Twentieth Century League—main object to support Reformatory. Captain W. D. Hargwood, superintendent of the Boys' Reformatory at Mount Meigs, Ala., was in the city Tuesday, and returned the same night with a youthful criminal that had been turned over by the court to the custody of the reform school.

The transportation expenses of the superintendent and boy were paid by the Woman's Twentieth Century League.

When it was learned that the little unfortunate was very scantily clad, and had neither shoes nor stockings on, a christian-hearted mother donated a complete outfit of good clothing and underwear, besides shoes and stockings. —Mobile, Ala.

Our Woman's Club of this city is not yet able to give full support to any particular work. We care for a few old and sick people. Our plan is to have a reading-room and to look after the young children of the laboring class of women during the day while they are away from home at work.—Gainesville, Fla.

The City Federation of Colored Women care for the sick and needy and are trying to raise funds to build an Orphans' Home and an Old Folk's Home.— Pensacola, Fla.

Sojourner Truth Club aims to build a Home for Working Women and Girls. They have succeeded in raising money enough to purchase a lot upon which to erect a building.—Los Angeles, Cal.

The Woman's Loyal Union owes its formation to an unusually large meeting held in New York city, in aid of Miss Ida B. Wells, now Mrs. Barnett, at that time editor and publisher of a paper in Memphis, Tenn., whose press on account of her fearless utterances had been destroyed and her life threatened. At this gathering a generous purse was secured for Miss Wells. The meeting proved such a success, and the enthusiasm aroused among the people was so great, that it was considered wise and fitting to found a permanent organization embodying the sentiments elicited by the meeting.

The Woman's Loyal Union was therefore organized December 5, 1892. The motto of the club is, "Vigilant, Patriotic, Steadfast." This association, whose initial effort was the defense of the oppressed, continued to work along race lines. In accordance with the clause of the constitution, "The object of this Union shall be the diffusion of accurate and extensive information relative to the civil and social status of that class of American citizens of African descent—i. e., Afro-Americans—that they may be led to an intelligent assertion of their rights," etc., a circular letter containing questions for information respecting the condition of the people was widely distributed throughout the South. Toward the dissemination of race literature Congressman White's speech delivered in the House of Representatives was sent to the celebrated Union League of Manhattan, to the Christian League, and to other prominent parties; and leaflets issued by the Afro-American Council were also sent to white clubs and to liberal-minded people.

Also when the mentioned Council was soliciting funds to try a test case in the courts of the South, the sum of $10 was given by the club to assist this worthy cause, and a like amount to the Citizens' League to protect the sufferers in the race riots which took place in New York city in 1900. An account of these riots, issued in pamphlet form, was circulated in the convention of the Northeastern Federation of Women's Clubs, held in Brooklyn in the summer of 1902.

When refugees from Oklahoma, the unfortunate victims of a Liberian scheme, in a destitute and helpless condition, were stranded in cars in Jersey City, the Women's Loyal Union came to their relief, placing the matter in the hands of the Ways and Means Committee of the association. The amount of $20 was furnished this cause and the needy ones were supplied with temporary homes and otherwise succored in the hour of their great distress.

In relation to further financial assistance rendered by this club, a sum of money was given to the school at Manassas managed by Miss Deans, and $10 to the Waller Fund created by the New York Press toward the relief of Ex-Consul Waller, then confined in a French prison on the island of Mauritius.

From a feeling of reverence and affection for the memory of John Brown, money was also, at one time, sent to his daughter, then in dire need. The club gave a substantial amount toward the purchase of the Northfield Home, a building at Northfield, Mass., which the Northeastern Federation had agreed to secure as a center of rest and recreation for club members during the summer.

In the line of educational work two children were supported for several years in a kindergarten in Florida, and money contributed toward the maintenance of a school in Georgia.

Emphasizing the desire to keep in memory the heroes of the race, the death of Frederick Douglass was observed by appropriate exercises, including a memorial poem written by the recording secretary.

Under the third section of article two of the constitution of the Union, in the autumn of 1905, a Protective and Industrial Home for Working Girls was established by the club, and continued for nearly two years with a reasonable degree of success; its object was to shelter and protect girls who come North to secure employment, and to aid them in the accomplishment of their plans. The Home was suitably equipped, provided with a competent matron and managed by an efficient House Committee; and effective work was accomplished during the period of its activity; but it has been temporarily suspended on account of changes made by the owner in the premises where it was located. The aim of the association, however, is to re-open the Home as soon as sufficient funds can be obtained and proper accommodations secured, when the work can be developed on a larger scale and with greater facilities for usefulness.

The membership of the Woman's Loyal Union is not as large as it has been on account of various changes made in the community where the club has worked since its organization. The present enrollment is twenty-five.—New York.

The Semper Fidelis is a club composed of twenty-five married ladies. It was organized about ten years ago, mainly as a literary club, but added the charitable feature at once. Some years it has given scholarships to deserving pupils in the Negro High School. It has also made large donations to the Industrial Department of the High School. Each year it makes donations of money, clothing, and other necessities to the Old Folks and Orphans' Home of this city, besides helping other needy persons in the city. Since the beginning of the State Reformatory for Negro Boys, several years ago—and which does not receive any State aid as yet—it has taken a very active part in helping to establish and maintain the same.—Birmingham, Ala.

The Anna M. Duncan Club was organized in September, 1898. The first work they did was to issue a call for the organization of a State Federation of clubs, which was effected December 26, 1898. After this organization was perfected, the clubs seeing the need of a city federation, they organized one. They took as their work the building of a State Reformatory. Each Sunday afternoon different members would visit the jail, and seeing how our young men and boys were being sent to the chain-gang and farms for the least offense, they determined if possible to save our boys from being placed in prison cells with hardened criminals, and by this means coming from prison much worse than when put in; in fact, becoming full-fledged criminals. They worked at this for two years, until they finally interested the State Federation to adopt the work. Of this State Federation Miss Anna M. Duncan was the first president. She was also president of the club until her death. Her undying devotion to the work of saving the boys, and her untimely death, caused the club in honor of her memory to adopt the name of the Anna M. Duncan Club. At first the number of members was unlimited and the club met from church to church; then the number was limited. We have now thirty active members. Our special work is the Reformatory that has been established in this city by the State. We have one building, a cottage of about eight rooms, and a farm of twenty acres that has all been paid for by the Federation. The cottage cost something over twelve hundred dollars. This club is an important factor in the running of the Reformatory, the president of the club being chairman of the Board of Managers and its corresponding secretary being a member of the Committee.

These women are untiring in their efforts to make the Reformatory work a success. While the Reformatory is their chief work, other objects of charity have not been neglected. A child has been kept in the kindergarten, another in the Normal School of this city by the paying of tuition and furnishing books; another has been sent to and from Talladega College, she having a scholarship but unable to pay the railroad fare to and from school.

In this city is the Hale Infirmary, a large and commodious building built by Mrs. Ann Hale in memory of her husband and children. While Mrs. Hale gave the building, the running of the house depends upon the donations given it. To this object the clubs give thirty dollars a year. Clothing, food and fuel have been given to the needy poor during the year to the amount of thirty or forty dollars.

During last year the Club collected three hundred and sixty dollars. Of this amount two hundred and fifty was given to the Reformatory. The Club hopes to be able to double this amount during the present year.

We study different authors for our own improvement. Papers are read and events of interest to the race are discussed. At different times we have had men of note to lecture for us, and the money so raised has gone into our Reformatory Fund.—Montgomery, Ala.

The Woman's Club of Marietta was organized in September, 1900, with eleven members. One of the objects of the club is to help the needy in and about Marietta. For several years the charity of this club was shown by donations of raw food, wood, bed-clothing, garments and medicine to the poor and needy. In very rare instances money was given, with which to buy a needed article. Many yards of cloth have been bought and made into garments by the ladies for orphans and sick people. Once we gave a Christmas tree for orphan children. About twenty-five children received two and three presents each. A neat little program was rendered by the children and added much interest to the occasion. But we have stopped this promiscuous giving. We help an individual now, only when he is in extreme need and applies to us. We are keeping our pennies together for the purpose of establishing a "Home." At first we thought an Orphanage, but now we think a Home for the Friendless, orphans included.

We have in the bank about eighty dollars and it is drawing interest. We have just decided to buy a two-acre tract of woodland in a good Negro settlement three miles from the center of town. Before thirty days I think it will be in our possession. Then we shall go to work to build on it.

Our membership is small, never having been more than twenty at any one time. Being purely philanthropic, women are not very anxious to join.—Marietta, Ga.

The Woman's Club was organized with ten members. The number has grown to thirty. There are various departments: the Child Culture Department, the Juvenile Department, the Domestic Science Department, the Prison Department, the Sick and Aged Committee and the Orphan Committee. All of the departments and committees are active except the Domestic Science Department which has been closed for some time on account of lack of funds. Through these various committees we are brought in touch with all classes. Mothers' Meetings are held from time to time in the different churches some time during the week, also sometimes on Sunday afternoons. They are held to suit the convenience of the people.

Many are the needy ones who have been relieved at the hands of the Woman's Club.

To help us in our charitable work twenty members have taken stock in a millinery project. The value of each share is five dollars. Some have taken half of a share. Ten per cent of the undivided profits will be given to the club to further its work of charity. The little millinery store was opened last month and we are praying for success.—Athens, Ga.

The St. Pierre Ruffin Club, the oldest club here, is composed of twenty-five married ladies, who are engaged in the work of social and benevolent uplift. We feel that the social side of life has been greatly improved through this agency.—South Bend, Ind.

The Daisy D. Walker Club is composed of twelve young ladies. They make a specialty of supplying the sick with milk and fruit and giving of flowers to the dead. They are also engaged in literary work.—South Bend, Ind.

The Mothers' Society studies and discusses home-making, the rearing of children, etc. They have in hand the building of a hospital for Negroes, and have collected a considerable amount. They are receiving generous support from the race.—Frankfort, Ky.

The Francis E. W. Harper Club of Portland, Me., was organized in 1902 as a literary club. It has fourteen active members and one honorary member.

Since its organization the club has been engaged in philanthropic work. Our object is to build a home for women—a place where the aged may pass their last days in comfort and where young women may find a home for small compensation.

Although the field here is very small we find plenty of work at hand, and in many cases co-operate with one of the ladies connected with the Associated Charities of this city.

We have a small bank account which is increasing gradually. I am also pleased to add that this year the club has been unusually prosperous.—Portland, Me.

The New Bedford Mothers' Club is carrying on work for neglected and homeless children. This work was started in 1904. We are doing a good work which is limited only by our means. We have a sum of money in the bank which is known as the Children's Home Fund, and will be used when the work warrants it in building a home for these waifs. This work appeals especially to a mother's heart.—New Bedford, Mass.

The Ann Arbor Women's Club was organized in 1898 with ten members. From the first we have felt that there was need of an organization to help over the rough places, and we ten went to work. We have given nearly $700 to aid the needy, possibly not all in ready cash—although much of it has been cash—but we have given clothes, food, fuel, bedding and flowers to the poor of our own city, to say nothing of having sent quilts, rugs, food (including canned goods, fruit, vegetables, sugar, etc.), clothing and money to the Phillis Wheatley Home in Detroit. We also placed an inmate at the Home for which we paid $200. Each year we give to each of the two churches, besides when we have our annual sermon preached in October we give a special collection to every church. Our club now numbers twenty active and two honorary members, and as we are making up our report for the State Convention we feel proud of the work done this year, as it has been the most successful one during our existence. We are contemplating having a flag day. We have not purchased any real estate yet, but that is the point that we are aiming for, and hope before long to make the first payment on a piece of property. We also contribute toward the support of a district nurse in our city. At the Christmas Tide we send dinners to the poor that we know of and fruit to the sick.—Ann Arbor, Mich.

The women of Vicksburg, after several attempts, succeeded in 1905 in effecting a permanent organization. These club women were banded together to do charity work, but for a long time could not decide what work was most necessary. They finally concluded that some provision for caring for the old folks and orphans should be made. This work was immediately undertaken by them. They began at once to solicit funds from the people of this immediate vicinity for the purpose. They had to overcome the difficulties common to all incipient work. Many felt that nothing would ever come of the movement and refrained from taking a part.

Notwithstanding this, they selected a suitable lot about a mile from Vicksburg, containing a large ante bellum residence, and contracted to buy the same for $1,200.

They have now paid for the place. They have bought also two smaller lots in the same locality, and are now collecting funds to repair the Home, after which they intend to open it for the reception of the aged poor.

They have no permanent source of support. Their collections have been made solely in this community.—Vicksburg, Miss.

In January, 1903, having for some time seen the necessity for a club in our city whose object would be the help and uplift of the women and girls of our race along many lines of usefulness, I asked a number of women to meet at my residence to organize such a club. Nine responded and we formed what is known as the Afro-American Woman's Industrial Club. We decided to meet twice a month, the first meeting being a strictly business meeting and the second a social meeting to which our friends are invited; the meetings being held at the different members' homes.

During the first year of our organization we joined the Northeastern Federation of Women's Clubs. Last year we were incorporated under the laws of New Jersey and in May, 1908, we purchased a small house situated at 104 Harrison avenue, the lot being 25 feet by 108 feet. Our very efficient treasurer, who is a widow with her aged mother to care for, was installed as housekeeper. The house is a modest one, having only six rooms; these have been occupied ever since we opened. We hope to be able to enlarge the building soon, as we desire to be able to care for all or at least a large part of the girls and women who come to our city from various parts of the country seeking employment and often, unfortuuately, falling into bad hands.

From a membership of nine we have steadily grown until we number forty earnest workes.—Jersey City, N. J.

We have the E. L. Davis Club, which is a part of the Pennsylvania State Federation of Negro Women's Clubs. We have raised over two hundred dollars in the last two years for the Home for Destitute Negro Children, located at New Castle. We have assisted in paying the funeral expenses of a poor woman, given clothes to the poor, flowers to the hospital. We send three dollars each month to the home at New Castle towards the maintenance of the Home.—Johnstown, Pa.

The Mothers' Club was organized September, 1903, for the purpose of aiding struggling mothers. In May, 1904, we opened a day nursery—a small place of four rooms, for we were poor and few in number. We saw the great need for such a place for mothers—those who must go out to work—to leave their little ones to be cared for, instead of having them roam the streets uncared for. We have struggled hard to carry on the work. The meetings are very helpful to all. We have very often a program, and topics for discussion which are usually Child Training, Housekeeping, Village Improvement, or some race subject, or temperance.—Providence, R. I.

We have been organized four years. During this time we have made donations to any and every needy person, regardless of denomination. We are laboring now to raise means to establish an Old Folk's Home, which we hope to be able to do in the near future. Our membership is fifty-nine, with seven officers. We meet twice during the month. Our treasury is maintained by the monthly dues paid by each member, together with donations given at the different mass meetings held by the club.

The preamble of the constitution is as follows:

"Whereas, a nation's standard is measured by that of its women, and seeing great need of improvement in the race in general: we the women of Jackson, State of Tennessee, being sensible of the great responsibility resting upon us as women, have organized ourselves under the name of a Woman's Club.

"We believe that in union or friendly co-operation in the work of 'lifting as we climb,' we can best elevate our homes and the race by developing ourselves along various lines, we do hereby adopt the following Constitution and By-Laws for the Woman's Club of Jackson, Tennessee."—Jackson, Tenn.

Different men, lawyers, doctors, ministers, also visiting men of note, address the club at each meeting; dues and other moneys are turned over to the church; we have sent barrels to different industrial schools in the South, and also make up baskets and boxes for one or two orphan asylums and Old Folk's Homes.—St. Paul, Minn.

The first summer or vacation school to be maintained by any Woman's Club in the State was organized by the Koffee Klatsch in 1906. The children received instruction in sewing, picture-framing and cooking. The smaller ones were kept interested in blackboard work, story telling, etc. These classes, with an average attendance of eighteen and twenty, were maintained for two years.

Aside from the general relief work, specific attention is given twice yearly to the Home for Aged and Infirm Colored People. During the early autumn a special day is given over to the club, at which a good program is arranged at one of the churches and a collection is lifted solely for the purpose of buying fuel for the Home. This is known as "Coal-fund day."

When the fruit season is at its best a day is set apart and known as "Canning day." The members of the club take the fruit and sugar out to the institution and put the fruit up for the winter. Over one hundred and fifty quarts have been put up by their exertions at different times. At various times money has been raised to assist in placing an inmate in the Home.

Miscellaneous relief work has included cases like the following: the purchase of fuel, groceries, and miscellaneous provisions; the distribution of clothing and shoes and medicine, also services of a physician; helping to purchase an invalid chair, and occasionally a special church donation.

We feel that we have been wonderfully blessed in our endeavors, as no case reported to us during our existence has been passed over on account of lack of funds.

A committee of four ladies are delegated to visit the sick and bring reports of cases to be looked after.—Chicago, Ill.

The College Aid Society of Wilberforce, Ohio, have to their credit thirty years' support of aiding needy students. The Twentieth Century Club of Xenia, Ohio, has pursued a course of study of American and English literature, and fostered the kindergartens for colored children in Xenia, Ohio.

The women of St. Louis, Missouri, under the leadership of Mrs. M. L. Harrison, have completed seven years of successful work in caring for the St. Louis Colored Orphans' Home, which they founded May 19, 1901, at a cost of $6,700. Mrs. Susan Paul Vashon, of St. Louis, has been successful in arousing the interest of a large number of mothers in forming mothers' clubs and holding mothers' meetings.

The colored women in Indianapolis have a club which has been interesting itself to secure opportunity for colored women to get work. Arrangements have now been made by which more than 150 colored women have secured work in one of the canning factories of that city, the managers having agreed to take only women and girls recommended by clubs.

The Harriet Tubman Club, of Boston, Mass., has been successfully conducting a Home for Working Girls on Holyoke street. This property is in a good part of the city and has sheltered a large number of women, giving them a good comfortable Christian home. Ruth Circle of King's Daughters of Boston has done much to assist in the charitable work of the city. The Woman's Era Club of the city of Boston has covered a wide field of work along literary, musical, and other lines. The Woman's Loyal Union, New Bedford, is engaged in the work of a Home for the Aged, irrespective of race or religion (see souvenir program and historical sketch). The Woman's Progressive Club of Worcestor, Mass., is also the founder of a Home for Aged People in that city.

Through the efforts of Judge Feagin and the work of an organization composed of the better class of Negro women in Birmingham, Ala., an industrial school has been started and to this eighteen little waifs have already been sent. During the past year these women have raised $2,000, with which they purchased twenty-five acres of land near Montgomery, Ala. Upon this they have built a six-room cottage which now serves as a home for these eighteen little waifs. The superintendent chosen for this school is W. B. Tyrrell, a Negro of unusual ability and peculiar history. After being educated in the schools of his native State, Virginia, he was sent by a priest to a classical school in England to be trained for the Catholic priesthood. He was seven years in England, then was graduated from Bonn University in Germany and went as a missionary to Abyssinia. Failing health compelled him to return to this country. He has taken up the work for colored youth with great zeal.

The Yates Woman's Club of Cairo, Ill., recently pnrchased land on which to build a hospital. Within three years the club has raised more than $2,100, paying in cash $900 for their land and $1,200 on a two-story brick building.

The Phyllis Wheatley Club, Chicago, Ill., has a Home for Working Girls and has been very successful in securing funds for the land and for buiding and maintaining the work; in fact, all of the clubs in Chicago, as well as in the State of Illinois, are all well organized and working along many lines for the uplifting of humanity.

The State of Texas is well organized. At the recent meeting of the State Federation, "The Mother's Part in Preventing Diseases" was discussed; also many pertinent ideas concerning the responsibility which rests upon mothers to train their children in hygienic living; "What the wash-women have done for us as a race," was another subject presented. Special mention was made of the great work and influence of those great workers who have humbled themselves that their children might rise to higher plains of usefulness. In fact, the women of Texas are alive to the demands which the spirit of the times has placed upon colored womanhood.

The Woman's Industrial Club of Louisville, Kentucky, is a business, charitable and industrial club, quartered in a well-equipped twenty-room building on one of the most popular thoroughfares of the city. Various industries are carried on under its roof, and it has given impetus to the business life of the city of Louisville.

From the millinery department have gone out scores of young women who are doing high-class work. Louisville has a large number of clubs, and the next biennial of the National Association of Colored Women is to be in the city, the guest of forty clubs of that city.

The White Rose Mission of New York city, organized about twelve years ago by Mrs. Victoria Earle Matthews, has done much good work in that city. A large number of needy ones have found shelter within its doors and have been able to secure work of all kinds. This club has a committee to meet the incoming steamers from the South and see that young women entering the city as strangers are directed to proper homes. Mrs. Frances Keyser, who has charge of the work, is the right woman in the right place.

The Dorcas Home Mission Society of Brooklyn, N. Y., which numbers two hundred good earnest working women under the leadership of Mrs. Alice Wiley, has done much to relieve the sick and distressed in that city.

Last year the clubs of Minnesota issued a State Federation calendar, which was a most beautiful calendar of all the clubs, with the date of their organization, federation days, hours of meetings, their presidents and those in the National Association of Colored Women. It was a beautiful design and reflected much credit on the women of Minnesota.

A Mothers' Reception was held by the clubs of Colorado, fifty invitations on postal cards having been issued for the same. "Ventilation and Sanitation," also "The Mother's Influence in the Home," were the subjects discussed, each telling of some of her experiences in her own home. The key note sounded by the mothers was, pure mothers for pure children; they advocated patience for the children, reasoning, and less whipping, thereby gaining their confidence and making them companionable.

The W. C. T. U. used to be strong among colored women and is still influential; it is, for instance, "a strong influence for good" in Dallas, Texas.

The King's Daughters and Sons have many colored circles:

In New York city there is a Circle which has done very earnest work, and also the Gould Circle, the Rest-Room Circle, the Aunt Jane Circle, Home for Aged Colored People, St. John's Place, Brooklyn, also do splendid work.

In Toledo and in other Ohio cities the colored people have done some very fine work. In Michigan, also, the colored people have accomplished a great deal. There is a Circle of colored people in Frankfort, Kentucky.

There are, of course, other Circles, but, as I say, we cannot give you a complete list and can only indicate here and there some of the better known workers.

Other reports follow:

Our club, the Faithful Few Circle of the King's Daughters, belongs to the International Order of the King's Daughters. While we operate under their constitution and laws and labor for the same cause, we belong to the Mississippi State Federation of Women's Clubs.

We have a membership of twenty-five persons, with about twelve active workers. Our work is confined to the unfortunate, "In His name." We use the Silver Cross Journal and keep in touch with the great Order throughout the world.

We are now attempting to build an "Old Folk's Home," with a nursery and a kind of headquarters for working girls, somewhat on the order of a rescue home.—Natchez, Miss.

We have the King's Daughters Society, which has been organized seventeen years. We have a membership of fifty-two, and our work is to care for old people who can not help themselves. During the past year we gave as much as $68 in money, and each week we make up baskets of food and clothing and send to the needy. We have also helped to bury a number of poor persons.—Austin, Tex

The following are the kinds of program rendered by these Women's Clubs:

Ohio State Federation, Dayton, O.

Subject: Light on the Work of the Ohio State Federation.

Program

The Local Clubs.
The Model Club.
The Ohio Federation, its Weak Points and How to Overcome Them.
Helpful Echoes from the World's Fair and Club Life in Missouri.
Hints on Club Literature.
Our Children. Shall the Ohio Federation form Clubs among its Children?
Race Pride as Manifested in Club Life.
The Entertaining Hostess, and Appropriate Decorations and Souvenirs or Favors.
To What Extent Should our Federation be Public-Spirited? Have we a Voice in the School, the Republic, the Nation?

The Wheel of Progress, Cincinnati, O.

Philanthropical and Economical Department

SECOND TUESDAY

November 14: Original poem, "The Forest." Music. Discussion, "Misplaced Charity."

December 12: "What is the Greatest Evil that Retards the Commercial Progress of the Negro?" Music. Industrial Work.

January 9: Discussion, "The Best Education for our Girls." Music. Industrial Work.

February 13: Paper, "Should Social Games be Enconraged in the Home, and to What Extent?" Music. Industrial Work.

March 13: Discussion, "What Can the Club Woman Do to Raise the Intellectual Status of our Young Men?" Music. Industrial Work.

April 10: "Influence of Aesthetic Decoration in the Home." Music. Industrial Work.

May 8: "Reverence for Holy Things." Music. Industrial Work.

June 12: "The Attitude of the Club Woman Toward Her Less Fortunate Sisters." Music. Industrial Work.

July 10: "Development of Domestic Economy." Music. Industrial Work.

August 14: "Checks to Evil Influences of Environment." Music. Industrial Work. "Duties of a Good House-wife." Music. Industrial Work.

September 11: "Economy and Taste in Dress." Music. Industrial Work.

October 9: Annual Reports. Election of Officers.

Literary and Musical Department

FOURTH TUESDAY

November 28: Queries and Current Events. Instrumental Music. Lecture, "A Trip to Sicily." Song.

December 26: Queries and Current Events. Paper, "Negro Writers and Their Best Productions." Music.

January 23: Queries and Current Events. Lecture, "Development of Political Economy." Vocal Music.

February 27: Queries and Current Events. Paper, "Anti-Slavery Heroes of the Nineteenth Century." Instrumental Music.

March 27: Discussion, "How Can We Dignify the 'Jim Crow' Car?" Paper, "The Most Potent Influences Tending Toward the Eradication of Color Prejudice." Song.

April 24: Queries and Current Events. Instrumental Music. Paper—Prose Fiction, "Ramona." Music.

May 22: Queries and Current Events. Paper, "Characteristics of the Poetical Triad.' Instrumental Music.

June 26: Queries and Current Events. Paper, "The Story of Toussaint L'Ouverture." Music.

July 24: Queries and Current Events. Paper, "Harriet Beecher Stowe and Her Writings." Music.

August 28: Queries and Current Events. Paper, "Natural Curiosities of Our Country." Music.

September 25: Cullings from Vacation Experiences. Lecture, "The Great Religions of the World." Music.

October 23: Greetings from Distant Members. "The Club Outlook." Song.

Section 11. Old Folk's Homes. The most characteristic Negro charity is the Home for Old People. Nothing appealed from the earliest days more strongly to the freedmen than the care for the old people.

In slavery days the old were, in many cases, carefully taken care of by the masters, especially in cities and towns and on the home plantations, but in numberless other cases, particularly on the great absentee plantations of the Black Belt, the old and decrepit were shamefully treated and neglected. The breaking up of families in slavery by sale and during the war and Reconstruction times, greatly aggravated the sufferings of the old, while the loosened family ties, due to the slave system, left in post-bellum times numbers of neglected old folk. Even loose family ties, however, were not able to overcome the native African reverence for parents, and before the war began Old Folk's Homes for Negroes had begun to be established, some by Negroes themselves, others by their friends.

The chief Homes now existing are noted below:

The Women's Twentieth Century Club of New Haven, Conn., was organized March 18, 1900, at the residence of Mrs. J. W. Stewart, 65 Edgewood, with a membership of nineteen.

At first we met for the study of race literature and to become better acquainted with the history and life-work of our celebrated men and women. The idea of charitable work was an after consideration.

Some of our members, in making sick calls, had visited the Hannah Gray Home and our attention had been called to the condition of the same.

Right here it would be well to state that this property, located at 158 Dixwell avenue, was formerly the home of a colored woman by the name of Miss Hannah Gray. She died in the early sixties and left the property in the hands of white trustees for the use of aged colored females. From what we have been able to learn, it was the first piece of trust property left for a home in the city. Unfortunately, Miss Gray had little or no money to leave as an income, to care for the home, and the inmates paid a small sum for the use of the rooms.

The club in 1903 appointed a committee to wait on Lawyer Henry White, the only living trustee, and found that the back taxes amounted to two hundred dollars, and the property would soon be disposed of to pay the same. We informed Mr. White of our willingness to try to save the property. At our request three colored trustees were appointed. The back taxes were abated and by appeals we have been successful in having them abated each year. Since the club took control we have had the house painted inside and out, walls and ceilings scraped, wood and coal put in each year, and in many ways we have been the mainstay of the old ladies.

Since 1903 four of our old friends have died, and the club assumed all responsibility for burial expenses.

At the present time we have five in the home; two being dependent upon us. At the holiday season they have been given regular holiday dinners, and the public schools have at Thanksgiving sent money and vegetables. Through the kindness of a white friend last year the five enjoyed a Christmas tree and each received a small gift of money.

For nearly two years we have employed a woman to go to the home daily and look after things.

The club annually elects a board of directors to look after the affairs of the home and report same to club. Our other officers look after the program, club business, finances, etc.

We have now a membership of over fifty. We meet weekly and have a program every Wednesday, except the last in the month; this we devote to business.

We are now making an appeal for funds for a new building, and have already in hand money for a new fence; circulars are out for donation day and two days' fair, June 2nd and 3rd.—New Haven, Conn.

St. Monica's Home is an old and well-known charity of Boston, Mass., supported in part by Negroes.

Home for Aged Men, Springfield, Mass., founded by Primus Mason for all races (cf. p. 38).

Home of the Aged, New Bedford, Mass.

The idea of having the New Bedford Home for the Aged was planned nearly twelve years ago by Miss Elizabeth C. Carter, who had been accustomed to making friendly visits to several aged people in this city, and who was previously interested in the Home for Aged People in Brooklyn, N. Y.

In this way she knew many aged ones; knew their needs, sufferings and joys. Here and there many were being provided for by private bounty. Miss Carter came in contact with several cases of this kind, and it caused her to study how something could be done to let the old people really get the benefit of the money that was being paid regularly for them, yet some of them too feeble to care for themselves properly.

So, after studying the question from every point of view, she planned the work, relying upon the co-operation of the persons supporting the old people to secure a pleasant house, furnish it invitingly, and gather the old people into it, with the hope of making it in the truest and sweetest sense a home for them.

The Woman's Loyal Union indorsed the idea and voted to unite their efforts for the maintenance of the Home. After trying to secure several houses for the work, the house at the corner of Cedar and Mill streets was secured by Miss Carter paying one hundred and five dollars of her personal money for six months' rent in advance, the society at this time having no money in its treasury.

The members of the union took books and solicited money, furniture and groceries, with the result that everything in the house was donated.

The Home was opened to the public March 25, 1897, and, like all other charitable work, it has had its "toils and conflicts," but by generous contributions it has continued. In 1898 a building fund committee was formed. After remaining in the house at the corner of Mill and Cedar streets nearly two years the work was moved to 121 Cedar street, which the society has rented until moving into its present building. January 14, 1902, the organization was incorporated under the general laws of the State of Massachusetts. In December of the same year the first large gift—$500, which was continued until last year—was received from a friend for the current expenses.

In 1904 one thousand dollars was received from the estate of Robert C. Billings, of Boston, and the same year land at the corner of Chancery and West Middle streets purchased. In 1904, by the terms of the will of the late Sarah E. Potter, ten thousand dollars and a part of the residue of the estate of Mrs. Potter was left to the Home. It is by this beneficent gift that the present building has been erected. Ground was broken in August, 1907, during

Old Home Week. The estimated cost of the building was $8,625, but with some necessary additions the building has cost $9,000. It contains twenty-one rooms. The furnishing cost between one and two thousand dollars, all of which is paid for at present. They have invested in stock $11,780, in bonds $12,951.68, cash $8,895.06; total amount, $33,626.74.

The future efforts of the management will be to secure funds for the current expenses; also an endowment fund, so that the work may become self-supporting.

During the work of eleven years nearly all of the charitable organizations of the city, also several churches as well as individuals, have assisted in some way.

Home for Aged Colored Women, Providence, R. I.

The Lincoln Hospital and Home, New York, N. Y., is an old charity supported by whites mainly. Cares for old people.

Home for the Aged, Brooklyn, N. Y.

Home for Aged and Incurable, Atlantic City, N. J.

Dr. Fayerman, seeing the need of such an institution occasioned by the peculiar conditions of Atlantic City, some years ago worked very hard for the establishment of it. As most of the cottagers there fill their houses with lodgers, a sick person, or aged one, would necessarily receive scant attention.

Colored Aged Home Association, Irvington, N. J.:

This Home was opened in 1895 at Coe's Place, Newark, where we paid rent for ten years. The association then thought it time for them to buy a place, so we moved to Ivington in 1905. We have a nice place which cost $4,500. We paid down $2,000, and are now in the building and loan association and pay $32 a month and we are doing the best we can. Since we opened we have had about 42 inmates, and would have had more if we could have taken them for nothing, but you know it takes money to run a place of this kind. In such a work the laborers are few, still we are doing the best we can and at the last meeting twenty-five names were enrolled, which means something. We have very little income. There are fifteen inmates now.

Annual Report for Year ending December 31, 1908

RECEIPTS

Agents	$ 760 70
Churches......................................	104 60
Donations.......................................	33 75
Admission fees...............................	400 00
Societies	40 00
Entertainments.............................	121 49
Received by the Matron....................	48 94
Joining fees.	15 00
Total......	$1,524 48
Drawn from Bank.........................	234 00
	$1,759 48

DISBURSEMENTS

Matrons	$ 324 00
Insurance	60 00
Butcher	240 00
Gas	7 82
Water	21 27
Telephone	5 62
Coal	147 50
Extra help	21 00
Plumber	37 03
Building and Loan Association	384 00
Dry Goods	8 25
Furniture	15 00
Groceries	211 00
Incidentals	66 16
Percentage to agents	167 25
Stationery and printing	8 00
Doctors	30 00
Total	$1,753 90
Balance in hand	5 50
Balance in Bank to date	234 00

Home for Aged and Infirm Colored Persons, Philadelphia, Pa., was founded by Stephen Smith and organized September 14, 1864. The Home has sheltered seven hundred and seventy inmates and had, in 1908, one hundred and forty inmates. The income from the estate of Smith amounts to about $3,760 annually, representing a capital of nearly $100,000. The total income is $21,000 and the property is worth $400,000. The home is controlled by twenty-eight trustees, of whom five are colored.

Home for Aged Colored Men and Women, Philadelphia, Pa.

Colored Masonic Home and Orphanage, Linglestown, Pa.

The Grand Lodge of Colored Free and Accepted Masons of this State has recently formed a corporation known as the "Trustees of the Colored Masonic Home and Orphanage of Pennsylvania," and has purchased near Lingles-town, nine miles from Harrisburg, a farm of some sixty or more acres for which they paid $4,500.

The purpose of this corporation and the farm which they have purchased, is to maintain a home for aged and indigent Masons, their widows and orphans.

Home for Aged and Infirm Colored Women, Pittsburgh, Pa., is "said to be the best in the country conducted entirely by our people."

The Sarah Ann White Home, Wilmington, Del.

The will of Sarah Ann White said:

"I give, devise and bequeath to the Rev. Edward H. Chippey in trust for a home for the colored aged women, all of my property of whatever kind, real, or personal, or mixed, wherever it may be found, and that as soon as an institution is incorporated that he may make over said property to the incorporation to be theirs and their successors so long as they shall continue to carry out this, my last will and testament.

"It is my desire that the Rev. Edward H. Chippey shall organize an association to be known by the name and title of the Sarah A. White Association, composed of male members and female members, with a Board of not less than five Trustees nor more than seven male members of African descent, said members shall compose the incorporation (corporators)."

The faithful adherence by the executor and the Association to the program laid down by this public-spirited woman was the occasion of constant remark on the day the Annex was dedicated. The failure on the part of the heirs after a long contest to break the will left the executor and his associates free to develop the provisions of the "trust."

May 4th, 1896, found the institution incorporated under the name of the Sarah Ann White Home for the Aged and Infirm Colored Persons, and conducting a Home in the old homestead house, which soon became crowded and necessitated the building of the annex at a cost of four thousand dollars completed with modern improvements.

The corporation is absolutely without endowment, and receiving no aid from the State; these facts are eloquent evidence of the magnitude of the struggle which has maintained this institution, housing, feeding, clothing, nursing, and providing for the many wants of as many as twenty old people at a time, with recourse to nothing but public charity. It is this condition of things which impels us to new endeavor to pay off the mortgage and lay the basis of permanent endowment.

Aged Men and Women's Home (Lee street), Baltimore, Md. Property $3,000. Inmates, 16. State aid, $250.

Bethel Old Folk's Home, Baltimore, Md. Property, $10,000. Inmates, 16.

The Stoddard Baptist Home, District of Columbia.

Some ten or twelve years ago Mrs. Maria Stoddard, a white woman, saw fit to set apart a small portion of ground in a very fashionable part of Washington, D. C., for a Baptist Home. But the gift was accompanied with conditions and limitations, which caused it to be of little service for a long while. Then the city cut off a portion of the lot to widen and improve a public street. This so reduced the size of the place that it was too small for such a home as the Baptists of the District of Columbia desired to have. Moreover, the heirs of Mrs. Stoddard came forward at this juncture and claimed both the money, which the District was about to pay for what it had taken for public use, and the remainder of the property. Consequently, the matter was thrown into court, and the heirs agreed with the trustees of the property, the court consenting, to sell the property, then divide all money coming from the disposition of any and all parts of the gift as follows, after deducting all legal and court expenses: to the heirs of Mrs. Stoddard 40%, to trustees of the Home 60%. It was further provided, that the trustees of the Home should invest their portion of the money in property elsewhere, for a Baptist Home, and so carry out the desire and intention of Mrs. Maria Stoddard in making the gift. Accordingly a tract of land, consisting of four and a half acres with a ten-room house on the same, was purchased about May 20, 1901, and a few months later put in proper condition and opened to Baptist ministers, their widows and orphans, and such other persons as the trustees see fit to admit. June 15, 1901, five and a half acres more were purchased by the trustees of the Baptist Home, giving them in all a total of ten acres. For this addition the sum of $2,750 was paid.

The Home is the property of the Baptist Ministers' Union of the District of Columbia, and is held in trust for the purpose and persons to which it is set apart by fifteen trustees who are appointed by the Baptist Ministers' Union of the District of Columbia.

The institution is situated on Hamilton Road, in the southeastern section of District of Columbia. At present there are ten inmates in the Home, four men and six women.

The management of the Home is in the hands of a body of women, consisting of ten delegates from each Baptist church in the District of Columbia and vicinity.

The property of the Home is free of debt, but the struggle to maintain the Home in a becoming manner and pay the expenses of every kind arising from its care, gives the management daily concern. It requires about one hundred and ten dollars monthly to meet all the requirements of the Home and its management.

I am not in a position to give you any exact statement as to the amount of money which has been raised for the Home since it began. The truth is we are mere learners in the conduct of work of this kind. The churches have their special work of many kinds, and are slow to take hold of this, but the future is sure, under God.

Old Folk's Home, Richmond, Va. Conducted by the Afro-American Emancipation Association.

Negro Baptists' Old Folk's Home, Richmond, Va.

The Negro Baptist Old Folk's Home, West Baker street, is the property of the Negro Baptist churches of Richmond and vicinity, and supported by the same with the aid of white and colored friends. Rev. R. V. Peyton is president and his church does much for its support.

Old Folk's Home, Westham, Va.

At Westham, Va., the True Reformers support not only a home for the aged but also one for the orphans. This institution is in excellent condition and the inmates, old and young, are being taken from all parts of the country.

Old Folk's Home, Portsmouth, Va.

The Old Folk's Home at Portsmouth is about four years old. It is supported entirely by Negroes. It was their first intention to locate the home in the suburbs of the city, where they purchased two acres of land. Since then they purchased a plot in the city at a cost of $4,000. At present there are no inmates, as the promoters want to get the home paid for before they admit any.

Old Folk's Home, Hampton, Va.

The Old Folk's Home at Hampton is a very interesting institution. It was organized in May, 1897, under the auspices of a society of women called "Tents." The head of the Order was the first to suggest that the Order have a home where the orphan children and the disabled sisters of the Tents might be cared for. She gave the ground and the sisters gave what they could to build and furnish the home.

This home is supported by contributions from the sisters, and no sister of the Order is allowed to solicit aid from the public. Last year it cost a fraction over $500 to care for the home. Since its organization in 1897 at no time has anything been bought on credit. This society not only supports its home but aids in other philanthropic work.

The home is controlled by a board of directors consisting of nine sisters of the Order. At present there are seven inmates.

Old Folk's Home, Norfolk, Va.

At Norfolk there is an Old Folk's Home, which was organized in 1894. Up to the present time it has cared for forty-two persons. Last year the expenses were $388, one-half of which was contributed by Negroes. At present the home has but three inmates.

Old Folk's Home, Gloucester, Va.

There is in Gloucester, Va., an Old Folk's Home, which was established in

1907. It has twenty acres of land. The main building is not yet completed, but on June 3, 1909, there was a special rally to raise money for its completion. So far, the home has cost $890, all of which was raised by the Negro women of Gloucester county.

Old Folk's Home, Alexandria, Va.—Non-sectarian and supported by voluntary contributions, with some city aid. There are from six to twelve inmates. It owns no real estate.

Tent Sisters' Old Folk's Home, Raleigh, N. C.

This is, perhaps, the most interesting experiment in the country. The secretary writes:

A few years ago I opened a school, of a business nature, but soon realized the class who really needed aid did not reach that standard. This school I closed, and a work has been quietly going on that I know God is well pleased with, for we daily see His blessings.

By becoming a member of four secret orders—you know the masses like such—I am in sympathetic touch with a great number, and can visit them in numbers. Through some of the women's earnest work, about two years ago we began to fix and fit a home for old people who are in a suffering condition. Since that time we have had nine inmates. Some of these came from neighboring towns. We have also had one death. None of these inmates have given us five cents for expenses.

This work is done through our club known as Tent Sisters in North Carolina.

Two hundred and fifty working women pledge one pound of food a month and at the least twenty-five cents per year in cash and more when dire necessity demands.

We borrowed from the building and loan association $200. The donations to this work are as follows:

Raleigh, N. C.—Furniture, bedding, crockery, clothes, and twenty-five dollars.
Cary, N. C.—Food, clothing, and ten dollars.
Apex, N. C.—Food, clothing, and seven dollars.
Holly Spring, N. C.—Food, clothing, and eight dollars.
Willow Spring, N. C.—Food and five dollars.
Durham, N. C.—Nine dollars.
Johnson, N. C.—Three dollars.
Wake Forest, N. C.—Two dollars.

Individuals, thirteen dollars and seventy-five cents; also, we have entertainments to meet many expenses.

DISBURSEMENTS

Repairs of home	$300 00
Furniture, etc	70 00
Wood for the two years	96 50
Heaters	4 50
Cook stove	4 00
Water, per month	1 25
For work in garden	1 00
To motherless children	15 00
For medicine and burial	31 00
Paid on debt of $200	113 00
Paid to matron during two years	18 50
Paid for washing	6 00
Paid for nursing sick	4 00
Paid for lights, etc	9 60

PRESENT INDEBTEDNESS

On borrowed money	$ 87 00
For medicine and burial	20 75

The matron has no stated salary, but we are obligated to pay her more for past services.

Mrs. Lucy Fikes has given her life to this work without a penny from us. She is a woman who has to earn her bread daily. I, the secretary, being busy in different working quarters, have no itemized account of everything done but this will give you an insight of the work.

About one hundred of the two hundred and fifty persons helping are more than sixty years of age. Some are feeble, yet they help carry on this work with their means.

One who knows the work but is unconnected with it says:

They are all Negroes. It is run by the poor working class of Negroes; has no endowment, and the inmates come though they have not a penny to help them. People make bed clothes for them. They need money to help pay someone to care for them. They have one wooden building which was once known as Business School and is owned by Miss Sallie A. Upperman. She has kindly given it to the people for the purpose of charitable work. She is trying to help the boys and girls, the women and men, who walk the street because they do not know'how to do what is required of them to make an honest living. I believe that God will help her. I shall do all I can in this noble work. She needs encouragement.

The Centenary Church Home of Charleston, S. C., is suppored by a Negro church.

Ashley River Asylum, Charleston, S. C.:

Is an institution entirely supported by the city government for aged colored people, male and female. The institution is excellently conducted by very competent officers (colored) and the inmates receive the best treatment in food, clothing, and the ordinary comforts of life.

Masonic Home, Columbus, Ga.

Carter's Old Folk's Home, Atlanta, Ga.

Old Folk's Home, Augusta, Ga.

Evergreen Old Folk's Home, Savannah, Ga.:

The Evergreen Old Folk's Home was organized April 7, 1908. I am very sorry that I am not able to speak of it as I would like, but I am thankful to the Lord for what He has done and is still doing. It was incorporated May 2, 1909.

We have nine inmates and could have had one hundred and nine, but on account of the way in which we had to provide for them we decided we would go slowly until we could do better.

Rescue Home for Orphans and Old Folks, Jacksonville, Fla.

The Colored Old Folks and Orphans' Home, of Mobile, Ala., was organized in 1871. One piece of property was bought and lost, and a second piece bought for $4,000 cash. It contains two acres of land, with fourteen pecan trees. The college has nine rooms, running water, and $120 a year is earned from pecans and pears. They have a cow and chickens, and own other real estate.

The Priscilla Brown Mercy Home, Selma, Ala.:

A charitable organization of the city of Selma was organized October 9, 1902, irrespective of denomination. They were at first a committee auxiliary to the U. A. Charity Association which after a few meetings drifted into obscurity, and the Daughters of Mercy, seeing the good work to be done and having already begun, became an incorporated body. The first donation given was two lots of land nearly paid for by Sister Priscilla Brown, a woman well known for her good deeds and charitable works, and her devout Christian spirit, and for whom our home is named. This band begun by seven women afterward grew to nine and now to forty-five, all mostly volunteers.

Our meeting days are the second and fourth Thursdays in each month, at the home of the president. We have now an honorary board of trustees composed of all of the ministers of the different denominations, and their successors, with Principal R. B. Hudson as chairman. We have not space to place before the public the many needy poor we have relieved with clothing, food, medicine, coal, shoes, books and tuition for orphans, during our organization. Each year at Thanksgiving the city school children give to us a great amount of food to be distributed among the poor.

The Priscilla Brown Mercy Home was opened and dedicated last October. We now have a matron and four inmates in the home. We are, however, prepared to accommodate comfortably about twelve. Our means are limited, and one of our rules for entrance is that all persons coming to us must be recommended by the pastor and officers of some church or officers of some society. Those organizations sending to us inmates partially support them. Our standard age for receiving persons is sixty years of age and upward.

The house is furnished throughout with single iron beds. The sanitary conditions are good. The property is valued at $2,500.

Old Folk's Home, Birmingham, Ala.

The Lafon's Home of the Holy Family, New Orleans, La.

The Lafon's Home of the Holy Family, corner Tonti and Hospital streets, is largely the gift of the late Thomy Lafon, who left over $100,000 for this institution. Before he died he also gave them their chapel. This home has 71 inmates and is the home for the old indigents. The city contributes $30 per month to this home.

The Lafon's Old Folk's Home, New Orleans, La.

The Lafon's Old Folk's Home is operated by the Protestant people. The late Thomy Lafon left $11,000 and Aristide Marie left $1,000 for this home. The city contributes $120 towards the support of this institution. For maintenance the institution depends almost wholly upon the colored Methodist and Congregational churches of this city. It has on an average about 25 to 30 inmates, both male and female, old indigents.

The Widow's Faith Home for Colored Destitutes, New Orleans, La.

The Faith Home, corner Robert and Pitt streets, is maintained and operated by the colored Baptist churches of this city, and is also aided to a small extent by the city. It is now taking care of 18 colored women, some of whom are over a hundred years old.

The Liner's Harvest Home, New Orleans, La.

The Liner's Harvest Home is for men, women and children. It was established over twenty years ago by the late Edward Liner, who gave the lots and building. The institution is in charge of Mrs. Fanny Taylor, who is aided by an organization of charitably disposed colored persons. There are now 16 inmates, five of whom are men, six women and five children. It depends entirely upon subscriptions for its maintenance and support. The property is valued at $6,000.

Woman's Home Mission Society Home, Baton Rouge, La. Conducted by Baptist women.

M. W. Gibbs Colored Old Ladies' Home, Little Rock, Ark.

Our work at present is the furnishing of one room at the Old Ladies' Home. A new building is being erected by the citizens of our city, and the different clubs are furnishing it. The site for the building was given by Judge M. W. Gibbs, and the home is named for him.

St. James Old Folk's Home, Louisville, Ky.

The St. James Old Folk's Home was founded in 1887, or thereabouts; flourished a few years, got on the toboggan and went to the bottom in 1893. A younger set, together with two or three of the old managers, reorganized the Society of St. James and under the leadership of Miss N. L. Frye undertook the purchase of the present $10,000 property at a set-up price of $3,500 on a five years' basis at six per cent. By paying in advance and saving, or discounting the interest, we bought it for a little more than $2,900. The lot is 200 feet by 200 feet, with a seven-room frame dwelling. We have erected a handsome little chapel seating about 150 comfortably. There are all necessary out-buildings—stables, chicken-houses, etc.

The institution is owned and controlled exclusively by colored people, and we owe not a cent on it. It is the only institution of its kind in the city that is strictly and unconditionally owned by colored people.

Widows and Orphans' Home, Jackson, Miss.

Old Ladies and Orphans' Home, Memphis, Tenn.

Old Folks and Orphans' Home, Memphis, Tenn.   Property, $15,000.

Masonic Widows and Orphans' Home, Nashville, Tenn.; property, $7,000.

Old Folks and Orphans' Home, Kansas City, Mo.

About fifteen years ago a colored man, Samuel Eason, undertook to care for a number of aged people in a frame dwelling at 1308 Vine street. This was the beginning of what is now known as the Old Folks and Orphans' Home in Kansas City, Mo.

Mr. Eason was soon assisted by some good women from the different churches, a number joining them after a charter was obtained in 1896.

As time went on Mr. Eason withdrew from the association, which was composed of women assisted by seven trustees.

A building with a lot of fifty feet was purchased at 2446 Michigan avenue where the present home is yet located. The cost, which was $2,500, was paid by the efforts of the association and the Codaya Circle (a literary club).

A building permit has just been granted to the association to erect a $4,000 home on the present site. The association has been enabled to do this by the generosity of Mr. T. Benoist, who left to the Old Folk's Home Association $4,000 in his will.

The old building will be pushed to the rear of the lot and the new home of brick will be erected in front.

The Home is supported entirely by voluntary subscriptions. During the past two years over forty old people and children have been cared for. Good homes are obtained for the children as fast as possible. Over one thousand dollars were given to maintain the Home during the past year.

The association is composed of fifty influential women and seven men trustees.

The erection of the new Home will double the capacity of the present quarters.

Old Folk's Home, St. Louis, Mo. Maintained by the Central Baptist Church.

Old Folk's Home, St. Louis, Mo. Maintained by the Wednesday Afternoon Serving Club.

Taborian Home for Aged and Indigent Members, Topeka, Kan. For members of the Knights of Tabor, a secret organization.

Home for Aged and Infirm Colored People, Chicago, Ill.

Probably no institution in Chicago is more entitled to the consideration of the charitably inclined than is the Home for Aged and Infirm Colored People, now located at No. 610 Garfield Boulevard (West Fifty-Fifth street).

These old people, from no fault of their own, were forced to spend the best years of their lives in the service of others, deprived of the right to make a home for themselves, or to provide for the coming of old age and infirmities. Bred in ignorance and reared in oppression, it is but a common act of humanity that they be allowed to spend their declining years in an atmosphere more hospitable and congenial than is usually accorded in a county alms-house.

Several years ago the present superintendent, Mrs. Gabriella Smith, gathered together several of these homeless old people and, at great personal sacrifice, cared for them as best she could. She succeeded in interesting a number of her race in the work to the end that on the second day of April, 1898, an association bearing the name as above was incorporated and the home permanently established.

The first to come to the assistance of the Home in a substantial way was Mrs. Bena Morrison, to whose splendid philanthropy the organization is indebted for the gift of the property now occupied as a home, together with its furnishings; also the piece of property known as No. 620 Fifty-seventh street, as the nucleus of an endowment fund. She has also made donations of cash which more fully appear in the treasurer's report. This gracious act on the part of Mrs. Morrison has made it possible to comfortably house and provide for fifteen old men and women during the past pear.

The secretary's report gives a list of other donations received by the home for which the board of directors desire to make acknowledgement.

Too much can not be said concerning the economical management of the Home during the recent year. The report of the treasurer shows that $1,147.95 passed through his hands and that the deficit for the year amounts to $61.52. While this does not include donations of food, etc., yet it is remarkable that so much could be done for so little money.

The superintendent, Mrs. Gabriella Smith, served the year without any compensation whatever; such heroic self-sacrifice is rare, and while the board of directors make grateful acknowledgement, they can but feel humiliated; such sacrifices should not be demanded of her, nor is it fair to accept them. She is a working-woman, with no means other than what she daily earns.

The Volunteer Workers for this home were organized in 1904 and give an annual bazaar. They have installed a steam-heating plant, and raised $1,000 in 1909.

Lincoln Old Folks and Orphans' Home, Springfield, Ill.

Green Memorial Home for the Aged and Infirm, Evansville, Ind.

It is yet in its infancy, but promises to be of much benefit to those whom it is intended to help.

Alpha Home Association, Indianapolis, Ind. For aged colored people.

Phillis Wheatley Home, Detroit, Mich.

The Labor of Love Circle was organized on February 26, 1907, and confirmed March 5, 1907. Its main work is in the interests of a charity and maintenance of the inmates of The Phillis Wheatley Home, an organization for old and infirm colored ladies.

The value of real estate on which the Phillis Wheatley Home is located is estimated at $7,000, and accommodates twelve inmates, and is always taxed to its capacity.

Home for Aged Colored People, Cleveland, O.

Mrs. Eliza Bryant, one of our oldest and most highly respected citizens (now deceased), was impressed with the thought of establishing a home for worthy aged colored people of this city. In July, 1893, Mrs. Bryant expressed the thought to a few friends, and this led to a call through the colored churches to women to meet for the purpose of forming an organization to devise plans for the accomplishment of the work. At a preliminary meeting nothing more was done than to get the work before the people. After a few meetings the women formed themselves into a permanent organization, the condition of membership being the payment of one dollar each year.

The work moved on encouragingly the first year, and at the expiration of two years, by means of membership fees, socials and entertainments the faithful few in the organization had in the bank $407.85. A constitution and by-laws were adopted and the home was incorporated under the name of "The Cleveland Home for Aged Colored People," September 1, 1896.

After these two years of earnest work and much sacrifice on the part of the few that faithfully stood by the work of establishing the home, a small but comfortable structure was opened for inspection and reception September 2, 1897, at 284 Giddings avenue. The attendance was large and the daily papers commented favorably upon the project. The original cost of the Giddings avenue home was $2,000. September 9, 1896, the first payment of $400 was made, leaving a balance of $1,600 to be paid in five notes.

Through the efforts of Mr. Welcome T. Blue, the property at 186 Osborn street, containing eleven rooms and all improvements, was purchased. One thousand dollars was paid on this property as a down payment and the house thoroughly renovated in hope that the inmates might eat their Thanksgiving dinner at their new home. But this was not to be, for on Monday morning, November 25, 1901, the house was burned by an incendiary. This was a dreadful blow, but the earnest workers had the Home rebuilt and in such a manner as to make it more suitable for an institution of its kind, and the inmates were moved into it the first week of March, 1902.

Mrs. Mina Harris, present secretary of the Home, gives the following statement of the year ending 1907. Total money received from the Men's Auxiliary, Board of Lady Managers, donation, entertainments and dues $759.44, from Admission Committee $450.00, making a total of $1,209.44. Total expenditures $844.57, leaving a balance at the beginning of 1908, $364.87. The report for 1908 up to September 1st, is as follows: Received from all sources $768.74, total amount on hand $1,133.61; total expenditures $969.92, leaving a balance in treasury September 1, 1908, of $163.69.

Old Folk's Home, Columbus, O.

Crawford's Old Folk's Home, Cincinnati, O. Property, $25,000.

Home for Aged Colored Women, Cincinnati, O.

Iowa Home for Aged and Orphans, Des Moines, Ia.

Home for Destitute Children and Aged Persons, San Antonio, Texas.

Beside the 61 homes mentioned above there are many others, while numbers are being started, as, e. g., in Anniston, Ala. :

The colored women have started a fund to build a home for old women and orphaned children. Quite a good deal has been collected. They hope to start this home very soon.

These efforts are of all degrees of efficiency and betterment, and receive considerable contribution from whites.

Section 12. Orphanages. Next to homes for the aged the Negroes have felt the need of orphanages and refuges for children. Of the homes mentioned above many also receive children, notably those at New Orleans, La., Kansas City, Mo., Springfield, Ill., Des Moines, Ia., San Antonio, Tex., Jackson, Miss., Memphis, Tenn., Jacksonville, Fla., and Linglestown, Pa.

The care of destitute children of freedmen and refugees especially appeals to the white friends of the Negroes. In cities like New York and Philadelphia there were, before the war, many such charities. Numbers of these still survive, especially in Philadelphia.

The Home for Destitute Colored Children, 541 Berks street, was founded in 1855 and has forty young children.

The Shelter for Colored Orphans, Forty-fourth and Wallace streets, was founded about 1836 and has eighty-four children.

Each institution appears very cold and business-like, and seems to regard their chief function to be the training of servants. One report says:

Besides our usual visiting we have full written reports during the winter from the families in which our children are placed and thus keep in touch at all times with their welfare. It is always interesting to watch the development of the children, and we are often surprised to see how useful and dependable they become. There is an old saying: "Good mistress—good maid," and it is often so with these children, when they have conscientious, painstaking caretakers the children grow naturally into good habits.

Other institutions, like the House of the Holy Child, seem a little more human:

The object of this House is to provide a happy Christian home, permanent or temporary, for Colored Children of any age, who have been deprived by death, sickness or other adversity of a home with their relations. The House has the sanction of the Bishop of the Diocese, but has no connection with any parish, no endowment, no wealthy patron, and therefore asks for gifts, large or small, from any one who pities little children suffering for want of care.

Next come a class of orphanages supported by the devotion of single individuals who conduct them and solicit funds. One such institution is the Leonard Street Home, Atlanta, Ga., conducted by one frail

English woman, and conducted not like a charity but like a loving human home.

The Home was founded in April, 1890, and chartered September, 1890.

Our three buildings were once used as barracks for soldiers, later for dormitories at Spelman Seminary. For the last nineteen years they have served as a home for needy children.

As our work is undenominational and without the help of any organization, we are dependent on donations from Christian people. Last year $1,596.18 was received in this way, the rest of the support coming from the relatives of the children who, when it is possible, pay four and a half dollars per month for board, but of our present family of fifty-five (55), ten (10) are paying this full amount. Fifteen are paying half, and twenty-four (24) are entirely dependent on the home, while six (6) large girls are working full time for board and tuition. We are very anxious to increase the spirit of "self-help," and therefore do not wish to relieve any relative of responsibility by having them legally bind their children to the Home, though the Home does have legal claim to deserted children.

Colored workers took up such homes first as agents of philanthropists, as are these two cases:

Laing Orphans' Home for Colored Children is located at Mt. Pleasant, S. C. (a suburban town of Charleston). This institution is under the charge of Miss A. Munes, who also has charge of the public school of the town. This institution is supported largely by a Society of Friends in the North.

In Richmond, Va.:

The Friends' Orphan Asylum was a gift of the Friends to the colored people. Some money was left to it by a white friend and it is in very good condition. It is supported by the colored churches here, aided by the generous gifts of white merchants and friends.

Gradually there has arisen with the Negro race the call and work of this sort. The woman who founded the Tent Sisters' Home in Raleigh, N. C., writes:

A place is needed to protect the children. Oh, that you could see the condition of social affairs here in the State.

I am in close touch with four little girls, ages from ten to thirteen, from homes where the helping hand is necessary. I have them interested in music, so they gladly come within my reach, and I have been repaid for my effort.

Another girl about eighteen is living in our home as one of our family, and her interest is now aroused for an education.

Somebody must do this great work. The respect and confidence of the street urchins and of individuals of the different classes have been gained, but some place to gather them in and with interesting work lead them to be true and honest men and women should be provided.

I have not yet been permitted to personally speak with those who can and will do great things for us financially, "But think on me when it shall be well with thee, and shew kindness, I pray thee, unto me and make mention of me unto Pharaoh [your wealthy and generous friends] and bring me out of this house."

Some of the promoters entering the field to do this work have been doubtful characters. In one Western city, for instance, is "another

small orphans' home, managed by a man named ———. It is small—
has about a dozen children—is supported by ' prayers and subscriptions.' Through the efforts of this man (many have no confidence in
his honesty) the condition of the little waifs that he finds is improved,
even if he does get his own living by the subscriptions.''

Other men succeed in getting State aid, and develop great executive
ability. For instance, in Charleston:

The Orphan Aid Society was organized by Rev. D. J. Jenkins, December
16, 1891, for the purpose of establishing an orphan house for colored orphan
children. However, this was the first step in the great philanthropic work
to be organized and operated by individual efforts of the African race. The
object is to maintain and educate the orphan and destitute children of the
colored race. This work began with four children. From January 4, 1892, to
May 1, 1896, we had on the roll five hundred and thirty-six children, eight
teachers and two laborers. A farm of one hundred acres of land was given
to the society by Deacon Joseph Wild, of the Greenwood Baptist Church, Brooklyn, N.Y., for the purpose of training the children in the industrial line as well
as educational.

The gift brought to the mind of the Orphanage Man the idea of establishing
a reformatory for little orphan and destitute boys who are convicted in the
Police Court for menial offences. The work has grown rapidly. The Judge
of the Recorder's Court has been very favorably impressed with the work
and has been a very staunch friend to it from its incipiency. The City Council
has been very much impressed with the work of the Jenkins' Orphanage and
Industrial School for Colored Children; their interest is manifested by what
they appropriate annually. They appropriated $200 in 1897; $250 in 1898; $300
in 1899; $300 in 1900; $300 in 1901; $500 in 1902; $500 in 1903; $500 in 1904; $1,000 in
1905; $1,000 in 1906; $1,000 in 1907.

A similar case is that of Amanda Smith, a notable character.

The Amanda Smith Industrial Orphan Home.

The above named industrial home has been founded by Mrs. Amada Smith
for the purpose of caring for colored children who, by death of parents, or
otherwise, have been left without homes or natural protectors.

Her plan is to keep the children in this Home only until they can be suitably provided for in permanent homes elsewhere.

There are at the present time thirty-one boys and girls in the Home, and
since it was opened in 1899 sixty have been received and cared for. Several
of those who have been trained here are now employed in household work.

The Home is located at Harvey, about twenty miles south of Chicago, on the
line of the Illinois Central Railroad.

The property consists of eight lots of ground, 25 by 100 feet each, in Harvey, on which the buildings stand, leaving sufficient space for playground,
garden, etc.

The founder, Mrs. Amanda Smith, is a widely-known colored evangelist
whose history is, in several respects, remarkable.

She was born in slavery but, while she was yet a young girl, her father by
hard work and self-denying economy was able to purchase his own freedom
and that of his wife and children. Amanda's educational advantages were
very meager, consisting of only three months' schooling. She was converted
in 1856, and some twelve years later she began work as an evangelist. Her
success from the beginning was marvelous. Everywhere crowds attended

her services, sinners were converted and believers were led into a deeper experience of the things of God.

Her labors were not confined to America, but extended to England, India and Africa. Wherever she went God signally blessed her work, as thousands of witnesses can testify.

She is now sixty-six years of age and can not reasonably expect to continue many years more in active service. This Home is the object to which she is devoting the closing years of her unselfish life. It is her ambition and earnest desire to place it on a permanent basis of support before she dies.

Financial Statement

ENDOWMENT FUND

Amount received to May 1, 1903.....$3,140 77	
Lot, gift of McFadden............... 400 00	
Rent of house on Desplaines street. 72 00	
	$3,612 77

EXPENDITURES

Cost of lots 17, 18, 19 and 24...........$ 699 63	
Cost of two Homes.................... 1,800 00	
Assessments, insurance, etc........ 325 10	
Total expenditures..................	$2,824 73
Balance on hand	$ 788 04

Current Expense Account

RECEIPTS		EXPENSES	
Cash donations from July, 1901, to June, 1903..................	$2,993 92	Printing to June, 1903............	$ 988 68
From the "Helper" to June, 1903.	1,298 50	Postage (domestic and foreign).	134 05
" Children's board..........	454 75	Publishing book	378 39
" Sale of book..............	132 39	Repairs on property.............	1,608 84
		Furnace, etc.....................	82 75
Total cash receipts......	$4,879 56	House exp., fuel, laundry, etc....	1,624 95
		Shoes and dry goods.............	68 64
		Incidentals—express, freight,etc.	657 88
Deficit...................	$ 664 12	Total expenses..............	$5,543 68

Another case is the Louise Juvenile Home of Chicago. Its founder and manager, Elizabeth McDonald, writes:

For fifteen years I have been engaged in the rescue work, in this State and in other States. In the North as far as Minnesota, west as far as Omaha, Neb., and east as far as New York, and to the southern extremity of Illinois.

Seeing that in the prisons the larger majority were colored according to population; knowing that we have always had prisons and dungeons, and people have been burned at the stake and have been hanged by the neck and nothing seemingly to have done any good in regards to reforming one that has fallen, experience in my rescue work has taught me that it would be easier to prevent crime than it is to reform hardened criminals. So after serious and prayerful study to Almighty God I was convinced that a Christian Home for the training, both spiritually and temporally, was needed. So on October 3, 1907, we established the Louise Juvenile Home for dependent and neglected children in my own private home, in which we care for fifty-six children and two mothers, through the assistance of a very grand young woman by the name of Miss Elizabeth Scott, a student of Walden University, giving her entire assistance as matron free. She has really been the only help that we have had. She also taught school in the common schools of Kentucky and is worthy of support, but our institution being a charitable one we are unable to give her any salary.

Our first anniversary was held last October, and then we were able to show to our friends what we had accomplished in one year's time. This is what we had done: purchased an eleven-room house costing $2,400, and by renting the upper flat we were able to occupy the lower flat and furnish it up nicely for our work.

Our Home is industrial. The children are taught washing, ironing, cooking, sewing (such as plain sewing), embroidering, hemstitching, etc.

The children attend the public school, which is two blocks from the Home.

We hope to have very soon all the material that it takes to train the children. We have girls and boys. The boys are not over twelve years of age.

I am a member of the Institutional Church, and have been a probation officer of the Juvenile Court ten years; giving my time and labor free of charge among my people; also Evangelist of the A. M. E. Church and of the Iowa Conference for the past eleven years.

Our work was supposed to be supported by charitable donations, but we have failed absolutely along that line, and the most support we have is my lecturing and evangelistic work, with a few exceptions; the parents pay $1.00 to $1.50 and $2.00 for their children, sometimes.

The North Georgia Industrial Orphanage has this story; the founder says:

I came here from Atlanta as pastor of the B Street Baptist Church June 1, 1907, and being insisted on by some of our members who had tried, we set to work, and on September 19, 1907, effected an organization in an old two-room house which the city had used for a schoolhouse which we secured free of charge. We soon found a larger house of nine rooms at 303 Blossom Hill. Here we had a fire which did us thirty or forty dollars damage. Finding that we did not have room enough we bought two acres out near the Calhoun road, and are now erecting a cottage where we hope the Lord will help us to finish our work. The best colored people are with us, and our property will aggregate when finished about eight hundred dollars. Our work is strictly industrial.

We moved into the new home on the 22d of March, 1909, and although we have had some very rough nights the Lord has helped us. We depend absolutely on charity. We are still in need, but believe and trust help will come to us.

Mrs. —— gave us a goat, and we have a pig and some chickens.

We hope to teach cooking, sewing, and other things that will be necessary for life, that they may be the people sought after, and we anticipate a splendid future.

The Weaver Orphan Home for Colored Children, at Hampton, Va.:

Was opened for the reception of children in June, 1904. It is managed and controlled by Mr. W. B. Weaver, his wife and another helper. At present there are thirty-nine children in the home. It costs $1,500 a year to support the home, including clothing. The colored people give two-thirds of the money and about nine-tenths of the donated groceries.

Cash receipts for 1905...................... $ 947 50
Donations for 1906.........................$ 643 14
Received from parents....................   267 00
Sales of articles............................   14 12
Miscellaneous 28 50   952 76

          Total.................. .. .. $1,900 26

Perhaps the most interesting of all this class of orphanages is the
Reed Home and School, Covington, Ga.:

I was among the first pupils at Knox Institute. As soon as I was old enough
to know and understand what slavery meant to my people it was a great
grievance to me. The non-freedom of speech was one of the first awakenings
of my mind to the fetters of bondage. My mother and her sister were owned
by different masters, and when they visited each other I noticed they conversed in whispered tones; and even after the war-whoop was hushed, "the
river crossed" (meaning freedom in their unwritten language), the sunlight
of liberty shone in our home, around our own fireside, the two devoted sisters
still whispered; the habit had become so fixed that it was as unbreakable as
a cable, and I often wept when I heard them, for I knew that freedom in its
true sense could never be realized by them. In 1868 we moved to Atlanta, Ga.
I attended Storr's School. From there I went to Atlanta University and
graduated from the normal course in 1883. While a student at Atlanta University I taught school during my vacation, in the rural districts, and there
got an insight of the general needs of my people. These experiences I received while teaching helped much in fixing my purpose in life. I grew more
anxious to finish my course in school that I might go out and be of some service to my people. The thing that most inclined my heart and made me more
determined than ever before was something that I saw while a student at
Atlanta University. I could not, if I should try to, explain this scene, for
there are no words to express my sad feeling that day.

There is a street cut through the campus of the Atlanta University and a
bridge across this street was being dug out by chain-gang hands. One cold, icy
morning I was crossing the bridge and heard a pitiful scream below. I looked
down and there stood a poor little boy of about nine or ten years old, with the
lash being applied to his back. There was no one to say a word of comfort to
this dear little fellow. It pressed my heart and caused me to weep bitterly
in classroom. When school was dismissed I hastened to my room, for I didn't
want to see any one. I at once pleaded with the Lord and asked him for
strength to complete my course, that I might go out to save at least one boy
from the chain-gang. I soon felt the comforter and went about my school
duties as before.

In July, 1883, I began teaching school in Covington, Ga. The school term
at that time was only three months, from July to October. I closed school
the last week in September, as most of the children had to help pick cotton.
The first of November I opened private school and taught through the winter. In June, 1884, I set up housekeeping for the purpose of caring for one
little girl. I made most of my furniture of dry goods boxes, and now and
then a friend gave me a plate, a cup and saucer or some little piece necessary
for housekeeping, and we did our cooking in ovens and frying-pans on the
fireplace, as we had no stove. I set up housekeeping in one room, and lived
in this room until there were five little ones in the family. I then moved
where we could have two rooms and lived there until there were eleven in
the family. I then bought a place in 1887 on which stood an old log cabin of

three rooms. In 1891 the family numbered fifteen and a friend, Mrs. H. C. Reed, from whom comes the name of the Home, gave a thousand dollars. This, with the aid of others, enabled us to have a building of ten rooms. This building is now so crowded that we haven't a spare room for the sick when such is our lot. My salary for teaching was not sufficient to support the work, so I had a farmer to teach me how to hoe cotton, so that I could have something for the children to do to help themselves, and at the same time have them do the kind of work so that I could be with them while at work. In the spring we all went out to work in the field and earned all we could toward our own support; in the fall we picked cotton. This, with the aid of friends, helped much. Three years ago we finished paying for a hundred acres of land. On this place we hope to permanently settle the home.

At the beginning I only took girls, but now I have a large number of boys as well as girls. It makes the work doubly hard, but the boys must be cared for. We need men in the race, and it is very necessary that we take greater interest in the boys than we have before, so that there shall be better homes and better citizens. When I took the first boy into the family I felt now I had kept my agreement with the Lord. The boys are a great help, too, for they do all of the farm work.

Our school is not kept up by the county, State, or any educational fund, and we have to depend on our farm for our main support. We also help other planters gather in their crops, and during the months of September and October we are more than busy in this way, picking cotton and doing other things every day except Saturday, when we work for ourselves. The children seem to realize that this outside work is teaching them how to do for themselves, hence they are very diligent little workers.

Since 1905, however, we have purchased 75 acres of land, four mules, two oxen, a brick machine, and we are buying a sawmill, paying for it with money we earn by sawing timber. We make brick, saw lumber from our land, and farm.

The Home owns at present:

175 acres of land	$6,125 00
Four mules	475 00
Two oxen	80 00
Three wagons	115 00
Farming implements	75 00
House and lot in town	2,000 00
Library	500 00
Household furniture	500 00
Total	$9,870 00

At present there are forty children in the Home.

In case a strong character like this dies the work is apt to suffer, as in the case of the Garred Orphanage, Columbia, S. C.

The Orphanage is a poor, struggling institution. During the life of its founder it did very well; but since her death it has been in very bad shape.

Out of these which we might call personal homes have grown the institutional orphanages conducted by boards, trustees, etc. One of the best is in Lexington, Ky. This institution is sixteen years old and shelters thirty to forty inmates. The children attend school and are taught sewing, cooking, blacksmithing, shoemaking, laundering, chair-bottoming, etc. Their income in 1908 was $7,826.

In New Castle, Pa., is a Home for Destitute Negro Children supported by the State Federation of Colored Women's Clubs.

The Colored Orphan Home of Western North Carolina has thirty-five children, and is controlled by eight colored directors.

The Dickson Colored Orphanage of Gilmer, Texas, is partly a State institution and partly supported by colored people. It is said to be doing an "admirable work."

In New Orleans are several Shelters, mostly due to the munificence of the Negro philanthropist, Lafon.

The Waifs' Home.—The Waifs' Home is located on City Park avenue and Conti street. It has been in operation for about seven years. It is under the general supervision of the Louisiana Society of Prevention of Cruelty to Children; and the City of New Orleans, through the above-named organization, maintains it. This Home is for boys only, who are sent here by the Juvenile Court for petty offenses. The institution is in charge of Mr. and Mrs. J. G. Jones, two very estimable Christian persons, who are doing their best to reform the boys in their charge. The City of New Orleans also provides the Home with a competent teacher, and Sunday-school instruction is given by the Catholics as well as the Protestants. At the time I visited the Home there were 63 boys who were committed therein.

House of Good Shepherd.—The House of Good Shepherd Convent, located at corner of Bienville and Broad, has 78 girls, nearly two-thirds of whom are colored. This is a Catholic institution and is in charge of Catholic sisters. The main buildings were provided for by the Catholic church of this city. However, the late Thomy Lafon in his will left $20,000 which was used for the erection of the Lafon Memorial Building, at a cost of $37,000. The City of New Orleans contributes $400 a month towards the current expenses. Two hours are devoted each day to class instruction, and quite a good deal of industrial work is given. The convent gets its inmates from the Juvenile Court, which sends the girls here for reformation.

The Frances Joseph Gaudet Home.—The Frances Joseph Gaudet Home is located out on Gentilly Road, a few miles out in the suburbs of the city. This reformatory is the result of the self-sacrificing efforts of Mrs. Frances Joseph Gaudet, our most notable social worker. The property and buildings are the gifts of philanthropic white citizens of this city. It has a farm and derives quite a good deal of support in this way. The inmates are both boys and girls, quite a number of whom are sent here by the Juvenile Court of this city.

The Lafon's Boys' Asylum.—The Lafon's Boys' Asylum was founded by the late Thomy Lafon, who made several gifts to it during his life. In his will he left $10,000, which later was increased approximately to $20,000 by Mr. Lafon's executor. It is located on Gentilly Road on the outskirts of the city, and has quite a number of inmates, both boys and girls, a large number of whom are mere babies. It, too, is aided by the city, to a small amount.

St. John Berchmann Asylum for Girls.—The St. John Berchmann Asylum for Girls is under the care of the Holy Family. It is maintained and operated by the Catholic Church. The late Thomy Lafon gave over $25,000 to this asylum. It is located at 717 Orleans street.

Other Negro Orphanages are:

Colored Orphan Asylum, Oxford, N. C.

Masonic Orphans' Home, Bennettsville, N. C.

St. Francis Orphan Asylum, Baltimore, Md. Property, $60,000; inmates, 94.

Friends' Orphan Asylum, Richmond, Va.

Georgia Colored Industrial and Orphans' Home, Macon, Ga. Inmates, 35; income, $4,350; property, $10,000. New building nearly ready.

General State Reformatory, Macon, Ga.:

RECEIPTS, 1906

Balance	$ 291 60
Cash donations from the public	3,425 70
Other donations, value	399 30
Amount of produce raised on farm by inmates	415 00
Total	$4,531 60

Masonic Home, Rock Island, Ill. Income, $960.

Orphans' Home, Huntington, W. Va. Inmates, 65. The State has been paying two teachers. Ten years.

Jenkins Orphanage, Courtland, Va. Seven years.

Shiloh Orphanage, Augusta, Ga.

Orphanage, Austin, Tex.

Colored Orphans' Asylum, Cincinnati, Ohio. Property, $100,000; endowment fund, $25,000; income, $2,010; inmates, 72; receipts, $3,123.45.

INMATES

	Males	Females	Total
Number remaining May 1, 1906	19	16	35
Admitted	19	18	37
Placed in homes	5	13	18
Died	—	2	2
Cared for during year	38	34	72
Remaining	33	19	52

Total income from Negroes about $300.

Universal Progressive School for Orphans, Baltimore, Md. Property, $1,950; inmates, 35.

Children's Orphans' Home, Kansas City, Mo. Inmates, 100; expenditures, $65 per month.

Rescue Home, Kansas City, Mo.

Baptist Orphanage, Baltimore, Md. Inmates, 25.

Orphanage, Richmond, Va.

Gad. S. Johnson's Orphanage, Macon, Ga. Inmates, 25; income, $1,500.

Home for Parentless Children, Petersburg, Va.

Maryland Home for Friendless Children, Baltimore, Md. Property, $2,000; inmates, 52; State aid, $250.

RECEIPTS

Brought forward from the year 1905	$ 269 47
Loans	850 00
Mortgage	1,950 00
City aid	826 20
State aid	500 00
Sale of property	1,000 00
Legacy	97 50
General contributions, etc	648 71
Total	$6,141 88

St. Louis Colored Orphans' Home, St. Louis, Mo.

Carrie Steele Orphanage, Atlanta, Ga. Inmates, 97; income, $2,200 ($100 from Negroes directly; the balance from taxes on both races).

Bridges Orphanage, Macon, Ga.

State Protective Home and Mitchell Hospital, Leavenworth, Kansas. Income, $2,320.60 during 1883.

Home for Destitute Children and Aged Persons, San Antonio, Texas. Inmates, 18.

TWO YEARS' INCOME

Total amount collected by subscription............... ..... $	114 45
Total amount of special donations	120 82
Total amount collected for building purposes........... .	68 55
Total amount from Bexar county and Board of Children.	794 20
Total amount from tables and entertainments........	173 16
Total amount collected from railway employees..........	85 65
Total amount collected from churches	1 19
Total collected for two years............................	$1,564 22

There are other orphanages in Pensacola, Fla., Jacksonville, Fla., Bellevue, Fla., Topeka, Kan., St. Louis, Mo. (two), Baltimore, Md. (three), Louisville, Ky., beside other places.

Section 13. Hospitals. The old folk's homes are mainly and the orphanages are largely supported by Negroes themselves. The hospitals, on the other hand, being newer enterprises and appealing to the educated few, are usually promoted and conducted by Negroes, but get their main support from the State or from whites.

The hospitals are the result of two impulses: the philanthropic desire to help the sick, which arose especially after the Civil War, and the scientific efforts of the new Negro physicians,who found themselves cut off from all clinical advantages.

The older type of hospital is represented by the Freedmen's Hospital of Washington, D. C. This is supported by the United States Government, but is otherwise a Negro institution. The Lincoln Hospital and Home, of New York, an old and well-endowed institution, takes Negro patients and trains Negro nurses, but admits no Negro physicians. Another type of hospital has arisen out of the colored wards of Southern city institutions. Colored associations are often formed to help these wards:

The Charity Organization is engaged in helping the colored department of the hospitals.—Frankfort, Ky.

The Colored Women's Hospital Aid Society was organized in last January. We have thirty active members. The object of the society is to assist in the maintenance of the colored ward of the John Sealy Hospital. At each monthly meeting of the society the small sum of ten cents is collected from each member. It is the custom to disband in June for the summer, beginning work again in October. During this interval dues are paid as if in session. Since our organization we have supplied the hospital with six sanitary beds at twelve dollars apiece; and the women with nineteen garments. The interest has never lagged, and as the society grows older we hope to accomplish much more.—Galveston, Tex.

In Jersey City, N. J.:

The Charity Club is composed of fifty ladies. The club was organized three years ago for the purpose of assisting Christ Hospital, a charitable institution which admits colored patients without any discrimination. Since our organization three years ago we have given the hospital $850. This money is raised by an annual charity entertainment which is heartily supported by all our people.

In the Galveston Colored High School are two hospital clubs.

Often such wards are erected into separate hospitals and given city aid or subscriptions. In some cases such hospitals have been endowed. Specimens of such hospitals are:

Good Samaritan Hospital, Charlotte, N. C.

The Roper Hospital, supported partly by the Roper Fund and an annual appropriation from the city government, has ample accommodations for the colored pauper patients but has no accommodations for colored people who wish a private room.—Charleston, S. C.

Lincoln Hospital, Durham, N. C.

Lamar Hospital, Augusta, Ga.

The most interesting hospitals have come from the efforts of physicians and nurses:

Dr. Matilda A. Evans, of Columbia, S. C., has the distinction of being the first licensed woman physician in that State. She is a Negro and the founder of a hospital and nurses' training school for colored people in Columbia. She was graduated from the Woman's medical college in Philadelphia.

The undersigned physicians respectfully announce that on and after September 20, 1909, Fair Haven Infirmary, 197 West Mitchell street, Atlanta, Ga., will be open for the reception of medical and surgical patients. We sincerely solicit your patronage.   Drs. A. D. Jones,   H. R. Butler,
                                            W. F. Penn,   T. H. Slater,
                                            L. P. Walton,   L. B. Palmer.

McKane's Hospital, Savannah, Ga., is supported by Negro physicians.

The Richmond Hospital is a child of a number of the colored physicians. It is located at 409 E. Baker street. It gets some help ($150 a year) from the city. The other support comes from charity. Dr. M. B. Jones is chief surgeon and Dr. D. A. Ferguson is secretary of the Board.—Richmond, Va.

The Woman's Central League Hospital is run at 414 N. Third street by Dr. R. E. Jones. For its support it depends largely upon the colored churches and societies.—Richmond, Va.

Such hospitals have a hard struggle to live, but on the whole are succeeding and multiplying.

The Red Cross Sanatarium operates a nurse training department which might be called strictly charitable, as it is not operated for private gain. The Red Cross Sanitarium owed one thousand dollars several months ago on the purchase debt, but the leading white women of the city (representing its culture and aristocracy) came together, and a public appeal to the citizens with their signatures attached quickly raised the amount and settled the incumbrance.—Louisville, Ky.

Charity Hospital of Savannah, Ga., was organized by several practicing physicians, and chartered June 1, 1896, by a few hard-working, energetic women anxious to take up and learn nurse training, that they might assist others of the less fortunate with whom they come in contact to better living and conditions of health.

Assisted by their friends in soliciting donations by personal appeal to the public, and through entertainments, sufficient funds were raised by December, 1896, to make the first payment on the purchase price of a two-story dwelling of five rooms in the southwest portion of the city. About five years later, through means from the same sources and the free services of Negro mechanics, an annex was made to the building, giving two large wards accommodating about twelve patients each. A year later we sought and were successful in getting a monthly appropriation from the city of $25 per month for taking care of their pauper patients, which amount was increased some years later to $75, but not before a thorough inspection and investigation of our work.

The county a year later, after an investigation, made an appropriation of $25 per month by our taking care of their pauper patients.

In 1906 one of our founders and charter members donated a two-story building, which we rolled up to and joined to our building, forming an "L." This we repaired, and fitted up for five private rooms and four nurses' rooms. We have accommodations for eight nurses for the training school, governed and controlled by a head nurse who is also matron.

We have graduated through a two years' course some twenty-five well-trained nurses, who are sought by white families and physicians as well as by those of their own color.

A regular course of lectures is given by our physicians, who compose the medical staff.

For the past two or three years our people, who have always had a horror for hospitals, are waking up to the fact that it is the best place for them when sick, and the demand for applications for admittance to private as well as ward room is more than we have accommodation for.

It has also come directly under our notice that the time spent in the hospital has taught them that fresh air and sunshine instead of keeping them sick with colds, etc., helps and benefits them in every way, and they return home with some ideas of simple sanitary measures which should be in all homes.

While soliciting donations for this work from our own people is in itself uphill work, we have found it much harder to get them to give any amount promised with any degree of system and regularity.

As our building is not so well constructed, a certain temperature can be maintained in the wards only at a very large cost for fuel, and we need more room for private as well as pauper patients. Several lots adjoining us have been secured at the cost of $2,000, and we are now planning a campaign for soliciting this from our churches and organizations, as we wish to get the ground paid for, at least, before starting the building.

Our own people, generally very superstitious and especially so of hospitals and what they call the "Black Bottle" used there, are becoming more and more enthused over their hospital and the work it is doing, and have no hesitancy as heretofore in coming, and in fact request it of their attending physician.

Below is our report to the city for the year 1908.

	CHARITY PATIENTS		PAY PATIENTS		Total No. Patients	Total days
	Number	Hospital days	Number	Hospital days		
January	12	208	7	73	19	281
February	16	284	10	120	26	404
March	22	288	25	175	47	463
April	22	269	20	169	42	438
May	32	336	15	153	47	489
June	19	308	19	149	38	457
July	17	192	13	151	30	343
August	17	215	8	52	25	267
September	22	333	21	157	43	490
October	24	262	20	163	44	425
November	18	199	18	239	36	428
December	22	303	28	234	50	637
Total	243	3197	204	1825	447	5022

Patients in hospital January 1, 1908 9
Number of patients admitted during year 1908 447
Number of patients discharged during year 1908 402
Number of patients died during year 1908 54
Number of patients remaining January 1, 1909 17
Number of births 5
Total number of days, charity patients 3197
Total number of days, pay patients 1825
Total number of days, all patients 5022
Total expenses $2,960.91

RECEIPTS

Appropriation from the city .... $ 900 00
Appropriation from the county 300 00
From pay patients 1,563 96
Donations—Churches, societies, individuals 472 09
       $3,236 05

EXPENSES

Salaries........................... ....$ 549 00
Groceries 495 61
Meats, vegetables, milk, etc................... 294 97
House supplies 408 70
Medical and surgical supplies 740 06
Undertakers 47 96
Fuel... 158 05
Insurance, telephone, and printing 65 85
Repairs and improvements................... 200 72
     $2,960 01
Deficit January 1, 1908 .... 372 04
       $3,332 95

Deficit January 1, 1909 .... $ 96 90

One of the most interesting buildings in Charleston, S. C., is:

The Hospital and Training School for Nurses, an institution devoted to the preparation of colored women for the profession of trained nurses.

The building itself is an old residence erected in the year 1800. Its solid walls, despite wars, storms and earthquakes, are as firm to-day as when first erected more than a century ago. In the year 1897, Dr. A. C. McClennan saw that trained nurses were needed in Charleston and that it would be well to establish a training school. After consultation with some of the other colored practitioners a course of lectures was arranged and, a room having been secured, the school was opened.

The large attendance showed that the school was destined to fill a long-felt want, but it soon became apparent that didactic instruction alone could not accomplish the desired end. The nurses needed practical instruction in a hospital ward. An attempt was made to arrange for such instruction in one of the public charitable institutions of the city; but after conference with the various boards having these institutions in charge, it became clear that nothing could be accomplished along that line, and that the school must have a hospital of its own. A meeting of citizens was called and an association was formed and incorporated.

The building which the school now occupies was for sale, the price being $4,500. By means of entertainments and subscriptions $500 was raised, and upon this small margin the building was purchased. Ten years have worked a wonderful change. The building, old and dilapidated, has been repaired and remodeled, and equipped to meet the needs of the work; the grounds have been leveled and drained, and outside and inside both buildings and grounds are in keeping with the character of the work. Meanwhile the debt upon the property has been reduced from $4,000 to $500.

Forty-five trained nurses, representing ten graduating classes, have been sent out and all of them have found employment and have given satisfactory service. Thirteen are residing and working in Charleston; the others are widely scattered, one of them being in northern New York, one in Florida, one in Ohio and one in California.

One of the most noteworthy cases treated at this institution was that of the family of Fraser Baker, postmaster at Lake City, S. C. Baker was killed and the members of his family seriously wounded by a mob, who set fire to their home and fired on them as they were making their escape from the burning building. These people were brought to Charleston and treated at the hospital free of charge. The expense of caring for them was considerable, and the institution could ill afford such a drain upon its resources, but it was done nevertheless. They were all discharged cured, and afterwards removed to Boston, Mass.

The hospital has been of great benefit to the people living in the country districts near Charleston, where it is difficult and at times impossible to obtain medical treatment. The charge made for patients in the hospital is very small, barely enough to cover the cost of food and medicines. There is a constant demand for the services of the nurses connected with the training school, and the fees paid for their services constitute the principal source of income for the institution. The great need of the work is money to erect additional buildings. A nurse dormitory is especially needed. There are always a large number of applicants for admission for nurse-training, but owing to the limited space only a small number can be accommodated. Yet with all the disadvantages the work still grows; those in charge of it are doing the best they can with the limited means at their command, and hoping that the time may come when some wealthy philanthropist may become interested in the work and supply the funds needed to enlarge the building.

In Pittsburgh:

The B. T. Washington Hospital and Nurse - Training School was organized October 30, 1907, by a few women.

In July, 1908, we purchased a twelve-room building located on La Place street at the cost of $7,000. We have two wards fitted up for male and female ready for operation. We have a head chief nurse, the staff and resident physician.

In Dallas, Tex.:

The Wright Cuney Memorial Nurse-Training School is an association of the best element among the Negroes of this city for the purpose of conducting a school for the training of sick nurses.

In Kansas City, Kan.:

The Douglass Hospital is kept up largely by the citizens and church of this city and Kansas City, Mo. The organization has been taken in charge by the A. M. E. Church.

In Houston, Tex.:

The Feagan Hospital is a new enterprise, but within the past year it has done a vast amount of good for our people. Patients are received at a very small cost, by week or month. Medical services are given free and Mrs. Feagan, a trained nurse, is in constant attendance.

Frierson & Co.'s ambulance conveys patients to and from the hospital, free of cost.

In Greenville, Miss.:

There is one Circle of the King's Daughters in Greenville, Miss., and they together with the white Circles of that city have built and operate a hospital.

Out of such beginnings have grown several large well-equipped hospitals; perhaps the best in the country is the Provident Hospital and Training School of Chicago:

Provident Hospital and Training School for Nurses has been in successful operation more than ten years. It was founded through the united efforts of a few earnest colored men. A building at the corner of Dearborn and 29th streets was rented, 14 beds were installed and its mission of caring for the sick poor regardless of race or creed was inaugurated.

In its early days it passed through gloomy and anxious periods. Several times it looked as though the doors would have to be closed, but renewed and sustained efforts on the part of the trustees averted the calamity.

The men who founded the institution were poor. The race it most sought to benefit is the humblest and most ostracized of races, yet the earnest and heroic struggles to maintain the institution won the confidence of many of Chicago's foremost men. The splendid generosity of Philip D. Armour, Nathan M. Freer, Herman H. Kohlsaat, George M. Pullman, George H. Webster and others made it possible to build and maintain a hospital which in administration, method, equipment, appointments and convenience is equal to the best in Chicago. Here over 3,000 sick persons mostly among the poor have already been scientifically cared for.

Five of the hospital staff of physicians and surgeons are colored men of education and attainments. To the hospital every year or two is admitted as an interne a bright colored doctor just graduated from one of the medical schools. These men otherwise could not secure the benefit of a hospital connection or experience. And in this hospital, although 65 per cent of the patients are white, a colored man can at all times be sure of advanced medical skill and sympathetic trained nursing.

The hospital and its allied charities is incorporated and is managed by a board of eighteen trustees of different creeds. Six only of the trustees are white. As the result of ten years of effort the association has accumulated property worth $100,000 upon which there is no encumbrance whatever. Notwithstanding the most rigid economy, there is, however, an annual deficit of about $3,500 which is made up by voluntary contributions and the revenues from associate memberships which call for the payment of ten dollars on the first of May in each year. These memberships are open to all and the aim is by this means to secure the interest of a great number of men and women who feel that they should be doing something for a people who are as yet financially unable to extricate themselves from conditions which have been imposed upon them by others.

When Provident Hospital was opened but one training school in America would receive colored women as students. With this exception it was then impossible for these women to be trained in the art of scientific nursing. This condition produced the training school, the hospital being in fact a means to this end. Colored nurses only are admitted. It has been in successful operation since the founding of the hospital. For the first five years the school suffered for lack of proper accommodations and equipment, but the few nurses the institution was able to accommodate, by their great patience, self-denying interest and earnest work, fixed the future not only of the training school but of the hospital. Now the early prejudice against the colored nurse has almost entirely disappeared. Patients are sent to the hospital by eighty physicians in addition to those of the staff, many of them believing that here more uniform and intelligent attention is given than can be secured elsewhere. The term is two years of actual service; the requirements for admission, good health, good moral character, and a high-school education or its equivalent. The selection of nurses is made after careful investigation, only one out of twenty applicants on the average being received and then upon three months probation.

Forty-one nurses have graduated. They have come from all parts of the United States, thus making the training school national in character. However, a majority of them have been from the South where their advancement would be especially difficult, and, in accordance with the wish of the trustees, they have returned to that part of the country as helpers and workers in the perplexing problem of uplifting the downtrodden of their people. Earnestness, intelligence, patience and sympathy must be combined in the nurse who would graduate from this school.

"Esther Freer Home," the dormitory for the nurses, is probably the most complete and artistic of its kind to be found anywhere and the young colored women, always poor, who are admitted feel during life the refining influence of this comfortable home with its atmosphere of benevolence.

When Armour Mission was founded, among its other activities was a free dispensary. This was transferred to Provident Hospital and became one of its departments. The aim has been to charge each patient ten cents for a prescription, a nominal payment being thought consistent with the wisest charity. None, however, who cannot pay is refused attention or medicine. More than 25,000 persons have been treated.

District visiting is an interesting feature of the training-school work. Into the more neglected sections of the city Provident nurses go daily, ministering to the poor and sick of both races. This service is attended with most gratifying results. The influence for good which these young women carry into many homes cannot be calculated. Practical instruction is given in the care of the sick, in house ventilation, in the preparation of food, in cleanliness of home and body, all in a gentle and effective manner. The work is of the utmost importance and when sufficient funds are available will be widely extended.

Provident Hospital was founded with a subscription of $350.

We may judge the results from the following figures:

Number of patients in the wards and private rooms in 10 years. 3,000
Number of homes visited by the nurses in 5 years................ 679
Number of visits made in 5 years................................ 2,927
Amount of property accumulated...................... $100,000
Donations received for operating expenses........... 33,147
Amount collected from patients for hospital service 52,524
Total revenue for operating expenses................. 85,672

These figures are gratifying. They show the peculiar merit of the institution in accomplishing so much with comparatively small means. They indicate how much more might be accomplished with ample means. They mean that there is maintained among the 35,000 colored people of Chicago a permanent object lesson to all who are struggling upward, teaching that the best hope of rising lies in doing a thing well.

The Frederick Douglass Hospital of Philadelphia:

Was founded in 1895 and incorporated the following year under a charter by the legislature of Pennsylvania. It has done and is still doing a much-needed work in the care and treatment of the humble and indigent sick, especially of the colored race, and also in the training and equipment of colored young women for the important functions of the professional nurse, and also giving a large field of practical service and usefulness especially to the thirty-five colored physicians of Philadelphia.

A post-graduate course is planned for doctors of medicine.

The hospital, while largely under colored control, has leading white and colored physicians on its staff, and its doors are open to all, without discrimination either of race or religion. The young women in its training school for nurses have been drawn from States North and South, and they are proving themselves evangels of mercy and helpfulness in the homes of the afflicted in various parts of the country.

Since its founation the hospital has treated nearly 2400 in-patients and upwards of 30,000 out-patients. Such work as this must command the confidence of any community.

Some hospitals are connected with schools, as those at Hampton, Spelman Seminary, and especially the one at Louisville connected with the Colored Medical School:

The Citizens' National Hospital is a part of the Louisville National Medical College. It was first organized in conformity to the laws governing medical schools. In 1904 we moved into our present quarters. The new home was given the present name.

The hospital is supported by board money from patients and tuition from medical students.

We have a training class for nurses (girls only), seven in class.

We do all the charity work our friends will permit. This is not much.

Hospital on grounds with College, combined value about $8,000.

We receive no help from the city and a very little from the public, perhaps about three hundred dollars from all sources in the last five years.

Capacity, twelve beds.

Other Negro hospitals are said to exist as follows:

Mercy Hospital and Nurse Training School, Ocala, Fla.

Mercy Hospital and School for Nurses, Philadelphia, Pa. Total income to November, 1907, $6,474.02; patients, $4,232.00; received from Negroes, $4,390.69, and from the State $5,000 every two years.

Mitchell Hospital, Leavenworth, Kansas. Income, $2,320.60.

Taylor Lane Hospital, Columbia, S. C.

Mercy Hospital, Nashville, Tenn. Patients, 394; total income, $1,873, all from Negroes.

Harris Sanitorium, Mobile, Ala. Patients, 25.

Colored Hospital, Petersburg, Va.

Provident Hospital, Baltimore, Md. Property, $15,000.

Burrus Sanitorium, Augusta, Ga.

Colored Hospital, Evansville, Ind.

Provident Hospital, St. Louis, Mo.

State's Hospital, Winston, N. C.

Colley's Hospital, Cincinnati, O.

Hairston Infirmary, Memphis, Tenn.

Dr. J. T. Wilson's Infirmary, Nashville, Tenn.

Colored Hospital, Dallas, Tex.

Woman's Central League Hospital, Richmond, Va.

Slater Hospital, Winston-Salem, N. C.

Hale Infirmary, Montgomery, Ala.

One interesting work is the Dispensary connected with the First Baptist Church of West Washington, D. C.

We have treated about one hundred and fifty persons at the Dispensary. We have not been open for business quite three months, yet the work is growing, however, and we feel that much more will be accomplished as the community becomes acquainted with the work.

Section 14. Young Men's Christian Association and Young Women's Christian Association.—These Christian Associations reveal in their history the curious complications of the Negro problem in America. In the South there is, in the recent abolition of slavery, an historical if not a logical excuse which lets the color separate Christians.

In the North there is no such excuse, and yet Negroes have been gradually excluded from Young Men's Christian Association buildings in New York, New Haven, Philadelphia, Chicago, and other large cities and segregated in separate bodies, while from the first they were in nearly all cases refused admittance to Young Women's Christian Associations. These separate Negro bodies are now growing and flourishing, but they are and are felt to be monuments to a miserable unchristian and unmanly prejudice. Of course if they represented voluntary segregation like the German associations or the Railroad men the case would be different; but this separation is compulsory and humiliating. The colored bodies have flourished because earnest and self-sacrificing secretaries have urged them on and counseled them to ignore the stigma. In this way they have done great good. But the good accomplished is no excuse for the insult offered.

Figures for the Colored Young Men's Christian Associations follow:

The Colored Men's Department now has 136 associations—96 in educational institutions and 40 in cities—with an aggregate membership exceeding 11,000 young men. Notwithstanding the financial stringency of the past year, two new city associations and six new student associations were added to the list, a new building was dedicated at New Orleans, and the corner-stone of the $100,000 building for Washington, D. C., was laid by President Roosevelt. The year was specially characterized by the splendid advances made in night-school work and by the increased attendance upon religious meetings. Ten colored student associations sent delegates to the first International Student Bible Conference at Columbus, Ohio.

Colored Young Men's Christian Associations

Alabama.—Mobile.

California.—Los Angeles.

Connecticut.—New Haven.

District of Columbia.—Washington: real estate, $52,000; debt on same, $2,000.

Georgia.—Americus. Atlanta: real estate, $4,500. Augusta. Columbus: value of real estate, $26,600.

Illinois.—Normal.

Indiana.—Indianapolis.

Iowa.—Buxton: Colored population, 5500; value of building and lot, $23,500; other real estate, $500; value of boys' building and lot, $10,000.

Kansas.—Topeka.

Kentucky.—Louisville: value of building and lot, $10,000; debt on same, $2,750.

Louisiana.—New Orleans: value of building and lot, $6,400; debt on same, $1,200.

Maryland.—Baltimore: value of building and lot, $3,000.

Missouri.—Kansas City: value of real estate, $7,200; debt on same, $6,000. St. Louis: value of building and lot, $5,500; debt on same, $2,000.

New Jersey.—Atlantic City. Montclair. Orange.

New York.—Brooklyn: value of building and lot, $6,400. Elmira. New York city: value of building and lot, $32,060.

North Carolina.—Asheville: value of building and lot, $35,000; debt on same. $4,580. Charlotte. Winston-Salem.

Ohio.—Springfield: building, $5,000; debt on same, $1,200.

South Carolina.—Charleston. Columbia.

Tennessee.—Chattanooga: building and lot, $8,800; debt on same, $4,175. Knoxville: building and lot, $2,000. Nashville.

Texas.—Dallas. Fort Worth.

Virginia.—Charlottesville. Norfolk: value of building and lot, $16,000, debt on same, $1,600. Portsmouth: funds paid in, $1,070; pledged in addition, $10,930. Richmond: value of building and lot, $7,000; funds paid in, $175; pledged, $730.

West Virginia.—Bluefield. Wheeling.

Colored City Associations

39 colored city associations exist.

28 of these report officers or statistics.

28 report 5,379 members.

26 report 2,836 active members.

24 report 1,300 serving on committees.

24 report a total amount paid out for current expenses, $41,947.

22 report a total average daily attendance at rooms of 1,070.

22 report 211 socials and receptions.

20 report 103 paid lectures and entertainments.

16 report 373 situations secured.

13 report gymnasiums, with 512 using same.

15 report 68 athletic teams or clubs, with 589 members.

7 report 289 enrolled in gymnasium classes, and 47 in leaders' corps.

7 report 56 matched games with outside teams.

EDUCATIONAL

22 associations report some educational information.

20 report reading-rooms with 499 periodicals on file.

16 report 188 educational lectures and practical talks (not including popular courses).

9 report 22 educational clubs, with 489 members.

16 report 49 educational classes, attended by 391 different students.

12 report 22 paid teachers.

19 report $1,322 total expenses of all educational work.

10 report $597 total receipts from class tuition fees.

BIBLE STUDY

18 associations report Bible study statistics.

18 report 708 different students in Bible classes: men, 523; boys, 185.

16 report 22 miscellaneous Bible classes of men, with 394 students.

1 reports 1 evangelistic Bible class, with 8 students.

6 report 8 Bible training classes, with 113 students.

7 report 11 boys' Bible classes, with 220 students.

14 report a total Bible-class attendance for the year of 13,922.

RELIGIOUS MEETINGS

24 associations report statistics of religious meetings, etc.

20 report 355 men serving on religious-work committees or doing personal religious work.

16 report $963 paid out for religious work.

3 report 192 shop meetings with a total attendance of 4,452.

22 report 808 evangelistic meetings for men, with a total attendance of 68,111.

22 report 1,121 all meetings for men, with a total attendance of 84,292.

4 report 148 meetings for boys, with a total attendance of 3,425.

22 report 1,620 average per week at all-men's meetings.

4 report 67 average per week at all-boys' meetings.

17 report 283 total professed conversions: men, 245; boys, 38.

10 report 156 of the above united with churches as a result of the work: men, 120; boys, 36.

24 report 102,784 a total attendance at all religious meetings and Bible classes.

Student Associations

91 associations in colored institutions are in existence.

2 have been organized this year.

72 report statistics of their work.

62 report 11,360 young men, students in their institutions.

61 report 7,821 young men, students in their institutions, members of evangelical churches.

68 report a total membership of 5,081.

66 report an active membership of 3,795.

66 report 1,389 men serving on committees.

30 report $1,650 paid out last year for current expenses.
46 report 1,595 young men's meetings, with a total attendance of 94,225.
25 report 1,234 Bible-class sessions, with a total attendance of 28,000.
26 report 188 missionary meetings; 6 report 361 men in mission study.
43 report 253 lectures.
15 report 545 volumes in libraries.

Items Common to City and Student Sections

130 colored associations are in existence; 100 send in reports.
96 report a total membership of 10,460.
92 report an active membership of 6,631.
90 report working committees, with a membership of 2,689.
54 report cash paid out for current expenses, $43,597.
37 report libraries, containing 6,281 volumes.
28 associations employ 29 secretaries.
16 associations own buildings, valued at $201,700.

As to the individual Young Men's Christian Associations, the following facts may be noted:

Kansas City, Mo., is arranging to put up a $10,000 building.

The Association in Louisville, Ky., has a handsome building which cost $10,000; of this the whites gave $7,000 and the colored people $3,000.

The Baltimore Association sold the old building for $3,500 in October, 1908, and is now in rented quarters with $8,000 in bank toward a building fund. They spend $1,800 a year and have a gymnasium, shooting gallery, pool table, etc.

The St. Louis Association has a building worth $5,000. They raised $2,100 last year; almost entirely among Negroes.

The Chattanooga Association raised $2,600 in 1907; over half of this came from Negroes.

The Knoxville Association has property valued at $3,000 and raises $800 a year.

Among the most interesting associations is that at Buxton, Ia. Buxton is a colored mining town of five thousand; three-fourths of the population being colored. This is the largest association for colored people in the world and has a building for men and one for boys. They have Sunday services, Bible class, night schools, reading-room, and theatrical entertainments in a hall which seats six hundred; about 150 men and boys use the gymnasium. At night after working hours from 150 to 200 men can be found in the buildings. The total membership is 369 and the buildings and furniture are worth $40,000.

The New Orleans Association has property worth $10,0000.

The association at Portsmouth, Va., has property worth about $5,000.

The association in Richmond, Va., has property worth $6,000 and a membership of 275; a good library of 1600 volumes; visits are made to the penitentiary and the sick, and there is a night school.

At Asheville, N. C., Mr. George W. Vanderbilt put up a building at a cost of $32,000. It contains four storerooms, three sleeping-rooms, a hall seating 600, four office-rooms, a parlor, reading-room, and a large room for night school, with baths in the basement. This proved to be too heavy a burden for the colored people to support, but when Mr. Vanderbilt threatened to foreclose the mortgage on the property and meet no more deficits coming from expenditures, the colored people rallied and bought the place by paying $2,400 in cash and securing a loan of $8,000. It then became a regular Young Men's Christian Association, and now has the debt down to $6,000. There is a membership of 200 and a night-school, also a library of 500 volumes and gymnasium work.

The Young Women's Christian Association has never flourished so well among the colored people, on account of social prejudice; but separate associations are beginning to be formed now.

There is an association in St. Paul, two sectional conferences in South Carolina and Alabama, and there are the following other associations:

Alabama, seven: Talladega College, Tuskegee Institute, Selma University, State Normal School, Miles Memorial College, A. & M. College.

Georgia, three; Spelman Seminary, Paine College, Haines Institute.

Kansas, two: The Western College, The Topeka N. & I. Institute.

Louisiana, one: Straight University.

Mississippi, four: Southern Christian Institute, Tougaloo University, Jackson College, Alcorn A. & M. College.

Missouri, three: Western College & Ind. Institute, Lincoln Institute, George R. Smith College.

Arkansas, three: Philander Smith College, Branch Normal College, Arkansas Baptist College.

District of Columbia, one: Howard University.

North Carolina, one: Bennett College.

Ohio, one: Wilberforce University.

Oklahoma, one: A. & N. University.

South Carolina, three: Claflin University, Benedict College, Allen University.

Tennessee, four: Walden University, Roger Williams University, Lane College, Knoxville College.

Virginia, one: V. N. & I. Institute.

Pennsylvania, one: The Philadelphia Association.

New York, two: The Fifty-third Street Branch, New York city, The Lexington Avenue Branch, Brooklyn.

Minnesota, one: The St. Paul Branch.

District of Columbia, one: The Washington Association.

The branch in New York, Fifty-third Street, has a dormitory, parlors, reading-room, library, an employment bureau, and serves meals. There is also instruction in sewing, millinery, cooking, physical culture and elocution.

The branch in Brooklyn has a regular night-school with instruction in 21 industries.

The association in Washington raises about $700 a year and has a building fund.

Section 15. Refuges and Rescue Homes for Women. These institutions fall into two classes: those that seek to protect decent girls and those that try to reform fallen women. Among the first are a series of homes for servant girls, supported mainly by colored people.

The Phyllis Wheatley Home of Chicago reports:

The home is established to solve the problem of befriending the colored girls and women who come into this great city seeking work, often without relatives, friends or money.

1st. By providing a comfortable home surrounded by Christian influences.

2nd. To elevate the standard of domestic service; to provide a social center for homeless girls and women, where they can improve their opportunities, be assisted in securing employment, and feel sure at all times of friendly help, mutual help and encouragement.

The home is open for the reception of visitors daily from 10 a. m. to 5 p. m.

Terms: $1.25 per week for lodging. Transient, 25 cents per night.

The winter has been one long struggle to keep things going and to help the many girls and women who come to us. We feel that our work is one of practical value to any community, especially one like this great cosmopolitan city where our people come in on every train and among them many women and girls seeking to better themselves in various ways. Of the hundred or more homes established here for working girls, not one of them offers a shelter to our girls except the Beulah Home and the Erring Girl's Refuge; both of them open their doors after the first false step has been taken.

Many of our girls coming from small towns and the Southland are unused to life in a great city and find themselves stranded and helpless, ready to fall an easy prey to the human vultures ever ready to destroy young womanhood.

Again, conditions in domestic service are vastly different from those they were familiar with in their homes, and they are labeled incompetent when often they are willing but "green," and ignorant of the ways of service in city homes.

The Phyllis Wheatley Woman's Club, organized thirteen years ago, has always felt the importance of its mission to better community conditions. We have during those years supported a sewing-school, a day nursery in a much-needed district, etc. Three years ago we determined to do something toward helping the stranger girl and woman especially, as well as those in our midst who needed it, to a standard of higher womanhood and usefulness.

We began the purchase of the Home at 3530 Forest avenue at a cost of thirty-four hundred dollars, with an incumbrance of twenty-five hundred dollars. We kept it rented until May 1st, 1908, turned the rentals over to the payment of the property until we had paid $2,029, which includes the equity, interest on mortgage, taxes, insurance, and reduction of mortgage by $500.

We opened the Home May 31st, 1908, and have never been without an inmate a single day. We have housed thirty girls, have secured employment for over one hundred, and have given encouragement, sympathy, and in a few cases financial aid, to many more. We have done very little soliciting. We have a membership of forty earnest Christian women.

A Home of this kind ought to be in every large city, and notices of the same given wide publicity in every town and city throughout the country, in order to safeguard our women and girls.

In Indianapolis, Ind., there is a Young Colored Women's Protective Association.

Something had to be done. There was a Young Men's Christian Association for the white boys, there was one for the colored boys; there was a Young Women's Christian Association for white girls, but there was none for the colored girls.

The work started in a four-room cottage and now they have bought a three thousand dollar house.

But the most hopeful feature of all, the most encouraging sign of the times, is that the responsibility and the burdens of the work have been borne by young women for their future development and for the benefit of other young women who might wish to share the privileges of upbuilding which this association has planned to provide. It was pioneer work, and all the hardships incident to pioneer work they have endured bravely and wonderfully. No pen can do justice to the loyalty, to the sacrifice, to the real heroism that has been manifested by the young women interested in the support and management of this work.

It has over one hundred members, and is designed among other things:

To provide literary, musical, social and industrial centers for the pleasure and improvement of young women.

To establish training-schools in domestic science for the improvement of conditions in the home, and from which young women who prefer house-keeping or cooking may graduate.

To recognize with respect, intelligent, moral, competent, cultured workers in whatever honorable avocation engaged.

To secure for working women better hours and bring before their employers the desirability of giving their woman employes half-holidays at least during the summer months.

To maintain an employment committee, which shall assist in procuring desirable positions for women who are out of employment.

To become acquainted with other women who are strangers in our city and to be helpful to them in any way possible.

To assist women desiring an education to find help along the particular lines in which they are interested.

To encourage commercial enterprise among Negroes by patronizing the same and thus to help make opportunities for other girls.

A Negro Working-Girls' Home will soon be opened in Springfield, Mass.

One in Boston, called the Harriet Tubman House, at 37 Holyoke St.,

Was established by a number of colored women of the W. C. T. U. of Boston, who have made many sacrifices for its maintenance during the past three years. On November 10th, 1904, the house was open to the public for inspection. It is designed to furnish protection and home comforts to young colored women who come to our city from various parts of the country and at a nominal cost to them. It is the only one of this kind in our city. At present the house has accommodation for twelve young women. There is a lecture-room, parlor, sleeping-rooms, dining-room, kitchen and laundry. This work is carried on by voluntary contributions, and it is not connected with any denomination or religious sect. It is the purpose of the management to open classes in the domestic arts, such as cooking, sewing, laundering, etc., as soon as sufficient funds are in hand to carry on the work.

The immediate need of the House is $10,000 for the purpose of paying for and equipping a permanent building:

The House takes respectable working girls and gives them a home. It has sheltered 77 girls last year, and raises about $1,000 a year for its support.

There are two such homes in Michigan: one in Grand Rapids which, with the aid of white friends, purchased a small building for $1,600, partially paid for. The other, in Detroit, was organized in April, 1906:

We have for the past two years been very successful in having millinery, dressmaking, and embroidery classes. We employed one of our race to instruct us in each class. We give ten lessons for $1.00 in advance. Our expenses for the millinery class has been about $90.00 or more, and dressmaking class expenses $50.00.

This year they are trying to buy property.

One of the most extensive efforts to help colored girls is the National Association for the Protection of Colored Women, started by the white women of New York. There are local associations in NewYork, Philadelphia, Baltimore, Norfolk and Washington. The local work is largely or wholly in the hands of colored people and supported by contributions from both races.

The Philadelphia association is perhaps the most active. Its object is to provide a settlement and protection for migrating colored women, to study conditions and disseminate information.

Mrs. H. F. Lanning, our dock worker, daily meets the boats at the Ericsson Line (Baltimore Boat Company) and the Merchants' and Miners' Line (Charleston and Georgia boats) bringing passengers from the Southern States. The courtesy of the boat companies is yet accorded to our worker. Following is a report of the total number of persons met during the year:

Virginia	458
Maryland	368
West Virginia	213
New Jersey	47
South Carolina	46
Pennsylvania	60
Delaware	59
Georgia	55
North Carolina	45
Total	1351

Employment agencies are looked after, and there is a working-girls' home established in Philadelphia.

There are also working-girls' homes in Lynchburg, Va., and Richmond, Va., and a movement for one in Columbia, S. C.

Next to this work comes attempts to rescue girls who are already fallen into vice, or liable to. There is, for instance, an industrial home for colored girls at Pittsburgh, Pa., now three years old. It raises $3,350 a year, of which $2,250 comes from the State of Pennsylvania.

The Dorcas Home Society of Yonkers, N. Y., is doing reformatory work among Negro women, and maintains a home and an employment office.

The White Rose Mission in New York has done considerable rescue work.

In Topeka, Kan., is a rescue home for fallen women and girls, and the Colored Hebron Rescue Association maintains a home in St. Louis.

In Kansas City, Mo., the legislature failed to decide on an industrial reform home for girls, and the Federation of Women's Clubs took up the matter and established a home in 1908, known as the Jackson County Home for Negro Girls.

Forty girls have been sent by the Court to the Home, of whom seven have been sent to homes out of the city, six paroled by the Court, nine discharged, and sixteen are now in the Home. We feel proud of the fact that not one has attempted to escape, and at no time has it been necessary to call an officer to quiet any disturbance.

The girls are taught cooking and laundry work, the latter bringing in quite a deal of revenue to the Home. We have also tried to improve them morally and religiously, sixteen having been induced to join the church. All attend church and Sunday-school regularly. Besides this influence, the Board of Education provides us a half-day school, conducted by Miss Doshia Johnson, a very kind and earnest young woman, who has done much good toward the progress of the girls.

We feel grateful to Mr. Lee and Mr. Ross, our probation officers, for their untiring efforts for the success of the Home, and to the public for its generous support of our work. Our board of managers meets monthly to settle the accounts of the Home, and its secretary is able at a moment's notice to give a complete and accurate statement of the financial condition of the institution and its working throughout.

The income of the Home has been as follows:

County Court ($10 per month for each inmate..$	826 78
Juvenile Improvement Association............	240 00
Board of Education..............................	75 33
Laundry Work of Girls	135 53
Subscriptions	556 61
	$1,834 25

In Philadelphia there is a Home for the Homeless where any woman may apply for temporary aid.

In Los Angeles, Cal., there is a Sheltering Arms Home:

Its doors are open night and day to any homeless woman, girl or child in need of shelter. We are renting, as yet, and caring for twelve persons at the present. We have sheltered fifty-six since opening, October 28, 1907. The growth has been slow because the people have not felt the real need of such an institution. We are beginning to awaken now, and are looking forward to great progress in the near future. We have donated five lots and a small three-room house which we hope to improve this fall.

In Washington there is a Home for Friendless, and also a National Association for the Relief of Destitute Women and Children supported by the Government at the cost of $10,000 a year, but conducted entirely by colored women. It had 103 women and children in 1907.

One woman, Mrs. Elizabeth McDonald, has been probation officer in Chicago, and does considerable lecturing on the subject of rescue work among women and children.

Section 16. Social, Literary and Art Clubs. All over the country there are a number of private and some public clubs among the colored people devoted primarily to literature or some form of art work. They are the remains of the more flourishing literary societies of ante bellum days in the free Negro settlements, but have changed considerably in character and kind of work.

The Friday Afternoon Study Club of Cleveland, O., consists of women who assemble once in two weeks to listen to papers and the discussions of general subjects. As, for instance, in 1905-06 they took the history of the United States and discussed different periods in sixteen different meetings, taking up not simply the formal history but the rise and fall of slave power, the development of American literature and art, the development of education, etc.

The Booklovers' Club of Washington, D. C., discussed the same year the principal religions of the earth and their effect on civilization. They held two meetings a month for seven months and took up the religion of Egypt and other ancient places, including Brahminism, Buddhism, Judaism, including a comparison of Jews and Negroes, Mohammedanism, Roman Catholicism, Protestantism, with discussions of the Negro and the Catholic Church and of American Negro religion.

Nearly all the larger churches throughout the United States have one or more literary societies connected with them; perhaps the most noted of these church literary societies is the Bethel Literary and Historical Association of Washington, D. C., organized in 1881 and commanding large audiences. Probably few organizations have had a more distinguished list of speakers, including Frederick Douglass, J. C. Price, John M. Langston, Alexander Crummell, Dr. E. W. Blyden, George W. Williams, Senator Blair, Richard T. Greener, and others.

Examples of some of the present societies follow:

The Dunbar Reading Circle of Newport News, Va., studies Negro history.

The Bowen Reading Circle of Washington, D.C., meets twice a month to read different authors.

The Royal Club of Houston, Tex., has a literary programme once a month and spends the rest of their time in charity work.

The Ladies' Reading Circle of Dallas, Tex., pursues certain lines of reading from year to year.

The Ladies' Literary Digest Club of Danville, Ky., is to encourage the reading of race literature and current events, and contribute to good causes.

The Macon Art and Social Club of Macon, Ga., consists of married women organized to do fancy work, and does some charity work also.

The West Indian Literary Club of Cambridge, Mass., does both literary and charitable work.

The Union of Haverhill, Mass., conducts a literary course.

The Detroit Study Club of Michigan is studying the lives of English and American poets.

The Scotia Reading Club of Jersey City, N. J., encourages the study of literature and maintains a scholarship at Scotia Seminary.

The Minervia Club of Cleveland, Ohio, is literary and musical, with some charitable work.

The American Girls' Culture Club of Newport, R. I., writes:

The American Girl's Culture Club was organized January 13, 1905, by Mrs. Bessie Jamison. There are at present twenty-two members. Our object is to work along various lines of charity and to help the Colored Old Folk's Home and the Working-Girls' Home in Providence. The first week in June the club is planning to give a star concert and the proceeds will be sent to a young colored man who is working his way through Brown University in Providence. Nearly all the girls in our club are talented, and very often the churches call upon us to help them out in their entertainments. We send flowers, fruits and other delicacies to the sick. We have made a number of visits to the hospital. We go and see the blind, and read to them. Easter-time we took several potted plants to a number of old ladies. In the last two or three weeks we have sent two large baskets of groceries to two poor old women. The club has given several dramas and concerts, and all proved to be successful. The ministers and all the churches seem to take a great interest in us. We have been very lucky in not losing any members by death. Nearly all of the girls attend the High School; some have graduated and are away to college.

In several cities there are organizations which maintain lectures and discussions on Sunday afternoon specially for men. Among these are the Men's Forum of Cambridge, Mass., the Sunday Forum of Minneapolis, Minn., and the Young Men's Christian Sunday Club, of Savannah, Ga. This latter club reports:

Its purpose is for the economic and hygienic development of Negroes. They do their work: (a) by having Sunday meetings at which men of ability give lectures; (b) they issue literature on hygiene to afflicted sections of the city; they make contributions to the poor, sometimes to the colored hospital. Any one willing to take part may become a member; no monthly fees required. Its finances come from collections from those who attend.

Various cities maintain regular lecture bureaus. One of the most successful of these is the People's Lecture Association of Little Rock, Ark. The following is a report of this organization:

Organization effected November 11, 1903, with about twenty-five members; seventy members in 1909.

Dues, one dollar per year, in quarterly payments.

During six years of its existence it has had forty-two lectures, two concerts by local talent, two concerts by professional talent, and one stereopticon lecture.

We have raised about $500.

Our earlier lecturers were colored college presidents of the city; later, white ministers of the city, politicians, teachers, educators of standing, not forgetting two lectures by Father Lucy, of Pine Bluff (white Catholic priest and writer of newspaper articles in State papers, advocating better treatment of Negroes), nor omitting Rabbi Wolsey (Jewish Priest, travelling orator; now of Cincinnati), nor Professor Dayne, State Superintendent of Public Instruction.

Our colored lecturers embrace names widely known and appreciated. Of these are Prof. W. E. Burghardt DuBois, Atlanta University; Prof. Wm. Pickens, Talladega College; Mrs. Mary C. Terrell, Hon. Edward Morris, of Chicago; Hon. J. T. Settles, lawyer of Memphis, Tenn., Archdeacon G. Alexander McGuire, of Cambridge, Mass.; Rev. Maximo Duty, of Memphis, Tenn.; Rev. D. LeRoy Ferguson, of Louisville, Ky.; Prof. Kelley Miller, Washington, D. C.

There are a number of small men's clubs like the Monday Club of Atlanta, Ga., and Advance Club of Birmingham, Ala. These are chiefly social clubs, but are also places of discussion and centers of various civic movements. For instance, members of the Atlanta Monday Club were largely called upon in the Atlanta riot to join with the whites in reconstruction.

Many social clubs are formed with the distinct purpose of beautifying and bettering social life. The Owl Club of Little Rock, Ark., consisting of nineteen married couples, was organized in 1894. Its object is to "uplift our race socially, and we have succeeded in bettering it morally as well."

There are a number of so-called art clubs whose object is chiefly social, and who do some drawing and painting and embroidery. They are chiefly valuable in keeping alive and encouraging the love for beautiful things; although the actual work accomplished is usually small and unimportant.

Silver Spray Art Club of Houston, Tex., is trying to beautify the homes of its members and also do some charitable work.

The most important developments in the line of art have been naturally toward music. Nearly all the large churches have organized choirs, and there are numbers of amateur musical associations, instrumental and vocal.

The work of Mr. Coleridge-Taylor, of England, led to the establishment of the Coleridge-Taylor Choral Society, in Washington, D.C. This society had a chorus of 200; among its patrons were Reginal DeKoven, Eugene E. Stephens, Henry Handzer, Lieutenant Santelmann.

It was organized in 1901 (incorporated 1903), under the stimulus of a proposed visit to Washington of the eminent composer. In a conference of our more prominent musicians, which met at the home of Mrs. A. F. Hilyer, it was discovered that the formation of a choral society among the colored singers of Washington had long been in the minds of many of them, and only needed the stimulus of the proposed visit of the composer and the opportunity to sing "Hiawatha" to give it tangible shape and permanent form. Its object is to develop a wider interest in the masterpieces of the great composers and especially to diffuse among the masses a higher musical culture and appreciation of works that tend to refine and elevate.

Since its organization the society has rendered "Hiawatha" on seven different occasions—four times in Washington, twice in Baltimore, and once in Philadelphia at the Academy of Music. It has also rendered Mr. S. Coleridge-Taylor's "Atonement" and the Choral Ballads (the latter having been dedicated to the society by the composer) and other compositions.

In November, 1904, the society had Mr. S. Coleridge-Taylor as its special guest, when it gave a Musical Festival consisting of three great concerts—two in Washington and one in Baltimore—rendering Hiawatha and the Choral Ballads under the direction of the composer, with the U. S. Marine Band Orchestra of 52 pieces accompanying, and other selections directed by Prof. John T. Layton. These concerts were attended by prominent musicians (white and colored) not only from this city, but from New York, Philadelphia, Boston, Baltimore, Chicago, Richmond, and other cities.

The most remarkable effort, perhaps, is the Foreign Scholarship Association established by Mme. E. Azalia Hackley. Mrs. Hackley, who herself has an unusual voice and was trained abroad, said in taking up her work in 1907:

I thoroughly believe that there is a future for colored musicians abroad, providing they take rank with white artists. I may not live to see it, but even in ten years, if something is done to encourage such a condition, I believe that several first-class companies—not coon shows—could have seasons in various countries. I also believe that white managers will engage colored artists, providing they can sing in foreign languages. I believe that there could even be colored managers abroad within the next ten years, but they would be obliged to offer real attractions.

If we encourage our young people generally throughout the country, every five or six years, some one of them will leap out of the circle of mediocrity and push his way to the front, and perhaps represent us musically as we have never been represented.

If the colored musicians in each place would unite as enthusiastically as people do to start a new church, or establish a lodge, there could be some one helped each year.

Who is doing anything for a colored genius? Well, of course, the race is comparatively poor, but there are some wealthy ones, and we could help a couple a year, at least, if we tried.

I heard abroad of about six students whom Mr. Schwab, the steel magnate, is helping. He does not even know the beneficiaries. Mr. Rockefeller and Mrs. Vanderbilt are educating several each, and many others are helping talented people.

Thereupon Mrs. Hackley established what she called the Foreign Scholarship, and induced two hundred or more colored people to contribute a scholarship of two or three hundred dollars a year. She then took a trip through the South, and reported an orchestra of thirty members in Richmond, Va., and a festival; a remarkable soprano at Atlanta University, and a good violinist; fine choral work at Tuskegee; a very competent piano teacher at Montgomery; an amateur cornetist at Mobile; a chorister in New Orleans and four exceptional voices, and a tenor soloist at Jacksonville. In the West she found a good soprano at Harrisburg, chorister in Pittsburgh, three violinists in Detroit and Chicago, a good soprano voice in Chicago together with a musical-study club, a good musical director in Kansas City, a rare contralto in Omaha, a chorus of thirty-five voices in Denver, a good baritone in Colorado Springs, a pianist in Oakland, Cal., and a study club in Los Angeles.

In the pursuance of this plan Mrs. Hackley has sent her first beneficiary abroad during 1908-9 in the person of Clarence C. White, a violinist of rare ability; the next beneficiary is to be Carl R. Diton; three hundred dollars is to be raised for him.

In her last report Mrs. Hackley says:

In June I finished the last payment of the five hundred dollars I had promised to Mr. Clarence Cameron White, to assist him in his studies abroad for one year. Mr. White sailed for London in June, 1908.

It has been a difficult task to collect this amount, but it has been accomplished, and the scholarship establishes a precedent. I am highly gratified with all results. If those who have contributed could understand how arduously Mr. White has worked, and how much he has improved in his playing, they would be as pleased as I am. If he had to return at this date, he will have profited to a remarkable extent, and the money has been well spent.

To have one colored artist presented abroad every five years would cost less than $5,000, an average of $1,000 a year. What a pittance this is if it scores one point in favor of ten millions of people. One department store in any large city expends that much in less than a week for advertising, because the results of advertisement are evident.

How can the race expect the world to believe that it has rare musical talent, the one line in which it can excel if given opportunity, if the fact is not continually advertised and evidence produced? Must there be no change of opinion because of a few dollars that might be easily given?

Another interesting musical association is the Viotti Association of Boston. Its founder says:

I went from house to house one day and saw as many mothers as I possibly could find at home, told them what my object was, that I wanted them to help me in getting the boys and girls off the streets at night and give them something to do at home, something all colored people, as a rule, are very fond of, and that is music. I started out with five other women and we organized a club called the Viotti Club of Boston. For one year it grew to fifteen, then I entered the club into the Northeastern Federation of Women's Clubs of New England, and we now number twenty-five. The club was named for Henry Viotti, of London, a professor of music. We have a Junior Department of twenty boys, who are organized into a brass band and orchestra. They are doing nicely. It is conducted by a colored woman of my club. Last year we raised one hundred and twenty-nine dollars from concerts given by the boys. I paid $150 for the instruments. We give the instruments to the poorer boys who are not able to pay for them.

There is one National Association which seeks to encourage literature and art among Negroes. This is the American Negro Academy, founded by Alexander Crummell in 1897. Its objects are "the promotion of literature, science and art; the culture of a form of Intellectual Taste; the fostering of Higher Education; the publication of scholarly work; the defense of the Negro against vicious assaults."

It has a limited number of selected members and has published thirteen pamphlets on Sociological and Historical subjects.

Section 17. Literature and Newspapers. Only a brief sketch of the attempt to better social conditions by means of newspapers, books and periodicals can here be attempted.

As early as the eighteenth century, and even before the Revolutionary War, the first voices of Negro authors were heard in the United States.

Phyllis Wheatley, the black poetess, was easily the pioneer, her first poems appearing in 1773, and other editions in 1784 and 1793. Her earliest poem was in memory of George Whitefield. She was followed by the Negro, Olaudah Equiano—known by his English name of Gustavus Vassa—whose autobiography of 350 pages, published in 1787, was the beginning of that long series of personal appeals of which Booker T. Washington's Up From Slavery is the latest.

Benjamin Banneker's almanacs represented the first scientific work of American Negroes, and began to be issued in 1792.

Coming now to the first decades of the nineteenth century we find some essays on Freedom by the African Society of Boston, and an apology for the new Negro church formed in Philadelphia. Paul Cuffe disgusted with America wrote an early account of Sierra Leone, while the celebrated Lemuel Haynes ignoring the race question dipped deeply into the New England theological controversy about 1815. In 1829 came the first full-voiced, almost hysterical, protest against slavery and the color line in David Walker's Appeal, which aroused Southern legislatures to action. This was followed by the earliest Negro conventions which issued interesting minutes, and a strong appeal against disfranchisement in Pennsylvania.

In 1840 some strong writers began to appear. Henry Highland Garnet and J. W. C. Pennington preached powerful sermons and gave some attention to Negro history in their pamphlets; R. B. Lewis made a more elaborate attempt at Negro history. Whitfield's poems appeared in 1846, and William Wells Brown began a career of writing which lasted from 1847 until after the war. In 1845 Douglass's Autobiography made its first appearance, destined to run through endless editions up until the last in 1893. Moreover it was in 1841 that the first Negro magazine appeared in America, edited by George Hogarth and published by the A. M. E. Church.

In the fifties William Wells Brown published his "Three Years in Europe"; James Whitfield published further poems, and a new poet arose in the person of Frances E. W. Harper, a woman of no little ability who is still alive; Martin R. Delaney and William Nell wrote further of Negro history, Nell especially making valuable contributions to the history of the Negro soldiers. Three interesting biographies were added in this decade to the growing number: Josiah Henson, Samuel G. Ward and Samuel Northrop; while Catto leaving general history came down to the better known history of the Negro church.

In the sixties slave narratives multiplied, like that of Linda Brent, while two studies of Africa based on actual visits were made by Robert Campbell and the revered Alexander Crummell; William Douglass and Bishop Daniel Payne continued the history of the Negro church, while William Wells Brown carried forward his work in general Negro history. In this decade, too, Bishop Tanner began his work in Negro theology.

Most of the Negro talent in the seventies was taken up in politics; the older men like Bishop Wayman wrote of their experiences. William Wells Brown wrote the Rising Son, and Sojourner Truth added her story to the slave narratives. A new poet arose in the person of A. A. Whitman, while James M. Trotter was the first to take literary note of the musical ability of his race. Indeed, this section might have been begun by some reference to the music and folk-lore of the Negro race; the music contained much primitive poetry and the folklore being one of the great contributions to American civilization.

In the eighties there are signs of unrest and different conflicting streams of thought. On the one hand the rapid growth of the Negro church is shown by the writers on church subjects like Moore and Wayman. The historical spirit was especially strong. Still wrote of the Underground Railroad; Simmons issued his interesting biographical dictionary, and the greatest historian of the race appeared when George W. Williams issued his two-volume history of the Negro race in America. The political turmoil was reflected in Langston's Freedom and Citizenship, Fortune's Black and White, and Straker's New South, and found its bitterest arraignment in Turner's pamphlets; but with all this went other thought: a black man published his first Greek lessons, Bishop Payne issued his Treatise on Domestic Education, and Stewart studied Liberia.

In the nineties came histories, essays, novels and poems, together with biography and social studies. The history was represented by Payne's History of the A. M. E. Church, Hood's History of the A. M. E. Zion Church, Anderson's sketch of Negro Presbyterianism and Hagood's Colored Man in the M. E. Church; general history of the older type by R. L. Perry's Cushite, and the newer type in Johnson's History and DuBois's Suppression of the Slave Trade, while one of the secret societies found their historian in Brooks; Crogman's essays appeared and Archibald Grimke's biographies. The race question was discussed in Frank Grimke's published Sermons, while social studies were made by Penn, Wright, Mossell, Crummell, DuBois, Majors, and others. Most notable, however, was the rise of the Negro novelist and poet with national recognition; Frances Harper was still writing and Griggs began his racial novels, but both of these spoke primarily to the Negro race; on the other hand, Chesnutt's six novels and Dunbar's inimitable works spoke to the whole nation.

Since 1900 the stream of Negro writing has continued: Dunbar has found a worthy successor in the less-known but more carefully cultured Braithwaite; Booker T. Washington has given us his biography and Story of the Negro; Kelly Miller's trenchant essays have appeared in book form and DuBois's Souls of Black Folk and John Brown; Sinclair's Aftermath of Slavery has attracted attention, as have the studies made by Atlanta University. The forward movement in Negro music is represented by Frederick J. Work in one direction and Rosamond Johnson in another.

On the whole the literary output of the American Negro has been both large and creditable, although, of course, comparatively little known; few great names have appeared and little work that could be called first-class, but this, of course, is not a peculiarity of Negro literature.

A Chronological List of Some Notable Works in Negro Literature

Phyllis Wheatley—Poems on various subjects, religious and moral. 1773. 8vo.

Equiano, Olaudah (Gustavus Vassa)—Autobiography. 1787. 350 pp.

Benjamin Banneker—Almanacs, 1792-1806.

African Society. Essay on Freedom. Boston, 22 pp. 1808.

Act of Incorporation, Causes and Motives of the African Episcopal Church. Philadelphia, 1810.

Paul Cuffe—Brief Account of Sierra Leone. New York. 12 pp. 1812.

Lemuel Haynes—Sermons. 1815(?).

Walker, David—Appeal, in four articles, together with a Preamble to the Colored Citizens of the World, etc. 66 pp. Boston, Mass. 1829.

Minutes of the First Annual Convention of the People of Color Philadelphia. 1831. Pamphlet.

Appeal of forty thousand colored citizens threatened with disfranchisement to the people of Pennsylvania. Phila., 1838. 18 pp. 8vo.

Lee, Jarena—Journal. Cincinnati, 1839. 24 pp. 12mo.

J. W. C. Pennington—Origin and History of the Colored People. 1841. 100 pp.

African M. E. Church Magazine. (George Hogarth.) 1841.

Lewis, Robert Benjamin—Light and Truth, etc. Boston, 1844. 400 pp. 16mo.

Douglass—Autobiography, 1845.

Whitfield's Poems, 1846.

Brown, William Wells—Narrative of a fugutive. Boston, 1847. 110 pp. 16mo.

Garnet, Henry Highland—The Past and Present Condition and the Destiny of the Colored Race. Troy, 1848. 29 pp. 8vo. Plates.

W. W. Brown—Three Years in Europe. London, 1852.

W. W. Brown—Sketches of Places and People Abroad. New York, 1855.

Martin R. Delaney—Condition, Elevation, Emigration and Destiny of the Colored People of the United States. Phila., 1852. 215 pp. 12mo.

James M. Whitfield—Poems. America, and other poems. Buffalo, 1853.

Harper, Frances E. W.—Miscellaneous poems. Boston, 1854.

William Cooper Nell—The Colored Patriots of the American Revolution. Intro. by H. B. Stowe. Boston, 1855. 396 pp. 12mo.

Ward, S. G.—Autobiography of a Fugitive Negro. London, 1855.

Catto, W. T.—History of the Presbyterian Movement. Phila., 1857. 8vo. A semi-centenary discourse and history of the first African Presbyterian church, Phila., May, 1857, from its organization, including a notice of its first pastor, John Gloucester; also appendix containing sketches of all the colored churches in Philadelphia.

Henson, Josiah (Uncle Tom)—Father Henson's story. Boston, 1858.

Twenty Years a Slave. Northrup. 1859.

Incidents in the Life of a Slave Girl (Linda Brent). 1861.

Robert Campbell—A Pilgrimage to my Motherland. Phila., 1861.

Crummell, Alexander—The Future of Africa. 1862.

Douglass, William—Annals of St. Thomas's First African Church. Philadelphia, 1862. 172 pp. 8vo.

Brown, William Wells—The Black Man, his Antecedents, etc. New York, 1863. 288 pp. 12mo.

Payne, D. A.—The Semi-Centenary and the Retrospection of the A. M. E. Church. 1866.

Brown, William Wells—The Negro in the American Rebellion. Boston, 1867. 380 pp. 8vo.

Tanner, Bishop Benjamin T.—An Apology for African Methodism. Baltimore, 1867. 468 pp. 8vo.

Cyclopedia of African Methodism. Bishop Wayman.

Brown, William Wells—The Rising Son. Boston, 1874 (1873). 12mo. Portrait.

Truth, Sojourner—Narrative. Boston, 1875.

Whitman, A. A.—Not a Man and Yet a Man. Springfield, O., 1877.

Trotter, James M.—Music and some highly musical people. Boston, 1878. 353, (1) 152 pp. 12mo.

Moore, J. J.—History of the A. M. E. Zion Church. York, Pa., 1880.

Williams, Geo. W.—History of the Negro race in America from 1619 to 1880. New York, 1883. 2 vols. 8vo.

Wayman, A. W.—My recollections of A. M. E. Ministers. Philadelphia, 1881. 250 pp. 8vo.

Scarborough, W. S.—First Greek Lessons. New York, 1881. 150 pp.

Langston, J. M.—Freedom and Citizenship, 1882. 286 pp.

Still, Wm.—The Underground Railroad. Phila., 1883.

Fortune, T. Thomas—Black and White. New York, 1884.

Turner, H. M.—The Black Man's Doom. 1884, 1896. 90 pp.

Turner, H. M.—Methodist Polity, or the Genius and Theory of Methodism. Philadelphia, 1885.

Payne, Daniel A.—A Treatise on Domestic Education. Cincinnati, 1885.

Scarborough—The Birds of Aristophanes. 1886. 36 pp.

Stewart, T. Mc.—Liberia, the Americo-African Republic. New York, 1886.

Simmons, Wm. Johnson—Men of Mark: eminent, progressive, rising. Cleveland, 1887 1141 pp. 8vo.

Straker, D. Augustus—The New South Investigated. Detroit, 1888.

Hagood, L. M.—The Colored Man in the Methodist Episcopal Church. 1890. Cincinnati.

Gaines, W. J.—African Methodism in the South. Atlanta, 1890.

Recollections of Seventy Years—Bishop D. A. Payne.

Jamieson, Dr.—Minden Armais, the man of the new race. Phila., 1890. 110 pp.

Crummell, Alexander—Africa and America. Springfield, 1891. 466 pp. 8vo.

"Aunt Lindy"—Victoria Earle.

Penn, Irvine Garland—The Afro-American Press and its Editors. Springfield, 1811. 565 pp. 12mo.

Johnson, Edward A.—A School History of the Negro Race in America from 1619 to 1890, with a short introduction as to the origin of the race; also a short sketch of Liberia. Raleigh, 1891,

Payne, Daniel A.—History of the A. M. E. Church. Nashville, 1891. 498 pp.

Grimke, Archibald H.—William Lloyd Garrison. New York, 1891.

Grimke, Archibald H.—Charles Sumner. New York, 1892. 515 pp. 8vo.

Harper, Frances E. W.—Iola Leroy: a novel. 3d ed. Phila., 1892. 281 pp.

Perry, Rufus L.—The Cushite. Springfield, 1893.

Majors, M. A.—Noted Negro Women. Chicago, 1893.

Brooks, C. H.—Manual and History of the Grand United Order of Odd Fellows. Philadelphia, 1893. 260 pp. 8vo.

Smith, Mrs. Amanda—Autobiography of Amanda Smith. Chicago, 1893.

Mossell, Mrs. N. F.—The Work of Afro-American Women. Phila., 1894.

Jones, Robert—Fifty Years in the Lombard Street Central Presbyterian Church. Philadelphia, 1894.

Wright, Richard R.—Brief Historical Sketch of Negro Education in Georgia. Savannah, 1894.

Hood, W. J.—History of the A. M. E. Zion Church. New York, 1895.

W. H. Crogman—Talks for the Times. Atlanta, 1896.

DuBois, W. E. B.—Suppression of the Slave Trade. New York, 1896.

Anderson, Matthew—Presbyterianism and its relation to the Negro. Phila., 1897.

Griggs, Sutton E.—Imperium in Imperio. Cincinnati, 1899.

Chesnutt, Charles W.—
    The Conjure Woman. Boston, 1899.
    Frederick Douglass. Boston, 1899.
    The House Behind the Cedars. Boston, 1900.
    The Marrow of Tradition. Boston, 1901.
    The Wife of his Youth. Boston, 1899.
Grimke, Francis J.—The Lynching of Negroes in the South. Washington, 1899.
DuBois, W. E. B.—The Philadelphia Negro. Phila., 1899. 520 pp.
Dunbar, Paul Lawrence—The Sport of the Gods. New York, 1901.
Atlanta University Publications—The College-bred Negro. Atlanta, 1900.
Atlanta University Publications—The Negro Artisan. Atlanta, 1902.
Washington, B. T.—Up from Slavery. New York, 1901.
Penn, I. G., and J. W. E. Bowen, Editors—The United Negro; His Problems and His
    Progress. Containing the Addresses and Proceedings of the Negro Young Peo-
    ple's Christian and Educational Congress, held August 6-11, 1902. Atlanta, 1902.
Gibbs, M. W.—Shadow and Light. Washington, 1902.
Wright, R. R.—Negro Companions of the Spanish Explorers. From "American
    Anthropologist," vol. 8. 1902.
Work, Frederick J.—New Jubilee Songs, as sung by the Jubilee Singers of Fisk Uni-
    versity. 1902.
DuBois, W. E. B.—The Souls of Black Folk. Chicago, 1903.
Atlanta University Publications—The Negro Church. Atlanta, 1903.
The Negro Problem—A series of articles by representative Negroes of to-day. New
    York, 1903.
Braithwaite—Poems and Anthologies.
Grimshaw, Wm. H.—Official History of Freemasonry, etc. New York, 1903.
Cromwell, John W.—The Early Negro Convention Movement. Washington, 1904.
    (The American Negro Academy.)
Sinclair, William A.—The Aftermath of Slavery, etc., with an introduction by T. W.
    Higginson. Boston, 1905.
Miller, Kelly—Race Adjustment. 1908.
Washington, B. T.—Story of the Negro. 1910.

Turning now to the newspapers we quote from L. M. Hershaw:

Negro journalism in the United States had its origin in the aspiration for
freedom. The first Negro newspaper in the United States was begun in New
York city, March 30, 1827, and was called The Journal of Freedom. Its editor
was John B. Russworm, a graduate of Dartmouth College of the class of 1826,
perhaps the first Negro to receive a degree from an American institution of
learning. Associated with him in the editing was the Rev. Samuel E. Cornish,
a controversialist of no mean powers.

This journal had an existence of but three years, and other attempts by
Negroes to publish newspapers failed of notable success until Frederick
Douglass started The North Star at Rochester, N. Y., in 1847. The name was
subsequently changed to Frederick Douglass's paper, and Mr. Douglass
continued it up to the opening of the Civil War. For length of life, extent
of circulation, ability of matter contributed and commanding talents of its
editor, the publication was one which occupies a conspicuous chapter in the
history of Negro journalism.

From these beginnings the Negro newspaper has grown until to-day
there are over three hundred periodicals published, most of which are
in the form of weekly papers. Since the establishment of the Journal
of Freedom in 1827 thousands of Negro journals have lived and died.

Among these papers the most notable was the Voice of the Negro, an excellent magazine which lasted several years. At different times small Negro daily papers have been started. The only surviving one at present seems to be the Daily Metropolitan of Dallas, Tex. At present there have been received in this office specimen copies of 185 papers and 9 magazines. Besides these we have the names of 76 other weekly papers which either are being published or have been until quite recently.

The 185 papers actually received have been tabulated according to the year of founding, the number of pages, the size of the page and the number of columns of "live matter," i. e., of matter actually set up in type by the paper each week and not received in printed form from some printing or advertising agency:

Name	Published	Year	Pp.	L. M.	Size
Christian Recorder	Philadelphia	1852	8	36	15x22
Southwestern Christian Advocate	New Orleans, La.	1866	16	42	11x15
Christian Index	Jackson, Tenn.	1870	16	32	9x13
Star of Zion	Charlotte, N. C.	1877	8	27	12x21
Afro-American Presbyterian	Charlotte, N. C.	1878	4	11	16x22
The Washington Bee	Washington, D. C.	1879	8	15½	15x22
Georgia Baptist	Augusta, Ga.	1879	8	23	13x20
Western Star	Houston, Dallas, Tex.	1881	8	10	15x22
Baptist Vanguard	Little Rock, Ark.	1881	8	19	13x20
The World	Indianapolis, Ind.	1881	8	11	15x22
Pioneer Press	Martinsburg, W.Va.	1882	4	11½	11x20
Gazette	Cleveland, O.	1883	4	10	18x24
Normal Index	Normal, Ala.	1883	4	13	11x16
Appeal	St. Paul, Minn.	1884	4	8	18x24
Southern Letter	Tuskegee, Ala.	1884	4	7	9x12
Savannah Tribune	Savannah, Ga.	1885	8	13	15x22
Philadelphia Tribune	Philadelphia	1885	8	24	15x24
Brotherhood	Cincinnati, O.	1886	8	10½	15x22
Crusader	Baltimore, Md.	1886	8	5½	15x22
Florida Sentinel	Pensacola, Fla.	1886	8	15	15x22
New York Age	New York	1887	8	33	16x20½
The Light	Vicksburg, Miss.	1887	4	7	18x24
The Freeman	Indianapolis, Ind.	1887	8	23	15x22
Steelton Press	Steelton, Pa.	1888	4	2	18x24
Tuskegee Student	Tuskegee, Ala.	1888	4	9½	11x16
New Light	Edwards, Miss.	1888	8	12½	15x22
Statesman	Denver, Col.	1888	16	25	11x15
Southern Christian Recorder	Columbus, Ga.	1889	4	22	18x23
Baptist Leader	Birmingham, Ala.	1889	4	9½	15x22
Christian Banner	Philadelphia	1889	4	20	18x24
The Christian Hope	Demopolis, Ala.	1891	4	6	15x22
Dallas Express	Dallas, Tex.	1892	8	18	18x24
Griffin Echo	Griffin, Ga.	1892	4	2½	18x24
Oklahoma Guide	Guthrie, Okla	1892	4	4	18x24
People's Recorder	Orangeburg, S. C.	1892	4	20	15x22
Oklahoma Safeguard	Guthrie, Okla.	1893	4	12	18x24
Iowa Bystander	Des Moines, Ia.	1893	4	15	18x24
Baptist Truth	Cairo, Ill.	1894	4	7½	18x24
Plaindealer	Palestine, Tex.	1894	8	6	15x21
Weekly Express	Mobile, Ala.	1894	6	11	15x22
Charleston Messenger	Charleston, S. C.	1894	4	13	18x24
The Standard	Lexington, Ky.	1894	4	9	18x24
The Journal	Huntsville, Ala.	1894	4	12	15x22
Seattle Republican	Seattle, Wash.	1894	8	8	11x16
Western Outlook	San Francisco, Los Angeles and Oakland, Cal.	1894	4	10	18x24

Name	*Published*	*Year*	*Pp.*	*L.M.*	*Size*
Rock Hill Messenger	Rock Hill, S. C.	1895	4	5½	18x24
Colored Citizen	Memphis, Tenn.	1895	8	10	15x22
Advance Citizen	Springfield, Ill.	1895	4	5	15x22
Detroit Reformer	Detroit, Mich.	1895	4	11	18x24
The Reformer	Richmond, Va.	1895	4	18½	20x26
Broad Ax	Chicago, Ill.	1895	4	9	16x22
Odd Fellows' Journal	Philadelphia, Pa.	1896	8	15	13x20
The Advance	Jamestown, N. C.	1896	4	1	15x22
Recorder	Indianapolis, Ind.	1896	4	12	18x24
The Educator	Huntsville, Ala.	1896	8	3	11x16
Taborian Visitor	Little Rock, Ark.	1895	8	40	15x22
Enterprise	Omaha, Neb.	1896	8	10	15x22
The Helping Hand	Paris, Tex.	1896	8	27	15x22
Louisiana Baptist,	Alexandria, La.	1897	9	22½	18x20
Informer	Urbana, O.	1897	4	10	15x22
Oakland Sunshine	Oakland, Cal.	1897	4	13½	18x24
News-Enterprise	Shreveport, La.	1897	8	13	15x19
Nashville Clarion	Nashville, Tenn.	1897	4	10	17x19
Weekly Gazette	Metropolis, Ill.	1897	8	14½	13x20
City Times	Galveston, Tex.	1897	4	4½	18x24
Mission Herald	Louisville, Ky.	1897	4	19	12x19
National Protest	St. Joseph, Mo.	1897	8	16½	15x22
Texas Freeman	Houston, Tex.	1898	–	–	18x24
Western Enterprise,	Colorado Springs	1898	8	13	15x22
Plaindealer	Topeka, Kan.	1898	8	13	12x20
Baptist Sentinel	Raleigh, N. C.	1898	8	13	11x16
Durham Reformer	Durham, N. C.	1898	8	15	15x22
Kentucky Standard	Louisville, Ky.	1898	4	6	18x24
Missionary Seer	Philadelphia.	1898	8	14	9x12
Independent	Savannah, Ga.	1899	8	8	15x22
Southern Reporter	Charleston, S. C.	1899	4	14½	15x21
Kentucky Reporter	Owensboro, Ky.	1899	4	8	15x22
Advocate,	Charleston, W. Va.	1900	8	31½	18x22
Western Messenger	Macon, Jefferson City and St. Louis, Mo.	1900	4	15	15x22
The Demonstrator	Mound Bayou, Miss.	1900	4	7½	18x24
St. Luke Herald	Richmond, Va.	1900	4	9	13x21
Florida Reporter	Tampa, Fla.	1900	8	10	13x20
American Star	Tuscumbia, Ala.	1900	8	6	11x15
National Star	Vicksburg, Miss.	1900	4	6	18x24
Pythian Monitor	Cincinnati, O.	1901	8	30	15x24
Bluff City News	Memphis, Tenn.	1901	12	12	17x22
Friendship Banner	Rock Hill, S. C.	(?)	4	10	11x17
Wilkes-Barre Advocate	Wilkesbarre, Pa.	1901	4	11½	15x22
The Star	Newport News, Va.	1901	8	18½	15x22
The Courant	Philadelphia.	1901	4	9	15x22
Professional World	Columbia, Mo.	1901	8	22	15x22
The Guardian	Boston, Mass.	1901	8	35	18x24
The Torchlight	Danville, Ky.	1901	4	10½	15x22
Florida Labor Temple	Jacksonville.	1901	8	12	18x24
Baptist Rival	Ardmore, Okla.	1901	8	11	15x22
Industrial Era	Beaumont, Tex.	1902	4	4½	16x22
Seattle Searchlight	Seattle, Wash.	1902	4	17	16x22
The Truth	Birmingham, Ala.	1902	4	3	12x18
Missionary Presbyterian	Washington, Ga.	1902	4	6	13x20
Portland Advocate	Portland, Ore.	1902	4	12	18x24
Vox Populi	Albany, Ga.	1902	8	8	13x20
Fisherman's Net,	Hampton, Va.	1903	4	10	15x22
The Forum	Springfield, Ill.	1903	8	7	12x16
Cleveland Journal	Cleveland, O.	1903	8	14	15x22
Southern Age	New Orleans	1903	4	8½	18x22
The Echo	Red Bank, N. J.	1903	4	7½	15x22
The Signal	Memphis, Tenn.	1903	4	7	15x22
Birmingham Reporter	Birmingham, Ala.	1903	8	12	15x22
Illinois Idea	Chicago	1903	4	7	18x24
National Watchman	Topeka, Kan.	1903	8	9	15x22
The Defender	Sumter, S. C.	1903	8	9	15x22
The Advocate	Portland, Ore.	1903	4	15	18x24
Springfield Leader	Springfield, Ill.	1904	8	11	15x22
Interstate Reporter	Helena, Ark.	1904	4	7	15x22
Staunton Reporter	Staunton, Va.	1904	4	8	11x15
Beaufort County News	Beaufort, S. C.	1904	4	3½	13x20
Boley Progress	Boley, Okla.	1904	4	8	15x22
Florida Standard	Jacksonville	1904	4	6	15x22
Negro Fortune Teller	Huntsville, Ala.	1904	4	11½	11x16
Atlanta Justice	Atlanta, Ga.	1904	6	9 9½x19½	
Colorado Times	Pueblo, Col.	1904	4	7	18x24
The Messenger	Tuskegee, Ala.	1905	4	10	11x16

Name	*Published*	*Year*	*Pp.*	*L.M.*	*Size*
American Problem	Newport News, Va.	1905	4	4½	15x22
Nashville Globe	Nashville, Tenn.	1905	8	27	13x18
Light of the Race	Newport News, Va.	1905	4	15	15x22
Farmers' Courier	Darlington, S. C.	1905	4	4½	15x22
Southern Plowman	Columbia, S. C.	1905	4	22½	15x22
The Messenger	Atlantic City, N. J.	1905	4	8	15x22
Chicago Defender	Chicago, Ill.	1905	4	14	18x24
Richonnd Planet	Richmond, Va.	1905	8	12	18x24
Mid-weekly Progress	Memphis, Tenn.	1905	4	6	15x22
Colored Alabamian	Montgomery, Ala.	1906	4	10	11x16
Waycross News	Waycross, Ga.	1906	4	8	15x22
Wisconsin Weekly Defender	Milwaukee, Wis.	1906	4	5½	15x22
The Advance	Providence, R. I.	1906	4	7½	15x22
Saturday Evening News	Columbus, O.	1906	4	14	11x14
The Union	Cincinnati, O.	1906	8	6	15x22
Union Messenger	Dothan, Ala.	1906	4	8	15x22
Macon Dispatch	Macon, Ga.	1906	8	8	15x22
The Daily Metropolitan	Dallas, Tex.	1906	4	9	14½x10½
San Antonio Inquirer	San Antonio, Tex.	1906	4	3	15x22
National Industrial Enterprise	Washington, D. C.	1906	8	16½	15x22
The American Citizen	Atlanta, Ga.	1907	8	8½	15x22
Kansas City Son	Kansas City, Mo.	1907	8	7½	15x22
Yonkers Standard	Yonkers, N. Y.	1907	4	11	15x22
Fessenden Academy Herald	Fessenden, Ala.	1907	8	11	9x12
New York Eye	Brooklyn, N. Y.	1907	8	8½	13x20
Union Ledger	Anniston, Ala.	1907	4	3½	13x20
The Light	Columbia, S. C.	1907	8	9	15x22
Mississippi Odd Fellow	Holly Springs, Miss.	1907	4	13	15x22
Southern Indicator	Spartanburg, S. C.	1907	8	15	13x22
The Advocate	Boston, Mass.	1907	8	19	15x22
The Plaindealer	Helena, Mont.	1907	4	16	15x22
Muskogee Cimeter	Muskogee, Okla.	1907	8	14	15x22
Conservative Counselor	Gonzales, Tex.	1907	4	5	15x22
The New Century	Norfolk, Va.	1908	4	7	15x22
Spokane Citizen	Spokane, Wash.	1908	8	15	11x16
Atlantic City Weekly Topic	Atlantic City, N. J.	1908	4	8	15x22
Washington American	Washington, D. C.	1908	4	10	18x24
Allen Student	Columbia, S. C.	1908	4	15	16x22
Wagoner Lantern	Wagoner, Okla.	1908	4	3	13x20
Supreme Circle News	Albany, Ga.	1908	4	15½	15x22
Bath Times	Hot Springs and Covington, Va.	1908	4	3½	18x24
The New Age	Los Angeles, Cal.	1908	4	10	15x22
The Sentinel	Richmond, Ky.	1908	6	15	11x17
The College Journal	Savannah, Ga.	1908	4	16	11x17
Baltimore Times	Baltimore, Md.	1909	8	14	15x22
Appreciator Union	Ft. Smith.	1909	4	12	13x20
Negro Leader	Uniontown, Ala.	1909	4	6½	8½x14
St. John Herald	Montgomery, Ala.	1909	4	9	8½x12
Baptist Herald	Lynchburg, Va.	1909	8	10	13x20
Ethiopian Phalanx	Covington, Ga.	1909	4	6½	15x22
The Caret	Philadelphia.	1909	4	8	15x22
The U. B. F. Searchlight	Sedalia, Mo.	1909	4	13	15x22
Fort Valley Uplift	Ft. Valley, Ga.	1909	4	5½	9½x12
New York Defender	New York	1909	-	-	-
The Forum	Spokane, Wash.	1909	4	11	16x22
Wadesboro Enterprise	Wadesboro, N. C.	1909	4	10	18x24
Indiana Register	Richmond, Ind.	1909	4	12	15x22
Zanesville Advocate	Zanesville, O.	1909	8	8	15x22
National Aspect	Chicago, Ill.	1910	4	12	18x24
Jackson Gazette	Jackson, Tenn.	1910	4	8	15x22
The Enterprise	Muskogee, Okla.	1910	8	12½	18x24
Illinois Chronicle	Chicago, Ill.	1910	4	15½	15x24
Pittsburgh Courier	Pittsburgh, Pa.	1910	8	18	16x22

Magazines

Name	*Published*	*Year*	*Pp.*	*L.M.*	*Size*
A. M. E. Church Review	Nashville, Tenn.	1882	100	99	6x9
A. M. E. Z. Quarterly	Charlotte, N. C.	1889	91	182	6x9
Gazetteer and Guide	St. Paul, Detroit, Richmond,Va., and Montreal.	1900	24	9½	11x16
Business League Herald	Washington, D. C.	1908	12	34½	9x12
The Horizon	Washington, D. C.	1907	12	24	10½x8
McGirt's Magazine	Philadelphia.	(?)	40	60	6x9
The Liberator	St. Louis.	(?)	96	145	7½x9½
Negro World Echo	Hot Springs, Ark.	1910	64	36	6¾x10
The Sixth Race Magazine	Orlando, Fla.	1910	20	19	6x8¾

Papers Not Received, but Reported as Being Published

The Tribune, Bessemer, Ala.
The Selma News, Selma, Ala.
Voice of the 20th Century, Argenta, Ark.
Union Trumpet, Montrose, Ark.
Reporter, Little Rock, Ark.
Fraternal Union, Fort Smith, Ark.
Echo, Hot Springs, Ark.
Eagle, Los Angeles, Cal.
The Forum, San Jose, Cal.
The Light, Colorado Springs, Colo.
Delaware Advocate, Wilmington, Del.
Afro-American Ledger, Wilmington, Del.
Masonic Forum, Jacksonville, Fla.
Florida Tribune, Marianna, Fla.
Christian Recorder, Orlando, Fla.
Advocate, Covington, Ga.
Baptist Truth, Macon, Ga.
Enterprise, Pulaski, Ga.
Standard World, Columbus, O.
Ohio Standard, Xenia, O.
Republican, Muskogee, Okla.
Sun, Ardmore, Okla.
The Western Age, Langston, Okla.
The Gazette, Buxton, Ia.
The Enterprise, Salina, Kan.
The Searchlight, Wichita, Kan.
American Baptist, Louisville, Ky.
Blue Grass Bugle, Frankfort, Ky.
Reporter, Mt. Sterling, Ky.
The Watchman, Shreveport, La.
Republican Liberator, New Orleans, La.
Louisiana Searchlight, Shreveport, La.
The Guide, Evansville, Ind.
The Sun, Columbia, S. C.
The Monitor, Greenville, S. C.
The Blade, Chattanooga, Tenn.
The Conservator, Memphis, Tenn.
The Signal, Memphis, Tenn.
The Paul Quin Weekly, Waco, Tex.

The Wiley Reporter, Marshall, Tex.
The Witness, Houston, Tex.
The Watchman, Austin, Tex.
Texas Pythian Journal, Waco, Tex.
The Searchlight, Austin, Tex.
The New Idea, Galveston, Tex.
The Item, Fort Worth, Tex.
The Louisiana Record, New Orleans, La.
The Advocate, Baltimore, Md.
The Appeal, Meridian, Miss.
The Baptist Reporter, Jackson, Miss.
The Herald, Natchez, Miss.
The News Journal, Laurel, Miss.
Delta Light House, Greenville, Miss.
The National Mirror, Kansas City, Mo.
The Western Christian Recorder, Kansas City, Mo.
The Sentinel, East St. Louis, Ill.
The Signal, Kansas City, Mo.
The Palladium, St. Louis, Mo.
The American Citizen, Kansas City, Mo.
The Advance, St. Louis, Mo.
The Appeal, Jersey City, N. J.
The Industrial Watchman, Paterson, N. J.
Voice of Missions, New York.
The Statesman, New York.
The National Review, New York.
The Gazette, Charlotte, N. C.
The Piedmont Advocate, Salisburg, N. C.
The True Reformer, Littleton, N. C.
The Bee, San Antonio, Tex.
The Utah Plaindealer, Salt Lake City, U.
The National Pilot, Petersburg, Va.
The Virginia Baptist, Richmond, Va.
The Colored Union, Clifton Forge, Va.
The Westerner, Spokane, Wash.
Fair Play, Parkersburg, W. Va.
The Wisconsin Advocate, Milwaukee, Wis.

Section 18. Libraries. Most of the public libraries of the South exclude Negroes, even though they pay taxes; for instance, in Atlanta there is a Carnegie public library and a branch library supported by public taxation, to which Negroes have no access. This and the natural desire for books have led to movements for Negro libraries.

In Montgomery, Ala., the Sojourner Truth Club was organized about twelve years ago by a number of young women.

It has always stood for personal improvement and for social service. It meets twice a month, having one meeting devoted to business and the other to a literary program. For a number of years its benevolences were of a general character. For the past five years the strength of the club has been given mainly to the maintenance of a Free Reading-Room and Library. The establishment of the Reading-Room grew out of the fact that our people here were refused admission to the Carnegie Library. Appeals were made, in the churches and to the citizens in general, and about three hundred dollars collected to be used for furnishings. The present rooms were rented and the doors thrown open. At first the public was invited simply to come and read; later, as books were accumulated, books were loaned for use in the home. The expense of maintaining this work is between twenty and twenty-five dollars a month. It would be more, but the rooms are open for six hours daily instead of all day. There are about five hundred volumes of good literature.

The Sojourner Truth Club also gives an annual prize for the best paper written by a student of our Junior or Senior class on a subject connected with the history of the development of the race.

Our money is raised by entertainments and contributions. In having entertainments to raise money for even so laudable an undertaking as the Reading-Room and Library, we are scrupulous as to the character of these entertainments. We seek to have them at all times uplifting and elevating. Many of the most distinguished persons of the race have come to Montgomery under the auspices of this club. Among them are Prof. Kelly Miller, Dr. W. E. B. DuBois, Mrs. Mary Church Terrell, Dr. Booker T. Washington, Mr. Joseph Douglass, Mr. Clarence White and Madame Anita Patti Brown of Chicago.

Only thirty women compose this faithful little band. They have always stood for the highest and best things in club life, and have never shirked duties because they were hard.

From Guthrie, Okla., we learn:

The colored people of Guthrie have an organization known as the Excelsior Club, which is conducting a library for the Negroes. The city has appropriated a part of the taxes for its maintenance, but since it is conducted wholly and partially supported by Negroes, it ought to be counted. It is called the Excelsior Club Library.

There is also a colored library in Dallas, Tex., and one has just been incorporated in Jacksonville, Fla.; besides this, Jacksonville has a colored department to her public library.

The number of books loaned from the colored department has increased from 5,031 in 1907 to 7,182 in 1908, an increase of 2,151. The registration has nearly doubled, being 121 in 1907 and 234 in 1908. Even with this increase, however, the use of the department is still very small when the large colored population of the city is considered. If the time should come when a separate branch library for the colored people could be conducted, we are convinced that the registration and circulation could quickly be very greatly increased. For the present, however, the finances of the library forbid this important step. In November the librarian gave an address at the Florida Baptist Academy, a colored school, on the subject "What Books are For."

The Colored Branch of the Louisville, Ky., public library says:

In outlining the library system for Louisville the Trustees wisely planned a special library for the 40,000 colored citizens. After the opening of the main library the Colored Branch came next on September 23, 1905, in temporary quarters. At the same time the Board purchased a site at Tenth and Chestnut streets, where one of the Carnegie branch buildings was erected, and opened October 29, 1908.

The new building is 77 feet long and 45 feet wide, two stories high, built of brick with some trimmings and tile roof. On the main floor near the entrance is the delivery desk and back of it are large tables with abundant space for reading and reference; to the left on entering is a newspaper alcove, an office and the special children's room; to the right is a magazine alcove, a special room for adults and a small study-room. The ground floor contains a large lecture-room, two class-rooms, and supply and boiler rooms.

Site...$ 3,180 00
Improving grounds 1,048 68
                                        ——————— $ 4,228 68
Building proper,...... .... 27,511 74
Light fixtures.. 433 55
Furniture.. 8,395 84
                                        ——————— 81,340 63
Books and periodicals 6,139 71

    Total...$41,709 02

CIRCULATION

The number of volumes drawn for home use was:
    First fiscal year... 17,888
    Second fiscal year 80,259
    Third fiscal year...... 85,910
    September 1, 1908 to May 1, 1909 89,754

    Total... 123,761

The library contains 6,882 volumes of books and 65 current magazines and periodicals, all of which are free. New books are being added constantly. The branch serves as a reference library for the colored schools. Books are distributed free, not only at the branch proper but also at various public schools.

The opening of its doors marked an epoch in the development of the race. It is the only institution of its kind in existence and has been a success from the beginning. Since its opening 123,761 volumes have been drawn for home use; of these only 38 per cent were fiction and 67 per cent were children's books. It is at present in such high favor that the Library Trustees in May 1909 voted to establish a Second Colored Branch in the eastern portion of the city.

Besides these Hampton Institute sends out Traveling Libraries, and the number sent from Atlanta University has been increased this year to twenty-five.

Section 19. Day Nurseries. We now come to a set of specialized and more scientific charities, and many of which the Negro population as a whole is just learning. There are, therefore, comparatively few examples of these among them, but the few that are arising are very significant.

The Day Nursery is a widespread and crying need among Negroes. There ought to be not only several in each city and town, but also in country districts. It is a potent field for philanthropic enterprise.

The Women's Union Day Nursery in Philadelphia is one of the most successful.

The Women's Union Day Nursery was first opened November, 1898, at 1508 Lombard street, and so is now in its tenth year. It is entirely conducted by an organization of colored women of every religious denomination. Its support has come almost entirely from our own people. The children of parents whose work calls them from home are taken care of from 6.30 a.m. to 6.30 p.m. for five (5) cents a day. They receive excellent care, and three wholesome meals are provided. All children of the proper age are sent to the kindergarten or school.

The Nursery is now located at 707 S. 19th street, this property having been recently secured by the Women's Union Missionary Society as a permanent home. Since moving into the new location, May 10th, an aggregate number of three thousand four hundred children have been cared for. The largest attendance in one day was forty.

This increase in work has made a corresponding increase in expenses, and we strongly appeal to all, particularly the church, to help to carry on this most excellent charity.

The society that carries this on has a membership of 200 and has spent about $2,000 annually. The property at 707 S. 19th street cost $4,000, and $1,000 worth of repairs put upon it. The work is purely charitable and no one in the organization receives any remuneration.

The Day Nursery in Columbus, O., on the other hand, was begun and is still supported largely by white people.

This institution was inaugurated by the Woman's Educational and Industrial Union, a corporation of Christian women (white) of this city, February 4th, 1901, in a two-story five-room frame building, at 231 N. Ohio avenue.

At the opening of the Nursery a matron and cook were employed and three children constituted their first care, which number has gradually increased until at the present time they number 58.

Realizing the necessity of some assistance from the colored people in carrying on this work, on April 19th, 1901, an auxiliary board of managers was organized among them, consisting of four members, who worked in conjunction with the white board.

Owing to the rapid growth of the institution the auxiliary board was, in 1902, increased to twelve members.

About this time it became apparent that this building was not adequate for the growth of the Nursery. As the necessity for more room and increased facilities for doing the work became evident, it was decided by the board to purchase larger quarters, which they did by securing the present quarters, a seven-room brick house, modern, with two large lots at 162 N. Ohio avenue, in the name of The Woman's Educational and Industrial Union.

In Lexington, Ky., there is a Day Nursery just beginning:

The Woman's Improvement Club has purchased a four-room cottage with nice playground, in which to begin this work. The house is now undergoing repairs, and I was so successful as to solicit the material necessary for said repairs. Lumber, paint, paper, roofing and guttering have been given. The workmen readily responded to the request to give a portion of their labor. As soon as the house is ready for use we have the promise of furniture.

The Nursery in Washington, D. C., at 69 O street, is supported almost entirely by white people.

The Nursery at Pittsburgh, Pa., reports:

Some ladies of the Baptist church have established a Day Nursery at 3211 Penn avenue, which is filling a long-felt want. They also take children temporarily, which has been a great help to the Juvenile Court work.

The Douglass Club of Austin, Tex., is seeking to establish a nursery and there are other nurseries established on Rodman street, Philadelphia, and Bainbridge street, in the Lincoln Settlement of Brooklyn, N. Y., in Richmond, Va., Athens, Ga., Louisville, Ky., and Los Angeles, Cal. There are probably a number of others unreported.

Section 20. Social Settlements. There are a few Social settlements among the Negro city populations, and considerable unorganized slum work like that of the Women's Twentieth Century League in Mobile, Ala.

The Presbyterian Colored Missions maintained by the Southern white Presbyterians of Louisville, Ky., is a specimen of settlement work. They report as follows:

The Presbyterian Colored Missions celebrated the tenth anniversary of their organization on April 14, 1907, and the work has now passed the experimental stage and is a firmly established factor for good in this community. The year which closed on March 31, 1907, was one of marked progress and some permanent results were achieved. There were more pupils enrolled, more religious services conducted, and more industrial classes instructed each week, than ever before in their history.

The average weekly attendance for the year was as follows:

	Pupils	Teachers
First quarter, April-June, 1906	445	52
Second quarter, July-Sept., 1906	427	25
Third quarter, Oct.-Dec., 1906	539	47
Fourth quarter, Jan.-Mch., 1907	677	54

The average weekly attendance for first three weeks in April, 1907, showed 744 pupils and 54 teachers.

They maintain a cooking-school, carpentry shop, sewing-school and public playgrounds. This work is supported almost entirely by Southern whites.

On San Juan Hill, New York city, a noted Negro quarter, is a missionary settlement work supported by the white Episcopalians and carried on by colored priests and workers, known as St. Cyprian's Chapel. This settlement ministers to over 1,500 families, and has a new parish house and four workers.

The new building has made it possible to assemble our congregation under healthier and more churchly conditions, and so our services have continued to grow, not only in numbers but in heartiness and reverence. With our new gymnasium, our shower baths and lockers, we have been enabled to carry out our long-cherished desire to enlarge the scope of our work among our boys and girls as well as that with young men and women of the neighborhood. For six afternoons and evenings of each week, under safe and competent instruction, our young folks are carried through exercises that will tend to give them strong and vigorous bodies. In this connection I ought to mention also the excellent work done by four young women, communicants of St. Cyprian's, as visitors, nurses, or model home-keepers in our district.

Several doctors, white and colored, meet the mothers in our rooms, and after examining the infants give talks as to their proper feeding and clothing. The New York Milk Committee has kindly supplied pure milk to such as were too poor to buy it. Some 200 children have been handled. Of this number not six died during the summer.

Four hundred and twenty girls are enrolled in cooking and sewing-schools. The cooking-school has grown into a lunchroom where poor and hungry school children and other sick folk are fed.

During the month of October 156 meals were given to the poor, while the 400 sold to school children about covered the total expenses. Once a month our young people have donation parties, at which time they bring gifts of groceries, canned goods and vegetables for the lunchroom. In the sewing-school our girls continue to make underwear and dresses which when finished are given or sold to them. Out of the sewing-school has come an industrial exchange which gives sewing to worthy women who come to us seeking employment. The garments made by these workers are sold through our Clothing Bureau, as are second-hand shoes and other clothing. We repair our shoes through our cobbling classes.

Chicago furnishes a settlement of a different type—the Frederick Douglass Center, on Wabash avenue. This work was founded by Celia Parker Woolley, and its object is stated to be: to promote a just and amicable relation between the white and colored people; to remove the disabilities of which the latter suffer in their civil, political and industrial life; to encourage equality irrespective of race, color, or other arbitrary distinction; to establish a settlement of friendly helpfulness and influence in which to gather useful information, and for mutual co-operation for the needs of right living and higher citizenship. One of the reports says:

The Frederick Douglass Center is increasingly busy on old and new lines. Its work is educational and philanthropic.

The Negro in this country suffers not only those hindrances that spring from his former enslavement, but he suffers even more from the obstacles imposed in race and caste feeling. Our treatment of the colored people in this country constitutes the greatest charge that can be made against our patriotism, our religion, our humanity. The civilized world stands aghast at the crimes committed almost daily by race hatred in this country, the most advanced civilization under the sun.

The darkest spot on our national escutcheon is race prejudice. This feeling exists in other parts of the world: in Russia against the Jew, in Great Britain against her Irish, Boer and East Indian subjects, but nowhere does this feeling find more brutal expression than with us. Nowhere is it a greater travesty on the general creed and profession than in our free republic.

This attempt to establish a center of friendly influence and co-operation between the races has met the approval of representative men and women of highest standing on both sides the color line. Its demand for the colored people is equal opportunity. Its plea to the white is for simple justice, while its labors for the moral uplift of the people in its vicinity are incessant.

The workers are both colored and white, and the activities consist of a woman's club, sewing-class, children's singing-class, study-class, an orchestra, quartette and religious services Sunday afternoon; besides this there are social meetings of colored and white people with lectures and talks. A building worth $5,500 has been bought, and no salaries are paid except to the sewing teacher, the janitor and the housekeeper.

One of the best social settlements along regular lines is the Colored Social Settlement on M street, Washington, D. C. It is conducted by colored and white people and is doing an excellent work.

In the year 1902 Mr. Charles F. Weller, former secretary of the Associated Charities of this city, founded in southwest Washington a colored social settlement. The object of this organization was to place before the neglected and unfortunate colored people such principles of industry and right living as would remove the causes of dependeñce which exists so prominently among a great number of the people in southwest Washington.

In two small meanly-provided houses situated at 116–118 M street S.W., this institution has been located since it was founded. These houses are without even water. Besides visiting the neglected homes of the unfortunate colored people of this district, teaching them morality, temperance, religion, and neatness in domestic life, this settlement maintains a day nursery where the babies of working mothers are cared for through the day, while the mother provides for house-rent and other necessities of life. We are also giving instructions in housekeeping, cooking, sewing and drawing. Again, the settlement has managed a stamp savings bank where, in the year of 1908, over a thousand dollars, mostly in pennies, were deposited by children and adults who had probably never saved a cent before: now they were learning their first lesson in thrift.

The public can little imagine the immense good this work has done for the colored people of southwest Washington, and little can they imagine the great work that yet remains to be done. The problem is a difficult one, but if the generous-hearted and Christian people of this city support us, in time the desired work will be accomplished.

At present there is under erection a sixteen room building which will better accommodate the work. And there will be carried on in this building in· addition to the industries taught at the present Settlement House, carpentry, shoe-repairing and chair-caning. A library and gymnasium will also be provided. The cost of this building is $6,000, $1,000 of which will go for the equipment. There must also be raised $200 per month for the running expenses.

As this institution is supported entirely by voluntary contributions, we must look to the public for the money with which to pay this debt and at the same time keep the work in progress.

Philadelphia has three colored settlements. The Eighth Ward Social Settlement has three residents and 22 workers.

The Starr Center, an old work, has a branch of the city library and a coal club of a thousand members who pay in over three thousand dollars a year; medical visitation, a dispensary, kindergarten, penny lunches and a savings bank. This is supported very largely by white people and most of the workers are white.

The Spring Street Settlement has both colored and white managers and workers. It has the following departments of work:

Gymnasium class for large boys, in which wholesome talks are given.

Cobbler class. To teach older boys to mend and to make shoes.

Chair-caning class. To teach younger boys to cane chairs.

Dressmaking class. For older girls.

Domestic science class. To teach girls plain house-keeping duties.

Social evenings for small boys and girls. Some preliminary work is done, after which games are played, lantern talks given, etc.

Social evenings for large girls. Same as above.

Mothers' meetings. To discuss helpful topics of home-life and care and training of children.

Savings fund.

Library.

Fuel savings fund.

First-day (Sunday) school.

Colored probation officer.

Visiting nurse. Colored trained nurse who calls on families when illness is reported and sees that medical attendance, medicines and proper diet are obtainable; also that cleanliness, ventilation, etc., are observed. Visits and assists daily or when necessary.

The Lincoln Settlement is in Brooklyn, N. Y. It has a kindergarten, day nursery, visiting-nurse, and physician. It is supported by white and colored people—the president, Miss Mary W. Ovington, being white and the head worker being colored.

The eleventh ward of Brooklyn for nearly a century has been the home of colored people, and it remains so to-day despite the encroachment of business houses. Fleet, Prince, Navy and Fair streets and Hudson avenue are largely populated by the Negro race.

Poverty dwarfs the life of this ward, and vice and crime thrive on some of its streets. Myrtle avenue has a crowd of loafers who corrupt its neighboring boys, and a decent girl avoids Hudson avenue at night. Disease breeds in the rear tenements and in the frame houses, too dilapidated to be worth repairing. Sometimes the nights are noisy with carousing, and the worthy families whom necessity forces to live with the bad, see their children in contact with much that they can not remedy but deeply deplore.

In this neighborhood, at 105 Fleet place, the Lincoln Settlement was opened in May, 1908. Its organizers hope that it will stand for a center of social service to the neighborhood, and especially to the colored people who are not reached by other philanthropic organizations.

The Flanner Guild, of Indianapolis, Ind., is a neighborhood home established about ten years ago. The properties were given to the Negroes of Indianapolis by a prominent white undertaker, Frank. W. Flanner. The first property given had on it a double house of four rooms, two on a side, which was repaired, furnished and made comfortable for the work and used for two years. The work grew so rapidly that it was necessary to have a larger building. Mr. Flanner then gave another piece of property and the building now occupied was erected. It has an office, reading-room, a large convenient kitchen, an assembly-hall with a seating capacity of two hundred; joining this building is a four-room residence.

The Guild is a charitable institution for the moral and industrial uplift of the Negro boys and girls, and is struggling and striving to do its duty in the neighborhood. In the office we have a telephone for the accommodation of the public; an employment agency is managed by the matron. The reading-room has games and literature for the children and they spend their idle hours here, and each evening from seven to nine o'clock the room is crowded.

We have a boys' club with a membership of thirty-five. On Wednesday evening of each week these boys are instructed in military drilling by Captain James Anderson.

The kitchen is large and properly equipped for the instruction of cooking classes, or the preparations of serving clubs, receptions and social gatherings.

The assembly is bright and cheerful, with a large platform and a piano. On Sunday afternoons during the winter months we have one hour's devotional service and a short program, which are usually well attended, owing to the fact that some of the best talent participate from time to time. We know that great good has been accomplished in the neighborhood. Clubs and literary societies have the privilege of using the hall at any time, and our entertainments and social gatherings are held with great satisfaction.

We have an orchestra of nine pieces under the direction and management of Mr. Smith, with Ruth E. Guthrie, aged fifteen years, as pianist. They rehearse Tuesday and Friday evenings of each week.

Sewing and millinery are taught the girls by the matron and the voluntary service of women interested in the success of the work.

The day nursery for the little tots adds much to the work; ten cents each per day furnishes lunch for them. Many mothers are compelled to work away from home, and the larger children are in school; but their minds can be at ease, for they know that their little tots are kept warm, have something to eat and are out of danger of the evils of the city.

We have a choral society with an enrollment of seventy-five, under the direction of Professor Robert Anston. This gives those musically inclined a chance to learn all the rudiments of music and voice culture.

After the present matron had been in the work about a year it was deemed necessary to open another branch of work that we might have a place to care for fallen Negro girls; there being no place in the city among the white institutions that would accommodate them. March 1, 1908, the first cottage mentioned was comfortably fitted and furnished for a maternity home. This has a sitting-room, dining-room, dormitory and kitchen. Friendless fallen girls ranging in age from 15 to 21 years are placed in this cottage, nursed and cared for until they are able to return to work.

Medical assistance is donated by the different physicians of the city. Drs. A. J. King and A. H. Wilson were the first to serve us. We also accept young girls with their little ones from the city hospital, as they are discharged in two weeks after their illness regardless of where they are to go. We encourage the girls to keep their babies, and do everything in our power to find homes for the girls and their little ones. We endeavor to surround these girls with Christian and motherly influence, with kindness and sympathy to make them feel they have friends, and though they have sinned they can be forgiven and may improve their lives by being honest Christian girls. Ten girls have been nursed in the Home and ten from the city hospital with babies have been cared for.

This work is wholly dependent upon the generosity of the public for maintenance, and so far we have been able to successfully carry it on. There is a Ladies' Board of Managers who work earnestly to help us.

A nine-room house and lot was given the Guild by Rev. Moses Dixon. This property was not convenient for the work here, it being in another locality. The board of trustees decided it best to sell this property and pay off the indebtedness of the Guild. This was done and the Guild proper is free from debt.

The county appropriates $500 each year, which is used for current expenses.

Much and lasting good has been accomplished since the establishment of this institution in this neighborhood; as the time goes on the results become more evident.

Some of the colored schools are doing settlement work. The Institutional Church of Atlanta, for instance, with its various settlement activities, has a membership composed largely of Atlanta University graduates. Atlanta Baptist College supports a Neighborhood Guild. There is a large Baptist church doing institutional work in Jacksonville, Fla. There are two settlements at Hampton, Va.

The two settlements in which the school takes an active part are located in the town of Hampton and in the country near-by. Both are in charge of resident workers who are not directly connected with the school. The former is the larger. It has a clubhouse and makes use of the home and grounds of Mrs. Harris Barrett, who founded and still carries on the work. Six girls' and women's clubs meet here—five every week and one every month. The membership is from one hundred twenty-five to one hundred fifty. They meet "to learn sewing, to do quilting, to talk about the care of the home, to cultivate the love for flowers, and to do other useful things which make for a better and happier life." Four boys' clubs with a membership of about sixty-five and a night-school with an average attendance of twelve also use the Barrett home regularly. The object of the club is to create a desire for healthful pleasures, such as singing, reading, table and athletic games. One club has a bank account of thirty dollars.

In some cases the associated charities have colored auxiliaries or workers who are doing systematic charitable work; in Harrisburg, Pa., for instance, there is a ladies' auxiliary to the Associated Charities, with 54 members and a bank account. They think of opening a social settlement.

At Columbus, O., the Associated Charities reported in 1909:

For several years past a full third of all our families have been colored families. Believing that a properly-qualified visiting agent of their own race would be more helpful in tracing out the causes of their distress and stimulating them to self-help, we secured last fall the services of Miss Bowles, whose work this past year has proven the truth of our contention beyond a doubt. We feel that this is one of the most important advances we have made during the year.

Section 21. Kindergartens. The most elaborate effort at systematic free kindergartens is that of the Gate City Free Kindergarten Association of Atlanta, Ga. Some years ago some colored people of the city started a free kindergarten association. It ran a kindergarten for two years and then getting into financial difficulties suspended. Later, at one of the Atlanta University Conferences, Miss Gertrude Ware, the white superintendent of kindergarten methods in the Atlanta University Training School, suggested a new beginning of the work. The colored women rallied again, and the result has been five free kindergartens here in operation; four of them since 1905 and the fifth started last year. The following are the figures concerning these kindergartens:

	Raised	Expended
1905-06	$ 1,043 60	$ 443 19
1906-07	689 63	950 00
1907-08	546 05	921 15
1908-09	1,089 86	1,041 00

Average attendance each kindergarten, 25 in a.m., and 15 in p.m.
Total average attendance .... 200 children
           At such times as Christmas 400 children are reached.

No aid is received from the State, although the white kindergartens receive such help.

In Columbus, Ga., on the other hand, the colored association began and supported the kindergartens, but they were eventually taken over by the city.

In Gainesville, Tex., the Women's Reading Club is about to establish a free kindergarten.

Many of the settlements, like the Lincoln Settlement, Brooklyn, the Star Centre, Philadelphia, and the Washington Settlement, have kindergartens connected with them.

In Anderson, S. C., the only club or institution doing wholly charitable work is the Thurman Kindergarten Club which has established and maintained a free kindergarten for the past seven months, paying a teacher forty dollars per month and purchasing material and furniture. The president of this club is also president of the W. C. T. U., of which the kindergarten club is an auxiliary.

The colored women of Harrisburg, Pa., are planning to establish a kindergarten and a day nursery.

It will thus be seen that the kindergarten idea is new and being developed only in a few centers.

Section 22. Civic Reform. The continued charges of criminality against the Negroes have aroused sentiment among them in many places. These charges are known to be exaggerated and unjust, but, at the same time, it is recognized that by reason of economic transition and racial prejudice it is much easier for colored boys and girls to fall into crime than for most white children. Effort, therefore, is being put forth here and there to reclaim criminals, stop crime, and spread some knowledge of civic duties. These efforts, however, are dependent for their successes very largely upon the attitude of the authorities. In the South, and especially the lower South, the colored people are almost helpless; they have few or no representatives on the police force; no influence in the police courts; no control over the jail and methods of punishment. Personal influence may do something, but, for the most part, they have to sit by and see children punished unintelligently and men and women unjustly. In the Border States and in some of the large cities of the North, however, constructive work is being done. In Johnstown, Pa., for instance:

We have a probation officer in the person of your humble servant, appointed by a Democrat judge of this county. I am a member of the Civic Club (white) and was recommended by the said club. We have several white probation officers and they wanted someone to look after the dependent colored children. All children sent by the Cambia Civic Club to the various schools, our county pays $1.50 for their board.

Pittsburgh, Pa., reports:

Our Juvenile Court Association was formed about three years ago to help care for the colored Juvenile Court children who were without friends. Heretofore we have been paying for some boys and girls in different institutions and have found private homes for many others. We have now decided to pay the salary of a probation officer instead of paying board for children in institutions, thinking that we can the better serve our race thereby. In Pittsburgh the county does not pay the salaries of probation officers, but they are paid by private organizations, clubs, etc. The Juvenile Court Association (white) pay five; the Catholics pay two; the Jews pay one, and the Colored Association pays one. The legislature now sitting in Harrisburg may pass a bill providing for the payment of the salaries and this association will provide only for the charitable end of the cases, for there is much destitution attending many cases.

Kansas City, Missouri, has the Negro Civic League, an organization composed of about forty of the leading colored men, ministers, teachers, business men, etc., devoted to the social, moral, physical, political, economic and intellectual betterment of the race. A part of the work of this civic league is extremely interesting. It has taken over a sub-organization called the "Brotherhood."

The society was formed at the request of the Board of Pardons and Paroles, with which it works as a committee on Negro cases. This Board, at the outset of its work, found it impossible to deal justly and intelligently with Negroes brought before them, because of a lack of information concerning their cases. Hence, a few of our prominent public-spirited citizens were called in and formed into a committee, whose duty should be to examine and report upon all Negro cases before action by the Board. Our committee felt a great responsibility resting upon its shoulders, in fact we feel now that we are on trial, as our attitude toward each case is scrutinized carefully, and never before has such an opportunity been given to us to protect and encourage our unfortunate masses.

To systematize and make our work efficient, the committee divided the city into fifteen districts, each having from one to five workers—members of the Brotherhood—all of whom were selected with special attention to their moral worth in the communities in which they reside. The duty of these members is to keep in close touch with the life of their districts and report upon all cases of crimes and misdemeanors or any irregularity to our executive committee of seven—five men and two women—who after due deliberation forwards its result to the Board.

The work of the Brotherhood does not end there. Each person paroled must report weekly to our secretary and tell us what he is doing, and we are to encourage him by visits and advice, keeping always in touch with him.

Up to this writing we have secured some fifteen pardons, none of whom has broken his faith with the Board. But even more, we have been able to prevent many petty cases from going on record by using our influence for a good, healthy moral tone in our districts. Disorderly houses, illicit practices and many other offenses have been checked by bringing quiet but forceful pressure to bear upon them.

There are no salaried positions and no money is solicited or required by us whatever. Each worker feels that the opportunity to do something for our more unfortunate brethren, and the opportunity of coming in contact with the best element of the white men and women of our city, is ample reward for our services.

In Baltimore the Colored Law and Order League has been waging a fight against disreputable saloons, with considerable success.[1]

---

[1] cf. Waring: Work of the Colored Law and Order League, Baltimore, Md. Cheney, Pa., 1910.

Springfield, Ill., has a Law and Order League formed since the disgraceful race riot.

In various Southern States there have been efforts to establish reformatories. In Richmond, Va., a colored man, the Hon. John R. Smythe, formed a Negro Reformatory Association.

He secured subscriptions and laid his plans before the Prison Association of Virginia and received their endorsement. He then organized and incorporated the Negro Reformatory Association of Virginia, of which he was president until his death. With the money obtained by his efforts from philanthropists, north and south, the association purchased 405 acres of the old plantation known as Broad Neck Farm. The remaining 1,200 acres was later purchased by Mr. C. P. Huntington and leased to my father for the use of the school.

In 1898 the school was started with six boys from the penitentiary pardoned by the Governor, and committed to the institution for the remainder of their terms. The State then made an appropriation for the support of 100 boys at 83 cents per day for clothing and 25 cents per day for board. Out of this annual income, together with subscriptions, my father was able to clear up the land, build dormitories, start farming operations on a large scale, and pay all the employees, about 14 in number.

The work of the school has been excellent from a moral standpoint. The percentage of lapses into former errors have been, I believe, less than ten per cent. These lapses have been mostly among the older boys. The work carried on at the Reformatory is mostly agricultural. It was my father's hope to ultimately establish a first-class trades school, but as yet it has been impossible to start this school with the limited means at the command of the institution.

In Alabama, as has been noted, the State Federation of Women's Clubs opened a Negro Reformatory at Mt. Meigs, and has been supporting it, hoping for eventual State aid.

In Arkansas the Women's Clubs have done a similar piece of work.

In Georgia there have been several small reformatories started. One in Macon reports:

We are styled the Delaney Mission and Reformatory Club. We were organized February 19, 1906, with five members, and have now an enrollment of over sixty. The Reformatory which we help to support is situated three miles from the city of Macon. It is an institution for wayward boys and girls. The school is not a denominational school, but its founders and chief supporters are Baptist ministers and the laymen of their churches. We meet once a week and put our little mites together, and by that means we have been able since we were organized to raise in actual cash $375 for the Reformatory, part of which we gave to the Convention to be used for erecting a large building at the Home and with the other we bought a buggy for them and a cow and paid for both. We have given them aid aside from the things mentioned above, by way of clothing and food, giving picnics, etc.

The Johnson's Orphanage of Macon, Ga., and the Carrie Steele Orphanage of Atlanta, Ga., are partially reformatory; the latter is aided by the City of Atlanta.

The National Association of Colored Women's Clubs has been interested in juvenile work in various parts of the country.

The Unity Political Club of Haverhill, Mass., aims
"to encourage political, economic and educational activity among colored
citizens of Essex county." This club has only been organized nine months.
It is pledged to no one party, but is simply pledged to the good of the city
and State and race.

In Paducah, Ky., there was a movement in this line:

The Forum movement was begun in our town, but everything is dormant
at present. I was connected with a similar movement in Bowling Green, Ky.
The Forum there had an interesting career of four or five years, bringing the
colored people together monthly for the discussion of vital matters incident
to our race life, working up a spirit of racial co-operation, and culminating in
the opening of a grocery which did a creditable business. I should mention
also that through the agency of the Forum the city council abolished certain
nuisances repugnant to the better element of our people.

While I have been active in the above mentioned organizations, yet the
idea came to us (as well as I can remember) from Chicago and Kansas City,
Kan.

The following extract from a set of resolutions show the purpose of the
Organization:

"Further be it resolved, that we organize ourselves into a body to be styled
"The Forum," which shall meet monthly, on a Sunday afternoon convenient
to the coming together of all the congregations of our city churches, and
whose object shall be to take constant note of the conditions and needs of our
people; to allow opportunity for free and open discussion of these conditions
and needs; and to take such steps and measures, and to initiiate such enterprises and movements, as will promote the religious, moral, educational, civic
and temporal welfare of our people."

In Lynchburg, Va., there is a Civic League, and also one in Washington, D. C.:

The Civic Club of Washington, D. C., was organized about five years ago. As
its name implies, its scope is civic rather than charitable. Like all other
organizations among the colored people of whatever kind, it has shown a
lively interest in matters pertaining especially to the race. We have endeavored to oppose and remedy the discrimination that is shown in nearly all
public places in this city against colored people. We have accomplished very
little on account of the lack of suffrage. We have no building, but meet at
the homes of members.

The Equal Suffrage League of the National Association of Colored
Women has sent out literature and circulated petitions.

Section 23. Miscellaneous. Among miscellaneous efforts which
may be noted are boys' clubs, summer camps, and efforts at securing
work, humane bands and tuberculosis leagues.

There is a Boys' Club in Indianapolis, Ind., and in Louisville, Ky., a
society for the reclamation and improvement of newsboys.

The Boys' Culture Club of St. Paul, Minn., reports:

The Boys' Culture Club of St. Paul, Minn., was organized in January, 1904.
The object of this club is to promote a feeling of brotherhood among its members, to teach them the principles of honest, intelligent self-government, to
encourage good citizenship among them; also to be directed in Physical Cul-

ture, that they may become strong, mental and physical men. During which time we have given several literary, gymnastic and athletic entertainments, among which we have given three annual, gymnastic and athletic expositions, in 1907, 1908 and 1909, respectively. We also have baseball, football and basket-ball teams in connection with the club. Each of the teams have made good records during the four years they have been playing. Neither team has lost more than two games out of the season.

The Wissahickon School Club, conducted by white people near Philadelphia for Negroes, has manual training class, out-door athletics, lectures and entertainments, and spends over $1,000 a year; some 4,500 boys attend its various functions.

The Empty Stocking and Fresh Air School of Baltimore has a summer home for poor colored children.

The Summer Outing Home of Washington, D. C., maintains a camp of about 1500 children at a cost of $650. This enterprise was supported by white and colored people.

The Woman's Employment Company of Indianapolis, Ind., maintains a Summer Camp for the sick, and the Lincoln Settlement of Brooklyn has summer outings.

In the line of increasing opportunities for employment there are numbers of benevolent efforts, among which might be mentioned the Farmer's Conference at Hampton and Tuskegee, the Georgia State College, Calhoun and other places, and the Farmer's Union at Waugh, Ala.

There are two or three women's exchanges. one in Richmond, Va.

In New York and Philadelphia, through the Armstrong Association, there is a special effort to secure opportunities for competent Negro artisans to work; money and advice for this has been furnished by white and colored contributors. The actual work has been done by Negro executive officers. In Philadelphia, for instance, there was reported in 1908:

SUMMARY OF NINE MONTHS' WORK

Number of jobs given up to date since April, 1908	85
Number of men employed through such jobs	81
Amount of cash of such jobs, material and all, about	$ 17,500
Number of jobs estimated on since April, 1908, i. e., over $500 or in which there was a competitor, or in which an estimate was especially asked for by patron	46
Amount of cash in such, about	$133,000
Jobs given to colored architects	4
Number of meetings held by Carpenters' Association	20
Number of meetings held by General Association	16
Manual training introduced in three public schools.	
Public meetings held in churches	4

The following is an outline of the work of the Armstrong Association for the colored people of Philadelphia from April, 1908, to January 1, 1909.

The chief work of the Association has been to secure work for competent colored mechanics, and thus to help them help themselves. Up to date nearly $18,000 worth of work has been secured. More than 80 different men have thus been helped. The jobs ranged from 75 cents to $3,000. As a direct result of the Association's activity, more colored mechanics are at work this winter than any winter before in this city. For every dollar which has been spent by the Association for this branch of its activity, twenty dollars have come to the men whom it is designed to help. Among those from whom work has been secured are Mr. J. Henry Scattergood, Mr. John T. Emlen, Miss Ellen Morris, the Octavia Hill Association, the City of Philadelphia, Herman Voigt, Frank I. Wintz, contractors, and others. Many jobs have come from the colored people themselves. Opportunities to bid have been given by Savery, Scheetz & Savery, Bailey & Bassett and other architects.

The Association especially urges upon its patrons to assist in this feature of the work by permitting its mechanics to estimate on their work, thus helping the colored people to help themselves. The Association has as its members an ex-foreman on Panama canal work, a half dozen men who worked on the Rockefeller Hall, Bryn Mawr College, and on the University of Chicago, two foremen who worked on the well-equipped Rockefeller barn, Long Island; a former instructor in Tuskegee Institute, and another in Clark University; also graduates from various industrial schools, including Hampton and Tuskegee. Only first-class mechanics will be recommended.

Equally as good work has been accomplished by the Armstrong Association of New York.

There has been some effort to organize Humane Bands to teach children humanity in the care of animals, etc. In New Orleans, for instance, there are reported 47 such bands with 5,300 children connected with them.

Encouragement to buy homes is furnished in California by the Home Promoters' Association.

The recent agitation about tuberculosis has resulted in a number of anti-tuberculosis societies.

There is an anti-tuberculosis league in Georgia with headquarters at Savannah, and one in Washington, D. C.:

Our society was organized November 11, 1908. A recent report of the Health Officer of this District contained such appalling figures with regard to the death-rate among colored people that in the eyes of many it amounted to an actual stigma on the race. In connection with many other observing persons, however, Dr. Wilder considers this death-rate due not so much to constitutional weakness as to unhygienic housing, natural carelessness, and lack of sanitary information. This he proposed to remedy by the formation of a society to conduct an educational campaign among the people in need of it. Necessarily our work is conducted mostly among colored people; more than 2,000 having been reached by lectures and house to house visits alone.

We have also very pleasant relations with "The Society for the Prevention of Tuberculosis," some of its members having visited our society during the progress of an entertainment and one of whom addressed us.

Our members are: first, honorary, which include all the pastors in the city who will accept membership, together with such men as Commissioner McFarland, the late Dr. Reyburn and President Thirkield of Howard University; second, any one who will join. The names on the Board of Directors and Chairmanships show you the class of persons who are doing the work.

We are supported by voluntary contributions and entertainments.

We give a pledge for framing and a neat little button to all who join.

Section 24. Conclusion. From this general and very imperfect review of efforts for social betterment among Negro Americans it is clear that the evolution is in the right direction and that Colored people are more and more largely becoming interested in practical work for their own social uplift and are also to an increasing extent bearing the cost of this work., The most obvious criticisms and suggestions would be:

(1) A hope that the Negro church will in the future become more and more institutional and reformatory, and will call to its aid trained social workers. There are some small beginnings in this line already and they need encouragement.

(2) The economic foundation of the Negro school should be changed and changed quickly. To-day it rests partly on public aid, partly on the local efforts of Negro patrons, partly on general charity, and to a very small extent upon endowments. It should rest on general local taxation, aided by grants of the National Government. Higher cultural and technical work should be supplied by National and State aid and endowments. This would free the benevolent public from the burden of Negro schools and also the Negro churches and organizations, and would enable the benevolence of black and white alike to be directed toward the pressing need of social reform in all the various lines indicated in this study.

(3) The work of women's clubs has been tremendous, both in its actual accomplishments and in its educational value. These clubs should be greatly multiplied and especially encouraged to take up local benevolent work.

(4) Old folk's homes, orphanages and hospitals are greatly needed. So far as possible orphanages should be made places of temporary detention only, and homes for the children obtained in good families. There is a pressing call for the spread of hospital work in country districts.

(5) The work of rescue among women and children especially and also among men and boys is greatly needed, particularly among city Negroes, and has been neglected too long.

(6) In the direction of art and literature much can be done which has not been done for Negroes. It is difficult for the people of America to understand that the Negro is essentially an artistic being, whose rich emotional nature can be made to contribute much to the world's enjoyment and appreciation of beauty. To this end greater opportunity in drawing and music and other art-training should be opened to Negro children.

(7) Day nurseries, social settlements and kindergartens, together with other of the newer forms of uplift work, like public play-grounds, should be furnished for the right training of the black workingman's children to a much larger extent than now. In fact, in these lines, only the beginnings of work can be noted.

(8) While something can be accomplished by organizations for civic reform among Negroes themselves, yet so long as the race is deprived of the ballot it is impossible to make such organizations of the highest efficiency in any avenue of life, whether it be education, religion, work, or social reform; the impossibility of the Negro accomplishing the best work so long as he is kept in political serfdom is manifest even to the casual student.

There would seem to be for the philanthropists no more inviting field for work than in helping on some of the efforts for social uplift which Negroes have instituted and are carrying on.

Efforts for Social Betterment among Negro Americans

Index

The Atlanta University Publications, No. 15

THE
COLLEGE-BRED
NEGRO AMERICAN

Report of a Social Study made by Atlanta University
under the patronage of the Trustees of the John F.
Slater Fund; with the Proceedings of the 15th Annual
Conference for the Study of the Negro Problems, held
at Atlanta University, on Tuesday, May 24th, 1910

Edited by

W. E. Burghardt Du Bois, Ph.D.
*Director of Publicity and Research, National Association for
the Advancement of Colored People*

and

Augustus Granville Dill, A.M.
Associate Professor of Sociology in Atlanta University

The Atlanta University Press
ATLANTA, GA.
1910

A LL that a man does outwardly is but the expression and completion of his inward thot. To work effectually, he must think clearly; to act nobly, he must think nobly. Intellectual force is a principal element of the soul's life, and should be proposed by every man as the principal end of his being.

—*Channing.*

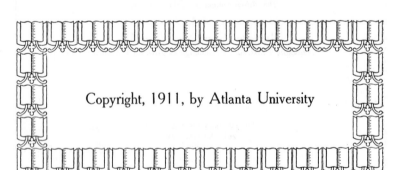

The College=bred Negro American

Contents

The Fifteenth Annual Conference

The Higher Education of Negro Americans

PROGRAM

First Session, 10:00 a. m.
(Ware Memorial Chapel)

President E. T. Ware presiding.
Subject: "Relation of Higher Education to Other Kinds of Training."
Address: President J. H. Dillard of the Jeanes Fund.

Second Session, 11:30 a. m.

Subject: "Education and Health."
For women: Ware Memorial Chapel.
For men: Room 13, Stone Hall.

Third Session, 3:15 p. m.

Thirteenth Annual Mothers' Meeting. (In charge of the Gate City Free Kindergarten Association.) Mrs. David T. Howard presiding.
Subject: "The Education of the Child."

1. Kindergarten songs, games and exercises by 125 children of the five free kindergartens.
2. Address: Report of the year's work in each school—Mrs. John Rush.
3. Explanation of Kindergarten Exhibit—Miss Minetta Sammis.
4. Report of Treasurer—Mrs. Lizzie Burch.
5. Collection.

Fourth Session, 8:00 p. m.

President E. T. Ware presiding.
Subject: "The College-bred Negro American."
Short addresses by presidents and representatives of Negro colleges.
Stereopticon exhibit of Higher Education.

Special Sessions
(Suite 16, Stone Hall. Admission by invitation only.)

8:00-10:00 a. m.

"Methods and Results of the Present Investigation." Dr. DuBois, of Atlanta University, in charge.

11:00 a. m.-1:00 p. m.

"The Need and Supply of Negro College Students." President Kumler, of Walden University, presiding.

1:30-3:30 p. m.

"The Curriculum of Negro Colleges." President Gates, of Fisk University, presiding.

4:00-6:00 p. m.

"The Financial Support of Negro Colleges." President Dunton, of Claflin University, presiding.

Preface

In 1900 the Atlanta University Negro Conference made an investigation of the college graduates among Negro Americans. The study received widespread publicity and did much towards clearing up misapprehension in regard to educated colored people.

Ten years later we return to the same investigation aided by an appropriation of $1,000 from the Trustees of the John F. Slater Fund. The results are based on college catalogs, letters of officials and the reports of 800 Negro graduates. This is, therefore, far from an exhaustive study, but it has much value.

This study is, therefore, a further carrying out of the Atlanta University plan of social study of the Negro American, by means of an annual series of decennially recurring subjects covering, so far as is practicable, every phase of human life. The object of these studies is primarily scientific—a careful research for truth, conducted as thoroly, broadly and honestly as the material resources and mental equipment at command will allow. It must be remembered that mathematical accuracy in these studies is impossible; the sources of information are of varying degrees of accuracy and the pictures are wofully incomplete. There is necessarily much repetition in the successive studies, and some contradiction of previous reports by later ones as new material comes to hand. All we claim is that the work is as thoro as circumstances permit and that with all its obvious limitations it is well worth the doing. Our object is not simply to serve science. We wish not only to make the truth clear but to present it in such shape as will encourage and help social reform.

Our financial resources are unfortunately meager: Atlanta University is primarily a school and most of its funds and energy go to teaching. It is, however, also a seat of learning and as such it has endeavored to advance knowledge, particularly in matters of racial contact and development, which seem obviously its nearest field. In this work it has received unusual encouragement from the scientific world, and the published results of these studies are used in America, Europe, Asia and Africa. Very few books on the Negro problem, or any phase of it, have been published in the last decade which have not acknowledged their indebtedness to our work.

On the other hand, the financial support given this work has been very small. The total cost of the fifteen publications has been about $17,000, or a little over $1,000 a year. The growing demands of the work, the vast field to be covered and the delicacy and equipment needed in such work, call for far greater resources. We need, for workers, laboratory and publications, a fund of $6,000 a year, if this work is going adequately to fulfill its promise. Three years ago a small temporary grant from the Carnegie Institution of Washington, D. C., greatly helped us; and for three years our work has been saved from suspension by an appropriation from the John F. Slater Fund.

In past years we have been enabled to serve the United States Bureau of Labor, the United States Census, the Board of Education of the English Government, many scientific associations, professors in nearly all the leading universities, and many periodicals and reviews. May we not hope in the future for such increased financial resources as will enable us to study adequately this the greatest group of social problems that ever faced America?

Resolutions of the Fifteenth Atlanta Conference

1. There is an increased and pressing demand for college trained Negroes.
2. The Negro graduates are at present, with few exceptions, usefully and creditably employed.
3. The course of study in these colleges does not call for any peculiar modification, but should, on the whole, conform to the general type of curriculum designed for the preparation of broadly educated men to take their places in modern civilization.
4. There should be at least one college for Negro students in each state, liberally endowed.
5. There should be every effort towards co-operation between colleges in the same locality, and towards avoidance of unnecessary duplication of work.
6. We believe that Negro public high schools in the South are greatly needed.
7. We believe in perfect honesty in living up to catalog requirements of admission.
8. We believe the amount of Greek and Latin in college should be gradually reduced.
9. We believe that time given to Natural Science, English, History and Sociology should be increased.
10. We believe that vocational training is a pressing need of Negroes but that it should be preceded by as much cultural training as possible.

President John Hope, Atlanta Baptist College.
President E. T. Ware, Atlanta University.
Dr. W. E. B. DuBois, Atlanta University.
Prof. B. W. Valentine, Benedict College.
President W. E. Holmes, Central City College.
President L. M. Dunton, Claflin University.
President W. H. Crogman, Clark University.
President George A. Gates, Fisk University.
Dean L. B. Moore, Howard University.
Mr. H. S. Dunbar, Paine College.
President Lucy Hale Tapley, Spelman Seminary.
President J. M. P. Metcalf, Talladega College.
Rev. A. W. Partch, Tougaloo University.
President John Kumler, Walden University.
Chaplain T. G. Stewart, Wilberforce University.

A Select Bibliography of Higher Education for Negro Americans

Part I

Arranged alphabetically by authors

Archer, William. Through Afro-America. New York, 1910.

Atlanta University Publications, The. The College-bred Negro. Atlanta, 1900 (1902), 115 (33) pp. 8vo.

Beard, A. F. A Crusade of Brotherhood. Boston and New York, 1909. 334 pp.

Brousseau, Kate. L' education des Negres aux Etats Unis. Paris, 1904. xvi, 396 (1) pp. 8vo.

Bruce, Roscoe Conkling. Service by the Educated Negro. Tuskegee, 1903, 17 pp. 12mo.

Bumstead, Horace. Higher Education of the Negro—its practical Value. Atlanta, 1870. 15 pp. 24 mo.

Corey, Chas. H. A History of the Richmond Theological Seminary. Richmond, 1895. 240 pp. 12mo.

Crummell, Alexander. The attitude of the American mind toward the Negro intellect. Washington, 1898. 12 pp.

Curry, J. L. M. Difficulties, complications and limitations connected with the education of the Negro. Baltimore, 1895. 23 pp. 8vo. J. F. Slater Fund papers.

Curry, J. L. M. Education of Negroes since 1860. Baltimore, 1890. 32 pp. 8vo. J. F. Slater fund papers.

Douglass, H. P. Christian Reconstruction in the South. Boston, 1909. 407 pp.

DuBois, W. E. B. The Souls of Black Folk. Chicago, 1903. viii (1), 264 (1) pp. 8vo.

Easton, Hosea. A treatise on the intellectual character and condition of the colored people of the United States. Boston, 1837. 54 pp. 8vo.

Eaton, John. Report of freedmen's schools for 1864-1865. (Contained in report of the General Superintendent of Freedmen. Department of the states of Tennessee and Arkansas. 1864-5.)

Goodwin, M. B. History of schools for the colored population in the District of Columbia. U. S. Bureau of Education. Special report on District of Columbia for 1869. Pp. 193-300.

Gregoire, H. Enquiry concerning the intellectual and moral faculties, etc., of Negroes. Brooklyn, 1810. 253 pp. 8vo.

Hartshorn, W. N. An Era of Progress and Promise. Boston, 1910. 576 pp.

Haygood, Atticus Green. Our Brother in Black, etc. New York, 1881. 252 pp. 12mo.

Haygood, Atticus Green. The case of the Negro, as to education in the southern states, etc. Atlanta, 1885. 59 pp. 8vo.

Lovinggood, R. S. Why *hic, haec, hoc* for the Negro? Marshall, Tex., 1900. 56 pp. 16 mo.

Mayo, Amory Dwight. How shall the colored youth of the South be educated? Boston, 1897. (1), 213-224 pp. 8vo.

Mayo, Amory Dwight. Northern and Southern women in the education of the Negro in the South. U. S. Bureau of Education. Circular of Information, No. 1, p. 71. 1892.

Mayo, Amory Dwight. The opportunity and obligation of the educated class of the colored people in the Southern states. N. p., 1899 (?). 32 pp. 8vo.

Miller, Kelly. Race Adjustment. New York and Washington, 1908. 306 pp.

Miller, Kelly. The Education of the Negro. Washington, 1902. U. S. Bureau of Education Reports, 1900-01. Vol. I, pp. 731-859.

Mitchell, E. C. Higher Education and the Negro. N. p., 1896. 19 pp. 12mo.

Negro Young People's Christian and Educational Congress, Atlanta, 1902. 600 pp. 8vo. The United Negro. Atlanta, 1902.

Richings, G. F. Evidences of Progress among Colored People. ——, 1896.

United States Bureau of Education. Education of the colored race. Negroes in America. Washington, 1896. (In report of Commissioner for 1893-94. Vol. I, 1038-1061 pp.)

United States Bureau of Education. Education of the colored race. Washington, 1901. Report 1899-1900.

United States Bureau of Education. Education of the colored race. Washington, 1902. Report 1900-1901.

Wright, Richard R. Brief Historical Sketch of Negro Education in Georgia. Savannah, Ga., 1894. 58 pp. 8vo.

Part II. Periodical Literature

American Journal of Social Science:
Higher education of Negroes. H. L. Wayland. 34:68.
Present problem of the education of Negroes. W. H. Baldwin. 37:52.
Education of Negroes. C. D. Warner. 38:1.
Education of Negroes. K. Miller. 39:117.

American Negro Academy: Occasional Papers.
No. 3. (a) Civilization the primal need of the race. (b) The attitude of the American mind toward the Negro intellect. Alexander Crummell.
No. 8. The educated Negro and his mission. W. S. Scarborough.

Atlantic:
Education of Negroes. W. T. Harris. 69:721.

Training of black men. W. E. B. DuBois. 90:289-97.
Charities Review:
Atlanta University Conferences. W. E. B. DuBois. 10:435.
Dial:
Function of the Negro college. K. Miller. 32:267.
Education:
Education of Negroes. C. G. Andrews. 6:221.
Training of the Negro teacher. N. B. Young. 21:359.
Educational Review:
Education of the Negro in its historical aspects. D. L. Kiehle. 27:299.
Forum:
Negro and higher learning. W. S. Scarborough. 33,349.
Gunton's Magazine:
Atlanta: the center of Negro education of the world. M. G. Anderson. 25:433-41.
Independent:
Negro graduates. 53:1147-8.
Education of white and black. E. A. Alderman. 53:2647-9.
Higher education for the colored youth. A. F. Hilger. 54:1500-2.
Missionary Review:
What intellectual training is doing for the Negro. W. E. B. DuBois. 27:578-82.
Nation:
Education of Negroes of the South. 24:276.
Higher education for the colored youth. 74:381.
South and the educated Negro. 76:324.
Educated Negro and the South. 78:143.
National Quarterly Review:
Intellectual position of the Negro. R. T. Greener. 41:164.
New England Magazine:
Education of Negroes. A. D. Mayo. 17:213.
North American Review:
Education and civilization of freedmen. E. E. Hale. 101:528.
Negro intellect. W. Matthew. 149:91.
Will education solve the race problem? J. R. Straton. 170:785-801.
Outlook:
Training of Negroes for social power. W. E. B. DuBois. 75:409-14.
Popular Science Monthly:
Higher education for the colored youth. A. F. Hilger. 57:437-8.
Slater Fund, Proceedings and Occasional Papers of the:
No. 3. Curry: Education of Negroes since 1860.
No. 5. Curry: Difficulties connected with education of Negroes.
Southern Literary Messenger:
Capabilities of Negroes. W. H. Holcombe. 33:401.
Spectator:
Capacity of Negroes. 75:927.

THE COLLEGE=BRED NEGRO

Section 1. Scope of the Inquiry

In 1900 Atlanta University made a study of the colored colleges in the United States and colored graduates of them and other colleges. Ten years later we come back to the same study, made essentially on the same plan.

The first work was to determine which of the Negro institutions were to be considered colleges. This was done by testing the entrance requirements of these institutions according to the "Carnegie units," i. e. the units of work laid down by the Carnegie Foundation for the Advancement of Teaching.

The next work was to correspond with the colleges of the land and find out the number of colored graduates. This gave only approximate results as the color was not always a matter of record.

Finally a list of living colored college graduates was obtained and a blank with the following questions was sent them.

DEAR SIR or MADAME:

The Atlanta University Conference is repeating this year the inquiry made into the work and condition of college-bred Negro Americans, which it made first in 1900. This study was used, quoted and read all over the world, and the present study will be equally in demand.

I ask your earnest and prompt co-operation. Please fill out and return the enclosed blank immediately. All answers are strictly confidential.

THE COLLEGE-BRED NEGRO AMERICAN, 1910

1. No . . .   2. Sex . . . .   3. Address . . . .
4. Born in (State and place) . . . . in the year . . .
5. Single, married, widowed or divorced . . . . ; year of marriage . . . .
6. Number of children: living . . ; dead (including still born) . .
7. Early life and training.
8. Education (school, college, professional school, etc.)
9. Honorary degrees.
10. Occupation since graduation, with terms of service.
11. Membership in learned societies.
12. Publications: Essays and books.
13. Public offices held, and political activity.
14. Activity in charitable work and work of social reform.
15. Amount of land owned.
16. Assessed value of real estate, land and houses.

17. Total property owned (market value—confidential).
18. How shall you educate your children?
19. What have been your chief hinderances?
20. Briefly, what is your present practical philosophy in regard to the Negro race in America?

About 800 answers to these blanks were received.

Section 2. The Negro College

The first annual report of the President and Treasurer of the Carnegie Foundation for the Advancement of Teaching lays down the following standard requirements for admission to college: at least fourteen units, "a unit being a course of five periods weekly throughout the academic year of the preparatory school. For the purposes of the Foundation the units in each branch of academic study have also been quantitatively defined, the aim being to assign values to the subjects in accordance with the time usually required to prepare adequately upon them for college entrance."

The fourth annual report suggests as a statement that a unit "represents a year's study in any subject in a secondary school, constituting approximately a quarter of a full year's work." This statement assumes "a well ordered high school course" and "limits to four units the amount of credit possible to attain within a given year."

In accordance with this we may arrange the following tables of Negro colleges. In these tables students are graded according to work done. If, for instance, a student has finished the 12th grade and is studying regularly in the institution he is counted as Freshman College, altho he may be in the Normal school. Professional students are not included in these tables.

FIRST GRADE COLORED COLLEGES

(14 or more units of entrance requirements and more than 20 students of college rank).

1. Howard 238		7. Clark 35
2. Fisk 117		8. Knoxville 29
3. Atlanta 78		9. Spelman 27
4. Wiley 50		10. Claflin 23
5. Leland 43		11. Atlanta Baptist . 22
6. Virginia Union . . 36		

SECOND GRADE COLORED COLLEGES

(12 to 14 units of entrance requirements and over 20 students).

12. Lincoln 132
13. Talladega 30
14. Wilberforce . . . 19

OTHER COLORED COLLEGES

(A)   Those with 14 or more units of entrance requirements, but 20 or fewer students.

15. Lane 20
16. G. R. Smith . . . 20
17. State, Louisville,
    Ky. 18
18. Bishop 18
19. Walden 16
20. New Orleans . . . 15

21. Bennett 13
22. Morgan 10
23. Straight   9
24. Lincoln Institute .   4
25. Hartshorn   3
26. Miles Memorial .   2

(B)   Those with less than 12 units of entrance requirements and more than 20 students.

27. Shaw 51
28. Benedict 36

(C)   Colleges with less than 12 units of entrance requirements and few college students.

29. Morris Brown . . . 20
30. Paine 7

31. Langston 6
32. So. Carolina State . 3

To these we may append the rank of the best industrial schools:

9-12 units.

Kentucky (Frankfort)
A. & M. College (N. C.)
Hampton (Va.)
Tallahassee (Fla.)

Princess Anne (Md.)
Prairie View (Tex.)
Institute (W. Va.)

4-6 units.

Tuskegee (Ala.)

Pine Bluff (Ark.)

The standard of the leading colored colleges, as shown in the above groupings, may be compared with that of the leading white colleges of the South.

Institution	Requirements for admission in units, 1907-8[1]
University of North Carolina	14.7
West Virginia University	14.3
Randolph-Macon College	14
Trinity College	14
University of Georgia	12
University of Virginia	11.5[2]
University of South Carolina	11.2
Washington and Lee University	11
University of Alabama	10.5
Roanoke College	7.5

[1] Third Annual Report of the President and Treasurer of the Carnegie Foundation, pp. 92, 93.   [2] In 1909, 14.5 units.

The date of founding and the number of students in Negro colleges appear in the following table. Where there are several courses, such as college, normal, academic, etc., the students are all classified according to the grade of work which is being done:

1909—

TABLE GIVING DATE OF ESTABLISHMENT OF COLLEGE DEPT.,

INSTITUTION	LOCATION	Date of establishment of college department	Number students in college classes							Number students in high school					
			Graduate	Senior	Junior	Sophomore	Freshman	Special	Total	12th	11th	10th	9th	Special	Total
1. Miles Memorial College	Birmingham, Ala.	1907		1		1			2	1	11	12	14		38
2. Talladega College	Talladega, Ala.	1885		7	6	7	5	5	30	18	12	31	55		116
3. Howard University	Washington, D.C.	1868	1	35	35	46	82	39	238	46	58	113	167	18	402
4. Atlanta Baptist College	Atlanta, Ga.	1890		2	8	7	5		22	14	10	9	23		56
5. Atlanta University	Atlanta, Ga.	1872	2	6	10	15	43	2	78	35	48	70	145		298
6. Morris Brown College	Atlanta, Ga.	1894			8	12			20	28	31	37	49		145
7. Spelman Seminary	Atlanta, Ga.	1897		1	2	12	12		27	11	12	26	56		105
8. Paine College	Augusta, Ga.	1888			3	1	3		7	21	28	29	30		108
9. Clark University	South Atlanta, Ga.	1879		4	8	2	21		35	9	29	43	71		152
10. State University	Louisville, Ky.			2	2		13	1	18	12	18	27	43		100
11. Leland University	New Orleans, La.	1870	24		4	3	2	10	43	15	9	15	31		70
12. New Orleans University	New Orleans, La.	1874		5	2	1	7		15	10	19	33	63		125
13. Straight University	New Orleans, La.	1869	4				5		9	12	9	15	40	10	86
14. Morgan College	Baltimore, Md.	1884			3	2	5		10	17	16	15	19		67
15. Lincoln Institute	Jefferson City, Mo.	1890			2				4	57	49	36	71		213
16. Geo. R. Smith College*	Sedalia, Mo.	1898				5	15		20	20	38	28	45	6	137
17. Bennett College	Greensboro, N.C.				5	3	5		13	8	14	16	29		67
18. Shaw University*	Raleigh, N.C.	1870			8	11	18	14	51	16			27		43
19. Wilberforce University	Wilberforce, O.	1856	a												
20. Col. A. & M. College*	Langston, Okla.				2	1	3		6	2	8	22	26	4	62
21. Lincoln University	Lincoln Univ., Pa.	1864		28	30	45	29		132						
22. Benedict College	Columbia, S.C.	1894	2	5	4	12	13		36	48	40	61	32		181
23. Claflin University	Orangeburg, S.C.	1878		6	1	1	15		23	42	40	52	56	24b	214
24. S. C. State College	Orangeburg, S.C.	1896		3					3	24	32	39	43		138
25. Lane College	Jackson, Tenn.	1900		2	3	6	9		20	25	6	19	44	1	95
26. Knoxville College	Knoxville, Tenn.	1877		5	4	9	11		29	29	24	36	32	25	146
27. Fisk University	Nashville, Tenn.	1871	6	20	28	20	43		117	42	47	39	58	1	187
28. Walden University	Nashville, Tenn.	1873		3		7	3	3	16	17	18	29	76	19	159
29. Bishop College	Marshall, Tex.			4	4	4	6		18	18	23	25	55		121
30. Wiley University	Marshall, Tex.			11	9	13	17		50	19	35	35	34	2	125
31. Hartshorn Mem. Col.	Richmond, Va.	1892			1	1	1		3	3	5	8	15		31
32. Virginia Union Univ.	Richmond, Va.	1898	1	8	5	8	14		36	23	23	42	21		109
Total			40	162	189	245	432	64	1131	642	722	962	1470	110	3896

*Catalog 1908-9.

aExact information unobtainable.

bIncluding 7 taking "Special Courses" and 17 in Business College (Catalog p. 79).

-1910
WITH THE NUMBER OF STUDENTS BY CLASSES AND GRADES

				Number students in grades						Profes-sional	Indus-trial	Music	Total in whole school
8th	*7th*	*6th*	*5th*	*4th*	*3rd*	*2nd*	*1st*	*Special*	*Total*				
21	33	24	38	20	18	13	12		179			49	268
38	54	57	75	73	73	72	42	70c	554	28			728
										592			1232
25	26	31	24					1	107	38			223
													376
41	52	62	84	81	77	79	85		561	39			765
45	59	64	89	51	54	40	25	16d	443	28	43	2	648
35	41	37	18	15				1	147	16			278
48	55	54	41	27	32	13	11	9	290				477
21	11								32	8			158
17	44	32	40	48	16	7	4	2	210	26			349
38	34	64	55	59	44	29	37	22e	382	2	1		525
39	48	72	85	79	96	56	58	20f	548			6	649
													77
72	34	43	10					29	188				405
22	15	2	5	2	1				47				204
28	29	53		21	9	2	8		150				230
69	69	75	29						242	206	19	4	565
67	45	42	115					4	273		26		367
										62			194
44	52	94	31	45	40	26	41		373	57			647
48	48	57	71	81	73	23	7	103g	511				748
50	92	88	81	79	65				455		6		602
24	50	53							127	42			284
38	28	35	24	38	17	6	11		197	8	29		409
11	14	13	12	12	8	10	9		89		13	51	457
45	32	19	18						114	402	2		693
54	34	22							110				249
54	54	61	65	42	30			35	341	22			538
28	23	32	39					3	125				159
21	29								50	26			221
1043	1100	1186	1049	773	653	376	350	315	6845	1602	139	112	13725

cThirty-five in night schools and 35 in kindergarten.
dStudents in night school.
eStudents in night school.
fStudents in kindergarten.
gIn afternoon free school.

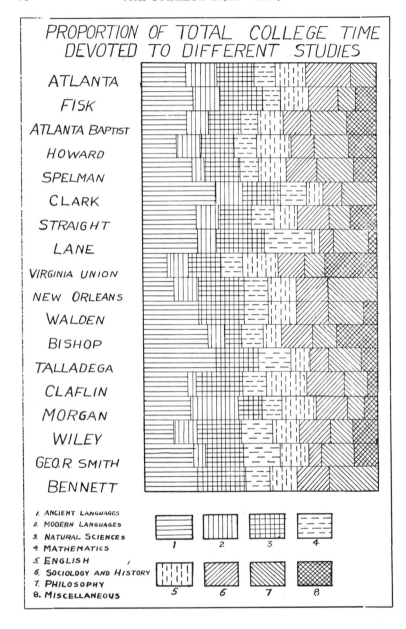

PROPORTION OF TOTAL COLLEGE TIME
DEVOTED TO DIFFERENT STUDIES

ATLANTA
FISK
ATLANTA BAPTIST
HOWARD
SPELMAN
CLARK
STRAIGHT
LANE
VIRGINIA UNION
NEW ORLEANS
WALDEN
BISHOP
TALLADEGA
CLAFLIN
MORGAN
WILEY
GEO. R. SMITH
BENNETT

1. ANCIENT LANGUAGES
2. MODERN LANGUAGES
3. NATURAL SCIENCES
4. MATHEMATICS
5. ENGLISH
6. SOCIOLOGY AND HISTORY
7. PHILOSOPHY
8. MISCELLANEOUS

As has been shown, there are about thirty-two colored institutions doing college work; but the leading colleges, according to the Carnegie Foundation units, which have a reasonable number of students are:

Howard University	Knoxville College
Fisk University	Spelman Seminary
Atlanta University	Claflin University
Wiley University	Atlanta Baptist College
Leland University	Lincoln University
Virginia Union University	Talladega College
Clark University	

In addition to their college work, nine of these institutions are carrying on work in one or more of the professional departments. These are Howard, Wiley, Leland, Virginia Union, Knoxville, Spelman, Atlanta Baptist College, Lincoln and Talladega. And almost all of them are doing work also in the High School or Academy—which work corresponds to "College Preparatory." Because of this latter fact, adverse criticism has often been pronounced against these institutions of higher learning. These institutions have been accused of going under the name of *college* when so much of their work was actual high school work. A more careful study of educational conditions in the South, however, would present the case in a different light. To be sure, much of the energy of these institutions has been devoted to training in high school branches; but this has been absolutely necessary. The South has been slow in providing public high schools for the education of her Negro children and even today comparatively little is being done in that direction. The report of the United States Commissioner of Education for the year ending July, 1909, showed that in the whole South there were but one hundred and twelve public high schools for Negroes. Even the larger cities which provide something of primary and grammar school education for Negroes make little or no provision for their high school training. The results here are two: first, Negro children graduating from the grammar school are unable to find public instruction in high school work; and second, the Negro colleges are without public feeders. To meet this situation the Negro colleges have been compelled to provide in large part their own feeders. The rise of the Negro secondary schools thruout the South, for the most part established and directed by graduates of these higher institutions and supported by voluntary contributions, has been of great help in this direction. To insure the best and largest results in the future the South must take a more liberal view of public education for Negroes.

To find the predominant character of these institutions we may make the following table:

INSTITUTION	Total	Profes-sional	College	All other students	Total college and lower students	Per cent of college to college and lower students
Howard . .	1232	592	238	402	640	37.2
Fisk . . .	457	. . . .	117	340	457	25.6
Atlanta . .	376	. . . .	78	298	376	20.7
Wiley . . .	538	22	50	466	516	9.6
Leland . .	349	26	43	280	323	13.3
Virginia Union . .	221	26	36	159	195	18.4
Clark . .	477	. . . .	35	442	477	7.3
Knoxville . .	409	8	29	372	401	7.2
Spelman . .	648	28	27	593	620	4.3
Claflin . .	748	. . . .	23	725	748	3.07
Atlanta Baptist . .	223	38	22	163	185	11.8
Lincoln . .	194	62	132	. . . .	194	68.04
Talladega . .	728	28	30	670	700	4.2

By giving the per cent of college students to total college and lower students the preceding table also shows with some considerable degree of accuracy what share of each institution's work is being devoted to college training.

In order to determine the grade of college students more carefully we may make the following table of Negro institutions doing college work. This table is based upon the catalogs of the various institutions, those of 1909-10 being used in almost all cases, and shows the distribution of students of college rank by grade and class. The table is as follows:

1909-1910

Number of Students of College Rank According to Catalog

INSTITUTION	Graduate	Senior	Junior	Soph.	Fresh.	Special	Others of college rank	Total
1. Miles Memorial College			1		1			2
2. Talladega College		7	6	7	5	5		30
3. Howard University	1	23	30	38	53	4	89	238
4. Atlanta University	2	6	10	15	20	2	23	78
5. Atlanta Baptist College		2	8	7	5			22
6. Morris Brown College			8	10	7		2	27
7. Spelman Seminary		1	2		3		21	27
8. Paine College		3	1	3	8			15
9. Clark University		4	8	2	14		7	35
10. State University (Kentucky)		2	2			1	13	18
11. Leland University	24	4	3	2	7		3	43
12. New Orleans University		5	2	1	7			15
13. Straight University	4						5	9
14. Morgan College			3	2	5			10
15. Lincoln Institute			2		2			4
16. Geo. R. Smith College *					5	15		20
17. Bennett College				5	3	5		13
18. Shaw University *			8	11	18	16	14	67
19. Colored A. & M. College *				2		2	2	6
20. Lincoln University		28	30	45	29			132
21. Benedict College	2	5	4	12	13			36
22. Claflin University		6	1	1	15			23
23. South Carolina State College		3						3
24. Lane College		2	3	6	9			20
25. Knoxville College		5	4	9	11			29
26. Fisk University	6	20	28	20	17		26	117
27. Walden University		3		3	7	3		16
28. Bishop College		4	4	4	6			18
29. Wiley University		11	9	13	17			50
30. Hartshorn Memorial College		1	1	1				3
31. Virginia Union University	1	8	5	8	14			36

* Catalog 1908-9.

Section 3. Curricula in Negro Colleges

The studies in Negro colleges can best be illustrated by the following schedule which shows also the general division of time between these subjects. The diagram which appears on page 16 is a graphic presentation of the proportion of the total college time (i. e. the total recitation time of a full college course) devoted by these institutions to the different studies:

Comparison of college studies, number of hours devoted to each (by classes),

Subject	Class	V.U. Hrs	V.U. %	Lane Hrs	Lane %	Straight Hrs	Straight %	Clark Hrs	Clark %	Spelman Hrs	Spelman %	Howard Hrs	Howard %	Atl. Baptist Hrs	A.B. %	Fisk Hrs	Fisk %	Atlanta Hrs	Atlanta %
Ancient Languages	Senior		10.1	180	23.2	192	22.9	128	31.6	256	21	102	14.7	256	19	198	21.7	136	19.1
	Junior	256		180		256		288		256		102		256		288		306	
	Sophomore			360				288				102							
	Freshman																		
Modern Languages	Senior	128	9.4	90	8.7	64	9.8	128	11.5	128	5.2	102	9.8	128	9.5	90	12	170	13.2
	Junior	112		180		128		128				102		128		180		136	
	Sophomore																		
	Freshman																		
Natural Sciences	Senior	160	13.9	180	20.3	128	13.9	96	15.8	192	15.7	102	14.7	192	14.2	180	17.7	102	16.1
	Junior	192		180		48		128		64		102				90		136	
	Sophomore			90		96		128		128		102				126		136	
	Freshman			180															
Mathematics	Senior	80	9.4	180	20.3	64	9.8	96	11.5	64	7.8	102	9.8	64	7.1	180	8	68	8.8
	Junior	160		270		128		160		128		102		128				136	
	Sophomore			180															
	Freshman																		
English	Senior	96	15.1	36	3.4	128	9.8	64	7.1	64	11.8	102	14.7	64	10.7	180	12	170	13.2
	Junior	96		72		64		96		128		102		128		54			
	Sophomore	96								64		102				36			
	Freshman	96								32									
Sociology and History	Senior	160	11.3	90	5.8	224	13.9	112	7.9	128	13.1	102	9.8	64	11.9	180	12.9	136	19.1
	Junior	64		90		48		64		128		102		128		108			
	Sophomore	64								64				64					
	Freshman													32					
Philosophy	Senior	160	8.8	486	15.6	176	9	192	14.3	288	17.1	204	14.7	128	15.4	72	7.2	136	10.2
	Junior	64						128		128		102		128		90		306	
	Sophomore													64					
	Freshman																		
Miscellaneous	Senior	192	21.5	72	2.3	112	10.6			64	7.8	204	11.4	288	11.9	18	8	170	
	Junior	96				32				64				128		54		68	
	Sophomore	128				32				64						108			
	Freshman	128										34							

per cent of total college time (full college course) devoted to each

Subject	Class	Bennett %	Bennett Hours	Geo. R. Smith %	Smith Hours	Wiley %	Wiley Hours	Morgan %	Morgan Hours	Claflin %	Claflin Hours	Talladega %	Talladega Hours	Bishop %	Bishop Hours	Walden %	Walden Hours	New Orleans %	N.O. Hours
Ancient Languages	Senior	23.6	270	21.2	300	12.7	160	19.7	68	18.7	150	31.2	18	27.8	304	23.6	288	13.1	160
	Junior		270		300		160		136		150		144		320		288		160
	Sophomore								204		150		198						
	Freshman								136				360						
Modern Languages	Senior			5.3	150	10.1	128	20.9	238	3.7	90	17.9	180	7.1	160			10.5	256
	Junior						128		102				90						
	Sophomore								102				144						
	Freshman								136										
Natural Sciences	Senior	19.7	120	15.9	150	19.1	128	9.8	102	20	150	14	180	7.1	160	19.7	128	19.7	128
	Junior		90		150		96		102		150		144				96		96
	Sophomore		150		150		160				90						160		160
	Freshman		90				96				90						96		96
Mathematics	Senior	10.5	90	15.9	150	13.3	80	8.6	68	10	120	8.5	18	9.2	80	10.5	96	10.5	96
	Junior		150		150		160				120		126		128		160		160
	Sophomore				150		96						18						
	Freshman												36						
English	Senior	11.8	90	12.4	200	11.4	96	14.8	102	17.5	120	7.8	180	7.8	96	11.8	96	11.8	96
	Junior		90		156		96		136		120				80		96		96
	Sophomore		90				96				90						96		96
	Freshman										90								
Sociology and Hist.	Senior	13.8	90	5.3	100	13.3	176	13.5	68	16.2	90	14	324	13.5	144	13.8	96	13.8	96
	Junior		225		50		160		102		150				80		240		240
	Sophomore								102		150				80				
	Freshman								136										
Philosophy	Senior	20.3	330	14.1	300	9.5	160	7.4	68	10	150			10	176	15.1	288	20.3	352
	Junior		135		100		80		102		90				48		80		144
	Sophomore								136										
	Freshman								68										
Miscellaneous	Senior			9.5	220	10.1	192	4.9	34	3.7	90	6.2	36	17.1	320	6.2	64		
	Junior				50		64		34				36		32		64		
	Sophomore								34				36		32				
	Freshman								34				36						

Section 4. A Personal Evaluation

A student of social and educational conditions among Negroes, who has had opportunity thru frequent visits to form an opinion of the work done in Negro colleges, makes the following tabular statement of his evaluation of some twenty odd institutions:

NAME OF INSTITUTION	Thoroness of work done				Adherence to catalog announcements				Quality of work done
	Excellent	*Good*	*Fair*	*Poor*	*Excellent*	*Good*	*Fair*	*Poor*	
A. and M. College (N. C.)...			X					X	Fair
Arkansas Baptist College ...			X					X	Poor
Atlanta Baptist College	X				X				Good
Atlanta University	X				X				Good
Benedict College........			X			X			Fair
Bennett College				X			X		Poor
Bishop College		X				X			Good
Claflin University		X				X			Fair
Clark University		X				X			Fair
Fisk University	X				X				Good
Georgia State College			X			X			Fair
Howard University			X			X			Fair
Knoxville College	X				X				Good
Lane College			X				X		Fair
Miles Memorial College			X					X	Poor
Morris Brown College ...				X				X	Poor
New Orleans University ...			X			X			Fair
Paine College		X				X			Fair
Paul Quinn College				X			X		Poor
Shaw University			X			X			Fair
South Carolina State College .				X			X		Poor
State University				X			X		Poor
Straight University		X				X			Fair
Tougaloo University		X				X			Good
Walden University			X				X		Fair
Wilberforce University			X			X			Fair
Wiley University		X					X		Good

Excellent—About 90 to 99 per cent.
Good—About 75 to 89 per cent.
Fair—About 60 to 74 per cent.
Poor—Below 60 per cent.

Section 5.   The Attitude of other Colleges towards Negro Students

Negroes have attended northern colleges for many years, both as graduate and undergraduate students. As early as 1826 a Negro was graduated from Bowdoin College and almost every year from that time till today has added to the number of Negro graduates from such schools. Many of the largest and best colleges of the North welcome Negroes to their student bodies—a welcome which has been taken advantage of by many young men and women of the Negro race. The rise in the standard of the Negro college has created, among other desires, the desire for more knowledge; so that each year we find many graduates from the Negro colleges applying for admission to the large colleges of the North— sometimes as graduate, sometimes as undergraduate students. Too, many Negro teachers of the South take advantage of the summer quarter to do further educational work. Harvard, Columbia and the University of Chicago have enrolled many such students.

In collecting data for this study the following letter was sent to officials of other colleges:

MY DEAR SIR:—

Atlanta University is making a study of Negro college graduates similar to one made in 1900. May I ask your co-operation?

1. Can you furnish me the names, class and addresses of such of your graduates as are of Negro descent?

2. In general what has been their success and what is the attitude of the institution and student body toward them?

Some replies are given here:

"Princeton University has never had any graduates of Negro descent."

"The Johns Hopkins University has not yet conferred a degree upon a Negro; none have ever applied for a degree, tho to be sure but two men have studied here."

Wells College, Aurora, N. Y.—"We have never graduated a student of Negro descent."

"We have never had a Negro woman as a student in Bryn Mawr College."

Mills College, California.—"There are no graduates of Negro descent on our rolls."

Rockford, Ill.—"We have never had any graduates of Negro descent from Rockford College."

"We have reason to believe that we have at one time had among the students at Barnard College a girl of Negro descent."

Yale University.—"The success of these graduates has varied considerably. Many of them, such as ——— '04, ——— '03 Law, ——— '96, have made most creditable records in every way. Yale University has never tried to attract Negro students and, on the other hand, has never felt justified in refusing admittance to those who became qualified to enter."

Beloit College, Wisconsin. — "These young people were treated with unfailing courtesy by the faculty and students of the college. Mr. ——— was a man of some ability as a speaker, and of fair ability as a student. He has not made much of a record since graduation. Mr. ———, while not a thoro student when in college, is a man of unusually attractive qualities, and was a decided favorite while here. He won a large reputation by his rendering of the part of King Oedipus in Sophocles' drama, Oedipus Tyrannus, and also won the second place in the interstate contest in oratory, including twelve states of the interior. On his return from this triumph he was met by the students of the college and I had the pleasure of seeing them carrying him on their shoulders from the train to the carriage which the students then drew themselves instead of the horses doing it. I have often said that this was a sight that could be seen nowhere excepting in an American college.

"Miss ——— was a faithful worker, but had hardly mental power enough for her college work. She was favored by the faculty on account of her handicaps, and was graduated; but her health was not good after graduation and she accomplished nothing before her death."

Leland Stanford University. — "I have never been aware of any hostile attitude on the part of the student body toward Negro students. Of course, we have never had but an occasional Negro student in the University."

Fordham University, New York. — "We have had no applicants for admission from the black race. What we should do were the applicants to come I just cannot say."

St. Vincent College, Beatty, Pennsylvania. — "I cannot tell what the attitude of the student body should be towards Negroes, but we shall not risk a trial of it. Applications are very rare—one during the last four years. We do not think it wise here under the prevailing conditions to accept any distinctively colored students into the college."

Hanover, Indiana—"For obvious reasons we have no colored students in Hanover College."

Park College, Parkville, Mo. — "Never a Negro graduate nor a student. Couldn't do it in Missouri if we wanted to."

Missouri Valley College, Marshall, Mo. — "We have never had any graduates of Negro descent and are not likely to ever have."

Carleton College, Farmington, Mo. — "We have never had any Negro or any person with Negro blood graduate from Carleton College in its history. I have not found a student in the state that would tolerate a Negro in the college. And it is even worse since the Johnson-Jeffries fight."

Tarkio College, Tarkio, Mo. — "We have had one Negro student who spent a year in our Preparatory Department. I do not suppose any other white college in the state would receive a Negro student. This young man remained in the school for a year with credit to himself and the school, was a member of its glee club and never an individual intimated to me any objection to his presence. I regard this as a remarkable experience for a Missouri college."

Greenville College, Illinois. — "There is no attitude either for or against them. We do not have applications from members of the colored race."

Union College, College View, Nebraska. — "We have had several Negro students in the past and accept them in our school at the present time. As far as we are able to judge there has not been much distinction made among our students between the Negro students and the others. It depends very largely upon the student himself how he is received by the student body."

"The University of North Dakota is open to all students of any rank or race who are prepared."

South Dakota State College, Brookings, S. D. — "The attitude towards Negro students is not favorable with the student body."

Simpson College, Indianola, Iowa. — "The sentiment of the students seems to be along the line of being willing to help these students in any way possible and, of course, we are far enough North so that race prejudice is not very manifest."

Occidental College, Los Angeles, Cal. — "So far as I know a Negro applying for admission would receive a cordial welcome from the student body. We have Japanese, Koreans and Chinese, and there is no race prejudice in this school so far as I know. The question has never been raised."

Thiel College, Greenville, Pa. — "Should any apply for admission they would be welcome."

Earlham College, Richmond, Ind. — "So far as I know Negro students here are treated with respect by the student body. We never have many of them and they are not thrown closely with the other students in a social way, but all students are measured by their work whether they are white or colored."

Oskaloosa College, Iowa. — "We have had at various times Negro students who have made excellent records in their class-room work."

Upsala College, Kenilworth, N. J. — "We have had some Negro students and they have been treated with same respect as other students."

Hope College, Holland, Mich. — "Hope College has never been favored with having Negro graduates nor even Negro students. I feel confident, however, that if young men of that blood should present themselves as students they would be kindly treated.''

Salina Chautauqua Association, Kansas. — ''As far as I know the attitude of the student body towards the Negro student has been in most respects at least the same as their attitude toward other students. Our student body, so far as I know, holds no prejudice against the Negro.''

Worcester Polytechnic Institute, Mass. — ''There has been one [Negro] student in the Freshman Class this year, and, so far as I have been able to notice, no discrimination of any sort has been made either in his favor or against him by the student body.''

Oregon Agricultural College, Corvallis, Oregon. — ''There were two Negro students registered during the past year and I understand they have been making very good records. One of the young men in question is very active in certain student enterprises, particularly the Cosmopolitan Club, and is popular with the students generally. The attitude of the student body of the Oregon Agricultural College towards colored students, so far as the writer's observation and experiences are concerned, has been very friendly.''

Franklin and Marshall College, Lancaster, Pa. — ''I am sure such a student would be well received and have courteous treatment from our student body.''

Pittsburg College of the Holy Ghost. — ''There was within my recollection a Negro student in the college. Our boys treated him as they did the other boys.''

Des Moines College, Iowa. — ''There has never been any objection on the part of faculty or students toward the presence of Negro students in our institution.''

The University of Nebraska. — ''We have had a number of Negro graduates and so far as I know the general student body feels very kindly towards them and towards our Negro undergraduates. On commencement days a Negro usually receives a little more applause than a white boy when he walks over the stage. I presume some things happen in his personal relations with his fellow students that are not entirely pleasant, but they never come to the surface. I doubt if there is a school in the country which is freer from race prejudice than the University of Nebraska.''

Section 6.   Negro Alumni of the Colleges of Iowa (by *Prof. Paul S. Peirce*)

So far as the writer has been able to determine, there are thirty-four colored alumni of Iowa colleges and universities and these persons hold some forty degrees taken *in cursu*. Of the thirty-four, twenty-six are males and eight are females; of those receiving more than one degree in Iowa institutions, three are men and two are women (one man holding three degrees).

These alumni are distributed among eleven institutions, the State University claiming eleven of them, Drake University six, Iowa Wesleyan University five, Tabor College three, Iowa State College and Coe College two each, and Grinnell, Cornell, Penn, Amity and Highland Park colleges one each. It is a curious coincidence that no one of these institutions seems to have graduated both colored men and colored women, altho all are co-educational; seven have graduated only men of this race and four only women.

The colored alumnus of Iowa colleges seems to be a phenomenon peculiar to the last three decades, and it is interesting, tho not surprising, to note the progressive increase in the number of graduates from decade to decade: during the first decade (1880-1890) six degrees were conferred upon colored candidates; during the next (1890-1900) thirteen; during the decade just closing twenty-one, that is, more than during both the other two.

Equally interesting and reassuring is the increasing range and diversity of courses pursued. During the first decade law and liberal arts held the whole field (law 2, liberal arts 4); during the second decade law and liberal arts were still in the center of the field, but medicine, agriculture and graduate work have entered (law 4, liberal arts 4, medicine 1, graduate 3 and agriculture 1); while during the last decade no less than seven lines of study were completed by colored men and women (law 3, liberal arts 10, pharmacy 4, medicine, dentistry, agriculture and graduate courses one each). The distribution by courses for the entire period is as follows: liberal arts 18, law 9, graduate 4, pharmacy 4, agriculture 2, medicine 2, dentistry 1.

Geographical Distribution

1. As to place of birth, data were secured from twenty-five of the total thirty-four, some neglecting to reply at all and others, who replied to most questions, omitting the answer to this one. Of those reporting ten were born in Iowa, seven in Missouri, two each in North Carolina and South Carolina and one in each of the following states: Alabama, Texas, Virginia and Nebraska.

2. As to migration, several have lived in more than one state since graduation, but as data concerning such movements are quite incomplete we will simply compare birthplaces with present locations. Of the ten born in Iowa five are now in that state, two in Oklahoma, one in Wyoming, one in Minnesota, and one in Venezuela; of the seven born in Missouri two are in Iowa, two in Mississippi, one in Missouri, one in Alabama and one in Oklahoma; of the two born in North Carolina one is in Illinois and one in Missouri; the native of Virginia is a resident of Iowa; the native

of Texas is in Tennessee; the native of Alabama lives in Texas; the native of Nebraska is in Iowa; and of the two South Carolinians one is in
Illinois and the other in Georgia.

3. By way of summary of present location, it may be noted that of
the thirty-four, twelve have settled in Iowa, four in Missouri, three each
in Oklahoma and Illinois, two each in Mississippi and Tennessee, and one
in each of the following: Minnesota, Georgia, Texas, Wyoming, Alabama,
Venezuela, District of Columbia; and one died in Liberia.

4. These figures show a pretty even division between the northern
states on the one hand and the southern and border states on the other,
so far as place of birth is concerned and so far as present location goes.
But statistics of birthplace and migration are too fragmentary to warrant
very definite conclusions as to movements from the one section to the
other.

Age Statistics

1. As to age of graduation some facts are perhaps noteworthy:
First, that the average age is earlier for women than for men, that of
the former being $21\frac{1}{3}$ and of the latter $22\frac{3}{16}$; second, the average has
slightly increased from decade to decade, being 21 years for men and
women from 1880-1890, 22 years from 1890-1900 and $22\frac{4}{11}$ from 1900-1910.
This increase seems much more noticeable among the men than among
the women.

2. As to present age, of the twenty-four reporting sixteen are still
under thirty-five and only one is over fifty.

The Family

In view of the fact that so large a proportion of the alumni studied•
are recent graduates, it is not surprising to find a large proportion of
them still unmarried. Of the twenty-six reporting twelve were married—
ten men and two women, twelve were single—eight men and four women;
one is a widower, and one woman is separated from her husband. That
is, about one-half have married and one-half remained single, with a very
low percentage of separated. Among the men the percentage of marriages was naturally much greater among graduates of the first two decades, while the proportion of marriages among the women was highest
for graduates of the last decade.

Of the thirteen who have been married the average age of marriage
was for men 30 years, for women 25 years; of the wives of graduates the
average age at marriage was 23 years, and of husbands of graduates
(only three reported) the average age at marriage was 35 years.

The total number of children of these marriages was twenty-two, of
whom seventeen are living and five dead. These children were distributed
among seven of the thirteen marriages, four reporting no children, three
reporting one child each, two reporting two children each, three reporting
three children each and one reporting six children.

Occupation

The thirty-three living alumni studied are at present distributed among the following pursuits: teachers 8, lawyers 5, clergymen 4, physicians 3, pharmacists 3, homemakers 3, editors 2, students 3, dentists 1, civil service 1, railway service 1, restaurant work 1, parcel message delivery 1 (three duplicates).

In addition it should be noted that nine have previously served as teachers for a longer or shorter period, two have been lawyers, one a book agent, one has run a carpet-cleaning establishment and one has been an editor, while fourteen have never had any other than their present occupation.

Testimony of College Authorities as to Negro Students

Amity College. — "Miss B. was a girl of excellent conduct and good scholarship. Her mother (a widow) is still a resident of College Springs, their home for many years. She was a slave, can not write and reads only a little with difficulty. Her livelihood for herself and children has been earned by hard toil washing and ironing."

Central University. — "I will say that while Negroes are admitted to the college freely, but few have attended and none have graduated. We had one year, 1902-1903, a young woman, a quadroon, who received a prize for highest scholarship in the entire school. That was an unusual experience, however. As a rule our Negro students have not done a high grade of work."

Cornell College. — "We have had but one Negro graduate from Cornell College and he made a very fine record as a student while in college. During his college course he was a member of our base ball team and was elected to membership in one of our literary societies."

Coe College. — "So far as I can learn only two Negroes have graduated from Coe College. One was a good student and gave class poem on commencement day. Unfortunately he is a dwarf physically — a hunchback — and for that reason chiefly, I presume, he has not been able to secure such a position as his scholarship would merit. The other was a student of fair ability and fine athlete (football)."

Des Moines College. — "We have none. Within the last twenty years we have had only two students of that race. Neither of them went beyond the freshman year. Both were good students. One of them is doing an excellent work now as pastor of one of the strongest Negro churches in this city. The other, a young woman, who was with us last year, passed perfect examination in her Latin, a thing that had probably never occurred in that class before."

Highland Park College. — "We have never had but one Negro graduated from the regular college of pharmacy. We have had very few Negroes in the past and two years ago, you will probably remember, we announced that we would not receive Negroes any longer, not that we had anything against the Negro, on the other hand we shall be glad to do anything that we can to further Negro education; but it became humiliating to the Negro and compromising to the school; the students would not sit by them in school and would have no communication with them, and since we had only one or two each quarter, we thot it would be better for all parties concerned to have the Negro seek his education under more favorable circumstances."

Leander Clark College.—"We have had a number of Negro students in past years. Some of them did good, creditable work, and have made useful citizens. We have never had a graduate from any of the departments."

Penn College.—"There has been only one Negro graduate. This one was a student of fair ability. Since graduation she has been teaching and has met with excellent success. We have one Negro woman in school at the present time; she is a fair student, above the average in language courses."

Parsons College.—"We have never had a Negro graduate. To my knowledge no Negro has attended this school."

Tabor College.—"We have reason to be proud of our Negro alumni: Mr. Hightower T. Kealing, A. M., editor of A. M. E. *Review*, Nashville, Tenn.; Mr. Edward L. Blackshear, A. M., principal of Texas State Industrial School at Prairie View, Texas; and the Rev. W. H. Speese, B. L., pastor of A. M. E. church of Brookport, Illinois. These men have all demonstrated their worth and are an honor to our institution."

State University.—"The Negro graduates of this University have varied in point of scholarship widely as have the white alumni. But their average has been quite as high as the general average for all alumni, and among their number have been some of marked superiority. A former teacher of logic here said of one of them that he had never had a keener mind in his class room. And another, Mr. S. Joe Brown, was elected to the local chapter of Phi Beta Kappa."

Appreciation of College Training

All are confident that their college training has benefited them. To this question the response is always a positive *yes*. But two of the number addressed felt that it would have been better if their liberal arts work had been supplemented by some commercial or manual training. The rest believed that no other than the course pursued would have been better for them.

Work of Teachers

No vocation has claimed so many of the Negro graduates of Iowa institutions as teaching, and thru no other channel has the influence of college training reached so far. About one-fourth of the total number are now teachers, and more than one-half have been teachers at some time in their lives. In the aggregate they represent more than one hundred and thirty years of teaching, and judging from their own estimates which are, of course, only rough at best their educational endeavor has, either thru themselves personally or thru their pupils who have become teachers, touched nearly a hundred thousand lives. For the most part these lives have been those of Negroes, altho there is at least one notable instance of a colored graduate conducting a school for whites and several instances where some whites have been taught by persons of color. The grade of teaching done has varied from primary to collegiate. At present three of the alumnæ are teaching in the grades of Kansas City and Buxton; while of the alumni one has recently established a small industrial institute in Mississippi, another has been for five years professor in the state colored agricultural and normal university at Langston, Oklahoma, one has been for fourteen years principal of the State Normal at Prairie View, Texas, and two are trained agriculturalists, directing that line at Tuskegee and Clark University.

The Work of Lawyers

Of the nine who have completed courses in law seven seem to have undertaken the practice of that profession. Of this latter number two failed to respond to the questionnaire; one reports that after eight years' practice in Des Moines and St. Joseph he has gone into the messenger delivery business; another after four years' practice in Des Moines entered the consular service; a fifth, a young attorney in St. Joseph, reports that his cases are mostly criminal and chiefly colored; the sixth, located in Des Moines, combines law with journalism, and says fully one-half his practice consists of white cases; and the seventh, the only one with a solid collegiate training as a basis for legal studies, after nine years' experience, reports a practice of $1,500 to $2,000, largely criminal but including several civil rights cases; he has some white clients, has practiced in state and federal courts in three states and has usually been successful.

Work of Physicians

Of the three physicians in the list two completed liberal arts courses before entering upon the study of medicine. Two are located in northern states and one in Tennessee. Only one has thus far responded to the questionnaire, but this one is no doubt the most successful of all. He made an enviable record at the State University of Iowa, first in liberal arts and then in medicine; he was the first Negro graduate of the college of medicine in that institution and in the examination by the State Board of Medical Examiners he ranked second in a class of fifty-six. For three years he has been practicing at Buxton, Iowa, his home town, a mining community of some 4,500 inhabitants, mostly colored. He is assistant surgeon for the Northwestern Railway and surgeon for the local mining company. He reports a plentiful and varied practice among both whites and blacks. He has recently been chosen state vice-president of the National Medical Association, consisting of the Negro doctors, dentists and pharmacists of the United States.

Work of Pharmacists

Of the four graduates in pharmacy, all had received high school training before beginning the pharmacy course; one had spent a year at Drake University and two held bachelor's degrees from Fisk University. Two are men and one is a woman. One, a graduate of last year, has not yet begun work as a pharmacist; one is proprietor of a drug store and two are managers of drug companies. All are located in communities having a considerable colored element: one in Oklahoma, one in Mississippi and one at Buxton, Iowa. All, however, report patronage from both races. None of these is a graduate of more than three years' standing, so none has a long business record, but the reports of all are hopeful and reassuring:

"I have met with much success since I have broken the barrier of prejudice againt a woman pharmacist by accuracy, neatness and promptness."

"I have only been in business a few months, yet I get patronage from both races and the white druggists give me many professional courtesies."

"The fact that a number of whites from this place took the board examination in October and all failed, while I passed, gave me a high professional standing."

The Work of Dentists

The only dental graduate and practitioner completed his course one year ago. He has located in St. Joseph, Mo., and reports that he has been very successful thus far and has a number of white patients.

Work of Ministers

Of the three who have gone into the ministry two were born in North Carolina and one in Iowa. Two took their first degree in liberal arts and one in law. All had good records as students. One followed his collegiate course with theological seminary training, another entered the ministry only after seven years' experience as a school principal, the third and youngest became a pastor after several years of small-scale business experience. They are located in three separate states: Iowa, Illinois and Missouri. Each represents a different decade of Negro graduation in Iowa. Two are identified with the A. M. E. Church and one with the M. E. Church. The oldest of the three has won recognition in his profession as shown by the fact of his appointment as district superintendent in the M. E. Church.

Work as Editors

The transition from minister to editor is easy and natural, since the most notable figure in the editorial group is the editor of the A. M. E. Church *Review*, Nashville, Tenn., Mr. H. T. Kealing, the oldest colored alumnus of an Iowa college and an editor and lecturer for fifteen years. The only other journalist in the group is John L. Thompson, editor of the one colored journal in the state of Iowa (*The Iowa State Bystander*) and president of the Western Negro Press Association.

Civil Service

Two of the Iowa Negro alumni have entered the civil service: Alexander Clark, one of the older men, died in Liberia, whither he was sent as United States Minister; H. R. Wright, one of the more recent graduates, has been in the consular service five or six years and is now consul at Puerto Cabello, Venezuela.

Political Activity

Most of the male graduates stated that they vote and that their votes are counted. The only exceptions are those living in Alabama, Mississippi and Georgia; they have either failed to reply to questions relating to voting practice and experience or have stated that they do not vote.

Very few have held public office and none has attained to other than minor elective and appointive positions in the state of Iowa, viz: deputy county treasurer, township clerk, file clerk of the general assembly of the state senate, clerk in the hall of archives, judge of election and candidate for nomination for city councilman Des Moines.

Real Estate Ownership

For the seventeen who stated the assessed value of real estate which they owned the holdings ranged in value from $500 to $10,000, and showed an average of $3,000. This number includes a few of the recent graduates, whose property accumulations were naturally small.

Literary Work

Only two seem to have published books, both on religious and moral themes. A dozen or more have contributed articles to magazines, newspapers and bulletins with a wide range of topics and titles, short stories for children, orations and poems, industrial training, agricultural bulletins, abridgment of rights of Negro citizens, discourses on temperance and other social, moral and religious themes.

Advanced Degrees

At least thirteen have taken more than one degree, the second or third degree being in most cases A. M., in some cases professional and occasionally honorary. At least three others have pursued post-graduate study.

Learned Societies

At least ten belong to learned societies, including Phi Beta Kappa, N. E. A., A. A. A. S., National Medical Association, state teachers' associations, etc.

Group Leadership

Aside from the pursuit of their regular vocations most of these men and women have been more or less active in various lines of social and civic service. Many have engaged in religious activities and some have figured rather prominently as laymen in religious organizations, one as a conference delegate and president of Iowa Sunday-school Institute, another as district superintendent of A. M. E. Sunday-schools, another as director of the boys' department of a local Y. M. C. A. and lecturer on physiology and hygiene, one lady has been prominent as a speaker before religious and educational meetings and active in W. C. T. U. and juvenile improvement work, several have turned their attention to leadership in local religious and moral needs. A number have solicited and raised money for schools in which they were interested. One helped in the settlement of the Alton school fight. A few have addressed themselves to the agricultural and industrial uplift of their people and have conducted farmers' congresses or organized farmers' institutes and otherwise led in instruction in agricultural lines. One was former national legal adviser and is now state president of the Afro-American Council. A few have been identified with local business enterprises, such as banks, drug companies, real estate companies, etc.; and one claims the distinction of starting the movement for a Semi-Centennial of Negro Progress since 1863.

The Future

Nearly all these men and women have come up thru adversity and have triumphed despite the heavy odds against them. All express themselves as hopeful for the future of their people in this country. Their suggestions as to the solution of the problems of their race vary widely and reveal diverse philosophies, but for the most part they vouch for the usefulness of these alumni to the communities of which they form a part and to the race whose leadership they in part provide.

Section 7. Colored Students and Graduates of the University of Kansas [1] (by Mr. Larry M. Peace)

Thirty-nine years ago, when old North College was the University, among the few lank youths and bronzed haired maidens who came from the prairies of Kansas to begin their college careers with the study of grammar, geography, arithmetic, and the like, there was a single dusky face. The enrollment of the colored people in the University of Kansas

---

[1] Printed in *The Graduate Magazine*, University of Kansas.

began then, in 1870, when just one student, a woman, entered the freshman class of the preparatory department. It was not until 1873, however, that this same woman, upon entering what is now the college of liberal arts and sciences, became also the first colored person to do real university work.

During the years subsequent to 1870, there has been no session of the University which has not been attended by colored students. From 1870 to 1890 the number of such students was small; only one, or occasionally two new ones would come each year. From 1890 to 1909 their enrollment has been from four or five to ten new persons each year, the greater numbers having come within the five years just passed. The University register shows that of the forty-four enrolled for the year 1908-1909, nine are in the school for the first time.

The total registration of colored people in the University has been two hundred and eleven: one hundred and forty-three men and sixty-eight women. The six—all, in fact—who came prior to 1876, were women. Beginning with two men in 1876, by far the majority of those who came later were men.

Excepting two, who registered only in the normal department, the twenty-two colored students who came first to the University began their work in the preparatory department. Only six of these, however, remained long enough to enter the collegiate department, where three of them continued to graduation, receiving the degree of bachelor of arts. To one of these three, as will be seen later, was granted the additional degree of bachelor of didactics, the only normal degree ever granted to a colored person by the University of Kansas.

At some time during the past forty years the University has had colored students in every school and in almost every department. At present the writer does not have in mind any course for which some colored person has not enrolled. Just how many have done some work in the graduate school is uncertain, but there have been several, one of whom—a man—received credit for full work leading to a degree. Counting the students of the preparatory department there have been altogether, in what is now the college of liberal arts and sciences, one hundred and eighteen: fifty-nine men and fifty-nine women. In the school of engineering ten men have studied at least thru the freshman year. Thirty men have studied in the school of law, while only two men and seven women have enrolled in the school of fine arts. In the school of pharmacy twenty-six men and two women have been registered, as compared with a total of sixteen men in the school of medicine.

A glance at the following simple table will show the number of men and women who have been enrolled in the various schools of the University, together with the number of degrees granted to each sex.

It will be noticed that no colored women have ever studied in the schools of medicine, law and engineering, and that no colored person has ever graduated from the schools of medicine and fine arts. It will also be noticed that very few colored women have enrolled for the professional courses, while in the courses in the college they have kept pace with the men not only in number but also in the quality of their work.

	Enrollment			Degrees granted		
	Total	Men	Women	Total	Men	Women
All schools	211	143	68	60	45	15
The Graduate School	(?)	Several	Several	1	1	. . . .
The School of Liberal Arts and Sciences	118	59	59	31	16	15
The School of Engineering	10	10	. . . .	2	2	. . . .
The School of Law	30	30	. . . .	18	18	. . . .
The School of Fine Arts	9	2	7	. . . .	. . . .	. . . .
The School of Pharmacy	28	26	2	8	8	. . . .
The School of Medicine	16	16	. . . .	. . . .	. . . .	. . . .

By far the majority of the colored students who have come to the University did not remain thru the sophomore year. Three-fourths of the preparatory students left before reaching the freshmen year of the college. Nearly all of those who passed the sophomore year continued to graduation. This statement is true only for the college.

To the sixty degrees just listed must be added the degree of bachelor of didactics which, together with the degree of bachelor of arts, was granted in 1885 to one man who then became the first colored graduate of the University of Kansas. The table shows that no colored women have been enrolled in the schools of engineering, law or medicine, and that only two have been enrolled in the school of pharmacy; neither one of the latter, however, continued to graduation.

Of the thirty-one degrees granted by the college fifteen were received by women, all bachelor of arts degrees. No other degrees have ever been received from the university by colored women.

During the attendance of such students at the University for forty years the number to graduate at any one time has varied, sometimes one, sometimes two, and at a few commencements there has been none. The greatest number to graduate at any one time finished in 1901, when eight degrees were granted to colored persons: five by the College, two by the School of Pharmacy and one by the School of Law. During all these years only one person has appeared for a higher degree, one man having received the degree of master of arts in 1908.

Taking no account of gymnasium work, voice culture, theme writing and hygiene, the following table of subjects will show in detail the number of men and women enrolled in any subject in the list; the total credits given for that subject, and the number of credits received by men and women respectively, the greatest number of credits received by men and women; and finally, the number of each sex who received three or more credits in any one subject:

SUBJECTS	Enrollment			Credits			Greatest credit		Three or more credits	
	Total	Men	Women	Total	Men	Women	Men	Women	Men	Women
English	28	13	15	130	45	85	10	10	5	13
Mathematics	23	12	11	63	34	29	3	3	6	5
Physical sciences	41	23	18	57	39	18	8	2	5	
Chemistry	22	11	11	37	25	12	4	1	5	
Physics	3	3		3	3		2			
Geology	16	9	7	17	11	6	2	1		
Biological sciences	38	27	21	89	63	26	15	6	7	
Zoology	19	12	7	33	26	7	7	1	2	
Botany	22	11	11	45	30	15	6	2	5	
Entomology	5	4	1	8	7	1	2	1		
Physiology	2		2	3		3		2		
Philosophy	15	8	7	36	18	18	4	7	3	2
History	24	11	13	77	34	43	10	8	5	6
Economics	3	3		10	10		8		1	
Foreign languages	71	32	39	220	90	140	25	27	12	22
Latin	16	8	8	47	21	26	7	8	3	3
Greek	7	3	4	22	13	9	6	4	3	2
German	26	13	13	98	42	56	8	8	6	11
French	18	6	12	46	10	36	2	5		6
Spanish	4	2	2	7	4	3	2	2		
Astronomy	1	1		1	1		1			
Education	12	5	7	36	17	19	5	4	3	4
Evolution	8	5	3	9	5	4	2	1		
Sociology	16	10	6	43	24	19	5	6	4	3

A glance at the table will show that when arranged in the order of their popularity, which is determined by the number of credits given in each case, the subjects stand as follows: foreign languages, first; English, second; biological sciences, third; history, fourth; mathematics, fifth; physical sciences, sixth; and social sciences, seventh. In making the calculations economics and sociology are combined. The two subjects are so closely related that they were not carefully kept separate in the table. A few of the credits, therefore, which are assigned to sociology should be given to economics.

It may be seen from the table that the ratios of the credits received by men in the various subjects, to those received by women, can be expressed as follows: English, 1:1.8; mathematics, 1.1:1; physical sciences, 1.2:1; biological sciences, 2.5:1; philosophy, 1:1; history, 1:1.3; social sciences, 1.4:1; foreign languages, 1:1.5. The women clearly outclassed the men, from the standpoint of credits, in the languages and in history, while the men took the lead in biological, physical and social sciences and in mathematics. Upon the whole, the number of men to have received credits in the various subjects is well balanced by that of women.

Three subjects, astronomy, physics and economics, were taken by men only. No subject, however, was taken by women only. Credits in physiology were not assigned to men in the table because such students took the work in the School of Medicine.

An examination of the grades of all colored students who hold degrees from the College of Liberal Arts and Sciences shows no special fitnesses or abilities peculiar to either men or women. Excellent students, as well as very poor ones, were found among those of both sexes in every course. The grade records show that the men must have taken the sciences and the women the languages for other reasons than special ability along these particular lines of work. Excepting the great disparities in the biological sciences and also the physical sciences the number of individual credits by men and women in any particular subject is almost the same for one sex as it is for the other.

Summing up the grades of all colored people who hold degrees from the college and arranging them in the order, grade I, grade II and grade III, the aggregate of I's, II's and III's, sustain the relation 8:12:4. This is an easy but unsatisfactory way of obtaining a notion of the scholarship as a whole.

To compare their standing with that of the white people who hold degrees from the same school is more difficult and even more unsatisfactory. In fact, there is no method of comparison which would be fair to both.

A preliminary comparison was made by selecting from the entire list of those who hold degrees from the college the names of white men and women equal in number to those colored men and women who hold degrees from the same school. One or two names were selected from nearly every class list, by dropping the pencil point upon it and taking the name nearest the point. Thus the records of thirty-one white students, out of a total of seventeen hundred, were secured to be compared with the records made by the thirty-one colored students. Summing up their grades it was found that in the order of grades, I, II and III, as before, they presented the relation 8:9:3—not a great deal different from the 8:12:4 upon the part of the colored students.

In the list of white students was one man who made a complete record of grades one. This standard was not quite reached by any colored student. A few, however, came very near to it, one reaching a total of thirty-two grades one out of thirty-eight credits. Upon the other hand, no individual colored student received quite as many grades three as did an individual white student.

It has already been pointed out that the total number of colored people to attend the University is two hundred and eleven. The total number of white people is said to have been nearly twenty-five thousand. The ratio of the attendance of colored students to that of white students is accordingly about 1:123. The ratio of the number of colored students to finish to the total number to enter is 1:3. The ratio of the number of white students to finish to the number to enter is 1:7.3. The ratio of the number of colored students to graduate to the number of white students to finish is 1:56. An interesting fact to be noticed here is that while there has been one colored student among every one hundred and twenty-three to enter the University there has been an average of one in every fifty-six to finish.

Something of interest pertaining to the colored student in the College of Liberal Arts and Sciences may be gleaned from what has already been said but not a great deal has been said concerning him in the other schools of the University.

The School of Engineering, with only two colored graduates, and the School of Medicine, with none, will be passed without further comment. The School of Law, in the matter of degrees granted, ranks next to the college but owing to the manner of keeping the records no exact data could be obtained. Like the college, however, it has sent out a few excellent students along with the poor ones.

It has been only within the past ten years that any number of colored students have undertaken work in the School of Pharmacy. A few of these have done creditable work.

Whatever have been the accomplishments of the colored student in the class-room, he has taken an insignificant part in university affairs in general. A few have been identified with the various university literary societies, and have even represented the university in debate. This literary inactivity is only a seeming one, for the colored students have done quite creditable things in the town literary societies which they have always maintained. They have generally supported two or three of such societies, holding weekly meetings where all the various literary programs could be rendered. They have maintained exclusive clubs for both men and women, one of the most progressive of which is a girls' club of some years' standing. This one is strictly a university girls' club, in which, to quote from their current year book, such subjects as "Macaulay as a Critic," "Religious Troubles in England" and "Warren Hastings" are discussed.

Like their literary powers, the religious talents of the colored students have been little exercised on Mount Oread. Upon the other hand, these same students have taken the lead in the down-town churches. In times past the Sunday-school, the Christian Endeavor, the Baptist Young People's Union and various other church societies would have suffered without their help. They have held all church offices, from Sunday-school teacher and chorister to minister.

While the colored students do not take any part in the social life of the University, in conjunction with the town people they provide themselves with all the latest fads and luxuries of social enjoyment. They have their receptions, their banquets, their club dances, and their annual spring parties.

Tho they have looked well to their literary, religious and social training, they have had very little to do with athletics. Aside from one or two baseball men and a football player the colored students have had very little interest in university sports. This athletic inactivity is due in part to the circumstances under which nearly every one of these students must acquire his education. Aside from the disparity of their numbers it may be found that one of the great differences between white and colored students in the University lies in the circumstances under which each race accomplishes what it does.

If it is more difficult for some colored students to rank high in scholarship from a standpoint of grades than it is for white students it may be owing to the fact that this excellence is not expected of them. Good work on the part of a colored student nearly always calls forth comment or even expressions of surprise. The white students do not necessarily have to meet a condition of this nature.

For reasons too obvious to be discussed the associates of the colored student are not men and women schooled and highly cultured, both at home and abroad. He has not the lure of the Phi Beta Kappa or other honorary society, with friends and relatives to assist him, to advise and direct him, as well as to scheme for him, in order that he may make an enviable record. The white student may have all of these favors.

Again, nearly all of the colored students are wholly or in part self-supporting. This was the case with fifty-three out of the sixty who now hold degrees from the University. It may be that the earning of one's way through school does not need to be a handicap. Those reporting upon the subject differ in opinion. Indeed an examination of the records of the colored students shows that the students who labored most strenuously to meet expenses while in school often far surpassed the students who were not at all self-supporting.

It may be, however, that the colored student is somewhat handicapped because of the nature of the work which he must perform for a living. He is usually able to obtain an abundance of work and is willing to do it, but the work is, as a rule, not very remunerative and often takes his time inopportunely. There were no clerks, stenographers, bookkeepers, and the like, among those fifty-three people who worked their way through the University. They were table-waiters, janitors, porters, farmers, maids and laundresses.

In addition to these employments they were bound to their social duties. The white student can forego any social demands with impunity and applause while he is at school. This is not true of the colored student; his social opportunities and obligations increase with his schooling. If he is not brave enough to ignore adverse criticism and remain loyal to his studies his scholarship must suffer. It is true he is needed in society; he is from the best of homes, perhaps, so that much is expected of him; nevertheless, he has yet to learn that toil for a living, society and scholarship do not make an harmonious trio. Twenty-five of the graduates have been happily married. Of this number only one couple have been united as the result of a college romance.

Again, it is more difficult for the colored student to succeed because of his home life. In most cases he comes from parents whose opportunities have not fitted them for assisting him in an educational way. Often they are innocently indifferent, unsympathetic, and in some cases, even antagonistic.

However well or ill those two hundred former students and graduates fared while in school all are emphatic in their loyalty to a great university where men and women from the humblest walks of life and without money can tarry and get wisdom.

So far as is known all but fourteen of these former students and graduates are still living and doing well. The dead are eleven women and three men. Of these, three—one woman and two men—were graduates. Of the former students eight are practicing physicians, holding degrees from other universities. Three of those holding degrees from the University of Kansas are now studying in other universities for higher degrees. Of the remaining graduates of the University, one, having obtained his degree of doctor of medicine from another school, is practicing medicine; three bachelors of law and twenty-one bachelors of arts are teaching. Of the latter, three are college professors, two are high school teachers and three are ward principals. Two bachelors of art are foreign missionaries. With one exception those holding degrees from the School of Pharmacy are practicing their profession. One law graduate is a minister of the gospel, while another is in the diplomatic service of the United States. Eleven bachelors of law and one bachelor of arts are practicing law. One bachelor of arts and a pharmacist are in the civil service department of the United States. One former student is a successful manufacturer.

Communications from nearly all of these graduates insist that a college training is worth while.

Section 8.   Attitude Toward Negro Students at Oberlin

Oberlin College is especially notable because it was the great pioneer in the work of blotting out the color-line in colleges. During the early thirties Lane Seminary in Cincinnati became a center of anti-slavery enthusiasm. The trustees of the seminary attempted to prohibit the discussion of the slavery question in the institution and this led to a great secession of students. Many of the seceders proposed to go to Oberlin College which had been established in 1833 and there form a theological department, on condition, however, that they have Charles G. Finney, the noted revivalist, as their teacher. Mr. Finney says:

"I had understood that the trustees of Lane Seminary had acted 'over the heads' of the faculty; and, in absence of several of them, had passed the obnoxious resolution that had caused the students to leave. I said, therefore, ... that I would not go at any rate, unless two points were conceded by the trustees. One was, that they should never interfere with the internal regulation of the school but should leave that entirely to the discretion of the faculty. The other was, that we should be allowed to receive colored people on the same conditions that we did white people; that there should be no discrimination made on account of color.''[1]

These conditions were met, Finney entered upon his work in Oberlin, and the college thus became an anti-slavery stronghold. Each year since that time has found a considerable number of Negro students enrolled in Oberlin College; and the institution has graduated more Negroes than any other institution of its kind. There have been the following Negro graduates from Oberlin:

NEGRO GRADUATES FROM OBERLIN

	Living		Dead		Total
	Male	Female	Male	Female	
1844–49	2	. . . .	2	. . . .	4
1850–54	. . . .	. . . .	1	3	4
1855–59	2	1	1	3	7
1860–64	2	3	2	3	10
1865–69	. . .	3	6	. . . .	9
1870–74	1	3	2	2	8
1875–79	3	5	2	. . . .	10
1880–84	7	5	1	. . . .	13
1885–89	5	4	1	1	11
1890–94	10	9	2	3	24
1895–99	7	1	. . . .	. . . .	8
1900–04	10	6	. . . .	. . . .	16
1905–09	13	11	1	. . . .	25
Total	. 62	51	21	15	149

Lately the color line has appeared at Oberlin, as the following quotations show:[2]

'' . . . Like any other condition which depends upon the undergraduate state of mind it changes with the changing classes. Under normal conditions the attitude of the senior class determines the attitude of the student body and there is some reason to think that the feeling against having colored men in the literary societies is stronger in the present senior class than in the other classes. If the present attitude were merely sporadic—a temporary aberration of the men of 1910—it would not be

[1] Memoirs of Rev. Charles G. Finney, written by himself, p. 333. New York, 1876.
[2] From the *Oberlin Alumni Magazine.*

worth comment. That this is not the case is clear from several facts. In 1905 Alpha Zeta refused to admit a man because of his color. (This action was reversed under pressure from alumni of Alpha Zeta.) Since the graduation of this man no colored men have been members of the literary societies. . . .

"This feeling against the colored men is, of course, not shared by all of the men of the college and we are glad to print here articles from the undergraduates expressing their beliefs on both sides of the question."

" . . . Phi Delta is not a reformers' club; it is an association of men for literary and social purposes. I know that to me one of the most treasured factors of my society life has been the fellowship and good feeling so evident all thru our work, the feeling of friendship and brotherliness for every fellow member. And this element has had its very important influence on the grade of our literary work, first for Alma Mater, next for the honor of Phi Delta. And, to speak plainly, the presence of a colored man in our ranks would for many of us spoil utterly the social side of society life. It may be a sign of narrowness, but many of us have a very strong feeling in that respect and knew that this step would be a cruel blow at Phi Delta.

"As for the man himself this same feeling would have injured him. Personally, I have nothing but respect and good will toward this individual nor had any of us, but few of us would have been able to give him the glad hand of fellowship and the social equality which would have been his due if admitted. Furthermore, even if he had been taken in and made one of us in every way, many of you older men know full well how small a degree of any such treatment he could have outside Oberlin walls. Would you tantalize a human soul with the vision of a promised land from which an impassable gulf will soon shut him off? And, inasmuch as there are few, if any others of his race, worthy of admission to Phi Delta this step would have isolated him from those with whom his future must be linked."

" . . . For what greater opportunity could come to a society organized to orate and debate on current problems than actually to help solve one of these problems? And how can this particular problem be solved except by the co-operation of the better classes of each race and the encouragement on the part of the dominant race of those who are struggling to overcome the handicap given them by fortune?

"It is hard, of course; for race prejudice is no thing of the imagination, but is real and deeply rooted. But merely because it is hard is no reason why we should shrink from it, but is all the more reason for facing the matter squarely whenever the opportunity is presented. To face the matter squarely is not to hope for some act of congress or other miracle but to make the problem a personal one, for each individual to use his education to supplant prejudice with reason. For race prejudice is directly opposed to reason in that it regards each member of the race as a type rather than as a person. And if college men have not the foresight to look at the situation in its entirety and the justice to judge a college man on his own manly qualities rather than on the traditional qualities of his race, then these men need not be horrified at the cruelties which the same prejudice may lead mobs of their ignorant brothers to perform.''

"In your March issue (p. 224) you announce 'that it has become generally understood' that men like Frederick Douglass, Paul Lawrence Dunbar and Booker Washington 'are not wanted' in the literary societies of the progressive Oberlin of today.

''Is this a fair representation of the 'modern scholarship' of Oberlin, or is it a slanderous fiction? Has color and not character or talent become the 'open sesame' to literary honory on the campus once graced by Tappan Hall, and once the inspiring center of impulse to heroisms of self-sacrifice for men of every color and clime? Has the Missionary Arch, the memorial of men and women who lived and died for those of an off color, crumbled into dust and been forgotten, or has the spirit of some Legree been permitted to come back from the realm of Pluto to misrepresent the Oberlin of today?''

'' . . . I hardly know which surprises me most; the existence of the state of feeling here recorded, or the matter-of-fact way in which the article seems to accept it as something in the order of natural development and progress. Can it be that the present generation of students and instructors have cut themselves loose from the past history and traditions of Oberlin so that they do not realize the foundations on which its present prosperity rests? Oberlin during its early history stood out from other colleges for two fundamental principles, the higher education of women and the brotherhood of man, including the black man. These two ideas gave her friends and prestige in every state of the union and in many foreign countries. It is because of these that Oberlin has a national reputation instead of being a small, local Ohio college. Its liberal and progressive policy has attracted students, friends and money, and so has made its present success possible.''

'' . . . I belonged to Phi Delta in the years 1875 to 1878. If I remember correctly every man in college except three or four belonged to a society, and some colored men were the strongest members. It was not the custom to solicit members for one society rather than another, but new students were expected to visit society meetings and to make their own choice. I never knew of any one being rejected. Any man whose character and scholarship enabled him to stay at Oberlin College could be sure of admission to the society of his own choice. The democratic spirit of all the societies was unquestioned. . . . . .

"If it is true that colored young men who desire to join a college society refrain from applying because they fear they will not be welcome, this is a serious misfortune for them, and still more serious for the societies if such an unwillingness to admit them really exists. I can appreciate the sensitive and gentlemanly attitude of those who quietly hold back from going where they suspect they may not be wanted, but I am alarmed for those who are willing to have any share in barring out any of their fellow students from the valuable opportunities of our Oberlin College societies."

Section 9. The Number of Negro College Graduates

The number so far as can be ascertained of persons of Negro descent who have been graduated from American colleges may be arranged in the following tables:

NEGRO COLLEGE GRADUATES BY YEARS

1823 1	1861 3	1879 48	1895 130
1826 1	1862 3	1880 . . . , 50	1896 104
1828 1	1864 2	1881 55	1897 128
1841 1	1865 . . . ·. 6	1882 . . . · 39	1898 144
1844 2	1867 4	1883 74	1899 89
1847 1	1868 9	1884 64	1900 92
1849 3	1869 11	1885 100	1901 145
1850 1	1870 26	1886 94	1902 128
1851 1	1871 15	1887 90	1903 148
1852 1	1872 26	1888 . . . 87	1904 139
1853 1	1873 29	1889 85	1905 . : . . 267
1854 1	1874 27	1890 95	1906 182
1856 5	1875 25	1891 99	1907 133
1858 1	1876 37	1892 70	1908 224
1859 1	1877 43	1893 137	1909 155
1860 6	1878 37	1894 130	Total . . 3,856

The following table shows the increase by decades from three graduates during the decade 1820-1829 to 1,613 graduates during the decade 1900-1909:

Decade	Number of Negro college graduates
1820–1829	3
1830–1839	. . .
1840–1849	7
1850–1859	12
1860–1869	44
1870–1879	313
1880–1889	738
1890–1899	1,126
1900–1909	1,613
Total	3,856

NEGRO GRADUATES OF OTHER COLLEGES (BY SEX)

INSTITUTION	Male	Fe-male	Total	INSTITUTION	Male	Fe-male	Total
Oberlin	83	66	149	University of Illinois	7	...	7
Dartmouth	14	...	14	University of Wooster	1	...	1
Ohio State	9	4	13	University of Vermont	3	...	3
Radcliffe	...	4	4	Middlebury	3	1	4
Smith	...	4	4	Southwest Kansas	1	...	1
Iowa State	2	...	2	St. Stephens	4	...	4
Vassar	...	1	1	Trinity	1	...	1
Western Reserve	9	4	13	Otterbein	1	1	2
Indiana	8	...	8	Tabor	3	...	3
University of Pittsburg	10	...	10	Moravian	1	...	1
College of the City of N.Y.	2	...	2	Mt. Union	1	...	1
University of Minnesota	8	...	8	Ohio Wesleyan	2	1	3
Harvard	41	...	41	Marietta	6	...	6
Yale	37	...	37	McKendree	...	1	1
Columbia	3	...	3	Ohio	3	...	3
Univ. of Pennsylvania	29	...	29	Denison	6	1	7
Amherst	14	...	14	University of Rochester	1	...	1
University of California	2	1	3	Purdue	3	...	3
Northwestern	4	1	5	Pomona	1	...	1
Boston	3	...	3	Wesleyan (Conn.)	5	...	5
Coe	2	...	2	Bloomington	...	1	1
Iowa Wesleyan	5	...	5	Iowa State College	2	...	2
Bowdoin	1	...	1	Lafayette	1	...	1
Butler	3	1	4	Albion	3	...	3
Case	2	...	2	Amity	...	1	1
Catholic	2	...	2	Franklin	3	...	3
Cornell College	1	...	1	Bates	12	1	13
Dickinson	1	...	1	Rutgers	1	...	1
Beloit	2	1	3	Westminster	2	...	2
Bucknell	7	...	7	Eureka	1	...	1
Rhode Island State	1	...	1	Hiawatha	1	...	1
Baldwin	2	...	2	Hiram	3	...	3
Washington and Jefferson	2	1	3	Heidelberg	1	...	1
Hillsdale	3	...	3	Lawrence	...	1	1
Monmouth	1	...	1	Lebanon	2	...	2
University of Cincinnati	1	2	3	Wittenburg	2	2	4
Kansas	4	2	6	Lombard	1	...	1
Armour	5	...	5	Univ. of Washington	1	...	1
University of Nebraska	5	1	6	Univ. of So. California	1	...	1
New York	3	...	3	Lake Forest	1	...	1
Illinois	1	...	1	Grove City	1	...	1
Mt. Holyoke	...	2	2	Geneva	7	3	10
Shurtliff	2	...	2	Syracuse	2	...	2
Bellevue	1	...	1	Berea	31	4	35
Adrian	1	1	2	New Hampshire	1	...	1
Allegheny	1	...	1	University of Kansas	45	15	60
Colby	3	...	3	Wheaton	2	1	3
De Pauw	1	...	1	Wellesley	...	3	3
Penn	...	1	1	Williams	7	...	7
Olivet	1	1	2	University of Denver	3	1	4
Washburn	4	3	7	Grinnell	1	...	1
Omaha	1	...	1	Hamilton	1	...	1
University Park	3	1	4	Cornell University	7	3	10
Upper Iowa	...	1	1	Total	549	144	693

The above table is made from the reports of 107 colleges (not Negro) and shows the total number of Negro graduates to be 693; 549 or 79.2 per cent of them are men while 144 or 20.8 per cent are women.

GRADUATES OF NEGRO COLLEGES (BY SEX)

INSTITUTION	Male	Fe-male	Total	INSTITUTION	Male	Fe-male	Total
New Orleans	36	14	50	Wilberforce	114	24	138
Branch	10	2	12	Bennett	68	71	139
Georgia State	4	. . .	4	Geo. R. Smith	6	. . .	6
Paul Quinn	37	18	55	Spelman	. . .	13	13
Bishop	28	2	30	Atlanta Baptist	42	. . .	42
Wiley	35	5	40	Benedict	22	4	26
Clark	57	36	93	Tougaloo	9	3	12
Knoxville	54	18	72	Paine	15	4	19
Howard	159	23	182	Shaw	136	82	218
Tillotson	1	. . .	1	Walden	62	15	77
Hartshorn Memorial	. . .	2	2	Straight	28	9	37
Morris Brown	27	3	30	Virginia Union	46	. . .	46
Shorter	18	14	32	Colored A. & M. (Okla.)	2	1	3
Claflin	61	18	79	St. Augustine	42	15	57
Atlanta	129	34	163	Arkansas Baptist	11	4	15
Biddle	275	. . .	275	Central City	3	. . .	3
Fisk	187	58	245				
Lincoln	617	. . .	617	Total	2450	514	2964

The above table is made from the reports of 34 Negro colleges and shows a total of 2,964 graduates; 2,450 or 82.7 per cent of them are men, while 514 or 17.3 per cent of them are women. Most, tho not all, of these schools are co-educational. Biddle, Lincoln, Atlanta Baptist College and Virginia Union University are schools for male students, while Spelman and Hartshorn Memorial are for female students only.

It is shown that the following Negro colleges have sent forth a hundred or more graduates:

Atlanta University 163
Bennett College 139
Biddle University 275
Fisk University 245
Howard University 182
Lincoln University 617
Shaw University 218
Wilberforce University 138

NEGRO GRADUATES OF OTHER COLLEGES BY TIME GROUPS

NAME OF COLLEGE	1820-1829	1830-1839	1840-1849	1850-1854	1855-1859	1860-1864	1865-1869	1870-1874	1875-1879	1880-1884	1885-1889	1890-1894	1895-1899	1900-1904	1905-1909	Class not given	Total
Oberlin			4	4	7	10	9	8	10	13	11	24	8	16	25		149
Dartmouth								1	1	1	1		3	2	5		14
Ohio State											2		4		7		13
Radcliffe													1	1	2		4
Smith														3	1		4
Iowa State												1		1			2
Vassar																1	1
Western Reserve												1	2	4	6		13
Indiana													4	1	3		8
Univ. of Pittsburg												1	2	2	5		10
College City of N.Y.															2		2
Univ. of Minnesota										1	1	2	1	2	1		8
Harvard								1		2	1	3	4	10	20		41
Yale									1	3	1	2	6	9	15		37
Columbia										1		1	1				3
Univ. of Penn										2	2	9	6	6	4		29
Amherst										1		3	1	3	6		14
Univ. of California															3		3
Northwestern															5		5
Boston												3					3
Coe														1	1		2
Iowa Wesleyan											2	2	1				5
Bowdoin	1																1
Butler											1		1	1		1	4
Case																2	2
Catholic																2	2
Cornell College														1			1
Dickinson														1			1
Beloit												1	1	1			3
Bucknell								1	1	2			2	1			7
Baldwin										1			1				2
Rhode Island State													1				1
Washington & Jeff'n													2		1		3
Hillsdale											1		2				3
Monmouth													1				1
Univ. of Cincinnati													1	1	1		3
Kansas State													1	3	2		6
Armour Institute													2	2	1		5
Univ. of Nebraska													2	1	3		6
New York													1		2		3
Illinois													1				1
Mt. Holyoke											1		1				2
Shurtliffe									1							1	2
Bellevue											1						1
Adrian								1			1						2
Allegheny											1						1
Colby											1		1			1	3
De Pauw													1				1
Penn													1				1
Olivet								1								1	2
Washburn													1	2	3	1	7
Omaha													1				1
University Park													1	2		1	4
Upper Iowa													1				1
University of Illinois														2	5		7
Univ. of Wooster													1				1
Univ. of Vermont																3	3
Middlebury	1		1							1						1	4
Southwest Kansas											1						1
St. Stephens													1			3	4
Trinity																1	1
Otterbein													1			1	2
Tabor																3	3

NEGRO GRADUATES OF OTHER COLLEGES BY TIME GROUPS— CONTINUED

NAME OF COLLEGE	1820-1829	1830-1839	1840-1849	1850-1854	1855-1859	1860-1864	1865-1869	1870-1874	1875-1879	1880-1884	1885-1889	1890-1894	1895-1899	1900-1904	1905-1909	Class not given	Total
Moravian															1		1
Mt. Union															1		1
Ohio Wesleyan														1	2		3
Marietta								1			1	3			1		6
McKendree												1					1
Ohio	1				1										1		3
Denison										1	1	1	1		3		7
Univ. of Rochester												1					1
Purdue												1		1	1		3
Pomona														1			1
Wesleyan (Conn.)						2									3		5
Bloomington															1		1
Iowa											1			1			2
Lafayette			1														1
Albion																3	3
Amity																1	1
Franklin			1									1		1			3
Bates								1	1	1	2	2	5	1			13
Rutgers												1					1
Westminster								1	1								2
Eureka														1			1
Hiawatha											1						1
Hiram								1			1		1				3
Heidleburg															1		1
Laurence															1		1
Lebanon																2	2
Wittenburg													2	1	1		4
Lombard											1						1
Univ. of Washington																1	1
Univ. of So.California																1	1
Lake Forest																1	1
Grove City																1	1
Geneva							1	2	2	2	1				2		10
Syracuse																2	2
Berea																35	35
New Hampshire											1						1
Univ. of Kansas																60	60
Wheaton																3	3
Wellesley														1		2	3
Williams											1	2	1	1	2		7
Univ. of Denver												1	2		1		4
Grinnell														1			1
Hamilton											1						1
Cornell University																10	10
Total	3		7	5	7	12	13	15	19	33	36	78	81	89	149	146	693

GRADUATES OF NEGRO

NAME OF COLLEGE	Before 1876	1876	1877	1878	1879	1880	1881	1882	1883	1884	1885	1886	1887	1888	1889	1890
New Orleans				3		2		2		2				1	2	
Branch Normal								1	1	4	2				1	
Georgia State																
Paul Quinn															2	
Bishop										1	1				1	
Wiley													1			
Clark								1	1	2		3	3	1	4	
Knoxville								2	1	1			1	5	5	3
Howard	5	2	2	1	2	4	6		4	2	3	3	2	6	5	4
Tillotson																
Hartshorn Memorial																
Morris Brown																
Shorter																
Claflin																
Atlanta		6	3	4	5	5	5	2	3	3	2	4	4		3	3
Biddle		1	4	2	4	2	6	3	1	3	6	7	3	3	3	2
Fisk	4		2	2	4	6	5	1	7	4	13	3	8	7	12	12
Lincoln	48	8	6	6	4	4	5	5	8	17	14	23	23	20	19	17
Wilberforce	11	1	1	2	1	3	4	1	3	5	5	2	5	3	4	1
Bennett											1	2	1	3	7	
George R. Smith																
Spelman																
Atlanta Baptist																
Benedict																1
Tougaloo																
Paine																
Shaw				6	5	12	5	4	6	4	10	12	4	13		19
Walden				1	5	5	1					4			3	3
Straight		2	1	3	8			5		5	1		1	2		
Virginia Union																
Colored A. and M. (Okla.)																
St. Augustine													11			
Arkansas Baptist																
Central City																
Total	68	20	19	30	33	43	50	23	50	45	69	75	53	62	69	54

It is impossible to ascertain the exact number of Negroes who have graduated from colleges in the North for many of these institutions keep no record of race or nationality of their graduates. We quote from the replies from Brown University and from the University of Michigan which are typical of such cases:

University of Michigan.—"I find that in our alumni records no mention is made as to the color of graduates."

Brown University.—"There is no one who can give a list of the Negro graduates of Brown University. We have never kept any list of students according to race or nationality. While from one point of view

COLLEGES BY YEARS

1891	1892	1893	1894	1895	1896	1897	1898	1899	1900	1901	1902	1903	1904	1905	1906	1907	1908	1909	Class not given	Total
4			1	2	1	1	2	1	2	5	2	3	5	1	2	2	1	1	2		50
	1		1			1					2										12
							1	1		2											4
4	1	1	1	3	1	2	4	2	1	1		7	3	4	2	7	5				55
										1			2	5	6	13					30
1	1	1			1		2	2	1	4	1	3	4	4	3	7	3				40
1	3		2			2		3	2	2	4	6	8	8	8	9	5	15			93
1		2	3	1	2	3	8	2	1	5	4		7	2	4	3	4	2			72
2	2	5	5	3	3	2	8	5	4	11	7	7	6	11	10	6	17	17			182
																	1				1
																2					2
							2	3	2	3	3	1			8	1	3	2	2		30
																			32	32
																			79	79
5			2	7	4	5	4	3	9	4	6	4	10	6	8	7	10	10	7		163
7	7	9	10	12	9	6	8	10	15	13	13	14	14	21	22	13	13	11		275
12	6	14	8	11	15	9	11	11	8	13	13	22	21	22	23	16	20	34		376
19	18	20	36	27	19	19	18	21	26	27	23	28	18	24	19					617
1	2	2	4	2	5	6	5	8	6	3	5	2	10	8	7	9				138
	2	4	5	8	3	14	15			15	8	8		2	7	11	5	4	10		139
																			6	6
									2		4			1	1	3	2			13
						3	3			4	3	1	3	2	7	5	2	9		42
	2			1			1	4		1	1	2	1	1	6	1	1	3		26
									1	3	1	3	1		1	2				12
	1	3	2	3	2				1	2	3	2								19
	6	18	10	9	5	6	3	5	3	10	3	5	1	7	∘6	4	17				218
4				1	2	4	2	10	2	4			3	2	2	3	3	1	4	8	77
1					1				2	3			1			1				37
											4	7	4	5	3	9	9	3	5		46
																3				3
2	2	1	1			2	2	1	2	3	2	1	6	4	5	7				57
								3				2				4	2	1	3		15
																			3	3
64	54	83	99	88	76	85	107	93	105	122	116	129	127	158	160	150	137	128	120	2,964

such distinctions are valuable, from another point of view it may be said that the constant effort of the college should be to ignore such distinctions, and replace them with the distinctions of ability and character. It is possibly for this reason that we have never kept any record of race distinctions among our alumni."

It is similarly true of other schools, which consequently do not appear in the above tables, tho they are known to have graduated Negroes. The University of Chicago, Columbia University and Tufts College are but a few additions to this list—all of which have sent forth Negro graduates of power and efficiency. There are also a few notable cases of American Negroes who have been graduated from colleges abroad.

It is probably safe to say that 5,000 Negro Americans have graduated from college.

Section 10.   Statistics of Certain Living Negro Graduates

In answer to the questionnaire sent to Negro college graduates about eight hundred answers were received. These answers come from graduates of eighty-one colleges as follows:

NEGRO COLLEGES

Allen	Morris Brown
Atlanta Baptist	New Orleans
Atlanta University	Paine
Bennett	St. Augustine
Biddle	Shaw
Bishop	Shorter
Central City	Spelman
Claflin	State (Georgia)
Clark	Straight
Fisk	Talladega
Geo. R. Smith	Tougaloo
Gilbert	Virginia Union
Howard	Walden
Knoxville	Wilberforce
Leland	Wiley
Lincoln	

OTHER COLLEGES

Adelbert	New York University
Albion	Oberlin
Allegheny	Ohio State
Amherst	Olivet
Amity	Otterbein
Armour	Pomona
Bates	Rutgers
Bellevue	Shurtliff
Berea	Stanford
Boston University	Tabor
Brown	University of Cincinnati
Bucknell	University of Denver
Colby	University of Illinois
Cornell	University of Indiana
Dartmouth	University of Iowa
Denison	University of Kansas

Dickinson
Franklin
Harvard
Hillsdale
Kansas State
Lawrence
Massachusetts Agr. Col.
Middlebury
Nebraska State University

University of Minnesota
University of Pennsylvania
University of Rochester
University of Vermont
Washburn
Wesleyan
Western Reserve
Williams
Yale

NEGRO GRADUATES REPORTING, BY COLLEGE AND TIME OF GRADUATION

INSTITUTION	1850–1869	1870–1889	1890–1899	1900–1909	Total	INSTITUTION	1850–1869	1870–1889	1890–1899	1900–1909	Total
Adelbert				1	1	Nebraska State Univ.				1	1
Albion				2	2	New Orleans				1	3	4
Allegheny		1			1	New York University				1	1
Allen		1			1	Oberlin	3	4	6	13	26
Amherst			1		1	Ohio State	1		3	4	8
Amity				1	1	Olivet			1		1
Armour				1	1	Otterbein			1		1
Atlanta Baptist			5	26	31	Paine			3	8	11
Atlanta University		14	12	29	55	Pomona				1	1
Bates			3		3	Rutgers			1		1
Bellevue			1		1	St. Augustine		2	2	4	8
Bennett		1	7	11	19	Shaw		15	9	15	39
Berea		4	4	2	10	Shorter			1	3	4
Biddle		13	16	19	48	Shurtliff				1	1
Bishop		1		2	3	Spelman				7	7
Boston University			1		1	Stanford			1		1
Brown		1	3	2	6	State (Georgia)			1		1
Bucknell			1		1	Straight		1	1	2	4
Central City			1	1	2	Tabor		1	1		2
Claflin		5	7	12	24	Talladega				13	13
Clark		4	4	5	13	Tougaloo				9	9
Colby			2		2	Univ. of Cincinnati			1		1
Cornell			2	2	University of Denver		1			1
Dartmouth			4	4	University of Illinois			4	4
Dennison			2	2	4	University of Indiana			1	1	2
Dickinson			1	1	University of Iowa			1	1
Fisk		23	36	58	117	University of Kansas	1	3	2	6
Franklin			1	1	2	Univ. of Minnesota			1	1
Geo. R. Smith			3	3	Univ. of Pennsylvania		1		1
Gilbert			1	1	Univ. of Rochester		1		1
Harvard	1		3	4	Univ. of Vermont		1		1
Hillsdale	1			1	Virginia Union			17	17
Howard	7	4	6	17	Walden		2	7	3	12
Kansas State		1	1	Washburn			2	2
Knoxville	6	9	14	29	Wesleyan	2	1	4	7
Lawrence	1		1	Western Reserve		1	1
Leland	2	7	8	17	Wilberforce	8	7	7	22
Lincoln	1	21	19	20	61	Wiley	2	7	9
Massachusetts Ag. Col.			1	1	Williams		1	1
Middlebury	1			1	Yale	1	3	1	5
Morris Brown		1	6	7						

TABLE SHOWING PLACE OF BIRTH AND PRESENT RESIDENCE OF NEGRO GRADUATES REPORTING

LIVING IN → BORN IN ↓	*New England States*	*Southern North Atlantic States*	*Northern South Atlantic States*	*Southern South Atlantic States*	*Eastern North Central States*	*Western North Central States*	*Eastern South Central States*	*Western South Central States*	*Rocky Mountain States*	*Basin and Plateau States*	*Pacific States*	*Outside United States*	*Unknown*	*Total*
Louisiana	1		1	1			4	24					1	32
Kentucky	1		2	1	5	2	14	1					1	27
Illinois	2		2			3	1	1						9
Ohio		1	4	4	14	4	2	3						32
Tennessee	3	2		3	4	5	43	6				1	1	68
Virginia	1	6	28	6	5	5	11	3					5	70
South Carolina		9	7	62	6	1	4	7				1	2	99
North Carolina		4	12	86	4		3	4					2	115
Florida		1	1	2			1	2						7
Kansas	1	1				7							1	10
Indiana					3			1						4
Mississippi		3	2			1		15	7					28
Texas						1	2	14						17
Michigan			1		3		1							5
Maryland	1	2	9		3	1		3					1	20
Missouri			1		2	7		1	1				2	14
Arkansas			1	1	1		1	7					1	12
Ontario							1							1
Canada		1		1			1							3
Nova Scotia				1										1
South Africa				1										1
British West Indies	1													1
Alabama	6	1	2	8	2	1	20	7	1					48
Georgia	1	2	4	89	4	4	12	6			1			123
Iowa					1	4		1						6
Massachusetts		1					1							2
Connecticut	1													1
New Jersey		1			1									2
New York			3				1							4
Pennsylvania		3	1	2	1	1	2	1			1			12
West Virginia			3				1				1			5
District of Columbia		1	8			2								11
West Indies				2			1							3
Rhode Island		1			1									2
Unknown		1		4				1					1	7
Total	19	42	92	276	61	47	141	99	2		3	2	18	802

From the above table the following facts concerning birth-place of these 802 graduates are noted:

South Atlantic States*

Maryland	20	2.5	per cent
District of Columbia	11	1.4	" "
Virginia	70	8.7	" "
West Virginia	5	.62	" "
North Carolina	115	14.3	" "
South Carolina	99	12.3	" "
Georgia	123	15.2	" "
Florida	7	.87	" "
Total	450	56.1	per cent

South Central States

Kentucky	27	3.3	per cent
Tennessee	68	8.5	" "
Alabama	48	5.9	" "
Mississippi	28	3.5	" "
Arkansas	12	1.5	" "
Louisiana	32	4.	" "
Texas	17	2.1	" "
Total	232	28.9	per cent
Total South	682	85	" "

The leading states of the North on the basis of birth of Negro college graduates reporting are as follows:

Ohio. . . . 32 | Missouri. 14 | Pennsylvania. 12 | Kansas . 10 | Illinois . . 9

Further using the census nomenclature we draw the following facts concerning present residence of these 802 graduates:

Present residence	Number	Per cent of total
New England States	19	2.4
Southern North Atlantic States	42	5.2
Northern South Atlantic States	92	11.5
Southern South Atlantic States	276	34.4
Eastern North Central States	61	7.6
Western North Central States	47	5.9
Eastern South Central States	141	17.6
Western South Central States	99	12.3
Elsewhere	25	3.1
Total	802	100

The following table is a clear statement of the movements of these graduates:

---

* Census nomenclature used.

BORN IN	Total	LIVING IN			
		North	South	Places out-side U. S.	Unknown
North	103=100%	65=63 %	35=34 %	1=1 %	2=2 %
South	682=100%	102=15 %	563=82.5%	2= .3%	15=2.2%
Places outside United States .	10=100%	3=30 %	7=70 %	. . . . . .	. . . . . .
Unknown	7=100%	5=71 %	1=14 %	. . . . .	1=14 %
Total	802=100%	175=21.8%	606=75.6%	3=3 %	18=2.2%

The above table shows that of 103 graduates born in the
North, sixty-five or 63 per cent of them remained in the
North, while thirty-five or 34 per cent went to the South to
labor among their people.   Of 682 graduates born in the South
102 or 15 per cent of them went to the North, while 563 or
82.5 per cent of them remained in the South.

These statistics cover only about one-fourth of the living
Negro college graduates but they are typical of the whole
group.   Three facts are clearly shown:

1.   The greater part of the labors of college-bred Negro
Americans is expended in the South where the great masses
of Negroes dwell.

2.   The great majority of southern born Negro college
graduates have remained in the South to labor among their
people.

3.   There has been a continuous stream of northern born
college-bred Negroes who have come to the South and joined
in the work of lifting black people to higher planes of culture
and intelligence.

There has been a rapid and encouraging development in the
family life of the American Negro since the emancipation.
For more than two hundred years the Negroes in America
suffered the social evils of the slave regime.   It may be said
that the greatest evils of slavery in America were the breaking up of family ties and the consequent premium placed
upon promiscuous sexual relations.   The evident tendencies
then were toward uncertainty of and disregard for the marriage vow.   During the forty odd years of freedom great

progress has been made in the eradication of these evils as is evidenced by the number of well ordered Negro homes built upon constant family relations. In this great work the college-bred men and women of the Negro race have had a large share.

The statistics are meagre but they show something of present tendencies.

CONJUGAL CONDITION

	Male	Female	Total
Married	465=67.3%	34=31.1 %	499= 62 %
Single	207=30 %	72=66.05%	279= 35 %
Widowed	17= 2.4%	2= 1.88%	19= 2 %
Divorced	1	1	2
Total	690=100 %	109=100 %	799=100 %

The above table shows that 67.3 per cent of the males and 31.1 per cent of the females reporting are married. It must be remembered that many of these reports come from graduates of quite recent years. The per cent of divorced is exceedingly low.

AGE AT MARRIAGE

AGE AT MARRIAGE	Males	Females	Total
Under 20 years	3	. . . . .	3
20-24 years	49	10	59
25-29 years	170	17	187
30-34 years	151	3	154
35-39 years	53	. . . . .	53
40-44 years	19	. . . . .	19
45 years and over	9	1	10
Not given	11	3	14
Total	465	34	499

The above table shows that of the 465 male graduates reporting themselves as married the majority have married between the ages of twenty-five and thirty-four, and of the thirty-four female graduates reporting themselves as married the majority have married between the ages of twenty and twenty-nine.

The tables which follow contain statistics of children born to families of Negro college graduates reporting themselves as having been married. The first of these tables shows that the families of 134 male graduates and of seven female graduates are childless. Here also it must be remembered that not a few of these reports come from graduates of quite recent date. The families of the remaining graduates reporting themselves as having been married report from one child to fourteen children each; that is, the families of 378 graduates report 1,411 children or roughly speaking an average of four children per family. The average for all families of graduates reporting themselves as having been married would be slightly less.

The following table shows:

CHILDREN BORN TO FAMILIES OF GRADUATES REPORTING

CHILDREN	Number Families of		CHILDREN	Number Families of	
	Male graduates	*Female graduates*		*Male graduates*	*Female graduates*
No children	134	7	Eight children	9	. . . . .
One child	82	7	Nine children	10	. . . . .
Two children	55	4	Ten children	6	. . . . .
Three children	63	4	Eleven children . . .	2	1
Four children	44	. . . . .	Twelve children . . .	3	1
Five children	36	3	Thirteen children . .	2	. . . . .
Six children	24	2	Fourteen children . .	1	. . . . .
Seven children	17	2			

The following tables combine the number of children born to and the number of children lost by families of Negro graduates reporting. The death statistics include still-birth. It is seen that the families of 208 graduates reporting children have lost none. The remaining 170 families report the loss of one child to eight children each; that is, a total loss of 344 children or an average loss of barely one child per family of the families reporting children.

It is no small part of the mission of the educated to see to it that children are well born. The college-bred Negro American has helped in this direction. Meagre as these statistics are they are nevertheless of value.

FAMILIES OF MALE GRADUATES REPORTING

Families having born / Families losing by death (including still-birth)	One child	Children													Total
		2	3	4	5	6	7	8	9	10	11	12	13	14	
	82	55	63	44	36	24	17	9	10	6	2	3	2	1	354
No children	68	41	39	23	11	6	2	3	3	.	.	.	.	.	196
One child	14	10	15	12	6	4	5	1	4	.	.	.	.	..	71
Two children	..	4	7	5	12	8	5	2	1	3	1	..	1	..	49
Three children	..	..	2	3	4	4	2	1	1	..	1	..	..	..	18
Four children	..	..	..	1	2	2	2	..	..	1	..	1	..	..	9
Five children	..	..	..	..	..	1	..	1	1	2	..	..	..	1	6
Six children	..	..	..	..	..	..	1	1	..	..	..	2	..	..	4
Seven children	..	..	..	..	..	..	..	..	..	..	..	..	..	..	..
Eight children	..	..	..	..	..	..	..	..	..	..	..	..	1	..	1
Total	82	55	63	44	36	24	17	9	10	6	2	3	2	1	354

FAMILIES OF FEMALE GRADUATES REPORTING

Families having born / Families losing by death (including still-birth)	One child	Children											Total
		2	3	4	5	6	7	8	9	10	11	12	
	7	4	4	..	3	2	2	..	..	..	1	1	24
No children	6	2	1	..	3	..	..	..	..	..	..	..	12
One child	1	..	3	..	..	..	1	..	..	..	..	..	5
Two children	..	2	..	..	..	1	1	..	..	..	..	..	4
Three children	..	..	..	..	..	1	..	..	..	..	1	..	2
Four children	..	..	..	..	..	..	..	..	..	..	..	1	1
Total	7	4	4	..	3	2	2	..	..	..	1	1	24

Section 11.   Early Life and Training

Reports of early life and training do not lend themselves to ready tabulation. The following quotations are taken from the reports of these Negro college graduates and are both typical and interesting—showing as they do something of the childhood and youth thru which these men and women have passed.

Men

"I was carefully reared by parents who had been slaves, attended public schools, removed to Ohio and attended high school."

"I was born and reared on a cotton farm. My early training was such as could be received in an ex-slave home and three-months-in-the-year school. Mother and father were honest tho unlettered and strove to make the best of their opportunities and left that impression upon their children. Best of all, I was reared in a Christian home."

"I went from Virginia to Vermont December 23, 1863. I worked on the farm nine months during the year and attended common school three months. I did this till 1872. I then went to Andover, Massachusetts, March 7, 1872. Attended Phillips Andover Academy from 1872 to 1875; then to Middlebury College, Vermont, 1875 to 1880; Boston University, 1880 to 1883."

"My early life was spent on the farm. My early training was two months of public school each year and studying at night by lightwood knots. I went from this to the graded school of Wilson, North Carolina, and from there to Lincoln University, Pennsylvania."

"I was born of poor, hard-working parents and was left an orphan at eleven years. I went to night school in the town where I was being reared by a family of white people who were the ex-owners of my parents. I entered school as a day student at age of seventeen, completed the academic course at twenty and then went to college."

"Being born a slave, my early training was quite meagre until I was eleven or twelve years old, having simply learned to read and spell well up to my twelfth year. My literary training was obtained in Tennessee, to which I was brought in very early life."

"My early life was one of poverty and longing for better things."

"I was born on a farm and remained there until I was well up in age. I have chopped cotton, worked corn, pulled hay, because I had no scythe to cut it, peddled wood at the Fayetteville, North Carolina, market many a winter with no shoes on and clothing extremely scarce. . . . My life was one of struggle from the time I could remember but in the future I saw a star of hope and pushed in that direction every time I saw an opportunity to advance. I went to a country school in a log house in Cumberland county, North Carolina. I went to Wilmington to live and there went to night school four or five months."

"My father deserted home when I was about five years old. My mother died when I was twelve years old, leaving me in the care of an illiterate foster mother. She was very kind to me and did laundry work that I might be allowed to attend school. I finished the public school course in 1895. In the summer of 1896 I went to Rhode Island to work. From that time until I finished school in 1905 I paid my own expenses by doing hotel work in summer."

"I was born a slave. I learned the alphabet in 1868 near Nashville, Tennessee, and graduated from college in 1878."

"Early life on a plantation amid surroundings incident to slave life. Attended public school more or less irregularly."

"I was a slave until eleven years of age. I learned the bricklayer's trade. I entered college in 1875."

"I was born in the country, worked on farm till eighteen years old, then worked for railroad three years. I went to school about four months before I was twenty."

"I passed my early life on the farm near the town of Franklinton, North Carolina, and was trained in the Christian Institute and Albion Academy. I never had the support of a father but was obedient to the direction of a loving mother to whom I owe all I am and all I hope to be."

"I worked on a farm and attended rural schools until I was sixteen and then entered Fisk University."

"I was born a slave and was freed by the Emancipation Proclamation of Abraham Lincoln."

"I went to a private school when quite young. My father and mother died when I was nine years old. I lived then with white people, working for my board and clothes several years. While there I lacked one year of completing the high school course. I went from there to Lincoln Institute and completed the two years' Normal course. From Lincoln Institute I went to Fisk University and completed the bachelor of arts course."

"I was born on a sugar plantation; spent early life as a farmer. I had some advantages of public school instruction."

"I assisted my father on the farm and in his winter work as the town butcher during school vacations in the summer and on Saturdays. I attended the public schools of Macon, Mississippi, during their sessions of nine months. I was taught first by those whites who came from the North as teachers during the seventies; then by Fisk and Rust University graduates until I came to Fisk in 1887. I pushed my own way forward mostly, i. e. with the occasional lift my father would give when I called upon him, which I reluctantly did as he evidently had succeeded some in his teaching of self-reliance—not running up the white flag upon every occasion."

"I was born on my father's farm in the traditional log cabin. Early training was received in the country public school."

"My childhood and youth were spent in Atlanta. Most of my time I was working to help support my family. Now and then I went to night school and the summer country school. In 1876 I got desperate and broke away from my family and entered Storr's School. Finishing there in the spring of 1877, in the fall of the same year I entered Atlanta University and there I remained till I was graduated in 1884."

"I was eighteen months old, the youngest of six children, when my father died. My mother was left with a home and six children too young to work. Having nothing left me and with brothers and sisters to be supported by my mother, my early life was one of denial. I had the necessary things of life—nothing else. When I became old enough to work I secured a route on an afternoon paper and sold papers Sunday mornings. I did this all the time I was attending school in this city, making from one and a half to three and a half dollars per week. My people were free, able to read and write, and with a knowledge of refinement above the average, therefore my home surroundings were above the average. I had a good training along religious lines.''

"During vacations and holidays I worked in the shop with my father who was a wheelwright and wagon and carriage builder. I worked some with an uncle on the farm when work in the shop was slack.''

"I was born in slavery and came into freedom under the terms of Lincoln's Emancipation Proclamation. While a slave I did various kinds of light work for my master's family or for other white people to whom I was often hired. From 1865 to 1867 I tried to help my mother support her large family of children. From 1867 to 1880 I was in school in Atlanta, Georgia, and Andover, Massachusetts.''

"Beginning at the age of six I attended the country district school, terms averaging about two and one-half months per year. I worked on farm with my father until I was fifteen; then a few months on the railroad; but my chief work up to the age of twenty-one was in tobacco factories.''

"I worked at any and all kinds of common work, such as waiting table and barber shop porter, attending the common schools and also taking advantage of such private schools as were offered.''

"I was sixteen when the war closed. I learned to read and write in night school in Albany, Georgia, in 1866. I plowed all day and walked a mile and a half at night to school.''

"I was born a slave on a farm in Franklin county, Virginia. When I was eight years old I walked with my parents to Kanawha county, West Virginia, a distance of two hundred and fifty miles, in the month of March. My father died when I was twelve. I never attended school until after that time.''

"I was a slave until I reached the age of thirteen years. I was taken from my parents at ten years of age. I have been compelled to support myself since 1865. I had about nine months of schooling before reaching the age of twenty-one years. I have received most of my education since I became twenty-one years of age.''

"I was born and reared on a farm, attended the country schools during my boyhood days. I have done all kinds of laboring work, both on the farm and on the railroad. I acted as a clerk in a supply department at a summer resort for eighteen years during summer vacations while a student and since I have been teaching.''

"I was brought up on a farm with no chance to educate myself. I had to work for what I could eat and wear, having no one to help me in life. Father was dead; mother could not help me because she was not able. I had no chance to go to school until I was nineteen years old.''

"I jobbed around in summer and attended winter school, maintained by my parents; taught generally by students from Oberlin College. I was hired out as house-boy for a while; carried clothes back and forth as my mother took in washing. I was naturally studious. I studied Latin and Algebra myself. I went to Louisville, Kentucky, before the war and assisted my brother-in-law in teaching free Negro children and slaves who could get a permit. From there I went to Ohio University, Athens, Ohio, in 1849 and graduated there in 1853.''

"I was educated largely by my own efforts, being left an orphan in the state of Vermont after 1865.''

"My mother died when I was six months old, father when I was seven years old. Between the city and country I lived, survived and did not perish. At the age of nineteen I was janitor of graded school in Durham, North Carolina. I received ten dollars per month and my schooling. At the end of the school term I passed the fourth grade, the proudest boy in the world. I clerked in store that summer and in the fall I entered Fisk with a vim to win.''

"I was born a slave. I was bound out for four years. I was taught at nights by the daughters of the man to whom I was apprenticed for four years. Lived and worked on farm most of the time till nineteen years of age.''

"I was born a slave and left an orphan. I was sent adrift empty-hand without parents or guardian. I began education in night school. I entered day school under Quakers at age of seventeen. I attended two months during session for four years. Meanwhile I continued to burn the midnight oil. I became clerk, bookkeeper, deputy sheriff, policeman, public school teacher.''

"I attended public schools of Augusta, Georgia, and worked between times as a newspaper carrier and later on as a printer. I was graduated from Ware High School in 1886 and then entered Atlanta University.''

"I grew up on a farm with a 'scrapped up' education in fitful public and private schools and private instruction.''

"My early life and training was that of the ordinary youth of our race: one of a large family of children, on a little farm, a few months' attendance every year at public schools until large enough to work. At the age of twenty I left for the North and by hard work by day and private study by night I prepared to enter Lincoln University.''

"I was born a slave and was a farm boy until twenty-four years old.''

"I was born in the country in Missouri. Up to nine years of age I had no schooling. I learned my A, B, C's from the Bible in my tenth year. I had two terms of school, one three months, one five months in

Missouri. My family emigrated to Nebraska when I was in my twelfth year. Farmed there and finished common and high school at Seward, Seward county, Nebraska."

"I was a farm boy until twenty-four years of age. I was born a slave."

"Sea life for eight or ten years. I traveled much. I attended district school in Massachusetts in winter. My academic training was received at Pierce Academy, Middleboro, Massachusetts; college work at Atlanta University."

Women

"I attended public school in a rural district until sixteen years old. I then went to a small town and entered graded school. I made a good average with attendance daily the first term and was promoted. The next term I became tutor. My parents being dead my teachers became interested in me and made it possible for me to enter college in 1893."

"I was reared on the farm until old enough to earn wages; then I was hired out until about twenty years old, when I entered school for the first time. Steady work and interested parties put me thru school."

"I was reared on a farm. My parents were poor yet they kept me supplied with books and saw to it that I attended our rural school regularly. At the age of fourteen I entered Tougaloo University."

"I was reared on a large farm owned by my father, who was one of the most extensive cotton planters in Ouachita Parish. My parents were not educated but both could read and write; and knowing the advantage of an education they spent a fortune in educating their children, giving thirteen—all who did not die in early childhood—a fair English training. When I was nine years of age they employed a tutor in the home to prepare me to be sent off to school, since educational advantages for Negroes were so poor in that part of the state. The next year I entered Straight."

"I was born in a cabin and attended a country school."

"The child of a college-bred mother and fairly intelligent father, my home life and early training were good; I had every opportunity and encouragement to acquire an education."

"I had a good home and intelligent parents, who were free people before the war, hence I enjoyed some educational advantages before the Civil War. My father was a barber and a lawyer, the first colored man admitted to the bar in Tennessee. My mother was a skilled dressmaker who served for Mrs. President Polk and others high in social life."

"I attended the public school of Oberlin, Ohio, for two years. We moved South in 1883. From then I was taught in the home until I went off to school in 1890."

"I was a pupil in the public school of Gainesville, Florida, until about sixteen years of age. Then I entered the State Normal School at Tallahassee, Florida, from which I graduated in 1902. While a student at Tallahassee I taught each summer in rural schools. During each school year I earned my board entirely by services rendered in the president's family. After graduating I taught two consecutive terms in city schools and in 1904 spent the summer studying at the University of Chicago. In the fall of 1904 I returned South and entered Clark University."

"I was educated in Iowa. I earned my way thru the University."

"My father was a man of fair education; mother not formally educated but a great reader from her youth up. Both were actively interested in the education of their children."

Section 12. Occupations

The value of any educational scheme is seen in the life and work of the men and women who have enjoyed the opportunities afforded by the same. In estimating the value of college training for the Negroes of America it is quite natural, therefore, to ask, What are the college-bred Negro Americans doing? As a matter of fact this is the first and in some degree the crucial question asked concerning college-bred Negroes. The Conference finds that these Negro graduates are at present, with few exceptions, usefully and creditably employed and that there is an increased and pressing demand for college trained Negroes.

The statistics set forth in this section are compiled from the reports of only about one-fourth of the total number of living Negro college graduates in the United States. While not exhaustive they are of much value, since they may be regarded as typical of the whole group.

The following table compiled from the returned blanks of the Negro college graduates reporting shows the various occupations in which these graduates are engaged and the number engaged in each occupation:

OCCUPATION OF NEGRO COLLEGE GRADUATES REPORTED BY
THEMSELVES

Architect	1	Mail carriers	5
Banker	1	Matron	1
Barbers	3	Mechanical drawing	1
Bookkeeper	1	Merchant	1
Bookkeeper and editor	1	Merchant and real estate dealer	1
Business	1	Miner	1
Business manager of school	1	Missionaries	6
Cashier in bank	1	Music teachers	2
Caterer	1	Newspaper correspondent	1
Census worker	1	Physicians	46
Civil engineer	1	Physician and druggist	2
Civil service	1	Planter and real estate dealer	1
Clerical workers	6	Post office clerks	12
Clerk general Land Office (U. S.)	1	Preachers	97
Clerk Treasury Department (U. S.)	1	Preacher and editor	2
Dean of college	1	Preacher and farmer	1
Dentist	2	Preacher and physician	1
Director of publicity and research	1	Preacher and teacher	47
Domestic	1	Preceptress	2
Draftsman	1	Preceptress and matron	1
Draftsman (U. S.)	1	President of bank	1
Dressmaker	1	President of college	1
Druggists	3	Railway mail service	10
Druggists and physicians	2	Real estate dealers	3
Editors	2	Secretaries	2
Editor and preacher	1	Shoe dealer	1
Electrical engineers	2	Stenographers	2
Elevator operator	1	Students	28
Farmers	6	Superintendents	4
Farmer and preacher	1	Superintendent manual training	1
Foreman	1	Surgeon and physician	2
Government service	1	Tailor	1
Grocer	1	Teachers	353
Housekeepers	6	Teacher and editor	1
Housewives	13	Teacher and lawyer	1
Insurance	2	Teacher and matron	1
Internal revenue collector	1	Teacher, preacher, farmer	1
Janitors	2	Undertaker	1
Judge	1	United States clerkship	2
Lawyers	26	United States deputy marshal	1
Lawyer and teacher	1	United States Pension Bureau	2
Librarian	1	Waiters	2
Lumber dealer	1		

It is seen from the table that the occupations which draw the largest numbers of these graduates are teaching, preaching, the practice of medicine and the practice of law. Of those reporting occupations the numbers so engaged are as follows:

OCCUPATION	Number engaged	Per cent of total reporting
Teaching	407	53.8
Preaching	151	20
Medicine	53	7
Law	29	3.8

Here indeed is shown the particular mission of the Negro college: the training of teachers and leaders and professional men and women for the black people of America. The work of the educated Negro is largely the work of leadership

Teachers

The crying need of the four million Negroes at the close of the Civil War showed itself in the call for teachers. In response to this call came the early Negro colleges, established primarily for the training of Negro teachers. That has been and is today their chief mission.

The above statistics show that 407 or 53.8 per cent of the total number of Negro college graduates reporting occupation are engaged in the profession of teaching. These men and women are scattered thruout the South and are engaged in teaching in all kinds of institutions—from primary to collegiate. It can be truly said that the progress of the American Negro during the forty-seven years since emancipation has been due largely to the wholesome and helpful influence of these Negro college graduates who have labored as teachers of their people.

Preachers

The Negro church and the Negro preacher have occupied a unique place in the social development of the black people of this country. Both during and since the slave regime the church has been the chief social center of the Negro people. The church and the people alike have suffered from an ignorant ministry and the end of the suffering is not yet. It is encouraging, however, to find that many educated Negroes have entered and are entering this sphere of activity. Of the number reporting occupation, 151 or 20 per cent are engaged in the ministry. This indicates to some extent the work of the Negro college in this important field and it likewise gives hope for the future.

Most of these ministers have been trained in the Negro theological schools, chief of which are the following:

Gammon Theological Seminary, Atlanta, Georgia
Payne Theological Seminary, Wilberforce, Ohic

Virginia Union, Richmond, Virginia
Lincoln, Lincoln University, Pennsylvania
Atlanta Baptist, Atlanta, Georgia
Talladega, Talladega, Alabama
Fisk, Nashville, Tennessee

Many of these ministers have done work in theological schools of the North. Among those reporting are graduates of the following northern schools:

Yale Divinity School, New Haven, Connecticut
Andover Theological Seminary, Andover, Massachusetts
Hartford Theological Seminary, Hartford, Connecticut
Auburn Theological Seminary, Auburn, New York
Drew Theological Seminary, Madison, New Jersey
Oberlin Theological Seminary, Oberlin, Ohio
Princeton Seminary, Princeton, New Jersey
Western Theological Seminary, Allegheny, Pennsylvania
Boston University School of Theology, Boston, Massachusetts

It is encouraging to note here that most of these ministers have completed college before entering upon their theological training. The Negro ministry is rapidly changing from an uneducated to an educated factor in Negro life in America.

Physicians

The Negroes of the South are looking to the members of their own race for medical attention and so the demand for Negro physicians is great. Social conditions, too, have increased this demand. There is, therefore, an ever widening field for the Negro doctor. The above table shows that fifty-three or seven per cent of the total number reporting occupations are engaged in the practice of medicine. The influence of this profession upon the masses of Negroes cannot be over-estimated. These men and women have done much to raise the physical and moral tone of the communities in which they have worked and their influence upon the cultural standards of their people has been marked. These physicians report themselves as graduates from the following medical schools:

Negro Medical Schools

Leonard Medical School, Raleigh, North Carolina
Howard Medical School, Washington, District of Columbia
Meharry Medical School, Nashville, Tennessee

Northern Medical Schools

Harvard Medical School, Boston, Massachusetts
University of Pennsylvania, Philadelphia, Pennsylvania
Albany Medical College, Albany, New York
Northwestern University Medical School, Chicago, Illinois
University of Michigan, Ann Arbor, Michigan
Chicago Medical School, Chicago, Illinois
Indiana Medical College, Indianapolis, Indiana
College of Physicians and Surgeons, Chicago, Illinois
Illinois Medical College, Chicago, Illinois
College of Physicians and Surgeons, Boston, Massachusetts
Denver Medical College, Denver, Colorado
University of Pittsburg, Pittsburg, Pennsylvania
University of Iowa, Iowa City, Iowa
Bennett Medical College, Chicago, Illinois
National Medical University, Chicago, Illinois

Lawyers

The lot of the Negro lawyer has not been on the whole a pleasant one. While the need for his services has been great he has not been given a fair chance to meet this need. Many things have militated against him. In the first place the discriminating laws of the South have so circumscribed the ordinary and customary forms of legal procedure that the Negro lawyer from the very start finds the odds against him. The very laws under which he must practice and upon which he must build his methods of procedure are in many instances aimed directly against the people from whom he must draw his clientele. In the second place the injustice which the Negro meets all too frequently in the courts of the South has made the success of the Negro lawyer all the more uncertain. With judge and jury afflicted with racial prejudice he cannot always be sure of receiving justice at their hands, even tho the evidence in the case and the accepted forms of judicial procedure seem to assure success to his efforts. Lastly, the Negro lawyer must meet the prejudice, the antipathy and the lack of confidence on the part of his own people. The latter, however, may be due largely to the conditions mentioned above. When we note the confidence placed by Negroes in their teachers, their preachers and their doctors it is only natural to presume that they would place similar confidence in the lawyers of their race did social, political and economic customs but give them an opportunity for doing so.

Nevertheless there have been many college-bred Negroes to enter the legal profession. Of the number reporting occupations, 29 or 3.8 per cent are engaged in the practice of law. The following schools of law have trained these men:

> Howard University Law Department
> Wilberforce University Law Department
> Walden University Law Department
> Allen University Law Department
> Harvard University Law School
> Boston University Law School
> Yale University Law School
> University of Minnesota Law School
> Ohio State University Law School
> Columbia University Law School
> Kansas State University Law School
> University of Michigan Law School
> Chicago College of Law
> Cleveland Law School
> Kent Law School (Chicago)
> Western Reserve University Law School
> University of Iowa Law School

These lawyers are practicing in the following states:

Ohio	Massachusetts
Connecticut	Kentucky
Illinois	Tennessee
Iowa	South Carolina
Minnesota	Georgia
Kansas	Texas
Missouri	Oklahoma
Pennsylvania	District of Columbia
New York	West Virginia

The work of the Negro professional men has been and is of great importance in the educational, social and economic uplift of the Negro race in America. By precept and by example these men have taught the lessons of sacrifice and perseverance—lessons so much needed by the newly emancipated race. Likewise their example of thrift and economy cannot be overestimated; it has indeed made for progress of the Negro American.

Section 13. Ownership of Property

It is difficult to collect reliable statistics concerning the ownership of property but the results here are worth the effort. In collecting data for this study the Negro college graduates were asked the amount of land owned, the assessed value of real estate, lands and houses in their possession and the market value of total property owned.

The statistics on landownership cover the ownership of farm land and the ownership of lots and from these the following tables are compiled:

LANDOWNERS—FARM LAND

CLASS OF FARMS	No. of owners	Total acreage
Under three acres	45	44
Three and under 10	23	117
Ten and under 20	21	260
Twenty and under 50	36	1,179
Fifty and under 100	28	2,007
One hundred and under 175	30	3,858
One hundred and seventy-five and under 250 .	11	2,402
Two hundred and fifty and under 500	10	3,599
Five hundred and under 1,000	4	2,606
One thousand and over	2	3,233
Total	210	19,305

LANDOWNERS—LOTS

NUMBER OF LOTS	No. of owners	Total lots
Under 5 lots	150	293
Five and under 10	19	113
Ten and under 15	15	179
Fifteen and under 25	9	157
Twenty-five and under 45	2	65
Forty-five and over	2	719
Total	197	1,526

The tables show that two hundred and ten of the graduates report the ownership of 19,305 acres of farm land, an average of ninety-two acres per graduate reporting ownership, while one hundred and ninety-seven graduates report the ownership of 1,526 lots, which is an average of eight lots per graduate reporting ownership.

The reports of assessed value of real estate, land and
houses, owned by Negro college graduates reporting are com-
compiled in the following table which shows total assessed
value of real estate of 458 graduates reporting ownership to
be $1,640,750.68 or an average of $3,582.42 per individual so
reporting:

ASSESSED VALUE OF REAL ESTATE

	Number	Amount
Less than $100.	5	$ 280 00
$100–$250	11	1,770 00
$250–$500	25	6,757 68
$500–$1,000	49	33,450 00
$1,000–$1,500	67	73,019 00
$1,500–$2,000	42	66,680 00
$2,000–$2,500	46	93,970 00
$2,500–$3,000	39	99,330 00
$3,000–$4,000	50	157,430 00
$4,000–$5,000	35	144,236 00
$5,000–$10,000	57	357,900 00
$10,000–$15,000	23	252,178 00
$15,000–$20,000	5	80,000 00
$20,000–$30,000	4	96,000 00
$30,000–$40,000	5	176,850 00
Total	458	$ 1,640,750 68

Average per individual reporting $3,582.42.

The following table is compiled from the reports of total
property owned by 495 graduates reporting and shows a total
of $2,794,537 or an average of $5,645.53 per individual:

TOTAL PROPERTY

	Number	Amount
Less than $500	26	$ 7,180
$500–$1,000.	40	27,035
$1,000–$1,500	43	46,782
$1,500–$2,000	43	68,250
$2,000–$3,000	78	177,850
$3,000–$4,000	60	190,900
$4,000–$5,000	40	165,500
$5,000–$7,500	64	370,000
$7,500–$10,000	25	203,450
$10,000–$15,000	30	322,890
$15,000–$20,000	18	288,800
$20,000–$25,000	9	188,900
$25,000–$30,000	6	153,000
$30,000–$40,000	7	228,000
$40,000–$50,000	3	126,000
$50,000–$100,000	2	110,000
More than $100,000	1	120,000
Total	495	$ 2,794,537

Average per individual reporting $5,645.53.

It is difficult to estimate from these meagre statistics the amount of property in the possession of the Negro college graduates. In the first place many who are known to be in possession of property did not make answer to these questions and so are not included in the above tables. Then, too, the usual ratio between assessed value and real value taken into consideration here alters the figures to the advantage of the whole group. Lastly, it must be remembered that the total replies to the conference questionnaire cover only about one-fourth of the total number of living Negro college graduates. All things taken into consideration it is probably safe to say that the college-bred Negro Americans are in possession of $15,000,000 worth of property.

Some conclusions may be drawn from this phase of the study:

1. The Negro college graduates have made and are making a good showing in the accumulation of property, both personal and real estate.

2. By precept and by example these men and women are teaching their people the virtues of thrift, economy and saving.

3. No small measure of the value of these men and women may be seen in the impetus they have given to their people in the building of homes and the accumulation of property.

Section 14. Avocations

The work of the educated Negro is largely the work of leadership. The college-bred Negro, therefore, finds great opportunity for telling activity among his people and that in addition to his regular vocation. A study of the avocations of these educated men and women reveals much of interest and shows in a striking way the place of the college-bred in the Negro race. In like manner it gives some idea of the social value of the college-bred Negro to America.

Learned Societies

The Negro college graduates have reported themselves as members of the following learned societies:

Academy of Science, St. Louis

African Society (London)

Alpha Kappa Literary
Alpha Phi Alpha
American Academy for Advancement of Science
American Academy of Political and Social Science
American Archæological Association
American Association of Electrical Engineers
American Breeders' Association
American Civic Alliance
American Economic Association
American Geographic Society
American Historical Association
American Institute for Psychic Research
American Library Association
American Medical Association
American Nature Study Society
American Negro Academy
American Ornithologists' Union
American Philological Association
American Statistical Association
Arkansas Medical, Dental and Pharmaceutical Surgical Association
Association of Collegiate Alumnæ
Chicago Medical Society
Classical Association of the South and Middle West
Constitution League
Eastern Manual Training Association
Entomological Society of America
Illinois Academy of Science
Illinois State Medical Society
Inter-State Literary Society of Kansas and the West
Massachusetts Medical Society
Medical Society, Essex County, New Jersey
National Bar Association
National Educational Association
National Medical Association
National Sociological Society
Niagara Movement
Phi Beta Kappa
Physics Club of Indiana University
Rock City Academy of Medicine and Surgery
Sigma Chi Fraternity (Chicago Chapter)
Society of Arts (England)
Standard Literary Society, Chicago
State Medical Association (Tennessee), Colored

Publications

The college-bred Negro has contributed in a small way to the literature of America. In this contribution we find some works of considerable importance whether viewed from the standpoint of literature, or history, or science, or sociology. We find also, in addition to the larger publications, numerous pamphlets, essays and smaller works of importance such as those issued by the American Negro Academy, the Committee of Twelve for the Advancement of the Negro Race, the different religious organizations and numerous individuals.

The official organ of each of the leading Negro religious bodies is directed in large part by college-bred men.

Almost all of the leading magazines have published articles written by Negro college graduates—the *Atlantic*, the *Forum*, the *North American Review*, the *World's Work*, the *Century*, the *Independent*, the *Outlook*. Something has been done in the field of poetry as is evidenced by James W. Johnson's "O Black and Unknown Bards" and "Mother Night"; by Kelly Miller's "Mors Vincta" and "A Moral Axiom"; and by Silas Xavier Floyd's "Floyd's Flowers" and "Not by Bread Alone."

Atlanta University Publication, Number 14, Efforts for Social Betterment among Negro Americans, gives a list of newspapers and magazines which have been published by Negroes. Many of these have been controlled wholly or in part by college-bred men.

The following bibliography, by no means exhaustive, is some indication of the literary activity of the college-bred Negro American:

Anderson, Matthew. Presbyterianism and its Relation to the Negro. Philadelphia, 1897. 12mo., 263 pp.
Barber, J. M. One Hundred One Eminent Negroes.
Bowen, J. W. E. Sermons. Philadelphia. 88 pp.
    Africa and the American Negro. Atlanta. 250 pp.
    Addresses. Atlanta. 300 pp.
Brawley, B. G. The Negro in Literature and Art. 1910.
Broughton, Mrs. J. A. O. Women's Work. 52 pp.
    Twenty Years' Experience of a Missionary. 140 pp.
    Christian Homes the Hope of the Race.

Byrd, W. A.   Reply to German Criticism on Bible.   30 pp.
    Exposition of Kinosis.   50 pp.
    Commentary on Joel.   30 pp.
Camphor, Rev. A. P.   Missionary Story Sketches and Folk Lore from
    Africa.   346 pp.   Cincinnati and New York.
Camphor, Rev. R. A.   Papers and Addresses.   50 pp.   Atlanta.
Coffin, A. O.   A Land without Chimneys.   Cincinnati.   352 pp.
Cooper, A. J.   A Voice from the South.   Xenia, O., 1892.   30 pp.
Crogman, W. H.   Talks for the Times.   Atlanta.   330 pp.
Crummell, Alexander.   Africa and America.   Springfield, Mass., 1891.
    466 pp.
Du Bois, W. E. B.   Suppression of the Slave Trade.   New York, 1896.
    335 pp.   (Harvard Historical Series, No. 1.)
    The Philadelphia Negro.   Philadelphia, 1899.   520 pp.
    The Souls of Black Folk.   Chicago, 1903.   264 pp.
    John Brown.   Philadelphia, 1909.   406 pp.
    Editor Atlanta University Studies of the Negro Problem.
Dyson, Walter H.   Syllabus on U. S. History and Civics.   Washington,
    1910.
Floyd, S. X.   Life of C. T. Walker.
    Gospel of Service and other Sermons.
    Floyd's Flowers.
    National Perils.
Gilmer, John C.   History of Alabama.
    A Guide to English Oration.
Gregory, J. M.   Frederick Douglass. Springfield, Mass., 1890.   300 pp.
Grimke, A. H.   William Lloyd Garrison. (American Reformers Series.)
    New York, 1891.   405 pp.
    Charles Sumner. (American Reformers Series.)   New York, 1892.
    515 pp.
Grimke, F. J.   The Negro, his Rights and Wrongs.   Washington, D. C.,
    1899.   100 pp.
Henderson, G. W.   Essays on Negro Citizenship.
    Plantation Life in Louisiana.
Hubert, J. W.   *Syllabi:*
    (1) Seven Studies in Physiography.
    (2) Seven Studies in Right Living.
    (3) Seven Studies in Geology.
    (4) Life's Ten Richest Blessings.
Johnson, C. J.   Pilgrimage of a Race.   1910.
Kealing, H. T.   History of African Methodism in Texas.
    Fortune Telling in History.
    The Minor Prophets.
    How to Live Longer.
Langston, J. M.   From the Virginia Plantations.   Hartford, 1894.   544 pp.

Lawson, Jesse. How Solve the Race Problem. Washington, D. C. 297 pp.

Ethics of the Labor Problem. Washington, D. C. 14 pp.

Lewis, W. H. A Primer of College Foot-ball. New York. 205 pp.

Long, F. A. Across the Continent. Danville, Va. 60 pp.

Lovinggood, R. S. Why *hic, haec, hoc* for the Negro? Marshall, Tex., 1900. 56 pp.

The Negro Seer, his Mission and Preparation.

McWilliams, B. F. The Needs of the Negro. Univ. Press, Richmond. 1903. 16mo.

The Negro Church of Virginia, its Condition and Needs. 1905.

Miller, Albert P. The Black Man's Burden or the Two Sides of the Negro Problem.

Miller, Kelly. The Education of the Negro. Washington, 1902.

Race Adjustment. New York and Washington, 1908. 306 pp.

Mossell, C. W. Toussant L'Ouverture.

Ousley, B. F. Gospels and Acts translated into African Tongue. New York. 371 pp.

Paisley, J. W. The Voice of Mezraim. New York. 122 pp.

Payne, D. A. History of the A. M. E. Church. Nashville, 1891. 498 pp.

Paynter, J. H. Joining the Navy. Hartford. 330 pp.

Pegues, A. W. Our Baptist Ministers and Schools. Springfield, Ohio. 680 pp.

Pettus, J. W. Home Again. Fort Smith, Ark. 34 pp.

Vagaries of Substitute. Indianapolis. 127 pp.

Phillips, C. H. History of the Colored Methodist Episcopal Church.

Scarborough, W. S. First Greek Lessons. New York. 150 pp.

Birds of Aristophanes. Boston.

Scruggs, L. A. Afro-American Women of Distinction. Raleigh, N. C.

Sinclair, William A. The Aftermath of Slavery. Boston, 1905. 358 pp.

Talbert, H. The Sons of Allen. 286 pp.

Turner, C. H. Numerous biological publications, the result of scientific research.

Work, F. J. New Jubilee Songs. Nashville, 1902. 50 pp.

Folk Songs of American Negro. Nashville. 64 pp.

Some American Negro Folk Songs. Boston, 120 pp.

Among the interesting pamphlets published by Negro college graduates are the following:

Bruce, Roscoe Conkling. Service by the Educated Negro.

Carver, G. W. Bulletin of Tuskegee Experiment Station.

Cook, C. C. Study of the Negro Problem.

Crummell, Alexander. Sermons and Addresses.

Dammond, W. H. Factoring.

Davis, M. T. The South the Negro's Door of Hope (An Essay).

The Education of Negro Youth of Texas.

Grimke, A. H.　Why Disfranchisement is Bad.

Harris, Eugene.　Social Purity.

McClellan, G. W.　Poems.　Nashville.

Miller, Kelly.　A Review of Hoffman's "Race Traits and Tendencies,"
　　etc.　Washington, 1897.　36 pp.

　　As to the Leopard's Spots, etc.　Washington, 1905.

　　The Primary Need of the Negro Race.　Washington, 1899.　18 pp.

　　The Political Capacity of the Negro.

Steward, T. G.　Black St. Domingo Legion.

Talley, T. W.　A Natural Trinity.

Wesley, A. A.　The Spanish-American War.

Williams, D. H.　Reports of Surgical Cases.

Wright, R. R.　Historical Sketch of Negro Education in Georgia.　Sa-
　　vannah.　58 pp.

Public Office

The following is a partial list of public offices which have
been held by Negro college graduates:

Seven Alderman (N. C., Pa., Mass., Ky., S. C.)

Nine Members Board of Education (N. C., S. C., Ohio, Tenn., D. C.,
Ga., Kan.)

Two Assistant Attorney Generals (N. Y.)

Members of State Legislatures (N. C., Miss., Ill., Ga., Tenn., Minn.)

Four Clerks in District Courts (Kan., Okla., D. C.)

One Member of Congress

Three served in Spanish-American War (Major and Paymaster,
Chaplain, and Captain)

Two Judges of Civil Courts

Two United States Deputies

Four Tax Assessors (Ill., Ark., Miss., N. C.)

Five Officials in Custom Houses (La., Tenn., Va., Ga.)

Two State Superintendents of Public Instruction (La., Ala.)

Two Medical Inspectors (Pa., Col.)

One Special Land Agent

One City and State Health Officer (Col.)

Assistant Corporation Counsel (New York City)

Inspector of Customs

Member of Grand Jury (Ark.)

United States Jail Physician

Justice of Peace

Deputy Auditor

Engrossing Clerk, General Assembly

Deputy Collector of Customs (La.)

Prosecuting Attorney (Ill.)

Secretary of Haytian Legation
Tax Collector (Pa.)
Chaplain House of Representatives (S. C.)
Registrar of Births and Deaths (West Indies)
Registrar of Deposits, U. S. Mint (La.)
United States Minister to Hayti
United States Minister to Liberia
Assistant United States District Attorney (Mass.)

Charitable Work

The Atlanta University Publication, Number 14, Efforts for Social Betterment among Negro Americans, gives an elaborate account of the charitable work being done by the Negroes of this country. The field is broad and the phases of this activity are many: church, school, general charity, women's clubs, old folk's homes, orphanages, hospitals, young men's Christian associations, young women's Christian associations, refuges and homes for women and children, libraries, day nurseries, social settlements, kindergartens, civic reform.

The college bred Negroes have done and are doing a large share of the work along these charitable lines. The following list shows in a general way the charitable activity of these men and women:

Church work	Old folks' homes
Y. M. C. A. and Y. W. C. A.	Hospitals
Trustees of institutions	Labor organizations
Anti-tuberculosis leagues	Boys' reform societies
Charitable societies	Jail and slum work
Day nurseries	Temperance and prohibition movement
Social settlements	
Secret societies	White Cross society
Prison reform	American Health League
Mission work	Jeanes Fund
Play grounds	Associated charities
Civic leagues	Libraries
Mothers' clubs	Social reform

The following extracts from reports received will show something of the charitable work of individual graduates:

Originator of movement to investigate sanitary conditions of our people in New Orleans.

Home for friendless girls, Washington, D. C.

Associated Charities, Washington, D. C.

Work in slums of Providence, R. I.

Member of Oberlin Improvement Society.

Entire time in connection with .——— College devoted to relieving needy students and promoting the welfare of the institution. Actual money given $3,967.90.

United Charities for Colored People, Nashville, Tenn.

Vice-president North Carolina Reform School Association.

Chairman of Negro branch of Associated Charities, Gallipolis, Ohio.

Member of board of directors National Home-finding Society and of Library and Improvement Association; member of Anti-tuberculosis Committee, of Play Ground Association, of Colored Orphan Society, Louisville, Ky.

Working girls' home, Columbia, S. C.

United Charities, Rochester, N. Y.

Member of board of directors of State Orphan Society, Oxford, N. C.

Member Associated Charities, Raleigh, N. C.

Association for Protection of Colored Women; Old Ladies' and Orphans' Home, Memphis, Tenn.

Home for Aged Men; Association for Prevention of Tuberculosis; Trustee of Mutual Housing Company, the object of which is the improvement of housing conditions in Springfield, Mass., and vicinity.

Volunteer work in connection with probation officer of the juvenile court of St. Louis, Mo.

Member of Consolidated Charities of New Albany, La.

Secretary of Galveston Relief Association.

Trustee of Orphan and Old Ladies' Home; chairman Domestic Science Board; Association for Relief of Colored Women; organizer social settlement work, Memphis, Tenn.

Negro school improvement league; Teachers' and Citizens' Co-operative Association; social settlement, Petersburg, Va.

Superintendent of Mercy Hospital, Nashville, Tenn.

Member of Committee for Improving Industrial Conditions among Negroes in New York City; member of N. A. A. C. P.

Colored Orphan Home, Huntsville, Ala.

Chairman board of directors of Provident Hospital and Training School for Negroes, Arkansas.

President of Galveston Relief Association.

United Charities, Nashville, Tenn.

Civic Improvement Club; Farmers' Union and Protective League, Okmulgee, Okla.

Associated Charities; Director of Slater Hospital, Winston, N. C.

Secretary Civic League; Board of Directors of Anti-tuberculosis League, Portsmouth, Va.

Secretary Social Uplift Society for Colored People, Jersey City, N. J.

Built the Pickford Sanitorium for Tuberculous Negroes, Southern Pines, N. C.

Editor and Investigator Atlanta University Publications; member of Committee of Forty, N. A. A. C. P.; American Secretary Universal Races Congress.

Director of Public Play Grounds for Colored Youths; Volunteer Probation Officer of Juvenile Court; Association for Prevention of Tuberculosis, St. Louis, Mo.

Trustee of Amanda Smith Industrial Home; Probation Officer, Cook county, Ill.

President Board of Managers for Reform School for Girls, Kansas.

Legal and general adviser of the Cleveland Home for Aged Colored People; Probation Officer of Juvenile Court of Cuyahoga county, Ohio. (No compensation.)

Director of the Sarah Ann White Home for Aged and Infirm Colored People, Washington, D. C.

Organizer of state teachers' association; organizer fair association; organizer colored anti-tuberculosis league, Georgia.

State Superintendent of Department of Anti-narcotics, W. C. T. U., North Carolina.

Trustee of Provident Hospital and Training School for Negroes, Chicago; director of Douglass Center, Chicago; director of Juvenile Court League, No. 4, Chicago; trustee Peace Haven Institute, Blackville, S. C. Personal work. For the past eight years I have been assisting Negro physicians in the establishment of infirmaries of their own thruout the South and instructing them along surgical lines.

Old Folks' Home, Selma, Ala.

Associated Charities, Augusta, Ga.

Colored Orphan Home, Columbus, Ohio.

Business

The Negro college graduates report themselves as engaged in the following business enterprises, in almost every case in addition to the regular vocation:

Real estate	38	Merchandise	4
Banking	19	Home association	1
Drug business	5	Plumbing	1
Shoe business	3	Newspaper business	5
Gardener	1	Trust company	3
Farming	8	Mining company	6
Building and loan association	11	Contractor	1
Editors	5	Insurance	4
Construction	2	Coal business	1
Co-operative business league	1	Fair association	1
Land improvement	4	Publishing	3
Investment	4	Grocers	2
Fruit farming	2	Millinery	1
Warehouse	1	Steam laundering	1
Manufacturing	4	Mercantile company	1
Cotton ginning	2	Realty company	3
Lumber business	1	General store business	1
Book store	1	Printing	2
Mail order	1	Poultry raising	2
Music publisher	2		

Section 15. Education of Children

How shall you educate your children? The answers received in reply to this question are interesting. By far the greater number of those making reply are planning to give their children the advantages of a college education, hoping thereby to properly equip them for life's work, whether in the trades or in the professions. Many of these answers are grouped as follows:

College	101
College and professional	101
Trade, college and professional	48
College training and trade	45
According to their ability	44
According to their inclination	41
Professional	24
College, trade or professional	20
Industrial and professional	9
Trade	7
College or professional	3
Some industrial and some college	2
Academic and trade	2
Technical	1
Head, hand and heart	1
Liberal education	1
College and professional or business	1
Professional or trade	1
College and business	1
Literary education and domestic work	1
Academic	1

The following quotations, none of which is included in the above grouping, are taken from the replies to this question concerning the education of children:

"It is my present intention to give my boys a full university training in order that they may be equipped to take high rank in whatever calling or profession they may choose."

"I believe in educating the child to make the best citizen; a college education to those who will take it."

"In obedience to their inclinations and gifts and without prejudice for or against any particular training. Technical, agricultural, mercantile, professional training are of equal importance if preparation and research are sufficient, there being urgent need for real high grade leadership in every avenue for the Negro. If then any offspring from my household manifest special taste for and high merit in any worthy line, I shall only ask God to enable me to assist them to the highest in that line."

"First public school, secondly college, third university, then if possible provide for her to study abroad. I shall teach the importance of attainment of the highest possible type of culture and refinement and the importance of possessing something that people who have money want."

"I have but one daughter. I plan to give her a college education in southern, eastern and European institutions."

"I am striving to be in shape to give my children a thoro, practical education which will best fit them for the daily pursuits of life."

"I shall endeavor to give that training which in my judgment will be of the highest good to him."

"I want my daughter to make music her specialty but will allow her to choose her literary course."

"Each is to receive at least a normal and academic education. Two or three may take the university course, one in music, one in theology."

"It is my intention to give them the very best education that they can assimilate."

"I desire to have them brought up at a school such as Fisk after they have reached puberty and later at a northern university. But first of all I shall teach them the fundamentals of politeness, hygiene, and the art of doing work assigned them smoothly and with polish."

"The education of my children will probably depend largely upon their own wishes but I should like them to receive training equivalent to the four years' college course at Atlanta University and professional or special training for some particular line of work."

"If I should be so fortunate as to have any children I would send them to Phillips Exeter, Harvard and Lawrence Scientific School."

"Some in trade, some in college and some in a profession. One is already a dressmaker, another is a trained nurse and still another has finished in theology and is doing good pastoral work at Albany, Georgia."

"I expect to send my boys thru college and my daughter thru a normal training school."

"I propose to give them as complete an education as they can receive."

"As their talent seems to· indicate. The best is none too good. Broadly as men and as American citizens and not narrowly as Negroes."

"I dont know as to a trade or a profession but most certainly I shall give my boy a college education and my daughter a good normal training."

"College and technical as far as my influence can bring this about; ultimately, of course, the child must decide."

"This would depend largely upon the natural tendency of the children but my desire would be for them to have a college education and, if possible, for the boys to take a profession afterwards. Both boys and girls should work at some trade during vacation seasons while in public school as I believe no boy or girl should be permitted to grow up without learning how to do some kind of work proficiently with the hands."

"I favor college education because then they are better prepared to succeed; then to his trade or profession well equipped."

"I shall give them a higher Christian literary education as a foundation and allow them afterwards to study any trade or profession they may wish."

"I shall educate my girls to be school teachers."

"I am giving my son academic and professional and my daughter academic and trade."

"In the way that shall best fit them as individuals to be of greatest service to themselves and to others. I desire them to have a three-fold education."

"Train their early years in some form of handicraft or trade; give them a college course in an institution for Negroes; and the boys a professional course in one of the best schools without regard to color."

"I will try to educate my children according to their inclinations. I am not partial; to any kind of education which fits men and women for true service."

"For profession if they show inclination and ability sufficient to indicate that they will be successful in such work. For trades or business if they show special adaptability for that class of work."

"I would give him a broad and comprehensive college training and leave it to his own inclination as to trade or profession."

"I shall endeavor to study the aptitude of the child. If he or she is best fitted for an industrial life or a profession I desire to root that industry or profession into a fertile, college-trained brain."

"Boys to a trade or a profession, according to their respective inclinations and apparent adaptability. Girls in college and domestic science."

"Some trade along with their preparatory training. College course, a part of which shall be in some Christian institution. Their professional training shall be the outgrowth of their natural adaptation together with the aid and direction of parents."

"Intend to make teachers of some of them. The boys wish to be scientific farmers."

"In college and in the ministry with some industrial training, with the hope that he may become a missionary to Africa."

"Intend to make a dentist of my boy and a musician of my girl."

"Hope to have them learn trade, go thru one of the northern colleges and learn some profession."

"Boy, to trade or medicine; girl, to domestic science and music."

"I am striving to give my children a thoro practical education which will best fit them for the daily pursuits of life."

Section 16. Hindrances

What have been your chief hindrances? Most of the hindrances which were reported in the replies to this question find a place in the following grouping:

1. Lack of money.
2. Race prejudice against the Negro.
3. Prejudice of Negroes themselves.

The following quotations are taken from the replies:

"Prejudice has all along hindered me in getting what I have merited. On the other hand, it has been a negative good, doing for me in some measure what a rough sea does for a mariner: bringing out whatever of good stuff there is in me."

"My chief hindrance has been a lack of funds. I have always had to hustle for what I have attained and having become accustomed to it I hardly consider that a hindrance now. I have found a certain amount of prejudice everywhere I have been but I have also found that ambition and energy with integrity can override prejudice."

"I have no reason to complain. While opportunities for the young Negro are fewer than for the young white man in this country, the young men of our race are neglecting opportunities which would seem golden to the young men of other lands."

"I find that a desire to work, when based on a good foundation, educational and moral, is appreciated and encouraged by all classes of people."

"My chief hindrance has been a lack of capital with which to carry out my plans. Prejudice cuts very little figure in the business world if you have what the white man wants or if he can use you in any way. He will look you up."

"I think sometimes people of our own race who are in position to do so throw obstacles in your way of progress. I think to a certain extent I have been such a victim."

"In getting into close, vital relation with my people in order to be of real service."

"I could say poverty; but it has been the spur that made me move when I would have fallen by the wayside. Prejudice and lack of opportunity: I cannot be harsh on either. Where prejudice existed I strove to soften by acquaintance and have never failed. Opportunity: so far I have always been able to be ready when it made its appearance to step in and get my share."

"Poor salary. Prejudice on account of progress and satisfactory conditions of my surroundings."

"Prejudice has militated against increase of salary in service of city."

"Prejudice has been a great hindrance but not any more so than is usual with colored people. My greatest hindrance has been lack of opportunity as I have had to meet heavy obligations since leaving school."

"Lack of opportunity thru prejudice both among the more ignorant of my race as well as among the white people has been a great hindrance to my advancement. I have never been able to receive pay adequate to my qualifications."

"Southern prejudice has helped rather than hindered me."

"Prejudice has been a great hindrance. The things which would tend to advancement for white men have been overlooked in my case on account of color."

"The same every colored man meets. Menial positions; poor pay as a teacher; fidelity to my race, which led me to decline a high position on a railroad in Georgia which I could have had by passing for white. I could get only about two-thirds the salary paid to a white teacher of the same grade."

"While I have no great complaint to make, I think perhaps my life would have been larger and far different but for my color, tho the fact that I was elected to public office in a white community shows that I have escaped much of the race prejudice with which the race has to contend.''

"The lack of money has been one of the drawbacks in my case. I never allowed prejudice to worry me. I always attended to my own business and let other people do the same.''

"My opportunities have been very good. I have often been able to cross the bounds set by prejudice.''

"I have not had access to hospital and clinical facilities to keep up and perfect myself in my professional work.''

"Prejudice has hindered me from becoming head physician here. I am oldest in point of location here.''

"I have never allowed prejudice to crush me. With me it has been more of a stimulus. It is an awful fact and works with a maliciousness that is wilful and premeditated but it is wanting in substance; it is not founded on the rock of reason and truth. It is unthinking and blind and will, therefore, ultimately work its own destruction.''

"Chief hindrance perhaps is my desire to always draw salary rather than take chance in business. Prejudice has made me less prominent as an engineer, kept me from good paying positions and forced me to accept less pay for the same work. All of my classmates who are white are drawing larger salaries than I.''

"Doing same or more work for less money than my white comrades. No incentive to be anything better than what I am. Difficulty in obtaining promotion over white competitors or even along with them.''

"Prejudice among colored people against their own college men is a hindrance.''

"I have gone steadily on and have done whatever has been my duty so far as I have been able to see my duty. I have not been directly hindered in my work, hence prejudice has hindered me in a general way in proportion as it has impeded my race.''

"I have succeeded fairly well in my profession but have been prevented from reaching that prominence in it which I might have otherwise reached by the awful race prejudice that exists here as elsewhere. Then the colored lawyer does not have the stimulus to exertion the white lawyer has because he knows the honors and emoluments of the profession are denied him because of his race. No matter what his excellence or fitness he can never reach the bench or have retainers from large corporations. The truth is that the colored lawyer to succeed at all must be far beyond the average white lawyer.''

"Prejudice circumscribed the sphere of activities for broader culture and for increased efficiency.''

"Race prejudice has undoubtedly lessened my opportunities but on the other hand has served indirectly to make me use such opportunities as I have had to a better advantage than I would otherwise have done possibly."

"Lack of means to procure needed facilities to carry out and plan my line of work for myself and for my pupils. A desire on the part of school boards to restrict us in our efforts to secure a sufficient number of, and capable, efficient teachers, well equipped laboratories and libraries. I taught physics and chemistry in a laboratory in —— furnished by ourselves."

"In some places silent opposition to Negro college graduates on the part of white and colored."

"Prejudice is always present but I have found far more opportunity than prejudice, i. e. prejudice that hindered in any vital sense. The greatest hindrance is the indifference of my own people to the necessity for unity and increased, well-directed activity. Prejudice has made me work harder and so has proved many times a blessing in disguise."

"It is my belief that prejudice is a spur to serious endeavor on the part of intelligent colored men."

"Prejudice and proscription have operated to my disadvantage to the extent of cooling ardor and chilling aspiration."

"Prejudice and lack of opportunity have retarded my progress but by industry, economy, conservatism and perseverance I have in a measure overcome them."

"Prejudice against the higher education of Negroes."

"Prejudice denies us the privilege of enjoying the confidence and association of many superior minds. It has denied me the opportunity to enjoy or be benefited by the large number of programs and meetings of a public or semi-public nature where a great deal of information and inspiration may be obtained."

"My chief hindrance has been lack of opportunity. There is not enough business among colored people to employ their young men and women when they finish school."

"It is hard to specify the ways in which prejudice has worked against one. No man who has been hampered by or has been compelled to contend against prejudice has been able to reach his best and biggest self."

"Prejudice has been from the very beginning the chief hindrance in my life. I have been turned from printing establishments because of objection to my color. I have been engaged for clerical work and then discharged when my color became known. It has operated against me in oratorical contests at college."

"I cannot complain of lack of opportunity. I find the old adage holds true: Where there is a will there is a way."

"Prejudice has been no barrier when it came to acquiring property, but it often crushes my spirit."

"In my estimation my chief hindrance has been that I have never had all the equipment which I felt should be mine to make the greatest possible success in the tasks which have been mine. Tho measurably successful in all my career I have so often felt the need of more mastery over the immediate problem or business. Prejudice has had to do with my life and experience as with others. Promotions which would have been given freely and early to a man of another racial identity, I have had to labor long for. Yet in all fairness I must say that whereas prejudice, damnable and low, is continually operating against me, yet I have won so far. I have got what I went after, after a fight nevertheless, yet I got it."

"I cannot buy or rent respectable property without the greatest embarrassment and sometimes not even then. This gives a set-back to my dignity and influence."

"Prejudice has closed several doors of opportunity along the line of educational advantages; was responsible for a low wage for some years; and caused much embarrassment in ways whose name is legion."

"My chief hindrance has been the treachery and vanity of the namby-pamby Negro.   .   .   .   . To put it another way my chief hindrance has been my inability to play the hypocrite."

"Prejudice is the chief hindrance in the way of all college-bred Negro men who want to make the most of life. Prejudice, I think, has made me suspicious of all white people, sometimes with injustice to them, I fear, and with injury to myself."

"My chief hindrance is that I am deprived of the enjoyment of my rights as a free citizen."

"I feel that only half the measure of the possibilities of my career has been filled because prejudice has been a handicap to the full and free prosecution of my professional labors. Most of the Negroes believe that to succeed in our courts they must have a white advocate."

"There is in this community a kindly growing sentiment on the part of the whites toward the colored people and so prejudice does not interrupt much. My chief hindrance is due to the fact that it is difficult to get my own people to appreciate in a large way our opportunities for growth and power."

"Lack of confidence among our people to intrust their business with one another and to do business with each other generally. I might term it 'race pride.' I think it is due more to absolute ignorance. However, we are coming to a better understanding of each other and business confidence in each other is being developed both on account of oppression and prejudice and the preaching of self-help among ourselves."

"Prejudice and lack of opportunity have been at once my handicap and my constant stimulant. Daily experience with them has kept me keyed up to constant exertion and the doing of my best. Expecting no quarter it has been with me a fight to the finish and a point of manhood and honor to succeed."

"Lack of proper aspiration among the masses. Failure of the people to appreciate real ability. Jealousy and prejudice among certain leaders."

"My greatest hindrance was lack of public school opportunity early in life. A lot of good time was lost in those days."

"Prejudice hinders a man all the time and everywhere in doing a man's work. No man can do his best while hampered by senseless prejudice."

"Prejudice of ignorant blacks as well as whites does a great deal to hinder. The uneducated black is very jealous of his educated brother and will do lots to hinder his progress."

"In my work I have felt perhaps more than anything else the prohibition from public library facilities in such a city as Atlanta."

"Prejudice has played so small a part that it can be considered a negligible quantity. Perhaps I have not followed the paths in which one would meet it so keenly. My chief hindrance has possibly come from within: the ignorance of the big opportunities that await the average young Negro man of education and energy in the business world provided he works eternally."

"A very limited field to choose positions from, as compared to many of my white fellow students whose academic standing was below mine. Social conditions in my home state shut me out of the career I would have naturally sought there."

"Prejudice has made me fight the harder to overcome the disabilities of caste. It has kept me alive and made me yearn to accomplish something, nerved me to live and endure suffering and sorrow of any kind in order to see the ultimate triumph of righteous civic ideals."

"Rather difficult to answer as I have worked all the while under conditions that I saw little hope of changing hence gave little thot to what I might have done under different conditions. I feel sure the lack of opportunity for full exercise of ability in certain lines has, perhaps in some cases unconsciously, served to stifle ambition and prevent activity that might have been useful to communities in which I have lived. In some instances I think prejudice has nerved me to more persistent effort."

"The color line has prevented a chance for scientific and literary work."

"Race prejudice prevents me being retained as counsel where otherwise I would be employed. It keeps away the most remunerative class of business. It compels me to accept a smaller fee for work done and services rendered than would otherwise be the case. It often causes me to contest in court for fees after they have been earned, when but for the 'previous condition of servitude' of my ancestors said fees would be cheerfully paid. No one is able to estimate the damage inflicted upon him by the forces which make for ostracism and which impose a perennial and continued boycott because of race."

"1. Prejudice which debars me from work in institutions for which my training fits me.

"2. Superficially trained Negroes who, like the dog in the manger, have ever tried to hinder my progress.

"3. The false notion that the Negro scholar does not deserve as much pay for intellectual work as a white man does for the same work.

"4. Poor salary which has made it necessary for me to abandon many of my researches at an early stage. Indeed what little I have accomplished has been at the expense of the comforts and often of the necessities of life."

Section 17.   Philosophy of Life

What is your present practical philosophy in regard to the Negro race in America? This question was asked the Negro college graduates and to it varying answers were received. The following quotations are taken from the replies and are indicative of the attitude of the Negro American of college training:

"The hope of the Negro is a Christian education of heart, head and hand."

"In my opinion the Negro needs nothing so much as to be let alone. He wants not special attention either in the legislative hall or out. He wants to be treated and regarded as an American citizen in fact. He asks for no more than he merits but he wants all he does merit. To reach this point he must contend for all the term implies. Life is a battle and every man must be a fighter.   .   .   .   . Playing the baby-act will not accomplish anything. Brave men will not only suffer hardships in maintaining their rights but will face dangers. Long since I came to the conclusion that right living on our part would not alone solve the problem. It is not the worthless, ignorant spendthrift among us that arouses the white man's opposition, repression, oppression and prejudice. That class knows 'his place.'   .   .   .   ."

"I have an abiding hope for the future of the race. But great suffering and loss are in store for the race thru error. There is an attempt in a large part of the country to establish a caste system of education for the Negro. .   .   . In the state institutions they are taking out the higher studies and promoting mediocre men and women, paying them in proportion much larger salaries than they are paying college-bred Negro teachers."

"I firmly believe that the destiny of the American Negro lies largely in his own hands. I have never yet seen a self-respecting, honest and industrious Negro, educated or uneducated, who did not have the respect and good-will of the better class of whites with whom he comes in contact. .   .   .   .   I believe that we as individuals must take as our weapons honesty, industry and economy and wage a war against prejudice."

"The Negro race in America is fortunate. The country is still far from being developed or crowded. Tho race prejudice is rampant it is still too weak to suppress any class which has the determination to rise. There is still plenty of room. Less complaint and more effort will pull us up with the dominant class. We should seek and develop all the thinly settled parts of this country."

"The Negro must continue to contend for all the rights, privileges and opportunities accorded other American citizens. He must be unyielding in this respect. He ought to ally himself with any political party that will further these ends."

"I feel that the Negro has many reasons to be hopeful. Of course there are many things that are deplorable; but on the other hand there are so many opportunities already open to us that we do not take advantage of that we would do well to spend less time in finding fault and complaining and use that time preparing ourselves for larger activities and more usefulness."

"My own confident hope is that there will be ultimately a satisfactory issue to all present race difficulties."

"I regard it as essential that political privileges be granted to men regardless of color, the same qualifications demanded of all in an absolutely impartial manner. I regard education as indispensable and believe in absolutely equal facilities for it. .   .   .   .   The problem of the American Negro is difficult to solve upon a basis of perpetual segregation. It is particularly desirable that there shall be no segregation in the higher institutions of learning. Industrial and manual activities should be elements in the course of study for colored people as for all people but not the only elements nor even the principal ones. I think that the colored people should be stimulated to acquire property and to become fixed in their communities. In order that this may happen it is necessary to secure for the Negro greater protection of life and property."

"With education and the right to vote—for both of which the Negro must work and fight daily—he will win the place which is his here in America."

"Persistent, definite and determined effort along all legitimate lines of education, coupled with an all-controlling desire to stick to the right, will not only win for the Negro the respect of America but will give him a place immortal in the history of the world."

"Educate him in the highest and best way possible so as to enable him to successfully compete with every other element of Americanism in every walk of life."

"The accumulation of property will do more to relieve the American Negro of many hardships and disadvantages than any other agency. This should not be the case but it is. The ability to think well (generally the result of thoro training) should outrank the ability to live well (the result of accumulated wealth). First train the mind; then in order to be highly regarded by Americans own some of the world's goods."

"The Negro race would be much stronger if there were more who could see the benefit of a college education, be it in the professional line or in a trade. I think the higher education of the Negro race will tend towards reducing race prejudice."

"1. The Negro must be an active voter.

"2. He must be encouraged to engage in what he is by nature fitted to follow, this not to be determined by one man or set of men but by the individual.

"3. He should study the conditions of his community and enter such activities as he can. He should strive to establish himself in every line of business possible.

"4. He should study mining and manufacturing. He should become an intelligent farmer, vegetable raiser and cotton producer.

"5. He should be more thoroly grounded in mechanics that he may become an inventor. Our colleges could look out for this. There should be no cheap course in mechanics.

"6. Our schools and other institutions should teach everything that is necessary to make the pupils serviceable and life enjoyable.

"7. The Negro should be urged to contend peaceably and earnestly for everything that is needed to make him a man."

"The Negro is passing thru a critical period of his existence in America and no one can say with certainty what the result will be. To my mind, however, it is clear that he will come out with a loss of political power and interest, but greatly strengthened in wealth, intelligence and manhood which will ultimately force political recognition and consideration and the full enjoyment of his civil rights. The Negro is undergoing a refining and hardening process which tho humiliating and painful will in the end make him stronger and better and will prove a blessing to him and to his posterity.''

"If the Negro is given protection and an equal opportunity in the industrial world he will succeed as a race.''

"I think that with better rural schools, longer terms, better teachers, a more practical education for the masses and a higher and more thoro education for the leaders, more effective and aggressive religious training with a practical religion that we live and not simply talk and shout, we shall ultimately build for ourselves character and accumulate wealth, a combination which merits and demands respect. This done the future will take care of itself.''

"I believe the Negro should secure all the training the American school system, public and private, can give. He should then enter some occupation, business or professional, for which he seems fitted individually regardless of tradition or prejudice. As he labors he should link himself to every movement for the betterment of the social and economic life of the community in which he casts his lot. He should preserve a manly, courageous attitude on all questions pertaining to the future of his race to the end that the traditions and ideals of his people become a significant and serviceable factor in American civilization. He must seek to show that his uplift, political, social and religious, is necessary to the progress of all America.''

"The Negro should occupy and improve every worthy position attainable. In a manly and honorable way he should protest against any racial discrimination shown against him. He should study carefully his white neighbor and strive in every honest way to live in harmony with him. He should qualify himself politically as well as otherwise and become interested in all questions affecting humanity in general and himself in particular.''

"The ideal must be reached after: not on the basis of color or race or any such physical divisions or distinctions, but on the basis of humanity. Only by the way of frank, full, free opportunities can we hope for the ideal. The Negro American must be accorded absolute social and political equality and all the rights guaranteed under a pure democracy.''

"All kinds of activities are essential to the growth and proper development of a people. Diversification in education and pursuit is necessary if a people is to be of the highest good to the country.''

"Strong, well-trained leadership for the masses. Educational opportunities unrestricted for all as the case may demand. Retention of the right of suffrage and the display of more independence in the matter of voting. A better trained ministry to inculcate sound moral teaching. The organizing in cities of clubs for civic improvement and for demanding better grammar school training for Negro children and for teaching the masses, as far as possible, the proper meaning and duties of citizenship.

Encouraging business enterprises. Vigorously opposing the doctrine of servility and submission—but not service. Co-operation as far as possible and wherever warranted with fair and right-minded whites for civic improvement."

"If the Negro is given a chance and equal rights as a citizen he will eventually climb as high and accomplish as much as any race or people has accomplished. A college training is not bad for him nor does it unfit him for usefulness as is often said; but he is better able to meet the demands and responsibilities of the times."

"In spite of the evidences of prejudice everywhere in our country, I believe that the Negro will some day become a big factor in the political life of the nation and occupy an enviable place in the economic development of the United States. He has already made a marvelous record— a record that should give every man with Negro blood in his veins the highest hope for the future."

"I believe that the American Negro must live and die in America. Africa is not his home for he would be an absolute stranger there. I believe in the ultimate triumph of right. I believe that we will receive our rights and be given full citizenship when we as a people demand the same and not until then."

"If the Negro will be wise and educate himself in the trades and the professions, get homes and own land and build up a strong moral character, he will eventually come into his own and be fully recognized as an American citizen."

"The Negro must work and fight and fight and work. He must scorn peace earned at the price of his self-respect. He must deport himself as a man and he must insist on being treated as a man in America. Much time must be given to the bettering of his environment so that he can will to his children far better surroundings than he himself has inherited. Finally, he must cultivate more of the religion of self-respect and less of the religion of fear."

"The Negro should be given every opportunity and encouraged to get the very best education possible—college education in every possible case before entering a professional school. I think Negroes should enter professions and trades, after college, as their tastes lead them and wherever there is likely to be a demand for such professions and trades. They should own homes and acquire additional property as much as they can. They should have a better educated ministry and more thoroly trained teachers."

"I think that full political rights and a more modified social code may be inaugurated in the future. These higher attainments are not possible until the Negro catches the true spirit of the commercial age in which he lives and lays an economic substructure as his foundation. We must produce a substantial capitalist class. Such a state of economy admits of a leisure class. If this leisure class is composed of persons who are cultured, thrifty and energetic I see no reason why full, political rights should not be attained and a widely modified social code substituted for the sham of ignorance under which we are now living. I think education can help ameliorate conditions."

"A leadership more broadly educated. An intelligent and consistent agitation for the securing of our citizenship rights. A manly stand in all things pertaining to civil, social and moral questions. A right-about-face with regard to the matter of the education of the youth of our race; that is, less industrialism and more intelligence."

"I most strenuously urge that our people, all of them, get the best possible training in the best colleges and universities of the country and affiliate with all the forces and organizations making for the moral and religious development of all the people. In the meantime, I would add, encourage in every way possible all the organizations for the material growth of the country."

"Undoubtedly prejudice is increasing rather than diminishing. This has been brought to our minds more forcibly by the passage of the 'grandfather clause' amendment to the constitution of this state. We who are here in Oklahoma feel that colonization has brought it about as much as anything. Wherever our people congregate in large numbers there very soon begins the agitation for disfranchisement. Were it possible for the race to be widely diffused over the United States, so that they might acquire wealth like the so-called superior race, and be found only a few in any one place, there would be no race problem."

"I believe that the acquirement of education and wealth, the teaching of a saner and purer religion, performance of duties and a demand for all our rights under the law will bring a brighter day for the Negro in America."

"I believe that education coupled with a good moral and religious training will be the main factor in the solution of the Negro problem in America."

"I am rather an enthusiast on the return of a goodly portion of the Negroes to Africa as a final solution, by his voluntary and gradual move as he realizes that he can hardly expect to attain to a full measure of citizenship in all that the word implies in this country."

"The Negro will ever remain in America. Citizenship and opportunity will increase as the Negro grows in stability, wealth and intelligence. Prejudice will be forced to abate as slavery recedes and the Negro acquires independence."

"I believe that as the Negro and the white man are educated up to the truth of the legal equality of all men under our American government each will come to see that all must enjoy the same privileges. Neither is yet equal to the occasion. There are few Negroes who are aggressive and demand, and a few philanthropic whites who acknowledge and concede equal opportunities for all men."

"The Negro is growing more assertive and manly. Every day gives us new evidences of the fact that he is becoming more appreciative of his right to life, liberty and property. He is beginning to meet imposition with opposition, even with his life."

"The Negro needs leaders and instructors who will teach that he is a man and therefore must have all the aids to the better life and good citizenship that other men require; that to become a citizen in the true sense he must enjoy the same opportunities and benefits as other citizens."

"The Negro must measure up to the standard of a man in all respects if he hopes to gain what other races have gained. Hence he must be impressed with the necessity of preparing himself. The young Negro must be inspired with reminders of what other Negroes have accomplished. He must be taught not to close the door of hope upon himself, even in thot. He must be made to feel that competency must win, has won."

"To me, the outlook for the Negro race in America is bright or dark owing to the deportment of the Negro himself. If he will make use of the opportunities he has in educating himself, saving his money, acquiring property and in being a law-abiding citizen there is no law that can successfully stop him."

"Let him cease to be a cringing suppliant; assert his manhood intelligently; speak out against unjust discrimination and laws that affect him; demand a competent leadership in pulpit, school training and politics; give his children the highest possible training and repudiate the stigma of being fit only for the workshop; demand the rights guaranteed to citizens by the Constitution; get property; migrate from the South to all parts of the country."

"The Negro came to America not by his own volition and is here to stay. I believe he should contend for all his rights as an American citizen and enter all lines of competition with the other races in this country."

"The Negro in America should be educated just as any other race in America. One phase of education should not be too much emphasized above another. All phases are necessary for the highest realization of any race. Negroes should demand their rights. It is nonsense to expect perfect harmony between two races so situated as the Negroes and whites of America. The day which brings perfect harmony in America must bring at the same time amalgamation."

"Persecution is a friend of progress. The very things that are denied us we shall still want—and we shall supply them ourselves. Whatever community tries to keep the Negro down must stay there with him. The two things indispensible to the Negro's advance are money and education, both of which things are being slowly but surely acquired by individuals and by Negro communities.   .   .   .   . I have no doubt that prejudice is growing but I do believe it is a jealous prejudice and an outgrowth of the desire to keep the Negro in a slave's position."

"I believe that the ultimate solution of the race problem is amalgamation."

"We ought now to have all the rights and privileges which are guaranteed by the Federal Constitution. We must agitate and fight to the last ditch for them. Nothing is worth having if it is not worth fighting for."

"With the highest possible training, the acquisition of property and the launching out into all kinds of business enterprises, the Negro in America will succeed and become a mighty power in the affairs of this country."

"Industry, economy, obedience to all just laws—in short, the same principles which are helpful to any other race; morality, wealth and education being big factors in the solution of our problem; business enterprises of various kinds which will give employment to the average boy and girl of our race, allowing him to aspire to the highest place in the business."

"The Negro needs simply the proper training and a fair chance in the business world along with a square deal before the law and he will find a way or make one along by the side of America's best citizens. We must insist on a thoro education however. No limited education in any particular will suffice."

"The Negroes in America will never develop to the extent of their capacity, will never become a great people, not even a free people, until they have political rights equal to the white race. The man who has no political rights has no way of protecting himself and family."

"While he must give all due attention to his duties, the Negro must not so act now or at any time as to give the impression that he is satisfied to give up even temporarily any of the rights that belong to him as a man. In the present swift revolving scheme of industrial America, the right to vote is paramount."

"The Negroes ought to have every right guaranteed by the Constitution of the United States. We are American citizens and should accept no treatment that does not apply equally to every other American citizen."

"The masses should be trained in such a way as to know well their rights and duties as citizens and should be urged to faithfully perform their duties and quietly, firmly, persistently demand their rights.   .   .   .   . The Negro men who are really qualified to speak should take a bold, manly stand for the race."

"The future of the Negro in this country will depend upon the kind of training given to the Negro youth. The same kind of training which has made other races great is also necessary to make the Negro race great."

"The Negro must become a part of all the life about him. He must become Americanized in the best and largest sense. He should be led out of the consciousness that he must have anything less than other citizens enjoy. All kinds of education, all forms of wealth and a knowledge of the ways of the American world are his needs for this achievement. Each one of us must refuse to turn from any avenue of life because other men think it is not for Negroes. We must work, think and live independent of the dictates of those who regard us as less than other men. The best of us should give of our means, our time and ourselves to leaven the whole. College-bred Negroes should live these ideas among the masses and teach them to their children."

A careful reading of the above quotations from the replies of the Negro college graduates discloses on the whole a hopeful and encouraging attitude on the part of these educated men and women. Tho hampered by prejudice and its accompanying discriminations as well as by lack of opportunity these men and women are for the most part hopeful of the future of the Negro race in America.

The suggestions which these replies contain fall in the main under the following groups:

1. Equality before the law.
2. Full citizenship rights and privileges.
3. The right to vote.
4. Unrestricted educational opportunities.
5. Well trained leadership.

Indeed these suggestions are not to be ignored nor even treated lightly if we hope to bring the Negroes of America to a higher place in the scale of social values; and that not alone for their own sake but for the sake of the American people as a whole.

Section 18. Conclusion

The conference, in studying the college-bred Negro for the second time, concludes that the work of the Negro college and that of the college-bred Negro American have been of inestimable value.

While a few Negroes were graduated from Northern colleges prior to 1860, the great work began with the Emancipation. The Negro college came in response to the call for teachers for the freedmen and their children. For less than fifty years then the work has been carried forward and that with remarkable results. From the ranks of the college-bred have come many of the teachers and leaders and professional men and women of the Negro race in this country.

The demand for such workers has always been and is now greater than the supply. The educational field is constantly in need of thoroly equipped teachers and leaders. In fact the whole educational system must be built upon the college else the system suffers from the lack of competent leadership and direction. So, too, in business and in the professions: the man of training will ever be the controlling factor.

These statements have a special significance when applied to the life of the eleven million Negroes in America. Not only for them but also for all America, the colleges of this country have done a great service in sending forth these five thousand Negro college graduates; men and women who by precept and by example have been of great service in lifting the moral, the social and the economic tone of the American people.

The College=bred Negro American

Index

The Atlanta University Publications, No. 16

THE

COMMON SCHOOL

AND THE

NEGRO AMERICAN

Report of a Social Study made by Atlanta University
under the patronage of the Trustees of the John F.
Slater Fund; with the Proceedings of the 16th Annual
Conference for the Study of the Negro Problems, held
at Atlanta University, on Tuesday, May 30th, 1911

Edited by

W. E. Burghardt Du Bois, Ph.D.
Director of Publicity and Research, National Association for
the Advancement of Colored People

and

Augustus Granville Dill, A.M.
Associate Professor of Sociology in Atlanta University

The Atlanta University Press
ATLANTA, GA.
1911

I AM thankful to-day for the Pen of Lincoln and the Sword of Grant; but more thankful by far for the patient Schoolmarm who taught the Negro his letters and set a million of us to reading.

—William H. Crogman.

The Common School and the Negro American

Contents

The Sixteenth Annual Conference

"The Negro Common School"

PROGRAM

First Session, 10:00 a. m.

President Ware presiding.

Subject: "The Negro Rural School."

"Methods of the Present Investigation." Mr. A. G. Dill, of Atlanta University.

Address: Mr. Henry A. Hunt, Principal of the Fort Valley High and Industrial School, Fort Valley, Ga.

Second Session, 11:30 a. m.

Subject: "The Common School and Health." (Separate meetings for men and women.)

Address to men: Dr. W. F. Penn.

Address to women: Mrs. H. R. Butler.

Third Session, 3:00 p. m.

Fourteenth Annual Mothers' Meeting. (In charge of the Gate City Free Kindergarten Association.) Mrs. I. E. Wynn presiding.

Subject: "The Kindergarten and the Common School."

1. Kindergarten songs, games and exercises by 125 children of the five free kindergartens:
    East Cain Street—Mrs. Ola Perry Cooke.
    Bradley Street—Mrs. Hattie Sims Fountain.
    White's Alley—Miss Leila Golden.
    Martin Street—Mrs. John Rush.
    Leonard Street Orphanage—Miss Rosa Martin.
2. Address: Mrs. Anna E. Murray, Washington, D. C.
3. Explanation of Kindergarten Exhibit: Miss Gertrude H. Ware.
4. Report of the Treasurer: Mrs. Lizzie Burch.
5. Collection.

Fourth Session, 8:00 p. m.

President Ware presiding.

Subject: "The Common School as a Key to the Problem."

Address: Mrs. Anna E. Murray, Washington, D. C.

Address: "The Importance of the Public School." Rev. Silas X. Floyd, D.D., of Augusta, Ga.

Preface

In 1901 the Atlanta University Negro Conference made an investigation into common schools for Negro Americans. The publication which resulted from this investigation was quoted and discussed especially because of the questions which it raised in regard to the contributions of Negroes for their own elementary education and in regard to the meagre school facilities afforded Negro children.

Ten years later we return to the same investigation aided by an appropriation of $1,000 from the Trustees of the John F. Slater Fund. The results are based on national and southern state school reports, local reports and studies and reports from school officials. The study is not exhaustive and much material information is missing; but even this partial survey is of much value.

This study is, therefore, a further carrying out of the Atlanta University plan of social study of the Negro American, by means of an annual series of decennially recurring subjects covering, so far as is practicable, every phase of human life. The object of these studies is primarily scientific—a careful research for truth; conducted as thoroly, broadly and honestly as the material resources and mental equipment at command will allow. It must be remembered that mathematical accuracy in these studies is impossible; the sources of information are of varying degrees of accuracy and the pictures are wofully incomplete. There is necessarily much repetition in the successive studies, and some contradiction of previous reports by later ones as new material comes to hand. All we claim is that the work is as thoro as circumstances permit and that with all its obvious limitations it is well worth the doing. Our object is not simply to serve science. We wish not only to make the truth clear but to present it in such shape as will encourage and help social reform. The resolutions which follow this preface are the expression of the members, delegates and attendants upon the sessions of the sixteenth annual Conference.

Our financial resources are unfortunately meagre: Atlanta University is primarily a school and most of its funds and energy go to teaching. It is, however, also a seat of learning and as such it has endeavored to advance knowledge, particularly in matters of racial contact and development, which seem obviously its nearest field. In this work it has received unusual encouragement from the scientific world, and the published results of these studies are used in America, Europe, Asia and Africa. Very few books on the Negro problem, or any phase of it, have been published in the last decade which have not acknowledged their indebtedness to our work.

On the other hand, the financial support given this work has been very small. The total cost of the sixteen publications has been about $18,500, or something over $1,000 a year. The growing demands of the work, the vast field to be covered and the delicacy and equipment needed in such work, call for far greater resources. We need, for workers, laboratory and publications, a fund of $6,000 a year, if this work is going adequately to fulfill its promise. Four years ago a small temporary grant from the Carnegie Institution of Washington, D. C., greatly helped us; and for four years our work has been saved from suspension by an appropriation from the John F. Slater Fund.

In past years we have been enabled to serve the United States Bureau of Labor, the United States Census, the Board of Education of the English Government, many scientific associations, professors in nearly all the leading universities, and many periodicals and reviews. May we not hope in the future for such increased financial resources as will enable us to study adequately this the greatest group of social problems that ever faced America?

Resolutions

The Sixteenth Atlanta Conference feels great concern over the condition of common school training among Negro Americans.

In the North the Negro children usually have the same facilities for schooling as other children have but they often lack encouragement and inspiration.

In the larger cities of the border states, Negroes have good tho crowded schools. In Texas, their town schools are good and the county schools fair. But in South Carolina, Georgia, Florida, Alabama, Mississippi, Louisiana and Arkansas and in the country districts of the border states, elementary training for Negroes is in a deplorable condition. In the larger part of this area it is our firm belief that the Negro common schools are worse off than they were twenty years ago, with poorer teaching, less supervision and comparatively few facilities. In Virginia and North Carolina there are signs of improvement and in isolated instances in other states; but on the whole, thruout the lower South and to a large degree thruout the whole South these things are true:

1. The appropriations for Negro schools have been cut down, relatively speaking.

2. The wages for Negro teachers have been lowered and often poorer teachers have been preferred to better ones.

3. Superintendents have neglected to supervise the Negro schools.

4. In recent years few school houses have been built and few repairs have been made; for the most part the Negroes themselves have purchased school sites, school houses and school furniture, thus being in a peculiar way double taxed.

5. The Negroes in the South, except those of one or two states, have been deprived of almost all voice or influence in the government of the public schools.

Summarizing then: As a result of such conditions it is certain that of the Negro children 6 to 14 years of age not 50 per cent have a chance today to learn to read and write and cipher correctly. Unless we face these facts the problem of ignorance in the race question will soon overshadow all other problems.

The Negroes themselves are making heroic efforts to remedy these evils thru a wide-spread system of private, self-supported schools and philanthropy is furnishing a helpful but incomplete system of industrial, normal and collegiate training for children of the black race. In many parts of the South Negroes are paying into the school fund in the way of taxes much more than they are receiving in actual appropriations for their school facilities. Wherever this is true it may be said that the Negroes are helping to pay for the education of the white children while the states are depriving the Negro children of their just share of school facilities.

In order to secure the best results it is necessary to take a more liberal view concerning Negro education and to provide adequate facilities for the instruction of Negro youth. The Conference feels that in the case of continued failure on the part of the South to provide adequate school facilities for Negro children, permanent relief can be secured only from national aid to education with such safeguards as will insure the fair treatment of black children.

(Signed)   MRS. A. E. MURRAY, Washington, D. C.
            H. A. HUNT, Fort Valley, Ga.
            A. G. DILL, Atlanta, Ga.
            W. E. B. DUBOIS, New York, N. Y.

A Select Bibliography of Common School Education for Negro Americans

Part I

Arranged alphabetically by authors

Atlanta University Publications, The Negro Common School. Atlanta, 1901. ii (2), 120 pp. 8 vo.

Baskerville, W. M. Shall the Negro be educated or suppressed? Nashville, 1899. 24 pp. 8vo.

Boston, Mass., Grammar school committee. Report of a special committee of the Grammar school board. Abolition of the Smith colored school. Boston, 1849. 71 pp. 8vo.

Boston, Mass., Primary school committee. ·Report. Abolition of colored schools. Boston, 1846. 38 pp. 8vo.

Boston, Mass., Public school. Report of the minority of the committee of the primary school board on the caste schools of Boston (E. Jackson and H. I. Bowditch) with remarks by Wendell Phillips. Boston, 1846. 36 pp. 8vo.

Boston, Mass., School committee. Report of the minority of the committee upon the petition of J. T. Hilton and other colored citizens of Boston, praying for the abolition of the Smith colored school. Boston, 1849. 13 pp. 8vo.

Brousseau, Kate. L'education des Negroes aux etats unis. Paris, 1904. xvi, 396 pp. 8vo.

Brown, M. H. A plea for industrial education among the colored people. New York, 1884. 30 pp. 16mo.

Brown, William Wells. The rising son. Boston, 1874 (1873). 12 mo. Portr.

Bumstead, Dr. Horace. Secondary and higher education in the South for whites and Negroes. 1910.

Coon, Charles L. Public taxation and Negro schools. Twelfth annual conference for education in the South. Atlanta, Ga., April 14-16, 1909.

Curry, J. L. M. Difficulties, complications and limitations connected with the education of the Negro. Baltimore, 1895. 23 pp. 8vo. J. F. Slater fund papers.

Curry, J. L. M. Education of Negroes since 1860. Baltimore, 1890. 32 pp. 8vo. J. F. Slater fund papers.

Delaware association for the moral improvement and education of the colored people. Annual reports, 1868, 1869, 1870. Wilmington, Del.

Douglass, H. P. Christian reconstruction in the South. Boston, 1909. 407 pp.

Eaton, John. Report of freedmen·'s schools for 1864-1865 (contained in report of the general superintendent of freedmen. Department of the states of Tennessee and Arkansas. 1864-5.)

Finger, S. M. Educational and religious interests of the colored people of the South. U. S. Bureau of Education. Circular of information, No. 2. 1886. Pp. 123-133.

Fletcher, Hon. Richard. Opinion as to whether colored children can be lawfully excluded from free public schools. Boston, 1846 (?).

Friends. A brief sketch of the schools of the black people and their descendants, established by the religious society of Friends. Philadelphia, 1867. 32 pp. 8vo.

Goodwin, M. B. History of schools for the colored population in the District of Columbia. U. S. Bureau of Education. Special report District of Columbia for 1869. Pp. 193-300.

Greogoire, Ḩ. Enquiry concerning the intellectual and moral faculties, etc., of Negroes. Brooklyn, 1810. 253 pp. 8vo.

Harris, Wm. T. Education of the Negro. An address made to the students of Atlanta University, Atlanta, Ga., Oct. 29, 1895.

Hartshorn, W. N. An era of progress and promise. Boston, 1910. 576 pp.

Haygood, Atticus Green. Our brother in black, etc. New York, 1881. 252 pp. 12mo.

Haygood, Atticus Green. The case of the Negro, as to education in the southern states, etc. Atlanta, 1885. 59 pp. 8vo.

Institute for colored youth, Philadelphia. Objects . . . . list of officers and students, etc. Philadelphia, 1860-65. 12mo.

Massachusetts general court. Petitions. Equal schools for all without regard to color or race. Boston, 1851.

Mayo, Amory Dwight. How shall the colored youth of the South be educated? Boston, 1897 (1). 213-224 pp. 8vo.

Mayo, Amory Dwight. The northern and southern women in the education of the Negro in the South. U. S. Bureau of Education. Circular of information, No. 1, p. 71, 1892.

Miller, Kelly. The education of the Negro. Washington, 1902. U. S. Bureau of Education Reports. 1900-1. Vol. I. Pp. 731-859.

Miller, Kelly. The primary needs of the Negro race. Washington, 1899. 18 pp. 8vo.

Orr, Gustavus. The education of the Negro. Atlanta, Ga., 1880. 15 pp. 8vo.

Report of the actuary of the Delaware association for the education of the colored people (1877-78). Wilmington, 1878. 8vo.

Ruffin, Frank G. The cost and outcome of Negro education in Virginia. Richmond, 1889. 20 pp. 8vo.

Smith, Thos. P, An address before the colored citizens of Boston in opposition to the abolition of colored schools, 1849. Boston, 1850. 12 pp. 8vo.

Stetson, Geo. R. The problem of Negro education. Boston, 1884. 21 pp. 8vo.

Triumph of equal rights in Boston. Meeting in honor of W. C. Nell. Boston, 1856. 24 pp. 12 mo.

United States Bureau of Education. Education of the colored race. Washington, 1901. Report, 1899-1900.

United States Bureau of Education. Education of the colored race. Washington, 1902. Report, 1900-1901.

United States Bureau of Education. Education of the colored race. Negroes in America. Washington, 1896. (In report of commission for 1893-94. Vol. I, pp. 1038-1061.)

United States: Report of the Industrial Commission, 1901-1902. 19 Vols. Washington. Vol. 15: On immigration and on education. 259 pp.

Wright, R. R., Jr. Self-help in Negro education. Cheney, Pa.

Wright, R. R., Sr. Brief historical sketch of Negro education in Georgia. Savannah, Ga., 1894. 58 pp. 8vo.

Part II. Periodical Literature

American Journal of Political Economy: Education of Negroes. A. A. Gundy. 1:295.

American Journal of Social Science:
   Education of Negroes. C. D. Warner. 38:1.
   Education of Negroes. K. Miller. 39:117.
   Negro schools in Virginia. O. Langhorne. 11:36.
   Present problem of the education of Negroes. W. H. Baldwin. 37:52.

American Magazine of Civics: Education of Negroes. J. L. M. Curry. 8:168.

Andover Review:
   Negroes at school. H. Bumstead. 4:550.
   Education of Negroes. A. Salisbury. 6:256.
   New basis of education of Negroes. G. R. Stetson. 14:254.

Annals of the American Academy of Political Science: Negro education in the South. W. B. Hill. 22:320-9.

Anthropological Review: Brain in the Negro. J. D. Davis. 7:190.

Arena:
   Education of Negroes. C. M. Blackford. 23:24-30.
   Educational possibilities of the Negro. B. T. Washington. 21:445.

Atlantic:
   Education of Negroes. W. T. Harris. 69:721.
   Negro schoolmaster in the new South. W. E. B. DuBois. 83:99.

Catholic World: Education of Negroes. J. R. Slattery. 63:265.

Century: Yankee teacher in the South. E. G. Rice. 62:151.

Crisis: Colored high schools. Mason A. Hawkins. June, 1911.

Current Literature:
   Blow at Negro education. 36:491.
   South's verdict on Negro schools. 36:425.

Education: Education of Negroes. C. G. Andrews. 6:221.

Educational Review:
   Education of the Negro in its historical aspects. D. L. Kiehle. 27:299.
   New education in the South. P. B. Barringer. 21:233.

Forum: Expenses of the education of Negroes. Does the Negro pay it? G. W. Cable. 13:640.

Gunton's Magazine: Education of Negroes and New Orleans. 20:66.

Harper's Weekly: Education of freedmen. D. H. Strother. 49:457.

Independent:
    Burden of Negro schooling. W. E. B. DuBois. 53:1667-8.
    Education of Negroes, symposium. April 7, 1892.
    Education of white and black. E. A. Alderman. 53:2241-9.
    New Orleans and Negro education. 53:1630.
    South's dual system of education. N. B. Young. 52:314-16.
Lend a Hand:
    Educational statistics of Negroes. 6:149.
    Education of Negroes. Report of Calhoun school. C. R. Thorn and
      W. M. Dillingham. 13:52.
Lippincott's Magazine: Education of Negroes of the South. W. R.
    Hooper. 4:671.
Methodist Quarterly Review: Education of freedmen. S. G. Arnold.
    38:48.
Missionary Review: What intellectual training is doing for the Negro.
    W. E. B. DuBois. 27:578-82.
Nation:
    Education of Negroes of the South. 24:276.
    First colored school in Philadelphia. 72:316.
    Negro education and the South. 78:62-3.
New England Magazine: Education of Negroes. A. D. Mayo. 17:213.
New World: Education of Negroes. H. B. Frissell. 9:625.
Niles Register: Negro school at New Haven. 41:74-88.
North American Review:
    Education and civilization of freedmen. E. E. Hale. 101:528.
    Education of Negroes. J. R. Gilmore. 143:421.
    Education of Negroes of the South. F. B. Stowe. 128:605; 129:81.
    Negro intellect. W. Matthew. 149:91.
Old and New: Education of Negroes of the South. S. Andrews. 1:200,
    373.
Outlook:
    Aims of Negro education. H. B. Frissell. 74:937-9.
    Education of the Negro in the United States. 78:96-7.
    Educational solution of the Negro problem. 74:632-5.
    Negro Common Schools. 71:675-7.
    Popular education and the race problem in North Carolina. J. W.
      Bailey. 68:114-16.
    Shall the Negro be educated? 68:13-15.
    Should southern whites aid Negro schools? C. H. Poe. 71:1010-13.
    Training of Negroes for social power. W. E. B. DuBois. 75:409-14.
Public Opinion: Negroes and schools. 3:526.
Putnam's Monthly Magazine: Negro schools. E. Kilham. 15:31.
Review of Reviews: Alabama Negro schools. O. G. Villard.
Slater Fund:
    Proceedings and occasional papers of the, No. 3. Curry: Education
      of Negroes since 1860.
    Proceedings and occasional papers of the, No. 5. Curry: Difficulties
      connected with education of Negroes.
Southern Workman: The outlook in Negro education. W. T. B. Wil-
    liams.

The Common School and the Negro American

Section 1. Scope of the Inquiry

In 1901 Atlanta University made a study of the Negro Common School. Ten years later we come back to the same study. The present investigation is based on the following data in addition to other miscellaneous sources:

1. The annual reports of the United States commissioner of education.
2. State school reports as follows:

Alabama 1910	Mississippi . . 1907–1908, 1908–1909
Arkansas (Adv. sheets) . . 1910	Missouri. 1910
Delaware. 1910	N. Carolina. . 1908–1909, 1909–1910
Florida 1908–1910	South Carolina 1910
Georgia. 1909–1910	Tennessee. 1909–1910
Kansas 1907–1908	Texas. 1909–1910
Kentucky . . . 1908–1909, 1910–1911	Virginia . . . 1907–1908, 1908–1909
Louisiana. 1908–1909	Washington, D. C. . . . 1907–1908
Maryland. 1909–1910	West Virginia. 1908–1910

3. Replies of city superintendents to the following circular:

DEAR SIR:

Atlanta University is making a study of Negro public schools. Will you kindly answer the following questions and return the blank to us at your earliest convenience?

1. City . . . . State . . . .
2. Number of Negro school buildings?
3. Seating capacity?
4. Number of Negro pupils enrolled?
5. Number of Negro teachers employed?
6. Where were these teachers educated?
7. Do they make efficient teachers?
8. What are their chief defects?
9. Salaries of Negro teachers?
10. What is your opinion of the work of the Negro schools?

NOTE. Will you write on the back the names and addresses of the principals of the Negro schools in your system?

4. Replies to the following general questionnaire sent to teachers and citizens thruout the South:

DEAR FRIEND:

Will you kindly answer the following questions as well as possible and return the blank to Atlanta University? We will hold your answers in strict confidence and use the information only to help the schools of our race. Please be prompt in replying.

1. State and county.

2. Are there any printed school reports published in your county? If so, can you send us copies, or tell us whom to write?

3. How many colored schools and how many white schools are there in your county?

4. What was the length of the term of the colored schools and of the white schools last year?

5. How many grades are there in the colored schools? How many grades in the white schools?

6. How many colored and how many white teachers are there in your county?

7. How well are the teachers educated and where?

8. What salaries do the colored teachers get a month? What salaries do the white teachers get a month?

9. What is the total amount spent annually on colored schools and on white schools in the county?

10. How many colored and how many white children regularly attend school?

11. How do the school facilities now compare with ten years ago?

12. Are there any separate town school systems in the county?

13. Do they lay a special school tax? If so, how much of this goes to colored schools?

14. Do the colored people support any schools of their own or do they supplement the school term?

15. In general what is the condition of Negro public school education in your county?

Section 2.   Illiteracy

The Negro population in America had its beginning in 1619, when nineteen Negroes were landed upon the Virginia coast and sold as slaves to the settlers in that region. For more than two hundred years this importation of Negroes continued. As a rule the imported slaves were kept in ignorance for the unwritten law of the land was that Negroes should receive no instruction. In the main this was accomplished by acts of legislation. For instance, South Carolina, in 1740, declared: "Whereas, the having of slaves taught to write or suffering them to be employed in writing may be attended with inconveniences, be it enacted, That all and every person and persons whatsoever, who shall hereafter teach or cause any slave or slaves to be taught, or shall use or employ any slave as a scribe in any manner of writing whatever, hereafter taught to write, every such person or persons shall for every such offense forfeit the sum of one hundred pounds current money."

Louisiana, in 1830, declared that "All persons who shall teach, or permit or cause to be taught, any slave to read or write shall be imprisoned not less than one month nor more than twelve months."

Georgia, in 1770, fined any person who taught a slave to read and write 20 pounds. In 1829 the State enacted: "If any slave, Negro or free person of color, or any white person, shall teach any other slave, Negro or free person of color to read or write, either written or printed characters, the same free person of color or slave shall be punished by fine and whipping, or fine or whipping, at the discretion of the court; and if a white person so offend, he, she, or they shall be punished with a fine not exceeding $500 and imprisonment in the common jail at the discretion of the court."

Virginia, in 1819, forbade "all meetings or assemblages of slaves or free Negroes or mulattoes, mixing or associating with such slaves, ... at any school or schools for teaching them reading or writing, either in the day or night." Nevertheless free Negroes kept schools for themselves until the Nat Turner Insurrection, when it was enacted, 1831, that "all meetings of Negroes or mulattoes at any school house, church, meeting house or other place for teaching them reading and writing, either in the day or night, under whatsoever pretext, shall be deemed and considered an unlawful assembly." This law was carefully enforced.

The other slave states had similar laws. To be sure, there were individual slaves who learned to read and write despite these prohibitions, and many of the house servants, who came in closer contact with the master class, came into possession of the knowledge of these arts. Nevertheless at Emancipation the percentage of illiteracy among the colored population was probably about ninety per cent. The following table gives the census figures for Negro illiteracy:

ILLITERACY BY PER CENT

STATES	Negroes 10 years of age and over			
	1870	1880	1890	1900
District of Columbia. . . .	70.5	48.4	35.0	24.3
Missouri . .	72.7	53.9	41.7	28.1
West Virginia.	74.4	55.0	44.5	32.3
Florida	84.1	70.7	50.5	38.4
Maryland	69.5	59.6	50.1	35.1
Delaware	71.3	57.5	49.5	38.1
Arkansas	81.2	75.0	53.6	43.0
Texas	88.7	75.4	52.5	38.2
Tennessee	82.4	71.7	54.2	41.6
Kentucky	83.8	70.4	55.9	40.1
Virginia	88.9	73.2	57.2	44.6
North Carolina	84.8	77.4	60.1	47.6
Mississippi	87.0	75.2	60.8	49.1
South Carolina	81.1	78.5	64.1	52.8
Georgia	92.1	81.6	67.3	52.4
Alabama	88.1	80.6	69.1	57.4
Louisiana	85.9	79.1	72.1	61.1
Massachusetts	18.5	15.1	14.3	10.7
United States	79.9	70.0	57.1	44.4

It is probable that at present something over one-third of the Negro population of the United States is illiterate.

Section 3.   Beginnings of the Negro Common School

The first school for Negroes so far as is known was the one established by Elias Neau in New York City in 1704. Anthony Benezet opened a school in Philadelphia in 1770. The free Negroes of Charleston had an established school as early as 1774. This school was taught by a Negro and was intended for free Negroes only, altho some slaves who hired their time managed to send their children there. The colored people of Boston began a school for themselves in 1798. From these beginnings private schools multiplied rapidly during the early nineteenth century among the free Negroes and fugitive slaves in the District of Columbia and the border states and to a more limited extent among the free Negroes of the South. By the time of the opening of the Civil War there were perhaps twenty schools for free Negroes in Washington, D. C., and about as many in New Orleans. In the country districts, on the other hand, where more than nine-tenths of the Negroes lived, there were no schools for either free Negroes or slaves.

During the war the first complication that confronted the armies was the continual arrival of fugitive slaves within the Union lines. At first the commands were rigid against receiving them. "Hereafter," wrote Halleck early in the war, "no slaves should be allowed to come within your lines at all." Other generals, however, thot differently. Some argued that the confiscating slaves would weaken the South, others were imbued with abolition sentiment for right's sake. Twice attempts were made to free the slaves of certain localities by proclamation, but these orders were countermanded by the President. Still the fugitives poured into the lines and gradually were used as laborers and helpers. Immediately teaching began and gradually schools sprang up. When at last the Emancipation Proclamation was issued and Negro soldiers called for, it was necessary to provide more systematically for Negroes. Various systems and experiments grew up here and there. The freedmen were massed in large numbers at Fortress Monroe, Va., Washington, D. C., Beaufort and Port Royal, S. C., New Orleans, La., Vicksburg and Corinth, Miss., Columbus, Ky., Cairo, Ill., and elsewhere. In such places schools immediately sprang up under the army officers and chaplains. The most elaborate system, perhaps, was that under General Banks in Louisiana. It was established in 1863 and soon had a regular Board of Education, which laid and collected taxes and supported eventually nearly a hundred schools with ten thousand pupils under 162 teachers. At Port Royal, S. C., were gathered Edward L. Pierce's "Ten Thousand Clients." After the capture of Hilton Head in 1861 the Sea Islands were occupied and the Secretary of the Treasury designated this as a place to receive refugee Negroes. Mr. Pierce began the organization of relief societies in the North and established an economic system with schools. Eventually these passed under the oversight of General Rufus Saxton, who sold forfeited estates, leased plantations, received the camp-followers of Sherman's march to the sea and encouraged schools. In the West, General Grant appointed Colonel John Eaton, afterwards United States Commissioner of Education, to be Superintendent of Freedmen in 1862. He sought to consolidate and regulate the schools already established and succeeded in organizing a large system.[1]

[1] Atlanta University Publication, No. 6, p. 22.

In the border states the development of the Negro schools was somewhat different. Missouri and West Virginia established free schools about the time that the other states did and made provisions for Negroes. Tennessee was slower, while Delaware, Kentucky and Maryland refused to provide for colored children at first and for a long time granted them only the taxes raised among themselves. Not until 1880 were the colored children put on a legal footing with other children. The decisive reason for so doing, as given by one superintendent was, "The elevation of this class is a matter of prime importance since a ballot in the hands of a black citizen is quite as potent as in the hands of a white one."

The activities in the various states may illustrate the differing conditions:

GEORGIA. — In December, 1865, the colored people of Savannah, within a few days after the entrance of Sherman's army, opened a number of schools, having an enrollment of 500 pupils and contributed $1,000 for the support of teachers. Two of the largest of these were in Bryant's Slave Mart.

In January, 1866, the Negroes of Georgia organized the Georgia Educational Association, whose object was to induce the freedmen to establish and support schools in their own counties and neighborhoods.

In 1867, 191 day schools and 45 night schools were reported as existing. Of these, 96 were reported either wholly or in part supported by the freedmen, who also owned 57 of the school buildings.

ARKANSAS. — After 1865 they established the first free schools that ever were in Arkansas. This they did at Little Rock, where, after paying tuition for a short time, they formed themselves into an educational association, paid by subscription the salaries of teachers, and made the schools free.

FLORIDA. — Among the various agencies engaged in the work of educating the freedmen of the South are two, consisting of colored people in the southern states, and known respectively as the African Civilization Society, and the Home Missionary Society of the African Methodist Episcopal Church. . . .

Several schools were opened at Tallahassee and other places in Florida shortly after the close of the war.

In 1866 the freedmen erected school houses at their own expense, besides contributing from their scanty means towards the support of teachers. They formed "school societies" and co-operated with the Bureau in furnishing school lots and erecting buildings.

KENTUCKY.—After the war, the thirty schools which were established, in spite of great obstacles, were mainly supported by the freed people themselves.

NORTH CAROLINA.—In 1867 the State Superintendent of Education reported that many instances had come under his notice where the teachers of a self-supporting school had been sustained until the last cent the freedmen could command was exhausted, and where these last had ever taxed their credit in the coming crop to pay the bills necessary to keep up the school.

The Freedmen's Bureau found many schools for freedmen already in existence maintained by tax commissioners, by Negroes and by the army. The original Freedmen's Bureau Act made no provision for Negro education; but notwithstanding this the funds derived from the rent of abandoned property were used for education and government buildings were turned into school houses. Transportation was given to teachers and subsistence granted. By an act of 1866 the educational powers of the Bureau were greatly enlarged and co-operations with benevolent associations, teachers and agents were sanctioned, buildings were leased, etc. The sum of $521,000 was appropriated for school purposes and other sums provided by the sale and lease of property formerly belonging to the confederate government. The next year Congress voted $500,000 for schools and asylums, and during the next two years they made liberal provisions. The Bureau school system now assumed a more comprehensive and stable character. Grading of city and village schools began. The number of Bureau schools still increased, and in November, 1867, they had a wide-reaching system. Higher schools then began to be established, and thus in many ways the Freedmen's Bureau fostered and organized the Negro school system.

The Freedmen's Bureau published the following figures:

School report for the last six months in 1868:

Day schools	1,198
Night schools	228
Total	1,426
Tuition paid by freedmen	$65,319 75
Expended by Bureau	67,208 48
Total cost	$180,247 44

```
Schools sustained wholly by freedmen . . . . . . . . . . . . . . .    469
Schools sustained in part by freedmen . . . . . . . . . . . . . . .   531
School buildings owned by freedmen . . . . . . . . . . . . . . .     364
School buildings furnished by Bureau . . . . . . . . . . . . . .     417
White teachers . . . . . . . . . . . . . . . . . . . . . . . . . .  1,031
Colored teachers . . . . . . . . . . . . . . . . . . . . . . . . .    713
Total enrollment . . . . . . . . . . . . . . . . . . . . . . . . . 81,878
Average attendance . . . . . . . . . . . . . . . . . . . . . . . . 58,790
Pupils paying tuition . . . . . . . . . . . . . . . . . . . . . . . 26,139
```

The summary for 1866-1870 was as follows:

INCREASE OF EDUCATION

DATE	Schools	No. of Teachers	Pupils
1866	975	1,405	90,778
1867	1,839	2,087	111,442
1868	1,831	2,295	104,327
1869	2,118	2,455	114,522
1870	2,677	3,300	149,581

EXPENDITURES FOR SCHOOLS

YEAR	Expended by			Total
	Freedmen's Bureau	Benevolent Associations	The Freedmen	
1866	$ 123,655 39	$ 82,200 00	$ 18,500 00	$ 224,359 39
1867	531,345 48	65,087 01	17,200 00	613,632 49
1868	965,896 67	700,000 00	360,000 00	2,025,896 67
1869	924,182 16	365,000 00	190,000 00	1,479,182 16
1870	976,853 29	360,000 00	200,000 00	1,536,853 29
Total	. . . .	. . . .	$ 785,700 00	$ 5,879,924 00

The annual amount which the Bureau voted to school purposes increased from $27,000 in 1865 to nearly $1,000,000 in 1870 and reached a total from 1865 to 1871 of $5,262,511.26. In July, 1870, there were 4,239 schools under their supervision with 9,307 teachers and 247,333 pupils. Notwithstanding this, of the 1,700,000 Negro children of school age in 1870 only about one-tenth were actually in school.

So much has been said lately about the Fifteenth Amendment that we are apt to forget that in all human probability the passage of this amendment was decisive in rendering permanent the foundation of the Negro public school. If the Negroes had been left a servile caste, personally free, but politically powerless, it is not reasonable to think that a system of common schools would have been provided for them by the southern states.[1]

[1] Atlanta University Publication, No. 6, p. 38.

The Negro carpet bag governments may be said to have established the public schools:

Altho recent researches have shown in the South some germs of a public school system before the war, there can be no reasonable doubt but that common school instruction in the South, in the modern sense of the term, was founded by the Freedmen's Bureau and missionary societies, and that the state public school systems were formed mainly by Negro reconstruction governments. The earlier state constitutions of Mississippi from 1817 to 1865 contained a declaration that "Religion, morality and knowledge being necessary to good governments, the preservation of liberty and the happiness of mankind, schools and the means of education shall forever be encouraged." It was not, however, until 1868 that encouragement was given to any general system of public schools meant to embrace the whole youthful population. In Alabama the reconstruction constitution of 1868 provided that "It shall be the duty of the Board of Education to establish thruout the state, in each township or other school district which it may have created, one or more schools at which all the children of the state between the ages of 5 and 21 years may attend free of charge." In Mississippi the constitution of 1868 makes it the duty of the legislature to establish "a uniform system of free public schools, by taxation or otherwise, for all children between the ages of 5 and 21 years." Arkansas in 1868, Florida in 1869, Louisiana in 1868, North Carolina in 1869, South Carolina in 1868 and Virginia in 1870 established school systems. The constitution of 1868 in Louisiana required the General Assembly to establish "at least one free public school in every parish," and that these schools should make no "distinction of race, color, or previous condition." Georgia's system was not fully established until 1873.

The school systems established in the carpet bag period were of varied degrees of efficiency. There were speculation and ignorance, but notwithstanding, as time passed, they gradually improved. In Florida, for instance, a Negro, Jonathan C. Gibbs, a graduate of Dartmouth, later State Superintendent of Schools in Florida, succeeded in founding an excellent system of schools. In other states Negro officials worked hard. After the fall of the carpet bag governments, a period of doubt ensued, and for a while it was feared that the system would be paralyzed. Finally, however, the Negro school system was left standing. Too, the effect of these governments upon public education in general is worth noting:

The reorganization of their [the southern states] system of public education grew out of the complete enfranchisement of the colored race, and became necessary in order to adjust their new political relations to this race under the amendments to the Constitution of the United States.[1]

As Albion Tourgee said of the Negro voters of reconstruction times: "They instituted a public school system in a region where public schools had been unknown."

Colonel Richard P. Hallowell adds: "The whites had always regarded the public school system of the North with contempt. The freedman introduced and established it and it stands today a living testimony to his faith that education is necessary to social welfare."[2]

Section 4.   Enrollment

On January 1, 1866, the total enrollment as near as could be ascertained of Negro children in all colored schools was 90,589.   In 1880, the total enrollment of Negro children, according to the report of the United States Bureau of Education was 784,709, while in 1890 it was 1,296,959.   The figure rose to 1,560,070 in 1900.   The Negro school population (5 to 18 years of age) in the sixteen former slave states and the District of Columbia for the scholastic year 1908-9 was 3,038,710.   Of this number, 1,712,137, or 56.34 per cent, were enrolled in the public schools.   The average daily attendance was 1,116,811, that is 65.22 per cent of the total enrollment and 36.75 per cent of the total Negro school population.   The enrollment of white children and colored children since 1890 is given in the following table:

YEAR	Common School Enrollment		YEAR	Common School Enrollment	
	White	Colored		White	Colored
189:-91	3,570,624	1,329,549	19 0-01	4,30 ,954	1,594,308
1891-92	3,6 7,549	1,354,316	1901-02	4,386,322	1,575,659
1892-93	3,697,899	1,3 i7,5i5	19:2-03	4,428,842	1,578,632
1893-94	3,848,541	1,432,198	19 3-04	4,522,744	1,577,3*5
1894-95	3,846,267	1,423,593	19 4-05	4,564,798	1,602,194
1895-96	3,943,801	1,449,325	19 5-i 6	4,6 8,5i1	1,617,998
1896-97	3,937,992	1,460,i 84	19 6-'7	4,671,135	1,672,725
1897-98	4,145,737	1,54 ',749	1907-08	4,692,927	1,665,781
1898-99	4,144,643	1,509,275	19 8- 9	4,9 9,283	1,712,137
1899-19 0	4,261,369	1,560,070			

[1]Report of U. S. Bureau of Education, 1888.
[2]Why the Negro was Enfranchised, p. 33.

From the reports of the United States Bureau of Education come the following statistics:

COMMON SCHOOL STATISTICS, CLASSIFIED BY RACE

1899-1900

STATE	Average daily attendance	Per cent of persons 5 to 18 years enrolled	
	Colored	White	Colored
Alabama	99,342	66.54	47.26
Arkansas	52,656	68.29	64.49
Delaware	2,947	71.74	54.58
District of Columbia	11,611	68.49	60.76
Florida	28,736	68.48	53.83
Georgia	119,276	70.79	51.25
Kentucky	43,074	75.22	70.38
Louisiana	56,136	53.53	30.60
Maryland	22,989	68.07	60.61
Mississippi	102,898	73.71	58.09
Missouri	23,001	75.22	62.32
North Carolina	64,505	64.86	51.80
South Carolina	110,947	67.94	49.88
Tennessee	67,904	74.39	57.70
Texas	83,904	55.16	50.46
Virginia	61,754	66.05	44.99
West Virginia	5,480	72.40	63.55
Total, 1899-1900	957,160	68.28	51.46
Total, 1889-1890	813,710	67.15	32.85

1900-1901

STATE	Average daily attendance	Per cent of persons 5 to 18 years enrolled	
	Colored	White	Colored
Alabama	99,342	71.12	50.62
Arkansas	53,011	73.78	67.55
Delaware	3,800	76.70	69.09
District of Columbia	11,883	76.41	77.74
Florida	30,123	71.17	59.75
Georgia	122,887	74.72	55.32
Kentucky	40,225	73.98	72.84
Louisiana	49,817	52.95	33.06
Maryland	22,712	66.04	68.82
Mississippi	102,898	80.08	61.62
Missouri	22,631	76.86	71.78
North Carolina	80,747	69.79	63.85
South Carolina	113,566	69.27	54.94
Tennessee	67,904	78.44	64.51
Texas	89,012	63.18	60.87
Virginia	61,754	67.38	51.92
West Virginia	5,480	78.84	72.15
Total, 1900-1901	977,192	71.57	57.22
Total, 1889-1890	813,710	67.15	32.85

COMMON SCHOOL STATISTICS, CLASSIFIED BY RACE

1901-1902

STATE	Average daily attendance	Per cent of persons 5 to 18 years enrolled	
	Colored	White	Colored
Alabama	90,000	69.24	42.71
Arkansas	56,290	75.98	70.88
Delaware	3,800	76.70	69.09
District of Columbia	12,206	76.54	77.90
Florida	29,881	70.59	57.00
Georgia	124,553	76.56	56.39
Kentucky	40,314	73.11	71.84
Louisiana	49,817	51.85	32.36
Maryland	22,712	66.04	68.82
Mississippi	119,190	83.23	64.69
Missouri	21,079	74.90	68.22
North Carolina	83,405	74.12	66.31
South Carolina	109,699	68.46	49.58
Tennessee	71,779	79.09	67.61
Texas	91,016	67.65	63.41
Virginia	69,440	70.26	54.11
West Virginia	5,200	78.48	68.65
Total, 1901–1902	1,000,381	72.49	56.97
Total, 1889–1890	813,710	67.15	32.85

1902=1903

STATE	Average daily attendance	Per cent of persons 5 to 18 years enrolled	
	Colored	White	Colored
Alabama	90,000	69.04	42.59
Arkansas	54,147	74.92	68.42
Delaware	3,800	74.67	67.24
District of Columbia	12,120	77.00	76.27
Florida	29,881	69.99	56.51
Georgia	120,732	74.42	53.51
Kentucky	41,116	72.73	71.10
Louisiana	53,605	55.66	31.30
Maryland	22,712	64.62	67.32
Mississippi	118,096	86.89	63.46
Missouri	20,191	74.31	67.28
North Carolina	83,405	73.45	65.26
South Carolina	111,681	71.29	52.31
Tennessee	68,331	77.38	61.29
Texas	88,718	64.44	60.54
Virginia	67,694	68.70	51.63
West Virginia	5,924	76.59	75.29
Total, 1902–1903	991,453	71.63	55.55
Total, 1889–1890	813,710	66.28	51.65

COMMON SCHOOL STATISTICS, CLASSIFIED BY RACE

1903-1904

STATE	Average daily attendance	Per cent of persons 5 to 18 years enrolled	
	Colored	White	Colored
Alabama	90,000	69.24	42.71
Arkansas	58,177	73.80	69.48
Delaware	3,800	76.70	69.09
District of Columbia	12,565	74.28	76.16
Florida	32,338	74.28	59.64
Georgia	120,032	77.42	53.51
Kentucky	41,116	72.73	71.10
Louisiana	53,605	55.66	31.30
Maryland	14,420	65.44	41.30
Mississippi	118,096	86.89	63.45
Missouri	20,173	76.07	69.49
North Carolina	1 2,151	77.41	66.90
South Carolina	113,929	70.92	52.35
Tennessee	69,621	77.80	62.12
Texas	92,157	65.42	58.91
Virginia	67,694	68.70	51.03
West Virginia	5,686	76.56	69.57
Total, 1903-1904	1,015,560	72.38	55.14
Total, 1899-1900	957,160	68.28	51.46
Total, 1889-1890	813,710	66.28	51.65

1904-1905

STATE	Average daily attendance	Per cent of persons 5 to 18 years enrolled	
	Colored	White	Colored
Alabama	75,000	69.95	49.07
Arkansas	53,329	72.67	66.07
Delaware	3,800	76.70	69.09
District of Columbia	13,005	77.85	77.85
Florida	32,338	74.28	59.64
Georgia	119,705	71.94	51.72
Kentucky	41,116	72.73	71.10
Louisiana	46,201	56.25	28.22
Maryland	21,886	65.57	60.47
Mississippi	118,096	86.89	63.45
Missouri	20,432	74.86	67.53
North Carolina	83,390	73.72	63.41
South Carolina	107,800	73.03	53.21
Tennessee	71,151	77.95	61.66
Texas	94,605	67.05	59.29
Virginia	62,621	66.01	46.54
West Virginia	6,251	76.02	74.03
Total, 1904-1905	970,726	71.89	55.01
Total, 1899-1900	981,026	72.32	57.67
Total, 1889-1890	813,710	66.28	51.65

COMMON SCHOOL STATISTICS, CLASSIFIED BY RACE

1905-1906

STATE	Average daily attendance	Per cent of persons 5 to 18 years enrolled	
	Colored	White	Colored
Alabama	75,000	69.95	49.07
Arkansas	54,564	73.56	67.50
Delaware	3,800	76.70	69.09
District of Columbia	13,075	77.85	77.85
Florida	34,446	74.47	58.59
Georgia	119,705	71.94	51.72
Kentucky	41,116	72.73	71.10
Louisiana	46,201	56.25	28.22
Maryland	24,067	65.08	60.02
Mississippi	118,096	86.89	63.45
Missouri	22,580	76.61	68.40
North Carolina	83,390	73.72	63.41
South Carolina	114,490	74.95	55.71
Tennessee	72,791	77.12	60.70
Texas	94,605	67.05	59.29
Virginia	62,621	66.01	46.54
West Virginia	6,251	76.02	74.03
Total, 1905-1906	986,728	72.18	55.27
Total, 1899-1900	981,026	72.32	57.67
Total, 1889-1890	813,710	66.28	51.65

1906-1907

STATE	Average daily attendance	Per cent of persons 5 to 18 years enrolled	
	Colored	White	Colored
Alabama	86,093	70.24	49.42
Arkansas	55,083	71.73	65.22
Delaware	3,830	76.70	69.09
District of Columbia	14,031	77.08	78.82
Florida	36,032	71.35	58.16
Georgia	119,150	71.91	50.34
Kentucky	41,116	72.73	71.10
Louisiana	53,692	56.54	31.01
Maryland	23,199	66.26	58.98
Mississippi	150,271	81.08	76.57
Missouri	22,190	74.28	67.23
North Carolina	88,795	73.45	62.62
South Carolina	118,885	72.78	54.56
Tennessee	70,421	74.51	57.94
Texas	94,186	66.43	59.90
Virginia	62,333	66.23	46.28
West Virginia	6,491	74.95	75.46
Total, 1906-1907	1,045,698	71.42	55.49
Total, 1899-1900	981,026	72.32	57.67
Total, 1889-1890	813,710	66.28	51.65

COMMON SCHOOL STATISTICS, CLASSIFIED BY RACE

1907=1908

STATE	Average daily attendance	Per cent of persons 5 to 18 years enrolled	
	Colored	White	Colored
Alabama	86,093	69.34	39.91
Arkansas	59, 87	76.39	68.76
Delaware	4,069	76.90	69.02
District of Columbia	14, 06	77.42	77.72
Florida	37,814	72.22	57.31
Georgia	119,5(4	7 .46	49.64
Kentucky	36,659	59.79	61.96
Louisiana	59,125	64.72	32.83
Maryland	22,897	66.95	57.69
Mississippi	132,732	86.81	72.10
Missouri	21,931	69.43	60.30
North Carolina	88,117	75.40	61.82
South Carolina	124,135	72.89	54.92
Tennessee	66,798	76.(6	56.72
Texas	9 ,277	67.91	53.82
Virginia	65,758	66.96	46.45
West Virginia	6,745	74.19	75.33
Total, 1907-1908	1,035,747	70.34	54.36
Total, 1899-1900	981,(26	72.32	57.67
Total, 1889-1890	813,710	66.28	51.65

1908=1909

STATE	Average daily attendance	Per cent of persons 5 to 18 years enrolled	
	Colored	White	Co'ored
Alabama	9),930	76.27	44.46
Arkansas	59,597	73.04	67.95
Delaware	4,(69	76.90	69.(2
District of Columbia	14,098	77.75	77.18
Florida	39,876	85.93	68.16
Georgia	145,856	77.47	56.07
Kentucky	33,521	74.94	64.52
Louisiana	57,386	61.(7	32.(1
Maryland	24,522	68.78	59.25
Mississippi	145,153	91.78	66.11
Missouri	24,205	73.61	64.54
North Carolina	95,09)	82.48	68.96
South Carolina	123,481	76.14	57.30
Tennessee	83,536	78.28	59.83
Texas	95,(35	68.00	55.97
Virginia	72,667	69.51	47.59
West Virginia	7,789	85.25	9).57
Total, 19(8-1909	1,116,811	74.76	56.34
Total, 1899-19)0	981,026	72.32	57.67
Total, 1889-1890	813,710	66.28	51.65

The official reports give the following figures:

SCHOLASTIC YEAR	Negroes 5 to 18 years of age	Enrolled	Per cent of persons 5 to 18 years enrolled	Daily attendance	Per cent of enrollment	Number of Teachers
1889–90	2,510,847	1,296,959	51.65	813,710	62.74	24,072
1899–1900	2,705,142	1,560,070	57.65	981,026	62.88	27,313
1908–09	3,038,710	1,712,137	56.34	1,116,811	65.22	30,334

We find that in 1908-9 only 36.75 per cent of the Negro school population was actually in school and the proportion of teachers to children enrolled is less than it was twenty years ago.

From these official figures it seems clear:

1. That the official statistics especially in the earlier years were poorly kept and hence are of very questionable reliability. This is proven by the internal evidence of the figures.

2. That there has been in recent years no marked increase in the average daily attendance of Negro children in the public schools.

3. That the percentage of Negro children of school age (5 to 18 years) enrolled in the public schools has decreased in the last twenty years.

4. That without doubt the proportion of Negro school children in average daily attendance in the public schools has greatly decreased in the last decade and in the last two decades.

Section 5. General Conditions

The first fact that the student must notice concerning the public school system of the South is that it is a dual system and so necessitates a double set of schools. Such an arrangement is costly and involves various peculiar difficulties. If the black and white population were evenly distributed or perfectly segregated, the double system school could bring no particular race discrimination or waste. This, however, very seldom occurs, and usually if there are in districts few white people or few Negroes, they are very apt under this double system to be left entirely without schools. There are districts in Missouri, Kentucky, Maryland and in the hill counties of the gulf states where the segregated Negro population is left practically without schools. The poor whites in the black belt and in the mountains are sometimes similarly neglected.

First, with respect to school funds: The total school fund in the South is small as compared with that of the North and the following table for 1908-9 will illustrate this:

GEOGRAPHIC DIVISION	Income of permanent school funds and rent of school lands	From state tax or appropriations	From local tax or appropriation	From other sources, state and local	Total revenue (including balances on hand and proceeds of bond sales)
United States	$ 13,446,826	$63,547,354	$ 288,642,500	$38,010,609	$ 403,647,289
North Atlantic Division .	1,082,421	18,551,670	114,456,578	16,357,897	150,448,566
South Atlantic Division .	285,'11	9,390,959	14,191,928	2,216,761	26,084,659
South Central Division . .	3,328,278	12.167,929	16,195,256	2,040,496	33,731,959
North Central Division . .	7,04'',129	15,150,358	116,450,435	14,688,214	153,329,136
Western Division	1,710,987	8,286,438	27,348,303	2,707,241	40,052,969

But even this does not tell the full story because there is open and acknowledged discrimination in the distribution of the school funds between white and Negro schools.

If we consider the total cost of Negro schools, we mày select these typical figures:

Cost of schools		Persons of school age (5-18), 1908-9
South Carolina, 1909—		
White.	$1,590,732.51	201,868
Negro	308,153.16	316,007
Alabama, 1909—		
White	$2,143,662.15	364,266
Negro	287,045.43	311,552
North Carolina, 1908—		
White	$1,851,376.57	437,376
Negro.	366,734.28	232,624

If the Negro schools of South Carolina had been equal to the white schools they would have cost $2,985,000 instead of $300,000. If the Negro schools of Alabama had been equal to the white schools they would have cost $1,833,000 instead of

$287,000. In North Carolina, if the Negro schools had been equal to the white schools they would have cost $984,000 instead of $367,000. There seems to be similar discrimination in Virginia, Georgia, Florida, Mississippi, Louisiana and Arkansas. The discrimination is very nearly as large in Maryland, Kentucky and Tennessee. It is somewhat less in Texas and Missouri.

The same conditions may be gotten at by considering the per capita cost of educating children. In South Carolina in 1899 the yearly cost per capita for educating white children was $4.98 and for colored children, $1.42. In 1909 South Carolina spent $10.34 on each white child and $1.70 on each Negro child. Further evidence of similar discrimination is found if we take the state county by county. In Charleston, for instance, the white children received $35.70 per head and the Negro children $2.55 a head. In Richland county the whites received $25.15 per head, while the Negroes got $3.21. There were six counties where the per capita expenditure for Negroes was less than one dollar a head.

In 126 counties of Georgia the average monthly cost of tuition for white children was $1.16; for colored children, $0.66; in 19 counties, white, $2.05; colored, $0.66; in the other 56 counties of the state, white, $1.70; Negroes, $0.78.

In Mississippi the per capita yearly expenditure for educating each white child was in 1909 $13.37; for each Negro child, $4.21.

In the number and cost of schools there are great differences between the races:

In South Carolina for 180,882 white children there were 2,712 schools; for 283,865 colored children there were 2,354 schools. The white schools ran 25 weeks; the colored schools, 15 weeks. White school houses built during the year 1909 cost $255,180.85; the colored school houses built in that year cost $7,061.80. For building and repairing the white schools and buying fuel, $1,590,752.51; colored schools, $308,153.16.

In North Carolina the white school property was worth $4,282,255; Negro school property was worth $635,057. The white rural schools each served a district of 9 square miles; the colored rural schools each served a district of 22 square miles.

Georgia has almost equal numbers of white and colored school children. In 1909 the whites had 4,560 schools and the Negroes 2,803. In those schools there were 7,384 white teachers and 3,512 colored teachers. The various boards of education had furnished 3,116 school houses for the white schools and 400 for the colored schools.

In Alabama, 1909, 381,460 white children had 4,360 schools; 305,938 colored children had 1,880 schools. Of these schools 1,190 of the white schools were graded and 257 of the colored schools were graded. The white schools had 6,147 teachers; the colored schools had 2,126 teachers. The average length of white schools was 128 days; of colored schools 98 days. Three thousand nine hundred and ninety-five (3,995) of the white schools continued five months or more; 1,065 of the colored schools continued five months or more. The public school houses of the whites were worth $4,217,045; of the Negroes, $374,835. The furniture of the white schools was estimated to be worth $459,142; that of the colored schools $74,095.

In Mississippi, 1909, there were reported 301,548 white children of school age and 410,089 colored children of school age. The white children had 4,238 schools and the colored children had 2,987 schools. During the year, 202 white school houses were built and 75 Negro school houses. One hundred and nine thousand, eight hundred and eighty-five (109,885) white children attended school on an average and 132,672 colored children. There were 5,089 white teachers employed and 3,236 Negro teachers.

The wages offered white and colored teachers differed greatly:

In South Carolina, the average salary of white men was $479.79, white women, $249.13. The total salary paid white men was $419,390.36; the total salary paid white women, $799,679.54. The average annual salary paid colored men was

$118.17; colored women, $91.45. The total salary paid colored men was $100,948.26; the total salary paid colored women, $172,566.69.

In North Carolina, 1908, the average annual amount paid each white teacher was $176.73; each colored teacher, $113.12.

The average salary of teachers in 126 counties of Georgia: first grade, white, $45.47; Negroes, $26.37; second grade, white, $35.39; colored, $21.53; third grade, white, $28.31; colored, $17.33.

In Alabama the average monthly salaries of teachers were: white men, $60.63; colored men, $27.18; white women, $45.65; colored women, $24.

In Mississippi the average monthly salary for white teachers was $41.49; colored teachers, $20.58.

To this general discrimination there are local exceptions, especially like Washington, D. C., and to a less extent Baltimore, Md., St. Louis, Mo., and the states of West Virginia and Texas. In the schools of the District of Columbia there is no discrimination in the pay of teachers or in the requirements for teachers or in the course of study laid down. In the expenditures for the white and colored schools the colored schools have often gotten poorer buildings but even here the discrimination is not glaring. The colored people of the District have representatives on the board of education and one assistant superintendent is a colored man, who has charge of the colored schools under the superintendent.

In West Virginia, which is rather a western than a southern state, the colored schools have been on the whole well treated, the only difference arising in parts where there are comparatively few colored children.

Cities like Baltimore and St. Louis discriminated considerably in the past against colored schools but have lately made amends. In St. Louis, for instance, a new colored high school costing $100,000 has recently been erected but only after a long fight made by the colored people. Baltimore is now asking for a new colored high school.

Texas, which has a large school fund from the vast endowment of public land, is treating the colored schools with considerable fairness. There is no discrimination in the per capita amount of money appropriated to the white and colored children but there is considerable discrimination in the amount paid the teachers and in matter of school houses and supplies.

Section 6. Delaware

The early attempts at the education of the colored youth of Delaware were made by the Negroes themselves and it was not until 1875 that schools for Negroes had any recognition by the state. By personal taxes, tuition fees and voluntary contributions these people were able to keep up the work of education until the general assembly of the state assumed the responsibility in 1881. Since that date the work of educating Negroes has been a matter of public concern.

The following table of school statistics for the state of Delaware is compiled from the annual reports of the United States Bureau of Education:

DELAWARE

YEAR	School population, colored	Enrollment	Per cent	Daily attendance	Per cent of enrollment attending
1899–1900	8,900	4,858	54.58	2,947	60.66
1900–1901	8,888	6,141	69.09	3,800	61.88
1901–1902	8,888	6,141	69.09	3,800	61.88
1902–1903	9,133	6,141	67.24	3,800	61.88
1903–1904	8,888	6,141	69.09	3,800	61.88
1904–1905	8,888	6,141	69.09	3,800	61.88
1905–1906	8,888	6,141	69.09	3,800	61.88
1906–1907	8,888	6,141	69.09	3,800	61.88
1907–1908	9,510	6,564	69.02	4,069	61.99
1908–1909	9,642	6,564	69.02	4,069	61.99

In 1900, thirty-three (33.84) per cent of the colored children of Delaware were in regular attendance at the public schools whose average length was 141 days in the year. In 1909 the attendance had advanced to forty-two (42.2) per cent. It is reported that there is a decided improvement in the school facilities over what they were ten years ago, especially in Wilmington. Outside of Wilmington Negro public school education is reported to be considerably behind.

The following summary of school statistics is compiled from the report of the state board of education of Delaware for the year 1910:

New Castle County:

```
Number of Negro students . . . . . . . . . . . . .        1,272
Number of Negro teachers . . . . . . . . . . . .             29
Average salary of Negro teachers . . . . . . . . . $   31.20
Average number of days . . . . . . . . . . . . . .      142.31
Average attendance of students . . . . . . . . . .      70.7%
```

Kent County:

```
Number of Negro students . . . . . . . . . . . .         1,864
Number of Negro teachers . . . . . . . . . . . .            38
Average salary of Negro teachers . . . . . . . . . $   31.36
Average number of days . . . . . . . . . . . . . .      141.1
Average attendance of students . . . . . . . . . .     62.17%
```

Sussex County:

```
Number of Negro teachers . . . . . . . . . . . .            39
Number of Negro students . . . . . . . . . . . .         1,920
Average salary of Negro teachers . . . . . . . . . $   33.69
Average number of days . . . . . . . . . . . . . .      145.45
Average attendance of students . . . . . . . . . .     52.07%
```

According to the census reports of the last four decades Negro illiteracy for Delaware has been as follows:

PER CENT OF ILLITERACY

	1870	1880	1890	1900
Delaware	71.3	57.5	49.5	38.1

Section 7. Maryland

The report of the United States Commissioner of Education for the year 1870 says: Nothing was done during this year by the state [Maryland] for the education of colored children, but the colored people, aided by benevolent associations, particularly the "Baltimore Association," established schools of their own.   The schools under the Baltimore Association made remarkable progress, having always trained teachers, who were subject to rigid examination before receiving their appointment.

The revised law of 1870 required "that all the taxes paid for school purposes by the colored people of any county shall be used for maintaining schools for colored children."

The revised law of 1872 directed that schools for Negroes be established in each county. It is said, however, that many of these schools, even where established, were not well provided for, so that the law was imperfectly carried out.

The state board of education is composed of six members appointed by the governor. The schools in each county are controlled by a board of county commissioners. The county boards in turn appoint district school trustees.

The school laws of Maryland contain the following clauses:

Section 42.—In every school house district in each county, established as hereinbefore provided, there shall be kept for ten months in each year, if possible, one or more schools, according to population, which shall be free to all white youths over 6 and under 21 years of age. 1872, Ch. 377.

Section 124.—It shall be the duty of the board of county school commissioners to establish one or more public schools in each election district for all colored youths, between 6 and 20 years of age, to which admission shall be free, and which shall be kept open as long as the board of county school commissioners shall determine; provided, the colored population of such district shall warrant said board in establishing said schools. 1904, Ch. 584.

The following table of school statistics for the state of Maryland is compiled from the annual reports of the United States Bureau of Education:

MARYLAND

YEAR	School population, colored	Enrollment	Per cent enrolled	Daily attendance	Per cent of enrollment attending
1899–1900	77,290	46,852	60.61	22,989	49.07
19 0–1901	70,120	48,257	68.82	22,712	47.06
1901–1902	70,120	48,257	68.82	22,712	47.06
1902–19 3	71,686	48,257	67.32	22,712	47.06
1903–1904	72,508	29,940	41.30	14,420	48.16
19 4–1905	73,355	44,355	60.47	21,886	49.34
19 5–19 6	74,161	44,514	60.02	24,067	54.50
1906–1907	75,420.	44,475	58.98	23,199	52.16
1907–1908	75,925	43,802	57.69	22,897	52.27
1908–1909	74,818	44,330	59.25	24,522	55.32

In 1900, twenty-nine (29.74) per cent of the Negro children of Maryland were in regular attendance at the public schools whose average length was less than 188 days. In 1909 the attendance had advanced to thirty-three (33.77) per cent. The following summary of the school statistics is compiled from the report of the Department of Public Education, state of Maryland, for the year 1910:

MARYLAND
1909-1910

Expenditures

Whites . . . .
Negroes. . . . .

Total $4,060,341.29

Number of Schools

Whites. 1,952
Negroes 522

Total 2,474

Number of Teachers

Whites. 4,691
Negroes 823

Total 5,514

Average Salary, all Teachers

White and Colored . $ 51.93

Length of Term

	Counties	City of Baltimore
Whites.	. 9.4 Mos.	10 Mos.
Negroes	. 6.9 Mos.	10 Mos.

Enrollment

Whites. 154,263
Negroes 35,651

Total 189,914

Per Cent of Attendance

Whites. 89
Negroes 84

The following statistics for the Negro schools of Baltimore are compiled from the Eighty-second Annual Report of the Board of School Commissioners of Baltimore:

Negro Schools of Baltimore, Md., 1910

Total number of schools 15

Teachers

High school 24
Training school 2
Ward schools 175

Total 201

Average Enrollment

High school 508
Training school 88
Ward schools 8,078

Total 8,674

Average Attendance

High school 489
Training school 86
Ward schools 6,696

Total 7,271

Per Cent of Attendance

High school 96
Training school 98
Ward schools 82
All schools 84

Night School

Number of teachers 32
Average enrollment 778
Average attendance 545
Per cent of attendance 70

Total cost Negro high schools . . . $ 37,105.14
Per capita cost of Negro high and
  training school 56.20

According to the census reports of the last four decades Negro illiteracy for Maryland has been as follows:

PER CENT OF ILLITERACY

	1870	1880	1890	1900
Maryland	69.5	59.6	50.1	35.1

Section 8.   District of Columbia

Public education in the District of Columbia is in the hands of a board of education, which appoints one superintendent of all schools with two assistants, one of whom is in charge of the Negro schools.   Schools for Negro children in the District of Columbia were instituted under authority of an act of Congress of 21 May, 1862, and amended in July of the same year; also acts of 25 July, 1864, and 23 July, 1866, which provided for a board of trustees for the colored schools and directed that the pro rata of school monies should be apportioned to the Negro schools according to population.   "It was not until the year 1867 that these trustees obtained sufficient funds to undertake the establishment of any considerable number of schools.   Previously to that time, for about three years, from 60 to 80 colored schools had been maintained at a large expense by various benevolent associations in the northern states."[1]

The following table of school statistics for the District of Columbia is compiled from the annual reports of the United States Bureau of Education:

DISTRICT OF COLUMBIA

YEAR	School population, colored	Enrollment	Per cent enrolled	Daily attendance	Per cent of enrollment attending
1899–1900 . . .	25,110	15,258	60.76	11,611	76.09
1900–1901 . . .	20,041	15,580	77.74	11,883	76.27
1901–1902 . . .	20,428	15,914	77.90	12,206	76.70
1902–1903 . . .	20,660	15,758	76.27	12,120	76.91
1903–1904 . . .	21,030	16,017	76.16	12,565	78.45
1904–1905 . . .	21,370	16,630	77.85	13,005	78.20
19 5–1906 . . .	21,370	16,630	77.85	13,005	78.20
1906–1907 . . .	22,054	16,791	76.13	13,039	77.65
1907–1908 . . .	22,362	17,379	77.72	14,006	80.59
1908–1909 . . .	22,935	17,703	77.18	14,098	79.63

In 1900 forty-three (42.84) per cent of the colored children of the District of Columbia were in regular attendance at the public schools.   In 1909 this attendance had advanced to sixty-one (61.46) per cent.   The following summary of school statistics is compiled from the report of the Board of Education of the District of Columbia for 1907-8:

---

[1] Report of United States Commissioner of Education, 1870, p. 313.

Negro Enrollment		Night School Enrollment	
Male	7,712	Male	770
Female	9,667	Female	1,048
Total	17,379	Total	1,818
Average attendance	14,006		
Teachers		Night School Teachers	
Male	108	Male	21
Female	415	Female	28
Total	523	Total	49

Negro School Buildings

Owned	47
Rented	19
Total	66

The Conference has also been able to gather the following statistics for the District of Columbia:

APPROPRIATIONS FOR PUBLIC SCHOOL BUILDINGS AND GROUNDS—
DISTRICT OF COLUMBIA

FISCAL YEAR	White	Colored	Colored per cent
1901	$ 221,800	$ 156,000	41
1902	243,000	155,000	39
1903	173,000	61,944	26
1904	180,300	. . . .	0
1905	170,000	9,713	5
1906	150,000	40,800	21
1907	331,158	55,200	14
1908	410,000	125,000	23
1909	469,000	122,000	21
1910	772,000	35,000	4
Totals	$3,120,258	$ 760,657	20

WHOLE NUMBER OF PUPILS ENROLLED IN THE PUBLIC SCHOOLS OF THE
DISTRICT OF COLUMBIA DURING THE SCHOOL YEAR
ENDING JUNE 30, 1909

DAY SCHOOLS	White	Colored	Total	Per cent colored
Normal schools	180	119	299	40
High schools	3,063	718	3,781	19
Manual training	884	660	1,544	43
Grammar and primary	30,869	15,120	45,989	33
Kindergartens	1,720	985	2,705	36
Ungraded schools	173	101	274	37
Totals	36,889	17,703	54,592	32
Night schools	1,896	1,896	3,792	50
Aggregate	38,785	19,599	58,384	34

According to the census reports of the last four decades Negro illiteracy for the District of Columbia has been as follows:

PER CENT OF ILLITERACY

	1870	1880	1890	1900
District of Columbia	70.5	48.4	35.0	24.3

Section 9. Virginia

The public schools of Virginia are under the control of the following: a state board of education, a superintendent of public instruction, division superintendents of schools and county and district school boards. The state board of education consists of the following: the governor, the attorney-general, the superintendent of public instruction and three experienced educators. These are chosen quadrennially.

The division superintendent, together with the school trustees of each county, including those in separate town districts, constitute a corporate, authoritative body, subject to higher authority.

The public schools of the state of Virginia are supported by permanent fund, taxes, gifts and bequests of the state.

The state has a compulsory school law.

The following table of school statistics for the state of Virginia is compiled from the annual reports of the United States Bureau of Education:

VIRGINIA

YEAR	School population, colored	Enrollment	Per cent enrolled	Daily attendance	Per cent of enrollment attending
1899–1900 . . .	260,320	117,129	44.99	61,754	52.72
1900–1901 . . .	225,600	117,129	51.92	61,754	52.72
1901–1902 . . .	227,940	123,339	54.11	69,440	56.30
1902–1903 . . .	232,144	118,463	51.03	67,694	57.14
1903–1904 . . .	232,144	118,463	51.03	67,694	57.14
1904–1905 . . .	236,503	110,059	46.54	62,621	56.89
1905–1906 . . .	236,503	110,059	46.54	62,621	56.89
1906–1907 . . .	241,272	111,677	46.28	62,333	55.81
1907–1908 . . .	243,472	113,102	46.45	65,758	58.14
1908–1909 . . .	246,797	117,471	47.59	72,667	61.86

ALBEMARLE COUNTY:

Here the facilities are much improved. The colored people have been running an industrial school as well as supplementing the school term. In general the condition is poor but better than it has been.

ELIZABETH CITY COUNTY:

There are 17 colored schools, which have six months term in some districts and seven in others. The white schools have eight and nine months. The colored schools have only six grades while the whites have a full high school course, ten grades, to which all white children have access. There are 17 colored teachers and 49 white, the colored receiving $17 and the whites $45 per month.

Sixty-seven thousand seven hundred and thirty dollars are spent annually, $4,348.90 going to the colored schools and $63,381.09 to the white. One thousand three hundred and eighty-five colored and 1,775 white children attend school regularly. The school facilities for the colored are almost as poor as they possibly could be, but the reverse is true of the white. All the colored children attend the county school while all the whites except 470 attend schools in the towns, brot in by conveyances furnished by the town. For years the Negroes have supplemented the school funds in several of the schools. There is no private school now tho for eight or ten years there was a large denominational school. In general the condition of Negro public school education is at the lowest possible ebb. No special part of the special school tax goes to the colored schools.

HENRICO COUNTY:

Nothing is wanted for the whites but the school facilitiés for the colored children are in need of attention. In general the Negro public school education is sadly deficient.

PRINCE GEORGE COUNTY:

The colored schools have a term of three months and the whites a term of five months; 1,608 Negro children and 1,700 whites attended school regularly; 25 Negro teachers and 36 white for three Negro schools and five white; seven grades in each. Appropriation for whites annually $20,000, for the colored $10,000. Yet there is a marked improvement over ten years ago. Not much of the $1.00 per capita tax goes to the colored schools. In general Negro public school education here is above the average, and the teachers are well fitted for the work.

In 1900 twenty-five per cent of the Negro children of Virginia were in regular attendance upon the public schools whose annual length was less than 119 days. In 1909 the attendance had advanced to twenty-nine (29.44) per cent but the term length had increased only to 122 days.

The following summary of statistics is compiled from the biennial report of the superintendent of public instruction of the commonwealth of Virginia for 1907-08 and 1908-09:

Expenditures

	1906-7	1907-8	1908-9
Whites			
Negroes			
Total	$3,308,086.14	$3,648,615.00	$4,431,370.45

Number of Schools

	1906-7	1907-8	1908-9
Whites	7,098	7,263	7,570
Negroes	2,284	2,285	2,340
Total	9,382	9,548	9,940

Number of Teachers

	1906-7	1907-8	1908-9
Whites	7,248	7,410	7,754
Negroes	2,220	2,242	2,339
Total	9,468	9,652	10,093

Length of Term in Days

	1906-7	1907-8	1908-9
Whites	133.2	132.5	133.3
Negroes	124.0	121.0	122.6

Enrollment

	1906-7	1907-8	1908-9
Whites	257,654	263,598	276,836
Negroes	111,677	113,147	177,577
Total	369,331	376,745	394,413

Average Attendance

	1906-7	1907-8	1908-9
Whites	158,891	168,555	185,057
Negroes	63,676	65,758	72,667
Total	222,567	234,313	257,724

Average Salary of Teachers

	1906-7	1907-8	1908-9
Whites . . . . $	41.75	$ 43.45	$ 47.18
Negroes	27.78	29.37	28.82

According to the census reports of the last four decades Negro illiteracy for Virginia has been as follows:

PER CENT OF ILLITERACY

	1870	1880	1890	1900
Virginia	89.9	73.2	57.2	44.6

Section 10. West Virginia

The schools of West Virginia are controlled by a state board of education, composed of the state superintendent and five commissioners chosen one each from the five districts of the state. The state legislature provides for county superintendents and such other officers as are necessary to carry out the aims and purposes of free education.

It is the duty of the board of education to establish one free school and more if necessary in any district for colored children where there are ten or more children and if possible where there are fewer children. School monies are divided between schools for white and colored children according to numbers of white and colored children enumerated.

The state has a well administered compulsory school law.

The following table of school statistics for the state of West Virginia is compiled from the annual reports of the United States Bureau of Education:

WEST VIRGINIA

YEAR	School population, colored	Enrollment	Per cent enrolled	Daily attendance	Per cent of enrollment attending
1899–1900 . . .	12,760	8,110	63.55	5,480	67.57
1900–1901 . . .	11,240	8,110	72.15	5,480	67.57
1901–1902 . . .	11,487	7,886	68.65	5,200	65.94
1902–1903 . . .	11,951	8,998	75.29	5,924	65.84
1903–1904 . . .	12,155	8,456	69.57	5,686	67.24
1904–1905 . . .	12,385	9,168	74.03	6,251	68.18
1905–1906 . . .	12,385	9,168	74.03	6,251	68.18
1906–1907 . . .	12,743	9,605	75.46	6,491	67.58
1907–1908 . . .	13,057	9,836	75.33	6,745	68.57
1908–1909 . . .	12,288	11,130	90.57	7,789	69.98

FAYETTE COUNTY:

There are 67 colored and 306 white schools in this county. The average term for both is six months. The students are taken as far as the eighth grade. There are 67 colored teachers and 306 white teachers. Almost all of the teachers, both white and colored, are educated in the state normal schools of West Virginia. All teachers, colored and white, receive salaries from $30 to $60 according to the grade of the certificate. A No. 3 certificate, $30; No. 2, $45; No. 1, $60. We have two funds in the county, the building fund and a teachers' fund. For the year 1910 there were $90,850.29 spent. The teachers' salaries, including white and colored, for the year 1910 amounted to $129,447.52.

There are 1,870 colored and 9,740 white children in regular attendance for the year 1910.

Much improvement has been made in the white schools and some in the colored, but not nearly so much as in the white.

KANAWHA COUNTY:

Three hundred and twenty-two white and 23 colored schools. The whites have a term of six months. Both the white and colored schools have eight grades.

The colored teachers receive from $40 to $60 in the rural districts and $32 to $75 in the city. The whites receive from $40 to $150.

Last year $123,221 was appropriated for teachers' fund; $16,979 for colored teachers and $66,744 for building fund for the entire county. The facilities have improved a great deal as to buildings, salaries, length of term, quality of teachers and equipments. Yet Negro public school education here is not on a par with that of the whites.

In general the condition of Negro public school education in West Virginia is very good, equal to or better than that of any state in the union.

In 1900 forty-nine (48.81) per cent of the Negro children of West Virginia were in regular attendance upon the public schools whose average annual length was 111 days. In 1909 the attendance had advanced to sixty-three (63.38) per cent. In 1910 the average annual length was 6.7 months.

The following summary of statistics is compiled from the biennial report of the state superintendent of free schools of West Virginia for the two years ending June 30, 1910:

Expenditures	1909	1910
Whites		
Negroes		
Total	$4,341,972.00	$4,542,611.67
Number of Schools		
Whites	6,726	7,010
Negroes	261	303
Total	6,987	7,313
Number Teachers		
Whites	8,186	8,417
Negroes	313	365
Total	8,499	8,782
Average Annual Salary of Teachers		
Whites	$ 305.17	$ 309.75
Negroes	359.68	331.90
Term Length		
All schools	6.78 months	6.70 months

Enrollment

Whites	264,823	265,049
Negroes	11,035	11,309
Total	275,858	276,358

Average Attendance

Whites	185,564	181,877
Negroes	7,789	7,596

According to the census reports of the last four decades Negro illiteracy for West Virginia has been as follows:

PER CENT OF ILLITERACY

	1870	1880	1890	1900
West Virginia	74.4	55.0	44.5	32.3

Section 11. North Carolina

The schools of North Carolina are under the control of a state board, consisting of the governor, the lieutenant governor, the secretary of state, the treasurer, the auditor, the attorney general and the superintendent of public instruction, hence fully elected by the people. County boards and county superintendents manage affairs in the individual counties.

The compulsory school law is left to the discretion of the county boards who act in accordance with the votes of the people.

The following table of school statistics for the state of North Carolina is compiled from the annual reports of the United States Bureau of Education:

NORTH CAROLINA

YEAR	School population, colored	Enrollment	Per cent enrolled	Daily attendance	Per cent of enrollment attending
1899–1900	250,970	130,005	51.80	64,505	49.61
1900–1901	221,120	141,180	63.85	80,747	57.19
1901–19 2	225,900	149,798	66.31	83,4 5	55.68
1902–1903	228,526	149,798	65.26	83,405	55.68
1903–1904	231,507	154,884	66.90	102,151	65.95
1904–1905	234,693	148,821	63.41	83,390	56.04
1905–1906	234,693	148,821	63.41	83,390	56.04
19 6–1907	238,373	152,4′0	63.51	87,529	57.43
1907–19 8	244,473	151,141	61.82	88,117	58.30
1908–1909	232,624	160,427	68.96	95,090	59.27

ALAMANCE COUNTY:

Thirty-four colored schools, 90 white. The term of the colored schools ranges from 100 to 170 days and of the white from 150 to 170 days. There are 39 colored and 118 white teachers. The colored teachers receive $20 to $28, and the whites $25 to $35. Total amount spent annually on colored schools, $6,000, and on the white, $27,000. One thousand and nine hundred colored and 4,950 white children attend school regularly. The school facilities for the whites are much improved over what they were ten years ago, but those of the colored are poorer, tho the taxes of the colored are increased from 150 to 300 per cent. There are large and commodious buildings for the white graded schools while the colored are conducted in old dilapidated structures, the only equipments being what has been used by the white schools. The colored schools get from ten to fifteen per cent of the special school tax. The colored people do very little toward supporting schools aside from public taxes.

CALDWELL COUNTY:

Twelve colored and 74 white schools, each having a term of 81 days, seven grades in each. There are 15 colored and 87 white teachers. The amounts appropriated for 1910-11 were: for the colored, $1,180, and for the white, $16,566. In general the condition of Negro education is much better than formerly, but there is room for improvement. The houses are comfortable, teachers fairly good.

CRAVEN COUNTY:

The colored teachers get from $15 to $30 and the whites from $25 to $75. The colored schools receive annually about $3,000 and the whites $10,000. In the country the school facilities are not even as good as they were ten years ago, but 300 per cent better for the whites. In the city they are about twenty-five per cent better. The colored schools receive about twenty per cent of the school tax. The colored people both support schools of their own and supplement the public school terms. The general condition of Negro public school education is very common indeed.

EDGECOMBE COUNTY:

There are 39 rural white and 35 rural colored schools, the terms being 154 and 103 days respectively. There are 64 white and 42 colored teachers. Colored teachers having first grade certificates, 7; second grade, 28; normal training, 16; those having four years' experience, 35; those having college diplomas, 7. The colored teachers receive $129.50 for the whole school term and the whites $328.35.

HALIFAX COUNTY:

Thirty-nine colored and 50 white schools. White school population, 4,107; colored, 7,859. Colored school term, 108 days; white school term, 144 days. First grade teachers, 26; second grade, 30; those having normal training, 43; those having four years' experience, 49; those having college diplomas, 5. The white teachers receive $236.62 for term of 144 days and the colored $134.17 for term of 108 days. The total amount spent annually on colored schools is $8,820.96 and on the white $20,822.54. The average attendance of colored pupils is 2,402 and that of the whites 1,779. The enrollment of colored is 4,438 and of the white 2,697.

The school facilities, buildings and equipments are very much better than they were ten years ago. In some places the colored people supplement the schools. In general the condition is very good considering the facilities, but they ought to have closer and more helpful supervision. The colored people themselves are not using all of their opportunities. They simply pay their school tax and seem to think they have done enough and show no interest whatever in repairs, etc.

GRAHAM COUNTY:

The intensity of the fight against Negro education seems to have been broken by the division of the dominant political party on county and state financial conditions. Yet the colored people cannot take full advantage of these conditions since they are affected with so many moral cowards posing as leaders. The average text book is poor, but the so-called school histories are "positive insults" to the colored teachers and pupils.

GUILFORD COUNTY:

Here the colored teachers are paid about $25 a month and the whites $40.

HERTFORD COUNTY:

Thirty-three colored, 32 white. The colored teachers receive $25 and the whites $30 per month. The total amount spent on colored schools is $3,076 and on the white $5,146. There are 3,235 colored and 2,165 white children of school age, with 1,311 colored and 754 whites attending school regularly. There is scarcely any improvement in the facilities of the Negro schools, but the white schools are about 100 per cent better than they were ten years ago. There are two separate town school systems for the whites. Special school tax has been levied in two districts, but for the whites only. The colored people give from $1,000 to $3,000 a year to help a normal school and they have one public school about four months in the year. In general the condition is poor with very inefficient teachers and short terms; the best trained young men and women refuse to teach for the salary offered.

MECKLENBURG COUNTY:

The term for the colored school is four months and for the white six. The colored schools have only one grade and the white two. Colored teachers receive $20 and white $40 per month. In some instances the school facilities are slightly better than they were ten years ago, but on the whole they are very poor.

NASH COUNTY:

There are 54 white and 41 colored schools for school populations of 4,522 and 3,096 respectively. The whites have a school term of 105 days and the colored 90 days. There are 84 white and 41 colored teachers. Colored teachers having first grade certificates, 9; second grade certificates, 30; third grade certificates, 2; those having four years' experience, 32; college graduates, 5. The colored teachers receive $121.82 for 90 days and the whites $247.86 for 105 days. The white schools receive annually $27,264.71, while the colored receive only $5,846.66. There is an average attendance of 1,332 colored and 2,544 white children.

The school facilities here are much improved over what they were ten years ago, but they are not yet adequate nor in any way equal to the whites. In some places the colored people pay a special school tax but they derive no benefit from it. In some places they supplement the school terms but only for a few weeks. In general the condition is very good considering the bad facilities most of the schools have. In some cases repairs have been made and the money paid for them was the regular appropriation for the teachers' salaries. Teachers put up with poor school houses because generally improvements mean a short school term.

WAYNE COUNTY:

There are 41 colored and 69 white schools. Except in four cases the length of the term in the colored country schools was four months. These four were given six months. In the town they had from eight to nine months. The county schools of the whites had from four to six months. In the town schools the grades run from the first to the eighth. The elementary white schools have seven grades, and there are four high schools. There are 85 white and 40 colored teachers. The colored teachers receive from $20 to $25 per month and the whites from $25 up. One white teacher gets $100 per month. Twelve thousand six hundred and thirty-five dollars are appropriated annually for the white and $3,845.13 for the colored schools. Two thousand one hundred and eighty white and 1,308 colored children attend school regularly.

There is a decided improvement in the facilities for both white and colored schools. Of the special school tax laid last year, the Goldsboro colored graded schools received for all purposes $3,796.40 and the white, $16,563.30. In general the condition of Negro public school education here is fair.

In 1900 twenty-nine (28.61) per cent of the Negro children of North Carolina were in regular attendance in the public schools.

In 1909 forty-one (40.83) per cent of the Negro children of North Carolina were in regular attendance in the public schools. In 1900 the average school term was 68.3 days a year but in 1910 the term had increased to 93.7 days a year.

The following table of statistics is compiled from the biennial report of the superintendent of public instruction of North Carolina for the scholastic years 1908-09 and 1909-10:

	1908-09	1909-10
Total expenditures	$3,069,260.36	$3,178,950.50
Number of Schools		
Whites	5,362	5,325
Negroes	2,308	2,284
Total	7,670	7,609
Number of Teachers		
Whites	8,129	8,369
Negroes	2,828	2,793
Total	10,957	11,162
Salaries of Teachers		
Whites	$ 34.80	$ 37.02
Negroes	24.70	25.26
Length of Term in Days		
Whites	105.0	104.6
Negroes	91.9	93.7
Total School Population		
Whites	490,710	497,077
Negroes	236,855	238,091
Total	727,565	735,168
Enrollment		
Whites	360,775	360,121
Negroes	160,427	160,283
Total	521,202	520,404
Average Attendance		
Whites	240,879	235,872
Negroes	95,090	95,463
Total	335,969	331,335
Per Cent of Total School Population Enrolled		
Whites	73.3	72.4
Negroes	67.7	67.3

According to the census reports of the last four decades Negro illiteracy for North Carolina has been as follows:

PER CENT OF ILLITERACY

	1870	1880	1890	1900
North Carolina	84.8	77.4	60.1	47.6

Superintendent J. Y. Joyner, in his biennial report of the public schools of North Carolina for 1908-09 and 1909-10 speaks as follows of the education of the Negro:[1]

As the conditions have not changed since my last report, and as I have seen no reason to change my views upon the subject of the education of the Negro, I shall repeat here the views expressed in my preceding biennial report, changing only the figures used in that report so as to conform to the correct figures of this biennial period.

It would be easier and more pleasant for me to close this report without undertaking to discuss this most perplexing problem of the education of the Negro, about which there are so many conflicting and divergent views among my people. This is a part, however, of the educational problem of the state and, in some respects, the most difficult part. It is, therefore, my duty to study it and to give to you and thru you to the general assembly and to the people my honest views about it. He is a coward that basely runs away from a manifest duty.

In considering this question of Negro education it is necessary to lay aside so far as possible, prejudice on the one hand and maudlin sentimentality on the other. There has been too much of both. For an expression of my general views upon this question I beg to refer you to my report for 1900-1902, pages 6 to 12. I have seen no reason to change or materially to modify these general views.

In justice to the Negro and for the information of some of our people who have been misled into thinking that too large a part of the taxes that the white people pay is spent for the education of the Negro, it may be well in the outset to give a brief statement of the facts in regard to the apportionment of the school fund. As is well known, under section 4116 of the School Law, the apportionment of the school fund in each county is practically placed absolutely under the control of the county board of education, the only restriction laid upon the board therein being that the funds shall be apportioned among the schools of each township in such a way as to give equal length of term as nearly as possible, having due regard to the grade of work to be done, the qualifications of the teachers, etc. The Constitution directs that in the distribution of the fund no discrimination shall be made in favor of either race. This report shows that in 1910 the Negroes of city and rural districts received for teachers' salaries and building school houses $373,390.55 for 238,091 children of school age. The whites received for the same purpose for 497,077 children of school age $1,924,704.40. The Negroes, therefore, constitute about thirty-two per cent of the school population and receive in the apportionment for the same purposes less than seventeen per cent of the

[1]Biennial Report of the Superintendent of Public Instruction of North Carolina for 1908-9 and 1909-10, p. 54 et seq.

school money. This report shows that the Negroes paid for schools in taxes on their own property and polls about $163,417.89, or nearly one-half of all that they received for school purposes. Add to this their just share of fines, forfeitures and penalties and their share of the large school tax paid by corporations to which they are entitled under the Constitution by every dictate of reason and justice, and it will be apparent that the part of the taxes actually paid by individual white men for the education of the Negro is so small that the man that would begrudge it or complain about it ought to be ashamed of himself. In the face of these facts, any unprejudiced man must see that we are in no danger of giving the Negroes more than they are entitled to by every dictate of justice, right, wisdom, humanity and Christianity.

. . . . The Negro is here among us thru no fault of his own, and is likely to remain here. There are but two roads open to him. One is elevation thru the right sort of education; the other is deterioration and degradation thru ignorance and miseducation, inevitably leading to expulsion or extermination. We must help him into the first if we can. If we do not our race will pay the heaviest penalty for the failure.

. . . . There is another phase of this problem of Negro education worthy of the serious consideration of our people. It is manifest to me that if the Negroes become convinced that they are to be deprived of their schools and of the opportunities of an education, most of the wisest and most self-respecting Negroes will leave the state, and eventually there will be left here only the indolent, worthless and criminal part of the Negro population. Already there has been considerable emigration of the Negroes from the state. There is no surer way to drive the best of them from the state than by keeping up this continual agitation about withdrawing from them the meager educational opportunities that they now have. Their emigration in large numbers would result in a complication of the labor problem. Some of our southern farms would be compelled to lie untenanted and untilled. The experience of one district in Wilson county illustrates this. The county board of education found it, for various reasons, impossible to purchase a site for a Negro school house. Before the year was out the board received several offers from farmers in the district to donate a site. Upon inquiry by the chairman of the board as to the reason of these generous offers, he was told that when it was learned that no site for the school house could be secured and that the Negroes were to have no school in that district, at least one-third of the best Negro tenants and laborers there moved into other districts where they could have the advantages of a school. This is a practical side of this question that our people would do well to consider. What happened in this district will happen in the entire state if we give the best Negroes reasonable grounds to believe that their public school privileges are to be decreased or withdrawn.

Section 12. South Carolina

The Constitution of 1868 established the state school system, providing for free schools regardless of race or color. For the next few years there was but slow progress in these schools. The year 1873, however, showed "marked progress and improvement."

The following table of school statistics for the state of South Carolina is compiled from the annual reports of the United States Bureau of Education:

SOUTH CAROLINA

YEAR	School population, colored	Enrollment	Per cent enrolled	Daily attendance	Per cent of enrollment attending
1899-1900 . . .	311,900	155,602	49.88	110,947	71.30
1900-1901 . . .	287,540	157,976	54.94	113,566	71.89
1901-1902 . . .	292,000	144,786	49.58	109,699	75.77
1902-1903 . . .	294,962	154,383	52.31	111,681	72.34
1903-1904 . . .	299,129	156,588	52.35	113,929	72.75
1904-1905 . . .	303,125	161,272	53.21	107,800	66.84
1905-1906 . . .	307,121	171,022	55.71	114,490	66.94
1906-1907 . . .	311,111	169,731	54.56	118,885	70.04
1907-1908 . . .	314,931	172,967	54.92	124,135	71.77
1908-1909 . . .	316,007	181,095	57.30	123,481	68.18

CHARLESTON COUNTY:

There 42 teachers in the Negro schools of Charleston city, forty of whom are white and two colored. In the county schools there are 59 colored teachers. The salaries of the two Negro teachers in Charleston are the same as those of the white teachers but the salaries of the Negro teachers in the county schools are always considerably less than those of the whites. For the scholastic year 1909-10 there were 2,426 Negro children enrolled in the schools of the city of Charleston, while 5,073 were enrolled in the county schools.

The school facilities seem adequate in the city. It is reported that all are accommodated who apply in the county, the enrollment reaching as high as 125 to 140 in single schools. This comes from the schools being not widely dispersed in some districts. The school buildings are very good in the city, fair in the county but with decided need of improvement. Appropriate furniture is almost entirely lacking in all but a few instances. This state of affairs may be remedied to some extent by the efforts of the teachers in making demands of the trustees. The Negroes of the county help to support three or four parochial schools.

The greatest need is for colored teachers in the schools. The buildings are good and the instruction equals that given the whites in the grammar schools; but until there are Negro teachers for Negro children the very essential thing in the education of the Negro youth is lacking—inspiration. There is need of a public high school; the only high school in the community is Avery Normal Institute, supported by the American Missionary Association.

NEWBERRY COUNTY:

There are six Negro teachers in the city schools and 66 in the county schools. The average salary paid the male teachers in the county is $121 per year, for female teachers $105 per year. The average salary paid Negro male teachers is a little more than one-fourth that paid white male teachers, while the average salary of the Negro female teachers is not quite one-third that paid white female teachers. According to the report for 1909-10 the Negro enrollment was 5,329 for the county and 475 for the city. Thus the average number of pupils per teacher is 81, a large number in itself not to mention the lack of facilities. It is estimated that at least 500 Negro children are unable to get into schools because of lack of facilities.

It has happened in the city school proper and happens quite often in the different county districts that the Negro patrons have to supplement the fund allotted them to extend or in some cases even to run the school for the whole of the otherwise short school term. It is being done this year in some districts, while in some instances this year the school term has been greatly shortened.

I consider it to be almost impossible for the schools in our community to do very effective work because of a lack of sufficient number of teachers, many of them having 100 or more scholars. They have no equipment for modern school work.

The Negro public schools in my community are doing in a little way much good in shaping the character of the Negro youth. I believe if more financial aid were given them, and to this employ competent teachers who are prepared to teach intelligently, much more good than at present would be forthcoming.

PICKENS COUNTY:

There are 23 colored and 43 white schools here. Last year the term of the city schools for Negroes was from four to five months and of the rural schools from two to two and one-half months. In the city the term of the whites was from six to eight months and in the rural districts from four to six months. The colored schools have an average of six grades and the whites an average of eight. There are 23 colored and 63 white teachers. The colored teachers receive an average salary of $20 and the whites $40. The improvement in the school facilities is decidedly good, for ten years ago there was scarcely a colored school in this county. The colored schools are supposed to get the special tax collected from the colored people. Usually the colored people supplement the school term. There seems to be very little improvement in the condition of Negro public school education here.

RICHLAND COUNTY:

There are 55 colored and 49 white schools with 72 colored and 135 white teachers, the colored receiving from $143 to $196 a year and the whites from $394 to $576 a year. Fifteen thousand five hundred and ninety dollars and twenty-five cents ($15,590.25) are spent on the colored schools annually and $61,746.02 on the white. Five thousand three hundred and ten colored and 4,584 white children attend school regularly. In a few instances the colored people supplement the school term. In general the Negro public school education is poor.

UNION COUNTY:

The colored schools average five grades and the white seven. The colored teachers receive an average of $25 and the whites an average of $60. The general condition of Negro public school education is very poor.

Many of the colored teachers of South Carolina are not at all prepared to do the most elementary work. Many of the facilities are not so good as they were ten years ago but in a few cases they are better. The general condition of Negro public school education has been fair but it is going back.

In 1900 thirty-five (35.23) per cent of the Negro children of South Carolina were in regular attendance upon the public schools whose annual length was 75 days. In 1909 the attendance had advanced to thirty-nine (39) per cent but the term length was only 70 days.

Summary of facts as reported in the Forty-first Annual Report of the State Superintendent of Education of the State of South Carolina, 1909:

Whites, 5-17, 1900 180,882
Negroes, 5-17, 1900 283,165

	White	Colored
Public school houses	2,334	1,442
Private school houses	254	718
Public schools	2,712	2,354
Men teachers (white: 1st grade, 2,487; 2nd grade, 610; 3rd grade, 150); (colored: 1st grade, 317; 2nd grade, 377; 3rd grade, 170)	933	894
Women teachers: (white: 1st grade, 2,487; 2nd grade, 610; 3rd grade, 150); (colored: 1st grade, 638; 2nd grade, 775; 3rd grade, 389)	3,247	1,802
Total teachers	4,180	2,896
Pupils	153,807	181,095
Average attendance	107,368	123,481
Pupils to a school	55	77
Pupils to a teacher	35	63
Average number of weeks of school	25.19	14.7
School houses built last year, (white: wood, 117; brick, 17); (colored: wood, 49; brick, 0)	134	49
Value of school houses built last year	$ 255,180.85	$ 7,061.80
School houses with grounds enclosed	105	3
Districts that levy an extra tax	656	. . . .
Districts that do not levy an extra tax	1,177	. . . .
Town schools	282	193
Country schools	2,430	2,161

HOUSES, TEACHERS AND PUPILS

School Houses

	White	Colored
Public	2,334	1,442
Private	254	718
Public schools	2,712	2,354

Teachers

First Grade

Men	672	347
Women	2,487	638

Second Grade

Men	186	377
Women	610	775

Third Grade

Men	75	170
Women	150	389

Enrollment

Boys	74,034	83,164
Girls	79,773	97,931
Average number of pupils to school	55	77
Average number of pupils to teacher	35	63
Average number of weeks session	25.19	14.7
Average number of weeks of town schools	33.63	23
Average number of weeks of country schools	23.36	13.5
Total revenues (for both whites and Negroes)	$2,345,647.72	
Total expenditures	1,590,732.51	$308,153.16
Balance on hand July 1, 1909	446,762.05	
Average yearly salary paid men teachers	479.79	118.17
Average yearly salary paid women teachers	249.13	91.45
Institutions of higher education	27	11

EXPENDITURES

Average salary paid teachers	White	Colored
Men	$ 479.79	$ 118.17
Women	249.13	91.45
Total salaries paid teachers		
Men	419,390.36	100,948.26
Women	799,679.54	172,566.69
Building school houses	141,144.02	7,132.66
Repairing school houses	43,816.37	7,015.91
Rent of school houses	2,747.54	2,138.02
Land for school purposes	27,775.37	579.75
Fuel and incidentals	37,476.29	10,945.86
Other purposes	118,703.02	6,826.01
Total	$1,590,732.51	$308,153.16

The following statistics are for Charleston county for school year 1908-09:

Enrollment

Whites	3,912
Negroes	7,866
Total	11,778

Number of Schools

Whites	30
Negroes	52
Total	82

Number of Teachers

Whites	155
Negroes	61
Total	216

Average Number of Pupils to a Teacher

Whites	35
Negroes	76

Average Length of Term in Weeks

Whites	34
Negroes	25

Average Yearly Salaries

Whites	
Males	$ 1,248
Females	402
Negroes	
Males	$ 213
Females	184

Total Expenditures

Whites	$139,666
Negroes	20,100

Per Capita Expenditure (Enrollment)

Whites	$ 35.70
Negroes	2.55

It is well to note here the per capita expenditures on white and Negro children for educational purposes. The following figures for the state cover the period from 1899 to 1909:

Per Capita Expenditure for South Carolina According to Enrollment

YEAR	White	Negro
1899	$ 4.98	$ 1.42
1900	5.55	1.30
1901	5.82	1.30
1902	6.01	1.53
1903	6.11	1.45
1904	6.88	1.47
1905	7.49	1.51
1906	7.83	1.47
1907	7.93	1.57
1908	9.00	1.60
1909	10.34	1.70

Per Capita Expenditures for Certain Counties in South Carolina According to Enrollment, 1908-1909

COUNTY	White	Negro
Bamberg	$ 18.59	$ 0.89
Beaufort	31.86	3.09
Calhoun	14.89	0.58
Charleston	35.70	2.55
Fairfield	13.26	0.78
Laurens	11.05	0.97
Marlboro	12.14	0.95
Richland	25.35	3.21

The following summary of statistics is compiled from the annual report of the state superintendent of education of the state of South Carolina for the year ending June 30, 1910:

Expenditures

	[1]1909	[2]1910
Whites	$ 1,509,732	$1,684,796.85
Negroes	308,153	368,802.64
Total	$ 1,817,885	$2,053,599.49

Number of Schools

Whites	2,712	2,702
Negroes	2,354	2,386
Total	5,066	5,088

Number of Teachers

Whites	4,180	4,352
Negroes	2,696	2,616
Total	6,876	6,968

Salaries, Average Yearly

	[1]1909	[2]1910
Whites (male) . . .	$ 480	$ 539.46
Whites (female) . .	249	258.26
Negroes (male) . . .	118	118.18
Negroes (female) . .	91	94.34

Length of Term

Whites	25.19 weeks	24.4 weeks
Negroes	14.7 weeks	14.0 weeks

Enrollment

Whites	153,807	156,051
Negroes	181,095	184,364
Total	334,902	340,415

Average Attendance

Whites	107,368	114,731
Negroes	123,481	129,170

[1]Estimated school population of South Carolina for 1908-9 was: whites, 201,868; Negroes, 316,007.

[2]Census for 1910 gives the following figures for the total population of South Carolina:
Whites . . . . 679,162 | Negroes 835,843

State Aid for Summer School		Appropriations to Higher Education	
	1909 1910		1908-09
Whites	$ 5,168	Whites	$ 355,994.88
Negroes	Nothing	Colored	12,000

It is reported that

. . . . of the $20,000 appropriated last year [1909] by the state legislature to aid weak schools 256 white schools in 31 counties have shared in the appropriation but no colored. And of the $60,000 appropriated to aid rural high schools 131 white high schools were helped in 40 counties but no colored.

Thus it will be seen . . . . that the colored schools of South Carolina do not share on an equality with the whites. The revenue received from Negro property tax and Negro poll tax to say nothing about the money received from other sources more than pays for the running of Negro schools in this state. The Negro public schools are surely no burden to the white tax-payers here who are not interested in these schools which are being supported by the Negroes themselves.

According to the census reports of the last four decades Negro illiteracy for South Carolina has been as follows:

PER CENT OF ILLITERACY

	1870	1880	189)	1900
South Carolina . . .	81.1	78.5	64.1	52.8

Section 13. Georgia

The Negro school system of Georgia started in the memorable conference at Savannah in December, 1864, when Stanton, secretary of war, and General Sherman met five or six of the leading Negro ministers, and after a dramatic interchange of opinion, free schools were decided upon. An old slave market was bought, the bars which marked the slave-stalls broken and a school opened.

The provisional government under the constitution of 1865 gave the legislature power to establish schools, but did not contemplate schools for Negroes. The new constitution of 1868 provided for schools for both races, but none were opened until the summer of 1871. In 1872 lack of funds compelled the suspension of the schools, but they were finally started permanently in 1873. [1]

The state board of education for the state of Georgia consists of the governor, the attorney-general, the comptroller-

---

[1] Atlanta University Publication, No. 6, p. 67.

general, the state school commissioner and four other persons appointed by the governor.

The following table of school statistics for the state of Georgia is compiled from the annual reports of the United States Bureau of Education:

GEORGIA

YEAR	School population, colored	Enrollment	Per cent enrolled	Daily attendance	Per cent of enrollment attending
1899–1900	380,970	195,276	51.25	119,276	61.08
1900–1901	363,050	200,848	55.32	122,887	61.18
1901–1902	363,050	204,706	56.39	124,553	60.84
1902–1903	376,445	201,418	53.51	120,032	59.59
1903–1904	376,445	201,418	53.51	120,032	59.59
1904–1905	387,166	200,238	51.72	119,705	59.79
1905–1906	387,166	200,238	51.72	119,705	59.79
1906–1907	387,166	200,238	51.72	119,705	59.79
1907–1908	405,948	201,512	49.64	119,504	59.30
1908–1909	393,638	220,699	56.07	145,856	68.35

BIBB COUNTY:

There are 20 colored schools and 35 white. Each has a nine months' term. The colored schools have six grades. The whites have high and normal schools. There are 58 colored and 144 white teachers. Three thousand seven hundred and seventy-eight colored and 8,874 white children attend school regularly. The school facilities for colored children are about the same as they were ten years ago.

CHATHAM COUNTY:

There are 10 city and 12 county schools for the whites and 3 city and 28 county schools for Negroes. In the city the terms for both white and colored are nine months long, but in the county the colored have only six months. The grammar schools for both the white and colored have eight grades. In the city schools there are 129 white teachers and 43 colored, and in the county schools 15 white and 28 colored teachers. The salaries of the county white teachers are $40 and those of the colored $30.

The total amount spent on all schools annually is $310,915; Negro schools, $19,413. Nothing for new buildings or improvements for the colored.

The facilities for the colored schools remain practically the same as they were ten years ago. The whites have been provided with a new high school costing $135,000, three grammar buildings and large additions to several old buildings.

On the whole the colored teachers are well qualified. Buildings and equipments for Negroes are poor.

Two thousand and thirty-five colored and 4,284 white children attend the city schools, and 978 colored and 319 white children attend the county schools.

FULTON COUNTY:

Thirteen colored, 30 white schools. Term of each nine months with eight grades in both. Twenty colored and 75 white teachers. The white teachers receive salaries from $45 to $75 and the colored from $20 to $40. There are 997 colored and 2,480 white children attending school. Thru the efforts of the Negroes conditions have been improved over what they were ten years ago. The Negroes do not pay a very large share of the school tax. The general condition of Negro education is growing better.

The following extracts are taken from the printed report of the superintendent of schools of Fulton county, Georgia, for 1909, and show something of Negro self-help in public school education:

College Park.—The Negroes of this town made a deed to a half-acre lot to the board of education and besides, met them half way in the building of a $1,200 house.

Bethlehem.—The following lines which appear in the *School and Home* tell the tale of this building: This school, valued at $800, was constructed by a dozen Negroes of a community, 10 miles from Atlanta, none of whom owned more than $300 or $400 worth of property. There are hundreds of schools for white children in Georgia that would suffer by comparison.

Pittsburg.—Since the beginning of the last term the Negroes here, with the aid of only $75 from the county board of education, have bought a lot worth $200 and built a $1,800 house. It has been hard to get this accomplished, mainly, because of difficulties which they apprehended from the city extension movement, but it is done at last and this work reflects great credit on the teachers and community.

Springfield.—This building has been continually improved since it was constructed a year ago and it is now in very good condition. This is largely due to the leadership of the teacher.

South Atlanta.—The house and lot cost $3,200 and was raised almost entirely by the Negroes of the community.

By way of summary the report says:

Our Negro schools have done excellent work in the way of improvement during the last year. But little help has been given by the county authorities, the Negroes for the most part desiring to own their buildings themselves. Building plans are furnished them, together with much inexpensive advice and insistence upon comfortable quarters for teachers and pupils. Here and there, as an incentive, some small part of the building material used has been given them, but they have met nearly all the expense connected with the new schools.

GREEN COUNTY:

Thirty-seven colored and 58 white schools. Term of colored schools five months and of white schools nine months. The colored schools have six grades and the white ten. There are 41 colored teachers and 66 white. The colored teachers receive from $15 to $20 and the white from $40 to $75.

The total amount spent annually on colored schools is $3,485 and on the white, $26,730. One thousand and twenty-five colored and 1,650 white children attend school regularly. Two-tenths of the school tax goes to colored schools. The colored people support schools of their own. In general the system is very poor.

MACON COUNTY:

There are today 28 Negro public schools in the county. There are about three times as many for white children. For Negro children the average number of schools in each township is one. There are many country communities which do not boast of even one public school for Negroes. This part of Macon county has suffered so much for lack of public school facilities. The schools are few and far between, the children often being obliged to walk five or six miles to attend school.

It would seem that these few schools would be well provided for since there are so few of them, but this is not the fact. In the rural communities the same building serves for the double purpose of school building and church. The building is often built and kept up by the Negroes in that community who are members of that particular denomination. There are no desks in these buildings and no backs to the seats. The windows have no glass, but are opened and shut with wooden shutters.

In these rural communities there is an average of one teacher per school. At times the teacher may press into service one of the advanced scholars as an assistant. The assistant is sometimes given as much as $10 per month.

In Macon county there is often no effort made by the county superintendent to secure the best teachers. All one has to do to secure a position in the rural schools is to "stand in with the authorities." Thus the county fails to secure efficient Negro teachers for the Negro schools.

The salaries of the county school teachers range from $17.50 to $37.50. The county schools are taught for five or six months at a time. They have from one to five grades. Some of them do not seem to be graded at all.

There are 40 Negro teachers in the county. The schools for Negroes in the towns and villages are somewhat better than those in the country districts, altho there is not enough difference to show any startling contrast.

The school buildings in the towns and villages often serve for both school and church purposes. The teachers in the town schools range from one to six, the smallest number of teachers being in the largest town in the county (Montezuma) and the largest number being in the smallest town in the county (Marshallville).

These town schools have eight grades and they have a school year of nine months. The salaries of the teachers range from $20 to $40 per month. The Negroes themselves give no aid to any private schools for their children. That is one thing they have not as yet been taught to do.

In one town (Marshallville) the Negro children pay $0.25 per year into the town treasury for school purposes, but they pay nothing at all for the support of the private schools in the county.

The number of children attending school in the county is 2,005. The number kept out of school on account of lack of facilities is said to be about 400. The number of students in each room in these schools is very large. There are at times as many as 150 in one class.

Altho these Negro teachers have about twice as many children to teach, they get about one-third as much salary as the white teachers who teach the same classes.

There is no high school for Negroes in this county. There are many for white children.

The salaries of the white teachers range from $60 to $100 per month. The teachers in the Negro schools were educated in such schools as Fisk, Howard and the Atlanta universities, Talladega, Ballard and the schools of the county.

The progress of these schools is very slow. The great need for the Negroes of the county is a high school. It would be an inspiration for the large boys and girs of the community.

Many stop school for the reason that they are obliged to work, others because they are ashamed to go to a school where there are so few large boys. The county is a good field for energetic young men who are willing to work.

Putnam County:

There are 25 colored and 15 white schools. Term of colored school 5 months and of white 7 months. The colored schools are not graded. Ten grades in white schools. There are 26 colored teachers and 24 or more white, the colored teachers receiving from $12.50 to $22.50 per month and the whites from $35 to $50.

The annual report of the county school commissioner, March 20, 1911, says: "By the local tax plan the Negroes get exactly what they pay in and no more." The school population of the county shows 688 white and 3,172 Negro children of school age. The expenditures were $8,842.35 for white schools and $1,641.34 for colored schools.

RICHMOND COUNTY RURAL SCHOOLS:

	Expenditures[1]	1910
Whites		$ 129,145.21
Negroes		

Number of Schools		Length of Term	
Whites	25	Whites	7.9 months
Negroes.	14	Negroes	6.3 months
Total	39	Enrollment[2]	
Number of Teachers		Whites	6,554
Whites	28	Negroes.	2,970
Negroes.	14	Total	9,524
Total	42	Average Attendance	
Average Salaries		Whites	70 per cent
Whites	$ 41.14	Negroes.	See Note 3
Negroes.	25.40		

City Systems

Atlanta (1910-11)

The city of Atlanta has eleven public schools for Negroes. Five of these schools are suburban schools and have only recently been incorporated into the city system by the extension of the city limits. Since 1890 but one public school for Negroes has been added to the list, tho the school population has steadily increased. A new school is now being built for Negroes. The Negro enrollment in the city system is 5,122. There are 80 teachers. The attendance in these schools is good, averaging about ninety-two per cent. This is accounted for in part by the fact that irregularity in attendance results in the loss of one's seat, for almost every one of these eleven schools has its waiting list of those who are desirous of attending but are unable to do so because of lack of school facilities.

The work of the teachers is good, for the greater part of them have had excellent training. The schools for higher education in Atlanta have trained these teachers for efficient service. Atlanta University alone has trained about seventy-five per cent of the public school teachers of the city.

At least 250 pupils who apply for admission each year are turned away for lack of seats. Hundreds do not apply at all because of the crowded condition of the schools, and still others do not concern them-

---

[1] The figures for expenditures for whites were taken from the Thirty-ninth Annual Report of the Department of Education of Georgia for the year 1910. The figures for expenditures of Negro schools do not appear.

[2] Thirty-ninth Annual Report of the Department of Education of Georgia, page 261.

[3] Among the Negro schools the enrollment is generally large, several schools having 50 to 60 pupils on roll, five or six as many as 40 pupils and the smallest among them not less than 30. We generally estimate that a little more than half the Negro children in the rural districts are in school.—Annual Report of Public Schools of Augusta and Richmond County, Georgia, 1910, page 70.

selves. Many are enrolled in the private schools of the city and many are taught in the afternoon sessions provided by the Gate City Free Kindergarten Association, an organization supported by Negroes. Usually the first four or five grades of the Negro public schools are running double sessions. The same teacher has two sets of children, usually 60 in a set, one coming in the morning and the other in the afternoon. Thus the children are doing about half time in school, an injustice to both the teacher and the students.

The salary of the colored teachers, even of those doing double session work, is considerably less than the salary of the white teachers doing the same grade work.

The teachers' salaries in the public school system of Atlanta are shown by the following schedule:[1]

	Salary Per Year	
	White	Negro
Principals,[2] eight grades:		
First year, ...	$ 1,066.50	$ 666.50
Second year.	1,075.00	675.00
Third year.	1,116.50	675.00
Fourth year.	1,125.50	675.00
Fifth year.	1,166.50	716.50
Sixth year.	1,175.00	716.50
Seventh year	1,216.50	725.00
Eighth year.	1,225.00	725.00
Ninth year	1,266.00	750.00
Tenth year	1,300.00	758.50
Assistant Principals:		
First year	660.00	
Second year.	670.00	
Third year	715.00	
Fourth year.	725.00	500.00
Fifth year.	770.00	
Sixth year.	780.00	
Seventh year	825.00	
Grade Teachers:		
First year.	. . . . [3]	310.00
Second year.	558.50	310.00
Third year	584.00	336.00
Fourth year.	610.00	336.00
Fifth year.	636.00	361.50
Sixth year.	661.50	361.50
Seventh year	687.50	387.50
Eighth year.	713.50	387.50
Ninth year	721.50	413.50
Tenth year	730.00	413.50
Eleventh year	738.50	439.00

In 1908 Atlanta had a school fund of $395,730.89. Of this fund $65,492.24 came from the state. The rest was raised by local taxation.

[1]From the *Atlanta Constitution*, 25 March, 1911. [Since this study was made an increase of 5 per cent in all salaries has been reported.]

[2]Principals are paid $25 a year extra for each grade above eight.

[3]Grade Teachers: First half of the first year $40 month (rate, year $400), $55 month ($550 year); increase $15 month. Second half of first year, $45 month (rate, year $450), $55 month ($550 year); increase $10 month.

Negroes paid taxes on property assessed at $1,028,290. It would seem that almost all of the tax raised on the property went to the support of white schools while the Negro schools got simply the state tax.

Not long since the city voted $600,000 for additional school houses and repairs. The board of education apportioned $35,000 of this amount for one new Negro school building.

The Negro school buildings are in bad condition and sorely in need of improvements. Some of them could be improved as they now stand. Others should be razed to the ground. All are in need of better equipment. One of these schools has a curious environment: On one side stands an orphan home, beyond is the city stockade, on a third side is a slaughter pen, while a pest house occupies the fourth. A recent observer remarks that, notwithstanding these conditions, every Negro school building in the city is as neat and tidy as possible under the circumstances.

Since this study began a new public school has been built for Negroes, the only thoroly modern building devoted to them.

The work done in the Negro common schools of Atlanta is of the same grade as that done by the white schools thru the eighth grade. The whites have two public high schools, one for boys and the other for girls, but the city makes no provision for the high school education of its black children. The whites have also a night school.

Under adverse circumstances the Negro public schools of Atlanta are doing a great work, not only for black Atlanta, but for the city as a whole.

Augusta

There are 4 public schools for Negroes in the city of Augusta with 30 teachers. The total enrollment in these schools is 1,479. Fully 1,000 Negro children are unable to get into the public schools because of lack of facilities and in addition to this about 500 are on half time. The city has 5,736 Negro children between the ages of 6 and 18 years. The white schools have eight grades and in addition two high schools are provided. The Negroes have seven grades and no provision for public high school work, the eighth grade having been abolished in order to introduce domestic art and domestic science.

Salaries: The white principals receive $1,500 per year. Two Negro principals receive $802 per year; four less than $600, i. e. from $580 down. As for other teachers, the lowest salary for the white teachers is $46 per month, while the lowest salary for Negro teachers is $27.50. The highest salary for whites, except those doing special work, is $85; for Negroes, including those doing special work, $40 per month.

Columbus

The first public school for Negroes in Columbus, Ga., was established in the early seventies. Today they have three well-kept buildings, two owned and one rented by the city, and all under the control of the Columbus public school system.   The value of these buildings according to the assessors' valuation for 1910 is $35,000.   The value of the equipment for the three schools (one rented) is estimated at $4,200.

Especial mention must be made of the Fifth Avenue school for colored people which was completed in 1908.   This school was built in place of the Sixth Avenue school which was sold by the city.   It is a handsome two-story brick structure, having a basement which is used for industrial work and modern improvements and conveniences.   The value of this building alone is $20,000 and the estimated value of its equipment is $2,400.   In commenting upon this school one correspondent said: "Our Fifth Avenue school is among the best in the city, white or colored, having shower baths and other conveniences for cleanliness."   In short, the common answer as to the condition of the Negro public school buildings in Columbus is "very good."

There are enrolled in these schools 1,225 children between the ages of 6 and 18 years.   Each child upon entering school pays a fee in accordance with his grading.   From first to the fourth grade inclusive his fee is $1.50 per year.   From fifth to seventh inclusive, $3.00 per year.   From the eighth to ninth inclusive, $6.00 per year.   For this fee the school furnishes each child with all books, paper and pencils that he needs thruout the year.   There is no delay in supplying the needs of any child.   On the day that school opens every child sits at his desk which is fully supplied.

The school term is nine months.   These schools have nine grades, the eighth and ninth grades going into high school work for a little way. Besides the academic work enough industrial work is offered to give each child a practical turn of mind.   The industrial work as well as the academic work of the first, second, third and fourth grades is done by the grade teacher.   Above these grades special teachers have charge of the work.   The boys spend one hour per day in carpentry and blacksmithing on alternate days.   For instance, those boys who spend one hour in blacksmithing today, spend one hour in carpentry tomorrow.   The girls spend equal time cooking, sewing and laundering.   When a class leaves the academic department it is divided, one part taking cooking, another sewing and the other laundering, and the next day the classes change occupations.   Thus each child receives five hours of industrial work for five years.

As to the number of Negro children unable to get into school because of lack of school facilities, the answers received vary from twenty-five to almost thirty-five (35) per cent.   According to the catalog of the Columbus public schools, 1910, seventeen (17.35) per cent of the school population was out of school.   Therefore, I should say that a little over twenty (20) per cent of the Negro children are kept out of schools because of lack of school facilities.   There are 5 male and 22 female teachers. These teachers were educated at Morris Brown College and Atlanta University, Atlanta, Ga.; at Haines Institute, Augusta, Ga.; Tuskegee Institute, Alabama; Fort Valley High and Industrial School, Fort Valley, Ga.; at Ballard Institute, Macon, Ga., and at the Columbus public schools. Their salaries range from $22.50 to about $85 per month, which is about fifty (50) per cent of what the white teachers receive.

Only seventy-four (74) per cent of the school population of Columbus is enrolled in the public schools. About nine (9) per cent is enrolled in private schools. Among the colored people there are three or four such schools which are helping to supplement the work of the public schools. The work in such schools can be bettered, but it well illustrates the fact that the Negroes are eager for an education.

The value of schools to a community and the work done by them can best be estimated from the comments of the people of that community. One sums up his opinion in the terse statement, "Best in the South." Another says, "My opinion of the Negro public schools in my community is that they are very good. Much stress is being placed on the industrial features, which are proving to be very helpful in the early training of the youth."

Says a third, "We have about the average teachers and I believe we are doing some of the best work."

Still another says, "It is said by some of the best people that the public school system in Columbus, Ga., ranks second of those in the United States, Philadelphia coming first."

Macon

There are eight public schools for Negroes in the city of Macon with 47 teachers. The total enrollment in these schools is 2,852. Fully 800 Negro children in the city are unable to get into the schools because of lack of facilities. The white schools have seven grades and a high school. The Negro schools have but six grades and no high school. The Negro school buildings are kept up very well and are fairly comfortable.

Salaries: The white principals receive $1,000 per year. The Negro principals receive $62.50 per month. The lowest salary for white teachers is $45 per month, while the lowest salary for Negroes is $30 per month. The salary of the white teachers is increased $5 per month every two years up to $60 per month, while that of the Negroes is increased $2.50 per month every two years up to $37.50.

Savannah

The following school statistics are taken from the forty-sixth annual report of the public schools of Savannah:

Number of Teachers		Average Number Belonging	
Whites	129	Whites	4,736
Negroes	43	Negroes	2,152
Total	172	Total	6,888

Number of Pupils Enrolled		Average Daily Attendance	
Whites	5,328	Whites	4,335
Negroes	2,365	Negroes	1,992
Total	7,693	Total	6,327

Per Cent of Daily Attendance

Whites	91
Negroes	93
Total	92

Sylvester

Sylvester is a small town with about 2,000 inhabitants, about sixty per cent white. The colored people have a two-story framed building, the upper story used as an auditorium and the ground floor as class rooms of which there are four. This school is run by the city government, the school site having been donated by the colored people at a cost of $300. Three teachers are supplied for nine months at a salary of $20 to $50 each.

The rural schools are not so good. Terms about four months with poorly prepared and poorly paid teachers. Salaries from $15 to $20. No school houses but unfinished church houses are used. The colored people are buying and building nice homes in city and country districts.

In 1900 twenty-nine per cent of the Negro children of Georgia were in regular attendance upon the public schools whose annual length was less than 117 days. In 1909 the attendance had advanced to thirty-seven per cent.

The following summary of school statistics is taken from the thirty-eighth and thirty-ninth annual reports of the Department of Education of the state of Georgia:

Expenditures

	1909	1910
Whites	$3,556,089.25	. . . .
Negroes	449,235.40	. . . .
Total	$4,005,324.65	$4,417,695.88

Number of Schools

Whites	4,805	4,891
Negroes	3,023	3,055
Total	7,828	7,946

Number of Teachers

Whites	8,408	8,714
Negroes	3,823	3,911
Total	12,231	12,625

Average Salaries (Counties)

Whites (males)	$ 58.34	$ 59.56
Whites (females)	37.48	39.28
Negroes (males)	26.37	45.90
Negroes (females)	19.55	26.96

Average Salaries (Systems)

	1909	1910
Whites (males)	$ 104.32	$ 117.40
Whites (female)	47.76	49.34
Negroes (male)	45.53	45.90
Negroes (female)	25.83	26.69

Length of Term in Days (Counties)

Whites	121	123
Negroes	108	106

Length of Term in Days (Systems)

Whites	171	173
Negroes	156	162

Enrollment

Whites	316,315	334,994
Negroes	213,386	220,800
Total	529,701	555,794

According to the census reports of the last four decades Negro illiteracy for Georgia has been as follows:

PER CENT OF ILLITERACY

	1870	1880	1890	1900
Georgia	92.1	81.6	67.3	52.4

Section 14. Florida

The public school system of Florida is controlled by the state board of education, consisting of the governor, the secretary of state, the state treasurer, the attorney-general and the state superintendent of public instruction. There are also county superintendents, county boards of education and district trustees.

The impetus to public school education in Florida was given by the "carpet bag" government in its act of 30 January, 1869.

Jonathan C. Gibbs, a Negro graduate from Dartmouth, was state superintendent of public instruction during the years 1873-1874, and under his administration the schools of the state became well established.

The following table of school statistics for the state of Florida is compiled from the annual reports of the United States Bureau of Education:

FLORIDA

YEAR	School population, colored	Enrollment	Per cent enrolled	Daily attendance	Per cent of enrollment attending
1899-1900	77,640	41,797	53.83	28,736	68.75
1900-1901	72,933	43,578	59.75	30,123	69.12
1901-1902	75,160	42,843	57.00	29,881	69.75
1902-1903	75,812	42,843	56.51	29,881	69.75
1903-1904	78,121	43,568	59.64	32,338	69.44
1904-1905	78,121	46,568	59.64	32,338	69.44
1905-1906	83,456	48,992	58.59	34,446	70.31
1906-1907	83,456	48,992	58.59	34,446	70.30
1907-1908	88,659	50,812	57.31	37,814	74.42
1908-1909	78,506	53,512	68.16	39,876	74.52

CLAY COUNTY:

This county has 6 colored and 22 white schools, 10 grades in the colored and 12 in the white. The salaries of the colored teachers range from $25 to $60 per month; those of the whites from $45 to $100. Seven thousand five hundred dollars per year are spent on white schools, while the colored receive only $2,400. Three hundred colored children attend school and 600 whites.

The school facilities are very much better, better school houses, longer terms and better equipment for teaching. The colored people supplement the school term. In general the condition of Negro public education here is hopeful.

LEON COUNTY:

There are 35 white and 41 Negro schools here. Both the white and colored schools have five grades, with 201 pupils in the higher grades of the colored and 466 pupils in the higher grades of the white.

Thé salaries of the colored teachers are: male, $32.60; female, $25; and those of the white teachers, male, $76; female, $42.80. The average term of the white schools is 116 days and of the Negro schools 93 days, with an average daily attendance of white children of 769 and of colored children 3,862. The amount spent annually on colored schools is $11,861.48 and on the white $24,303.84.

There is no decided advance in school facilities except that made by individual teachers themselves. The status of the county schools, especially the Negro schools, remains almost a constant quantity. There are several night schools and several private schools for Negroes and they have supplemented the school term in several instances.

The general condition averages a little above the typical county conditions for the following reasons: 1st, the county has one of the four high schools for Negroes; 2d, the Florida Agricultural and Mechanical College sends teachers into the county; 3d, the only training school for teachers is conducted in this county. However, the county does not provide adequately for Negro public schools.

In 1900 thirty-seven (36.59) per cent of the Negro children of Florida were in regular attendance upon the public schools whose annual length was 87 days. In 1909 the attendance had advanced to thirty-nine (39) per cent in schools whose average annual length was 90 days.

The following table of school statistics is compiled from the biennial report of the superintendent of public instruction for the state of Florida for the two years ending June 30, 1910:

Expenditures	1908-09	1909-10
Whites	$1,469,436.94	$1,521,778.49
Negroes	245,501.44	257,369.11
Total	$1,714,938.38	$1,779,147.60

Number of Schools	1908-09	1909-10
Whites	1,819	1,848
Negroes	724	714
Total	2,543	2,562

Number of Teachers	1908-09	1909-10
Whites	2,912	3,338
Negroes	966	1,131
Total	3,878	4,469

Length of Term	1908-09	1909-10
Whites	108 days	110 days
Negroes	90 days	96 days

School Population	1908-09	1909-10
Whites	136,773	125,343
Negroes	104,877	86,187
Total	241,650	211,530

Enrollment	1908-09	1909-10
Whites	88,416	92,834
Negroes	53,512	55,255
Total	141,928	148,089

Average Daily Attendance	1908-09	1909-10
Whites	61,904	63,243
Negroes	39,876	40,649
Total	101,780	103,892

Salaries	1908-09	1909-10
Whites (male)	$ 65.40	$ 68.13
Whites (female)	48.20	55.80
Negroes (male)	33.80	33.68
Negroes (female)	29.40	30.18

According to the census reports of the last four decades Negro illiteracy for Florida has been as follows:

PER CENT OF ILLITERACY

	1870	1880	1890	1900
Florida	84.1	70.7	50.5	38.4

Section 15. Alabama

The public school system of Alabama was established by the state constitution of 1867 and organized in the following year. Owing to a continual lack of funds and non-payment of local taxes, as well as other opposing conditions, the schools were stopped altogether in 1873-74. The following year, however, the system was resumed and since that day the schools have been at work.

The public schools of Alabama are today under the control of the following:

1. The state superintendent of education.
2. County superintendent in each county.
3. District trustees in each school district. ·
4. County board of education in each county.

The following table of school statistics for the state of Alabama is compiled from the annual reports of the United States Bureau of Education:

ALABAMA

YEAR	School population, colored	Enrollment	Per cent enrolled	Daily attendance	Per cent of enrollment attending
1899-1900	301,300	142,423	47.26	99,342	69.75
1900-1901	281,348	142,423	50.62	99,342	69.75
1901-1902	295,250	126,116	42.71	90,000	71.36
1902-1903	296,136	126,116	42.59	90,000	71.36
1903-1904	295,250	126,116	42.71	90,000	71.36
1904-1905	305,663	150,000	49.07	75,000	50.00
1905-1906	305,663	150,000	49.07	75,000	50.00
1906-1907	305,663	150,000	49.07	75,000	50.00
1907-1908	319,451	127,480	39.91	86,093	67.53
1908-1909	311,552	138,533	44.46	90,930	65.64

TALLADEGA COUNTY:

The colored schools vary from three to six months per year and run to the fourth or fifth grades, while in the white schools there are twelve

grades. The salaries of the colored teachers are from $20 to $30, sometimes less. White 'teachers receive from $40 upward as a rule. As a
rule the school facilities for the colored are poorer than those for the
whites. Negro public school education in this county seems not to have
advanced for the past twelve years.

WILCOX COUNTY:

There are in this county 50 colored schools and 57 white. Last year
the colored schools had a term of only 80 days, while the white schools
had 140 days. The colored schools seem to be ungraded. The white
schools have seven grades. There are 50 colored teachers and 73 white,
the colored teachers receiving a salary of $18.75 and the white $66.80.

Thirty thousand six hundred and twelve dollars and seventy-five cents
are spent annually on the white schools, while the colored schools receive
$3,339.70.

Number of colored children in county	10,758
Number of white children in county	2,000
Enrollment colored children	2,963
Enrollment white children	1,772
Average attendance of colored children	1,948
Average attendance of white children	1,452

The colored people support a few schools of their own and almost in
all cases supplement the school term. The general condition of Negro
education in this county is very poor indeed. Were it not for six United
Presbyterian and two or three Baptist schools education would be at a low
ebb.

The following summary of statistics is compiled from the
annual report of the Birmingham public schools for the year
ending June 30, 1910:

Public Schools of Birmingham, Ala., 1910

Expenditures

Whites	$ 220,598.69
Negroes	35,467.96

Number of Schools

Whites	35
Negroes	20
Total	55

Number of Teachers

Whites	393
Negroes	101
Total	494

Actual Enrollment

Whites	13,870
Negroes	6,390
Total	20,260

Average Membership

Whites	10,879
Negroes	4,646
Total	15,525

Average Daily Attendance

Whites	10,080
Negroes	3,982
Total	14,062

Length of Term

Whites	178 days
Negroes	178 days

Average Annual Salaries

Whites	$ 448.01
Negroes	299.88

Total Value of School Property

Whites	$1,374,002.87
Negroes	81,680.51

In 1909 twenty-nine (29.18) per cent of the Negro children
of Alabama were in regular attendance upon the public schools

whose annual length was 98 days. In 1910 the annual length for Negro schools was reduced to 90 days. Prof. Harry C. Gunnels, state superintendent of education in Alabama, says in his annual report for 1910:

So far as this office is aware, there is no reason to justify the shortening of the term for the Negro schools the past year over the year before. [1]

The following summary of school statistics is compiled from the annual report of the Department of Education for the state of Alabama for the scholastic year ending September 30, 1910:

Expenditures	1908	1909	1910
Whites	....	....	$2,417,378.57
Negroes.	....	....	329,094.83
Total	....	....	$2,746,473.40
Number of Schools			
Whites	4,207	4,360	4,424
Negroes.	1,813	1,880	1,965
Total	6,020	6,240	6,389
Number of Teachers			
Whites	5,740	6,147	6,434
Negroes.	2,023	2,136	2,243
Total	7,763	8,283	8,677
Salaries of Teachers			
Whites (male)	$ 57.03	$ 60.63	$ 61.12
Whites (female)	43.85	45.65	46.41
Negroes (male)	28.23	27.18	30.14
Negroes (female)	23.37	24.00	24.81
Length of Term			
Whites	123 days	128 days	131 days
Negroes.	95 days	98 days	90 days
Enrollment			
Whites	258,998	271,910	279,982
Negroes.	127,480	133,316	142,813
Total	386,478	405,226	422,795
Average Attendance			
Whites	162,937	176,500	176,562
Negroes.	86,093	89,000	89,008
Total	249,030	265,500	265,570

According to the census reports of the last four decades Negro illiteracy for Alabama has been as follows:

PER CENT OF ILLITERACY

	1870	1880	1890	1900
Alabama	88.1	80.6	69.1	57.4

[1] Annual Report of the Department of Education of Alabama, 1910, page 6.

Section 16.   Mississippi

The public school system of Mississippi was established in accordance with a clause of the state constitution of 1868 which made it the duty of the legislature to establish "a uniform system of free public schools, by taxation or otherwise, for all children between the ages of 5 and 21 years."

Many difficulties were encountered in the early life of Mississippi's school system and its progress was naturally slow.   Objections to Negro education were early apparent.

The school report of 1873 says: "Again it is objected that a general tax compels white men of the state to educate the children of the Negro.   But as the Negro forms a majority of the entire population of the state, and in an eminent degree a majority of the producing classes, as such classes of every population—the laborer, tenant and consumer—indirectly bear the burdens of taxation, it follows that an assessment upon the property of the state would be principally paid by the Negro and, therefore, the ground of complaint, if any, against a general tax is with the colored people and not with the white."

The following table of school statistics for the state of Mississippi is compiled from the annual reports of the United States Bureau of Education:

MISSISSIPPI

YEAR	School population, colored	Enrollment	Per cent enrolled	Daily attendance	Per cent of enrollment attending
1899-1900	331,330	192,493	58.09	102,898	53.45
1900-1901	312,400	192,493	61.62	102,898	53.45
1901-1902	322,07)	208,346	64.69	119,190	57.21
1902-1903	210,766	210,766	63.45	118,096	56.03
19 3-1904	332,141	210,766	63.45	118,096	56.03
1904-1905	332,141	210,766	63.45	118,096	56.03
1905-1906	332,141	210,766	63.45	118,096	56.03
1906-1907	353,471	270,659	76.57	150,201	55 49
1907-19)8	358,806	258,697	72.10	132,732	51.31
1908-1909	3 30,925	238,639	66.11	145,153	60.83

BOLIVAR COUNTY:

One hundred and ten colored and 35 white schools.   Both the white and colored schools have eight grades.   There are 160 colored and 39 white teachers, the colored receiving an average of $25 and the white $50 per month. The colored receive $15,000 annually and the white $25,000. Four thousand colored children and 1,000 white attend school regularly. The general condition of Negro public school education is poor. By supplementing the school terms the colored people have been able to extend several schools to six or eight months.

WARREN COUNTY:

The terms for both the white and colored schools are eight months in the country and nine in the city, each having eight to nine grades in the country and twelve in the city, also special departments such as music, drawing, etc. The colored teachers receive from $23 to $33 and the whites $55. There is in the city some improvement in the school facilities over what they were ten years ago, but none in the country. In general the condition of Negro public school education is poor. This, however, does not apply to the schools of our city (Vicksburg). Aside from buildings, they are very good. Our curriculum embraces ten grades and two years in what is known as the high school department. While we have no high school building, these two classes are taught by the two principals of the colored public schools. We are supposed to have the highest curriculum of any separate school district in the state.

In 1900 thirty-eight (38.27) per cent of the Negro children of Mississippi· were in regular attendance upon the public schools whose average annual length was less than 101 days. In 1909 the attendance had advanced to forty per cent. The following summary of school statistics is compiled from the biennial report of the state superintendent of public education of Mississippi for the scholastic years 1907-08 and 1908-09:

Mississippi 1908-09

Expenditures

Whites	
Negroes	
Total	$2,756,082.45

Number of Schools Taught Exclusive of Separate Districts

Whites	4,238
Negroes	2,987
Total	7,225

Number of Teachers

Whites	6,099
Negroes	3,552
Total	9,651

Average Salaries in Separate Districts

Whites	$ 58.84
Negroes	29.57

Average Salaries Exclusive of Separate Districts

Whites	$ 41.49
Negroes	20.31

Term Length

Average number of days excluding separate districts	123
Average number of days including separate districts	163

School Population

Whites	301,548
Negroes	410,089
Total	711,637

Enrollment

Whites	221,392
Negroes	238,639
Total	460,031

Average Attendance

Whites	138,813
Negroes	145,153

Per Cent of School Population Enrolled

Whites	73
Negroes	58

The Conference has been able to compile the following tables of school statistics for eleven typical counties of the state of Mississippi for the year 1908-09:

SCHOOL STATISTICS FOR ELEVEN TYPICAL COUNTIES IN MISSISSIPPI, 1908-09

COUNTY	Total Enrollment		Total Attendance	
	White	Colored	White	Colored
Attala.	3,693	3,491	2,580	2,047
Bolivar	1,217	10,627	740	6,366
Claiborne	947	3,761	584	1,591
Copiah	3,356	5,147	2,095	2,730
Greene	1,787	479	1,024	398
Issaquena	185	2,2 2	160	1,835
Itawamba	3,792	406	2,404	195
Madison	974	4,016	815	7,324
Noxubee	1,022	6,330	730	4,970
Washington	555	6,387	402	4,114
Yazoo	2,800	7,633	1,238	3,428

COUNTY TREASURERS' REPORTS

Receipts

Attala	$24,794.48	Itawamba	$18,107.38
Bolivar	40,992.82	Madison	26,205.05
Claiborne	36,850.23	Noxubee	32,529.44
Copiah	43,505.48	Washington	58,643.12
Greene	24,233.17	Yazoo	53,131.93
Issaquena	16,883.03		

Attala County

	White	Colored
Number of districts established	101	54
Number of schools taught	101	54
Number of school houses built		
Average monthly salaries paid teachers ,	$ 31.40	$ 16.68
Per capita each child enrolled	3.42	1.02
Per capita each child in average attendance	5.48	1.74

Bolivar County

Number of Educable Children

White	1,360
Negro	10,707

Total Receipts and Disbursements

Total receipts	$40,992.82
Total disbursements	31,999.12

	White	Negro	Total
Number of pupils enrolled	1,217	10,627	11,844
Number in average attendance	740	6,366	7,106
Number of districts established	38	106	144
Number of schools taught	38	105	143
Number of school houses built			
Average monthly salaries paid teachers	$ 49.13	$ 24.28	$ 30.67
Per capita each child enrolled	7.26	1.18	1.81
Per capita each child in average attendance	11.95	1.98	3.02

Claiborne County

	White	Colored
Number of districts established	30	41
Number of schools taught	29	40
Number of school houses built	1	1
Average monthly salary paid teachers	$ 40.14	$ 19.77
Per capita each child enrolled	1.61	0.27
Per capita each child in average attendance	2.61	0.62

Copiah County

	White	Colored
Number of districts established	76	71
Number of schools taught	76	71
Number of school houses built	2	1
Average monthly salary paid teachers	$ 41.00	$ 18.09
Per capita each child enrolled	7.43	2.51
Per capita each child in average attendance	11.90	0.59

Greene County

	White	Colored
Number of districts established	48	13
Number of schools taught	48	13
Number of school houses built	2	
Average monthly salary paid teachers	$ 43.58	$ 28.80
Per capita each child enrolled	9.22	4.59
Per capita each child in average attendance	15.10	5.51

Issaquena County

Number of Educable Children	Total Receipts and Disbursements
White 191	Total receipts $16,884.03
Negro 3,634	Total disbursements 11,530.76

	White	Negro	Total
Number of pupils enrolled	185	2,202	2,387
Number in average attendance	160	1,835	1,995
Number of districts established	20	28	48
Number of schools taught	20	28	48
Number of school houses built	1		1
Average monthly salaries paid teachers	$ 55.00	$ 20.00	$ 33.00
Per capita each child enrolled	30.00	1.00	4.00
Per capita each child in average attendance	31.00	2.00	4.00

Itawamba County

	White	Colored
Number of districts established	72	8
Number of schools taught	72	8
Number of school houses built	4	
Average monthly salaries paid teachers	$ 35.80	$ 21.00
Per capita each child enrolled	3.76	1.70
Per capita each child in average attendance	5.65	3.50

Madison County

	White	Colored
Number of districts established	44	64
Number of schools taught	44	64
Number of school houses built	2	
Average monthly salaries paid teachers	$ 49.30	$ 21.26
Per capita each child enrolled	2.22	0.18
Per capita each child in average attendance	2.66	0.33

Noxubee County

Number of Educable Children

White 1,528
Negro 13,048

Total Receipts and Disbursements

Total receipts . . . . $ 32,529.44
Total disbursements 30,219.39

	White	Negro	Total
Number of pupils enrolled	1,022	6,330	7,352
Number in average attendance	730	4,970	5,700
Number of districts established	55	61	116
Number of schools taught	55	61	116
Number of school houses built	7		7
Average monthly salaries paid school teachers	$ 43.62	$ 20.91	$ 32.26
Per capita each child enrolled	14.08	1.69	7.88
Per capita each child in average attendance	21.09	2.14	11.61

Washington County

	White	Colored
Number of districts established	32	82
Number of schools taught	32	82
Number of school houses built		1
Average monthly salaries paid teachers	$ 59.13	$ 32.91
Per capita each child enrolled	12.29	2.50
Per capita each child in average attendance	21.50	3.84

• Yazoo County

	White	Colored
Number of districts established	67	89
Number of schools taught	67	89
Number of school houses built	3	7
Average monthly salaries paid teachers	$ 42.72	$ 22.49
Per capita each child enrolled	8.40	1.83
Per capita each child in average attendanae	19.02	4.08

Brooksville (Separate Town District in Noxubee County)

	White	Negro	Total
Enrollment	87	172	259
Average daily attendance	71	143	214
Teachers employed	3	3	6
			Average
Number of days taught	180		
Average salaries paid	$ 75.37	$ 21.11	$ 48.24
Per capita each child enrolled	23.40	3.32	13.36
Per capita each child in average attendance	23.40	3.32	13.36

Receipts . . . . $ 3,531.32
Disbursements 3,108.89

Macon (Separate Town District in Noxubee County)

	White	Negro	Total
Enrollment	195	475	670
Average daily attendance	180	410	590
Teachers employed	10	4	14
			Average
Number of days taught	180		
Average salaries paid	$ 69.92	$ 30.21	$ 50.31
Per capita each child enrolled	22.61	4.09	13.35
Per capita each child in average attendance	24.47	4.72	14.59

Receipts	$7,403.15
Disbursements	7,179.94

Shuqualak (Separate Town District in Noxubee County)

	White	Negro	Total
Enrollment	111	175	286
Average daily attendance	85	135	220
Teachers employed	3	3	6
			Average
Number of days taught	180		
Average salaries paid	$ 65.00	$ 20.00	$ 41.50
Per capita each child enrolled	15.81	3.09	9.45
Per capita each child in average attendance	20.65	4.00	12.37

Receipts	$2,613.07
Disbursements	2,585.81

According to the census reports of the last four decades Negro illiteracy for Mississippi has been as follows:

PER CENT OF ILLITERACY

	1870	1880	1890	1900
Mississippi	87.0	75.2	60.8	49.1

Section 17. Louisiana

The public school system of Louisiana was made a state institution by the constitution of 1868. All children were admitted to the public schools regardless of color and in fact the law provided for compulsory mixed schools. This condition prevailed until 1877.

The public school system is at present under the control of a state board of education composed of the governor, the state superintendent of public instruction, the attorney-general and eight others. Parish superintendents have charge of the schools in the various parishes.

The following table of school statistics for the state of Louisiana is compiled from the annual reports of the United States Bureau of Education:

LOUISIANA

YEAR	School population, colored	Enrollment	Per cent enrolled	Daily attendance	Per cent of enrollment attending
1899–1900 . . .	242,590	74,233	30.60	56,136	75.62
1900–1901 . . .	222,730	73,624	33.06	49,817	67.66
1901–1902 . . .	227,500	73,624	32.36	49,817	67.66
1902–1903 . . .	230,830	72,249	31.30	53,605	74.19
1903–1904 . . .	230,830	72,249	31.30	53,605	74.19
1904–1905 . . .	238,827	67,387	28.22	46,201	68.56
1905–1906 . . .	238,827	67,387	28.22	46,201	68.56
1906–1907 . . .	247,331	76,703	31.01	53,692	70.00
1907–1908 . . .	250,896	82,367	32.83	59,125	71.78
1908–1909 . . .	257,058	82,286	32.01	57,386	69.74

EAST BATON ROUGE:

There are 23 Negro and 29 white schools. In the rural districts the term of the colored schools is only four months but in the city it is nine months, the same as the white schools. The colored schools have seven grades while the white have eleven. There are 20 Negro teachers and 84 white. There are 11 Negro teachers with first grade, 6 with second grade and 3 with third grade certificates, and 79 white teachers with first grade and 5 with second grade certificates. The amount spent annually on white schools is $42,800 and on the colored, $3,700. Nine hundred and thirty Negro children and 1,829 white attend school regularly. In general the condition of Negro public school education is very poor.

GRANT COUNTY:

The length of the colored school term is two months; of the white from nine to ten months. The colored schools run to seven grades. The white schools run thru the high school course. There are 5 colored and 75 white teachers. The salaries of the colored teachers run from $25 to $35 and those of the whites from $40 to $150. Only $1,000 are spent annually on the colored schools, while the white schools receive from $60,000 to $80,000.

Five hundred colored children attend school regularly and from 1,500 to 2,000 whites. The school facilities for the colored are the same as they were ten years ago with one exception, where the improvement has been made by the colored people themselves. The white schools are much better with regard to equipment and the addition of high schools and colleges. The colored schools receive no part of the school tax. In a few cases there are private schools for the colored which are inefficient, and in only one case do the colored people supplement the school term. The general condition of Negro public school education is very poor indeed.

ORLEANS PARISH:

There are 14 colored and 70 white schools (elementary). The school term for both the white and colored is nine months. The colored have six grades and the white eight. There are 115 colored teachers and about 1,000 white. The colored teachers receive from $40 to $60 and the white from $45 to $70. The white principals receive much higher salaries than the colored. The amount appropriated annually for the salaries of white teachers is $717,240 and for the colored $53,703.95.

The average attendance of the colored children is 4,222 and of the white 21,523. The educational facilities are very little better than they were ten years ago. The colored people support many schools of their own and in many cases supplement the school term by three or four months. The city is doing very little toward bettering conditions of Negro education. Were it not for the denominational and private schools the educational facilities for Negro children would be meagre indeed.

SABINE COUNTY:

There are 27 colored and 80 white schools. The term of the colored schools is from three to six months and of the white from four to eight months. Both the white and colored schools have eleven grades. There are about 41 white and 150 colored teachers, the colored receiving from $30 to $55 and the white from $40 to $125. The general condition of Negro education is fairly good compared with other counties.

In 1900 about one-fifth of the Negro children of Louisiana were in regular attendance upon the public schools whose annual length was reported as six months. In 1909 the attendance was twenty-two (22.32) per cent and the annual term length was 92.6 days. The following summary of school statistics is compiled from the biennial report of the state superintendent of public education of Louisiana for 1908-09:

Louisiana

Expenditures	1908	1909
Whites	....	....
Negroes	....	....
Total	$3,604,992.63	$3,932,939.20

Number of Schools

Whites	3,178	2,315
Negroes	1,119	897
Total	4,297	3,212

Number of Teachers

Whites	5,269	4,865
Negroes	1,287	1,185
Total	6,556	6,050

Average Monthly Salaries

Whites (male)	$78.89	$75.01
Whites (female)	54.52	51.84
Negroes (male)	29.75	32.84
Negroes (female)	26.34	28.13

Length of Term	1908	1909
Whites	156 days	156 days
Negroes	96 days	92.6 days

Enrollment

Whites	172,694	176,479
Negroes	82,367	82,367
Total	255,061	258,846

Per Cent of School Population Enrolled

Whites	62.8	64.51
Negroes	37.1	32.64

Average Attendance

Whites	120,188	111,166
Negroes	59,125	54,724

The following school statistics are taken from the official report of the Department of Education of the state of Louisiana for the year July 1, 1909, to July 1, 1910.   The census population of Louisiana for 1910 was:

Whites 941,125
Negroes 713,874

School Statistics—Louisiana

July 1, 1909=July 1, 1910

Disbursements

Teachers' salaries, white $2,404,062.54	Total number of teachers employed, colored male	426
Teachers' salaries, colored . . . 202,251.13		
Total number of teachers employed, white male 921	Total number of teachers employed, colored female	859
Total number of teachers employed, white female 4,080		

Certificates Issued by Virtue of Examination

First grade, white 511	Second grade, colored	127
Second grade, white 605	Third grade, colored	384
Third grade, white 429		
	Total number of certificates issued, first, second and third	546
Total number of certificates issued, first, second and third 1,545		
First grade, colored 35	Total number of certificates issued to white and colored	2,091

Average Monthly Salary of Teachers

White, male $75.29	Average salary of white teachers, both male and female	$56.16
White, female 50.80		
Colored, male 34.25	Average salary of colored teachers, both male and female	29.87
Colored, female 28.67		

Enrollment and Attendance

Average length of session of high schools, in months 8.82	Per cent of educable children enrolled, white	75.9
Average length of session of elementary schools, white 7.64	Per cent of educable children enrolled, colored	45.3
Average length of session of elementary and high schools, white . . . 8.23	Per cent of children attending school, based on enrollment, white	70.3
Average length of session of elementary schools, colored 4.6	Per cent of children attending school, based on enrollment, colored	68.3
Enrolled in high schools, male . . . 4,142	Per cent of children attending school, based on educables, white	53.1
Enrolled in high schools, female . . 5,629	Per cent of children attending school, based on educables, colored	36.8
Male and female 9,771	
Enrolled in elementary schools, white male 89,632	Average monthly cost of each child, based on average attendance, white . $ 2.90
Enrolled in elementary schools, white female 85,352	Average monthly cost of each child, based on average attendance, colored	1.21
Male and female 174,984	Average monthly cost of each child, based on enrollment, white	2.00
Enrolled in high and elementary schools, white, male and female . . 184,755	Average monthly cost of each child, based on enrollment, colored	.82
Enrolled in elementary schools, colored, male 36,800	

Value of School Property

Value of all school houses, sites and furniture, white $6,503,019.57

Value of all school houses, sites and furniture, colored 273,147.50

Value of all school libraries, white 104,500.68

Value of all school libraries, colored 2,503.90

Value of all school wagonettes in the state, white 21,624.95

Value of all office fixtures in the state, white 15,270.25

Approximate value of sixteenth sections owned by parishes . . $ 867,966.00

Total value of school property, white 7,539,145.45

Total value of school property, colored 266,281.40

Total value of all school property $7,805,926.85

School Houses

Schools having one teacher, white . . 1,559

Schools having one teacher, colored . . 1,005

Schools having two teachers, white . . 367

Schools having two teachers, colored . 87

Schools having three teachers, white . 99

Schools having three teachers, colored . 15

Schools having four teachers, white . . 64

Schools having four teachers, colored . 8

Schools having five or more teachers, white 211

Schools having five or more teachers, colored 12

Brick school houses owned by parishes, white 111

Brick school houses owned by parishes, colored 3

Frame school houses owned by parishes, white 1,717

Frame school houses owned by parishes, colored 156

Houses rented by parish boards, white . 34

Houses rented by parish boards, colored 13

Houses furnished free to parish boards, white 435

Houses furnished free to parish boards, colored 672

Houses used this session, white . . . 2,352

Houses used this session, colored . . . 1,043

Houses built this session, white 141

Houses built this session, colored . 10

Cost of sites and houses, including furniture, built this session, white . . . . $ 631,403.53

Cost of sites and houses, including furniture, built this session, colored 4,272.96

Expended for libraries this session, white 10,047.73

Expended for libraries this session, colored 80.00

Total number of volumes in all libraries, white 203,912

Total number of volumes in all libraries, colored 3,755

Total number of volumes bought this session, white 19,348

Total number of volumes bought this session, colored 258

Number of school houses supplied with patent desks, white . 1,826

Number of school houses supplied with patent desks, colored 72

Number of school houses not supplied with patent desks, white 530

Number of school houses not supplied with patent desks, colored 749

According to the census reports of the last four decades Negro illiteracy for Louisiana has been as follows:

PER CENT OF ILLITERACY

	1870	1880	1890	1900
Louisiana	85.9	79.1	72.1	61.1

Section 18. Texas

The constitution of Texas, adopted near the close of 1869, provided that the legislature shall "make suitable provisions for the support and maintenance of a system of free public schools for the gratuitous instruction of all the inhabitants of this state, between the ages of 6 and 18 years." It also provided the basis of an ample school fund and for district taxation for school purposes. The difficulties encountered by this free school system were many. The report of the United States Bureau of Education for 1880 says:

> The free school system instituted in 1870 under the constitution of 1868 encountered the strong prejudices then prevailing in the South against northern methods and laws that bore traces of their northern stamp. These prejudices were especially intense against including the Negro population among those entitled to free schooling by the state, and against local taxes for the maintenance of any schools. Hence there were in the first years, besides the burning of the school houses for colored people and a social ostracism of the teachers, efforts to prevent, by legal processes, the collection of the local tax for educating either white or colored youth.
>
> In spite of these hindrances the new school officers worked on. A better feeling on the part of many of the people soon came to aid their efforts, and the record of the first three years showed a substantial gain. For the next two years there was a superintendency, more of the soil, and hence in better favor with the people, under which some advance was made. But opposition was not silenced, and in 1875, 1876 and afterwards it showed its strength by breaking down the reconstruction constitution of 1868, by the obliteration of the school system founded on it, and by the institution of a wholly new one, which made the opening of schools in any community entirely voluntary; made attendance on them, if established, likewise wholly so; did away with the supervision of educated officers; shortened from twelve years to six years the ordinary time for free schooling by the state; allowed this to be shortened still more by permitting communities to use a year's school funds for a school house instead of for teaching; and, except in cities and towns, made no provision for allowing even those who wished to do so, to tax themselves for the extension of their educational advantages beyond mere elementary studies and a four months' annual term of school. This is the system that in 1880 still existed, but which had so demonstrated its inherent weaknesses that the chief state officers were urging its improvement.

Finally, a system was organized which gave the state a commendable educational scheme. At present the state board of education consists of the governor, the comptroller, the secretary of state and the state superintendent of public instruction. The state has a large school fund from the vast endowment of public land. The school law provides as follows:

All available public school funds of this state shall be appropriated in each county for the education alike of white and colored children, and impartial provisions shall be made for both races.[1]

The following table of school statistics for the state of Texas is compiled from the annual reports of the United States Bureau of Education:

TEXAS

YEAR	School population, colored	Enrollment	Per cent enrolled	Daily attendance	Per cent of enrollment attending
1899–1900	250,860	126,538	50.46	83,904	66.28
1900–1901	224,350	136,556	60.87	89,012	65.18
1901–1902	227,660	144,362	63.41	91,016	63.05
1902–1903	234,655	142,075	60.54	88,718	62.44
1903–1904	240,689	141,805	58.91	92,157	64.99
1904–1905	246,490	146,161	59.29	94,605	64.73
1905–1906	246,490	146,161	59.29	94,605	64.73
1906–1907	252,301	142,416	56.44	91,229	64.73
1907–1908 . . .	264,208	150,121	56.82	90,277	60.14
1908–1909	271,579	152,038	55.97	93,035	62.50

BEXAR COUNTY:

The general condition of Negro education here is poor because of short terms, poor buildings and poor equipments. In the city it is in excellent condition.

BRAZOS COUNTY:

There are 1 Negro town school and 40 county schools. Six teachers in the town and 41 in the county. Salaries vary from $40 to $80, from a third to a half lower than those of whites. About 400 enrolled in the city, over 1,200 in the county schools. None unable to get in on account of lack of facilities. Eleven grades in city, five to eight grades in country school. The building in the city is good; in the county the buildings are fair. In some cases the country schools are taught in the Negro church houses. Negroes in the county have contributed money for the purchase of school sites and the building of school houses.

Under the supervision of an efficient county superintendent our schools have taken on new life and are partly fulfilling the purpose for which they were established. They are introducing as rigidly as possible the modern features of the best schools in the country.

HARRIS COUNTY:

There are 45 districts, many of which have two or three schools; many of the white schools having two or three teachers. As a rule the white schools have eight months and most of the colored six. Some of the colored schools have been known to have no term at all. Very little

---

[1] School Laws of Texas. Section 66.

attention is paid to the grading of the colored schools, but the whites fare better as more teachers are allowed them.

The colored teachers receive from $25 to $60 per month and the whites from $45 to $70. Principals of both races get more. There is great improvement in the facilities of the white schools but the colored schools show very little improvement.

Aside from a few feeble private schools the colored people have only Houston College. They do not supplement the school term.

MILAM COUNTY:

There are 40 Negro schools with 50 teachers. Salaries $40 to $65, which is about two-thirds the salary of the white teachers. The city schools have twelve grades and county schools seven grades. Buildings in town are fair but poor in the country. The Negroes help to support a private school and have contributed money to extend the school term in this county.

NAVARRO COUNTY:

The white schools have a term of six months and the colored schools about five. There is a considerable improvement in the white school. The colored schools are not doing much.

TARRANT COUNTY:

There are 15 colored and 80 white schools. The colored schools have a term of from three to six months and the whites four to ten. Both have eleven grades. The colored teachers receive an average salary of $40 and the whites an average of $75. The annual appropriation ranges from $5.50 to $6.25 per capita. The facilities are fifty per cent better than they were ten years ago. Under the separate school system the Negro schools may be considered as doing as good work as the system will permit.

TRAVIS COUNTY:

The average length of the school term is seven months and the schools of both races run to eleven grades. The white teachers are generally well educated and the colored teachers generally have second or third grade certificates. An effort is being made to compel all to have first grade certificates. The colored teachers receive $40 or less per month and the whites from $75 to $100.

The annual appropriation is about $80,000. Two thousand four hundred colored and 6,400 white children attend school regularly. The school facilities are much improved. The colored schools receive practically none of the special school tax. In general the Negro public school education is at a low ebb because while the value of education is recognized few are willing to tax themselves. They support with some enthusiasm the church schools.

VICTORIA COUNTY:

There are 1 city and 9 county schools. Eleven teachers in the town and 9 in the county. Salaries range from $30 to $70. Five hundred and forty children are enrolled; none unable to get in because of lack of facilities. Eleven grades in the city and seven in the county. The Negro school at Victoria is a two-story brick building with ten rooms and compares favorably with the best Negro school building anywhere. The Negroes in this county help to support private schools.

WILLIAMSON COUNTY:

There are 13 Negro schools and 22 teachers. The average salary is $40, about two-thirds that of the whites. About 1,300 children enrolled. About twenty-five per cent of the scholastic population unable to get into school because of a lack of facilities. Ten grades where graded. Buildings in the town fair or good, in the country poor. Negroes have contributed to buy a school site and build a house. The Negro schools in this county need improvement: better buildings, furniture, salaries, efficient teachers.

City Systems

Dallas[1]

Scholastic Census, May, 1910		Average Daily Attendance	
Whites	12,890	Whites	8,000
Negroes	3,706	Negroes	1,703
Total	16,596	Total	9,703

Enrollment		Number of Schools	
Whites	10,670	Whites	19
Negroes	2,511	Negroes	6
Total	13,181	Total	25

Average Number Belonging		Number of Teachers	
Whites	8,700	Whites	294
Negroes	1,944	Negroes	61
Total	10,644	Total	355

Salaries, White

Principal high school	(a) $2,400, (b) $1,800
Principal grade schools	$1,200 to 1,800
Teachers high school	1,200 to 1,800
Supervisor of music	1,500
Supervisor of penmanship and drawing	1,500

Teachers Elementary Schools

One year's experince	$55
Two years' experience	60
Three years' experience	65
And so on to a maximum	85
Probationary teachers	40

---

[1] Compiled from the Thirteenth Biennial Report of the Public Schools of Dallas, Tex.

Salaries, Negroes

Principal of high school (who shall be also inspector of Negro schools)	$135
Principal of Wright Cuney School	80
Principal of Booker T. Washington School	95
Principal of Fred Douglass School	100
Principal of Pacific Avenue School	80
Principal of Ninth Ward School	80
High school teachers	$75 to 85
Supervisor of penmanship, drawing and music	85

Teachers in Elementary Schools

One year's or less experience	$ 40
Two years' experience	43
Three years' experience	46
And so on to a maximum of	70
Probationary teacher	30

Length of session	180 days

Per Capita Cost

White high schools	$ 47.00
Negro high school	36.00
White elementary schools	26.00
Negro elementary schools	19.00

Value of School Property

Whites	$ 1,115,030
Negroes	70,985
Total	$ 1,186,015

Houston

The following extracts are taken from a recent report of the superintendent of schools for the city of Houston:

The superintendent feels that this report would not be even measurably complete if it were to be closed without some special reference to the work done in our colored schools. So many and so varied opinions are held on the subject of the education of the Negro, that the public is entitled to have a clear report as to the results being obtained from it. On the principle that the best way to judge the quality of a carload of apples is to taste a number of apples selected at random from the car, it is my purpose to tell some four or five true stories of the work done in our colored schools and let you judge of the schools by these examples.

First story. This is the story of Nicodemus:

Readers of our local papers are familiar with the name of Nicodemus, or used to be. He was not exactly a headliner, but his name was formerly good for a few inches of space in the police columns almost any day. By the time he was twelve years old he was a professional jail bird. He was a petty thief, housebreaker and general juvenile offender. Incidentally he didn't know A from B. He was too young to send to the penitentiary and too bad to leave out of it. Our juvenile court law had gone just far enough to make it impossible to do anything with him. He had been arrested repeatedly, jailed and turned loose again. The officers were hopefully awaiting the time when he would be old enough to send to the penitentiary.

While matters were in this condition it came about one day that the teachers of the ―― School became interested in Nicodemus. They asked why he did not go to school. He told them that he had once tried to enter one of our colored schools and had been refused admittance on account of his general record as an undesirable. They told him that the ―― School would be glad to take him and to keep him so long as he behaved himself. Nicodemus decided that the experiment might be worth trying; at any rate he didn't see how it could make matters much worse with him. The result was that he secured a primer and entered the low first grade along with the little tots who were just starting. They knew as much as he did, about books at any rate.

He not only started but he stuck. It caused a mild sensation among colored circles when it was learned that Nicodemus had been in school a month and had not burned the school house down or stolen it. The man for whom he did odd jobs, in return for which he was given a place to sleep, was one of the first to notice the change and to comment upon it. The superintendent heard of it and began to take a little friendly interest in Nicodemus. He sent word that when the boy could read every lesson in the book he would give him another. That book was soon called for and was delivered with the word that when this was finished there would be another one sent. Soon after the superintendent heard him read the last lesson in this book and gave him another with the inscription: "To Nicodemus. As a reward for good conduct."

This inscription seemed to please Nicodemus tho the idea was rather a novel one to him. It was probably about the first time he had ever been told that his conduct was good. He spoke of these books as "the ones the boss man gave me."

When Nicodemus was forced on account of sickness to be absent a day from school he anxiously sent word as to the cause lest his teacher might think he had gone back to his old ways. In one year's time he has been transformed from an incorrigible thief and jail bird to an industrious, hard-working Negro boy. One excellent feature is that he is not proud of his past record. He has even dug up another name which he says is his right one. He refuses to be known any longer as Nicodemus. I do not give his new name because it is not right that he should be embarrassed by his past. I predict that he will make a useful, intelligent, industrious man of his race. . . . . If our colored schools can work such changes with boys like Nicodemus, they are worth all we are paying for them and more. Incidentally, it may be added, that the money the state would have paid out in trying Nicodemus, convicting him, sending him to the penitentiary and keeping him there off and on thruout the term of his natural life would pay the expense of maintaining the ―― School for quite a time to come.

Story Two. This is the story of Lettie Smith. I do not know that I can tell it better than by quoting the exact words of a personal letter which I received last winter from a Houston lady of culture and refinement:

"I think that as superintendent of the Houston schools you would perhaps be interested if I were to tell you some of the things I have noticed about Lettie Smith, the little colored girl who now works for me as nurse and house girl. She is a pupil of the high third grade at the —— School.

"My attention was first called to her school work by the respectful manner in which she spoke of her teacher and her childish longing for school. Next I found her recognizing the portraits of Longfellow, Whittier and other American poets, which she saw on the walls of our library. She would tell little stories of their childhood which she said she had read at school. She noticed some raffia mats that I have and readily told how and of what they are made. She often sings little patriotic songs to the baby and tries to teach her rhymes and memory gems. She usually gets good grades on her report cards, and she says she can't bear to hear children 'mouth' over their reading.

"She has evidently had a good, earnest, sensible teacher. It is remarkable to me that the public schools are doing so well for the colored children. . . . . I think that Lettie compares at least fairly well in advancement with the average white child of her age and grade."

The fact that an educated Houston woman, a housekeeper and the wife of one of Houston's good citizens, thot it worth while to write the superintendent this letter speaks well, not only for her own kind heartedness and appreciation, but also for the work our colored schools are doing.

*   *   *   *   *   *   *   *   *   *

Story Four. This also will be told only in briefest outline. It is about one of our colored teachers, who told me that she expected to raise $100 to help establish some form of industrial work at her building. The climax of the story is that after continued effort she raised it. She did so by a number of concerts, musical entertainments, etc., gotten up chiefly with the help of the children, given for an admittance fee of ten cents. It takes quite a time to raise $100 in ten-cent sums, but this Negro woman accomplished it. It must have been a cause of heaven helping them who help themselves. She remarked to me last year that if the school board would, next year, give her enough equipment to teach laundry work she would be glad to teach it. I most heartily recommend that the equipment be provided.

Such stories as these could be continued indefinitely. I could tell of the woman who teaches Latin in the colored high school. In order to prepare herself better for her work some years ago she resigned her position, went abroad and used the little money she had saved up in spending a year in Rome and studying. How many white teachers could or would have accomplished this feat?

Of course there is another side to this picture. Not all of our Negro teachers are as intelligent or as faithful as those mentioned. Some of them hold low grade certificates and are not deeply interested in their work. It is impossible to obtain all of high grade. There are not enough of this kind to go around. Even the best of them work under marked disadvantages. . . . . It is my firm opinion that our Negro teachers, working under many very adverse circumstances, are doing faithful, earnest work, are making an honest effort to help their race and are reaching results that are abundantly worth all that is paid for their schools.

Salaries—Grade Teachers

	Whites	Negroes
First year	$ 45	$ 40
Second year	50	45
Third year	55	50
Fourth year	60	50
Fifth year	65	50
Sixth year		55
Seventh year	75	60
Eighth year	80	. . .
Ninth year	85	. . .
Supernumeraries	20	15

Ward Principals—White Schools

In buildings of less than six rooms the salary is set by the board in each instance.

In buildings of six or seven rooms the principals are paid for their first, second and third years $1,000, $1,100 and $1,200, respectively.

In buildings of eight rooms and more the principal is paid $1,200 for the first year, $1,300 for the second, $1,400 for the third and $1,500 for the fourth year, $1,600 for the fifth year and each year thereafter.

High School Principal—White School

The high school principal is paid $2,200 for a year of nine months.

Women teachers are paid $85 a month for the first year and thereafter are raised $5 each year until the fourth year, when they receive $100, which is their maximum.

Heads of departments in the high school receive $300 a year in addition to these rates.

Ward Principals—Negro Schools

Two-room building	$ 65
Four-room building	75
Six-room building	80
For each additional room, per year	15

High School—Negro

Principal	$105
Vice-principal	75
First assistant	70
Second assistant	60

In 1900 thirty-one (30.88) per cent of the Negro population, 5 to 18 years of age, were in regular attendance upon the public schools of Texas. In 1909 the attendance had advanced to thirty-four (34.25) per cent.

The following table of statistics is compiled from the seventeenth biennial report of the Department of Education of the state of Texas:

Total Expenditures

	1908-09	1909-10
Whites		
Negroes		
Total	$9,938,993.41	$10,850,923.27

Number of Schools

Whites	9,894	10,072
Negroes	2,454	2,409
Total	12,348	12,481

Number of Teachers

Whites	16,893	18,062
Negroes	3,205	3,215
Total	20,098	21,277

Length of Term

Whites	135.20 days	138.82 days
Negroes	132.05 days	135.07 days

Salaries

	1908-09	1909-10
Whites	$ 61.25	$ 62.07
Negroes	48.09	46.34

Scholastic Population

Whites	727,257	756,770
Negroes	187,371	192,236
Total	914,628	949,006

Enrollment

Whites	625,132	664,804
Negroes	145,653	156,827
Total	770,785	821,631

Average Attendance

Whites	423,398	664,804
Negroes	89,460	156,827
Total	512,858	821,631

According to the census reports of the last four decades Negro illiteracy for Texas has been as follows:

PER CENT OF ILLITERACY

	1870	1880	1890	1900
Texas	88.7	75.4	52.5	38.2

Section 19. Arkansas

Several special laws for the establishment of schools in Arkansas were passed between 1840 and 1843. In the latter year a general law was passed, entitled "An Act to Establish a System of Common Schools in the State of Arkansas." In 1866 the state legislature passed the first law for free schools based on taxation of the people. This law provided thall all white children between the ages of 6 and 21 years should be entitled to the provision of the law, thus excluding Negro children.[1] Another section provided for the election of a superintendent of public instruction.

"The gain of this law of March 1, 1867, was: first, schools based on the taxed wealth of the state; second, the state

[1] Twentieth Biennial Report of the Superintendent of Public Instruction of Arkansas, p. 27.

superintendent of public instruction, and third, a county school commissioner for each county. Its weakness was a limitation to the white children and the tax limitation to two mills on the dollar.''[1] The reconstruction constitution of 1867 made it obligatory upon the General Assembly to establish and maintain a system of free schools for all persons in the state between the ages of 5 and 21 years and provided for an unlimited levy upon the taxable property of the state for the support of these schools. Thus the limitation was removed from Negro children.[2]

Mr. J. C. Corbin, a Negro graduate of Oberlin, was state superintendent of public instruction for Arkansas from 6 January, 1873, to 30 October, 1874.

The following table of school statistics for the state of Arkansas is compiled from the annual reports of the United States Bureau of Education:

ARKANSAS

YEAR	School population, colored	Enrollment	Per cent enrolled	Daily attendance	Per cent of enrollment attending
1899–1900 . . .	130,740	84,317	64.49	52,656	62.45
1900–1901 . . .	125,066	84,481	67.55	53,011	62.75
1901–1902 . . .	127,120	90,109	70.88	56,290	62.47
1902–1903 . . .	128,458	87,895	68.42	54,147	61.60
1903–1904 . . .	130,148	90,437	69.48	58,177	64.33
1904–1905 . . .	131,871	87,125	66.07	53,329	61.21
1905–1906 . .	133,594	90,185	67.50	54,564	60.50
1906–1907 . . .	135,317	88,255	65.22	55,083	62.41
1907–1908 . . .	137,124	94,292	68.76	59,087	62.66
1908–1909 . . .	145,325	98,755	67.95	59,597	60.35

PHILLIPS COUNTY:

There are about 150 colored schools and 40 white. The average length of the term of the colored school is six months per year and the white schools eight months. The rural colored schools have five grades and those in the villages eight. There are four eight grade schools. All the white schools have seven grades and one or two nine.

There are 160 colored teachers and 40 white, the colored teachers receiving an average salary of $40 and the whites $60 per month. The class of work seems higher than it was ten years ago. The length of the terms and the salaries are about the same.

[1] Twentieth Biennial Report of the Superintendent of Public Instruction of Arkansas, p. 32.
[2] Ibid, p. 32.

A special school tax is laid of which the colored people pay about one-half, altho the ratio of white children to colored is about 1 to 5.

In the uplands the school system is good. The village schools there are carefully graded and are doing splendid work. At Trenton, Marvell, Helena and Poplar Grove pupils finish yearly from the seventh or eighth grade, and the majority are able to make the second grade teacher's certificate which requires an average of seventy-five per cent on nine English branches. In the lowlands the prospect is not so good. The schools in their general management are controlled often by those unfriendly to intellectual training for the Negro; the selection of teachers, etc., is less a matter of care, with the resulting conditions.

In 1900 thirty-seven (36.77) per cent of the colored children of Arkansas, or less than two in every five, were in regular attendance upon the public schools whose average annual length was less than 70 days. In 1909 the attendance had advanced to forty-one per cent and the annual length to 94 days.

The following summary of school statistics is compiled from the twentieth biennial report of the superintendent of public instruction of the state of Arkansas:

Expenditures	1907	1908
Whites		
Negroes		
Total	$2,413,767.85	$2,537,122.43

Number of Schools		
Whites		
Negroes		
Total	5,714	5,411

Number of Teachers		
Whites	6,462	6,681
Negroes	1,651	1,616
Total	8,113	8,297

Length of Term		
Average	93.32 days	93.95 days

Salaries	1907	1908
Average	$ 38.02	$ 38.80

Scholastic Population		
Whites	381,779	386,976
Negroes	152,044	157,543
Total	533,843	544,519

Enrollment		
Whites	258,614	271,762
Negroes	89,538	94,292
Total	348,152	366,054

Average Attendance		
Whites	165,538	173,583
Negroes	55,083	59,087
Total	220,621	232,670

According to the census reports of the last four decades Negro illiteracy for Arkansas has been as follows:

PER CENT OF ILLITERACY

	1870	1880	1890	1900
Arkansas	81.2	75.0	53.6	43.0

Section 20. Tennessee

The public school system of Tennessee was firmly established by an Act of 1873. At present the system is under the control of a state superintendent, nominated by the governor and confirmed by the senate, county superintendents elected by the county courts, and district officers. The state board of education consists of the governor, the state superintendent and six members appointed by the governor.

The following table of school statistics for the state of Tennessee is compiled from the annual reports of the United States Bureau of Education:

TENNESSEE

YEAR	School population, colored	Enrollment	Per cent enrolled	Daily attendance	Per cent of enrollment attending
1899–1900	174,510	100,705	57.70	67,904	67.42
1900–1901	156,103	100,705	64.51	67,904	67.42
1901–1902	157,885	106,747	67.61	71,779	67.24
1902–1903	161,919	99,234	61.29	68,331	68.86
1903–1904	163,926	101,811	62.12	69,621	68.39
1904–1905	165,881	102,288	61.66	71,151	69.56
1905–1906	167,836	101,863	60.70	72,791	71.46
1906–1907	167,836	101,863	60.70	72,791	71.46
1907–1908	171,801	97,453	56.72	66,798	68.54
1908–1909	167,532	100,248	59.83	83,536	24.15

GILES COUNTY:

There are 39 colored and 74 white schools, each having a term of six months. Each has five grades in the rural districts and eleven in the city. There are about 50 colored and 100 white teachers. The colored teachers receive from $25 to $30 per month and the whites from $30 to $112.50. About $35,000 is spent annually for all schools and only one-third of that amount goes to the colored schools. The total number of pupils attending schools is 11,500, and of colored 4,543. The facilities are fifty per cent better than they were ten years ago. About one-third of the special school tax goes to the colored schools. The colored people support a small private school by paying tuition where about 20 pupils attend.

HAMILTON COUNTY:

There are 17 county schools for Negroes with 39 teachers. The school term is eight months. Average salaries of these teachers are: male $68.43, female $44.21, about three-fourths those of the whites. There are 1,770 Negro children enrolled in the county schools. The buildings are in good condition.

Chattanooga

Chattanooga has three Negro schools with 45 teachers. The term is 9 months long. About 2,263 Negro children are enrolled. The teachers' salaries are: Negro principals $85 to $135 per month, white principals $100 to $200; Negro high school teachers $50 to $80, white high school teachers $65 to $100; Negro primary and grammar teachers $30 to $55, whites $35 to $75. The buildings are good.

In 1900 forty-one (40.9) per cent of the Negro children of Tennessee were in regular attendance upon the public schools whose average annual length was 89 days. In 1909 the attendance had advanced to fifty (49.86) per cent.

The following table of school statistics is compiled from the biennial report of the superintendent of public instruction of Tennessee for the scholastic years 1909 and 1910:

Expenditures			Term Length (All Schools)		
	1909	1910		1909	1910
Whites.	. . . .	. . .	Counties	120 days	121 days
Negroes.	. . . .	. . .	Cities	178 days	180 days
Total.	$3,404,555.17	$4,402,574.40	General average	128 days	130 days

Number of Schools			Scholastic Population		
Whites	5,683	5,821	Whites	587,088	578,287
Negroes.	1,406	1,422	Negroes.	184,646	188,562
Total	7,089	7,243	Total	771,734	766,849

Number of Teachers			Enrollment		
Whites	8,763	8,466	Whites	411,910	423,947
Negroes.	1,687	1,820	Negroes.	100,248	97,806
Total	10,450	10,286	Total	512,158	521,753

Average Salaries			Average Attendance		
Counties.	$ 39.05	$ 39.25	Whites	274,377	293,487
Cities	54.27	55.00	Negroes.	68,358	70,466
General average	$ 40.75	$ 40.90	Total	342,735	363,953

According to the census reports of the last four decades Negro illiteracy for Tennessee has been as follows:

PER CENT OF ILLITERACY

	1870	1880	1890	1900
Tennessee	82.4	71.7	54.2	41.6

Section 21. Missouri

The constitution of Missouri declared that "A general diffusion of knowledge and intelligence being essential to the preservation of the rights and liberties of the people, the

general assembly shall establish and maintain free schools
for the gratuitous instruction of all persons in this state
between the ages of 5 and 21 years.'' The first general act
upon the subject was passed in 1824 and improved in 1835.
The next few years saw several new laws and revisions. The
constitution of 1865 and the enactments of the following year
made good schools possible for both whites and Negroes, and
the movement was strengthened by the new constitution of
1874.

The report of the United States commissioner of education
for 1870 says:[1]

This state has a larger proportion of schools for colored children than
any former slave state. . . . . Opposition to the education of the
colored people is rapidly disappearing. Their rapid improvement and
good conduct help to disarm prejudice.

The report speaks as follows of Lincoln Institute, a school
for the training of Negro youth:[2]

Lincoln Institute owes its origin to the liberality of colored soldiers
enlisted from Missouri. In the spring of 1866 a subscription of $4,000
was made by the enlisted men of the Sixty-second United States colored
infantry, to aid in the foundation of an educational institution in Missouri
for the especial benefit of the colored people. Afterward another colored
Missouri regiment added to it the sum of $1,325; and $2,000 were subsequently received from the Freedmen's Bureau.

The school laws of Missouri provide for the education of
all the children and require that the school privileges accorded
the colored children shall be equal those enjoyed by the white
children.

The establishment of a colored school in some old tumble-down shed
of a building, with little or no furniture, and situated in a remote and
inaccessible part of the district, while the white children in the same
district are provided with a comfortable well-furnished school building,
does not comply with the spirit of this law. Instances have been reported
in which it is claimed that the enumerator returned a false enumeration
in order to avoid the establishment of a school for the colored children.
In doing this, the enumerator not only violated his oath of office, but is
guilty of a misdemeanor, punishable by a fine of $100. [3]

[1]Report of United States Commissioner of Education, 1870, page 202.
[2] Ibid, page 204.
[3] Revised School Laws of Missouri, 1909 and 1911, page 24, note.

The law further provides that the expense of maintaining colored schools shall be paid in the same manner and out of the same funds drawn upon for the maintenance of the white schools.

The supervision of public instruction in Missouri is vested in the state board of education, consisting of the governor, the secretary of state, the attorney-general and the state superintendent of schools. Local matters concerning education are under the control of county superintendents and district directors.

The following table of school statistics for the state of Missouri is compiled from the annual reports of the United States Bureau of Education:

MISSOURI

YEAR	School population, colored	Enrollment	Per cent enrolled	Daily attendance	Per cent of enrollment attending
1899–1900 . . .	55,420	34,540	62.32	23,001	66.59
1900–1901 . . .	45,295	32,511	71.78	22,031	67.76
1901–1902 . . .	45,971	31,360	68.22	21,079	67.22
1902–1903 . . .	46,459	31,257	67.28	20,191	64.60
1903–1904 . . .	47,121	32,745	69.49	20,173	61.50
1904–1905 . . .	47,736	32,234	67.53	20,432	63.39
1905–1906 . . .	48,350	33,070	68.40	22,580	68.28
1906–1907 . . .	48,965	32,796	67.23	22,190	68.28
1907–1908 . . .	49,647	29,937	60.30	21,931	73.26
1908–1909 . . .	47,131	30,406	64.54	24,205	4.88 *

* Evidently an error. Should be 79.60.

St. Louis

The city of St. Louis is offering excellent advantages to its Negro children. There are nine district schools and also a high school. The high school is a new building of excellent construction and modern equipment. Its contract price was $297,827 and its equipment is listed at $69,-307.91. Negro teachers are paid according to the same schedule as the white teachers.

As a means of holding the children in school, a scheme of scholarship aid has been in use for four years. The scheme provides for the payment of a weekly wage to the parents of the child whose services are needed in the support of the family, upon a satisfactory report of the teacher regarding the child's attendance, scholarship and conduct during the week. In granting this scholarship aid "there is no discrimination on account of creed or color."[1]

The following statistics are taken from the Report of the Board of Education of St. Louis for 1909-1910 :

[1] Report of Board of Education, St. Louis, 1909-1910, page 191.

Cost	1910
White	$ 2,247,517.51
Negro	171,562.12
Total cost	$ 2,419,079.63

Scholastic Population

Whites	187,886
Negroes	8,080
Total	195,966

Enrollment (Day Schools)

Whites	91,844
Negroes	6,698
Total	98,542

Number of Teachers

Whites	2,010
Negroes	172
Total	2,182

Salaries (Principals and Teachers)

Whites	$ 1,578,949.05
Negroes	117,778.65
Total	$ 1,696,727.70

Average Membership per Teacher

High School

White	23
Negro	20

District School

White	43
Negro	34

Kindergarten

White	36
Negro	38

Expenditure per capita of pupils
enrolled . . . . $ 48.78

Columbia

Columbia has two schools for Negroes, enrolling during the last year 418 pupils under nine teachers. The salaries of the teachers vary from $40 to $65 for the assistant teachers and $100 for the principal. The schools are doing a good work.

Kansas City

Kansas City, in keeping with other Missouri towns and cities and in accordance with the spirit of the state, is making large provision for the education of its colored children. The city provides twelve ward schools and one high school for Negroes, also an evening school. During the scholastic year ending June 30, 1911, 3,521 Negro children were enrolled in the public schools of the city under 72 teachers. The Negro high school has graduated twenty-five classes, the total number of graduates being 384.

The average cost per pupil in the Negro high school, not including permanent improvements, was $94.16, which is an excellent showing; for the average cost per pupil in all high schools of the city was $76.15. The average cost per pupil in the Negro ward schools ranged from $27.56 to $42.66.[1]

In 1900 twenty-eight per cent of the Negro children of Missouri were in regular attendance upon the public schools whose annual length was 141 days. In 1909 the attendance had advanced to fifty-one (51.33) per cent. The term length in 1910 averaged 155 days.

---

[1] From the Fortieth Annual Report of the Board of Education, Kansas City, Missouri, 1911.

The following table of school statistics is compiled from the sixty-first report of the public schools of Missouri for the school year ending June 30, 1910:

Expenditures		Number of Teachers	
Whites		Whites	17,582
Negroes		Negroes	783
Total	$13,905,188.80	Total	18,365
Enrollment		Number of Schools	
Whites	677,469	Whites	10,415
Negroes	29,562	Negroes	409
Total	707,031	Total	10,824
Average Length of Term		Average Daily Attendance	
All schools . . . . 155 days		All schools	490,374

Average Yearly Salaries
All teachers . . . . $ 442.49

According to the census reports of the last four decades Negro illiteracy for Missouri has been as follows:

PER CENT OF ILLITERACY

	1870	1880	1890	1900
Missouri	72.7	53.9	41.7	28.1

Section 22. Kentucky

The schools of Kentucky are under the control of the state board of education, while local officials have charge of local educational matters. The law provides that graded schools shall be established for all white children within the common school age whenever at least ten legal voters who are tax payers in the school district shall petition for the same. In like manner colored graded schools shall be organized when at least ten colored legal voters make a petition to that effect.

No school shall be deemed a common school or be entitled to any contribution out of the school fund unless it has been actually kept or is under contract to be kept for six or more months. The state has a compulsory school law.

The following table of school statistics for the state of Kentucky is compiled from the annual reports of the United States Bureau of Education:

KENTUCKY

YEAR	School population, colored	Enrollment	Per cent enrolled	Daily attendance	Per cent of enrollment attending
1899-1900	98,490	69,321	70.38	43,074	62.14
1900-1901	86,399	62,934	72.84	40,225	63.92
1901-1902 . . .	87,654	62,975	71.84	40,314	64.02
1902-1903	88,580	62,981	71.10	41,116	65.28
1903-1904	88,580	62,981	71.10	41,116	65.28
1904-1905	88,580	62,981	71.10	41,116	65.28
1905-1906	88,580	62,981	71.10	41,116	65.28
1906-1907	88,580	62,981	71.10	41,116	65.28
1907-1908	94,128	58,319	61.96	36,659	62.86
1908-1909	90,353	58,301	64.52	33,521	57.50

FRANKLIN COUNTY:

School term eight months for both white and colored. Both the white and colored schools have eight grades. There are nine colored and fifty white teachers. The salaries of teachers depend on the number of pupils. Teachers are graded according to the class certificate they hold. The schools are classed as 1st, 2d, 3d, according to number of pupils in the district: 1st class, 75 pupils or more; 2d class, 55 to 74; 3d class, not exceeding 54. Example: If a district has one hundred pupils and the per capita is $4.00, 400÷8=$50.00 per month.

The amount spent annually on white schools is $11,180.40, and on colored schools, $1,446.96.

One thousand two hundred and forty white and 136 colored children attend school regularly.

School facilities are a great deal better than they were ten years ago, both as to buildings and equipments.

Each school district receives its pro rata of school tax according to the number of children of school age. The fund is divided according to the number of each race. The general condition of Negro education is much improved, the grades have been extended from five to eight and the grading has been systematized.

HANCOCK COUNTY:

Tho much improved over what they were ten years ago there is vast room for improvement in the school facilities. The general condition of Negro education is not good owing to the domination of a set of comparatively ignorant trustees. Dishonesty, bribery, unfairness in a large measure have been practiced in many cases where Negroes are in charge, but on the whole conditions are improving.

WARREN COUNTY:

Both white and colored teachers receive from $50 to $67 per month. The average amount spent annually on colored schools is $7,000 and on the white $23,000. Nine hundred colored children are enrolled and 450 attend regularly. There is an enrollment of 4,050 white children with a regular attendance of 2350. The school facilities are 60 per cent better than they were ten years ago. The general condition is above the average.

In 1900 forty-five (44.59) per cent of the Negro children of Kentucky were in regular attendance upon the public schools whose annual length was 115 days. In 1909 the per cent of Negro children in regular attendance upon the schools was but thirty-seven (37.1).

The following summary of school statistics is compiled from the biennial reports of the department of education of the state of Kentucky for 1908-9 and 1910-11:

	Expenditures			
	1907-8	1908-9	1909-10	1910-11
Whites.........	......	......	......	......
Negroes.........	......	......	......	......
Total........	$3,081,616.10	......	$5,779,739.59	$6,150,768.06

	Scholastic Population			
Whites...........	521,392	521,609	652,183	648,073
Negroes...........	65,470	65,551	87,723	85,749
Total.........	586,862	587,160	739,906	733,822

	Enrollment			
Whites...........	381,984	404,803	442,710	501,825
Negroes...........	44,108	44,026	54,064	65,218
Total.........	426,092	448,829	496,774	567,043

	Average Attendance			
Whites............	...	233,389	199,907	245,777
Negroes.........	...	24,054	25,650	27,783
Total...........	...	257,443	225,557	273,560

According to the Census reports of the last four decades Negro illiteracy for Kentucky has been as follows:

PER CENT OF ILLITERACY

	1870	1880	1890	1900
Kentucky	83.8	70.4	55.9	40.1

Section 23.   Superintendents and Teachers

One of the great difficulties in the dual public school system of the South is seen in the lack of intelligent superintendence for the Negro schools. The superintendents are usually elected by white voters. In only a few of the southern states, notably the District of Columbia, West Virginia, Kentucky and Texas, is there any attempt to give the colored people any voice in the direction of the colored school system, either as members of the boards of trustees or as assistant superintendents.   On the whole, then, the colored schools are apt to be neglected.   In addition to this, in many cases there is positive hostility on the part of the school authorities toward the Negro schools. ' For instance, in a meeting of county commissioners in south Georgia in 1906, this resolution was introduced: That whenever two or more colored teachers apply for the same school, it should be the policy of the county commissioner to give the school to the least competent.   This resolution did not pass but it was discussed and strongly supported; and indeed it is the working policy in many of the country districts of the South.

The alarming neglect of and discrimination against the Negro schools are plainly evident to any one who reads the reports of educational officers in the southern states.   For instance, in the state of Mississippi where there were 410,089 educable Negro children and 301,548 educable whites, the report of the state superintendent of education for 1907-8 and 1908-9 makes absolutely no mention of the Negro school system in his narrative report and recommendations.   About the same time (1908) the school superintendent of Butts county, Georgia, said:

So far as I have been able to ascertain every white boy and girl within school age, except three, was enrolled some time during the last year.

The superintendent of Jones county, in the same state, said:

From our experience we are assured it is useless to try to have a longer term than five or six months for the Negroes.   In this county there is no town for them to congregate in; they are entirely agricultural and need their children to chop and pick cotton and will not send regularly longer than the time mentioned.   But we propose to run the white schools full nine months.

The report of Pike county in the state report of Georgia for 1910 says:

We have twenty-nine white schools wholly in the county, besides the public school system in Barnesville, and several line schools in adjoining counties to which some of our children go. We employ in these twenty-nine schools about forty white teachers for the common school grades at an average salary of $50 per month. There are twenty-seven Negro schools with an average attendance of forty pupils each. We pay them an average salary of $20 per month. . . . . . All of our white schools have been supplied with blackboards, charts, maps and globes.

In 1909, the official report of Houston county in Georgia showed the division of school funds as follows:

	Children	Teachers	Amount received
Negro.	3,165	63	$ 4,509.25
White.	1,044	33	10,678.28

The report of the state superintendent of public instruction of Alabama for 1910 shows that in Wilcox county there were 10,758 Negro children of school age and 2,000 white children. During that year the school expenditure in that county was $33,952.45, of which $3,339.70 was spent on the 10,758 Negro children and $30,612.75 was spent on the 2,000 white children. The expenditure for the Negro children in the county was according to these figures less than 32 cents per capita, while for the white children it was about $15.30 per capita. The report further shows that in the seven counties surrounding and touching Wilcox county there were 64,285 Negro children of school age, for whom $47,719.24 was appropriated. These same counties reported 21,841 white children of school age, for whom $224,842.32 was appropriated. The following tabulated report indicates the distribution of this money:[1]

COUNTIES	Negro Children		White Children	
	Population	Apportionment	Population	Apportionment
Monroe	5,107	$ 3,605.08	3,568	$24,309.12
Dallas	15,860	14,567.10	2,629	45,734.58
Lowndes	11,633	8,694.94	1,304	28,371.20
Butler	6,919	4,800.00	5,088	34,000.00
Clarke	6,054	4,584.12	4,323	27,706.06
Marengo	10,060	3,945.50	2.742	39,380.54
Perry	9,452	7,522.50	2,239	25,340.54
Total	64,285	$47,719.24	21,843	$244,842.32

[1] From "The Crisis," Vol. III, No. 6, p. 229.

Mr. W. K. Tate, state supervisor of elementary rural schools of South Carolina, says in the forty-second annual report of the department of education of the state:

It has been my observation that the Negro schools of South Carolina are for the most part without supervision of any kind. Frequently the county superintendent does not know where they are located and sometimes the district board can not tell where the Negro school is taught.

It is true that many reports can be cited showing better treatment of the Negro schools. But certainly the cases similar to the ones quoted here are alarmingly plentiful. The situation, moreover, is often a good deal worse than the published reports would indicate. For instance, when Wilcox county in Alabama in 1909 reported 10,000 Negroes and 2,000 whites there were reported fifty-five schools for whites and forty-eight schools for Negroes. Even with this official report, reliable Negro citizens of the county declared that they had absolutely no knowledge of more than six schools for colored people taught in that county during the year, and that the public school system for Negroes in that county had practically been given up. In those six schools the teachers received from $16 to $18 per month. In that county the United Presbyterian Church had established six private schools for Negroes and in presenting their statistics the school authorities of the county counted these private schools.

In order to study the city schools for Negroes from the superintendents' point of view, the Conference addressed a questionnaire[1] to the superintendents in two hundred and sixty-two (262) cities in fourteen southern states, the cities being chosen on the basis of population. The questionnaire asked, among other things, if the Negro teachers in these city systems were efficient; and the answers are in the main encouraging. The following summary of answers is self-explanatory:

Best I ever saw 1
Very good 3
Yes 71
In the majority of cases 14
The average good 1

[1] The questionnaire to city superintendents appears on page 13 of this publication.

Fairly 13
Satisfactory 1
Yes, in low grades 1
Moderately well 1
Half 1
Comparatively 1
Fair; some excellent 1
Reasonably 1
Yes, for Negroes 1
Some, but nearly all are earnest 1
Some 10
Few 4
Not altogether 1
No 1

The superintendents in many places, however, criticize these teachers. Their first criticism is indeed strangely naive: thirty-five of them complain of "lack of education," "lack of broad learning," "lack of culture," etc., on the part of the Negro teachers. This is undoubtedly a just criticism. But what is the cause of this condition? The cause may be stated as follows:

1. The Negro public schools of the South are so curtailed in curriculum that they are less and less providing students for the higher schools.

2. The graduates of the higher private schools are not usually desired by the school authorities because:

(a) These authorities put especial stress on technical teaching. Twenty-two superintendents ask for more manual training to replace other work. One wishes all to be industrial work after the fourth or fifth grade, one after the fourth grade, and one wants Negro schools to be "almost wholly industrial." For this reason, teachers are employed who can teach cooking and sewing, while but little attention is paid to their other qualifications or their qualifications in other lines. Small wonder that, as one superintendent complains, the work in domestic science is "good" but the "regular" school work is unsatisfactory!

Moreover, strong outside pressure is being applied to improve the industrial work while very little and in many places practically nothing is said about learning to read and write and cipher.

The Anna T. Jeanes Fund, which is doing excellent work in many ways and is proving an educational blessing to many a rural community in the South, experiences great difficulties in its work as the resultant of local school conditions. It is not surprising then that some curious results are evident. A statement of the work in Brookland district, Henrico county, Virginia, for 1910-11, will bear out the point:

No. of teachers in school group	Average monthly roll	Average daily attendance	Money Raised 1910-11	INDUSTRIAL WORK DONE OUTSIDE THE REGULAR STUDIES
3	88	65	$100.81	Planted flowers, laid a walk around side of school, whitewashed fence, purchased two lamps, clock, tables, dishes, kitchen articles; cooking, sewing, carpentry, preserving, canning.
			40.27	Taught sewing, woodwork, paper cutting, gardening. Garden plot 30x15 feet.
			34.53	Sewing, paper cutting, cardboard work. Put pictures on walls. Helping fix kitchen. Gave shells to beautify yard.
1	33	17	$82.66	Taught caning, basketry, paper folding, sewing, canning and preserving.
1	26	21	$17.01	Taught cabinet making from boxes, sewing, paper folding. Pictures donated by Dr. King, of the Virginia Union Univ. A rented building.
1	27	21	$40.00	Taught sewing, basketry and woodwork. Built woodhouse and improved interior of building.
1	43	35	$65.93	Cement walks and improved toilets. Made work bench and cooking table. Improved grounds. Taught sewing, canning, preserving, box furniture making.
2	53	41	$50.00	Painted building, laid cement walks, planted hedge and flowers. Taught cooking, sewing, canning, preserving and raffia work.
			60.00	Bought curtains for school and flag. Taught paper cutting, sewing, raffia and woodwork.
2	67	47	$102.00	Taught cooking, sewing, woodwork and basketry. Bought flag, water coolers and individual drinking cups, shades, curtains, tools. Set out hedge and whitewashed trees and fences. Built woodhouse. Repaired outhouses.
			14.66	Taught sewing, raffia, paper cutting and woodwork. Whitewashed trees, planted flowers and helped keep yard clean.

When one considers this work there are certain things plain. These teachers have enough to do in nearly all cases if they teach the children to read and write and cipher. If in addition to that they do this other work well in all probability the regular work of the school will suffer. It is asking too much of one to teach common school branches to thirty-five or forty children each day and in addition raise money, repair the school house and teach sewing, canning and preserving, etc. We have the word of the district superintendent that the industrial work was unusually well done. One cannot feel so sure concerning the efficiency of the regular school work.

When now the layman objects to such a system he is by no means an enemy of industrial and manual training. Most of the industrial work done here is good in itself and well worth doing. But when it is done at the expense of teaching children to read and write and cipher well, it would seem that the system is not the best. It is quite natural, then, that there should be and is a demand for a larger teaching force and a longer school term.

(b) Broadly trained Negro teachers are feared by many school authorities because they have "too much egotism" or "individuality" and because they can not be depended upon "to teach the Negro his place." The result is that many superintendents and trustees will, therefore, hire a half-trained graduate of an industrial school who can teach a few industries and then complain that the teacher lacks education and culture.[1]

3. The colored graduates of colleges and normal schools of high grade cannot afford to teach in most of the public schools of the South because of the wretched wages paid. Teachers from outside of the community often find it absolutely impossible to live on these wages. In many of the larger towns of the South the pay of Negro teachers is so small that many of the best teachers are being forced into other lines of work.

---

[1] The following is a reprint of a note received by the principal of a private Negro institution in Georgia from a colored teacher of the largest school in the county. This teacher's salary is $14 a month and she teaches more than one hundred children:

my 12, 19011.

Prof. ———————— I drop yo this card to let yo know that i will be in on that early train munday morning tell mrs. markos to meet the train.

yours

In addition to the question concerning the efficiency of the colored teachers in the city schools, the superintendents were asked their opinion of the work done by these Negro city schools. Some of the answers are printed here:

School Superintendents' Answers
Alabama

Birmingham.—Opinion: Far from satisfactory.

Gadsden.—Defects: Lack of experience and more training. Opinion: When we can pay more and hence enable them to improve we will get fine results.

Huntsville.—Defects: Lack of enthusiasm for the work and indifference to further preparation and thoro self-improvement. Methods are poor in many instances. Opinion: Our school is far above the average. The work is very satisfactory.

Mobile.—Defects: Lack of scholarship; overcrowded grades; lack of vital interest in the welfare of the child. Salary the chief concern. Need of better teachers. Opinion: Work is good considering the salaries paid to inexperienced teachers and the irregularity of the attendance. The average colored teacher does not realize the responsibility resting upon her.

New Decatur.—Defects: Lack of education, positiveness and personality. Opinion: Some good accomplished. Very good considering the opportunities. Manual training needed.

Selma.—Defects: Lack of scholarship, individuality. Too much imitative work. Opinion: Have no fixed opinion.

Talladega.—Opinion: Gradually improving. Teachers more efficient than they were ten years ago. A large element of Negroes improving.

Tuscaloosa.—Defects: Lack of suitable preparation; indifferent natural ability. Opinion: In clerical and memoriter subjects the quality is quite good.

Florida

Live Oak.—Defects: None. Opinion: They are the best things to help make better people of the Negroes.

Ocala.—Defects: None well defined. Opinion: Probably most are doing good work and some are trifling away time. The worst feature that we have to handle is that of tardiness.

Georgia

Albany.—Opinion: The work is unusually good. In addition to literary work, cooking and sewing is taught all the older girls and woodwork to the boys.

Americus.—Opinion: Excellent.

Athens.—Defects: I do not know that they have any defects that would differentiate them from other teachers. Opinion:—Under the circumstances they are doing very well.

Columbus.—Opinion: We are doing efficient work for the Negro.

Dalton.—Defects: Lack of technical training. Opinion: Often the education received by Negro children is such as to unfit them for useful lives.

Dublin.—Defects: Inability to use their time most advantageously. Opinion: Unusually good here.

Macon.—Defects: In a small percentage, indifference, laziness, lack of conscientiousness. Opinion: They are doing excellent work. On the whole the teachers are capable, conscientious, and earnestly striving to uplift their race. They are teaching the Negro youth to adapt themselves to conditions and environments.

Marietta.—Defects: Each has his own. One in general is too great a tendency to become mechanical. Opinion: Good beyond a doubt.

Newnan.—Defects: The teachers are good enough for the salary paid. Opinion: They do good work for their race.

Savannah.—Defects: Broader scholarship is needed. Teachers work under adverse circumstances. Opinion: I think it is very good. I have very little trouble with them.

Thomasville.—Defects: Common to all teachers. Opinion: Compares favorably with the work of whites.

Kentucky

Ashland.—Opinion: Considering the amount of work the teachers are doing, I think the results from our colored schools are very favorable.

Bowling Green.—Defects: Their race and blood are against them. They lack originality and initiative. Opinion: They are doing some good, but not an amount commensurate with the time and money. They should have more training in agriculture, manual and domestic sciences.

Covington.—Defects: Lack of accurate scholarship and professional courtesy. Opinion: In upper grades more attention needs to be given to the industrial and vocational, less to the purely academic.

Henderson.—Defects: Too mechanical; lack of originality; lack of ambition. Opinion: Doing good work, especially when the handicap under which they have to work is considered—the indifference of a number of Negroes.

Lexington.—Defects: Lack of initiative and broad learning. Opinion: Very good considering opportunities.

Louisville.—Opinion: Good.

Maysville.—Defects: Lack of progressive ideas and willingness to put such ideas into effect. Lack of sympathy for each other. Poor scholarship. Opinion: Our schools are doing good creditable work.

Middlesboro.— Defects: They possess fewer of these than any faculty of Negroes I ever had. Opinion: Ours is doing fine work, but so far as I know, we are an exception to the rule. Industrial training very beneficial.

Newport.—Defects: Characteristic of the general defects of the race. Opinion: The work is fairly good and the progress of the pupils satisfactory thru the primary and intermediate grades. In the higher intermediate department and in the high school subjects, the results show a greater difference between the colored pupils and white pupils of the same department. At the point where reason and judgment are required the colored child falls behind the white child in degree very much more noticeable than in the primary and intermediate departments.

Owensboro.—Opinion: Fairly good.

Paris.—Defects: A knowledge of what it means to be a teacher. Genuine interest in the race and its improvement. Opinion: It is doing much good. No educated Negro has been in jail or fined in police court.

Louisiana

Baton Rouge.—Defects: Lack of scholarship; lack of professional training. Opinion: Rather unsatisfactory.

New Orleans.—Defects: Lack of education and moral instruction. Opinion: Should be vocational after fourth grade. There should be regular high school and college opportunities for teachers and other leaders of the race.

Maryland

Annapolis.—Defects: Disposition to ape white people's ways and instill them into their pupils. Opinion: In the city they are doing very satisfactory work, but in the country it is very hard to follow them as they have no efficent supervision owing to the schools being scattered over such a large area.

Cumberland.—Defects: The properly educated Negro teacher can accomplish much by persistent effort and personal detachment. The most prominent obstacle in the way is the desire to claim acquaintance with the higher studies and disinclination to all that tends to local efficiency.

Mississippi

Columbus.—Defects: Their defects are not so great as their lack of opportunity to do good work. Opinion: The schools are doing good work. Lack of appreciation on the part of adults and the consequent poor attendance prevent schools having a fair chance. Negroes are not productive enough to keep their children in school.

Corinth.—Defects: Lack of education and professional training, and race development. Opinion: Of very little value both as to efficiency and results.

Greenville.—Defects: Hunger for the dollar instead of benefit to the children. Opinion: The Negro school is essential to qualify the Negroes for manhood and womanhood, and the results are encouraging.

Hattiesburg.—Opinion: Very good.

Laurel.—Defects: Lack of sound scholarship. Opinion: Fairly good. It is our intention to introduce domestic training.

Natchez.—Opinion: Very good.

Vicksburg.—Defects: Lack of education; lack of power to govern except by brute force.

Missouri

Boonville.—Opinion: Some of the work is of a high order.

Cape Girardeau. —Opinion: Work should be almost wholly industrial.

Carthage. —Defects: Lack of critical knowledge of the subjects they have to teach. Opinion: Not satisfactory. Lack of harmony between the work of the school and the life of the Negro people.

Chillicothe.—Opinion: Work as good as in the schools for white.

Clinton.—Defects: Restricted scholarship. Opinion: Rather poor.

Independence. —The defects are a matter of detail. Opinion: Schools are doing good work.

Jefferson City. —Opinion: Schools are doing good work considering the handicap of such a small number of well-ordered homes.

Lexington.—Defects: Indifference. Lack of sympathy with the people. Lack of creative power as teachers. Opinion: Too much time spent on things that are not practical. Need of more industrial training.

Marshall.—Defects: Individual defects—not general. Opinion: Doing good work. More industrial training needed.

Maryville.—Defects: Inexperience; ineffective teaching. Opinion: Stronger teachers and more industrial work needed.

Mexico. —Defects: Do not read enough. Opinion: Good under conditions.

Poplar Bluff. —Opinion: Doing just as efficient work as the white schools.

Springfield.—Defects: Haven't any. Opinion: Excellent.

St. Joseph.—Opinion: Most of them are faithful and sincere, others do not regard the calling of much importance. Better support from parents needed.

Trenton. —Defects: Too much rote work. Opinion: Work as well done as one could expect with one teacher for all grades.

Warrensburg.—Defects: Not sufficiently interested in the culture of their race. Opinion: Slowly improving.

Webb City.—Opinion: Only ten Negro children of school age out of three thousand six hundred and sixty-six school children. These are sent to Joplin schools.

North Carolina

Asheville.—Defects: Lack of thoroness, breadth of view and training in methods. Opinion: Doing fairly good work which is improving every year. Compulsory attendance is helping greatly.

Burlington.—Defects: Chief trouble lies in the parents. They are ignorant and do not appreciate the school. Opinion: Until this year the teachers were not efficient, thus making the work very unsatisfactory. At present the work is progressing.

Charlotte.—Opinion: Very good.

Kinston.—Defects: Lack of thoro preparation. Opinion: They are doing good work.

Newbern.—Defects: Initiative. Opinion: Work is very creditable. Attendance irregular. Should have more practical training, manual training.

Salisbury.—Defects: Lack of sympathy. Opinion: More manual training and domestic science should be given.

Washington.—Opinion: Work very satisfactory, some excellent.

Winston-Salem.—Defects: Lack of preparation. Opinion: Very good.

Oklahoma

Chickasha.—Defects: Morality and discipline. Opinion: Efficient, considering conditions a few years back. Room for vast improvement.

El Reno.—Defects: Inability to put into execution suggestions. Failure to realize the importance of small matters. Opinion: Quite effective. Our school is doing much for the Negro of this community.

Enid.—Defects: Egotism. Opinion: They are successful teachers.

Guthrie.—Defects: None. Opinion: The Negro schools in this city are not excelled anywhere. My teachers are gentlemen and ladies and they are developing the boys and girls along this line. The colored children are crowding the whites for supremacy.

McAlester.—Defects: Lack of system, defective education. Opinion: The schools should furnish industrial training but do not.

Ponca City.—Opinion: The work is good.

Shawnee.—Defects: Lack of academic education and professional training. Opinion: Domestic science department doing good work. Regular work of the grades unsatisfactory, due to poorly prepared teachers.

Tulsa.—Opinion: It is not as good as the rest of the work on the whole and yet two or three of the teachers are doing a high grade of work. The rest of the work is fair to good.

South Carolina

Abbeville.—Defects: Lack of discipline and preparation. Opinion: The Negro schools would accomplish more if domestic science were introduced, even at the expense of high school work.

Anderson.—Opinion: Not perfect but good.

Newberry.—Opinion: They attempt to do too much with the classics instead of those studies which increase the earning capacity of the race and make them better citizens.

Union.—Opinion: A very high grade of work.

Tennessee

Chattanooga.—Defects: Lack of education; parrot-like adaptation of what they are taught; lack of individuality.

Columbia.—Defects: Lack of ambition as to character building; aversion to the various avocations, and stressing too strenuously the year of Jubilee.

Knoxville.—Defects: Lack of practicability. Opinion: Not up to standard of white. Work inclined to abstract.

Nashville.—Defects: Lack of broad scholarship; poor judgment. Opinion: The work on the whole is fair. More manual and less literary work should be given.

Texas

Austin.—Defects: Difficult matter to write out defects of a teacher. Opinion: To prepare the children for best citizenship.

Beaumont.—Defects: Tactful discipline. Opinion: The work is excellent and Negroes are uplifted thru these schools.

Belton.—Defects: Lack of sufficient funds renders work of teachers defective. Opinion: Work compares favorably with that of other schools of the state.

Bonham.—Defects: Lack of scholarship; lack of native capacity; lack of energy. Opinion: Results far inferior to the average white school.

Brownwood.—Opinion: Doing a good work and a good thing for the colored people.

Corpus Christi.—Opinion: Doing good work and are well thot of by the white population.

Corsicana.—Defects: Such as are peculiar to their race. Opinion: The work is fairly satisfactory considering all the difficulties. The attendance is irregular, co-operation of parents not good, pupils not well provided with books, clothing, lack of refinement in the home.

Denison.—Defects: Lack of experience; lack of ability; lack of personality. Opinion: The work should consist largely of the industrial and the mechanical.

Denton.—Defects: Just being Negroes. Opinion: Our schools improve the morals of colored children.

El Paso. —Defects: Lack of application; lack of self control. Opinion: Not enough attention paid to practical work. This is being obviated by the introduction of manual training and domestic economy.

Gainesville. —Opinion: Good.

Galveston. —Defects: They will compare favorably with white teachers of the same educational advantages.

Greenville.—Opinion: There should be more industrial work in the high schools.

Hillsboro.—Defects: Superficiality. Opinion: After the fourth and fifth grades the schools should be largely industrial.

Marlin.—Opinion: The schools should be such as to help the Negro to live cleanly and make an honest and sufficient living and do good unto his race.

Marshall.—Defects: Lack of thoro knowledge of subject matter and of correct methods. Laziness. Lack of pride in work. These defects are not universal. Opinion: Some of the work is good, but there is not enough preparation for making a living. The children get good moral training.

Navasota.—Opinion: The work should be more vocational than the public schools are.

Orange.—Opinion: Too much superficiality. More practical courses needed and better preparation of teachers, also industrial training.

Palestine.—Defects: Lack of culture and professional training. Opinion: More good would come to the individual and to the state if agriculture, domestic science and vocational subjects were added, these to be determined by local conditions.

Paris.—Opinion: Doing good work. More practical work needed. Negro children do not attend school regularly.

San Antonio.—Defects: Lack of scholarship; deficiency of morals; lack of regard for merit. Opinion: The character of the work is good.

Taylor.—Defects: Too much "pedagoguery," too little "practicality." Opinion: "The education of the Negro should give him high moral ideals and train him to strive after their realization; moreover, it should fit him for the work he must do to make a livelihood and a good citizen. What we now offer them does *not* do much of this."

Terrell.—Defects: Lack of scholarship and professional training. Opinion: Very good.

Texarkana.—Defects: Politics. Opinion: They do very well.

Victoria.—Opinion: The work is good, and whatever fault there is is with the plan of work.

Waco.—Defects: Not enough earnestness. Opinion: Excellent work in every respect.

Waxahachie.—Defects: Lack of discipline. Opinion: Not good. There should be more manual and less literary instruction.

Weatherford.—Defects: Lack of scholarship and personality. Opinion: Fairly good.

Virginia

Alexandria.—Defects: I think our colored teachers are above the average. I am in favor of individual training of Negroes. Opinion: I am of the opinion that we have too little domestic science and manual training in our colored schools. Am making every effort to carry out my ideas along this line but am very much handicapped by lack of funds.

Charlottesville.—Opinion: Work splendid.

Danville.—Defects: They hold themselves aloof. It is not a defect in teaching but of the government of the schools. Opinion: The work in our Negro schools is very good. We have manual training and domestic science in which they excel. We have no white teacher in Negro schools.

Norfolk.—Defects: They are well qualified, enthusiastic and efficient. Opinion: The work here is very satisfactory, the spirit is good and the attendance excellent—about 93 per cent.

Portsmouth.—Defects: Imitation without discretion; roughness toward pupils. Our schools show good results in scholarship and. manners, and we hope in morals as the teachers stress this. While the attendance is fair there is a vast number of absences, cases of tardiness, with numberless truancies. Opinion: We feel here that the work is good and the results satisfactory. Compulsory education and free text books might secure very much better results.

Radford.—Opinion: One of our schools is doing good work. It is taught by graduates of Hampton. They give a good school and so far as I can see teach the Negro public and practical service.

Richmond.—Opinion: Negro schools are doing good but we need more industrial work so that the Negro may realize the dignity of service.

Staunton.—Opinion: The work of the Negro schools is good.

West Virginia

Bluefield.—Defects: Poor disciplinarians; weak scholarship; teachers talk too much themselves; some teach for money and not for the good they may do.   Opinion: As yet the work of the majority of the Negro schools is below the average.   Too often the teachers lack in scholarship and too often politics tend to keep that class of teachers in as they can be used for political purposes.   The Negro schools in this state are improving fast.

Moundsville.—Defects: Lack of discipline.   Opinion: It is very good and ranks fairly with the same work of the white schools.

Parkersburg.—Opinion: The course of study should allow quite a selection and provide manual training and domestic science.

Wheeling.—Defects: Lack of professional interest.   Desire for ease. Opinion: The work at present is of good quality.   This is mainly due to the principal who is a very capable man and maintains a high standard of effort for his teachers and his school.

Section 24.   Disfranchisement and the Public School

Since 1890 five and a half million Negroes, over half of whom can read and write and who own fully $150,000,000 worth of property, have been practically deprived of all voice in their own government.   The restrictions by which this has been accomplished are eight in number: 1. Illiteracy: The voter must be able to read and write. 2. Property: The voter must own a certain amount of property. 3. Poll tax: The voter must have paid his poll tax for the present year or for a series of years.   4. Employment: The voter must have regular employment.   5. Army service: Soldiers in the Civil War and certain other wars, or their descendants, may vote. 6.   Reputation: Persons of good reputation who understand the duties of a citizen may vote.   7. "Grandfather" clause: Persons who could vote before the freedmen were enfranchised or descendants of such persons may vote.   8. Understanding clause: Persons may vote who understand some selected clause of the Constitution and can explain it to the satisfaction of the registration officials.

The states have adopted these qualifications apparently as follows:[1]

---

[1] This table is but approximately accurate as the laws are often obscurely drawn and not easily understood in some cases.

1890—Mississippi (1 or 8) +3.
1895—South Carolina 1 or 2 or 8.
1898—Louisiana (1+2) or 7.
1901—North Carolina (1+3) or 7.
1901—Alabama (1+4) or 2 or 5 or 6.
1902—Virginia (1+3 or 5) or 8 or 2.
1909—Georgia 1 or 2 or 5 or 6.

To illustrate the immediate effect of these disfranchising laws, the following statistical tables are given:

LOUISIANA

		White	Negro
1900	Population	729,612	650,804
1900	Males 21 years or over	178,595	147,348
	Literate	146,219	57,086
	Illiterate	32,376	90,262
1908	Registered voters	152,135	1,743

LOWNDES COUNTY, ALABAMA

	Males of Voting Age		Total
	Whites	Negroes	
Total, 1900	1,138	6,455	7,593
Illiterate	81	4,667	4,748
Literate	1,057	1,788	2,845
Total registered 1902	1,097	39	1,136
Total registered 1906	1,142	52	1,194

From the latter table we may conclude that nearly ninety-nine (99) per cent of the Negroes in Lowndes county, Alabama, 21 years of age and over have been disfranchised and over ninety-seven (97) per cent of those who can read and write. Taking these two cases as typical and considering the general movement of disfranchisement, the question arises: *What effect has this had on the Negro public schools?*

After the disfranchisement laws were passed, the next step which the radical South wished was the overthrow or distinct curtailment of Negro schools. The argument, of course, of the better South had always been: If you take the Negro out of politics you will leave us free from the fear of Negro domination and put us upon our honor to treat this dependent race with fairness and good will. The better South,

however, forgot to reckon with its masters. Its masters are
the mass of white voters who come more or less into economic
competition with the Negroes and who are the historic enemies of the black man.

In order to get the votes of these white workingmen, the
better class of the South has not hesitated to cater to their
anti-Negro bias, and the southern demagogs have done
more than cater to it—they have distinctly encouraged it. The
result is that since disfranchisement it has been quite impossible for the best class of southerners to stop the wave of determination to curtail the facilities for Negro education. A
very frequent argument in the South to induce the whites to
better themselves is to point out the shameful consequences
of allowing Negroes to surpass them in any respect. And
this, instead of resulting in increased efforts on the part of
the whites to excel, is apt to result in increased determination to keep Negroes down. This determination is voiced in
various ways. Sometimes it is evidenced by sheer physical
force. For instance, the county school commissioner of Pulaski
County, Ga., reports for 1909 that during one year "five school
houses for colored children, with their contents, have been
burned. All of these fires are reported to be the work of the
incendiary." During the last few years the burning of Negro
school houses, churches and lodge houses by white neighbors
has been frequent in the gulf states. Further than this, deliberate effort has been made by school authorities to cut down
school appropriations. In the rural schools of North Carolina,
for instance, the colored teachers were paid $224,800 in 1907
and $221,800 in 1908; during this same time the amount paid
white teachers in the rural districts was increased by $50,000.
In South Carolina the per capita increase of school money spent
on Negro children has been less than twenty per cent, while
that for whites has increased over one hundred per cent. In
Alabama the average length of the public school for Negroes
was cut from 95 days in 1908 to 92 days in 1909 and to 90
days in 1910, while the average salary paid Negro school
teachers was also decreased. At the same time the private

schools for Negroes, supported largely by northern benevolence, were reduced thirty-four per cent. In spite of these three
facts the state school superintendent, evidently with his eyes
simply on the whites, says that it is "interesting to note the
increased efficiency of the Alabama school system." While
there were in 1908-9, 647,914 more white children in school in
the South than there were in 1899-1900, there were only 152,067
more Negroes and the percentage of enrollment for the total
school population had decreased among the Negroes from
fifty-seven (57.67) per cent to fifty-six (56.34) per cent; the
percentage of enrollment in average daily attendance had decreased for these years. In North Carolina the average term
of the colored schools decreased during that year and so had
the average monthly salary of the teachers.

Not only has the general enrollment and attendance of
Negro children in the rural schools of the lower South and to
a large extent of the city schools been at a standstill in the
last ten years and in many cases actually decreased but many
of the school authorities have shown by their acts and in a few
cases expressed declaration that it was their policy to eliminate
the Negro schools as far as possible.

Another phase of the situation presents itself. Using the
official reports of about the same time, if in Mississippi you
take eleven counties where the white children are receiving
$20 or more per capita for their education you find that
these counties are in every single case counties where the
black children are in large majority. On the other hand,
taking the thirty-three counties where the white children
are receiving less than $10 a head, one finds that in all but
eight of these counties the white children are in the majority, and in three of the eight the numbers of white and
black children are about the same. This means, of course,
that in the black belt of Mississippi the counties draw their
share of the state money according to the number of white
and black children and then that money is spent almost
exclusively upon the white children, giving them a per
capita as high as $50 a head in one county. On the other

hand, in the white belt of Mississippi where there are more white children and fewer blacks the white school fund sinks to from $3 to $5 a head.   Now the white children of the black belt are largely children of rich land owners, while those of the white belt are the children of the poor whites.   If, however, the white belt objects to this per capita distribution of the school money, immediately the black belt threatens to let black folk vote, and to give them schools; and as much as the white belt desires education for itself, it hates education for blacks enough to refrain from radically changing this peculiar situation.   In other words, we have here in the center of the South a peculiar result of disfranchisement analogous with the increased power of the white voter of the South as compared with the white voter of the North.   Thus the situation is so anomalous that it explains much of the bitterness of Mississippi politics.

There is a distinct endeavor to curtail the facilities of education which the Negroes already possess.   This can be seen in the persistent campaigns carried on in the North and directed toward the North which say in effect, that the Negroes' education as carried on by northern philanthropists has been a mistake, that it is an interference with the local conditions in the South, and that the stream of benevolence ought to be stopped.   There is no doubt but that this argument has had tremendous influence upon the benevolent public.

Again there has been a continual effort to curtail Negro education by reducing the number of grades in the Negro public schools.   Macon and Augusta, Georgia, and New Orleans, Louisiana, are typical in this connection.   The lack of public high schools for Negroes is one of the greatest drawbacks of the southern school system.   This, however, is spoken of elsewhere in this study.

The only remedy for this state of affairs and for discrimination, retrogression and paralysis of the whole school system of the South is democracy—the putting into the hands of all men of the South the weapon of self-defense which will not leave them merciless beneath the blows of prejudice and ignorance.

Section 25.   The Cost of Negro Schools

What do the Negro schools of the South cost and who pays for them?   It is frequently charged that Negro education is a burden on the white tax-payer of the South; similarly it is urged that only such amounts should be expended on the Negro schools as are collected from Negroes in the way of taxes.   Such is the reply, alike to the student who seeks to investigate the condition of public education in the South and to the Negro citizen who asks for more and better facilities for the training of black children.

It is difficult to secure exact statistics of expenditures according to race.   However, such data as the Conference has been able to present in this study are worth while and give evidence of the fact that the Negroes are bearing, and that in a larger way than is generally supposed, a considerable share of the expense of public education in the South.

Mr. Charles L. Coon, for some time superintendent of schools in Wilson, North Carolina, has made a study of public taxation and Negro education.   We quote freely in the following pages from his "Public Taxation and Negro Schools," a paper read before the twelfth annual conference for education in the South, held in Atlanta, Ga., in April, 1909, and published by the Committee of Twelve for the Advancement of the Negro Race:

I shall confine this paper to the investigation of the question, *"Is the Negro public school in the South a burden on the white tax-payer, and if so, to what extent?"*   For the purpose of this investigation, I shall include the eleven southern states which, in 1900, contained 7,199,374 of the 8,840,789 Negroes then living in the United States, or 81.4 per cent of the Negro population of the country.   These states are Virginia, North Carolina, South Carolina, Georgia, Florida, Alabama, Mississippi, Louisiana, Texas, Arkansas and Tennessee.   In these eleven states the total population in 1900 was 18,975,665, of which 11,776,391 was white and 7,199,374, or 40.1 per cent was Negro.

First.   In order to find out whether the Negro public school is a burden on the white tax-payer in these states, it is necessary, first of all, to ascertain what these states are spending for public schools, both white and colored.   The latest reports of the several departments of education indicate that these eleven states are now spending about $32,068,851 for elementary and secondary public education. This sum represents every item of expense. . . . .

Second. The South is spending $32,068,851 on her public schools, both white and black, but what part of this sum is devoted to Negro public schools, which must serve at least forty per cent of her school population? It is not possible to answer this question with absolute accuracy. But it is possible, from the several state reports, to find out the whole amount spent for teachers, and, in all the states except Arkansas, what was spent for white and Negro teachers separately. The aggregate amount now being spent for public school teachers of both races in these eleven states is $23,856,914, or 74.4 per cent of the whole amount expended. Of this sum not more than $3,818,705 was paid to Negro teachers, or twelve per cent of the total expenditures. And here let me call your attention directly to the fact that nearly three-fourths of our total public school expenditures are for teachers, but that Negro teachers receive only twelve per cent of the total expended, while white teachers receive sixty-two (62.4) per cent. It is also evident that the amount spent for Negro teachers is by far the largest item of expense of the Negro public schools.

EXPENDITURES FOR TEACHERS AND TOTAL COST OF NEGRO SCHOOLS

STATE AND YEAR	Total expenditure	Spent for white teachers	Spent for Negro teachers	Per cent spent for white teachers	Per cent spent for Negro teachers	Spent for Negroes above teachers	Cost of Negro schools	Cost of Negro schools in per cent	Per cent of population Negro
Virginia, 1907	$ 3,308,086	$ 1,761,264	$ 389,945	53.2	11.7	$99,283	$ 489,228	14.7	35.7
North Carolina, 1908	2,958,160	1,374,143	313,914	46.4	19.6	88,744	402,658	13.6	33.3
South Carolina, 1908	1,595,986	1,102,094	254,161	69.0	16.0	20,798	274,959	17.3	58.4
Georgia, 1907	2,850,211	1,819,321	420,664	63.8	14.7	85,506	506,170	17.7	46.7
Florida, 1908	1,584,043	864,214	153,062	54.5	9.6	82,428	235,490	14.9	43.7
Alabama, 1908	2,195,325	1,712,898	240,179	78.0	10.9	32,822	273,001	12.4	45.3
Mississippi, 1907	2,631,790	1,515,685	469,073	57.5	17.7	107,890	576,963	21.9	58.7
Louisiana, 1907	3,481,276	1,810,474	196,411	52.0	5.6	104,438	300,849	8.6	47.2
Texas, 1906	6,344,739	4,527,877	782,412	71.3	12.3	142,183	924,595	14.5	20.4
Arkansas, 1907	2,413,768	1,784,519	189,300	73.9	7.8	72,414	261,714	10.8	28.0
Tennessee, 1907	2,705,457	1,765,720	409,584	65.2	15.2	81,164	490,748	18.2	23.8
Total	$32,068,851	$20,038,209	$3,818,705	62.4	12.0	$917,670	$4,736,375	14.8	40.1

NOTE.—In the Virginia report the amount paid Negro teachers is not given, but the number of Negro teachers and their average salary is given. In the Tennessee report the average salary of all teachers and the number of Negro teachers is given. The amount credited to Negro teachers, is, therefore, likely too large. The amount credited to Negro teachers in Arkansas is based on the average tuition and enrollment in Negro schools. The average tuition is likely too high for Negro schools. In all calculations the Negro teachers are credited with such amounts as the face of the reports indicates. Investigation would undoubtedly lower the figures of some states.

Third. But aside from the expense of Negro teachers, what is the additional cost of the Negro public schools? This additional cost cannot be accurately determined from the data now available. But South Carolina, Florida, Alabama, Mississippi and Texas—five states—report the total cost of Negro schools. In these states the additional cost of Negro schools above the cost of teachers is as follows: South Carolina, 1.3 per cent of total expenditures; Florida, 5.3 per cent; Alabama, 1.5 per cent; Mississippi, 4.2 per cent; Texas, 2.2 per cent. These figures indicate that between two and three per cent of the total expenditures for public schools in the South is being devoted to the Negro schools above the cost of Negro teachers. This means that about $917,670 is to be added to the cost of Negro teachers to get the entire cost of the Negro public schools in the South. The aggregate cost of the Negro public schools is, therefore, near $4,736,375, or 14.8 per cent of all expenditures. The significance of these figures is that, while the Negro race has, at least, forty per cent of the children to educate, not quite fifteen per cent of the money expended on public education is being devoted to their schools.

Fourth. It is generally assumed in the discussion of the cost of the Negro public schools, that the white race bears all the cost or nearly all; that the Negroes of the South are truly the white man's burden when it comes to paying the bills for public education.   .   .   .   .   .

And this brings me directly to the main inquiry: Is the Negro public school of the South a burden on the white tax-payer? But here again, complete data with which to work cannot be had. However, this question can be answered for Virginia, North Carolina and Georgia, with some degree of accuracy.

First. Is the Negro public school of Virginia a burden on the white tax-payer of that state? (a) The state auditor for 1908 reports the total assessed value of Virginia property at $702,503,778, divided as follows: Listed by whites, $521,612,627, or 74.3 per cent; listed by railroads and other corporations, $155,262,815, or 22.1 per cent; listed by Negroes, $25,628,326, or 3.6 per cent. Thus it will be seen that the state of Virginia does not assess 22.1 per cent of its property as either *white* or *black*. This is a fact worth remembering in any discussion of this question. On page 14, Advanced Sheets, State Superintendent's Report, 1907, it is said that Virginia raised for public schools during that year the sum of $3,473,048, of which amount $2,855,871 was raised by state and local taxation, while $450,000 was directly appropriated out of the state treasury. The income of the literary fund was $60,127, leaving the sum of $107,050 raised from other sources. If we assume that the $450,000 directly appropriated to the schools was raised by taxation, then Virginia raised by taxation for schools in 1907, $3,305,871. Bear with me, then, while I set forth what I conceive to be the part the Negro should have of this school fund, if we assume that it is to be divided on the color line and not on the basis of the actual needs of the children to be educated.

(b) Property does not raise all this Virginia school fund. The Negroes pay something like $120,000 school poll taxes, after deducting insolvents and commissions. It is fair to assume that some of the literary fund income belongs to Negroes, but what part? This fund is neither white nor black. It was not created by white property. Negroes constitute 36 per cent of the population of Virginia, and I take it they should be given 36 per cent of the income of the literary fund, which amounts to $21,649. The ten cents state school tax on Negro property after deducting commissions amounted to at least $22,500 more. The ten cents state school tax on the $155,262,815 railroad and other corporation property would not all, in fairness, belong to the white children. Not many of us, I think, would, after the last few years of agitation, charge the railroads and other corporations with being altogether *white*. I take it, therefore, that 36 per cent of the proceeds of the ten cents state school tax Virginia levies should be given the Negro schools. This would add about $50,000 more to the Negro school fund.

Now we must consider the $1,913,760 raised by Virginia cities, counties and districts. If this sum were all raised by property taxation, and we shall so assume, then 3.6 per cent of it was raised on Negro property, 22.1 per cent of it was raised on corporation property, and the remainder on white property. The 3.6 per cent raised locally on Negro property would add $68,895 to the Negro school fund. Then we shall have to add $152,259 more to the account from the corporation property taxed locally, or 36 per cent of the total amount raised on that kind of property.

Finally, if the $450,000 directly appropriated to the schools was raised by taxation, then 3.6 per cent of that sum belongs to the Negroes' school fund, also 36 per cent of 22.1 per cent of this $450,000 raised on railroads and other corporation property. These two items will add $16,200 and $35,802, respectively, to the Negroes' part of the school fund of Virginia, not taking into account the balance from 1906 or the fund raised from other sources.

Summarizing, the Negroes' part of the school fund raised in 1907 will stand as follows:

From poll tax	$ 120,000
From literary fund	21,649
From state corporation tax	50,000
From state tax on Negro property	22,500
From local tax on Negro property	68,895
From local tax on corporations	152,259
From 3.6 per cent direct state appropriation	16,200
From 36 per cent direct state appropriation (corporations)	35,802
Total due to Negroes	$ 507,305

I have shown before that Virginia is spending only about $489,228 on her Negro schools. If my figures are correct, then $18,077 of the amount which should be devoted to their schools, if we assume the race division of the funds, does not reach the Negro schools of Virginia. I assume that the Negroes' part of the balance from 1906 and their part of the fund from other sources will cancel any balance carried over from 1907 to 1908, so far as the Negro fund is concerned.

Second. Is the Negro public school of North Carolina a burden on the white tax-payer of that state?

(a) The total assessed value of all property in North Carolina is $593,485,331, divided as follows: Listed by whites, $440,669,472; listed by Negroes, $21,716,922, or 3.7 per cent; corporations, $111,098,937, or 19.3 per cent.

(b) The state superintendent reports for 1908 the school fund as follows:

Balance from 1907	$ 413,214.63
Local taxes	650,739.40
Literary fund	100,534.00
Bonds and loans	208,018.56
Fines, polls, licenses	631,007.00
State fund	1,045,263.10
State apportionment	198,547.00
Other sources	46,907.11
Total	$3,294,231.70

(c) If this fund had been divided on the race basis, I think a fair division would be as follows:

33⅓ per cent of 19.3 per cent of $650,740, local tax (corporation)	$ 41,864
33⅓ per cent of literary fund of $100,534	33,511
3.7 per cent of $198,548, state appropriation (Negro property)	7,346
33⅓ per cent of 19.3 per cent of $198,548, state appropriation (corporations)	12,773
33⅓ per cent of $254,834 licenses and fines	84,834
Poll taxes actually paid	80,000
3.7 per cent of $1,045,263 (Negro property)	38,675
33⅓ per cent of 19.3 per cent of $1,045,263 (corporation property)	67,245
3.7 per cent of $413,215, balance of 1907 (Negro property)	15,289
33⅓ per cent of $413,215, balance of 1907 (corporation property)	26,583
3.7 per cent of $208,018, bonds (Negro property)	7,696
33⅓ per cent of 19.3 per cent of $208,018, bonds (corporation property)	13,381
Total due to Negroes	$429,197

I have shown before that North Carolina is likely spending only $402,658 on her Negro schools. This leaves $26,539 of the North Carolina fund which never reached the Negro in 1908. But, it may be objected, there is no account taken in this calculation of the balance carried over from 1908 to 1909. It may be further objected that these calculations take no account of the fact that local taxes are not levied on all the property of the state under consideration, but only on the property in certain communities; also that local taxes are derived from polls as well as property. But the excess of the amount calculated as due Negroes in North Carolina will nearly provide for the balance in question. Local taxes are generally levied in the richer communities and there Negroes own more property and there is more corporation property than in poorer communities. It will hardly make much difference in the final result, if the actual facts were in hand and the calculations made from them. As to the local poll taxes, there is no injustice done in these calculations when it is remembered that the local taxes are all considered as raised on property. The thing to remember here is, that the funds are not all put in a common treasury and distributed. My calculations are made as if such were the case. The practical result of such not being the case would be that the funds for Negroes in this state would be largely increased in many communities and reduced in others. Hence, I conclude that the Negro school is likely not a burden on the white tax-payer of North Carolina.

Third. Finally, is the Negro public school of Georgia a burden on the white tax-payer of that state?

(a) On page 397 of the state superintendent's report for 1907 the following is set forth as the school fund of that year:

Balance, 1906	$ 180,190.33
State appropriation	1,744,461.47
Convicts	199,659.71
Local tax	750,577.59
Other sources	136,789.36
Total	* $3,011,678.46

(b) On page 8, comptroller's report, 1907, the sources of the state school appropriation are given as follows:

Poll tax	$ 275,000.00
Liquor	242,000.00
Fertilizer	21,000.00
Oil	1,600.00
Shows	9,616.00
Georgia Railroad	2,046.00
W. & A. Railroad	210,000.00
Prison farm	16,639.71
School lands	8,680.62
Property tax	1,000,000.00
Total	$1,786,588.33

(c) It will be observed that $42,126.86 of the state fund is not accounted for in the State Superintendent's report. But this small item may be overlooked for the present. I think a fair division of the school fund of Georgia for 1907 would be as follows:

Negro poll tax	$ 111,898.00
46.7 per cent of income, W. & A. R. R.	98,072.76
46.7 per cent of income from liquor	113,014.00
46.7 per cent of income from fertilizer	9,807.00
46.7 per cent of income from oil	747.20
46.7 per cent of income from shows	4,481.67
46.7 per cent of income from Georgia R. R.	955.48
46.7 per cent of income from prison farm	7,770.88
46.7 per cent of income from school lands	4,053.56
15 cents tax on $25,904,822 Negro property	38,857.23
46.7 per cent income 15 cents tax, $123,588,172 (corporation property)	86,552.50
46.7 per cent income from convicts	93,241.22
3.7 per cent of $887,367, local tax, etc. (Negro property)	32,832.58
46.7 per cent of 19.1 per cent of local tax, etc. (corporation property)	45,568.46
Total due to Negroes	$ 647,852.54

* The total assessed value of all property in Georgia is $699,536,879, divided as follows: White, $540,073,885; Negro, $25,904,822, or 3.7 per cent; corporation, $123,588,172, or 19.1 per cent.

I have shown above that Negroes actually received about $506,170 of the Georgia school fund of 1907.   This leaves $141,682.54 to the credit of the Negro fund, upon any fair race division.   If we count the $42,126.82 not accounted for in the school report and the Negroes' part of the balance carried over to 1908, and also the Negroes' part of the balance due them from 1906, we shall still have a comfortable sum over and above the actual expenditures made for Negro schools by Georgia in 1907. Therefore, I think the Negro schools of Georgia are not a burden on white tax-payers.

I do not wish it understood, however, that I favor any such race division of the public school funds as I have suggested above.   My object is to show, first of all, that upon any fair division of the present school funds of the three states under consideration, the Negro would likely fare as well as he does at present, in the absence of any such division.   I am confident, whether my figures are absolutely accurate or not, that any one who takes the pains to ascertain the present sources of the public funds of these states and then tries to make a fair division of them between the races will come to the conclusion that the Negro school is not very much of a white man's burden, in at least three states, unless the white man is ready to say that the division I suggest is not a fair one. And, in view of the facts set forth for these three states, will the white man be able to maintain successfully that he pays nearly all the cost of the Negro public schools in these states?

Time is not at hand to make a detailed study of this question for all the eleven states under consideration.   What is true of the school funds of the three states considered above is probably true of all the others.   A somewhat careful study of this question for several years leads me to the conclusion that the Negro school of the South is no serious burden on the white tax-payer.

*   *   *   *   *   *   *   *   *   *   *   *   *   *   *   *

In concluding this section on the cost of Negro schools, we quote from "Self Help in Negro Education," by Dr. R. R. Wright, Jr.:

It is probably also true that the Negroes pay possibly a larger percentage of the cost of their schools than any other group of poor people in America.

The Negroes have paid in direct property and poll taxes more than $45,000,000 during the past forty years.

The Negroes have contributed at least $15,000,000 to education thru their churches.

The Negro student possibly pays a larger percentage of the running expenses of the institutions which he attends than any other student in the land.

Section 26. High Schools

The work of Negro public education in the South is seriously handicapped by the wholesale neglect of high school facilities for colored children. Recent years have witnessed a notable extension of high school facilities in the South, as is evidenced by the official reports; but the white population has been the fortunate recipient. It seems almost incredible that Atlanta with a Negro population of 51,902, Savannah with a Negro population of 33,246 and Augusta with a Negro population of 18,344, should make no provision for the high school training of their black children.

There are some cities in the border, western and southwestern states which are making large provision for the high school education of their Negro youth, notably Washington, D. C., Baltimore, Md., St. Louis and Kansas City, Mo., and Dallas and Houston, Texas, but these are happy exceptions. The widespread indifference to public high school education for Negroes in the South is an injustice to both parents and children of the Negro race and a serious handicap to the intellectual efficiency of the whole South.

(1) It deprives the ambitious Negro youth of that preparation for college which a good high school course gives. The result here is that the schools for the higher education of the Negro, maintained chiefly by northern philanthropy, must carry preparatory departments in order to fit the Negro youth for college.

(2) Many young minds are denied that cultural training which none should be denied and which may be gained from a four years' course of high school rank. Many of these young people will never attend college and it is only fair that there should be some provision for their high school training at public expense.

(3) The withholding of public high school education denies the Negro youth that incentive to perseverance which is of so much importance during the period of adolescence.

(4) The Negro is in a sense double taxed for this type of education, since he pays his share of the public school tax

and in addition is forced to pay tuition charges for his high school training in private institutions of learning.

(5) The sum total of intelligence, culture and refinement is less for the whole South than it would be if high school facilities were afforded the Negro youth at public expense.

In 1906 the General Assembly of Georgia passed a bill authorizing the establishment of one agricultural high school in each of the eleven congressional districts of the state. All eleven of these schools were established and opened for work by September, 1908. These schools are supported from a fertilizer tax, much of which comes from the pockets of Georgia Negroes. Yet not a single one of these schools has been provided for the instruction of Negro youth, tho the Negroes form 45.1 per cent of the population of the state and fully 80 per cent of them live in the rural districts.

The thirty-ninth annual report of the department of education of the state of Georgia, in speaking of these agricultural high schools, which, it must be remembered, are provided only for the white youth of the state, says:

The agricultural high schools have now gone beyond the experimental stage. They are not yet what we hope to make them, but they are proving a success. . . . . . "The latest philosophy of education shows that that which fits a child best for his place in the world as a producer tends to his own highest development physically, intellectually and morally." It is upon this philosophy that these schools are founded. Secondarily, they are preparatory schools, but most of our graduates will not go to the colleges. The chief purpose is to make the citizen—farmer—to give the boys and girls that are to develop the high rural civilization of succeeding generations a liberal education in terms of country life. They train both the head and the hand and in requiring labor of every one they teach the dignity of labor. The sturdy young farmer graduate of one of these schools will not live in town and farm by proxy, but he will live in the country and till his own land. He will build up around him a progressive, intelligent and prosperous community. By precept and example he will encourage better farming, the use of better farm machinery and more home conveniences. His home will be neat and attractive, kept by one who is as well trained in her department as he is in his. Good roads, a better school and a better church will be found. The young people will have the best of social, educational and religious advantages. There we will see a happy, independent, prosperous country community, the people living on their own fertile and well tilled farms, enjoying the bountiful gifts of nature. There we will find a rural civilization in the highest, broadest sense of the word.[1]

This work is deserving of the highest praise and commendation. It is deplorable, however, that the Negro youth of the state are not offered similar opportunities for education and training.

The table which appears on the following page, showing the public high schools for Negroes in the United States, is compiled from the annual reports of the United States Commissioner of Education. This table is misleading, however, owing to the curricula of the alleged *high* schools. Many of the public schools have taken the name of "high school," tho no high school work is done in them. Others are called by that name from the fact that some work above the ordinary grammar grades is done in them. Georgia, for instance, is credited with eleven public high schools for Negroes. As a matter of fact there is not in the whole state a single public high school for Negroes with a four years' course above the eighth grade; and so far as the Conference has been able to ascertain only the following public schools for Negroes in the state of Georgia have any work at all above the eighth grade:

Athens	Milledgeville
Columbus	Vienna

Superintendent Charles L. Coon, who is quoted in the preceding section, estimates that during the year 1907 the Negroes of Georgia should have received from the school fund of the state, upon any fair race division, $141,682.54 more than they actually received in the way of school facilities for their children. This sum if wisely expended would have given high school opportunities to thousands of Negro children of the state. Not only the Negro children but also the whole state would have reaped the benefits.

What is true of Georgia in this respect is also true of other southern states. As a rule, the high school education of

---

[1] Thirty-ninth Annual Report of the Department of Education of the State of Georgia, pages 162-164.

Negro children is wofully neglected. In order to insure the largest and best results in the future the South must make provision for the high school training of its colored youth.

PUBLIC HIGH SCHOOLS FOR NEGROES

STATE	1899-1900	1900-01	1901-2	1902-3	1903-4	1904-5
Alabama	1	1	1	3	3	4
Arkansas	4	4	3	5	6	7
Delaware	. .	. .	. .	. .	1	1
District of Columbia	1	1	1	2	2	2
Florida	2	2	2	3	4	4
Georgia	4	4	4	4	7	6
Illinois	2	2	2	2	2	2
Indiana	3	3	5	6	6	6
Indian Territory	. .	. .	. .	. .	1	1
Kentucky	8	8	7	6	6	7
Louisiana	. .	. .	1	1	1	1
Maryland	2	2	1	1	1	1
Mississippi	7	7	8	7	8	10
Missouri	15	18	17	19	19	21
North Carolina	3	3	2	1	. .	1
Ohio	. .	. .	1	2	1	2
Oklahoma	. .	. .	1	3	3	3
Pennsylvania	1	1	1	1	1	1
South Carolina	7	7	5	6	9	9
Tennessee	8	8	8	11	9	10
Texas	16	19	19	29	32	37
Virginia	5	7	6	7	5	6
West Virginia	3	3	4	4	4	4
Total	92	100	99	123	131	146

STATE	1905-6	1906-7	1907-8	1908-9	1909-10
Alabama	3	4	1	3	4
Arkansas	7	7	5	5	6
Delaware	1	1	1	1	1
District of Columbia	2	2	2	1	1
Florida	2	2	2	3	6
Georgia	6	6	5	7	11
Illinois	3	4	4	4	4
Indiana	6	7	4	4	6
Indian Territory	1	. .	. .	. .	. .
Kansas	. .	. .	. .	. .	1
Kentucky	5	6	4	6	7
Louisiana	1	1	1	1	1
Maryland	1	1	1	1	1
Mississippi	8	8	6	7	8
Missouri	22	17	15	13	21
North Carolina	1	1	. .	. .	. .
Ohio	1	1	1	2	2
Oklahoma	3	3	4	2	3
Pennsylvania	1	1	1	. .	1
South Carolina	4	2	2	2	4
Tennessee	9	8	10	9	7
Texas	31	31	30	32	36
Virginia	5	5	5	6	5
West Virginia	4	3	2	3	5
Total	129	121	106	112	141

Section 27. The Outlook

It is unfortunate that definite conclusions as to the Negro public schools of the United States must be made on such a fragmentary and partial basis of fact as has been presented in this study. It is nothing less than a shame that the United States Bureau of Education is not given funds and authority sufficient to enable it to tell the whole truth concerning our efforts to educate the children of the freedmen as well as of our general educational system. The figures supplied at present bear on their face the evidence of inaccuracy, carelessness and ignorance, as may be plainly seen. We do not as a matter of fact know definitely the facts concerning public education in the South.

The Conference has made every effort to secure reliable information upon which to base this study and the resulting evidence speaks for itself. The difficulties which have been met are those difficulties which are common to every attempt at a scientific study of any phase of an intricate social problem.

The findings of the Conference are in agreement with the authoritative statements of other educational investigators, a few examples of which will suffice. The following quotations are from Mr. W. T. B. Williams, who is field agent of the John F. Slater Fund.[1]

In the greater portion of the country the colored people are cut off from the ordinary incentives to interest in education. Aside from teaching they share not at all, or but little, in the management of the schools or in the popular movements for school improvement. And when the Negro is considered at all, too often it is merely to be told that his education is a burden to other men, and at best that he ought not expect to reap the same rewards from education as others. In so far as Negro education receives popular favor generally it is with the idea that thereby the Negro may be of greater service to others. That he should be trained for his own best self-development meets but scant popular favor. As a result the Negro is often charged with having no interest in education, or when he makes indifferent use of the public schools, he is blamed for being a passive recipient of what they have to give.

The apparent indifference of the colored people to public education is

---

[1] From "The Outlook in Negro Education," a paper read by Mr. W. T. B. Williams before the National Association of Teachers in Colored Schools in the summer of 1911.

due in the main to the ineffectiveness of their schools. And in so far as there is any other real indifference, it is to be overcome mainly thru larger participation in the affairs of the schools. It is not reasonable to expect that the colored people, or any people, will give enthusiastic support to any feature of government or of social uplift upon which they have scarcely an opportunity to express an opinion, and from the administration of which they are almost entirely excluded.

.   .   .   .

A cursory review of colored schools in seven southern states where most of the colored people live will give a fair idea of general educational conditions in the colored schools of the South. The seven states are Virginia, North Carolina, South Carolina, Georgia, Alabama, Mississippi and Louisiana.

.   .   .   .

South Carolina, with 27,288 more colored than white children, employs only 2,696 colored teachers against 4,180 white teachers. And Mississippi, with 17,247 more colored than white children enrolled in her schools, employs 2,547 more white than colored teachers.

In all these states the number of colored children enrolled per teacher is greater for the colored than for the white teacher. With an average of 58 pupils to a colored teacher and 46 to a white, they are nearer together in Louisiana than elsewhere. In Mississippi and in South Carolina they are farthest apart, each colored teacher having an average of 67 and each white teacher an average of only 36.

About seventy per cent of the white school population of these seven southern states is enrolled in the schools. The figures from five of them show, however, that the enrollment of the colored children in one state only, North Carolina, reaches as high as sixty-five per cent, while in Alabama and Louisiana it drops to forty-one and thirty-nine per cent respectively. In this group of states the highest average of white school population per teacher is sixty-eight in Louisiana. From this it runs down to fifty and forty-nine in Virginia and Mississippi respectively. On the other hand, the lowest average of colored school population per teacher is eighty-three, in North Carolina. And it goes up steadily to 152 children of school age per colored teacher in Alabama.

.   .   .   .

While salaries in all southern schools are relatively low, it is at this point that the colored school suffers most. Colored teachers usually receive from one-half to two-thirds the monthly pay of white teachers, and that, outside of the cities, for shorter periods than the whites. And there are but few signs of improvement in these conditions. From many indications it actually seems that the states are going backward in the matter of salaries for colored teachers. North Carolina furnishes a significant example in point. In 1885 the average salary of a colored country teacher was $23.30. Twenty years afterwards, in 1905, the average salary was only $22.20.

.   .   .   .

The following comment of the superintendent will suffice. He says: "It will be observed that the above table shows that considerable more was spent on rural Negro schools in 1895 than in 1905, and that almost as much was spent in 1885 as in 1905. Suppose our white schools showed the same results for the past twenty years, would we not be necessarily alarmed at that evidence of lack of progress?"

In his report for 1906, and there has been no material change since, this superintendent says: "In thirty counties (of North Carolina) the Negro country teachers are now paid less than $20 per month each. .   .   .   . The country school population of the thirty counties which pay Negro teachers less than $20 per month is 59,665, or nearly one-third of all the Negro country school population of the state."

.   .   .   .

The tendency is toward a rapid increase in the salaries of white teachers without any perceptible increase in the salaries of colored teachers. In Virginia, for example, the average pay for white women teachers has risen in the last one or two years to $39, while the salaries of colored women teachers have remained stationary.

.   .   .   .

As small as the amounts are in each southern state for every child of school age, still they are greatly in excess of the actual amounts spent upon the education of each colored child. In scarcely one of the southern states does a colored child receive half of what goes to each white child. In North Carolina each white child's education costs $3.81 per year, while each colored child gets $1.58; in Mississippi each white child gets $7.63 and each colored child $1.89; in South Carolina, where the greatest disparity seems to obtain, there is an average expenditure of $10.34 for each white child and $1.70 for each colored child enrolled in the schools.

.   .   .   .

As has been well said, Negro education has never been actually tried in the South.

.   .   .   .

The average salary paid colored women teachers in nineteen counties of South Carolina is less than $80 per school year. And in five counties of this state the terms of colored schools are given as seven, eight, nine and ten weeks respectively.

As for the physical conditions of rural school houses for colored youth, Dr. Dillard of the Jeanes Fund reports to the United States Commissioner of Education as follows after visits in Virginia, North Carolina, South Carolina and Alabama: "With rare exceptions I found wretched conditions in the way of school houses and school equipment."

The following official description given four years ago of school houses for colored youth in North Carolina still holds good, for most rural schools at least: "These children are provided with 2,198 school houses valued at $124.37 each. Only sixty-four of these houses have any patent desks, and the sixty-four thus equipped are found in seventeen different counties. All the other Negro school houses are furnished either with home-made desks or with benches. Nearly half of these Negro school houses, 964 in all, have no furniture except benches, which of itself makes it next to impossible to do any very effective teaching in the primary grades."

What is true generally of our rural schools is too often almost as true of many of our city schools. They are usually, however, better housed, tho often they are badly overcrowded. They have longer terms, richer courses of study, and sometimes are better supervised. It is disheartening, tho, to see how poor and inadequate many of the colored school buildings are in a number of our otherwise progressive southern cities. Indeed it is not difficult to point out important little southern cities with no colored school buildings at all. In such cases, however, some public money is given to the county school outside or to one or more private colored schools operating in the city. In their excellent provisions for colored schools such cities as Louisville, Nashville, Chattanooga and Little Rock are deserving of great praise, to say nothing of the splendid equipment and the admirable administration of the schools for colored youth in Washington, Indianapolis, St. Louis and other cities of Missouri and Texas. But the conditions reported by the superintendent of schools of Augusta, Georgia, in 1904 obtain still only too frequently in most of our southern cities. The report reads: "Altogether we can accommodate not more than 2,100 pupils in our Negro schools, out of the 6,500 in the school population. This seating capacity is possible only by having two sessions a day in the lower grades, giving the teachers as many as 100 pupils to teach in two sections, one-half in the morning and the other half in the afternoon."

The remarkable movement during the last few years for increased high school facilities has hardly touched the colored people at all. The United States Commissioner of Education reports for 1910 only 141 public high schools in the whole United States for the colored race. This is a smaller number than the number of new high schools created during the present school year in a dozen southern states; fewer, too, than were created recently in Virginia alone in eighteen months. Virginia has raised her full number of high schools for whites from 75 to 400 within the last half dozen years.

As a southern authority on high schools regretfully says, there are practically no public high schools for colored people. Generally there is but one public institution in a state giving normal training to prospective colored teachers. This school is generally a part of the agricultural and mechanical college, where the emphasis is usually upon industrial or technical training with but little or no attention to special training for actual work in the classroom. And there does not exist for the training of colored youth a single public institution of full college rank in all the Southland.

It is not generally known, for instance, even among colored people, to say nothing of whites, that from 1884 to 1900 the A. M. E. Church raised and appropriated for schools $1,140,013.31; that the A. M. E. Zion Church during a recent quadrennium, raised for schools $71,585.21; that several C. M. E. conferences in the South raise for similar purposes about $10,000 annually; that the expenditures for sixty-one Baptist schools, supported almost entirely by Negroes for the single year 1906, amounted to $148,883.50; that the colored Baptists of North Carolina alone raised $22,000 last year for the smaller Baptist schools of that state, and that the Negroes contribute annually in nearly every southern state thousands of dollars as supplements to the inadequate public school funds. In Virginia the records show that from $5,000 to $8,000 are raised for this purpose annually by the colored people. For the school year 1910-11 the colored people of Macon county, Alabama, are reported to have raised $4,000 for school supplements. And there are hundreds of dollars given by the colored people every year of which no official records are made. To make these facts known will encourage our friends and stimulate us to greater efforts in behalf of Negro youth.

Likewise, we quote from "Suggested Solutions for Some Rural School Problems in South Carolina," by Mr. W. K. Tate, State Supervisor of Elementary Rural Schools. The reprint from the forty-third annual report of the state superintendent of education is issued by the University of South Carolina in its quarterly bulletin, No. 28, Part VI, January, 1912.

During the current year the Negro schools of the state enrolled 193,440 pupils. The greater part of the pupils are in the country schools of the state and these schools show an increased enrollment of Negro pupils every year. The education of the Negro in South Carolina is in the hands of the white race. The white trustees apportion the funds, select the teachers, and receive the reports. The county superintendent has the supervision of these schools in his hands. We have expended this year $349,834.60 in the support of Negro schools. I never visit one of these schools without feeling that we are wasting a large part of this money and are neglecting a great opportunity. The Negro school houses are miserable beyond all description. They are usually without comfort, equipment, proper lighting, or sanitation. Nearly all the Negroes of school age in the district are crowded into these miserable structures during the short term which the school runs. Most of the teachers are absolutely untrained and have been given certificates by the county board not because they have passed the examination, but because it is necessary to have some kind of a Negro teacher. [1]

Mr. Tate speaks further of the Negro schools:

The Negro school buildings in the state are in most cases a serious reflection on our civilization. They are without adaptation to school work, are destitute of all proper furniture and equipment, frequently without window sash, usually unceiled, often without any kind of heating arrangements, and comfortless and unsanitary in the extreme. They are usually erected by private effort and without any sort of suggestion or direction from any competent authority. Frequently the same money spent wisely would secure a cheap but decent building. In my opinion, simple plans for very inexpensive school buildings should be prepared and distributed for the guidance of trustees in the erection of Negro buildings, and the Negroes should be encouraged to provide school buildings as convenient and attractive as the churches which they are erecting all over the state. I believe that comfortable and sanitary school buildings for the Negroes would go far toward raising their standards of living and would awaken new wants and the consequent incentives to labor which now seem to be so sadly lacking. In my journeys over the state this fall I have seen thousands of acres of cotton unpicked. It is useless to expect labor beyond that necessary to supply the wants of the laborer. The wants connected with a well-kept home are the most constant and the most insistent. A comfortable and attractive school house for the Negro children will help set for them a better standard of living, and will secure for the landowner a more steady and more reliable tenantry. [2]

One of the most potent factors making for the educational advancement of the South during recent years has been the Southern Education Board. As to the scope of its work, we quote from "A Review of Five Years," published by the board in 1907: [3]

In this movement, divisive questions have been avoided and those of common concern have received chief attention, in the belief that unity is essential to the greatest efficiency, and that every advance in the cause of popular education is of universal significance.

[1] "Suggested Solutions for Some Rural School Problems in South Carolina," by W. K. Tate, State Supervisor of Elementary Rural Schools. Page 31.

[2] *Ibid*, 13-14.

[3] Southern Education Board: A Review of Five Years. 1907. Page 38.

The white people seem to have reaped the greatest immediate advantage. The conferences have been almost confined to them in the attendance; they have caught the spirit of these occasions, have put themselves into the new efforts suggested and carried them into practical demonstration; naturally the schools for white children have been the first to feel the influence.

From these and other evidences adduced it seems fair to conclude:

1. That the overwhelming majority of Negro children of school age are not in school.

2. That the chief reason for this is the lack of school facilities; and a further reason is the poverty and ignorance of parents.

3. That those Negro children who are in school are as a rule poorly taught by half-prepared and poorly paid teachers and thru short terms of three to six months a year.

4. That the school houses and equipment for Negro schools are for the most part wretched and inadequate.

5. That the Negro schools as a rule receive little or no helpful superintendence from the school authorities.

6. That the result and apparently one of the objects of disfranchisement has been to cut down the Negro school fund, bar out competent teachers, lower the grade and efficiency of the course of study and employ as teachers in the Negro schools those willing tools who do not and will not protest or complain.

7. That in the attempt to introduce much needed and valuable manual and industrial training there has been introduced into the curriculum of the Negro common school a mass of ill-considered, unrelated work which has overburdened the teacher and pushed into the background the vital studies of reading, writing and arithmetic. In a large measure this has been done with the avowed object of training Negroes as menials and laborers and of cutting them off from the higher avenues of life.

8. That the forward movement in education in the South during the last ten years has been openly confined almost

entirely to white people. The movement for local school taxes, better high schools, consolidation of schools and transportation of children has with small exception been encouraged and made possible among the whites and not among the Negroes. In many cases the Negroes have been taxed for the improvement of white school facilities, while their own schools have not been allowed to share in these improvements.

9. That along with this curtailment of elementary public education for Negroes has gone a tendency to decry the work of those schools which are devoted to the higher training of the Negro youth, to lower their curricula, to cut off northern benevolence and to decrease the supply of intellectual leaders for the Negro race.

To the editors of this study, these facts seem incontrovertible. If they are not true the evidence for them is of such a character as to call for federal investigation. It would seem, therefore, of prime necessity that the United States Bureau of Education be so enlarged and extended as to investigate the status of elementary education in the United States; that federal inspectors be put in the field to make regular and searching reports; further than this that a large annual fund be provided to aid common school education in parts of the United States where the need is greatest, such aid to be so given as to encourage the largest amount of local effort and to discourage discrimination on account of race or poverty.

This is surely a modest and reasonable program and its carrying out in the immediate future would be a work of far-seeing statesmanship. The United States of America permitted the enslavement of millions of black folk and then freed them in ignorance and poverty. From that day to this there has been no systematic attempt to give the masses of those people systematic elementary school training. It is time to make such an attempt.

ADDENDUM.—Page 32 gives the cost of the new high school for Negroes in St. Louis as $100,000. It should be $300,000. The exact figures are given on page 96.

Index

The Atlanta University Publications, No. 17

THE

NEGRO AMERICAN

ARTISAN

Report of a Social Study made by Atlanta University
under the patronage of the Trustees of the John F.
Slater Fund; with the Proceedings of the 17th Annual
Conference for the Study of the Negro Problems, held
at Atlanta University, on Monday, May 27th, 1912

Edited by

W. E. Burghardt Du Bois, Ph.D.
Director of Publicity and Research, National Association for
the Advancement of Colored People

and

Augustus Granville Dill, A.M.
Associate Professor of Sociology in Atlanta University

The Atlanta University Press
ATLANTA, GA.
1912

IT IS something more than mere prediction to suggest that along the lines of liberal surroundings, education, and culture lies the ultimate solution of the labor problem.

—*Thomas Nixon Carver.*

The Negro American Artisan

Contents

The Seventeenth Annual Conference

"The Negro Artisan"

PROGRAM

First Session, 10:00 a. m.

President Ware presiding.

Subject: "The Training of Artisans."

"Methods of the Present Investigation." Mr. A. G. Dill, of Atlanta University.

Address: Mr. Chester A. Coles, of Atlanta, Ga.

Address: Mrs. Florence Kelley, of New York City.

Second Session, 11:30 a. m.

Subject: "Health and Efficiency." (Separate meetings for men and women.)

Address to men: Dr. Stephen A. Peters.

Address to women: Dr. Shelby Boynton.

Third Session, 3:00 p. m.

The Fifteenth Annual Mothers' Meeting. (In charge of Gate City Free Kindergarten Association). Mrs. I. E. Wynn presiding.

Subject: "The Kindergarten and the Artisan."

1. Address: Mrs. Florence Kelley, New York City.
2. Report of the Treasurer: Mrs. Lizzie Burch.
3. Collection.
4. Kindergarten songs, games and exercises by one hundred and fifty children of the five free kindergartens:
   East Cain Street—Mrs. Ola Perry Cooke.
   Bradley Street—Mrs. Hattie Sims Fountain.
   White's Alley—Mrs. Idella F. Hardin.
   Allen's Alley—Miss Willie Kelley.
   Leonard Street Orphanage—Miss Rosa Martin.

Fourth Session, 8:00 p. m.

President Ware presiding.

Subject: "The Artisan and the Artisan's Problems."

Address: Mrs. Florence Kelley, New York City.

Music.

Address: Mr. Alexander D. Hamilton, Atlanta, Ga.

Discussion.

Preface

There is only one sure basis of social reform and that is Truth—a careful, detailed knowledge of the essential facts of each social problem. Without this there is no logical starting place for reform and uplift. Social difficulties may be clear and we may inveigh against them, but the causes proximate and remote are seldom clear to the casual observer and usually are quite hidden from the man who suffers from, or is sensitive to, the results of the snarl.

To no set of problems are these truths more applicable than to the so-called Negro problems. Perhaps the most immediate of these problems is the problem of work. To many superficial men the problem is simple: *The Negro is lazy; make him work.* Hence peonage, vagrancy laws and the like. To other men, broader minded, but unacquainted with the facts, the matter, while not simple, is clear: *Negroes have a childish ambition to do work for which they are not fitted. Let us train them to do work for which they are fitted.*

This study is an attempt to get at the facts underlying such widespread thot as this by making a study of the trained Negro laborer, his education, opportunity, wages and work. The first attempt at this was made in 1902 and the results appeared in No. 7 of the Atlanta University Publications. The present study seeks to go over virtually the same ground after an interval of ten years.

The study is, therefore, a further carrying out of the plan of social study of the Negro American, by means of an annual series of decennially recurring subjects covering, so far as is practicable, every phase of human life. This plan originated at Atlanta University in 1896. The object of these studies is primarily scientific—a careful research for truth; conducted as thoroly, broadly and honestly as the material resources and mental equipment at command will allow. It must be remembered that mathematical accuracy in these studies is impossible; the sources of information are of varying degrees of accuracy and the pictures are wofully incomplete. There is necessarily much repetition in the successive studies, and some contradiction of previous reports by later ones as new material comes to hand. All we claim is that the work is as thoro as circumstances permit and that with all its obvious limitations it is well worth the doing. Our object is not simply to serve science. We wish not only to make the truth clear but to present it in such shape as will encourage and help social reform. In this work we have received unusual encouragement from the scientific world, and the publisht results of these studies are used in America, Europe, Asia and Africa. Very few books on the Negro problem, or any phase of it, have been publisht in the last decade which have not acknowledged their indebtedness to our work.

We believe that this pioneer work in a wide and important social field deserves adequate support. The Trustees of the John F. Slater Fund have given us generous aid in the last five years, which aid has been supplemented by the general funds of the University. These latter funds are limited, however, and needed in many other directions. What we earnestly ask is an endowment for this research work. A fund yielding $5,000 a year might under proper supervision yield incalculable good and help the nation and the modern world to a righteous solution of its problems of racial contact.

Resolutions

The following resolutions are the expression of the members, delegates and attendants upon the sessions of the seventeenth annual Conference:

The Seventeenth Annual Atlanta Conference has considered the subject of the Negro artisan in a manner similar to the study of ten years ago. We have come to the following conclusions:

1. Negro American skilled labor is undoubtedly gaining ground both North and South.

2. This advance however is in the face of organized opposition and prejudice. The organized opposition is illustrated by the determined effort of the white locomotive firemen to displace Negro firemen, not for inefficiency or any cause but race and color. Race prejudice is shown by both employers and laborers in every line of skilled labor where the Negro is seeking admission. On the other hand, in the Miners' Union and in some building trades where the colored man has an assured footing, he is well treated and is achieving economic independence.

3. What, then, should be the black man's attitude toward white laborers and the labor movement? Some people advise enmity and antagonism. This is a mistake. The salvation of all laborers, white and black, lies in the great movement of social uplift known as the labor movement which has increased wages and decreased hours of labor for black as well as white. When the white laborer is educated to understand economic conditions he will outgrow his pitiable race prejudice and recognize that black men and white men in the labor world have a common cause. Let black men fight prejudice and exclusion in the labor world and fight it hard; but do not fight the labor movement.

We call attention to the advantages derived by the working class from co-operation in every form in which it has been practiced—in the building of homes, in buying the necessaries of life, in the selling of farm products and in bargaining for wages. We note the gain made thru teachers' associations and mothers' clubs, medical associations and farmers' unions and building and loan associations. We recommend to the Negro American in general and to the Negro artisan in particular the study of the principle of association as it has been applied in other countries as well as our own.

4. Manual training and industrial and technical education are great needs of the colored people; but the movement in this line today, excellent

as it is, is in some respects deficient. There are points to be remembered in this connection:

(1) Industrial training cannot be made a substitute for intelligence.

The effort to abolish illiteracy receives great encouragement from the figures of the thirteenth census which shows that from 1870 to 1910 illiteracy among Negro Americans had been reduced from eighty per cent to thirty per cent, while the Negro population had more than doubled.

Illiteracy, however, is still so extensive that we call upon the government of city, state and nation to work together to provide sufficient schools for the elementary education of all persons below the age of twenty-one years. Of equal importance with universal elementary education is the need of higher and technical education in preparation for the professions and industries, including the great and fundamental industry of home-making. For this education, also, the active participation of city, state and nation is urgently needed.

(2) Technical training for trades which are not in economic demand is not a good investment.

There is an attempt in many quarters to restrict the training of Negroes in general intelligence—even in reading, writing and arithmetic—to the narrowest possible limits and to substitute industrial training. This will not make intelligent working men but will encourage ignorance. It is not good business to train a race simply in the poorly paid, the declining and the undesirable vocations. This will increase poverty and discontent.

5. Finally, this Conference notes with pride and satisfaction the increase of property-holding among Negro Americans, which fact so effectually sets at naught the familiar charge of laziness and inefficiency.

(Signed)   W. E. B. Du Bois, New York, N. Y.
Florence Kelley, New York, N. Y.
A. G. Dill, Atlanta, Ga.

A Select Bibliography of the Negro American Artisan

Part I

Arranged alphabetically by authors

A Brief Sketch of the schools for black people and their descendants, established by the Society of Friends, etc. Phila., 1857. 32 pp.

Agricola (pseudonym). An impartial view of the real state of the black population in the U. S., etc. Phila , 1824. 26 pp.

Allen, W. G. The American prejudice against color. London. 107 pp. 1853.

Alvord, J. W. Letters from the South relating to the condition of the Freedmen, addressed to Gen. Major O. O. Howard. Washington, 1870. 42 pp.

America's Race Problems. N. Y., 1901. 187 pp.

Atlanta University Publications: No. 2: Social and physical condition of Negroes in cities. 1897. 72, 14 pp.

No. 3. Some efforts of American Negroes for their own social betterment. 1898. (2) 66 pp.

No. 4. The Negro in Business. 1899. (3) 77pp.

No. 5. The College-bred Negro. 1900. (2), 115 (3) pp.

No. 6. The Negro Common School, etc. 1901. ii, (2), 120 pp.

No. 7. The Negro Artisan. 1902. 192 pp.

No. 9. Notes on Negro Crime, Particularly in Georgia. 1904. 68 pp.

No. 12. Economic Co-operation among Negro Americans. 184 pp. 1907.

No. 13. The Negro American Family. 152 pp. 1908.

No. 14. Efforts for Social Betterment among Negro Americans. 136 pp. 1909.

No. 15. The College-bred Negro American. 104 pp. 1910.

No. 16. The Common School and the Negro American. 140 pp. 1911.

Bacon, Benjamin C. Statistics of the colored people of Philadelphia, taken by and published by order of the Board of Education of the Pennsylvania Society for the Promotion of the Abolition of Slavery. Philadelphia, 1856. Second ed. Phila., 1859. 24 pp.

Baker, Ray Stannard. Following the Color-line. New York, 1908.

Banks, Chas. Negro Town and Colony. Mound Bayou, Miss. 10 pp.

Barringer, Dr. Paul. The American Negro: his past and future. Raleigh, 1900. 23 pp.

Bassett, John S. Slavery and Servitude in the Colony of South Carolina. Johns Hopkins Press, Baltimore, 1896.

Slavery and Servitude in the Colony of North Carolina. Balt., 1896. 86 pp. Series 14. No. 4, 5. Authorities cited, p. 3.

History of Slavery in North Carolina. Johns Hopkins University Studies. Balt., 1899. 111 pp. Studies in historical and political science. Authorities, pp. 110-111. Series 17, No. 7, 8.

Blair, Lewis H. The prosperity of the South dependent upon the elevation of the Negro. Richmond, Va., 1889. 147 pp.

Boas, Franz. Commencement Address at Atlanta University, May, 1906. Atlanta University Leaflet, No. 19. 15 pp.

Brackett, Jeffrey Richardson. The Negro in Maryland. A study of the institution of slavery. Balt., 1889. (5) 268 pp. (Johns Hopkins University Studies, extra vol. 6).

The status of the slave, 1775-1789. (Essay V. in Jameson's Essays in the constitutional history of the United States, 1775-1789). Boston, 1889. Pp. 263-311.

Notes on the progress of the colored people of Maryland since the war; a supplement to the "Negro in Maryland: a study of the institution of slavery." Johns Hopkins Press, Balt., 1890. Pp. 96.

Brousseau, Kate. L'education des Negres aux Etats-unis. Paris, 1904. 396, (1) pp.

Brown, Frederick John. The northward movement of the colored population. A statistical study. Balt., 1897. 50 pp.

Brown, H. M. A plea for industrial education among the colored people. New York, 1884. 30 pp.

Bruce, P. A. Economic History of Virginia in the 17th century. New York, 2 vol. 1896.

The plantation Negro as a freeman. New York, 1889. 262 pp.

Bruce, Roscoe Conkling. Service by the educated Negro. Tuskegee, 1903. 17 pp.

Bruce, W. Cabell. The Negro problem. Balt., 1891. 33 pp.

Buckingham, J. S. Slave States of America. London, 1842.

Buecher, Carl. Industrial Evolution. Translated by S. M. Wickett, New York, 1904. 393 pp.

Bumstead, Horace. Higher education of the Negro, its practical value. Atlanta, 1870. 15 pp.

Cable, George Washington. The Negro Question. New York, 1888, 32 pp. New York, 1890. 173 pp.

Campbell, Robert F. Some aspects of the race problem in the South. Pamphlet, 1899. Asheville, N. C. 31 pp.

Chandler, J. W. This is a white working-man's government Washington, 1866. 14 pp. U. t. p.

Cincinnati Convention of Colored Freedmen of Ohio, Proceedings, Jan. 14-19, 1852. Cincinnati, 1852.

Colored People's Blue Book and Business Directory of Chicago, Ill. 1905.

Commons, John R. et al. Documentary History of American Industrial Society. 10 Vols. Cleveland, 1910.

Condition of the people of color in Ohio. With interesting anecdotes. Boston, 1839. 42 pp.

Cooley, H. S. Slavery in New Jersey. Johns Hopkins University Studies. Balt., 1896. 60 pp. Series 14. Bibliography, pp. 59, 60.

Crisis, The. Organ of the National Association for the Advancement of Colored People. New York, 1910 et seq.

Curry, J. L. M. Education of Negroes since 1860. Balt., 1894. 32 pp.
J. F. Slater Fund Papers.
Difficulties, complications and limitations connected with the education of the Negro. (Trustees of the John F. Slater Fund. Occasional papers, No. 5.) Balt., 1895. Pp. 23.

De Bow, J. D. B. Industrial resources of the southern and western states. New Orleans, 1852-1853.

Denniker, J. The Races of Man. New York, 1904. 611 pp.

Douglass, H. Paul. Christian Reconstruction in the South. Boston, 1909. 407 pp.

Dowd, Jerome. The Negro Races. New York, 1907. 491 pp.

Du Bois, W. E. B. The Negro in the black belt: Some Social Sketches. In the Bulletin of the Department of Labor, No. 22.
The Philadelphia Negro. Phila., 1896. 520 pp.
The Negroes of Farmville, Va. U. S. Dept. of Labor Bulletin, Jan., 1898. Vol. III, No. 14. Pp. 1-38. Washington.
The Study of the Negro Problems. Annals of the American Academy of Political Science. Phila., 1898. 29 pp.
The Negro land-holders of Ga. U. S. Dept. of Labor Bulletin, No. 35, 1901. Pp. 647-777. Washington.
The relation of the Negroes and Whites in the South. Phila., 1901.
Souls of Black Folk. Chicago, 1903. 264 (1) pp.
The Quest of the Silver Fleece. Chicago, 1911. 434 pp.

Education and Employment Statistics of the colored people of Philadelphia. (In Library of Penn. Historical Association).

Eggleston, Edward. The Ultimate Solution of the American Negro Problem.

Ely, R. T. The Labor Movement in America. 1890.

Finger, S. M. Educational and religious interests of the colored people of the South. U. S. Bureau of Education circular of information, No. 2, 1886. Pp. 123-133.

Fortune, T. Thomas. Black and White. New York, 1884. Pp. 311.

Freedmen's Bureau. Annual Reports of the Bureau for Refugees, Freedmen and Abandoned Lands. 1866-1872.

French, Mrs. A. M. Slavery in South Carolina. New York, 1862. 312 pp.

Gannett, Henry. Occupations of the Negroes. (Trustees of the John F. Slater Fund. Occasional papers, No. 6). Balt., 1895. Pp. 16.
Statistics of the Negroes in the U. S. Balt., 1894. 28 pp.

Garnet, Henry Highland. The past and present condition and the destiny of the colored race. Troy, 1848. 29 pp.

Goodwin, M. B. History of schools for the colored population in the District of Columbia. U. S. Bureau of Education. Special Report on District of Columbia for 1869. Pp. 193-300.

Hammond, Isaac W. Slavery in New Hampshire. Concord, 1883.

Hampton Negro Conference. Reports, 1897-1911.

Hand, Daniel. A sketch of the life of, and of his benefaction to the American Missionary Association for the education of the colored people in the Southern States of America. New York, 1889. 31 pp.

Harris, William T. Education of the Negro. An address made to the students of Atlanta University, Atlanta, Ga., Oct. 29, 1895.

Hart, Albert B. Southern South. New York, 1910. 445 pp.

Haygood, Atticus G. Our Brother in Black: his freedom and his future. New York, 1881. 252 pp.

Haynes, George Edmund. The Negro at work in New York City. New York, 1912. 158 pp.

Helper, Hinton Rowan. The impending crisis of the South: how to meet it. New York, 1860. 420 pp.

Hickok, Chas. T. The Negro in Ohio, 1802-1870. A Thesis, etc. Cleveland, 1896. 182 pp.

Index to acts and resolutions of Congress and to proclamations and executive orders of the President, from 1861-1867, relating to the refugees, freedmen, etc. Washington.

Ingle, Edward. The Negro in the District of Columbia. Johns Hopkins University studies, Vol. XI. Balt., 1893. 110 pp.

Johnston, Sir Harry. Negro in the New World. New York, 1910. 499 pp.

Juge, M. A. The American planter, or the bound labor interest in the U. S. N. Y., 1854. 43 pp.

Kemble, Fanny. A journal of a residence on a Georgia plantation. N. Y., 1863. 337 pp.

Kirk, Edward Morris. Educated labor, etc. N. Y., 1868. 11 pp.

Labor and Capital. Investigation of Senate committee. (Blair committee). Washington, 1885. 5 vol.

Laws, J. B. The Negroes of Cinclaire central factory and Calumet plantation. U. S. Dept. of Labor Bulletin, 1902.

Levasseur, E. The American Workman. Translated by T. S. Adams, edited by T. Marburg. Balt. Johns Hopkins Press, 1900. 517 pp.

Livingstone, W. R. The Race Conflict. A study of conditions in America. London, 1911.

Lyell, Chas. A second Visit to U. S. New York, 1849. 2 vol.

MacAfee, C. B. Some Southern Problems. Parksville, Mo., 1898. 30 pp.

Macaulay, T. B. Social and Industrial Capacities of Negroes. Critical and misc. essays. 6:361-404.

Martin, T. H. Atlanta and her Builders. 1902.

May, Samuel. The right of colored people to education vindicated. Brooklyn, 1833. 24 pp.

Mayo, Amory Dwight. How shall the colored youth of the South be educated? Boston, 1897. (1), 213-224 pp.

The future of the colored race. Wash., 1900. U. S. Bureau of Education. Report, 1898-99, Vol. I. Pp. 1227-1248.

The opportunity and obligation of the educated class of colored people in the Southern states. N. P., 1899 (?). 32 pp.

McCrady, Edward. Slavery in the province of South Carolina. (In American Hist. Ass. Reports. 1895). Wash.

McNeill, G. E. The Labor Movement: the problem of today. Boston and New York, 1887. 670 pp.

Miller, Kelly. Race Adjustment. New York and Wash., 1908. 306 pp.
The education of the Negro. Wash., 1902. (U. S. Bureau of Education Reports, 1900-01, Vol. I. Pp. 731-859).
The primary needs of the Negro race. Wash., 1899. 18 pp.

Mitchell, S. C. Higher education and the Negro. (In Report of U. S. Bureau of Education, 1895. Pt. 2, p. 1360).

Moxom, Phillip Stafford. Our problem with the Negro in America. N. Y., 1903. 16 pp.

Needles, Edward. Ten years' progress, or a comparison of the state and condition of the colored people in the city and county of Philadelphia from 1837 to 1847. Phila., 1849.

Negro Exodus. Report and Testimony of the select committee of the U. S. Senate, etc. 3 vols. Wash.

Negroes of Litwalton, Va. In Bulletin of the Department of Labor, No. 37.

Negroes of Sandy Springs, Md. In Bulletin of Department of Labor, No. 32.

Negroes of Xenia, Ohio. In Bulletin of the Bureau of Labor, No. 48.

Oliver, Sir Sidney. White Capital and Colored Labor. London, 1906.

Olmstead, Frederick Law.
A Journey in the Seaboard Slave States. N. Y., 1856. Pp. 723.
Our Slave States. London, 1856.
A Journey in the Back Country. N. Y., 1861. Pp. 492.
A Journey Thru Texas. N. Y., 1857. Pp. 516.
The Cotton Kingdom. N. Y., 1861. 2 vol.

Orr, Gustavus. The education of the Negro. Atlanta, Ga., 1880. 15 pp.

Ovington, M. W. Half-a-Man. N. Y., 1911. 236 pp.

Page, T. N. The Negro, the Southerner's problem. N. Y., 1904. 316 pp.

Penn, I. G., and J. W. E. Bowen, editors. The United Negro: His problems and his progress. Containing the addresses and proceedings of the Negro Young People's Christian and Educational Congress, held August 6-11, 1902. Atlanta, 1902. 600 pp.

Phillips, Ulrich B. The plantation and frontier, 1649-1863. (Vols. 1 and 2 of the Documentary History of American Industrial Society). Cleveland, 1909.

Powderly, T. V. Thirty years of labor. 1889. 693 pp.

Proceedings of the Select Committee of the United States Senate to investigate the causes of the removal of the Negroes from the Southern states to the Northern states. 3 parts, 1486 pp. Wash., 1879-1880.

Ratzel, F. History of Mankind. N. Y., 1904. 3 vols.

Reed, William B. A Race between two Straits. Newport, 1912. 77 pp.

Report of the condition of the colored people of Cincinnati, 1835.

Report of the Industrial Commission on the relations and conditions of capital and labor, etc. 19 vols. Wash., 1901. (Consult especially Vols. VII, VIII, XII, XIV and XVII).

Schneider, Wilhelm. Der Culturfaehigkeit des Negers. Frankfurt, 1885. 220 pp.

Scober, J. Negro apprenticeship in the colonies. London, 1837. 44 pp.

Shaler, Nathaniel Southgate. The Neighbor. The natural history of human contrasts. (The problem of the African.) Boston, 1904. 342 pp.

Sharpe, H. Ed. On the abolition of Negro apprenticeship in a letter to Lord Brougham. London, 1838. 27 pp.

Sinclair, W. A. Aftermath of slavery. Boston, 1905. 358 pp.

Social and industrial condition of the Negro in Massachusetts. Boston, 1904. 319 pp.

Southern Workman, 1871-1912. 41 vols.

State convention of colored men of South Carolina. Proceedings at Columbia, 1883. Columbia, 1883. 6 pp.

Statistical inquiry, A, into the condition of the people of color of the city and the districts of Philadelphia. 1849. 44 pp.

Stetson, Geo. R. The problem of Negro education. Boston, 1884. 21 pp.

Still, Wm. The underground railroad. Phila., 1883.

Sturge, James. Horrors of the Negro apprenticeship system in the British colony. Glasgow, 1837. 20 pp.

Talbot, Henry. Manual Training, Art and the Negro. An experiment. (Reprinted from Pub. Sch. Journal, 1894). 34 pp.

The Economic Position of the American Negro. Reprinted from papers and proceedings of the seventeenth annual meeting of the American Economic Association, Dec. 1904.

Thompson, Geo. English Abolitionist. Speech at a great meeting for the extinction of Negro apprenticeship. London, 1838. 58 pp.

Tillinghast, Joseph Alex. The Negro in Africa and America. N. Y., 1902. 231 pp.

Trades of the colored people. Phila., 1838.

Trustees of the John F. Slater Fund. Occasional papers, 10 numbers. Balt., 1891-1897 (Nos. 1-6 partly reprinted in Report Bureau of Education, 1894-95, chap. 32).

United States Census Bureau. Censuses of 1850, 1860, 1870, 1880, 1890, 1900.

United States Department (Bureau) of Labor Bulletin: No. 10. Conditions of the Negro in various cities. No. 14. The Negroes of Farmville, Va., a social study, by W. E. B. Du Bois, Ph.D. No. 22. The Negro in the black belt: Some social sketches by W. E. B. Du Bois, Ph.D. No. 32. The Negroes of Sandy Spring, Md., a . social study by W. T. Thomas, Ph.D. No. 38. The Negroes of Cinclaire Central Factory and Calumet Plantation, La., by J. Braddford Laws. No. 48. The Negroes of Xenia, Ohio, by R. R. Wright, Jr., 1892. 31 pp.

United States Bureau of Education.   Education of colored race.   Negroes in America.   Wash., 1896.   (In report of commissioner for 1893-94. Vol. I, pp. 1038-1061).

United States Bureau of Education.   Annual Reports, 1887-1911.

United States Bureau of Education.   Education of the colored race. Wash., 1901.   Reports, 1899-1900.

United States Bureau of Education.   Education of the colored race. Wash., 1902.   Reports, 1900-1901.

United States Census.   Reference to the Negro American:
Volume on cotton production and land and labor.   Volume on population, part II: Ages, illiteracy, occupations.
Special reports: Volume on occupations.
Statistical Atlas Bulletins.
No. 8.   Negroes in the United States, by W. F. Willcox and W. E. B. Du Bois.   Wash., 1904.   333 pp.

United States: Report of the Industrial Commission, 1901, 1902.   19 vols. Wash.
For references to Negroes, see particularly:
7.   On the Relation and Condition of Capital and Labor in Manufactures and General Business.   1071 pp.
8.   On the Chicago Labor Disputes of 1900.   612 pp.
12.   On the Relations and Conditions of Capital and Labor in the Mining Industry.   747 pp.
14.   On the Relations and Conditions of Capital and Labor in Manufactures and General Business.   809 pp.

Vance, W. R.   Slavery in Kentucky.   1896.

Vass, S. N.   The Progress of the Negro Race.   Raleigh, 1906.   31 pp.

Washington, B. T.   Address delivered at the opening of the Atlanta Exposition, Sept. 18, 1895.   In Atlanta *Constitution*, Sept. 19, 1895.
Future of the American Negro.   Boston, 1899.   244 pp.
Education of the Negro.   Albany, 1900.   44 pp.
Negro Education not a Failure.   Tuskegee, Ala., 1904.   13 pp.
Working with the Hands.   New York, 1904.   246 pp.
The Story of the Negro.   New York, 1909.

Washington, B. T., and Du Bois, W. E. B.   The Negro and the South.

Weatherford, W. D.   Negro Life in the South.   New York, 1910.

Webster, Noah, Jr.   Effects of Slavery on Morals and Industry.   Hartford, 1793.

Weeden, William B.   Economic and Social History of New England, 1620-1789.   Boston, 1890.

West, Gerald M.   The Status of the Negro in Virginia during the Colonial Period.   New York, 1897.   76 pp.

Williams, George W.   History of the Negro Race in America.   New York and London, 1882.

Work, Monroe N. Negro Year Book. Tuskegee, Ala., 1912. 215 pp.
Wright, Carroll D. The Industrial Evolution of the United States. Chatauqua, 1897. 362 pp.
Wright, R. R., Jr. The Negro in Pennsylvania. Phila., 1912. 250 pp.

Part II. Periodical Literature

A. M. E. Church Review: The Negro as an inventor. R. R. Wright. 2:397.
American: Trade schools for Negroes. 19:353.
American Historical Review: Problem of Southern economic history. A. H. Stone. 13:779-97.
American Journal of Political Economy:
  Education of Negroes. A. A. Gundy. 1:295.
  Solution of Negro problem. W. A. Curtis. 3:352.
American Journal of Political Science: Philadelphia Negroes. K. B. Davis. 8:284.
American Journal of Social Science:
  Negro exodus (1879). 11:1, 22.
  Higher education of Negroes. H. L. Wayland. 34:68.
  Present problem of the education of Negroes. W. H. Baldwin. 37:52.
  Education of Negroes. C. D. Warner. 38:1.
  Education of Negroes. K. Miller. 39:117.
American Journal of Sociology:
  The Negro Artisan. W. E. B. Du Bois. 8:854-6.
  Industrial reorganization in Alabama after the Civil War. W. L. Fleming. 10:473-500.
American Magazine of Civics: Education of Negroes. J. L. M. Curry. 8:168.
American Missionary: 56 vol. 1856-1912.
American Statistical Association, Publications of: American Negroes. M. M. Dawson. 5:142.
Andover Review:
  Negroes at school. Horace Bumstead. 4:550.
  Education of Negroes. A. Salisbury. 6:256.
  Industrial education of Negroes. 14:254.
Annals of the American Academy of Political Science:
  Philadelphia Negro. W. E. B. Du Bois. 5:100-2.
  Study of Negro problems. W. E. B. Du Bois. 11:1.
  Race problem. 15:807-10.
  Relation of the Whites to the Negroes in the South. W. E. B. Du Bois. 18:121-40.
  Evolution of Negro labor. C. Kelsey. 21:55-76.
  Negro education in the South. W. B. Hill. 22:320-9.
  Negroes in the trade unions in New York. M. W. Ovington. 27:551-8.

Training of the Negro laborer in the North. H. M. Browne. 27:579-89.

Industrial conditions of the Negro in New York City. W. L. Bulkley. 27:590-6.

Relation of industrial education to national progress. B. T. Washington. 33:1-12.

Negro mine labor, central Appalachian coal field. G. T. Surface. 33:338-52.

Negro labor and the boll weevil. A. H. Stone. 33:391-8.

Economic needs of the South. W. H. Glason. 35:167-71.

Labor supply and labor problems of the South. E. M. Banks. 35:143-9.

Arena:

The race problem of Negroes. W. C. P. Breckinridge. 2:39.

The race problem of Negroes. Wade Hampton. 2:132.

Progress of the Negro. G. W. Forbes. 2:134-41.

The race problem of Negroes. J. T. Morgan. 2:385.

The race problem of Negroes. W. S. Scarborough. 2:560.

Negroes in the United States. N. S. Shaler. 2:660.

Educational possibilities of Negroes. B. T. Washington. 21:455.

Atlantic:

The Freedmen of Port Royal. Edward L. Pierce. 12:291.

Problems of Negroes. N. S. Shaler. 54:696.

Negroes: What they are doing for themselves. S. J. Barrows. 67:805.

Education of Negroes. W. T. Harris. 69:721.

Awakening of the Negro. 78:322.

Strivings of the Negro people. W. E. B. Du Bois. 80:194.

Training of Black Men. W. E. B. Du Bois. 90:289-97.

Fruits of industrial training. B. T. Washington. 92:453-62.

Bankers' Magazine: Economical aspects of the Negro. 33:933.

Cassier's Magazine: American Negro Artisan. T. J. Calloway. 25:435-45.

Catholic World:

Education of Negroes. J. R. Slattery. 56:28.

Present and future conditions of Negroes in the United States. J. R. Slattery. 58:219.

Negroes in Baltimore. J. R. Slattery. 66:519.

Century:

Signs of progress among Negroes. B. T. Washington. 37:472.

Industrial color line in the North. J. S. Stemons. 60:477.

Charities:

The Negro in the cities of the North. 15:1.

Kowaliga, a community with a purpose. W. E. Benson. 15:22-4.

Industrial conditions among Negro men in Boston. J. Daniels. 15:35-9.

Negro in times of industrial unrest. R. R. Wright, Jr. 15:69-73.

Manual training for Negro children. D. E. Gordon. 15:84.

Christian Examiner: Freedman and free labor at the South. 76:344.

Conservative Review: Social condition of the Negroes before the war. 3:211.
Contemporary:
    The race problem of Negroes. G. W. Cable. 53:443.
    American Negro of today. P. A. Bruce. 77:284.
Cosmopolitan: Problems in education. B. T. Washington. 33:506.
Crisis, The. Organ of the National Association for the Advancement of Colored People. 1910 et seq.
Current Literature: Economic work of the Negro. B. T. Washington. 32:85.
DeBow's Review:
    Importation of African laborers. 24:421.
    The South demands more Negro labor. E. Deloney. 25:491.
Education:
    Industrial education of Negroes. W. P. Johnston. 5:636.
    Education of Negroes. C. G. Andrews. 6:221.
Educational Review:
    New education in the South. P. B. Barringer. 21:233.
    Education of the Negro in its historical aspects. D. L. Kiehle. 27:299.
    Social and industrial capacities of Negroes of the South. 45:383.
    Negro apprenticeship system. J. Spedding. 66:477.
Forum:
    Progress of the Negroes of the South. A. D. Mayo. 10:335.
    The Negro and Education. K. Miller. 30:693.
Gunton's Magazine:
    Coleman cotton mill. Sept., 1902.
    Colored men as cotton manufacturers. J. Dowd. 23:254-6.
    Negro as an artisan. 24:452.
    Georgia State Industrial College for Negroes. L. B. Ellis. 25:218-26.
Harper's Weekly:
    Georgia race strike. 53:5.
    Georgia strike arbitration. July 3, 1909.
Independent:
    Industrial education for the African. J. E. Rankin. April 2, 1891. 43:3.
    Condition of the Negro: What he is doing for himself and what is being done for him. Testimony from both races. (A symposium). 43:477.
    Negro manual training experiment in Texas. 47:5552.
    Industrial training. W. E. Hutchison. 58:92-4.
International Monthly: American Negro and his economic value. B. T. Washington. 2:672-86.
    Negro as an industrial factor. 2:672.
International Review: Negro exodus (1879). 7:373.
Lippincott: Industrial question. 59:266.
Manufacturers' Record: Colored help for textile mills. (Baltimore, Md.), Sept. 22, 1893.
Methodist Quarterly: Negro exodus (1879). 39:722.

Missionary Review:
  What industrial training is doing for the Negro. H. B. Frissell.
    27:574-8.
  What intellectual training is doing for the Negro. W. E. B. Du Bois.
    27:578-82.
Nation:
  Negro exodus (1879). 28:242, 386.
  Negro labor in Southern manufactures. 53:208.
  Negro and the trade unions. 76:186.
  Rural industrial school. 88:401-2.
N. Ecclesiastical Review: Freedmen and Southern labor problems.
    3:257.
New World: Education of Negroes. 9:625.
New York Times: The black North. (Studies of Negroes in Northern
    cities). 1901.
North American Review: Negro as a mechanic. 156:472.
Our Day: Industrial education of Negroes. B. T. Washington. 16:79.
Outlook:
  Negroes an industrial factor. C. B. Spahr. 62:31.
  Negro cotton mill. 67:468.
  Savings of black Georgia. W. E. B. Du Bois. 69:128-30.
  Negro in business. J. T. Montgomery. 69:733-4.
  Aims of Negro education. H. B. Frissell. 74:937-9.
  Training of Negroes for social power. W. E. B. Du Bois. 75:409-14.
  Negro enterprise. B. T. Washington. 77:115-8.
  Helping the Negro to help himself. C. C. Smith. 78:727-30.
  Economic future of the Negro. 82:102-3.
  New phase of industrial education. Kowaliga. J. C. Barrows.
    83:896-8.
  Work and education. 88:526-7.
  Forced labor in America and the Alabama contract law. 90:846-8.
  Definite progress among Negroes. 92:770-1.
  Georgia Railroad strike. 92:310-2.
Political Science Quarterly:
  Negro artisan. 9:699-701.
  Slave labor problem in the Charleston district. U. B. Phillips.
    22:416-39.
  Local study of the race problem in Georgia. R. P. Brooks. 26:193-221.
Popular Science Monthly:
  Negro artisan. W. E. B. Du Bois. 19:699-701.
  Negro since the Civil War. N. S. Shaler. 57:29-39.
Public Opinion: Knights of Labor and Negroes. 2:1.
Review of Reviews: Negro progress on the Tuskegee plan. Albert
    Shaw. 9:436.
  American Negro at Paris. W. E. B. Du Bois. 22:575-7.
Science: Industrial training and the Negro problem in the United States.
    E. L. Blackshear. 23:606-7.

Scribners: Negroes of the South under free labor. D. C. Barrows, Jr. 21:830.

Slater Fund:

    Proceedings and occasional papers of.

    No. 3. Education of Negroes since 1860. Curry.

    Proceedings and occasional papers of. No. 6.

    Occupations of Negroes. Gannett.

South Atlantic Quarterly: Industrial development in Alabama during the Civil War. W. L. Flemings. 3:260.

Southern Workman:

    Industrial training and the race question. E. L. Blackshear. July, 1906.

    The industrial opportunity for Negroes in Philadelphia. J. B. Leeds. July, 1911.

    Some labor tendencies in the South. G. S. Dickerman. Oct., 1907.

    Industrial condition of Negro women in New York. Samuel H. Bishop. Sept., 1910.

    The Negro in Chicago. R. R. Wright, Jr. Oct., 1906.

    Value of educating the Negro. B. T. Washington. Oct., 1904.

    Local conditions among Negroes in four counties of Georgia. W. T. B. Williams. Nov., 1906.

    Negro craftsmen in New York. Helen A. Tucker. Oct., Nov., 1907.

    New York Negro Colony. M. W. Ovington. Nov., 1909.

    Pleas for Negro trade schools in cities. R. C. Bruce. Dec., 1904.

    Relation of industrial education to the economic progress of the South. T. J. Jones. Dec., 1908.

    The Negro in Gloucester county, Virginia. W. T. B. Williams. Feb., 1906.

    Economic progress of the South. T. J. Jones. March, 1909.

    Forty years of Negro progress. R. R. Wright, Jr. March, 1907.

    Place of industrial training in higher Negro education. W. E. Hutchison. April, 1906.

    Relation of industrial education to the nation's progress. B. T. Washington. April, 1908.

    Industrial education in schools of Columbus. C. B. Gibson. May, 1908.

Spectator:

    Capacity of Negroes. 75:927.

    Progress among Negroes. 63:852.

Tradesman (Chattanooga, Tenn.):

    Negro labor. July 15, 1889.

    Negro labor. July 20, 1891.

    The Negro skilled laborer in the South. Oct. 15, 1902.

World's Work:

    Negro as he really is. W. E. B. Du Bois. 2:848-66.

    Successful training of the Negro. B. T. Washington. 6:3731-51.

    Georgia Negroes and their fifty millions of savings. W. E. B. Du Bois. 18:11550-4.

The Negro American Artisan

Section 1. Scope of the Inquiry

In 1902 Atlanta University made a study of the Negro artisan. Ten years later we come back to the same study, with a desire to ascertain the present condition of the Negro American artisan, to inquire into his training and experience, and to set forth in positive, scientific statements the actual economic and social conditions of this important group of American citizens,—their problems and their prospects.   The present investigation is based upon the following data in addition to other miscellaneous sources:

1.   Studies of African life.
2.   Ante-bellum American historical studies.
3.   Local studies.
4.   The Reports of the Census Department of the United States.
5.   The catalogs of Negro institutions.
6.   Replies to the following general questionnaire sent to interested citizens thruout the United States:

DEAR FRIEND:

Atlanta University is making a study of the Negro Artisan. Will you kindly answer the following questions and return the blank to us at your earliest convenience?

1.   Name of place . . . .   State . . . . . .
2.   Are there many Negro skilled laborers here?
3.   What trades do they follow chiefly?
4.   Is the Negro gaining or losing as a skilled laborer?   Why so?
5.   What results can you see of industrial school training?
6.   Are young men entering the trades?
7.   What success are the Negro artisans in your community having?
8.   Will you kindly write on the other side of this paper the names and addresses and trades of all the Negro artisans in your city or town? Your name and address.

NOTE.—An Artisan is a skilled laborer—a person who works with his hands but has attained a degree of skill and efficiency above that of an ordinary manual laborer—as, for instance, carpenters, masons, engineers, blacksmiths, etc. *Omit* barbers, ordinary laborers in factories, who do no skilled work, etc.

7.   Replies to the following questionnaire sent to the heads of Negro institutions:

Dear Friend:

Atlanta University is making a study of the Negro Artisan. Will you kindly answer the following questions and return the blank to us at your earliest convenience?

  1.   Name of institution
  2.   Address.
  3.   How many of your graduates or former students are earning a living entirely as artisans?
  4.   How many of the above mentioned are: Carpenters, blacksmiths, brickmakers, masons, engineers, firemen, dressmakers, iron and steel workers, shoemakers, painters, plasterers, coopers, tailors?
  5.   Where are most of these artisans located at present?
  6.   How many of the rest of your graduates or former students are earning a living partially as artisans?
  7.   What trades and other work do they usually combine?
  8.   What difficulties do your graduates meet in obtaining work as artisans?
  9.   Do they usually join trades unions?
  10.   How many of them teach industries in schools?
  11.   Will you kindly furnish us with a list of your graduates from industrial courses, with occupations and present addresses?

8. Replies to the following questionnaire sent to Negro Artisans:

Dear Friend:

For several years past Atlanta University has made an annual study of some phase of Negro life in America. The results of these studies have been published in book form and have received the attention of thinking people thruout the civilized world. In this way we have been able, we believe, to help the entire Negro race. This year the University is making a study of the Negro Artisan. Your name has been sent to us as one of the leading artisans in your community. Will you kindly answer the following questions and return the blank to us at your earliest convenience? By so doing you will greatly help this work.

  1.   Name?
  2.   Address?
  3.   Age? Sex?
  4.   Married, single, widowed or divorced?
  5.   Trade?

6. (a) Do you work for yourself?
         Do you own your own tools?
         Do you hire other workers?
         What is your average income?
    (b) Do you work for wages?
         What wages do you receive?
         Time unoccupied per year?
         What wages do the whites receive for the same kind of
         work?
7. How did you learn your trade?
8. Did you attend a trade school?
    How long?
    Where?
9. Do you belong to a trade union?
    If so, what union?
    Do whites belong?
    Can you join with the whites?
    If you do not belong to a union, why not?
10. Do you work with whites?
    Do you work chiefly for whites or for Negroes?
    What is the feeling between the white and colored workers in
    your trade?
11. Education: Common school? Higher training?
12. Do you own real estate?
13. Are the conditions for the Negro skilled worker growing better?
    Why?
14. Remarks.

9. Study of Negro skilled labor, thru employer and employee.

10. Study of the relation of the Negro artisan to organized labor in the United States. This study was made by means of a blank questionnaire sent to labor organizations, national, state and local, thruout the country.

The statements of present conditions which are made in these pages under the various state headings are taken from the replies of interested friends and correspondents of the Atlanta Conference, both North and South. The Negro artisans themselves have also contributed much valuable information concerning local conditions.

Section 2.   The African Artisan

A Select African Bibliography

Africanus, Leo: "Geographical Historie of Africa." London, 1600.
Barth, Heinrich: "Travels and Discoveries in the North and Central Africa." New York, 1859.
Bowen: "Missionary Labor in Africa." Charleston, 1857.
Deniker: "The Races of Man." London, 1900.
Dowd, Jerome: "The Negro Races." New York, 1907.
Featherman: "Social History of the Races of Mankind. Nigritians, etc." London, 1887.
Kingsley: "Travels in West Africa." London, 1900.
   "   "West African Studies." London, 1901.
Livingstone: "Missionary Travels and Researches in South Africa." New York, 1858.
Park: "Life and Travels." New York, 1858.
Quatrefages: "The Pygmies." New York, 1895.
Ratzel: "The History of Mankind." 3 Vols. London, 1897.
Reclus: "The Earth and its Inhabitants." New York, 1892.
Rohlfs: "Reise von Mittelmeer noch dem Tschad-See und Golf von Guinea." Leipzig, 1875.
Schweinfurth: "The Heart of Africa." New York, 1874.
Stanley: "In Darkest Africa." New York, 1890.
Staudinger: "Im Herzen der Haussa Lander." Oldenburg and Leipzig, 1891.
Stuhlmann: "Mit Emin Pasha ins Herz von Africa." Berlin, 1894.

A study of the Negro American artisan quite naturally begins with the entrance of the Negro into American life. Twelve years after the founding of Jamestown in Virginia and one year prior to the landing of the Pilgrims at Plymouth, the first cargo of Negro slaves was brot to the American continent. Sold to the settlers in the Virginia colony, these Negroes joined in the work of building the nation, a work which demanded both brain and brawn. Endowed with physical strength, this new American group was no mean asset to the economic forces of the new world, considered especially in the light of the strenuous demands of the strenuous period.

What had been the experience of the members of this group, so rapidly increasing by birth and by the activities of slave-catcher and slave-trader? Had there been anything in the African life which would render the Negroes capable of taking a part in the building of homes, the acquiring of wealth, the developing of the new land, the building of the nation? Is there any evidence of mechanical skill among the African natives? A glimpse into African life may help us to answer these questions; for among the Pygmies, the Hottentots, the

Bushmen, the Ashantis and in practically all parts of the continent of Africa, we find concrete evidences of that ability which makes for artisanship.

While the Pygmies, still living in the age of wood, make no iron or stone implements, they seem to know how to make bark cloth and fibre baskets and simple outfits for hunting and fishing. Among the Bushmen the art of making weapons and working in hides is quite common. The Hottentots are further advanced in the industrial arts, being well versed in the manufacture of clothing, weapons and utensils. In the dressing of skins and furs as well as in the plaiting of cords and the weaving of mats we find evidences of their workmanship. In addition, they are good workers in iron and copper, using the skeepskin bellows for this purpose. The Ashantis of the "Gold Coast" know how to make "cotton fabrics, turn and glaze earthenware, forge iron, fabricate instruments and arms, embroider rugs and carpets, and set gold and precious stones."[1] Among the people of the banana zone we find rough basket work, coarse pottery, grass cloth, and spoons made of wood and ivory. The people of the millet zone, because of uncertain agricultural resources, quite generally turn to manufacturing. Charcoal is prepared by the smiths, iron is smelted and numerous implements are manufactured. Among them we find axes, hatchets, hoes, knives, nails, scythes and other hardware. Cloaks, shoes, sandals, shields and water and oil vessels are made from leather which the natives have dressed. Soap is manufactured in the Bautschi district, glass is melted, formed and colored by the people of Nupeland, and in almost every city cotton is spun and woven and dyed. Barth tells us that the weaving of cotton was known in the Sudan as early as the eleventh century. There is also extensive manufacture of wooden ware, tools, implements and utensils.

Leo Africanus writing of Timbuctu in the sixteenth century said: "It is a woonder to see what plentie of Merchandize is dayly brought hither and how costly and sumptuous all

---

[1] Reclus: "The Earth and its Inhabitants," Vol. 3, p. 241.

things be. . . . . Here are many shops of artificers and merchants and especially of such as weave linnen and cloth."[1]

Kuka, on the west shore of Lake Tchad, and Sokoto, in the northwestern part of the empire of the same name, are the principal manufacturing centers of this district. Here cotton is spun and woven into cloth; skins are tanned and manufactured into boots, shoes and saddles; and implements, ornaments and tools are wrot of iron.

Thruout the continent of Africa we find evidences of the industrial ability of the natives. Anthropologist and geologist, scientist and man of letters, alike record the achievements of the African people along this line.

The industries of the native Africans were greatly disturbed during the activities of the slave trade. Dowd in his sociological study, "The Negro Races," says:

> During the activities of the slave trade there was a noticeable decline in native manufactures thruout Africa, especially along the coast regions. The natives gave up to a large extent their primitive industries and depended upon the sale of slaves as a means of supplying what they wanted in the line of manufactured goods.[2] . . . . During the flourishing days of slave exportation to America, the industrial arts declined as well as the cultivation of the soil. One of the effects of the contact with European peoples and products was at first to cause the natives to imitate the articles of foreign manufacture, such as glass and gunpowder, and but for the slave trade and other mistaken policies of the white man which disorganized the whole economic life of the natives there is no telling what strides would have been made in all lines of industry. Since the abolition of the external slave trade, the revival of industrial activities among the people of the Sudan has been hindered by the wars between the pastoral Fellatahs and native blacks. [3]

Dr. Franz Boas, whose knowledge of man has been a source of inspiration to many a social reformer, in speaking of the African Negro, says:

> The achievements of races are not only what they have done during the short span of two thousand years, when with rapidly increasing numbers the total amount of mental work accumulated at an ever increasing rate. In this the European, the Chinaman, the East Indian, have far outstripped other races. But back of this period lies the time when mankind struggled with the elements, when every small advance that seems

---

[1]Africanus: "Geographical Historie of Africa," pp. 287-29).
[2]Dowd: The Negro Races, Vol. 1, p. 94.   [3]*Ibid.* P. 108.

to us now insignificant was an achievement of the highest order, as great as the discovery of steam power or of electricity, if not greater. It may well be, that these early inventions were made hardly consciously, certainly not by deliberate effort, yet every one of them represents a giant's stride forward in the development of human culture. To these early advances the Negro race has contributed its liberal share. While much of the history of early invention is shrouded in darkness, it seems likely that at a time when the European was still satisfied with rude stone tools, the African had invented or adopted the art of smelting iron.

Consider for a moment what this invention has meant for the advance of the human race. As long as the hammer, knife, saw, drill, the spade and the hoe had to be chipped out of stone, or had to be made of shell or hard wood, effective industrial work was not impossible, but difficult. A great progress was made when copper found in large nuggets was hammered out into tools and later on shaped by melting, and when bronze was introduced; but the true advancement of industrial life did not begin until the hard iron was discovered. It seems not unlikely that the people that made the marvelous discovery of reducing iron ores by smelting were the African Negroes. Neither ancient Europe, nor ancient western Asia, nor ancient China knew the iron, and everything points to its introduction from Africa. At the time of the great African discoveries towards the end of the past century, the trade of the blacksmith was found all over Africa, from north to south and from east to west. With his simple bellows and a charcoal fire he reduced the ore that is found in many parts of the continent and forged implements of great usefulness and beauty. . . . . Nothing, perhaps, is more encouraging than a glimpse of the artistic industry of native Africa. I regret that we have no place in this country where the beauty and daintiness of African work can be shown; but a walk thru the African museums of Paris, London and Berlin is a revelation. I wish you could see the scepters of African kings, carved of hard wood and representing artistic forms; or the dainty basketry made by the people of the Kongo river and of the region near the great lakes of the Nile; or the grass mats with their beautiful patterns. Even more worthy of our admiration is the work of the blacksmith, who manufactures symmetrical lance heads almost a yard long, or axes inlaid with copper and decorated with filigree. Let me also mention in passing the bronze castings of Benin on the west coast of Africa, which, altho perhaps due to Portuguese influences, have so far excelled in technique any European work, that they are even now almost inimitable. In short, wherever you look, you find a thrifty people, full of energy, capable of forming large states. . . . . In place of indolence you find thrift and ingenuity, and application to occupations that require not only industry, but also inventiveness and a high degree of technical skill.[1]

---

[1]Atlanta University Leaflet, No. 19.

Section 3. The Ante-bellum Negro Artisan

The Negro slave was the artisan of the South before the war.   Both on the plantation and in the towns and cities there was a constant demand for his service.   While the average workmanship was low and suited only to rough plantation life, it is nevertheless true that on many of the better plantations and in many of the towns and cities there were first-class Negro skilled workmen.

Prior to the war there were a large number of Negro mechanics in the southern states; many of them were expert blacksmiths, wheelwrights, wagon-makers, brick-masons, carpenters, plasterers, painters and shoemakers.   They became masters of their respective trades by reason of sufficiently long service under the control and direction of expert white mechanics.   During the existence of slavery the contract for qualifying the Negro as a mechanic was made between his owner and the master workman.[1]

The South was lacking in manufactures, and used little machinery. Its demand for skilled labor was not large, but what demand existed was supplied mainly by Negroes.   Negro carpenters, plasterers, bricklayers, blacksmiths, wheelwrights, painters, harnessmakers, tanners, millers, weavers, barrelmakers, basketmakers, shoemakers, chairmakers, coachmen, spinners, seamstresses, housekeepers, gardeners, cooks, laundresses, embroiderers, maids of all work, were found in every community, and frequently on a single plantation.   Skilled labor was more profitable than unskilled, and therefore every slave was made as skillful as possible under a slave system.[2]

Bruce in his economic history of Virginia in the seventeenth century speaks as follows of the Negro mechanics in that colony:

The county records of the seventeenth century reveal the presence of many Negro mechanics in the colony during that period, this being especially the case with carpenters and coopers.   This was what might be expected.   The slave was inferior in skill, but the ordinary mechanical needs of the plantation did not demand the highest aptitude.   The fact that the African was a servant for life was an advantage covering many deficiencies; nevertheless, it is significant that large slaveholders like Colonel Byrd and Colonel Fitzhugh should have gone to the inconvenience and expense of importing English handicraftsmen who were skilled in the very trades in which it is certain that several of the Negroes belonging to

---

[1] Ex-Governor Lowry, of Mississippi, in *North American Review*, 156:472.

[2] G. T. Winston in Annals of American Academy, July, 1901, p. 111.

these planters had been specially trained. It shows the low estimate in which the planters held the knowledge of their slaves regarding the higher branches of mechanical work.[1]

It is stated that among the slaves of the first Robert Beverly was a carpenter valued at £30, and that Ralph Wormeley of Middlesex county owned a cooper and a carpenter each valued at £35. Colonel William Byrd mentions the use of Negroes in iron mining in 1732. In New Jersey slaves were employed as miners, iron-workers, sawmill hands, house and ship carpenters, wheelwrights, coopers, tanners, shoemakers, millers and bakers, among other employments, before the Revolutionary War. As early as 1708 there were enough slave mechanics in Pennsylvania to make the freemen feel their competition severely. In Massachusetts and other states we hear of an occasional black artisan.

During the early part of the nineteenth century the Negro artisans increased. In the District of Columbia many "were superior mechanics, ... Benjamin Banneker, the Negro astronomer, assisting in surveying the District in 1791." Olmsted, in his journeys thru the slave states, just before the Civil War, found slave artisans in all the states. In Virginia they worked in tobacco factories, ran steamboats, made barrels, etc. On a South Carolina plantation he was told by the master that the Negro mechanics "exercised as much skill and ingenuity as the ordinary mechanics that he was used to employ in New England." In Charleston and some other places they were employed in cotton factories. In Alabama he saw a black carpenter—a careful and accurate calculator and excellent workman; he was bought for $2,000. In Louisiana he was told that master mechanics often bot up slave mechanics and acted as contractors. In Kentucky the slaves worked in factories for hemp-bagging, and in iron works on the Cumberland river, and also in tobacco factories. In Mobile an advertisement read: "good blacksmiths and horse-shoers for sale on reasonable terms."[2]

[1] Bruce: Economic History of Virginia in the Seventeenth Century. II., pp. 405-6.
[2] Atlanta University Publications, No. 7, pp. 13-14.

An official register of free persons in Richmond county, Ga., 1819, printed in the Augusta (Ga.) *Chronicle*, March 13, 1819, furnishes the following statistics:[1]

Boat corkers	1
Carpenters	12
Harnessmakers	1
Millwrights	2
Saddlers	2
Seamstresses	31
Weavers	9
Total	58

The entire labor in a cotton factory located in Maury county, Tennessee, in 1827 was performed by slaves.

Thruout the slave states there seems to have been a constant demand for Negro apprentices. The following advertisements are but examples:

APPRENTICES WANTED.—The subscriber carrying on the blacksmith's business in all its branches on Reynold street, near Calffrey and Bustin's hotel, would willingly receive three Negro fellows as apprentices. The owners may confidently rely that every necessary attention will be given to their instruction. J. J. PERIN. [Advertisement from the Augusta (Ga.) *Chronicle*. March 2, 1811].[2]

WANTED IMMEDIATELY—As an apprentice to the blacksmith's business, a smart, active boy, of from twelve to fifteen years of age, who can come well recommended. A black boy of this description will be taken. Wanted also, a Journeyman who understands his business and has good recommendations for honesty, industry and sobriety. A black man would not be rejected. ELLIS MADDOX, Nashville. [Advertisement from the Tennessee *Gazette and Mero District Advertiser* (Nashville), October 24, 1804].[3]

In many places in the South, white mechanics and Negro mechanics worked side by side with little or no friction. A letter of H. Crowell to the editor of the *Federal Union*, Milledgeville, Ga., dated March 18, 1836, speaks of a boat building establishment on the Flint river where there were "ten or fifteen white mechanics, and some twenty or more Negroes, working well." Buckingham in discussing labor in the cotton mills at Athens, Ga., in 1839, says:

[1] Documentary History of American Industrial Society, Vol. II, pp. 143-147.
[2] Printed in Documentary History of American Industrial Society, Vol. II, pp. 348-9.
[3] *Ibid.* P. 349.

. . . There is no difficulty among them on account of color, the white girls working in the same room and at the same loom with the black girls; and boys of each color, as well as men and women, working together without apparent repugnance or objection. . . . . The Negroes here are found to be quite as easily taught to perform all the required duties of spinners and weavers as the whites, and are just as tractible when taught.[1]

Of the Negroes in New York City from about 1835 until 1841, it is said:

The occupations included three carpenters and joiners, five boot and shoemakers, five tailors, ... one engraver, one watch and clock maker, one sign painter, two dress and cloakmakers.[2]

The slave mechanics were often hired out by their masters and in many cases were allowed to hire their own time. Such encouragement naturally resulted in the growth of a privileged class among the slaves and this class produced many of the Negro leaders of the ante-bellum days: Vesey, Nat Turner, Richard Allen and Absalom Jones, as examples. Among this class were many who, free in everything but name, acquired property, reared families and often lived in comfort.

The lot of these slave mechanics was by no means an easy one, for they had continually to encounter the opposition of white mechanics. The legislatures of Pennsylvania and Maryland were prevailed upon by white mechanics to pass enactments aimed at the Negro mechanics and thruout the South were concrete evidences of such opposition.

The jealousy of the white artisans toward Negro competition is shown by the following open letter from a citizen of Athens, Ga., printed in the *Southern Banner* (Athens), January 13, 1838:

To the Contractors for Mason's and Carpenter's Work, Athens:

GENTLEMEN:—I desire your candid consideration of the views I shall here express. I ask no reply to them except at your volition. I am aware that most of you have strong antipathy to encourage the masonry and carpentry trades of your poor white brothers, that your predilections for giving employment in your line of business to ebony workers have so cheapened the white man's labor, or expatriated hence with but a few solitary exceptions, all the white masons and carpenters of this town.

[1] Buckingham, J. S.: Slave States of America, Vol. II, p. 112.
[2] Haynes, George Edmund: "The Negro at Work in New York City," p. 67.

The white man is the only real, legal, moral and civil proprietor of this country and state. The right of his proprietorship reaches from the date of the studies of those white men, Copernicus and Gallileo, who indicated from the seclusion of their closets the sphericity of the earth: which sphericity hinted to another white man, Columbus, the possibility by a westerly course of sailing, of finding land. Hence by white man alone was this continent discovered; by the prowess of white men alone (tho not always properly or humanely exercised), were the fierce and active Indians driven occidentally: and if swarms and hordes of infuriated red men pour down now from the northwest, like the wintry blast thereof, the white man alone, aye, those to whom you decline to give money for bread and clothes, for their famishing families, in the logic matter of withholding work from them, or employing Negroes, in the sequel, to cheapen their wages to a rate that amounts to a moral and physical impossibility for them either to live here and support their families—would bare their breasts to the keen and whizzing shafts of the savage crusaders—defending Negroes, too, in the bargain, for if left to themselves without our aid, the Indians would or can sweep the Negroes hence, ''as dew drops are shaken from the lion's mane.''

The right, then, gentlemen, you will no doubt candidly admit, of the white man to employment in preference to Negroes, who must defer to us since they live well enough on plantations, cannot be considered impeachable by contractors. It is a right more virtual and indisputable than that of agrarianism. As masters of the polls in a majority, carrying all before them, I am surprised the poor do not elect faithful members to the legislature, who will make it penal to prefer Negro mechanic labor to white men's. But of the premises as I have now laid them down, you will candidly judge for yourselves, and draw a conclusion with me, that white bricklayers and house-joiners must henceforward have ample work and remuneration; and yourselves and other contractors will set the example, and pursue it for the future without deviation.

Yours respectfully,   J. J. FLOURNOY.

In 1845 the Georgia legislature passed an act aimed at Negro mechanics.

''An act to prohibit colored mechanics and masons, being slaves or free persons of color, being mechanics or masons, from making contracts for the erection of buildings, or for the repair of buildings, and declaring the white person or persons directly or indirectly contracting with or employing them, as well as the master, employer, manager, or agent for said slave, or guardian for said free person of color, authorizing or permitting the same, guilty of a misdemeanor.

''Section 1. Be it enacted by the Senate and House of Representatives of the state of Georgia in General Assembly met, and it is hereby enacted by the authority of the same, That from and after the first day

of February next, each and every white person who shall hereafter contract or bargain with any slave mechanic, or mason, or free person of
color, being a mechanic or mason, shall be liable to be indicted for a misdemeanor; and on conviction, to be fined, at the discretion of the court,
not exceeding two hundred dollars."

Then follows another clause imposing the like penalties on
the owners of slaves, or guardians of free persons of color,
who authorize the contracts prohibited by this statute.

Charles Lyell, commenting upon the law said:

I may first observe, in regard to this disgraceful law, which was only
carried by a small majority in the Georgian legislature, that it proves that
not a few of the Negro race have got on so well in the world in reputation and fortune, and in skill in certain arts, that it was worth while to
legislate against them in order to keep them down, and prevent them
from entering into successful rivalry with the whites. It confirms, therefore, most fully the impression which all I saw in Georgia had left on my
mind, that the blacks are steadily rising in social importance in spite of
slavery or, to speak more correctly, by aid of that institution, assuming,
as it does, in proportion as the whites become civilized, a more and more
mitigated form. . . . .

I have heard apologists in the North endeavoring to account for the
degraded position which the Negroes hold, socially and politically, in the
free states, by saying they belong to a race which is kept in a state of
slavery in the South. But, if they really desired to accelerate emancipation, they would begin by setting an example to the southern states,
and treating the black race with more respect and more on a footing of
equality. . . . . Many white mechanics who had emigrated from the
North to the slave states, declared to me that every opening in their
trades was closed to them, because the black artisans were employed by
their owners in preference. Hence, they are now using in Georgia the
power given to them by an exclusive franchise, to pass disabling statutes
against the blacks, to prevent them from engaging in certain kinds of
work. In several states, Virginia among others, I heard of strikes where
the white workmen bound themselves not to return to their employment
until the master had discharged all his colored people. Such combinations
will, no doubt, forward the substitution of white for Negro labor, and
may hasten the era of general emancipation. But if this measure be prematurely adopted, the Negroes are a doomed race, and already their situation is most critical.[1]

Another evidence of white opposition to Negro mechanics
is seen in the petition signed by about two hundred mechanics

[1] Lyell, Charles: "A Second Visit to the United States."

and laborers and presented to the city council of Atlanta, Ga.,
March 5, 1858.

We, the undersigned, would respectfully represent to your honorable
body that there exists in the city of Atlanta a number of men who, in the
opinion of your memorialists, are of no benefit to the city. We refer to
Negro mechanics whose masters reside in other places, and who pay
nothing toward the support of the city government, and whose Negro
mechanics can afford to underbid the regular resident citizen mechanics
of your city to their great injury, and without benefit to the city in any
way. We most respectfully request your honorable body to take the
matter in hand, and by your action in the premises afford such protection to the resident mechanics of your city as your honorable body may
deem meet in the premises, and in duty bound your petitioners will ever
pray.

In Ohio about 1820 to 1830 and thereafter the white mechanics' societies combined against Negroes. In Philadelphia
the series of fearful riots against Negroes was due in large
part to the jealousy of white working men and several riots
and disorders on the part of white mechanics aimed against
Negroes occurred in New York, Washington and other cities.

Notwithstanding great opposition, the Negro artisan managed to keep in evidence. The following letter is of interest:[1]

During the days of slavery the Negro mechanic was a man of importance. He was a most valuable slave to his master. He would always
sell for from two to three times as much in the market as the unskilled
slaveman. When a fine Negro mechanic was to be sold at public auction,
or private sale, the wealthy slave owners would vie with each other for
the prize and run the bidding often up into high figures.

The slave owners early saw the aptitude of the Negro to learn handicraft, and fully appreciating what vast importance and value this would
be to them (the masters) selected their brightest young slavemen and had
them taught in the different kinds of trades. Hence on every large plantation you could find the Negro carpenter, blacksmith, brick and stone
mason. These trades comprehended and included much more in their
scope in those days than they do now. Carpentry was in its glory then.
What is done now by varied and complicated machinery was wrot then by
hand. The invention of the planing machine is an event within the
knowledge of many persons living today. Most of our wood-working
machinery has come into use long since the days of slavery. The same
work done now with the machine, was done then by hand. The carpenter's chest of tools in slavery times was a very elaborate and expensive

---

[1] From Mr. J. D. Smith, stationary engineer, Chicago, Ill.

outfit. His "kit" not only included all the tools that the average carpenter carries now, but also the tools for performing all the work done by the various kinds of "wood-working" machines. There is little opportunity for the carpenter of today to acquire, or display, genius and skill in his trade as could the artisan of old.

One only needs to go down South and examine hundreds of old southern mansions, and splendid old church edifices, still intact, to be convinced of the fact of the cleverness of the Negro artisan, who constructed nine-tenths of them, and many of them still provoke the admiration of all who see them, and are not to be despised by the men of our day.

There are few, if any, of the carpenters of today who, if they had the hand tools, could get out the "stuff" and make one of those old style massive panel doors,—who could work out by hand the mouldings, the stiles, the mullions, etc., and build one of those windows, which are to be found today in many of the churches and public buildings of the South; all of which testify to the cleverness of the Negro's skill as artisan in the broadest sense of the term. For the carpenter in those days was also the "cabinet maker," the wood turner, coffin maker, generally the pattern maker, and the maker of most things made of wood. The Negro blacksmith held almost absolute sway in his line, which included the many branches of forgery, and other trades which are now classified under different heads from that of the regular blacksmith. The blacksmith in the days of slavery was expected to make any and everything wrot of iron. He was to all intents and purposes the "machine blacksmith," "horseshoer," "carriage and wagon ironer and trimmer," "gunsmith," "wheelwright;" and often whittled out and ironed the hames, the plowstocks, and the "single-tree" for the farmers, and did a hundred other things too numerous to mention. They were experts at tempering edge tools, by what is generally known as the water process. But many of them had secret processes of their own for tempering tools which they guarded with zealous care.

It was the good fortune of your humble servant to have served his time as an apprentice in a general blacksmithing shop, or shop of all work, presided over by an ex-slave genius known thruout the state as a "master mechanic." In slavery times this man hired his own time,—paying his master a certain stipulated amount of money each year, and all he made over and above that amount was his own.

The Negro machinists were also becoming numerous before the downfall of slavery. The slave owners were generally the owners of all the factories, machine shops, flour-mills, saw-mills, gin-houses and threshing machines. They owned all the railroads and the shops connected with them. In all of these the white laborer and mechanic had been supplanted almost entirely by the slave mechanics at the time of the breaking out of the Civil War. Many of the railroads in the South had their entire train crews, except the conductors, made up of the slaves—including engineers and firemen.   The "Georgia Central" had inaugurated just such a movement, and had many Negro engineers on its locomotives and Negro machinists in its shops.   So it will be seen at once that the liberation of the slaves was also the salvation of the poor white man of the South.   It saved him from being completely ousted, as a laborer and a mechanic, by the masters, to make place for the slaves whom they were having trained for those positions.   Yet, strange as it may seem to us now, the great mass of poor white men in the South who were directly and indirectly affected by the slave mechanic, —being literally forced out of the business, took up arms and fought against the abolition of slavery.

While the poor whites and masters were fighting, these same black men were at home working to support those fighting for their slavery. The Negro mechanic could be found, during the conflict, in the machine shops, building engines and railroad cars, in the gun factories making arms of all kinds for the soldiers, in the various shops building wagons, and making harness, bridles and saddles, for the armies of the South. Negro engineers handled the throttle in many cases to haul the soldiers to the front, whose success, in the struggle going on, meant continued slavery to themselves and their people.   All of the flour mills, and most of every other kind of mill of the South, was largely in charge of black men.

Much has been said of the new Negro for the new century, but with all his training he will have to take a long stride in mechanical skill before he reaches the point of practical efficiency where the old Negro of the old century left off.   It was the good fortune of the writer once to fall into the hands of an uncle who was master of what would now be half a dozen distinct trades.   He was generally known as a millwright, or mill builder. A millwright now, is only a man who merely sets up the machinery, and his work is now confined mostly to the hanging of shafting, pulleys and belting.   In the days of slavery the millwright had to know how to construct everything about the mill, from foundation to roofs.   This uncle could take his men with their "cross-cut saws" and "broad axes" and go into the forests, hew the timbers with which to build the dams across the rivers and streams of water, to erect the "mill house" frames, get out all the necessary timber and lumber at the saw-mill.   Then he would, without a sign of a drawing on paper, lay out and cut every piece, every mortise and tenon, every brace and rafter with their proper angles, etc., with perfect precision before they put the whole together.   I have seen my uncle go into the forest, fell a great tree, hew out of it an immense stick or shaft from four feet to five feet in diameter, and from twenty to thirty feet long, having as many as sixteen to twenty faces on its surface, or as they termed it, "sixteen" and "twenty square."   He would then take it to the mill seat and mortise it, make the arms, and all the intricate parts for a great "overshot" water wheel to drive the huge mill machinery.   This is a feat most difficult even for modern mechanics who have a thoro knowledge of mathematics and the laws of mechanics.

It is difficult for us to understand how those men with little or no knowledge of mathematics, or mechanical rules, could take a crude stick · of timber, shape it, and then go to work and cut out a huge screw and the "Tap-blocks" for those old style cotton presses.

Section 4. The Economics of Emancipation

Emancipation found many Negro artisans of varying degrees of skill and efficiency scattered thruout the United States. So far as the South was concerned, the Negro slave had been for years the actual artisan; and it was the black artisan who met peculiar conditions in the readjustment which followed the war measure by which four million black men were set free. For a time, of course, the old conditions remained and the Negro artisan, not infrequently patronized by his former master, still held undisputed sway. Three circumstances, however, soon disturbed the situation:

(1)   The competition of white mechanics.

(2)   The efforts of the Negro for self-protection.

(3)   The new industrial development of the South.

First: The opposition of white mechanics to Negro workmen which was evident in ante-bellum days became more intense after the emancipation of the slaves and in the competition which followed, the untutored, inexperienced black mechanic found himself outdistanced by his thriftier white competitor, sometimes by fair means, sometimes by foul. Without the protection, and with less and less of the patronage of his former master, the Negro artisan found himself being gradually supplanted by the white working man.

Secondly: The Negro artisan found himself at a political disadvantage. Having no political power with which to defend himself, he was still at the mercy of his white competitor, who was armed with the ballot. Seeing that his safety and, in the long run, his very economic existence depended upon the possession of the ballot, the Negro made desperate efforts to secure that power. These efforts of the Negro to secure the ballot further complicated his economic position.

Thirdly: The new industrial development of the South made new demands upon the mechanic. Old methods of production gave way to new ones and the Negro mechanic, schooled in the economy of the ante-bellum days and knowing so little of mills and machinery, found himself unprepared to meet the demands of the new economy. Nevertheless into this field he made his way. How far he has been able to take his place in the ranks of the American artisans, the census reports from 1870 to 1910 will show.

The Negro American after slavery made four distinct and different efforts to reach economic safety. The first effort was thru the preferment of the selected house servant class; the second was by means of competitive industry; the third was by means of land-holding; and the fourth was by means of what may be called the group economy.

(1) The one person who under the slave regime came nearest escaping from the toils of the system and the disabilities of the caste was the favorite house servant. This arose from four reasons:

> (a) The house servant was brot into closest contact with the culture of the master's family.
>
> (b) He had more often the advantages of town and city life.
>
> (c) He was able to gain at least some smattering of an education.
>
> (d) He was frequently a blood relative of the master class.

It is not surprising, then, that the natural leadership of the emancipated race fell to this class. Indeed the brunt of reconstruction fell on their shoulders. When the history of the reconstruction period is written according to truth and not according to our prejudices it will be clear that no group of men ever made a more tremendous fight against more overwhelming odds.

It seemed natural at this time that this leading class of upper servants would step into the economic life of the nation from this vantage ground and play a leading role. This they did in several instances, the most conspicuous being the barber, the caterer and the steward. For the most part, however, economic society refused to admit the black applicant on his merit to any place of authority or advantage. He held his own in the semi-servile work of barber until he met the charge of color discrimination from his own folk and the strong competition of Germans and Italians; while the caterer was displaced by the palatial hotel in which he could gain no foothold. On the whole, then, the mass of house servants found the doors of advancement closed in their faces. The better tenth, both themselves and thru their better trained children, escaped into the professions and thus found economic independence. The mass of servants remained servants or turned toward industry.

(2) The second attempt of the freedmen was made along the lines of industrial co-operation. It was a less ambitious attempt than that of the house servants and comprehended larger numbers. It was characterized by a large migration to cities and towns and entrance into work as teamsters, railway section hands, miners, saw-mill employees, porters and hostlers, etc. This class met and joined in the towns the older class of artisans, most of them connected with the building trades, and together these classes attempted economic advance. Excepting the farmers, it is this class that has attracted most attention, that has met all the brunt of the economic battle and that is usually referred to in studies of this sort. What the outcome of this second attempt at economic freedom will be can only be divined by calling attention to the third method by which the Negro has searched for the way of life.

(3) Meantime, however, the freed hands had started forward by a third way: that of land ownership. Most of those who got any start became share tenants and a fourth of these succeeded in buying land. Those who bot land approximated economic independence, formed the closed plantation economy of the olden times, but with colored owner, colored laborers, and colored tenants. In an increasing number of cases the

colored store came in to help them and thus a complete system of what may be called the group economy was established.

(4)   The group economy, the fourth method, is of striking importance.   However, outside the country districts it is little understood.   It consists of such a co-operative arrangement of industries and services within the Negro group that the group tends to become a closed economic circle largely independent of the surrounding white world.   The recognition of this fact explains many of the anomalies which puzzle the student of the Negro problems.

One used to see numbers of Negro barbers; one is tempted to think that they are all gone.   Yet today there are more Negro barbers in the United States than ever before but at the same time a larger number than ever before cater solely to Negro trade, where they have a monopoly.   Because the Negro lawyer, physician and teacher serve a colored clientage their existence is half forgotten.   The new Negro business men are not successors of the old; there used to be Negro business men in New York, Philadelphia and Baltimore catering to white trade.   The new Negro business man caters to Negro trade.   So far has this gone that today in every city of the United States with a considerable Negro population the black group is serving itself with religious ministration, medical care, legal advice and education of children; and to a growing degree with food, houses, books and newspapers. So extraordinary has been this development that it forms a large and growing part in the economy in the case of fully one-half of the Negroes of the United States and in the case of between 50,000 and 100,000 town and city Negroes.   Representing at least 300,000 persons, the group economy approaches a complete system.   To these may be added the bulk of the 200,000 Negro farmers who own their farms.   They form a natural group economy and they are increasing the scope of it in every practical way.

Section 5.   The Occupations of Negroes

I recommend to them (the people so declared to be free) that, in all cases when allowed, they labor faithfully for reasonable wages.[1]

The entrance of the Negro into gainful occupations in a large way followed the abolition of slavery.   Handicapped by lack of previous training and beset by desperate economic conditions, the freed blacks launched forth as free workers on a paid labor basis.   The census figures from 1870 to 1900 have given evidence of the Negro's place in gainful occupations.   The following statistics are taken from the census of 1900:[2]

Occupations of American Negroes, 1900

Agricultural pursuits	2,143,154	or 53.7 per cent.
Professional service	47,219	" 1.2 "
Domestic and personal service	1,317,859	" 33.0 "
Trade and transportation	2'8,989	" 5.2 "
Manufacturing and mechanical pursuits	275,116	" 6.9 "

Occupations of Native Whites (Native Parents), 1900

Agricultural pursuits	6,004,039	or 43.3 "
Professional service	80ϳ,288	" 5.8 "
Domestic and personal service	1,841,853	" 13.3 "
Trade and transportation	2,4'00,018	" 17.3 "
Manufacturing and mechanical pursuits	2,823,131	" 20.3 "

Occupations of Native Whites (Foreign Parents), 1900

Agricultural pursuits	1,100,608	or 20.8 "
Professional service	259,434	" 4.9 "
Domestic and personal service	913,645	" 17.2 "
Trade and transportation	1,225,351	" 23.1 "
Manufacturing and mechanical pursuits	1,801,886	" 34.0 "

Occupations of Foreign Whites, 1900

Agricultural pursuits	1,074,211	or 18.7 "
Professional service	143,893	" 2.5 "
Domestic and personal service	1,435,407	" 25.0 "
Trade and transportation	915,151	" 16.0 "
Manufacturing and mechanical pursuits	2,168,153	" 37.8 "

These statistics show that the per cent of Negroes engaged in agricultural pursuits is greater than the per cent of any other group of American citizens so engaged.   The same is true for domestic and personal service.   The former is explained, of course, by the large rural Negro population; the latter, by the strenuous economic conditions which confront the ever increasing mass of black people who move to the urban centers.   Professional service claims 1.2 per cent of the Negro workers, an appreciable increase over 1890.

---

[1] From the Emancipation Proclamation.   [2] The figures for 1910 are not yet available.

SEX, GENERAL NATIVITY AND COLOR	Agricultural Pursuits		Professional Service		Domestic and Personal Service		Trade and Transportation		Manufacturing and Mechanical Pursuits	
	Number	Per Ct.	Number	Per Ct.	Number	Per Ct.	Number	Per Ct.	Number	Per Ct.
Both sexes (all persons)*	10,381,765	100.0	1,258,538	100.0	5,580,657	100.0	4,766,964	100.0	7,085,309	100.0
Native white—native parents	6,004,039	57.8	806,288	64.1	1,841,853	33.0	2,400,018	50.4	2,823,131	39.8
Native white—foreign parents	1,100,608	10.6	259,434	20.6	913,645	16.4	1,225,351	25.7	1,801,886	25.4
Foreign white	1,074,211	10.4	143,896	11.4	1,435,407	25.7	915,151	19.2	2,168,153	30.6
Negroes	2,143,154	20.6	47,219	3.7	1,317,859	23.6	208,989	4.4	275,116	3.9
Males—										
Native white—native parents	5,685,429	60.4	530,570	64.1	1,258,045	36.1	2,168,869	50.9	2,305,779	39.9
Native white—foreign parents	1,071,210	11.4	146,357	17.7	554,424	15.9	1,020,507	23.9	1,324,889	23.0
Foreign white	1,032,484	11.0	117,973	14.2	967,838	27.8	852,035	20.0	1,886,769	32.7
Negro	1,561,153	16.6	31,625	3.8	635,933	18.2	204,852	4.8	241,934	4.2
Females—										
Native white—native parents	318,610	32.6	275,718	64.0	583,808	27.9	231,149	45.9	517,352	39.4
Native white—foreign parents	29,398	3.0	113,077	26.3	359,221	17.1	204,844	40.7	476,997	36.4
Foreign white	41,727	4.3	25,923	6.0	467,569	22.3	63,116	12.6	281,384	21.4
Negro	582,001	59.5	15,594	3.6	681,926	32.6	4,137	0.8	33,182	2.5

*Including Chinese, Japanese and Indians.

Dividing the Negro wage-earners by sex we have:

	Males	Females	Total
Professions	1.2	1.2	1.2
Agriculture	58.3	44.2	53.7
Trade and transportation	7.7	0.3	5.2
Manufacturing and mechanical pursuits	9.0	2.5	6.9
Domestic and personal service	23.8	51.8	33.0
Total	100.0	100.0	100.00

These statistics show that in 1900 about twelve per cent of the Negroes engaged in gainful occupations were engaged in trade and transportation and manufactures and mechanical pursuits, an increase of about two per cent over those so engaged in 1890. There is shown a decrease of about three and one-half per cent in agricultural pursuits, largely explained by the cityward movement of the Negro, which also explains in part the slight increase in the number of Negroes engaged in domestic and personal service. Taking all the states of the union we have the following figures for 1900:

Negro Wage-earners, 1900

BY STATES	All Occupations		Trade and Transportation		Manufacturing and Mechanical Pursuits	
	Males	Females	Males	Females	Males	Females
United States	2,682,091	1,316,872	205,017	4,137	241,963	33,186
Continental United States	2,675,497	1,316,840	204,852	4,137	241,934	33,182
Alabama	256,452	150,294	13,639	225	26,140	1,453
Arizona	1,175	167	40	. . . .	57	15
Arkansas	116,594	46,546	5,431	82	7,159	445
California	3,903	1,349	603	19	410	130
Colorado	3,273	1,344	527	10	571	55
Connecticut	4,923	3,047	1,026	28	648	138
Delaware	9,764	3,864	770	17	865	67
District of Columbia	25,115	23,448	5,999	214	2,565	1,691
Florida	74,528	26,844	6,293	94	11,403	1,202
Georgia	302,616	163,234	19,004	468	23,021	2,680
Idaho	135	30	7	1	10	1
Illinois	31,757	9,725	5,119	184	4,326	753
Indiana	19,566	6,838	2,941	47	2,617	339
Indian Territory	11,293	2,283	401	6	1,078	39
Iowa	4,801	1,083	582	14	1,430	60
Kansas	15,892	4,430	1,661	34	2,955	220
Kentucky	87,766	36,712	9,654	123	9,975	1,165
Louisiana	194,386	100,888	9,899	164	11,331	2,498
Maine	455	171	92	1	68	10
Maryland	70,728	35,658	8,682	147	7,780	1,146
Massachusetts	10,864	5,747	2,325	99	1,555	532
Michigan	5,510	1,678	618	19	656	146
Minnesota	2,224	568	429	23	114	67
Mississippi	275,925	150,041	10,301	196	9,687	1,188
Missouri	52,294	21,272	7,260	79	5,917	614
Montana	700	212	74	2	55	18
Nebraska	2,508	903	381	14	289	48
Nevada	58	17	5	. . . .	6	5
New Hampshire	242	156	40	2	35	11
New Jersey	23,035	13,211	3,839	67	2,065	369
New Mexico	833	129	71	. . . .	238	3
New York	34,011	23,059	7,669	137	4,419	1,401
North Carolina	179,139	87,178	9,250	143	15,924	2,609
North Dakota	127	3	13	. . . .	12	1
Ohio	33,180	10,449	4,751	115	5,366	715
Oklahoma	5,560	1,262	405	12	199	20
Oregon	568	159	71	3	59	13
Pennsylvania	55,805	24,624	9,033	201	9,150	1,277
Rhode Island	2,978	1,928	764	19	362	148
South Carolina	224,561	138,560	8,238	219	13,807	2,237
South Dakota	197	55	26	. . . .	19	1
Tennessee	146,013	65,744	16,281	233	15,892	1,808
Texas	175,382	67,709	10,886	107	6,906	813
Utah	376	71	16	1	20	8
Vermont	305	105	39	. . . .	31	2
Virginia	187,726	80,239	16,930	548	27,835	4,869
Washington	1,289	216	121	. . . .	348	29
West Virginia	17,424	3,273	2,455	18	6,376	99
Wisconsin	1,019	235	106	2	74	21
Wyoming	522	55	85	. . . .	109	3

According to the twelfth census there were in the United States in 1900 215,369 skilled Negro artisans distributed by occupations as follows:

Negro Artisans in the United States—Census of 1900

Occupations	No.	Occupations	No.
Architects, designers, etc.	52	Clock and watch makers and repairers.	109
Electricians	185	Gold and silver workers.	66
Engineers (civil, etc.), and surveyors.	120	Tin plate and tinware makers.	924
Carpenters and joiners	21,114	Other metal workers	353
Masons (brick and stone)	14,357	Bookbinders	86
Painters, glaziers and varnishers	5,784	Boxmakers (paper)	60
Paper hangers	586	Engravers	22
Plasterers	3,757	Paper and pulp mill operatives	261
Plumbers and gas and steam fitters	1,193	Printers, lithographers and pressmen.	1,221
Roofers and slaters	3.8	Bleaching and dye works operatives.	446
Mechanics	377	Carpet factory operatives	43
Brick and tile makers, etc.	9,970	Cotton mill operatives	1,425
Glassworkers	427	Hosiery and knitting mill operatives	36
Marble and stone cutters	1,257	Silk mill operatives	136
Potters	212	Woolen mill operatives	169
Blacksmiths	10,104	Other textile mill operatives	330
Iron and steel workers	12,327	Dressmakers	12,572
Machinists	1,2 3	Hat and cap makers	22
Steam boiler makers	335	Milliners	180
Stove, furnace and grate makers	248	Seamstresses	11,538
Tool and cutlery makers	198	Shirt, collar and cuff makers	181
Wheelwrights	376	Tailors and tailoresses	1,845
Wireworkers	144	Other textile workers	159
Boot and shoe makers and repairers	4,574	Broom and brush makers	213
Harness and saddle makers and repair-		Charcoal, coke and lime burners	3,870
ers	273	Engineers and firemen (stationary)	10,227
Leather curriers and tanners	1,073	Glove makers	15
Trunk and leather case makers	23	Model and pattern makers	24
Cabinet makers	342	Photographers	247
Saw and planing mill employees	33,266	Rubber factory operatives	44
Coopers	2,964	Tobacco and cigar factory operatives.	15,349
Other woodworkers	2,803	Upholsterers	1,045
Brass workers	110	Other miscellaneous industries	21,939

It is seen here that the occupations which claim the largest numbers of male Negro artisans are those connected with the building trades: milling, carpentering, masonry and working in iron and steel. The female workers classed as artisans are engaged chiefly as dressmakers and seamstresses. When one remembers, in the first place, the Negro's physical endowment, and in the second place, the economic conditions which prevailed during the slave regime, these statistics are rather as one would expect. These two hundred thousand and more Negroes engaged as skilled or semi-skilled workers occupy an important place in their own racial group and are indeed no small asset to the economic forces of the nation. Had their training been better their social value, great as it is today, would be even greater.

Taking the sixteen former slave states and the District of Columbia we have the following table:

Negro Skilled Laborers by Selected States—1900

OCCUPATIONS	Alabama	Arkansas	Delaware	Dist. of Columbia	Florida	Georgia	Kentucky	Louisiana	Maryland	Mississippi	Missouri	North Carolina	South Carolina	Tennessee	Texas	Virginia	West Virginia	Totals
MALE—																		
Barbers	657	411	40	611	352	1,116	812	515	551	486	91.	707	537	993	1,.58	1,094	255	11,105
Brick and tile makers	544	93	13.	16.		639	342	339	559	430	275	825	567	532	279	863	12	6,625
Blacksmiths and wheelwrights	898	323	13	109	196	1,230	539	70.	167	663	187	719	8.3	980	523	1,222	83	9,358
Boot and shoe makers	335	81	15	171	99	664	116	304	102	152	55	33.	340	315	95	623	31	3,828
Butchers	217	71	1	62	120	353	98	195	88	183	116	166	267	160	170	239	10	2,516
Carpenters and joiners	1,807	569	34	23.	1,150	3,385	701	1,711	29	1,497	219	1,5.0	2,695	1,308	764	1,619	76	19,561
Cabinet makers			2	14		54	11	45	7		5	13		30	9	69	1	430
Cotton and other textile mill operatives	168	1	4		6	305	117	22	11	14	6	157	343	31	29	10	1	1,280
Engineers (civil and mechanical)	7			.3		6		14	4	3	2	2	3	5	4			74
Engineers and firemen (stationary)	714	278	32	227	394	835	431	504	303	479	411	903	657	709	3.6	797	92	8,073
Iron and steel workers	4,439	39	19	25		281	370	36	645	48	243	9	40	1,242	107	1,173	11	8,979
Machinists	8	41	56	32	39	154	35	33	11	52	23	52	54	87	62	86	9	851
Marble and stone cutters and masons	859	184	5	337	287	1,5.8	757	877	589	392	798	1,112	1,069	1,387	309	937	1.1	11,589
Millers	73	103	6			126	76	31	16	15	29	81	87	1.0	19	112	4	778
Painters	389	4		149	218	865	234	354	86	227	66	382	693	340	164	250	19	4,545
Plasterers	204			134		309	285	271	76		212	169	125	235	3.	508	30	2,588
Plumbers and gas fitters	82	29	2	85	37	139	27	27	16	27	30	48	47	45	61	55	5	905
Printers	43	26	2	83	29	68	21	60	37	27	37	39	54	94	44	12	6	676
Steam boiler makers	60					33	5	7	1		3				30		1	246
Steam railway employees	6,313	2,318	89	196	2,118	6,366	2,384	3,086	599	4,681	769	3,268	2,93.	5,542	4,353	5,418	1,555	51,985
FEMALE—																		
Dressmakers and seamstresses	1,318	399	45	1,611	891	2,234	721	2,241	990	1,112	412	753	1,992	1,377	751	1,445	76	18,368
Milliners	6	7	1	2	2	7	7	12	3	8	2		3	7	5	2	2	78
Printers				19		5	2				2	8			6	6	1	39
Tailoresses			1	6		25	4	99	8		4			6	3	8		172
Total	19,213	4,977	675	4,272	5,983	20,706	8,1.9	11,483	5,159	10,526	4,816	11,326	13,3.9	15,662	9,184	16,913	2,381	164,649

Negro Skilled Laborers (by Selected Cities) — 1900

OCCUPATIONS	New York, N. Y.	Wilmington, Del.	St. Louis, Mo.	Richmond, Va.	Pittsburg, Pa.	Philadelphia, Pa.	New Orleans, La.	Nashville, Tenn.	Memphis, Tenn.	Louisville, Ky.	Kansas City, Mo.	Cincinnati, O.	Chicago, Ill.	Charleston, S. C.	Baltimore, Md.	Atlanta, Ga.
MALE—																
Engineers (C. and M.)	7		1		2	7	3	1	1	1			2		3	1
Barbers	215	36	359	222	176	444	238	182	206	142	148	154	362	154	358	168
Engineers and firemen (S.)	227	21	238	52	143	133	145	113	167	147	54	120	112	99	174	79
Steam railway employees	70	28	232	237	52	105	661	278	984	242	33	27	67	148	79	415
Blacksmiths and wheelwrights	34	3	13	117	24	30	147	99	159	61	31	18	33	101	32	113
Boot and shoe makers	19	10	19	102	2	60	64	72	64	14	5	14	17	90	55	134
Brick makers	2	49	137		97	183	62	91		112	30	5	8		339	
Butchers	31		49	42	3	36	598	21	31	6	21	4	30	108	63	33
Carpenters	94	13	49	125	26	96	20	163	462	110	37	21	55	616	67	372
Cotton and other textile mill operatives	1	4	3			4				3		9	1			30
Iron and steel workers	40	144	213	191	373	176	9	20	59	223	15	21	34	35	56	57
Machinists	47	1	12	12	9	47	532	10	38	14	4	4	30	7		34
Marble and stone cutters and masons	107	41	192	142	227	345	227	314	242	165	289	115	79	163	431	239
Painters	177	5	26	27	21	57	45	83	133	50	20	24	137	186	44	100
Printers	53	2	13	13	21	81	122	20	32	13	13	10	47	14	35	13
Cabinet makers and upholsterers	24	6	13	15	6	76	3	25	5	8	3	3	15		69	15
Harness, saddle and trunk makers	9		2			5	32	4		8			5			6
Plasterers	51	3	18	129	25	24	255	60	82	74	38	14	43	89	8	77
Tailors	69	3	16	14	6	34	40	30	27	11	6	6	46	43	34	59
Tinners and tinware makers	10	2	2	5	4	5	37	10	12	3	1	3	4		107	2
FEMALE—																
Dressmakers, milliners and seamstresses	1,071	38	200	379	101	851	1,459	396	557	197	79	152	556	1,023	858	348
Printers			1			4	96	2		1			3		7	1
Tailoresses	17	1	2							3		12	6	14		9
Negro population, 1910	60,666	9,733	35,516	32,230	17,040	62,613	77,714	30,044	49,910	39,139	17,567	14,482	30,150	31,522	79,258	35,727

The Ages of Negro Employees — 1900

Ages	Manufacturing and Mechanical Industries	Trade and Transportation
10-15	8,901	8,146
16-24	74,357	61,385
25-34	79,496	62,787
35-44	51,696	39,756
45-54	33,652	22,238
55-64	16,301	8,999
65 years and over . . .	8,3(2	3,652
Age unknown	2,444	2,191

Negro Artisans by Age Periods—1900

AGE PERIODS	10-14 Yrs.	15-24 Yrs.	25-34 Yrs.	35-44 Yrs.	45-54 Yrs.	55-64 Yrs.	65 yrs and over	Total
MALE—								
Blacksmiths and wheelwrights	133	1,505	2,070	1,882	1,927	1,656	1,179	10,352
Boot and shoe makers	46	538	839	791	970	831	451	4,466
Butchers	75	833	869	531	350	172	70	2,900
Carpenters and joiners	118	2,196	4,155	4,627	4,672	3,201	1,910	20,879
Cotton mill operatives	72	380	283	178	116	29	14	1,072
Machinists	9	277	420	310	160	58	19	1,253
Masons	67	1,792	3,920	3,633	2,680	1,429	720	14,241
Miners and quarrymen	1,348	11,825	11,915	6,191	3,400	987	260	35,926
Printers	45	414	387	166	65	29	12	1,118
Steam railway employees	495	18,272	20,223	9,802	4,067	1,076	261	54,196
Tailors	48	575	510	185	100	60	42	1,520
Textile mill operatives	68	261	2(9	132	111	55	17	853
Tobacco and cigar factory operatives . .	1,298	3,608	2,562	1,496	788	295	124	10,171
FEMALE—								
Dressmakers, milliners and seamstresses	256	6,819	8,311	4,914	2,378	976	410	24,064
Tobacco and cigar factory operatives . .	478	2,056	1,214	823	368	114	40	5,093
Tailoresses	13	99	80	65	34	15	7	313
Total	4,569	51,450	57,967	35,726	22,186	10,983	5,536	188,417

The table on page 45 shows the Negro artisans in the sixteen former slave states and the District of Columbia. In view of the constant migration of Negroes to urban centers it is interesting to note the distribution of Negro artisans in such places. The table which appears on page 46 is compiled from the twelfth census and gives the Negro artisans of sixteen large cities in both the North and the South. The figures show that the skilled Negro workers are to be found chiefly in the southern cities, which fact accounts in large part for the attitude of the local trades unions toward Negro laborers. The table appearing on page 47 shows the ages of Negro artisans. The average age among the Negro workers is quite low and argues that the Negro youths are started to work at an early age and so are denied the opportunities for that education which should be afforded them in their formative years of adolescence.

Section 6. Alabama

The state of Alabama had 827,307 Negroes in 1900 and 908,275 in 1910. According to the census of 1900 the state had the following skilled and semi-skilled Negroes: [1]

Alabama

Male—

Engineers (civil and mechanical) . .	7
Barbers	657
Steam railway employees	6,313
Brick and tile makers	544
Blacksmiths and wheelwrights . . .	898
Boot and shoe makers	335
Butchers	217
Carpenters and joiners	1,807
Cotton and other textile mill op's . .	168
Iron and steel workers	4,439
Machinists	8
Marble and stone cutters and masons .	859

Male—

Millers	73
Painters	389
Plasterers	204
Plumbers and gas fitters	82
Printers	43
Steam boiler makers	(?)
Engineers and firemen (stationary) .	714

Female—

Dressmakers and seamstresses . . .	1,318
Milliners	6

General Conditions[2]

BIRMINGHAM: Many skilled Negro laborers here—carpenters, masons, blacksmiths, plasterers and machinists. Negro skilled laborers are losing because of unions and poor pay. Industrial school training has made very little improvement on the old, self-made artisan. Not many of the young men from this district are entering the trades. Negro artisans are not having much success when compared with the white artisans. It is hard for a colored man to get skilled labor here under a white contractor.

FLORENCE: There are not many skilled Negro laborers here. They follow chiefly, blacksmithing, carpentering and shoemaking. Negro skilled labor is losing here, because those most skilled are carried elsewhere because of better wages and steadier work. Industrial school training has made very little if any difference here. The young men are not entering the trades but those already in are succeeding well.

MOBILE: Many Negro skilled laborers are here—brick masons, blacksmiths, carpenters, horseshoers and wheelwrights. The Negro skilled laborers are gaining here, because the requirements for skilled labor are met by industrial school training. The young men enter the trades previously named, in great numbers, and are taking the place of the old-time workmen, thereby showing the public the need of more industrial schools since modern times demand new ideas.

MONTGOMERY: Many Negro skilled laborers here—carpenters, brick masons and painters. Negro skilled laborers are gaining, because they

---

[1] The figures given in this section and following sections are taken from the "Twelfth Census of the United States, 1900. Special Reports. Occupations." They are the only available figures.

[2] The statements of general conditions given in this and following sections are taken from the replies received from correspondents of the Conference.

are increasing in number and doing more work for their own race. Industrial school training helps in acquiring wealth, but it does not make one liberal and unselfish. The young men are entering the trades and the artisans in this community are having more than medium success.

TALLADEGA.—Average number of Negro artisans here—carpenters, blacksmiths and brick masons. Negro skilled laborers are not gaining fast, because of common race prejudice and general lack of steadiness. Very little results of industrial school training visible outside of schools founded by industrial school graduates. The young men are entering the trades and the colored artisans on the whole are successful.

TUSKEGEE.—Many Negro skilled laborers here—carpenters, brick masons, blacksmiths, wheelwrights, shoe makers and cabinet makers. They are gaining because they are becoming more and more efficient in the trades. The results of industrial school training are that many men and women are being sent out as skilled workers. The young men are entering the trades in large numbers. The Negro artisans in this community are doing well.

Replies of Artisans[1]

BIRMINGHAM.—Contracting Electrician. I do not belong to a union, tho I have been asked to join. The unions are not particular about colored electricians and they would not furnish me with help should I belong to them, which would handicap my business. I am now wiring the Alabama Penny Savings Bank building ($50,000) and a dormitory ($30,000). I just finished the Sixteenth Street Baptist Church ($50,000) and Sixth Avenue Church ($40,000), besides many residences ranging from $500 to $10,000 for both white and colored people.

MONTGOMERY.—Painter. Conditions are growing better for the Negro skilled worker because the men who are entering the trades now are steady and intelligent. The local trade conditions among Negroes are encouraging. Practically all of the brick work, lathing and plastering is done by Negroes. In painting and carpentering the whites and blacks are about equal. Plumbing is practically a white trade here. Electricians are divided with a big white majority.

SELMA.—Merchant Tailor. I employ sixteen workmen and do an average business of $16,000 or $17,000 per year. I work five white tailors and the rest colored. Conditions are growing better for the Negro skilled workers because they are growing more proficient.

---

[1]The replies printed in this section and following sections are taken from the questionnaires which were filled out and returned by Negro artisans.

Section 7.   Arizona, Colorado, Nevada, New Mexico and Utah

The Negro population of these states in 1900 and 1910 was as follows:

STATES	1900	1910
Arizona	1,848	2,067
Colorado	8,570	11,453
Nevada	134	513
New Mexico	1,610	1,628
Utah	672	1,143
Total	12,834	16,804

The census of 1900 recorded the following Negro skilled or semi-skilled workmen in these five states (and territories):

Male—
Barbers	202
Steam railway employees	8)
Brick and tile makers	10
Blacksmiths and wheelwrights	21
Boot and shoe makers	10
Butchers	4
Carpenters and joiners	38
Iron and steel workers	165
Machinists	5
Marble and stone cutters and masons	1(9

Male—
Painters	9
Plasterers	18
Plumbers and gas fitters	5
Printers	6
Engineers and firemen (stationary)	22

Female—
Dressmakers, seamstresses and milliners	73
Printers	2

Section 8.   Arkansas

Arkansas had 366,856 Negroes in 1900 and 442,891 in 1910. According to the census of 1900 the state had the following skilled and semi-skilled Negro laborers:

Arkansas

Male—
Engineers (civil and mechanical)	1
Barbers	411
Steam railway employees	2,318
Brick and tile makers	93
Blacksmiths and wheelwrights	323
Boot and shoe makers	81
Butchers	71
Carpenters and joiners	569
Iron and steel workers	39
Machinists	41

Male—
Marble and stone cutters and masons	184
Millers	4
Painters	103
Plumbers and gas fitters	29
Printers	26
Engineers and firemen (stationary)	278

Female—
Dressmakers and seamstresses	399
Milliners	7

General Conditions

FORT SMITH.—Not many skilled Negro laborers here; a few carpenters, masons and blacksmiths. He is gaining as a skilled laborer because of manual training in schools. As results of industrial school training, the boys who enter are inclined to work and remain in school longer, and when out, readily find employment. There is a perceptible increase in the number of young men entering carpentry. The Negro artisans are having fair success here.

POPLAR GROVE.—Not many Negro skilled laborers here; a few carpenters and brick-layers. Skilled labor among Negroes is gaining because their work is proving more efficient. A vindication of Negro labor in the trades is a result of industrial school training. The young men are entering the trades very slowly. The artisans in this community are earning a livelihood and stand second to none. Our best buildings are the work of Negro artisans. Our near-by villages have discarded all other artisans where the Negro skilled labor can be obtained.

TEXARKANA.—Many Negro skilled laborers here—tailors, carpenters, masons and smiths. The Negro is gaining as a skilled laborer because of the sharpness of competition. Industrial school training causes marked efficiency and steady employment with good pay for service. The young men are entering the trades. The artisans are receiving good pay and steady employment.

Replies of Artisans

BRINKLEY.—Builder and Contractor. I can build anything from a pier to a bank. I am a member of the B. and M. I. U. of America, which organization admits both white and Negro members. Conditions are hardly growing better because bias, selfish interests tend to push the Negro hard.

ENDORA.—Tailor. Conditions are growing better here because the people in this section are looking for the real artisan regardless of color and learning to appreciate the substantial rather than the superficial.

Section 9. California

The state of California had 11,045 Negroes in 1900 and 21,645 in 1910. The census of 1900 recorded the following skilled or semi-skilled Negro laborers for the state:

California

Male—

Engineers and firemen (C. and M.)	1
Barbers	170
Steam railway employees	46
Brick and tile makers	9
Blacksmiths and wheelwrights	31
Boot and shoe makers	19
Butchers	7
Carpenters and joiners	41
Cotton and other textile mill operatives	1
Iron and steel workers	8
Machinists	2
Marble and stone cutters and masons	33

Male—

Painters	23
Plasterers	20
Plumbers and gas fitters	3
Printers	7
Steam boiler makers	1
Engineers and firemen (stationary)	6

Female—

Dressmakers and seamstresses	98
Milliners	2
Printers	3
Tailoresses	8

General Conditions

OAKLAND AND SAN FRANCISCO.—Few Negro skilled laborers here—carpenters, painters and plasterers. Negro skilled labor is gaining as a result of industrial training because the industrial schools add more skill to all lines of work. A few young men are entering the trades. The Negro artisans are not having very great success here because they are barred by union labor organizations.

Section 10. Connecticut and Massachusetts

The Negro population of these states in 1900 and 1910 was as follows:

STATES	1900	1910
Connecticut.	15,226	15,174
Massachusetts	31,974	38,042
Total.	47,200	53,216

The census of 1900 recorded the following skilled or semi-skilled Negro laborers in these two states:

Connecticut and Massachusetts

Male—
Engineers (civil and mechanical)	5
Barbers	383
Steam railway employees	114
Brick and tile makers	19
Blacksmiths and wheelwrights	55
Boot and shoe makers	203
Butchers	28
Carpenters and joiners	148
Cabinet makers	3
Cotton and other textile operatives	46
Iron and steel workers	101
Machinists	63
Marble and stone cutters and masons	236

Male—
Millers	2
Painters	125
Plasterers	9
Plumbers and gas fitters	39
Printers	45
Steam boiler makers	3
Engineers and firemen (stationary)	144

Female—
Dressmakers and seamstresses	438
Milliners	16
Printers	2
Tailoresses	26

General Conditions

NEW HAVEN.—Not many Negro artisans here in proportion to the population. They are mostly carpenters, masons and painters. The Negro skilled laborer is just about holding his own because the younger element is not looking toward the trades. The success of the Negro artisan, on the whole, is fair.

HAVERHILL.—Fair number of Negro skilled laborers here. They are engaged chiefly in the manufacture of shoes and are just holding their own. Industrial school training would give the Negro a decided advantage here. The young men are not entering the trades very fast; they are more inclined to do menial labor. The artisans are having fair success.

PITTSFIELD.—Not many Negro skilled laborers here. The Negro skilled laborer is losing because race prejudice discourages him.

Section 11. Delaware, District of Columbia and Maryland

The Negro population of these geographical divisions in 1900 and 1910 was as follows:

STATES	1900	1910
Delaware	30,697	31,181
District of Columbia	86,702	94,446
Maryland	235,064	232,249
Total	352,463	357,876

The census of 1900 recorded the following skilled or semi-skilled Negro workers:

Delaware, District of Columbia and Maryland

Male—

Engineers (civil and mechanical)	7
Barbers	1,202
Steam Railway employees	884
Brick and tile makers	855
Blacksmiths and wheelwrights	289
Boot and shoe makers	288
Butchers	151
Carpenters and joiners	560
Cabinet makers	23
Cotton and other textile mill operatives	15
Iron and steel workers	860
Machinists	44
Marble and stone cutters and masons .	982

Male—

Millers	22
Painters	241
Plasterers	210
Plumbers and gas fitters	103
Printers	122
Steam boiler makers	1
Engineers and firemen (stationary) . .	562

Female—

Dressmakers and seamstresses	2,646
Milliners	6
Printers	19
Tailoresses	15

General Conditions

WASHINGTON.—Not many Negro skilled laborers here. They are losing because of labor unions. Very little results of industrial school training is perceptible save in the increase in school attendance. A few young men are becoming engineers. Those in the trades are doing well.

BALTIMORE.—Not many Negro skilled laborers here—carpenters, cement layers, shoemakers and printers. The Negro is losing as a skilled laborer because of insufficient opportunity for intensive industrial training. Industrial school training has caused an awakened interest of educated classes in the need for artisans in the community. The young men are entering the trades in a very slight degree only. The Negro artisans are producing satisfactory results because they show possibility of performing employment in practically any line.

Section 12. Florida

There were 230,730 Negroes in Florida in 1900 and 308,669 in 1910. The census of 1900 recorded the following skilled or semi-skilled Negro laborers:

Florida

Male—

Engineers (civil and mechanical) . . .	6
Barbers	352
Steam railway employees :	2,118
Blacksmiths and wheelwrights	196
Boot and shoe makers	99
Butchers	120
Carpenters and joiners	1,150
Machinists	39
Marble and stone cutters and masons .	287

Male—

Painters	218
Plumbers and gas fitters	37
Printers	29
Engineers and firemen (stationary) . .	394

Female—

Dress makers and seamstresses	891
Milliners	2

General Conditions

GREENVILLE.—There is a friendly feeling between the white and colored laborers here, largely due to the Negro's preparation. The conditions are growing better for the Negro skilled workers because they can do more work and in many cases better work.

Section 13. Georgia

The state of Georgia had a Negro population of 1,034,813 in 1900 and of 1,176,987 in 1910. According to the census of 1900 there were the following skilled and semi-skilled Negro workers in the state:

Georgia

Male—		Male—	
Engineers (civil and mechanical) . . .	6	Millers	126
Barbers	1,116	Painters	855
Steam railway employees	6,366	Plasterers	3,09
Brick and tile makers	639	Plumbers and gas fitters	139
Blacksmiths and wheelwrights	1,230	Printers	68
Boot and shoe makers	664	Steam boiler makers	33
Butchers	353	Engineers and firemen (stationary) . .	836
Carpenters and joiners	3,385		
Cabinet makers	54	Female—	
Cotton and other textile mill operatives	3 5	Dressmakers and seamstresses	2,234
Iron and steel workers	281	Milliners	7
Machinists	154	Printers	3
Marble and stone cutters	1,508	Tailoresses	25

General Conditions

ALBANY.—Many skilled Negro laborers here—carpenters, masons and blacksmiths. Negro skilled labor is gaining because the number is increasing. Industrial school training has caused very marked results. Many young men are entering the trades. The success among the artisans at present is much better than it has been in many years.

AMERICUS.—Not many skilled Negro laborers here; a few carpenters, masons and blacksmiths. The Negro is gaining as a skilled laborer. Industrial school training has produced good results. Few young men are entering the trades. The artisans are having good success.

COVINGTON.—Not many skilled Negro laborers here; a few carpenters. The Negro skilled laborer is gaining because the attendance in trade departments is increasing. Industrial school training has caused improvement in the homes. Many young men are entering the trades. The artisans find ready employment.

DAWSON.—Many skilled Negro laborers here—carpenters, brickmasons, blacksmiths and tailors. They are gaining because of the increase in intelligence. Very little results of industrial school training evident in this community. The young men are entering the trades. The Negro artisans are succeeding well.

FORT VALLEY.—Many skilled Negro laborers here. They are chiefly builders. The Negro skilled laborer is losing here because he does not fit himself to compete with the trained white artisan. Those who are able to hold their own are those who have had some industrial school training. A great many young men are entering the trades, but they are going in as apprentices and can hardly attain the efficiency to cope with the trained artisan. The Negro trained laborer is having splendid success.

HARLEM.—Many skilled Negro laborers here for the size of the town—carpenters, printers, masons, blacksmiths and engineers. They are gaining because of competency and reliability. As results of industrial school training there are better buildings, better kept homes and scientific farming. The young men enter the trades now and then and are having great success. They are all kept busy.

HARTWELL.—Many skilled Negro laborers here—carpenters and masons. In many instances they are losing because of the lack of constancy. Industrial school training creates thrift and industrial habits. Not many young men in this section entering the trades. The Negro artisan is having moderate success here.

LA GRANGE.—About a dozen Negro skilled laborers here—carpenters, bricklayers and plasterers. They are losing here because of race antipathy and a love for their own by the other race. Not many results of industrial school training visible as yet. Few such students have come here. Not very many young men are entering the trades. The artisans are making a moderate living.

MACON.—Many skilled Negro laborers here—brickmasons, carpenters, tailors, blacksmiths, plasterers and painters. I am unable to say whether or not he is gaining, but the demand is much greater than the supply. The majority of the graduates of industrial schools are either in the civil service or studying or practicing some profession. Not many young men entering the trades. Most of the brick work and plastering is done by colored artisans. Can find them at work on the largest and finest buildings. We have at least two Negro contractors, whose patrons are almost exclusively of the other race.

STANFORDVILLE.—Not many Negro skilled laborers here. They follow farming chiefly. The Negro skilled laborer is losing here, because before the Civil War it was customary to put Negro boys under a good artisan as apprentices to learn certain trades. With freedom these conditions passed away and Negro men as a whole are not inclined for their boys to learn trades. Very little results of industrial training perceptible. The sewing and cooking departments of many of the American Missionary Association schools produce very marked results among the Negro women. The Negro artisans receive all the patronage of the community from both races. Efficient work is all that is required.

Replies of Artisans

ALBANY.—Contractor and Builder. There are more colored workmen here than white, hence the feeling is fairly good. Conditions are growing better for the Negro skilled worker. This is the day of the survival of the fittest in the mechanical world and especially here in southwest Georgia.

AMERICUS.—Contracting Plasterer and Brick Mason. I am a member of Union No. 19, Georgia, B. and M. I. U. of the United States of America. Conditions are improving slightly. The Negro can do more and better work in a given time and have less to say about it and give the contractor less trouble. While some contractors favor the white mechanic as a general thing the work is more progressive with the Negro at his post. The Negro workers need to learn about plan reading and thoroly fit themselves for their work.

AMERICUS.—Contractor and Builder. Conditions seem to be standing because white workers are coming in and preventing the Negro workers from having so much to do. Perhaps the colored workman would do better if he possessed more stability and reliability. There would be a greater demand for his work.

ATLANTA.—Bricklayer. Conditions are growing better for the Negro skilled worker because the class of work done at present demands the skilled workman. I was secretary of B. and M. I. U. No. 6 of Georgia for five years, said union being colored. Whites and Negroes have separate unions but their laws and government are the same, each receiving charter and regulations from the executive board of the B. and M. I. U. of America.

ATLANTA.—Plumber. I have made several attempts to join the union but have been refused because of my color. Conditions are growing better for the Negro workers because skill is able to compete with skill and the men of the other race who are in the field find that they must forget prejudice, etc., in order to keep abreast with their rivals. A few years ago the supply houses in Atlanta would not sell material of any kind to a Negro master plumber but now they vie with each other in giving us the best of goods at the lowest possible wholesale prices.

ATLANTA.—Brick Mason. There is the same prejudice and discrimination as in other fields of labor. Negro contractors are barred even from the architects' offices. About one per cent of these offices are open to Negroes. In some cases it has come under my observation that even if a Negro has equal ability and in some instances a lower bid he is barred or the job is given to his white opponent.

BAINBRIDGE.—Horse Shoer. There is a very good feeling between the white and colored workers here. There is a class of white and colored people here that can get together and settle any difference. I came to this town about ten years ago by an invitation from the mayor and chief of police to establish a business. They have stood by me as they would stand by a white man.

GIBSON.—Blacksmith and Buggy Builder. So far as blacksmithing is concerned it is simply a matter of efficiency of the workman. Conditions are growing better because the masses are being educated to the immediate needs of their community, thus making themselves useful. I have been establisht here four years. All of the county's work in general repairing on road machines, carts, dumps, wheelers is done at my place.

OXFORD.—Carpenter and Builder. Conditions are growing better because the richer and better class of whites has now reached the place where the skill of the workman and not the color of his skin is considered. I finished one of the finest white churches in Covington and a twelve-room dwelling for a white banker's son. I can use any man's blue print if it can be worked by the scale.

Section 14.   Illinois, Indiana, Michigan, Minnesota, Wisconsin

The Negro population in these states in 1900 and 1910 was as follows:

STATES	1900	1910
Illinois	85,078	109,041
Indiana	57,505	60,280
Michigan	15,816	17,115
Minnesota	4,959	7,084
Wisconsin	2,542	2,900
Total	165,900	196,420

According to the census of 1900 these states had the following Negro skilled or semi-skilled workers:

Illinois, Indiana, Michigan, Minnesota, Wisconsin

Male—
Engineers (civil and mechanical) . . . 7
Barbers 2,135
Steam railway employees 1,030
Blacksmiths and wheelwrights 226
Brick and tile makers 187
Boot and shoe makers 82
Butchers 147
Carpenters and joiners 353
Cabinet makers 18
Cotton and other textile mill operatives 20
Iron and steel workers 441
Machinists 83
Marble and stone cutters and masons . . 824

Male—
Millers 38
Painters 289
Plasterers 257
Plumbers and gas fitters 63
Printers 94
Steam boiler makers 6
Engineers and firemen (stationary) . 575
Female—
Dressmakers and seamstresses 1,179
Milliners 24
Printers 7
Tailoresses 14

General Conditions

CHICAGO.—Not many Negro skilled laborers here—carpenters, plumbers, brick-layers and plasterers. The Negro artisan is losing because of labor unions and competition. Industrial school training is producing good results where skilled workmen are turned out. Very few young men are entering the trades. The artisans are having small success in a general way. Some few are doing excellently.

MINNEAPOLIS.—Not many skilled Negro laborers here—carpenters, plasterers and contractors. As a skilled laborer the Negro is gaining because of his superior work. Not many young men are entering the trades. The artisans are succeeding well.

ST. PAUL.—Not many Negro skilled laborers here—shoe makers, tailors, cleaners and pressers. The Negro skilled laborer is not gaining because of a lack of "get up." No results of industrial school training are evident. The Negro young men are not entering the trades.

Section 15. Iowa and Kansas

The Negro population of Iowa and Kansas for 1900 and 1910 was as follows:

STATES	1900	1910
Iowa	12,693	15,078
Kansas	52,003	54,504
Total	64,696	69,582

According to the census of 1900 these two states had the following skilled or semi-skilled Negro laborers:

Iowa and Kansas

Male—

Barbers	496
Steam railway employees	540
Brick and tile makers	96
Blacksmiths and wheelwrights	128
Boot and shoe makers	44
Butchers	79
Carpenters and joiners	127
Cabinet makers	2
Iron and steel workers	80
Machinists	17
Marble and stone cutters and masons	291
Millers	20

Male—

Painters	55
Plasterers	157
Plumbers and gas fitters	20
Printers	30
Steam boiler makers	3
Engineers and firemen (stationary)	138

Female—

Dressmakers and seamstresses	199
Printers	5
Tailoresses	1

General Conditions

DES MOINES.—About thirty Negro skilled laborers here—two carpenters, six masons, three linotypers, one printer, five chauffeurs, one lathe worker, five modistes and seven manicurists. Very few young men are entering the trades. The artisans are succeeding very well.

ATCHISON.—The Negro skilled laborer is in evidence here. The largest blacksmith and repair shop in the state of Kansas is in this city. It is kept by a Negro whose income is said to be more than $8,000 a year.

LAWRENCE.—Not many skilled Negro laborers here—blacksmiths, marble cutters, electric wirers, plumbers and carpenters. The Negro is gaining as a skilled laborer because he has begun to recognize the need for efficiency in order to be steadily employed. The results of industrial school training are very apparent—increased efficiency, increased self respect and aspiration, and respect from the opposite race. The artisans here are successful in keeping busy all of their time. They are promoted and their salaries are frequently raised.

Replies of Artisans

DES MOINES.—Dressmaker. There is no union here of members of my trade. If there were, I could join along with the white workers.

They treat me as well as they treat each other and the Negro woman who learns her trade well has the same chance that the white girls have. I have worked at my trade for more than ten years. I have held positions in some of the largest white establishments in this state as manager and as head waist maker and have always been well treated.

DES MOINES.—Mechanic. Conditions are growing better. Negroes hold good positions when competent, providing they are self-respecting and stick to business. I am hopeful for Negro skilled workmen. We should have more of them. I believe, tho, the Negroes should organize and own and operate business for themselves.

Section 16. Kentucky

The state of Kentucky had 284,706 Negroes in 1900 and 261,656 in 1910. According to the twelfth census the state had the following skilled or semi-skilled Negro laborers:

Kentucky

Male—		Male—	
Engineers (civil and mechanical) . . .	4	Millers	76
Barbers.	812	Painters . :	234
Steam railway employees	2,384	Plasterers.	285
Brick and tile makers	342	Plumbers and gas fitters	37
Blacksmiths and wheelwrights	539	Printers	21
Boot and shoe makers	116	Steam boiler makers	5
Butchers	98	Engineers and firemen (stationary) . .	431
Carpenters and joiners	701		
Cabinet makers.	11	Female—	
Cotton and other textile mill operatives	117	Dressmakers and seamstresses	721
Iron and steel workers	370	Milliners	7
Machinists	35	Printers	2
Marble and stone cutters and masons .	757	Tailoresses	4

General Conditions

BOWLING GREEN.—Many skilled Negro laborers here—carpenters, blacksmiths and stone masons. They are gaining because the skilled laborer has no trouble in getting work. All who desire to work are kept busy. Those artisans coming from our industrial schools are doing well; the better prepared they are the better they succeed. Not very many young men entering the trades, but a surprising number considering the sentiment. Sentiment is getting better and they are succeeding.

FRANKFORT.—Many Negro skilled laborers here in proportion to the population—carpenters, plasterers, engineers, stone masons, firemen, shoe makers, paper hangers and decorators. The Negro skilled laborers are losing slightly because they are not as steadily employed as heretofore and many have moved to other towns and cities. Industrial school training causes those having trades to receive better wages and to be more self-sustaining and independent. Few young men are entering the trades; not enough, tho. Most of the artisans are substantial citizens, possessing homes of their own besides other property. Many of these homes are unusually modern, commodious and good.

HAWESVILLE.—Three Negro skilled laborers here—two blacksmiths and a tinner. They are gaining because the demand for their labor is increasing. Industrial school training causes better pay and greater demand for their service. The young men are entering the trades slowly but the success is encouraging.

HENDERSON.—An average number of Negro skilled laborers here—carpenters and blacksmiths. They are seemingly holding their own. Few young men enter the trades. The artisans are succeeding when efficient.

LEBANON.—Few Negro skilled laborers here—plasterers, carpenters and stone masons. They are losing because the older skilled laborers are dying and the young men have not learned the trades. The young men are not entering the trades. The success of the artisans is only moderate.

LEXINGTON.—Many skilled Negro laborers here—plumbers, blacksmiths, tinners, carpenters, painters, brick-layers, stone masons, silver smiths and tailors. The Negro is gaining as a skilled laborer because there are more here now than fifteen years ago. Industrial school training has produced good results. The people are learning that labor is honorable, understanding that by the sweat of the brow you must earn what you eat. The artisans are succeeding finely.

RICHMOND.—Many skilled Negro laborers here—carpenters, masons, engineers, blacksmiths, tailors, upholsterers and tinners. The skilled laborer is gaining because he is much in demand. If a Negro can do good work he need not fear the white man, but he loses when his work does not come up to the white man's. We need more skilled laborers here. There are wide fields open to the skilled laborer here. We have to give our work to the white man because the Negro cannot do it. The industrial school training is doing a great thing for the young Negro. He is going out into the world and doing business for himself. He is his own boss and is making good money. Where he at one time worked under a boss for three dollars per week, he is now making under his own management ten and fifteen dollars per week. Many young men are entering the trades. The Negro artisans are succeeding very well.

Replies of Artisans

FRANKFORT.—Shoe Maker and Repairer. There is a friendly feeling between the white and colored workers in my trade here. I have had white shoe makers work for me. My shop is equipt with modern machines and I made them pay for themselves. I enjoy a nice trade from both white and Negro patrons.

FRANKFORT.—General Contractor and Builder. Conditions are not so good here because of growing race prejudice and because there are not young men enough learning the trade. I came to Frankfort in 1883 and for eight years thereafter my work was for white contractors. Since that time I have been contracting for myself and have had as many as seventy-five men under my employ at one time. None of the white contractors in Frankfort now will employ colored mechanics.

HAWESVILLE.—Blacksmith. There exists a friendly feeling here between colored and white workers. I think conditions are growing better for the Negro laborer because he does better work with less contention with contractors.

HENDERSON.—Blacksmith. There is an exceedingly friendly and congenial feeling between the white and colored workers here, hardly any prejudice existing as far as trade relations are concerned. As I see it the country is demanding efficiency and satisfactory results and if the Negro mechanic can produce these he is sure to get recognition and consideration.

Section 17. Louisiana

The state of Louisiana had 650,804 Negroes in 1900 and 713,874 in 1910. The twelfth census (1900) recorded the following skilled or semi-skilled Negroes for the state:

Louisiana

Male—		Male—	
Engineers (civil and mechanical)	14	Millers	31
Barbers	515	Painters	354
Steam railway employees	3,086	Plasterers	271
Brick and tile makers	339	Plumbers and gas fitters	27
Blacksmiths and wheelwrights	700	Printers	60
Boot and shoe makers	304	Steam boiler makers	7
Butchers	195	Engineers and firemen (stationary)	504
Carpenters and joiners	1,711		
Cabinet makers	45	Female—	
Cotton and other textile mill operatives	22	Dressmakers and seamstresses	2,241
Iron and steel workers	36	Milliners	12
Machinists	33	Tailoresses	99
Marble and stone cutters and masons	877		

General Conditions

BATON ROUGE.—Many skilled Negro laborers here—carpenters, brick masons, plasterers, painters and decorators. The Negro artisan is holding his own here because there are not so many white artisans and the Negro gives full satisfaction. Very many young men are entering the trades. The Negro skilled laborers are having fair success.

MONROE.—Many skilled Negro laborers here—carpenters, masons, painters, plasterers, etc. The Negro skilled laborer is gaining because of his efficiency in whatever he has a chance to do. Whenever the trained man is given work he does it commendably no matter where trained, in school or out. The training is the necessity and should be given to all. The young men are entering the trades. The Negro artisan is having such success as should be reasonably expected from one who does his duty with an open chance before him.

Replies of Artisans

BATON ROUGE.—Contractor and Brick-layer. I do not belong to a trade union at present for the union went to the bad here more than a year ago. At that time we had quite a number of whites in our organization, tho we Negroes had the majority. I think conditions are growing better for the Negro skilled worker. He does his work as a rule with more taste and does more in an allotted time. That within itself is the solution of the work problem. The man who has work to be done employs as a rule the man who puts up the most complete package. The majority of the mechanics in Baton Rouge are colored and they own an enormous amount of real estate. We have any quantity of jack-leg white carpenters who dislike working with the colored brother but they need his assistance to such an extent that they work with him, tho with reluctancy. In other words, they simply can't do without the colored man in the trades. We have two colored men here who have been contracting for twenty years. They are highly considered by the white people and do principally all of the city work. They are now engaged in putting another story on one of the largest hotels in the city.

MONROE.—Plasterer. I do not belong to a trade union because I do not endorse the methods adopted by trade unions to enforce their claims. An amicable relation exists between the white and colored workers of my trade in this place. I fear conditions are not growing better for the Negro skilled worker because of the very small number with a liberal education that are engaged in the trades.

NEW ORLEANS.—Electrician. I do not belong to a trade union because the union here will not admit a Negro. I believe the conditions for the Negro skilled worker are growing better because the world is now looking for the man who can deliver the goods. My experience in this city has been interesting. My work is inspected and approved by a board known as the Louisiana Fire Prevention Bureau. The city electrician also approves my work.

Section 18.   Maine, New Hampshire, Rhode Island, Vermont

The Negro population in these states in 1900 and 1910 was as follows:

STATES	1900	1910
Maine	1,319	1,364
New Hampshire	662	564
Rhode Island	9,092	9,529
Vermont	826	1,621
Total	11,899	13,078

According to the census of 1900 these states contained the following skilled or semi-skilled Negro workers:

Maine, New Hampshire, Rhode Island, Vermont

Male—
Barbers 106
Steam railway employees 33
Blacksmiths and wheelwrights 19
Brick and tile makers 1
Boot and shoe makers 13
Butchers 11
Carpenters and joiners 34
Cabinet makers 2
Cotton and other textile mill operatives . 24
Iron and steel workers 16
Machinists 17
Marble and stone cutters and masons . . 59

Male—
Painters 38
Plasterers 3
Plumbers and gas fitters 6
Printers 3
Steam boiler makers 1
Engineers and firemen (stationary) . . . 25

Female—
Dressmakers and seamstresses 136
Milliners 3
Printers 1
Tailoresses 4

Section 19. Mississippi

The state of Mississippi had a Negro population of 907,630 in 1900 and of 1,009,487 in 1910. According to the census of 1900 there were the following skilled or semi-skilled Negro workers in the state:

Mississippi

Male—
Engineers (civil and mechanical) . . 3
Barbers 486
Steam railway employees 4,681
Brick and tile makers 460
Blacksmiths and wheelwrights 663
Boot and shoe makers 152
Butchers 183
Carpenters and joiners 1,497
Cotton and other textile mill operatives 14
Iron and steel workers 48
Machinists 52

Male—
Marble and stone cutters and masons . 392
Millers 15
Painters 227
Plumbers and gas fitters 27
Printers 27
Engineers and firemen (stationary) . . 479

Female—
Dressmakers and seamstresses 1,112
Milliners 8

General Conditions

HOLLY SPRINGS.—Not many Negro skilled laborers here — blacksmiths, carpenters and brick masons. The Negro is gaining as a skilled laborer because his services are always in demand. Industrial school training has produced efficiency and reliability. Only a few young men are entering the trades.

INDIANOLA.—Many Negro skilled laborers here—contractors, foremen, carpenters, brick-layers, electricians, engineers, blacksmiths, agriculturists, etc. The Negro artisan is gaining in proportion to his skill. There are more demands for laborers trained in industrial schools than for the unskilled. Some of the young men are entering the trades. The artisans of this community are attaining competence and material and business rating of a high order.

NATCHEZ.—About twenty Negro skilled laborers here—carpenters, masons, plasterers, painters, blacksmiths and chauffeurs. The skilled

Negro laborers are gaining here because of proficiency. Industrial school training turns out better workmen. The young men are entering the trades. The Negro artisans are having fair success here.

VICKSBURG. —Many skilled laborers here—carpenters, blacksmiths, masons, paper hangers, cement workers, plasterers, painters and upholsterers. In some respects they are losing because of prejudice. First, eleven years ago there was not a contractor here who did not work Negroes, now the leading contractor does not employ a single Negro carpenter. Secondly, because the Negro as a carpenter does not acquire the skill of the finished workman. There are more Negro brick-layers than white and they get work with all the contractors. The best cement worker and plasterer in town is a Negro. The third reason that the Negro is losing is that there are no young men entering the trades to fill the old workmen's places. Not many workmen here who have attended industrial schools. The Negro artisans are having fair success; that is, they make money. The brick masons and cement workers do not accumulate very much.

Replies of Artisans

INDIANOLA.- Carpenter. A fairly good feeling exists between the white and colored workers in this section. Conditions are growing better for the Negro skilled worker because ability is the thing needed and most contractors (private parties) have seen that the skilled Negro mechanic is a money saver.

NATCHEZ. Mason. I am a member of Natchez Union, No. 7, being permitted to join with the white workers. I think conditions are growing better for the Negro skilled laborer.

VICKSBURG. Contracting Brick-layer. There is a good feeling between the white and colored workers here and the conditions are growing better for the Negro skilled workers. I am president of the Brick-layers' Union, to which both whites and Negroes belong.

VICKSBURG. Decorator. Conditions are growing better for the Negro skilled laborer because thoro training is giving him confidence in himself and is demonstrating the Negro's ability to render competent service. When I began this work I had no intention whatever of remaining in the trade; but finding it a lucrative trade I applied myself diligently, always with a desire to excel. As a result my reputation as a workman grew and today I cannot accept all the work offered me.

YAZOO CITY. --Contractor and Builder. Conditions are growing better for the Negro skilled worker because he is learning to see how well he can do what is entrusted to him instead of how little he can do for the money that is paid him. I teach my men to do their work so well that no one else can improve upon it; the importance of doing their best at all times. I believe it is largely this that keeps me busy.

Section 20. Missouri

The state of Missouri had a Negro population of 161,234 in 1900 and of 157,452 in 1910. The census of 1900 recorded the following skilled and semi-skilled Negro workers for the state:

Missouri

Male—

Engineers (civil and mechanical)	2
Barbers	910
Steam railway employees	769
Brick and tile makers	275
Blacksmiths and wheelwrights	187
Boot and shoe makers	55
Butchers	116
Carpenters and joiners	219
Cabinet makers	5
Cotton and other textile operatives	6
Iron and steel workers	243
Machinists	23
Marble and stone cutters and masons	798

Male—

Millers	29
Painters	66
Plasterers	212
Plumbers and gas fitters	30
Printers	37
Steam boiler makers	3
Engineers and firemen (stationary)	411

Female—

Dressmakers and seamstresses	412
Milliners	2
Printers	2
Tailoresses	4

General Conditions

BOONVILLE. Several Negro skilled laborers here—two carpenters, two masons, two engineers and a plumber. The Negro is gaining as a skilled laborer. The number has increased slightly in ten years. As results of industrial school training we have an engineer and a carpenter. Only three young men are entering the trades. The artisans here are succeeding well.

CHILLICOTHE. Not many Negro skilled laborers here a few blacksmiths, engineers and masons, a few gardeners and farmers, while the majority are day laborers. The Negro is losing as a skilled laborer because he is not pursuing it extensively. In this section he is not taking up the work. Those who do follow it find employment readily. There are no persons here from an industrial school. The young men are not entering the trades. The Negro skilled laborer is succeeding where he can do the work.

DALTON. Not many Negro skilled laborers here—carpenters, plasterers and painters. The Negro is gaining as a skilled laborer because of large openings. Many results visible in every way of industrial school training, especially in the trained farmers. Some young men are entering the trades. The Negro artisan is succeeding well in this community.

MARYVILLE. —Practically no Negro skilled laborers here a few plasterers and house-cleaners. Those laboring in these occupations are very proficient. There is no gain in the number because organized white labor does all of the skilled work and there are too few Negroes to organize. There are no Negro workmen trained in industrial schools in this city. The young men are not entering the trades. What Negro artisans there are are having splendid success.

ST. LOUIS.—Not many Negro skilled laborers here—brick-layers, carpenters, plumbers, blacksmiths, paper-hangers and plasterers. The Negro is not gaining as a skilled laborer because of lack of motive and inclination. Industrial school training promises much. Not many young men are entering the trades. The Negro artisan as far as he is efficient is succeeding splendidly.

Replies of Artisans

BOONVILLE.—Contracting Brick-layer and Plasterer. There is a good feeling here between the white and colored workers in my trade. I frequently hire white plasterers. Conditions are growing better for the Negro skilled laborer.

DALTON.—Carpenter. I do not belong to a union, tho I could join with the whites. An agreeable feeling exists between the races in my trade. Conditions grow better as the Negro workers master their trades.

ST. LOUIS.—Stone Cutter. I am a member of the Building Laborers' International Protective Union, Local No. 3, a Negro union. Negroes cannot join with the whites. The conditions can hardly be said to be growing better here for there are not enough Negroes in the trades to make it so. I could put many to work if they were qualified. We have a few plasterers and brick-layers working here, but they cannot get into the unions here on account of past dealings with white unions in regard to colored hod carriers' union. We have seven-tenths of the work here now.

ST. LOUIS.—Electrician. I do not belong to the union because Negroes are not admitted to Electrical Workers' Union in the state of Missouri. Conditions are growing better because the Negroes are building more homes and business places for themselves in St. Louis. Negro plumbers are in great demand here, there being only one finished plumber here at present. The Negro tradesmen need a leader to go to the front for them and I think they will be able to get into the unions then. I could get three times as much work if I could join the Electrical Workers' Union. As I am the only finished Negro electrician here I cannot fight the union alone. There are six other unfinished Negro electricians here who do very good work.

Section 21. New York, New Jersey and Pennsylvania

The Negro population of New-York, New Jersey and Pennsylvania in 1900 and 1910 was as follows:

STATES	1900	1910
New York	99,232	134,181
New Jersey	69,844	89,760
Pennsylvania	156,845	193,908
Total	325,921	417,849

The census of 1900 recorded the following Negro skilled or semi-skilled laborers for these three states:

New York, New Jersey and Pennsylvania

Male—		Male—	
Engineers (civil and mechanical)	26	Millers	20
Barbers	2,461	Painters	430
Steam railway employees	674	Plasterers	172
Brick and tile makers	2,744	Plumbers and gas fitters	119
Blacksmiths and wheelwrights	244	Printers	200
Boot and shoe makers	169	Steam boiler makers	9
Butchers	112	Engineers and firemen (stationary)	797
Carpenters and joiners	438		
Cabinet makers	22	Female—	
Cotton and other textile mill operatives	43	Dressmakers and seamstresses	2,754
Iron and steel workers	1,764	Milliners	24
Machinists	157	Printers	4
Marble and stone cutters and masons	1,644	Tailoresses	32

Two recent studies of the economic status of the Negro in York City[1] show that in the skilled trades "the Negro is conspicuous by his absence. Only four in every thousand where there should be eighteen. . . . . The census division of mechanical pursuits shows only a few colored men working at trades, and the paucity of the numbers is often attributed by the Negro to a third obstacle in the way of his progress, the trade union."[2]   Hence in New York City "Negroes are crowded into these poorer paid occupations because many of them are inefficient and because of the color prejudice on the part of white workmen and employers. Both of these influences are severe handicaps in the face of the competition in this advanced industrial community."[3]   As to the wages and efficiency of the Negro workers in New York City, Dr. Haynes says:[4]

> The wages of skilled trades do not affect the larger part of the Negro population, because so small a percentage are engaged in these occupations. . . . . It is evident that compared with the large number of Negro workers few are engaged in the skilled trades, join the unions, and thus enter into the more highly-paid occupations. . . . . The small number of skilled artisans who are equal to or above the average white workman and can get into the unions receive the union wages.

The following statistics for Negroes in New York City are of interest:

---

[1] Miss Ovington: Half a Man.   Dr. Haynes: The Negro at Work in New York City.
[2] Ovington: Op. cit., pp. 89, 95.   [3] Haynes: Op. cit., pp. 76, 77.
[4] Haynes: Ibid, pp. 82, 83, 89.

OCCUPATIONS OF NEGROES—NEW YORK CITY, 1900	Number of Negroes in each occupation	Number of Negroes to each 1,000 workers in each occupation
Engineers, firemen (not locomotive)	227	14
Masons (brick and stone)	94	7
Painters, glaziers and varnishers	177	6
Plasterers	51	12
Blacksmiths	29	4
Butchers	31	2
Carpenters and joiners	94	3
Iron and steel workers	40	4
Paper-hangers	18	19
Photographers	22	14
Plumbers, gas and steam fitters	31	2
Printers, lithographers and pressmen	53	2
Tailors	69	1
Tobacco and cigar factory operatives	189	16
Fishermen and oyster-men	65	45
Miners and quarry-men	21	64
Machinists	47	3

Ovington, M. W.: Half a Man. P. 90.

Negro Wage=earners, 10 Years of Age and Over, Engaged in Selected Occupations—New York City, 1890 and 1900

OCCUPATIONS	1890	1900	Per cent increase
Steam railway employees	28	70	150.0
Blacksmiths	9	29	222.2
Masons (brick and stone)	20	94	370.0
Painters, glaziers, varnishers	99	177	78.8
Plasterers	10	51	410.0
Plumbers, gas and steam fitters	11	31	181.8
Carpenters and joiners	33	94	184.8
Tobacco and cigar factory operatives	146	189	29.4
Tailors	20	69	245.0
Upholsterers	11	18	63.3
Engineers and firemen (stationary)	61	227	272.1
Machinists	7	47	571.4
Total	455	1,096	140.8

Haynes, G. E.: The Negro at Work in New York City. P. 71.

Occupations of Negro Wage=earners, 15 Years of Age and Over—Manhattan, 1905

Pursuits	No.	Pursuits	No.
Male—		**Male—**	
Asphalt layers	6	Masons (brick)	8
Blacksmiths	5	Masons (not specified)	5
Carpenters	18	Painters and decorators	26
Confectioners	3	Plasterers	7
Drill runners	5	Plumbers (steam and gas fitters)	5
Electricians	3	Printers and compositors	14
Engineers (stationary)	48	Shoe makers and repairers	6
Firemen (stationary)	19	Tailors	20
Factory employees (not specified) . . .	6	Miscellaneous	22
Hod carriers	9	**Female—**	
Harness and saddle makers	2	Dressmakers	164
Cigar makers	32	Garment workers	18
Kalsominers	8	Milliners	5
Machinists	12	Seamstresses	16
Mechanics (automobile, bicycle, etc.) . .	9	Tailors' assistants	3
Masons (stone)	2	Miscellaneous	6

Haynes: *Ibid.* Pp. 74-76.

General Conditions

NEW ROCHELLE.—Not many Negro skilled laborers here—a few carpenters. The Negro is gaining as a skilled laborer because the number has increased within the last four years. The young men are not entering the trades. The artisans are succeeding fairly well.

ORANGE.—Not many Negro skilled laborers here—a few masons and carpenters. The Negroes have nothing to gain or lose because the labor unions won't admit them and the few who are acting independently are either incompetent or unreliable or both. Apparently there are no Negroes of industrial school training here; a few industrious or "industrially" trained would undoubtedly be of service. The young men are not entering the trades. The artisans who are willing to work are kept busy.

SCHENECTADY.—Not many skilled Negro laborers here—a few carpenters and masons. The Negro is gaining as a skilled laborer. The young men are not entering the trades. The artisans are having fair success.

Replies of Artisans

ORANGE.—Painter and Decorator. We have tried hard to get into the painters' union but have been held out on account of color. However, I use union men. As a rule the white workers do not like to see Negroes on the job, but no better for them. If you can do the work you will get it to do.

ORANGE.—Carpenter. I could join with the whites in the union if I wished to do so. I have no need to as I am kept busy, being my own boss. If a workman is capable he can work anywhere. I take contract for all manner of mechanical work and furnish men for any and all lines as well as all materials, such as painting, brick-laying, plastering, slating, excavating and macadamizing.

ORANGE.—House Painter. I do not belong to a union. Probably I could join. Out of the union, I have a better chance to work colored men on my jobs and a better chance to get jobs. The white man in my trade seems to be satisfied so long as the colored man will content himself in doing those little jobs down the alleys. Only in part are the conditions growing better. It is seldom the Negro worker gets a chance to show his ability to do things as well or better than the white man. I find more prejudice existing among the white tradesmen toward the colored tradesmen than from any other source. It remains, however, for the majority of our mechanics to gain the confidence of the employer thru honesty and punctuality, being always true to the trust however large or small it may be as were our fathers.

Section 22. North Carolina

The state of North Carolina had a Negro population of 624,469 in 1900 and of 697,843 in 1910. The twelfth census recorded the following skilled and semi-skilled Negro workers for the state:

North Carolina

Male—		Male—	
Engineers (civil and mechanical)	2	Marble and stone cutters and masons	1,112
Barbers	707	Millers	81
Steam railway employees	3,268	Painters	382
Brick and tile makers	825	Plasterers	169
Blacksmiths and wheelwrights	719	Plumbers and gas fitters	48
Boot and shoe makers	330	Printers	39
Butchers	165	Engineers and firemen (stationary)	9 3
Carpenters and joiners	1,500		
Cabinet makers	13	Female—	
Cotton and other textile mill operatives	157	Dressmakers and seamstresses	753
Iron and steel workers	9)	Milliners	2
Machinists	52	Tailoresses	8

General Conditions

CHAPEL HILL.—Many skilled Negro laborers here—masons and carpenters. The Negro is gaining as a skilled laborer because he seems to have a love for the trades. The results of industrial school training are good. Many young men are entering the trades. The artisans are succeeding in that they have all they can do.

KINGS MOUNTAIN.—Few Negro skilled laborers here—carpenters, masons, engineers and blacksmiths. The Negro is gaining as a skilled laborer because he is in demand. Industrial school training is causing more and better work to be done by our race. The young men are entering the trades. The artisans are having good success here.

WINTON.—Not many skilled Negro laborers here—a few masons, painters, carpenters and farmers. The Negroes are gaining in farming but losing in the other pursuits. The reason for this is not known unless it is that farming is the leading industry of this section. No industrial school training has been given to the boys. The girls are doing well in cooking and sewing. Only a few young men are entering the trades. The Negro artisans make a comfortable living.

Section 23. Ohio

There were 96,901 Negroes in the state of Ohio in 1900 and 111,443 in 1910. According to the twelfth census the state had in 1900 the following skilled and semi-skilled Negro workers:

Ohio

Male—
Engineers (civil and mechanical) . . .	5
Barbers	1,359
Steam railway employees	202
Brick and tile makers	135
Blacksmiths and wheelwrights	233
Boot and shoe makers	101
Butchers	44
Carpenters and joiners	242
Cotton and other textile mill operatives	16
Iron and steel workers	699
Machinists	55
Marble and stone cutters and masons .	692
Millers	9

Male—
Painters	205
Plasterers	305
Plumbers and gas fitters	25
Printers	37
Steam boiler makers	7
Engineers and firemen (stationary) . .	369

Female—
Dressmakers and seamstresses	573
Milliners	17
Printers	2
Tailoresses	22

General Conditions

GALLIPOLIS.—Not many Negro skilled laborers here. They are losing because work of all sorts is scarce. There are no graduates of industrial schools here. The young men are entering the trades very slowly. Two or three engineers and two carpenters have establisht excellent reputations in their respective trades.

IRONTON.—Not many skilled Negro laborers here—carpenters, plasterers and brick masons. The Negro is losing as a skilled laborer because of old age, death and the failure of the young men to take up the trades. The Negro artisans are having very little success.

OBERLIN.—Not many skilled Negro laborers here—a few carpenters, painters, shoe makers and masons. The Negro is losing as a skilled laborer because it requires time, energy, money and encouragement to acquire skill. Pleasure and amusement are more sought after. The young men are not entering the trades. The Negro artisans are having good success.

PORTSMOUTH.—Many Negro skilled laborers here—stationary engineers, blacksmiths, horse-shoers, automobilists, plasterers and tinners. The Negro is holding his own as a skilled laborer. No artisans trained in industrial schools here. A few young men are entering the trades. The artisans here are generally employed.

SPRINGFIELD.—Many skilled Negro laborers here—carpenters, iron molders, blacksmiths, brick masons, stone masons and plasterers. The Negro as a skilled laborer is decidedly gaining because there are many more than formerly and in different trades. A few years ago we had no iron molders, now we have more than fifty who are making their living at this trade and the number in the other trades has increased. There are some from training schools here who seem to be prospering. The young men are entering the trades, but not in as large numbers as they should. The artisans here seem to be making a living from their trades. A few are making more than a living. There is a colored contracting carpenter who takes rank second to none in his trade. He builds the best houses in the city.

Replies of Artisans

IRONTON.—Plasterer. There exists a jealous feeling on the part of the white workers toward the colored. We have to bid a little cheaper or be very superior in workmanship to the whites. Conditions are growing worse because of prejudice.

OBERLIN.—Carpenter. The union would be open to Negroes. An agreeable feeling exists between the white and colored workers here. For efficient men conditions are growing better. I would say conditions in Oberlin are all one could expect.

PORTSMOUTH.—Plasterer. I do not belong to a union because I think them detrimental to our race. The feeling between white and colored workers is fairly good where there is no union. I think conditions are growing better for the Negro skilled worker. Thru negligence the condition of the Negro here is not what it could be but there are some who are progressing rapidly.

PORTSMOUTH.—Horse-shoer. There is no union here for my trade. I could join if there were. The feeling between white and colored workers is good. I think conditions are growing better because capital does not care for texture of hair or color of skin. Good, fast work is wanted. The better and faster the work, the more money for the employer. I am serving time as apprentice but my wages are good.

SPRINGFIELD.—Piano Plate Molder. I do not belong to the union because I can not be recognized by the molders' union in this state but I can in Illinois. There is an ill feeling between the white and colored workers in my trade. I can work only in open shops. Yet conditions are growing better because the Negro is grasping every opportunity and the manufacturers are giving him a show in order to hold down strikes. I have been working at the trade for eleven years. I have been making plates for parlor grand pianos for some time.

SPRINGFIELD.—Molder. I cannot join the molders' union. The unionization of men in this trade was to oppose the Negro as well as to protect the trade against unskilled labor. At the present time it is purely prejudice that operates against us. In many localities the feeling between the white and colored workers is bitter, while in others there seems to be the best of feeling. Universally there is much bitterness. I think conditions are growing better for the Negro skilled worker because: (1) He is English speaking. (2) He is obedient. (3) He is trusty. (4) He will not strike. (5) He is not hard to satisfy. (6) He is the best mechanic where the opportunity is allowed him. I truly advocate schooling not only in this but in all branches of trades, especially for the Negro. It is not only expected of you to know more and to do better work than the white man. It is required of you. So to go into the trade world equipt you will be able to confront and battle down every opposition.

Section 24. Oklahoma[1]

There were 55,684 Negroes in Oklahoma in 1900 and 137,612 in 1910. The census of 1900 recorded the following skilled or semi-skilled Negro workers:

Oklahoma

Male—		Male—	
Barbers	131	Millers	1
Steam railway employees	341	Painters	9
Blacksmiths and wheelwrights	56	Plasterers	13
Brick and tile makers	10	Printers	9
Boot and shoe makers	17	Engineers and firemen (stationary)	22
Butchers	18		
Carpenters and joiners	61	Female—	
Machinists	3	Dressmakers and seamstresses	50
Marble and stone cutters and masons	54	Milliners	2

General Conditions

CLARKSVILLE.—Not many Negro skilled laborers here—a few are carpenters. They are gaining because they have increased in number and efficiency. Industrial school training opens more and better opportunities for labor. The young men are not entering the trades. The artisans are meeting with medium success.

GUTHRIE.—Few Negro skilled laborers here—carpenters and blacksmiths. They are gaining because they are able to compete with the white laborers. Industrial school training causes better homes and more pride. Not many young men are entering the trades. Prejudice and labor unions hinder the success of the Negro artisans.

HENNESSEY.—Not many Negro skilled laborers here—painters, carpenters, paper-hangers, plasterers and automobile repairers. They are gaining because of their superior skill. Industrial school training gives the Negro the necessary technical knowledge of his trade. Few young men are entering the trades. The artisans are succeeding fairly well here.

OKMULGEE.—Many Negro skilled laborers here—plumbers, painters, blacksmiths, carpenters, engineers and tailors. The Negro is holding his own as a skilled laborer. This being a new place most of those in the trades gained knowledge of them elsewhere. As results of industrial school training the younger men give evidence of more intelligence in their work. Not many young men are entering the trades. The artisans are succeeding well.

Replies of Artisans

GUTHRIE.—Carpenter. I do not belong to a union because I cannot join with the whites and the Negro workmen are so divided they will not come together and form a union among themselves. The feeling between the white and colored workers in my trade is not good. When a Negro

---

[1] Including statistics for Indian Territory.

is classed as a good workman the white workmen at once plan to get him out of town. Conditions for the Negro skilled worker are growing better because there are enough of them getting together to support each other which is enabling them to take contracts of much value. The greatest pull back to the Negro is the lack of preparation.

HENNESSEY.—Brick and Cement Contractor. I am barred from the union on account of color. A bad feeling exists between the white and colored workers. Extreme prejudice seeks to exclude us from employment.

Section 25. Oregon and the Northwest (Idaho, Montana, Nebraska, North Dakota, Oregon, South Dakota, Washington, Wyoming)

The Negro population of these states in 1900 and 1910 was as follows:

STATES	1900	1910
Idaho	293	646
Montana	1,523	1,834
Nebraska	6,269	7,689
North Dakota	286	617
Oregon	1,105	1,519
South Dakota	465	817
Washington	2,514	6,058
Wyoming	940	2,235
Total	13,395	21,415

According to the census of 1900 these states had the following skilled or semi-skilled Negro laborers:

Idaho, Montana, Nebraska, North Dakota, Oregon, South Dakota, Washington, Wyoming

Male—

Engineers (civil and mechanical)	1
Barbers	310
Steam railway employees	72
Blacksmiths and wheelwrights	19
Brick and tile makers	9
Boot and shoe makers	7
Butchers	24
Carpenters and joiners	24
Iron and steel workers	10
Machinists	5
Marble and stone cutters and masons	59
Millers	1

Male—

Painters	21
Plasterers	47
Plumbers and gas fitters	5
Printers	12
Steam boiler makers	2
Engineers and firemen (stationary)	44

Female—

Dressmakers and seamstresses	87
Milliners	8
Tailoresses	1

Section 26. South Carolina

The state of South Carolina had a Negro population of 782,321 in 1900 and of 835,843 in 1910. According to the census of 1900 there were the following skilled and semi-skilled Negro workers in the state:

South Carolina

Male—

Engineers (civil and mechanical) . . .	5		
Barbers	537		
Steam railway employees	2,939		
Brick and tile makers	567		
Blacksmiths and wheelwrights	803		
Boot and shoe makers	340		
Butchers	267		
Carpenters and joiners	2,695		
Cotton and other textile mill operatives	346		
Iron and steel workers	40		
Machinists	54		

Male—

Marble and stone cutters and masons .	1,069
Millers	87
Painters	693
Plasterers	125
Plumbers and gas fitters	47
Printers	54
Engineers and firemen (stationary) . .	657

Female—

Dressmakers and seamstresses	1,992
Milliners	3

General Conditions

AIKEN. —Many Negro skilled laborers here—carpenters, masons, painters and smiths. They are gaining. Industrial school training causes them to secure homes and property; to educate the young and surround themselves with more of the comforts and in some instances the luxuries of life. The young men are not entering the trades as they should. The artisans are succeeding well.

BEAUFORT. —Not many Negro skilled laborers here—brick-layers, blacksmiths, carpenters, engineers, painters, plumbers, shoemakers, tailors, tinners and wheelwrights. The Negro is gaining as a skilled laborer because he does four-fifths of all the work in his line. He has proven his efficiency and hence gets the work. Those who have had training in industrial schools are in greater demand than the others. Many young men are entering trades in industrial schools. The artisans are succeeding well here.

FLORENCE. —Many Negro skilled laborers here—blacksmiths, carpenters, masons, painters, tinners and firemen. The Negro is holding his own as a skilled laborer because he is in demand for the work. Industrial school training has caused some improvement in the quality of the work done by men with technical knowledge of the subject. The young men are not entering the trades as fast as the times demand. The Negro artisans are having very good success.

LIBERTY HILL.—Not many Negro skilled laborers here—carpenters, painters, engineers, masons and blacksmiths. The majority are farmers. The Negro is gaining as a skilled laborer and is receiving higher wages. Industrial school training causes more skilled laborers. The young men are entering the trades. The Negro artisans are having considerable success because they have no white competition.

McCORMICK.—Not many Negro skilled laborers here—farming and carpentry are their chief trades. They are gaining because they are awakening to the fact that skill and competency are required in order to survive. Where the Negro goes with industrial training he is preferred and appreciated. The physical poise and carriage are conspicuous. The young men are entering the trades. The Negro artisans are having good success. They work with the white artisans with great acceptability.

NEWBERRY.—Not many skilled Negro laborers here—carpenters, blacksmiths, bricklayers and painters. The Negro is losing as a skilled laborer because the other races are taking to the trades. Very little results of industrial training are evident. The young men are not entering the trades. The artisans are having fair success here.

Replies of Artisans

AIKEN.—Blacksmith. The conditions are growing better for the Negro skilled workers here because they are doing the best and practically all of the work around here.

BEAUFORT.—Tinsmith and Plumber. Conditions are growing better as the Negro workers prove themselves efficient and responsible. I find that the trained or skilled workman is always in demand.

CHARLESTON.—Horse-shoer and Farrier. There is a good feeling existing between the white and colored workers. Conditions are growing better for the Negro skilled laborers because all avenues are open to them. The Negro is the controlling workman in Charleston along all trades.

Section 27. Tennessee

The state of Tennessee had a Negro population of 480,243 in 1900 and of 473,088 in 1910. According to the census of 1900 there were the following skilled and semi-skilled Negro workers in the state:

Tennessee

Male—
Engineers (civil and mechanical)	5
Barbers	993
Steam railway employees	5,542
Brick and tile makers	532
Blacksmiths and wheelwrights	980
Boot and shoe makers	315
Butchers	160
Carpenters and joiners	1,308
Cabinet makers	30
Cotton and other textile mill operatives	31
Iron and steel workers	1,242
Machinists	87
Marble and stone cutters and masons	1,387

Male—
Millers	100
Painters	340
Plasterers	235
Plumbers and gas fitters	137
Printers	45
Steam boiler makers	94
Engineers and firemen (stationary)	709

Female—
Dressmakers and seamstresses	1,377
Milliners	7
Tailoresses	6

General Conditions

JOHNSON CITY.—Not many Negro skilled laborers here. There are a few brick masons. The Negro is gaining as a skilled laborer because those desiring skilled labor would rather have a Negro, all things being equal. The results of industrial school training are very evident in all departments of service. The young men are entering the trades. The Negro artisans are succeeding. They have all they can do. Some of the largest and best houses in the city were built by Negro artisans.

MEMPHIS.—There are many Negro skilled laborers here—carpenters, brick masons, engineers, blacksmiths, printers and painters. They are gaining because of the growing demand for them and because of their efficiency. Industrial school training has made a very little improvement over the old artisan. Not many young men of this district are entering the trades. Negro artisans are having much success here.

NASHVILLE. — Many skilled Negro laborers here — carpenters, painters, blacksmiths, machinists and florists. They are gaining because they are increasing in number and efficiency. Industrial school training has made a vast improvement over the old self-made artisan. Many young men are entering the trades. The artisans in this district are having much success.

Replies of Artisans

JOHNSON CITY. — Brick-mason. I do not now belong to a union tho I formerly belonged to one. We failed to get a square deal from our white brother workmen and after fifteen years of failure along this line I withdrew from the union. Conditions here are not so good for the feeling between the white and colored workers is very bad and growing worse.

MEMPHIS. — Brick-mason. I belong to the Brick-layers, Stone-masons and Plasterers' International Union, No. 1, being permitted to join with the whites. In my trade and union a good feeling exists between the races. Memphis, according to my observation, is the best city in the world for a colored mechanic. Here he is recognized by every union except the plumbers' union, altho there are at least seventy-five or eighty extra good colored plumbers here doing nicely.

MEMPHIS. — Contractor. I formerly belonged to the Carpenters' Union, No. 152, the whites and blacks having separate unions. Conditions are growing better for the Negro skilled workers because they are delivering the same goods that the whites are. They are more careful with their work now than ever before.

Section 28. Texas

There were 620,722 Negroes in Texas in 1900 and 690,020 in 1910. According to the twelfth census the state had the following skilled or semi-skilled Negro laborers:

Texas

Male—		Male—	
Engineers (civil and mechanical)	4	Millers	19
Barbers	1,058	Painters	164
Steam railway employees	4,353	Plasterers	30
Brick and tile makers	279	Plumbers and gas fitters	61
Blacksmiths and wheelwrights	526	Printers	44
Boot and shoe makers	95	Steam boiler makers	30
Butchers	170	Engineers and firemen (stationary)	306
Carpenters and joiners	764		
Cabinet makers	9	Female—	
Cotton and other textile mill operatives	29	Dressmakers and seamstresses	751
Iron and steel workers	107	Milliners	5
Machinists	62	Printers	6
Marble and stone cutters and masons	309	Tailoresses	3

General Conditions

BEAUMONT.—Not many skilled Negro laborers in this community—chiefly carpenters and blacksmiths. As a skilled laborer the Negro is losing because of the numerous labor organizations of the whites. Industrial school training has evident results here. Young men are entering the trades in goodly numbers. The artisans here are having much success.

CAMERON.—A few skilled Negro laborers here. The Negro is losing as a skilled laborer because he cannot meet the overwhelming competition of the white laborers. Industrial school training is helping the situation greatly. Young men are entering the trades steadily. Negro artisans are succeeding fairly well.

CORSICANA.—Not many skilled Negro laborers here—chiefly carpenters and plasterers. The Negro is losing as a skilled laborer here because they are few in number and the work mostly has to be done by white laborers. Industrial school training has very apparent results here. Young men are entering the trades slowly. Negro artisans are having medium success.

DALLAS.—Not many skilled Negro laborers in this community—mostly carpenters. They are losing because the white laborers are more efficient. No results of industrial school training can be seen here. The Negro artisans are having very poor success.

HOUSTON.—Many skilled Negro laborers here—carpenters, harness makers, plumbers and contractors. They are gaining because of the increasing demand for their services and their high efficiency. The majority of these skilled laborers have had industrial school training. Many young men are entering the trades. Negro artisans of this community are having much success, being employed by both races.

NAVASOTA.—Not many skilled Negro laborers here—carpenters, blacksmiths, engineers, harness makers, painters and tailors. Because of the increased demand the Negro as a skilled laborer is gaining. Industrial school training has many good results—increased efficiency, more self-respect and higher aspirations. Young men are steadily entering the trades. Negro artisans are prosperous.

SAN ANTONIO.—Many skilled Negro laborers here—carpenters, painters, plumbers and masons. The skilled Negro laborer is gaining because of higher proficiency, the greater need for his services and the general building up of this section. The results of industrial school training are excellent. Many young men are entering the trades. The Negro artisan here is succeeding fairly well.

WACO.—Many Negro skilled laborers here—carpenters, blacksmiths, brick-masons, tailors and butchers. The skilled Negro laborer is holding his own here. The results of industrial school training are very poor. A fair number of young men are entering the trades. Negro artisans are having medium success.

WAXAHACHIE.—Many Negro skilled laborers in this district—carpenters, plasterers and blacksmiths. Negro skilled laborers are gaining because of the great increase in their number. Industrial school training has made a great improvement on the old self-made artisan. A fair number of young men are entering the trades. Negro artisans are having fair success.

Replies of Artisans

BEAUMONT.—Carpenter. I believe conditions are growing better for the Negro skilled worker. Several real estate companies here have all their building done by colored workmen. The employers say that the Negro is honest in his work and that it is not necessary to stand over him to make him work.

DALLAS.—Paper-hanger and Decorator. There is a great demand for Negro skilled labor because in Dallas there is a great deal of local work such as repair work. If you can do the work your color doesn't matter. This applies to all trades. I have been contracting here for twelve years and today I have the largest resident trade of any workman, white or black, in Dallas. In the spring and fall I can't secure help enough to keep up with my work. I could work a dozen men six months in the year.

HOUSTON.—Contractor and Builder. Negroes have no union here and the whites do not allow Negroes to join their unions. A good feeling exists between the white and colored workers. There is no trouble at all. I employ white and Negro laborers and they work together peacefully. Conditions are growing better for the Negro skilled laborer because he is proving that he is able to do the work and is doing his work the very best.

Section 29. Virginia

The state of Virginia had 660,722 Negroes in 1900 and 671,096 in 1910. The census of 1900 recorded the following skilled and semi-skilled Negro workers for the state:

Virginia

Male—

Engineers (civil and mechanical)	10
Barbers	1,094
Steam railway employees	5,418
Brick and tile makers	863
Blacksmiths and wheelwrights	1,222
Boot and shoe makers	623
Butchers	239
Carpenters and joiners	1,619
Cabinet makers	239
Cotton and other textile mill operatives	69
Iron and steel workers	1,173
Machinists	86
Marble and stone cutters and masons	967

Male—

Millers	112
Painters	250
Plasterers	508
Plumbers and gas fitters	96
Printers	55
Steam boiler makers	12
Engineers and firemen (stationary)	797

Female—

Dressmakers and seamstresses	1,445
Milliners	2
Printers	6
Tailoresses	8

General Conditions

BRISTOL.—Not many skilled Negro laborers here—carpenters, brick-masons and blacksmiths. They are losing as skilled laborers, being barred out of the trades unions. The results of industrial school training are fairly good. Young men are entering the trades very slowly. Negro artisans here are succeeding fairly well.

CHARLOTTE.—Not many skilled Negro laborers here—chiefly carpenters and blacksmiths. The Negro is gaining as a skilled laborer because he competes favorably with the white artisans. Many good results of industrial school training are evident. Young men are entering the trades in increased numbers. Negro artisans are having much success.

FARMVILLE.—Many skilled Negro laborers here—chiefly carpenters and masons. They are gaining because of the great demand for their efficient service. Industrial school training has made very poor results here. Many young men are entering the trades. Negro artisans here are having excellent success.

PETERSBURG.—A fair number of skilled Negro laborers here—chiefly painters, carpenters and blacksmiths. ·There is very little to indicate that we are near a great industrial school, tho we are. Young men are not entering the trades. The Negro artisans here are kept busy. I recently noticed on a large building being erected that all of the plasterers working on it were Negroes.

Replies of Artisans

CHARLOTTE.—Blacksmith. I have never cared to consider the unions for I own and operate my own shop and have all the work I can do. There is no color line here for first-class workers. The Negro youth seems to be leaving the trades to the white people. Proficient workers are in demand. My advice to the young men of my race would be to learn to be masters of the trades and then stick to them.

FARMVILLE.—Blacksmith. There is a very good feeling providing one knows and does well what he is doing in the trades. I think conditions are growing better for the Negro skilled workers because in most cases they can do just as good work as any and their expense is not so great, therefore they are engaged.

FARMVILLE.—Painter and Decorator. There is a reasonably fair feeling with the best white workmen. I think conditions are growing better because the Negro workman who is thoroly prepared seems to give better satisfaction in this community.

PETERSBURG.—Practical Horse-shoer. I do not belong to a union because I think it does not profit a black workman to belong. It would be better for him, I believe, if no union had ever existed. The Negro skilled laborers are meeting improving conditions because so many of them are learning under skilled workmen and hence doing good work. I know my business from start to finish and can make any patent of shoes from my anvil that is on the market.

Section 30. West Virginia

The state of West Virginia had a Negro population of 43,499 in 1900 and of 64,173 in 1910. The twelfth census recorded the following skilled and semi-skilled Negro workers for the state:

West Virginia

Male—		Male—	
Barbers	255	Millers	4
Steam railway employees	1,555	Painters	19
Brick and tile makers	12	Plasterers	30
Blacksmiths and wheelwrights	83	Plumbers and gas fitters	5
Boot and shoe makers	31	Printers	6
Butchers	10	Steam boiler makers	1
Carpenters and joiners	76	Engineers and firemen (stationary)	92
Cabinet makers	1		
Cotton and other textile mill operatives	1	Female—	
Iron and steel workers	11	Dressmakers and seamstresses	76
Machinists	9	Milliners	2
Marble and stone cutters and masons	101	Printers	1

General Conditions

BLUEFIELD.—Not many skilled Negro laborers here—a few carpenters. The Negro is losing as a skilled laborer because he is not allowed to enter the trades unions. Industrial school training has made no improvement here. Young men are entering the trades very slowly. The Negro artisan is having very poor success.

CHARLESTON.—Many skilled Negro laborers here—chiefly carpenters, brick masons and paper-hangers. As a skilled laborer the Negro is gaining because of the increase in number and efficiency. Industrial school training has added to the efficiency of the Negro. A fair number of young men are entering the trades. The success of Negro artisans here is fairly good.

HILL TOP.—Not many skilled Negro laborers here—chiefly carpenters, brick masons, painters and printers. The Negro is gaining as a skilled laborer because of the increased opportunities in the trades. Industrial school training has produced some very apparent results. Young men are entering the trades in large numbers. Negro artisans are having moderate success.

Replies of Artisans

CHARLESTON.—Machinist and Lineman. Conditions are not so good as they should be because the whites are banded together in a union which strictly bars Negroes. The trade which I have mastered best is that of lineman and telephone work in general but owing to such a great opposition in this section by the linemen's union to Negro labor I have been completely barred from the telephone work after having served nine years in that capacity. My experience in this matter is the experience of others of my race.

CHARLESTON.—Painter and Decorator. I do not belong to a union because of the race prejudice as displayed by whites and because I feel that trade unions as now conducted are detrimental to Negro workmen. Conditions are growing better for the Negro skilled workers because locally the field is ample for more workers and the Negro is preferable when he can meet the demands. The young men of our race must not grow discouraged in the trades because they do not meet with immediate success but must learn to "stick to their bush" for results.

INSTITUTE.—Carpenter. I have never tried to join the unions for I have always received the wages for which I asked. Negro skilled workers are meeting better conditions. What the Negro needs now is higher practical training so as to be able to measure arms with any one.

Section 31.   The Negro and Organized Labor

The Negro workman has had to encounter racial prejudice on the part of his white fellow workmen from early colonial days until the present time.[1]   In the present study an attempt has been made to ascertain:

(1) The attitude of Negro workmen toward labor organizations.

(2) The attitude of labor organizations toward Negro laborers.

The results of the former have appeared in the replies of Negro artisans printed in sections 6-30.[2]   The results of the latter are collected in this section (Section 31.)

Some unions admit Negroes in considerable numbers as the following selected reports show:

The Tunnel and Sub-way Constructors' International Union, New York City, reports about two hundred Negro members. "In our trade they are as good as there is in the business."

The Tobacco Workers report four or five hundred Negro members, but this is a decrease from the one thousand five

---

[1] See Atlanta University Publications, No. 7, pp. 153-157.   Also pages 28-37 of this study.
[2] See pages 48-82.

hundred which they had in 1900.   They report that the Negro workmen "do fairly well."

The United Mine Workers of America report that there are twenty-five thousand colored members and that eighty per cent of the largest local union in the organization, with one thousand, five hundred and eight members are Negroes. The secretary-treasurer reports that the Negro workers are "intelligent, honorable, progressive and good workmen." The United Mine Workers of America place a fine on any local which discriminates on account of color.

The Brotherhood of Railroad Freight Handlers has fifty Negro members.

The Hod Carriers' and Building Laborers' Union reports "about a thousand members," but gives no further information.

The International Union of Pavers, Rammermen, Flaggers, Bridge and Stone Curb Setters reports one hundred and fifty Negro members as against four hundred in 1900.

The Brick-layers, Masons and Plasterers' Union reports several hundred Negro members.   The Negroes make "average and fair" laborers.   "Our constitution provides that any discrimination against a man on account of color subjects the offending union to a one-hundred dollar fine.   The chief and only objection to colored men was on account of color.   This objection is likely to be overcome in time."

There are other unions that have Negro members.   In some cases, however, the whites are not elated over the Negro membership.   A union man from central Indiana writes as follows:

I take more than a mere passing interest in the Negro race, more especially those of them who are wage-earners.   No true trade unionist will object to the Negro belonging to a labor union.   I mean by a true trade unionist one who understands the economic or industrial question. All the men whom I have heard object to the Negro joining a labor union or refusing to work with a Negro, were in all cases men who did not understand or comprehend the first principles of the so-called "labor question."   In my own craft (cigar making) as far back as 1867 we expunged the word "white" from our International Constitution.   There are many Negroes who are members of the Cigar Makers' International Union and we who believe in the uplift of humanity are pleased to have them with us.   For a number of years a Negro, William Jones by name, was international treasurer of the Cigar Makers' International Union. His home was in Mobile, Ala., but of course he was elected largely by the votes of northern men.   This objection to the Negro in unions is not only ridiculous but is criminal and is born of hatred, jealousy and ignorance. The Negro wage-earner is a competitor with his white brother (or sister) and in order for us whites to maintain our standard of living and secure anything approaching humane conditions of labor, we must of necessity organize and educate the Negro wage-earner.

This clap-trap about race superiority is silly.   If the white man is so much superior to the Negro in a given calling or in all industrial pursuits he need fear nothing from his Negro competitor.   I have seen specimens of mechanism and other tests of the Negro's ability and I say without fear of successful contradiction that where the Negro is industrious and temperate in his habits he is capable of advancing and becoming proficient in the same proportion as any other race.   I find again that in those unions where Negroes are admitted to membership and are given and guaranteed all privileges with any other member, that they make loyal and trustworthy union men.   One of the staunchest unions we have in Indiana is the Negro Building Laborers' Union of Indianapolis.   Among the miners are some of the most active and loyal union men in the United Mine Workers of America.   I might mention among these Charles Griffin and John Adams of Brazil, Ind., and James Bishop of Clinton, who was treasurer of his local union for a number of years and who turned over every penny to his successor in office when he retired from the position: more than could be said of several of his white predecessors.

In this city we have not a great many Negroes but we have lots of Negro haters, I regret to say.   In the Trades Assembly that has nineteen affiliated unions, Brother E. L. James (Negro) has held the position of statistician of the organization for four years.   In the barbers' union here the whites (not all of them) refuse to turn out on Labor Day because of the presence of the Negro, but I am pleased to state that their course in this is not approved of by the unionists in the other unions and the active white members of the barbers' union do not join the others in this matter.   As I said in the beginning, the men and women who really understand the economic question do not hold this prejudice against the Negro and the people who do hold this prejudice would be just as bitter against the Italian, Polish or any other race if the Negro were not here. You are at liberty to make whatever disposition of this letter you may deem proper.

Wishing God-speed to all who are striving for the uplift of humanity, I am,   Yours sincerely,

A few Negro members are scattered here and there in a number of unions.

The Amalgamated Society of Carpenters and Joiners' secretary writes:

Our constitution does not discriminate against Negro membership, altho to the best of my knowledge, so far as the United States is concerned, they are a very rare exception, probably owing to the fact that we have but very few locals establisht in the South. I have never heard any uncomplimentary remarks made against any Negro that has been admitted into our organization, either as a trade unionist or as to his ability as a carpenter, but as previously stated they have been so few in number that it would be impossible for me to attempt to give you any reliable information regarding this matter.

The secretary-treasurer of the International Typographical Union is a little non-committal in his answers:

Competent persons of both races have always been eligible to membership in our organization. This office does not keep any record showing how many males, females or Negroes are connected with the organization. All persons, under our laws, must receive the same wages, pay the same dues and enjoy the same benefits. A local union can reject any applicant for membership if it so desires. The rejected applicant has the right of appeal to the executive council and that body has authority to order his admission if it believes he has been dealt with unjustly by the local union. In some of our southern unions there are objections to the admission of Negroes. This is a natural condition which time will probably eliminate.

The Boot and Shoe Makers' Union has a few Negro members.

Some unions are composed of city or state employees. In such cases few colored members are usually admitted. There are, for instance, three members of the Firemen's Association of Chicago, Ill., and eight members of the City Firemen's Protective Association in Wilkinsburg, Pa.

Four union men are reported in Carlinville, Ill.; six union pavers are reported in Cleveland, Ohio; a very few belong to the Western Federation of Miners; twelve belong to the Granite Cutters; twelve belong to the Newspaper and Mail Dealers' Union, New York; twelve to the Building Laborers of Portland, Oregon; twenty-five to the Paving Cutters' Union.

Quite a number of Negroes belong to Wood, Wire and Metal Lathers' International Union; a few belong to the German Tailors' Union; the Metal Polishers' Union has one colored member; the Tobacco Strippers' Union of Tampa, Fla., has seventeen colored members; the Janitors' Protective Union of San Francisco, Cal., has three colored members; the American Brotherhood of Slate Workers has fifty; the International Brick, Tile and Terra Cotta Workers' Alliance has forty or fifty; the Quarry Workers' International Union has a "small number;" the International Brotherhood of Foundry Employees probably has a few. The International Brotherhood of Book Binders has four.

The International Ladies' Garment Workers' Union writes:

There are few if any Negroes in our trade. At least I don't know of any just now. I knew that in Philadelphia two years ago some Negro women were taken in shirt waist factories to replace strikers. I do not know if they are still there.

A typical attitude of the unions with a few Negro members is that of the molders. The editor of the *International Molders' Journal* writes:

The International Molders' Union of North America, now in its fifty-third year of existence, has never in its laws discriminated against the Negro molders. As membership in the organization depends upon the votes of the members in the local union where application for membership is made, it has followed that very few, in fact an inconsiderable number, have been initiated by our local unions in the South where the Negro molders are to be found. Here and there, in the east, north, central west and Pacific coast Negroes have been taken into membership and placed on an equality with the other members so far as the union was concerned.

During recent years a large number of Negroes have worked at molding in Chattanooga, Tenn., and many efforts have been made to organize them. Some eleven years ago I made strenuous efforts to organize the Negro molders of Chattanooga but failed. We found considerable prejudice on the part of our membership and a suspicion as to the genuineness of our motives by the Negro. Within the last year we have placed a southerner, Mr. ——— ———, in the southern field and he gave special attention to the matter of organizing the Negroes in Chattanooga with considerable success and also with much opposition from the foundry men. In fact, the foundry men informed the Negroes that if they joined our organization they would no longer work at the trade in Chattanooga. We have struck several foundries to protect the Negro to membership in our organization and at present we are paying strike benefits to a number.

Our first difficulty which we had to overcome in connection with the Negro molder was to impress upon the southern molder that the question was one of economics, it was a question of industrial equality and not one of social equality, and that our organization did not exist for any purpose except to educate the workmen, regardless of their race or color, to act collectively in the industrial field for the purpose of improving their term of employment.

Some of our unions in the South who a few years ago would have refused to initiate Negro molders have since that time not only done so, but placed themselves on record as favoring the initiation of Negroes.

It is interesting to consider the replies made by the labor organizations. Many answer directly, many give evasive answers, others say that the question of Negro members has not been considered, and still others reply simply no Negro members. In other cases it is reported that few or no Negroes work at the trade. Illustrations follow:

Gardeners' Protective Union.--We have only a small membership and up to this time no Negro has applied for admission to our union. However, in my experience of years as a gardener, I have never heard of a good Negro gardener.

Watch Case Engravers' International Association of America.—The Negroes, in my opinion, should receive as much consideration and as good treatment as any other human. They have dark skin, but have all other faculties the same as the best white man that ever lived. They are neglected in education due to the fact that there is so much pride and vanity in too many of our own race and color.

Gas and Water Workers, Oakland, Cal.—Our business comprises the manufacture and distribution of gas, and in the event of a Negro being employed, he would be welcomed to membership in our local.

Wire Drawers.—No religion or color deprives any body from belonging to our union and it should not in any union.

United Cloth Hat and Cap Makers of North America.—During the existence of our organization no Negroes have ever applied for admission to our union. As a matter of fact we are not aware of any Negroes employed in the cap industry, as it is a more or less skillful trade. As a matter of principle we do not draw any line between race and race; we consider all races alike and it is my firm belief that Negroes can make good workers and good union members.

International Association of Steam, Hot Water and Power Pipe Fitters and Helpers.—In place of objections it is necessary that they should join to attain the results desired.

International United Brotherhood of Leather=workers in Horse Goods.—No discrimination. Every local union is competent to pass upon the applicants for membership, can reject or accept for reasons satisfactory to the local.

Stove Mounters' International Union.—We have no laws concerning this question.

Flour and Cereal Mill Employees.—"Have not had to make a test." They state the objections to Negroes "because they belong to a class of themselves" and do not see how these objections are likely to be overcome.

The Fur Dressers' Union of Brooklyn, N. Y., says the question has not yet been considered.

The International Union of Elevator Constructors says: Our locals have the right to refuse any candidate, let him be black or white. All candidates are balloted on and are questioned as to their qualifications.

The undecided attitude is represented in the case which follows:

The Machinists' Helpers and Laborers' Union of Washington, Ind., says that Negroes cannot join their union "at present." The reply further gives an interesting history. "We have not had any Negroes in this shop until six months ago. Some of them are good workmen. Like all classes of people there are bad workmen. As for the objections, we have not had any applications yet, and the people here have not been used to working with the Negroes and the northern folks are stubborn about going into any union with the Negro. When these shops were built they went into a contract not to hire any Negroes or foreign men for twenty years and the contract was lived up to until the strike here two years ago. Since the strike was settled they have been hiring some Negroes, but the most of the Negroes that are living here are well-to-do and own good farms and they do not bother with the shops much; but those that are working in the shops are good, well-to-do folks and peaceful; but as far as organizing there has not been anything said to them about going in and they do not know anything about the federation. There are not more than about twenty Negroes working in the shops."

The same union in St. Thomas, Ontario, has no Negro members but declares "our constitution will take a candidate irrespective of creed, color or nationality."

Other difficulties are hinted at:

The Journeymen Tailors' Union of America says that Negroes may join their union: "Negro tailors are principally in the southern states. We have some members in Macon, Augusta and a few other towns in the Carolinas and one or two in Chicago. We have discovered that in some instances the man who employs a few colored tailors discriminates against them if they join the union, hence it is hard to interest them to become members."

The separate Negro local is one method of solution:

The International Union of Steam Engineers has one colored local in Washington, D. C. "Colored men whom I have met in our craft have been able mechanics and good trade unionists."

The American Brotherhood of Cement Workers has this provision in its constitution: "In localities where colored men are working at cement work colored locals can be formed, provided, however, such membership shall be granted transfer to colored locals only."

The Wood, Wire and Metal Lathers' International Union says: "With one or two exceptions we have found the colored men unable to maintain an exclusive colored organization. We have establisht several colored locals in the South, but only two of them have ever made a success, one in Savannah and the other in Charleston, the one in Savannah having been in existence since our international was formed. I attribute much of its success to the influence of one strong character in their ranks, W. E. Searles, who has been secretary for a number of years. We establisht an exclusive colored local in Philadelphia, at the request of both the white and colored lathers in that city; but it was an absolute failure."

The Building Employees' Union of New York has no Negro members and explains: "In 1909 we had about twelve Negro members (janitors) in our union. We had trouble getting or rather keeping a meeting hall on account of them and formed them in a branch as we do have branches of different languages. They met two or three times and dropt out. We are quite willing to help in forming a branch again."

Outside forces sometimes compel separation as hinted at here:

There are no Negro members connected with the unions in Herrin, Ill. The secretary writes: "Being a miner mysef will say there is no objection to Negroes in the miner's organization as long as they can find towns or cities where there is no objection to them living. Our contract with the operators provides for no discrimination on account of creed, color or nationality. So does our constitution provide the same."

The general argument is often put in this way:

The Negro is employed by the large packing industries extensively for in many cases he has the highest paid positions, notably in Kansas City, Kan., and East St. Louis, Ill. He is equally as skillful as the white man and in many cases the employer prefers him. It would thus be the height of folly for our organization to legislate against him. As to the number we have with us we cannot state as in the smaller cities they are affiliated directly with the local union and no mention is made of color in their report to the general office.   Of course there are localities in the South and Southwest where local prejudice prevents their becoming members of the local union, but in all cases they can form locals by themselves and be chartered by the international organization.

Personally I might say that so long as a man is competent to take my situation I care not what his color may be—white, black or yellow. I want him to become a member of the organization as the rules and usages make it possible for him to do.   In our organization (the Amalgamated Meat Cutters and Butcher Workers of North America) the Negro stands on the same plane with the white man.   Our obligation states emphatically that a member of our organization agrees not to discriminate against a fellow worker on account of his creed, color or nationality.

Many unions frankly exclude Negroes.

Negroes are not admitted to membership in the **Order of Railway Conductors of America.**   Eligibility to membership in this order is governed by the laws as adopted by the Grand Division of said order and which provides that "any white man shall be eligible to membership who is at the time of making application actually employed as conductor of a train of a steam surface railway."

The Cutting, Die and Cutter Makers answer, "Nothing doing on the Negro."

The Brotherhood of Railway Car Men of America has never had any Negro members at all and does not admit them now.   An officer writes: "I have never lived in the South myself and do not know very much about them.   Will say that I think the reason Negroes have never been admitted into the order is because our southern brothers will not agree to it. We have never had any application for admission that I ever heard of."

The Brotherhood of Locomotive Firemen and Engineermen denies Negroes admission by their constitution and by-laws.   The general secretary says: "Our delegates in convention have always objected to them becoming members."

The International Brotherhood of Boiler Makers, Iron Ship Builders and Helpers of America reports that Negroes are not admitted to the union and that their membership is provided "by secret work."   Some of the officers, however, are working to organize in Newport News, Va., ship builders who are colored into a separate union.   "Our laws, at the present time, would not permit the organizing of the Negro, but we hope to see that lodge.   I expect the future generations to provide a better way so that we can be together in one local.   Of course, if they organize under the banner of this order their traveling cards will only be in colored locals.   This is for the beginning, but in future years I expect this will be eliminated.   There is only color against them, that is all anyone can say and we cannot work it out by violent or drastic measures; we must take time to work it out. I am a southern man out and out, raised and educated in ———. I worked with the Negroes and they made good union men, and always in their places when called on. There is a future for the race but it must not be forced on the white race."

The Federation of Labor of Madison, Wis., reports no colored members in any of the local unions and says that they bar Negroes from membership and that some of them refuse to recognize the traveling card of the Negro mechanic. This is on account of color and the objection "is not likely to disappear. These men form their own local unions if there are enough to do so," says the secretary, and then he launches forth: "I also wish to state that the American Federation of Labor does not bar any nationality no matter what creed, color or sex, and separate charters may be issued to unions composed exclusively of colored members. The American Federation of Labor spends large sums to organize all wage-earners without regard to class, race or sex, etc. These people, if organized, will become better workmen."

The American Wire Weavers' Protective Association admits only white males.

The Paving Cutters' Union of the United States and Canada: An officer of that union says: "We have no law against them. Haven't had much experience with the Negro. I think there are good and bad among them as there are among the whites. But what colored men I have observed in our trade, they do not seem to have the same proficiency in handling the tools as the white man. From our members in the South, particularly in Georgia, whose minds on the Negro question possibly may be biased to a more or less extent, I am led to believe that the Negro is unable to grasp the principles of unionism. He (the Negro) believes in the theory that half a loaf is better than none. He is not capable, they say, of being a good union man, working out his own salvation. Possibly the day is coming when he will equal the white man, mentally. The Negro, speaking in connection with his chances industrially, labors under great disadvantages. In the first place, the white man will not, especially those in the South (I refer especially to our own members), tolerate the Negro to be on the same level as himself. The fact is that the Negro is not wanted in the trades. He is all right as long as he is satisfied to occupy a position less than or below that occupied by the white man; under such conditions he and the white man get along very well together. When I speak of the colored man not seemingly being able to handle the tools with the same proficiency as the white man, I perhaps should qualify that statement by mentioning the fact that in order that a man—any man—be proficient at a trade it is necessary for him to learn in his young days, — grow up with the trade as it were. Those of the colored people who have been able to a more or less degree to learn our trade have done so under adverse conditions. They, as far as I know, have never been trained in their young days. Those who have managed to break into the trade have picked it up as best they could while working as helpers to the mechanics.''

It is probable that ninety per cent of the Negroes of the United States are residents of the South and so it is of interest to note the attitude of unions in that section. The reports from the South are of special interest.

The Waycross, Ga., Trade and Labor Assembly reports that half of the brick-layers and forty-seven of the carpenters are Negroes. Negroes are, however, refused admission to many of the unions and some of the unions refuse to recognize the traveling card. The secretary thinks Negro workers are ''treacherous and unreliable—can't make mechanics and are poor imitators.'' These objections will ''never'' disappear.

Sedalia, Mo., has no Negro union men, but the secretary of the labor organizations writes: ''In some localities perhaps there still exists that race prejudice kept alive by the employing class in order that they may array race against race for the exploitation of both. Economic pressure will eventually compel a closer union between all races—including the Negro—for their emancipation from wage slavery; and the Negro will be found fighting just as valiantly for the emancipation of the toilers as those who fought to break the shackles from four million blacks.''

The Georgia Federation of Labor has one Negro local. The secretary says: ''The Georgia Federation does not bar Negro locals or mixt locals. In a good many of the carpenters' and painters' unions there are Negro members. I have only one local that is composed entirely of Negroes. Some of the locals absolutely bar Negroes from membership. The chief objection that I hear urged against them is the difficulty experienced in controlling them in case of strike and in preventing them from working under the standard wage scale in their locality.''

The Trade Assembly at Fort Worth, Tex., has no Negro members altho it has had them in the past. The objections are said to be ''social.'' ''Negro delegates of common labor and hod carriers and mortar mixers have been admitted to the Trade Assembly and Building Trades Council when affiliated with the American Federation of Labor, but in the skilled trades Negroes have not been admitted.''

The Federal Labor Union of Dallas, Tex., ''keeps Negroes out'' by a provision in the by-laws and by the refusal of members to elect Negroes. The reason for this is thus stated by the secretary: ''The ingrained prejudice towards anything that looks to the members like an approach towards social equality. I think that this prejudice against allowing Negroes to join unions is unreasonable and that the pressure of economic forces will remove it. As Negroes become more skilled they will become more and more the competitors of the whites in the labor market and if they are not organized, either in unions with whites or in unions parallel with the whites and bound by the same obligations and getting protection from corresponding white unions, they will cut the throats of the whites just as very poor immigrants do in the East or the North. The rise of Negro unions for self-protection will probably hasten this day. Time and education will go far to produce co-operation among Negroes and whites for self-protection just as the progress of industry has forced them to co-operate in all sorts of work for the bosses."

There are no Negro members in the **Central Trades and Labor Councils of Roanoke, Va.**, and none in the local unions. If any applied there might be objections on account of color, but such objections are "likely to arise" as time goes on.

From a town in Oklahoma where there are no Negro union men comes the following account: "In general we have not had much dealings with the Negro. One Negro was refused admission to the halls who carried a card fully paid up. That was when we were under a charter of the International Liberty Union. The most important part was that the Negro referred to above was a deputy organizer whose commission had not yet expired."

The **Trades and Labor Council of Memphis, Tenn.**, has twenty-five or thirty Negro members in affiliated unions. The writer thinks that prejudice against Negro union men will disappear in time.

On the other hand, the secretary of the **Marshall, Texas, Trades and Labor Council** does not think these objections will disappear. He says that one "cannot make them stick as union men; will scab in spite of all that can be done." This council has no affiliated Negro unions.

The **Central Labor Union of Miami, Fla.**, also has no Negro members. The secretary says that admitting Negroes has a "tendency to lower wages and self-respect of white mechanics and casts a stigma of association," and he hopes that these objections will never disappear.

The **Labor Assembly of Lawton, Okla.**, has no Negro union men and says "we are not troubled with them to any extent."

In **Greenville, Texas,** Negroes cannot join the unions but may have unions of their own. The secretary writes: "The Negro makes a first-class union man when organized and properly instructed. In times of strikes and trouble he is a stayer. I long to see the day when all of the colored people are organized industrially and politically and cease to be thrown about by every ism that comes along; but this will continue until he is organized and educated."

From Temple, Texas, we learn that Negroes are kept out of unions:

The objection is the color-line, caused by southern traditions. Nearly all men raised south of Mason and Dixon's line do not want to give the Negro any chance to become expert mechanics. The South needs a great awakening to its own necessities from the laboring man's standpoint. I have been successfully connected with the labor movement for several years in all parts of the country as far as the southern born mechanic is concerned. First, they will not attend their local meetings; second, they want someone else to take the lead and bear all the brunt of battle. If an important subject is to come up on meeting night just a quorum is present perhaps out of thirty or forty members. It's the lack of union interest and principle. Have worked hard here for a year and only with the help of rounders have been able to organize the printers and musicians; clerks and bookkeepers, stenographers, factory employees seem to be afraid of losing their jobs.

The Teachers' Union of San Antonio, Texas, says no Negroes may join this union. "They would not think of applying here. It is unthinkable because it means social equality which saps the foundations of race purity. Neither mongrel Negroes nor mongrel whites are desirable." The writer does not think that these objections are likely to be overcome in time and "certainly hopes not."

An officer of the **Texas State Federation of Labor** writes as follows: "It is generally understood that the white trades unions of Texas do not admit colored people to membership. Once in a while a Federal Labor Union is organized which admits on equal terms both races, but no such organization has ever lasted long and there is none now in the state. There are a few Federal Unions, Longshoremen's Unions and Barbers' Unions composed entirely of colored people. These are admitted to membership and representation in the Texas State Federation of Labor on equal terms with white unions. Colored people, however, do not apply for membership in white unions and therefore none has ever been refused admission. Legally unions cannot refuse to admit a Negro if he is otherwise qualified, but a majority of no union would admit that a Negro was qualified for membership. Unions cannot legally refuse to recognize the traveling card of a union man, no matter if he is colored, but they would scarcely tolerate his attending meetings or working on the same job with other members. In some trades they make good workmen, which creates all the more enmity against them. If they were not capable of becoming skilled workers in any trade they would be more cheerfully tolerated by the average union membership. The foundation objection to admitting them to membership in unions is racial prejudice, which again is based almost wholly on the competition for jobs which is so keenly felt by working men of both races. The Negro is marked with a color that distinguishes him from other poor working men and he is condemned because he often works cheaper, is more docile (servile), takes abuse without quitting and lives cheaper than white men. He also has inherited from slavery days a lack of discrimination as to what is honestly his and is inclined to retaliate for cruel treatment by petty pilfering to help out his starvation wages. The poor white man starves and helps himself to any little thing he can pick up when he can no longer secure anything by servility, beggary or cajolery. The situation is quite deplorable and you see the poor white man must have some one to kick. And there he is! Look at the color of his skin.

"These objections will disappear with a general uplift of the conditions of the poor. When the economic conditions are such that poverty will be abolisht and there is no man without plenty of jobs at good wages, racial prejudices will entirely disappear. Make monopoly get off the back of the worker and no longer will any bad feeling exist between the races. Until this is done thru an equitable system of taxation, relieving labor of the burden and placing it upon monopoly, there is no hope of relief from the present deplorable situation.

"Apply the single tax and racial prejudice will disappear and not before. I have no time to elaborate this statement, but it is true.

"Yours truly,   ——————— "

The reports from the various city centrals furnish perhaps the best conspectus of conditions and states of mind.

California

The Alameda County, California, Central Labor Council has Negro members in the Teamsters, No. 1015 Clay street, Oakland; Cooks and Waiters, No. 31, 128½ Telegraph avenue, Oakland; Journeymen Barbers, No. 134, 1512 Broadway, and United Laborers, No. 13018, 311 Fourteenth street. Applicants have not been refused to their "knowledge," altho "there is a strong racial prejudice evidenced in some of the so-called skilled craft unions. I have known some very good Negro workmen who were blacksmiths, carpenters, brick-layers, plasterers, painters and printers. My experience is that there is no line of skill in which the Negro may not attain efficiency. The chief objection is racial; the cause of this is the tendency toward miscegenation which is the natural outgrowth of social assimilation in the union meeting. I do not believe that these objections will disappear in time from the fact that they invariably enhance with result of experience in both white and black races. Personally I sympathize with the Negro rather because his presence here is the result of the white man's greed to which I find myself and all wage workers victims. I feel no personal animosity toward him, tho I must confess to aversion to social intercourse of a very close nature, possibly based in the belief that when nature created the races it was with the intent that they be kept separate. I owe the race a debt of gratitude which inspires a sympathy with all who are mentally fit and morally my equal. I believe that as time goes on with education and the inculcation of race responsibility in industrial affairs men will prove the economic friends of the Negro. The only bar that now stands between him is his preference to supplant the white man in industry at a lesser price than that establisht by unions; in short, his allowing himself to be misled into scabbing by those who have even less use for him than his white union brother has. I believe that the American Federation of Labor plan to induct him into separate unions where race prejudice prevents him joining where white men dominate will raise the Negro in the estimation of all union men. Thru organization into unions he will be taught our inter-responsibility.

The secretary of the Central Labor Council of Los Angeles, Cal., says: "We have one local union of Negro building laborers and hod carriers of about one hundred and fifty members that is not affiliated with the American Federation of Labor and for that reason is not affiliated with the central body. Yes, there are Negro members in the locals. Cannot give the number but not a great many. Brick-layers, hod carriers, plasterers, carpenters, cigar makers, boot-blacks, teamsters, electrical workers. Negroes are barred from only those whose international constitution prohibits. We have done our best to get Negro workmen interested but have not had a great deal of success. They seem to be afraid to get into the organization for some reason or other. Thru the locals we have taken the matter up with the international unions that have a clause in their constitutions that bar Negroes, urging them to remove the clause."

The Richmond, Cal., Contra Costa Central Labor Council has fifteen cement workers and ten hod carriers. These are Negroes. They also admit that the unions do bar Negroes from membership and have refused admission to Negro applicants and that they do refuse to recognize the traveling card of a Negro mechanic. "I organized the Cement Workers' Union; at the beginning sent for the regular organizer to come from San Francisco. His comment after looking over the men assembled among whom I had six Negroes was, 'It looks too dark for me.' This remark of the organizer expresses the only objection I have ever heard. I would put it, not in his language, but in my own, which is prejudice against race and color. This man, a naturalized citizen, proposed to bar these men who were born citizens. I told him to go back home and that I would organize the union myself. He said that I would not get a charter but I knew our rights under the law and put the application for a charter up to headquarters in such a way that they knew I understood. Well, we got the charter and have a very harmonious mixt union which has been in existence now for three years. I state this case at some length, believing it would be the best explanation I could make. Prejudice is all I can see against the race. The colored men are doing their work and satisfying the employer and are good union men, live strictly up to the rules, pay their dues and attend meetings. The large cities of San Francisco and Oakland, an hour and a half from Richmond, bar them wherever they can. I am president of the Central Labor Council of this county; am also a veteran of the Civil War and am still on the firing line for principles I advocated over forty years ago.''

The Sacramento, Cal., Trades and Federation Council has one hundred Negro barbers as members, one hundred and fifteen in the cement workers, forty-five hod carriers and fifty teamsters.

The San Francisco, Cal., Labor Council has no Negro members. The secretary writes: "Whatever objections there may have been in the past was due to race prejudice which has been overcome, the white members realizing that if the Negro is going to live he must work and if they don't let him work alongside of them during the time they are enjoying industrial peace it is only natural for the Negro to take the place of the white man when he is on strike. Also the Negro has stood the test as a union man wherever he has been on strike and the local men here know it. There are not many Negroes in San Francisco and very seldom do we hear of a Negro artisan coming along. They generally make their home in Los Angeles, where the climate is warmer. There they have a strong membership in the unions and some very active representatives in the central councils.''

Colorado

The Colorado State Federation of Labor of Denver, Col., replies that "there are Negro members in the local numbering one hundred. Several Negroes are employed in coal mines in this state.''

The Pueblo, Col., Trades and Labor Assembly is "composed of Negroes to about thirty in number. The Steam Engineers' local, No. 21, has one member. Brother ——, of the steam engineers, is considered a first-class workman. Negroes make good building trades laborers.''

Connecticut

The Central Labor Union of Derby, Conn., says: "There are fourteen locals connected with this organization and about seven have Negro members. They are the carpenters, brick-layers, stone masons, iron molders, machinists, hotel employees and hod carriers. No Negro applicant has been refused admission as far as I am able to find out; it's too dangerous. As the capitalist does not look at color, we have to use the same rules to play the game. Formerly in industry when all industries were small, ideas were small, and the boss usually worked beside his men and what the boss thot the men usually agreed with, and he was particular whom he had to work with and, of course, that to a large extent kept the Negro out. But as industries became diversified and the workers were divorced from the boss and, in fact, never saw the boss, he did not care who did the work so long as his profits were not interfered with; so when his employees struck he filled their places with Negroes, who had been denied membership in unions, and that is what will make every union eventually open its doors to the Negroes. One of the most optimistic signs of the times I know of is the growing feeling in the trades union movement for economic justice for the Negro. I will state from personal experience on the Negro that up to four or five years ago no one was more prejudiced against the Negro than myself and I thot it was just and proper to keep him out of my union if possible. However, I have since that time joined the Socialist party and have found out my mistake, that as the capitalist class is no respecter of persons, neither can the workers be divided in sex, race or color, but must constitute themselves into a political party separate and distinct unto themselves and take over all the means of production and distribution, thus insuring every man a job and means of livelihood with time for recreation and self-culture. Then and then only will the Negro worker and white worker be able to pave the way for the real brotherhood of man."

The Central Labor Union of Waterbury, Conn., has no Negro members.

Illinois

The Aurora, Ill., Trades and Labor Assembly has "twenty-five Negroes in Building Laborers' Union, about six in Teamsters' Union; both unions are composed of white and black members. No objections as to color. As a rule there is a good class of Negroes in Aurora."

The Carlinville, Ill., Trades and Labor Assembly has "about fifteen Negro members in the Federal Labor Union."

The Carrier Mills, Ill., Central Labor Union has "probably about one hundred and fifty altogether in Miners' Unions, Nos. 1059, 1112 and 2837. Have no objections here at this place, but there are places in this country where they are not allowed."

The Chicago Federation of Labor is a central body comprising over two hundred and seventy local unions. "We have one local union comprising all Negro members,—the Asphalt Pavers and Helpers' Union, No. 25,—who are regularly affiliated with the international, who are affiliated with the American Federation of Labor. We have Negro delegates from several other organizations. I know of no union affiliated with the federation that prevents Negroes from joining; at least this office has never received any complaint from that direction. We often try to organize the Negro but find it difficult for one reason or another, principally, the employer is successful in always getting some Negro to tell others that organized labor is not their friend, etc. The employer always has in mind it is to his best interest to keep the Negroes unorganized."

The Danville, Ill., Trades and Labor Council has about seven hundred Negro members in Miners' Union and forty in the Brick, Tile and Terra Cotta Workers' Alliance, but admits that they do bar Negroes from membership and have had Negroes as applicants. "We recommend that the Negro join the trades union of his trade whenever possible. We also recommend that the Negro make a study of the different political parties so when voting to vote intelligently and to back up his union with political action."

The Springfield, Ill., Federation of Labor has Negro members in the local unions, consisting of miners, barbers, hod carriers and cement workers. Some local unions do "bar Negroes from membership and Negro applicants have been refused admission to the unions."

Indiana

From the Indianapolis, Ind., Central Labor Union comes the word that they have Negro members composed of "hod carriers, building laborers, plasterers and the structural iron workers. The plasterers number five, the structural iron workers one, and the hod carriers and building laborers about one hundred and seventy-five. Once the bricklayers refused a Negro member but the international lodge fined the local $150. Color is sometimes an objection but the chief objection is the fact that once the doors are opened wide too many would come and cause an over supply of mechanics for the work in view. The objections will certainly disappear in time. The objection held against the colored race is the same as is held against the foreign races who are generally brot into sections where labor troubles abound and the prejudice is more deep seated against the colored man on account of the fact that he understands the English language; but for every colored man who, to use a harsh term, scabs there are two white men who do the same. The best solution is to see that the mechanic or artisan is thoroly schooled in all branches of whatever trade he may learn and ability will certainly do more for him than any agitation either for or against organizing him can offset."

The Logansport, Ind., Trades Assembly has "twenty-one Negro members in the Journeymen Barbers' Union, No. 48, out of a total of forty-three; from four to five in Building Laborers' Union, according to state of the trade." The railway orders do bar Negro members. The secretary has never heard of the traveling card being refused in that city nor that the electrical workers would bar Negroes. "There are many objections offered, but I have failed so far to hear a valid one. I am persuaded that it is pure hatred and race prejudice in most instances. Ignorance lies at the bottom of it all. The railway men put forth the rather weak argument that the Negro is not reliable and cannot be trusted. This, of course, pertains to railway train service. I hope these objections will disappear."

In Richmond, Ind., the Central Labor Union has no Negro members and "there has been very little race trouble here; in fact, not as much as occurs in the average northern city of this size. Negroes have not applied for admission into the unions, therefore we have never heard any objections."

Iowa

The Dubuque, Ia., Trades and Labor Congress has no Negro members "at present." The secretary writes: "Whilst quite a number of colored people are employed in this city yet they do not seem to be impregnated with unionism as we would like."

Kansas

The Emporia, Kansas, Trades and Labor Council has no Negro members. The secretary-treasurer writes: "Negroes should be treated white but kept separate."

The Girard, Kansas, Industrial Labor Council has four Negro members belonging to the Federal Labor Union, No. 12756. Unions do bar Negroes from membership.

Massachusetts

The State Branch American Federation of Labor of Boston, Mass., sends the following message: "We know no race, no creed and no color."

The Haverhill, Mass., Central Labor Union has twenty-eight Negro members in the Boot and Shoe Workers' Union. No Negro applicant has ever been refused "on account of color." The chief objection to them is "their willingness to take unfair jobs." These objections may disappear "by trade union education."

The Central Labor Union of North Adams, Mass., has no Negro members "at present." The objections being "none outside of not desiring social intercourse. But in the broad field of labor and labor organization I know of no objection, either to work with or to hold membership in the same organization."

The Central Labor Union of Springfield, Mass., has Negro members in unions of brick-layers, builders, laborers, carpenters, painters and coal handlers. The secretary says: "From answers received from ninety-five per cent of the local unions affiliated with their central body, not one barred a Negro from membership if he was a capable mechanic and could pass the regular examination given to all applicants. A case came to my attention: Several on a job in a small town where a number of brick-layers refused to work with a Negro and the labor union of which they were members was fined $100."

Michigan

The Ann Arbor, Mich., Trades Council has one Negro member, a carpenter.

Missouri

The Springfield, Mo., City Central Union has "a colored local of building laborers and hod carriers with a membership of eighty. The barbers have twenty members, but they do bar some applicants for membership. We have Negro workmen in the harness craft, molders and blacksmiths that I know of and they are fair mechanics; and also barbers and team drivers. Their color is the most often used in the rejecting of colored men in a white local. The objections are not likely to disappear altogether but they are not as common as formerly."

Montana

The secretary of the Anaconda, Mont., American Federation of Labor writes that they have "twenty-one Negro members at present as compared with six in 1900. The average Negro of this vicinity makes a first-class citizen as a whole and the Negroes are very industrious. There are about forty-five Negro members of the Mill and Smeltermen's Union employed by the Anaconda Copper Mining Company as engine drivers and switchmen."

Federal Labor Union, No. 12968, of Miles City, Mont., has no Negro members, objection being "color." "At present I am working with a colored man and have been for two years past for the street department. I find him a good working man. All crafts, including electricians, teamsters, engineers and common laborers, are organized and all members paid up. He sent in his application two years ago and was turned down on account of color, but we recognized his rights and therefore he is working right amongst strictly union men and is not bothered."

Nebraska

The Omaha, Neb., State Federation of Labor has no Negro members "at present" altho in 1900 they had "several in building laborers." "No," the unions cannot refuse to recognize the traveling card of a Negro union man. "We want the Negroes to feel that we will protect them if they will stand with us."

The Central Labor Union of Lincoln, Neb., has "probably ten" Negro members in the Plasterers' and Federal Labor Unions. The secretary writes: "The only objection that I know of is the old story: 'A Negro is not as good as a white man.'"

The South Omaha, Neb., Central Labor Union has Negro members, numbering one in the barbers' union and one in the printers. The secretary writes, "They are not usually good union men."

New Hampshire

"The State Branch of the New Hampshire Federation of Labor in Manchester, N. H., is a voluntary federation of unions in this state and I do not know of any union in the state that bars the Negro workman from membership, neither do I believe that there is any good reason to bar any worker because of his color, if he is otherwise eligible to membership. I do not know how many Negroes are members of locals in this state. We meet in convention once a year, and we have had a Negro delegate twice from a local of paving cutters, he being the only colored man in the local."

New Jersey

The Central Labor Union of Camden, N. J., sends the following message: "We never have had any application from any local union that was composed of colored people."

New York

The New York State Federation of Labor says: "This is a delegate body and there is no distinction as to color or creed. Negro delegates have been seated and none rejected."

Berlin, N. Y., Central Labor Union sends the following word: "If we had more Negro members as good as the one we have I think it would be better for the unions."

In Ithaca, N. Y., the Central Labor Union has Negro members in the brick-layers and masons to the number of five and the barbers two. "No objections and from experience I think it is general thruout the North. In our Central Labor Union we have one colored delegate. He is from the Barbers' Union; he is one of our best workers and highly appreciated by all."

The Central Labor Council of Jamestown, N. Y., has Negro members in the Barbers' Union. The secretary writes: "The objections are 'color.' I believe this is a serious mistake. I myself have more respect for the Negro than for the aliens who come to this country, as the Negro is an American citizen and we should help to uplift him and respect him."

Central Trades and Labor Council of Kingston, N. Y., has a Negro member "and he is recording secretary of the Butchers' Union; also one who belongs to the Hod Carriers' Union and he is a hustler."

The Lancaster, N. Y., Central Labor Union has no Negro members and says "there are some members here who do not like to come in contact with the Negro as a member to our different locals. But the general feeling is this way: If he is a man, black or white, and can show us good credentials, we take him in."

In the Poughkeepsie, N. Y., Trade and Labor Council there are Negro members—two carpenters, one sheet metal worker and one hod carrier.

The Salamanca, N. Y., Central Labor Council has no Negro members "at present," the reasons given being "social."

The Federation of Labor, Troy, N. Y., has Negro members in the barbers, waiters, teamsters and other unions. The objections are none. "A delegate in this body, Mr. Adams, is one of our most efficient and respected members. He is a full-blooded Negro and represents the Barbers' Union, composed mainly of whites."

The White Plains, N. Y., Central Labor Union has Negro members: "Laborers' Local Union, No. 9, has fifteen members. Also the hod carriers have ten members. The members of this body that have worked with them say they are apt to be careless in their work. The Negro members that attend this body attend meetings better than some of the white men."

Ohio

The Akron Central Labor Union of Akron, Ohio, has Negro members in the unions of barbers, steam engineers and lathers, altho there are "very few." The traveling card of a Negro mechanic is not refused recognition "any more than whites." "There are no objections to the Negro if he should want to be a union man, so far as I know. What few Negro members we have in this city are good mechanics and make good members."

In Columbus, Ohio, the Federation of Labor has Negro members, consisting of the musicians, who have fifteen members. The Hod Carriers' Union has all Negroes. The secretary writes: "I have never heard of any objection in this community unless it is one of association. The brewery workers have two Negro members in the powers' department as firemen. We have no Negro problem in this state to amount to anything, the chief objection being that of the whites not wanting to associate with the Negro."

The Central Labor Union of Fremont, Ohio, has no Negro members altho they used to have Negro members in the local unions. "When you find one good one you will find one bad one."

The Mansfield, Ohio, Trades Council has no Negro members. The secretary-treasurer says he does not know the objections. "What few unions do bar them do so on orders from headquarters. What their objection is I do not know."

The Middletown, Ohio, Trades and Labor Council has Negro members in the "hod carriers only."

The East Palestine, Ohio, Trades Council "has two locals partly composed of Negroes; that is, about fifty members per local. There are two in the barbers and four in the brick-layers and masons. We do not think it would be policy to bar any nationality or color from labor organizations as long as they conduct themselves in the right manner and use the organization to which they belong in the right manner and for the cause which it advocates—the uplift of the working man and wages."

The Steubenville, Ohio, Trades and Labor Assembly has Negro members in the unions of barbers, hod carriers and teamsters. The barbers have thirteen, the hod carriers sixteen and the teamsters eight. The local unions do bar Negroes from membership and Negro applicants have been refused admission to the unions and the traveling cards are refused in most cases.

Oregon

The Trades and Labor Council of Salem, Ore., has no Negro members. "The bar-tenders' locals require that the Negroes form a separate union and will not allow them in with the whites. The chief objection being, as far as I know, simply the fact that they are black."

Pennsylvania

The Bradford, Pa., Trades Assembly has one or two Negro members. They say some unions do bar Negro applicants, not all. "There are so many lazy, worthless Negroes, who bring the whole race into disrepute. The honest working Negro is treated squarely as far as my observations go. They have been delegates to this body but the union they belonged to disbanded. Whether the objections will disappear or not depends on the Negro himself, I think."

The secretary of the Chester, Pa., Federation of Labor says: "I don't know of any objection, as we have never yet been up against the question of admitting them. The Negro in this section is as a rule usually working at cart driving or laboring work in general, and as yet they have made no attempt to get into the trades in general. But I must say if they tried to join the unions in this city, I think we would have to be shown before they would be taken in, as color prejudice is rather strong."

The Lancaster, Pa., Central Labor Union has no Negro members "at present;" there were hod carriers but they have withdrawn and are now a lodge. I can give no reason at all for objections, because we have no applications from them and not many work in our own crafts that are organized. We have had a national treasurer from Tampa, Fla., who was a Negro artisan of my own craft of the International Cigar Makers' Union of America, and have thousands of good union men of his race and we don't bar them in any place. As for other crafts in other localities, I could not say; but here we never get any applications for membership as yet." He hopes these objections will disappear.

The Nanticoke, Pa., Federation of Labor has Negro members. They state that local unions make their own rules, but they think none is excluded in this state.

The Royersford and Spring City, Pa., Trades Council has no Negro members. "The only objections that I ever heard of amongst the various trades unionists here was because they are Negroes. What few Negroes that I have ever had occasion to come in contact with in any of our public works, I can personally say that I would much rather work with the colored man than the majority of the dumpings of Europe that land on our shores every day."

The Williamsport, Pa., Trades Union Assembly has Negro members in the hod carriers' and barbers' unions. The secretary says: "In this city I notice in particular the race is lazy and indifferent, as probably in other sections of which I know not. On the other hand, we have with us a few Christian gentlemen—black faces, but white hearts, and who may be trusted in the extreme."

In Wilkesbarre, Pa., the Central Labor Union has no Negro members but has Negro delegates. Negro applicants can "form unions of Negroes in all that do refuse to admit and get charters from international unions. Most of the objections are racial and will disappear the more the Negro takes part in the union movement."

Rhode Island

The Woonsocket, R. I., Central Labor Union has no Negro members and the secretary writes "there has never been any Negroes who applied for admission to any of our local unions."

Wisconsin

The Central Labor Union of Ashland, Wis., has no Negro members. The secretary writes: "Some unions admit only white men, barring Indians and Chinese as well as Negroes. Lower plane of living makes these willing to work at a lower wage and consequent lowering of standards. Racial prejudice is at the bottom. Race problem has no bearing at so northern a point as this and receives little attention."

The Fond du Lac, Wis., Trades and Labor Council says: "Some have one member or so, among whom are masons and brick-layers. The objections are none because we are all wage slaves regardless of creed or color."

The Milwaukee, Wis., Federated Trades Council has Negro members in the carpenters, hod carriers and cement workers. "There is no objection to admitting them to trade unions here. In fact they are engaged in any trade. Every attempt is made to get them to join."

The Waukesha, Wis., Trade and Labor Council has no Negro assembly. The secretary says: "We have no Negroes in our locals and never had any applications."

Washington

The Central Labor Council of Seattle, Wash., has "some Negro members, number unknown, but a sprinkling in painters, building laborers, federal (common) labor and carpenters. This being a northern country and the racial problem being of an oriental nature there is very little objection to the Negro on any grounds."

Porto Rico

The Central Labor Union of Porto Rico sends the following message: "Our organization has ninety per cent Negro members. As a state we have unions composed of ninety per cent of colored people. There are Negro members in locals; in fact, more than three thousand are colored members in the trades of carpenters, masons, janitors, printers, machinists and all trades.   We have no division or difference of color lines in our country.   We could not tolerate such divisions of race anyway in this country.   Here in Porto Rico there are two classes of people, the rich men and the poor men, and there are no other differences among the people than those which come of social standing.   We fight against the ignorance of the people and against the exploitation and tyranny put in practice for those who make capital."

The Caguas Central Labor Union of Porto Rico says: "Our members are one thousand and we have three per cent of Negroes in the unions. There are some in all unions."

Ontario

The Hamilton, Ontario, Trades and Labor Council has Negro members but cannot state the exact number.   They include cigar makers, tobacco workers, lathers, barbers, teamsters and letter carriers.   The secretary writes: "I am instructed to inform you that Negro artisans are not discriminated against in this city; that, if so, it has never been brot to our notice."

Section 32.   Some Results of the Attitude of Unions

What are some of the results of the attitude of organized labor toward Negro members?   As mentioned before, the separate Negro local is one method of solution.   The secretary of a Negro local in New Orleans, the Street Track Repairers' Union, writes:

In answer to your question blank, let me say that I am a Negro, filling the office of corresponding secretary of our local union, working hard by day and attending to my official duties at night, not feeling the least impatient in so doing because I have the union at heart.   I have been and always will be for the union cause even if this local sinks.   I shall be with one that is above the tide if I have to send my application to some other local of the American Federation of Labor.   I always try to keep my conscience clear with my fellow mates and brethren so that they may not point the finger of scorn at me.

On the other hand, many Negroes are working peacefully as members of mixed unions.   Numerous instances of this are noted in the replies of artisans printed in sections 6-30. From Sheridan, Wyoming, comes the following message:

I would like to state that I have been a member in good standing of Local No. 12696 for the past four years.   I am a charter member and have been a regular attendant upon the meetings save when I was absent from the city. During this period there has never been the slightest objection raised whenever a Negro candidate was presented for membership. You are at liberty to use this in any way you choose.

The relation of the Negro to organized labor in Pennsylvania is discussed at length in Dr. Wright's "The Negro in Pennsylvania." The following selections are taken from that valuable study in economic history:[1]

The great mass of Negro laborers are unorganized and come in contact but little with the labor union. There are a few Negroes in Philadelphia who are members of some of the unions, viz., the carpenters, stone masons, brick-layers, painters, cement layers, asphalt pavers, etc. On the other hand, there are some unions which do not admit or have not admitted Negroes, such as the machinists, locomotive engineers, etc. In the more skilled trades the Negro union laborers number less than two hundred in Philadelphia and less than three hundred in Pennsylvania. Of unskilled labor the most thoroly organized group is that of the hod carriers. Thruout the state there are Negro hod carriers. In Philadelphia there is a local union composed chiefly of Negroes, with a Negro president. This union, the Light Star Lodge, owns a four story brick hall, valued at about $20,000. In Pittsburg also the Hod Carriers' Union is composed predominantly of Negroes, but is not as large as the Philadelphia lodge. Next to the hod carriers come the miners. All of the Negro miners in the state are union men and members of the United Mine Workers of America. These are located chiefly in the western part of the state, having their district headquarters at Pittsburg. The United Mine Workers is one of the few unions in which the Negroes agree that they receive fair treatment. In some of these miners' unions there are Negro officers and Negroes are always in attendance at the annual meetings.

Negroes have made some attempts at independent organizations. The most successful of these is that among the hoisting engineers, steam and gas engineers, started in Pittsburg in 1900 and incorporated in 1903 under "The National Association of Afro-American Steam and Gas Engineers and Skilled Laborers in America." While the intention is to organize Negro labor on a racial basis, there is no antagonism to the general labor movement. It is merely believed by the promoters to be better for Negro workmen. This union has been of slow growth, however. There are only three locals in the state; two at Pittsburg, having fifty members, and one at Reading. In Philadelphia there is an organization of hoisting engineers which as yet is not connected with the Pittsburg union. There are numerous societies and clubs among Negroes which are organized along labor lines; but which are more social and beneficial clubs than labor unions. The largest of these is the Hotel Brotherhood, establisht at

[1] Wright, Dr. R. R., Jr.: The Negro in Pennsylvania, pp. 94-95, 98-100.

Philadelphia in 1881, and including present or former hotel employees. It pays sick and death benefits and acts as a kind of clearing house for hotel labor. In 1906 the brotherhood purchased a club house at the cost of $15,000. The bell-men, the Pullman car porters, the janitors, the private waiters, the caterers, the coachmen and others in domestic and personal service, have similar but smaller organizations. These organizations serve largely as aids in securing work, but have made but little attempt to regulate wages and apprentices. . . . .

The general opinion of the Negro workers in the Pittsburg steel mills who were interviewed by the writer is that the unions are a hindrance rather than a help to the Negro. Several have been members and one had been president of a southern union and a delegate to the National Convention of Steel Workers; some had gone out on strikes for the union. Their testimony is summarized as follows:

1. The organizations out of which the Amalgamated Association of Steel and Iron Workers was formed did not admit Negroes.

2. After the Amalgamated Association was formed white union men refused to work with Negro union men or to help protect Negro work-men, thus making union membership of no industrial value to the Negro workers.

3. All the new opportunities secured by Negroes have been gotten in spite of the union, not with its aid.

4. Membership was offered to Negroes only after they had success-fully won their places against unions and the pledges of membership gen-erally broken by the white members. . - . .

. . . When the present investigation was made . . . very few Negroes could be found who had recently applied to the unions for ad-mission. . . . The . . . investigator . . . found a very pro-nounced opinion prevalent among the Negroes that they were not welcome in the unions. Now instead of applying for admission to the unions, the Negroes take for granted that the unions are hostile and they do not seek to join.

This attitude has the effect of preventing many Negroes from at-tempting to follow their trade. The newcomer who has probably worked at the trade of a carpenter in the South is informed as soon as he reaches the state that he cannot work at his trade because of the hostility of the labor unions. Having probably heard this also before he left the South, after a desultory search he gives up under the impression that the union is the cause of his inability to get work at his trade. The fact, however, is that it is not always the union as much as the increased competition and higher standard of efficiency of the more complex community into which he has come.

The leaders of the labor movement both in Pittsburg and in Philadel-phia are agreed that there is in theory no hostility on the part of the union against the Negro. Most of them see clearly what a disadvantage

to the labor movement it would be to have Negroes hostile to the movement or the movement hostile to the Negroes. They complain that the
Negroes have been used in many instances to injure their cause and they
know that, with increasing intelligence and skill, Negroes will be more
capable of retarding the movement for the uplift of labor. Most labor
leaders have to contend very largely with mediocre intelligence and often
gross ignorance among white men; with greed and selfishness, with human
nature as it is. They claim that as the ordinary white man who joins the
Christian church is not revolutionized in his idea about the Negro, so the
one who joins the union probably has undergone but little change in regard to the Negro. They point out also that non-union white men are as
averse to working with Negroes as union white men. At any rate as
the situation now is the majority of Negroes are non-union and will
probably so remain until they develop enough strength independently so
that they can be of more definite help or hindrance to the union cause.
By keeping Negroes out of the trades competition is lessened for the men
in the union. As long as Negroes wait to be invited in by the unions
they will remain outside. Only by succeeding in spite of the indifference
of the union and even its occasional hostility can Negroes hope to be
recognized.

The situation in New York City is discussed by both Miss
Ovington and Dr. Haynes, whose interesting and valuable
works have been referred to in former pages. Miss Ovington
says:[1]

To the colored man who has overcome race prejudice sufficiently to
be taken into a shop with white workmen the walking delegate who
appears and asks for his union card seems little short of diabolical; and
all the advantages that collective bargaining has secured, the higher
wage and shorter working day, are forgotten by him. I have heard the
most distinguished of Negro educators, listening to such an incident as
this, declare that he should like to see every labor union in America destroyed. But unionism has come to stay, and the colored man who is
asked for his card had better at once get to work and endeavor to secure
it. Many have done this already and organized labor in New York, its
leaders tell us, receives an increasing number of colored workmen. Miss
Helen Tucker, in a careful study of Negro craftsmen in the West Sixties,
found among one hundred and twenty-one men who had worked at their
trades in the city, thirty-two, or twenty-six per cent in organized labor.
The majority of these had joined in New York. Eight men out of the
one hundred and twenty-one had applied for entrance to unions and
not been admitted. This does not seem a discouraging number, tho we
do not know whether the other eighty-one could have been organized or

---

[1] Ovington, M. W.: Half a Man, pp. 95-98.

not. Many probably were not sufficiently competent workmen. In 1910, according to the best information that I could secure, there were one thousand three hundred and fifty-eight colored men in the New York unions. Eighty of these were in the building trades, one hundred and sixty-five were cigar makers, four hundred were teamsters, three hundred and fifty asphalt workers and two hundred and forty rock drillers and tool sharpeners.

Negroes in Unions—New York City

Occupations	1906	1910
Asphalt workers	320	350
Teamsters	300	400
Rock drillers and tool sharpeners	250	240
Cigar makers	121	165
Brick-layers	90	21
Waiters	90	
Carpenters	60	40
Plasterers	45	19
Double drum hoisters	30	37
Safety and portable engineers	26	35
Eccentric firemen	15	0
Letter carriers	10	30
Pressmen	10	. . .
Printers	6	8
Butchers	3	3
Lathers	3	7
Painters	3	
Coopers	1	2
Sheet metal workers	1	1
Rockmen	1	
Total	1,385	1,358

Entrance to some of the local organizations is more easily secured than to others, for the trade union, while part of a federation, is autonomous or nearly so. In some of the highly skilled trades, to which few colored men have the necessary ability to demand access, the Negro is likely to be refused, while the less intelligent and well paid forms of labor press a union card upon him. Again strong organizations in the South, as the brick-layers, send men North with union membership who easily transfer to New York locals. Miss Tucker finds the carpenters, masons and plasterers' organizations easy for the Negro to enter. There is in New York a colored local, the only colored local in the city, among a few of the carpenters with regular representation in the Central Federated Union. The American Federation of Labor in 1881 declared that "the working people must unite irrespective of creed, color, sex, nationality or politics." This cry is for self-protection, and where the Negroes have numbers and ability in a trade their organization becomes important to the white. It may be fairly said of labor organization in New York that it finds and is at times unable to destroy race prejudice, but that it does not create it.

The following account is gleaned from the circumstances in the recent New York hotel situation, at which time Negroes were called in to take the places of striking white waiters. Tho not dealing primarily with Negro skilled laborers, it is illustrative of the relation existing between the Negro and organized labor.[1]

Now that the strike is in progress, representatives of the International Hotel Workers hasten to say that they are not interested in the betterment of conditions for the white man alone, but that also they want to help the colored man. This statement, coming just at this time, is received by the colored waiters "with a grain of salt." The men recall what took place among the colored molders of Chattanooga some time ago. The white molders struck and colored men were put at the strikers' work. Whereupon the white men took the Negroes into their union. Shortly after this the colored molders, one by one, found that they were losing their jobs until all the Negroes had been replaced by the original strikers. Soon after these events a similar situation arose in Louisville and the colored molders who had lost their jobs in Chattanooga were given the jobs of the striking molders in Louisville. Immediately, as in Chattanooga, the white men offered to take the Negroes into their union, but this time the Negroes refused absolutely to enter into negotiations with them. The result was that the colored men kept those jobs.

In the present situation in New York there seems to have been little or no attempt on the part of the International Hotel Workers to bring the Negroes into this organization. To be sure Negroes are not rejected by the union and there are possibly two hundred and fifty colored members, but they seem to have gained little for themselves or their racial group by this membership. Even tho he is a union member the Negro is not permitted to work with white waiters; he can get a job only where all the waiters belong to his own color group.

The colored men who are taking the white men's places are being paid the same amount, three dollars a day, which the white men had been receiving.

The Molders' International Union of America, which has made a long fight for excluding Negroes from membership, is considering the question of admitting them. In their last convention one speaker said:

The Negro has demonstrated that he is a capable mechanic and is quite able to fill the place of the white laborer. The southern foundry managers are making capital out of the race prejudice between the white and the colored molders and if we do not raise the colored worker to our standard he will drag us down to his.

We can hardly find language strong enough to express our opinion of

---

[1] Special investigation made for the Conference.

the feudal lords when we consider the days when the laborer was bot and sold with the land. Our evolution from a condition of slavery to the freedom that we now enjoy was slow, but we now withhold our aid from the Negro, who is trying to gain the same freedom.

How can you get the Negro organized unless you are willing to meet with him? His interests are identical with yours. Everyone knows that this condition will have to be met, yet some of us want to postpone the day and let others take the responsibility. Do not let your race prejudice warp your judgment.

We find the following observation in the "Negro Year Book, 1912:"[1]

Negroes during the year made gains in the field of organized labor. At the 1910 annual meeting of the National Council of the American Federation of Labor a resolution was unanimously passed inviting Negroes and all other races into the Labor Federation. The officers of the Federation were instructed to take measures to see that Negro workmen as well as workmen of other races were brot into the unions. Following out this policy steps were taken to unionize the Negro working in the Pittsburg district. At New Orleans in October the Negro longshoremen were admitted to the International Longshoremen's Union. T. V. O'Connor, president of the International Union, was present and in his address urged fair play between white and black laborers. He said: "We are not going to take up social equality but we can if we achieve the proper organization bring about industrial equality. To you colored men I will say that the white man is ready and willing to assist you to get the same wages and working conditions that he enjoys, but you must stand ready to assist yourselves."

The following interesting passages, illustrative of the better attitude towards Negro workers, are taken from "An Appeal to Timber and Lumber Workers," by Jay Smith, secretary Brotherhood of Timber Workers:

The constitution of the Brotherhood of Timber Workers declares our purpose to be the organization of all wage workers employed in and around the timber and lumber industry into one big union regardless of creed, color or nationality. . . . .

Failing to split the workers' forces on craft lines, the next cry raised by the bosses and their stool pigeons is the "Negro question," and so we are often asked how will the Brotherhood handle the Negro and the white men in the same organization. Answer: How do the capitalists or employers handle them?

To the employer a working man is nothing but a profit-producing animal and he doesn't care a snap of his finger what the animal's color

[1] Work, Monroe N.: The Negro Year Book, 1912, pp. 18-19.

is—white, black, red, brown or yellow; native or foreign born, religious or unreligious—so long as he (the worker) has strength enough to keep the logs coming and the lumber going—that is all the bosses want or ask. It is only when we see the slaves uniting, when all other efforts to divide the workers on the job have failed, that we hear a howl go up as to the horrors of "social equality." Not until then do we really know how sacred to the boss and his hirelings is the holy doctrine of "white supremacy."

This is always the tactics of the bosses: First, prevent the workers from organizing any kind of union; failing in this, split them on craft lines into as many so-called unions as possible, each with a separate contract expiring on a different date with sympathetic strikes strictly prohibited; and, then, failing in this, appeal to their race and religious hatred, for, if the bosses can divide the workers, the bosses can win every time; but if the bosses cannot divide the workers then the workers will win, and win, and win until there are no more bosses. In fighting the workers the age-long motto of the bosses has been: "Divide and conquer." . . . .

As far as the "Negro question" goes it means simply this: Either the whites organize with the Negroes or the bosses will organize the Negroes against the whites, in which last case it is hardly up to the whites to damn the "niggers." . . . .

As to the "race question": Once upon a time a butcher threw a bone out in the alley; a white dog and a black dog made a rush for it, reached it at the same time and started a fight for its possession. While they were making fools of themselves a big, lazy red dog sneaked up, grabbed the bone and lit out with it. The white dog was a "white supremacy" sucker, the black dog was a "social equality" sucker and the red dog that got the bone was one of those gentlemen who in one breath call the timber and lumber workers "pals" and "freemen" and in the next threaten to shut down the mills and starve the workers to death if they dare to think and act for themselves—in other words, a capitalist, a boss.

An officer of the Free Federation of Workingmen of Porto Rico, a union affiliated with the American Federation of Labor, who visited America recently as a delegate to the convention of the Federation, makes an interesting reply to the Conference:

. . . . I must say emphatically that there is not such a struggle of color distinction in our country. We have, of course, the universal distinction of classes.

Here a person is worth nothing in the commercial, industrial or professional life if he has not sufficient intelligence and money. Money and intelligence, without regard to the color, are the real forces moving the whole mechanism of our society, may a man be white or colored, red or yellow. . . . .

The working shop, the university, the theater, the library, the social hall and every institution that promotes the welfare of mankind and the happiness of the spirit, are here opened to all men in accordance with their financial positions.

Our labor movement has more ideal than material basis. The organizations in America are fighting for greater salary, less hours and sanitary conditions; the Latin worker follows the brilliant ideal of founding societies and nations upon the rock of fraternity and absolute harmony to secure the real emancipation, may it be social, economical or political. Our struggles are noticed by two opposing bands: those who are rich and well fed and those who are poor and misfortunate; those who oppress and those who are oppressed.

The distinction of races, the social and political differences are doing nothing but dividing mankind into opposite groups to bring forth the Universal War. The only place in the world where a man is superior to another on account of skin, is the United States of America. No other country has such an inferior war, such an unchristian fight, tho it is true that the Americans have a deep love for liberty, that they have admirable institutions, a great commercial development and a monument of rights unsurpassed in the world, i. e., the constitution that declares that all men are equal, that they possess certain inalienable rights to work and promote their welfare, but this constitution and all the free institutions of the American people and the splendorous sun of their liberty is totally eclipsed by the barbarous struggle of races with the inhuman division of the white and the black.

"America, the cradle of liberty, is being the theater of the most barbarous and atrocious war." This is what they say in Europe among the Latin and Saxon races of that old continent. It is what they say in Japan, even in China, in India and in Northern Africa, where, as you know, the first civilization was born. . . . .

I certainly regret that I have had to extend these remarks, but I was compelled to do it because your letter shows that you have the idea that in Porto Rico exists the same hateful distinction of races. I wanted to give you the right idea. We have struggles between the rich and the poor, between capital and labor.

Hoping that this information may give you some light and help in the work initiated by Atlanta University, and hoping also that the division of races in some of the southern states may soon cease, I beg to remain,   Yours in humanity,
                                                         _____

Section 33.   The Training of Negro American Artisans

The success of the man who labors with his hands, even as the success of any other worker, depends in no small degree upon his training and his capability for the work to be performed. The question of fitness is the determining factor under a truly competitive economic system and in the long run all other superficial barriers must pale into insignificance. This will be more and more apparent in the case of the Negro worker as the superficial barriers of race and color are done away with and he is allowed to enter unhampered into the fair field of economic competition.

In a social study of the Negro American artisan the question of the training of these workers is of vital importance. The Negro artisans studied were asked: How did you learn your trade? The answers to this question fall into three heads: (1) By apprenticeship (41 per cent.); (2) Picked up trade (37 per cent.); (3) Attended trade school (21 per cent.).[1] Many of the best and most successful of the Negro artisans are among those who come under the first two classes, those who learned their trades under the system of apprenticeship and those who "picked up" their trades. Numerous evidences of this fact may be seen both in antebellum days and during the years that have passed since emancipation.

Recent years have witnessed a marked increase of interest in industrial school training for Negroes. Most of the higher institutions of learning as well as the secondary schools for Negroes have included industrial courses in their curricula. The following tables, compiled from the Report of the United States Commissioner of Education for 1911, give statistics for those secondary and higher schools for the Negro race that had students enrolled in the industries:

---

[1] These percentage figures apply to the artisans making reply to the Conference questionnaire and not to all the Negro American artisans. Taking all Negro artisans the percentage figures for the first two classes would be larger. The third class would show a smaller percentage.

Secondary and Higher Schools for Negroes having Students in Industries, 1910-11

LOCATION	NAME OF SCHOOL	Total Enrollment	Students in Industries	Value of Grounds and Buildings	Gifts	State, U.S., or Municipal Aid	Tuition	Interest	Other Sources	Total
Alabama										
Athens	Trinity School	269	269	15,000			515		675	1,190
Birmingham	St. Mark's Academic and Industrial School	358	198	40,000			1,593		2,700	4,298
Corona	Corona Normal and Industrial Institute	336	186	20,010		500	3,780	320	200	4,800
Florence	Burrell Normal School	247	76	8,000			675		2,170	2,845
Marion	Lincoln Normal and Industrial Institute	422	372	15,000			700		1,300	2,000
Miller's Ferry	Miller's Ferry Normal and Industrial School	316	206	14,000					4,426	4,426
Mobile	Emerson Institute	391	310	30,000			2,646		3,480	6,126
Normal	State Agr. and Mech. College for Negroes	333	301	141,000		4,000	1,380		35,280	40,660
Selma	Knox Academy	849	317	21,000			1,200	300	7,400	8,900
Talladega	Talladega College	768	647	267,091	115		5,950	6,992	30,622	43,679
Tuskegee	Tuskegee Normal and Industrial Institute	1,702	1,702	1,295,214	464,133	4,740	17,047	71,788	138,725	696,433
Arkansas										
Little Rock	Arkansas Baptist College	424	125	75,000			2,500		2,000	4,500
Little Rock	Philander Smith College	483	175	71,000			3,900		10,100	14,000
Pine Bluff	Branch Normal College	320	230	92,000		9,000	550		12,273	21,823
Southland	Southland College and Normal Institute	400	330	32,000			500	3,000	6,500	10,000
Delaware										
Dover	State College for Colored Students	146	130	35,000		3,000	168		220	3,388
Dist. of Columbia										
Washington	Howard University	1,382	273	1,265,244		104,700	47,781	13,825	3,896	170,202
Florida										
Eatonville	Robert Hungerford Nor. and Ind. School	145	109	48,760		245	345	740	1,025	2,355
Fessenden	Fessenden Academy	288	288	30,000		1,750	1,800		2,000	5,550
Jacksonville	Florida Baptist Academy	431	132	2,000			2,105		14,013	16,118
Pensacola	Pensacola Normal and Industrial School	268	148	5,600			1,560		578	2,138
Tallahassee	Florida Agr. and Mech. College for Negroes	324	324	69,463		5,000			23,221	28,221
Georgia										
Americus	Americus Institute	223	150	30,000			682			
Athens	Knox Institute and Industrial School	426	350	60,000					10,451	11,133

State / Town	Institution			$	$	$	$	$	$	$
Georgia—Continued										
Atlanta	Atlanta Baptist College	266	97	120,000	5,100		1,145	1,000	10,804	12,949
Atlanta	Atlanta University	394	308	273,505			6,306	2,798	40,175	54,379
Atlanta	Morris Brown College	805	139	100,010	2,003		3,425		2,000	5,425
Atlanta	Spelman Seminary	664	546	306,720			5,113	542	33,015	40,673
Augusta	Paine College	291	279	47,910			874	3,138	11,600	15,612
Brunswick	Selden Normal and Industrial Institute	156	86	6,540	12,500	50	840		1,658	15,108
Macon	Ballard School	435	344	250,000			3,200		3,120	6,220
Sandersville	Sandersville Industrial School	233	104	4,000			500		300	1,661
Savannah	Georgia State Industrial College	541	541	65,000		861	8,000		15,000	23,000
Social Circle	Negro Normal and Industrial School	154	80	10,000		600	200	400	375	1,575
South Atlanta	Clark University	407	96	250,000	310		3,439	200	9,703	13,642
Thomasville	Allen Normal and Industrial School	334	255	4,700			1,175		2,750	3,925
Waynesboro	Haven Academy	200	65	15,010			600		515	1,115
Kentucky										
Danville	Danville Polytechnic Seminary	178	130	20,000			360	510	6,580	7,450
Frankfort	Kentucky Normal and Industrial Institute	292	237	113,000	12,256		334		6,525	19,175
Louisiana										
Alexandria	Peabody State Normal and Industrial School	766	766	18,000	1,210	1,600	300	250	89	2,239
Converse	Sabine Normal and Industrial School	186	118	15,000	414	1,000	250	1,200	250	3,900
Homer	Homer College	86	40	6,000			500		414	1,328
New Orleans	Leland University	1,715	1,068	499,000					31,000	31,000
New Orleans	New Orleans University	62	436	250,000			2,752		10,427	13,179
New Orleans	Southern Univ. and Ag. and Mech. College	434	426	102,803		10,750			21,047	31,797
New Orleans	Straight University	607	325	150,000			6,000		7,200	13,200
Maryland										
Baltimore	Morgan College	284	182	100,000	19,601		4,568	207	16,822	41,198
Princess Anne	Princess Anne Academy	130	130	29,900					11,000	11,000
Mississippi										
Alcorn	Alcorn Agricultural and Mechanical College	616	598	246,500		15,500	45	12,592	22,180	50,317
Holly Springs	Mississippi Industrial College	391	105	200,000			1,509		24,081	25,590
Holly Springs	Rust University	438	231	130,000	149		3,498		7,640	11,247
Okolona	Okolona Industrial College	338	338	84,150		827	4,942		9,348	15,117
Tougaloo	Tougaloo University	496	435	130,000			1,860	100	18,000	19,900
West Point	Mary Holmes Seminary	204	204	50,000					6,000	6,000
Missouri										
Jefferson City	Lincoln Institute	402	297	170,000	1,000		893		1,740	3,633
Macon	Western College and Industrial Institute	101	101	25,000					5,000	6,600
Sedalia	George R. Smith College	193	80	6,500			1,600			

Secondary and Higher Schools for Negroes having Students in Industries, 1910-11

LOCATION	NAME OF SCHOOL	Total Enrollment	Students in Industries	Value of Grounds and Buildings	INCOME, 1910-1911					Total
					Gifts	State, U.S., or Munici-pal Aid	Tuition	Interest	Other Sources	
New Jersey					$	$	$	$	$	$
Bordentown	Manual Training and Industrial School	142	142	$ 90,000		$ 22,000				$ 22,000
North Carolina										
Burgaw	Burgaw Normal and Industrial School	250	145	10,000		600	75		2,000	2,675
Edenton	Edenton Normal and Industrial School	115	115	10,000			360		600	960
Enfield	Joseph Keasby Brick Ag., Ind. and Nor. Sch.	279	223	127,000			900	8,000		8,900
Fayetteville	State Colored Normal School	327	187	28,000		3,333				3,333
Franklinton	Albion Academy, Nor. and Ind. School	323	323	45,000					10,000	10,0 0 0
Greensboro	Ag. and Mech. College for the Colored Race	339	268	122,485		14,350	716		13,473	28,539
High Point	High Point Nor. and Ind. Institute	502	110	35,00		2,490	22			2,512
Kings Mountain	Lincoln Academy	272	110	20,000		130	300		2,948	3,378
Lumberton	Thompson Institute	169	122	10,500			5'0		1,080	1,580
Newbern	Newbern Collegiate Industrial Institute	150	150	75,000			2,500		8,500	11,000
Oxford	Mary Potter Memorial School	429	389	35,000			280		5,100	5,380
Raleigh	St. Augustine's School	339	339	38,000				2,040	15,951	17,991
Raleigh	Shaw University	549	300	260,000			10,449	1,422	17,219	29,80
Sedalia	Palmer Memorial Institute	123	70	19,000	1,0'0	210		60	4,000	5,270
Wilmington	Gregory Normal Institute	280	157	10,000	2,900		1,5'0		700	5,100
Winston-Salem	Slater Industrial and State Normal School	395	184	25,000		6,C00	330			6,330
Winton	Water's Normal Institute	245	58	20,000		225	233		2,040	2,498
Ohio										
Wilberforce	Wilberforce University	313	201	300,000	42,000	16,000	3,335	1,724	15,450	78,509
South Carolina										
Aiken	Schofield Normal and Industrial Institute	500	211	75,0 0	5,000	350	700	3,000	4,000	13,050
Chester	Brainerd Institute	223	223	50,000						
Columbia	Allen University	685	40	20,000			5,0C0		32,000	37,000
Cowpens	Providence Nor., Ag. and Ind. School	317	141	10,000		400	150		930	1,450
Greenville	Sterling Normal and Industrial College	160	95	28,000			1,128		1,414	2,542
Greenwood	Brewer Normal School	593	279	42,5 1			1,009		4,000	5,C09
Greer	Bailey View Academy	105	105	3,825			25		766	791

So. Carolina—Cont'd				$	$	$	$	$	$	$
Lancaster	Lancaster Nor. and Ind. Institute	315	98	13,000	3,000	805	286	1,240	1,508	3,839
Mayesville	Mayesville Educational and Ind. Institute	511	418	24,950		250	50	3,021	4,462	11,233
Mount Pleasant	Laing Normal and Industrial School	340	104	3,000		800	75	251	2,000	3,126
Orangeburg	Claflin University	683	683	300,000	6,000	19,000	6,172		26,218	38,390
Orangeburg	Colored Normal, Ind., Ag. and Mech. College	584	584	260,000		305	350		8,146	27,146
Rock Hill	Clinton Normal and Industrial College	334	75	12,000		250	2,000		845	1,500
Rock Hill	Friendship Normal and Industrial College	395	90	20,000						2,250
Tennessee										
Cleveland	Cleveland Academy	117	115	5,000					2,300	2,300
Jackson	Lane College	310	243	85,000			1,350		5,000	6,450
Knoxville	Knoxville College	427	212	180,000		10,350	2,100	100	12,500	25,450
Memphis	Le Moyne Normal Institute	702	702	55,000		250	5,085	500	3,217	12,012
Morristown	Morristown Normal and Industrial College	324	240	100,000	4,378		1,886	3,470	14,590	20,854
Nashville	Fisk University	479	305	337,312	3,091		9,766	2,707	46,493	62,057
Nashville	Walden University	733	140	147,780		30,000	31,967	1,758	8,755	42,480
Shelbyville	Turner Normal College	129	92	8,500	3,750		120	575	2,605	7,050
Texas										
Austin	Samuel Huston College	381	80	48,650			2,537		10,834	13,371
Austin	Tillotson College	312	250							
Crockett	Mary Allen Seminary	228	228	50,000			10,000		331	10,331
Ladonia (R. 1)	Farmers' Improvement Society Ag. College	90	90	15,000			480		1,000	1,480
Marshall	Wiley University	603	375	200,000			2,525		3,900	6,425
Prairie View	Prairie View State Nor. and Ind. College	860	860	256,750		30,000	10,000			32,000
Seguin	Guadalupe College	161	161	65,000			850	2,000	1,269	16,269
Tyler	East Texas Academy	185	160	20,000					2,500	3,350
Tyler	Phillips University	366	100	100,000			2,300	5,000	10,000	12,300
Virginia										
Cambria	Christiansburg Industrial Institute	297	78	75,000	45,000	635	232	250	6,500	7,617
Claremont	Temperance, Indust. and Collegiate Inst.	421	281				1,497		1,784	48,281
Dinwiddie	Dinwiddie Ag. and Ind. School	66	66	31,000			2,360		2,150	5,010
Hampton	Hampton Normal and Agricultural Inst.	1,399	1,399	1,030,000	128,827		3,203	103,699	152,462	384,988
Lawrenceville	St. Paul Normal and Industrial School	529	214	161,023	35		2,400	1,417	30,544	35,199
Norfolk	Norfolk Mission College	634	233	92,000			484		12,780	15,180
Ozeana	Rappahannock Industrial Academy	73	73	6,000					1,088	1,572
Petersburg	Virginia Normal and Industrial Institute	605	605	197,000		21,000	3,637			24,637
Richmond	Hartshorn Memorial College	211	187	100,000			2,411		5,619	8,030
Richmond	Virginia Union University	246	60	300,000			2,289	3,500	18,000	23,789
West Virginia										
Harper's Ferry	Storer College	207	207	75,000	1,000	2,500	472	2,096	8,000	14,068
Institute	West Virginia Colored Institute	265	235	104,965		33,550	265		9,000	42,815

The industrial courses offered in these schools are as follows:

Industry	Number of Schools Offering
Carpentry	35
Dressmaking and Sewing	30
Blacksmithing and Forging	24
Printing	23
Cooking	23
Mechanical Drawing	18
Tailoring	14
Millinery	14
Painting	13
Shoe and Harness Repairing	12
Wheelwrighting	12
Bricklaying	12
Plastering	12
Laundering	10
Sheet Metal and Machine Shop Work	7
Electrical Engineering	6
Plumbing	5
Upholstery	4
Brickmaking	4
Steam Engineering	3
Basketry	3
Broom Making	2
Tinsmithing	2
Mattress Making	2
Mechanical Engineering	2

How far are these courses preparing and how far are they designed to prepare Negro youth for the organized industry of the South? During the twenty years from 1880 to 1900 there was in the South a relative decrease in the importance of agricultural and personal service and a large increase in trade and transportation, manufacturing and professions. The theory of the industrial training of Negro youth is that Negroes should be trained to take skilled and intelligent part in this development of trade and transportation and manufacturing. How far is this true in application?

If we carefully scan the list of industries taught we may divide them into:

(1) Repair work and tinkering.
(2) House work.
(3) Trades and industries.

In nearly all cases the following courses are training simply in repair work and tinkering:

Carpentry.
Blacksmithing and forging.
Tailoring.
Shoe and harness repairing.
Wheelwrighting.

Sheet metal and machine shop work.
Plumbing.
Upholstering.
Tinsmithing.
Mattress making.

Modern wood-working involves elaborate machinery and training in machine methods. In nearly all these schools "carpentry" is confined to hand tools and bench work. Blacksmithing and forging are taught by the simplest tools and not by modern power methods. Tailoring is not taught as modern garment making but as individual cutting and mending. Shoe repairing is taught but there is but little or no use made of shoe making machinery which is universally in vogue. Wheels and wagons are made chiefly by hand and at a cost which would make competition with machine made wagons impossible. The same thing is true of most of the other industries. *Negro youth are being taught the technique of a rapidly disappearing age of hand work.* The training has undoubtedly good physical and mental results but if used as a means of livelihood it will command the poor and decreasing wages of tinkers and repairers; and those who follow these methods will be completely shut out of modern machine industry.

Happily there are some exceptions to this general rule. At Hampton, Tuskegee, Wilberforce and a few other schools machine industry along modern lines is being taught in some branches of wood-working and metal-working. For the most part, however, the courses offered in this division are not modern or remunerative.

The next group comprises the house industries,—dressmaking, sewing, cooking and laundering. Here we see little of settled idea or aim. These subjects might be taught with the idea of training the mistresses of small homes, or with the idea of training servants in rich homes, or with the idea of making professional cooks and dress makers. These three aims call for widely different courses of study. Usually, however, a single course is laid down, the aim of training servants is widely advertised and the net result is dubious.

The third set of industries taught comprises the following: Printing, mechanical drawing, millinery, painting, bricklaying, plastering, brickmaking, mechanical engineering, both steam and electric, basketry and broommaking.

In the case of printing, brickmaking and broommaking there is the same difficulty as in the first group, save that here hand work is still in fair demand. The linotype and the monotype have not as yet displaced the hand typesetter, and brickmaking and broommaking by hand are still able to compete with machines. Nevertheless a proper training in the industries cannot long omit machine teaching. In the case of bricklaying hand work seems secure. Still, re-inforced cement work should receive attention. In drawing, painting and basketry industry touches upon the work of the artist and in this field these schools need strengthening. The Negro is humanly the artist and yet little is being done to develop his sensitive perceptions.

The engineering courses are nearly all misnamed, being much too short and elementary to deserve the larger designation.

To sum up: The industrial school is facing an age of machinery. The teaching of mere hand work, save in limited amounts and for educative purposes, is not training for modern industry. The machine equipment for the larger teaching is expensive; but how, for example, can modern printing be taught without the linotype and the cylinder press, and how can modern shoemaking be taught without shoemaking machines? These are the difficult problems facing Negro industrial schools.

The whole plan of study in these schools needs overhauling. Simply to accept the fact that schools should train for practical vocations and then put in any industries taught any way is not enough. Modern plants are necessary for the teaching of modern industry and intelligent common school training must precede it. It is possible that the different schools could specialize. One might give instruction in mechanical engineering and have a complete and modern machine shop; another could have woodworking with the complete and modern machinery necessary for the same. Certainly the present incomplete makeshifts cannot long survive.

The soundness of this criticism is shown by the results of industrial teaching. Hampton has given four hundred and sixty-seven trade certificates. Of these one hundred and sixty-nine are following their trades, thirty-eight are still studying, and sixty-three are teaching their trades. It would seem then that economic industrial demand was at present sufficient to absorb between thirty-six per cent and forty-nine [1] per cent of those trained at the best Negro trade school.

A recent publication from Tuskegee Institute, Tuskegee, Alabama, makes the following observation:

Almost two-thirds of its 1,508 graduates and three-fourths of its 12,000 former students are directly or indirectly engaged in some form of industrial work. . . . . Three hundred and seventy-four persons, 173 graduates and 201 former students have been considered. They were distributed in the trades as follows: 2 bakers, 33 blacksmiths and wheelwrights, 5 bookkeepers, 56 brickmasons, 1 cabinetmaker, 42 carpenters, 2 carriage makers, 1 chauffeur, 1 cook, 1 cooking demonstrator, 1 cotton classer, 5 in domestic service, 31 dressmakers, 3 stationary engineers, 8 electricians, 1 elevator operator, 4 firemen, 9 harnessmakers, 1 hostler, 5 janitors, 1 laundress, 3 laundrymen, 9 machinists, 10 miners, 3 molders, 42 trained nurses, 11 painters, 6 plumbers, 10 printers, 3 sawmill workers, 19 shoemakers, 26 tailors, 8 tinsmiths, and 2 woodturners. . . . . One hundred and two graduates and former students are carrying on business in connection with trades. Five are architects, one is in the bakery business, eighteen are conducting blacksmithing and wheelwrighting businesses, eighteen are in the contracting and building business, one is in the electrical business, one in the florist business, eleven are milliners, five are in the printing business, eight in the shoemaking business, and two are in the tinsmithing business. [2]

An examination of the catalogs of other industrial schools reveals the following facts concerning the number of graduates and those of them at present following trades: [3]

---

[1] According as one does not or does count those teaching trades as following their trades. There is argument on both sides.

[2] Work, Monroe N.   Industrial Work of Tuskegee Graduates and Former Students.   Pages 5, 25, 28.

[3] These tables are not exhaustive. However, the figures of present occupations are taken from the replies of the schools to the Conference questionnaire or compiled from the lists of graduates contained in the catalogs.

Alabama

TALLADEGA COLLEGE

Total graduates	400
Carpenters 5	
Masons 1	
Engineers 1	
Dressmakers 1	

BURRELL NORMAL SCHOOL

Total graduates	—
Dressmakers 1	
Tailors (app) 1	

LINCOLN NORMAL SCHOOL

Total graduates	—
Blacksmiths 1	
Painters 4	
Masons 6	
Plasterers 6	
Dressmakers 8	
Tailors 3	

PAYNE UNIVERSITY

Total graduates	152
Seamstresses 1	
Blacksmiths 1	

Florida

PENSACOLA NORMAL AND
INDUSTRIAL SCHOOL

Total graduates	—
Carpenters 1	
Dressmakers 2	

ROBT. HUNGERFORD NORMAL
AND INDUSTRIAL SCHOOL

Total graduates	—
Carpenters 3	
Blacksmiths 2	
Dressmakers 4	
Printers 2	

THE FLORIDA A. & M. COLLEGE

Total graduates	154
Dressmakers 1	
Carpenters 3	
Masons 1	
Tailors 3	
Printers 1	

Georgia

ATLANTA UNIVERSITY

Total graduates	678
Dressmakers 6	

MORRIS BROWN COLLEGE

Total graduates	349
Dressmakers 5	
Tailors 1	

FT. VALLEY HIGH AND
INDUSTRIAL SCHOOL

Total graduates	50
Dressmakers 3	
Machinists 1	
Masons 3	
Carpenters 2	

SPELMAN SEMINARY

Total graduates	416
Dressmakers 31	
Milliners 1	

BALLARD NORMAL SCHOOL

Total graduates	227
Carpenters 1	
Tailors 1	
Dressmakers 2	

ATLANTA BAPTIST COLLEGE

Total graduates	355
Carpenters 1	

SELDON INSTITUTE

Total graduates	—
Carpenters 4	
Painters 3	
Masons 7	
Plasterers 5	
Dressmakers 14	
Coopers 2	
Tailors 6	

ALLEN NORMAL AND
INDUSTRIAL SCHOOL

Total graduates	55
Dressmakers 2	
Shoemakers 1	

SANDERSVILLE INDUSTRIAL SCHOOL

Total graduates	—
Carpenters 4	
Engineers 4	
Painters 4	
Blacksmiths 3	
Shoemakers 2	
Plasterers 6	
Masons 10	
Dressmakers 12	
Tailors 2	

Kansas

WESTERN UNIVERSITY AND
STATE INDUSTRIAL DEPT.

Total graduates	244
Shirtmakers 1	
Dressmakers 7	
Tailors 4	
Carpenters 1	

Louisiana

STRAIGHT UNIVERSITY

Total graduates	439
Dressmakers 1	
Contractors 1	
Carpenters 1	

SABINE NORMAL AND
INDUSTRIAL INSTITUTE

Total graduates	—
Carpenters 15	
Masons 3	
Firemen 1	
Dressmakers 14	
Blacksmiths 2	
Shoemakers 5	
Iron and Steel Workers 1	
Brickmasons 3	
Painters 4	
Plasterers 3	
Tailors 4	

Mississippi

LINCOLN SCHOOL

Total graduates	—
Carpenters	9
Dressmakers	12
Painters	8
Plasterers	2

ALCORN A. & M. COLLEGE

Total graduates	469
Carpenters	4
Shoemakers	3
Cabinet Makers	1
Mechanics	2
Painters	1
Tailors	1

MERIDIAN ACADEMY

Total graduates	187
Dressmakers	1
Milliners	1
Mechanics	1

CAMPBELL COLLEGE

Total graduates	48
Dressmakers	7

North Carolina

WATERS NORMAL AND INDUSTRIAL INSTITUTE

Total graduates	—
Dressmakers	3

ST. AUGUSTINE'S SCHOOL

Total graduates	235
Carpenters	1
Dressmakers	4
Masons	5

STATE COLORED NORMAL SCHOOL

Total graduates	208
Carpenters	11
Masons	7
Shoemakers	3
Blacksmiths	4
Firemen	1
Painters	2
Tailors	2
Brickmakers	2
Dressmakers	8
Plasterers	4

KITTRELL COLLEGE

Total graduates	227
Mechanics	1
Seamstresses	1
Printers	1

J. K. BRICK AGRICULTURAL, INDUSTRIAL AND NORMAL SCHOOL

Total graduates	—
Painters	1
Carpenters	2
Blacksmiths	2
Dressmakers	2

A. & M. COLLEGE

Total graduates	152
Mechanics	3
Engineers	1
Tinners	1
Carpenters	1
Contractors	1

BIDDLE UNIVERSITY

Total graduates	1,075
Mechanics	1
Printers	1

ROANOKE COLLEGIATE INSTITUTE

Total graduates	74
Painters	1

HENDERSON NORMAL INSTITUTE

Total graduates	54
Carpenters	2

Ohio

WILBERFORCE UNIVERSITY

Total graduates	706
Engineers	1
Milliners	1
Dressmakers	1
Carpenters	1
Brickmasons	1

South Carolina

BETTIS ACADEMY

Total graduates	—
Carpenters	12
Engineers	3
Dressmakers	37
Blacksmiths	10
Firemen	1
Shoemakers	3
Tailors	4
Masons	25
Painters	8
Plasterers	13

HARBISON COLLEGE

Total graduates	—
Carpenters	4
Blacksmiths	2
Masons	2
Shoemakers	1
Dressmakers	18

FRIENDSHIP COLLEGE

Total graduates	—
Carpenters	4
Painters	2
Masons	1
Plasterers	1
Dressmakers	4
Tailors	1

AVERY INSTITUTE

Total graduates	—
Carpenters	6
Tailors	7
Cabinet Makers	1
Dressmakers	28
Ship Carpenters	1
Machinists	1
Patternmakers	1
Electricians	1

BENEDICT COLLEGE

Total graduates 1	587
Printers. 1	
Carpenters 2	

COLORED NORMAL, INDUSTRIAL,
    AGRICULTURAL AND MECHANICAL
    COLLEGE

Total graduates	527
Tailors 2	
Masons 7	
Blacksmiths. 1	

Tennessee

LANE COLLEGE

Total graduates	—
Carpenters 3	
Blacksmiths 1	
Dressmakers 2	
Iron and Steel Workers 2	

KNOXVILLE COLLEGE

Total graduates	417
Carpenters 4	
Masons 5	
Dressmakers 8	
Plasterers 1	
Blacksmiths 6	
Engineers. 4	
Iron and Steel Workers 4	
Tailors 1	
Brickmakers 1	
Firemen 1	
Shoemakers 1	
Printers 2	

FISK UNIVERSITY

Total graduates	795
Tailors 1	
Painters 1	
Masons 1	
Dressmakers 5	

Texas

PRAIRIE VIEW STATE
    NORMAL AND INDUSTRIAL
    COLLEGE

Total graduates	762
Contractors and Builders 1	
Mechanics. 1	
Tailors 1	

PAUL QUINN COLLEGE

Total graduates 158	
Printers. 1	

GUADALUPE COLLEGE

Total graduates	130
Mechanics 1	

WILEY UNIVERSITY

Total graduates	143
Painters 3	
Plumbers 1	
Dressmakers 36	
Carpenters 4	
Brickmakers 6	
Masons 6	
Engineers. 3	
Firemen 3	
Plasterers 2	

BISHOP COLLEGE

Total graduates	275
Tailors. 1	
Printers. 2	

Virginia

CHRISTIANSBURG INDUSTRIAL
    INSTITUTE

Total graduates	67
Carpenters 3	
Painters 3	
Masons 1	
Dressmakers 1	

VIRGINIA NORMAL AND
    INDUSTRIAL INSTITUTE

Total graduates	9.16
Printers. 1	
Blacksmiths 1	
Dressmakers 3	
Carpenters 2	
Tailors. 1	
Milliners. 1	

West Virginia

STORER COLLEGE

Total graduates	439
Dressmakers 6	
Carpenters 3	
Masons 1	
Mechanics. 2	

WEST VIRGINIA
    COLORED INSTITUTE

Total graduates	274
Carpenters 7	
Engineers. 1	
Blacksmiths 6	
Dressmakers 8	
Masons 4	
Painters. 7	
Tailors. 1	
Iron and Steel Workers 1	

The following table showing the number of Negro pupils receiving industrial training in the school year 1910-11 is taken from the Report of the United States Commissioner of Education:

Negro Pupils Receiving Industrial Training, 1910-11 *

STATES	Male	Female	Total
Alabama	2,252	3,129	5,381
Arkansas	322	616	938
Delaware	156	60	216
District of Columbia	287	261	548
Florida	427	608	1,035
Georgia	1,327	2,531	3,858
Indiana	35	20	55
Kentucky	223	316	539
Louisiana	1,386	1,948	3,334
Maryland	132	210	342
Mississippi	1,245	1,222	2,467
Missouri	210	268	478
New Jersey	53	89	142
North Carolina	1,560	2,457	4,017
Ohio	57	144	201
Oklahoma	42	18	60
South Carolina	1,314	1,933	3,247
Tennessee	851	1,223	2,074
Texas	730	1,637	2,367
Virginia	1,524	2,137	3,661
West Virginia	233	209	442
Total	14,366	21,036	35,402

* U. S. Commissioner of Education, Report of 1911.

It would seem fair to conclude that from half to two-thirds of the Negroes trained in industrial schools do not follow their trades. This may be on account of other offers made to them, such as teaching in rural schools. However, considering the poor pay in such competing occupations and the rising wages of and growing demand for skilled artisans, one cannot help reaching the conclusion that the Negro industrial schools are not yet meeting the demands of modern industry.

Section 34.   The Economic Future of the Negro American

What are the questions in the present problem of the economic status of the Negro American? They may be summed up in four groups:

1. The relation of the Negro to city and country.
2. The relation of the Negro to group and national economy.
3. The influence of race prejudice.
4. The question of efficiency.

City and Country

A fact of great importance in regard to the economic conditions of the Negro American is his cityward movement. According to the Thirteenth Census 2,689,229 or 27.3 per cent of the Negroes in the United States lived in urban centers in 1910, a decided increase over 1900. The cityward movement of the Negro is explained by: [1]

1. The divorce of the Negro from the soil.
2. The trend of the Negro to industrial and commercial centers.
3. Secondary or individual causes:
   (a) Attractiveness of urban centers.
   (b) Labor legislation.
   (c) Desire for economic improvement.
   (d) Family relationships.
   (e) Desire to escape from restrictive and oppressive legislation and social customs.

This means an intensifying of the urban economic problem. This group of 2,689,229 town Negroes presents preeminently all of the economic problems outside of those connected with land holding and agriculture.

Moreover, the city Negroes include more than a third of the intelligent Negroes of the United States and have a rate of illiteracy of probably less than 25 per cent. Unquestionably it is in the city that the more intricate problems of economic life and race contact are going to be fought out. On the other hand, the very presence of seven million Negroes in the country districts makes the economic problem there, tho simple in quality, of tremendous proportions in quantity and of added significance when we see how the country is feeding the city problems.

Group Economy and National Economy

Present conditions show that while the force of competition from without is of tremendous economic importance in the economic development of the Negro American it is by no means final. In an isolated country the industry of the inhabitants can be supported and developed by means of a protecting tariff until the country is able to enter into international trade with fully developed resources; that a similar thing can be accomplisht in a group not wholly isolated but living scattered among more numerous and richer neighbors is often forgotten. There is therefore a double question in

---

[1] See Haynes, G. E. The Negro at Work in New York City, pp. 13-44.

regard to the Negro's economic advance.   The first question is: How far is the Negro likely to gain a foothold as one of the economic factors in the nation's industrial organization? The second is: How far can the Negro develop a group economy which will so break the force of race prejudice that his right and ability to enter the national economy are assured?

Race Prejudice

Race prejudice, more than any other single factor, retards the Negroes' development in the economic world.   Outside of all question of ability an American of Negro descent will find more or less concerted effort on the part of his white neighbors:

(1) To keep him from all positions of authority.
(2) To prevent his promotion to higher grades.
(3) To exclude him entirely from certain lines of industry.
(4) To prevent him from competing upon equal terms with white workingmen.
(5) To prevent his buying land.
(6) To prevent his defence of his economic rights and status by the ballot.

Efforts in these directions have been prest with varying degrees of emphasis and have had varying degrees of success. Yet they must all be taken into account in any economic study of the Negro American.   Strikes have repeatedly occurred against Negro firemen, of whose ability there was no complaint.   The white office boy, errand boy, section hand, locomotive fireman all have before them the chance to become clerk or manager or to rise in railway service.   The Negro has few such openings.   Fully half of the trade unions in the United States, counted by numerical strength, exclude Negroes from membership and thus usually prevent them from working at the trade.   Another fourth of the unions while admitting a few black men here and there practically exclude most of them.   In only a few unions, mostly unskilled, is the Negro welcomed, as in the case of the miners. In a few others the economic foothold of the Negro has been good enough to prevent his expulsion, as in some of the building trades. Agitation to prevent the selling of land to Negroes has for a long time been evident over large districts of the South and is still spreading. In an Atlanta campaign in the not far distant past the most telling cartoon for the influence of white voters was one which represented the house of a particular candidate in process of erection by black men. The black vote was of course disfranchised in this contest, as it is in a large part of the South.

Negro Efficiency

The last element in the economic condition of the Negro is the great question of efficiency. How efficient a laborer is the Negro and how efficient can he become with intelligent technical training and encouragement? That the average Negro laborer today is less efficient than the average European laborer is certain. When, however, you take into account the Negro's past industrial training, his present ignorance, and the social atmosphere in which he works it is not exactly fair to condemn him nor is it easy to say offhand what is his possible worth. Certainly increasing intelligence has made him increasingly discontented with his conditions of work; the determined withdrawing of responsibility from the Negro has not increased his sense of responsibility; the systematic exploitation of black labor has decreased its steadiness and reliability. Notwithstanding all this there never were before in the world's history so many black men steadily engaged in common and skilled labor as in the case of the American Negro. Nor is there today a laboring force which seems capable, under judicious guidance, of more remarkable development.

Economic Groups

The Negroes of America may be divided into three distinct economic groups:

(1) The independents farmers, teachers, clergymen, merchants and professional men and women.

(2) The struggling artisans, industrial helpers, servants and farm tenants.

(3) The common laborers.

The Independents

The independents number possibly 300,000 Negroes and include 225,000 farmers, 25,000 teachers, 17,000 clergymen, 15,000 merchants and numbers of professional men and women of various sorts. They are separated sharply into a rural group of farmers and an urban group and are characterized by the fact that with few exceptions they live by an economic service done their own people. This is least true in regard to the farmers but even in their case it is approximately true, for they, to an increasingly large degree, raise their own supplies and use their produce as a surplus crop. Usually thru this alone do they come into national economy. This group is the one that feels the force of outward competition and prejudice least in its economic life and most in its spiritual life. It is the head and front of the group economy movement, comprehends the spiritual as well as the economic leaders and is bound in the future to have a large and important development, limited only by the ability of the race to support it. However, in some respects this group is truly vulnerable. Many of the teachers, for instance, depend upon educational boards elected by white voters and many depend upon philanthropy. There has been concerted action in some of the rural districts of the South to drive out the best Negro teachers and even in the cities the way of the independent black teacher who dares think his own thots is made difficult. In many cases Negro teachers under the great philanthropic foundations are being continually warned that their bread and butter depend on their agreeing with present public opinion in regard to the Negro. There is growing up however, silently, almost unnoticed, a distinct Negro private school system officered, taught, attended and supported by Negroes. Such private schools have today at least 30,000 pupils and are growing rapidly—another example of group economy as produced by the Negro American.

If we regard exclusively the urban group of these independents we find that the best class of this group is fully abreast in education and morality with the great middle class of Americans. They have furnisht notable names in literature, business and professional life and have repeatedly in Boston, New York, Philadelphia, Chicago, Washington and other great urban centers proved their right to be treated as American citizens on a plane of perfect equality with other citizens. Despite this fact and despite the fact, too, that this group is numerically small and without much inherited wealth, it has been struggling under two overwhelming burdens: First, upon this group has been laid the duty and responsibility of the care, guidance and reformation of the great stream of black rural immigrants from the South simply because they happen to be of the same race. There is no claim or vestige of a claim that this small city group of risen Negroes is responsible for the degradation of the plantation, yet upon this small group the great work is placed. In the case of other immigrants to our urban centers, each race must care for its own and be responsible for its advancement, but the helpers are given all aid and sympathy in their undertakings and their hands are upheld. In the case of the Negro however, every disability, every legal, social and economic bar placed before the new immigrant must be endured by the city group on whom the immigrants have been dumped. And that group must be judged continually by the worst class of those very immigrants whose uplift is calmly shifted by the city at large.

What is the result? The talented tenth is submerged under the wave of immigration. And this is the second burden under which the group has labored. This has been the experience in many cities of the North. In the South, however, the beating back of the leading group has not awaited the excuse of immigration. On the general ground of impudence or indolence members of this class of economic and social leaders have been repeatedly driven out of the smaller towns, while in the larger cities every possible combination and tool from the Jim Crow laws to the secret society and the boycott has been made time and time again to curtail the economic advantages of the members of this class and to make their daily life so intolerable that they would either leave or sink to listless acquiescence.

What then, in view of these conditions, can this town group do in self defence? It can organize the Negroes about it into a self supplying group. This organization is actually going on. So far has it gone that in cities like Washington, Richmond and Atlanta a Negro family which does not employ a Negro physician is in danger of social ostracism; in the North this is extending to grocery stores and similar businesses. Whereas only a few years ago Negroes transacted insurance business with white companies, today more than half of that business has passed to black companies.

There are persons who see nothing but the advantages of this course. But it has grave disadvantages, too. It intensifies prejudice and bitterness. For example: White insurance agents and collectors in the South, for fear of white opinion, would not take off their hats when they entered Negro homes. The black companies have harpt on this, publisht it, called attention to it and actually capitalized it into cold cash. Again, this movement narrows the activity of the best class of Negroes, withdraws them from much helpful competition and contact, perverts and cheapens their ideals—in fact provincializes them in thot and deed. Yet it is today the only path of economic escape for the most gifted class of black men and the development along this line is certain to be enormous.

Turning to the rural group of this independent class the Negro land owners are to be considered. Here first one runs against one of those traditional statements which pass for truth because unchallenged, namely, that it is easy for the southern Negro to buy land. The letter of this statement is true but the spirit of it is false. There are vast tracts of land in the South that anybody, black or white, can buy for little or nothing for the simple reason that such tracts are worth little or nothing. Eventually these lands will become valuable. But they are almost valueless today. For the Negro, land to be of any value must have present value for he is too poor to wait. Moreover it must be

1. Land which he knows how to cultivate.
2. Land accessible to a market.
3. Land so situated as to afford the owner protection.

There are certain crops which the Negro farmer knows how to cultivate; to these can be added certain food supplies. Gradually intensive cultivation can be taught but this takes a long time. It is idle to compare the South with Belgium or France for the agricultural economy of those lands is the result of centuries of training aided by a rising market and by law and order, while the present agricultural economy of the South is but a generation removed from the land murder of a slave regime. No graduate of that school knows how to make the desert blossom as the rose and the process of teaching must be long and tedious. Meantime he must live on such crops as he knows how to cultivate. In addition to the poverty of the soil, bad roads, comparatively few railroads and few navigable rivers throw much of this land out of usefulness. But even more important than all this: the Negro farmer must seek the protection of community life with his own people and this he finds in the black belt. It is precisely in this black belt, however, that it is most difficult for him to buy land. For there it is that the capitalistic culture of cotton with a system of labor peonage is so profitable that land is high. In addition, in many of these regions it is considered bad policy to sell land to Negroes because a fever of land owning "demoralizes" the labor system; so that in the densest black belt of the South the percentage of land holding among Negroes is alarmingly low, a fact that has led to curious moralizing on the shiftlessness of black men.

The increase of the average size of farms in many parts of the South is illustrative of the astounding and dangerous concentration of land holding in that section which is itself more appalling when it is noted that many of these farms do not belong singly to single owners but are owned in groups of as high as forty or fifty by great landed proprietors. Many of these landed proprietors refuse to sell a single acre of land to black men. While there are of course large regions where black men can buy land on reasonable terms, it is usually land poorly situated as regards markets, or unhealthful in climate, or so placed as to afford the owners poor schools and lawless, overbearing white neighbors.

Add to these facts the results of the training and the character of the Negro farmers. Black farmers are often discust and criticised as tho they were responsible, trained men who carelessly and viciously neglect their economic opportunity. On the contrary they are for the most part unlettered men, consciously and carefully trained to irresponsibility, to whom all concepts of modern property and saving are new and who need benevolent guardianship in their upward striving. Such guardianship they have in some cases received from former masters and in this way a considerable number of the present land owners first got their land. In the great majority of cases however, this guardianship has consisted in deliberately taking the earnings of the Negro farmer and appropriating them to the use of the landlord. The argument was this: "These Negroes do not need this money. If I give it to them they'll squander it or leave the plantation; therefore I will give them just enough to be happy and keep them with me. In any case their labor rightfully belongs to me and my fathers and was illegally taken from us." On the strength of this argument and by such practices it is a conservative estimate to say that three-fourths of the stipulated wages and shares of crops which the Negro has earned on the farm since emancipation has been illegally withheld from him by the white landlords, either on the plea that this was for his own good or without any plea at all.

Would this wealth have been wasted if given the laborer? Waiving the mere question of the right of any employer to withhold wages, take the purely economic question: Is the community richer by such practices? It is not. The South is poorer. The best Negroes would have squandered much at first and most would have squandered all, but this would have been more than offset by the increased responsibility and efficiency of the resulting Negro landholders. Nor is this mere pious opinion. There is in the South in the middle of the black belt, a county of some 700 square miles, Lowndes County, Alabama. It contained in 1910 28,125 Negroes and 3,769 whites. It was formerly the seat of the most strenuous type of American slavery—with absentee owners, living at ease in Montgomery, great stretches of plantations with 500 to 1000 slaves on each driven by overseers and riders. There was no communication with the outside world, little passing between plantations. The Negroes were slothful and ignorant—even today, fifty years after emancipation, the illiteracy among those over ten is about 51 per cent. It would be difficult to find a place where conditions were on the whole more unfavorable to the rise of the Negro. The white element was lawless, the Negroes thoroly cowed, and up until recent times the body of a dead Negro did not even call for an arrest. In this county during the last twenty years there has been carried on a scheme of co-operative land buying under the Calhoun School. It was asked for by a few Negroes who could not get land; it was engineered by a Negro graduate of Hampton; it was made possible by the willingness of a white landlord to sell his plantation and actively further the enterprise by advice and good will. It was capitalized by white northerners and inspired by a New England woman. Here was every element in partnership and the experiment began in 1892. It encountered all sorts of difficulties: the character and training of the men involved; the enmity of the surrounding white population with a few notable exceptions; the natural suspicion of the black population born of a regime of cheating; the low price of cotton; several years of alternate flood and drouth; and the attempts of the neighboring whites to secure the homesteads thru mortgages.

The twentieth annual report of the Principal of the Calhoun Colored School of Calhoun, Lowndes County, Alabama, says:

While in 1892 the majority of the people lived in rented one-room cabins, now by far the larger number are in cottages of from two to four rooms and in some cases as many as six to eight rooms. Many of these cottages were put up and are owned by the Negro occupants on land they have bot thru the school.

The improvements have come slowly and by daily almost imperceptible growth, but just as truly have they come to stay and to increase. . . . . All the land the school had for sale near its own locality has been bot by the Negroes. Several men have this year finisht their payments on land and on houses, and have paid in full the mortgages they were under. Only a few men have still a debt remaining before they can really say, "These are our own homes." In several instances a man has sold a few acres of his land to lessen the debt upon the whole, and this is a double help. It reduces his financial burden and forces him into more intensive farming.

Not only from an economic point of view but from the standpoint of the sociologist as well the experiment here in Lowndes County has been both interesting and successful. The Negroes call it the "Free Land." There are no overseers and riders roaming about whipping the workers and seducing black wives and daughters; there is an eight months' school in their midst, a pretty new church, monthly conferences, a peculiar system of self government, and a family life of high moral tone.

What has been done in Lowndes County under the Calhoun School and the sensible guardianship of its wise leaders could be duplicated in every single black belt county in the South. It is to be hoped that such will be done and on that hope is based one's faith in the economic future of this black rural group.

The Struggling

The second great economic group among the Negroes of America may be called "the struggling." It includes the artisans, the industrial helpers, the servants and the farm tenants. This group is characterized as follows:

1. It is sharply divided into a city and a country group.

2. While it has a large significance in the group economy of the Negro American, its overwhelming significance is for the industry of the nation as a whole.

3. Its great hindrance is the necessity of group substitution in the place of individual promotion.

4. Its greatest enemy is the organized opposition of its white fellow workmen.

The rural group of this class of Negro Americans consists of farm tenants. In a large number of cases farm tenancy has been an aid to land buying; in many cases farm tenancy has been a school of thrift and saving; in the majority of cases it was the only available system after the war when the Negroes were set free without landed possessions of their own. Yet, when all this is said, it remains true that the system of farm tenancy as practiced over the larger part of the South today is a direct encouragement to cheating and peonage, a means of debauching labor, and a feeder of crime and vagrancy. It demands for its support a system of mortgage and contract laws and a method of administration which are a disgrace to twentieth century civilization. For every man whom the system has helped into independence it has pushed ten back into virtual slavery. It is often claimed that honest and benevolent employers and landholders have made this system a means of uplift, development and growth. In thousands of cases this is perfectly true; but at the same time it remains true and terribly true that any system of free labor where the returns of the laborer, the settlement of all disputes, the drawing of the contract, the determination of the rent, the expenditure of the employees or tenants, the price they pay for living, the character of the houses they live in, and their movements during and after their work are left practically to the unquestionable power of one man who owns the land and profits by the labor and who is in the exercise of his power practically unrestrained by public opinion or the courts and who has no fear of ballots in the hands of the laborers or their friends—any such system is inherently wrong. If men complain of its results being shiftlessness, listlessness and crime, they have themselves to thank. To the man who declares that he is acting justly and treating his tenants and employees even better than they treat themselves, it is sufficient answer to say that he is an exception to the rule; that the majority of the landholders are as indifferent to the welfare of their men as are employers the world over; and that a deplorably large minority consciously oppress and cheat them. The best employer or landholder suffers therefore for the sins of the average.

The only salvation for these Negro tenants lies in landholding, and in this the Negroes have made commendable strides. In 1890 Negro Americans owned 120,738 farms; in 1900 they owned 187,799 farms; in 1910 they owned about 220,000 farms, an increase of over 82 per cent. If the Negroes thruout the whole of the rural South had been encouraged by such wise economic leadership as was the case in Lowndes County, Alabama, referred to above, the record would be even more encouraging.

The city group of this class of Negro workers consists of perhaps 130,000 skilled artisans, 600,000 semi-skilled and ordinary industrial helpers, and 500,000 servants. The servant class has lost most of its best representatives because it offers a narrower and narrower method of uplift. This is due in part to foreign competition and in part to the fact that the temptations to Negro girls in domestic service are greater than in any single industry. It must be remembered that the mulatto is the product of house service in the South.

With the skilled and semi-skilled Negroes the industrial history has been this: Groups of Negroes have been excluded entirely from certain trades and admitted to others. Unfortunately they have been able to hold their place in the second set by working for lower wages, tho in certain industries they have forced themselves without resorting to the lever of low wages. This gave the trade unions a chance to fight Negroes as scabs. In some battles the unions won and so continued to exclude Negroes. In other cases the Negroes won and were admitted to the unions. Even in the union, however, they have been and are today discriminated against in many cases. In the near future the members of this class of Negro workingmen are going to have the struggle of their lives and the outlook indicates that by the fulcrum of low wages and the group economy, coupled with increasing efficiency, they will win. This means that the Negro is to be admitted to the national economy only by degrading labor conditions.

The alternative offered is shameful and could be easily avoided if color prejudice did not insist upon group substitution for Negroes in industry. That is, under present conditions a single individual or a few men of Negro descent cannot usually gain admittance to an industry. Only when they can produce workmen enough to supply the whole industry or the particular enterprise can the black man be admitted. Then immediately this substitution is made the occasion of a change in labor conditions—lower wages, longer hours and worse treatment. It thus often happens that by refusing to work beside a single black man, the workmen in an industry suffer a general lowering of wages and working conditions. The real economic question in the South is: How long will race prejudice supply a more powerful motive to white working-men of the South than decent wages and industrial conditions? Today the powerful threat of Negro labor is making child labor and the fourteen-hour day possible in southern factories. How long will it be before the white workingmen of the South discover that the interests that bind them to their black brothers are greater than those that artificially separate them? The answer is easy: That discovery will not be made until the present wave of extraordinary prosperity and exploitation passes and the ordinary every day level of economic struggle begins. If the Negro can hold his own until then his development is certain.

The Common Laborers

The third distinct economic group of American Negroes is the group of common laborers numbering more than two millions. A million and a quarter are farm laborers and the remainder are common laborers of other sorts. This group includes half the breadwinners of the race and its condition is precarious. In many of the country districts of the South the laws concerning contracts, wages and vagrancy are continually forcing the lower half of these laborers into pauperism and crime. In most of the southern states the law concerning the breaking of a contract to work made between an ignorant farm hand and a land owner and covering a year's time is enforced to the letter and the breaking of such a contract by the laborer is a penitentiary offense.   A large proportion of the homicides in the country districts of the South in which Negroes are the slayers or the victims arise from disputes over wage settlement.   So intolerable has the condition of the farm laborer of the South become, that he is running away from the country and entering the cities, there to add to the already complex problems of city life.   One frequently hears the demand for immigrants to fill the places of these fleeing Negro farm hands.   Notwithstanding all efforts in this direction it is safe to say that no group of immigrants will stand the present contract and crop lien system.   Certain it is that they will not stand the lawlessness of the average country district of the South where every white man is a law unto himself and where no Negro has any rights which the worst white man is bound to respect.   So bad has this lawlessness become in some parts of the South that concerted and commendable action has been taken against white cappers and night riders and a few peonage cases have reached the courts.   These efforts, however, have but scratched the surface of the real trouble—a trouble which lies deep-seated in the social fabric of the South, a trouble which so seriously retards the whole South in its economic advancement and development.

On the whole there are four general cures for the economic submersion of this class of Negro Americans.   First, the classes above must be given every facility to rise so as not to bear down upon them from above.   Secondly, the system of law and law courts in the South by which it is practically impossible in the country districts and improbable even in the cities for a black laborer to force justice from a white employer must be changed.   Thirdly, Negro children must be given common school training.   The states are not doing their duty in this respect and the tendency in some of them is to do less. [1]

---

[1] See Atlanta University Publication, No. 16, The Common School and the Negro American.

Finally, the black laborer must have a vote. It is impossible for these two million and more black workingmen to maintain themselves when thrust into modern competitive industry so long as the state allows them no voice or influence in the making of the laws or the interpretation and administration of the same.

The value of land and buildings owned by Negroes in the South in 1910 was $272,992,238, an increase of nearly 90 per cent in a single decade. This does not include land owned by Negro farmers and rented out. On a basis of the value of farm property the total Negro wealth today may be estimated at $570,000,000. Yet in much of the South the holders of this wealth are as absolutely disfranchised as the worst criminal in the penitentiary. They cannot say a word as to the condition of the roads and highways which pass their property, or as to the location or supervision of their schools or the choice of teachers, or as to the selection of the government officials or the fixing of the rate of taxation.

Summary

Half the Negro breadwinners of the nation are partially submerged by a bad economic system, an unjust administration of the laws, and enforced ignorance. Their future depends on common schools, justice, and the right to vote. A million and three-quarters of men just above these are fighting a fierce battle for admission to the industrial ranks of the nation—for the right to work. They are handicapped by their own industrial history which has made them often shiftless and untrustworthy; but they can, by means of wise economic leadership, be made a strong body of artisans and land owners. Three hundred thousand men stand economically at the head of the Negroes, and by a peculiar self protecting group economy are making themselves independent of prejudice and competition.

What can be said of any one of these groups of black working men can be said of them all. *In so far as they are given opportunity and assured justice, in so far can the world expect from them the maximum of efficiency and service.*

Index

The Atlanta University Publications, No. 18

MORALS AND MANNERS

AMONG

NEGRO AMERICANS

Report of a Social Study made by Atlanta University under the patronage of the Trustees of the John F. Slater Fund; with the Proceedings of the 18th Annual Conference for the Study of the Negro Problems, held at Atlanta University, on Monday, May 26th, 1913

Edited by

W. E. Burghardt DuBois, Ph.D.
Director of Publicity and Research, National Association for
the Advancement of Colored People

and

Augustus Granville Dill, A.M.
Some time Associate Professor of Sociology in Atlanta University

The Atlanta University Press
ATLANTA, GA.
1914

A T any rate, we must depend for the peace and progress of the world upon the formation of a horizontal upper layer of cultured persons among all the more civilized peoples—a cross-section, as it were, of the nations, whose convictions and sentiments shall supply the moral force on which international arbitration courts and similar agencies will have to depend.

—*Felix Adler*

Morals and Manners among Negro Americans

Contents

The Eighteenth Annual Conference

"Morality and Religion among Negro Americans"

PROGRAM

First Session, 10:00 a. m.

President Ware presiding.

Subject: "Social Service and the School."

"Methods of the Present Investigation." Mr. A. G. Dill, of Atlanta University.

Address: Prof. L. H. Williams, of Macon, Ga.

Address: Dr. W. E. B. DuBois, of New York City.

Second Session 11:30 a. m.

Subject: "Health and Service." (Separate meetings for men and women.)

Address to men: Dr. Loring B. Palmer, of Atlanta, Ga.

Address to women: Mrs. Dinah Watts Pace, of Covington, Ga.

Third Session, 3:00 p. m.

The Fifteenth Annual Mothers' Meeting. (In charge of Gate City Free Kindergarten Association.) Mrs. I. E. Wynn presiding.

Subject: "Social Service and the Child."

1. Kindergarten songs, games and exercises by one hundred and fifty children of the five free kindergartens.

    East Cain Street—Mrs. Ola Perry Cooke.

    Bradley Street—Miss Willie Kelly.

    White's Alley—Mrs. Idella F. Hardin.

    Presbyterian Mission—Miss Rosa Martin.

    Leonard Street Orphanage—Miss Sadie Anderson.

2. Symposium: Social Work among Children.

    Mrs. Ruth Greenwood Carey, Atlanta, Ga.

    Mrs. Dinah Watts Pace, Covington, Ga.

    Miss Lucy C. Laney, Augusta, Ga.

    Miss Amy Chadwick, Atlanta, Ga.

    Mrs. John Hope, Atlanta, Ga.

Fourth Session, 8:00 p. m.

President Ware presiding.

Subject: "Social Service and the Negro American."

Address: Miss Lucy C. Laney, of Augusta, Ga.

Music.

Address: Dr. W. E. B. DuBois, of New York City.

Discussion.

Preface

There is only one sure basis of social reform and that is Truth — a careful, detailed knowledge of the essential facts of each social problem. Without this there is no logical starting place for reform and uplift. Social difficulties may be clear and we may inveigh against them, but the causes proximate and remote are seldom clear to the casual observer and usually are quite hidden from the man who suffers from, or is sensitive to, the results of the snarl.

To no set of problems are these truths more applicable than to the so-called Negro problems.

One of the most fundamental of these problems is that of the manners of the Negro race. On this question the most diverse and contradictory opinions are confidently exprest, leaving the real inquirer for truth in great bewilderment.

There is without a doubt a deep-seated feeling in the minds of many that the Negro problem is primarily a matter of morals and manners and that the real basis of color prejudice in America is the fact that the Negroes as a race are rude and thotless in manners and altogether quite hopeless in sexual morals, in regard for property rights and in reverence for truth.

This accusation, which has been repeated for decades, is the more easily made because manners and morals lend themselves but seldom to exact measurement. Consequently, general impressions, limited observations and wild gossip supply the usual data; and these make it extremely difficult to weigh the evidence and to answer the charge.

This study is an attempt to collect opinion on the general subject of morals and manners among Negro Americans from those who ought to know. It is by no means complete or definitive, but it is to some degree enlightening.

The first attempt to study the moral status of the Negro was made in 1903, the results of the study appearing as No. 8 of the Atlanta University Publications, bearing as its title "The Negro Church". The present study goes over a part of this ground after an interval of ten years.

The study is, therefore, a further carrying out of the plan of social study of the Negro American, by means of an annual series of decennially recurring subjects covering, so far as is practicable, every phase of human life. This plan originated at Atlanta University in 1896. The object of these studies is primarily scientific—a careful research for truth; conducted as thoroly, broadly and honestly as the material resources and mental equipment at command will allow. It must be remembered that mathematical accuracy in these studies is impossible; the sources of information are of varying degrees of accuracy and the pictures are wofully incomplete. There is necessarily much repetition in the successive studies, and some contradiction of previous reports by later ones as new material comes to hand. All we claim is that the work is as thoro as circumstances permit and that with all its obvious limitations it is well worth the doing. Our object is not simply to serve science. We wish not only to make the truth clear but to present it in such shape as will encourage and help social reform. In this work we have received unusual encouragment from the scientific world, and the publisht results of these studies are used in America, Europe, Asia and Africa. Very few books on the Negro problem, or any phase of it, have been publisht in the last decade which have not acknowledged their indebtedness to our work.

We believe that this pioneer work in a wide and important social field deserves adequate support. The Trustees of the John F. Slater Fund have given us generous aid in the last six years, which aid has been supplemented by the general funds of the University. These latter funds are limited, however, and needed in many other directions. What we earnestly ask is an endowment for this research work. A fund yielding $5,000 a year might under proper supervision yield incalculable good and help the nation and the modern world to a righteous solution of its problems of racial contact.

Resolutions

The following resolutions are the expression of the members, delegates and attendants upon the sessions of the eighteenth annual Conference:

The eighteenth Atlanta Conference has reviewed the moral and religious condition of the American Negroes and its changes during the last decade. It finds a decided strengthening of the home life, a betterment in the habits of courtesy, cleanliness and thrift and a wider conformity to the rules of modern morality. The Conference finds two great hindrances still in the path of advance: the persistence of older habits due to slavery and poverty and racial prejudice. It is not to be expected that a people whose original morality had been wholly destroyed by slavery and but partially replaced should not show in a single generation of freedom many marks of the past in sexual irregularity, waste, irresponsibility and criminal tendencies. The Conference finds that much has been done in the last decade to improve these habits; and that much more could be done if racial prejudice did not operate to leave colored women unprotected in law and custom, to invade colored residence districts with vice and bad sanitary conditions and to degrade and make inefficient the Negro public school system. We regard it as the burning shame of the decade that of three and a half millions of colored children of school age two millions were not even enrolled in school last year.

The Conference is glad to note in the Negro church some signs of awakening to new duties and larger responsibilities. New institutional work of social uplift is appearing here and there under trained men. The majority of Negro churches remain however financial institutions catering to a doubtful round of semi-social activities. The Negro church must, if it survives, adopt a new attitude towards rational amusement and sound moral habits.

The Conference is pleased to call the attention of the country to the fact that much of the real work of social uplift and moral awakening is being carried on by Negro women in their clubs and institutions. No group of women in the world have amid studied insult and race discrimination made so brave a fight for social betterment or accomplisht so much of actual, tangible good.

The hope of the future in moral uplift lies in thoro common school training for Negro children, respect and protection for Negro women, widened industrial opportunity for Negro men and systematic effort to lessen race prejudice.

(Signed)

W. E. B. DuBois, New York, N. Y.
L. H. Williams, Macon, Ga.
A. G. Dill, Atlanta, Ga.

A Select Bibliography

Arranged alphabetically by authors

American Academy of Political and Social Science:
The Negro's Progress in Fifty Years. Philadelphia, 1913. 244 pp.

Atlanta University Publications:
No. 9. Notes on Negro Crime, particularly in Georgia. 1904. 68 pp.
No. 12. Economic Co-operation among Negro Americans. 1907. 184 pp.
No. 13. The Negro American Family. 1908. 152 pp.
No. 14. Efforts for Social Betterment among Negro Americans. 1909. 136 pp.
No. 15. The College-bred Negro American. 1910. 104 pp.
No. 16. The Common School and the Negro American. 1911. 140 pp.
No. 17. The Negro American Artisan. 1912. 144 pp.

Autobiography of an Ex-Colored Man. Anonymous. Boston, 1912. 207 pp.

Baker, Ray Stannard. Following the Color-Line. New York, 1908. 314 pp.

Barnes, Albert. The Church and Slavery (with Appendix). Philadelphia, 1857. 204 pp.

Blyden, Edward Wilmot. Christianity, Islam and the Negro Race. Introduced by Samuel Lewis, London, 1887 (4) VII (1) 423 pp.

Boas, Franz. Commencement Address at Atlanta University, May, 1906. Atlanta University Leaflet, No. 19. 15 pp.
The Mind of Primitive Man. New York, 1911. 294 pp.

Brawley, B. G. A Short History of the American Negro. New York, 1913. 242 pp.

Crawford, Daniel. Thinking Black. New York, 1913. 16,485, 17 pp.

Crisis, The. Organ of the National Association for the Advancement of Colored People. New York, 1910, et seq.

Crummell, Alexander. A Defense of the Negro Race in America, etc. Washington, 1883. 36 pp.

Douglass, H. Paul. Christian Reconstruction in the South. Boston, 1909. 407 pp.

Du Bois, W. E. B. The Philadelphia Negro. Philadelphia, 1896. 520 pp.
The Quest of the Silver Fleece. Chicago, 1911. 434 pp.
Souls of Black Folk. Chicago, 1903. 264 (1) pp.

Dunbar, Paul Lawrence. The Sport of the Gods. New York, 1901.

Ferris, William H. The African Abroad. 2 Vols. New Haven, 1913.

Hare, Maud Cuney. Norris Wright Cuney. New York, 1913. 230 pp.

Hartshorn, W. N. An Era of Progress and Promise. Boston, 1910. 576 pp.

Haynes, George Edmund. The Negro at Work in New York City. New York, 1912. 158 pp.

Johnston, Sir Harry. Negro in the New World. New York, 1910. 499 pp.

Krehbiel, H. E., Editor. Afro-American Folksongs. New York and London, 1914. 176 pp.

Laidlaw, Walter, Editor. The Federation of Churches and Christian Workers in New York City, N. Y.
   Sociological Canvasses 1896, First, 112 pp. Second, 116 pp.

Miller, Kelly. Race Adjustment. New York and Washington, 1908. 316 pp.

Negro Young People's Christian and Educational Congress. The United Negro. Atlanta, 1902. 600 pp.

Ovington, M. W. Half-a-Man. New York, 1911. 236 pp.
   Hazel. New York, 1913. 162 pp.

Spiller, G., Editor. Inter-Racial Problems. London, July, 1911. 485 pp.

Stewart, William and T. G. Gouldtown. Philadelphia, 1913. 237 pp.

United States Census. Vol. on Churches, 1904.
   Thirteenth Census, 1910.

Washington, B. T. and Du Bois, W. E. B. The Negro in the South. Philadelphia, 1907. 222 pp.

Williams, George W. History of the Negro Race in America from 1619 to 1880. New York, 1883. 2 Vols.

Wright, R. R., Jr. The Negro in Pennsylvania. Philadelphia, 1912. 250 pp.

Morals and Manners among Negro Americans

Section 1. Scope of the Inquiry

The results of the eighth annual social study of the Negro American were publisht as "The Negro Church". The largest volume yet issued by the Conference, it was an historical and institutional inquiry into the moral and religious condition of Negro Americans. The historical and institutional phase of the subject does not as yet call for further investigation. On the other hand, one section of the report, the moral status of Negroes, is a large field for inquiry. The problem before the social investigator is this: How can such an inquiry be made scientifically? The chief sources which suggest themselves for such an inquiry are birth statistics, crime statistics, and statistics of religious bodies. All of these we have endeavored to find, but there are comparatively few available. Birth statistics are not kept in the localities where the masses of Negroes live, save in the District of Columbia. Crime statistics are too general and too much mingled with extra-moral causes and motives to be trustworthy. In this connection we have used the report issued in 1904 by the Department of the Census. The statistics of religious bodies from the same source have seemed sufficient for our purposes, since the later figures reported by the churches are liable to exaggeration.

The reports of the Department of the Census served as a basis for the following studies made by the members of the class in Sociology in Atlanta University:

Negro Americans in the United States.

The Negro American Farmer.

Marital Conditions among Negro Americans.

Religious Bodies among Negro Americans.

Using the following questionnaire, the class also made an intensive study of:

The Negro Church in Atlanta, Georgia.

1. City—Atlanta.   State—Georgia
2. Name and denomination of church.
3. Location.
4. Name of pastor.
    Address of pastor.
    Where educated.
5. Membership.   Number under twenty years of age.
6. What is the proportion between male and female members?
7. Value of church property.
8. Total expenditures of church last year.
    Amount expended for missions.
    Amount expended for education.
    Amount expended for buildings and repairs.
    Amount expended for charitable work.
9. What is the church doing along the following lines:
    Caring for old people.
    Encouraging young people.
    Holding to young men.
    Other social service.
10. Where does the church encounter its greatest difficulty?

Investigator . . . .

In addition to the above sources, the only, and in some respects the best, available material for the use of this investigation seemed to be the opinions of trustworthy persons in various parts of the United States who ought to know of the morals and manners of Negro Americans. Such a study was attempted in the use of the following questionnaire sent to interested persons thruout the United States:

1. City . . . .   State . . . . . .
2. What is the condition of colored people whom you know in regard to the following?
    (1) Good manners.
    (2) Sound morals.
    (3) Habits of cleanliness.
    (4) Personal Honesty.
    (5) Home life.
    (6) Rearing of children.
    (7) Wholesome amusement for young people.
    (8) Caring for old people.
3. What is the church doing along these lines?

4. How do present conditions in these respects compare with conditions ten (or twenty) years ago?

Name . . . .

Street Address . . . .

The questionnaire was sent to four thousand people residing in all parts of the country and engaged in all walks of life. Ten per cent of those questioned made replies to this questionnaire, the answers coming from thirty states and from persons classed under the following groups:

Preachers:
  Bishops (2)
  Presiding Elders (5)
  Ministers (125)
Teachers:
  Presidents of Colleges (1)
  Principals of Public Schools ⎰ (36)
  Principals of Private Schools ⎱
  Teachers in Public Schools ⎰ (80)
  Teachers in Private Schools ⎱
Social Workers:
  Y. M. C. A. Secretaries (7)
  Nurses (2)
Artisans:
  Contractors and Builders (5)
  Bricklayers (3)
  Tailors (3)
  Painters (4)
  Blacksmiths (4)
  Dressmakers (4)
  Cigar Manufacturers (1)
  Harness Makers (1)
  Stationary Engineers (1)
Professionals:
  Physicians (40)
  Dentists (14)
  Lawyers (7)
  Unclassified (40)

Section 2. The General Problem

When we consider the ten million American Negroes from the standpoint of their daily conduct and personal morality, what sort of folk are they? How far have they assimilated and presumably how far are they able to assimilate modern culture of the average kind?

Two elements would, to most minds, enter into the final answer to these questions: The general racial morality of the Negro and the social environment of the American Negro. The general racial morality of any great group is exceedingly difficult to determine, if indeed there is any such thing. The Negro race, like all great races, is, even in Africa, widely divergent in type, largely mixt with other races, and the result of widely differing influences of climate and contact. To speak of a single racial morality under such conditions is not to speak intelligently. We can, however, quote with advantage the judgment of competent and careful observers as to particular tribes and nations. A few such judgments are subjoined:

It is therefore by no means difficult to account for the deep impression made by the Niam-niam on the fantastic imagination of the Soudan Arabs. I have seen the wild Bishareen and other Bedouins of the Nubian Deserts; I have gazed with admiration upon the stately war-dress of the Abyssinians; I have been riveted with surprise at the supple forms of the mounted Baggara: but nowhere, in any part of Africa, have I ever come across a people that in every attitude and every motion exhibited so thoro a mastery over all the circumstances of war or of the chase as these Niam-niam. Other nations in comparison seemed to me to fall short in the perfect ease—I might almost say, in the dramatic grace—that characterized their every movement.[1]

The numerous skulls now in the Anatomical Museum in Berlin are simply the remains of their repasts which I purchased one after another for bits of copper, and go far to prove that the cannibalism of the Monbuttoo is unsurpassed by any nation in the world. But with it all, the Monbuttoo are a noble race of men; men who display a certain national pride, and are endowed with an intellect and judgment such as few natives of the African wilderness can boast; men to whom one may put a reasonable question, and who will return a reasonable answer. The Nubians can never say enough in praise of their faithfulness in friendly intercourse and of the order and stability of their national life. According to the Nubians, too, the Monbuttoo were their superiors in the arts of war, and I often heard the resident soldiers contending with their companions and saying, "Well, perhaps you are not afraid of the Mon-

---

[1]Schweinfurth: Heart of Africa, Vol. 2, p. 12.

buttoo, but I confess that I am; and I can tell you they are something
to be afraid of". [1]

Ratzel says: [2]

Agreeably to the natural relation the mother stands first among the
chief influences affecting the children. From the Zulus to the Waganda,
we find the mother the most influential counsellor at the court of ferocious sovereigns like Chaka or Mtesa; sometimes sisters take her place.
Thus even with chiefs who possess wives by hundreds the bonds of blood
are the strongest. The father is less closely bound up with the family.
He is indeed the head, and is recognized as such; it is said too that the
Negro is in general a lover of children and therefore a good father. But
even here he often rules more by force than by love. Among the institutions recalling Roman law which Hubbe-Schleiden, an expert on that
subject, found among the Mpongwes, he mentions their domestic or
family life: "We find among them the *patria potestas* equally comprehensive and equally strict, if not carried into such abstraction. Wives,
children, servants, are all in the power of the *pater-familias* or *oga*. He
alone is quite free; a degree of independence to which a woman among
the Mpongwes can never attain". Yet that woman, tho often
heavily burdened, is in herself in no small esteem among the Negroes is
clear from the numerous Negro queens, from the medicine-women, from
the participation in public meetings permitted to women by many Negro
peoples.

Sweinfurth says: [3]

Parental affection is developt among the Dyoor much more decidedly
than among the other tribes. A bond between mother and child which
lasts for life is the measure of affection shown among the Dyoor.

Parents (among the Dinkas) do not desert their children, nor are
brothers faithless to brothers, but are ever prompt to render whatever
aid is possible. Family affection is at a high ebb among them".

Miss Kingsley says: [4]

The House is a collection of individuals; I should hesitate to call it a
develovt family. I cannot say it is a collection of human beings,
because the very dogs and canoes and so on that belong to it are a part
of it in the eye of the law, and capable therefore alike of embroiling it
and advancing its interests. These Houses are bound together into
groups by the Long ju-ju proper to the so-called secret society, common
to the groups of houses. The House is presided over by what is called
in white parlance, a king, and beneath him there are four classes of

[1] Ibid, p. 94-95.
[2] Ratzel: History of Mankind.
[3] Sweinfurth: Heart of Africa.
[4] Kingsley: West African Studies, 2d ed., p. 365

human beings in regular rank, that is to say influence in council: firstly, the free relations of the king, if he be a free man himself, which is frequently not the case; if he be a slave, the free people of the family he is trustee for; secondly, the free small people who have placed themselves under the protection of the House, rendering it in return for the assistance and protection it affords them service on demand; the third and fourth classes are true slave classes, the higher one in rank being that called the Winnaboes or Trade boys, the lower the pull-away boys and plantation hands. The best point in it, as a system, is that it gives to the poorest boy who paddles an oil-canoe a chance of becoming a king.

Section 3.   The American Environment

The environment of the American Negro has not been in the past and is not today conducive to the development of the highest morality. There is upon him still the heritage of two hundred and fifty years of the slave regime. Slavery fosters certain virtues like humility and obedience, but these flourish at the terrible cost of lack of self-respect, shiftlessness, tale bearing, theft, slovenliness and sexual looseness.

Ignorance and poverty have been the greatest and most influential facts for the freedmen, and to these must be added the disadvantage of a strong caste system. The average Negro child must be educated in poor schools, if indeed in any school at all; he must grow up in an atmosphere where he can scarcely escape humiliation, contempt and personal insult; his chances for work are narrowly restricted; as a man he lives in a world limited by law and custom in such ways that he is liable to violent punishment for acts involving no moral turpitude or to excessive punishment for peccadillos. His general outlook on life is apt to be distorted by such surroundings and his tendency, if he is thotful, is to become surly in temper, or pessimistic or hypocritical. If he is careless he becomes more so and tends to shiftlessness and irresponsibility. The history and environment of the American Negro have brot their marked results.

Section 4.   Good Manners

We subjoin one hundred and twenty-three answers from twenty-nine states as to the manners and general courtesy of Negro Americans.

Alabama

The educated class of our people shows a certain degree of culture and refinement; but the masses do not. The latter need especially to be careful about their manners and general deportment in public places.

The manners of the colored people whom I know are fair. They are about as good as can be expected in the present state of intelligence. They often are rude, but mean well.

The manners of the majority of our people are very good and they are making improvement, of which we are very proud.

There are two distinct classes of colored people in Birmingham: (1) the mining class,—a very poor and ignorant set of miners; (2) the better class,—the people who own homes and are engaged in the professions and paying occupations. The manners of class (1) are sometimes rowdy in public places. The manners of class (2) are practically irreproachable.

As a whole their manners are not up to the standard, but this is due very largely to the lack of proper training. In cases where they have had the proper training they are as a rule very good.

The general manners of the colored people in the district where I preside is 75 per cent better now than what it was five years ago. It is the Tuscaloosa district and covers about 50 square miles of territory.

A few not unusually good—fair; a smaller number, good; a number by far greater than aggregate of other two classes, bad.

The majority of colored people of this vicinity have very good manners. They are very kind and courteous to each other and to strangers. They work to the advantage of each other.

Fairly good, can be a great deal better.

For uneducated people their manners are harmless enough.

All sorts of manners, from the best to the worst. The best educated have the best manners as a rule. On the whole they are better mannered than their white friends.

In the presence of whites timid, then obsequious; for the most part selfish with regard to themselves. Lack of ease due to restricted contact.

In most cases where the proper influences have been brot to bear and most especially where a thoro school training has been given the individual, my people exhibit remarkably good manners.

As a rule I find them very polite, but the rougher element, such as we find hanging around pool rooms and barber shops, is not so polite.

The happy, cheerful, care-free disposition of the Negro makes him at times seem loud and ill-mannered but this must be charged as often to his peculiarities as to persistent bad manners. One has only to note the courtesy and consideration shown to women in public places to become convinced that there is improvement in both the lettered and unlettered Negroes.

Good manners are inborn instincts in Negroes everywhere, especially in the South.

There are a number with very good manners but they are sadly in the minority. It seems not because they do not know good manners but rather that they prefer to be rude.

Arkansas

I cannot say that our young people are as careful as they might be, certainly not as much so as I would like.

Among the more enlightened and cultured the number of those who exhibit good manners is large. But there is a large class of careless, rude and coarse-mannered people yet untoucht by the influences of culture.

The manners are not what they should be.

Fair. There is room for a great deal of improvement.

California

Very much improved.

Connecticut

As time goes on they are improving along this line. Education and the refinement associated with it are doing their work well.

Among the lower element there is a real lack of good manners but among those of training, that is of ordinary training, there is a fine sense of fitness of things and conduct.

Delaware

Good.

District of Columbia

Generally good.

This varies with the social grade and opportunities for contact with cultured people. Judged by the American standard they are governed by fear of disapproval rather than by habits of regard for the presence and feeling of the other man, and are better mannered than a class of whites of a better economic condition. They imitate the bizarre and unusual rather than the spirit of social intercourse. They inquire for your health not because they appreciate the value of it but to be pleaseable. They remove their hats and bow to position and authority rather than to indicate conscious courtesy.

Not at all such as was to be expected, considering that manners should improve with the acquisition of knowledge. The lack of good manners among us supplies a cursed prejudice with a specious excuse for "Jim-Crowing" the race, and makes of the "Jim-Crow" a hell.

Excellent with a large majority of the people but very reprehensible with a great portion of the lower class.

Florida

Sixty per cent of them very poor. Perhaps have been instructed but not introduced into practice. Especially is this true of the young men.

We have gentlemanly and lady-like manners among the boys and girls that have attended our good schools. But there is much rudeness and even coarseness among the young ones who have not enjoyed, or rather have not availed themselves of, school privilege.

Compare favorably with the other race.

I think they are improving as they become more and more educated. Good speakers and leaders help our people very much. They are all eager to learn and improve their condition.

The people in general have very good manners as far as they really know, while there is room for improvement.

We have many that are fair, yet there are many who seem to know or care very little about good deportment.

With few exceptions manners very poor. Polite enough, but manners poor except very small minority. Young men as a rule have no respect for their girls but seek their down fall. They keep company with the lewd and best at one and the same time. They are boisterous and loud, they are given to clog dancing and the reel. They feel that they are privileged in every home on equal terms and will bloat if they are restrained from their street manners.

About as they are elsewhere. A shade better than average American who has a reputation for bad manners.

Georgia

The better class of people have very good manners and are still improving.

While the condition is not as general as desirable, yet there is progress toward good manners.

Good in many instances; majority exceeding poor. The tendency among the young (after going thru the 4th, 5th and 6th grades in city schools) is to live in the streets and their manners and street behavior are very, very bad. We might as well face the music, for here I think you have toucht a key that will make a very harsh note. Some of these young people come from the homes of parents that have good homes and fair surroundings and fair education, too.

In general the manners of the Negro are good when alone, but when in crowds he usually becomes boisterous, rough and impolite.

Great improvement. There have been wonderful changes during the last decade. The improvement is greatest among the young women.

I have an extensive acquaintance with all classes of colored people in the city of Atlanta. I think their general manners compare favorably with those of any people among whom I have lived.

There is much room for improvement along the line of good manners among the colored people, especially towards one another. Yet there are marks of improvement. Our young men and women do not seem to use as good manners towards one another as the older people.

The colored people of my acquaintance have about as good manners, if not a little better, than any other people of equal education and refinement.

Thoro manners are scarce among the colored people here. The percentage of forct manners, that is manners from a selfish standpoint, is somewhat greater. There is much need of improvement and the schools here are giving the subject more attention.

The colored people whom I know, as a rule, have very good manners. They are polite and respectful. Of course, there is a class who are not so polite and respectful, but the majority of the people have very good manners.

Illinois

It seems to me that we are losing our good manners in cities. Parents take too little time to train their children. The older folks are selfish and to a very large degree don't regard the feelings of people they don't know. There seems to be an effort to break away from the old ways.

I am inclined to think that the large city Negro suffers by comparison with the Negroes of the smaller populated cities and towns and the rural district. As to manners I am not sure the race is any improved by its education over the first generation removed from slavery.

Indiana

Fair. It must be admitted while the manners of our populace is fairly good there is room for vast improvement. Our bumptious Negro is ever present.

Kansas

Are lacking on account of false standard of morals. Much is being done to build a foundation for good manners.

Kentucky

Good when not molested.

I find much improvement, a steady growing better along this line. Good when restricted by fitting rules and regulations provided they are properly executed; otherwise uncouth.

The manners of many of our young people, particularly women from the ages of twenty-four to thirty-seven years of age are not just what they should be in regards to politeness.   They seem to forget what appreciation of small favors means.   "Thank you" is obsolete.

Need more culture.

Markt improvement during the last ten years, in public, especially. The schools in these parts have succeeded in supplying the training often neglected in the home.   The results both apparent and pleasing.

Not so good.   They need more training in that line.   Young people have not got the manners they should have.   They should be trained in the churches and in the schools.   Good manners will help us at any time and any place.

Louisiana

The great mass of Negroes possesses excellent manners, but you would be surprised to know that a goodly number of those who attend and finish school assume an air of importance and fail to look up to their superiors.

They are very generous in every stage of life so far as I have seen in business with quite a deal of them.

Manners are comparatively good.   I have always found them so, individually.   In crowds they are noisy but, as a rule, good natured.

Majority seem very polite.

Manners among our young boys and girls who are attending school and college are not what they should be.   Truthfully, there is room for improvement.

Sorry to admit but the average is poor here.

Maryland

They are improved wonderfully.

I find among people with whom I work no great lack of manners. As a rule they are kind, polite and respectful.

This phase of development of the Negro here is very good.   However, something must be done to touch the boys and girls along this line or we may have to soon change our statement.

Minnesota

The manners of the race here are good and compare favorably with those of the dominant race.

Mississippi

They are growing much better thruout this community, as our people educate themselves.

Negroes here are very well behaved.   I find them too ready to resent minor insults from one another while they calmly suffer any indignity or insult from whites,—possibly due to lack of protection before the law.

Missouri

Manners are good. Boisterousness and rowdyism are exceptional in public conveyances or in halls and on the streets.

I should think it might be called a result practiced by those who are educated to know and trained to practice the rules of good morals. Our people are gradually emerging from ignorance, thus the counteracting forces of good manners are gradually lessening.

St. Joseph, a city of possibly eighty thousand, has not more than four or five thousand Negroes. These are scattered over the city and there is no one street where the rough element congregates in large numbers. I would say the people are well mannered as a whole. Few are seen on the streets. They are admitted to public parks and receive courteous treatment.

Show markt improvement yet uncertain as to what constitutes same. Standard rising.

New Jersey

Among the older people fair to good. Among the youths rather below fair.

On par with the average American.

New York

Fairly good in this section of the state. Of course, the colored people here mostly, as to the number of them, came direct from the South here. They compare favorably with any others of any other race here.

Considerable carelessness, thotlessness as to manners but noticeable improvement constantly seen. Little viciousness, teachable with the jolly spirit so overflowing that it is difficult to get them to be seriously thotful. Spirit of reverence greatly lacking among the young people.

Generally good. Somewhat conceited.

The majority of the colored people whom I know have very good manners, especially toward strangers.

There are between 700 and 800 colored persons in the city of Troy sharply divided into two classes: The one made up almost wholly of members and adherents of the (colored) Presbyterian and A. M. E. Zion and of the various white churches. The other, non-church goers. About 300 of the former and 400 of the latter. Class A, good; class B, poor.

North Carolina

Are generally good among the colored people. Are very much improved. Their deportment is much better now than in the past.

A few have good manners but the greater number are rough and uncouth. This has been neglected in the homes by the parent. Politeness and refinement are lacking in the most of our young people. Respect for the aged and those in authority is not adhered to as it should be. We find one here and there with refinement, showing it in their daily deportment and life.

Improving. They have not reacht the stage of the most cultured as a mass but quite a number are refined. The masses need to be improved in this respect.

Our town is divided into two very distinct elements, viz., the factory and non-factory elements. The former is exceedingly good; while the latter would not get as high an averge their manners could not be considered bad.

Ohio

I would say that they are far in advance of many other races of people. In our city the condition is not one that gives us fear only on a few streets where the saloons are located.

The colored people here use good manners with one exception and that is a tendency toward boisterousness. I mean by this loud talking and laughing which seems to be a trait of character not yet overcome by culture.

Oklahoma

The truth and nothing but the truth:—There are a few who possess this grace. Every day I see the Bible is more and more true. We are truly living in the last days according to II Timothy, 3:1-17. Read St. Matthew, 7:13-14. "Few there be that find it".

There is, I think, a steady improvement. There seems to be a decrease in boisterous conduct.

They have improved 50 per cent over five years ago and I can candidly say that the condition of my people along the above line is very hopeful.

The manners of the Negroes of this community are not far below standard. Their street manners and conventional etiquette are fairly commendable.

Pennsylvania

I am living in the North for the first time. I am a Virginian by birth. The colored people of the North have not the good manners of the colored people of the South. Of course, there are exceptions to this rule.

The manners of the middle class are what one would expect from such a class. The lower strata are vulgar and loud and sometimes annoying.

Not very good except that quite a number imitate in a superficial manner the manners of the upstart white people.

The more cultured classes behave themselves like others in like situation and so with the less cultured.

I find the great majority with good manners.

Viewing the colored people of today from but two classes, viz., the upper and the lower, or the professional or laboring classes, I find myself inclined to believe that with the different social, and intellectual advantages at their respective doors, the laboring class exhibits a greater and a more pleasing degree of conventional good manners than the professional class, whose exhibition savors of a veneer.

Rhode Island

Boisterous manners from the class very recently from rural parts of the South. Among the best class the manners are typically New Englanders: formal, cold and precise.

South Carolina

A majority of young people are rude.

As a whole the colored people in this section of the country are very polite, charitable, sympathetic.

My impression respecting the matter of good manners among our people is that they are about the same as among other people of similar intellectual and social standing. While there are, of course, markt instances of the woeful lack of what are usually called good manners—and these make so profound an impression upon us that we are likely to note and remember them—there are many, a very great many, who are of polish and culture in these particulars; and those having a reasonable degree of these graces are in my opinion in the large majority.

Among some very good. Among a large number of others bad, especially on the part of our men toward our women.

They behave as well as the whites who have had equal advantages; and I think better.

Tennessee

Clarksville is a small town of about ten thousand inhabitants, over half of them being colored. In manners and culture our people excel most places of its size. Our public entertainments are frequently visited by some of our best white citizens who always commend them.

As a rule children get but little teaching or drill as to good manners in the home. The school teachers in the schools do most of the teaching along this line. While there is but little uncouthness there is on the other hand not much real politeness.

Texas

While the manners of our people here are not as good as desired there is a constant tendency toward improvement in this respect and it is hoped that conditions of this character will soon be second to none.

The old people are exceedingly polite. The Negro who has had school advantages is polite. The unchurcht and uneducated Negro is rough and ugly in manners.

Texas is still in that period known as the condition of the wild and woolly West. People are not as polite here as in the East. I am a Virginian by birth and have lived all my life in the East. I do not think the folks here measure up to the folks in the East in manners, still there are some here who are up to the standard of any race.

The colored people have great respect for the white people but they are greatly wanting in manners for their own people.

The older colored people are ostensibly more defferential in matters of salutation, etc. There seems to be a general lack of good manners now a days among all classes of the younger generation both white and colored, but the colored people of the South are inclined to have good manners.

On the streets, in the churches and at other public places, fairly good.

When sober the conduct of the average Negro is kind, thotful, restrained and considerate. When under the influence of strong drink or excitement he is noisy, boisterous and sometimes dangerous. The decent people are always decent.

Among educated Negroes good; varying from fair to bad among the less fortunate.

Far above that of the average southern Negro due to the fact that this city is an educational center for whites and the schools furnish work for between 300 and 500 young men and women. Thru such sources they gain much uncommon knowledge.

Always kindly disposed, growing. It has always been so with the older members of the race. The charge that the younger elements of the race are gross, insulting, uncouth, is false. He is actually demonstrating to the world his great susceptibility to good manners and practicing them.

I live in an exceptional town. The colored people are very kindly disposed toward each other. They are trying to raise their children to honor and respect everybody; but the newcomer is so very much different in his life and manners until we hate to see the new class come among us.

Virginia

Some of them excellent. Many very deficient.

My impression is that on all of these subjects improvement can be seen in proportion to the amount of education and proper home training. Of course, much depends on environment.

Some have excellent manners, all that anyone might desire. Others that I know are sadly lacking in this particular. In some instances the lack of good manners is due to home training. In other cases it is not due to home training.

Adults have become more formal and affected and young people are less respectful than formerly.

West Virginia

A large percent are still very much too loud in public places, but the Negro as a whole is improving in his manners.

Generally speaking the Negroes of Clarksburg have good manners. Among the transient element we sometimes meet with the coarse, insolent Negro.

They are up to the average. The younger people seem to be more careless in other things than in good manners.

The condition of our people in regards to manners is excellent. They surpass the Anglo-Saxon in many respects.

Section 5. Sound Morals

Morals are matters of vaguer speculation and more variable judgment than manners. There are few figures by which sexual morals can be judged. The record of illegitimate births in Washington, D. C., is as follows:

Washington, D. C.

Year	Total Negro Births Reported	Percentage of Illegitimate Births Reported	Negro Population
1870			43,404
1879	1,659	18.8	
1880	1,793	18.1	59,596
1881	1,536	18.6	
1882	1,592	19.7	
1883	1,397	21.1	
1884	1,482	20.2	
1885	1,500	22.2	
1886	1,584	22.9	
1887	1,761	19.5	
1888	1,756	22.3	
1889	1,804	26.2	
1890	1,848	26.4	75,572
1891	1,891	25.0	
1892	1,910	27.1	
1893	1,963	26.7	
1894	2,001	25.7	
1895	1,942	26.8	
1896	1,842	27.0	
1897	1,875	25.9	
1898	2,043	25.1	
1899	1,737	27.6	
1900	1,867	25.5	86,702
1901	1,735	24.3	
1902	1,846	24.7	
1903	1,817	22.7	
1904	2,224	24.6	
1905	2,275	24.7	
1906	2,199	22.1	
1907	2,322	21.4	
1908	2,205	20.9	
1909	2,220	21.9	
1910	2,392	19.9	94,446
1911	2,260	20.7	
1912	2,273	21.8	

One hundred thirty-two answers from twenty-six states giving general impressions as to moral conditions among Negroes are printed here:

Alabama

Medium.

They have not got real good morals.

The majority have good morals.

Both classes should awake to a deeper sense of true morality. We should commend the right as right and condemn the wrong as wrong. Too much illegitimacy still exists.

The standard of morality practiced is not what it ought to be. Flagrant and open immorality is not tolerated. The standard is high but few live up to it.

The people in this city have made and are making rapid improvement along the line of sound morals. I note a wonderful improvement during the last fifteen years.

Their morals are very bad in places.

Depending on circumstances among them. Poverty, low wages and home conditions have all to do with them.

Condition as to this feature poor, especially females. Larger element of "grass widows" here than any place I have lived. Cause, most usually, infidelity. Adultery common. Larger number of bastards born since 1870 I think than any other town in the state—proportionately. Miscegenation has been the order of the day—changing however for better. Most products of this mating among females are some of our worst characters. Been low white trash and Negro, mostly mulattoes, concerned.

All sorts of morals from the best to the worst. The best educated have the best morals as a rule. On the whole their morals are better than those of their white friends.

It is a well known and lamentable fact that the code of laws subscribed to by a large percentage of our people has not brot as good results as we might have wisht. But on the whole this was largely consequential. The Negroes' morals status is about as good as the conditions and possibilities will admit.

I think we are improving in morals. The same crowd that hangs around bar rooms, pool rooms and barber shops furnishes our darkest side as to morals. Girls who work out and come home after dark are subjected to too much temptation for lack of the proper protection along this line.

The general feeling is that the Negroes have not grown as rapidly in sound morals as in economic lines. My feeling is that this is not true. One, you can see and tabulate the data; the other is ethical and cannot be so readily recorded, but I believe it is as real nevertheless.

Very poor. The old Spanish treaty insured exemption from slavery to the Creoles in this section of the state, opened an avenue for white men to make inroads upon the morals of Negro women who were anxious for their children's future. The effects still last.

I am sorry to say that I find colored people very lax in their morals but not more so than the other races.

Arkansas

Those I know personally and those with whom I most often come in contact are of good morals.

Among the more enlightened and cultured the number of those who exhibit sound morals is large. But there is a large class of careless, rude and coarse mannered people yet untoucht by the influences of culture. Far too many seem to be without proper sense of right and wrong both as to honesty and chastity.

I find many with sound morals, but about the city the masses are very weak.

I find that the moral condition of the people, generally speaking, is at a very low ebb. There are so many children born and reared in the slums who know nothing else but that kind of life. Some have never heard the Gospel of Jesus Christ.

So far as the better class is concerned it is O. K., but not as a whole; understand this part.

California

Our people are acquiring good morals in social and religious organizations.

Connecticut

I think in this there is an improvement.

For the most part here there is a rather low standard of morals due to the fact that a large percent of the colored population is constantly coming and going.

District of Columbia

More honest thru fear and ignorance than morality. Less restrained in sex contact than desired. Not sufficiently capable of sustained reaction to idea of "I ought". Average higher than ten years ago.

The partaker and sharer of the general deterioration of morals so alarmingly characteristic of our day. "Evil communications corrupt good morals" but comparatively in my opinion, strange to say, the Negro has yielded less to the tendency sweeping downward. He is more conservative.

Good in a very heavy majority. Still there is need for improvement.

Florida

The morals are good and sound except one family and we had them leave the settlement.

It is lamentable that there is not more emphasis placed on sound morals. The people are not classified in this particular. Character does not count, if one has money and can dress well and put on a good exterior. There are only a few exceptions in this particular city. The majority is weak. There are very few that have that unblemisht morality. Since our state has collected a mass of floating element from all other states to do public labor in Florida and in this mass it has brot a large number of immoral characters.

Quite an improvement over the past ten years among the people I have moved and been laboring with. Sound morals count for everything and they look upon it as such.

The morals of our young people are very much corrupted. Their highest ambition seems to be this rag-time dancing which in my estimation is very degrading.

About as good as their neighbors, especially in sex morality. The Negro (thru ignorance of course) washes his dirty linen in public and hangs it on the front yard fence. Their white neighbors more or less *vice versa*.

Sound morals are much in the minority and it should be taught that good morals go far in summing up a race. Of course, here, the white man in our section is trying to place a colored liquor bar on every corner.

Georgia

Very sound. You can depend upon them in business.

It is very burdensome for the few who possess them to bear the blame of the masses who lack them. It is alarming that our educators have shown weakness in some cases.

As good as that of the community in general.

To this question many claim that there is a going back but I do not. I think that, when a fair examination is given them, under conditions, etc., the Negro is holding his own. I am fifty-three years old and have been teaching twenty-three years and twenty years in the ministry and I can speak for this part of the state.

The morals of the older of the race are very good. Those of the younger set are very bad. To my personal knowledge we have many young girls from twelve to eighteen who are morally wrong and yet they have good moral parents and good homes. The under class (from whom these children take lessons in public schools), they number the sands. They are to be found in every city I have traveled, North, South, and East and West, (the West not so much as the other sections and none so prolific as the Southern cities). I find them in the country also. Poor public schools are the cause in my opinion.

The Negro is making progress toward sound morals but is at present far from the desired goal.

Much better than formerly. A high sense of moral purity is dominant and apparent.

Their morals are improving and the future is bright.

Quite a deal of improvement may be made and yet I do not regard the condition as one not readily susceptible to the proper kind of training and help.

There is much room for improvement along the line of sound morals among the colored people, especially towards one another. Yet there is markt improvement. Our young men and women do not seem to have as good morals towards one another as the older people.

In this respect our people have greatly advanced.

I would say the same about sound morals that I said in inquiry one about thoro manners. I believe, however, that there is an earnest effort in this community to improve substantially along moral lines. The percentage of morals is much lower than it ought to be, so it seems.

Judging my race by its best element, I consider the moral standard of the race a good one. In our schools the children are taught morality by action as well as word. We have organizations connected with the various churches that tend to raise the moral standard of our people and better them in every way.

Their morals are something better than a few years back. They are beginning to manifest shame for wrong-doing.

Illinois

The crowded conditions, fashions, pleasures, resorts, etc., seem to be making hard against our sound morals. Temptations are carrying us away. The high cost of living and small opportunities for earning money have a great deal to do with lowering our standard.

Bad; town wide open to vices led by white citizens and imitated by black.

Poor, but as compared to the white people of this community and of whom I know, they are good.

Not worse than other races but much room for improvement in this branch. Thirst for gold and luxuries seems to affect sound morals.

I do not think the Negro is wholly to blame. The whole country seems to suffer from the hypnotism of debauchery. The Negro is not more to be charged than the white race that invented the debased system.

Kansas

Misconception of morals is generally found. Strong men and women have been kept in the back-ground. While it is a slow process, the condition is changing.

Kentucky

Is very good and really growing better each and every day.

I think they are progressing along these lines.

While the morals of our people are not as sound as we should like to have them, not by any means, yet, I am frank to confess that there seems to be progress and improvement and upon the whole our people are doing about like other folks with similar environments.

Much improvement is needed, yet the standard has been perceptibly raised.

There is a small but growing number who show sound morals. Too many have questionable morals or bad associations.

Each generation more solid.

Not prepared to speak authentically, yet considering the general moral laxity of both races in their search for pleasure and desire for fine clothes, there is a reasonable proportion of colored homes who uphold purity and foster morality.

Bad in some places. Leading men are doing bad along this line.

Young people should be taught that they will kill the race by not having sound morals. It should be imprest upon them to be sound in morals.

Making rapid progress, but far from "A" No. 1.

Louisiana

Considering the poverty of our people, their craze for fine dress, the low wages paid, their recent deliverance from slavery, etc., we have among us a goodly number of young people whose morals are as sound as those of any people.

Would say that when we classify, there are marked improvements, but when we consider the masses, of course, there is a deficiency; yet, generally speaking, there are evidences of progress.

I think the majority are immoral but I am glad to say that I have noted a change for the better in the last few years. Where there has not been actual improvement, they have grown less careless.

In my personal estimation, they are worse than cannibals, altho they are only imitating their white brothers.

Maryland

The question of morals is rather a grave one due mostly to the fact that girls are not taught to be strong of volition in order to resist the snares set for them. I think much can be done along this line, too, by teaching colored women and girls their rights and privileges when insulted by white men. My attention has been called often to cases where white men have insulted colored women and the women feeling the sting refrained from calling public attention when they should have gone as far as the law would protect them in the case.

Minnesota

The moral status of the race is good, tho there is much room for improvement.

Mississippi

The morals of the people of Indianola and community are decidedly better than in former years. Marriages among those of higher moral training and the building of homes with purer surroundings are considerably on the increase.

Of course, there are a great many Negroes of my acquaintance whose moral character is without reproach. I know too.many colored people however, not a majority, whose morals will not stand close inspection.

Some of our women and men stand for absolute purity. I regret to say, as a whole, Negro men have not and do not accord our women that respect and attention so much in evidence in Southern white men. Again a Negro woman, self-respecting and good looking, is too often the target of attack for white men and when Negro women fall, they seem to be cheaper and fall lower and are more common than white women.

Missouri

Sound integrity is somewhat lacking; the spirit of getting by on appearances and covering up ends and short-comings pervades much of our atmosphere. Conceptions of sexual morality are low with a class of our people.

In all essentials poor.

The schools and churches are popular here. All of the teachers and most of the people are church going people. The ministers are above the average and the teachers are of sound morals generally. I can't say so much for the younger set; seems to be a reign of loose morals. I believe children are trusted too much alone. The wants of the parents have increast; the mothers leave home to work; charity no longer begins at home. The mothers give their time to churches and clubs.

There is also some improvement here, tho not so "sound". I feel justified in saying that in proportion to the intelligence, morals are good. Some are pulling upward—many are pulling downward.

New Jersey

Among the masses, there are low moral standards, consequently loose living. There is a better element, fewer in number, who have sounder morals.

New York

The law governing immorality is quite rigidly enforced for such a large summer resort like Niagara Falls. The Negro has his weak spots here morally, but on the whole his comparison with the other races who live here, is not odious.

About with the average as noted generally in other places—in most places. Fidelity to the marriage vow, with probably but few exceptions.

Depends entirely upon training, grade for grade.

North Carolina

The majority are very much improved for the last ten years and they are doing much better on this line.

Some improvements among the masses.

The standards are not high in this community—about an average. The leaders are at times immoral and illiterate, prejudiced and superstitious. There are no lines of demarkation of morality drawn plainly here and it will be some time before this will be a strong healthy place with good sound morals. But we can see a slight improvement here and there and a desire for a purer and a higher life. Reformation is taking place here and there and we hope for a better time and believe it will come in the near future.

Very poor but is kept within the race.

The moral condition seems above the average of the race; conditions have greatly improved in the last ten years.

I think the moral tendency is better than in previous years.

Ohio

Far from perfect but need have no immediate concern as long as our organizations for good are at work.

It is below the average of the white race. The sexual instinct seems not to be governed by high respect for female chastity.

Oklahoma

This is hard to report; and yet we must admit the steady thumping they are getting is having its effect.

Their morals have kept pace with their manners and I feel much encouraged at the rapid advance of my people.

Am sorry that I cannot say as much for the morals in a general way as may be said for their manners. The ministry in these parts is far from clean. In fact, it has been so vile that the reaction among the people has been far from healthy. Our people have not been trained to a proper conception of the worth of feminine virtue and the rigid fidelity in domestic relations.

Much improved over conditions ten years ago. When properly trained, our people seem to be more steadfast. Much improvement needs to be made yet.

Pennsylvania

The morals of this city are fairly good but sadly imperiled by flat and tenement housing. The localities in which many of the colored people have to live are not conducive to the best morals.

The superficial are prone to imitate the degenerate society of the whites in evenings of debauchery.

The moral aspect is not just what it might be considering the educational and social advantages to which they have access.

The morals are undergoing quite a change due to the influx of people from the South. That is, it is a common thing for the better class as well as the lower, to be mistresses of white men. This is a serious matter here.

My observations and dealings especially in connection with Jews, Italians and middle class of white Americans, convince me that there is no essential difference between them and Negroes of the same class.

About four-fifths of the number that I have had dealings with, I have found morally sound.

From all points of vantage the morals of the people deserve favorable comment, despite adverse criticism from many sources. Morality from the civilized viewpoint receives less insulting thrusts from the Negro than from the Caucasian, for the simple reasons that: First—the former adopts principles somewhat foreign to those of his ancestral teachings. Second—he is forct to adopt idealistic theories which are inconsistently practict by their creator, the latter. Hence, the questionable exemplary effect on the imitator. Ethnologists have satisfied us that the primitive peoples, and those slightly more fortunate, enjoy a more serene phase of "Sound Morals" than do the so-called highly civilized.

Rhode Island

Reformed municipal government has driven to the wall open houses of shame. Divorces on the ground of adultery or desertion are rare. There are few instances of illicit relations openly practiced. On a whole, there is room for improvement.

South Carolina

Not very good but some improvement noticed in recent years, and as they grow intelligent their morals improve.

In morals, I believe we are making fair headway in an upward tendency. The thousands of good and pious people are likely to be overlookt in considering the large number of the vicious and the criminal who are members of the race. One very bad man will very frequently attract more attention than a thousand good people.

Morals are good among those who have been trained, but a large number who have had little or no training of home or school are very low in morals.

Tennessee

I think the moral conditions of our people might be improved upon. However, they are quite as good as are found elsewhere and much better than are found in some places.

Sorry to say that sound morals are at a low ebb. There are some who are moral in the strictest sense of the word but the majority are very slack. Here, as every where else, a great many rank in society as moral people who are not. I am answering your questions to the letter.

I know a large number of Negroes whom I believe to be thoroly sound in morals, but not a large per cent. Many seem to be moral along certain lines but not so on others.

Much the same as above but the baneful influence of immoral men of prominence among the colored people is alarming.

Texas

Unsound as to high morals. Have almost lost respect for truth.

Few if any people can boast of entirely sound morals. To be sure, our people here must make great advances before reaching anything like perfection in the moral standard.

There are many Negroes who are pure in character; who live in a pure atmosphere; they are true and honest. There are many who are immoral.

The moral question is lookt into and unless they stand for what they pretend, they are set aside and set to themselves.

Morals in the masses are not so good. The failure to enforce the laws has caused many to go astray. Here in our city colored women are allowed to remain in the red-light district for the exclusive use of white men. Many of the leading people are divorct. Improper causes are at the bottom of the trouble. Many of our women will get fine clothes at any cost and by any means. I consider their morals below par.

From my study and observation, I am prepared to pronounce the morals of the colored people sound. The refinements of vice render vice really insidious. Vice among the Negroes, where it appears, is very coarse and brutal and therefore repulsive. Only the brutalizing laboring and housing conditions are responsible for the lack of sound morals among certain classes. Religion in its peculiar aspects has inculcated a fear of evil into the average Negro's mind; beside this the virgin moral nature of the colored people has not yet been infected by the pernicious virus of refined and perverted instinct and habit.

Not common. Even the ministers are some of them not above reproach. Divorces are very common.

Seventy-five per cent of the colored people, I believe, might be clast as morally sound.

Conduct mixt; good morals in all classes; bad morals in all.

The moral conduct of the Negroes of this city is highly complimented by the whites.

Much sounder in their life than formerly. The race is becoming less spotted. Virtue and uprightness greater elements in its life. It is less wavering; stability and firmness greater watchwords.

The morals among our people could be better. As a poverty-stricken race, a great many of our people are led away and their morals become unsound like other races. I note that the morals of our people are about as good as those of other races.

I am afraid to speak along that line. Great improvement can be made along that special line. I sometimes fear we are retrograding, while I know we are improving but not fast enough for me.

Virginia

Improving, but still standards are low even in many from whom better things would be expected. Some are excellent.

They have sound morals in proportion to their education and environment.

Lack exalted ideals of morality. For some reason the lower classes speak lightly of the morals of the more favored.

For the most part, according to the educational advantages the people have had, there ought to be a higher moral standard. The women and girls are not as chaste as they ought to be.

The standard is not as good as we would like it to be altho some are all right.

I don't think the advance in morals has been commensurate with that in other respects.

The moral standing of the people is very low.

West Virginia

Above the average of a mining settlement.

I fear that the people feel that they have done well by their children when they are properly sheltered, fed and clothed. My impression is that but little time is spent in moral instruction. It seems that this is one of Clarksburg's greatest weaknesses.

On par with those of other races around them. Above the average you will find in any industrial section composed of a changing population.

The morals of the young people, I am sorry to say, do not favorably compare with the older generation.

Morality seems to be at a stand-still, or at its critical stage with the scales waiting to tip for better or for worse.

How far has the moral condition of Negroes shown itself in crime?

This is, despite general opinion, a question difficult to answer. Previous to 1904 our data were gathered at the time of the decennial census and were estimated on a counting of all persons in prison on a particular day. These figures for Negroes were:

	Number of Prisoners	Ratio per Million of Negro Population
1870	8,056	1621
1880	16,748	2480
1890	24,277	3250

In 1904 the number of prisoners enumerated did not include those unsentenct and awaiting trial. Subtracting those from 1890 and estimating the Negro population for 1904 we have the following data:

	Number of Prisoners	Ratio per Million of Negro Population
1890	19,808	2649
1904	26,087	2783

Taking the proportion of prisoners by color, we have the following percentages:

	White	Negro
1890	69.6	30.4
1904	67.4	32.6

In other words, according to the method of enumerating prisoners on a certain day every ten years, the Negro American forming one-eighth of the population seemed responsible for nearly one-third of the crime; and his criminal tendencies increase rapidly from 1870 to 1880, enormously from 1880 to 1890, and perceptibly from 1890 to 1904.

It was pointed out, however, in 1890 that this method of estimating crime was misleading and erroneous. Such a method furnisht no basis for estimating the increase or decrease of crime; and without doubt it exaggerated Negro crime. For example: If in communities A and B five men a year are arrested but B punishes her men by twice as long terms as A, by the method of enumeration of prison population on a certain day community B appears on a given day with twice as many criminals as community A, when as a matter of fact there is no difference in the number of crimes ocmmitted. The better method is to count the number of prisoners committed within a certain time period. Dr. R. B. Falkner estimated that if such a method had been used the Negro would be found responsible for nineteen per cent of the crime in 1890 instead of thirty per cent.

The report of 1904 counted not only the prison population but also the commitments. It is striking and reassuring to black men to find that instead of being responsible for thirty-three per cent of American crime, the report shows them responsible for only fifteen and eight-tenths per cent.

Prisoners Committed in 1904

	Number	Per Cent
Whites	125,093	83.6
Negroes	23,698	15.8

Or in other words one-eighth of the population furnisht one sixth of the crime, —a condition not unfavorable to the Negro, considering his past history.

Why is it that Negroes formed so much smaller a proportion of the commitments than of the prison population? This is because of their longer sentences. In 1890 the average white prisoner had a sentence of three and one-half years, the average Negro of nearly five years. So, too, one-third of the white prisoners were in for less than a year; while only one-fifth of the Negroes were thus favored. The figures for 1904 show that this condition still continued. First note the curious discrepancy in numbers:

Color	Prisoners Enumerated June, 1904	Prisoners Committed 1904
White	55,111	125,093
Negro	26,087	23,698

Then the reason:

Sentences	Total Number	Number Negroes	Percent of Negroes
For Life	640	343	53.5
15 Yrs. and Over	808	408	50.5
Under 1 Yr.	116,129	7,363	6.3

Or again in the North Atlantic States only one-tenth of one per cent of all sentences were for life, while in Mississippi, where nearly all convicts were Negroes, six per cent were for life; in the North Central States forty-two per cent sentences were for less than a month; but in Georgia only one per cent were for so short a time. Why is it that Negroes were so severely punisht? The editors of the census bulletin, while admitting the possibility of "A somewhat greater severity in dealing with colored criminals than white" were disposed to think that a part of the cause is that the Negro is guilty of the more aggravated forms of crime.

They divided all prisoners committed in 1904 into major and minor offenders and found that Negroes contributed thirty-one per cent of the graver and thirteen per cent of the minor offenses.

Two difficulties present themselves in this argument:

1. Length of sentence to some extent determines the classification into graver and minor offenses.

2. Negroes are indicted often for the graver of two possible offenses: To strike a white woman is for a white man "Assault"; for a Negro it may be "Attempted Rape".

The classification leads to apparently inexplicable results: If, for instance, we take the prisoners committed in 1904, we find that of all offenses the following proportion are major offenses:

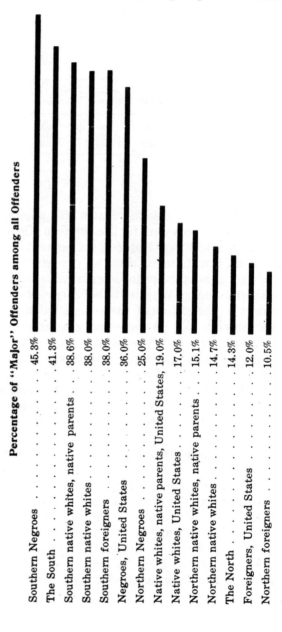

Percentage of "Major" Offenders among all Offenders

Southern Negroes 45.3%

The South 41.3%

Southern native whites, native parents . . . 38.6%

Southern native whites 38.0%

Southern foreigners 38.0%

Negroes, United States 36.0%

Northern Negroes 25.0%

Native whites, native parents, United States, 19.0%

Native whites, United States 17.0%

Northern native whites, native parents . . . 15.1%

Northern native whites 14.7%

The North 14.3%

Foreigners, United States 12.0%

Northern foreigners 10.5%

This would look as tho the South was a veritable school of graver crime for all colors unless we go back of the figures and remember:

1. Southern whites are not arrested and punisht for smaller misdemeanors.

2. The number of foreigners in the South is very small.

3. The Negroes suffer from race discrimination.

The criminologist passes no judgment on the right or wrong of this discrimination. He simply recognizes it as a fact; but he knows:

(a) That many economic forces of the South depend largely on the courts for a supply of labor.

(b) That public opinion in the South exaggerates the guilt of Negroes in certain crimes and enforces itself thru police, jury, magistrate and judge.

(c) That southern public opinion over-looks and unduly minimizes certain other Negro misdemeanors, which lead to immorality and crime.

Of the truth of these statements there can be no reasonable doubt in the mind of any careful student.

In crimes against society (unchastity, perjury and violating United States laws) the Negro is less seldom committed than whites. This is because his crimes against chastity, when his own race are victims, are seldom punisht properly in the South. His proportion of crimes against property are larger, due to his past economic history. His proportion of crimes against the person are greatest because right here, in his personal contact with his fellows, prejudice and discrimination, exasperation and revolt show themselves most frequently; and also because his masses are reaching the brawling stage of self-assertion.

While the proportions vary the actual number of those committed for bigamy, perjury, arson, adultery and violating United States laws is small. Of the more frequent delinquencies, vagrancy, drunkenness, and fraud show the Negroes less guilty than whites. The cases of disorder are but a little larger than the Negro's proportion. The cases of stealing are more seriously in excess, but this excess is hardly more than would be expected from the heritage of slavery, the custom of partial payment in kind and very low wages contrasted with rapidly expanding wants. The cases of rape, altho absolutely few in number, are relatively large, but here the influence of racial prejudice is large: Any insult or suspected insult to white women by a Negro in the South is liable to be denominated and punisht as attempted rape. How much real guilt therefore lies back of the figures can only be conjectured. The really dangerous excess of Negro crime would appear to be in assault and homicide, fighting and killing. Here again interpretation is difficult: How much of these are aggressions on whites, repelling of white aggressions on Negroes, and brawling among Negroes themselves? Undoubtedly the majority of cases belong to the last category, but a very large and growing number come under the other heads and must be set down to the debit of the race problem.

Any Negro tried for perjury, assault, robbery, rape, homicide, arson, burglary, larceny or fraud is going to get a severer penalty in the South than a white man similarly charged. This the white community judges to be necessary and its decisions are carried out by police forces, police magistrates and juries drawn from the white classes whose racial prejudices are strongest. The higher judges tend toward greater independence but even they must stand in fear of the white electorate, whose power is exercised at short intervals.

Next to this stands the fact that in the South road-building, mining, brickmaking, lumbering and to some extent agriculture depend largely on convict labor. The demand for such labor is strong and increasing. The political power of the lessees is great and the income to the city and state is tempting. The glaring brutalities of the older lease system are disappearing but the fact still remains that the state is supplying a demand for degraded labor and especially for life and long term laborers and that almost irresistibly the police forces and sheriffs are pusht to find black criminals in suitable quantities.

If this is so, many ask, how can crime in the North be explained? Northern Negro crime is different in character and cause. It arises from:

(a) A sudden change from country to city life.

(b) Segregation in slums.

(c) Difficulty of obtaining employment.

The proof of (a) is seen among the whites: Massachusetts and Iowa are of similar grade of culture, yet Massachusetts, a state of towns and cities, has 846 annual commitments per 100,000 of population while Iowa, a state of farms, has 402. Thus prejudice and economic demand account for much of the excess of Negro crime. But they do not account for all of it. Another factor as shown by the census is: *Ignorance.* Of native white criminals ninety-three per cent could read and write; of foreigners seventy-eight per cent; of Negroes only sixty-two per cent. This minimum of education it is the duty of the state to furnish; and since this is not done, the Negro, more than any other criminal element has the legitimate but costly excuse of sheer ignorance. Another factor is: *Neglect of the young.* The South sent to prison in 1904 sixteen hundred children of both races under twenty years of age, nine hundred and fifty of whom were under fifteen years of age. Yet, North and South Carolina, Alabama, Mississippi, Texas, and Oklahoma made no provision whatsoever for juvenile delinquents among Negroes; and Florida, Georgia, Louisiana, Tennessee and West Virginia had each one small institution with from thirteen to fifty-four inmates. Probably a thousand delinquent Negro children in the South to-day are being trained in prisons by companionship with the worst grown criminals. And this thing has been going on for years.

This is the more serious because Negro crime is peculiarly the crime of the young. The following table is explicit:

Ages by Percentages

	Native Whites	Negroes
Under 20 years of age . . .	10	19
20-3.) years	35	52
30 years and over	55	29

The cause of this youthful crime is:

(1) The difficulty of adjusting the young to a caste system.

(2) The poor home training.

(3) The demand for strong young convict labor.

Other causes of crime not shown in these figures are:

(1) Poverty.

(2) Discouragement arising from lawless treatment and withdrawal of civil and political rights.

(3) Lack of self-respect under a caste system.

What now is the remedy for Negro crime?

1. Justice in southern courts; Negroes on the police force and in the jury box.

2. Abolition of the economic demand for criminals in the South.

3. Better housing and free chance to work in the North.

4. National aid to Negro education.

5. Better wages.

6. Full civil and political rights for Negroes, on the same basis as they are granted to whites.

There is a theory held by many persons and often openly exprest, that Negroes are especially guilty of crimes against white women. The facts do not bear this out. In the West Indies, with an overwhelming preponderance of Negroes in the population, such crimes are practically unknown. In the United States lynching has long been excused by many as the only cure for these crimes. But of 2855 lynch law murders done, between 1885 and 1913, the accusation of assault on women was made in only 706 or 24.4 per cent, less than a fourth, of these cases. It is moreover fair to assume that in these 706 alleged cases the proportion of guilty persons was small. It must be remembered that in a condition of inflamed racial hatred, where sexual intercourse between colored men and white women is regarded as a crime in many sections under any circumstances and where fear and suspicion are in the air, the general accusation of rape may include much that is not criminal at all. Personal insult of all degrees, wrongful suspicion, lying and disguise, accident, self defense, circumstantial evidence, burglary in a woman's room, exaggeration, illicit relations and sheer mental suggestion may all go to swell the charge of rape. A few actual newspaper clippings are given below as illustrations:

Insult:

Estherwood, La., Oct. 8.—Two men with the aid of a blacksnake whip gave a strange Negro a sound thrashing at Mr. Breaux's thrashing outfit, where all were working, for making remarks about some white girls. He was ordered to leave at once.
Galveston, Tex., News.

Ed Wren, a young white man of Ensley, is dead and Aaron Duncan, a 16-year-old Negro boy, is in the county jail charged with his murder, as a result of the young man resenting an alleged insult offered a young lady whom he was escorting at the fair last night.

While details are lacking and stories regarding the cause of the murder differ greatly, it seems from all accounts that the Negro brushed against the lady and Wren turned to resent it. After a word or two was passed the Negro drew a knife and made a slash at Wren, cutting him in the neck, severing the jugular vein.
Birmingham, Ala., Age-Herald.

Hope, Ark., Oct. 17.—Charley Lewis, a Negro, died near here this afternoon from the effects of wounds received this morning while his capture was being made.

Lewis went to the home of Mr. Lewellan,
a prosperous white farmer, who resides a
few miles south of Hope, this morning, and
used very insulting and abusive language
to Mrs. Lewellan, who was alone at home,
threatening to kill her. She secured a gun
and fired several shots at him, all of which
went wide of their mark, and he escaped.
He then went to the home of Will Byrom,
a white farmer, and, securing an ax, tried
to kill him, again making his escape. Constable Steve Berry, of this place, was notified, and with a number of armed citizens
started for the scene of the trouble. In
the meantime a posse of armed citizens
had been formed and the Negro's capture
effected before Constable Berry reached
them, but his capture was not made until
his body was riddled with bullets.

Memphis, Tenn., Commercial-Appeal.

Suspicion:

Clinton Glover, a young Negro of St.
George, charged with attempted rape, was
convicted last Tuesday and sentenced to
on be hanged on the 10th inst. There was
no direct testimony to convict this man.
He was only seen in the street opposite
the house where the assault was attepmted
at about 3 o'clock, whereas the attempt·
was made about 10 o'clock that evening.
The lady is reported to have said that she
did not know the man, did not know
whether he was white or colored. She
only felt the touch of some hand.

Charleston, S. C., Southern Reporter.

Lying:

Cumberland, Md., Oct. 22.—After she
had stabbed her sweetheart, Clarence Button, because he teased her about another
girl, Mrs. Walter Williams set her umbrella up over his head to keep the rain off
him, and knelt beside him and talked to

him lovingly during the few minutes that
he lived. * * * * * He talked to her
affectionately and begged her to get rid of
the knife and say he had been attacked by
a Negro who had insulted her.

"For God's sake get rid of that knife!"
he said as he died.

New York World.

Washington, Pa., Wednesday.—Publicly
repudiating the story told by Miss Beatrice
Burr of an attack by Negro highwaymen
near her home November 15, in which the
automobile she was driving was damaged,
the young girl's father today announced
that he would pay damages to W. H.
Adams, of Philadelphia, whose buggy he
says was smashed by his daughter's machine.

New York Herald.

Entering a Room:

Irwinton, Ga., October 10.—Because he
entered the room of Miss Effice Chappell,
the daughter of a planter, last Sunday
night, after she had retired, and approached her bed, Andrew Chapman, a
Negro, to-day was hanged from a tree near
here by a mob and his body riddled with
bullets.

Miss Chappell awoke, as the Negro approached her bed, and screamed. Her
cries aroused the family, and the Negro
fled.

Cincinnati, O., Enquirer.

Revenge:

Caruthersville, Mo., Oct. 11.—Shortly
after midnight last night a mob broke into
the city jail and dragged therefrom two Negroes, carrying them to the baseball park,
on the edge of the Mississippi river, north
of town, and from there sounds of lashing
and screams of the blacks were heard. An

hour or so later flames were seen bursting from an ancient frame building, which has for several years been used as a Negro boarding house, and which has long been the rendezvous of many tough characters of the race. It is evident the building was saturated with oil, and before the fire company could respond the old landmark was a glowing bed of coals.

Early yesterday evening a Negro known as High Pockets followed two young lady clerks of the supply store, Miss Josie Faulk and Miss Bessie Gee, to their homes. It was growing dark and the Negro hid in the shrubbery of the J. H. McFarland place, near the home of the girls. The girls called the attention of J. W. McClanahan to the threatening actions of the Negro, and the police were telephoned for. The Negro was found where he had hidden, and was placed in the city jail. In some way the suspicious action of the Negro became known, but to the public there appeared no evidence of the gathering of a mob.

*   *   *   *

There has been smouldering excitement in this city since last week when Lee Fleming and Albert Dugger were slashed nearly to death by a knife in the hands of a bad Negro. This Negro was arrested and carried to Kennett, the county seat of Dunklin county. Excitement ran high and a mob captured a train and made the Kennett jailer a midnight call, but Kennett was wired and the Negro taken from jail and hidden.

Memphis, Tenn., Commercial-Appeal.

Illicit Intercourse:

These headlines tell their story.

NEGROES IN A
BOLD OUTRAGE

BREAK INTO WOMAN'S HOME AND
ASSAULT AND ROB HER

SUSPECT IS CAPTURED IN THE CANADIAN SOO

ATTACK UPON LITTLE GIRL IS
UNSUCCESSFUL

**One of Two Thieves Remained in House
for Two Hours After Assault and
Robbery Had Been Com-
mitted—Other Flees**

*Sault Ste. Marie Evening News
Tuesday, Oct. 24, 1911*

SENSATIONAL STORY

Might Have Led to Lynching in
Many Communities

A MOUNTAIN OF A MOLE HILL

**"Social Call" Stamped as "Most Das-
tardly Crime Ever Committed
in This Community"**

Soo Times, Oct. 28, 1911

Imagination:

Several days ago a very sensational story
of an assault on two little girls at Rocky
Mount was told in the papers, and the
man who was suspected was arrested, and
he was identified by the girls, one of them
11 years old and the other 10. Nothing
has been said of the matter lately, it was
left like the sensational stories in the
paper, right where it was the most sensational. The mob was after the Negro and
it was uncertain whether the sheriff could
protect him or not.

The sheriff was suspicious of the story
when it was told by the children but the
mob believed it and thought that they
were doing their duty by their families
and the race in trying to lynch the Negro.
It is understood that the children had
been hearing and reading sensational stories
throughout the country which have been
very frequent in the papers recently and
they thought that they would get up a sensation on their own account, so they made
up the tale and only the fact that the
sheriff was a level headed man saved that
section of the country an outbreak of lawlessness.

The sheriff got the story from the children after some persuasion.

Florence, (S. C.) Times.

Section 6.   Cleanliness

The dirt and squalor of the slaves was often spoken of,
altho there was much difference between house servants and
field hands in this respect.   One hundred nineteen selected
answers from twenty-six states indicate general improvement.

Alabama

Our people have made great progress in this particular.   We are
realizing that cleanliness of person, home and general surroundings is essential to good health.

Habits of cleanliness are far above the average.   The homes and surroundings and general appearance are clean, generally speaking.

As a rule our people do not use all the soap and water that they
should but some very earnest efforts are being made to get them to form
habits of cleanliness.

Many of the wives and mothers do the washing for most of the city
in a most acceptable way.   As compared with the Jews and Italian in
the city they are decidedly superior in the matter of cleanliness.

The majority of our people present themselves to the public in a very
decent manner.

As a whole they don't come up to the mark; but the better trained
people here are very careful along this line.

Improving.

They are growing better every day along this line of cleanliness. The ministers and teachers are doing more along this line than ever before in the history of this state.

Fair proportion have habits of cleanliness. That class, however, is not in number large enough to appreciably affect health status of the race generally.

The most of the people of the vicinity wear good clothes and they go neat and tidy. Also they are very neat in their homes.

Habits of cleanliness are very much improved over what they were five years past. People want to know and daily apply them more and more. Pleasingly remarkable. Can easily be denominated.

Habits of cleanliness have their bearing on morals; and if living conditions were better for colored people most assuredly their morals would be better. On the whole where conditions are favorable the habits of cleanliness are all that could be expected of them. We cannot make brick without straw even in this field.

There is a wonderful improvement among them as to cleanliness. They are more cleanly both as to their homes and person.

Arkansas

Not as good as it should be. Much improvement is needed among the uneducated class.

For the most part habits of neatness in home and business obtain.

The percentage of those who observe a fair degree of personal and home cleanliness is encouragingly large.

Our people are learning this rapidly and are building sanitary homes and keeping them in sanitary condition. There are few exceptions.

They are fairly clean because the city is demanding that everything be kept in a sanitary condition. There are some homes yet that could do better along that line.

They have made wonderful progress along sanitary lines.

California

The people here take a pride in adopting modern sanitary practice.

District of Columbia

Tho, perhaps, if not contradictory, then somewhat paradoxical, yet it is a fact that the Negro has improved appreciably in habits of cleanliness while in morals and manners he has not.

Growth of self pride seems to go hand in hand with increase in cleanliness in small particulars. High standard here. Public assemblies display tastefully drest, clean people in numbers as large as 5000 at one time. Alley, drinking population below the standards of any whites in the city in filth. Bodies, clothes, houses, neighborhoods and relations all indicate shiftlessness which demands continued training to induce the feeling of cleanliness. Our dictum to graduates is: "Wherever you go, clean up first, teach afterwards".

Florida

As clean as their neighbors will encourage them to be. Not as dirty as they seem.

In housekeeping and cleanliness there is a wonderful change. You seldom see many real dirty colored people. You see the most dirt among the very ignorant colored people.

The sanitary conditions of our people are poor on the public works and around some of the little towns; while in some of our cities they are pretty good.

There is little to complain of in this respect. I presume physical cleanliness is meant by your question.

Georgia

Habits of cleanliness are growing better on all lines.

The more enlightened our people are, the cleaner they are inclined to be. Contact with the best class of white people has improved my race. In most parts fairly good, but much improvement can be made.

There has been a markt change in the last ten years toward general habits of cleanliness. They are as a rule clean. They delight to clean up and parade the streets. They are clean on the outside, clothing fairly good tho cheap. I have nothing to say on the subject of cleanliness. They are doing well along that line.

Not what it should be. As to the masses they are not so clean but about one third of them are clean.

That the Negro is making progress along the lines of cleanliness is evident to the most casual observer. He is tidy in dress, especially on Sundays, and neat in his home.

Great improvement both in homes and personal habits. Less snuff and tobacco is used among the women but no decrease among the men.

The majority that I come in contact with seem to be clean with their person and in their appearance.

They are not as clean as they could be under the circumstances because they have not been taught the importance of it. I think, however, conditions are better than when I came here eight years ago.

Advance in this particular is very encouraging. The homes of the people from kitchen up are up to the average in this community to that of his white brother. You will find the screens very much in use and the people are fond of the baths. Much work to do yet, however.

The people, as a rule, are very clean. A great number of the colored citizens of Dublin own their homes which are well kept. Dublin should be proud of the cleanliness of her colored people.

The more intelligent people are aiding the City Board of Health in enforcing the laws of cleanliness.

In this section, the country people are more tidy than those in town, but all are improving in this respect.

Illinois

Bath tubs and shower baths are becoming very fashionable. Most all try to be clean and appear well. Large numbers of hair dressing and manicure parlors are establisht among them.

As a whole, the race is superior in personal cleanliness and dress.[3] I find many unsanitary homes tho.

Indiana

Exceedingly good. No city of its size in the country can present as well drest clean looking people. A stranger notices this and soon gets the habit.

Kansas

In the mining towns of Kansas, Missouri and Oklahoma poor. Better conditions prevail in Kansas City, Kansas and Missouri.

Kentucky

Are good with the majority of Negroes and this is growing better among the young race.

Outwardly good; but the laws of health and rules for cleanliness are not strictly obeyed by far.

We have a cleaner and healthier community than we had five years ago.

Great and daily improvement along this line. It is a rare thing to see a dirty child in a school of this city. Our people have begun to realize the true worth of the bathtub. Not fine clothes but clean clothes and clean bodies has begun to be the slogan of the humblest homes.

Still greater progress. No race in this section, under similar conditions, ranks higher.

Louisiana

Our people are arranging their homes so as to include bath rooms and are equipping them with the necessary paraphernalia to serve water and keep themselves clean. They are learning quite rapidly to be clean.

Ordinary. Some excellent.

Most of them have clean habits. This is due in a large measure to being servants and the campaign against tuberculosis.

There is a markt improvement along this line among the better classes. The poorer classes could do much better.

Exceptional cases are good but the average is poor.

Maryland

I find that their habits of cleanliness are not wofully lacking tho they could improve.

The Negroes here have made considerable development along this line. They have very good homes, etc., yet we have the alley to contend with. The Colored Doctors' Medical Association is helping along this line.

Minnesota

Habits of personal cleanliness are splendid and taken as a whole I think they excel those of their fellow citizens.

Mississippi

Much improved.

Evidences of cleanliness can be seen in most of the homes.

Good. There are a few Negroes who still cling to the weekly bath but as a rule the sporty and the honest striving Negroes look after their bodies and clothes beyond their means in certain cases.

A little better. We have some that are all O. K. but they are in the minority.

Missouri

The people are divided into classes with respect to cleanliness. The movement is toward better homes and greater cleanliness. The schools, with their bathing facilities, strengthen this movement.

Decidedly on the increase for the better.

Habits of cleanliness are necessary to fit a young man or woman for good society. This is generally being aspired for by young Afro-Americans.

There has been great improvement along this line. There have been so many lectures during the past ten years. The public school teachers are required by the Board to attend such lectures. Our people are clast as intelligent people. The children from the second grade up visit regularly the Public Library. A reading people cannot but improve along this line.

Ninety per cent of all the families here are exceptionally clean with their persons and their homes. Out of about thirty families only three or four are indecent as to clean linen.

New York

Their showing in this direction is commendable.

Much carelessness among many but very good among many others. Progress so general that it can be constantly noted along this line. General personal appearance favorable. Generally well develop physically and healthy.

Comeliness the rule with few exceptions.

Among the improved, excellent. Worse than twenty-five years ago among the laboring people in the cities.

Good; far above the average of the same class of whites with whom

I come in contact.

These people are surprisingly clean, especially in keeping their homes. Many colored people take pride in the cleanliness of their homes and not of their bodies.

North Carolina

Very good. Improvement on this line and striving to do better all of the time to make themselves a nation.

Not as great among the people as we should like it to be. Bodily cleanliness is adhered to at times, but lacking greatly. Some put on clean clothing, bathing weekly, generally Saturday nights for Sunday, while others don't put on clean clothing at all unless compelled to do so. Sanitation and general cleaning up around the house is lacking much indeed. Some have neat and clean homes while others have not. This can be improved on much in this community. Practical sanitation is much needed and there are some who regard this as a very important matter and practice it in their lives.

Good for a rural section. It is said that the people here dress neater and look cleaner than you find them anywhere else similarly situated.

Very much improved. I speak from personal knowledge. I am in a position to come in contact with almost every family here.

Ohio

Some among the poorer classes, perhaps because of poor accommodations for living, are not as clean as one would wish; but as a general thing I find homes exceedingly clean.

I think here while there is much room for improvement we are on a par with any nationality who have to labor in the same occupations as ourselves. The whites sometime raise the question but as far as I can see, and I have lookt closely, it is about all prejudice.

Oklahoma

There are quite a few who are clean and tidy in their persons and homes and a great multitude who are not.

Just fairly clean, generally our homes are not furnisht with bath tubs. We are not provided with public baths and the daily sponge off is none too familiar with the rank and file of our citizens. Still, most of them put on a veneer of cleanliness when they go to church and other gatherings. They are gradually improving in the conditions of their homes.

Naturally reasonably clean and according to their means, I believe, surpass the other races here, i. e. white and Indian.

Pennsylvania

The colored people here are generally neat when they appear in public but their home surroundings are not always clean.

We are rising.

On the whole very clean.   I would say that the average about eighty per cent.

My observation is that there is no difference between the Negro and other races of the same class.

This depends upon the class and the environment.   If the class is low and the environment bad, you must expect dirt and filth.   This is not peculiar to the Negro but to any race with similar conditions.   The best classes and the middle classes are as clean as anybody.

Some very clean while others are to the opposite.

In this measure, the American Negro compares favorable with Negroes in England, Canada, West Africa and the West Indies from the point of class and education.   Thru long years of social relationship, the example with the more fortunate members of the human race, the Caucasian, he has imbibed and exhibits traits of innate tendencies toward a love for what is clean.   Hence, my comparison as the result of personal experience in the above-mentioned countries.   I defy contradiction, that, taking it class for class, the colored people in America are in no way behind the whites in habits of cleanliness.

Rhode Island

Fair, but the old fashioned houses make personal cleanliness difficult. Most of them maintain pleasant surroundings.   The best is exceptiontionally good.

South Carolina

They are good in their habits of cleanliness; homes are nicely kept with some exceptions of course, and the women in town and country dress nicely and fashionably.   One used to be able to tell just when a country girl struck town by her seven primary colors but not so now.   The R. F. D. carries the style to the country as well as to the town.

The increast instruction given in the schools regarding hygiene and sanitation, and the attention given in the pulpit, press and on lecture platform to "Gospel of Cleanliness" and to matters involving the question of good health, and the removal of the belief that it is "Saintly to be sickly and sinful to be healthy and strong," are having good results among the rank and file of our people.

For the last ten or fifteen years, I have found this to be a growing habit among our people both in town and cities and the country places.

Good where the facilities are favorable.   We have many communities where the houses are almost packt upon each other with almost no front or back yards.   Cleanliness is not to be found in such places.

Tennessee

The sanitary conditions of our people are good.   We have an infirmary owned and controlled by Dr. R. T. Burt which is a credit to the race. Proud to say the colored people are ahead of the white people in that respect, there being not an infirmary for the white people in the city. Dr. Burt is called by all one of the finest surgeons in the country.

This is the most rapid advance that I have noticed in the race.

They are as clean as their occupations and means allow.

People here practice personal cleanliness and also take pride in caring for their homes, most of which they own. They have habits of beautifying their homes and churches.

Progress. More pride and attention are being manifested and progress made.

I know many who are personally clean and whose houses are kept in a beautiful fashion. Many who would like to be neat housekeepers are out at service and do not have the time or strength.

Texas

Are not what they ought to be. There can be no excuse for filth.

As to cleanliness, conditions are fair in this city among our people There seems to be improvement in this respect. The city enforces some regulations as to cleanliness also.

Of course, here the Negroes are divided again into two classes. Both as to their personal appearance and home life some are scrupulously clean, others are not.

Clean-up days have been instituted among the colored people and there are few yards that are not overgrown with beautiful flowers and fern. They vie with each other in their yards of beautiful flowers. Their homes are beautiful thruout.

About seven-eighths of the colored people here seem to try to keep very clean around them. There are some who are not concerned.

They are generally coming to this great virtue.

The colored people take pride in cleanliness.

Uncleanliness is forst upon them by their occupations and lack of the means of keeping clean. They are really clean as far as their knowledge of cleanliness and their means allow them to be. The Negro is not apt to appear as tidy as he is, when seen in his working clothes, but when the nature of his work is considered he is as clean as he can be. He has much to learn in this line for the modern idea of cleanliness is in advance of that of colored people generally; but the most uncleanly and unsanitary conditions are forst upon them.

The Public School system of our State has done and is doing a good work among the young; and race pride has taken root and produced a great people whose habits lead to cleanliness and virtue.

Considering their homes and advantages, they are exceedingly good.

Greatly improved both as to person, dress and homes.

The white Civic League takes much interest in the general cleanliness, hence, thru the Negro Civic League, many lectures and suggestions are given by the leading whites.

The masses are putting more stress upon cleanliness. They are understanding that prolongation of life is guaranteed more to a clean body than to a filthy body.

Virginia

Taking conditions of our city under consideration, the best class of our people are very clean.

Generally, people here are cleanly both in their homes and on their person.

In this particular with many it is all that could be desired. I am acquainted with a few who are not so particular as they might be.

I should say good. The habits of the older heads of cleanliness appear to have been good.

Good and still improving.

Medium, due to the fact that the city has no sewerage.

West Virginia

They are gradually growing more cleanly. They are growing quite rapidly in their adherence to sanitary laws.

There is, to my knowledge, one section where Negroes of careless habits live contrary to all habits of cleanliness; but in the main they are clean.

Not the best. Due to segregation, high rents, obliged to live in unsanitary districts and several families live in one house to enable them to pay their rent.

In most cases good. There are those as are found in every community who are filthy.

A great deal of training needs to be done along this line. Yet the outlook is hopeful.

Section 7.   Personal Honesty

Slavery meant compulsory poverty and the lack of incentive to thrift. The result was the encouragement of petty thievery. Among the house servants this took the form of taking food and clothes. Gradually this grew to be a tacitly recognized custom. After emancipation the "wages" promist house servants were arranged with the mutual understanding more or less clearly made that cold food and old clothes together with small quantities of other perquisites would periodically disappear. In this way the distinction between *meum* and *teum* grew slowly and vaguely among the freedmen and caused much harsh and unmerited criticism among outsiders trained to the modern commercial code. Our correspondents were therefore askt about habits of personal honesty among Negro Americans. We select one hundred twenty-two answers from twenty-six states and print them here.

Alabama

Very good.

Below par.

Some are honest and some are not.

We can see the remarkable results of this virtue in the fact that many Negroes hold honorable positions not only on the farm but even in the government service. The court records are also more favorable.

The colored people are much more honest now than some years back. They are becoming much more reliable in the matter of paying their debts.

As a rule they will do to depend upon.

Not reliable at all.

They are not honest as a rule. We have some honest people here but the dishonest outnumber the honest by far.

All of the best families are real honest and a few of the other class.

I am sorry to say but I do not think that honesty stands as firm and prominent as it should.

As to their personal honesty I am inclined to the opinion that not more than seventy per cent of them are real honest in their general dealings. My opinion comes from personal contact and general observation.

Rated equal in comparison to other race, I say good. Conclusion from observation of cases in police court. Cases calendared are as a rule disorderly conduct or something more or less trivial.

Poor among all classes but improving wonderfully.

There is room for improvement along this line but the disposition to be dishonest has decreast wonderfully in the past ten years. Poor pay is partly responsible for a good bit of the dishonesty.

Very little. The Negro here is divided and it is impossible to look for personal honesty where each one of any race feels that his success depends upon the destruction of all else besides and that he has a right to a part of whatever the other fellow has, his own improvidence notwithstanding.

Arkansas

One rarely hears of dishonesty.

Those with whom I have had dealings are ninety per cent honest.

I don't suppose this city is any worse than the general run of cities. I think I can safely say that the larger per cent is honest.

The younger ones seem to have a higher sense of honesty than the older ones.

California

I think our police court records show us to be above the average in this respect and I can speak favorably of the race from this point of view.

Occupations circumscribed, wages small, cost of living high, standard of personal honesty low.

District of Columbia

Severe conditions of competition engender small peculations and lying; but standard of dependableness higher than ever before.

Florida

Good. I know whereof I speak.

They are not honest to themselves. Therefore cannot be to their fellowmen.

Good. So much so that even in a town as Dunnelton where I've taught some people never lock their doors. It is a rare thing to hear of any one being arrested for stealing in this section.

Generally speaking the average person is not as bold with his dishonest habits as was the case ten or twelve years ago, while we have some exceptions both ways.

No. Here again the tendency is quick and easy money with the least effort.

I can say we don't have very many cases in court for stealing.

Georgia

Decidedly honest considering their way of getting means.

Towards the white man is gradually improving but towards one another not much of a change.

Merchants say that in general they are more trustworthy than the whites, especially the women.

There is no doubt a general betterment, not as large as desirable, yet enough to mark progress.

The Negro is generally honest. As he accumulates he becomes more trustworthy and dependable.

Great development. The improvement is more noticeable among the women.

As a general thing we find that the colored people are very honest and have made a great improvement along this line in the last few years. On an average I believe they are ahead of the other races along this line.

They are not as honest and trust-worthy as they might be. A great deal of this is due to the leadership of many of those who have had better advantages than the masses trying to take advantage of the weaker and less fortunate to build up their own wealth.

A conscientious regard for keeping his word seems to be much below normal in this community. Promises made are not lookt upon with as much seriousness as in some other settlements I have observed.

There are many colored men here who can go security on bank notes who are not in real possession of property. Their honesty has gained for them a pretty good standing.

This is a thing that our people seem slow to learn; but I am very glad to say that they are showing a great deal of improvement along the line of personal honesty.

Illinois

A large number of "confidence men" have developt. They often have women confederates, but generally, with these two exceptions, they are honest. The waiters and porters and real estate agents make up the principal groups of "shrewd dealers".

Good toward the white but only fair toward each other.

Indiana

Judging from my practice I should say ninety per cent are honest; my accounts will bear out this statement.

Good. On a whole the people are hard-working, honest people. Much given to extravagance of dress and entertaining. This has a tendency to impair them financially.

Kansas

There is a growing tendency to individual pride and personal honesty.

Kentucky

I think they desire to be honest but cannot always act in accordance due to low wages, etc.

The people here are trust-worthy.

I find them about as honest, speaking of the masses, as other people.

Good. A large number carry snug bank accounts.

Has increast wonderfully.

For the past ten years I have taught in the public schools and have left my purse with sums as high as ten dollars in it lying on my desk and have left it unguarded often, yet never has it been toucht. The rogue in the room is a thing of the past generally. The colored servant is generally trusted by the employers.

As a general rule it is bad, more so among the young people. Something must be done to show our people that they should be honest in dealing with mankind. Some of them for a dollar will do almost anything or tell you any kind of a story to get a dollar. This must be stopt before we can be a good race and reliable.

Louisiana

Evidences of personal honesty are manifested in business relations one with the other, viz,—the faithful carrying out of contracts, agreements, etc.

I don't consider our people actually dishonest but their love to ape the white man in his more expensive living, dress, etc., compels the little money they make to give out and then that is the cause of the trouble. He means well but after getting into debt as a result of these things he finds he cannot get out. This is found more so among the so-called better class. They do but little stealing.

The masses are not educated in square dealing.

Minnesota

There is much personal dishonesty among us here and I often feel that this is the Negro's greatest weakness in the far North. It certainly closes the door of opportunity to him in many places where he might otherwise enter. He is lamentably wanting in reliability.

Mississippi

Yes, I feel safe in saying that the coming young citizens have more regard for their word and honesty is more evident among Negroes generally.

Personal honesty is prevalent among the colored people whom I know. Dishonesty is certainly an exception to the rule.

Good. In only a few cases have the servants around white homes or at the places of work violated any trust imposed. Whites have taken advantage of the Negro's honesty and his abnormal wants. They sell him cheap furniture at high prices on time and lend him money at exorbitant rates of interest and many are kept in real need due to poor management.

The majority are lacking in it. There are some notable exceptions.

Missouri

Vast improvement within the last ten years.

Personal honesty is a trait in the Negro lad that is growing, due probably to penalty for violated law inflicted by a prejudiced race and as a poison kills a poison thus the would-be suppression becomes an incentive and a blessing.

Since the general trend of our people is onward and upward religiously and intellectually, I believe that habits of personal honesty are unconsciously being formed and strengthened. They are trusted so completely by the opposite race that when one deceives they are shockt. While they claim all Negroes steal, yet, if they have ten servants, nine white and one Negro, the Negro is the trusty.

They are fairly honest but apparently the law is extreme with most of them. Within ten years only one Negro has been arrested and convicted for dishonesty.

New Jersey

Very good.

Promises not too reliable. Too little value put on their word. You will note that ninety-five per cent is recently from the South and over fifty per cent is from the worst instead of the best element of our southern folks.

New York

In this he is the equal of any here. The chief of police informed me the arrests made each month were one or two out of a population of 500 and this was for drinking, none for stealing.

The people, tho poor, work hard, spend freely—too freely, but as a rule are honest. Not inclined to idleness and idle only, as a rule, when they cannot find employment.

Much improved.

Their honesty is unsurpast by any race of people. This information comes to me, aside from personal knowledge, from credit houses with which colored people have dealt.

Good in both classes. Few arrests for larceny either grand or petit, but many for drunkenness and disorderly conduct,—that is proportionately.

North Carolina

Extra good compared with whites.

Many do not regard their word or promise as anything to be kept. Do not like to come up to their obligations. I find many who do not like to pay honest debts, especially to one another.

Along this line the improvement has been rapid. We can say truly that the people are generally honest and reliable. Perhaps the cashier of the Merchants' and Farmers' Bank of this place, who is a white man, can give you a better answer to this question.

They are learning to be honest. In proportion to the numbers and opportunities for training, quality, I mean, they are as honest as others.

Ohio

Excellent in places of trust and seldom betrays that trust.

I think, the percentage of petit thievery is too great. I think, too, that this is due to the fact that many Negroes think that the white race took all from them in slavery and that they are justified to get what they can from them now even by theft. Then too, the white race offers very little inducement to inspire the Negro to look upward.

Oklahoma

Am almost afraid to say. The wave of graft and money madness has also struck one section and I could not conscientiously say that there is any increase in that respect.

The per cent of our people who possess personal honesty is lower than it should be. They are not as truthful as they should be.

Very good.

Just fair. The majority are not reliable in their negotiations and their business promises do not amount to much. We are backward in this respect.

A good number of our people are as safe as a bank. The masses are not honest. Much improvement needs to be made for our welfare. Women are more honest than men.

Pennsylvania

Of course most of the people with whom I come in contact are honest but the grafting of the city must have infected our people also.

My observations and dealings especially in connection with Jews, Italians and the middle class of white Americans, convince me that there is no essential difference between them and Negroes of the same class.

Are better than they were ten years ago.

While there is a good deal of dishonesty in every race, I believe if this race is placed side by side with others and note made of financial and other losses that this race would be guilty of taking less.

Good as can be expected under the conditions.

Honesty in the sense of honor needs continuous and careful fostering by the representatives of the people so as to prevent deceptive encroachments; while honesty from the standpoint of business inter-relationships generally holds its own encouragingly well. Especially so among the bulwarks of the race—the women.

The greater part of them pay their debts.

Rhode Island

Excellent. I have no knowledge of a single case of a person having the reputation for dishonesty. Perhaps the explanation is that it is difficult to be dishonest here and not be caught.

South Carolina

I have had great experience with my people on the point of personal honesty and find that as a rule the people here have honest intentions even tho circumstances happen that they can't come up to their obligations. Give him a chance and treat him human and he will do all that is within his power to meet his obligations. I find that the high cost of living and the low price paid for labor are greatly responsible for the seeming dishonesty of the people of this community.

I am optimistic enough to believe that we are improving along this line also. It is true that we have as yet a long way to go before reaching perfection, yet that is not alone the case as to the black man. Shady transactions and graft as they exist among white and black these days are being given much notice in the press; and far too many among all people are failing to respect the vast difference between the "Meum and Teum" as regards property. But a candid and unbiast observation of the state of affairs as they exist forces me to believe that our race is really making more advancement along the line of recognizing and respecting that difference than are the whites.

The percentage of honesty is far greater than it was ten years ago. This is my experience and I have been interested in the subject for years.

Tennessee

Exceedingly good. They hold many positions of trust with credit to he race. All of our mail carriers are colored men and all of our sick nurses are colored ladies.

Generally good, many exceptions.

As a rule, honest. White people credit them for any reasonable amount and it is a rare thing that there is any trouble given. As to stealing, this town is almost free from that. A few years ago there were two Negroes and one white man nabbed on account of stealing and house breaking and since then there is but little stealing here.

Somewhat below the average. It will grow with other things.

When put under special trust they rarely fail to be true.

I know many whom I regard as eminently trustworthy. The distinctions between *meum* and *teum* are not as clear as might be, especially in small things.

Standard not so high as it ought to be.

Texas

Needs to be improved, could be better. When one is not honest to himself it is impossible to be honest to others.

The standard in this respect is not as high and hence not satisfactory as it should be. However, many of our people are the very soul of honesty and I am confident that the future will find much improvement along this direction.

Collecting from students and parents, I can say that eighty per cent of the colored people are honest.

Not much abuse of honesty—a pretty fair dealing set of people are found here and confidence of both races enjoyed.

About two-thirds who try to pay up and be true to their word.

Totally disregarded in all business affairs.

As a rule good. This applies especially to the lower class people. It is a fact that the only Negro bank here has gone to the wall. Many of the Negro business enterprises have gone down as a result of dishonesty. Our leading doctor and several of our leading colored wealthy men are now in the courts charged with stealing church money. It is a com-

mon saying here that "You must do this fellow or he will do you."
Here the Negro fails. The word has no meaning to the average
Negro.

As a whole the colored people are honest. It is wonderful to what
extent the servant class is trusted by their white employers. If it were
not for their honesty they would not be tolerated. Where a Negro ap
pears dishonest, it is more the fault of the economic and socia conditions
forst upon him than because of any real defect in his morality. A study
of the criminal Negro reveals more delinquency on the part of modern
society to give the Negro a chance to be honest than it reveals any disposition on the part of the Negro to be dishonest. He is forst into what
often appears dishonesty. The true morality of the Negro is found
largely in the awful conditions under which he is forst to live.

They are reliable.

There is a making for better in all walks and with all classes among
our people. They have learned that they must be honest if they would
have a place in the world among men.

Getting better. They have not reached perfection yet, but there is
a vast improvement. Defalcation in positions of trust are the exception.
Petty thieving is on the decrease. The average man's word means more
than it used to.

The general average is not so good. Tho there are some that are
safe and most worthy.

This one feature is to be especially complimented. When you can
hear many hundreds of Negroes say "Charge it to me" at the leading
institutions in the city it means a lot.

This is my thirtieth year in the college room and in that time there
have come to me more than ten thousand pupils. I am pleased to add my
personal testimony to the fact that the Negro is improving in integrity,
honesty and sobriety.

Bad pay masters make dishonest people. The Negro race is honest.

Virginia

Some absolutely trustworthy, but a very large part are careless
about paying debts, keeping contracts, meeting engagements, etc.

Depends upon the environment.

The following statement from the banker at this place answers your
question: "I have loaned colored people thousands of dollars and I have
never lost a cent either on a loan made to a colored person or on a loan
endorsed by one".

My experience does not justify me in thinking that there is more
honesty among those whom I know than there was twenty-five years ago.

Not able to say much on this line. The business men seem to not
run accounts, the people are required to pay as they go and I don't know

whether it is from dishonesty or from the fact that it is a strict cash business which is easier and safer.

West Virginia

So far as my observation serves me, the Negroes are quite honest. It is rare indeed to read of dishonesty among them here and the papers usually publish everything disparaging concerning the Negro.

Fair. Attempting to meet a false standard of living often contracts debts which they cannot pay even if they have the inclination to pay.

With himself good. I think with the trust of others he thinks all others are dishonest. He has some traits which lead up to personal dishonesty, altho I think he is in a fair way honest with himself.

Section 8. Home Life.

Africa is distinctly the land of the Mother. In subtle and mysterious way, despite her curious history, her slavery, polygamy and toil, the spell of the African Mother pervades her land. Isis, the Mother, is still titular goddess in thot, if not in name, of the dark continent. This does not seem to be solely a survival of the historic matriarchate thru which all nations pass. It appears to be more than this; as if the black race in passing down the steps of human culture gave the world not only the Iron Age, the cultivation of the soil and the domestication of animals but also in peculiar emphasis the Mother-idea. Schneider writes: "No mother can love more tenderly and none is more tenderly loved than the Negro mother". Robin tells of the slave who bot his mother's freedom instead of his own. Mungo Park writes:

"Everywhere in Africa I have noticed that no greater affront can be offered a Negro than insulting his mother. 'Strike me,' cried the Mandingo, 'but revile not my mother.'"

A student of the present Gold Coast life describes the Headman as head of the village:

It is the duty of the Head of the family to bring up the members thereof in the way they should go; and by "family" you must understand the entire lineal descendants of a head *materfamilias*, if I may coin a convenient phrase. It is expected of him by the State to bring up his charge in the knowledge of matters political and traditional. It is his work to train up his wards in the ways of loyalty and obedience to the powers that be. He is held responsible for the freaks of recalcitrant members of his family, and he is lookt to keep them within bounds, and to insist upon conformity on their part with the customs, laws, and traditional observances of the community.

It is a difficult task that he is set to, but in this matter he has all-powerful helpers in the female members of the family, who will be either the aunts, or the sisters, or the cousins, or the nieces of the Headman; and as their interests are identical with his in every particular, the good women spontaneously train up their children to implicit obedience to the Headman, whose rule in the family thus becomes a simple and an easy matter. "The hand that rocks the cradle rules the world." What a power for good in the Native State System would the mothers of the Gold Coast and Ashanti become by judicious training upon natives lines!

Upon this African Mother-idea, the westward slave trade and the regime of slavery in America struck like doom. Sex statistics of our early census reports indicate in a numerical way the social dislocation which the slave regime brot to the Negro population of this country. But beneath this numerical indication of social dislocation lay polygamy, polyandry, concubinage and moral degradation.

The crushing weight of slavery fell heavily on black women. Under slavery there was no legal marriage, no legal family, no legal control over the children. To be sure custom and religion here and there supplied what the law denied, yet one has but to read advertisements like the following to see the iniquity which lay beneath the system:

"One hundred dollars reward will be given for my two fellows, Abram and Frank. Abram has a wife at Colonel Stewart's in Liberty county, and a sister in Savannah at Capt. Grovenstine's. Frank has a wife at Mr. LeCont's Liberty County; a mother at Thunderbolt, and a sister in Savannah.

—*Wm. Roberts. Walthourville, 5th Jan., 1829.*"

"Fifty dollars reward—Ran away from the subscriber, a negro girl named Maria. She is of a copper color, between thirteen and fourteen years of age—bareheaded and barefooted. She is small for her age—very sprightly and very likely. She stated she was going to see her mother at Maysville.

—*Sanford Thomson*"

"Fifty dollars reward—Ran away from the subscriber, his negro man Pauladore, commonly called Paul. I understand Gen. R. Y. Hayne has purchased his wife and children from H. L. Pickney, Esq., and has them now on his plantation at Goose Creek, where, no doubt the fellow is frequently lurking.

—*T. Davis*"

The Presbyterian Synod of Kentucky said to the churches under their care in 1835:

Brothers and sisters, parents and children, husbands and wives, are torn asunder, and permitted to see each other no more. These acts are daily occuring in the midst of us. The shrieks and agony often witnessed on such occasions proclaim, with a trumpet tongue, the iniquity of our system.

There is not a neighborhood where these heart-rendering scenes are not displayed. There is not a village or road that does not behold the sad procession of manacled outcasts, whose mournful countenances tell that they are exiled by force from all that their hearts hold dear.

Such a system was bound to have its evil effects upon both sexes of the slave population. Certainly the greater burden was felt by the women of the black race.

Alexander Crummell in writing of his darker sister said:

In her girlhood all the delicate tenderness of her sex has been rudely outraged. In the field, in the rude cabin, in the press-room, in the factory, she was thrown into the companionship of coarse and ignorant men. No chance was given her for delicate reserve or tender modesty. From her childhood she was the doomed victim of the grossest passion. All the virtues of her sex were utterly ignored. If the instinct of chastity asserted itself, then she had to fight like a tiger for the ownership and possession of her own person, and ofttimes had to suffer pain and lacerations for her virtuous self-assertion. When she reacht maturity all the tender instincts of her womanhood were ruthlessly violated. At the age of marriage—always prematurely anticipated under slavery—she was mated as the stock of the plantation were mated, not to be the companion of a loved and chosen husband, but to be the breeder of human cattle for the field or the auction block.

Yet thru all this mire the Negro woman has come; and in thousands of cases has demonstrated superior qualities of character, intellect and ability. The names of Harriet Tubman, Sojourner Truth and Phyllis Wheatley stand out in the early records of the race.

One of the early workers in the Negro Church, Mary Still, writes quaintly in the forties:

When we were as castouts and spurned from the large churches, driven from our knees, pointed at by the proud, neglected by the careless, without a place of worship, Allen, faithful to the heavenly calling, came forward and laid the foundation of this connection. The women, like the women at the sepulchre, were early to aid in laying the foundation of the temple, and in helping to carry up the noble structure, and in the name of their God, set up their banner. Most of our aged mothers are gone from this to a better state of things. Yet some linger still on their staves watching with intense interest the ark as it moves over the tempestuous waves of opposition and ignorance. ***** But the labors of these women stopped not here, for they knew well that they were subject to affliction and death. For the purpose of mutual aid, they banded themselves together in society capacity, that they might be better able to administer to each other's sufferings, and to soften their own pillows. So we find the females in the early history of the church abounded in good works, and in acts of true benevolence.

The sacrifice of Negro women before the war for freedom and uplift is one of the finest chapters in their history. Such women it is, added to thousands of humbler black "Mammies", faithful servants, toiling housewives and self-sacrificing mothers, who have builded the womanhood of to-day.

In 1900 there were in the United States 4.447,447 females of Negro descent, of whom twelve thousand were children, about a million were girls and young women under twenty years of age and two million grown women. As a mass these women were intelligent,—only a third of those from fifteen to twenty-five years of age being unable to write. While their grandmothers had married at twelve and fifteen, thirty per cent of those over fifteen were single. In 1910 there were 4,941,882 Negro females in the United States of whom two and one-half million were grown. Of those ten years of age and over 30.7 per cent were illiterate and only 16 per cent of those between the ages of fifteen and nineteen. Marriage was more normal among them, 26.6 per cent of those fifteen years of age and over being single.

The economic foundation of the family, the abilty to support and keep the group intact is not yet certain, not simply because of moral laxness but principally because of low wages. This explains in large measure the fact that among Negro women in 1900 one woman in six was widowed or separated from her husband, while among whites there was but one in ten. In 1910 this condition had improved slightly. The corresponding figure for Negro women being 15.9 per cent.

That the Negro woman is compelled in so many cases to help in the support of the family, is a fact often overlookt by the casual observer of Negro life. In 1900 there were 1,832-818 Negro homes in this country. Out of these walkt daily one and one-third million women and girls over ten years of age to work—four out of every ten as against one out of each six white women. These then were a group of workers fighting for their daily bread like men, independent, approaching economic freedom. They furnisht a half million farm laborers, 70,000 farmers, 15,000 teachers and professional folk, 700,000 servants and washerwomen, and 40,000 in trades and merchandising.

Add to these those engaged in miscellaneous work and 200,000 school girls and we have nearly a million and a half. Subtracting the old and feeble, the defective and the idle and we have probably less than one and a half million housewives to manage nearly two million homes. This is a sad deficiency and it tells for harm. Black mothers who ought to be home training their children are away at work. Girls who ought to be at school must help earn bread and butter. But while toil holds their brothers in the small towns and country, higher wages call the sisters to the city. The result is that in cities like Washington and Baltimore the Negro women out number the men ten to nine.

It can be said without danger of contradiction that considering their poverty and lack of legal protection, no modern women have maintained and achieved greater purity of life and strength of worthy purpose—and this too without taking into account the horror of their past deliberate and forst degradation. Not only this but to-day this group is developing a social leadership and a sense of deep social responsibility. A glance at their work is almost bewildering. Not only do they furnish two-thirds of our teachers, an overwhelming majority of our church workers and no small proportion of our business folk, but they are the ones who, turning from the beaten paths to bread and butter and livelihood, have taken up definitely and successfully the inner burden of social reform. Their work takes the form of general charity, Women's Clubs, Old Folks' Homes, Orphanages, Hospitals, Christian Associations, Literary and Art Clubs, Day Nurseries, Settlements, Kindergartens and Civic Reform. It is a fact worthy of special note that much of the real work of social uplift and moral awakening to-day is being carried on by Negro women.

The census statistics show gradual improvement in home conditions. The disparity between the numbers of the sexes is less. In slavery days it was abnormal, there being only nine hundred sixty-seven colored women to every thousand men in 1820. Directly after the war the disparity went the other way and there were one thousand thirty-nine females to a thousand males of the Negro population. Since that the number has become more normal, being a thousand twelve females to a thousand males in 1910.

The figures for marital conditions in 1910 are:

MARITAL CONDITIONS AMONG NEGROES-1910

NEGRO POPULATION—15 YEARS AND OVER

	Total	Single	%	Married		Married	%	Widowed and Divorced		Divorced	%
				Total	%			Widowed	%		
Male...	3,059,312	1,083,472	35.4	1,959,344	64.0	1,749,228	57.2	189.970	6.2	20,146	0.7
Female .	3,103,344	823,996	26.6	2,269,066	73.1	1,775,949	57.2	459,831	14.8	33,286	1.1

The figures for 1890, 1900 and 1910 show a general improvement in marital conditions among Negro Americans. The following table is compiled from the census reports:

NEGRO MARITAL CONDITIONS

By per cent-1890, 1900, 1910

Per Cent Married, Widowed or Divorced

	MALE			FEMALE		
	1910	1900	1890	1910	1900	1890
15 Years and over . .	64.0	60.2	60.0	73.1	69.9	69.8
15 to 19 Years	2.3	1.8	0.9	18.1	16.6	15.0
20 to 24 Years	39.6	35.1	34.2	64.8	60.0	61.7
25 to 34 Years	74.5	71.6	74.7	85.3	82.4	84.8
35 to 44 Years	87.5	86.5	88.5	92.8	91.9	92.4
45 to 64 Years	93.7	93.3	93.9	95.4	95.1	95.2
65 Years and over . .	95.5	95.0	94.3	95.9	95.2	95.3

Some answers to our questions as to home life among Negro Americans follow:

Alabama

It is very good. The young people are making a more rapid progress along these lines than the older people in this section.

Very good but not as it should be.

In this particular great improvement is being shown. The size and appearance of the house, habits of cleanliness and industry and general intelligence all show a commendable degree of advancement.

The home life of the colored people of this city has wonderfully advanct in the last twenty years. They are building good and comfortable homes many of which have the latest improvements.

The home life of these people is especially notable for the maternal devotion which usually keeps the family together. The home life of the better class compares very favorably with that of the average white American family.

Family ties are alarmingly too loose, concubinage too common and divorces too popular.

They don't seem to know how to deport themselves in their home life in order to be happy and to have things in good shape around them but they are growing better.

Fair in some instances. Generally does not measure up to this rating.

There are several people here who own land and homes of their own. Some of them have very nice homes and nice conveniences around them.

Generally live in one room cabins.

Varies according to economic and intellectual conditions. Our colored people are growing encouragingly in good life.

Not what it should be but getting better.

More in evidence and becoming of greater moment in the thot and plans of the average Negro.

The home life among colored people in the South is so much like that other employment, farming, in which many of us are engaged without a clear knowledge of the rules governing it. For reasons which we will not discuss here, home has not meant and does not mean to the average colored man what it means to some others living under the same flag.

On a whole they live happily with few separations but a vast improvement can be made in building good homes.

Perhaps this is a line in which we will see most improvements in the cities and communities near the various industrial schools. Many ignorant people have comfortable homes and the home life is usually commendable.

Better homes in both town and country give us the best evidence that there is improvement along this line.

Marvelously improving from day to day. Education and increast earning capacity together with other things have lifted the ideal of home life among the Negroes thruout the South.

Arkansas

This among the religious and educational part of the Negro people according to my experience is fairly good, but much improvement is needed among the less fortunate.

Nearly every family owns a home and in many instances more than one so that a natural love of order, etc., is maintained.

About seventy-five per cent of the people lead fairly good sound congenial home life, care for their children and try to make home happy.

The majority of the people live well. Most of them own their own homes.

A great deal of the property of the city is owned by colored people.

Their home life is one hundred per cent better than it has been.

California

Very much up to modern requirements.

Connecticut

The majority of our people are lovers of home and while property is high yet they are making the struggle to make the home-life pleasant and agreeable. Recently in our daily paper an article appeared stating that we owned more property for our numbers than any other race.

There is little real home life due to long working hours and large numbers of secret organizations which take both men and women away from home. Their small wages prevent home from being made attractive.

District of Columbia

Every grade and condition of home-life is to be found. The fundamental sacredness of home is absent, however, in even the best. Pride of appearance extends to size of house rather than to condition; but the interiors are artistic and in many cases the reflection of keen artistic sense of owners. Desire for pleasure and lack of opportunities to labor for high returns change many homes to lodging houses with the attendant evils to young girls. Owned homes and homes on principal streets grow by leaps and bounds. No suburban life of any account.

Better classes of colored people have good home life. Among the lower elements it is deplorable.

Florida

They seem to take a great interest in home life.

Seem to be all one would wish according to their condition. Quite an interest manifested in getting good homes and all the things that go to make life happy.

The Negro home life is far from what it ought to be and that is very evident in the conduct of his children. Taking the Negro as a whole you find very rare cases where the father and mother are both proper examples for their children.

The Negro men in my community are among the working class and they spend all their leisure away from home while the women seem to be interested in home life.

The greatest change can be seen in home life. More persons are being built some very pretty homes; others comfortable. Children are being taught to love the home and respect their parents.

Industrial, economic home life is very encouraging.

The most of the people own their own homes, from forty to one hundred sixty acres and are making their living at home.

Most colored people here own their homes, which are very neatly kept in most cases.

A true and pure home is the crying need of this place. There is need of a proper conception of the relations of all the members of the household.

Georgia

They are trying to get homes and care for them.

Their home life seems to be very fair, with the majority of our people having their own stock and vehicles and some with their own homes

As they become home owners home life is showing constant improvement.

Too careless. Much rather the outer world see their greatness than use scant means at home where they are needed.

The Negro is building better and more attractive homes. Landlords are recognizing the fact that Negroes no longer live in any sort of hut and are building better tenements. I suppose this has some bearing on the subject of home life.

This is good in the majority of people in Atlanta who are striving to climb. There is great improvement in this line, but it seems to have little effect on the young in the homes.

He has more respect for the marriage vow than in former times; home and surroundings in general are more comfortable; therefore, home life is more ideal.

The average person seems desirous of having a nice well furnisht home.

Each year shows new interest and progress in home life.

Very fond of home life and they seem to strive to make home life more happy.

Most of the folk are renters and take little interest in where they live and how.

Their home life is not what it ought to be because in the main they are without homes of their own and do not try to improve their homes or home life.

Home life is not ideal, by any means. The conduct of the children in the school rooms and on the streets is the greatest proofs of this statement. Parents being in service has much to do with the great deficiency.

There is a decided improvement and progress is being made still. They do not pack in such small quarters as they used to.

Illinois

They, for the most part, have well furnisht, well kept houses. There is almost always music but seldom a proper supply of good books. Few comparatively subscribe for a daily paper.

Miserable; fifty per cent of which is due to poverty and lack of time to develop same in the struggle for an existence.

Negro home life at best is never ideal. It is too soon for him to boast of a family tree. I believe he measures up with many of the more favored races; is far superior to the various nationalities coming to our shores. His married life is on the up-grade. Behavior is very good considering the short time.

Kansas

Is not what it should be but much is being done by the schools in the vicinity; such as the extension work of Western University. In many cases an unwholesome one. Kansas is a prohibition state and the temptation to sell liquor in the home is very great.

Kentucky

They are greatly improved in regards to the comfort and government of their children on a whole.

Much improvement in the home life of the masses of our people.

Home life is becoming more cheerful and delightful.

Most families are industrious, prosperous and own homes with pleasant surroundings.

They need a little training on that line that must be done from the pulpit and the school room.

The past ten years in this city has been an era for acquiring homes on the part of the Negro population. They are taking pride in making their homes the center of their social and intellectual life.

Some of our people do not take the pride that they should in the home life. Some say they don't want any home and will let anything do and will try to have absolutely no progress along that line.

Far from the ideal but improving yearly.

Louisiana

Not improving much among the masses of our people. It is growing better and better among the trained.

In particular do we find evidences of progress along this line. Homes are more comfortable, hygienic and sanitary conditions show markt improvement.

We are learning the needs of the bath tubs, wire screens, etc., for the home.

Much better than it was five years back.

Simple but not very attractive, owing to a lack of proper knowledge.

The home life of the people of this section of the country is good. About half own their homes and are very industrious.

Exceptional cases good but the average is poor.

Maryland

This is a city that is rather characterized by attention given to home life.

The home life among the Negroes here is about as good as any large city in the Union. About forty per cent of the colored population is fairly well housed.

Minnesota

We are rapidly cultivating the highest ideals of home life and learning more and more the great responsibility imposed in the care and rearing of children.

Mississippi

Thirty per cent pretty fair, twenty per cent poor, fifty per cent indifferent.

They can greatly improve in their home life especially as it pertains to the mutual respect and honor of husband and wife and the careful training of their children.

Generally over crowded and living in poorly kept and dirty sections. A very large number of Negroes here own homes and have modest and otherwise very attractive homes. A large number here are forst to live in very undesirable sections because of small wages.

Missouri

St. Louis is a city of homes. The home life of those I know best is admirable. There are others with whom home life is not exemplary.

Is not keeping pace with other improvements.

Is improving. For a long time there was this complaint: few children were found in the homes of people of intelligence. There is great improvement along this line but most of the mothers are very young. They need mothers' clubs to instruct them for they send their children to school without any breakfast and give them money with which they buy pickles and doughnuts.

All homes except two or three are well kept. About eighty per cent own their own homes. They are peaceably quiet. Almost every house has a telephone.

New Jersey

Owing I think to the narrow quarters in which most of the people must live, home conditions are not good.

Improving among the home-buying element.

New York

In most cases good and in some cases exceptional.

Improving constantly and yet there is a large margin left for further improvement. At least a third own homes, but many are careless in their keeping of them. Just at this time there is a new awakening among the people in the matter of purchasing homes. This they do mostly thru Building and Loan Associations.

The average colored man and woman in this city, as far as my observation goes, takes very little advantage of home life. I have come in contact with very few families in proportion whose home life is ideal.

North Carolina

Their deportment on this line has improved very much indeed. They are looking ahead for better things.

Is far from what it should be. It is poor and meagre. Many have no personal pride and the home is not what it ought to be. Decoration

and adornment is lacking many a home. We find some homes that compare favorably with any home in town and city, rich or poor.

Sad lack of home discipline.

The homes are good—far above the average rural home. They are
well kept and furnisht and many families own two-story dwellings painted inside and out.

The home life of the people of this town is fairly good; of the people of the rural districts and most of the county—very good. I refer
to the county because I come into close contact with people all over the
county.

Ohio

Our city is called the city of homes and there are some very beautiful ones. Those who can find good homes usually keep them good.

On this subject, as far as their means will permit, they score as
high a percentage as any in the country. I think the whites here have
the greater number of divorces.

Oklahoma

Impure.

They are in the dark.

In poor condition—most generally with the untrained.

There is absolutely a betterment along this particular line.

None too good. Conjugal infidelity is common both with spouses and
divorces from that cause are very rare. Many of our people come in
here from those parts of the South where it is not considered a disgrace
for a young woman to bear an illegitimate child.

Much improved but too much freedom and not enough exactness and
punctuality.

Pennsylvania

There is very little real home life among the colored people in this
city because they have to live in tenements and flats. I speak of the
masses, not the exceptions.

Very much improved. Better perhaps than the home life of the
same class of whites.

I don't believe there is a race that loves home life much more than
the Negro.

I know of instances where a comparatively poor family has taken
some sick person or friendless one in to share their shelter and food.

Rhode Island

The males have many outside attractions, such as amusements, social life and lodges. On the whole, home life for the females is normal.

South Carolina

Both good and bad. Most of our people in this state do not pay sufficient attention to home life. Some few are making great efforts to improve along that line, others are almost totally indifferent.

Camden is noted for the anxiety of the colored people to own their own homes, and I think I am correct when I say that the majority of the town people own their homes and as a rule they are kept very nicely.

In this respect we are making only a very limited improvement in my judgment, altho I believe we are making some advancement in promoting and strengthening the sanctity of the home. For while the number who seriously fail in this respect is very large, there are evidences that as a whole we are making some headway in making the home in truth what it ought to be.

This is very good because many of them have their own homes and live in larger and better houses in town, cities and the country.

In the congested districts mentioned above—and many rural tenants locate there—the home life is very poor and disorderly.

Tennessee

Good and compares well with that of the best communities. A large percentage own their own homes which are beautiful and well kept.

In the majority of homes the men seem not to realize their responsibility.

As a rule when young people marry they begin to build up a home and rear their family. The town does not afford work for the men the year round and this makes it difficult to have the homes as they should be. The majority are happy and agreeable.

A decided progress shown. There is a growing pride and ambition to have better homes. These are signs of better living.

Becoming better, especially as shown in the children of our graduates.

Texas

Far below normal; many are impure and their habits of life are too bad for the public to know.

Parents could be stricter on children.

Very particularly guarded. A great rivalry exists in trying to make the homes inviting and cultured.

Practically thirty per cent property owners whose home life is fair but that of the remainder is questionable.

Turbulent, or there would not be so many divorce cases.

He does not understand the value of home. But little attention is given to this most essential of all his needs.

Simple and inadequate in too many instances. Hard work and late hours returning home and early hours to work undermine the home life. But the colored people are home loving and do much to have good homes. Economic conditions outside the home handicap the Negroes' homes.

Judging from the girls who come here, I should think that they did as they pleased and had no proper government.

Is broadening. Home-getting and home-keeping is the chief ambition. Happiness generally reigns in the home.

Home life is not what you would call ideal, but a majority are learning the importance of proper environment in forming character.

Rather better homes, cleaner and more comfortable.

Fairly good, most Negroes here own their own homes, and take a certain amount of pride in them.

Out of three thousand seven hundred seventy Negroes in this city, more than ninety-eight per cent read and write; eighty per cent own their own homes and among them are many nice ones.

Sad conditions—constantly moving, renting and mortgaging.

He is improving here very markedly. The roaming disposition is giving away to building up the home and making it more attractive.

Virginia

Great improvement.

Better homes and surroundings may be seen in the city and country, which indicate better home life.

Improvement. Often unlettered parents use advice of children in lower grades at school.

In those families where the parents are educated, the homes are as they should be—on a high plane. In lower classes, it is coarse and crude. There are exceptions to the latter.

Morally good. They devote their time mostly to work in and about the home.

Medium according to surroundings. This is a furnace and public-work town and women give most of their time to cooking and carrying meals, washing and ironing; consequently they have no time to care for their homes.

West Virginia

Is improving but not enough buying of homes.

Home life is improving rapidly especially during the past five years.

Decided improvement. Great interest is shown in purchasing homes, beautifying and keeping them.

Too much time is given to dressing, eating and hunting amusements to spend much time in trying to inculcate the principals of truth, virtue, honesty and cleanliness.

Poor. Have but little respect for home or how they live. Small rooms poorly ventilated. Have but little for the uplifting of those dependent upon them.

Compare favorably with all races in other parts of the country. The average American home life is below what it should be.

Section 9. Rearing of Children

The children of the slave families did not belong to their parents and discipline was lax. The selected answers which are here printed indicate present conditions. These answers come from twenty-five states.

Alabama

Is not as good as it should be.

Better families look after children well. Others are somewhat neglectful.

A deeper interest relative to the education of children is now being manifested. They are sent to school rather than to work. Sometimes a great sacrifice is made for the proper rearing of children.

Generally speaking the rearing of children is well done tho many fail thru ignorance and lack of character.

Greatly neglected in this city. Many parents allow their children to run at large at late hours of the night. They assemble in dives and hang around the corners in great numbers, especially the boys. Many of them are becoming gamblers and idlers.

The children are neglected in many cases from lack of facilities to rear them properly, inadequate schools, necessity of the parents to work and spend little time in the home.

They delight in education. Children have access to three good schools which run from eight to nine months in the year.

Four fifths of the children are improperly reared. The parents in equal numbers have never had the proper training themselves.

As a majority they are allowed to go too much undisciplined.

These people are gifted in loving their offspring to such an extent as not to bend them in time, so to speak, consequently so many stray.

The education ot more fathers and mothers proves to be of much improvement in the rearing of children.

Some improvement.

They are very careful in the rearing of their children. Some of them teach them how to work, send them to Sunday school and church and to the day schools.

Varies according to economic and intellectual conditions. Our colored people are growing encouragingly in the rearing of their children.

Improving but very slowly.

Rearing and training of children is the most difficult problem of any people and because of the colored man's financial and political status and because of having to battle with conditions which are imposed upon him the work of properly rearing his children has been far from satisfactory either to himself or to his best friends.

A little too careless and not taking the proper interest in schools.

Not very good. Few are being born and they are not provided for as they ought to be.

I fear that married couples are not inclined to rear large families as used to be the case with our fathers in the past. This is not due to natural conditions but to the crime of abortion in many cases. This is especially true of those who live in cities.

The fact that all the schools both public and private are each year overcrowded must indicate a corresponding interest in the home care and concern about the child.

I am not prepared to answer this question. I have given this subject considerable thot but am still undecided as to whether the Negro of my community is rearing his children in a way that could be improved under circumstances or not.

A very great falling off along this line. Children are allowed to be idle and slothful.

Arkansas

This needs much improvement among all classes.

There is a tendency to permit children to have too many liberties before they are really able to see for themselves or really know what are the consequences that result from too early taking upon themselves the responsibility which belongs to mature years and I believe the parent is wholly in error.

Think they are a little careless along this line as a majority; yet we have ample provision for schools, etc.

Some of the children are well reared. A large per cent of them attend Sabbath school and church, also the city schools. A great many of the children have little restraint and are allowed to run the streets.

It is not as good along all lines as it should be. While there are many of our people who try to raise their children right others let them come on as they can.

They bear children freely.

Connecticut

There is a decrease, I am sure, along this line. Some large families are left but not as many as formerly. The high cost of living and medical aids given women to prevent increase are the causes partly at least.

Children are much on the streets and in cheap places of amusement and are harmed.

District of Columbia

This, formerly considered the duty of parents, has been delegated to the public schools. Our children are longer in contact with their teachers and under their influence than with and under their parents. Modern conditions.

All grades of care and neglect are to be found in the children of the same schools. Proper feeding and hygiene are the deficiencies. Children of Negroes are dependent upon the schools to a greater extent than the whites for all ideals of living, even in the best homes. Too much dress and cheap pleasure and too little formation of right habits characterize the people as a whole.

Better classes of colored people rear their children properly. Among the lower elements the children are not reared properly.

Florida

Seem to be losing ground with quite a majority of our people.

Not as good as it ought to be, thanks(?) to their leadership(?).

Most children these days get no home training and the example of their parents is such as is sure to corrupt their morals and manners.

If there is any one thing that should be establisht it is a school to teach our people how to rear their children. For God knows they don't know and don't care.

They are somewhat careless with their children. The principle of their training comes from mothers and when the boys reach a certain age they are beyond her reach.

Children are being reared properly and sent to school. Mothers are one hundred per cent more intelligent than they were years ago, so I think they can rear the young better.

Very little stress is being put on the rearing of children and home culture.

Little attention is paid to the proper rearing of children in many homes.

Georgia

We do not. We turn them loose and let them go as they want to go.
He is taking greater interest in his children.

Anxiety is exprest by all to have their children come up under better conditions than their parents. Heretofore, parents have said that as they were raised the same conditions were good enough for their children,—but that idea is not the one now.

On a decline. Leave the children to assume duties beyond their abilities which ends disastrously.

Much care is exercised in many cases while some are careless.

There are but few or no children in the families of the younger set of educated people; but the children as a whole are given a better education and stay in school longer than in former years. There are two orphanages in the city.

I must admit that along this line there is slow progress yet nothing to cause hopelessness.

Very careless. Seems that they are taking new steps along this line.

Domestic influence is more wholesome, parents are more intelligent, therefore, children are receiving better training.

Less are being born but more care is given. Negro parents need to know better how to treat their children.

I do not think that parents are quite as strict with their children as they were when I was a child.

Another field for improvement. The condition of the working people hinders them in the rearing of their children. Among the better class it is good.

Improving rapidly along this line. It seems that they take great care in observing the health rules and have made great improvement along this line.

Not much care is taken along this line. Many mothers work out and children are left a great deal to themselves.

They are being educated and trained in better habits.

They are generally trained in schools and parents are rigid in having their children mannerly.

Entirely too lenient in rearing their children and hire them out to work too young.

Rapid improvement; care more for children; keep them in school and send them to Sunday school.

Illinois

Parents don't seem to be taking enough time to teach children what they ought to know and to encourage them to do what they ought to do. They tell them and just pass on, and then wonder why they do not get better results.

Reared in the streets. Some of our best citizens hardly know what their children are doing.

Not much rearing the children in the big cities; often children are what their parents wish them to be thru pride. Of course, there are many families in large cities who are earnest and direct their children properly, but they belong to a pitiable minority.

About the ordinary; some spoiled and over-fed; others neglected and go unwashed; nothing unusual.

There is a great laxity. Not enough education, especially in the higher branches. Too great a stress on dressing.

Indiana

Good. Family normal. No race suicide. The slogan is: "Fewer but better children".

Kansas

Upon the decline. Smaller families in most communities.

Very much neglected. Small houses and large families make a very perplexing problem.

Kentucky

We are spoiling our children with over indulgence.

They raise themselves.

They drift to the city too soon. They should be put to work.

Altho many of our children are neglected and allowed to run to the moving picture shows and public dances at night unaccompanied, yet the "Parent-Teachers' Association" is making a winning fight to give assistance to incompetent mothers.

Bad. Parents think too much of them when they are young and when they become men and women they are looking for some way to beat thru the world.

Louisiana

Below par. On account of not receiving that training which pertains to their religion and education. A four months' school term and no effort to have it lengthened is put forth by parent or church.

As the race improves in education, there is a tendency toward fewer children, but they are rearing the few they have better.

Among the lower classes, the children are left entirely to the teachers.

Maryland

Children are loved too dearly, if that is possible, and are allowed to get beyond control.

Finding difficulty along this line. For many instances, the mother is away all day from home. Yet the conditions along this line are very fair.

Mississippi

More wholesome environment than formerly.

Not so carefully raised as in former years. Parents of the second generation after slavery do not seem to be so expert in that art as their ex-slave parents.

It is really pathetic to see the sacrifices the humble Negroes are making to educate their children. There is very little companionship; while the parents work and strive to improve their children's condition, they very often take them in their confidence and talk with or advise them to live honestly and uprightly.

Missouri

Children are given too great liberties. There is not enough of the wise restrictions that aid positively toward the building of character.

Just waking up to the great importance.

Fair, but girls are cared for more than boys which is always a danger. Out of two hundred school children less than a dozen illegitimate ones among them.

Some of the best women we have in morals and education, are the poorest housekeepers. They are just now beginning to appreciate being taught sewing, cooking and manual training in the schools. They are not the equal of the older people in rearing children.

I know of only one family where the children were desired. Ninety per cent were either accidental or incidental. Very little pride. Sixty per cent are legitimate. Very little interest taken in them.

New Jersey

Very little; domestic services and "day's work" make it difficult for them to give the time they should to their children.

Most of the parents are rearing their children well, failing however, in many cases to teach them respect for elders and reverence for God.

New York

Conditions in this direction could be improved. They are not all that they should be but the many exceptional cases found form the basis of hope for the others.

Our people here marry early in life and as a rule have large and rapidly increasing families. There is probably no effort among any of them to prevent or to hinder rapid increase of children. There is much parental negligence and many of the children do not receive the proper home attention.

Discipline not as severe as formerly. Method of moral suasion more generally followed.

Like all other people except the Jewish, Negroes are not taking the proper interest in their children. Result: the children become immoral before they are matured.

As a race their one idea is to keep them healthy long enough to go to work for parents; there is no pressure brot to bear to force the child or encourage children to remain in school.

Ohio

Many are by far too easy with them. Even our curfew can hardly keep them off the street at night. Their entertainment is left too much for their selection.

The teachers and preachers need to thunder forth a change. There is too much laxity, children are not taught to obey their parents and superiors as they should; they are allowed to go and come too much at will without reporting to superiors; to visit pool rooms, saloons, dances and places of cheap notoriety.

Oklahoma

The children are left to themselves.

Their children are not cared for as they should be on account of our mothers being called from home much of the time to help make the living.

Educational interest is slowly but gradually growing. Ninety per cent of our children of school age are in school.

A radical change for the better has been wrot in the last ten or twenty years. More home interests and instructions should be given.

Pennsylvania

It is very difficult for the average colored people in this city to rear their children. They have no places in which they may play except the parks and streets; often the parks are far away.

A tendency not to have children; but when they have them they make an honest effort to educate them.

Rhode Island

The children have very little of a father's care and on a whole not enough of a mother's.

South Carolina

Some few properly reared. Most are allowed to come up as best they can; to have their own way. A majority of our boys and girls do not attend school. A large number do not attend any Sunday school.

I should say they are totally ignorant and this is one of their weakest points.

Children are very well cared for and attend school very largely but there should be some improvement along this line.

Imitating the whites in desiring small families. The high cost of living and the increast number of what were formerly regarded as luxuries, that only the rich were to have, but now must be supplied in even the more humble homes, had the same effect among our people as among the whites in making many of them consider a large number of children a burden. More colored children have school training and home instruction now than at any former time.

This is better because they are better trained, clothed and fed. Not brot up in one-room houses.

Quite a number of mothers in service thus leaving children to care for and rear themselves during the very time they need watching. Many children attend school from such homes having to prepare themselves. In many such cases the children are taught at home to defend themselves at all hazards.

Tennessee

The children of our town as a whole are well cared for. I regret to say that I do not think there is enough attention paid to the rearing of the boys in our town and many other towns I have visited.   We have a splendid school system but it carries only nine grades.   Every year we have from twenty to twenty-five very young children to finish school that might otherwise be held in school longer.

They are making a hard struggle to bring their children up right.

Children are rearing the parents.   The rule seems to be "Children make your parents obey you''.

People are too slack in the rearing of their children; seem to have no rule to conform to.   Do not see after them especially but send them to school until they are fourteen or fifteen and for the most part to Sabbath school; but after that age they go to the amusement halls, the cafes etc.

Suffer from ignorant and incompetent parents.   Do not get proper physical, mental and moral training.   Poor and but little parental government.   Much carelessness and neglect in essential things.   Need of reform.

The homes where children have the care and training which they ought are comparatively few but increasing in numbers.

Texas

Is a complete failure.   Lost almost without a remedy.   Indeed a sad state of affairs as the children are permitted to run the streets at will.

Some are rearing their children with great care as regards the cardinal elements of truth, honor, virtue and usefulness; many others extremely careless.   Some homes are without children.

Receives great attention among the people of our race and every school is supported by strong mothers' clubs who go side by side with teachers in the welfare of the children.

Only about one-half who seem to pay the right attention; some of them dress their children all right and try to school them and teach them how to work while others work themselves and let the children stray and go where they please.

Not so good in many.   I think this is because of the conduct of the children in the high school and the grades; also from their actions in the street.

The Father's Club is doing a grand work.   Pastor and people alike have united to see that the children are trained in the home and that good instruction is gently given them.

Smaller families or no families at all seems to be the general rule.

Not strict enough.   Children are given more liberty than is good for them.

This is fairly good altho there are some who do not take the proper interest along this line.

The teaching of the leaders and especially of teachers is having more weight in our state.   So that there is better family government.   Parents are firmer in seeing that home regulations are obeyed.

Virginia

The children are too frequently allowed too much latitude, but this is a weakness of the time among white and colored.

Parents seem anxious to put children forward and lose sight of the necessity of exacting strict obedience and respect to all.

Children have good educational advantages of which they avail themselves up to the grammar grades. Seventy-five per cent don't go beyond the grades.

Among the educated parents, the majority of the children are being beautifully reared. Some of the families are large and some small. There are ignorant families where the children are being neglected. This is easy to account for.

The children are comparatively behind as they have no high schools and the city school is run on the same basis as the county and district schools, from four to six months. Many are ill-mannered.

West Virginia

Parents are not giving the attention to their children that they should so as to have them grow up the most useful men and women. In the sections where it is possible to secure homes, that is, purchase homes, the conditions are much improved; but here in the coal fields where it is impracticable to purchase homes, the people have made but slight improvement. There is a large orphanage at Huntington, W. Va.

We have here a parents' union in which we aim to discuss the practical things of life such as amusements, associations and dress, in fact any phase of life which will benefit the child.

But very little done. Children left very largely to themselves. Lack of parental restraint. Mother and father so busy trying to secure a livelihood, children not thot of until the close of the day.

They are almost a failure in the rearing of children. Giving them too much liberty allowing them to roam the streets and keep late hours.

Section 10.   Amusements for Young People.

Few persons pause to consider how difficult is the problem of amusement for young Negroes in America. First, they are frankly shut out of most places of public amusement and most Negro parents are afraid to send their children where they would be admitted for fear that some veiled action or word would poison their pleasure. Secondly, these naturally joyous, dancing, singing people have received a puritanic training which continually thunders against "worldly" amusements. Small wonder is there that our answers here are strangely contradictory and that they reveal astonishing moral attitudes.

Alabama

Fairly good. There is no such thing as dancing in this section of the country.

As a rule the young people do not have a sufficiency of wholesome amusement. Hence, their minds are often wrongly influenst.

Very little wholesome amusement if any is provided for the young people, hence, they seek the amusement which is not best for them nor for any race.

Wholesome amusement for young people is insignificant when compared with the hurtful amusements, such as gambling, drinking intoxicating liquors, frequenting what is known as "Honky-tonks" etc.

The majority of them seem to take more delight in the unwholesome.

The communities are in poor condition as to wholesome amusement.

As to the wholesome amusement for the young people we use such as the Christian endeavor, Y. M. C. A. and Y. W. C. A. and libraries.

None, save what children from their own resources create at school.

Some of the people have musical instruments in their homes to amuse the young people. They give entertainments for the young people, and also have a society for the young people.

Very much needed. Very poor opportunities in this. Amusement places "for whites only" except cheap shows.

The lack of wholesome amusement among our people is having its unwholesome effect upon the church. The tendency also is to lessen the charms which a well ordered home should have for the child in its formative period.

I find that steps are being taken by many intelligent leaders to furnish the young people with wholesome amusements. Many are making the effort to eliminate the dance by the skating rink and such other amusements as will take up their time at times when they usually go to the dance halls.

There is almost none. Here is the greatest avenue for the service of the social worker.

We are wofully lacking in this. The most of the amusements for our young people are furnisht by white people whose interest is financial returns.

They are beginning to see the need of wholesome amusement for children.

Arkansas

In churches only.

There is no general movement in this direction but we feel the need of it and with the co-operation of the teachers another year we mean to start a work of this kind. Most young people are not among the uneducated class.

This important work is far below what it should be among the best of us.

The amusements are few, if any. The Y. M. C. A. does not afford any. There are no play grounds or public parks. The theatre is about the only place for amusement. This not very wholesome.

California

A beginning has been made along this line but lack of means is hindering progress.

Connecticut

Fraternal societies occupy much of their time. The theatre and dance halls form some amusement but ought to be engaged in by the young under parental guidance or ministerial advice, especially the dances.

Y. M. C. A. and churches are seeking to furnish wholesome amusement, but the masses are not attracted.

District of Columbia

The cheap picture shows more than neutralize the good done by the recent institution known as the play-ground.

School play-grounds are in existence but sex contact spoils most of their results for children over twelve. Y. M. C. A. and Y. W. C. A. are engaged in work which are giving better opportunities for adolescents, but fundamental racial feelings are being disregarded for imitation of methods in white institutions of same kind. Culture clubs exist among classes but are offset by cheap dances which attract splendid female possibilities with the usual results. Syncopated music with its sensual stimulus is in every house with a piano and dancing at any hour.

Our people are fairly well equipt in this regard but we are in need of more playgrounds.

Better classes of colored people have wholesome amusements. Among the lower classes the amusements are not wholesome.

Florida

Woefully deficient. Too much time devoted to getting ready for heavenly citizenship; too little for earthly citizenship.

There are no special arrangements made for amusements for children in and thruout this section. Hence, they seek their own amusements.

The church should furnish such but alas it seems that the church has partially joined the rag time amusements which seem to be the only kind which will draw a crowd. To build churches our people seem willing to sacrifice all.

What a fair-minded person would call none for persons between the ages of twelve and twenty years.

Vaudeville theatre and moving pictures are among the chief amusements of the young people.

The young people are free moral agents and are zealous in keeping up with every questionable fad that is brot into the city.

Very little amusement for young people.

The greatest amusement here for young people is dancing and I do not consider this wholesome.

There is nothing in an organized way. The ballroom is the most popular amusement; also cards. A good effort to do something in this line has been undertaken.

Georgia

Not being furnisht as it should be. Hence they amuse themselves with things that destroy them.

Leads our people away from education and refinement.

We need amusement for young folk. The manner of dancing and playing cards has misled many.

Only two playgrounds and these only recently establisht. No parks for them. They live in the streets or closed up in the homes. This is a condition found in practically every southern city.

Little or no wholesome amusement is held out to country children aside from hunting, fishing, etc. The Negro children hardly consider this amusement. Where the sexes are brot together socially they are off when it comes to wholesome amusement.

Our people go on too many excursions.

I don't think as much attention is given as should be to provide the young people with wholesome amusement.

Housekeepers are supplying their parlors with pianos and organs and are lavish in granting innocent amusements.

Very little effort in general is put forth to better conditions along this line. No group seems to be especially interested in this phase of development. Some individal efforts are being made to do something.

Illinois

The churches and Sunday schools and the Y. M. C. A. are furnishing a great deal of wholesome amusement in some places and the others are seeing the need of doing so.

None that I would call wholesome save a few selected church entertainments and settlement affairs.

Movies, I believe, have an unwholesome effect upon the young people. Roller skating, rag-time music, cabaret songs, and ugly suggestions of the big city are all pernicious. The dancing clubs in the big cities are also vicious.

Indiana

A little short on this point, I think, but thru public playgrounds connected with some of the schools, the junior department of the Y. M. C. A. and a constantly growing number of home-purchasers the condition is growing better.

Kentucky

Wholesome amusement has been so unwelcome that pleasing amusement has overwhelmed it.

The Mothers' Club and the Association mentioned above are trying to supply this great need, knowing that children are truly social beings.

Maryland

The Dunbar Athletic Club devotes a good bit of its time to provide wholesome amusement for the young. The children are trained in many athletic sports and have several meets a year.

Very good, but more stress should be put on them for the purpose of counteracting the improper amusements.

Practically none, other than incidental amusements of the church and school. Tendency to theatrical and house and ball dances harmful.

Minnesota

In the abstract, all public amusement (of which there is much here) is open to the race; yet, nevertheless, there is need and want of something more racial in character to bring them more closely together in social contact and intercourse.

Mississippi

None. Nor are there any arrangements being made. No choice as to the kind. Twenty-five per cent do not go or allow their children to go.

I know of nothing that I could call wholesome.

None. A moving picture place is their resort; that has a Negro gallery.

No play grounds, clubs nor a decent hall in the town.

Missouri

There is much being begun. The public dance hall is still the chief place of amusement.

Does not receive the attention that should be given it by the parents here. Very often as a result boys and girls are thrown with bad associations which have their demoralizing effects.

I think that we are a sleeping people when it comes to amusements for young people. Little or nothing is being done. Personal efforts were abandoned for lack of support.

New Jersey

Very little—too much of the unwholesome; the public dance hall, so-called dancing class, is the worst.

New York

Illiberal regulations must be abolisht.   Standards of many Christian bodies make hypocrites of the youth.

Many and a variety of which they readily take an active part.   Athletics among boys greatly encouraged and willingly and strenuously strive to excel.

North Carolina

Slow on this line, but they have improved.   Somewhat better for the past ten years.

No definite kinds—sometimes baseball, tennis, croquet, socials, etc. A few have them but this is greatly neglected in the home.   Therefore the streets and public places draw many of the young people to resorts of low repute and demoralizing habits.

Ohio

Partly answered in the preceeding.   There is lack of wholesome amusement and we can hardly blame them for their selection unless we present something else.

We have here a Y. M. C. A. which is being well patronized by them. The women, too, are making efforts along the same line.

Oklahoma

Real advancement—popular lectures, concerts, etc.

We encourage such games as baseball, tennis, croquet, basket ball and the indoor gymnastic exercises generally.   Our greatest struggle in this direction is to counteract the influence of the dive Negro as seen in the music and dancing.

Pennsylvania

The "Nickelodium" is the only amusement and often the children are compelled to seek their own amusement.

There are many clubs and centers for such but they need careful direction.

None but dancing, moving pictures and a low life of vaudeville, which is running riot here at the present, given by the better classes for the benefit of their institutions and which include all types of dancing.

The low dance hall has almost entirely disappeared before the commonly used vaudeville theatre and moving picture shows.

Unfortunately for the colored people in Philadelphia such amusement is limited.   Racial barriers act as retarding forces in the attaining of such desired goals.   The Y. M. C. A. and Y. W. C. A. are timely growing in numbers and in financial strength and so will soon be able to offer a variety of healthy pastimes.   Some of the theatres and dance halls accommodate colored patrons while others do not.   The public parks discriminate very little.

Rhode Island

Moving picture shows maintain a high level.   Vaudeville does not edify.   Shows generally fair.   Concerts and lectures uplifting.

South Carolina

None whatever.   No reading room, no Y. M. C. A., no Christian Endeavor or anything whatever to inspire the young and therefore, considering all things, Camden people succeed wonderfully well.

The development of a true home life and the increast personal care given to the young in the matter of educating them in mind and heart, both are, in my opinion, showing themselves also in the growth of a proper sense of the necessity that suitable and helpful as well as instructive and developing amusement be provided; such amusement as will polute not the mind and corrupt not the heart will attract and sustain the interest of the child.

Tennessee

Some are very strict.   There is absolutely nothing that could be called wholesome amusement.   Our best young people cannot mix with them at all, they are conducted in such a bad manner.

Not so much being done as might be done considering the increasing number of children who are not obliged to go into service early.

Very little done—a great need in this line.

Texas

Have about gone into rag-time.   No one has charge of affairs except the Police Recorder.

The places for wholesome amusements are few, especially for our people.

Social centres are in vogue thruout the city for pastime and amusement for our young and work a great benefit in training the young how to amuse themselves in wholesome games.

Poorest sort—poor concerts, moving pictures, etc.

None save that provided by church and school.

Dancing, ball playing.

Moving pictures and shows.

Question not yet reacht.   We have failed a long time along these lines of giving our young inviting fields of pleasure.

Literary meetings and church socials.

Not enough of it.   The children now are amused by contact as it were at so much per moving picture show, theatre, entertainments of various and questionable kinds.

The children select their own amusement.   The public schools furnish various games, such as basket ball, tennis, base ball, etc., and our church is attempting the same.

They are adopting a system of amusement as a substitute for rougher or coarser amusements with better results.

Virginia

Here is a weak spot.   It is hard to get the church people to see things with our new light.

Moving picture shows with vaudeville for those who delight in such things but the better class of our people are religiously inclined.

West Virginia

Has received but little attention but thru the Parents' Union we hope to arouse the parents.   Indiscriminate nickelodium attendance is common here.   Parents are careless about attending different places of amusement with their children.

None whatsoever.   No playgrounds, parks, gymnasiums even, connected with the school.

They are very poorly planned. Anything almost to be on the go. There are but few.   Too much night carousing, no outdoor or fresh air amusements.

In many sections they are few and far between.   The dance halls are the curse of the day.

Section 11.   Caring for Old People

A last measure of the family and group tie is the care bestowed on the old.   From early times Negroes in the United States have establisht old folks' homes and have now perhaps a hundred such homes thruout the nation.   Our correspondents send these answers to our question concerning the care of the old people.

Alabama

Much attention is given.   Have old people's homes here for colored supported by the colored people.

Most of the old people are cared for by relatives, friends, or some charitable institution.   Many of them have acquired enough to maintain their own support.

Each family is caring for its old people.

Nothing is being done for the old people by way of caring for them.

A committee of colored citizens have establisht an Old Folks' and Orphans' Home and an attempt is made to care for the old people.

The old people are cared for by the family and city.

There is no organized effort to care for the old people nearer than the city of Birmingham.

Old people who have homes or people who are able to see after them are cared for by their people. As a rule the old people who have not someone to care for them see a very hard time.

Those of the church are seen after.

There are several old people's homes being provided for and charitable donations for the benefit of the old people.

Poorly cared for old folks' home. Individuals take good care of aged parents in their respective homes.

The people are very nice in caring for old people. They have a society to help the people, a sick committee to visit and see after them and they take up collections in the church for the old people.

Our home with about six inmates.

Women's clubs here do a most commendable work in this respect. especially the Dunbar Club.

The churches and a number of benevolent institutions are turning their attentions more and more to this most needed work. Our local church here has a treasury from which it disburses monthly a stipend as to its worthy poor old people. The love and care are growing proportionately in the home and church as the people are being educated to it.

The principal way which I know of for caring for old people is in the various old folks' homes establisht thruout the country. Several cared for by contributions from churches and some by local contributions including money and clothing, supplies, etc.

I can point to a good many Old Folks' Homes started and maintained by colored women. Dozens of cases of young people giving up education and pleasures for aged parents come under my notice annually.

Very little is done along this line. We have an Old Folks' Home and Orphans' Home for the care of the aged and distrest but it is poorly provided for as there is no general awakening with interest in the care for the aged.

They are beginning now to reverence old age more and to make provisions for old people.

Arkansas

Very much neglected.

Our Women's Club and one or two of the churches assist the aged.

Much of it is done by the individual family. Very little organized work for that purpose. One Old Folks' Home.

There are homes built for old and decrepit people, also charitable hospitals.

There is a home for the aged but few ever go out to be cared for. At present there are no inmates.

California

Many organizations and the public at large seem to regard it their duty to contribute to this purpose.

Connecticut

Nothing at present is being done along this line.   Six years ago a home was started for such but about a year ago was closed for lack of funds.

There is a good one of some ten years' standing in New Haven.

Home for aged women supported by colored people but no provision made for the aged men.

District of Columbia

Ancestral worship is a cult which is not yet affected by our people. In return, for the missionaries of the Gospel sent to them, we hope that China will send to us, who will teach us the meaning of the fifth commandment.

Commendable efforts are made to care for the aged and indigent but much is needed to be done in these matters.

Florida

No provision made in this community for the care of old people and no effort being made to that end.

This subject seldom enters into their religion.   They do not even take care of their worn-out preachers, but appropriate these funds to suit their own conveniences.

Very little, if any, as yet.   There is a plan now on foot in this community that will soon have a comfortable home for the old and helpless.

The old people are cared for in an Old Folks' Home which is supported by the people here.

A philanthropic association by the name of the Buckingham-Smith Association left considerable cash, stocks, bonds, real estate, etc., all of which is very valuable to the old colored people of St. Augustine.   The value exceeds over a half million but it is now in the hands of a white man who gives a small pittance to a few now and then.   This gift is worthy of investigation but the colored people here seem afraid to tackle it.   The leading whites say that something should be done about it.

They die here before they get old.   Notwithstanding, Pensacola has begun to operate an Old Folks' Home and Orphan Home.

Georgia

A growing necessity.   The white people are saying the Negroes were better cared for in slavery than now.   Too much shiftlessness characterize the youths of to-day.   We should wake to our sense of duty.

We have two homes for old people; one dependent upon the general public and the other supported by the Steward A. M. E. Church.

Everybody is in societies which care for them.

There are quite a number of societies that are doing real good work in looking after and caring for the old and needy.

No place for old people supported by the city. The Carter Old Folks' Home is the only place in the city. It is largely sectarian in its admissions; not wholly so, however, I am told.

The old are pretty well cared for by church and society.

Good. Old Folks' Homes are being establisht in many places.

I know of only one place for the care of old people as an institution. In the homes the old people seem well cared for.

No arrangement is made for them. They are left to individual care of whoever may do for them. A number are cared for by their former white employers.

I know of several homes for the old, both North and South, and I think our race is as generously supporting them as any other race.

We have an Old Folks' Home.

Illinois

There seems to be a growing pride in the Old Folks' Home. The churches are establishing them and the Women's Clubs as well.

Dependent upon charity; no organized effort.

Kentucky

Cared for as best we can under present conditions. No home for them—yet they do not suffer.

I really believe better efforts would be put forth in this respect if the Negro's salary was better. His spirit is willing but his pocket weak.

No hospital nor home for the aged and helpless. Lodges and other charitable organizations contribute to the needy.

We have a home for the old and infirm which is fairly well supported by the race.

Louisiana

There are two homes in New Orleans for the old people: "The Lafon" and "Faith Home". In my home, committees are organized to erect an Old Folks' Home.

There are many benevolent societies whose mission is the care of the old and helpless. The churches are doing much along this line.

Maryland

Homes for aged conducted by the M. E. Church and another by Bethel A. M. E. Church. Then there is still another shelter or home for the aged.

Mothers, fathers and relatives are seldom neglected altho they are not as well lookt after as are the Hebrew parents. This should be lookt

after.
    I know of only one home not conducted under auspices of some church.

Mississippi

They are caring for old people all right in my churches.
    An Old Folks' Home managed by a club of Christian women; non-denominational. They have a small home and a few old people in it.

Missouri

An Old Folks' Home is maintained, but it is not at all creditable to the people.
    An old and invalid hospital home. In place of the old people going to the poor farm, we get the County Courts to let us have them in the Hospital and give us what it would cost to keep them at the poor farm and we beg the rest of the money necessary.
    Little generally done. As individuals, our people are proud and care for their old in a very creditable way. Our people remain young and we have very few real old and helpless people.

New Jersey

A home with limited improvements is being developt in Newark.

New York

In a community so small as this, the number of old people is, of course, not large. There is no "Old Folks' Home" here; yet, I know of none of the old people here that are not fairly well cared for. The churches here, regardless of color or race, look out for such.
    Great interest manifested in the past ten years due, I think, to the fact that white people are gradually withdrawing their support along this line.
    Seemingly indifferent except among the colored Catholics and Episcopalians.

North Carolina

Quite dutiful in way of Old Folks' Home.
    I have noted in many places that great care is given the old.

Ohio

All things considered, I think we are to be commended on the care given. I can call to mind a dozen families who are caring for their aged parents respectfully and not one where their parents are on charity. There are a few of the other kind however.

Oklahoma

This duty is performed very largely thru the church organizations.

Pennsylvania

Some commendable enterprises are on foot for caring for the aged which is very commendable for the colored people.   The Home for the Aged and Infirm Colored People is located here.

Philadelphia has, perhaps, the best home for old folks in the country. The churches are beginning to provide for their aged.

Satisfactorily met with.   Churches and small charitable bodies make provision for the aged.   This is a beautiful contrast to the lamentable neglect observed twenty or more years ago and as is met with in uncivilized countries.

Rhode Island

The state maintains an institution.   Our people have a home in Providence, which is supported in part by contributions from clubs run by leaders of the race.

South Carolina

The lessened number of our old people proportionately now found in poor houses and on the streets as beggars, and as subjects and objects of public charity, convinces me that they are being cared for more successfully by their own relatives than was the case some years ago.   Many of the secret societies and charitable orders among our people too, are largely supplementing what is being done in private homes for the support of the aged.

Tennessee

They are establishing and maintaining an Old Folks' Home.

Not much provision.   Even the county does not provide a place for them, altho it will appropriate a small sum for their maintenance if they are in some home.   Some lodges provide a home for the old and orphans. They are generally very kindly cared for by some member of the family or friend.

In the main, by the various benevolent organizations.   There is no special suffering here.   All things considered, they are lookt after very well.

Nothing systematic.   Personal response as occasion calls is most gratifying.

Texas

The fraternal and benevolent societies and church organizations are doing much in this direction, the sick and feeble being cared for and the dead being buried.

Greater interest being taken.   Old Folks' Homes being establisht.

Lookt after by various charity clubs but there is not an establisht institution in the city to care for the aged. That has been and is shamefully neglected.

Outside of societies, there is little care for the aged.

On a whole, there are a few old paupers among our people considering the large number of aged Negroes. Fine examples of filial loyalty to aged parents and relatives are not rare.

Most excellent. Now, more than ever, the Negro's Home is an old folks home as well as an orphan asylum.

In Texas, our people are becoming aroused on this subject. While several meagre attempts have been made to help the aged, last week the Baptist Conventions of Texas raised several thousand dollars to construct a building. Ten acres of land paid for here in Houston, Texas.

Virginia

My observation is that while many old people are neglected, in the majority of cases they are better cared for than formerly.

There is no organized charity but the aged are taken care of by their relatives. I do not know of a single case where an aged or helpless person has been neglected.

I know of numbers of old people who have been helpt and cared for. I have in mind also the caring for older parents by the children.

West Virginia

Only family care. No institutions.

A healthy sympathy is growing. The needs are being fairly well lookt after thru relatives, benevolent societies and the Church.

Section 12. The Church

Our publication of ten years ago, *The Negro Church*, went so thoroly into the subject of the history and function of the Negro church that little needs to be added.   In 1906 the United States government publisht a census of churches. The following tables were compiled from this government report. They present statistics of interest to this study.

Church organizations among Negro Americans

DENOMINATION	Number of Organizations	
	1906	1890
All denominations, consisting in whole or in part of colored organizations .	36,770	23,462
Denominations consisting wholly of colored organizations	31,393	19,158
Baptist Bodies		
Baptist National Convention	18,534	12,533
Colored Primitive Baptists in America	797	323
United American Freewill Baptists	251	
Church of God and Saints of Christ	48	
Churches of the Living God		
Church of the Living God (Christian Workers for Friendship)	44	
Church of the Living God (Apostolic Church)	15	
Church of Christ in God	9	
Evangelistic Associations		
Voluntary Missionary Society in America	3	
Free Christian Zion Church of Christ	15	
Methodist Bodies		
Union Amer. Methodist Episcopal Church	77	42
African Methodist Episcopal Church	6,647	2,481
African Union Methodist Protestant Church	69	40
African Methodist Episcopal Zion Church	2,204	1,704
Congregational Methodist Church	—	9
Colored Methodist Episcopal Church	2,381	1,759
Reformed Zion Union Apostolic Church	45	32
Reformed Methodist Union Episcopal Church	58	
Evangelist Missionary Church	—	11
Presbyterian Bodies		
Colored Cumberland Presbyterian Church	196	224
Denominations consisting in part of colored organizations	5,377	4,304
Adventist Bodies		
Advent Christian Church	2	—
Seventh-day Adventist Denomination	29	
Baptist Bodies		
Baptists—Northern Convention	198	406
Baptists—Southern Convention	—	7
Free Baptists	197	5
Primitive Baptists	4	
Two-Seed-in-the-Spirit Predestinarian Baptists	—	15
Christians—(Christian Connection)	92	63
Churches of God in N. Amer., Gen. Eldership of the	15	
Congregationalists	156	85
Disciples or Christians		
Disciples of Christ	129	⎫
Churches of Christ	41	⎬ 277
Independent Churches	12	⎭
Lutheran Bodies		
United Synod of the Evangelical Lutheran Church in the South	—	5
General Council of the Evangelical Church in North America	1	
Evangelical Lutheran Synodical Conference of America	6	5
Methodist Bodies		
Methodist Episcopal Church	3,750	2,984
Methodist Protestant Church	64	54
Wesleyan Methodist Connection in America	22	
Independent Methodists	—	2
Moravian Bodies		
Moravian Church (Unitas Fratum)	2	
Presbyterian Bodies		
Presbyterian Church in the United States of America	417	233
Cumberland Presbyterian Church	1	—
Presbyterian Church in the United States	44	45
Associate Reformed Synod of the South	1	
Synod of the Reformed Presbyterian Church of North America	—	1
Protestant Episcopal Church	198	49
Reformed Bodies		
Reformed Church in America	2	—
Reformed Episcopal Church	38	37
Roman Catholic Church	36	31
United Brethren Bodies		
Church of the United Brethren in Christ	10	—

Colored Organizations, Communicants or Members, 1906

DENOMINATIONS	ORGANIZATIONS REPORTING SEX		Total Number	COMMUNICANTS OR MEMBERS REPORTED BY SEX					
				Total		Male		Female	
	Number	Per Cent of Total	Total Number	Number	Per Cent	Number	Per Cent	Number	Per Cent
Total	34,648	94.2	3,685,097	3,527,660	95.7	1,324,123	37.5	2,203,537	62.5
Baptist National Convention (Col.)	18,034	97.3	2,201,549	2,201,599	97.3	822,162	37.3	1,379,387	62.7
African Methodist Church	6,486	97.6	494,777	481,997	97.4	177,887	36.9	304,160	63.1
Methodist Episcopal Church (Part)	3,183	85.9	308,561	271,821	88.1	102,740	37.8	169,081	62.2
African Methodist Episcopal Zion Church	2,156	97.8	184,542	180,501	97.8	67,096	37.2	113,405	62.8
Colored Methodist Episcopal Church	2,309	97.0	172,996	169,252	97.8	64,988	38.4	104,264	61.6
Roman Catholic Church (Part)	33	(2)	38,235	35,430	92.7	16,838	47.5	18,592	52.5
Colored Primitive Baptist in America	329	41.1	35,178	17,881	50.8	6,386	35.7	11,495	64.3
Baptist Northern Convention (Part)	98	90.7	32,639	29,802	91.3	10,694	35.9	19,108	64.1
Presbyterian in United States of America (Part)	356	85.4	27,799	23,898	86.0	8,935	37.4	14,963	62.6
Protestant Episcopal Church (Part)	151	76.3	19,098	15,487	81.1	5,414	35.2	10,041	64.8
Colored Cumberland Presbyterian Church	196	100.0	18,066	18,066	100.0	8,405	46.5	9,661	53.5
United American Freewill Baptist (Col.)	135	63.8	14,489	7,835	54.1	3,438	43.9	4,397	56.1
Congregationalist (Part)	155	99.4	11,960	11,952	99.9	4,613	38.6	7,339	61.4
Disciples or Christians (Part)	168	98.8	11,233	11,179	99.5	4,414	39.5	6,765	60.5
Free Baptist (Part)	175	88.8	10,876	8,951	82.3	3,397	38.0	5,559	62.0
All other Bodies (26)	604	94.5	43,051	42,059	97.7	16,734	39.8	25,325	60.2

Colored Organizations

DENOMINATION	Number		Per Cent Distribution		Increase from 1890		Rank in Number	
	1906	1890	1906	1890	Number	Per Cent	1906	1890
Total	36,770	23,462	100.0	100.0	13,308	56.7	—	—
Baptist National Convention (Col.)	18,534	12,533	50.4	53.4	6,001	47.9	1	1
African Methodist Episcopal Church	6,647	2,481	18.1	10.6	4,166	167.9	2	3
Methodist Episcopal Church (Part)	3,750	2,984	10.2	12.7	766	25.7	3	2
African Methodist Episcopal Zion Church	2,204	1,704	6.0	7.3	500	29.8	5	5
Colored Methodist Episcopal Church	2,381	1,759	6.5	7.5	622	35.4	4	4
Roman Catholic Church (Part)	36	31	0.1	0.1	5	(2)	15	18
Colored Primitive Baptist in America	801	323	2.2	1.4	478	148.0	6	7
Baptist, Northern Convention (Part)	108	406	0.3	1.7	298	78.4	14	6
Presbyterian Church in U. S. A. (Part)	417	233	1.1	1.0	184	79.0	7	9
Protestant Episcopal Church (Part)	198	49	0.5	0.2	149	(2)	9	12
Colored Cumberland Presbyterian Church	196	224	0.5	1.0	28	12.5	11	10
United American Freewill Baptist (Col.)	251	—	0.7	—	251	—	8	—
Congregationalist (Part)	156	85	0.4	0.4	71	(2)	13	11
Disciples or Christians (Part)	170	277	0.5	1.2	107	38.6	12	8
Free Bap tist (Part)	197	5	0.5	(6)	192	(2)	10	—
All Other Bodies (26)	724	368	2.0	1.6	356	96.7	—	—

(6) Less than one-tenth of one per cent.

(2) Base less than 100.

WHAT IS THE CHURCH DOING ALONG THESE LINES OF SOCIAL
UPLIIFT?

Alabama

It is trying to do and is doing much good.

Very little.

The church is doing well but since it is such a potent factor there is
still room for improvement. When other institutions fail in their appeal
the church can wield an influence.

Most of the churches do nothing for the colored citizens generally—
and little for their own denominations aside from annual picnics, occasionally supervising a colored lecturer but not settlement work outside
of their own churches of any note.

Nothing. She is asleep.

The churches are making an earnest effort to improve the people
along these lines but are progressing very slowly, by reason of the fact
that the majority of churches are being led by ignorant but zealous ministers—zealous avariciously, spectacularly and superficially.

The church is not doing very much along this line.

The churches are beginning to work to educate the people along
these lines.

I think really, churches should be the principal means to rectify these
conditions. They are somewhat asleep.

All branches of the Christian churches thruout this section seem to
have awakened along the lines of caring for the unfortunate old and
young.

Not as much as might be expected. More intelligence and a better
quality (not a bigger quantity) of religion is needed.

In the church we have a regular department which makes special
provision for its worn out ministers and the widows of deceast ministers.
The results are not as satisfactory as we would have them but we are
far from doing nothing. Thousands of dollars are distributed thru this
one department every year to widows and orphans of our church. This
is true of other churches right here in this state and southland.

The church is doing some good work.

All it can but it seems that very little good is done.

Many churches have benevolent societies connected with them. The
lodges are taking the lead in this respect, however.

Sorry to say that the church seems backward along these lines. The
Negro minister has not yet been trained for social service. He is a
slave still to the old individualism. At present the school is the chief
agency along these lines.

As such, the churches are doing nothing along these lines and becoming more interested in worldly things.

Arkansas

The churches, I think, are doing much to improve the above conditions.

Some of its duty but not all.   There is a vast room for improvement.

Nothing.   Our pastors are advising all the time but the people are far from us so we can't do anything but tell them and give the plans. The regular societies connected with all the churches do their part.   Nearly every church has its special young people's society and occasional concert or social—that is about all.   The churches mostly content themselves with frowning upon conditions without taking the lead in substituting better ones.

The churches are trying to do what they can to effect for good the lives of those within their reach.   Their influence is far-reaching.

California

The church is assisting nobly in all this general work of uplifting.

Connecticut

Altogether too little.   Individuals are helpt but many I fear go unaided.   The large Episcopal churches of this and other cities spend much money in rendering help but the smaller ones fail to do the little they might do.   Aside from ordinary church work we have Saturday morning classes for girls in sewing and physical culture with paid teachers; Saturday afternoon classes for boys in electrical experiments, photography and physical culture; weekly free socials for young people.   We continue to support our poor.

Delaware

All that is in its power.

District of Columbia

Rather, what effect have these conditions on the church?   The church is less concerned about the improvement of morals and manners and personal honesty, the home life, the rearing of children, etc., than about getting money and preaching the gospel of materialism.

Ministers as a whole are active social forces but the church as an institution is hardly maintaining its own as compared with ten years ago.

The young peoples' societies are largely literary in their nature and the Sunday school is perfunctory.   Intensive study of Bible history is neglected and little interest is manifested in social activities outside of the church as a unit of property.   Even church weddings are less common.   Catholic and Episcopal churches seem to be striving to imitate the activities of their parents.   Moving pictures and spectacular entertainments take much time formerly given to church activities.   The Negro Protestant church needs to learn the truth uttered by Van Dyke somewhere, "The man who aims to save his own soul is on the road to

Heaven but will never arrive; while he who serves his fellows cannot miss the goal".

The church is doing its part and in many instances more than its part along these lines.

Florida

Some of the churches are doing some good while most of the smaller ones only preach Heaven and Hell and never tell their people how to live each day.

Raises collections.

Failing sadly taken by and large.

Nothing worth while.

All she can do to better the conditions.

Nothing. The churches now are clamoring for money, money and are neglecting even the souls of men.

The church is failing miserably in every one of the above questions and should be severely held responsible. They fail to take proper action in matters pertaining to the best welfare of the people. The majority of the ministers are far from what they ought to be and the people very often complain to no purpose.

The church is a potent factor on these lines and is doing a deal of good in the uplift of our people.

Some churches are working faithfully while others are dead or dying.

The churches are helping all these organizations whenever called upon to do so. They also help the orphanage and rescue home for way ward boys and girls.

The indifference of the church is the result of its heavy denominational alliances. The minister theoretically exhorts, criticises, and denounces; but actively he is very busy in getting the money from any source to meet the claims of his denomination. Hence, the church is not doing anything along local lines but complaining and resenting insinuations.

Contributing to an undenominational city home for infirm also to Baptist State Home and then caring for our own aged by a Poor Saints' Fund, a free dinner on the first Sunday in each month, two benevolent and burial societies for members of the church.

Practically nothing. The spiritual life of most of the churches we regret to say is at a low ebb.

Georgia

Untold good toward helping to better their conditions on all lines.

Nothing. The societies have taken them away from the church and we can't get them to see that the souls of them are in need.

The church does not take, I think, altogether the right step on the lines of care. Why? Because we have too many poor preachers who look too hard for themselves and do not think of their friends.

I think the churches are carrying the greatest part of the burden.

Nothing. The pastors of the churches seem to have the idea that their only mission in life outside of making a loud noise in church service is to raise money for themselves. While this is not the case always the majority of them act in that manner and this is the bane of our peoples' progress as the ministers exercise the greatest amount of influence.

I think the church is doing the best it can along these lines.

The Methodist churches are doing nothing. The Baptists are doing a little; and when we take into consideration the great number of our people to be reacht, their work is but a drop in the great bucket. Here is where I think our churches are practically failures. Oh, the improvement that is needed in this line! And the strange thing about the whole matter is that so few ministers take time or have the time to think of these great questions that to my mind are to be found at the very bottom of the church work.

A little something, not much; but what is being done in this part of the Lord's world is being done by the church.

The church is doing most along these lines by establishing institutions of learning and the many small domestic schools which it maintains. The Negro pulpit is well up on teaching religion but deficient in the science of hygiene and the rules of right living.

Very little as the minister is almost alone so far as this work is concerned.

Practically nothing.

The churches seem to be doing all they can along these lines; the "higher-ups" ought to feel more in sympathy with those who are not so fortunate.

The church is the greatest force along many of these lines.

Untold good along these lines. We have very nearly all first class ministers in town and they are doing good, by meeting once a week and discussing the many things mentioned here.

Taking a very little interest.

Illinois

Lending their support quite freely to charitable institutions.

Nothing. City and state authorities protect places which are breeding crime and criminals and the preachers have made no organized effort to destroy these places.

Nothing. Absolutely nothing because they are too busy trying to see who can build the finest church and fighting among themselves, especially the Baptists. The Methodist some better, yet, not what they should be.

Cannot say as I believe in any religion that has a Jim Crow attachment.

Making some effort but accomplishing less than we would expect.

The church may be moving on. It does call for penny collections to devote to worthy charity but there is some doubt prevalent as to whether such collections are always devoted to the causes for which they are raised. The churches are still the great sun of Negro life. I think too much is intrusted to the preachers.

Not so much as possible, that is in my opinion.

Nothing to my knowledge.

Indiana

The Missionary Baptists of the state have just establisht a home for superannuated ministers and their wives and for worthy aged of that denomination. Once a month, the representative of the Alpha Home located here (Indianapolis) takes up in various churches a collection for that institution, which is establisht for aged colored women. Formerly, the superannuated and aged women were left to the poor house and public hospitals.

Practically nothing. Ladies' Club doing excellent work. Civic League also is especially interested in this work.

Kansas

Church leaders are selfish. Money getting is their chief interest. The Baptist church has a home for the aged but is neglecting it.

Here and there may be found a church which is wielding a definite, wholesome influence upon the community. There is a great field for constructive work by each church.

Kentucky

I think the churches are doing their best along this line.

Nothing special.

Not doing its full duty along these lines, yet, I find it taking a more positive stand for the general uplift of the people. To me the future seems bright.

Just enough to be well reprimanded and enforced to do better.

Some are doing much but most carry heavy debts and are trying to out do each other in raising money and erecting great church buildings.

Some excellent work on or along this line.

Not as active in actual work and endeavor as it should be.

Not much. Preachers mercenary.

Many are being helpt in all churches and yet, not as they should.

Louisiana

Great good, both religiously and morally. We have one main hindrance, that is, a deficient ministry. We will rejoice when the time will come that our ministers will be better prepared.

Take great interest in the work as to the interest of both old and young. The Methodist churches of this county are in lead of the work.

In some localities, manly efforts are made with ministers of churches and Sunday school teachers. The ignorance of the pulpit as to the duty of the minister with respect to his race is a great hindrance.

Its best; but there are not enough intelligent ministers in this community to do any real benefit to the colored people.

Maryland

They give as much attention as possible to the topics thru their leagues and other young people's meetings, Mothers' Day, and special exercises of this sort, as well as by missionary work.

Particularly M. E. and A. M. E. provide homes. The Baptists make donations of money, etc., to the needy.

Mississippi

All that is done.

Of the six colored churches at Indianola, all of them do something towards the caring for the aged.

Nothing in a general way. In a few personal or individual cases, it puts forth small efforts.

Not anything along these lines—only after all of the money they can get for the preachers.

Nothing as to amusement. Little as to the care of the aged.

Almost nothing. In fact, here there are by far too many churches. Most of them are heavily in debt and they are in a constant strain for a very humble existence. They beg the public regularly for support but do little moral or charity work. The Catholic and Episcopal churches have a school each.

Missouri

Practically nothing.

Only beginning to give attention to these things. Establishing itself and acquiring property has been the church's main object thus far.

Far less than it should be. Not yet awake to its duty along this line.

It has organized Missionary Societies, B. Y. P. U., Old Folks' Home and a Young People's League.

Only a feeble effort. We are mostly Baptists and Methodists.

Practically nothing. Our ministers are uneducated, well meaning but not seriously interested in anything except making a financial success with the church, upbuilding the parsonage, etc.

New Jersey

All that it can do. It is limited on account of the poverty and lack of appreciation on part of the non-church people, who will not accept the help of the church, who will not go to the church or permit the church to come to them.

New York

Not as much as it could have done. Heretofore, it has been handicapt with an ignorant ministry—a ministry without an ideal. However, better days are now expected along this line and better work can reasonably be expected.

The Mother Church here (white) of which mine (colored) is a mission, takes deep and active interest in the well being of the Negro citizens of this village and of those in the vicinity round about; ample facilities are provided for the general needs and well-being of the people.

Not much. If colored ministers would preach Christ crucified and the Bible, and discipline based upon the Ten Commandments, emphasizing the Seventh and Ninth, the church would be a better and a greater force.

The church cares for some of the sick and destitute, provides some amusements, but has no organized effort as to home life. The matter of church attendance and collections is emphasized by the churches.

A great work along the line of caring for the aged; along other lines, the church seems to fall far from doing much good. In my opinion, the reason for this is that too many young people in the church are immoral. Many old people in the church have immoral past lives.

Impossible to tabulate all of the activities of the churches even along these lines; but I believe I can say they are aware of the needs and up to their financial ability are seeking to meet them.

Catholics and Episcopalians something—others very little.

North Carolina

A good record on these things and looking for a brighter future.

Very little or nothing.

Does much in this direction. It makes offerings to the sick and poor as a free-will offering, yet, it does not do as much as it should.

Nothing in an organized way. Collections are raised regularly to aid the old and the sick.

Each one is doing some work in its own way. We have not an organization among them or among the ministers.

Scarcely anything except in a general way. There is not any united work of any consequence by the churches as I am aware of.

Introducing harmless and healthful games.

Nothing, except giving of contributions for the immediate relief of the poor, disabled and afflicted.

More for the general uplift of our people than ever before in all its history.

The Home Missionary societies have made efforts along these lines but really it seems that district schools, foreign missions, and orphans homes are the greatest problems of the church.

Ohio

Gradually awaking to the real sense of its real duty, rather than the Lodge doing it all. Our missionary societies are doing a grand work.

Not much. It cannot as it seems that all they can do is to meet current expenses and keep out of debt. There ought to be fewer churches and larger congregations. We need to study up in Church Economy. Our pastor can preach to a thousand as easily as to a hundred, then the salary of the other two pastors would be better.

Oklahoma

Absolutely nothing.

Nothing; they are for themselves and the preacher.

The church is very liberal toward its individual members.

More fine churches than any city in the Union and fighting every degrading influence.

The church is a negligible force in this section. The rank and file of our ministry is uneducated and immoral. Hence, no appeal is made to the younger classes of our people, and as a result there is no growth in our churches. The church in Western Oklahoma is almost entirely devoid of influence.

Pennsylvania

Practically nothing that is worthy of note. The average church is so deeply in debt that it takes all of its energies to look out for its debt.

Nothing but getting the money and the trustees are poor examples from a moral standpoint. The same holds true for the church leaders and on the whole those in church are more immoral than the non-church goers.

As a moral force, the church may be doing much, but as an organization, it is not so much felt. That is to say, it is difficult to get a united movement of it as an organization in a given direction for social or political betterment.

Found wanting "Money Crazy."

They are doing something, but might do more. I would say comparatively, the little church in the community, gives more than some wealthy congregations.

While the church makes a noble effort to combat existing evils, and to encourage good actions and intentions, yet, with the exercise of less sectarian selfishness and a leaning toward progressive lines, the masses would be more generally benefited, socially and industrially. The church, which has always been the pioneer in advancement, ofttimes, thru the changing of its leaders, lags by the wayside; and thus, allows science, the co-discoverer of truth, to surpass it by leaps and bounds.

Rhode Island

I believe all four churches here are working along these lines to the best of their knowledge and ability and they are heartily supported by the people; yet we are often guilty of more zeal than knowledge.

South Carolina

The best they can under the circumstances but much remains to be done.

More than they have ever done in helping on in the good work mentioned under the above questions. There is a less and less influence now being exerted by the ministerial hobo and vicious "whangdoodle" in the pulpit than before. The preacher who succeeds is finding that it requires more than a strong voice and a saintly moan and hallelujah groan to hold a respectable charge these days and that religious life must more and more show itself.

Recognizing and performing its duty.

The average church is not doing much.

Tennessee

We have seven handsome churches which are in a prosperous and thriving condition and are doing much good for the uplifting of our people. Each church has its B. Y. P. U. or other society for the uplift of our people.

Giving moral encouragement to all movements for the betterment of the race.

Along some lines, active. Along others, silent or indifferent.

Not as much as the lodges. There is a number of lodges and every one belongs to one or more lodges and insurances and in that way everybody is cared for; but the churches are doing very little altho people have church pride. We have seven good churches, four brick, three frame and people attend well and think a great deal of their churches.

Some do something, others nothing. It too often happens that those who could do the most good along these lines, afford an opportunity for immorality. Decency, morality and character are foreign to many. Piety is unpopular. I regret to say that their training and influence do not contribute to righteousness, edification and elevation.

Texas

Some do well, while others devote little, if any to same.

In connection with the societies mentioned, is doing a good, commendable work.

They help some along these lines but not as they could or should; this is due to the fact that out of ten churches, nine are led by ignorant, mercenary ministers, whose only aim is self gain. The secret orders do more for the uplift than the churches.

Positively doing the least of all.

Some of them are really retarding the progress of the race. Others are doing good work in the educational and moral uplift of the race. Many of them by the example of their preachers and leading men are sending more to hell than they are saving for heaven.

The church does very little more than collect money.

The church is the most active force working among our people. It is often pointed out that the church does too little, but however, the church does most and very often all that it can, and all that is done. The colored church is poor in money and workers, yet it does almost all that is done for our people along lines of moral uplift. Too little is being done; that is true; but the church alone deserves credit for what it is doing.

Our church is doing very little. It is in its infancy.

Very little. The churches have failed to unite their forces as a church. God only knows what will become of our aged. We hope that you may be able to awake our people along this line.

The church is trying to meet these conditions and fill them but has not been able to. I believe the church would, if it were not a question of money, prove to be the most effective agent in helping people to solve righteously and sensibly problems indicated by these questions.

Not what it might do for the reasons that too much attention is given to the secret societies to do this work.

The church is doing more than any other factor.

It is in the lead or at the head of all concerns for the uplift of our race and the betterment of mankind.

Virginia

Beginning to talk about and encourage improvement.

The churches are slowly awaking to their duty and are doing more work along a social line.

I speak for the church of which I am a member; collections are lifted on every second Sunday for the poor; strong sermons are preacht by our pastor in reference to unfavorable conditions.

Just about what the average Negro church does and that is not much. They seem to emphasize the spiritual rather than the social life.

The church here stands out strongly for all you have askt and preaches good manners, good morals, Christian honesty and cleanliness. It is strongly opposed to all questionable places. All of the churches give aid to its old and needy members.

A good deal of work and a great deal more of talk.

The church is a mighty factor in this community for the moral and spiritual uplift of the people.

West Virginia

Accomplishing something but there is very much room for improvement.

Thru Aid and Missionary Societies, the church is working to uplift the people of the community. The ministers are active in movements for the uplift of the race.

But little. An occasional collection after other church obligations have been met; would not get enough to feed a person for a week.

Something but not what they should or could. Too much pride in churches to consider the poor. The church is almost afraid to speak of the true condition of the people; they are weak along this line.

Sorry to say, the church seems to be doing very little along these lines due largely to our weak ministry, which is often a stumbling block to good efforts.

Very little, if anything and certainly, not as much as it might do along these lines.

THE NEGRO CHURCH IN ATLANTA

The students of the class in Sociology in Atlanta University made a study of the Negro churches in Atlanta. Data were secured for fifty-five of the sixty three churches. The following figures are compiled from the reports of the investigators:

Activities of Fifty-five Atlanta Negro Churches

Total membership 28,328
Number of members under twenty years of age 5,897
Value of church property 798,500
Total expenditure year 1912 . . . . $67,040.92
Spent for missions year 1912 . . . . $6,242.14
Spent for education year 1912 . . . . $7,677.68

The investigators report that the Ministers of the Negro churches in Atlanta were educated as follows:

    Public Schools
    Atlanta University
    Morris Brown
    Atlanta Baptist College
    Greely Institute
    St. Augustine School
    Paine College
    Fisk University
    Yale Divinity School
    Clark University
    Gammon Theological Seminary
    Philadelphia Divinity School of the Protestant Episcopal church
    Central City College

Normal School
Ballard
Claflin University
Union Theological Seminary
Biddle University
Lincoln University
Howard University

The investigators askt: Where does the church encounter its greatest difficulty? The following answers chosen from the reports are characteristic:

In securing the honest efforts of men.
In securing leaders to carry on the work.
In reaching and holding men.
In securing and maintaining the conscientious aid of men.
Lack of enthusiasm and devotion.
Lack of voluntary self-sacrifice in service, consecrated and systematic liberality. Lack of Bible study and home devotion, irregularity of attendance, lack of missionary fervor and ambition.
Lack of religious devotion.
Lack of regular attendance and devotion.
In finding freedom from an erroneous conception of the church and religion.
The church is hindered by the lack of attendance.
The poor wages paid the members for their work give them little money to contribute to the church.
Careless, unconcerned and disgruntled members.
In enlisting young Christians for active service.
In getting men to identify religion with life.
Getting hold of, and holding young people.
Getting the members to work together in a unit.
To my mind the Boy and Men problem presents the church's greatest difficulty.
Social evils together with Sunday sales of luxuries thruout the city from Greek stands and other business houses. In securing a regular attendance at eleven o'clock service by young people and attending weekly prayer meetings.
In meeting its financial obligations.
Poor preachers, bad management and factions in the church.
Weak pastor.
No particular difficulty, except ignorance of pastor and members.
Irregular attendance; lack of power to attract the people.
To get the men to manifest interest in the church.
In getting proper amount of money in order to do its full service.

Section 13.   Present Conditions compared with the past

We askt our correspondents how present conditions in these respects compare with conditions ten or twenty years ago.   These are their answers in part:

Alabama

In this section of the country it has greatly improved; at least fifty per cent.

Except for rearing of children, greatly improved, perhaps fifty per cent.

Better.

Pretty fair.   Above that of ten years ago.

No, they are not.

Conditions as a whole are ninety per cent better than twenty years ago.

Not as good.

There is a great change along this line.   More attention is being given to this line of work by our people.

Present conditions are indeed encouraging.   Ten or twenty years ago the situation was quite different.   "Let us then be up and doing" and success will crown our efforts.

They are two hundred per cent better now than they were twenty years ago.

There is not much general improvement in a general way over that ten years ago.   There is considerable improvement being done by individuals but no concerted efforts on the part of the people generally.

Conditions have improved greatly in the past ten years in that Birmingham was at that time considered unsafe on account of the preponderance of the mining class while now there are less of these people for they are gradually being considered in the better class.

There are much better lookt after and cared for by one hundred per cent.

Ten years ago church work was hardly known here, immorality was rampant, as a matter of course, but now the churches are growing in influence, the moral status is being considered, the schools are being improved and homes are being built and owned.

Things are much better now along some lines.   Schools and churches are better and the people are better educated.

I should say on the decline.

There is just as much difference in the conditions ten or twenty years ago as there is in day and night.

Now two hundred per cent better than twenty years ago.

About fifty per cent in advance.

People are much wiser but no better and we might truthfully say it might be worse, because much learning with a corrupted heart makes people more wicked.

Five hundred per cent improvement.

I think these people would be in worse condition than the heathen if there was no advancement in these conditions. There is some, of course.

Fifty or sixty per cent better.

The present conditions far excel the conditions ten or twenty years ago.

Forty per cent better, at least, along all lines.

I have been a public school teacher thirty-eight years. There is not less than seventy-five per cent improvement on the above questions. Seventy-five per cent is a big improvement since 1865, all things considered.

Can't speak for twenty years ago in this community. Have been here two years. According to information of others, conditions indicate improvement compared with ten or twenty years ago. A woman's club recently organized as a side issue distributed a little cheer to poor Christmas 1912. First in history, as far as "Old Timers"' know. Created much favorable comment. My answers refer to the Negroes of this community who are in the corporate limits of Demopolis, only.

It is seventy-five per cent better than it was ten or twenty years ago.

Much better.

In the present condition there is a vast change. The people have nice churches and schools, societies, good roads and nice homes which they did not have ten or twenty years ago.

Fifty per cent better.

Now in this respect they are a great deal better. They are somewhere about seventy-five per cent better in many degrees.

About twenty per cent better.

In some things a little better.

Improved. Much improved.

Not as good by a great deal.

All the way from sixty to one hundred and fifty per cent improvements.

Improved.

Conditions to-day compared with ten or even twenty years ago are almost too far ahead to suffer comparison. The almost innumerable benevolent, fraternal and church institutions have raised this question beyond the point of speculation or experiment.

Better than ten years ago.

They are much improved.

Much better.

I believe we were better then morally; now we excel along other lines.

Much more is being done now towards caring for the old than was done ten or twenty years ago.

Very much better in every respect.

Surpass them with exception of good morals and manners.

In this city the change in the past ten years has been wonderful. The backward tendency is due to poor school facilities and ante-bellum teachers. I regard conditions as being on a whole better than they were ten years ago.

There is an improvement over ten or twenty years ago.

Arkansas

There is quite an improvement.

To compare with ten years ago we are fifty per cent better; but some are just in the reverse.

They have changed for better all the way from twenty-five to seventy-five per cent.

About the same or worse.

Not favorably in many respects.

On the whole there is some improvement.

Better.

I believe that conditions are in advance of that time at least by fifty per cent.

It has increast eighty per cent.

Not as good as it was even ten years ago.

From twenty years the progress of our people is above the average.

They are far better.

California

The social and religious condition I regard as being far in advance of the past.

Connecticut

My hope is that the condition existing will arouse us to our sense of duty. The need is greater and greater. People from the Southland are flocking to the northern cities and the privileges as they call them are often engaged in to the detriment of their health. As a result age or disease siezes them and they become wards. This illustrates individual cases. On the other hand the man born on southern soil is the most thrifty class among us.

With reference to morals and training of children conditions do not seem as hopeful as ten years ago. This may be due to the fact that long residence has given us better knowledge.

Delaware

I think they are forty per cent better than they were ten years ago.

District of Columbia

Possibly,. we are in the midst of a period of transition which will not admit of comparison with conditions of other times.   But I cannot but confess to a sense of disappointment as regards conditions in some particulars.

The general average is higher than ten or twenty years ago but in different directions.   More effort is expended to make money for money's sake.   The standard of dressing is higher and more becoming.   The ambitions are more rational.   The morality is more conscious.   The chastity of girls is more deliberate.   The care of the body is gaining its respect. The preparations for living is longer and better.   Marriage is postponed and the size of families reduced thru regard for children as well as aim to live well.

About ten per cent improved.

Greatly improved.   Say about fifty per cent.

Marvelous advancement.   Momentary increases.   Leaning forward to better things.   Hope, courage, work are to be ceaselessly emphasized.

Very, very great improvement on the past and growing encouragingly better all the time.

Florida

It seems as if the race is short of competent leaders and is at a loss as to proper instruction.   Moving pictures and places of fun and amusement seem to be in majority on the Sabbath day.

Ten or twenty years ago the colored people were not as able as they are now to do what they desired to do.

Greatly improved.

I hope better.   It is only a hope, however.   My optimism compels me to think there is improvement along all lines tho imperceptible in places.

Very unfavorable in many respects.

Ten or twenty years ago, our people were in a better condition religiously and morally.   You askt me my cand.d opinion and I have given it.   I do not mean to say that this applies to every one in the race but the majority.

There has been quite an improvement along all lines to that of ten years ago excepting to that of old people.   They seem thrifty and progressive.

Seventy-five per cent better now than they were twenty years ago.

I think in many ways they are better while in some of them I think they have taken a decided fall especially in rearing their children and in sound morals.

They are improving.

I see a great improvement in the conditions of people within the last ten or fifteen years. Since the fire the city has been made the homes of people from all states and this has changed conditions considerably but there is a constant improvement along all lines.

A great improvement.

To differentiate is but to show what has been neglected and what has been subjected in the terms of years of moral activities. By comparison of conditions we have enough light to see the wrongs and virtues of the past, which are conclusive beyond a reasonable doubt that conditions are better than they were twenty years ago.

There is somewhat of an improvement along some lines.

Fairly well. Some of our people are improving themselves very well. Twenty years ago we had no church here but now we have also a school house and colored teachers. The condition is one hundred per cent better now than it was ten years ago.

Much better. One hundred per cent at least.

The way I understand it our churches twenty years ago were doing as much again for the old people as it is doing to-day.

There is progress. There would have been more had there been a better leadership in the church and in the school. Better pulpit leadership is the crying need of St. Augustine. The preachers are the veritable leaders of the people. The lives of only a very few are any pattern for the young people.

Georgia

Much better.

We are fifty per cent in advance.

They are far different now than twenty years ago. There was more union and we used more cordiality among ourselves and punctuality made us live better then than now in many ways; and in some ways we are better off; in some ways by having our own publications.

I feel that present conditions are much better than they were ten years ago.

A great improvement.

Now, as a matter of fact, I believe that the times are better but the church in some respects has lost his grip on young people and they no more go to church or enjoy themselves as they did in days gone by.

I think there is great improvement in twenty years along these lines. Just how much as a whole I could not say but they are better on all lines. As bad as they are now, they are better than they were in former years.

Some are in the front of that time and some are in the rear.

In the matter of homes, rearing of children and caring for the old there is decided improvement over the conditions that obtained ten years ago. The morals and manners of the children are also better.

Fifty per cent better.

I am candid in saying that I feel safe in telling you that there is a general sign of betterment in the questions askt in our town and county. I was born here fifty-three years ago and have spent my whole time here save a few years away at school.

To my judgment morals are growing worse and raising children the same; but other matters have improved ten to thirty per cent.

Very progressive. About seventy-five per cent compared with ten or twenty years ago.

When we speak as to the masses these conditions have been improved forty per cent.

The help which we are getting from white people, especially northern white friends, has lifted us to that degree.

There is a perceptible advancement along all worthy lines.

Things are so much better.

They compare very unfavorably in view of the vast educational adtages of to-day and ten or twenty years ago.

One hundred per cent in advance.

They are not as good. This is an exceptionally bad place. The morals are the lowest here of any place I have ever been.

Great improvement in my race over ten or twenty years ago.

Some improvement, I think.

Far surpass.

Some improvement, yet not what it should be.

I should think they have made at least seventy-five per cent improvement along these lines in the last fifteen years.

Cannot say. I have lived here only eight years and it seems that immediate circumstances are making the race restless and unstable. Of course, the older and wiser ones are careful and by their frugality are accumulating means and getting real estate.

There is a falling off.

Ninety per cent are worse than they were ten or twenty years ago.

He is better prepared to-day than he was twenty years ago.

I do not know so much about twenty years ago, but there is a wonderful improvement on forty years ago. Much of it is due to having more property. I do not know as the disposition to be upright and prudent is much more than forty years ago. Our people are making great strides in bettering their condition.

In my opinion, conditions as compared with ten years ago show markt improvement and progress.

Considerably advanced in comparison with those of ten years ago.

They are much better than they were ten or twelve years ago. Show markt improvement and progress.

Considerably advanced in comparison with those of ten years ago.

They are much better than they were ten or twelve years ago.

As to inquiry one and two, advancement is questionable; as to the other points, there has been a markt improvement.   To say at least thirty or thirty-five per cent would not be too liberal.

I would think that the conditions are much better, at least fifty per cent better, than twenty-five years ago.

I feel that our people are far in advance of what they were ten or twenty years ago and many testimonies here are to this effect.   This does not look like the same place it was twenty or ten years ago.

The people have made such rapid speed during the last ten years, until the fellow that was here ten years ago hardly favors himself and I must say they have outstript themselves since ten years.

The comparison is favorable.

Illinois

There seems to be less individual pride relatively and less individual feeling of responsibility, but greater effort collectively than we have had before.

This city is a Mecca for the criminals from other places and is growing worse.   The school advantages are excellent.

The conditions now are so far superior to the conditions of twenty years ago along these lines until there are few comparisons to make.

Children have less respect for parents than they did twenty years ago and lack the modesty and courtesy of long ago.

In this particular section of the city there has been some improvement along all lines, but the people are not very progressive as a whole and present conditions are not so improved over the past as they should be.

Some very great progress has been made in many different directions; I think the race has lost what it may not retrieve in a great many years by the easy acceptance of false standards—too much gaudy gloss, fine feathers, no fixt notions, excuses, promises, resolutions, determinations, etc.

They are very much better.

Greatly improved.

Can see markt improvement.

Great improvement in almost every line.

Indiana

Conditions are fifty per cent better than they were twenty years ago.   The people are living in better houses; some have bot homes; they are better drest; conditions are improved openly, while the high cost of living has impaired some.   The race has kept abreast of the time.

Kansas

Present conditions are fifty per cent better than ten years ago.   We have a community of which we are proud.

It seems fair to say that all conditions of life among our people have been changed for the better; I take it as a hopeful situation.

Much worse as the city increases in size.

Kentucky

It is three to one better at the present time than it was ten years ago, considering I can find no real low faults of more of the above conditions at present.

Not so much better in this town.

No improvement. All is left to private benefits and friends.

Much improvement in last twenty years.

Do not know but I am told much better now.

A decided improvement along all lines.

Better by far.

We are more easily discouraged, farther apart, more jealous, better educated, more restless and less persistent than we were ten years ago.

Conditions compare favorably with that of twenty years ago in many instances and much improved in others.

Very little advancement.

A slight improvement.

There is really no comparison at all—so much difference on all lines. Better.

In comparing conditions would say that in every respect, it is a great increase, except in rearing children. The new mother is too indulging.

Many are still in the dark and are a shame and disgrace to the race. Yet, in the past decade, the ranks of those going "Onward and Upward," have greatly increast.

They are worse today than they were ten or twenty years ago. People are thinking right on this point. Something should be done to help conditions along these lines

The last decade has been a decade of progress except probably along the lines of commercial honesty. The American greed has greatly influenct the Negro.

Louisiana

Greatly improved wherever the training, environment and example whether in the home, the school and the church has been of the right kind.

Compared with ten or twenty years ago there are evidences of progress.

Very much improved.

Conditions are seventy-five per cent ahead of that time. It might be well for me to say that, thinking closely on conditions, one hundred per cent would not be an exaggeration.

Fifteen per cent better.

Excellent.

There is no apparent improvement whatever.   Immorality and ignorance reign supreme.   The greatest impediment in the way of general improvement among the colored people is its poor public school system.

They are better.   Better school teachers, better preachers and more sincere Negro leaders are what we are most in need of and in my opinion we are gradually getting them.

I think conditions are better.

Better than ten years ago.

From what I can learn there is quite an advance in all of these lines during the past decade.

They are some better than they were but there is a tremendous amount of teaching and praying necessary for their salvation.

Maryland

The present conditions are fifty per cent better to-day in the uplift of the race.

Better.

Am not able to say.

Some improvement but not decidedly so.   I know all the homes are in the crowded blocks of the city.

General improvement, raising of standard along all lines.

Minnesota

The improvement has been so markt and wonderful that one would hardly realize that we are the same people.   Taking all in all, I think that you who carry the torch of advancement in these matters have reason to be exceedingly glad.

Better.

Mississippi

There is an improvement of fifty per cent.

There seems an improvement in all save in morals and personal honesty, in which there seems a decline.

The people have made great strides along both moral, religious and material lines since ten years ago.   This is evident on every hand.

Less is being done now.   The arrangements and privileges of to-day were begun or made ten or twenty years ago.

There has been some improvement along some lines—morals and honesty.

There is not as much love and care for religion and the churches and old people now-a-days as there was ten or twenty years ago.   All have backsliden.   Backsliding along these lines is mighty dark.

The conditions are better in everything except the "Rearing of Children," "Amusements of the young," and "Care for the old people."

Fifty per cent worse.

There is improvement in some things. Negroes have and are building better and more modern homes. Increast desire to educate the children. I regret to say there is not as yet any increasing demand for a high-class educated ministry.

I think there is improvement along all lines,—less in morals, in my judgment, than anywhere else.

They are improving fast; they are far beyond what they were years ago.

Much better.

Seventy-five per cent advance.

Missouri

Present conditions are worse.

From all I hear of former conditions they were far worse than anything we know of to-day.

Better.

They are worse in many respects. The Negro is being lured by the vanities and superficialities of life and is losing the seriousness of twenty years ago.

They are very much improved.

Much improved in every way. More homes owned and yards beautiful. Our people leaving the alleys at every chance. The two and three-room houses are almost gone.

Negroes in this city wearing better clothes, eating better food, living in better homes, buying more and better homes than they were twenty years ago.

In many respects, conditions are not as good as they were ten years ago and in some they are better. The young people seem to be disregarding church and are going after the evil things of life. It seems to be the home that is not discharging its duty to the children.

Speaking for this vicinity alone, there appears a seventy-five per cent advancement, except in religious worship. In this respect, there seems to be a strong tendency to "Stick to the oft-trodden path."

About the same.

Somewhat favorable.

New Jersey

Ten per cent better.

Very appreciably improved.

Improving from personal knowledge of five years' sojourn here.

There is some improvement; one good sign is, these people seem wiling to follow a competent leader.

Favorably.

Better.

New York

From what I can gather from those who are in a position to know the conditions of to-day are better than they were either ten or twenty years ago.

Have lived here only six years and note considerable improvement along all lines herein mentioned.

Greatly improved.

I think conditions are better. The ministers are of a higher class and the home life is better.

Getting better.

I have no personal knowledge of ten or twelve years back but information on the matter leads to the conclusion that there is an improvement.

There appears to be a gradual improvement along all lines, except it is now more difficult for colored men to secure good employment at fair wages.

The comparative conditions present a growing and healthy aspect. Very encouraging racially—indicating great progress and rapid strides. Tho morals of our young men and women should be lookt after more.

Public vulgarity should be discouraged in our youth.

North Carolina

The standard is at least twenty-five per cent higher than it was twenty years ago.

Over fifty per cent improved and we hope to reach the one hundred mark in the near future.

Much improved.

The conditions of say ten years ago are vastly different. The child has become the parent, therefore, it makes discipline wanting.

There are to my mind not as good as twenty years ago. People are careless and unconcerned about these things. Everybody must look out for himself, and not be interested in any one else much. Live if you can, if not, die. "Might is right" is the slogan now with the people.

They have more money, more property, live in better houses, have better schools and their opportunities along all lines are better; but they seem to lack ambition for those things to make them useful. Education, spiritual development, strict home rules are things of the past and held very cheap here; but money, fine dress, a big house to live in are the things they are striving for here, regardless of other things and at any sacrifice.

We note wonderful improvements. The changes seem almost miraculous.

As far as I can see and hear we are not doing as much.

Present conditions are a decided improvement on past ones.

Ten years has made quite a difference for the better, especially financially and intellectually. More could have been done on other lines.

Favorably.

They are far superior.

In home life, habits of cleanliness, good manners, the present conditions are better than they were ten years ago. In the others, I cannot see that any improvement has been made.

Conditions twenty years ago cannot be compared with the mighty upward trend of our people.

They compare favorably.

Ohio

Well—about fifty per cent better.

An improvement worth while. I speak directly for the Association work among our men and boys. A wonderful increase in the last three years.

There seems to me to be a steady growth in the right direction all along the line with the possible exception of rearing of children. I sometimes think of the past generation, how they were more on the Puritan line.

Oklahoma

Condition is improved.

Conditions in these respects compared with those ten years ago are entirely new.

I was not in this country ten years ago, but for the past four years of my life, which I have spent here, I can truthfully say there has been a great change in this place among the colored people.

In general, they seem to be more in earnest. The condition of the present to that of four years ago would be amazing to anyone who had not visited this country in four years.

Sound morals decreasing. Personal honesty decreasing. On the whole, I believe there is an improvement.

This is a new state and town. The town is a little more than eight years old. I judge conditions are about as they would be in any newly opened country where mines are opened. Hence, it requires time and patience, energy and money to bring about the needed reformations.

These conditions are better.

Ten or twenty years ago, this was the Indian Territory and conditions were bad. The new comers have been busy attending to their individual affairs but heroic efforts are being made by a few strong men and women and we are pleased to see progress along all lines.

They are improving slowly.

Quite an improvement.

Much improved.

Much better on the whole.   Quite fifty per cent better than it was twenty years ago.

Pennsylvania

I think there is an advance in this regard, but nothing to what it should be.   Colored people ought to learn to look after their own people as other races are doing.

All told, there is great improvement in everything save child bearing.   There is a distinct tendency among the higher classes not to have children.

Very much improved.

Present conditions are better than they were ten or twenty years ago.

As far as I can learn it compares very favorable.

They have made advancement along all lines and even in this they are like all American people.

Favorably, on a whole.

Great improvement.

The above conditions compare very favorably.

I think they are better than twenty years ago.

The developing sense of ownership, as is evident by the increasing number of home buyers; exhibition and cultivation of personal and racial pride; the markt decrease in illiteracy; and the attention, protection and forethot given to those who have braved the wars of time, and who scarce tell of their conflicts with varied vicissitudes; these conditions and more compare most favorably with those of a decade or two, thus giving hope to all.

Markt difference along all lines.   Much improvement.

Rhode Island

The progress is evident and the results are gratifying.

South Carolina

An improvement along all lines save in the home life and the rearing of children.

I have been in the practice of medicine for the last twenty years, and this work has given me a different insight into the real life of our people.   Previous to that I taught school, and thot then that we were making fair progress.   In this state everything is as bad as anyone should want to see it.   In my opinion, most if not the greatest progress that we have made has been in getting homes and farms etc.; but I am aware that the most valuable asset we can have is men and women of character and efficiency.

Conditions are changing and people seem to be waking up to the situation.   There are some influences at work for the betterment of conditions.

Very poor.

Not much better. If any a very little. I, personally, don't see any.

In all these respects there has been, in my opinion, a great advance. The thousands of lodge members, who in the secret meetings are taught valuable lessons of duty and destiny and receive therein earnest training in the matters involved in their relation to themselves, to their neighbor and their God, are having great influence in showing and setting good examples of the necessity of recognizing the moral obligations resting upon them in all their relations in life. The better schools and the cleaner pulpits are also helping ably in this great improvement that I believe is daily going on all around us.

Much improved, resulting from the progress of education and constant agitation along the above lines. The people are being aroused and are moving towards the light. They are knowing the truth, which is setting them free.

They appear about fifteen or twenty per cent better if not more.

About the same.

They are like the noon day sun over against the twilight.

Conditions are improving but not as fast as they should.

Tennessee

A gradual improvement on some things, such as finances, education, home improvements. Religion is on the decline.

Our people have improved religiously, intellectually and financially; but they have lost politically. We have been represented in the City Council by an alderman and have had a colored squire and constable; but we have neither now.

There seems to be improvement along all lines.

Considerable improvement.

Some improvement.

About the same.

An improvement on them.

Very little to be proud of.

There have been advancements in enlightenment along all lines except sound morals. There I cannot see much improvement owing I suppose, to transitory people who do not care for building up as they are not long in a place.

It seems to be a day of reaction. In some respects, they are better; and in some, apparently worse. There is more intelligence of a kind, but not the improvement in manners, morals, parental training that you would expect. The Negro has far to come. He had to go so far and reverse himself and begin again. Moral growth is very slow and the teaching, training and development of our young is a work of generations.

About fifty per cent better than they were twenty years ago.

Better in every way.

General improvement except in slums.

Very greatly improved at present.

Texas

They are not as good as they were a few years ago.

Conditions are growing worse; we have been flattered and we flatter ourselves with the idea of the contrast.

Not competent to judge conditions further back than eight years but there has been a decided change for the better in that time.

Not much improvement.

Conditions have taken a step in advance and there has been apparent improvement along the entire line.

Fifty per cent better.

The change for the better is so great that no comparison can be made, for with rapid strides all obstacles have been overcome and thousands upon thousands of dollars are possessed about here by our people.

There is a little fall off and all lines have gained in wealth; this part is better by two-thirds.

There is much change for the period in favor of the present.

I am thoroly acquainted with conditions in almost every city of Texas. Sorry to say, but I firmly believe the conditions in this city are worse today than formerly.

I am not able to speak of the conditions ten years ago. I was not in these parts. I am told that there is an improvement. I hope so.

They are worse.

Sixty per cent.

Very good; they are improving slowly.

This is a hard question to answer, but I think I may safely say that social and economic conditions are making it more difficult in every way for the Negro to make an excellent moral showing.

Perhaps some better.

They are much better now. For only five years ago we had nothing here; but now we have a beautiful church and a few members.

They are much better.

Quite a contrast. Much better now than it was ten or twenty years ago.

Better now by far.

There is on a whole some improvement made, say thirty-three and one-third per cent better over ten years ago; but there is a long field for improvement.

Ninety per cent better.

Some increase in each inquiry as I see it.

All are at least seventy-five per cent better.

Bad. The people seem to be wild and hard to civilize. Can't get many of the old people to church. Only a small percentage of the young people attend Sunday school.

On the whole an improvement is noted.

Somewhat for indifferent people.

We have less members more churches, more schools, more preachers and teachers.

Except the freedom of children, everything better. The strain is too great on the bodies and souls of the young people. If they could only find amusement and happiness in their own homes, instead of the public places, there would be less vice, disease and death.

I don't know definitely as I have been here only about nine months. I should think they were improving, tho.

They show a markt progress along every line.

Some improvement. The most markt is for better morals.

There have been remarkable changes along all lines in the last few years. Conditions are tending upwards. Agencies which were lifeless or silent ten or twenty years ago have awakened to see marvelous progress in every phase of the Negroes' life.

Better.

Eighty-five per cent better to-day than they were twenty years ago.

It is at least seventy-five per cent better now. They have grown more enlightened and think on higher things.

Some better.

They have made wonderful improvement in every respect. In property, in education, in banking, in tailoring, in claiming his rights.

Some improvements.

Much improvement.

Virginia

Great improvement in my judgment.

I am very gratified at improvements made and hope that the next decade will see evidence of still greater growth.

In some instances, conditions are better, while in others they are not as good.

Should say on the whole, conditions are improved.

About seventy-five per cent behind, so I am told.

There has been some improvement.

There is more affectation, more treachery, more frivolity and more selfishness.

Not as good to my mind, by twenty per cent. Our people need to be aroused along these lines.

Conditions, to my mind, are much better in many respects now.

Very little, if any improvement, has been made along this line. I am a new man here but those who have been here twenty-five years say very little improvement has been made; possibly in purchasing property, owning homes, etc., there has been some improvement, but education and religion are at a stand still.

I have been here four years.   The advancement for that time has been remarkable.

West Virginia

County schools are merely one-room shacks and the teachers employed are not prepared for the work.   One-third of the children of school age attend school.   Do not know how conditions were ten years ago.

A perceptible improvement.

Our present conditions are much better than they were ten years ago. In short, I would say, we are too far apart in all our lines of progress.

I can only say conditions are so different now from what they were ten years ago.   The colored population has increast rapidly and the majority coming to us have been a hindrance, rather than a help.   We have a large floating population.   They contribute nothing to our good.

The idea of separate districts for the race was not so distinct.   A person able to pay the rent or purchase property could do so and feel that he would not he molested.   Home life is better.   Sanitary conditions as well as morals, also; a general sign of uplift and higher ideals.

Conditions are not as good now as they were twenty years ago. Our leaders fear to speak of the true condition; they seem to think it will be detrimental to their financial gains.   In this section, I think conditions are a little better than they were five years ago.

I think they will continue better to some extent.

There is some improvement; but it is of such slow growth that we are impatient.

In some respects better and in other respects not so well.

All things considered, conditions are more hopeful due to education of the masses, and largely to civic organizations.

One hundred per cent better than it was ten years ago.

Generally, I think, I am safe in saying they are improving.

Conditions are very much better.

Section 14.   Conclusion

This study is fragmentary and impressionistic.   It had to be.   The subject does not easily lend itself to figures; and such parts as call for statistical study have few such collections of facts at hand.

And yet one cannot read this study without coming to some conclusions.   The Negro race in America is in spiritual turmoil.   It is self-conscious, self-critical, and has not yet grasped great and definite ideals.   On the other hand, its spiritual advance has been enormous.   One can sense this in the very terms of the criticisms exprest and in the ideals thus revealed.

It is manifest that the *Church* no longer holds the place of sole center of Negro activity. It is a social organization of large meaning but it does not speak *ex cathedra;* and there is a distinct tendency to bring it down to definite present social ends and to criticize it severely if it does not accomplish something in these lines.

The peculiar social position of the Negro is having its effect on his manners. The problem of the "second generation" is with him, with all its tendency to self-assertion, waywardness and revolt. But with this are coming new efforts and a new sense of responsibility toward the children. Here the older church, with its imported puritanism and theoretical crying down of amusements, stands in the way. But it must move. Dancing, games and organized play for young colored folk must be openly encouraged or they will be pushed, as they are to-day, into the furtive and questionable.

Moral standards are difficult to fix and fathom. For this very reason there is extraordinary divergence of judgment and expectation. Yet there cannot be in the mind of the patient unprejudiced observer any doubt but that the morals, sexual and other, of the American Negro compare favorably to-day with those of any European peasantry and that a large and growing class is in this respect the equal of the best in the nation.

There are, of course, the economic hindrances to sound moral life and these are tremendous in the case of the Negro. One can sense a strain to live according to the higher American standards on a wage below the American standard. This leads to crime and laxity. But the fight is being bravely made.

The criminality of Negroes is not large or dangerous considering their economic status; it calls, however, for far different treatment than it is receiving. Meantime, homes and home life are improving and there is wide spread effort in social reform.

With all its shadows and questions one cannot read this study without a distinct feeling of hope and courage.

Index

DATE

NOV 26 78	

GAYLORD